POSTCARDS

GERMANY

D0390159

The cathedral in Cologne is one of the finest in the world. See chapter 13. © Bob Krist Photography.

In the midst of one of Berlin's most bustling and fashionable districts stands the bombed-out shell of the Kaiser Wilhelm Memorial Church, a poignant reminder of the destruction of World War II. See chapter 3. © Doug Armand/Tony Stone Images.

The Brandenburg Gate, Berlin's most famous landmark, once marked the boundary between East and West Berlin. See chapter 3. © Tony Stone Images.

The Pergamon Museum in Berlin contains reconstructions of some of antiquity's greatest monuments. This frieze lies at the base of the classical Pergamon Altar. See chapter 3. © Gian Berto Vanni/Art Resource.

Sausages and beer: among the staples of the German diet. © Dave Bartruff Photography.

A "Ratskeller" is a restaurant in the basement of the town's Rathaus (Town Hall). Come here for good, moderately priced German food in a traditional setting. © Kevin Galvin Photography.

The Thomaskirche (St. Thomas Church) in Leipzig, where Johann Sebastian Bach served as cantor, is the home of the St. Thomas Choir. You can attend the choir's performances here when it's not on tour. See chapter 4. © Dave Bartruff Photography.

Rothenburg is the most popular stop on the well-traveled Romantic Road. See chapter 6. © Bob Krist Photography.

Munich's Oktoberfest (which actually starts in late September) attracts millions of beer-lovers every year. See chapters 2 and 7. © Sylvain Grandadam/Tony Stone Images.

The towers of the Peterskirche (St. Peter's Church) and the Frauenkirche (Cathedral of Our Lady) loom dramatically over Munich at night. See chapter 7. © Bob Krist Photography.

The Marienplatz is the center of Munich's historic district. See chapter 7. © Kevin Galvin Photography.

The Karwendel Mountains, near Mittenwald, have some of Germany's best hiking trails. See chapter 8. © Werner Muller/Tony Stone Images.

Extravagantly painted façades, like this one in Mittenwald, are common sights in the towns of the Bavarian Alps. See chapter 8. © Kevin Galvin Photography.

Oberammergau's world-famous Passion Play, performed only one year out of ten, was last shown in the summer of 2000. The actors are all members of the Oberammergau community. See chapter 8. © Kevin Galvin Photography.

A colorful cafe in the spa town of Baden-Baden. See chapter 10. © Bob Krist Photography.

The Black Forest has some of Germany's most scenic countryside. See chapter 9. © Paul Trummer/The Image Bank.

Imposing Sigmaringen Castle guards the Danube valley, south of Stuttgart. See chapter 5.
© Robert Everts/Tony Stone Images.

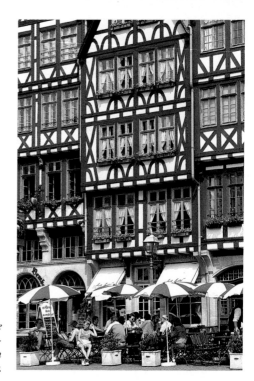

These half-timbered houses are in the Römerberg, the heart of old Frankfurt. See chapter 12. © Kevin Galvin Photography.

The best view of Heidelberg is from the Philosopher's Way, halfway up the hill on the north bank of the Neckar River. See chapter 11. © Bob Krist Photography.

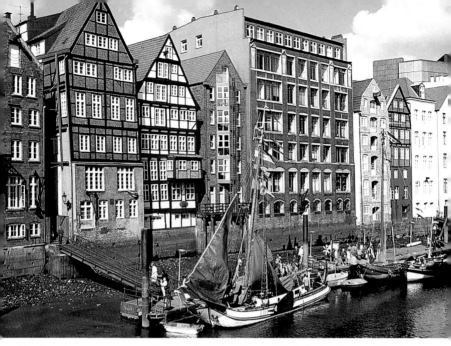

Merchant homes along a canal in Hamburg. See chapter 16. © Lothar Reupert/The Image Bank.

Another side of Hamburg: the gaudy Reeperbahn, the city's red light district. See chapter 16. © Romilly Lockyer/The Image Bank.

Vineyards line the banks of the picturesque Mosel River. You can take a river cruise between the towns of Cochem and Trier. See chapter 14. © Kevin Galvin Photography.

The Rhine is another popular cruise-ship route. See chapter 13. © Hans Wolf/The Image Bank.

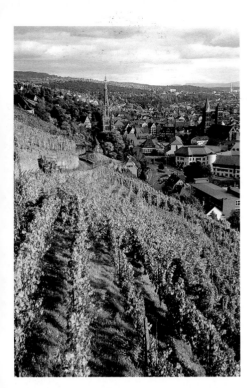

Esslingen is a stop on the Neckar Valley Cycle Path. See chapter 11. © Chad Ehlers/Tony Stone Images.

These vineyards are located in Bernkastel, the most colorful of the wine towns in the Mosel valley. See chapter 14. © Wolfgang Kaehler Photography.

A chapel nestled in the Bavarian Alps. See chapter 8. © Rose Dietrich/Tony Stone Images.

Other Great Guides for Your Trip:

Frommer's Portable Berlin

Frommer's Munich & the Bavarian Alps

Frommer's Europe

Frommer's Europe from $70 a Day

Frommer's Gay & Lesbian Europe

Frommer's Europe's Greatest Driving Tours

Europe For Dummies

Hanging Out in Europe

Frommer's Road Atlas Europe

Here's what the critics say about Frommer's:

"Amazingly easy to use. Very portable, very complete."
—*Booklist*

♦

"The only mainstream guide to list specific prices. The Walter Cronkite of guidebooks—with all that implies."
—*Travel & Leisure*

♦

"Complete, concise, and filled with useful information."
—*New York Daily News*

♦

"Hotel information is close to encyclopedic."
—*Des Moines Sunday Register*

♦

"Detailed, accurate and easy-to-read information for all price ranges."
—*Glamour Magazine*

Frommer's ®

Germany
2001

by Darwin Porter & Danforth Prince

IDG Books Worldwide, Inc.
An International Data Group Company
Foster City, CA • Chicago, IL • Indianapolis, IN • New York, NY

ABOUT THE AUTHORS

Veteran travel writers **Darwin Porter** and **Danforth Prince** have written numerous best-selling Frommer's guides, notably to Germany, France, Italy, England, and Spain. Porter, who was bureau chief for the *Miami Herald* when he was 21, wrote the first Frommer's guide to Germany and has traveled extensively in the country. Prince, who began writing with Porter in 1982, worked for the Paris bureau of the *New York Times*.

IDG BOOKS WORLDWIDE, INC.

An International Data Group Company
909 Third Avenue
New York, NY 10022

Find us online at **www.frommers.com**

ISBN: 0-7645-6139-1
ISSN: 1091-2827

Editor: Matthew Kiernan
Production Editor: Heather Gregory
Photo Editor: Richard Fox
Design by Michele Laseau
Cartographer: Nick Trotter
Production by IDG Books Indianapolis Production Department
Front Cover Photo: "Mad" King Ludwig's fairy-tale Neuschwanstein castle, along the Romantic Road

SPECIAL SALES

For general information on IDG Books Worldwide's books in the U.S., please call our Consumer Customer Service Department at 1-800-762-2974. For reseller information, including discounts, bulk sales, customized editions, and premium sales, please call our Reseller Consumer Service Department at 1-800-434-3422.

Manufactured in the United States of America.

5 4 3 2 1

Contents

List of Maps   ix

1   The Best of Germany   1

1 The Best Travel Experiences 1
2 The Best Museums 3
3 The Best Castles & Palaces 4
4 The Best Cathedrals 6
5 The Most Charming Small Villages 6
6 The Best Driving Tours 7
7 The Best Walks 7

8 The Best Biking 8
9 The Best Spas 8
10 The Best Luxury Hotels 9
11 The Best Small Inns & Hotels 9
12 The Best Restaurants 10
13 The Best Beer Halls & Taverns 11
14 The Best Shopping 11

2   Planning Your Trip: The Basics   12

1 The Regions in Brief 12
2 Visitor Information 18
3 Entry Requirements & Customs 18
4 Money 20
   The U.S. Dollar, the British Pound, the German Mark & the Euro 21
5 When to Go 22
   Germany Calendar of Events 22
6 The Active Vacation Planner 24

   Taking the Waters 26
   Germany for Jewish Visitors 29
7 Health & Insurance 30
8 Tips for Travelers with Special Needs 31
9 Getting There 33
   Flying for Less: Tips for Getting the Best Airfares 34
10 Getting Around 39
11 Tips on Accommodations 44
   Fast Facts: Germany 45

Planning Your Trip: An Online Directory   49

3   Berlin   63

1 Orientation 63
   Berlin Today & Tomorrow 64
   Neighborhoods in Brief 66
2 Getting Around 71
   Fast Facts: Berlin 72
3 Where to Stay 74
   Family-Friendly Hotels 78

4 Where to Dine 90
   Family-Friendly Restaurant 92
5 Seeing the Sights 100
   Frommer's Favorite Berlin Experiences 109
6 Organized Tours 114
7 Sports & Outdoor Pursuits 116

8 Shopping 117

*Treasures in the Barn
District* 121

9 Berlin After Dark 124

Life Is a Cabaret in Berlin 127

The Love Parade 128

10 A Side Trip: Potsdam &
Its Palaces 136

---

4   Saxony & Thuringia   140

1 Weimar 142

Goethe Gets a Touch-Up 146

*The Thuringian Forest:
Germany's Green Heart* 149

2 Leipzig 152

*Singing Through the Centuries:
The St. Thomas Boys'
Choir* 156

3 Dresden 164

4 Meissen 177

---

5   Franconia & the German Danube   180

1 Bayreuth 182

2 Bamberg 187

3 Nürnberg (Nuremberg) 191

*Albrecht Dürer & the German
Renaissance* 195

4 Regensburg 202

5 Passau 206

6 Ulm 210

---

6   The Romantic Road   213

1 Würzburg 215

2 Miltenberg 221

3 Amorbach 223

4 Bad Mergentheim 224

5 Weikersheim 226

6 Creglingen 227

7 Rothenburg ob der Tauber 228

8 Dinkelsbühl 235

9 Nördlingen 237

10 Donauwörth 239

11 Augsburg 240

12 Füssen 245

13 Neuschwanstein &
Hohenschwangau 248

The Fairy-Tale King 249

---

7   Munich   252

1 Orientation 252

Neighborhoods in Brief 256

2 Getting Around 256

Fast Facts: Munich 258

3 Where to Stay 260

Family-Friendly Hotels 261

4 Where to Dine 268

Family-Friendly Restaurants 273

Beer Gardens 278

5 Seeing the Sights 281

*Frommer's Favorite Munich
Experiences* 281

6 Organized Tours 293

7 Sports & Outdoor Pursuits 294

8 Shopping 295

9 Munich After Dark 300

François Cuvilliés 301

10 Side Trips from Munich 308

8   The Bavarian Alps   309

1 Berchtesgaden 313
2 Bad Reichenhall 318
3 Chiemsee 321
4 Bad Wiessee 323
5 Mittenwald 325

6 Garmisch-Partenkirchen 327
   Hiking in the Bavarian Alps 328
7 Oberammergau 334
   *Shopping for Wood
   Carvings* 336

9   Lake Constance (Bodensee)   340

1 Lindau 342
2 Friedrichshafen 346
3 Meersburg 349
4 Konstanz (Constance) 352

5 Reichenau 356
6 Überlingen 358
7 Ravensburg 359

10   The Black Forest (Schwarzwald)   362

1 Freiburg im Breisgau 362
   *An Excursion to the Upper
   Black Forest* 368
2 Badenweiler 369
3 Titisee 371
4 Triberg 375

*Wunderhiking in the Black
Forest* 376
5 Freudenstadt 377
6 Calw 380
7 Pforzheim 382
8 Baden-Baden 384

11   Heidelberg, Stuttgart & the Neckar Valley   392

1 Heidelberg 392
   Exploring on Two Wheels 395
2 Hirschhorn, Eberbach &
   Heilbrunn 403

3 Stuttgart 405
4 Tübingen 413
5 Schwäbisch Hall 416

12   Frankfurt   418

1 Orientation 418
2 Getting Around 419
   Fast Facts: Frankfurt 422
3 Where to Stay 423
   Family-Friendly Hotels 425
4 Where to Dine 428
   Family-Friendly Restaurants 431

5 Seeing the Sights 433
6 Sports & Outdoor Pursuits 437
7 Shopping 438
8 Frankfurt After Dark 439
9 Side Trips from Frankfurt 442
   Elvis in Bad Nauheim 453

13   The Rhineland   455

1 Speyer 457
   Cruising the Rhine 458
2 Worms 459

3 Mainz 463
4 The Rheingau 468
5 Koblenz 471

6 Bonn 475   9 Cologne 487
7 Bad Godesberg 481   *Beer Taverns* 496
8 Aachen (Aix-la-Chapelle) 482   10 Düsseldorf 500

14   The Mosel Valley   510

1 Cochem 512   4 Traben-Trarbach 516
2 Beilstein 514   5 Bernkastel-Kues 517
3 Zell 515   6 Trier (Treves) 518

15   Bremen, Lower Saxony & North Hesse   526

1 Bremen 526   6 Bad Pyrmont 548
2 Lüneburg 535   7 Goslar 550
   The Lüneburg Heath 537   8 Göttingen 553
3 Celle 538   9 Bad Wildungen 557
4 Hannover 540   10 The Fairy-Tale Road 559
5 Hameln 546

16   Hamburg   562

1 Orientation 562   4 Seeing the Sights 579
   Neighborhoods in Brief 564   5 Sports & Outdoor Pursuits 583
   Fast Facts: Hamburg 565   6 Shopping 584
2 Where to Stay 568   7 Hamburg After Dark 586
   Family-Friendly Hotels 570   *The Reeperbahn: A Walk on the
3 Where to Dine 574   Wild Side* 588
   Family-Friendly Restaurants 575

17   Schleswig-Holstein   594

1 Lübeck 595   4 The Island of Sylt 607
2 Kiel 602   *A Disappearing Playground* 609
3 Schleswig 605

18   A Scenic Drive Along the Baltic   613

1 Wismar 613   4 Stralsund 620
2 Schwerin 615   5 Rügen 622
3 Rostock 618

Appendix A: Germany In Depth   624

1 History 101 624   *The Best of the Wurst* 635
   Dateline 625   *O' Zapfstisl ("The Barrel Is
2 In Pursuit of Artistic Excellence 629   Tapped")* 636
3 A Taste of Germany 633   4 Recommended Books 638

| Appendix B: Useful Terms & Phrases | 640 |

1 Glossary 640   2 Menu Terms 641

Index   644

List of Maps

Germany   14

Berlin Neighborhoods   68

Western Berlin Accommodations &
  Dining   76

Berlin-Mitte Accommodations &
  Dining   87

Attractions in Charlottenburg   101

Attractions in Berlin-Mitte   105

Attractions Around the Tiergarten   107

Potsdam   137

Saxony & Thuringia   141

Weimar   143

Leipzig   153

Dresden   165

The Zwinger   167

Franconia & the German Danube   181

Nürnberg   193

The Romantic Road   214

Würzburg   217

Rothenburg ob der Tauber   229

Augsburg   241

Munich Neighborhoods   254

Munich U-Bahn & S-Bahn   257

Munich Accommodations &
  Dining   266

Munich Attractions   282

The Residenz   285

Deutsches Museum   288

The Bavarian Alps   311

Lake Constance   341

The Black Forest   363

The Neckar Valley   393

Heidelberg   397

Stuttgart   407

Frankfurt   420

The Rhineland   456

Cologne   489

Düsseldorf   501

The Mosel Valley   511

Lower Saxony & North Hesse   527

Bremen   529

Hamburg Accommodations &
  Dining   566

Attractions in Central Hamburg   581

Schleswig-Holstein   595

Driving Along the Baltic   614

AN INVITATION TO THE READER

In researching this book, we discovered many wonderful places—hotels, restaurants, shops, and more. We're sure you'll find others. Please tell us about them, so we can share the information with your fellow travelers in upcoming editions. If you were disappointed with a recommendation, we'd love to know that too. Please write to:

Frommer's Germany 2001
IDG Books Worldwide
909 Third Avenue
New York, NY 10022

AN ADDITIONAL NOTE

Please be advised that travel information is subject to change at any time—and this is especially true of prices. We therefore suggest that you write or call ahead for confirmation when making your travel plans. The authors, editors, and publisher cannot be held responsible for the experiences of readers while traveling. Your safety is important to us, however, so we encourage you to stay alert and be aware of your surroundings. Keep a close eye on cameras, purses, and wallets, all favorite targets of thieves and pickpockets.

WHAT THE SYMBOLS MEAN

✪ Frommer's Favorites

Our favorite places and experiences—outstanding for quality, value, or both.

The following abbreviations are used for credit cards:

AE	American Express	EC	Eurocard
CB	Carte Blanche	JCB	Japan Credit Bank
DC	Diners Club	MC	MasterCard
DISC	Discover	V	Visa

FIND FROMMER'S ONLINE

www.frommers.com offers up-to-the-minute listings on almost 200 cities around the globe—including the latest bargains and candid, personal articles updated daily by Arthur Frommer himself. No other Web site offers such comprehensive and timely coverage of the world of travel.

The Best of Germany

A unified, wealthy, industrial yet beautiful Germany awaits you, promising some of the most interesting travel experiences in Europe. Many of the country's historical and architectural treasures were lost during World War II, but much remains and much has been restored. In addition, German natural scenery, particularly in the Black Forest, the Mosel Valley, the Harz Mountains, and the Bavarian Alps, is a potent lure.

In the closing years of the 20th century, since East and West Germany were finally reunited in October 1990, the country has been growing and changing at an astonishing pace. The nation's capital has been relocated from Bonn to Berlin. Berlin's refurbished Reichstag, which in the spring of 1999 became the seat of German Parliament, in many ways represents the changing mood of the nation. Its new glass dome glitters as a symbol of modernity. Berliners celebrated the Reichstag's rededication, not with patriotic glory and pomp but with an oompah band, meatballs, and beer.

For those who want to see history in the making, we recommend visiting Potsdam, Leipzig, Dresden, Meissen, and Weimar, all centers of East Germany before unification. Keep in mind, however, that although political developments have been fast-paced, the infrastructure of the eastern states has not fully risen to western German levels, and living standards here are still different from those in the former West Germany.

Finally, remember that though this guide is meant to help you decide where to go in Germany and how best to enjoy its charms, ultimately the most gratifying rewards will be your own serendipitous discoveries—drinking beer in a yard shaded by chestnut trees, picnicking in a Bavarian meadow, or spending time chatting with a winemaker in the Mosel Valley. The German people are among the world's most sophisticated and interesting. You'll likely remember your experiences with them for years to come.

1 The Best Travel Experiences

- **Exploring the New Berlin:** Anyone who lived through the neuroses of the Cold War can't help but shudder at the memory of the Berlin Wall. Since reunification, civic planners, with almost manic enthusiasm, have demolished large sections of what stood for 40 years as a scar across the face of a defeated nation. The architectural changes and urban developments that are constantly updating the cityscape around Berlin's Friedrichstrasse and Potsdamer Platz can be confusing. But regardless of which renewal program is churning up rubble at the time of your visit, a pilgrimage through what used to be the most bitterly contested urban turf in Europe can't help but provoke powerful emotions. See chapter 3.

- **Dreaming on a Midsummer's Night in a Biergarten:** When the temperature rises, head immediately for the unpretentious cheer of the nearest biergarten. These watering holes, which often feature trellises, climbing vines, Chinese lanterns, and arbors, offer low-cost fun on soft summer nights. You can order platters of hearty food with your beer or bring your own picnic. Everybody in Germany seems to have his or her favorite, but some of the best are in Bamberg and Munich. See chapters 5 and 7.

- **Cruising the Elbe, the Danube, and the Rhine:** This trio of rivers, along with their tributaries, dominated German commerce for hundreds of years. Today, an armada of tugboats, barges, and cruise ships still ply the muddy waters beside riverbanks lined with the historic majesty (and sometimes the industrial might) of Central Europe. Cruises begin and end at large cities of historic interest and last anywhere from 6 hours to 7 days. **KD River Cruises of Europe (☎ 800/ 346-6525** in the U.S., or 0221/20881 in Cologne) offers the most services. See chapters 5 and 13.

- **Boating on the Königssee:** A romantic poet would praise this lake, near Berchtesgaden in Bavaria, for the forest-covered mountains that surround its cold, deep, dark waters. The baroque chapels and fairy-tale hamlets on its shores supplement its natural grandeur. The boat you ride will be powered by very quiet electric motors, so that you can hear the extraordinary echoes that bounce off the rock faces. See chapter 8.

- **Hiking in the Bavarian Alps:** In summer, alpine hiking is a major attraction in Germany. Hikers are able to observe firsthand a variety of wildlife, often including endangered species. One of the best areas for hiking is the 1,237m (4,060-foot) Eckbauer, lying on the southern fringe of Partenkirchen. The tourism office in Garmisch-Partenkirchen will supply maps and details. Many visitors come in summer to hike through the Berchtesgaden National Park, bordering the Austrian province of Salzburg. See chapter 8.

- **Ascending the Zugspitze:** If the gentle inclines of the Harz Mountains or the Thuringian forests aren't dramatic enough for you, ride the cable car from Garmisch-Partenkirchen to the top of Germany's tallest mountain at 2,963m (9,720 feet) above sea level. The view from the top is suitably panoramic, and you'll find an appealing aura of German-ness that comes from the many hill climbers and trekkers who fan out across the hiking trails. See chapter 8.

- **Taking the Waters at a Spa:** In Germany, the question isn't whether to visit a spa, but rather, which spa to visit? Each resort has its own virtues and historical associations and can supply a list of the health benefits associated with its awful-tasting waters. Regardless of your choice, you'll emerge from your treatment with a more relaxed attitude and a greater appreciation of German efficiency and German sensuality. The most famous spa is in Baden-Baden. See chapter 10.

- **Motoring Along the Neckar:** The Neckar River meanders through about 80km (50 miles) of some of Germany's most famous vineyards. But the real appeal of the winding road along the water is in the medieval castles scattered along the way. Highlights en route include Heidelberg, Neckarsteinach, Hirschhorn, Eberbach, Zwingenberg, and Burg Hornberg. Don't forget to stop en route for samplings of the local wines. See chapter 11.

- **Spending Harvest Time in the German Vineyards:** Springtime in Germany brings the promise of bounty to the legendary vineyards of the Rhine and Mosel Valleys, but the autumn harvest is truly the time to visit. Between late August and mid-October, the banks of the rivers turn gold and russet, and armies of workers gather buckets of grapes from the rows of carefully pruned vines. Most of the medieval villages and historic castles scattered between Koblenz and Trier are associated with estates where the new wines can be sampled. See chapters 13 and 14.

- **Touring the Fairy-Tale Road (Märchenstrasse):** This is one of the newer marketing ideas of the German tourist authorities, but considering its appeal, you'll wonder why they didn't think of it earlier. From the town of Hanau (a 30-minute drive northeast of Frankfurt), the route zigzags northward along the Weser River for about 600km (375 miles) through some of Germany's most evocative folkloric architecture, terminating in Bremen. Scores of well-marked detours pepper the way. Required reading for the trip is a collection of the fairy tales of the Brothers Grimm and the Nibelungen legends. Don't overlook the psychological implications of Goldilocks, the Big Bad Wolf, and the Pied Piper of Hameln. See chapter 15.

- **Lounging on the Island of Sylt:** Don't expect a lush or verdant island—the climate is temperamental, the setting is savage, the winds blow cold from the north even in summer, and the grasses that manage to survive in the sandy dunes are as weathered and sturdy as the soldiers in a Prussian regiment. Why is it wonderful? Because here, the no-nonsense residents of north Germany can preen, flutter, and show off to each other, far from the strictures of their workplaces and the hardworking grind of their economic miracle. See chapter 17.

2 The Best Museums

Financial prosperity, artistic flair, and academic curiosity have helped the Germans develop some of the finest museums anywhere.

- **Gemäldegalerie,** Berlin: This is one of Europe's leading art museums, with a celebrated collection of works from the 13th to the 18th centuries. Divided during the Cold War, since mid-1998 the collection has been reunited in one home. The lighting and the displays are better than ever. The cavalcade of major European masters ranges from Botticelli and Breughel to Vermeer and Velásquez. See chapter 3.

- **Pergamon Museum,** Berlin: Built in 1930 on an island in the Spree, this museum contains entirely reconstructed temples from ancient Assyria, Greece, Rome, and Sumer. And don't miss the sprawling exhibitions devoted to the ancient art of the Islamic world and the Far East. See chapter 3.

- **The Zwinger,** Dresden: A vast rectangular esplanade flanked with pavilions, heroic statues, formal gardens, and galleries, this museum was designed for Augustus the Strong (Elector of Saxony and King of Poland) by his favorite architect, Pöppelmann (1662–1736). The destruction of the Zwinger, one of Dresden's most beautiful buildings, in the final days of World War II was a great loss. Its postwar reconstruction was a triumph for the East German government. Among the treasures amassed inside are paintings, 18th-century Dresden porcelain, and an ornamental collection of antique weapons. See chapter 4.

- **Deutsches Museum,** Munich: Since 1925, this museum has been one of the most important showcases of science and technology in the world. Occupying an island in the Isar River, it features dozens of workable exhibits that go through their paces at the touch of a button. See chapter 7.

- **Old Pinakothek,** Alte Pinakothek, Munich: This massive and symmetrical building is one of the most visible in Munich, with a wraparound garden where urbanites like to walk during lunch hour. Inside is a staggering assortment of important paintings from every era, scattered over two sprawling floors of dignified splendor. See chapter 7.
- **Dachau Concentration Camp,** Dachau, near Munich: Heinrich Himmler first organized Dachau as a concentration camp for enemies of the Reich in 1933. An escaped inmate, Joseph Rovan, described it as "implacable, perverted, an organization that was totally murderous, a marvelous machine for the debasement and dehumanizing of man." Today, it's one of the most poignant museums in the world. See chapter 7.
- **Stadtische Galerie im Lenbachhaus,** Munich: Housed in the former villa of portrait painter Franz von Lenbach, this museum has a stunning and internationally renowned collection of modern art, including the Blaue Reiter ("Blue Rider") period, best represented by Kandinsky. It also has a rich collection of Gothic art works as well. See chapter 7.
- **Staatsgalerie Moderner Kunst,** State Gallery of Modern Art, Munich: In the west wing of the sprawling Haus der Kunst is the State Gallery of Modern Art for Bavaria. It has one of Germany's finest collections of 20th-century art and sculpture—everything from Klee to Kirchner. Its east wing is devoted to changing exhibitions, some of the most stunning in Europe. See chapter 7.
- **Gutenberg Museum,** Mainz: This museum is one of the most comprehensive tributes to printing and publishing anywhere in the world. The bulky presses on which Johannes Gutenberg used movable type (42 lines per page) and two of the earliest Bibles ever printed are the primary displays here. There's also a historical rundown on the science and technologies that have dominated the printing industry ever since. See chapter 13.
- **Wallraf-Richartz Museum/Ludwig Museum,** Cologne: This museum, with two intertwining collections on three floors of an 1880s building, is the oldest in Germany. It showcases German art from 1300 to the present. It's best to approach the sprawling collection with a firm notion of your own artistic priorities. The building also contains a museum of photography. See chapter 13.
- **Kunsthalle,** Hamburg: The leading art museum in Northern Germany, the Kunsthalle is one of the most important in Europe, with some 3,000 paintings in its treasure trove of art, along with some 400 sculptures. Some of its rare treasures date from the 14th century, including works by Bertram, the leading German master of the time. One section of the gallery also displays modern works, including art by such artists as Andy Warhol, Joseph Beuys, and Picasso. See chapter 16.

3 The Best Castles & Palaces

During the Middle Ages, Germany was divided into many intensely competitive feudal states and principalities. This unstable atmosphere encouraged the construction of fortified castles. As hostilities died down, architects began to design for comfort, style, and prestige, adding large windows, gilded stucco and plaster, frescoes, and formal gardens. As a result, Germany is full of all kinds and styles of castles (*burg*) and palaces (*schloss*).

- **Sans-Souci,** Potsdam: Frederick the Great's retreat, where he came to read, to listen to music, and generally to renew his allegiance to the principles of the Enlightenment, is Germany's most successful blend of landscape and architecture. The more than 120ha (300 acres) of intricately landscaped gardens have enough pavilions, fountains, orangeries, and heroic statues to keep a visitor intrigued for days. Its architectural highlight is the palace itself, approached by a terraced staircase of sublime beauty. See chapter 4.

- **Schloss Wartburg,** Eisenach: Built between 1067 and the 16th century, this was the headquarters of the Landgraves of Thuringia, a center of patronage for the troubadours (*minnesinger*) of Germany, and a place of refuge for Martin Luther, who completed his translation of the Bible within its massive walls. Wagner used it as inspiration for the setting of *Tannhäuser*, and Johann Sebastian Bach and Goethe both visited. Today, from its position on a rocky hilltop, it's a regional museum. See chapter 4.

- **Residenz,** Würzburg Palace, Würzburg: Built between 1720 and 1744 as the official residence of the powerful bishops of Würzburg, this is one of the most massive baroque palaces in Germany. It combines a chapel (*Hofkirche*) with gardens, a gallery of paintings, frescoes by Tiepolo, and enough decoration to satisfy the most demanding taste for ornamentation. Also within its showrooms are a worthy collection of ancient Greek and Roman artifacts and valuable paintings from the 14th to the 19th century. See chapter 6.

- **Neuschwanstein,** near Füssen: When the creators of California's Disneyland needed an inspiration for their fairy-tale castle, this is the model they picked. Neuschwanstein is the most lavishly romantic (and impractical) castle in the German-speaking world. A 19th-century theatrical set designer drew it up in a neofeudal style. The man who ordered its construction was (who else?) "Mad" King Ludwig II of Bavaria. See chapter 6.

- **Hohenschwangau Castle,** near Füssen: It was completed in 1836, and built on the ruins of a 12th-century fortress. Its patron was the youthful prince regent, Maximilian II of Bavaria, who used it to indulge his taste for "troubadour romanticism" and the life of the English country manor. See chapter 6.

- **Schloss Nymphenburg,** Munich: It was originally conceived and constructed between 1664 and 1674 as an Italian-inspired summer home for the Bavarian monarchs. Subsequent Bavarian kings added on to its structure until around 1780, by which time the building and its lavish park bore a close resemblance to the French palace at Versailles. A highlight of the interior is the green, gold, and white banqueting hall, whose frescoes and ornate stucco are among the most memorable in Bavaria. See chapter 7.

- **Schloss Linderhof,** near Oberammergau: This palace was built in the 1870s as a teenage indulgence by Ludwig II. Its architects created a whimsically eclectic fantasy, inspired by Italian baroque architecture. In the surrounding park, Moorish pavilions and Mediterranean cascades appear against alpine vistas in combinations that are as startling as they are charming. See chapter 8.

- **Altes Schloss,** Meersburg: Legend has it that its cornerstone was laid by Dagobert, king of the Franks, in 628. The castle remained a Catholic stronghold even during the Protestant Reformation, housing bishops who appreciated its 3m- (10-foot-) thick walls as a bulwark against the rising tempest around them. In the early 1800s, its owners threatened to tear the castle down, until a German Romantic, Baron Joseph von Lassberg, bought it and transformed it into a refuge for writers, poets, and painters. Although still a private residence, many parts can be visited. See chapter 9.

- **Heidelberg Castle,** Heidelberg: This castle originated as a Gothic-Renaissance masterpiece in the 1500s and was massively expanded as rival rulers competed for control of the Rhineland. After the French sacked and burned the town and the castle in 1689, it never regained its original glory. Today, from a position on a rocky hilltop high above the student revelry and the taverns of the folkloric city below, the ruins brood in dignified severity. See chapter 11.

- **Burg Eltz,** Moselkern, near Cochem: Its multiple turrets and towers, which rise amid a thick forest near the Mosel River, evoke the chivalry and poetry of the Middle Ages. This is one of the best-preserved medieval castles in Germany. See chapter 14.

4 The Best Cathedrals

- **Ulm Cathedral,** Ulm: The 160m (528-foot) spire of this cathedral is the tallest in the world. Although its foundations were laid in 1377, this skyscraper wasn't completed vertically until 1890. See chapter 5.
- **Speyer Cathedral,** Speyer: Partly because of their age, Romanesque churches are the most impressive symbols of early medieval Germany. This massive church, dating from 1030, has four bell towers, a cornerstone laid by one of Germany's earliest kings, Konrad II, and an undeniable sense of the (anonymous) architect's aesthetic links with the traditions of ancient Rome. See chapter 13.
- **Worms Cathedral,** Worms: The western chancel, completed in 1230, is the oldest Romanesque structure in Germany. The Diet of Worms, held here in 1521, condemned the beliefs of the young Martin Luther and banished him to the far boundaries of the Holy Roman Empire. See chapter 13.
- **Cologne Cathedral,** Cologne: Based on French Gothic models in Paris and Amiens, this cathedral was envisioned as one of the largest religious buildings in Christendom. It required 600 years to finish—work stopped for approximately 300 years (1560 to 1842), until the neo-Gothic fervor of the romantic age drove it to completion. In 1880 it was inaugurated with appropriate pomp and circumstance in the presence of the German kaiser. Today, its vast russet-colored bulk towers above the city, instantly recognizable from miles away. See chapter 13.
- **Imperial Cathedral,** Aachen: Its size and the stonework dating from 1414 are deeply impressive, but even more so is the cathedral's association with the earliest of the German emperors, Charlemagne. He was crowned in an older building on this site in A.D. 800. The cathedral's treasury contains gem-encrusted Christian artifacts from the 10th century whose heft and barbaric glitter evoke pre-Christian Germania. See chapter 13.

5 The Most Charming Small Villages

- **Quedlinburg:** Spared in part from the ravages of World War II, this Harz town still evokes the Middle Ages, with its 1,600 half-timbered buildings, more than any other town in the country. Named a UNESCO World Heritage Site, Quedlinburg is a gem of yesterday, and was an imperial residence for two centuries. Wander the cobblestone streets of Altstadt (old town) for a journey back in time. See chapter 4.
- **Meissen:** Some 26km (16 miles) north of Dresden, this is a romantic little town built along the banks of the River Elbe. It's celebrated for its porcelain, carrying a trademark of two crossed blue swords and valued by collectors the world over. Even without its porcelain factory, the town merits a visit for its quiet charm, its old buildings, and its 15th-century castle. See chapter 4.

- **Dinkelsbühl:** This beautifully preserved medieval town lies along the Romantic Road. It's not as grand as the more celebrated Rothenburg, but it manages to retain more old-time charm. See chapter 6.
- **Mittenwald:** This town has long been celebrated as the most beautiful in the Bavarian Alps. Its magnificently decorated houses have painted facades and ornately carved gables. In the mid–17th century it was known as "The Village of a Thousand Violins" because of the stringed instruments made here. See chapter 8.
- **Lindau:** This beautiful lakeside town lies at the eastern end of Lake Constance. It once sheltered Roman ships of war and trade. One part of Lindau is known as the "Gartenstadt," because of its luxuriant flowers and shrubs. See chapter 9.
- **Rüdesheim:** The Rhine Valley's most justifiably popular wine town is set along the edge of the mighty river. Rüdesheim is known for its half-timbered buildings and its Drosselgasse, or "Thrush Lane," a narrow cobblestone lane stretching for 200 yards and lined with wine taverns and cozy restaurants. See chapter 13.
- **Cochem:** The medieval riverside town is famous for its huge castle, which dates from 1027. With its many country inns serving a regional cuisine along with plenty of Mosel wine, this is your best bet for a stopover along the Mosel River, which many visitors prefer to the more commercial Rhine. See chapter 14.

6 The Best Driving Tours

The appeal of the open road is a prominent part of German culture today, much as it is in America.

- **The Romantic Road:** This well-traveled route, which stretches between the Main River and the beginning of the Bavarian Alps, is dotted with lovely medieval towns. See chapter 6.
- **Alpine Road (Deutsche Alpenstrasse):** Follow it for more than 480km (300 miles), through the foothills of the Bavarian Alps and the Allgäu. Scenic majesty and architectural charm combine for an unforgettable experience. See chapter 8.
- **Upper Black Forest:** Fairy tales always seem to be more believable when you're in the Black Forest. The twisting secondary roads that connect Freiburg with Lake Titisee pass through lots of charming scenery and architecture. See chapter 10.
- **Mosel Valley:** The road along this Rhine tributary passes by some of the country's most famous vineyards. At least a half dozen of the cities en route are worth visiting. See chapter 14.

7 The Best Walks

- **Mainau Island:** A walk across the footbridge to Mainau, in Lake Constance, is like a visit to a tropical country. Mainau is filled with exotic plants collected by the Baden princes and members of the Royal House of Sweden. Tropical brushwood and other botanical wonders still thrive in this mild climate. You'll hardly believe you're in Germany. See chapter 9.
- **Partnachklamm:** One of the most dramatic walks in all of the Bavarian Alps starts from the great winter sports resort of Garmisch-Partenkirchen. A signposted trail leads to the dramatic Partnachklamm Gorge. Carved from solid rock, the route passes two panoramic bottlenecks amid the thunder of falling water and clouds of spray. See chapter 8.
- **Cochem:** The Reichsburg castle, which towers over the little town of Cochem, can be reached on foot in about 45 minutes from the town's Markplatz, or market square. Although hardly an alpine climb, this walk is one of the

most rewarding you'll find in Germany, with panoramas in all directions. See chapter 14.

- **The Royal Castle Walk:** For one of the grandest panoramas in all of the Alps (in any country), hike up to the Marienbrücke, the bridge that spans the Pöllat Gorge behind Neuschwanstein Castle. From there, if you're up to it, you can continue uphill for about an hour for an amazing view of "Mad" King Ludwig's fantasy castle. See chapter 6.

8 The Best Biking

- **Munich by Bike:** So many locals can be spotted riding bikes that Munich at first appears to be the biking capital of Germany. If you'd like to join in the fun, pick up a copy of the pamphlet *Radl-Touren für unsere Gäste* (available at the tourist office), which outlines itineraries for touring Munich by bike. See chapter 7.
- **Lake Constance:** Rent a bike at the train station in the former imperial town of Lindau and set out in any direction to enjoy the views of this beautiful lake. The Lindau tourist office will provide you with a map and suggestions for the best routes to follow. See chapter 9.
- **The Neckar Valley Cycle Path:** This signposted path allows you to follow the source of the Neckar, beginning in Villingen-Schwenningen and going all the way to the confluence of the Rhine at Mannheim. Instead of going the whole way, many visitors prefer to pick up a bicycle in Heidelberg and cycle along the river banks until they find a good spot for a picnic. See chapter 11.
- **Lüneburg Heath:** This wild heath in northern Germany is one of the country's major natural attractions. Rent a bike and pick up a map at the Lüneburg tourist office and set out on your adventure. Some of Germany's greatest poets have waxed rhapsodic about this shrub-covered land. See chapter 15.

9 The Best Spas

- **Bad Reichenhall:** Many spa lovers head for this remote corner of Bavaria to "take the waters." Europe's largest saline source was first tapped here in pre-Christian times. There's a definite 19th-century aura to the place. See chapter 8.
- **Baden-Baden:** There's no better spa in all of Germany, and certainly none more fashionable or famous. Baden-Baden is also the site of the country's most celebrated casino. The spa's been going strong ever since the leisure class of the 19th century discovered its healing waters, although the Roman legions of the emperor Caracalla had discovered the springs here long before that. See chapter 10.
- **Wiesbaden:** One of Germany's oldest cities, Wiesbaden attracted Roman legions to its hot springs, and continues to lure today's fashionable traveler as well. It's not as chic as Baden-Baden, but Wiesbaden still has one of Germany's most elegant casinos and concert halls, along with two gourmet restaurants. In summer the beer garden at the Kurhaus is one of the most animated along the Rhine. See chapter 12.
- **Bad Homburg:** Bad Homburg lies at the foot of the Taunus Hills in a setting of medieval castles and luxuriant forests. There are more than 31 fountains in the town's Kurpark. The Bad Homburg Palace was once the summer residence of Prussian kings. See chapter 12.
- **Bad Nauheim:** What do Elvis Presley and William Randolph Hearst have in common? Both stayed at Bad Neuheim—the newspaper czar by choice, and Elvis by orders of the U.S. Army. The warm carbonic-acid springs are used in the treatment of heart and circulatory ailments and rheumatic diseases. See chapter 12.

10 The Best Luxury Hotels

German efficiency and cleanliness are legendary around the world, so it's not surprising that you can choose from a staggering number of well-managed hotels.

- **Four Seasons,** Berlin (☎ **800/332-3442** in the U.S., or 030/2-03-38): One of Germany's great new luxury hotels, this is all about opulence, superb service, and comfort. It's discreet, tasteful, reliable, and a brilliant addition to the roster of luxury leaders in Germany's capital. See chapter 3.
- **Kempinski Hotel Elephant,** Weimar (☎ **03643/80-20**): This is one of Germany's most interesting hotels because of its age (over 300 years), its name, its 50-year survival in Germany's eastern zone, and its associations with such luminaries as Schiller, Liszt, and Goethe. Today, it's a cost-conscious treasure chest of German history. See chapter 4.
- **Eisenhut,** Rothenburg ob der Tauber (☎ **09861/70-50**): This hotel's 16th-century walls and valuable collection of antiques enhance the appeal of the most authentic Renaissance town in Germany. See chapter 6.
- **Kempinski Hotel Vier Jahreszeiten München,** Munich (☎ **800/426-3135** in the U.S., or 089/2-12-50): Munich's most prestigious choice offers elegance and luxury. The wealthy and titled have checked in here for more than a century, enjoying the ambience, the antiques, the style, and the grace. See chapter 7.
- **Der Kleine Prinz,** Baden-Baden (☎ **07221/34-66-00**): This hotel's director once helped manage the New York Hilton and the Waldorf-Astoria. Today he and his wife run a century-old pair of neobaroque houses in the heart of Germany's most elegant resort, Baden-Baden. Der Kleine Prinz is among the most romantic of Germany's many Romantik Hotels. See chapter 10.
- **Krone Assmannshausen,** Rüdesheim-Assmannshausen (☎ **06722/40-30**): Sprawling along the banks of the Rhine in an oversized, grangelike, gingerbread-laden fantasy, this hotel has witnessed the arrival of many important Germans (including Goethe) in its 400-year history. The place also contains one of the best traditional restaurants in town. See chapter 13.
- **Park Hotel Bremen,** Bremen (☎ **0421/3-40-80**): Designed like an aristocratic manor house, this hotel lies within a 200ha (500-acre) city park. With infusions of grand bourgeois grace and impeccable service, it embodies the carefully maintained elegance of this North German trading port. See chapter 15.
- **Fürstenhof Celle,** Celle (☎ **05141/20-10**): This 17th-century manor, enlarged with half-timbered wings, stands out even in a town legendary for its medieval and Renaissance buildings. There's a cozy bar in the medieval cellar and one of the best dining rooms in Lower Saxony. See chapter 15.
- **Vier Jahreszeiten,** Hamburg (☎ **800/223-6800** in the U.S. and Canada, or 040/3-49-40): Its dignified interior is as opulent as its 19th-century facade. This hotel's appeal is correctly aristocratic, but it still has a touch of the saltwater zestiness that has made Hamburg a great city. See chapter 16.

11 The Best Small Inns & Hotels

- **Sorat Art'otel,** Berlin (☎ **030/88-44-70**): This hotel in the heart of Berlin is chic, discreet, and unique. The swirling action of the Ku'damm lies right outside the door, but inside the decor is soothing and serene, the work of some of the continent's top designers. See chapter 3.
- **Alstadt-Hotel Laubenwirt,** Passau (☎ **0851/33-70**): This inexpensive hotel stands at the convergence of three rivers—the Danube, the Ilz, and the Inn. But

the hotel offers more than river views. It's comfortably and traditionally furnished, and its regional cuisine and convivial pub attract the locals. See chapter 5.
- **Parkhotel Atlantic,** Heidelberg (☎ 06221/60-42-0): This 24-room inn is on the wooded outskirts of Heidelberg, near the famous castle. Comfort and convenience are found in every room, and in the afternoon you can go for long walks along the woodland trails surrounding the property. See chapter 11.
- **Admiral Hotel,** Wiesbaden (☎ 0611/5-86-60): A hotel of considerable charm, the Admiral offers the best value in this fashionable spa resort outside Frankfurt. Rooms are charmingly old-fashioned. The owner is a retired U.S. army officer. See chapter 12.
- **Das Kleine Stapelhäuschen,** Cologne (☎ 0221/2-57-78-62): This inn, which stands on the site of Cologne's old fish market, was originally constructed in the 12th century by Scottish Benedictine monks. Today, it offers a slightly faded old-fashioned charm and much comfort—all at a reasonable price. See chapter 13.
- **Römischer Kaiser,** Trier (☎ 06531/9-68-60): This small century-old building enjoys a prime location in Germany's oldest city. Formerly a patrician house, it has been skillfully converted to an attractive and well-kept hotel. See chapter 14.
- **Hanseatic Hotel,** Hamburg (☎ 040/48-57-72): This little hotel evokes a prim and proper English gentleman's club. Rooms are one of a kind, often containing antiques. In summer, the owner can be spotted out front tending his flower garden, getting ready to welcome you. See chapter 16.

12 The Best Restaurants

- **Rockendorf's Gourmet Restaurant,** Berlin (☎ 030/21-99-21-70): During the latter days of the Cold War, this restaurant was often photographed as a symbol of the "good life" available within West Berlin. Since reunification, it has moved but is still elegant and refined, offering a creative cuisine to a clientele that includes the most important movers and shakers in Germany. See chapter 3.
- **Essigbrätiein,** Nürnberg (tel. 0911/22-51-31): Food critics single this out as the best dining spot in Nürnberg, and we concur heartily. Its upscale Franconian and continental cuisine is reason enough to go to the city in the first place. The cuisine is inventive and refreshing, and we'd make a detour for this one. See chapter 5.
- **Weinhaus Zum Stachel,** Würzburg (☎ 0931/5-27-70): This is the oldest (ca. 1413) wine house in a town loaded with them. Portions are copious, the wine flows, and everyone has a wonderful time. It's old-time Deutschland at its most appealing. See chapter 6.
- **Tantris,** Munich (☎ 089/361-95-90): Savvy German food critics have honored Tantris's Hans Haas as the country's top chef. He serves some of the finest and most innovative food in Bavaria. See chapter 7.
- **Seehotel Siber,** Constance (☎ 07531/6-30-44): Bertold Siber remains one of the leading chefs of Germany, certainly without peer along the northern tier of Lake Constance. Both the service and the cuisine exhibit amazing attention to detail. See chapter 9.
- **Goldener Pflug,** Merheim, near Cologne (☎ 0221/89-55-09): The gold-plated building was once a modest tavern but now is a comfortable enclave of fine dining. The cuisine is sumptuous and sophisticated. See chapter 13.
- **Victorian Restaurant,** Düsseldorf (☎ 0211/8-65-50-22): Regulars know what a treasure they have in this restaurant. Market-fresh ingredients and a steady hand in the kitchen produce award-winning traditional and modern food. See chapter 13.

- **Fischereihafen,** Altona, near Hamburg (☎ **040/38-18-16**): Patrons from Tina Turner to Helmut Kohl have pronounced the food here delightful. From a window seat, you can overlook the boats that might have hauled in your sole, eel, turbot, herring, or flounder from the seas that very day. See chapter 16.

13 The Best Beer Halls & Taverns

- **Auerbachs Keller,** Leipzig (☎ **0341/21-61-00**): The most famous tavern in eastern Germany, this is where Goethe staged the debate between Faust and Mephistopheles. The tavern dates from 1530 and has a series of murals evoking the Faust legend. See chapter 4.
- **Hofbräuhaus am Platzl,** Munich (☎ **089/22-16-76**): The Hofbräuhaus is the world's most famous beer hall and can accommodate some 4,500 beer drinkers on any given night. Music from live bands and huge mugs of beer served at wooden tables combine to produce the best of Bavarian nighttime fun. See chapter 7.
- **Zum Roten Ochsen,** Heidelberg (☎ **06221/2-09-77**): Over the years, "The Red Ox" has drawn beer drinkers from Mark Twain to Bismarck. Students have been getting plastered here since 1703, and the tradition continues just as strong as ever. See chapter 11.
- **Ratskeller,** Göttingen (☎ **0551/5-64-33**): The beer in the town of Göttingen flows freely in many taverns, but this place is the most reliable. This 600-year-old spot lies in the cellar of the historic town hall. See chapter 15.
- **Bayrisch Zell,** Hamburg (☎ **040/31-42-81**): It doesn't quite have the charm of the fabled Hofbräuhaus in Munich, but after all, this is northern Germany. The bustling place seats 1,200, and on many nights there seems to be a lot more people here. It's one of the safe places in the notorious St. Pauli district. See chapter 16.

14 The Best Shopping

Germany is neither a shopper's mecca nor the bargain basement of Europe, but it has some good buys. The best way to approach shopping is to make it a part of your overall experience and not an end unto itself. Berlin and Munich are the major shopping centers.

- **Porcelain:** For centuries, Germany has been known for the quality of its porcelain. Names such as KPM, Rosenthal, and Meissen are household words. KPM, for example, has been a Berlin tradition for more than 2 centuries.
- **Timepieces:** Corny though they may be, carved Black Forest cuckoo clocks remain an enduring favorite. Germany, like Switzerland, is also known for its precision watches, which can be good buys. See chapter 10.
- **Cutlery:** WMF (Württembergische-Metalwaren-Fabrik) and J. A. Henckels are two of the country's premier producers of fine cutlery. Their knives are expensive, but longtime users say they last forever. WMF stores are found all over Germany.
- **Handcrafts:** In the Bavarian Alps, woodcarvers still carry on their time-honored tradition. The best place to purchase wood carvings is in the alpine village of Oberammergau. See chapter 8.
- **Optical Products:** German precision is best exemplified in its microscopes, binoculars, and other such precisely calibrated products.
- **Toys:** Nürnberg, the country's toy center, produces some of the most imaginative playthings in the world. See chapter 5.

2 Planning Your Trip: The Basics

This chapter covers everything you need to know to make trip-planning a snap, from when to go to how to shop for the best airfare. Browse through it to get started and make sure you've touched all the bases.

1 The Regions in Brief

Germany lies in the heart of Europe, bordered by Switzerland and Austria to the south; France, Luxembourg, Belgium, and the Netherlands to the west; Denmark to the north; and Poland and the Czech Republic to the east. The country encompasses 356,216 square km (137,535 square miles) and has a population of about 80 million.

BERLIN & POTSDAM

Berlin has once more taken its place as Germany's capital and cultural center. It beckons visitors with glorious museums, wonderful cultural offerings, and cutting-edge nightlife. Southwest of Berlin is Potsdam, with its famous palace and elegant gardens and parks, set in an idyllic landscape along the Havel River.

THURINGIA

Long a tourist mecca for workers from the Eastern bloc countries, Thuringia, with its untouched villages, churches, and medieval fortress ruins, is now being discovered by Westerners. If your idea of East Germany was nothing but grim industrial cities and cheap housing projects, be prepared for a surprise. Here you can still see the small towns once known to Luther, Bach, and Wagner. The region's densely forested mountains are prime hiking country. The cultural center, with many attractions, is the city of Weimar, once the bastion of such greats as Walter Gropius, Miës van der Rohe, Liszt, Goethe, and Schiller.

SAXONY: LEIPZIG & DRESDEN

Known for its annual trade fair that draws participants from around the world, Leipzig is the most important industrial center in the east after Berlin. But this city, once the home of Bach, is also a cultural treasure, with museums, old churches, and Thomanerchor (the famous boys' choir). For those who find Berlin too overwhelming, Leipzig offers an excellent alternative.

But if it's a choice between Leipzig and Dresden, make it Dresden, still one of the most beautiful cities in Germany, though 80% of its center was destroyed in an infamous 1945 Allied air raid. In fact, the remaining ruins form one of its attractions. Kurt Vonnegut's *Slaughterhouse Five* told the story of Dresden's destruction and makes good reading before heading here. Today, Dresden is bouncing back—and fast.

FRANCONIA & THE GERMAN DANUBE

Some of Germany's greatest medieval and Renaissance treasures came from this region, which gave the world such artists as Albrecht Dürer and Lucas Cranach. Come here to visit some of the most beautiful and historical towns in Germany, notably Regensburg, Bamberg, Nürnberg, and Bayreuth, where Wagner built his theater and created his Festspiel, the famous opera festival. But if you can only visit one town, head for Würzburg, Germany's baroque city. (Würzburg is also the ideal starting point of a tour of the Romantic Road; see below.) Located on the banks of the Main River, this glorious old city is overlooked by a fortified castle. Regensburg, 100km (62 miles) southeast of Nürnberg, is also worth a visit, though tourists often pass it by. It suffered no major bombings in World War II, and so remains one of the best preserved cities in Germany. Nürnberg, although it holds much of interest today with its many preserved art treasures, was heavily bombed and had to be virtually rebuilt. The Danube, which flows through this region, isn't blue and doesn't have the allure, dramatic scenery, or castles of the Rhine, but it's worth exploring for its own quiet charm.

THE ROMANTIC ROAD

One of the most scenically beautiful but also one of the most overrun attractions in Germany, the Romantic Road (Romantische Strasse) winds its way south from Würzburg to the little town of Füssen at the foot of the Bavarian Alps. Along the way, Rothenburg ob der Tauber is one of the most splendidly preserved medieval towns in Europe, and as if that weren't enough, the road comes to an end at "Mad" King Ludwig's most fantastic creation: Neuschwanstein Castle. The idea of the "Romantic Road," originally a bit of PR hype to promote the area, was launched in 1950. It was such a success that the road is now clogged with traffic in summer, so the trip is best made in spring or autumn, before the tour buses arrive. (If you want an admittedly less scenic, but still charming, "romantic road," try the "Fairy-Tale Road" in Lower Saxony and North Hesse.) The region of the Romantic Road is known for its folk traditions, old-world charm, and unspoiled medieval towns still surrounded by their original walls. Despite its drawbacks, the road remains one of the most beautiful and interesting trails in all Europe.

MUNICH & THE BAVARIAN ALPS

Rebuilt from the rubble of World War II, Munich is one of the most visited cities of Europe, and probably the best place in Germany for old-fashioned fun. It should be included even on the briefest of itineraries. As chic and cosmopolitan as Frankfurt or Berlin, Munich is also kitschy in the best sense of Bavarian tradition. A night at the Hofbräuhaus, Germany's most fabled beer hall, with its liter mugs and oompah bands, will get you into the spirit of Munich life. After strolling through the Englischer Garten and having a glass of Bavarian wine in Schwabing (the legendary artists' district), you can tackle Munich's vast array of museums and palaces. Save time for the Deutsches

Germany

Museum, the largest technological museum in the world. Munich also lies at the gateway to the Bavarian Alps. The best resorts are Berchtesgaden and Garmisch-Partenkirchen. Shimmering alpine lakes, half-timbered houses frescoed with paintings, picture-postcard towns like Mittenwald and Oberammergau are all here, plus hiking, nature, wildlife, and alpine-ski trails in winter.

LAKE CONSTANCE (BODENSEE)

The 260km (162-mile) coastline of the Bodensee is shared with Austria and Switzerland, but Germany got the best part, the lake's beautiful northern rim. A boat trip on the Bodensee, although not comparable to a Rhine cruise, is a major attraction. The tour takes in castles as well as towns built on islands near the shoreline. The best center is Lindau at the southeastern part, near the Austrian frontier. Reached by a causeway, this island town has the most luxuriant growth of flowers and shrubs of any resort along the lake. But Konstanz, the largest city on the lake, also merits a visit, since it's one of the best-preserved major medieval cities in Germany.

THE BLACK FOREST (SCHWARZWALD)

This dense fir forest, filled with beauty, charm, and myth, actually receives more sunshine than most other forests in Germany. The major center of the region is Freiburg, but the most visited city is the elegant resort, Baden-Baden. Black Forest cake and smoked ham might be reason enough to visit the area, but there are many other allures as well, including casino gambling, great spas, and plenty of hiking, bicycling, and cross-country skiing. Freiburg im Breisgau remains one of the most beautiful and historic towns in Germany and makes the best center for exploring the region. If you want a Black Forest cuckoo clock—just as good as the ones touted in Switzerland—head for Triberg and the Haus der 1,000 Uhren (House of 1,000 Clocks).

HEIDELBERG & THE NECKAR VALLEY

Except for the Bavarian Alps, there is no more tranquil and scenic part of Germany than the Neckar Valley. The area's Burgenstrasse (Castle Road) has more castles than any comparable stretch along the mighty Rhine, and the Neckar River Valley is just as romantically charming as the more overrun Romantic Road. Allow time to take detours into hidden side valleys to see sleepy little towns, most often with a protective castle hovering over them. Heidelberg, the apotheosis of romantic Germany, needs no selling. This famous medieval university town with its historic castle perfectly captures the spirit of south Germany and has attracted poets and composers over the decades. Goethe and hard-to-impress Mark Twain both fell in love here—Goethe with a woman of striking beauty, and the more cynical Twain with Heidelberg itself. Unfortunately, Heidelberg suffers from overcrowding, especially in July and August, when tourists descend by the busload.

STUTTGART & TÜBINGEN

The capital of the state of Baden-Württemberg, Stuttgart is an industrial giant, headquarters of both Mercedes and Porsche. It's also a city of world-class museums and home to the acclaimed Stuttgart Ballet and Stuttgart State Opera. Its setting, surrounded by green hills with vineyards and orchards, is attractive, but the town isn't a serious contender for visitors when compared to Berlin or Munich. If you can give Stuttgart a day, fine. If not, head at once to nearby Tübingen, the ancient university city on the upper Neckar that has been compared favorably to Heidelberg. It doesn't have Heidelberg's grandeur (or its hordes of visitors), but we prefer its youthful air, its tranquility, and the quiet beauty of its half-timbered houses and alleyways. Don't worry about rushing around to see a lot of attractions—just soak up the old-time atmosphere.

THE RHINELAND

After beginning in the mountains of Switzerland as a narrow stream, this mighty river of legend flows for some 1,370km (850 miles) through one of the most picturesque and most industrialized regions of Europe. For 2,000 years it has been a major trade route. Bonn, Cologne, Düsseldorf, and Koblenz all lie on its banks. For most visitors, the number-one attraction is a romantic cruise down the Rhine, through gorges and past ancient castles, vineyards, and the fabled Lorelei. The most panoramic stretch is between Rüdesheim and Koblenz. Start your Rhine cruise at Rüdesheim, Germany's favorite wine village, about 72km (45 miles) west of Frankfurt. If you have time for only one Rhineland city, make it Cologne rather than the more commercialized Düsseldorf. Cologne is dominated by its famous cathedral, the largest in Germany, but this ancient city is also filled with dozens of other attractions, including restored Romanesque churches, striking Roman ruins, and the best modern-art galleries in the country.

MOSEL VALLEY

Known as La Moselle in nearby France, the Mosel River weaves a snakelike path through the mountains west of the Rhineland. It doesn't have the Rhine's dramatic scenery, but we somehow prefer it, with its vineyards, castles, and fortresses that attract far fewer visitors. The swift-moving Rhine is filled with commercial traffic, but the Mosel is slow-moving, tranquil, and inviting, dotted with sleepy wine towns where you can sample some of the world's greatest vintages. Trains rumble all night along the Rhine, but not on the Mosel. (The inevitable tour buses do get through, however.) The best time to visit is during the annual fall grape harvest, centering in Cochem or Bernkastel-Kues. The very best for last: Near the Luxembourg border lies Trier, one of Europe's most fascinating antiques and the oldest city in Germany; it existed 1,300 years before Rome. Trier is a virtual theme park of Roman culture and architecture.

LOWER SAXONY & NORTH HESSE: THE FAIRY-TALE ROAD

Hansel and Gretel, Rumpelstiltskin, the Pied Piper, and even Cinderella list their addresses as "The Fairy-Tale Road." Frankly, the Fairy-Tale Road isn't as architecturally splendid as the Romantic Road, but it's also not as crowded, and it does have a wealth of treasures for visitors interested in German lore and legend or lovers of the tales of the Brothers Grimm, who lived and worked here. The road begins at Hanau, just east of Frankfurt, and stretches for 595km (370 miles) north, coming to an end in Bremen. The trail passes through colorful towns with half-timbered buildings and past plenty of castles. Naturally, it's haunted by witches and goblins and memories of the Pied Piper of Hameln.

SCHLESWIG-HOLSTEIN & THE BALTIC COAST

You're never far from the roaring waves in Schleswig-Holstein; the North Sea is to the west and the more peaceful Baltic to the east. This is a special world rarely visited by most Americans. It's as close as Germany comes to duplicating the charms of Denmark, to the north. The province contains Germany's most sophisticated beachside resort, the long narrow island of Sylt, whose capital is Westerland, Germany's northernmost point. The main features of the climate here are iodine-rich air and lots of rain. Sylt doesn't exactly live up to its reputation as the St. Tropez of the north, but it's still a cosmopolitan playground, a favorite with celebrities. But if North Sea resorts aren't your dream, the ancient 12th-century Hanseatic port of Lübeck is reason enough to visit. Surrounded by canals, the city was the home of the Mann family (both Heinrich and Thomas) and the setting for Thomas's novel *Buddenbrooks.* Although heavily restored after World War II, Lübeck is loaded with attractions, and its Aldstadt (old town) has been designated a UNESCO World Heritage Site. From Lübeck you can travel east along the Baltic coast, all the way to the Polish border. The German beach towns still haven't thrown off their Communist aura yet, but the sandy coastline and chalk cliffs give you a view of a world closed to most Westerners for many years.

2 Visitor Information

Nearly all larger towns and all cities in Germany have tourist offices. The **German National Tourist Board** headquarters is at Beethovenstrasse 69, 60325 Frankfurt am Main (☎ **069/21-23-8800;** www.germany-tourism.de).

You'll find a German National Tourist Board office in **New York,** 122 E. 42nd St., 52nd Floor, New York, NY 10168-0072 (☎ **212/661-7200**); **Toronto,** 175 Bloor St. E., North Tower, 6th Floor, Toronto, ON M4W 3R8 (☎ **416/968-1570**); **London,** Nightingale House, 65 Curzon St., London W1Y 8NE (☎ **020/7317-0908**); and **Sydney,** Sydney South, NSW 1235 (☎ **02/9267-8148**).

3 Entry Requirements & Customs

PASSPORTS & VISAS

Every U.S., Canadian, British, and Australian traveler entering Germany must hold a valid passport. You won't need a visa unless you're staying longer than 3 months. Safeguard your passport in an inconspicuous, inaccessible place like a money belt. If you lose your passport, visit the nearest consulate of your native country as soon as possible for a replacement. It is always a good idea to have a photocopy of your passport to expedite replacement.

CUSTOMS

ENTERING GERMANY   In general, items required for personal and professional use or consumption may be brought in to Germany duty-free and without hassle. No duty is levied for a private car, provided that it is reported. You can also bring in gifts duty-free up to a total value of 350DM ($175).

The following items are permitted into Germany duty-free from non-EU(European Union) countries: 200 cigarettes; 1 liter of liquor above 44 proof, or 2 liters of liquor less than 44 proof, or 2 liters of wine; 50 grams of perfume

Germany on the Web

For a list of great Web sites on Germany and its top cities and attractions, see **"Planning Your Trip: An Online Directory,"** following this chapter.

and 0.25 liters of eau de cologne; 500 grams of coffee; 100 grams of tea. From EU countries the duty-free limits are higher: 300 cigarettes; 1.5 liters of liquor above 44 proof, or 3 liters of liquor less than 44 proof, or 4 liters of wine; 75 grams of perfume and 0.375 liters of eau de cologne; 750 grams of coffee; 150 grams of tea. Duty-free allowances are authorized only when the items are carried in the traveler's personal baggage.

RETURNING TO THE U.S. Returning U.S. citizens who have been away for 48 hours or more are allowed to bring back, once every 30 days, $400 worth of merchandise duty-free. You'll be charged a flat rate of 10% duty on the next $1,000 worth of purchases. Be sure to have your receipts handy. You cannot bring fresh foodstuffs into the United States; tinned foods, however, are allowed. You can also mail gifts back to people in the U.S. duty-free if the value of the entire gift package does not exceed $100 (be sure to write on the package wrapping its dollar value and that it's a gift). For more information, contact the **U.S. Customs Service,** 1301 Constitution Ave., P.O. Box 7407, Washington, DC 20044 (☎ **202/927-6724**), and request the free pamphlet "Know Before You Go," also available on the Web at www.customs.ustreas.gov.

RETURNING TO CANADA For a clear summary of Canadian rules, write for the booklet "I Declare," issued by **Revenue Canada,** 2265 St. Laurent Blvd., Ottawa, ON K1G 4KE (☎ **613/993-0534**). Canada allows its citizens a C$750 duty-free exemption, which includes 200 cigarettes, 2.2 pounds of tobacco, 1.5 liters of liquor, and 50 cigars. In addition, you're allowed to mail gifts to Canada from abroad at the rate of C$60 a day, provided they're unsolicited and don't contain alcohol or tobacco (write on the package "Unsolicited gift, under $60 value"). *Note:* The C$750 exemption can only be used once a year and only after an absence of 7 days.

RETURNING TO THE U.K., IRELAND & OTHER EU COUNTRIES Citizens of the U.K. and Ireland who are returning from a European Union (EU) country will go through a separate Customs Exit (called the "Blue Exit") especially for EU travelers. In essence, there is no limit on what you can bring back from an EU country, as long as the items are for personal use (this includes gifts), and you have already paid the necessary duty and tax. However, customs law sets out guidance levels. If you bring in more than these levels, you may be asked to prove that the goods are for your own use. Guidance levels on goods bought in the EU for your own use are 800 cigarettes, 200 cigars, 1 kilogram smoking tobacco, 10 liters of spirits, 90 liters of wine (of this not more than 60 liters can be sparkling wine), and 110 liters of beer. For more information, contact **HM Customs & Excise, Passenger Enquiry Point,** 2nd Floor Wayfarer House, Great South West Road, Feltham, Middlesex, TW14 8NP (☎ **0181/910-3744;** from outside the U.K., 44/181-910-3744; www. hmce.gov.uk).

RETURNING TO AUSTRALIA The duty-free allowance in Australia is A$400 or, for those under 18, A$200. Citizens can bring in 250 cigarettes or 250 grams of loose tobacco, and 1.125 liters of alcohol. A helpful brochure, available from Australian consulates or customs offices, is "Know Before You Go." For more information, contact **Australian Customs Services,** GPO Box 8, Sydney, NSW 2001 (☎ **02/9213-2000;** www.customs.gov.au).

RETURNING TO NEW ZEALAND The duty-free allowance for New Zealand is NZ$700. Citizens over 17 can bring in 200 cigarettes, or 50 cigars, or 250 grams of tobacco (or a mixture of all three if their combined weight doesn't exceed 250 grams); plus 4.5 liters of wine and beer, or 1.125 liters of liquor. Most questions are answered in a free pamphlet, available at

New Zealand consulates and Customs offices, called "New Zealand Customs Guide for Travellers, Notice no. 4." For more information, contact **New Zealand Customs Service,** 50 Anzac Ave., P.O. Box 29, Auckland (☎ 09/359-6655; www.customs.govt.nz).

4 Money

The major cities of Germany are some of the world's most expensive. So if you want to see the country without breaking the bank, you may want to cut short your time in Frankfurt, Munich, or Berlin and concentrate on interesting regional capitals such as Freiburg in the Black Forest, where you can cut your travel cost by anywhere from 20 to 40%. Also, a moderately priced rail pass will allow you to see a lot of Germany in a short time.

But although prices in Germany are high, you generally get good value for your money. The inflation rate has remained low. Hotels are usually clean and comfortable, and restaurants generally offer good cuisine and ample portions made with quality ingredients. Trains are fast and on time, and most service personnel treat you with respect.

Many people come to Germany just for winter sports. The most expensive resorts are places like Garmisch-Partenkirchen. However, if you avoid the chic places, you can enjoy winter fun at a moderate cost. Some of the winter spots in the Bavarian Alps that haven't been overrun by the beautiful people give you great value for your money. And prices in a village next to a resort are often 30% lower than at the resort itself.

In Germany, many prices for children (generally defined as ages 6 to 17) are considerably lower than for adults. And fees for children under 6 are often waived entirely.

THE EURO

The **euro,** the new European currency, became the official currency of Germany and 10 other countries on January 1, 1999, but not in the form of cash. There are still no euro banknotes or coins in circulation—payment in euros can be made only by check, credit card, or some other bank-related system. The German mark will remain the only currency in Germany for cash transactions until December 21, 2002. The symbol of the euro is €; its official abbreviation is EUR. Although at this time, very few, if any, German hotel and restaurant bills can actually be paid in euros, there'll be an increasing emphasis on the new pan-European currency during the lifetime of this edition.

ATMS

ATMs worldwide are linked to a network that most likely includes your bank at home. **Cirrus** (☎ 800/424-7787; www.mastercard.com/atm) and **PLUS** (☎ 800/843-7587; www.visa.com/atms) are the two most popular networks; check the back of your ATM card to see which network your bank belongs to. Ask your bank for a list of overseas ATMs. Be sure to check the daily withdrawal limit before you depart and ask whether you need a new PIN for use in Germany.

CREDIT CARDS

Credit cards are invaluable when traveling. They are a safe way to carry money and provide a convenient record of all your expenses. Keep in mind that though credit cards are widely accepted throughout Germany, they're still not accepted quite as commonly as in the U.S., especially in smaller towns.

The U.S. Dollar, the British Pound, the German Mark & the Euro

The unit of German currency is the **deutsche mark (DM),** which is subdivided into **pfennig (pf).** Bills are issued in denominations of 5, 10, 20, 50, 100, 200, 500, and 1,000 marks; coins come in 1, 2, 5, 10, and 50 pfennig.

At this writing, **$1 = about 2DM** (or 1DM = 50¢), and this is the rate of exchange used to calculate the dollar values given throughout this book. Also at this writing, **£1 = about 3.20DM** (or 1DM = 31 pence), and this is the rate used to calculate the pound sterling values in the table below.

At this writing, **1 euro (€) = about .97 U.S. dollars and about 2DM.** To an increasing degree, prices in German hotels, shops, and restaurants are likely to be expressed in both deutsche marks and euros, though payment in euros, either in cash or by credit cards, is still relatively rare.

Note: The relative value of the deutsche mark to other world currencies fluctuates from time to time and may not be the same when you travel to Germany.

DM	U.S.$	U.K.£	Euro €	DM	U.S.$	U.K.£	Euro €
1	0.50	0.31	0.50	75.00	37.50	23.25	37.5
2	1.00	0.62	1.00	100.00	50.00	31.00	50.00
3	1.50	0.93	1.50	125.00	62.50	38.75	62.50
4	2.00	1.24	2.00	150.00	75.00	46.50	75.00
5	2.50	1.55	2.50	175.00	87.50	54.25	87.50
6	3.00	1.86	3.00	200.00	100.00	62.00	100.00
7	3.50	2.17	3.50	225.00	112.50	69.75	112.50
8	4.00	2.48	4.00	250.00	125.00	77.50	125.00
9	4.50	2.79	4.50	275.00	175.00	85.25	175.00
10	5.00	3.10	5.00	300.00	150.00	93.00	150.00
15	7.50	4.65	7.50	350.00	175.00	108.50	175.00
20	10.00	6.20	10.00	400.00	200.00	124.00	200.00
25	12.50	7.75	12.50	500.00	250.00	155.00	250.00
50	25.00	15.50	25.00	1000.00	500.00	310.00	500.00

You can also withdraw cash advances from your credit cards. At many banks, you don't even need to go to a teller; you can get a cash advance at the ATM if you know your PIN.

Almost every credit card company has an emergency 800-number that you can call if your wallet or purse is stolen. The company may be able to wire you a cash advance off your credit card immediately, and in many places, can deliver an emergency credit card in a day or two. **Citicorp Visa**'s U.S. emergency number is ☎ **800-336-8472. American Express** cardholders and traveler's check holders should call ☎ **800/221-7282** for all money emergencies. **MasterCard** holders should call ☎ **800/307-7309.**

TRAVELER'S CHECKS

Traveler's checks are something of an anachronism from the days before ATMs made cash accessible at any time around the world. But they still might be a good choice if you want to avoid the small fees charged whenever you use an ATM or if you value the added security they bring.

You can get traveler's checks at almost any bank. **American Express** offers denominations of $10, $20, $50, $100, $500, and $1,000. You'll pay a service charge ranging from 1 to 4%. You can also get American Express traveler's checks over the phone by calling ☎ **800/221-8472;** by using this number, Amex gold and platinum cardholders are exempt from the 1% fee. **AAA** members can obtain traveler's checks without a fee at most AAA offices. **Visa** offers traveler's checks at Citibank locations nationwide, as well as several other banks, in denominations of $20, $50, $100, $500, and $1,000. The service charge ranges between 1.5 and 2%. **MasterCard** also offers traveler's checks. Call ☎ **800/223-9920** for a location near you.

Be sure to keep a record of the checks' serial numbers, separately from the checks of course, so you're ensured a refund in an emergency.

5 When to Go

CLIMATE

Germany's climate varies widely. In the north, winters tend to be cold and rainy; summers are most agreeable. In the south and in the Alps, it can be very cold in the winter, especially in January, and very warm in summer, but with cool, rainy days even in July and August. Spring and fall are often stretched out—in fact, we've enjoyed many a Bavarian-style "Indian summer" until late in October. The most popular tourist months are May to October, although winter travel to Germany is becoming increasingly popular, especially to the ski areas in the Bavarian Alps.

Berlin's Average Daytime Temperature & Rainfall (inches)

	Jan	Feb	Mar	Apr	May	June	July	Aug	Sept	Oct	Nov	Dec
°F	30	32	40	48	53	60	64	62	56	49	40	34
°C	-1	0	4	9	12	16	18	17	13	9	4	1
Rainfall	2.2	1.6	1.2	1.6	2.3	2.9	3.2	2.7	2.2	1.6	2.4	1.9

Frankfurt's Average Daytime Temperature & Rainfall (inches)

	Jan	Feb	Mar	Apr	May	June	July	Aug	Sept	Oct	Nov	Dec
°F	34	36	42	49	57	63	66	66	58	50	41	35
°C	1	2	6	9	14	17	19	19	14	10	5	2
Rainfall	6.5	5.1	5.6	5.7	5.9	5.5	5.0	5.1	4.2	4.8	6.5	6.0

HOLIDAYS

Public holidays are January 1 (New Year's Day), Easter (Good Friday and Easter Monday), May 1 (Labor Day), Ascension Day (10 days before Pentecost/Whitsunday, the 7th Sunday after Easter), Whitmonday (day after Pentecost), October 3 (Day of German Unity), November 17 (Day of Prayer and Repentance), and December 25 to 26 (Christmas). In addition, the following holidays are observed in some German states: January 6 (Epiphany), Corpus Christi (10 days after Pentecost), August 15 (Assumption), and November 1 (All Saints' Day).

Germany Calendar of Events

Dates listed below are for 2001. All dates and events are subject to change. Contact the German National Tourist Board (see "Visitor Information," above) for more information. The Board publishes a free calendar of forthcoming events three times a year, in April, October, and January; the first two are half-yearly calendars and the last is a yearly preview. They give the dates of trade fairs and exhibitions, theatrical and musical performances, local folk festivals, sporting events, conferences, and congresses throughout Germany.

January
- **New Year's Day International Ski Jumping,** Garmisch-Partenkirchen. One of Europe's major winter sporting events. For more information, contact the tourist bureau on Dr.-Richard-Strauss-Platz (☎ **08821/ 18-06**). January 1.

February
- ✪ **International Film Festival,** Berlin (at various theaters; announced in local newspapers). Stars, would-be stars, directors, and almost anyone with a film to peddle show up at this well-attended festival. It lasts for 1 week and is a showcase for the work of international film directors as well as the latest German films. Tickets can be purchased at any box office. Contact the **Full House Service** (☎ **030/259-200**) or www.berlinale.de for more information. February 7 to 18.
- **Frankfurt International Spring Fair.** This is one of the principal consumer-goods trade fairs of Europe. Its origins go back centuries. For information, contact the **Messe Frankfurt Gubh** (☎ **069/7-57-50;** fax 069/75-75-64-33; 770/984-8023 in the U.S.). February 16-20.
- **Fasching.** Carnival festivals take place throughout Germany, reaching their peak on the Tuesday (Mardi Gras) before Ash Wednesday (February 28). Particularly famous Carnivals take place in Bonn, Cologne, Düsseldorf, and especially Munich.

March
- **Spring Fairs.** Highlights throughout Germany, especially in Augsburg, Münster, Nürnberg, Hamburg, and Stuttgart.

April
- **Walpurgis Festivals.** Celebrated in the Harz Mountains. Festivities occur on the night of April 30.

May
- **Hamburg Summer.** A whole series of cultural events, including concerts, plays, festivals, and special exhibitions throughout May, June, and July. For information, contact the **Hamburg Tourist Bureau,** im Hauptbahnhof (☎ **040/30-05-13-00**).
- **International May Festival,** Wiesbaden. This city near Frankfurt hosts a premier cultural event—a series of artistic celebrations lasting 1 month. For information, contact the **Wiesbaden Tourist Office,** Rheinstrasse 15 (☎ **0611/1-72-97-80**).
- **Mozart Festival,** Würzburg. Aficionados of the composer flock to this major cultural event in the baroque city of Würzburg. For more information, contact **Tourismus Zentrale** im Würzburg-Palais, am Congress-Centrum (☎ **0931/37-33-35**). May 28 to July 1.

June
- **Red Wine Festival,** Rüdesheim/Assmannshausen. This is held in Assmannshausen, the Rhine village most famous for red wines. For information, contact the **Rüdesheim Tourist Bureau,** Rheinstrasse 16 (☎ **06722/29-62**). June 1 to 4.
- **Floodlighting of the Castle,** Heidelberg. Fireworks enliven the display in this storied university city. For more information, contact the **Heidelberg**

Tourist Bureau, Pavillon am Hauptbahnhof (☎ **06221/1-42-20**). June 5, July 10, and September 4.

July

- **Freiburg Wine Tasting.** Local residents and visitors enjoy the first vintages from grapes grown in the Black Forest district. For more information, contact the **Freiburg Tourist Bureau,** Rotteckring 14 (☎ **0761/388-18-80**). July 4 to July 8.
- ✪ **Richard Wagner Festival.** Bayreuth Festspielhaus. One of Europe's two or three major opera events, this festival takes place in the composer's Festspielhaus in Bayreuth, the capital of upper Franconia. Note that opera tickets often must be booked years in advance. For information, contact Festival Administration, **Bayreuther Festspiele,** Am Festspiele, 95445 Bayreuth (☎ **0921/7-87-80**; www.festspiele.de). Late July to late August.

September

- ✪ **Oktoberfest,** Munich. Germany's most famous festival happens mainly in September, not October. Millions show up, and hotels are packed. Most activities are at Theresienwiese, where local breweries sponsor gigantic tents that can hold up to 6,000 beer drinkers. Contact the **Munich Tourist Bureau** (☎ **089/2-33-03-00**) or www.bavariashop.com/oktoberfest for particulars, or just show up. Always reserve hotel rooms well in advance. Mid-September to the first Sunday in October.
- **Berliner Festwochen.** One of the high points on the cultural calendar of Germany, the Berlin Festival brings an international array of performing artists to Berlin. It features opera and symphony performances as well as major theatrical presentations. Contact the **Berlin Tourist Information Office** (☎ **030/25-00-25**). September 1 to October 4.

October

- **Frankfurt Book Fair.** A major international event for publishers, book dealers, agents, and authors. Contact the **Frankfurt Tourist Office** (☎ **069/21-23-87-08**) or www.frankfurt-bookfair.com. October 10 to 15.

November

- **Jazz-Fest Berlin.** This annual festival staged at the Philharmonie attracts some of the world's finest jazz artists, ranging from traditional to experimental. Contact the **Berlin Tourist Information Office** (☎ **030/25-00-25**) for more information. November 1 to 4.
- **Winter Dom,** Hamburg. An annual amusement fair (sometimes called Hamburg Dom) at the Heiligengeistfeld. For more information, contact the **Hamburg Tourist Bureau,** Im Hauptbahnhof (☎ **040/30-05-13-00**). November 9 to December 9.

December

- **Christmas Fair,** Mainz. Mainz stages its Christmas fair on the Rhine for 4 weeks preceding Christmas. For more information, contact the **Mainz Tourist Bureau,** Vruckenturm Am Raphaus (☎ **06131/28-62-10**). Other German towns hold Christmas fairs in November.

6 The Active Vacation Planner

Himalayan Travel, 110 Prospect St., Stamford, CT 06901 (☎ **800/225-2380**; www.gorp.com/himtravel.htm), has a variety of German adventure trips, including hiking, walking, trekking, and cycling tours of such areas as the

Black Forest, Bavaria, and King Ludwig's Trail. The tours are self-guided, and luggage is transported by van from one hotel to the next. Rates include accommodations in two- and three-star hotels and some meals but not airfare.

Europe Express, 1940 116th Ave. NE, Bellevue, WA 98004 (☎ **800/ 426-3615**), offers a variety of self-guided walking and biking tours as well as cross-country skiing trips throughout Germany. It covers such areas as the Black Forest and King Ludwig's Trail, and will customize your trip if you wish.

Value Holidays, 10224 N. Port Washington Rd., Mequon, WI 53092 (☎ **800/558-6850**), will customize German walking tours for groups with special interests. Among its offerings are a Music Appreciation tour and a coach tour called "In the Footsteps of Luther."

Abercrombie & Kent, 15-20 Kensington Rd., Suite 212, Oak Brook, IL 60523-2141 (☎ **800/323-7308**), is well known for the exciting and extremely luxurious tours it offers around the globe. Its "Danube River Aboard the Magnificent M/S *River Cloud*" trip combines nostalgic, pre-war glamour with state-of-the-art engineering for a romantic 7-day voyage through Germany and then on to Austria and Hungary in the summer and fall.

BIKING

Pedaling through the Bavarian countryside is the way to go for many visitors. You can bike through green valleys and past rivers, such as the Danube, while enjoying rural landscapes and life in German villages. **Allgemeiner Deutscher Fahrrad-Club,** Hellerallee 23, 28209, Bremen (☎ **0421/34-62-90**), offers complete information on biking in Germany. For more information on touring Germany by bike, see "Getting Around," later in this chapter.

For the past 2 decades, **Classic Adventures,** P.O. Box 153, Hamlin, NY 14464 (☎ **800/777-8090**), has offered bike tours of such areas as the Romantic Road. **Euro-Bike Tours,** P.O. Box 990, DeKalb, IL 60115 (☎ **800/321-6060**), has a full range of bicycling and walking tours of Bavaria, as well as a 9-day biking tour of Germany, Switzerland, and France. The upscale outfitter **Butterfield & Robinson,** 70 Bond St., Toronto, ON, Canada M5B 1X3 (☎ **800/ 678-1147;** fax 416/864-5041), offers a new biking trip along the Romantic Road and along the banks of the Main, Tauber, and Neckar Rivers.

Dozens of companies in Britain offer guided cycling tours. One of the best is the **Cyclists Touring Club,** 69 Meadrow, Godalming, Surrey GU7 3HS (☎ **01483/417-217;** www.ctc.org.uk). It charges £25 a year for membership.

CAMPING & CARAVANNING

Germany boasts some 2,100 campsites, located in the most beautiful and popular resort districts and with all the necessary facilities. Blue signs bearing the international camping symbol—a black tent on a white background—make it easy to find campgrounds. Some 600 sites are kept open during the winter. You can obtain information on camping matters and campsites by writing to **Allgemeiner Deutscher Automobil Club (ADAC)** at Redaktion ADAC, Am Westpark 8, 81873 München (☎ **089/7-67-60**). You can also contact the **Deutscher Camping Club (DCC),** Mandlstrasse 28, 80802 München (☎ **089/380-14-20**).

FISHING

You can obtain information on fishing from any regional tourist office. In Germany, local catches include char, grayling, river and sea trout, carp, pike perch,

Taking the Waters

More than any other country in Europe, Germany developed the spa process to a high art. The heyday of German spa construction coincided with the rise of the bourgeoisie in the 19th century, when a lavish series of resorts was built around the dozens of mineral springs bubbling from the soil. Many of these springs had been known since the Middle Ages, or even Roman times, and to each was attributed specific cures for arthritis, gout, infertility, hypertension, and gynecological problems. (The German word *Ku—Kurort* means "spa"—is derived from the Latin *cura,* meaning "care.") Going to a spa became an intensely ritualized social experience.

There are basically four types of spas.

1. **Mineral & Thermal Spas/Springs.** Springs with at least 1 gram of dissolved mineral substances per liter of natural water are designated "mineral springs." If the water emerges from the ground at a temperature of 20°C (68°F) or more, it's called a "thermal spring." The treatment provided in mineral and thermal springs is as varied as the composition of the waters. Some of these waters are suitable for bathing.

2. **Climatic Health Resorts.** These health resorts lie in densely wooded area permeated with fresh air. Climatic therapy consists of open-air kinesitherapy and constitutional walks along paths.

3. **Seaside Spas & Health Resorts.** Seawater and mud from coastal shallows are much used in therapeutic treatments, often for treating circulatory disorders and cardiac defects, for rehabilitation after operations, and for skin diseases and other treatments.

4. **Kneipp (Hydropathic) Spas & Health Resorts.** This treatment was first developed by Sebastian Kneipp in 1849. It's based on a strengthening of the body's intrinsic immune system and on developing a proper macrobiotic rhythm. Warm water relaxes, cold water stimulates, and a natural way of life brings harmony—this is the basic Kneipp formula. Treatments consists of the following: (1) hydrotherapy for exercising the vascular and circulatory systems and for strengthening the immune system; (2) consumption of natural basic whole foods to ensure regular metabolism; (3) use of medicinal herbs to activate self-health powers; (4) physical training and kinesitherapy to improve cardiac activity and blood circulation; and (5) adjustment therapy to ensure a balanced way of life and a harmony of mind and body.

Don't expect frenzied nightlife or nonstop activities at a spa. Spas try to pad the emotional edges of life for their clientele and provide a soothing

rockfish, eel, and bream. An official license (*Fischereischein*) is required; it's available from local district or municipal authorities, and it's different in each area of Germany. Contact **Verband Deutscher Sportfischer,** Siemenstrasse 11–13 at 63071 Offerbach (☎ **069/85-50-06**).

Franconia has some of the best fishing in Germany, especially along the Main River and in the vicinity of Coburg. The **Coburg Tourist Information,** Herrngasse 4 (☎ **09561/7-41-80**), will supply complete information and hook you up with outfitters.

and unruffled environment that almost anyone can appreciate. The innards of the clinics often have a disturbing resemblance to hospitals, but you can avoid the interiors and still gain a fascinating insight into the ritualization of social life. Enjoy a leisurely meal in one of the resort's airy and elegantly formal restaurants, preferably one that overlooks a sprawling flower garden. Sit in a cafe, perhaps with a glass of wine, and watch the rituals of the prosperous bourgeoisie. And, if you choose, elect a spa treatment. Subject your travel-weary body to everything from mud baths to immersions in sulfur-rich water and endure the massages and skin treatments that will at least leave you more relaxed.

There are more than 300 health resorts in Germany today. The word *Bad* before the name in any town (for example, Bad Godesberg, Bad Orb) is a sure sign that the town has some sort of ritualized process for taking the waters. Most spa directors insist on a brief medical checkup—performed on site by resident doctors—before any treatment can begin.

In our view, no spa in Germany tops **Baden-Baden** in the Black Forest. It's where Elizabeth Taylor, Joan Collins, Plácido Domingo, or José Carreras might go to take a few years off. Heads of state often slip in. Baden-Baden has everything—not only the waters at its opulent Kurhaus, but also Germany's best casino. There're more sightseeing attractions than any other spa in Germany, more deluxe hotels, and better food.

Another fabled spa, though somewhat less grand than Baden-Baden, is **Wiesbaden,** which is located outside Frankfurt, in the shelter of the Rhine and the Taunus Mountains. It has one of the finest open-air thermal pools in the country, and its thermal baths include both indoor and outdoor pools, along with endless massage rooms and solariums.

After Wiesbaden and Baden-Baden, the other leading spas fall off a bit, attracting mostly those interested in specific cures. For example, **Bad Reichenhall** in the Bavarian Alps is known for its saline waters, and has a good reputation for the treatment of respiratory problems, skin ailments, and rheumatism. **Bad Kissingen** is known for mud baths, seawater Jacuzzis, and saunas—but it's a bit dull when stacked up against its more glamorous siblings. **Bad Homburg,** in the foothills of the Taunus mountains, is long past its 19th-century heyday, but it still enjoys a reputation for the treatment of heart and circulatory diseases.

Regardless of the various medical claims made at the spas of Germany, the real reason to go, in our view, regardless of which spa you select, is to escape momentarily the stress of everyday life.

GOLF

Most German golf courses welcome visiting players who are members of courses at home. Weekday greens fees are usually around 70DM ($35), rising to as much as 100DM ($50) on Saturday and Sunday. For information about the various golf courses in Germany, write to the **Deutscher Golf/Verband,** Victoriastrasse 16, 65185 Wiesbaden (☎ **0611/99-02-00**).

Here are a few of the country's best places to golf. The Swabian region of Allgau has several good courses. The **Golf Club Oberstaufen und Steibis**

(☎ 08386/85-29), at Oberstaufen, is an 18-hole golf course close to a forest and nature park. Oftrerschwang, a small, charmingly peaceful resort on the scenically beautiful Tiefenberger Moor, has **Golf Club Sonnenalp** (☎ 08321/27-20). **Golf Baden Baden** (☎ 07221/23-57-9), in the spa city of Baden-Baden, offers a good 18-hole course, as does **Golf Bodensee** (☎ 08389/89191) on Lake Constance in southern Germany. Farther north, the city of Augsburg has an 18-hole course at **Golf Augsburg** (☎ 08234/78-55).

HIKING & MOUNTAIN CLIMBING

These sports are popular in the German uplands. It's estimated that there are more than 80,000 marked hiking and mountain-walking tracks in the country. The **Verband Deutscher Gebirgs-und Wandervereine,** Wilhelmshöher Alle 157–159, 34121 Kassel (☎ 0561/938-730), services the trails and offers details not only about trails but also about shelters and huts and addresses of hiking associations in the various regions. The **Deutsche Alpenverein,** Von-Kahr-Strasse 2–4, 80997 München (☎ 089/14-00-30), owns and operates 50 huts in and around the Alps that are open to all mountaineers. This association also maintains a 15,000km (9,500-mile) network of alpine trails.

The best **alpine hiking** is in the Bavarian Alps, especially the 1,235m (4,060-foot) Eckbauer, on the southern fringe of Partenkirchen. The tourist office will supply hiking maps and details (see chapter 8). Another great place for hiking is **Berchtesgaden National Park,** Kurgarten, Maximilianstrasse 1, Berchtesgaden (☎ 08652/22-07), bordering the Austrian province of Salzburg (see chapter 8). This park also offers the best organized hikes and will hook you up with various groups offering hikes.

Waymark Holidays, 44 Windsor Rd., Slough, Berkshire SL1 2EJ, England (☎ 01753/516-477), owned by avid naturalists and mountaineers, offers **walking tours** that focus on particularly beautiful or folkloric regions of Germany. One popular trip is a 10-day walking tour through the Black Forest. The £595 ($1,011.50) price includes 10 nights lodging in a simple guest house, half board, round-trip transportation from Heathrow, and guided walking tours of around 5 hours a day. The tour is based in the alpine hamlet of Hinterzarten and includes trips to Lake Titisee and the Schlucksee (the largest lake in the Black Forest), as well as to Breitnau and nearby waterfall-filled gorges.

MOTORCYCLING

Guided motorcycle tours through Bavaria are the specialty of **Beach's Motorcycle Adventures,** 2763 W. River Pkwy., Grand Island, NY 14072 (☎ 716/773-4960). Two- to 3-week tours on BMW bikes begin and end in Munich, with accommodations at small hotels and inns. Maps are provided, as well as information and suggestions for sightseeing and independent cruising along the way.

SAILING SCHOOLS

In the southern German region of the Allgäu there are more sailing schools than anywhere else in Germany. Sailing enthusiasts can take lessons at the recreational resort of Immenstadt on the region's largest natural lake, the Grosser Alpsee at the nearby **Segelschule** (Sailing School) in Bühl am Alpsee (☎ 08325/346). Lechbruck, on the upper Lech lake, has classes at **Segel und Windsurfschule** (☎ 08862/84-97). On the beautiful

Germany for Jewish Visitors

In the last few years, Jews in Eastern Europe have decreased in population because of immigration; the Jewish populations in some Western countries have also decreased because of intermarriage. Germany's Jewish population, on the other hand, is slowly increasing, mostly through immigration. It's estimated that there are between 40,000 and 80,000 Jews now living in the country, a figure that's nowhere near the pre-war high of 500,000, but that still represents significant growth. The most prominent of the new arrivals are from the ex-Soviet Union. Some 70% of Jews in such cities as Bremen and Hamburg are native Russian speakers.

Berlin's Jewish community is the largest. Its 10,000 to 20,000 members are well served by several kosher restaurants, a Jewish high school, the new Mendelssohn Center at nearby Potsdam University, and both a weekly and monthly paper. Other important Jewish communities are located in Frankfurt (7,000), Munich (3,000), Düsseldorf (2,000), Stuttgart (1,600), Cologne (1,500), and Hamburg (1,500). Another 75 smaller communities are scattered throughout the country.

While anti-Semitism has not disappeared completely, in general, postwar Germany has worked hard to confront its past—far more so than Austria, for example. Some 30 museums today deal with Jewish issues, and former concentration camp sites display their grisly reminders to visitors. German high schools include Holocaust studies in their curriculum. In politics, there are about 80 extreme-right groups, 20 or so classified as neo-Nazi, with maybe 65,000 members, but this is in a country of more than 80 million people.

Berlin has the country's highest concentration of places of interest to Jewish visitors. The Jüdischer Friedhof at Weisensee, a suburb of Berlin, was Europe's largest Jewish cemetery, and today contains around 110,000 graves and a memorial to Jews murdered in the Nazi era. A darker sight is the chillingly elegant Wannsee Villa, overlooking the Wannsee lake, where the "Final Solution" was formally proposed in January 1942. The most hopeful landmark is the newly renovated Oranienburger Strasse Synagogue. Unlike the other five Berlin synagogues, this glorious and immense Moorish-style structure operates only as a memorial and museum. Berlin also has two museums dedicated to the city's Jews and many monuments, such as the Wives of Jewish Husbands Memorial, dedicated to the hundreds of non-Jewish women who demonstrated outside Gestapo headquarters in February 1943 after their husbands had been arrested.

lake Constance, sailors can take advantage of the **Bodensee Yachtshule** (☎ 08382/94-45-88) in the delightful resort of Lindau.

WINTER SPORTS

More than 300 winter-sports resorts operate in the German Alps and wooded hill country such as the Harz Mountains and the Black Forest. In addition to outstanding ski slopes, trails, lifts, jumps, toboggan slides, and skating rinks, many larger resorts also offer ice hockey, ice boating, and bobsledding. Curling is very popular as well, especially in upper Bavaria. The Olympic sports facilities at Garmisch-Partenkirchen enjoy international renown, as do the ski jumps of Oberstdorf and the artificial-ice speed-skating rink at Inzell. More than 250 ski lifts are found in the German Alps, the Black Forest, and the Harz Mountains. Information on winter-sports facilities is available from local tourist bureaus and the offices of the German National Tourist Board (see "Visitor Information," above).

Garmisch-Partenkirchen (see chapter 8), is Germany's most famous winter sports center. Set in beautiful alpine scenery, this picturesque resort is close to Zugspitze, Germany's highest mountain. A mountain railway and a cable car can take you to the peak. In the town itself is the Olympic Ice Stadium, built in 1936, and the Ski Stadium, which has two jumps and a slalom course. Skiers of every level will be satisfied with the slopes on the mountain above the town. For information, contact the **Verkehrsamt** on Richard-Strauss-Platz (☎ **08821/18-06**).

7 Health & Insurance

STAYING HEALTHY

German medical facilities are among the best in the world. If a medical emergency arises, your hotel staff can usually put you in touch with a reliable doctor. If not, contact the American embassy or a consulate; each one maintains a list of English-speaking doctors. Medical and hospital services aren't free, so be sure that you have appropriate insurance coverage before you travel.

The water is safe to drink throughout Germany; however, do not drink the water in mountain streams, regardless of how clear and pure it looks.

If you suffer from a chronic illness, consult your doctor before your departure. For conditions like epilepsy, diabetes, or heart problems, wear a **Medic Alert Identification Tag** (☎ **800/825-3785**; www.medicalert.org), which will immediately alert doctors to your condition and give them access to your records through Medic Alert's 24-hour hot line. Membership is $35, plus a $15 annual fee.

Pack prescription medications in your carry-on luggage. Carry written prescriptions in generic, not brand-name form, and dispense all prescription medications from their original labeled vials. Also bring along copies of your prescriptions in case you lose your pills or run out.

Contact the **International Association for Medical Assistance to Travelers (IAMAT;** ☎ **716/754-4883** or 416/652-0137; www.sentex.net/~iamat). This organization offers tips on travel and health concerns in the countries you'll be visiting, and lists many local English-speaking doctors.

INSURANCE

There are three kinds of travel insurance: trip-cancellation, medical, and lost luggage coverage.

Trip-cancellation insurance is a good idea if you have paid a large portion of your vacation expenses up front, say, by purchasing a tour. Trip-cancellation insurance should cost approximately 6 to 8% of the total value of your vacation. (Don't buy it from your tour operator, though—talk about putting all your eggs in one basket!)

Your existing health insurance should cover you if you get sick while on vacation (though if you belong to an HMO, you should check to see whether you are fully covered when away from home). If you need hospital treatment, most health insurance plans and HMOs will cover out-of-country hospital visits and procedures, at least to some extent. However, most make you pay the bills up front at the time of care, and you'll get a refund after you've returned and filed all the paperwork. Members of **Blue Cross/Blue Shield** can now use their cards at select hospitals in most major cities worldwide (☎ **800/810-BLUE** or www.bluecares.com/blue/bluecard/wwn for a list of hospitals). **Medicare** only covers U.S. citizens traveling in Mexico and Canada. For independent travel health-insurance providers, see below.

Check your existing policies before you buy additional insurance you might not need. But if you do require additional insurance, try one of the companies listed below: **Access America** (☎ **800/284-8300**), **Travel Guard International** (☎ **800/ 826-1300**), and **Travelex Insurance Services** (☎ **800/ 228-9792**). In the U.K., there's **Columbus Travel Insurance** (☎ **020/ 7375-0011** in London; www2.columbusdirect.co.uk). Companies specializing in accident and medical care include: **MEDEX International** (☎ **888/MEDEX-00** or 410/453-6300; fax 410/ 453-6301; www. medexassist.com); and **Travel Assistance International** (Worldwide Assistance Services, Inc.; ☎ **800/821-2828** or 202/828-5894; fax 202/828-5896).

8 Tips for Travelers with Special Needs

TIPS FOR TRAVELERS WITH DISABILITIES

Germany is one of the better countries for travelers with disabilities. In all the large cities, there are excellent facilities. The local tourist offices can issue permits for drivers, to allow them access to disabled parking areas. Older, smaller towns may pose more of a problem, however, especially where the streets are cobblestone.

In any case, a disability shouldn't stop anyone from traveling. There are more resources out there than ever before. *A World of Options,* a 658-page book of resources for disabled travelers, covers everything from biking trips to scuba outfitters. It costs $35 ($30 for members) and is available from **Mobility International USA,** P.O. Box 10767, Eugene, OR 97440 (☎ **541/343-1284,** voice and TDD; www.miusa.org). Annual membership for Mobility International is $35, which includes their quarterly newsletter, *Over the Rainbow.*

The Moss Rehab Hospital (☎ **215/456-9600**) has been providing friendly and helpful phone advice and referrals to disabled travelers for years through its **Travel Information Service** (☎ **215/456-9603;** www.mossresourcenet.org).

You can join **The Society for the Advancement of Travel for the Handicapped (SATH),** 347 Fifth Ave. Suite 610, New York, NY 10016 (☎ **212/447-7284;** fax 212-725-8253; www.sath.org) for $45 annually, $30 for seniors and students, to gain access to a vast network of connections in the travel industry. The Society provides information sheets on travel destinations, and referrals to tour operators that specialize in traveling with disabilities. Its quarterly magazine, *Open World for Disability and Mature Travel,* is full of good information and resources. A year's subscription is $13 ($21 outside the U.S.).

Travelers with disabilities may also want to consider joining a tour that caters specifically to them. One of the best operators is **Flying Wheels Travel,** 143 West Bridge, P.O. Box 382, Owatonna, MN 55060 (☎ **800/535-6790**). It offers various escorted tours and cruises, as well as private tours in minivans with lifts. Other reputable specialized tour operators include **Access Adventures** (☎ **716/889-9096**), which offers sports-related vacations; **Accessible Journeys** (☎ **800/TINGLES** or 610/521-0339), for slow walkers and wheelchair travelers; **The Guided Tour, Inc.** (☎ **215/782-1370**); and **Directions Unlimited** (☎ **800/533-5343**).

Vision-impaired travelers should contact the **American Foundation for the Blind,** 11 Penn Plaza, Suite 300, New York, NY 10001 (☎ **800/ 232-5463**), for information on traveling with seeing-eye dogs.

British travelers with disabilities might contact **RADAR** (Royal Association for Disability and Rehabilitation), Unit 12, City Forum, 250 City Rd., London EC1V 8AF (☎ **020/7250-3222;** fax 020/7250-0212), which publishes vacation "fact packs," containing information on trip planning, travel insurance, specialized accommodations, and transportation abroad.

TIPS FOR GAYS & LESBIANS

Although Germany is one of the "gayest" countries of Europe, there is also prejudice and hostility here. Violence against gays and foreigners (especially nonwhite) is not unknown. On the other hand, homosexuality is widely accepted by a vast number of the country's millions, especially young people. All major cities, especially Berlin, have a wide and varied gay and lesbian nightlife. Keep in mind western Germany is far more gay-friendly than the more isolated outposts of the former East Germany. The legal minimum age for consensual homosexual sex is 18.

Before you go, consider picking up a copy of *Frommer's Gay & Lesbian Europe,* which contains a fabulous chapter on Berlin.

The **International Gay & Lesbian Travel Association (IGLTA)** (☎ **800/ 448-8550** or 954/776-2626; fax 954/776-3303; www.iglta.org), with around 1,200 members, links travelers with appropriate gay-friendly service organizations or tour specialists. It offers quarterly newsletters, marketing mailings, and a membership directory. Most members are gay or lesbian businesses but individuals can join for $150 yearly, plus a $100 administration fee for new members. Members are kept informed of gay and gay-friendly hoteliers, tour operators, and airline and cruise-line representatives. Contact the IGLTA for a list of its member agencies, who will be tied into IGLTA's information resources.

General gay and lesbian travel agencies include **Family Abroad** (☎ **800/ 999-5500** or 212/459-1800; gay and lesbian); and **Above and Beyond Tours** (☎ **800/397-2681;** mainly gay men).

There are also two good, biannual English-language gay guidebooks, both focused on gay men but including information for lesbians as well. You can get the *Spartacus International Gay Guide* or *Odysseus* from most gay and lesbian bookstores; or order them from Giovanni's Room (☎ **215/923-2960**) or from **A Different Light Bookstore** (☎ **800/343-4002** or 212/989-4850). Both lesbians and gays might want to pick up a copy of *Gay Travel A to Z* ($16). **The Ferrari Guides** (www.q-net.com) is yet another very good series of gay and lesbian guidebooks.

Out and About, 8 W. 19th St., no. 401, New York, NY 10011 (☎ **800/ 929-2268** or 212/645-6922), offers guidebooks and a monthly newsletter packed with good information on the global gay and lesbian scene. A year's subscription to the newsletter costs $49. *Our World,* 1104 North Nova Rd., Suite 251, Daytona Beach, FL 32117 (☎ **904/441-5367**), is a slicker monthly magazine promoting and highlighting travel bargains and opportunities. Annual subscription rates are $35 in the U.S., $45 outside the U.S.

TIPS FOR SENIORS

Don't be shy about asking for discounts, and always carry some kind of identification, such as a driver's license, that shows your date of birth. Many hotels and airlines offer special rates for seniors; ask when you make your reservations. In many cities, seniors qualify for reduced admission to theaters, museums, and other attractions, and discounted fares on public transportation.

Members of the **American Association of Retired Persons (AARP),** 601
E St. NW, Washington, DC 20049 (☎ **800/424-3410** or 202/434-2277;
www.aarp.org), get discounts not only on hotels but on airfares and car
rentals, too. AARP offers a wide range of special benefits, including *Modern
Maturity* magazine and a monthly newsletter.

The National Council of Senior Citizens, 8403 Colesville Rd., Suite 1200,
Silver Spring, MD 20910 (☎ **301/578-8800**), a nonprofit organization, offers
a newsletter six times a year (partly devoted to travel tips) and discounts on hotel
and auto rentals; annual dues are $13 per person or couple.

Golden Companions, P.O. Box 5249, Reno, NV 89513 (☎ **800/
392-1256** or 631/454-0880), helps travelers 45-plus find compatible
companions through a personal voice-mail service. Contact them for more
information.

Another helpful publication is *101 Tips for the Mature Traveler,* available
from **Grand Circle Travel,** 347 Congress St., Suite 3A, Boston, MA 02210
(☎ **800/221-2610** or 617/350-7500; fax 617/346-6700).

Grand Circle Travel is also one of the hundreds of travel agencies specializing
in vacations for seniors, but many of these packages are of the tour-bus variety,
with free trips thrown in for those who organize groups of 10 or more. Seniors
seeking more independent travel should probably consult a regular travel agent.
SAGA International Holidays, 222 Berkeley St., Boston, MA 02116 (☎ **800/
343-0273**), offers inclusive tours and cruises for those 50 and older. SAGA also
sponsors the more substantial "Road Scholar Tours" (☎ **800/621-2151**), which
are fun-loving but with an educational bent.

If you want something more than the average vacation or guided tour, try
Elderhostel, 75 Federal St., Boston, MA 02110-1941 (☎ **877/426-8056;**
www.elderhostel.org), or the University of New Hampshire's **Interhostel**
(☎ **800/733-9753**), both variations on the same theme: educational travel for
senior citizens. On these escorted tours, the days are packed with seminars, lectures, and field trips, and all sightseeing is led by academic experts. Elderhostel
arranges study programs around the world for those aged 55 and over (and a
spouse or companion of any age). Most courses last about 3 weeks and many
include airfare, accommodations in student dormitories or modest inns, meals,
and tuition. Write or call for a free catalog, which lists upcoming courses and destinations. Interhostel takes travelers 50 and over (with companions over 40), and
offers 2- and 3-week trips, mostly international.

9 Getting There

BY PLANE

Flying time to Frankfurt is about 7¹/₂ hours from New York, 10 hours from
Chicago, and 12 hours from Los Angeles. There are also nonstop flights from
the U.S. to Munich and Düsseldorf (though not to Berlin).

Lufthansa (☎ **800/645-3880;** www.lufthansa-usa.com) operates the most
frequent service and flies to the greatest number of Germany's
airports. From North America, Lufthansa serves 16 gateway cities. In any sea-
son, there are more than 100 weekly flights from these cities to Germany. The
largest of the gateways is the New York City area, where flights depart from both
JFK and Newark airports. From JFK there are daily flights to Frankfurt. From
Newark, there are daily flights to Frankfurt, Munich, and Düsseldorf.
Lufthansa's other gateways include Atlanta, Boston, Chicago, Dallas/Fort
Worth, Detroit, Houston, Los Angeles, Miami, Philadelphia, San Francisco, and
Washington, D.C. Lufthansa also flies to Germany from Toronto, Vancouver,

Planning Basics

Flying for Less: Tips for Getting the Best Airfares

1. **Keep your eyes peeled for sales.** Check your newspaper for advertised discounts or call the airlines directly and ask if any promotional rates or special fares are available. If you already hold a ticket when a sale breaks, it may even pay to exchange your ticket, which usually incurs a $50 to $75 charge. You'll never see sales in summer or around the Christmas holidays, but there have been amazing bargains in late winter, spring, and fall for the last few years.

   Note, however, that the lowest-priced fares are often nonrefundable, require advance purchase of 1 to 3 weeks and a certain length of stay, and carry penalties for changing dates of travel.

2. **Ask the reservations agent lots of questions.** If your schedule is flexible, ask if you can secure a cheaper fare by staying an extra day or by flying midweek. Many airlines won't volunteer this information, so you've got to be persistent on the phone.

3. **Consolidators,** also known as bucket shops, are a good place to find low fares. Consolidators buy seats in bulk from the airlines and then sell them back to the public at prices below even the airlines' discounted rates. Their small boxed ads usually run in the Sunday travel section at the bottom of the page. Before you pay a consolidator, however, ask for a record locator number and confirm your seat with the airline itself. Be prepared to book your ticket with a different consolidator—there are many to choose from—if the airline can't confirm your reservation. Also be aware that bucket shop tickets are usually nonrefundable or rigged with stiff cancellation penalties, often as high as 50% to 75% of the ticket price.

   Council Travel (☎ 800/226-8624; www.counciltravel.com) and **STA Travel** (☎ 800/781-4040; www.sta.travel.com) cater especially to young travelers, but their bargain basement prices are available to people of all ages. **Travel Bargains** (☎ 800/AIR-FARE; www.1800airfare.com) was formerly owned by TWA but now offers the deepest discounts on many

Calgary, and Mexico City. The airline has a 10% discount for seniors over 60; the reduction applies to a traveling companion as well.

Lufthansa has an alliance with **United Airlines** and **Air Canada** to provide seamless air service to Germany and other parts of the globe from North America. Dubbed "Star Alliance," the union allows cross-airline benefits, including travel on one or all of these airlines on one ticket and frequent-flyer credit to the participating airline of your choice. The Star Alliance also includes Scandinavian Airlines System, Thai Airways International, and Varig.

American Airlines (☎ 800/443-7300; www.aa.com) flies nonstop to Frankfurt daily from both Dallas/Fort Worth and Chicago. Nonstop daily service is also available between Miami and Frankfurt. From Frankfurt, Düsseldorf, and London, among others, American's flights connect easily with ongoing flights to many other German cities on Lufthansa or British Airways.

Continental Airlines (☎ 800/231-0856; www.flycontinental.com) offers daily nonstop service between Newark and Frankfurt and Düsseldorf. The airline maintains excellent connections between Newark and its hubs in Cleveland and Houston. Continental also offers discounts and other benefits to seniors 62 and over and to their traveling companions, regardless of age.

other airlines, with a 4-day advance purchase. Other reliable consolidators are **1-800-FLY-CHEAP** (www.1800flycheap.com); **TFI Tours International** (☎ 800/745-8000 or 212/736-1140), which serves as a clearinghouse for unused seats; or "rebators" such as **Travel Avenue** (☎ 800/333-3335 or 312/876-1116).

4. **Consider a charter flight.** Most charter operators advertise and sell their seats through travel agents, so they're your best source of information for available flights. Before deciding to take a charter flight, however, check the restrictions on the ticket: You may be asked to purchase a tour package, to pay in advance, to be amenable if the day of departure is changed, to pay a service charge, to fly on an airline you're not familiar with (this usually is not the case), and to pay harsh penalties if you cancel—but be understanding if the charter doesn't fill up and is canceled up to 10 days before departure. Summer charters fill up more quickly than others and are almost sure to fly, but if you decide on a charter flight, seriously consider cancellation and baggage insurance.

Among charter-flight operators is **Council Charter,** a subsidiary of the Council on International Educational Exchange (CIEE), 205 E. 42nd St., New York, NY 10017 (☎ 800/226-8624 or 212/822-2700). This outfit can arrange charter seats to most major European cities on regularly scheduled aircrafts. Another big charter operator is **Travac,** 989 Sixth Ave., 16th Floor, New York, NY 10018 (☎ 800/TRAV-800 or 212/563-3303; fax 407/896-0014; www.travac.com).

Be warned: Some charter companies have proved unreliable in the past.

5. **Surf the Web for bargains.** (But always check the lowest published fare before you shop for flights online, so you know if you're getting a deal.) See "Planning Your Trip: An Online Directory," following this chapter, for lots of advice on how to use the Internet to your best advantage.

From the Delta Flight Center at JFK airport in New York, **Delta Airlines** (☎ 800/ 241-4141; www.delta-air.com) offers daily service to both Frankfurt and (via Brussels) Hamburg. Delta is especially strong in service to Germany from its home base in Atlanta, with two daily nonstops to Frankfurt and daily nonstops to Munich, as well as Hamburg via Brussels, and Stuttgart via Amsterdam. Delta also offers frequent nonstops to Frankfurt from Cincinnati (one of its major midwestern hubs).

If you fly one of **KLM**'s (☎ 800/374-7747; www.klm.nl) frequent nonstop flights into Amsterdam from New York's JFK and from Atlanta, you can include a stopover in Holland. From Amsterdam, many flights on both KLM and Lufthansa fly into all the major cities of Germany. Flights to Germany on **Northwest Airlines** (☎ 800/ 225-2525), KLM's partner, are available out of Boston and Washington, D.C.

United Airlines (☎ 800/538-2929; www.ual.com) offers daily nonstops from Washington, D.C., and Chicago to Frankfurt. Furthermore, because of the Star Alliance, discussed above, all German flights by Lufthansa or Air Canada will also be honored as a part of a United ticket. If you're interested in taking advantage of the Star Alliance, be sure to notify the United ticket agent when you are booking or inquiring about your flight.

From London, **British Airways** (☎ 0141/222-2345 in London, or 0345/222-111 in the U.K.; www.british-airways.com) and **Lufthansa** (☎ 0345/737-747 in the U.K.) are the most convenient carriers to the major German cities, including Düsseldorf, Cologne, Frankfurt, Munich, and Berlin. BA has seven flights a day to Cologne (flying time: 75 min.), five daily flights to Munich (1 hr. and 40 min.), and four nonstop and three one-stop to Berlin (1 hr. and 40 min.). It also services Bremen, Hannover, and Stuttgart. **British Midland** (☎ 0181/745-7321 in London, or 0345/554-554 in the U.K.) has two daily flights to Cologne, four daily to Frankfurt, and one daily to Dresden.

From Ireland, **Aer Lingus** (☎ 01/886-8888) flies between Dublin and Frankfurt and Düsseldorf; **Lufthansa** (☎ 01/844-5544) flies from Frankfurt to Dublin. From Australia, **Qantas** (☎ 008-112-121 in Australia) flies from both Melbourne and Sydney to Frankfurt via Asia. Lufthansa offers cheap fares in conjunction with Qantas.

BY TRAIN

Many passengers, especially holders of the **Eurailpass,** travel to Germany by train from other European cities. (See "Getting Around," below, for information on purchasing the Eurailpass and other rail passes.)

British Rail runs four trains a day to Germany from Victoria Station in **London,** going by way of the Ramsgate–Ostend ferry or jetfoil. Two trains depart from London's Liverpool Street Station, via Harwich–Hook of Holland. Most trains change at Cologne for destinations elsewhere in Germany. Tickets can be purchased through British Rail travel centers in London (☎ 0990/484-950 in the U.K., or 01603/764-776). See "Under the Channel," below, for information about the Eurostar service running between London and Brussels via the Channel Tunnel.

Train journeys can be lengthy. If you go by jetfoil, Cologne is $9^{1}/_{2}$ hours away from London; by Dover–Ostend ferry, it's $12^{1}/_{2}$ hours; and via the Ramsgate–Ostend ferry, it's 13 hours. Berlin can be reached in about 20 hours. Travel from London to Munich, depending on the connection, can take from 18 to 22 hours; it's often cheaper to fly than to take the train.

From **Paris** several trains depart throughout the day for points east, fanning out across eastern France to virtually every part of Germany. The most glamorous of these is the **Orient Express,** which departs from the Gare de l'Est around 6pm, arriving in Munich around 3am. For railway information on the French rail lines anywhere in Europe, call ☎ 08-36-35-35-39. Likewise, trains depart from throughout Austria, Italy, Holland, Denmark, and the Czech Republic for all points in Germany, interconnecting into one of the most efficient, and densely routed, rail networks in the world. For information and timetables prior to your departure, call **RailEurope** at ☎ 800/438-7245.

From Switzerland, the **Bavaria** (☎ 01-57-22-22) leaves Zurich at 7:30am daily, reaching Munich at 11:52am. The **Helvetia Express** (same phone number as the Bavaria) leaves Zurich daily at 11:57am, arriving in Hannover at 6:13pm and in Hamburg at 7:28pm.

BY CAR & FERRY

If you want to bring your car over from England, you face a choice of ports, from which you'll continue on driving to Germany. **P & O Stenna Lines** (☎ 800/677-8585 for North American reservations, or 0870/600-0611 in the U.K.) has 30 to 35 ferryboat crossings a day, depending on the season, between

Dover and Calais. The crossing can take as little as 1 hour, 15 minutes. Once in Calais, the drive to Cologne takes about 3 hours. Other options involve passage from Harwich to the Hook of Holland, a sea crossing of about 8 hours. You can also take your car via the Chunnel (see below).

BY BUS (COACH)

You can travel by bus to Germany's major cities from London, Paris, and many other cities in Europe. The continent's largest bus operator is **Eurolines,** 52 Grosvenor Gardens, London SW1W 0AU (☎ **0990/143-219**), which operates out of Victoria Coach Station in Central London. In Paris, Eurolines, 28, avenue du Général-de-Gaulle, 93541 Bagnolet (☎ **08/36-69-52-52;** Métro: Gallieni), is a 35-minute subway ride from the center. For information about Eurolines in Germany, contact **Deutsche Touring** (Eurolines Stadtböro), Am Römerhof 17, 60426 Frankfurt am Main (☎ **069/7-90-30**). Eurolines does not maintain a U.S.- based sales agent, but many travel agents can arrange for a ticket on the bus lines that link Europe's major cities.

Buses on long-haul journeys are equipped with toilets and partially reclining seats. They stop for 60-minute rest and refreshment breaks every 4 hours. Fares change without notice and often fluctuate from month to month. Discounts are sometimes available if you buy well in advance. In addition, discounts of around 20% are sometimes offered for bus passengers under age 26.

Buses from London to Frankfurt depart every evening; buses from London to Munich depart three times a week. The Frankfurt-bound itinerary from London leads through Ramsgate to Ostend and Brussels in Belgium, then to Aachen, Cologne, Bonn, and Koblenz in Germany.

BY THE CHUNNEL

The $15 billion **Channel Tunnel** (or "Chunnel"), one of the great engineering feats of all time, is the first link between Britain and the Continent since the Ice Age. The tunnel was built beneath the seabed through a layer of impermeable chalk marl and sealed with a reinforced concrete lining. The 50km (31-mile) journey between Britain and France takes 35 minutes, although actual time in the Chunnel is only 19 minutes. Once on the Continent, you can connect to Germany fairly easily.

Rail Europe sells tickets on the **Eurostar** direct train service between London and Paris or Brussels (☎ **800/94-CHUNNEL**). Round-trip first-class fare between London and Paris costs $329, regular second class $159. Round-trip first-class fare between London and Brussels costs $239, with regular second class at $159. In the U.K., make reservations for **Eurostar** at ☎ **0990/ 300-003;** in Paris at ☎ **01-44-51-06-02;** and in the U.S. at ☎ **800/ 387-67827.** A journey from London to Paris via the Chunnel takes about the same amount of time as flying, if you calculate door-to-door travel time. Trains leave from London's Waterloo Station and arrive in Paris at the Gare du Nord.

The tunnel also accommodates passenger cars, charter buses, taxis, and motorcycles from Folkestone to Calais. It operates 24 hours a day, 365 days a year, running every 15 minutes during peak travel times and at least once an hour at night. Tickets may be purchased at the toll booth. Contact **Eurotunnel** (☎ **800/4-EURAIL** in the U.S. and Canada; 08705/35-35-35 or 08000/38-83-88 in the U.K.).

BY ESCORTED TOUR

Escorted tours may not be the option for you if you like to go your own way and be spontaneous. But some people love them. They let you relax and take in the sights while a bus driver fights traffic for you; they spell out your costs up front; and they take you to the maximum number of sights in the minimum amount of time with the least amount of hassle. If you do choose an escorted tour, you should ask a few simple questions before you buy:

1. What is the **cancellation policy?** Do they require a deposit? Can they cancel the trip if they don't get enough people? Do you get a refund if they cancel? If you cancel? How late can you cancel if you are unable to go? When do you pay in full?
2. How busy is the **schedule?** How much sightseeing do they plan each day? Do they allow ample time for relaxing by the pool, shopping, or wandering?
3. What is the **size** of the group? The smaller the group, the more flexible the itinerary, and the less time you'll spend waiting for people to get on and off the bus. Tour operators may be evasive about this, but they should be able to give you a rough estimate. Some tours have a minimum group size and may cancel the tour if they don't book enough people.
4. What is included in the **price?** Don't assume anything. You may have to pay for transportation to and from the airport. A box lunch may be included in an excursion, but drinks might cost extra. Beer might be included, but wine might not. Can you opt out of certain activities, or does the bus leave once a day, with no exceptions? Are all your meals planned in advance? Can you choose your entree at dinner, or does everybody get the same chicken cutlet?

Note: If you choose an escorted tour, think strongly about purchasing travel insurance from an independent agency, especially if the tour operator asks you to pay up front. See "Insurance" earlier in this chapter. One final caveat: Since escorted tour prices are based on double occupancy, the single traveler is usually penalized.

American Express Vacations (☎ 800/241-1700 in the U.S. and Canada) is one of the biggest tour operators in the world. Its offerings are comprehensive, and unescorted customized package tours are available, too. **Brendan Tours** (☎ 800/421-8446) has a selection of 9- to 15-day tours. **Caravan Tours** (☎ 800/227-2826) offers tours of southern Germany and Austria, many of which begin and end in Berlin. Accommodations are at the better hotels, and rates include everything except airfare. **Collette Tours** (☎ 800/832-4656) has an Alpine Countries tour that covers southern Germany, Austria, and Switzerland. **Globus** (☎ 800/338-7092) offers 8- to 16-day tours of various parts of Germany. It also has a budget branch that offers tours at lower rates; all are escorted. **Maupintour** (☎ 800/255-4266) has a selection of upscale tours, such as a Rhine River tour of Berlin, Dresden, Meissen, Nürnberg, and Heidelberg, or an 18-day tour that goes from Vienna to Amsterdam. **Tauck Tours** (☎ 800/468-2825) has a wide selection of escorted tours, such as the 14-day Romantic Germany tour from Frankfurt to Berlin, with stops in Dresden, Heidelberg, and Oberammergau. Most meals are included in the rates, but airfare is extra.

Two companies offer superdeluxe tours (with prices to match). **Abercrombie & Kent** (☎ 800/323-7308 or 630/954-2944) provides group tours to various areas of Germany and will customize to suit your needs. **Travcoa** (☎ 800/992-2003) offers top-of-the-line coach tours, such as a 16-day tour of Ludwig's castles and the Romantic Road, which begins in Munich and ends in Strasbourg, France.

BY CRUISE

Germany's premier cruise carrier is **KD River Cruises of Europe.** For information, contact them at 323 Geary St., Suite 603, San Francisco, CA 94102 (☎ **800/858-8587** or 415/392-8817), or 2500 Westchester Ave., Suite 113, Purchase, NY 10577 (☎ **800/346-6525**).

Luxury 8- to 10-day cruises on the Rhine, Main, and Danube Rivers are also available through **Euro Cruises,** 303 W. 13th St., New York, NY 10014 (☎ **800/688-3876**). These cruises feature optional shore excursions. All cabins have twin beds and windows. **Jody Lexow Yacht Charter** rents hotel barges (including crew, food, and beverages) and smaller self-drive craft for touring the canals and rivers of Germany. For additional information, contact 26 Coddington Wharf, Newport, RI 02840 (☎ **800/662-2628**). **Extoile de Champagne,** 88 Broad St., Boston, MA 02110 (☎ **800/280-1492**), can arrange a 6-night luxury barge cruise that runs from Tier to Koblenz, with daily excursion stops along the way.

Groups of 12 to 16 people can arrange 7- to 14-day tours of European breweries, both well-known and off the beaten track, through **MIR Corporation** (☎ **800/424-7289**). The tours begin in many European cities.

BY PACKAGE DEAL

See "By Plane," above; most airlines offer packages that may include car rentals and accommodations in addition to your airfare. For example, **Delta Vacations** (☎ **800/ 221-6666**) offers both fly/drive and fly/rail packages, plus 3-day "city sprees" in Berlin, Frankfurt, and Munich.

DER Tours (☎ **800/782-2424**) offers discounted airfares, car rentals, hotel packages, short regional tours, and GermanRail, Eurail, and other rail passes.

10 Getting Around

BY PLANE

From Frankfurt, most **Lufthansa** (☎ **800/645-3880**) destinations in Germany can be reached in an average of 50 minutes, with at least four flights daily.

All German cities with commercial airports have an airport shuttle service, offering reduced fares and fast connections between the city center and the airport. Departure points are usually the airlines' town offices and the city's main rail terminal. Luggage can be checked at the DB (GermanRail) baggage counter at the airport for delivery to the railroad station at your ultimate destination.

The **Lufthansa Airport Express** is a high-speed train that travels between the Frankfurt and Düsseldorf airports, with stops at Bonn, Stuttgart, Dortmund, and Cologne, incidentally giving the traveler an opportunity to view the Rhine Valley.

BY TRAIN

Whether you travel first or second class, you'll find that the trains of **GermanRail (DER Rail)** deserve their good reputation for comfort, cleanliness, and punctuality. All are modern and fast. Both first- and second-class trains carry smoker and nonsmoker compartments. A snack bar or a dining car, serving German and international cuisine as well as good wine and beer, can usually be found on all trains except locals.

For city sightseeing, you can leave your baggage in a locker or check it at the station's baggage counter. In many cities, GermanRail provides door-to-door baggage service, allowing passengers to have luggage picked up at or delivered to their hotels. Accompanying baggage can be checked for a nominal fee. Suitcases, baby carriages, skis, bicycles, and steamer trunks are permitted as baggage. Insurance policies of various kinds, including a travel medical plan, are also available.

About 20,000 **InterCity (IC)** passenger trains offer express service every hour between most large and medium-size German cities. IC trains have adjustable cushioned seats and individual reading lights, and often offer telephone and secretarial services. Bars, lounges, and dining rooms are available too. A network of **EuroCity trains (EC)** connecting Germany with 13 other countries offers the same high standards of service as those of IC.

Germany's high-speed rail network, known as **InterCity Express (ICE)** trains, is among the fastest in Europe, reaching speeds of 265 kilometers per hour (165 miles per hour). One of these trains runs from Hamburg via Würzburg and Nürnberg to Munich; another from Frankfurt via Stuttgart to Munich; and yet another from Berlin via Frankfurt to Munich. Each train makes stops along the way. ICE significantly reduces travel time, making transits north to south across the country easily possible in the course of a single day. Some 200 east-west connections have been added to the GermanRail timetable to link the Deutsche Bundesbahn (west) and the Deutsche Reichsbahn (east). Additional connections make Leipzig and Dresden more accessible.

InterCity Night (ICN)—one of the most comfortable night trains in Europe—operates between Berlin and Bonn and Berlin and Munich. Even though the train doesn't depart until 10 or 11pm, you may board as early as 8 or 8:30pm. Arrival the next morning is between 6:55 and 7:55am, and you have the option of remaining aboard until 9 or 9:30am.

The ICN offers first and tourist class. Sleeping accommodations in first class include single or double compartments with shower and toilet, and equipped with key cards, phones for wake-up service, luggage storage, and other amenities. Tourist class offers open seating with sleeperettes (reclining seats). The ICN is equipped with a restaurant and bistro car, and breakfast buffet is included in the first-class fare. For an extra cost, a limited menu for dinner is offered. Advance reservations are mandatory for all sleeping accommodations.

DER Rail issues tickets for the ICN and also makes reservations. Eurail and GermanRail pass holders are accepted on this train but have to pay for the seat or sleeper reservation and also for meals. Youth-pass holders are only accepted in tourist class. Children under the age of 4 travel free, provided they do not require a separate seat; those between 4 and 12 are charged half fare.

Travelers wanting to avoid the fatigue of long-distance driving can reach their destination by taking themselves and their cars on car-sleeper **Auto Trains.** There are also some daytime automobile trains.

Before leaving for Germany, you can get complete details about the **German Federal Railroad** and the many plans it offers, as well as information about Eurailpasses, at 500 Mamaroneck Ave, Suite 314, Harrison, NY 10528 (☎ **800-4-EURAIL** in the U.S., or 800/555-2748 in Canada).

If you plan to travel a great deal on German railroads, it's worth buying a copy of the *Thomas Cook Timetable of European Passenger Railroads.* It's available exclusively in North America from **Forsyth Travel Library,** 226 Westchester Ave., White Plains, NY 10604 (☎ **800/FORSYTH**), at a cost of $27.95, plus $4.95 postage (priority airmail) in the United States or $6.95 to Canada.

GERMANRAIL TOURIST PASSES You can buy a **GermanRail Pass** from a travel agent before you leave home. The pass allows 4 days of travel in 1 month, and costs $252 first-class or $174 second class. Additional days cost $32 first class and $22 second class.

A youth version of the same pass, valid only for persons under 26 years of age and available only in second class, costs $138 for 4 days in 1 month, $156 for 5 days in 1 month, $162 for 6 days in 1 month, $174 for 7 days in 1 month, $186 for 8 days in 1 month, $198 for 9 days in 1 month, and $210 for 10 days in 1 month. Another bargain is a **Twinpass,** for two adults traveling together. This pass costs $378 for 3 days in 1 month for first-class or $261 for second class. Additional days cost $48 for two first class or $33 second class.

The passes also entitle the bearer to additional benefits, such as free or discounted travel on selected bus routes operated by Deutsche Touring/Europabus, including destinations not serviced by trains, or excursions along particularly scenic highways such as the Romantic Road and the Castle Road. The pass also includes free travel on **KD German Line steamers** (day trips only) along the Rhine, Main, and Mosel Rivers.

These passes are most conveniently available from **Rail Europe** (☎ 800/4-EURAIL in the U.S., or 800/361-RAIL in Canada). Rail Europe can also arrange cost-effective "Rail and Drive" packages that combine a certain number of days on the train with a certain number of days in a rental car. Here's an example of how it might work: Ride the train from Frankfurt to Munich, spend 3 days exploring the city, then rent a car for a 2-day excursion to Berchtesgaden and the Bavarian Alps. The GermanRail Flexipass is also sold by **DER Travel** (☎ 800/782-2424 in the U.S. and Canada) and by **CIT Travel** (☎ 800/248-7245 in the U.S. and Canada, or 847/318-7101 in Chicago).

EURAILPASSES The Eurailpass is one of Europe's greatest bargains, permitting unlimited first-class rail travel through 17 countries in Europe, including Germany. Passes are for periods as short as 15 days or as long as 3 months and are strictly nontransferable.

Your best bet is to buy a **Eurailpass** outside Europe (it's available in Europe but will cost more). It costs $554 for 15 days, $718 for 21 days, $890 for 1 month, $1,260 for 2 months, and $1,558 for 3 months. Children 3 and under travel free providing they don't occupy a seat (otherwise they're charged half fare); children 4 to 11 are charged half fare. If you're under 26, you can purchase a **Eurail Youthpass,** entitling you to unlimited second-class travel for $388 for 15 days, $499 for 21 days, $623 for 1 month, $882 for 2 months, and $1,089 for 3 months.

Seat reservations are required on some trains. Many of the trains have *couchettes* (sleeping cars), which cost extra. Obviously, the 2- or 3-month traveler gets the greatest economic advantages; the Eurailpass is ideal for such extensive trips. With the pass you can visit all of Germany's major sights, from Lake Constance to Saxony. Eurailpass holders are entitled to considerable reductions on certain buses and ferries as well.

If you'll be traveling for 2 weeks or a month, think carefully before you buy a pass. To get full advantage of a pass for 15 days or a month, you'll have to spend a great deal of time on the train.

The **Eurail Flexipass** allows you to travel through Europe with more flexibility. It's valid in first class and offers the same privileges as the Eurailpass. However, it provides a number of individual travel days that you can use over a much longer period of consecutive days. That makes it possible to stay in one city and yet not lose a single day of travel. There are two passes: 10 days of travel in 2 months for $654, and 15 days of travel in 2 months for $862. The **Eurail Youth Flexipass** is identical except that it's sold only to travelers under 26, and costs less: $458 for 10 days of travel within 2 months, and $599 for 15 days of travel within 2 months.

Another good option is the **Europass,** which is similar to the Eurailpass but covers fewer countries: Germany, France, Switzerland, Italy, and Spain (other countries may be added on at an additional cost). All passes are good for 2 months. Two adults can travel in first class for any 5 days during this period for $348; 6 days, $368; 8 days, $448; 10 days, $528; and 15 days, $728.

WHERE TO BUY RAIL PASSES Travel agents in all towns and railway agents in major North American cities sell all these tickets, but the biggest supplier is **Rail Europe** (☎ 800/438-7245; www.raileurope.com), which can also give you informational brochures.

For British travelers, an especially convenient outlet for buying railway tickets is opposite Platform 2 in Victoria Station, London. **Wasteels Ltd.** (☎ 020/7834-7066) will provide railway-related services and discuss the various types of fares and rail passes and their drawbacks; its staff generally spends a bit more time with a client while planning an itinerary. Depending on circumstances, Wasteels sometimes charges a £5 fee for its services, but for the information available, the money is well spent.

Many different rail passes are available in the U.K. for travel in Britain and continental Europe. Stop in at the **International Rail Centre,** Victoria Station, London SWIV 1JY (☎ 0990/848848 in the U.K., or 020/7834-2345). Some of the most popular passes, including Inter-Rail and Euro Youth, are offered only to travelers under 26 years of age; these allow unlimited second-class travel through most European countries.

BY CAR

British travelers who want to bring their own cars over should see "Getting There," earlier in this chapter.

Competition in the European car-rental industry is fierce, so make sure you comparison shop. You can make reservations by calling these toll-free numbers: **Avis** (☎ 800/331-1212), **Budget** (☎ 800/527-0700), **Hertz** (☎ 800/654-3131), **Kemwel Holiday Autos** (☎ 800/678-0678), and **Auto Europe** (☎ 800/223-5555). Cars can often be rented at one German city and returned at another for no additional charge.

There are some advantages to **prepaying rentals** in dollars before leaving the United States. You get an easy-to-understand net price (which you have to prepay at least 14 days before departure by credit card), the rental process is more streamlined, and you can avoid unpleasant surprises caused by sudden unfavorable changes in currency exchange rates. Remember, however, that if you opt to prepay and your plans change, you'll have to go through some rather complicated paperwork (and, in some cases, have to pay a penalty of around $25) for changing or canceling a prepaid contract.

A **collision-damage waiver (CDW)** is an optional insurance policy that can be purchased when you sign a rental agreement. For an extra fee, the rental agency agrees to eliminate all but a small percentage of your financial responsibility for collision damage in case of an accident. If you don't have a CDW and do have an accident, you'll usually pay for all damages, up to the cost of actually replacing the vehicle if the accident is serious enough. Some credit cards (especially gold cards) cover the CDW, so call your company to check on these benefits before you spend the extra money on additional insurance.

Note: Credit card companies do *not* cover liability if you injure someone, so unless you have your own car insurance that will cover you abroad, you may want to take the extra liability coverage.

GASOLINE   Gasoline is readily available throughout Germany, and service stations appear frequently along the Autobahns. The cheapest gasoline is at stations marked SB-TANKEN (self-service), but remember that gas will always be much more expensive than in the U.S. A liter (about a fourth of a gallon) costs 1.30DM to 1.70DM (65¢ to 85¢). Gasoline pumps labeled BLEIFREI offer unleaded gas.

DRIVING RULES   In Germany, you drive on the right side of the road. Both front-seat and back-seat passengers are required to wear safety belts. Children cannot ride in the front seat.

Easy-to-understand international road signs are posted, but U.S. travelers should remember that road signs are in kilometers, not miles. In congested areas, the speed limit is about 50 kilometers per hour (around 30 m.p.h.). On all other roads except the Autobahns, the speed limit is 100 kilometers per hour (about 60 m.p.h.).

In theory, there is no speed limit on the Autobahns (in the left, fast lane), but many drivers going too fast report that they have been stopped by the police and fined on the spot. So reasonable caution is recommended here, for safety if not other reasons. A German driver on the Autobahn can be a ferocious creature, and you may prefer the slow lane. The government recommends an Autobahn speed limit of 130 kilometers per hour (80 m.p.h.).

Note: Drinking while driving is a very serious offense in Germany. Be sure to keep any alcoholic beverages in the trunk or some other storage area.

BREAKDOWNS/ASSISTANCE   The major automobile club in Germany is **Automobilclub von Deutschland (AvD),** Lyoner Strasse 16, 60329 Frankfurt (☎ **069/6-60-60**). If you have a breakdown on the Autobahn, you can call from an emergency phone, each of which is spaced about a mile apart. On secondary roads, go to the nearest phone. If you don't belong to an auto club, call ☎ **01802/222-222.** In English, ask for "road service assistance." Emergency assistance is free, but you pay for parts or materials.

MAPS   The best maps, available at all major bookstores throughout Germany, are published by **Michelin,** which offers various regional maps. **Hallweg** also offers good maps.

DRIVER'S LICENSES   American drivers, and those from EU countries, need only a domestic license to drive. However, both in Germany and throughout the rest of Europe, you must also have an international insurance certificate, known as a green card (*carte verte*). Any car-rental agency will automatically provide one of these as a standard part of the rental contract, but it's a good idea to double-check all documents at the time of rental, just to be sure that you can identify the card if asked by border patrol or the police.

BY BUS

An excellent, efficient bus network services Germany. Many buses are operated by **Bahnbus,** which is owned by the railway. These are integrated to complement the rail service. Bus service in Germany is particularly convenient during slow periods of rail service, normally around midday and on Saturday and Sunday. German post offices often operate local bus services (contact local post offices for schedules and prices).

The most popular bus ride is along the Romantic Road (see chapter 6), where special green-and-white buses carry tourists regularly from town to town. For more information, ask a travel agent or call **Deutsche Touring GmbH,** Amrömerhof 17, Frankfurt (☎ **069/79-03-50**).

BY BOAT

Perhaps Germany's most beautiful features are its lakes and rivers. The mighty Rhine is the country's most traveled waterway. German cruise ships also run on the Main River between Mainz and Frankfurt; on the Danube from Nürnberg to Linz (Austria), going on to Vienna and Budapest; and on the Mosel between Cochem and Trier.

KD River Cruises of Europe, 323 Geary St., Suite 603, San Francisco, CA 94102 (☎ **800/858-8587** or 415/392-8817), or 2500 Westchester Ave., Suite 113, Purchase, NY 10577 (☎ **800/346-6525**), operates the most services. Eurailpasses are valid for most KD excursions. The company also offers luxury cruises, the most popular being a 5-day cruise along the Rhine from Amsterdam to Basel or vice versa.

BY BICYCLE

For information about biking, write to the association of German cyclists, **Allgemeiner Deutscher Fahrrad-Club,** Hellerallee 23, 28209, Bremen 71 (☎ **0421/34-62-90**).

Bicycles can be rented at more than 300 rail depots throughout the country, for 10DM to 16DM ($5 to $8) per day or 35DM ($17.50) per week. If you have a valid rail ticket, the cost is often reduced by 50%. You can make arrangements to rent a bicycle at one rail depot and return it at another.

11 Tips on Accommodations

In general, Germany has one of the highest standards of innkeeping in the world. However, many of the hotels in the eastern section of Germany—once geared to tourism from the old Eastern bloc countries—are not of the same standard as those in the west.

Hotels range from five-star palaces of luxury and comfort to plain country inns and simple guest houses (*Gasthäuser*), with a huge variation in rates. The cheapest accommodation is in pensions (*Fremdenheime*) or rooms in private homes (look for a sign saying ZIMMER FREI, meaning there's a room for rent). Hotels listed as *garni* provide no meals other than breakfast.

When you don't have time to make reservations on your own, you can call **Travel Interlink** at ☎ **800/888-5898.** Also, tourist offices will often book you into a room for a small charge. Obviously, the earlier you arrive in these offices, the more likely you are to get a good room at the price you want.

BUNGALOW, VILLA & APARTMENT RENTALS

Germans who own vacation homes or units often make them available for visitors when the homes are vacant. These villas, apartments, and bungalows—called *Ferienwohnungen* or *Ferienapartments*—shelter two to eight people in most cases. The longer you stay, the better the rate. Sometimes extra charges are imposed for utilities, but these matters have to be worked out, as does the arrangement for bed linens. Local tourist offices have details of rentals available in their areas.

EUROPEAN CASTLE HOTELS

A new breed of castle hotels has begun to pop up across what used to be Soviet-controlled territory of eastern and central Europe. The Mannheim-based

Gastemschloss Group, which is more of an affiliation than a chain, incorporates top-notch hotels with historic backgrounds, such as the Burg Hotel auf Schönburg in Oberwesel am Rhine, with newer contenders in Germany's eastern and Baltic zones. For information on these hotels contact **Euro-Connection,** 7500 212th St. SW, Suite 103, Edmonds, WA 98026 (☎ **800/ 645-3876**). This company also represents Romantik Hotels and Grandesétapes Françaises, a France-based affiliation of prestigious lodgings.

Fast Facts: Germany

Business Hours   Most **banks** are open Monday to Friday 8:30am to 1pm and 2:30 to 4pm (Thursday to 5:30pm). Money exchanges at airports and border-crossing points are generally open daily from 6am to 10pm. Exchanges at border railroad stations are kept open for arrivals of all international trains. Most **businesses** are open Monday to Friday from 9am to 5pm and on Saturday from 9am to 1pm. Store hours can vary from town to town, but **shops** are generally open Monday to Friday 9 or 10am to 6 or 6:30pm (to 8:30pm on Thursday). Saturday hours are generally from 9am to 1 or 2pm, except on the first Saturday of a month, when stores may remain open until 4pm.

Drug Laws   Penalties for illegal drug possession in Germany are severe. You could go to jail or be deported immediately.

Drugstores   Pharmaceuticals are sold at an *Apotheke*. For cosmetics, go to a *Drogerie*. German pharmacies take turns staying open nights, on Sunday, and on holidays, and each *Apotheke* posts a list of those that are open off-hours.

Electricity   In most places the electricity is 220 volts AC (50 cycles). A transformer and a plug that fits the German socket will be needed for your U.S. appliances. Many leading hotels will supply these.

Embassies & Consulates   In the life of this edition, embassy and consulate addresses are likely to change, in the move from Bonn to Berlin. Call before you set out for a particular address. The embassy of the **United States** is at Deichmannsaue 29, 53170 Bonn (☎ **0228/33-91,** or 0228/3-39-20-53 for visa applications); there's also a U.S. embassy office at Neustaedtische Kirchstrasse 4–5, 10117 Berlin (☎ **030/2-38-51-74**). U.S. consulates are located at Clayallee 170, 14195 Berlin (☎ **030/8-32-92-33**); at Siesmayerstrasse 21, 60323 Frankfurt (☎ **069/7-53-50**); at Wilhelm–Seyfferth-Strasse 4, 04107 Leipzig (☎ **0341/21-38-40**); at Königinstrasse 5, 80539 München (☎ **089/2-88-80**); and at Alsterufer 27-28, 20354 Hamburg (☎ **040/ 41-17-10**). The consular information hot line is ☎ **0130/82-63-64.**

The embassy of the **United Kingdom** is at Hardenbergstrasse 20, 10623 Berlin (☎ **030/311-09-90**). The British Consulate-General, handling passport and visa applications, is at Yorckstrasse 19, 40476 Düsseldorf (☎ **0211/9-44-80**); Harvestehuder Weg 8A, 20148 Hamburg (☎ **040/4-48-03-20**); Bockenheimer Landstrasse 42, 60323 Frankfurt (☎ **069/1-70-00-20**); Bürk–leinstrasse 10, 80538 Munich (☎ **089/21-10-90**); and at Breite Strasse 2, 70173 Stuttgart (☎ **0711/ 16-26-90**).

The embassy of **Australia** is at Godesberger Allee 105–107, 53175 Bonn (☎ **0228/8-10-30**), with a Berlin office on Kempinski Plaza, at

Uhlandstrasse 181–183, 10623 Berlin (☎ **030/8-80-08-80**), and a consulate at Gutleutstrasse 85, 60329 Frankfurt/Main (☎ **069/2-73-90-90**).

The embassy of **Canada** is at Friedrich-Wilhelm-Strasse 18, 53113 Bonn (☎ **0228/96-80**). Canada maintains a consulate at Friedrichstrasse 95, 23rd Floor, 10117 Berlin (☎ **030/2-03-12-470**); at Prinz-Georg-Strasse 126, 40479 Düsseldorf (☎ **0211/17-21-70**); at Tal 29, 80331 Munich (☎ **089/219-9570**); and at ABC Strasse 45, 20354 Hamburg (☎ **040/35-55-62-95**).

The embassy of **New Zealand** is at Bundeskanzlerplatz 2–10, 53113 Bonn (☎ **0228/22-80-70**). A consulate is at Heimhuderstrasse 56, 20148 Hamburg (☎ **040/4-42-55-50**).

Emergencies   Throughout Germany the emergency number for **police** is ☎ **110;** for fire or to call an ambulance, dial ☎ **112.**

Liquor Laws   As in many European countries, drinking laws are flexible, enforced only if a problem develops. Officially, you must be 18 to consume any kind of alcoholic beverage. Bars and cafes rarely request proof of age. Drinking while driving, however, is treated as a very serious offense.

Mail   General delivery—mark it POSTE RESTANTE—can be used in any major town or city in Germany. You can pick up your mail upon presentation of a valid identity card or passport. Street mailboxes are painted yellow. It costs 3DM ($1.50) for the first 5 grams (about one-fifth ounce) to send an airmail letter to the United States or Canada, and 2DM ($1) for postcards. To mail a package, go to one of the larger post offices, preferably the main branch in the area. All letters to the U.K. cost 1.10DM (55¢) or 1DM (50¢) for postcards.

Medical Assistance   Most major hotels have a physician on staff or on call. If you can't get hold of a doctor, dial the emergency service, ☎ **112,** which is open day and night. Medical and hospital services aren't free, so be sure that you have appropriate insurance coverage before you travel.

Pets   Dogs and cats brought into Germany from abroad will require a veterinary certificate stating that the animal has been vaccinated against rabies not less than 30 days and not more than 1 year before entry into the country. This certificate must be accompanied by a notarized translation of the document into German.

Police   Throughout the country, dial ☎ **110** for emergencies.

Rest Rooms   Use the word *Toilette* (pronounced twah-*leh*-teh). Women's toilets are usually marked with an "F" for *Frauen,* and men's toilets with an "H" for *Herren.* Germany, frankly, doesn't have enough public toilets, except in transportation centers. The locals have to rely on bars, cafes, or restaurants—and using them isn't always appreciated if you're not a paying customer. Toilets often have attendants who expect a small tip; if you need soap and a towel, give something extra.

Safety   Germany is a reasonably safe country in which to travel, although neo-Nazi skinheads, especially in the eastern part of the country, have sometimes attacked black or Asian travelers. One of the most dangerous places, especially at night, is around the large railway stations in such cities as Frankfurt, Munich, Berlin, and Hamburg. Some beer halls get especially rowdy late at night.

Taxes   As a member of the European Union, Germany imposes a tax on most goods and services known as a **value-added tax (VAT),** or in German, *Mehrwertsteuer.* Nearly everything is taxed at 15%, including vital necessities such as gas and luxury items such as jewelry. VAT is included in the prices of restaurants and hotels. Note that goods for sale, such as cameras, also have the 15% tax already factored into the price; but the listed prices of services, such as getting a mechanic to fix your car, don't include VAT, so an extra 15% will be tacked on to the bill. Stores that display a "Tax Free" sticker will issue you a Tax-Free Shopping Check at the time of purchase. When leaving the country, have your check stamped by the German Customs Service as your proof of legal export. You can then get a cash refund at one of the Tax-Free Shopping Service offices in the major airports and many train stations, even at some of the bigger ferry terminals. Otherwise, you must send the checks to Tax-Free Shopping Service, Mengstrasse 19, 23552 Lübeck, Germany. If you want the payment to be credited to your bank card or your bank account, mention this. There is no airport departure tax in Germany.

Telephone   The country code for Germany is 49. To call Germany from the United States, dial the international access code 011, then 49, then the city code, then the regular phone number. *The phone numbers listed in this book are to be used within Germany; when calling from abroad, omit the initial 0 in the city code.*

Local and long-distance calls may be placed from all post offices and coin-operated public telephone booths. The unit charge is 0.30DM or three 10-pfennig coins. More than half the phones in Germany require an advance-payment telephone card from **Telekom,** the German telephone company. Phone cards are sold at post offices and newsstands; they cost 12DM ($6) and 50DM ($25). Rates are measured in units rather than minutes. The farther the distance, the more units are consumed. For example, a 3-minute call to the United States costs 41 units. Telephone calls made through hotel switchboards can double, triple, or even quadruple the regular charge. Therefore, try to make your calls outside your hotel at a pay phone or post office. Post offices can also send faxes for you.

To call the U.S. or Canada from Germany, dial 01, followed by the country code 1, then the area code, and then the number. Alternatively, you can dial the various telecommunication companies in the States for cheaper rates. From Germany, the access for **AT&T** is ☎ **800-CALLATT;** for **MCI** ☎ **800/888-8000;** and for **Sprint** ☎ **800/888-0013. USA Direct** can be used with all telephone cards and for collect calls. The number from Germany is ☎ **01-30-00-10. Canada Direct** can be used with Bell Telephone Cards and for collect calls. This number from Germany is ☎ **01-30-00-14.**

If you're calling from a public pay phone in Germany, you must deposit the basic local rate.

Time   Germany operates on Central European time (CET), which means that the country is 6 hours ahead of eastern standard time (EST) in the United States and 1 hour ahead of Greenwich mean time (GMT). Summer daylight saving time begins in Germany in April and ends in September—there's a slight difference in the dates from year to year— so there may be a period in early spring and in the fall when there's a 7-hour difference between EST and CET. Always check if you're traveling during these periods, especially if you need to catch a plane.

Tipping   If a restaurant bill says *Bedienung,* that means a service charge has already been added, so just round up to the nearest mark.

If not, add 10 to 15%. Round up to the nearest mark for taxis. Bellhops get 2DM ($1) per bag, as does the doorperson at your hotel, restaurant, or nightclub. Room cleaning staffs get small tips in Germany, as do concierges who perform some special favors such as obtaining hard-to-get theater or opera tickets. Tip hairdressers or barbers 5 to 10%.

Water   Tap water is safe to drink in all German towns and cities. However, don't drink from rivers or mountain streams, regardless of how clean the water may appear.

Planning Your Trip: An Online Directory

by Lynne Bairstow

Lynne Bairstow is the editorial director of *e-com* magazine.

Day by day, the Internet becomes more integrated into our lives—including the way we plan and book our travel. By early 2000, one in every ten trips was being booked online, a trend that's sure to accelerate.

The Internet not only provides a wealth of destination information but also gives you the chance to compare experiences with fellow travelers, ask experts for pre-trip advice, seek out discounted fares once accessible only to travel industry insiders, and stay in touch via e-mail while you're away. The instant communication and storehouse of information has revolutionized the way travel is researched, reserved, and realized.

This Online Directory will help you take better advantage of the travel planning information available online, and it's most useful in conjunction with this book. Section 1 lists general Internet resources that can make any trip easier, such as sites for obtaining the best possible prices on airline tickets. In Section 2, you'll find some top online guides for Germany, organized by region.

Keep in mind this isn't a comprehensive list but a discriminating selection to get you started. Recognition is given to sites based on the value of their content and ease of use—unlike some publications' Web-site rankings, which are based on payment to the publisher rather than on merit. Finally, remember this is a press-time snapshot of leading Web sites—some undoubtedly will have evolved, changed, or moved by the time you read this.

1 Top Travel-Planning Web Sites

Though the Internet once featured a confusing jumble of travel sites with limited features, several key companies have emerged that offer comprehensive travel planning and booking. In addition to the Frommer's Online site (see box, above), we list the other top online travel agencies below, along with some more specialized services.

WHY BOOK ONLINE?

Online agencies have come a long way over the past few years, now providing tips for finding the best fare and giving suggested dates or times to travel that yield the lowest price if your plans are flexible. Other sites even allow you to establish the price you're willing to pay, and they check the airlines' willingness to accept it. However, in some cases, these

What You'll Find at the Frommer's Site

We highly recommend **Arthur Frommer's Budget Travel Online** (**www.frommers.com**) as an excellent travel planning resource. Of course, we're a little biased, but you'll find indispensable travel tips, reviews, monthly vacation giveaways, and online booking. Among the site's most popular features is the regular "Ask the Expert" bulletin boards, which feature one of the Frommer's authors answering your questions via online postings.

Subscribe to Arthur Frommer's Daily Newsletter (**www.frommers.com/ newsletters**) to receive the latest travel bargains and inside tips in your e-mail inbox every day. You'll read daily headlines and articles from the dean of travel himself, highlighting last-minute deals on airfares, accommodations, cruises, and package vacations. You'll also find great travel advice by checking our Tip of the Day or Hot Spot of the Month.

Search our Destinations archive (**www.frommers.com/destinations**) of more than 200 domestic and international destinations for great places to stay, tips for traveling there, and what to do while you're there. Once you've researched your trip, the online reservation system (**www.frommers.com/booktravelnow**) takes you to Frommer's favorite sites for booking your vacation at affordable prices.

sites may not always yield the best price. Unlike a travel agent, for example, they may not have access to charter flights offered by wholesalers.

Online booking sites aren't the only places to reserve airline tickets. All major airlines have their own Web sites and often offer incentives—bonus frequent-flyer miles or net-only discounts, for example—when you buy online or buy an e-ticket.

The new trend is toward conglomerated booking sites. By mid-2000, a consortium of U.S. and European airlines are planning to launch an as-yet-unnamed Web site that will offer fares lower than those available through travel agents. United, Delta, Northwest, and Continental have initiated this effort, based on their success at selling airline seats at their own online sites.

The best of the travel planning sites are now highly personalized; they store your seating preferences, meal preferences, tentative itineraries, and credit-card information, allowing you to quickly plan trips or check agendas.

In many cases, booking your trip online can be better than working with a travel agent. It gives you the widest variety of choices, control, and the 24-hour convenience of planning your trip when you choose. All you need is some time—and often a little patience—and you're likely to find that the fun of online travel research will greatly enhance your trip.

WHO SHOULD BOOK ONLINE?

Online booking is best for travelers who want to know as much as possible about their options, those who have flexibility in their travel dates and are looking for the best price, and bargain hunters driven by a good value who are open-minded about where they travel.

One of the biggest successes in online travel for both passengers and airlines is the offer of last-minute specials, such as American Airlines' weekend deals or other Internet-only fares you must purchase online. Another advantage is that you can cash in on incentives for booking online, such as rebates or bonus frequent-flyer miles.

More people still look online than book online, partly due to fear of putting their credit card numbers out on the Net. Secure encryption and increasing experience buying online have removed this fear for most travelers. In some cases, however, it's simply easier to buy from a local travel agent who can deliver your tickets to your door (especially if your travel is last minute or you have special requests). You can find a flight online and then book it by calling a toll-free number or contacting your travel agent, though this is somewhat less efficient. To be sure you're in secure mode when you book online, look for a little icon of a key (in Netscape) or a padlock (in Internet Explorer) at the bottom of your Web browser.

Business and other frequent travelers also have found numerous benefits in online booking, as the advances in mobile technology provide them with the ability to check flight status, change plans, or get specific directions from handheld computing devices, mobile phones, and pagers. Some sites will even e-mail or page passengers if their flights are delayed.

Online booking is increasingly able to accommodate complex itineraries, even for international travel. The pace of evolution on the Net is rapid, so you'll probably find additional features and advancements by the time you visit these sites. What the future holds for online travelers is increasing personalization, customization, and reaching out to you.

TRAVEL PLANNING & BOOKING SITES

Below are listings for sites for planning and booking travel. The sites offer domestic and international flight, hotel, and rental-car bookings, plus news, destination information, and deals on cruises and vacation packages. Free (one-time) registration is required for booking.

✪ **Travelocity (incorporates Preview Travel). www.travelocity.com; www.previewtravel.com; www.frommers.travelocity.com**
Travelocity is Frommer's online travel planning/booking partner. Travelocity uses the SABRE system to offer reservations and tickets for more than 400 airlines, plus reservations and purchase capabilities for more than 45,000 hotels and 50 car-rental companies. An exclusive feature of the SABRE system is its **Low Fare Search Engine,** which automatically searches for the three lowest-priced itineraries based on a traveler's criteria. Last-minute deals and consolidator fares are included in the search. If you book with Travelocity, you can select specific seats for your flights with online seat maps and also view diagrams of the most popular commercial aircraft. Its hotel finder provides street-level location maps and photos of selected hotels. With the **Fare Watcher** e-mail feature, you can select up to five routes and receive e-mail notices when the fare changes by $25 or more.

Travelocity's **Destination Guide** includes updated information on some 260 destinations worldwide—supplied by Frommer's.

Note to AOL Users: You can book flights, hotels, rental cars, and cruises on AOL at keyword: Travel. The booking software is provided by Travelocity/Preview Travel and is similar to the Internet site. Use the AOL "Travelers Advantage" program to earn a 5% rebate on flights, hotel rooms, and car rentals.

Expedia. www.expedia.com
Expedia is Travelocity's major competitor. It features several ways of obtaining the best possible fares: **Flight Price Matcher** service allows your preferred

airline to match an available fare with a competitor; a comprehensive **Fare Compare** area shows the differences in fare categories and airlines; and **Fare Calendar** helps you plan your trip around the best possible fares. Its main limitation is that, like many online databases, Expedia focuses on the major airlines and hotel chains, so don't expect to find too many budget airlines or one-of-a-kind B&Bs here.

TRIP.com. www.trip.com

TRIP.com began as a site geared toward business travelers, but its innovative features and highly personalized approach have broadened its appeal to leisure travelers as well. It is the leading travel site for those using mobile devices to access Internet travel information.

TRIP.com includes a trip-planning function that provides the average and lowest fare for the route requested, in addition to the current available fare. An on-site "newsstand" features breaking news on airfare sales and other travel specials. Among its most popular features are Flight TRACKER and intelli-TRIP. **Flight TRACKER** allows users to track any commercial flight en route to its destination anywhere in the United States by accessing real-time FAA-based flight monitoring data. **intelliTRIP** is a travel search tool that allows users to identify the best airline, hotel, and rental-car rates in less than 90 seconds.

In addition, the site offers e-mail notification of flight delays, plus city resource guides, currency converters, and a weekly e-mail newsletter of fare updates, travel tips, and traveler forums.

Yahoo! Travel. www.travel.yahoo.com

Yahoo! is currently the most popular of the Internet information portals, and its travel site is a comprehensive mix of online booking, daily travel news, and destination information. The **Best Fares** area offers what it promises, plus provides feedback on refining your search if you have flexibility in travel dates or times. There is also an active section of Message Boards for discussions on travel in general and specific destinations.

SPECIALTY TRAVEL SITES

Although the sites listed above provide the most comprehensive services, some travelers have specialized needs that are best met by a site catering specifically to them.

For adventure travelers, **iExplore** (www.iexplore.com) is a great source for information on booking adventure and experiential travel, as well as related services and products. The site combines secure Internet booking functions with hands-on expertise and 24-hour live customer support by seasoned adventure travelers for those interested in trips off the beaten path. The company is a supporting member of the Ecotourism Society and is committed to environmentally responsible travel worldwide.

Another excellent site for adventure travelers is **Away.com** (www.away.com), which features unique vacations for challenging the body, mind, and spirit. Trips may include cycling in the Loire Valley, taking an African safari, or assisting in the excavation of a Mayan ruin. For those without the time for such an extended exotic trip, offbeat weekend getaways are also available. Services include a customer service center staffed with experts to answer calls and e-mails, plus a network of over 1,000 prescreened tour operators. Trips are categorized by cultural, adventure, and green travel. Away.com also offers a Daily Escape e-mail newsletter.

Airline Web Sites

Below are the Web sites for the major airlines. These sites offer schedules and flight booking, and most have pages where you can sign up for e-mail alerts for weekend deals and other late-breaking bargains.

Aer Lingus. www.aerlingus.ie
Air Canada. www.aircanada.ca
American Airlines. www.aa.com
British Airways. www.british-airways.com
British Midland. www.britishmidland.com
Continental Airlines. www.continental.com
Delta. www.delta-air.com
KLM. www.klm.nl
Lufthansa. www.lufthansa.com
Northwest Airlines. www.nwa.com
Qantas. www.quantas.com.au
United Airlines. www.ual.com

Online Directory

GORP (Great Outdoor Recreation Pages; **www.gorp.com**) has been a standard for adventure travelers since its founding in 1995 by outdoor enthusiasts Diane and Bill Greer. Tapping their own experiences, they created this Web site that suggests unique travel destinations and encourages active participation by fellow GORP visitors through its sophisticated menu of online forums, contests, and discussions.

For travelers who prefer more unique accommodations, **InnSite** (**www.innsite.com**) offers listings for inns and B&Bs in all U.S. states and dozens of countries around the globe. Find an inn at your destination, have a look at images of the rooms, check prices and availability, and then send e-mail to the innkeeper if you have further questions. This is an extensive directory of bed-and-breakfast inns but includes listings only if the proprietors submitted them (*Note:* It's free to get an inn listed). The descriptions are written by the innkeepers, and many listings link to the inns' own Web sites, where you can find more information and images.

Another good resource for mostly one-of-a-kind places in the U.S. and abroad is **Places to Stay** (**www.placestostay.com**), which focuses on resort accommodations.

"Have Kids, Still Travel!" is the motto of the **Family Travel Forum** (FTF; **www.familytravelforum.com**), a site dedicated to the ideals, promotion, and support of travel with children. FTF is supported by memberships, which are available in flexible prices ranging from $2.95 per month to a heftier annual fee for more comprehensive services. Since no advertising is accepted, FTF provides its members with honest, unbiased information, informed advice, and practical tips designed to make traveling with children a healthier, safer, hassle-free experience, not to mention a better value.

TOP VACATION PACKAGE SITES

Both **Expedia** and **Travelocity** (see above) offer excellent selections and searches for complete vacation packages. Travelers can search by destination and desired dates coupled with how much they're willing to spend. Travelocity has a valuable "Cruise Critic" function, to help would-be cruisers obtain first-hand accounts of the quality and details of a cruise from recent passengers.

Travel wholesalers, like **Apple Vacations** (www.applevacations.com) and **Funjet** (www.funjet.com) are also good starting points, but they still require that the final booking be handled through a travel agent.

As travel agents tend to be more expert at sorting through the values in vacation packages, you might find **Vacation.com** (www.vacation.com) helpful in previewing packages and selecting an appropriate agent to help you book the deal. This site represents a nationwide network of 9,800 local travel agencies that specialize in finding the best values in cruises, vacation packages, tours, and other leisure travel services. To find a Vacation.com member agency, enter your zip code and the Vacation.com Agency Finder will locate a nearby office.

LAST-MINUTE DEALS & OTHER ONLINE BARGAINS

There's nothing airlines hate more than flying with lots of empty seats. The Net has enabled airlines to offer last-minute bargains to entice travelers to fill those seats. Most of these are announced on Tuesday or Wednesday and are valid for travel the following weekend, but some can be booked weeks or months in advance. You can sign up for weekly e-mail alerts at airlines' sites (for specific Web sites, see "Airline Web Sites," above) or check sites that compile lists of these bargains, such as **Smarter Living** or **WebFlyer** (see below). To make it easier, visit a site that'll round up all the deals and send them in one convenient weekly e-mail. But last-minute deals aren't the only online bargains; other sites can help you find value even if you haven't waited until the eleventh hour. Increasingly popular are services that let you name the price you're willing to pay for an air seat or vacation package and travel auction sites.

Cheap Tickets. www.cheaptickets.com
Cheap Tickets has exclusive deals that aren't available through more mainstream channels. One caveat about the Cheap Tickets site is that it'll offer fare quotes for a route and later show this fare isn't valid for your dates of travel—most other Web sites, such as Expedia, consider your dates of travel *before* showing what fares are available. Despite its problems, Cheap Tickets can be worth the effort because its fares can be lower than those offered by its competitors.

✪ 1travel.com. www.1travel.com
Here you'll find deals on domestic and international flights, cruises, hotels, and all-inclusive resorts like Club Med. 1travel.com's **Saving Alert** compiles last-minute air deals so you don't have to scroll through multiple e-mail alerts. A feature called "Drive a little using low-fare airlines" helps map out strategies for using alternate airports to find lower fares. And **Farebeater** searches a database that includes published fares, consolidator bargains, and special deals exclusive to 1travel.com. *Note:* The travel agencies listed by 1travel.com have paid for placement.

Bid for Travel. www.bidfortravel.com
Bid for Travel is another of the travel auction sites, similar to Priceline (see below), which are growing in popularity. In addition to airfares, Internet users can place a bid for vacation packages and hotels.

Go4less.com. www.go4less.com
Specializing in last-minute cruise and package deals, Go4less has some excellent offers. The **Hot Deals** section gives an alphabetical listing by destination of super discounted packages.

LastMinuteTravel.com. www.lastminutetravel.com
Suppliers with excess inventory come to this online agency to distribute unsold airline seats, hotel rooms, cruises, and vacation packages. It's got great deals, but you have to put up with an excess of advertisements and slow-loading graphics.

Moment's Notice. www.moments-notice.com
As the name suggests, Moment's Notice specializes in last-minute vacation and cruise deals. You can browse for free, but if you want to purchase a trip you have to join Moment's Notice, which costs $25. Go to **World Wide Hot Deals** for a complete list of special deals in international destinations.

✪ Priceline.com. travel.priceline.com
Even people who aren't familiar with many Web sites have heard about Price-line.com. Launched in 1998 with a $10-million ad campaign featuring William Shatner, Priceline lets you "name your price" for domestic and inter-national airline tickets and hotel rooms. In other words, you select a route and dates, guarantee your interest with a credit card, and make a bid for what you're willing to pay. If one of the airlines in Priceline's database has a fare lower than your bid, your credit card will automatically be charged for a ticket.

But you can't say when you want to fly—you have to accept any flight leav-ing between 6am and 10pm on the dates you selected, and you may have to make a stopover. No frequent-flyer miles are awarded, and tickets are nonre-fundable and can't be exchanged for another flight. So if your plans change, you're out of luck. Priceline can be good for travelers who have to take off on short notice (and thus are unable to qualify for advance-purchase discounts). But be sure to shop around first, because if you overbid, you'll be required to purchase the ticket—and Priceline will pocket the difference between what it paid for the ticket and what you bid.

Priceline says that over 35% of all reasonable offers for domestic flights are being filled on the first try, with much higher fill rates on popular routes (New York to San Francisco, for example). They define "reasonable" as not more than 30% below the lowest generally available advance-purchase fare for the same route.

Smarter Living. www.smarterliving.com
Best known for its e-mail dispatch of weekend deals on 20 airlines, Smarter Living also keeps you posted about last-minute bargains on everything from Windjammer Cruises to flights to Iceland.

SkyAuction.com. www.skyauction.com
This auction site has categories for airfare, travel deals, hotels, and much more.

Travelzoo.com www.travelzoo.com
Over 150 travel companies post special deals at this Internet portal. It features a Top 20 list of the best deals on the site, selected by its editorial staff each Wednesday night. This list is also available free via e-mail.

WebFlyer. www.webflyer.com
WebFlyer is a comprehensive online resource for frequent flyers that has an excel-lent listing of last-minute air deals. Click on **Deal Watch** for a round-up of

Online Directory

Know When the Sales Start

While most people learn about last-minute weekend deals from e-mail dis-patches, it can be best to find out precisely when these deals become avail-able. Because the deals are limited, they can vanish within hours—sometimes even minutes—so it pays to log on as soon as they're available. Check the pages devoted to these deals on airlines' Web pages to get the info. An example: Southwest's specials are posted at 12:01am Tues-days (Central time). So if you're looking for a cheap flight, stay up late and check Southwest's site to grab the best new deals.

One of the best sources of travel information is word-of-mouth from someone who has just been there. Internet discussion groups are offering an unprecedented way for travelers around the globe to connect and share experiences. The **Frommer's Online** site (**www.frommers.com**) offers these message boards and a section called "Ask the Expert," where you can pose questions to the guidebook writers themselves in the section. **Yahoo Travel, Expedia,** and **Travelocity** are other good sources of online travel discussion groups.

The granddaddy of specialized discussions on particular topics is **Usenet,** a collection of over 50,000 newsgroups. You'll find a comprehensive listing at **Deja News** (**www.dejanews.com/usenet/**) or at **www.liszt.com**.

weekend deals on flights, hotels, and rental cars from domestic and international suppliers.

ONLINE TRAVELER'S TOOLBOX

Veteran travelers usually carry some essential items to make their trips easier. The following is a selection of online tools to smooth your journey.

CDC Travel Information. www.cdc.gov/travel/index.htm
Here you can read health advisories and recommendations for inoculations from the U.S. Centers for Disease Control. The CDC site is good for an overview, but it's best to consult your personal physician to get the latest information on required vaccinations or other health precautions.

✪ Foreign Languages for Travelers. www.travlang.com
Here you can learn basic terms in more than 70 languages and click on any underlined phrase to hear what it sounds like. (*Note:* Speakers and free audio software are required.) It also offers hotel and airline finders with excellent prices and a simple system to get the listings you're looking for.

Intellicast. www.intellicast.com
Here you'll find weather forecasts for all 50 states and cities around the world. *Note:* Temperatures are in Celsius for many international destinations, so don't think you'll need that winter coat for your next trip to Athens.

✪ Mapquest. www.mapquest.com
The best of the mapping sites lets you choose a specific address or destination, and in seconds it provides a map and detailed directions. It really is easier than calling, asking, and writing down directions. The site also links to special travel deals and helpful sites.

Net Cafe Guide. www.netcafeguide.com/mapindex.htm
Stop here to locate Internet cafes at hundreds of locations around the globe. Catch up on your e-mail, log onto the Web, and stay in touch with the home front, usually for just a few dollars per hour.

Tourism Offices Worldwide Directory. www.towd.com
This is an extensive listing of tourism offices, some with links to these offices' Web sites.

Travelers' Tales. www.travelerstales.com
Considered the best in compilations of travel literature, Travelers' Tales is an award-winning series of books grouped by destination (Mexico, Italy, France, China) or by theme (Love & Romance, The Ultimate Journey, Women in the

Wild, The Adventure of Food). It's a new kind of travel book that offers a description of a place or type of journey through the experiences of many travelers. It makes for a perfect traveling companion.

The Travelite FAQ. www.travelite.org
Here you'll find tips on packing light, choosing luggage, and selecting appropriate travel wear—helpful if you always tend to pack too much or are a compulsive list maker.

Universal Currency Converter. www.xe.net/currency
Come here to see what your dollar or pound is worth in more than a hundred other countries.

U.S. Customs Service Traveler Information.
    www.customs.ustreas.gov/travel/index.htm
Wondering what you're allowed to bring into the U.S.? Check at this thorough site, which includes maximum allowance and duty fees.

U.S. State Department Travel Warnings. travel.state.gov/travel_warnings.
    html
You'll find reports on places where health concerns or unrest might threaten U.S. travelers. Keep in mind that these warnings can be somewhat dated and conservative. You can also sign up to receive State Department briefings via e-mail.

Visa. www.visa.com/pd/atm/
MasterCard. www.mastercard.com/atm
Use these sites to find ATMs in hundreds of cities in the U.S. and around the world. Both include maps for some locations and both list airport ATM locations, some with maps. *Tip:* You'll usually get a better exchange rate using ATMs than exchanging traveler's checks at banks, but check in advance to see what kind of fees your bank will assess for using an overseas ATM.

Web Travel Secrets. www.web-travel-secrets.com
If this list leaves you yearning for more travel-oriented sites, Web Travel Secrets offers one of the best compilations around. One section offers advice and tips on how to find the lowest prices for airlines, hotels, and cruises. The other section provides a comprehensive listing of Web links to airfare deals, airlines, booking engines, cars, cruise lines, discount travel and best deals, general travel resources, hotels and hotel discounters, search engines, and travel magazines and newsletters.

2 The Top Web Sites for Germany

Updated by Matthew Kiernan

Note: If you open a site that's in German and it's all Greek to you, don't panic. Many of them provide English translations. Look for the little British or American flag or the word *English*.

GENERAL GUIDES FOR GERMANY

German National Tourist Board. www.germany-tourism.de
This site gives you an online tour of several quaint, window-box-filled cities, and highlights attractions for educational excursions, romantic vacations, or youth trips. You can also access facts on weather, transportation, language, currency, accommodations, events, and so forth.

Check E-mail at Internet Cafes While Traveling

Until a few years ago, most travelers who checked their e-mail while traveling carried a laptop—an expensive and often technologically problematic option. Thankfully, Web-based free e-mail programs have made it much easier to check your mail.

Just open an account at any one of the numerous "freemail" providers—the original leaders continue to be **Hotmail** (www.hotmail.com), **Excite** (www.excite.com), and **Yahoo! Mail** (mail.yahoo.com), though many are available. AOL users should check out **AOL Netmail,** and **USA.NET** (**www.usa.net**) comes highly recommended for functionality and security. You can find hints, tips and a mile-long list of freemail providers at **www.emailaddresses.com**. Then all you'll need to check your mail is a Web connection, available at Net cafes and copy shops around the world. After logging on, just point the browser to your freemail's Internet address, enter your username and password, and you'll have access to your mail. From these sites, you can download all your e-mail—even from office accounts—or your local or national Internet Service Provider address. There usually will be a section generally called "check other mail" that allows you to add the names of other e-mail servers.

The downside is that most Web-based e-mail sites allow a maximum of only 3MB capacity per mail account, which can fill up quickly. Also, message sending and receiving isn't immediate; some messages may be delayed by several hours or even days.

Internet cafes have become ubiquitous, so for a few dollars an hour you'll be able to check your mail and send messages from virtually anywhere in the world. Interestingly, these cafes tend to be more common in very remote areas, where they may offer the best form of access for an entire community, especially if phone lines are difficult to obtain.

A to Z Hotels. reisen-mit-preisen.de
Within this chartreuse and typographically hip site are listings for 48,000 German hotels (or so it claims). Search by price and region, or link directly to the guide's half-dozen favorites.

Hotelguide Germany IHA Hotel Association. www.hotels-germany.com
Book a room at any of more than 750 German hotels through this site. Conduct a search according to location and amenity preferences, or check out the page of special offers for accommodations conducive to family, cultural activities, sports, biking, special events, or last-minute travel.

Eat Germany. www.eat-germany.net
Get started on the appealing, if daunting, task of eating Germany with help from this dining guide. Search for a schnitzel-filled *gasthaus* or other eatery by city, price, ethnicity, child-friendliness, level of festivity, wheelchair accessibility, or any of a slew of other criteria. If you're not sure what it is you're searching for, recommendations are listed.

BERLIN

✪ **Berlin.de. www.berlin.de**
Sporting a trendy Euro design, this guide to Germany's capital city features a cyber tour of more than two dozen Berlin attractions, complete with

virtual-reality panoramic images. The site also provides an online hotel reservation service, a virtual ticket counter for all kinds of shows and cultural events, and a wealth of information about Berlin's government, economy, ecology, and public services.

Berlin-Info. www.berlin-info.de
Though some sections of this Berlin guide are available only in German, others, such as the online sightseeing tour and the searchable accommodations directory, are full of useful information for English-speaking tourists.

Metropolis Berlin Scene. www.zitty.de/metact/m_guide2.htm
Metropolis magazine recommends Berlin hotels and hostels, bars, bookstores, cafes, night clubs, markets, restaurants, ticket agencies, car rental businesses, and tours. Each entry comes with a short but clear description of the establishment's attributes.

Net4 Berlin City Guide. www.net4berlin.com
This frills-free city guide encompasses the city's history, population, architecture, and culture. The site also gives tips on getting around and finding low-cost hostels and boarding houses. Best of all, Net4 Berlin breaks the city down into districts and describes the atmosphere and scene, as well as the best bars and restaurants, of each one.

Time Out Berlin: The Living Guide.
  www.timeout.com/berlin/index.html
The comfortable design of this Berlin travel site makes it easy to navigate. Check the front page to see what's going on in the city this month, or click on the sidebar menu for guides to accommodations, sightseeing, entertainment, kids' stuff, shopping, dining, and gay and lesbian culture. You can also check the weather and exchange rates or book a flight, hotel room, or rental car.

Berlin Hotel Discounts and City Guide.
  www.worldexecutive.com/cityguides/berlin
You can get discounts at Berlin luxury hotels when you book through this site. The guide also offers transportation and etiquette tips for travelers as well as photographs and attraction-marked maps of the city.

Public Transport and Traffic in Berlin. verkehr.epilog.de/traffic.htm
Whether you're traveling by plane, train, or automobile in Berlin, this site can help. You'll find road maps, bus fare rates, train and subway schedules, airport information, weather conditions, and a directory of useful phone numbers.

SAXONY & THURINGIA

Dresden Online. www.dresden-online.de
This guide provides a photo and short history of each of Dresden's important sights. You'll also find a simple directory of theaters and museums alongside searchable guides to hotels and restaurants.

Leipzig. members.aol.com/wksleipzig
Once an economic center of the East Germany, Leipzig has bloomed in recent years. The growth is illustrated by this site's extensive guide to the city's restaurants, nightlife, shopping centers, theaters, tourist attractions, and hotels.

Weimar Online. www.weimar.de
The site offers information and photos along with guides to hotels, restaurants, cultural sights, and day trips out of Weimar. There's even a special section suggesting things to do with your free time.

FRANCONIA & THE GERMAN DANUBE

Bayreuther Festspiele. www.bayreuther-festspiele.de
The official site of the Wagner Festival offers information on the festival, its history, and when tickets go on sale.

Hotel Bayerischer Hof Bayreuth. www.bayerischer-hof.com
This hotel wears three roofs: historic landmark, cozy inn, and home of the annual Richard Wagner festival. The site provides hotel photos and a festival program. You can reserve a room or buy tickets online.

MUNICH

Munich Guide. homepages.munich.netsurf.de/Nikolaus.Duttler/ munich.htm
A local resident offers insider tips, such as how to get free beer, as well as dining tips, a detailed guide to bars and nightclubs, lodging recommendations, more beer guides, photographs, and links.

The Munich Portal. www.perob.com
An Englishman now living in Munich shares his view of the German city. Click around and find information on attractions like the Glockenspiel, a multi-ethnic restaurant guide, a truly extensive beer guide, and a look at cultural quirks such as Munich's rampant graffiti art.

Munich Airport. www.munich-airport.de
Wondering how to get back to the airport after a long night at the beer garden? This site can help. The Munich airport's online guide directs travelers to and from the terminal, and provides timetables, parking information, and a virtual tour of the airport.

THE BAVARIAN ALPS

Bavaria Alpine Net Guide. www.bavaria.com
This guide to Bavaria covers culture, travel, entertainment, shopping, and business. Visit any of these sections to be led via narration and photos through the region, or, if you know what you're looking for, click on the index icon to go directly to opera, castles, rafting, or whatever strikes your fancy. *Note for revelers:* Extensive Oktoberfest coverage is available here.

Highlights around Munich. homepages.munich.netsurf.de/ Nikolaus.Duttler/bavaria.htm
This site offers a low-resolution but nonetheless enticing preview of what you'll find in the mountains outside Munich: beautiful peaks, lakes, and castles, including the famous Neuschwanstein and Linderhof.

LAKE CONSTANCE (BODENSEE)

Welcome to Lake Constance. www.bodensee-info.com
Find out how to arrange a holiday in orchard-filled, spa-speckled Lake Constance. Through this site, you can stay abreast of special travel packages and guided-tour offers, get to know the historic towns in the area, and take a peek at the museums and galleries.

HEIDELBERG, STUTTGART & THE NECKAR VALLEY

Visit-Heidelberg. www.visit-heidelberg.com
This hotel directory, which offers online booking, doubles as a brief guide to the city's events, museums, boat trips, and castle. Click on the side menu for

transportation information, currency exchange, or to send a friend a
virtual post card.

Welcome to Stuttgart. www.stuttgart-tourist.de
This perky tourists' guide claims that Stuttgart is always in season and then
proves it with a great deal of information about the city's cuisine, exhibitions,
festivals, markets, music, theater, museums, and sightseeing tours.

Stuttgart City-Guide. www.stgt.com/stuttgart/homee.htm
For a little Stuttgart appetizer, try this site's "pictorial walkabout," a photo tour
of the city's more notable buildings. The guide also lists hotels, restaurants,
museums and galleries, night spots, festivals, swimming pools, radio stations,
and other assorted tidbits.

Stuttgart Hotel Discounts and City Guide. www.worldexecutive.com/cityguides/stuttgart
You can get discounts at Stuttgart hotels when you book through this site. The
guide also offers travel, transportation, restaurant, and etiquette tips as well as
maps and photographs.

FRANKFURT
Frankfurt. www.frankfurt.de
Each major section (science, history, business, sports, etc.) of this busy guide
to the equally busy industrial metropolis is broken down into several sub-
groups. Under the culture heading, for example, you can find museums and
galleries, ballet, theater, literature, music, film, public art, and architecture.
The tourism section covers essentials such as hotels, sightseeing, and travel
packages.

Boomtown-Frankfurt. www.boomtown-frankfurt.com
Along with a look at Frankfurt's architecture, ranging from glorious historic
cathedrals to high-tech skyscrapers, this site provides a full city and travel
guide covering weather, lodging, transportation, city tours, museums, shopping, dining, nightlife, festivals, and the Rhine castles on the outskirts of town.

Frankfurt Airport. www.frankfurt-airport.de
It helps to have a lot of computer memory or a little patience when using this
directory for Germany's main airport. Once it's loaded, though, you can easily
find running announcements of arrivals and departures and a thorough guide
to the terminal and its facilities. See below for sites for the Munich and
Stuttgart airports.

THE RHINELAND
Middle Rhine River Valley Medieval Castles and Towers. www.rhineca tles.com
Have a look at dozens of towering castle hotels that speckle the Rhineland
countryside. You can even make reservations online to stay in one of these
grand dwellings. Too much? You can also find information on visiting some of
the castle museums and restaurants and on castle-seeing river cruises.

City of Cologne Tourist Office. www.koeln.org
You may know about the enormous Cologne cathedral and its climbable
spires, but have you heard of the city-on-the-Rhine's chocolate museum or its
thriving art and music centers? Learn about these and other attractions, as well
as Cologne's convention centers, online.

Online Directory

Landeschauptstadt Dusseldorf. **www.duesseldorf.de/f_tour_e.htm**
Take an online promenade through Dusseldorf's fashionable Königsallee district or on the banks of the Rhine. Or you can peek over the gate of the Benrath Palace. This site's photos and descriptive text will also give you a taste of the city's cultural scene, museums, restaurants, and shops. For the practical traveler, a chart with links and a breakdown of amenities helps you sort through hotel recommendations.

BREMEN, LOWER SAXONY & NORTH HESSE

Hannover Online. **www.hannover.de**
Search here to discover the city's rich history and masterful baroque gardens. This site directs you to attractions, events, city tours, historic buildings, parks, accommodations, restaurants, bars, night clubs, shops, and more.

Welcome to Bremen. **www.bremen-tourism.de**
There's more to see than the sea in Bremen, the City of the Town Musicians. This site will show you the town's art galleries, specialty museums, fairy tale theater, architecture, and bustling market place. You can also book travel packages and hotel rooms online.

HAMBURG

Hamburg. **www.hamburg.de**
Boasting that Hamburg is the greenest city in Germany, this guide urges visitors to visit parks and nature reserves as well as the museums and theaters listed here. The site also provides an overview of Hamburg's government, economy, harbor traffic, and educational institutions.

Hamburg Tourist Board. **www.hamburg-tourism.de**
Through this site, you can book a room at any of more than 190 Hamburg hotels or get help buying all sorts of theater tickets. You can also find information on guided tours aboard buses or boats. The shopping and dining guides are essentially ads, but the Info section bubbles over with photos and facts about Hamburg's history and culture.

The reunited city of Berlin is once again the capital of Germany. Berlin was almost bombed out of existence during World War II, its streets reduced to piles of rubble, its parks to muddy swampland. But the optimistic spirit and strength of will of the remarkable Berliners enabled them to survive not only the wartime destruction of their city, but also its postwar division, symbolized by the Berlin Wall.

Today, structures of steel and glass tower over streets where before only piles of rubble lay, and parks and gardens are again lush. Nonetheless, even in the daily whirl of working, shopping, and dining along the Ku'damm, Berliners encounter reminders of less happy days. At the end of the street stands the Kaiser Wilhelm Memorial Church, with only the shell of the old neo-Romanesque bell tower remaining. In striking contrast is the new church, constructed west of the old tower in 1961, and nicknamed "lipstick and powderbox" by Berliners because of its futuristic design.

Before the war, the section of the city that became East Berlin was the cultural and political heart of Germany, where the best museums, the finest churches, and the most important boulevards lay. The walled-in East Berliners turned to restoring their important museums, theaters, and landmarks (especially in the Berlin-Mitte section), while the West Berliners built entirely new museums and cultural Centers. This contrast between the two parts of city is still evident today, though east and west are more and more coming together within the immense, fascinating whole that is Berlin.

1 Orientation

ARRIVING

BY PLANE **Tegel** is the city's busiest airport, serving most flights from the west. Historic **Tempelhof** (made famous as the city's lifeline during the Berlin Airlift) has declined in importance, although it's still used for flights from Basel, Brussels, Copenhagen, Prague, and many cities within Germany. **Schönefeld,** the airport in the eastern sector, is used primarily by Russian and eastern European airlines. Private bus shuttles among the three airports operate constantly, so you can make connecting flights at a different airport.

Lufthansa (☎ **800/645-3880**) does not have direct transatlantic flights into Berlin; instead, it routes transatlantic passengers through its hubs at Frankfurt and Munich. Frequent connections can also be

Berlin Today & Tomorrow

Berlin is living up to its reputation as a dynamic, exciting hub of activity as never before. The city's nightlife is among Europe's best and wildest. And now that the German government has been transferred here from Bonn, Berlin is bidding to become the reborn capital not only of Germany but of all Europe.

As befits a new capital, the city is undergoing a major facelift. More than $120 billion has been invested in new streets, buildings, and railways. The former East Berlin is rapidly being restored and gentrified, particularly in the **Mitte** (central) district. Here new luxury hotels and shopping arcades compete with the litter of the Kurfürstendamm. The opening of the Hotel Adlon, overlooking the Brandenburg Gate, is particularly notable. **Prenzlauer Berg,** a blue-collar eastern neighborhood that escaped the worst of the wartime bombing, is becoming a chic district of cafes and boutiques. The downside of all this for Berliners has been the sharp increase in real estate prices, as well as the inconvenience of living in the world's largest construction site.

Many of Berlin's famous buildings have been restored. The rebuilt **Reichstag** has a glittering glass dome; upon the building stands not the old glowering imperial hunter, but the national symbol, the eagle (locals refer affectionately to the statue as "the fat hen"). The Oranienburger Strasse **synagogue,** wrecked on Kristallnacht and finished off by Allied bombers, has been rebuilt in all its splendor. Likewise, **Berlin Cathedral** and the five state museums on **Museum Island** have been painstakingly returned to their original glory.

Visitors often overlook Berlin's **natural attractions.** Few metropolitan areas are blessed with as many gardens, lakes, woodlands, and parks—these cover an amazing one-third of the city. First-time visitors are often surprised to learn that small farms with fields and meadows still exist within the city limits.

made into Berlin from dozens of other German and European gateways, including Paris, Rome, and Stockholm. Lufthansa offers 100 or more flights into Berlin every day from about a dozen German and European cities.

Delta (☎ 800/241-4141) has daily flights to Berlin-Tegel every evening from New York's JFK and from Atlanta. However, daily flights, depending on the season or on business, are not always a sure thing, so you'll need to check with a travel agent or else the airline itself.

The best and most convenient service into Berlin is available aboard **British Airways (BA)** (☎ 800/247-9292), which efficiently funnels dozens of daily flights from North America to Germany, including five a day into Berlin-Tegel, through its vast terminals at London-Heathrow. Connections to Berlin are excellent from at least 40 gateways in the U.S. and Canada, more than that offered by any other airline. Frequent transatlantic price wars keep fares to Berlin aboard BA lower than you might have thought, especially in off-season. Stopovers in London can be arranged at minimal cost, and deeply discounted hotel packages are available in either Berlin or London, at rates that are significantly less than what you'd have paid if you'd arranged them yourself. And if you opt for passage in Business Class (BA calls it Club Class), you'll ride on the most comfortable, and one of the largest, airline seats in the industry, in a configuration that can be transformed into something approaching a bed.

Berlin-Tegel Airport (☎ 01805/000186) is 8km (5 miles) northwest of the city Center. Public transportation by bus, taxi, or U-Bahn is convenient to all points in the city. BVG buses X9 and 109 run every 10 to 15 minutes from the airport to Bahnhof Zoo in Berlin's Center, departing from outside the arrival hall; a one-way fare is 3.90DM ($1.95). A taxi to the city Center costs 35DM to 40DM ($17.50 to $20) and takes 20 minutes. No porters are available for luggage handling, but pushcarts are free.

The main terminal has a **visitor information counter** where you can get a free map of the city. The counter is open daily 5am to 10pm. Facilities at the terminal include money-exchange Centers, luggage-storage facilities (and locker rentals), a police station, auto-rental kiosks, dining facilities, and a first-aid Center. Shops sell gifts, film, and travel paraphernalia. There's a hotel, the **Novotel Berlin Airport,** Kurt-Schumacher-Damm 202, 13405 Berlin (☎ 030/41060; fax 030/410-6700), with a connecting shuttle to and from the airport. Its 184 rooms cost 273DM ($136.50) for a double Sunday to Thursday, 158DM ($79) Friday and Saturday, including breakfast.

Berlin-Schönefeld Airport (☎ 01805/000186), once the main airport for East Berlin, now receives many flights from Asia, as well as Russia and other European countries. It lies in Brandenburg, 19km (12 miles) southeast of the city Center. The city Center is a 55-minute ride on the S-Bahn. You can also take bus 171 from the airport to Rudow, where you transfer to the U-Bahn. Either means of transport costs 3.90DM ($1.95).

Berlin-Tempelhof Airport (☎ 01805/000186) is the city's oldest, 6km (4 miles) southeast of the city Center. Tempelhof now receives several flights a day from German or European cities. Take the U-Bahn or bus 119. All bus trips from Tempelhof into the Center cost 3.90DM ($1.95).

BY TRAIN   As Berlin strengthens its role as capital, increasing numbers of trains are speeding their way into town. All points of the country, especially Frankfurt, Munich, Hamburg, and Bonn, maintain excellent rail connections, with high-tech, high-speed improvements being made to the country's railway system virtually all the time. Since reunification, Berlin has improved the facilities of railway stations in both the western zone (Bahnhof Zoologischer Garten) and eastern zone (Berlin Ostbahnhof), installing improved S-Bahn links to interconnect them. The station you'll use depends on the destination or origin of your train, or the location of your hotel within the city. Some, but not all, trains make arrivals and departures from both stations. A third station, Berlin Lichtenberg, within the city's eastern half, is used for trains pulling in from small towns. For information about any railway station, call ☎ **01805/996633.**

BY BUS (COACH)   Regularly scheduled buses operate from 250 German and continental cities, including Frankfurt, Hamburg, and Munich. Long-distance bus companies servicing Berlin include **Autokraft GmbH, Haru-Reisen,** and **Bayern Express & P. Köhn** (☎ 030/8-60-96-0 or 030/8-60-21-1). For information about any of these companies' routes into Berlin or anywhere else, call ☎ **030/302-52-94.**

Arrivals and departures are at the **ZOB Omnibusbahnhof am Funkturm,** Masurenalle, Charlottenburg. Taxis and bus connections are available at the station, U-Bahn at the nearby Kaiserdamm station.

BY CAR   From Frankfurt, take the E451 north until it connects with the E40 going northeast. Follow this Autobahn past Jena and then head north on the E51 into Berlin. From Nürnberg, also take the E51 into Berlin. From Dresden, take the E55 north to Berlin. Expect heavy traffic on the Autobahns on weekends and sunny days when everybody is out touring.

VISITOR INFORMATION

For visitor information and hotel bookings, head for the **Berlin Tourist Information Center,** Europa Center (near Memorial Church); the entrance is on the Budapesterstrasse side. It's open Monday to Saturday 8am to 10pm and Sunday 9am to 9pm. There's also a branch at the south wing of the Brandenburg Gate, open daily 9:30am to 6pm. Neither branch accepts telephone calls from the general public. Instead, dial ☎ **0190/75-40-40,** and expect to pay 2.42DM ($1.20) per minute. If you're calling from outside of Germany, you'll still pay the above-mentioned fee, but you'll have to access a different number: ☎ **01805/75-40-40.** The cheapest, and most up-to-date way to access tourist information about Berlin is on the Internet at www.berlin-tourism.de.

CITY LAYOUT

Berlin is one of the largest and most complex cities in Europe. Since it's so spread out, you'll need to depend on public transportation. No visitor should try to explore more than two neighborhoods a day, even superficially.

The Center of activity in the western part of Berlin is the 4km (2¹/₂-mile-) long **Kurfürstendamm,** called the Ku'damm by Berliners, who seem to have a habit of irreverently renaming every street and building in the city. Along this wide boulevard you'll find the best hotels, restaurants, theaters, cafes, nightclubs, shops, and department stores. It's the most elegant and fashionable spot in Berlin, but, like much of the city, it combines chic with sleaze in places. Walkers can stop off at one of the popular cafes lining the boulevard.

From the Ku'damm you can take Hardenbergstrasse, which crosses Bismarckstrasse and becomes Otto-Suhr-Allee, which will lead to the **Schloss Charlottenburg** area and its museums, one of your major sightseeing goals. The **Dahlem Museums** are in the southwest of the city, often reached by going along Hohenzollerndamm.

The huge **Tiergarten** is the city's largest park. Running through it is **Strasse des 17 Juni,** which leads to the famed **Brandenburg Gate** (just south of the Reichstag). On the southwestern fringe of the Tiergarten is the **Berlin Zoo.**

The Brandenburg Gate is the start of eastern Berlin's most celebrated street, **Unter den Linden,** the cultural heart of Berlin before World War II. It runs from west to east, leading to **Museumsinsel (Museum Island),** where the most outstanding museums of eastern Berlin, including the Pergamon Museum, are situated.

Unter den Linden crosses another major artery, **Friedrichstrasse.** If you continue south along Friedrichstrasse, you'll reach the former location of **Checkpoint Charlie,** a famous border site of the Cold War days. No longer a checkpoint, it now has a little museum devoted to memories of the Berlin Wall.

Unter den Linden continues east until it reaches **Alexanderplatz,** the Center of eastern Berlin, with its towering television tower (Fernsehturm). A short walk away is the newly restored **Nikolai Quarter (Nikolaiviertel),** a neighborhood of bars, restaurants, and shops that evoke life in the prewar days.

MAPS   Good maps of Berlin can be purchased at bookstores or news kiosks, such as the Europa Press Center (a magazine and newspaper store in the Europa Center). One of the best maps is the **Falk** map, which offers full-color detail and comprehensive indexes (consequently, it's sometimes awkward to unfold and refold). Be sure to obtain an up-to-date map showing the most recent changes.

Neighborhoods in Brief

Visitors who knew Berlin during the Cold War are amazed at the way traffic now zips between sectors that once were rigidly segregated by border guards. Today, your taxi will blithely drive beneath the Brandenburg Gate or along the Friedrichstrasse, without regard to barriers that once used to be virtually impenetrable. Names you're likely to hear as you navigate your way through the reunited city include the following:

Finding an Address

As for the numbering of streets, keep in mind the city sometimes assists you by posting the range of numbers that appears within any particular block, at least within major arteries such as the Kurfürstendamm. These numbers appear on the street signs themselves, which is a great help in finding a particular number on long boulevards. You won't find these numbers on street signs of smaller streets, however. Although some streets are numbered with the odds on one side and the evens on the other, many (including the Ku'damm) are numbered consecutively up one side of the street and back down the other. *Warning:* The names of some eastern Berlin streets and squares with links to the old East German regime have been changed.

IN THE WESTERN ZONE

Charlottenburg   Despite being renamed by Berlin wits as Klamottenburg (Ragsville) after the bombings of World War II, this is still the wealthiest and most densely commercialized district of western Berlin. Its Centerpiece is Charlottenburg Palace. One of the most interesting subdivisions of Charlottenburg is the neighborhood around **Savignyplatz,** a tree-lined square a short walk north of the western zone's most visible boulevard, Kurfürstendamm. Lining its edges and the streets nearby are a profusion of bars, shops, and restaurants, an engaging aura of permissiveness, and an awareness that this is the bastion of the city's prosperous bourgeoisie.

Dahlem   The university district, it was originally established as an independent village to the southwest of Berlin's center.

Ku'damm   In the 1950s and '60s, during the early stages of the Cold War, the Ku'damm emerged as a rough-and-tumble boomtown, bristling with boxy-looking new constructions, and permeated with a maverick sense of parvenu novelty. Since reunification, when vast neighborhoods within Mitte opened for real estate speculation and instant gentrification, the Ku'damm has reinvented itself as a bastion of capitalistic and corporate conservatism, with a distinct sense of old and established money that's waiting for public perceptions to grow bored with the novelties that have been associated with the opening of the former East Berlin. The poignancies of the Weimar Republic and the Cold War are not lost, however, even upon the corporate sponsors of the big money real estate ventures that line the Ku'damm. If you look at the Hochhaus entrance of the Europa Center, on the Tauentzienstrasse side, whose glossy chrome-trimmed interior decor might remind you of an airport waiting lounge, you'll find a plaque honoring the long-ago site of the private home of Weimar statesman Gustav Stresemann, which used to stand at 12A Tauentzienstrasse. Immediately adjacent to that plaque is an artfully graffitized chunk of the former Berlin Wall, encased in Plexiglas like an irreplaceable work of ancient archaeology. It is dedicated to the people who lost their lives trying to escape over the Wall during the peak of the Cold War.

Grunewald   Many newcomers are surprised by the sheer sprawl of Grunewald's 49 square km (19 square miles) of verdant forest. The area serves as a green lung for the urbanites of Berlin. It lies northwest of the city Center.

Hansaviertel   This neighborhood, northwest of Tiergarten park, contains a series of residential buildings designed by different architects (including Le Corbusier, Walter Gropius, and Alvar Aalto).

Kreuzberg   Originally built during the 19th century to house the workers of a rapidly industrializing Prussia, this has traditionally been the poorest and most

Berlin Neighborhoods

WEDDING

PRENZLAUER BERG

Fennstrasse

Chausseestrasse

Heidestrasse

NORDBAHNHOF
Ⓢ

Invalidenstrasse

Invalidenstrasse

Rosenthaler Strasse

Strasse

Schönhauser Allee

Prinzenstrasse

Greifswalder Strasse

LEHRTER
STADTBAHNHOF
Ⓢ

Wilhelm- Pieck-

Oranienburger Strasse
Ⓢ

BERLIN-MITTE

HACKESCHER
MARKT

Molls trasse

Karl-Liebknecht- Strasse

Museumsinsel
Ⓢ

Alexander-
platz

Karl-Marx-Allee

Spree

FRIEDRICHSTRASSE
Ⓢ

Karl-
Liebknecht-
Platz

Alexander- Strasse

Pariser
Platz
Ⓢ Unter den Linden

UNTER DEN
LINDEN

Mühlendamm

Nikolai-
viertel

JANOWITZ-
BRÜCKE

Tiergarten

Gertrauden-
strasse

Brücken-
strasse

Spree

Leipziger Strasse

POTSDAMER
PLATZ
Ⓢ Leipziger
Platz

Stresemann-

Friedrichstrasse

Lindenstrasse

Heinrich-Heine-
Strasse

Oranienstrasse

Landwehrkanal

Schöneberger Ufer

strasse

ANHALTER
BAHNHOF
Ⓢ

Gitschiner Strasse

Potsdamer Strasse

Bülow-
strasse

Tempelhofer Ufer

Landwehrkanal

YORCKSTRASSE
Ⓢ

Yorckstrasse

Gneisenaustrasse

KREUZBERG

Urbanstrasse

Hasenheide

Katzbackstrasse

Kolonnenstrasse   Dudenstrasse

Columbiadamm

Boelckestrasse

Flughafenstrasse

To Berlin-
Schönefeld
Airport ↓

Berlin-Tempelhof
Airport

S-Bahn stop Ⓢ

0   5 mi
0   5 km

69

overcrowded of Berlin's districts. Today, at least 35% of its population is composed of guest workers from Turkey, the former Yugoslavia, and Greece. Prior to the city's reunification, the district evolved into the headquarters for the city's artistic counter-culture. Since reunification, however, the fast-changing neighborhoods within Mitte, especially Hackescher Höfe (see below) have offered stiff competition.

Schöneberg   Like Kreuzberg, it was originally an independent suburb of workers' housing, but after the war it was rebuilt as a solidly middle-class neighborhood that also happens to include the densest concentration of gay bars and clubs (between Nol-lendorfplatz and Victoria-Luise-Platz).

Spandau   Set near the junction of the Spree and Havel Rivers, about 10km (6 miles) northwest of the city Center, Spandau boasts a history of medieval grandeur. Though it merged with Berlin in 1920, its Altstadt (old city) is still intact. The legendary Span-dau prison was demolished in the early 1990s.

Tiergarten   The name Tiergarten (which means "Animal Garden") refers both to a massive urban park and, to the park's north, a residential district of the same name. The park was originally intended as a backdrop to the grand avenues laid out by the German kaisers. The neighborhood contains the Brandenburg Gate, the German Reichstag (Parliament), the Berlin Zoo, and some of the city's grandest museums.

IN THE EASTERN ZONE

Mitte (Center)   Closed to capitalist investment for nearly 50 years, this monumen-tal district in the heart of Berlin is the one that's on every speculator's mind these days. It was originally conceived as the architectural Centerpiece of the Prussian Kaisers. Its fortunes declined dramatically as the Communist regime infused it with starkly angu-lar monuments and architecturally banal buildings. Although some of Mitte's grand structures were destroyed by wartime bombings, unification has exposed its remaining artistic and architectural treasures. The district's most famous boulevard is Unter den Linden. Famous squares within the district include Pariser Platz (the monumental square adjacent to the Brandenburg Gate), Potsdamer Platz (see below), and Alexan-derplatz (see below).

Alexanderplatz   The former East German regime threw up lots of rather ugly mod-ern buildings and defined Alexanderplatz as the Centerpiece of its government. Today the large and sterile-looking square is dominated by the tallest structure in Berlin, the Sputnik-inspired TV tower.

Hackesche Höfe   A warren of brick-sided factories during the 19th century, it's evolving into one of the city's most visible counterculture strongholds. Part of this derives from the fact that it wasn't too badly mangled by the former East German regime. Another factor in its renaissance involves a thirst by cutting-edge, often youth-ful, Berliners to re-colonize what used to be the heart of the DDR. You'll get a sense of rising real estate values and an aura that combines aspects of Paris's Latin Quarter and New York's Greenwich Village.

Museumsinsel (Museum Island)   This island in the Spree River hosts a complex of museums housed in neoclassical buildings that always seem to be under renovation. Its most famous museum, the Pergamon, contains magnificent reconstructions of ancient temples.

Nikolaiviertel   Near the Alexanderplatz, the Nikolaiviertel is the most perfectly restored medieval neighborhood in Berlin, and a triumph of the restoration skills of the former East German regime.

Potsdamer Platz   Before World War II, this was the thriving heart of Berlin. Blasted into rubble by wartime bombings, it was bulldozed into a "no man's land" when the Wall went up on its western edge. After reunification, it was transformed into the biggest building site in Europe, out of which emerged a glittering, hyper-modern square dominated by such corporate giants as Daimler-Chrysler. It's often cited as a symbol of the corporate culture of a reunited Germany.

2 Getting Around

BY PUBLIC TRANSPORTATION

The Berlin transport system consists of buses, trams, and U-Bahn (underground) and S-Bahn (elevated) trains. The network is run by the **BVG** or Public Transport Company Berlin-Brandenburg. Public transportation throughout the city operates from about 4:30am to 12:30am daily (except for 62 night buses and trams, and U-Bahn lines U-9 and U-12). For information about public transport, call ☎ **030/29-71-9843** or 030/19-449.

The **BVG standard ticket** (*Einzelfahrschein*) costs 3.90DM ($1.95) and is valid for 2 hours of transportation in all directions, transfers included. A 24-hour ticket for the whole city costs from 7.80DM to 8.50DM ($3.90 to $4.25) depending on the zone. Only standard tickets are sold on buses. Tram tickets must be purchased in advance. All tickets should be kept until the end of the journey; otherwise you'll be liable for a fine of 60DM ($30). Unless you buy a day pass, don't forget to time-punch your ticket into one of the small red boxes prominently posted at the entrance to city buses and underground stations.

If you're going to be in Berlin for 3 days, you can purchase for 29DM ($14.50) a **Berlin-Potsdam WelcomeCard,** which entitles holders to 72 free hours on public transportation in Berlin and Brandenburg. You'll also get free admission or a price reduction of up to 50% on sightseeing tours, museums, and other attractions, and a 25% reduction at 10 theaters as well. The card is sold at many hotels, visitor information Centers, and public-transportation sales points. It's valid for one adult and three children under the age of 14.

Two **excursion bus lines** make some beautiful scenic spots accessible. Bus 218 operates from the Theodor-Heuss-Platz U-Bahn station (near the radio tower) via Schildhorn, Grunewald Tower, and Wannsee Beach to the Wannsee S-Bahn station, and bus 216 runs from the Wannsee S-Bahn station to Pfaueninsel via Moorlake.

BY TAXI

Taxis cruise restlessly along the major boulevards, indicating their availability by an illuminated roof light. The meter begins ticking at 4DM ($2). A 2DM ($1) supplement is added if you call a cab to a specific address by phone. Within the city Center, each kilometer costs between 2.20DM to 2.40DM ($1.10 to $1.20), depending on the time of day. Prolonged taxi rides that you arrange to distant suburbs are factored at a per-kilometer rate of 1.80DM (90¢). Staff members at hotels and restaurants can easily summon a cab for you, in some cases simply by throwing a switch on their phone. Otherwise, dial toll-free, within Berlin, ☎ **0800/217-6544.** If that doesn't work, try 030/21-01-01, 030/26-10-26, or 030/69-022.

A Map Note

For a plan of Berlin's **U-Bahn and S-Bahn system,** see the inside back cover of this guide.

BY CAR

U.S. rental companies have outlets in Berlin. If possible, you should make reservations in advance. You'll find **Hertz** at Berlin-Tegel Airport (☎ **030/41-01-33-15**) and at Budapesterstrasse 39 (☎ **030/2-61-10-53**). **Avis** is also at Berlin-Tegel (☎ **030/4-10-13-148**) and at Budapesterstrasse 41 (☎ **030/23-09-370**).

But in general, touring Berlin by car is not recommended. Traffic is heavy and parking is very difficult to come by. Use the excellent public transportation network instead.

PARKING   If you're driving into Berlin, chances are that you'll want to safely store your car once you arrive. Many hotels offer parking facilities; otherwise, you'll find parking garages that remain open throughout the day and night. Those located near the Ku'damm and the Europa Center include the **Parkhaus Metropol,** Joachimstaler Strasse 14–19; **Parkhaus Los-Angeles-Platz,** Augsburger Strasse 30; **Parkhaus Europa Center,** Nürnberger Strasse 5–7; and the **Parkhaus am Zoo,** Budapesterstrasse 38. Charges start at 3.50DM ($1.75) per hour.

CITY DRIVING   One problem that often infuriates drivers in Berlin is that it's almost impossible to turn left on major avenues (except at major intersections in the east), because of the positioning of metal barriers and tram lines. Oversize signs tell you to drive straight on. Drivers have to make a right-hand turn, swing around the block, and then proceed straight across the tram lines wherever a traffic light will allow.

BY BICYCLE

Bicycling in Berlin's crushing traffic is not a very appealing prospect, but you might want to rent a bike to explore the city's outlying parks and forests. Both the U-Bahn and S-Bahn provide specific compartments for bicycles for an extra 5DM ($2.85). Transport of bicycles, however, is not permitted during rush hour: Monday to Friday before 9am and again in the afternoon between 2 and 5:30pm. In the city and suburbs, try to confine your bicycling to cycle zones, delineated with solid red lines running between the pedestrian sidewalks and the traffic lanes.

A good place for bike rentals is **Fahrradstation,** Rosenthalerstrasse 40–41 (☎ **030/28-38-4848;** S-Bahn: Hackescher Markt), open Monday to Friday 10am to 7pm, Saturday 10am to 4pm. A 24-hour rental costs from 20DM to 30DM ($10 to $15) on up.

Fast Facts: Berlin

American Express   Amex offices include locations at Bayreutherstrasse 37–38 (☎ **030/2149830;** U-Bahn: Wittenbergplatz), open Monday to Friday 9am to 6pm and Saturday 10am to 1pm; Alte Potsdamer Strasse 7 (☎ **030/25297474;** U-Bahn: Hüttenweg), open Monday to Friday 9:30am to 8pm and Saturday 9am to 4pm; Am Borsigturm 2 (☎ **030/43402060;** U-Bahn: Borischverger), open Monday to Friday 9:30am to 8pm and Saturday 9am to 4pm; and Friedrichstrasse 172 (☎ **030/2017400;** U-bahn: Friedrichstrasse), open Monday to Friday 9am to 6pm and Saturday 10am to 1pm.

Business Hours   Most **banks** are open Monday to Friday 9am to either 1 or 3pm. Most other **businesses and stores** are open Monday to Friday 9 or 10am to either 6 or 6:30pm and Saturday 9am to 2pm. On *langer Samstag,* the first Saturday of the month, shops stay open until 4 or 6pm. Some stores close late on Thursday (usually 8:30pm).

Currency Exchange   You can exchange money at all airports, at major department stores, at any bank, and at the American Express office (see above). There is also a currency exchange office at the Bahnhof Zoo; it's open Monday to Saturday from 8am to 9pm and on Sunday from 10am to 6pm. ATM machines proliferate in Berlin at virtually every branch of the Dresdner or Deutsche Bank, post offices, and railway stations. Two particularly convenient branches with 24-hour ATM service are **Deutsche Bank** at Wittenbergplatz (U-Bahn: Wittenbergplatz) and **Dresdner Bank** at Kurfürstendamm 237 (U-Bahn: Kurfürstendamm).

Dentists/Doctors   The Berlin tourist office in the Europa Center (☎ 030/264-7480; U-Bahn: Kurfürstendamm) keeps a list of English-speaking dentists and doctors in Berlin. For an emergency doctor, call ☎ 030/31-00-31; for an emergency dentist, call **030/890-04-333.**

Drugstores   If you need a pharmacy (*Apotheke*) at night, go to one on any corner and look for a sign in the window giving the address of the nearest pharmacy with nighttime hours (such postings are required by law). For a centrally located pharmacy, go to **Europa–Apotheke,** Tauentzienstrasse 9–12 (☎ 030/2-61-41-42; U-Bahn: Kurfürstendamm), located near the Europa Center; it's open Monday to Friday 9am to 8pm and Saturday 9am to 4pm. In Mitte, a few steps from Unter den Linden, and maintaining the same hours, is the **Dorotheenstadtische Apotheke,** Friedrichstrasse 154 (☎ 030/204-4817; U-Bahn: Friedrichstrasse).

Embassies & Consulates   See "Fast Facts: Germany," in chapter 2.

Emergencies   To call the police, dial ☎ 110. To report a fire or to summon an ambulance, dial ☎ 112.

Hospitals   Hotel employees are usually familiar with the locations of the nearest hospital emergency room. In an emergency, call ☎ 112 for an ambulance.

Hot Lines   In the incidence of rape or sexual assault, call **LARA,** Tempelhoferufer 14 (☎ 030/216-88-88). For problems relating to drug use or drug addiction, call the drug help line at ☎ 030/1-92-37. Gays seeking legal or health-related advice should call **Schwüles Uberfall** (☎ 030/216-33-36). Gays can also call the **Café Positif** (☎ 030/216-8654) for advice about AIDS and its treatment and prevention; and **Man-o-Meter** (☎ 030/216-8008) for information about anything to do with gay life or gay events in Berlin or the rest of Germany.

Internet Access   You can check your e-mail at the "Internet Café" on the lobby level of the **Radisson SAS Hotel,** Karl-Liebknechtstrasse 5 (☎ 030/23-828; U-Bahn/S-Bahn: Alexanderplatz). The charge, which requires a credit card, is 4.90DM ($2.45) for every six minutes of internet access.

Laundry/Dry Cleaning   Deluxe and first-class hotels offer laundry service, but prices tend to be high. You'll find Laundromats (*wascherei*) and dry-cleaning outlets (*reinigung*) all over town. One that's relatively convenient is **Wascherei Lindenberg,** Curtius Strasse 13–14 (☎ 030/833-1056; S-bahn Lichterfelder West).

Lost Property   For items lost on the bus or U-Bahn, go to **BVG Fündbüro,** Frauenhoferstrasse 33–36 (☎ 030/25-62-30-40; U-Bahn: Ernst-Reuter-Platz); open Monday to Thursday 9am to 6pm and Friday 9am to 2pm. For items lost on the S-Bahn, go to **Deutsches Bahn AG/8-Bahn Berlin GmbH,** Mittelstrasse 20 (☎ 030/2-97-296-12; U-Bahn: Friedrichstrasse), Monday, Wednesday, or Thursday 10am to 4pm, Tuesday 10am to 6pm, or Friday 8am to noon. The general lost-property office, **Zentrales Fündbüro,** is at Platz der Luftbrücke 6 (☎ 030/69-95; U-Bahn: Platz der Luftbrücke). Hours are Monday and Tuesday 7:30am to 2pm, Wednesday noon to 6:30pm, and Friday 7:30am to noon.

Post Office   The post office at Budapester Strasse 42 (U-Bahn/S-Bahn: Zoolo-gischer Garten) is open Monday to Saturday 8am to midnight, Sunday and holidays 10am to midnight. If you have mail sent there, have it marked *Haupt-postlagernd*, Postamt 120, Bahnhof Zoo, 10612 Berlin. An equivalently large post office in the city's eastern side is at Friedrichshain, Strasse der Pariser Commune 8–10 (U-Bahn: Oranienberger Strasse). It's open Monday to Friday 7am to 9pm and Saturday 8am to 8pm. For information about postal services, call ☎ **030/311-00-20.**

Radio   Radio programs in English can be heard on 87.9 FM (or 94 on cable) and 1197 AM for the American Forces Network, and on 90.2 FM (87.6 on cable) for the BBC.

Rest Rooms   A rest room is called a *Toilette* and is often labeled WC, with either F (for *Frauen*, "women") or H (for *Herren*, "men"). Public facilities are found throughout Berlin and at all terminals, including the Europa Center on Tauentzienstrasse. It's customary to tip attendants at least 50pf (25¢).

Safety   One unfortunate side effect of reunification has been an increase in muggings, bank robberies, bias crimes, and car break-ins. Residents of Berlin sometimes feel unsafe at night, especially in the dimly lit streets of Kreuzberg. Nonetheless, Berlin is still much safer than most large American cities. In case of a robbery or an attack, report the problem immediately to the police. You'll need a police report for any insurance claims.

Taxis   See "Getting Around," earlier in this chapter.

Telegrams/Fax   These can be sent from the post office (see "Post Office," above).

Water   The tap water in Berlin, as in all German cities, is safe to drink. However, most Berliners prefer to ask for bottled water, either carbonated or noncarbonated.

Weather   For a report on Berlin weather, call ☎ **0190/270-641.** The cost is 1.21DM (60¢) per minute.

3 Where to Stay

Berlin is the scene of frequent international trade fairs, conferences, and festivals, and dur-ing these times, vacancies in the city will be hard to find. The greatest concentration of hotels, from the cheapest digs to the most expensive, lies in the Center near the **Kur-fürstendamm** (Ku'damm), the main boulevard of western Berlin. Most good-value pen-sions and small hotels are in the western part of the city; note that many such accommodations are in older buildings where plumbing is rarely state-of-the-art.

The business convention crowd still anchors primarily in the west, as do the hordes of summer visitors on whirlwind tours of Europe. **Eastern Berlin** often attracts Ger-mans from other parts of the country who want a glimpse of the Berlin that was shut away behind the Wall for so long. The eastern sector still doesn't have the visitor struc-ture and facilities of the west, although several first-class and deluxe hotels have opened there, notably the Grand, Adlon, and Hilton.

Travelers can also head for hotels in **Grunewald,** close to nature in the Grunewald Forest, or **Charlottenburg,** near Olympic Park. If you like biking, jogging, and breathing fresh air and don't mind the commute into central Berlin for shopping and attractions, you'll enjoy both these areas.

ON OR NEAR THE KURFÜRSTENDAMM
VERY EXPENSIVE

Grand Hotel Esplanade. Lützowufer 15, 10785 Berlin. ☎ **030/25-47-80.** Fax 030/ 2-65-11-71. www.esplanade.de. E-mail: info@esplanade.de. 400 units. A/C MINIBAR TV TEL. 430DM–559DM ($215–$279.50) double; from 780DM ($390) suite. AE, DC, MC, V. Parking 30DM ($15). U-Bahn: Kurfürstenstrasse, Nollendorfplatz, or Wittenbergplatz.

Strikingly contemporary, this well-respected hotel was built in a quiet and verdant neighborhood near several foreign embassies, some prestigious concert halls, and the massively expanding the Potsdamer Platz. Thanks to river views and a swath of park, you might get the feeling that you're far from the city. It competes effectively with other five-star competitors in Berlin, with a well-conceived collection of modern art. The starkly contemporary, bright, sunflooded, and cheerful rooms pay strict attention to sound insulation. Baths are generously sized. Corner rooms are among the most spacious and have some of the best views of the surrounding area.

Dining/Diversions: The hotel's culinary showcase, the Harlekin (see "Where to Dine," below) benefits from a Michelin star. There's a cozy beerstube, the Eck-Kneipe, that provides a rustic and gutbürgerlich hideaway from the streamlined modernism that permeates the rest of the hotel. Harry's New York Bar, showcase for a live pianist, is famous as one of the city's most hip and sought after nightspots. During clement weather, the hotel maintains a restaurant on a converted barge, the *Esplanade,* docked on the river adjacent to the hotel. A lavish breakfast buffet is served in the festive-looking Orangerie.

Amenities: 24-hour room service, laundry and dry cleaning, in-house doctor and nurse, valet parking, massages, baby-sitting, triangular indoor pool, small fitness Center, whirlpool, solarium, three saunas, and full service hairdressing salon offering hair, nail, and facial treatments.

✪ **Kempinski Hotel Bristol Berlin.** Kurfürstendamm 2, 10719 Berlin. ☎ **800/426-3135** in the U.S., or 030/88-43-40. Fax 030/883-6075. www.kempinski-berlin.com. E-mail: ber1. reservations@kempinski.com. 301 units. A/C MINIBAR TV TEL. 435DM–585DM ($217.50–$292.50) double, 680DM–2,300DM ($340–$1,150) suites. AE, DISC, MC, V. Parking 35DM ($17.50). U-Bahn: Kurfürstendamm.

This hotel reigns as one of Berlin's most prestigious and visible hotels, enjoying a reputation equivalent to some of the best hotels in the world. It occupies a bulky, boxy-looking building that was originally erected during the peak of the Cold War, but whose interior has benefitted from ongoing improvements and renovations. The staff is superbly trained and the shamelessly rich-looking decor is more opulent and better-designed than many comparably priced five-star competitors. Rooms contain high-quality reproductions of English and continental antiques, enough insulation to retain an almost reverential hush, and spacious baths. Overall, this is probably the most opulent hotel in what used to be defined as Berlin's Western Zone.

Dining/Diversions: Elegant and expensive, the Kempinski Grill is one of the best hotel dining rooms in Berlin. Somewhat less formal is the Kempinski Eck, an upscale bistro whose most pleasant feature is an outdoor terrace, where you can get coffee, drinks, platters, and very fresh salads while watching the passersby on the Ku'damm

---

Dialing Germany

Remember that the phone numbers in this book contain an initial 0 in the German city code. That 0 is only used within Germany. Omit it when calling from abroad.

Western Berlin Accommodations & Dining

ACCOMMODATIONS
Ahorn Berlin **14**
Alpenland **23**
Ambassador Berlin **39**
Arco Hotel **38**
Art Nouveau **13**
Artemesia **2**
Bleibtreu Hotel **20**
Bogota **17**

Brandenburger Hof/
 Relais & Châteaux **31**
City Pension Alexandra **18**
Grand Hotel Esplanade **42**
Hecker's Hotel **19**
Hotel Crystal **21**
Hotel Domus **25**
Hotel-Pension Bregenz **15**
Hotel Sylter Hof Berlin **40**

Kempenski Hotel Bristol Berlin **27**
Kronprinz Berlin **4**
Palace Berlin **35**
Pension München **33**
Pension Niebuhr **12**
Pension Nürnberger Eck **38**
Ritz Carlton Berlin **3**
Savoy **26**
Sorat Art'otel **30**
Steigenberger Berlin **37**

DINING ◆
Alt-Luxemburg **7**
Ana e Bruno **8**
Bamberger Reiter **32**
Bierhaus Luisen-Bräu **9**
Daitokai **36**
Ernst-August **4**
Funkturm Restaurant **1**

Hard Rock Café **28**
Harlekin **43**
La Table **6**
Lubitsch **16**
Marjellchen **11**
Mensa
   (Markus Semmler) **41**
Paris Bar **24**

Paris-Moskau **34**
Ponte Vecchio **10**
Restaurant Mario **22**
Rockendorf's Gourmet
   Restaurant **44**
Vivaldi **2**
Vox **43**
Zlata Praha **29**

ℹ️ Family-Friendly Hotels

Ahorn Berlin *(see p.79)* Families like the large rooms that contain small kitchenettes.

Ambassador Berlin *(see p. 83)* Kids love the eight-floor heated tropical pool with a retractable dome and a waterfall. Rooms, for the most part, are spacious and exceedingly comfortable for families.

---

below. The rich-looking Bristol Bar seems to have been designed by proponents of the capitalistic dream, and features a pianist playing soft background music. And directly off the hotel's reception area is a gracefully large paneled room, the Gobelin-Halle, whose armchairs and deep sofas and lining of antique tapestries provides one of the city's most elegant spots for morning coffee, afternoon tea, or after dinner drinks.

Amenities: 24-hour room service, laundry, dry cleaning, an indoor swimming pool with a sauna, massage facility, steam bath, solarium, and fitness Center, and a concierge who can arrange virtually anything in Europe.

Steigenberger Berlin. Los-Angeles-Platz 1, 10789 Berlin. ☎ **800/223-5652** in the U.S. and Canada, or 030/21-27-0. Fax 030/2-12-71-17. www.steigenberger.com. E-mail: berlin@steigenberger.de. 397 units. A/C MINIBAR TV TEL. 360DM–540DM ($180–$270) double; from 850DM ($425) suite. AE, DC, MC, V. Parking 29DM ($14.50). U-Bahn: Kurfürstendamm.

One of Berlin's most visible luxury hotels lies on a formal, gracefully proportioned plaza a few steps from the Kaiser Wilhelm Memorial Church. Originally built behind a nondescript facade in 1981, it caters to a demanding clientele of relatively conservative clients. This place represents western Berlin's sense of the status quo more visibly than virtually any other hotel in town. Public areas are large, well-designed open spaces with high ceilings. Overall, expect a sense of bustling conservatism, plush and contemporary comfort, and corporate Europe at its most deeply entrenched. Rooms, for the most part, are medium in size, each maintained in good condition with a tasteful modern decor and generous-size beds. Baths have hair dryers, makeup mirrors, and robes.

Dining/Diversions: The culinary showplace is the Park Restaurant, a dinner-only hideaway that's permeated with warmth, contemporary style, and an intelligent ratio of value to quality. Less elaborate is the Berliner Stube, a street-level bistro that focuses on old-fashioned Prussian recipes. Near its entrance is the Destille Bar, whose theme duplicates in a more upscale form the trappings of a rough-and-tumble 19th-century distillery. There's also a champagne bar, plus a large and stylish street-level piano bar that's a magnet for off-duty residents of the surrounding neighborhood.

Amenities: 24-hour room service, dry cleaning, laundry, baby-sitting, massage, indoor pool, sauna, and solarium.

EXPENSIVE

✪ **Brandenburger Hof/Relais & Châteaux.** Eislebener Strasse 14, 10789 Berlin. ☎ **030/21-40-50.** Fax 030/21-40-51-00. www.brandenburger-hof.com. E-mail: info@brandenburger-hof.com. 82 units. A/C MINIBAR TV TEL. 345DM–465DM ($172.50–$232.50) double; 745DM ($372.50) suite. Rates include breakfast. AE, CB, DC, MC, V. Parking 25DM ($12.50). U-Bahn: Kurfürstendamm or Augsburger Str.; S-Bahn: Zoologischer Garten.

This hotel on a dignified street in the commercial heart of the city was built in 1991 in the classic Bauhaus style beloved by so many Germans. As a Relais & Châteaux property, it offers better food, service, and amenities than most hotels of its price. Rooms range from medium-sized to spacious and are among the most stylish in the city. The decor, with torchère lamps, black leather upholstery, and platform beds, may appear a touch minimalist, but everybody will appreciate the original artworks that adorn the walls. Another bonus is the state-of-the-art security system and the French doors that open up onto balconies on all but the top floor. The spacious baths have large shower/tub combinations, plenty of shelf space, scales, and hair dryers. House-keeping here is among the finest in Berlin. A popular gathering place for guests is the "Wintergarten," an unusual combination of Italian monastery garden and Japanese garden.

Dining/Diversions: Die Quadriga, a Frank Lloyd Wright design with cherry-wood walls and chairs, boasts French cuisine with an Asian influence and has received a Michelin star. The adjoining Wintergarten functions as both restaurant and piano bar.

Amenities: Room service (7am to 10pm), concierge, dry cleaning, laundry, twice-daily maid service, car-rental and tour desk, baby-sitting.

Savoy. Fasanenstrasse 9–10, 10623 Berlin. ☎ **800/223-5652** in the U.S. and Canada, or 030/31-10-30. Fax 030/31-10-33-33. www.savoy-hotels.com. E-mail: info@savoy-hotels.com. 140 units. MINIBAR TV TEL. 345DM–445DM ($172.50–$222.50) double; from 600DM ($300) suite. Children under 13 stay free in parents' room. AE, DC, MC, V. U-Bahn: Kurfürstendamm.

If you don't demand grand, full-service facilities, this might be the hotel for you. Built in 1929, the quiet, unassuming Savoy is a reliable and durable favorite. It's better than many in its category, and although it has lost some of its old-Berlin flavor, it remains the choice for the die-hard traditionalist. Its beautifully furnished rooms and luxuri-ous suites come complete with generous desk space, upholstered armchairs, and cock-tail tables as well as the usual hair dryers and trouser presses. There are also such amenities as private safes and double-glazed windows.

Dining/Diversions: In 2000, the hotel poured money into a restoration of its restaurant, Belle Epoque, moving it from street level to the 6th floor. Open daily for lunch and dinner, it serves well-prepared lunches and dinners in a somewhat staid room with touches of genuine charm. The street-level Times Bar (with the Casa de Habana Cigar Bar) is separately recommended in "Berlin After Dark," below.

Amenities: Room service, laundry, baby-sitting, sauna, fitness club.

MODERATE

Ahorn Berlin. Schlüterstrasse 40 (near the Ku'damm), 10707 Berlin. ☎ **030/8-81-43-44.** Fax 030/8-81-65-00. www.hotel-ahorn.com. E-mail: info@hotel-ahorn.com. 27 units. MINI-BAR TV TEL. 160DM–210DM ($80–$105) double; 180DM–240DM ($90–$120) triple; 30DM ($15) supplement for kitchenette. Discounts sometimes granted in Dec and Aug. Rates include continental breakfast. AE, DC, MC, V. Parking 10DM ($5). U-Bahn: Uhlandstrasse; S-Bahn: Savignyplatz.

This simple, clean, cost-conscious hotel is typical of those built during the Cold War era. Stay here more for the price than for grand comfort, but rooms are inviting nonetheless, with good though much-used furnishings, excellent mattresses, and tidy maintenance. Families often check in here, not only for the kitchenettes, but because many rooms are suitable for three. Nearby are many *Kneipen* (bars) and restaurants.

Artemisia. Brandenburgischestrasse 18 (near the Ku'damm), 10707 Berlin. ☎ **030/ 8-73-89-05.** Fax 030/8-61-86-53. www.frauenhotel-berlin.de. E-mail: frauenhotel-berlin@ t-online.de. 8 units, 6 with shower or bath. TV TEL. 170DM ($85) double without shower or bath; 200DM–220DM ($100–$110) double with shower or bath. Children under 8 stay free in mother's room. Rates include continental breakfast. AE, DC, MC, V. Free parking. U-Bahn: Konstanzerstrasse.

This hotel *for women only* occupies the fourth and fifth floors of a residential building with an elevator. In cold weather, there's often a cozy fire in one of the sitting rooms. Women's conferences and consciousness-raising sessions sometimes take place here. Rooms are medium in size and meticulously maintained, each with a quality mattress and fine linen, plus a good-sized bath with a hair dryer. On the premises are a bar and a rooftop terrace where a buffet breakfast is served on summer mornings. Children, including boys up to age 14, can stay here with their mothers.

✪ **Art Nouveau.** Leibnizstrasse 59, D-10629 Berlin. ☎ **030/327-74-40.** Fax 030/327-74-40. www.hotelartnouvweau.de. E-mail: hotelartnouveausnafu.de. 15 units. TV TEL. 210DM ($105) double, 350DM ($175) suite. U-Bahn: Adenauerplatz.

On the fourth floor of an art nouveau apartment house, this little known hotel is an atmospheric choice. Even the elevator is a historic gem of the upmarket and desirable neighborhood. Established in the late 1970s, Art Nouveau was fully renovated in 1998. The well-furnished and comfortable rooms are pleasantly decorated and high-ceilinged, filled with excellent beds. Rooms in the rear are more tranquil except when the schoolyard is full of children at play. There's an honesty bar in the lobby where guests keep track of their own drinks. A generous breakfast is the only meal served.

Bleibtreu Hotel. Bleibtreustrasse 31 (1 block south of the Kurfürstendamm). ☎ **030/88474-0** or 800/223-5652 for reservations in the US and Canada. Fax 030/88474-444. www.savoy-hotels.com. E-mail: info@bleibtreu.com. 60 units. MINIBAR TV TEL. 289DM–389DM ($144.50–$194.50) double. Rates include breakfast. AE, MC, V. S-Bahn: Savignyplatz.

The facade of this trend-conscious hotel isn't easily recognizable from the street, as the tiny lobby is accessible via an alleyway that leads past an avant-garde garden and a big-windowed set of dining and drinking facilities. The setting is the labyrinthine premises of what was built long ago as a Jugendstil-era apartment house. Rooms are small, minimalist, and furnished in carefully chosen natural materials. Extras include data ports and cordless phones. Baths are cramped but well-designed, and equipped with hair dryers. A flower shop, a restaurant that features vegetarian and organic cuisine, a bar, and a shop selling homeopathic remedies, vitamins, and New-Age health enhancements are on the premises, and an espresso bar abuts the sidewalk. Tables spill from the restaurant, cafe, and bar, into the tiny garden, where shrubs and flowers are surrounded with smooth-polished pieces of colored glass—a definite conversation piece.

Hotel Domus. Uhlandstrasse 49, D-10719 Berlin. ☎ **030/880-3440.** Fax 030/880344-44. 71 units. TV TEL 192DM–255DM ($96–$127.50) double; 265DM ($132.50) suite. Some discounts available some Fri-Sun, depending on bookings. AE, DC, MC, V. Parking 10DM ($5). U-Bahn: Hohenzollernplatz or Spichernstrasse.

Clean, streamlined, and unpretentious, this three-star hotel was created in 1975 from an older core whose elaborate detailing couldn't be salvaged. The result is an enduringly stylish, uncluttered piece of architecture that rises from a presigious neighborhood a few blocks from the Ku'damm. It's a favorite of business travelers, who appreciate its good value and respectability. As such, it has a high proportion of single rooms, which cost 145DM to 165DM ($72.50 to $82.50). Rooms are well-designed, well scrubbed, and although not particularly large, very comfortable. There are virtually no amenities on site, and other than breakfast and a drink that the receptionist might sell you within the lobby, no meals are served. But overall, it's a worthy, albeit simple choice, with good value and a helpful staff.

Kronprinz Berlin. Kronprinzendamm 1, 10711 Berlin. ☎ **030/89-60-30.** Fax 030/8-93-12-15. www.kronprinz-hotel.de. E-mail: reception@kronprinzhotel.de. 68 units. MINIBAR TV TEL. 260DM ($130) double; 380DM ($190) suite. Children 12 and under stay free in parents' room. Rates include buffet breakfast. AE, DC, MC, V. Free parking. U-Bahn: Adenauerplatz. Bus: 104, 110, 119, 129, or 219.

This hotel is located away from Berlin's Center at the far western edge of the Ku'damm. In spite of its many discreet charms and features, it remains relatively little known or publicized. All rooms have balconies and fine appointments (often tasteful reproductions of antiques). If you want a little extra comfort, ask for one of the Bel-Etage rooms. Many guests congregate in the cozy in-house bar, or in the garden under the chestnut trees in summer. Laundry and dry cleaning are available, as well as baby-sitting.

INEXPENSIVE

Alpenland. Carmerstrasse 8 (near the Ku'damm), 10623 Berlin. ☎ **030/3-12-39-70.** Fax 030/3-13-84-44. 40 units, 25 with bath (5 with shower only). TV TEL. 110DM–120DM ($55–$60) double without bath, 130DM–190DM ($65–$95) double with bath. Rates include breakfast. MC, V. S-Bahn: Savignyplatz. Parking 15DM ($7.50). U-Bahn: Zoologischer Garten.

This hotel is housed in a century-old building that was once an opulent private home. It's convenient to theaters, museums, pubs, and restaurants. Outside, it's ornately decorated with carvings and figures, though the stripped-down interior is almost monastically simple. Mattresses and towels are a bit thin, but there is reasonable comfort here, enhanced by good maintenance. On the ground floor is a tapas bar that caters to local office workers. There's also a pleasant terrace where guests can enjoy a drink as they watch the sun set over the city. Be warned that the building's four floors are not yet accessible via elevator.

Bogota. Schlüstrasse 45, 10707 Berlin. ☎ **030/8-81-50-01.** Fax 030/8-83-58-87. www.bogota.de. E-mail: hotel.bogota@t-online.de. 125 units, 60 with bath (12 with shower but no toilet). TEL. 130DM ($65) double without bath; 145DM ($72.50) double with shower but no toilet; 160DM–190DM ($80–$95) double with bath. Rates include continental breakfast. AE, CB, DC, MC, V. Parking 15DM ($7.50). U-Bahn: Adenauerplatz or Uhlandstr; S-Bahn: Savignyplatz.

The Bogota is one of the town's most popular budget hotels, though its facilities are less than state-of-the-art. The elevator and floor lobbies are old-fashioned, if not outdated. The small but tidy rooms are well maintained, if a bit dowdy. The best open onto an inner courtyard and are less noisy than those in front. Baths, though small, are efficiently organized. There's a cozy TV room. For an extra 5DM ($2.50) per night you can have a TV in your room.

City Pension Alexandra. Wielandstrasse 32, 10692 Berlin. ☎ **030/8-81-21-07.** Fax 030/ 88-57-78-18. E-mail: pension.alexandra@t-online.de. 9 units, 4 with shower only. TV TEL. 135DM ($67.50) double with shower only, 185DM ($92.50) double with bath. Rates include buffet breakfast. AE, DC, MC, V. Parking 10DM ($5). S-Bahn: Savignyplatz.

This three-floor hotel is comfortable, centrally located, and quiet. The building dates from 1900 and was converted into a hotel in the 1920s. The breakfast room, where a buffet is served, is lined with photographs of old Berlin—perfect for acquainting yourself with what to look for as you tour the streets of the city. Most rooms have modern furniture; some are more classic. The hotel provides laundry service, and baby-sitting is also available.

Hotel Crystal. Kantstrasse 144, 10623 Berlin. ☎ **030/312-90-47.** Fax 030/3-12-64-65. 33 units, 21 with bath (5 with shower only). TEL. 90DM ($45) double without bath, 110DM ($55) double with shower only, 130DM–150DM ($65–$75) double with bath. Rates include breakfast. AE, MC, V. Parking free. S-Bahn: Savignyplatz.

In a 19th-century building, the hotel rises six floors with an elevator. It's owned and operated by American John Schwarzrock and his German wife, Dorothée, who are always glad to welcome American visitors. The very basic rooms are comfortable and extremely clean, with eclectic furniture that you might think was gathered piecemeal. There's a small bar just off the lobby.

Hotel-Pension Bregenz. Bregenzer Strasse 5, 10707 Berlin. ☎ **030/8-81-43-07.** Fax 030/8-82-40-09. 14 units, 10 with bath. MINIBAR TV TEL. 110DM ($55) double without bath, 160DM ($80) double with bath. Rates include breakfast. MC, V. Parking 5DM ($2.50). U-Bahn: Adenauerplatz; S-Bahn: Savignyplatz.

This dignified pension occupies the fourth and sunniest floor of a four-story century-old apartment building, accessible by elevator. The owner, Mr. Zimmermann, works hard to maintain the cleanliness and charm of his comfortably furnished, relatively large rooms. Double doors help to minimize noise from the public corridors. A continental breakfast is served each morning in a small dining area. The staff gladly assists guests in reserving tickets for shows and tours.

Pension München. Guntzelstrasse 62 (close to Bayerischer Platz), 10717 Berlin. ☎ **030/ 8-57-91-20.** Fax 030/85-79-12-22. E-mail: hotel-pension.muenchen@arcormail.de. 8 units, 4 with bath. TV TEL. 95DM ($47.50) double without bath, 130DM ($65) double with bath. AE, DC, MC, V. On-street parking available. U-Bahn: Guntzelstrasse.

This pension occupies only part of the third floor of a massive four-story elevator building erected as an apartment house in 1908. It offers a simple but tasteful decor of modern furnishings accented with fresh flowers. Rooms are clean, with contemporary furniture and prints and engravings by local artists. Look for sculptures by the owner in some of the public areas as well. *Note:* If there are no rooms available here, you're likely to be recommended to a similar pension, **Pension Güntzel** (☎ **030/8-57-90-20**), on the building's street-level and cellar.

Pension Niebuhr. Niebuhrstrasse 74, 10629 Berlin. ☎ **030/3-24-95-95.** Fax 030/ 3-24-80-21. 12 units, 7 with bath. 120DM ($60) double without bath, 170DM ($85) double with bath. Rates include breakfast. AE, MC, V. Parking 5DM ($2.50). S-Bahn: Savignyplatz.

Clean, safe, and sophisticated, this gay-friendly hotel occupies one and a half floors of a century-old apartment building. Willi Heidasch is your amiable host, maintaining simple but clean rooms, seven with phone and TV. Beds are a bit worn but still have comfort in them, and baths are small. Paintings by aspiring Berlin artists (many for sale) decorate the public areas. Breakfast is served in your room anytime after 7am and is the only meal offered. About half the clientele is gay, a percentage that's growing, according to the owner.

Pension Nürnberger Eck. Nürnberger Strasse 24a (near the Europa Center), 10789 Berlin. ☎ **030/2-35-17-80.** Fax 030/235-178-99. 8 units, 5 with bath. TV TEL. 130DM ($65) double without bath, 160DM–180DM ($80–$90) double with bath. MC, V. Rates include breakfast. Parking 5DM ($2.50). U-Bahn: Augsburgerstrasse.

This reliable pension is refreshingly old-fashioned. It occupies the second floor of a four-story building on a relatively quiet side street. Rooms are large, with high ceilings, massive doors, and in many cases, reproductions of Biedermeier-style furniture, including comfortable beds with soft mattresses. This is the kind of place where Christopher Isherwood's Sally Bowles from *Cabaret* might have stayed.

NEAR THE MEMORIAL CHURCH & ZOO
VERY EXPENSIVE

Palace Berlin. Europa Center, Budapesterstrasse 45, 10789 Berlin. ☎ **800/457-4000** in the U.S. and Canada, or 030/2-50-20. Fax 030/2-502-1161. www.palace.de. E-mail: res@palace.de. 382 units. A/C MINIBAR TV TEL. 425DM-590DM ($212.50-$295) double; from 650DM ($325) suite. AE, DC, MC, V. Parking 30DM ($15). U-Bahn: Zoologischer Garten.

Although not at the level of the Kempinski or the Grand Hotel Esplanade, the stylish Palace from 1968 outranks such landmarks as the Berlin Hilton and the Steigenberger Berlin. The hotel is much improved over past years, and the staff is extremely pleasant. Rooms range from medium to spacious, all have fine beds, superb lighting, quality carpeting, hair dryers, and trouser presses. The best are in the newer Casino Wing. In some, even the good double glazing is unable to entirely shut out noise from the adjacent Europa Center. All of the seventh and part of the sixth floor are set aside for nonsmokers. Baths mostly feature tub/shower combinations (but some have showers only). Those in the Casino Wing have separate showers and tubs.

Dining/Diversions: Despite a lot of competition from restaurants nearby, the hotel maintains its own elegant dining room, the First Floor. It also operates two convivial bars and the Alt Nürnberg restaurant, located in the Europa Center.

Amenities: Room service, laundry, dry cleaning, massage, secretarial services, concierge, baby-sitting; adjacent to the hotel is the Thermen am Europa Center, a large health club with indoor and outdoor pools, exercise equipment, and a sauna. Admission is free to hotel guests.

EXPENSIVE

Ambassador Berlin. Bayreutherstrasse 42–43, 10787 Berlin. ☎ **030/21-90-20.** Fax 030/ 21-90-23-80. www.ambassador-berlin.de. E-mail: reservation@ambassador-berlin.de. 199 units. MINIBAR TV TEL. 260DM–290DM ($130–$145) double, 350DM ($175) suite. Rates include buffet breakfast. AE, DC, MC, V. Parking 18DM ($9). U-Bahn: Wittenbergplatz.

This hotel is an attractive choice if you'd like to lodge near the Ku'damm. The heated tropical pool on the eighth floor, with its retractable dome and a waterfall, is an unusual feature. Rooms are, for the most part, spacious and exceedingly comfortable and include traditional furnishings, trouser presses, robes, and hair dryers. Baths are rather small, and only a fifth have showers; the rest have tubs. Soundproof windows are always a relief in noisy central Berlin, and nonsmokers get a floor to themselves. The hotel is sometimes overrun with large groups.

Dining/Diversions: The elegant Schöneberger Krug restaurant serves tasty regional and international dishes. The hotel's Bar Ambassador is an attractive rendezvous.

Amenities: Same-day laundry, valet, baby-sitting, massage; heated tropical pool, sun lounge, Finnish sauna, solarium, pool bar.

Hecker's Hotel. Grolmanstrasse 35 (near the Ku'damm), 10623 Berlin. ☎ **030/8-89-00.** Fax 030/8-89-02-60. www.heckers-hotel.com. E-mail: info@heckers-hotel.com. 72 units. A/C MINIBAR TV TEL. 260DM–370DM ($130–$185) double. AE, CB, DC, MC, V. Parking 15DM–20DM ($7.50–$10). U-Bahn: Uhlandstrasse. Bus: 109 from Berlin-Tegel Airport to Uhlandstrasse.

For years this establishment enjoyed a reputation as a small, private hotel, but now it's been expanded. Although not in the same league as the Sorat (see below), this is still a winning choice. It's conveniently located near the Ku'damm and the many bars, cafes, and restaurants around Savignyplatz. The original 42 rooms are smaller than the newer units, which are medium-sized. The rather severe and somewhat somber modern style may not suit everyone—certainly not those seeking romantic ambience. Some rooms are exclusively for nonsmokers. There is a sterility here but also up-to-date comfort and top-notch maintenance.

Dining/Diversions: The hotel maintains a small restaurant and bar. The rooftop terrace is available for dining in summer and provides a great view of Berlin at night.

Amenities: Concierge, room service, dry cleaning and laundry, car-rental and tour desk, baby-sitting and secretarial services.

✪ **Sorat Art'otel.** Joachimstalerstrasse 28–29 (near the Ku'damm), 10719 Berlin. ☎ **030/ 88-44-70.** Fax 030/88-44-77-00. www.sorat-hotel-com. E-mail: headoffice@sorat-hotels. com. 133 units. A/C MINIBAR TV TEL. 230DM–355DM ($115–$177.50) double. Rates include buffet breakfast. AE, DC, MC, V. U-Bahn: Kurfürstendamm.

Chic, discreet, and avant-garde, the Sorat is unlike any other Berlin hotel. The location is ideal, in the heart of cosmopolitan Berlin, with the Ku'damm action virtually outside the front door. The decor, strictly minimalist, includes touches from top designers. You'll find Philippe Starck bar stools, Arne Jacobsen chairs, and artwork by Berliner Wolf Vostell. Modernists will be at home here, amid the pedestal tables evoking cable spools and the chrome-legged furnishings. Traditionalists might not be so pleased. Rooms are all comfortable, with soundproofing, deluxe mattresses on large beds, private safes, and tasteful lighting. Baths are generous in size. The service here is among Berlin's finest.

Dining/Diversions: The Anteo restaurant, adjacent to the hotel, is known for both its creative cuisine and its avant-garde decor.

Amenities: Concierge, room service, car-rental, laundry.

MODERATE

Hotel Sylter Hof Berlin. Kurfürstenstrasse 114–116, 10787 Berlin. ☎ **030/2-12-00.** Fax 030/2-14-28-26. www.sylterhof-berlin.de. 161 units. MINIBAR TV TEL. 256DM ($128) double; 326DM–386DM ($163–$193) suite. Rates include buffet breakfast. AE, DC, MC, V. Parking 20DM ($10). U-Bahn: Wittenbergplatz. Bus: 100 or X9.

Sylter Hof, built in 1966, offers rich trappings at good prices. The main lounges are warmly decorated in Louis XV style, with chandeliers, provincial chairs, and antiques. Well-maintained rooms—mostly singles—may be too small for most tastes but are good for business travelers. The bar-lounge features velvet armchairs and Persian rugs. The hotel has an American-style coffee shop that serves fresh-baked cakes and daily specials at reasonable rates. On the premises is a nightclub featuring burlesque shows (with discreet nudity). The staff pays special attention to your comfort.

INEXPENSIVE

Arco Hotel. Geisbergstrasse 30, D-10777 Berlin. ☎ **030/ 23-51-480.** Fax 030/ 21-47-51-78. www.arco-hotel.de. E-mail: arco-hotel@t-online.de. 22 units. TV TEL. 140DM–190DM ($70–$95) double. AE, MC, V. U-Bahn: Viktoria-Luise-Platz or Nollendorferplatz.

Although some of its competitors are more visible and more heavily promoted, this is one of the most consistently reliable and fairly priced gay hotels in Berlin. It occupies part of a former old-Berlin apartment building which was completely renovated in 1999. Rooms are mostly white, well-scrubbed, and well-organized, with tasteful albeit simple artwork and furnishings. There's a garden in back, site of breakfasts during clement weather. A polite and hardworking staff is alert to the location of emerging neighborhood bars and restaurants, many of whose owners recommend this place. Much of its business derives from repeat guests from as far away as Los Angeles.

IN GRUNEWALD
VERY EXPENSIVE

✪ **The Ritz Carlton Schlosshotel Berlin.** Brahmsstrasse 10, 14193 Berlin-Grunewald. ☎ 030/895-84800. Fax 030/89-58-48-07. www.ritzcarlton.com. 54 units. A/C MINIBAR TV TEL. 495DM–675DM ($247.50–$337.50) double; 795DM–5,500DM ($397.50–$2,750) suite. AE, DC, MC, V. Parking 29DM ($14.50). S-Bahn: Grunewald.

With only 54 gem-like rooms, this is the smallest Ritz-Carlton in the world, and also one of the most historic and plush. It was built in the 19th century by a friend and advisor of Kaiser Wilhelm II, who entertained him from time to time on the premises.

For anyone who can afford it, and who prefers a stay in the city's verdant suburbs, the experience can be elegant, historic, and charming. Service is superb and invariably cheerful. Although changes have been made to the decor since the hotel opened in the 1980s, its original inspiration was by German-born fashion superstar Karl Lagerfeld. The structure's monumental staircase, minstrel's gallery, and other belle époque trappings remain, but Mr. Lagerfeld's contributions have added an undeniable gloss to the hotel's interior. Beds are sumptuous, with deluxe mattresses, great pillows, fine linen, and elegant fabrics. Baths have shower and tub combos, plush towels, radiantly heated floors, slippers, scales, and robes.

Dining: The hotel contains a pair of restaurants. Vivaldi's is the more unusual (see "Where to Dine" below). The other, Le Jardin Wine Bistro, is somewhat less formal.

Amenities: Concierge, 24-hour room service, twice-daily maid service, health club with Jacuzzi and sauna, conference rooms, beauty salon and boutique, sun deck, babysitting, secretarial service, in-room massage, dry cleaning and laundry service.

IN BERLIN-MITTE
VERY EXPENSIVE

Berlin Hilton. Mohrenstrasse 30, 10117 Berlin. ☎ **800/445-8667** in the U.S. and Canada, or 030/2-02-30. Fax 030/20-23-42-69. www.infoberlin/hilton.com. 499 units. A/C MINIBAR TV TEL. 470DM–550DM ($235–$275) double; 480DM–1,500DM ($240–$750) suite. Special weekend packages available. AE, MC, V. Parking 25DM ($12.50). U-Bahn: Stadtmitte.

Set within one of the city's most expensive and desirable neighborhoods (Gendarmenmarkt), this deluxe hotel was the first to open in what was East Berlin following the collapse of the Berlin Wall. Today it's the third largest hotel in the city and one of the most popular. The seven-floor hotel contains enough accessories, bars, boutiques, upscale gift shops, and facilities to keep you jumping for a week. Thanks to all the visual distraction in the lobby, there's even a vague sense that you might be in a resort hotel that's eager to cater to the needs of both large groups and business travelers alike. Rooms are conservatively modern and very comfortable, with double-glazed windows, comfortable beds, bedside controls, private safes, and well-equipped baths with tub/shower combos and hair dryers. At least half overlook the twin churches of the dramatic Gendarmenmarkt.

Dining/Diversions: Restaurants include The Fellini, an Italian restaurant, and the Mark Brandenburg, with traditional cuisine. Bel Étage is the breakfast restaurant with a large American-style breakfast buffet. In the Wintergarten, you can order drinks, traditional snacks, light meals, and cakes. Restaurant Gendarmenmarkt is self-service, with an especially appealing salad buffet. Bars include the 7th floor's Kaminbar, which has an open fireplace, and the Mundi Bar, which strives to attract counter-culture artists and writers, thanks partly to an interior by German designer Charlotta Janse. For more raucous fun, there's a beer pub, Kaktus, with a bowling alley, and a disco is open from dusk until dawn.

Amenities: Concierge, 24-hour room service, laundry, baby-sitting, health club, saunas, pool with Jacuzzi, rooftop squash courts, bowling alley, and a business Center where the mechanics of international communications are made available to hotel guests.

EXPENSIVE

Alexander Plaza. Rosenstrasse 1, D-10178 Berlin. ☎ **800/223-5652** for reservations in North America, or 030/24001-0. Fax 030/24001-777. www.alexander-plaza.com. E-mail: info@alexander-plaza.com. 92 units. A/C MINIBAR TV TEL. 288DM–385DM ($144–$192.50) double, 325DM–575DM ($162.50–$287.50) suite. S-Bahn: Hackescher Markt.

Set a short walk from both Alexanderplatz and the historic district of Hackescher Höfe, this hotel originated around 1900 as an office building. In 1997, in combination with another building next door, it was converted into one of the neighborhood's most charming and best-managed hotels. A labyrinth of hallways open into rooms with unique floor plans. Each has parquet floors, high ceilings, and neo-Biedermeier blond-wood furniture. The larger "executive rooms" are very large. Low-end rooms are smaller and less dramatic, but still very comfortable. The staff here is among the most attentive in Berlin.

Dining: Bellini's restaurant, on the ground floor, is open daily for lunch and dinner. The hotel bar remains open daily noon to at least midnight. The breakfast buffet, set beneath a sunflooded atrium, is one of the most appealing in town.

Amenities: There's a business Center on the premises with computer facilities and everything you'd need to conduct affairs away from home. The cellar contains a small-scale health club, with exercise machines, a sauna, and a steam room.

✪ **Four Seasons.** Charlottenstrasse 49, 10117 Berlin. ☎ **800/332-3442** in the U.S., or 030/2-03-38. Fax 030/203-36-009. www.fourseasons.com. E-mail: kerstin.pundt@fourseasons.com. 204 units. A/C MINIBAR TV TEL. 440DM–560DM ($220–$280) double; from 640 ($320) suite. AE, MC, V. Parking 40DM ($20). U-Bahn: Französische Strasse.

One of Berlin's most opulent hotels was built in 1996 on the site of a bombed-out parking lot about a block from the Gendarmenmarkt. From the look of things, you'd never realize the venue is new, as everything about it evokes Versailles and an undeniable sense of well-established and very plush prosperity. Decor, illuminated with light from two separate courtyards, includes Viennese crystal chandeliers, antiques from throughout Europe, and the sense that you've entered a private and very upscale home. Rooms are furnished with timeless taste and elegance, with very large baths, each with walk-in showers, deep tubs, and a relentlessly upscale selection of toiletries.

Dining/Diversions: A crackling fire in winter adds to the intimate atmosphere of the Seasons Restaurant (see "Where to Dine," below).

Amenities: Health club, 24-hour room service, concierge, twice-daily maid service, newspaper delivery, dry cleaning, laundry.

✪ **Grand Hyatt Berlin.** Marlene-Dietrich-Platz 2, D-10785 Berlin. ☎ **030/25-53-12-34.** Fax 030/25-53-12-35. www.berlin.hyatt.com. 342 units. A/C MINIBAR TV TEL. 360DM–460DM ($180–$230) doubles; 80DM ($40) supplement, per room, for upgrade to Regency Club; 610DM–3,500DM ($305–$1,750) suite. AE, DC, MC, V. Parking 30DM ($15). U-Bahn: Potsdamer Platz.

This is the most exciting, best designed, and most iconoclastic hotel in Berlin, a five-star mecca. Don't expect rococo frills: Interior designer Hannes Wettstein permeated this hotel with a minimalist simplicity that might remind you of a Zen temple. Ceilings soar toward surreal-looking inverted pyramids, upstairs hallways run off into futuristic-looking infinities, and light derives from rambling expanses of glass or translucent slabs of alabaster. The large and sunflooded rooms are among the hotel's best features. Suites are often commandeered by fashion photographers as backgrounds for cutting edge fashion layouts. Hint: For the reasonable surcharge of 80DM, you can upgrade your accommodation to the 7th floor Regency Club. There, the value of free breakfasts, afternoon tea, evening cocktail hour, daytime snacks, and enhanced services will more than compensate you for the supplement you'll pay.

Dining/Diversions: Vox is the hotel's gourmet citadel and cocktail lounge (see "Where to Dine," below). Less grand options include the Tizian Italian Cafe, where an open-to-view kitchen prepares breakfast items throughout the morning and bistro/trattoria selections throughout the day and evening. Dietrich's Bistro serves pastries, salads, platters and stiff drinks in a setting that gets youth oriented and animated late at night, and downright voyeuristic during the frequent film festivals. During

Berlin-Mitte Accommodations & Dining

ACCOMMODATIONS ■
Alexander Plaza **14**
Berlin Hilton **1**
Four Seasons **21**
Hotel Adlon **6**
Hotel Hackenscher Markt **12**
Hotel Luisenhof **16**

Maritim Pro Arte **8**
Royal Dorint Hotel **22**
Westin Grand Hotel **19**

DINING ◆
Aigner **22**
Alexanderkeller **17**

Boon's **11**
Die Weltbühne **13**
Dressler **18**
Französischer Hof **5**
Ganymed **7**
Guy **4**
Keller Restaurant im Brecht-Haus-Berlin **9**

Langhans **2**
Mutter Hoppe **17**
Oren **10**
Restaurant Borchardt **20**
Reasurant Vau **3**
The Seasons Restaurant **21**
Zur Letzten Instanz **15**

✝ Church
Ⓢ S-Bahn Stop

clement weather, the hotel fills its nearby sidewalks with cafe tables, helping to transform this part of Potsdamer Platz into something akin to a small resort-style village.

Amenities: 24-hour room service, business Center with secretarial/translation services and the availability of rentable laptop computers, dry cleaning and laundry, and a concierge who can arrange virtually anything. On the hotel's 8th floor is Club Olympus, a private membership, state-of-the-art pool, sauna, spa, and fitness facility whose use is free for hotel guests, and whose view sweeps out over the rooftops of Berlin's most exciting architecture.

✪ **Hotel Adlon.** Unter den Linden 77, 10117 Berlin. ☎ **800/426-3135** in the U.S., or 030/22-61-0. Fax 30/22-61-1116. www.hotel-adlon.de. E-mail: adlon@kempinski.com. 337 units. A/C MINIBAR TV TEL. 390DM–690DM ($195–$345) double; 590DM–4,000DM ($295–$2,000) suite. AE, DC, MC, V. Parking 40DM ($20) per day. S-Bahn: Unter den Linden.

No other hotel sits as close to the Brandenburg Gate, at the top of an avenue that's reasserting its claim on the city's sense of chic. Grand and historic, and permeated with the legends of the glamour and tragedies that befell it during various eras of its life, it was originally built by legendary hotelier Lorenz Adlon in 1907, then reopened with a well-publicized flourish in 1997 after a massive expenditure of funds. Public areas, some of them illuminated with lavishly detailed stained-glass domes, contain coffered ceilings, mosaics, inlaid paneling, and lots of Carrara marble. Rooms are mostly large and have lots of state-of-the-art electronic amenities, such as CD players. Those on the top floor offer the best views but are a bit more cramped and lack some amenities. Overall, this hotel is one of the premier addresses of Berlin.

Dining/Diversions: There's a posh-looking bar on the premises, and three restaurants: the Adlon Bistro, the more folkloric-looking Adlonstübe, and a dinner-only enclave of gourmet-friendly charm, the Lorenz Adlon Restaurant.

Amenities: 24-hour room service, hair dryers, massage, spa services (including skin care and beauty treatments), concierge, an indoor swimming pool, health club, jogging path across the street, and access to bicycling, golf, and horseback riding within the city limits of Berlin.

Maritim Pro Arte. Friedrichstrasse 151–153 (across from Friedrichstrasse station), 10117 Berlin. ☎ **030/2-03-35.** Fax 030/20-33-42-09. www.maritim.de. E-mail: bpa@maritim.de. 403 units. A/C MINIBAR TV TEL. 298DM–528DM ($149–$264) double; from 530 ($265) suite. AE, DC, MC, V. Parking 25DM ($12.50). S-Bahn: Friedrichstrasse.

Set about a block from Unter den Linden, this hotel was built as an avant-garde architectural showcase in the mid-1970s by the then East German government. Today, despite frequent renovations, it still evokes a jazzy, "moderno," and vaguely dated kind of architecture that features lots of chrome and stainless steel. There's a bustle here, however, thanks in part to a hardworking and polite staff, and a regular clientele of business clients and conventioneers. Avant-garde artworks are exhibited throughout, and some of the furniture was created by Phillipe Starck. Rooms are individually designed, and are soothing, uncluttered, and comfortable. All have built-in safes and a reclining chair. Most provide a fax outlet.

Dining/Diversions: There are three restaurants: Bistro Media, the less formal Galerie Restaurant, and the premier à la carte restaurant, Atelier. There's also a bar.

Amenities: Room service, laundry, baby-sitting, indoor pool, fitness studio, sauna, solarium.

Royal Dorint Hotel. Charlottenstrasse 50–52. D-10117 Berlin. ☎ **030/20375-0.** Fax 030/20375-100. www.dorint.de. E-mail: info.Bergen@dorint.com. 92 units. A/C MINIBAR TV TEL. 355DM–515DM ($177.50–$257.50) double; 395DM–995DM ($197.50–$497.50) suite. AE, DC, MC, V. U-Bahn: Stadtmitte.

The shell that contains this unusual hotel was designed by the then-East German government in 1981 as a youth hostel, and set behind a faux-Jugendstil facade that has since then been declared a historic monument. After reunification, the Dorint chain carefully converted the structure into an upscale hotel of artfully simple, Zen-like minimalism. The result is a soothing blend of high-tech accessories and a restful kind of neutrality, all of it adminstered in a hip and upbeat way that usually appeals to anyone working in the field of media, the arts, or high-tech science. Small and choice, and presenting an ultra-hip version of "new Berlin" to the antique setting of the Gendarmenmarkt, it's one of the genuinely unusual five-star hotels in Berlin. Every room is different, but the best overlook the Gendarmenmarkt from behind tiny balconies.

Dining/Diversions: The ground floor contains the separately recommended Café Aigner. The Atrium Café is the site for breakfast.

Amenities: 24-hour room service, concierge, laundry, a 7th-floor health club with sauna and steam room, a meditation room with color therapy.

The Westin Grand Hotel. Friedrichstrasse 158–164, 10117 Berlin. ☎ **800/843-3311** in the U.S., or 030/2-02-70. Fax 030/20-27-33-62. www.westin-grand.com. E-mail: info@westin-grand.com. 357 units. A/C MINIBAR TV TEL. 445DM–570DM ($222.50–$285) double; 750DM–3,500DM ($375–$1,750) suite. AE, DC, MC, V. Parking 25DM–40DM ($12.50–$20). U-Bahn: Französische Strasse; S-Bahn: Friedrichstrasse.

Amazingly, this monument to capitalistic decadence was first constructed on socialist soil by the then communist East German government. Now under management by the Westin group, and devoid of its original sense of stiffness, it's one of Berlin's finest hotels. Belle époque features blend with contemporary styling. Rooms, radically renovated and upgraded in 1998, come in a wide range of styles, from beautifully appointed standard doubles all the way up to the lush-looking Schinkel Suite. Beds contain wonderfully soft linens, down pillows and comforters, and firm mattresses. Other features include terry-cloth robes, thick towels, and fresh flowers.

Dining/Diversions: Don't miss the public rooms one flight above lobby level. There's a bar and lounge in the lobby, Le Grand Restaurant, a formal eatery that's open daily for lunch and dinner, and the Stammhaus, a beer pub.

Amenities: 24-hour room service, fitness club, whirlpool, marble pool, saunas, solarium, deluxe hairdressing salon.

MODERATE

✪ **Hotel Hackescher Markt.** Grosse Präsidentenstrasse 8, D-10178 Berlin. ☎ **030/ 28-00-30.** Fax 030/ 28-00-31-11. www.hackescher-markt.de. E-mail: hohama@aol.com. 31 units MINIBAR TV TEL. 260DM–330DM ($130–$165) double; 290DM–340DM ($145–$170) suite. AE, MC, V. U-Bahn: Hackescher Markt.

You'd never know this nugget of charm was newly built in 1998, as everything about it evokes a late 19th-century landmark. Inside, there's a quiet, flagstone-and-ivy covered courtyard that clients use for reading, a richly paneled bistro and pub, and a polite and helpful staff that knows virtually everything about what's happening in the hotel's cutting edge neighborhood. There's a bar on street level where hipsters might feel supremely comfortable, and where live music is presented Wednesday and Saturday nights. Rooms are soothing, partially oak-paneled, and outfitted with comfortable and practical furniture. Standard singles tend to be just a bit small—a better bet might be one of the more upscale doubles. Baths have heated floors. Some guests appreciate the romantic overtones of rooms on the uppermost floor, whose walls are angled thanks to the building's mansard roof.

✪ **Hotel Luisenhof.** Köpenicker Strasse 92, 10179 Berlin. ☎ **030/2-41-59-06.** Fax 030/2-79-29-83. www.luisenhof.com. E-mail: info@luisenhof.de. 27 units. MINIBAR TV TEL. 265DM ($132.50) double; 380DM ($190) suite. Rates include breakfast. AE, DC, MC, V. Parking 14DM ($7). U-Bahn: Märkisches Museum.

This is one of the most desirable small hotels in eastern Berlin. It lies within a severely dignified house, built in 1822. Its five floors of high-ceilinged rooms have been outfitted in a conservative and traditional style, a welcome escape from modern Berlin. The upgraded units range in size from small to spacious, but all are equipped with fine beds, safes, and individual fax machines. Baths, though small, are beautifully appointed. The neighborhood around this hotel, like many other parts of the once-dour eastern zone, is undergoing a rapid renovation.

Dining/Diversions: Beneath the vaulted ceilings in the cellar, you'll find a very appealing restaurant, the Alexanderkeller (see "Where to Dine," below).

Amenities: Room service from 6am to midnight, laundry and dry cleaning, concierge.

4 Where to Dine

If it's true that optimism and appetite go hand in hand, Berliners must be among the most optimistic people in Europe. But just because Berliners like to eat, doesn't mean that they like to spend a lot on food. Locals know that you can often have a memorable dinner here in an unheralded wine restaurant or sidewalk cafe. Rising food costs in the east, however, mean that in the new Berlin, the eastern section can no longer be viewed as a bargain basement in the food department.

If a restaurant bill says *Bedienung,* that means a service charge has already been added, so just round up to the nearest mark.

Examples of typical dishes are the Berliner *Schlachteplatte* (cold plate), pigs' trotters cooked with sauerkraut and pea puree, and *Eisbein* (pickled knuckle of pork with sauerkraut). Venison, wildfowl, and wild boar also appear frequently, as do carp and trout, along with an infinite variety of sausages.

But Berlin does not limit itself to traditional cuisine. A new wave of restaurants has swept across the city, from east to west. More and more are going ethnic, everything from Indonesian to French to Thai or Japanese. Eastern European wines are now almost as popular as those from Germany itself.

ON OR NEAR THE KURFÜRSTENDAMM
VERY EXPENSIVE

✪ **Bamberger Reiter.** Regensburgerstrasse 7. ☎ **030/2-18-42-82.** Reservations required. Main courses 48DM–75DM ($24–$37.50); 5- or 7-course fixed-price menu 145DM–195DM ($72.50–$97.50). AE, MC, V. Tues–Sat 6pm–1am (last order 10:30pm). U-Bahn: Spichernstrasse. CONTINENTAL.

Bamberger Reiter, serving French, German, and Austrian dishes in the style of *neue Deutsche Küche,* is still the choice of savvy local foodies. Don't judge it by its location in an undistinguished 19th-century apartment house. The decor evokes old Germany, with lots of mirrors and fresh flowers. The quality is beyond question here—only Rockendorf's or Alt-Luxemburg can even pretend to have better food. The menu changes daily according to the availability of fresh ingredients and the inspiration of the chef, but might include a roulade of quail, bass with Riesling sauce, cream of fresh asparagus soup, lamb with beans and potato croutons, and date strudel with almond ice cream. The wine list is enormous, with a dozen varieties of champagne alone.

✪ **Harlekin.** In the Grand Hotel Esplanade, Lützowufer. ☎ **030/25-47-88-58.** Reservations recommended. Main courses 44DM–49DM ($22–$24.50); 4- to 6-course menu 165DM–170DM ($82.50–$85). AE, DC, MC, V. Tues–Sat 6–11pm. Closed Aug. U-Bahn: Nollendorfplatz or Wittenbergplatz. FRENCH/INTERNATIONAL.

This restaurant's rise to prominence chagrined jealous chefs at old favorites like the Kempinski. The menu is perfectly balanced between tradition and innovation. For example, appetizers are likely to include such dishes as calves' consommé with crayfish or osso bucco consommé with lobster Spätzle. For your main course, you might be won over by the saddle of lamb baked in a spring roll or turbot roasted with mixed root vegetables. All dishes are made with fresh local produce and are perfectly prepared. Set menus are always delightful and often pleasantly surprising.

Paris Bar. Kantstrasse 152 (between Savignyplatz and Fasenenstrasse). ☎ **030/3-13-80-52.** Reservations recommended. Main courses 27DM–55DM ($13.50–$27.50). AE. Daily noon–2am. U-Bahn: Uhlandstrasse. FRENCH.

This French bistro has been a local favorite since it cheered up the postwar years in dismal bombed-out Berlin. It's crowded with elbow-to-elbow tables like a Montmartre tourist trap, but is a genuinely pleasing little place on the see-and-be-seen circuit, close to the Theater des Westens. The food is invariably fresh and well prepared, but not particularly innovative.

✪ **Rockendorf's Gourmet Restaurant.** Passauerstrasse 5-7. ☎ **030/21-99-21-70.** Reservations required. Main courses 45DM–75DM ($22.50–$37.50). AE, DC, MC, V. Tues–Sat noon–2:30pm and 6–9:30pm. Closed last 2 weeks in July. U-Bahn: Wittenbergplatz. CONTINENTAL.

After 25 years in a villa in north Berlin, Rockendorf's, one of the best known of all the city's restaurants, has moved to newer and central quarters behind the landmark KaDeWe, near the Europa Center. This new 35- to 40-seat art deco restaurant mounts a serious challenge to frontrunners Bamberger Reiter and Alt-Luxemburg. Chef Siegfried Rockendorf achieves a happy wedding between nouvelle cuisine and classic specialties. Perhaps you'll try his memorable fresh jellied aspic with cucumber sauce. Other standbys include a fillet of turbot in Ricard sauce, and goose-meat pâté in Sauterne with cranberries. The service is exquisitely refined—attentive without being cloying. Everything is served on fine porcelain. Some of Germany's most visible names in show biz, journalism and politics come here.

The complex also contains a 30-seat cocktail/aperitif bar, a folkloric gutbürgerlich restaurant, Restaurant Berliner Original, wherein main courses cost from 25DM to 37DM ($12.50 to $18.50), and a Bistro & Café that's also a pastry emporium for very elaborate baked goods, where pastries, snacks, and small platters cost from 12DM to 30DM ($6 to $15). Berliner Original is decorated in a country alpine style, and the cafe in ersatz Jugendstil. The Berliner Original is open daily noon to 2:30pm and 6 to 9:30pm, and the bistro/cafe is open daily 10am to 10pm.

MODERATE

La Table. Damaschkestrasse 26. ☎ **030/3-23-14-04.** Reservations required. Main courses 24DM–30DM ($12–$15). MC. Mon–Sat 5pm–midnight. U-Bahn: Adenauerplatz. GERMAN.

La Table has gained a reputation as a select dining spot and social Center. Your host, Mr. Seidler, has a devoted local following among theater and media personalities. Savor the *Kohlroulade*, a stuffed cabbage roll—few chefs would want to compete with it. The *Tafelspitz*, boiled beef with vegetables, would have pleased Emperor Josef of Austria (it was his favorite dish). Another highlight is the rack of lamb with honey onions and rosemary potatoes. Look also for market-fresh daily specials. The chef

> ### ⓘ   Family-Friendly Restaurant
>
> **Funkturm Restaurant** *(see p. 95)*   Kids delight in ascending this radio tower on Messedam, open daily 10:30am to 11pm. The food at the restaurant is good, and later you can go to the observation platform for a truly grand view. The elevator costs 6DM ($3) for adults, 3DM ($1.50) for children.

believes in strong flavors and good hearty cookery. The ambience is that of a Berlin bistro, charmingly cluttered with kitsch from all over the world.

✪ **Marjellchen.** Mommsenstrasse 9. ☎ **030/8-83-26-76.** Reservations required. Main courses 19.50DM–39.50DM ($9.75–$19.75). AE, DC, MC, V. Mon–Sat 5pm–midnight. Closed Dec 23, 24, and 31. U-Bahn: Adenauerplatz or Uhlandstrasse. EAST PRUSSIAN.

This is the only restaurant in Berlin specializing in the cuisine of Germany's long-lost province of East Prussia, along with the cuisines of Pomerania and Silesia. The restaurant's unusual name comes from an East Prussian word meaning "young girl." Ramona Azzaro, whose East Prussian mother taught her many of the region's famous recipes, is the creative force here. Amid a Bismarckian ambience of vested waiters and oil lamps, you can enjoy a savory version of red-beet soup with strips of beef, East Prussian potato soup with shrimp and bacon, *Falscher Gänsebraten* (pork spare ribs stuffed with prunes and bread crumbs "as if the cook had prepared a goose"), marinated elk, and *Mecklenburger Kümmelfleisch* (lamb with chives and onions). This is the type of food Goethe or Schiller liked; perhaps you'll be a convert too. Of course, Marjellchen isn't the place if you want to keep tabs on the cholesterol intake.

Mensa (Markus Semmler). Am Lützowplatz 5. ☎ **030/25-79-93-33.** Reservations recommended. Main courses 47DM–49DM ($23.50–$24.50); set menus 99DM–145DM ($49.50–$72.50). AE, MC, V. Mon–Fri 11:30am–2:30pm; Mon–Sat 6:30–10:30pm. U-Bahn: Nollendorfplatz. CONTINENTAL.

This is one of the best culinary examples of new Berliner hip. Its creator is the youthful, much-talked-about entrepreneur Markus Semmler, who is likely to be working his way through the dining room throughout at least part of the evening, attending to service rituals, and gauging the responses received by his food. The setting is a large, off-white bistro-style room that's usually packed with residents of the surrounding well-heeled neighborhood. Similarities to a bistro, however, are deceptive, since the food is very grand, and much more elaborate than what a bistro might present. Examples include breast of quail in sesame with coriander-flavored noodles; a "froth" (more akin to a soup) of young spinach with a truffled lasagna of freshwater fish; carpaccio of beef with a mousse of black walnuts; fillet of turbot with melted gooseliver on a truffle-studded risotto; and a strudel of rabbit on a bed of turnip greens and cabbage.

Restaurant Mario. Carmerstrasse 2. ☎ **030/3-12-31-15.** Reservations recommended. Main courses 15DM–18DM ($7.50–$9) at lunch; 25DM–33DM ($12.50–$16.50) at dinner. AE, MC, V. Mon–Fri noon–midnight, Sat 4pm–1am. S-Bahn: Savignyplatz. NORTHERN ITALIAN.

Here you'll find Berlin's most imaginative northern Italian food. The innovative chefs shop for the best and most market-fresh ingredients. Begin with a platter of the most delectable antipasti in town. At least two different kinds of pastas are offered nightly, including a favorite made with a green-pepper pesto. Also on hand are more traditional dishes such as chicken breast stuffed with mozzarella and herbs, tantalizing herb-seasoned lamb cutlets, and fresh fish simply grilled and perfectly seasoned.

Zlata Praha. Meinekestrasse 4. ☎ **030/8-81-97-50.** Reservations recommended. Main courses 21DM–36DM ($10.50–$18). AE, MC, V. Daily 5–11:30pm. U-Bahn: Uhlandstrasse. BOHEMIAN/AUSTRIAN.

Zlata Praha is the top place for Bohemian cuisine. Many of the dishes evoke childhood memories for the restaurant's many regular clients. The Szegendiner goulash is as fine as any we've had during a tour of Hungary. Other specialties include a "Bohemian forest" goulash with spätzle and green salad, fillet stroganoff Paprikaschnitzel (an original version of Wiener schnitzel), and honey-glazed roast duck with red cabbage and dumplings. If you have room left after the gigantic portions, try the poppy seed strudel. German, French, and Austrian wines are featured, as well as the Czech beer Pilsner Urquell das Echte.

INEXPENSIVE

Hard Rock Cafe. Meinekestrasse 21. ☎ **030/88-46-20.** Reservations accepted for groups of 10 or more. Main courses 16DM–34DM ($8–$17). AE, MC, V. Sun–Thurs noon–midnight; Fri–Sat noon–2am. U-Bahn: Kurfürstendamm. AMERICAN.

This is the local branch of the familiar worldwide chain that mingles rock 'n' roll nostalgia with American food. Menu choices range from a veggie burger to a "pig" sandwich (hickory smoked pork barbecue) that you might find in rural Georgia. The food is unexceptional, but service is friendly.

Lubitsch. Bleibtreustrasse 47. ☎ **030/882-37-56.** Reservations not necessary. Main courses 12.50DM–34DM ($6.25–$17). AE, DC, MC, V. Daily 9:30am–midnight. S-Bahn: Savignyplatz. CONTINENTAL.

It's deeply entrenched in the consciousness of many local residents, and it's considered in some quarters to have a degree of conservative chic. That reputation was enhanced in 1999 when Chancellor Schröder dropped in for lunch and a photo-op, causing ripples of energy to reverberate through the neighborhood. Menu items include lots of cafe drinks, with glasses of wine priced at 7DM to 11DM ($3.50 to $5.50), and steaming pots of afternoon tea, but if you drop in for a meal, expect platters of chicken curry salad with roasted potatoes; Berlin-style potato soup; braised chicken with salad and fresh vegetables; a roulade of suckling pig; and Nürnberger-style *wursts*. Count on brusque, even hostile service, a black and white decor with Thonet-style chairs, and a somewhat arrogant environment that despite its drawbacks, is very, very *Berliner.*

NEAR THE MEMORIAL CHURCH & ZOO

EXPENSIVE

Daitokai. Europa Center. ☎ **030/2-61-80-99.** Fixed-price meals 28DM–38DM ($14–$19) at lunch, 78DM–128DM ($39–$64) at dinner. AE, DC, MC, V. Tues–Sun noon–2:30pm and 6–10:30pm. U-Bahn: Kurfürstendamm. JAPANESE.

Think of it as a less-institutionalized Benihana's. Vermilion carp lanterns illuminate the labyrinth of reflecting pools. Chefs prepare the meals before your eyes at several long tables. This teppanyaki restaurant offers some of the city's finest grilled steak—tender, juicy, and never overcooked. The seafood and vegetables are served with an artistic flair, and the fish is always fresh and beautifully presented. Quality is never skimped. The flawless service features kindly, almost overly polite waitresses in

---

A Map Note

For restaurants located in western Berlin, see the "Western Berlin Accommodations & Dining" map on pp. 76–77.

kimonos. To dine here inexpensively and still eat well, take advantage of the set luncheons.

NEAR THE TIERGARTEN
VERY EXPENSIVE

Paris-Moskau. Alt-Moabit 141. ☎ **030/3-94-20-81.** Reservations recommended. Main courses 34DM–43DM ($17–$21.50); fixed-price menus 90DM–140DM ($45–$70). No credit cards. Daily 6–11:30pm. S-Bahn: Bellevue. INTERNATIONAL.

The grand days of the 19th century are alive and well at this restaurant in the beautiful Tiergarten area, where good dining spots are scarce. Menu items are both classic and more cutting-edge. The fresh tomato soup is excellent. Some of the dishes are mundane—the grilled fillet of beef in mushroom sauce comes to mind—but other lighter dishes with delicate seasonings are delightful. We recommend the grilled North Sea salmon with herbs accompanied by basil-flavored noodles. The chef should market his recipe for saffron sauce, which accompanies several dishes. You'll receive attentive service from the formally dressed staff.

IN GREATER CHARLOTTENBURG
VERY EXPENSIVE

✪ **Alt-Luxemburg.** Windscheidstrasse 31. ☎ **030/3-23-87-30.** Reservations required. Main courses 46DM–53DM ($23–$26.50); 4-course menu 125DM ($62.50); 5–course menu 140DM ($70). AE, DC, MC, V. Mon–Sat 5–11pm. U-Bahn: Sophie-Charlotte-Platz. CONTINENTAL.

Bamberger Reiter is still the leader among Berlin restaurants, but Alt-Luxemburg is nipping at its heels. Karl Wannemacher is one of the outstanding chefs of Germany. Try the honey-glazed duck breast or the saddle of venison with juniper sauce. His Bavarian cream of eel and sturgeon terrine is also excellent. For dessert, don't miss the memorable semolina dumplings with orange ragout or the orange sorbet. The service is both unpretentious and gracious. The dark paneling, evenly spaced mirrors, antique chandeliers, and old-fashioned ambience create a belle époque aura.

EXPENSIVE

Ana e Bruno. Sophie-Charlotten-Strasse 101. ☎ **030/325-71-10.** Reservations recommended. Main courses 46DM–56DM ($23–$28); fixed-price menus 120DM–175DM ($60–$87.50). AE. Tues–Sat 6:30–10:30pm. U-Bahn: Bismarckstrasse. ITALIAN.

This is one of Berlin's most charming Italian restaurants. Ana and Bruno turn out a delectable cuisine that takes full advantage of the freshest ingredients and produce in any season. *Nuova cucina* is emphasized here more strongly than traditional Italian classics, and the chefs like to experiment. The combinations of food offer delicious flavors and the creations a harmonious medley. Expect dishes such as a radicchio-studded pasta with perfectly cooked shrimp or an Italian fillet of veal with a tuna sauce. Regular customers and gourmets keen on experimenting always seem satisfied with the results. A large wine selection, most of it reasonable in price, complements the well-chosen menus.

MODERATE

Bierhaus Luisen-Bräu. Luisenplatz 1, Charlottenburg (close to Charlottenburg Palace). ☎ **030/3-41-93-88.** Reservations recommended on weekends. Salads, snacks, and platters 10DM–35DM ($5–$17.50). MC, V. Sun–Thurs 9am–1am; Fri–Sat 9am–2am. U-Bahn: Richard-Wagner-Platz. GERMAN.

One of the city's largest breweries, Luisen-Bräu, established this restaurant in 1987. The decor includes enormous stainless-steel vats of the fermenting brew, from which the waiters refill your mug. There is no subtlety of cuisine here; it's robust and hearty fare. You serve yourself from a long buffet table. The seating is indoor or outdoor, depending on the season, at long picnic tables that encourage a sense of beer-hall *Bruderschaft* (camaraderie).

Ernst-August. Sybelstrasse 16. ☎ **030/3-24-55-76.** Reservations required. Main courses 23DM–34DM ($11.50–$17). No credit cards. Wed–Sun 6:30pm–1am (kitchen stops serving hot food at midnight). Closed July 15–Aug 15. U-Bahn: Adenauerplatz. FRENCH/INTERNATIONAL.

Although outclassed by dozens of grander establishments, this restaurant still maintains a special niche. It's the type of place a local might take a friend from out of town. The setting is quiet and unobtrusive. Antique bric-a-brac adorn the walls. The chef might prepare one of two variations of hare, a longtime German favorite in which he takes a special pride. Even a simple rump steak gets care and attention here.

Funkturm Restaurant. Messedamm 22. ☎ **030/303-829-96.** Reservations not necessary. Set-price lunch 39.50DM ($19.75); set-price dinner 59.50DM ($29.75). Main course 26DM–35DM ($13–$17.50). AE, DC, MC, V. Tues–Sun noon–3pm and 6–10pm. U-Bahn: Kaiserdamm.

This restaurant at the radio tower's 65m (213-foot) midway point provides both good food and sweeping, high-altitude views. You'll first have to pay 3DM ($1.70) for the elevator ride up. Inside the restaurant's metallic, glossy interior, every table sits near a window. Menu items include saddle of lamb with vegetables, pepper steak, and seafood. If you just want to enjoy the view without the food, consider paying 6DM ($3.40) for a ride up to the observation platform near the top of the 136m (446-foot) high tower. The higher platform is open daily 10am to 11pm. For information about the tower and its upper-tier observation platform, call ☎ **030/30-38-0996.**

Ponte Vecchio. Spielhagenstrasse 3. ☎ **030/3-42-19-99.** Reservations required. Main courses 30DM–50DM ($15–$25). DC. Wed–Mon 6:30–11pm. Closed 4 weeks in summer. U-Bahn: Bismarckstrasse. TUSCAN.

We've dined here many times before and were moderately pleased, but the place has so improved that we now view it as the finest Italian restaurant in Berlin. Market-fresh ingredients produce a winning cuisine with a Tuscan focus. If you don't opt for the excellent fresh fish of the day, you'll find any number of other tempting dishes, such as several variations of veal. Shellfish is deftly handled according to Tuscan style, with fresh basil and olive oil. For a pasta that's succulent, savory, and spicy, we'd recommend the *penne all'arrabiata,* that old Roman favorite.

IN GRUNEWALD
VERY EXPENSIVE

✪ **Vivaldi.** In the Ritz Carlton Schlosshotel Berlin, Brahmsstrasse 10. ☎ **030/89-58-40.** Reservations recommended. Main courses 52DM–65DM ($26–$32.50). Set-price 4-course dinner 155DM ($77.50); set-price 6-course dinner 196DM ($98). AE, DC, MC, V. Mon–Sat 6–10:30pm. S-Bahn: Grunewald. INTERNATIONAL.

This restaurant is the culinary showcase of one of the most unusual small hotels in Berlin, a neo-Renaissance palace built in 1912 by an advisor to Kaiser Wilhelm II. Vivaldi serves, with panache, some of the most elegant hotel food in Berlin, within a paneled and antique-strewn setting that's as grand as anything you're likely to find in Europe. Most diners opt for one of two set-price menus, although there's also a limited à la carte list. A clear soup of lentils with smoked duck breast might be followed by gratinated oysters and scallops resting on a bed of spinach salad. Turbot that's braised with green asparagus, U.S. fillet of beef in red wine sauce, and venison with black Perigord truffles are triumphs of subtle flavors. Service is impeccable. For dessert, consider a honey and clementine parfait.

IN BERLIN-MITTE
EXPENSIVE

Langhans. Charlottenstrasse 59. ☎ **030/20-94-50-70.** Reservations recommended. Main courses 28DM–45DM ($14–$22.50); set-price menus 80DM–90DM ($40–$45). AE, MC, V. Daily noon–11:30pm. U-Bahn: Stadtmitte. MODERN INTERNATIONAL.

Few other restaurants combine the culinary traditions of Italy and Japan with such skill and style. Named after the 18th-century designer of the Brandenburg Gate, and created by Detlef Bernhardt, a German-born long-time resident of Japan, it occupies two floors of a grandly proportioned building that flanks the Gendarmenmarkt. Downstairs is a convivial and hip bar loaded with well-dressed patrons, some of whom munch on Spanish-inspired tapas. The most visible culinary zest, however, is upstairs, within a long, minimalist dining room whose views sweep simultaneously out over the twin domes of the square's two churches and a panorama of the brightly lit kitchen. Here, an international team produces dishes whose flavors are as intriguing as they are delicious. They include lemongrass-and-coconut soup with shrimp; carpaccio of veal with sesame and arugula; spaghettini with salmon caviar, Japanese wakame, and lemongrass; braised dorado with green curry and mango; and a superb version of free-range hen with ginger-flavored risotto and sukiyaki sauce. Desserts, as well as virtually everything else on the menu, change frequently, but if it appears on the menu, you'd probably be richly satisfied with a pear charlotte with tonkabean ice cream.

Restaurant Borchardt. Französische Strasse 47. ☎ **030/20-39-71-17.** Reservations recommended. Main courses 34DM–50DM ($17–$25). AE, V. Daily noon–midnight. U-Bahn: Französische Strasse. FRENCH.

This restaurant is elegant, lighthearted, and popular with the city's artistic movers and shakers. It occupies a monumental dining area, complete with marble accents and partially gilded columns. You can order anything from a simple salad (as supermodel Claudia Schiffer often does) to more substantial fare, such as cream of potato soup with bacon and croutons, fillet of carp prepared with Riesling and herbs and finished with champagne, foie gras served with caramelized apples, chicken stuffed with morels and served with cream-and-herb sauce, and a pistachio mousse garnished with essence of fresh fruit.

✪ **Restaurant Vau.** Jägerstrasse 54. ☎ **030-202-9730.** Reservations recommended. Lunch main courses 20DM ($10) each, dinner main courses 48DM–68DM ($24–$34). Set dinner of 4 courses 129DM–198DM ($64.50–$99). AE, DC, MC, V. Mon–Sat noon–2:30pm and 7–10:30pm. S-Bahn: Hausvoigteiplatz. INTERNATIONAL.

This restaurant is the culinary showcase of up-and-coming chef Kolja Kleeburg. You can select from a menu based on fresh and seasonal ingredients. Choices include terrine of salmon and morels with rocket salad; smoked sturgeon with white beans and caviar; aspic of suckling pig with sauerkraut; salad with marinated red mullet, mint, and almonds; crisp-fried duck with marjoram; ribs of suckling lamb with thyme-flavored polenta; and desserts such as woodruff soup with champagne-flavored ice cream. The wine list is international and well chosen.

✪ **Vox.** In the Grand Hyatt Berlin, Marlene-Dietrich-Platz 2. ☎ **030/25-53-12-34.** Reservations recommended. Lunch main courses 25DM–36DM ($12.50–$18), dinner main courses 39DM–52DM ($19.50–$26); platters of sushi 20DM–60DM ($10–$30). AE, DC, MC, V. Daily 11:30am–2pm and 6–11pm. U-Bahn: Potsdamer Platz. INTERNATIONAL.

This is one of the most exciting and creative restaurants in Berlin, far outshining any competition within the vast architectural complex at Potsdamer Platz. One of Switzerland's best design teams created the minimalist decor, with lots of visual emphasis on a mostly stainless steel, open-to-view kitchen. Here, a team of uniformed chefs concoct artfully presented platters of braised goose liver with apple-flavored

A Map Note

For restaurants located in Berlin-Mitte, see the "Berlin-Mitte Accommodations & Dining" map on p. 87.

vinaigrette, fillet of lamb cooked in a wood-burning oven with goat cheese, pepper oil, and Mediterranean vegetables; rotisserie-cooked breast of Barbary duck with mango chutney; and roasted sturgeon on a frothy sauce of white rosemary. The culinary philosophy here combines Mediterranean with Asian cuisines in ways you might not expect. One corner of the restaurant features the best sushi bar in Berlin. The venue is enhanced by an attentive and very hip staff, some of whom shuttle between the restaurant and a stylish cocktail lounge that features jazz and blues every Tuesday to Saturday beginning at 10pm. During clement weather, tables spill out onto the terrace, beneath verdant rows of linden trees.

MODERATE

Aigner. In the Royal Dorint Hotel, Charlottenstrasse 50–52. D-10117 Berlin. ☎ **030/ 20375-0.** Reservations recommended. Main courses 21DM–38DM ($10.50–$19). AE, DC, MC, V. Daily noon–midnight. U-Bahn: Stadtmitte. CONTINENTAL.

In the late 1990s, the Dorint chain bought the furnishings from one of Vienna's oldest cafes, the Aigner, and moved them into the ground floor of of one of Berlin's newest hotels. The result is a black-and-white Jugendstil setting replete with Thonet chairs and reminders of Habsburg Austria. There's a lot of ambience here, thanks partly to a location that overlooks the Gendarmenmarkt, and a staff that presents old-fashioned service rituals with a hipster kind of flair. The restaurant's signature dish is *tafelspitz,* the boiled-beef-with-horseradish dish favored by Franz Joseph. Here, it's served in a big brass kettle with both haunch and shoulder of beef, with lots of soup, vegetables, savoy cabbage, crème fraîche, and apple-flavored horseradish. Other choices include baked and crusty pike perch; carpaccio of octopus; wienerschnitzel; and fillet of codfish with white beans and chorizo.

Die Weltbühne. Gormannstrasse 14. ☎ **030/280-094-40.** Reservations recommended. Main courses 29DM–39DM ($14.50–$19.50). AE, MC, V. Daily noon–midnight. U-Bahn: Rosenthalerplatz. INTERNATIONAL/MEDITERRANEAN.

This emerging restaurant maintains a bar—one of the longest in Berlin—where you're likely to get so distracted with visual input that you might find it hard to eventually move into dinner. You'll be glad you did, however, when you taste the well-flavored and sophisticated food that's churned out by chef Jens Heier. The dining room is divided into semi-private banquette areas outlined in hardwood paneling, forest green upholstery, elaborate Murano-glass chandeliers, and vague references to Bauhaus. Cuisine is superb, based on a changing set of visions influenced by the season and the inspiration of the chef. Examples include a galette of rabbit with arugula salad; carpaccio of duck breast with parmesan and vinegar; a salad of green asparagus with paprika mousse; mussels with baby onion risotto; and fillet of turbot with ratatouille, potato-filled ravioli, and champagne sauce. A particularly appealing, almost cleansing, dessert, is a kirsch-flavored praline with Campari-grapefruit sorbet.

Französischer Hof. Jagerstrasse 56. ☎ **030/2-04-35-70.** Reservations recommended. Main courses 29DM–42DM ($14.50–$21). AE, DC, V. Daily 10am–1am. Closed Dec 24. U-Bahn: Hausvogteiplatz. GERMAN.

If you want a reasonable meal in a relaxed atmosphere, this is the place. Französischer Hof fills two floors connected by a belle époque staircase, evoking a century-old Parisian bistro. The kitchen may not be the finest, but ingredients are fresh and deftly handled. One recent memorable dinner included roast duck breast with calvados along with zucchini and potato pancakes. You can begin with the delectable selection of fish canapés. Saddle of lamb is always admirably done, although you may prefer the rather theatrical flambéed fillet Stroganoff with almond-studded dumplings.

Ganymed. Schiffbauerdamm 5. ☎ **030/28-59-90-46.** Reservations recommended. Main courses 20DM–45DM ($10–$22.50). Set-price lunch 20DM ($10); otherwise, set menus 55DM–75DM ($27.50–$37.50). AE, DC, MC, V. Mon–Sat noon–1am; Sun 10am–3pm. U-Bahn: Friedrichstrasse. GERMAN/INTERNATIONAL.

There's nothing trendy or immediately fashionable about this restaurant, which occupied these premises beginning in 1929, and which stalwartly continued doing business within East Berlin throughout the Cold War. The setting includes two formal dining rooms, one with an ornate plaster ceiling of great beauty; the other a more modern, big-windowed affair that overlooks the Spree. Food arrives in worthy portions, with plenty of flavor, albeit without too much concern for modern culinary fancies or trends. Examples include the house assortment of appetizers (*vorspeisen*), laden high with smoked fish, smoked ham, stuffed dumplings, and fish mousse; goose liver terrine; Eisbein—the pork shank specialty of 19th-century Berlin; schnitzels made from organically raised veal; mussels in choron sauce; and breast of pheasant wrapped in Black Forest cured ham.

✪ **Guy.** Jägerstrasse 59–60. ☎ **030/20-94-26-00.** Reservations recommended. Main courses 36DM–49DM ($18–$24.50). Set-price lunches 34DM–44DM ($17–$22); set-price dinners 98DM–138DM ($49–$69). AE, DC, MC, V. U-Bahn: Stadtmitte or Französischer Strasse. INTERNATIONAL.

Few other topnotch restaurants in Berlin were designed with as strong a sense of gastronomy as theater. You'll understand this as you proceed to any of three separate balconies, each supporting at least one row of artfully decorated tables. The overall effect can be compared to the balconies of an old-fashioned opera house, where sight lines tend to focus on whatever's happening on the stage, or on the occupants of other balconies. Don't expect beer and schnitzels, as the cuisine is very *haute*, even to the point of seeming experimental. Examples change frequently, but might include a medley of marinated quail and goose liver; mussels served on a purée of arugula; lobster and sweetbreads cooked in puff pastry with tarragon-flavored cream sauce; and braised breast of goose with a roulade of potatoes and herbs. If you're in the mood for strong doses of *gemutlichkeit*, ask for one of the limited number of tables within its cozy wine cellar. During clement weather, there's additional seating on the terrace in front.

The Seasons Restaurant. In the Four Seasons Hotel. Charlottenstrasse 49. ☎ **030/2-03-38.** Reservations recommended. Lunch main courses 25DM ($12.50); dinner main courses 29DM–62DM ($14.50–$31). Set-price menus 81DM–107DM ($40.50–$53.50). AE, MC, V. Daily 11:30am–2:30pm and 6–11:30pm. U-Bahn: Französische Strasse. INTERNATIONAL.

One of the most appealing hotel dining rooms in Berlin exudes a sense of prosperity, thanks to a decor that might have been inspired by Versailles, a sheathing of carefully oiled and partially gilded oak, an open fireplace, and a color scheme of champagne and brown. Despite the upscale decor, the restaurant maintains a deliberately reasonable price-to-value ratio. An impeccably trained staff offers elaborate versions of tuna carpaccio with sesame; smoked breast of pheasant with wild mushrooms, black nuts, and farmer's salad; fillet and liver of veal with truffled mashed potatoes and glazed apples; and quail stuffed with goose liver baked in a clay pot. Consider prefacing a meal here with a drink in the hotel's supremely elegant bar.

Zur Letzten Instanz. Waisenstrasse 14–16 (near the Alexanderplatz). ☎ **030/2-42-55-28.** Soup 8DM–10DM ($4–$5); main courses 20DM–25DM ($10–$12.50); fixed-price dinner from 25DM–40DM ($12.50–$20). AE, DC, V. Mon–Sat noon–1am; Sun noon–11pm. U-Bahn: Klosterstrasse. GERMAN.

Reputedly Berlin's oldest restaurant, dating from 1525, Zur Letzten Instanz has been frequented by everybody from Napoléon to Beethoven. Prisoners used to stop off here for one last beer before going to jail. The place is located on two floors of a baroque building just outside the crumbling brick wall that once ringed medieval Berlin. Double doors open on a series of small woodsy rooms, one with a bar and ceramic *Kachelofen* (stove). At the back, a circular staircase leads to another series of rooms, where every evening at 6pm, food and wine (no beer) are served. The menu is old-fashioned, mainly limited to Berlin staples.

INEXPENSIVE

Alexanderkeller. In the cellar of the Hotel Luisenhof, Köpenicker Strasse 92. ☎ **030/2-75-01-42.** Main courses 12.50DM–30DM ($6.25–$15). MC, V. Daily 7am–midnight. U-Bahn: Märkisches Museum. GERMAN.

This reasonably priced, unpretentious restaurant is a lunchtime favorite of neighborhood residents and office workers. The generous meals might include fillet of roast beef served with potatoes and artichoke hearts; fillet of zander with parsley and new potatoes; or roast pork with red-wine sauce. Food is rich and the meat dishes heavy, but the people in this area love this type of food.

Boon's. Monbijouplatz 11–12. ☎ **030/28-53-98-90.** Reservations recommended. Main courses 22.50DM–34DM ($11.25–$17). AE, MC, V. Mon–Sat 5pm–midnight; Sun 2pm–midnight. U-Bahn: Hackescher Markt. CONTINENTAL.

It's crowded, it's hip, and its decor evokes the 1930s allure of what might have been a coffee plantation in the highlands of Africa. Many clients come here just for its bar scene, but if you're hungry, the food is firmly based on what's cooking in Germany and Austria, and served in generous portions. Come here for a chance to meet unattached residents of the surrounding neighborhood, a dialogue with a hip Berliner or two, and food items that include beef filet with braised arugula; all manner of fresh fish; homemade salmon with apples, roasted potatoes, and horseradish; and drinks that include raspberry daiquiris. Either before or after your experience here, you might want to play it like a local and drop into the also-recommended Kurvenstar Bar, which lies just across the street.

Dressler. Unter den Linden 39. ☎ **030/204-44-22.** Reservations recommended. Main courses 12.50DM–35DM ($6.25–$17.50). AE, DC, MC, V. Daily 8am–midnight. S-Bahn: Unter den Linden. CONTINENTAL.

No other bistro along Unter den Linden as successfully re-creates Berlin's pre-war decor and style. Designed to resemble an arts conscious bistro of the sort that might have amused and entertained tuxedo-clad clients in the 1920s, it's set behind a wine-colored facade, and outfitted with leather banquettes, black and white tile floors, mirrors, and film memorabilia from the great days of early German cinema. Waiters scurry around with vests and aprons, carrying trays of everything from caviar to strudel, as well as three kinds of oysters and hefty portions of lobster salad. You can always drop in to ogle the racks of elegant pastries, consuming them with steaming pots of tea or coffee. Otherwise, more substantial menu items include turbot with champagne vinaigrette; pheasant breast with Riesling sauce; local salmon trout with white wine sauce and braised endive; stuffed breast of veal; and calf's liver with apples.

✪ **Keller-Restaurant Im Brecht-Haus-Berlin.** Chausseestrasse 125. ☎ **030/2-82-38-43.** Reservations recommended. Main courses 18DM–35DM ($9–$17.50). AE, DC, MC. Daily 11am–midnight. U-Bahn: Zinnowitzer Strasse. SOUTH GERMAN/AUSTRIAN.

From 1953 until his death in 1956, Bertolt Brecht lived here with his wife, Helene Weigel. Today the building houses the Brecht-Weigel-Museum (see "Exploring Berlin-Mitte," below). The restaurant downstairs, with white plaster and exposed stone, is decorated with photographs of the playwright's family, friends, and theatrical productions. No one will mind if you just stop in for a glass or two of wine—the place specializes in eastern German wines, as well as French and New World wines. Traditional south German and Austrian food is also served, such as an Austrian recipe for *Fleisch Laberln,* meatballs made from minced pork, beef, green beans, and bacon and served with dumplings. In good weather, the seating area includes an enclosed courtyard upstairs.

Mutter Hoppe. Rathausstrasse 21, Nikolaiviertel. ☎ **030/241-56-25.** Reservations recommended. Main courses 19DM–30DM ($9.50–$15). MC, V. Daily 11:30am–11pm. U-Bahn/S-Bahn: Alexanderplatz. GERMAN.

This cozy, wood-paneled restaurant still serves the solid Teutonic cuisine favored by a quasi-legendary matriarch (Mother Hoppe) who used to churn out vast amounts of food to members of her extended family and entourage. Within a quartet of old-fashioned dining rooms, you'll enjoy heaping portions of such rib-sticking fare as sauerbraten with roasted potatoes; creamy goulash with wild mushrooms; filet of zander with dill-flavored cream sauce; and braised filet of pork in mushroom-flavored cream sauce. Wine is available, but most guests opt for at least one foaming mug of beer.

Oren. Oranienburger Strasse 28. ☎ **030/282-8228.** Reservations recommended. Main courses 17DM–19DM ($8.50–$9.50). No credit cards. Mon–Thurs noon–1am; Fri noon–2am; Sat 10am–2pm; Sun 10am–1am. S-Bahn: Oranienburger Tor or Hackescher Markt. ISRAELI/ARABIC.

You'll notice a similarity in architecture between this restaurant and the massive reconstruction of the Oranienburger synagogue, next door. The cream-colored, high-ceilinged premises are owned by, and rented from, Berlin's Jewish community, who permeate the place with the savory aromas and zests of old-fashioned Jewish cooking. As such, the site tends to exert a powerful and immediate emotional appeal on visitors, 90% of whom are visitors making a pilgrimage to the nearby synagogue. Prices are reasonable; and the vegetarian and fish platters are both wholesome and plentiful. The menu includes cream of garlic soup; vegetarian platters with hollandaise or choron sauce; fillet of zander with fresh cucumber salad; falafel with hummus and tahini, olives, and pita; cold gefilte fish with red beet salad; smoked trout; and a ragout of zucchini and mushroom with herbed rice. Red or white meat almost never appears on the menu.

5 Seeing the Sights

THE TOP MUSEUMS

The great art collections of old Berlin suffered during and after World War II. Although many paintings were saved by being stored in salt mines, many larger works were destroyed by fire. Part of the surviving art stayed in the east, including a wealth of ancient treasures that remind us of the leading role played by German archaeologists during the 19th and early 20th centuries. The paintings that turned up in the

Attractions in Charlottenburg

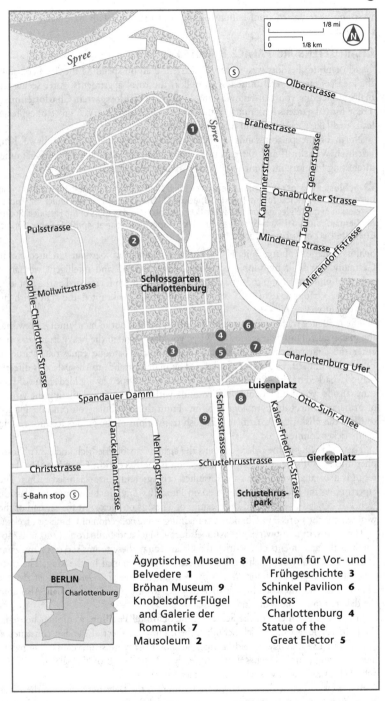

0 1/8 mi
0 1/8 km

Spree

Olberstrasse

Brahestrasse

Kamminerstrasse

Taurog-generstrasse

Osnabrücker Strasse

Mindener Strasse

Mierendorffstrasse

Pulsstrasse

Schlossgarten
Charlottenburg

Sophie-Charlotten-Strasse

Mollwitzstrasse

Charlottenburg Ufer

Luisenplatz

Spandauer Damm

Otto-Suhr-Allee

Kaiser-Friedrich-Strasse

Danckelmannstrasse

Nehringstrasse

Schlossstrasse

Gierkeplatz

Christstrasse

Schustehrusstrasse

Schustehrus-
park

S-Bahn stop Ⓢ

BERLIN
Charlottenburg

Ägyptisches Museum **8**
Belvedere **1**
Bröhan Museum **9**
Knobelsdorff-Flügel
    and Galerie der
    Romantik **7**
Mausoleum **2**

Museum für Vor- und
    Frühgeschichte **3**
Schinkel Pavilion **6**
Schloss
    Charlottenburg **4**
Statue of the
    Great Elector **5**

west and were passed from nation to nation in the late 1940s have nearly all been returned to Berlin.

CHARLOTTENBURG PALACE & MUSEUMS

Charlottenburg lies just west of the Tiergarten. Plan on spending the day here, since the area contains several museums as well as the royal apartments. After seeing the main attractions you can enjoy a ramble through **Schlossgarten Charlottenburg.** These formal gardens look much as they did in the 18th century. A grove of cypresses leads to a lake with swans and other waterfowl.

North of the palace stands the **Mausoleum,** which holds the tombs of King Friedrich Wilhelm II and Queen Luise, sculptured by Rauch, as well as several other interesting funerary monuments of the Prussian royal family.

✪ **Schloss Charlottenburg.** Luisenplatz. ☎ **030/32-09-11.** Combination ticket for all buildings and historical rooms 16DM ($8) adults, 11DM ($5.50) children under 14. English translation of guide's lecture on sale at the ticket counter. Guided tours of the Historical Rooms (in German), Tues–Fri 9am–5pm, Sat–Sun 10am–5pm (last tour at 4pm). U-Bahn: Sophie-Charlotte-Platz or Richard-Wagner-Platz.

Schloss Charlottenburg, one of the finest examples of baroque architecture in Germany, was built by Sophie Charlotte. This beautiful and intelligent woman, a patron of philosophy and the arts, was the wife of Friedrich I, crowned as the first king in Prussia (as opposed to "of") in 1701. He nearly bankrupted the state with his extravagant ways.

The residence was begun as a summer palace, but got out of hand until it grew into the massive structure you see today. When you pass through the heavy iron gates and enter the courtyard, you'll immediately encounter a baroque equestrian statue of Friedrich I himself, by Andreas Schlüter. The main entrance to the palace is directly behind, marked by the 48m-(157-foot-) high cupola capped by a gilded statue of Fortune. Inside, you'll find a columned rotunda with stucco reliefs depicting the virtues of Prussian princes in mythological terms. From this vestibule, you can take guided tours of the Historical Apartments. English translations of the guide's lecture are sold at the ticket counter.

The main wing of the palace contains the apartments of Friedrich and his "philosopher queen." Of special interest in this section is the **Reception Chamber.** This large room is decorated with frieze panels, vaulted ceilings, and mirror-paneled niches. The tapestries on the walls (1730) are based on Plutarch's *Lives;* included are such classical scenes as Pericles in battle and the sacrifice of Theseus on Delos. At the far end of the west wing is the **Porcelain Chamber,** containing a fine collection of Chinese porcelain.

The **new wing,** known as the Knobelsdorff-Flügel and built from 1740 to 1746, contains the apartments of Friedrich the Great. Today these rooms serve as a museum of paintings, many of which were collected or commissioned by the king. The treasures are on the upper floor. Works by Watteau include *The Trade Sign of the Art Dealer Gersaint,* purchased by Friedrich in 1745 for the palace's music hall. Also note the decoration on the walls and ceilings.

At the far eastern end of the Schloss is the **Schinkel Pavillon,** a summer house in the Italian style. Karl Friedrich Schinkel, the leading architect of the day, constructed this villa in 1825. Today it holds a small but noteworthy museum, containing paintings, drawings, and sketches from the early 1800s. Some of the sketches are by Schinkel himself, who was both an architect and an artist.

At the far end of Schlossgarten Charlottenburg is the **Belvedere,** close to the River Spree. This former royal teahouse contains exquisite Berlin porcelain, much of it from the 1700s.

✪ Ägyptisches Museum. Schloss-strasse 70. ☎ **030/32-09-11.** Admission 8DM ($4) adults, 4DM ($2) children; free admission 1st Sun of each month. Tues–Fri 10am–6pm, Sat–Sun 11am–6pm. U-Bahn: Sophie-Charlotte-Platz or Richard-Wagner-Platz.

The western Berlin branch of the Egyptian Museum is housed in the palace's east guard-house. It's worth the trip just to see the famous colored bust of Queen Nefertiti, which dates from about 1360 B.C. and was discovered in 1912. The bust, stunning in every way, is all by itself in a dark first-floor room, illuminated by a spotlight. It's believed that the bust never left the studio in which it was created but served always as a model for other portraits of the queen. In addition, look for the head of Queen Tiy, the world-famous head of a priest in green stone, and the monumental Kalabasha Gateway, built by Emperor Augustus around 30 B.C. Other displays feature jewelry, papyrus, tools, and weapons, as well as objects relating to the Egyptian belief in the afterlife.

Bröhan Museum. Schlossstrasse 1A. ☎ **32-69-06-00.** Admission 6DM ($3), free 11 and under. Tues–Sun 10am–6pm (until 8pm on Wed). U-Bahn: Sophie-Charlotte-Platz or Richard-Wagner-Platz.

Berlin's finest collection of Jugendstil (German art nouveau) is found here. When Professor Bröhan started the collection, Jugendstil was viewed as having little merit. It's a different story today. The objects include glass, furnishings, silver and gold, paintings, and vases. The outstanding porcelain collection ranges from Gallé to Sèvres and Meissen to Royal Copenhagen.

Museum für Vor und Frühgeschichte. Langhansbau. ☎ **030/32-09-11.** Admission 4DM ($2) adults, 2DM ($1) children. Tues–Fri 10am–6pm, Sat–Sun 11am–6pm. U-Bahn: Sophie-Charlotte-Platz or Richard-Wagner-Platz.

This museum of prehistory and early history is in the western extension of the palace, facing Klausener Platz. On display is the famous Schliemann collection of antiquities from Troy. The rooms have exhibits grouped into the ages of humankind, from 1 million B.C. through the first millennium A.D.

MUSEUMINSEL MUSEUMS

The **Alte Nationalgalerie** (behind the Altes Museum) is scheduled to reopen some time in 2001. The gallery displays paintings and sculpture from the end of the 18th to the beginning of the 20th century, including works by van Gogh, Manet, Monet, Renoir, and Cézanne. The gallery is especially proud to own the world's largest collection of Adolph von Menzel, a famous Berlin artist.

Altes Museum. Bodestrasse 1–3, Museumsinsel. ☎ **030/20-99-55-55.** Admission 8DM ($4) adults, 4DM ($2) children. Tues–Sun 10am–6pm. U-Bahn/S-Bahn: Friedrichstrasse. Bus 100 to Lustgarten.

Karl Friedrich Schinkel, the city's greatest architect, designed this structure, which resembles a Greek Corinthian temple, in 1822. On its main floor is the **Antiken-sammlung (Museum of Greek and Roman Antiquities).** This is a great collection of world-famous antique decorative art. Some of the finest Greek vases of the black-and-red-figures style, from the 6th to the 4th century B.C., are here. The best-known vase is a large Athenian amphora (wine jar) found in Vulci, Etruria. It dates from 490 B.C. and shows a satyr with a lyre and the god Hermes. One of several excellent bronze statuettes, the Zeus of Dodone (470 B.C.) shows the god about to cast a bolt of lightning. You can also see a rare portrait of Cleopatra (from Alexandria). In the Brandenburg-Prussian art collection is an exceptional bronze statue of the goddess Luna descending from the firmament. The Prussians called it "the pearl of the collection."

✪ **Pergamon Museum.** Kupfergraben, Museumsinsel. ☎ **030/20-90-5555.** Admission 8DM ($4) adults, 4DM ($2) children; free admission 1st Sun of each month. Tues–Sun 10am–6pm. U-Bahn/S-Bahn: Friedrichstrasse. Tram: 1, 2, 3, 4, 5, 13, 15, or 53.

The Pergamon Museum houses several departments, but if you have time for only one exhibit, go to the **Department of Greek and Roman Antiquities,** housed in the north and east wings of the museum, and enter the central hall to see the Pergamon Altar, (180–160 B.C.), so large that it has a huge room all to itself. Some 27 steps lead from the museum floor up to the colonnade. Most fascinating is the frieze around the base. It shows the struggle of the Olympian gods against the Titans and is strikingly alive, with figures that project as much as a foot from the background. If you explore further, you'll find a Roman market gate discovered in Miletus as well as sculptures from many Greek and Roman cities, including a statue of a goddess holding a pomegranate (575 B.C.), found in southern Attica, where it had been buried for 2,000 years. So well preserved was the statue that flecks of the original paint are still visible on her garments.

The **Near East Museum,** in the south wing, contains one of the largest collections anywhere of antiquities from ancient Babylonia, Persia, and Assyria. Among the exhibits is the Processional Way of Babylon with the Ishtar Gate, dating from 580 B.C., and the throne room of Nebuchadnezzar. Cuneiform clay tablets document a civilization that created ceramics, glass, and metal objects while Europe was still overrun with primitive tribes. The museum's upper level is devoted to the **Museum of Islamic Art.** Of special interest are the miniatures, carpets, and wood carvings.

TIERGARTEN MUSEUMS

✪ **Gemäldegalerie (Picture Gallery).** Mattäiskirchplatz 4. ☎ **030/20-90-55-55.** Admission 8DM ($4) adults, 4DM ($2) children. Tues–Fri 10am–6pm, Sat–Sun 11am–6pm. U-Bahn: Kurfürstenstrasse, then bus 148. Bus 129 from Ku'damm (plus a 4-min. walk).

This is one of Germany's greatest art museums. Several rooms are devoted to early German masters, with panels from altarpieces dating from the 13th to 15th centuries. Note the panel, *The Virgin Enthroned with Child* (1350), surrounded by angels that resemble the demons in the works of Hieronymus Bosch. Eight paintings make up the Dürer collection, including several portraits.

Most of the great European masters are represented. The Italian collection contains five Raphael Madonnas, along with works by Titian (*The Girl with a Bowl of Fruit*), Fra Filippo Lippi, Botticelli, and Correggio (*Leda with the Swan*). There are early Netherlandish paintings from the 15th and 16th centuries (van Eyck, van der Weyden, Bosch, and Brueghel) as well. Several galleries are devoted to 17th-century

A New Wall

Berliners aren't likely to forget the **Berlin Wall** any time soon, but just in case, their government has reconstructed a partial stretch of the wall at Bernauer Strasse and Ackerstrasse (U-Bahn: Bernauer Strasse), at a cost of $1.3 million. The 70m-long (230-foot-long) memorial consists of two walls that include some of the fragments of the original wall (those fragments not bulldozed away or carried off by souvenir hunters). The memorial is mostly made of mirrorlike stainless steel. Slits allow visitors to peer through. A steel plaque reads "In memory of the division of the city from 13 August 1961 to 9 November 1989." Critics have called the construction "a sanitized memorial," claiming it does little to depict the 255 people shot trying to escape its predecessor.

Attractions in Berlin-Mitte

Alte Nationalgalerie **10**
Altes Museum **8**
Berliner Dom **11**
Berliner Rathaus **14**
Brecht-Weigel-Museum **1**

Deutsche Staatsbibliothek **2**
Deutsche Staatsoper **6**
Equestrian statue of Frederick the Great **3**
Fernsehturm **13**
Friedrichwerdersche Kirche-Schinkelmuseum **5**

Hedwigskirche **4**
Humboldt-Universität **7**
Marienkirche **12**
Nikolaikirche **15**
Pergamon Museum **9**

✝ Church
Ⓢ S-Bahn Stop

Flemish and Dutch masters, with no fewer than 15 works by Rembrandt, such as his famous *Head of Christ*. *The Man with the Golden Helmet,* long famous as a price-less Rembrandt, was proven in 1986 to be by another hand. This remarkable painting is now accepted as a fine independent original.

Bauhaus-Archiv Museum für Gestaltung (Bauhaus Design Museum). Klingelhofer-strasse 14. ☎ **030/2-54-00-20.** Admission 5DM ($2.50) adults, 2.50DM ($1.25) children. Wed–Mon 10am–5pm. U-Bahn: Nollendorfplatz.

The Bauhaus Museum houses a permanent exhibition of photos and architectural designs relating to the Bauhaus school. Even if you're not a student of architecture, this museum is fascinating; it will bring you closer to the ideas and concepts that inspired modern design.

Kunstgewerbemuseum. Matthäikirchplatz (opposite the Philharmonie), Tiergartenstrasse 6. ☎ **030/2-66-29-02.** Admission 4DM ($2) adults, 2DM ($1) children. Tues–Fri 10am–6pm, Sat–Sun 11am–6pm. U-Bahn: Kurfürstenstrasse; S-Bahn: Potsdamer Platz.

This museum displays applied arts and crafts from the Middle Ages through the 20th century. Its outstanding exhibition is the Guelph Treasure, a collection of medieval church articles in gold and silver. The basement rooms show contemporary design from the Bauhaus school to Charles Eames and Memphis. Venetian glass, Italian majolica, German Renaissance goldsmiths' work, and 18th-century porcelain figurines are also displayed. Notable are such art-nouveau works as a translucent opal-and-enamel box by Eugène Feuillâtre. There's a cafeteria inside, open from 10am to 4:30pm.

Neue Nationalgalerie (Staatliche Museum zu Berlin). Potsdamerstrasse 50 (just south of the Tiergarten). ☎ **030/2-66-26-62.** Permanent collection, 10DM ($5) adults, 4DM ($2) children; temporary exhibitions, 12DM ($6). Tues–Fri 10am–6pm, Sat–Sun 11am–6pm. Closed Jan 1, Dec 24–25 and 31, and the Tues after Easter and Whitsunday. U-Bahn: Kurfürstenstrasse; S-Bahn: Potsdamer Platz.

In its modern glass-and-steel home designed by Ludwig Mies van der Rohe (1886–1969), the Neue Nationalgalerie is a sequel of sorts to the art at Dahlem. It contains a continually growing collection of modern European and American art. Here you'll find works of 19th-century artists, with a concentration on French impressionists. German art starts with Adolph von Menzel's paintings from about 1850. The 20th-century collection includes works by Max Beckmann and Edvard Munch, and E. L. Kirchner's *Brandenburger Tor* (1929), as well as paintings by Bacon, Picasso, Ernst, Klee, and American artists such as Barnett Newman. There's food service in the cafe on the ground floor, open 10:30am to 6pm.

OTHER MUSEUMS & SIGHTS

Deutsche Guggenheim Berlin. Unter den Linden 13–15 (at the intersection with Charlottenstrasse). ☎ **030/2020930.** Admission 8DM ($4) adults, 5DM ($2.50) children. Daily 11am–8pm. U-Bahn: Französische Strasse.

This state-of-the-art museum is devoted to modern and contemporary art. The exhibition space is on the ground floor of the newly restored Berlin branch of Deutsche Bank. The Guggenheim Foundation presents several exhibitions at this site annually, and also displays newly commissioned works created specifically for this space by world-renowned artists. The bank supports young artists from the German-speaking world by purchasing their work and displaying them throughout the company's offices and public spaces. Exhibitions have ranged from the most avant-garde of modern artists, to Picasso, Cézanne, and Andy Warhol.

Aquarium **11**

Bauhaus-Archiv Museum
für Gestaltung **10**

Brandenburger Tor **4**

Europa Center **12**

Gemäldegalerie **9**

Kaiser Wilhelm
Memorial Church **14**

Kongresshalle **2**

Kunstgewerbemuseum **8**

Museum für Gegenwart **1**

Neue Nationalgalerie **7**

Philharmonie **5**

Reichstag **3**

Staatsbibliothek **6**

Zoologischer Garten **13**

Die Sammlung Berggruen: Picasso und Seine Zeit (The Berggruen Collection: Picasso and His Era). Schlosstrasse 1 (entrance across from the Egyptian Museum, in Charlottenburg). ☎ **030/830-1466.** Admission 8DM ($4) adults, 4DM ($2) students and children. Tues–Fri 9am–5pm, Sat–Sun 10am–5pm. Closed Mon. U-Bahn: Sophie-Charlotte-Platz, followed by a 10-min. walk.

This unusual private museum displays the awesome collection of respected art and antiques dealer Heinz Berggruen. A native of Berlin who fled the Nazis in 1936, Berggruen later established a miniempire of antique dealerships in Paris and California before returning, with his collection, to his native home in 1996. Sometime during your visit, there's a good chance that 80-year-old Mr. Berggruen, who has an apartment nearby, will be conducting a lecture here on his favorite painter, or spontaneously strolling among his paintings. The setting is a renovated army barracks designed by noted architect August Stütler in 1859. Although most of the collection is devoted to Picasso, there are also works by Cézanne, Braque, Klee, and van Gogh. The Picasso collection alone, which covers all his major periods, is worth the trip.

Friedrichswerdersche Kirche-Schinkelmuseum. Werderstrasse (at the corner of Niederlagstrasse). ☎ **030/2-08-13-23.** Admission 4DM ($2) adults, 2DM ($1) children. Tues–Sun 10am–6pm. U-Bahn: Hausvogteiplatz.

This annex of the Nationalgalerie is located in the deconsecrated Friedrichswerdersche Kirche, which was designed in 1828 by Karl Friedrich Schinkel (1781–1841). It lies close to Unter den Linden, not far from the State Opera House. The twin Gothic portals of the old church shelter a bronze of St. Michael slaying a dragon. Inside, the museum is devoted to the memory of Schinkel, who designed many of Berlin's great palaces, churches, and monuments. Memorabilia and documents record his great accomplishments. There are also exhibitions of neoclassical sculptures, portraits, and tombs by Johann Gottfried Schadow, Christian Daniel Rauch, Friedrich Tieck, and Berthel Thorvaldsen, the Danish sculptor.

Käthe-Kollwitz-Museum. Fasanenstrasse 24. ☎ **030/8-82-52-10.** Admission 8DM ($4) adults, 4DM ($2) children and students. Wed–Mon 11am–6pm. U-Bahn: Hohenzollernplatz or Spichernstrasse.

This museum has been called a personalized revolt against the agonies of war. Many works express the sorrow of wartime separation of mother and child, inspired in part by the artist's loss of a son in World War I and a grandson during World War II. Berlin-born Käthe Kollwitz (1867–1945) was an ardent pacifist and socialist whose works were banned by the Nazis. The first woman ever elected to the Prussian Academy of the Arts, she resigned her position in 1933 to protest Hitler's rise to power. Her husband, Karl Kollwitz, was a physician who chose to practice among the poor on a working-class street (now called Kollwitzstrasse). In 1943, Allied bombing drove Käthe to the countryside near Dresden, where she died in 1945, a guest of the former royal family of Saxony in their castle at Moritzburg.

The lower floors of the museum are devoted to woodcuts and lithographs, the upper floors to particularly poignant sculptures. *Note:* The collection is closed twice a year for special exhibits.

Märkisches Museum. Am Källnischen Park 5. ☎ **030/30-86-60.** Admission 3DM ($1.60) adults, 1DM (55¢) children. Tues–Sun 10am–6pm. U-Bahn: Märkisches Museum. Bus: 147, 240, or 265.

The full cultural history of Berlin is displayed in one of the most prominent buildings on the banks of the Spree; 42 rooms contain collections of artifacts from excavations, plus such art treasures as Slav silver and Bronze Age finds. You can learn

---

✪ Frommer's Favorite Berlin Experiences

Strolling along Unter den Linden and the Kurfürstendamm. You can't know Berlin until you've strolled the Ku'damm, that glossy, store-lined showcase of Western capitalism, and Unter den Linden, the Prussian Centerpiece of the Berlin-Mitte district.

Kneipen Crawling. This is the Berlin version of "pub crawling." Whether you want breakfast or a beer at 4am, there's always a Kneipe waiting to claim you, no matter what neighborhood you're in.

Looking for a Touch of Culture. The baton of the late Herbert von Karajan is no longer raised, but the Berlin Philharmonic is still one of the world's leading orchestras.

Wandering the Nikolai Quarter. A symbol of Berlin's desire to bounce back after war damage, this charming 16th-century neighborhood has been completely rebuilt. Period taverns and churches make it ideal for a leisurely stroll down narrow streets illuminated by gas lanterns.

Picnicking in the Tiergarten. What better place for a picnic than the former hunting grounds of the Prussian electors? Wander through this 167ha (412-acre) park until you find the ideal spot, but first stop off at KaDeWe's sixth-floor food emporium at Wittgenbergplatz, 20 minutes away, for the makings of a memorable meal.

---

about Berlin's theaters and literature, the arts in Berlin and Brandenburg, and the life and work of Berlin artisans. Most visitors like the array of mechanical musical instruments that can be played Wednesday 3 to 4pm and Sunday 11am to noon, for an extra 2DM ($1.10).

Martin-Gropius-Bau. Stresemannstrasse 110. ☎ **030/25-48-60.** Admission 8DM ($4) adults, 4DM ($2) children. Tues–Sun 10am–8pm. U-Bahn: Potsdamer Platz; S-Bahn: Anhalter Bahnhof.

When this gallery opened in 1981, the *New York Times* called it one of the "most dramatic museums in the world." It contains the **Museum Berlinische Galerie,** with works of art, architecture, and photography from the 19th and 20th centuries; the **Jewish Museum;** and the **Werkbund Archiv.** On the ground floor are changing exhibitions. The building lies near the site of the former Berlin Wall, and its eastern section opens onto the leveled former Gestapo headquarters. It's fascinating to look at the adjoining building with its unrestored exterior terra-cotta friezes—damaged, destroyed, or left intact.

✪ Museum für Gegenwart. Invalidensrasse 50–51. ☎ **030/20-90-55-55.** Admission 8DM ($4.30) adults, 4DM ($2.15) children. Tues, Wed, Fri 10am-6pm, Thurs 10am-8pm, Sat-Sun 11am-6pm. U-Bahn: Zinnowitzer Strasse. Bus: 157, 245, 248, or 340.

This Museum of Contemporary Art opened in 1996 north of the Spree River in the old Hamburger Bahnhof or train station, the oldest in Berlin. The structure was the terminus of the 290km (180-mile) train run from Hamburg. Today, the 19th-century station no longer receives trains but is a premier storehouse of postwar art, a sort of Musée d'Orsay of Berlin. Traces of its former function still are evident, including the high roof designed for steam engines. The modern art on display is some of the finest in Germany, the nucleus of the collection a donation from the Berlin collector Erich Marx (no relation to Karl Marx). A multi-media event, you can view everything from Andy Warhol's now legendary Mao to an audio-visual Joseph Beuys archive. The museum houses one of the best collections of the work of Cy Twombly in the world because the curator, Heiner Bastian, was once his assistant. Other works are by Rauschenberg, Lichtenstein, and the recently deceased Dan Flavin. Beuys is also represented by 450 drawings.

Museum Haus am Checkpoint Charlie. Friedrichstrasse 44. ☎ **030/253-7250.** Admission 8DM ($4) adults, 5DM ($2.50) children and students. Daily 9am–10pm. U-Bahn: Kochstrasse. Bus: 129.

Exhibits in this small building evoke the tragic events connected with the former Berlin Wall. You can see some of the instruments of escape used by East Germans, including chairlifts, false passports, hot-air balloons, and even a minisub. Photos document the construction of the wall, the establishment of escape tunnels, and the post-war history of both parts of Berlin from 1945 until today, including the airlift of 1948 to 1949. One of the most moving exhibits is the display on the staircase of drawings by school children, who, in 1961 to 1962, were asked to depict both halves of Germany in one picture.

Olympia-Stadion. Olympischer Platz 3. ☎ **030/30-06-33.** Admission 1DM (55¢). June–Sept daily 9am–5pm; off-season daily 8am–4pm. U-Bahn: Olympia-Stadion.

Built in 1936 by Werner March for the XI Summer Olympic Games, the Olympia-Stadion, which seats 100,000 people, was the first in Europe to supply all the facilities necessary for modern sports. Hitler expected to see his "master race" run off with all the medals in the 1936 Olympics, but his hopes were dashed when an African American, Jesse Owens, took four golds for the U.S. team.

The stadium area covers a total of 136ha (330 acres), but the main attraction is the arena. The playing field in its Center lies 14m (47 feet) below ground level. For a panoramic view of Berlin, take the elevator to the top of the 80m (260-foot) platform, where the Olympic bell hangs. Sporting or cultural events are still presented here about once a week during spring, summer, and autumn. For ticket sales and information for sporting events within the stadium, call **Herta-BSC (Herta-Berlin Soccer Club)** at ☎ **030/3-00-92-80.** For information about the occasional live concerts, call **Conzert Concept** at ☎ **030/81-07-50.**

Schöneberg Rathaus. John-F.-Kennedy-Platz. ☎ **030/7-87-60.** Free admission. Daily 10am–6pm. Tower closed Nov–Mar. U-Bahn: Rathaus Schöneberg.

This former political and administrative Center of West Berlin is of special interest to Americans. It was the scene of John F. Kennedy's memorable (if grammatically shaky) "Ich bin ein Berliner" speech on June 26, 1963. Berliners have renamed the square around the building the John-F.-Kennedy-Platz. From the 72m-(237-foot-) high hall tower, a Liberty Bell replica is rung every day at noon. This Freedom Bell, a gift from the American people in 1950, symbolized U.S. support for the West Berliners during the Cold War. The document chamber contains a testimonial bearing the signatures of 17 million Americans who gave their moral support to the struggle.

EXPLORING BERLIN-MITTE

The best street for strolling in eastern Berlin is the famous **Unter den Linden,** beginning at Brandenburg Gate.

Alexanderplatz, named for Russian Czar Alexander I, was the Center of activity in the old East Berlin. This square has brightened considerably since reunification, though aesthetically speaking it's got a long way to go. Neon lights and bright murals now coexist alongside the dull and fading GDR-era structures, and street musicians and small markets give the area new life.

The massive 335m (1,100-foot) **Fernsehturm (TV tower)** on Alexanderplatz is the second-highest structure in Europe. It's worthwhile to take the 60-second elevator ride to the observation platform, 186m (610 feet) above the city. From this isolated vantage you can clearly distinguish most landmarks, and on the floor above, you can enjoy cake and coffee in the revolving Tele-Café. The elevator to the top costs 9DM ($4.50) for adults and 4DM ($2) for children. The tower is open daily March to October 9am to 1am, and November to February daily 10am to midnight.

At the foot of the Fernsehturm stands Berlin's second-oldest church, the brick Gothic **Marienkirche (St. Mary's Church),** Karl-Liebknecht-Strasse 8 (☎ 030/ 2-42-44-67), dating from the 15th century. Inside is the 1475 wall painting *Der Totentanz* (*The Dance of Death*), discovered in 1860 beneath a layer of whitewash in the church's entrance hall. Also worth seeing is the marble baroque pulpit carved by Andreas Schlüter (1703). The cross on the top of the church annoyed the Communist rulers of the former East Germany—its golden form was always reflected in the windows of the Fernsehturm. The church is open Monday to Thursday 10am to noon and 1 to 4pm, Friday to Sunday noon to 4pm. Free tours are offered Monday to Thursday at 1pm and Sunday at 11:45am.

Brecht-Weigel-Museum. Chausseestrasse 125. ☎ **030/282-99-16.** Admission 6DM ($3.00) adults, 3DM ($1.50) children and students. Tues–Wed and Fri 10am–11:30am, Thurs 10am–noon and 5–6:30pm, Sat 9:30am–1:30pm, Sun 11am–6pm. Visits by guided tour only. U-Bahn: Zinnowitzer Strasse.

This building was occupied by poet and playwright Bertolt Brecht (1898–1956) and his wife, noted actress Helene Weigel (1900–72), from 1953 until their deaths. Brecht, who lived in the United States during World War II, returned to East Berlin after the war. Here he created his own "epic theater" company, the acclaimed Berliner Ensemble. The museum is in an old apartment house. It displays the artists' living and working rooms and the Brecht and Weigel archives, containing 350,000 manuscripts, typescripts, collections of his printed works, press cuttings, and playbills. All visitors are guided around the museum by an attendant. There's a restaurant downstairs (see "Where to Dine," above).

THE HISTORIC NIKOLAI QUARTER

The historic ✪ **Nikolaiviertel** (U-Bahn: Klosterstrasse) was restored in time for the city's 750th anniversary in 1987. Here, on the banks of the Spree River, is where Berlin was born. Many of the medieval and baroque buildings in the neighborhood were completely and authentically reconstructed after World War II. Some of the city's old flavor has been recaptured here.

The area is named for the **Nikolaikirche (Church of St. Nicholas),** Nikolaikirchplatz, off Spandauerstrasse (☎ 030/24-00-20). The church, the oldest in Berlin, was originally constructed in the 14th century on the remains of a 13th-century Romanesque church. The restored building now displays the finds of postwar archaeological digs; during the reconstruction, 800-year-old skeletons were found. It's open Sunday 2pm to 4pm and Saturday noon to 3pm; a visit can be arranged on weekdays, if you call in advance. Admission to the church is free, but the tower is 2DM ($1).

OTHER ARCHITECTURAL SIGHTS

Just north of the Tiergarten is the **Hansaviertel,** or Hansa Quarter (U-Bahn: Hansaplatz). The architecture of this area was an outgrowth of the great INTERBAU 1957 (International Builder's Exhibition), when architects from 22 nations designed buildings for the totally destroyed quarter. The diversity here is exciting: 50 architects took part, including Gropius, Niemeyer, and Duttman.

Le Corbusier also submitted a design for an apartment house for INTERBAU 1957, but the structure was so gigantic that it had to be built near the **Olympic Stadium** (U-Bahn: Olympia-Stadion). The **Corbusier House,** called *Strahlende Stadt* (radiant city), is one of Europe's largest housing complexes—its 530 apartments can house up to 1,400 people. Typical of the architect's style, this tremendous building rests on stilts.

The architects of rebuilt Berlin were also encouraged to design Centers for the performing arts. One of the most controversial projects was the **Congress Hall (Kongresshalle),** on John-Foster-Dulles-Allee, in the Tiergarten, just west of Brandenburg Gate (S-Bahn: Unter den Linden). This building was conceived as the American contribution to INTERBAU 1957. The reinforced concrete structure has an 18m (60-foot-) high vaulted ceiling that reminds some viewers of an oversized flying saucer. Irreverent Berliners immediately christened it "The Pregnant Oyster." The building today is used mainly for conventions. More successful was the **Philharmonie,** new home of the Berlin Philharmonic, and its adjacent chamber-music hall, next to the Tiergarten. The tentlike roof arches up in a bold curve, and the gold-colored facade glitters.

Berlin's tallest building sits in the midst of the city's busiest area. The 22-story **Europa Center,** just across the plaza from the Kaiser Wilhelm Memorial Church (U-Bahn: Kurfürstendamm), is the largest self-contained shopping Center and entertainment complex in Europe. This town-within-a-town opened in 1965 on the site of the legendary Romanisches Café, once a gathering place for actors, writers, and artists in the flamboyant 1920s. Berliners immediately dubbed it "Pepper's Manhattan," after its owner, K. H. Pepper. In addition to three levels of shops, restaurants, nightclubs, bars, and cinemas, it contains dozens of offices, a parking garage, and an observation roof. At the Tauentzienstrasse entrance, you can find two pieces of the former Berlin Wall. The building is open daily 9am to midnight (to 10pm in winter). Admission to the observation roof is 3DM ($1.50).

SIGHTS IN THE ENVIRONS

Haus der Wannsee-Konferenz. Am Grossen Wannsee 56. ☎ **030/80-50-01-0.** Free admission. Mon–Fri 10am–6pm, Sat–Sun 2–6pm. S-Bahn: Wannsee, then bus 114.

This was the site of one of the most notorious conferences in history: a meeting of Nazi bureaucrats and SS officials to plan the annihilation of European Jewry. The minutes of the conference were kept by Adolf Eichmann, the sallow-faced SS functionary who later mapped out transport logistics for sending millions of Jews to their deaths.

The villa is now a memorial to the Holocaust. It includes a selection of photographs of men, women, and children who were sent to concentration camps. This exhibit is not for the squeamish. Nearly all the pictures on display are official Nazi photographs, including some of Nazi medical experiments. As noted at the trials at Nürnberg, "No government in history ever did a better job of photographing and documenting its crimes against humanity."

Jüdischer Friedhof (Jewish Cemetery). Herbert-Baumstrasse, Weissensee (a suburb east of Berlin). ☎ **030/9-25-33-30.** Mar–Nov, daily 8am–5pm; Dec–Feb, Mon–Thurs 8am–4pm, Fri 8am–3pm. Tram: 23 or 24, or taxi.

This famous Jewish cemetery was opened in 1880. It contains 110,000 graves of Jewish residents of Berlin. Many distinguished artists, musicians, and scientists, as well as religious leaders, are buried here. Some tombs are of Jewish soldiers who fought for Germany in World War I. A memorial honors Jewish victims murdered during the Nazi era. You may have a hard time finding the cemetery on your own, so we recommend a taxi.

The New Synagogue (Neue Synagoge Berlin-Centrum Judaicum). Oranienburger-strasse 31. ☎ **030/880-28-316.** Admission 5DM (2.50) adults, 3DM ($1.50) for children under 14. Sun-Thurs 10am-6pm; Fri 10am-2pm. Last entrance 30 minutes before closing. S-Bahn: Oranienburger Tor or Hackescher Markt.

The history of this building is almost as tragic and eventful as the saga of the Jews in Germany. Originally consecrated on Rosh Hashanah in 1866, and capped with what's remembered as one of the most spectacular domes in Berlin, it was vandalized in 1938 during Kristallnacht, torched by Berliners in 1944, blasted by Allied bombs in 1945, and finally, after about a decade of further deterioration, demolished by the Communist East Germans in the 1950s. During its heyday, with 3,200 seats and a design inspired by the Moorish architecture of the Alhambra in Granada, Spain, it was the largest synagogue in Germany. In recent times, it was partially rebuilt, and capped with a glided dome that's visible for many surrounding blocks. Inside, there's a replica, using some of the original carvings, of some of the original synagogue's entrance vestibules and anterooms, within which are exhibitions detailing the events that transpired in this building since its original construction. The bulk of the synagogue was never rebuilt. In its place is a gravel-covered plot of land where markers indicate the original layout of the building. Come here expecting a disturbing and unnerving insight into the destruction of a way of life that used to be, and a sense of the passion with which Berlin's Jewish and German communities commemorate the memory of their murdered kinfolk.

Spandauer Zitadelle (Spandau Citadel). Am Juliusturm. ☎ **030/354-944-200.** Admission 4DM ($2) Adults. Tues–Fri 9am–5pm, Sat–Sun 10am–5pm. U-Bahn: Zitadelle.

The citadel stands at the confluence of the Spree and Havel Rivers in northwestern Berlin. The Hohenzollern electors of Brandenburg used it as a summer residence, and in time it became the chief military Center of Prussia. The Juliusturm (Julius Tower) and the Palas, constructed in the 13th to 15th centuries, are the oldest buildings still standing. The main building, accessible by footbridge, houses a local-history museum. The citadel has been besieged by everybody from the French to the Prussians.

THE PARKS & ZOO

The huge **Botanischer Garten (Botanical Garden),** Königin-Luise-Strasse 6–8 (☎ **030/83-00-61-27;** S-Bahn: Botanischer Garten or Rathaus Steglitz), near the Dahlem Museums, contains vast collections of European and exotic plants. The big palm house is one of the largest in the world. There's a large arboretum here as well as several special collections, such as a garden for blind visitors and another with water-plants. Admission is 6DM ($3) for adults, 3DM ($1.50) for children, and free for children under 6. The garden is open daily 9am to 8pm (it closes at dusk in winter); the museum, Tuesday to Sunday 10am to 5pm. Free admission to the museum only.

The ✪ **Tiergarten** is the largest green space in central Berlin, covering 2.5km² (just under 1 square mile), with more than 23km (14 miles) of meandering walkways. It was originally laid out as a private park for the electors of Prussia by a leading landscape architect of the day, Peter Josef Lenné. The park was devastated during World War II—the trees that remained were chopped down for fuel as Berliners shivered through the winter of 1945–46. Beginning in 1955, trees were replanted, and walkways, canals, ponds, and flower beds were restored to their original patterns. The park is popular with joggers and (sometimes nude) sunbathers. Inside the park is the Berlin Zoo (see below).

Among the park's monuments is the **Siegessäule (Victory Column),** a golden goddess of victory perched atop a soaring red-granite pedestal. The monument stands in the Center of the wide boulevard (Strasse des 17 Juni) that neatly bisects the park. A

Fun for Kids

Children love the **Berlin Zoo-Aquarium** (see below). Its most famous residents, the giant pandas, are perennial favorites. The zoo also has playgrounds and a children's section, where the animals welcome a cuddle. Another place to take the kids is **Grips-Theater,** Altonaerstrasse 22 (☎ **030/39-74-74-77;** U-Bahn: Hansaplatz), known for its bright, breezy productions. Children are sure to enjoy the music and dancing (if not the simple German-language dialogue). Tickets cost 16DM ($8) for students and persons under 16, and 28DM ($14) for adults. Call to ask about current productions. Most performances begin at 7:30pm, although there are some matinees as well, depending on the production. The theater is closed from late June to mid-August.

48m (157-foot-) high observation platform can be reached by a climb up a 290-step spiral staircase. It's open on Monday 3 to 6pm and Tuesday to Sunday 9:30am to 6:30pm. Admission is 2DM ($1) for adults and 1DM (50¢) for children. For information, call ☎ **030/391-29-61.**

Zoologischer Garten Berlin (Berlin Zoo-Aquarium), Hardenbergplatz 8 (☎ **030/25-40-10;** U-Bahn/S-Bahn: Zoologischer Garten), founded in 1844, is Germany's oldest zoo. It occupies almost the entire southwest corner of the Tiergarten. Until World War II, the zoo boasted thousands of animals—many were familiar to Berliners by nickname. By the end of 1945 only 91 had survived. Today more than 13,000 animals live here, many of them in large, open natural habitats. The most valuable residents are giant pandas. The zoo also has Europe's most modern birdhouse, with more than 550 species.

The **aquarium** is as impressive as the adjacent zoo, with more than 9,000 fish, reptiles, amphibians, insects, and other creatures. The terrarium within is inhabited by crocodiles, Komodo dragons, and tuataras. You can walk on a bridge over the reptile pit (but don't lose your balance). There's also a large collection of snakes, lizards, and turtles. The "hippoquarium" is a new attraction.

Admission to the zoo is 13DM ($6.50) for adults and 7DM ($3.50) for children; to the aquarium, 13DM ($6.50) for adults and 7DM ($3.50) for children. A combined ticket costs 19DM ($9.50) for adults and 9.50DM ($4.75) for children. The zoo is open April to October daily 9am to 6:30pm; November to March, daily 9am to 5pm. The aquarium is open year-round daily 9am to 6pm.

6 Organized Tours

WALKING TOURS

For an excellent introduction to Berlin and its history, try one of the walking tours offered by **Berlin Walks** (☎ **030/301-9194** or e-mail: BerlinWalks@ compuserve.com for information). "Discover Berlin" is a 3-hour introductory tour that takes you past the New Synagogue, the Reichstag, and the Brandenburg Gate, among other major sites. This walk starts daily at 10am and 2:30pm (in winter at 10am only). "Infamous Third Reich Sites" focuses on the sites of major Nazi buildings in central Berlin, such as Goebbels' Propaganda Ministry and Hitler's New Reichschancellery; it starts at 10am, on Saturdays, Sundays, Tuesdays, and Thursdays in summer, less frequently in the off-season. "Jewish Life in Berlin" takes you through the pre-war Jewish community; sights include the Old Cemetery and the former Boys' School. The tour starts at 10am Monday and Thursday, April to mid-October. For all tours reservations are unnecessary—simply meet the guide, who will be wearing a Berlin Walks badge, outside the main entrance to Bahnhof Zoologischer Garten (Zoo Station), at the top of the taxi stand. Tours last from 2 ¹/₂ to 3 hours and cost 14DM ($7) for those under 26 and 18DM ($9) for everyone else. This summer, Berlin Walks will be inaugurating a new 5-hour tour to Potsdam, starting every Wednesday and Saturday at 9am; meet at the same place.

BUS TOURS

Berlin is a far-flung metropolis whose interesting neighborhoods are often separated by extended areas of parks, monumental boulevards, and Cold-War wastelands. Because of these factors, organized bus tours can be the best way to navigate the city.

Some of the best are operated by **Severin+Kühn,** Kurfürstendamm 216 (☎ 030/ 88-04-190; U-Bahn: Kurfürstendamm), located on the second floor of a building across from the Kempinski Hotel. This agency offers a half dozen tours of Berlin and its environs. Their 2-hour "12-Stops-City Tour" departs daily every half-hour April to October 10am to 4pm and November to March 10am to 3pm. Tickets cost 33DM ($16.50) per person. The tour passes 12 important stops in Berlin, including the Europa Center, the Brandenburg Gate, and Potsdammer Platz, provides taped audio commentary in eight languages, and offers the option of getting on and off the bus at any point during the hour. Retain your ticket stub to reboard the bus.

Severin+Kühn also offers the 3-hour "Big Berlin Tour," which departs at 10am and 2pm daily and costs 39DM ($19.50) per person. This tour incorporates more sites than the 12-stops Tour, including a live guide who delivers commentaries in both German and English.

One of the most interesting tours visits Potsdam, site of the famed World War II conference and of Sans Souci Palace, former residence of Frederick the Great. The price is 65DM ($32.50) per person. Departures are Tuesday to Sunday at 10am, May to September, and Saturday and Sunday at 2:15pm, April to October.

BOAT TOURS

It may not be the obvious choice for transportation in Berlin, but a boat ride can offer visitors a good change of pace. The networks of canals that bisect the plains of what used to be known as Prussia were an engineering marvel when they were completed in the 19th century. Today, transport through the lakes, locks, and canals around Berlin retains its nostalgic allure, and affords unusual vistas that aren't available from the windows of more conventional modes of transport. Berliners boast that their city has more bridges than Venice. Local waterways include the Spree and Havel Rivers—ranging in size from narrow channels to large lakes—as well as many canals. You can take short tours that offer close-up views of the city or daylong adventures along the Spree and Havel; the latter often turn into beer-drinking fests.

The city's best-known boat operator is **Stern- und Kreisschiffahrt,** Pushkinallee 60–70 (☎ 030/5-36-36-00). Since Germany's reunification, the company has absorbed the piers and ferryboats of its former East German counterparts. "Historische Stadtfahrt" is a ride along the banks of the Spree, the river that helped build Berlin. Two, three, and four-hour tours (in German only) depart at 10am and 2pm from a quay near Berlin's cathedral, Am Palast Ufer. These trips offer good views of the Reichstag, the Pergamon Museums, the Königliche Bibliothek (Royal Library), and the monumental heart of the former East Berlin. The tours lasting one hour cost 14DM ($7) per person; tours lasting two hours cost 16DM ($8); tours lasting four hours are 26.50DM ($13.25).

Stern- und Kreisschiffahrt also has a theme-derived cruising yacht, *Moby Dick,* that usually sails along the waters of the Eglersee and that's shaped like a whale as it might have been developed by the staff at Disneyland. It departs from a point near the Alt-Tegel U-Bahn station, on the city's northwestern edge. Walk for about 10 minutes through the suburb of Tegel to the Greenwich Promenade, and then to the Stern- und Kreisschiffahrt pier. Boats head southward from Tegel, passing along the Havel River and many of its lakes. Reservations are usually necessary for all boat rides described here. Rides operate only April to either late October or early December, depending on the tour. Prices and actual itineraries change seasonally; call for more details.

7 Sports & Outdoor Pursuits

BIKING

The best place to rent bikes in Berlin is at **Fahradstation,** GmbH, an outfit that maintains hundreds of bicycles and at least two locations within central Berlin. Two of their most central locations include Rosenthalerstrasse 40–41 (☎ **030/28-38-48-48;** S-Bahn: Hackescher Markt), in Hackescher Hofe, and Bergmannstrasse 9 (☎ **030/921-5156;** U-Bahn: Platz de Luftbrüke), in Kreuzberg. Rentals cost 20DM ($10) per day, plus a one-time rental fee of 5DM ($2.50). The city maintains a labyrinth of bike paths, marked by red bricks on the walkways, through the central core of Berlin and in its parks, especially the Tiergarten. The best places for biking are the Tiergarten in central Berlin, and farther afield in the Grunewald Forest (S-Bahn: Grunewald).

JOGGING

Head for the vast and verdant leafiness of the **Grunewald,** on the city's western edge, which is crisscrossed with pedestrian and cyclists' paths. This area is appropriate for very long endurance tests. Closer to the Center is the **Tiergarten,** which allows you to soak up a little history on your morning jog thanks to its many monuments and memorials. The grounds of **Schloss Charlottenburg** are also good for jogging.

SPECTATOR SPORTS

Among Berliners, **soccer** is the most popular sport. For information about which teams are playing, ask your hotel receptionist, or refer to a daily newspaper or the weekly magazine *Berlin Programm.*

SWIMMING & SAUNAS

Berlin has dozens of pools. One of the best equipped is the **S.E.Z. Landsberger,** Landsberger Allee 77 (☎ **030/421-820;** U-Bahn: Alexanderplatz). Here you'll find a swimming pool, a diving pool, a wave pool, an assortment of waterfalls, a jet pool, sauna and solarium facilities, a weight room, about half a dozen restaurants and snack bars, and a bowling alley. The cost is 8DM ($4) for adults and 4DM ($2) for children for 2 hours of swimming.

A worthy competitor (just east of Tempelhof Airport) is the **Club Paradise,** Buschkrugallee 64 (☎ **030/6-06-60-60;** U-Bahn: Grenzallee), which has indoor and outdoor pools, saunas, a steam room, solariums, and a 120-meter water slide. Its latest attraction, called "Crazy River," sends you down a river in water tubes. A 4-hour pass costs 21DM ($10.50) for adults and 16DM ($8)for children ages 2 to 12. It's open daily 10am to 11pm.

Perched on the top floor of the Europa Center's parking garage (*Parkhaus Europa Center*), you'll find a health and exercise club called **Thermen,** Nürnberger Strasse 9 (☎ **030/2-61-60-32;** U-Bahn: Wittenbergplatz), offering an array of heated pools, saunas, massage facilities, and solariums. A full-day pass costs 35DM ($17.50), but if you want to limit your exposure to just three hours, you'll pay 13DM ($6.50) for arrivals between 10am and 9pm, and 27DM ($13.50) if you arrive between 9pm and closing. Both men and women share the same saunas. If you just want to use the pool, and bypass the saunas and exercise facilities, you'll pay 15DM ($7.50) for a two-hour immersion, regardless of the time of day. Massages cost 38DM ($19) for 30 minutes. Hours are Monday to Saturday 10am to midnight and Sunday 10am to 9pm. For outdoor swimming during the hot months, head to one of Europe's largest lake beaches at **Wannsee.** Take the S-Bahn to Nikolaisee and follow the hordes of bathers heading toward the water's edge.

TENNIS & SQUASH

At **Sports Treffe,** Buschkrugallee 84 (☎ **030/6-06-60-11;** U-Bahn: Grenzall), indoor courts rent for 29DM to 53DM ($14.50 to $26.50) for a 45-minute session, depending on when you play. There are also five squash courts that each rent for between 10DM to 29DM ($5 to $14.50) for a 45-minute session. Somewhat closer to Berlin's Center is **Squash & Tennis Center,** Treuenbrietzenerstrasse 36 (☎ **030/4-15-30-11;** U-Bahn: Wittenau, then bus 124 or X-21), which has similar rates. Tennis or squash racquets at either establishment rent for around 5DM ($2.50) per 45-minute session. There are also courts in the **Preussen Park,** Kamenzerstrasse 34, Lankwitz (☎ **030/ 7-75-10-51;** U-Bahn: Mariendorfer), open during the day from April through October with rates beginning at 34DM ($19.40) per hour.

8 Shopping

The **Ku'damm** (or Kurfürstendamm) is the Fifth Avenue of Berlin. It's filled with quality stores but also has outlets hustling cheap souvenirs and T-shirts. Although Berliners themselves shop on the Ku'damm, many prefer the specialty stores on the side streets, especially between **Breitscheidplatz** and **Olivaer Platz.** You might also want to check out **Am Zoo** and **Kantstrasse.**

Another major shopping street is the **Tauentzienstrasse** and the streets that intersect it: **Marburger, Ranke,** and **Nürnberger.** This area offers a wide array of stores, many specializing in German fashions for women. Stores here are often cheaper than on the Ku'damm. Also on Tauentzienstrasse (near the Ku'damm) is Berlin's major indoor shopping Center, the **Europa Center** (☎ **030/3-48-00-88**), with around 75 shops, as well as restaurants and cafes. At the end of this street lies the **KaDeWe,** the classiest department store in Berlin and the biggest in continental Europe.

A new, upmarket version of the Europa Center is the **Uhland-Passage,** at Uhlandstrasse 170, which has some of the best boutiques and big-name stores in Berlin. Shoppers interested in quality at any price should head to **Kempinski Plaza,** Uhlandstrasse 181–183, a pocket of posh with some of the most exclusive boutiques in the city. Haute-couture women's clothing is a special feature here. More trendy and avant-garde boutiques are found along **Bleibtreustrasse.**

If it's serious bargains you're looking for, head to **Wilmersdorferstrasse.** Here you'll find a vast number of discount stores, although some of the merchandise is second-rate. Try to avoid Saturday morning, when it's often impossibly overcrowded.

In eastern Berlin, not that long ago, you couldn't find much to buy except a few souvenirs. All that is changed now. The main street, **Friedrichstrasse,** offers some of Berlin's most elegant shopping. Upmarket boutiques—selling everything from quality women's fashions to Meissen porcelain—are found along **Unter den Linden.** The cheaper stores in eastern Berlin are around the rather bleak-looking **Alexanderplatz.** Many specialty and clothing shops are found in the **Nikolai quarter.** The largest shopping mall in eastern Berlin, with outlets offering a little bit of everything, is at the **Berliner Markthalle,** at the corner of Rosa-Luxemburg-Strasse and Karl-Liebknecht-Strasse.

Most stores in Berlin are open Monday to Friday 9 or 10am to 6 or 6:30pm. Many stay open late on Thursday evenings, often to 8:30pm. Saturday hours are usually 9 or 10am to 2pm.

ANTIQUES

Astoria. Bleibtreustrasse 42. ☎ **030/8-83-81-81.** S-Bahn: Savignyplatz.

Astoria, whose buyers frequently scour the antique markets of France, England, and Germany, pays homage to the decorative objects of the 1920s and '30s. You'll find antique mirrors, lamps, tables, and jewelry here, as well as a handful of reproductions.

Harmel's. Damaschkestrasse 24. ☎ **030/3-24-22-92.** U-Bahn: Adenauerplatz.

Most of Harmel's inventory was gathered in England and France, a commentary on the relative scarcity of genuine German antiques because of wartime bombing. The carefully chosen collection stresses furniture, jewelry, and accessories from the Victorian and Edwardian eras.

Kunstsalon. Unter den Linden 41. ☎ **030/20-45-02-03.** S-Bahn: Under den Linden.

Don't expect everything in this shop to be tasteful. Instead, you'll find the kind of rococo art objects that Liberace might have used in a stage set, or that a hip Berliner nightclub or brothel might buy as a means of creating instant kitsch. Everything is a cast off from previous productions of the Komische Opera (Comic Opera), including both the stage props and the costumes. Come here for the wigs, gowns, and waistcoats that helped the partying during *The Merry Widow,* the candelabra that lit up Violetta when she died in *Traviata,* and the associated trash and treasures that evoke smiles from virtually anyone who understands their origin. The store also sells CDs, posters, and reproductions of rare portraits of Garbo, Dietrich, and Charlie Chaplin with Pola Negri during a holiday they enjoyed at the nearby Adlon Hotel in 1929.

L. & M. Lee. Kurfürstendamm 32. ☎ **030/8-81-73-33.** U-Bahn: Kurfürstendamm.

This is one of several sophisticated antiques stores on the Kurfürstendamm's eastern end. The inventory includes mostly German-made porcelain, silver, and glass from the early 20th century, and an assortment of 19th-century pieces from other European countries.

Stilbruch Antiquitäten & Schmuck. Bleibtreustrasse 50. ☎ **030/312-83-04.** S-Bahn: Savignyplatz.

It's far from being the largest antique store in Berlin, but something about its dense inventories of Biedermeier-era furniture, tableware, and jewelry might appeal to your sense of schmaltz and nostalgia. Owner Margareta Wojcieszak makes sure that objects are beeswaxed or polished to a high sheen. Everything seems to evoke a story about other places, other priorities, and other eras.

ART GALLERIES

Galerie Brusberg. Kurfürstendamm 213. ☎ **030/8-82-76-82.** U-Bahn: Kurfürstendamm

One of Germany's most visible and influential art galleries, Galerie Brusberg was established in 1958 by Dieter Brusberg. The gallery has handled the work of Max Ernst, Salvador Dalí, Paul Delvaux, Henri Laurens, Pablo Picasso, and René Magritte, plus German artists Altenbourg, Antes, and Klapheck. Long before unification, it promoted painters of the old Eastern bloc, notably Bernhard Heisig, Harald Metzkes, and Werner Töbke. No one will mind if you drop in just for a look.

You Paid What?

47,000 hotels, 700 airlines, 50 rental car companies. And a few million ways to save money.

Travelocity.com
A Sabre Company

Go Virtually Anywhere.

AOL Keyword: Travel

Will you have enough stories to tell your grandchildren?

Yahoo! Travel

Prüss & Ochs Gallery. Sophienstrasse 18. ☎ **030/28391-387.** U-Bahn: Weinmeisterstrasse.

Its setting resembles a fortress from the Industrial Revolution. It's built of red brick that's accessible via a labyrinth of alleyways that lead in from one of the oldest and most historic streets in the neighborhood. Art exhibitions change regularly, but regardless of what the temporary venue is, it's likely to be as offbeat and iconoclastic as the arts scene in Berlin itself. The company's main branch is in arts-conscious Cologne; this one gives the sense of exploring the artistic frontiers of Berlin, with special emphasis on counter-culture art that's being produced in Asia and the Balkans.

Galerie Pels-Leusden and Villa Grisebach Auktionen. Fasanenstrasse 25. ☎ **030/8-85-91-50.** U-Bahn: Uhlandstrasse.

This building, constructed in the 1880s by architect Hans Grisebach as his private home, is a historic monument in its own right. Two floors are devoted to 19th- and 20th-century art, mainly German. Prices begin at 175DM ($87.50) for the least expensive lithograph, and go much higher. The building also functions as headquarters and display area for an auction house. Sales are held every spring and fall.

Galerie Springer. Fasanenstrasse 13. ☎ **030/3-12-70-63.** U-Bahn: Uhlandstrasse.

The list of talent showcased in this gallery in recent years reads like a who's who of Central European artists: Dieter Appelt, François Bouillon, Christa Dichgans, Piero Dorazio, Agnes Maels, Vladimir Skoda, and two who prefer to be identified only by their first names: Marwan and Lucebert.

BOOKSHOPS

This literate and culture-conscious city boasts lots of bookshops catering to a multilingual clientele. For English and American literature and recent periodicals, go to the **British Bookshop,** Mauerstrasse 83–84 (☎ **030/2-38-46-80;** U-Bahn: Stadtmitte). An outfit richly stocked with works from German publishing houses is **Literaturhaus Berlin,** Fasanenstrasse 23 (☎ **030/8-82-50-42;** U-Bahn: Uhlandstrasse). The leading gay bookstore of Berlin, containing both erotica and upscale literature in several different languages, is **Prince Eisenherz,** Bleibtreustrasse 52 (☎ **030/3-13-99-36;** S-Bahn: Savignyplatz).

CHINA & PORCELAIN

✪ **KPM.** Kurfürstendamm 27 in the Kempinski Hotel Bristol. ☎ **030/88-67-21-10.** U-Bahn: Kurfürstendamm.

This prestigious emporium was founded in 1763, when Frederick the Great invested his personal funds in a lackluster porcelain factory, elevated it to royal status, and gave it a new name: **Königliche Porzellan-Manufaktur (Royal Porcelain Factory).** It was Prussia's answer to Meissen in Saxony. Since then, the factory has become world famous for its artistry and delicacy. Each exquisite, hand-painted, hand-decorated item is carefully packed in almost-unbreakable formats that can be shipped to virtually anywhere in the world. Patterns are based for the most part on traditional 18th- and 19th-century designs. All objects carry a distinctive official signature, an imperial orb, and the letters KPM. There's also an array of high-quality trinkets for visitors.

You can also visit the **factory** itself at Wegelystrasse 1 (☎ **030/39-00-90;** U-Bahn: Tiergarten). Guided tours let you look at the craftsmanship of the employees, and you can also buy pieces here. Tours are provided once a day from Monday to Thursday at 10am. The charge is 5DM ($2.50), which is applied to any purchase. Children under 16 are prohibited, as are video cameras and photography.

Meissener Porzellan. Kurfürstendamm 26A. ☎ **030/88-68-35-30.** U-Bahn: Kurfürstendamm.

This is one of the most famous porcelain outlets in Europe. It offers the finest array of exquisite Meissen dinner plates in Berlin, and also displays and sells sculptures and chandeliers. For a Meissen factory tour, see chapter 4.

Rosenthal. Kurfürstendamm 226. ☎ **030/8-85-63-40.** U-Bahn: Kurfürstendamm.

Head here for contemporary Rosenthal designs from Bavaria. In addition to Rosenthal porcelain, you'll find Boda glassware, along with elegantly modern tableware.

DEPARTMENT STORES

Kaufhaus des Westens (KaDeWe). Tauentzienstrasse 21. ☎ **030/2-12-10.** U-Bahn: Kurfürstendamm or Wittenbergplatz.

This huge luxury department store, known popularly as KaDeWe (pronounced kah-day-vay), was established some 90 years ago. It's best known for its sixth-floor food department, where more than 1,000 varieties of German sausages are displayed along with delicacies from all over the world. Sit-down counters are available. After fortifying yourself here, you can explore the six floors of merchandise. KaDeWe is more than a department store—one shopper called it a "collection of first-class specialty shops."

Wertheim. Kurfürstendamm 231. ☎ **030/88-00-30.** U-Bahn: Kurfürstendamm

This centrally located store is good for travel aids and general basics. It sells perfumes, clothing for the entire family, jewelry, electrical devices, household goods, photography supplies, and souvenirs. It also has a shoe-repair section. Shoppers can fuel up at a large restaurant with a grand view over half the city.

FASHION

Anette Peterman. Bleibtreustrasse 40. ☎ **030/323-2556.** S-Bahn: Savignyplatz.

This shop is noteworthy because of its limited number of carefully chosen dresses, each of which is displayed, and priced, like an art object in its own right. Sheer, shimmering, and undeniably sexy, they're the kind of design that might be worn to dinner at a posh schlosshotel in the country, or to the reading of a will where vast amounts of money are expected to be diverted your way.

Bleibgrün. Bleibtreustrasse 30. ☎ **030/885-0080.** S-Bahn: Savignyplatz.

It's small, its fashionable, and it's sought after by well-dressed and well-heeled women from Berlin and its suburbs. And best of all, the staff is charming and helpful. Come here for access to things that are terribly chic and contemporary, including dresses by Jean-Paul Gaultier, Paul Smith, Marithé François Girbaud, and a handful of other currently fashionable trend-setters.

Bogner-Shop Zenker. Kurfürstendamm 45. ☎ **030/8-81-10-00.** S-Bahn: Savignyplatz.

This three-story shop has sold garments to three generations of clients. Its selection of women's clothing includes everything from formal evening gowns to sportswear. Many of the items are made in Germany, Austria, or Italy.

Chaapeaux Hutmode Berlin. Bleibtreustrasse 51. ☎ **030/312-09-13.** S-Bahn: Savignyplatz.

There are only about ten hatmakers left in Berlin today, and of those ten, only two or three have earned the respect and patronage of the city's couture crowd. This is the most appealing of the lot, and also the most whimsical. Andrea Curti, owner and designer, draws her inspirations from vintage fashion magazines, old movies, and anything that looked good on Greta Garbo. The result is an artfully arranged inventory

Treasures in the Barn District

At the very heart and soul of Berlin's fashions and art revival is the Scheulenviertel, or "barn district" (S-Bahn: Hackescher Markt). The name comes from a period in the 17th century, when hay barns were built far from the city Center for fear of fires. In time the city's growth overtook the area, and it became Berlin's Jewish quarter. For some reason, many of its oldest buildings survived World War II bombing assaults.

The remains of a grand 1909 shopping arcade—which occupies most of the block formed by Oranienburger, Rosenthaler, Grosse Hamburger Strasse, and Sophienstrasse—have been turned into a series of galleries, studios, and theaters. Worth a visit is **Tacheles,** Oranienburger Strasse 53–56 (☎ **030/282-61-85;** S-Bahn: Hackescher Markt), or "talking turkey" in Yiddish. It's an alternative arts Center. One of the several cutting edge shops in the immediate Hackesche Hofe neighborhood includes **Lisa D.,** Hackescher Hof–Hof 4, Rosenthalerstrasse 40–41 (☎ **030/282-9061;** S-Bahn: Hackescher Markt), a sought after designer whose women's clothing comes in shades other than the black that has been favored in Berlin and New York for so long. Clothing includes a sophisticated mixture of sportswear, office wear, and evening wear, with an of-the-minute emphasis on stripes.

The more prestigious galleries are found along Auguststrasse. **Galerie Wohnmaschine,** Tucholskystrasse 34–36 (☎ **030/3087-20-15**), became the area's first gallery when it opened in 1988. Some of the best artists in the city are on exhibit here, mostly of a conceptual or minimalist bent. One of the most prestigious and respected of these is viewed today as a pioneer that made its way eastward within a few weeks of reunification: **Eigen & Art Gerd Harry Lybke,** Auguststrasse 26. (☎ **030/28-31-002;** U-Bahn: Rosenthaler Platz; S-Bahn: Oranienburger Strasse). They represent a roster of artists that include, among others, Leo Rauch and Carsten Nicolai.

Other shopping highlights include **Tools & Gallery,** Rosenthaler Strasse 34–35 (☎ **030/2859-9343;** U-Bahn: Weinmeisterstrasse), which sells both formal and elegantly casual clothes for both sexes, including exclusive labels such as Givenchy, Balenciaga, and Kenzo. **Johanna Petzoldt,** Sophienstrasse 9 (☎ **030/282-6754;** U-Bahn: Weinmeisterstrasse), sells handcrafts from the old Erzebirg region, including wooden toys and assorted curiosities, such as scenes fitted into a matchbox.

of veiled, feathered, or minimalist hats. Come here with a sense of glamour, a sense of humor, a sense of theatricality, and some open-ended ideas about what makes you look good.

Modenhaus Horn. Kurfürstendamm 213. ☎ **030/8-81-40-55.** U-Bahn: Kurfürstendamm.

Berlin is one of the world's most fashion-conscious cities, and here you'll see examples of what's *au courant* for chic women.

Sonia Rykiel. Kurfürstendamm 186. ☎ **030/8-82-17-74** for women, or **030/882-28-85** for children. U-Bahn: Adenauerplatz.

This stylish showcase is the only shop in Germany devoted exclusively to Ms. Rykiel, the successful French fashion mogul. She designed the store's interior herself. Beware:

even a Sonia Rykiel T-shirt is expensive. There's both a children's shop and a women's shop.

To Die For. Neue Schönhauser Strasse 10. ☎ **030/28-38-68-34.** U-Bahn: Rosenthaler Platz.

Clothing here follows trends so obsessively that you're likely to find inventories configured exclusively in tones of gray, black, and apple green. These examples are guaranteed to change before your visit, but unless you're relatively fit and in good shape, don't expect to find anything suitable. For any man or women who's relatively thin, you might find whatever you need to assimilate yourself into many of Mitte's emerging bars and hangout joints.

Triebel. Schönwalder Strasse 12, Spandau. ☎ **030/3-35-50-01.** U-Bahn: Rathaus Spandau; S-Bahn: Spandau.

This elegant store offers everything you might need for a weekend retreat at a private hunting lodge, such as clothing, shoes, boots, or sporting equipment. If you dream of looking like the lord of a Bavarian manor in a loden coat and feather-trimmed hat, or if you've been invited on a spontaneous fox hunt, come here first. The inventory includes a selection of hunting rifles and shooting equipment.

Werner Scherer. Unter den Linden 77. ☎ **030/22-67-98-93.** S-Bahn: Unter den Linden.

The arrival of this upscale menswear emporium symbolized to some extent the rebirth of the Unter den Linden as a glamorous shopping destination. Set on the street level of the Adlon Hotel, it's the showplace of Munich based designer Werner Scherer, who makes the kind of clothes that millionaires love to buy and, in some cases, touch. Expect access to the best-made shirts we've even seen, silk neckties, and curiosities that include bomber jackets crafted from a mixture of silk and linen, and buttery soft black leather coats. Despite its high prices, the shop does a roaring business with the glam crowd, many of whom wouldn't consider buying their shirts anywhere else.

JEWELRY

Galerie Lalique. Bleibtreustrasse 47. ☎ **030/8-81-97-62.** S-Bahn: Savignyplatz.

One of the more unusual jewelry stores in Berlin, this emporium stocks the original designs of about 50 German-based designers. Most pieces are modern interpretations, using diamonds and other precious stones. Even though the store's name is similar to that of the French glass designer, no crystal or glassware is sold here.

Würzbacher. Kurfürstendamm 36. ☎ **030/8-83-38-92.** S-Bahn: Savignyplatz; U-Bahn: Uhlandstrasse.

Everything this small store sells is crafted on site from either gold or platinum, often with accents of precious or semiprecious stones. Most designs are modern and streamlined. Some pieces are noteworthy for their heft. Most of the jewelry here is for women, although a scattering of rings, tie clips, and cuff links are for men.

KITCHENWARE

WMF. Kurfürstendamm 229. ☎ **030/8-82-39-41.** U-Bahn: Kurfürstendamm.

Its inventory is a restaurant owner's fantasy, with appealing kitchen gadgets that cooks will love. Be warned that most appliances here are incompatible with North American electric current. But if you're interested in glassware (from Nachtmann and Eich), stoneware, kitchen cutlery, and Hummel and Goebel porcelain figurines, you'll find this place fascinating.

MARKETS

Antik & Flohmarkt. Friedrichstrasse S-Bahn station, Berlin-Mitte. ☎ **030/2-08-26-45.** U-Bahn/S-Bahn: Friedrichstrasse.

You might want to check out the finds at this flea market in the S-Bahn station. Some 60 vendors try to tempt buyers with assorted bric-a-brac, including brassware and World War II mementos.

Berliner Trödelmarkt. Strasse des 17 Juni. ☎ **030/26-55-00-96.** S-Bahn: Tiergarten.

This flea market lies near the corner of the Bachstrasse and the Strasse des 17 Juni, at the western edge of the Tiergarten, adjacent to the Tiergarten S-Bahn station. It's the favorite weekend shopping spot of countless Berliners, who come here to find an appropriate piece of nostalgia, a battered semiantique, or used clothing. The market is held every Saturday and Sunday (also Easter Monday) 10am to 5pm.

MILITARY FIGURES

Berliner Zinnfiguren. Knesebeckstrasse 88. ☎ **030/315-700-0.** S-Bahn: Savignyplatz.

A mecca for collectors since 1934, this shop carries an impressive inventory of German-language books on military history and more than 10,000 different pewter figurines of soldiers from many different imperial armies, up to the Franco-Prussian War of 1870. Also included are hand-painted models of Roman and ancient Greek foot soldiers. Flat, hand-painted pewter figures are sold only in sets of 12 or more and cost from 150DM to 200DM ($75 to $100); fully detailed depictions of Prussian soldiers from the 1870s can range as high as 250DM to 300DM ($125 to $150) each, or even 1,800DM ($900) for special pieces.

MUSIC

Musik Riedel. Uhlandstrasse 38. ☎ **030/882-7395.** U-Bahn: Uhlandstrasse.

Most of the professional musicians of Berlin have a working familiarity with the layout of this well-established store, as it's been selling musical instruments and sheet music since 1910. Regardless of how esoteric, you're likely to find the score to whatever it is that interest you—sometimes in used folios that have some historic interest in their own right. There's a second branch of this outfit in the Schauspielhaus, on the Gendarmenmarkt (☎ **030/204-1136;** U-Bahn: Französische Strasse), but most of the old-time clients of this place continue to patronize the branch on Uhlandstrasse.

PERFUME

Harry Lehmann. Kantstrasse 106. ☎ **030/3-24-35-82.** U-Bahn: Uhlandstrasse.

This is the kind of shop where German mothers and grandmothers might have bought their perfume between the two world wars. Don't expect a standardized list of the big names you'd find at a duty-free airport shop. Most scents here are family recipes, distilled from flowers, grasses, and leaves. The reasonable prices might surprise you— 10 grams for as little as 4.5DM ($2.25). Coming here is a cheap and amusing way to experience the scents of a Prussian spring.

PUNK MEMORABILIA

Kaufhaus Schrill. Bleibtreustrasse 46. ☎ **030/882-40-48.** S-Bahn: Savignyplatz.

Few other stores mingle a sense of junkiness and kitsch with such artful abandon. Its stocks would gladden any punk-rocker's heart, especially if he or she were on the lookout for Elvis-era memorabilia, hair barrettes that glow in the dark, and jewelry that might appeal to Courtney Love for her date with a group of bikers. Don't come here expecting anything tasteful—that isn't its style. Partly because of that, and partly because the place evokes a vivid sense of the long-ago rebelliousness of the '60s, the place is something of an icon for disaffected, or counterculture, youth.

SCULPTURE

Gipsformerei der Staatlichen Museen Preussischer Kulturbesitz. Sophie-Charlotte-Strasse 17. ☎ **030/3267690.** S-Bahn: Westend.

This company has duplicated Europe's great sculptures as plaster casts since 1819. Today, there's an inventory of more than 6,500 of them, everything from busts of Queen Nefertiti to a faithful reproduction of the Farnese Bull. Prices begin at 25DM ($14.25). Objects can be crated and shipped around the world.

SHOPPING ARCADES

One of the many surprising aspects of the rebuilt and redesigned Postsdamer Platz is the **Potsdamer Platz Arkaden** (U-Bahn/S-Bahn: Potsdamer Platz), one of the most comprehensive shopping malls in Berlin. In a deliberate rejoinder to more outdated Ku'damm malls, such as the Europa Center, it contains at least 100 shops, with more being added all the time, scattered over three levels. Lots of the stores offer cost-cutting clothing and housewares, but two whose inventories are attractive to foreign short-term visitors include **The Museum Company** (☎ **030/25-29-69-21**), which sells high quality reproductions of the ancient Greek, Roman, and Egyptian sculptures and jewelry sold in Berlin's museums, and **La Bottega de Mamma Ro** (☎ **030/25-29-63-68**), which specializes in Tuscan pottery, linens, table settings, and kitchenware, much of it in bright Mediterranean colors.

9 Berlin After Dark

In Berlin, nightlife runs around the clock, and there's plenty to do at any time. There are at least three magazines that list happenings in the city. The English-language monthly, *Checkpoint Berlin,* is available free at hotel reception desks and tourist offices and sold at news kiosks. The German-language *Berlin Programm* is available at newsstands. The most detailed listings are found in *zitty,* a biweekly publication in German.

Berlin is famous not only for its opera, classical music, and theater, but also for its cabaret and nightclub entertainment. If you'd like to arrange tickets from America for shows and entertainment in Berlin, contact **Global Tickets,** (☎ **800/223-6108** or 212/332-2435; fax 914/328-2752; www.globaltickets.com). This company can mail actual tickets to your home in most cases, or leave tickets at the box office for you. There's a 20% markup (more for opera and ballet) over the box office price, plus a U.S. handling charge of up to $8. Tickets are available for musicals, cabaret, opera, and dance.

THE PERFORMING ARTS

OPERA & CLASSICAL MUSIC

✪ **Berliner Philharmonisches Orchester (Berlin Philharmonic).** Matthäikirchstrasse 1. ☎ **030/261-43-83.** Tickets 30DM–180DM ($15–$90). S-Bahn: Potsdamer Platz.

The Berlin Philharmonic, directed by Claudio Abbado, is one of the world's premier orchestras. Its home is the Philharmonie, noted for its excellent acoustics and unconventional interior design—the orchestra is in the middle of rising tiers of seats, and none of the 2,200 seats is more than 30m (100 feet) from the podium. The box office is open Monday to Friday 3:30 to 6pm, Saturday and Sunday 11am to 2pm. You can't place orders by phone, but if you're staying in a first-class or deluxe hotel, the concierge can usually get seats for you.

✪ Deutsche Oper Berlin. Bismarckstrasse 35. ☎ **030/3-43-84-01.** Tickets 30DM–125DM ($15–$62.50). U-Bahn: Deutsche Oper and Bismarckstrasse.

This opera company performs in Charlottenburg in one of the world's great opera houses, a notable example of modern theater architecture that seats 1,885. The company tackles Puccini favorites, Janácek rarities, or modern works, and has a complete Wagner repertoire. A ballet company performs once a week. Concerts, including Lieder evenings, are also presented on the opera stage.

Deutsche Staatsoper (German State Opera). Unter den Linden 7. ☎ **030/20-35-45-55.** Tickets, opera 15DM–300DM ($7.50–$150); concerts 15DM–65DM ($7.50-$32.50). U-Bahn: Französische Strasse; S-Bahn: Friedrichstrasse.

The German State Opera performs in the Staatsoper Unter den Linden. This was for years the showcase of the opera scene of East Germany. Originally constructed in 1743 and destroyed in World War II, the house was rebuilt in the 1950s, reproducing as closely as possible the original designs of Georg Knobelsdorff. Some of the world's finest opera as well as concerts and ballet are presented here. The box office is open Monday to Friday 10am to 6pm, Saturday and Sunday noon to 6pm. The opera closes from mid-June to late August.

Komische Oper Berlin. Behrensstrasse 55–57. ☎ **030/47-02-1010.** Tickets 16DM–160DM ($8–$80). U-Bahn: Französische Strasse; S-Bahn: Friedrichstrasse or Unter den Linden.

The Komische Oper has become one of the most highly regarded theater ensembles in Europe, presenting many avant-garde opera productions as well as ballet and musical theater. The box office is open Monday to Saturday 11am to 7pm and Sunday 1pm to 1¹/₂ hours before performance.

Konzerthaus Berlin. In the Schauspielhaus, Gendarmenmarkt. ☎ **030/203-09-21-01.** Tickets 15DM–135DM ($7.50–$67.50). U-Bahn: Französische Strasse.

This 1821 building was created by Friedrich Schinkel. It offers two venues for classical concerts, the Grosser Konzertsaal for orchestra and the Kammermusiksaal for chamber music. Its organ recitals are considered the finest in Germany. Performances are often daring and innovative. The Deutsches Sinfonie-Orchester is also based here.

THEATER

Berlin has long been known for its theater. Even if you don't understand German, you may enjoy seeing a production of a familiar play, or attending a musical.

Perhaps the most famous theater is the **Berliner Ensemble,** Am Bertolt-Brecht-Platz 1 (☎ **030/282-31-60;** U-Bahn/S-Bahn: Friedrichstrasse), founded by the late playwright Bertolt Brecht. His wife, Helene Weigel, played an important role in the theater's founding and was the ensemble's longtime director. Works by Brecht and other playwrights are presented here. Seats are reasonably priced.

The most important German-language theater in the country is **Schaubühne am Lehniner Platz,** Kurfürstendamm 153 (☎ **030/89-00-23;** U-Bahn: Adenauerplatz), at the east end of the Ku'damm, near Lehniner Platz. There are three different stages here.

Finally, **Theater des Westens,** located between the Berlin Zoo and the Ku'damm at Kantstrasse 12 (☎ **030/31-90-30;** U-Bahn/S-Bahn: Zoologischer Garten), specializes in plays, musical comedies, and the German equivalent of Broadway extravaganzas. The theater was built in 1896. Performances are held Tuesday to Saturday at 8pm and Sunday at 6pm. Ticket prices range from 32DM to 118DM ($16 to $59).

THE CLUB & MUSIC SCENE
CABARET

Very popular among visitors to Berlin is the kind of nightspot depicted in the musical *Cabaret*, with floor-show patter and acts that make fun of the political and social scene.

Die Stachelschweine. Tauentzienstrasse and Budapester Strasse (in the basement of Europa Center). ☎ **030/2-61-47-95.** Cover 25DM–45DM ($12.50–$22.50). U-Bahn: Kurfürstendamm.

Since the beginning of the Cold War, the "Porcupine" has poked prickly fun at the German and American political scenes. The performance is delivered in rapid-fire German and evokes the legendary Berliner sense of satire, which can often be scathing in its humor. Although you need to understand German to really appreciate what goes on here, you'll still recognize some of the names (George W., Al Gore, and Hillary), and there's likely to be a deliberately corny selection of popular ditties ("Life is a cabaret, old chum") thrown in. Shows take place Tuesday to Friday at 7:30pm and Saturday at 6pm and 9:15pm. The box office is open Tuesday to Friday 10am to 2pm and 3 to 7:30pm and Saturday 2 to 6:30pm. It's closed in July.

Wintergarten. Potsdamer Strasse 96. ☎ **030/23-08-82-30.** Cover Fri–Sat 74DM–98DM ($37–$49), Sun–Thurs 35DM–80DM ($17.50–$40) per person, depending on the seat. U-Bahn: Kurfürstenstrasse.

The largest and most nostalgic Berlin cabaret, the Wintergarten offers a variety show every night, with magicians, clowns, jugglers, acrobats, and live music. The most expensive seats are on stage level, where tiny tables are available for simple suppers costing from 25DM to 45DM ($12.50 to $22.50). Balconies have conventional theater seats, but staff members pass frequently along the aisles selling drinks. Shows last around 2¼ hours each and begin Monday to Friday at 8pm, Sunday at 6pm, and Saturday at 6 and 10pm.

DANCE CLUBS

Big Eden. Kurfürstendamm 202. ☎ **030/8-82-61-20.** Cover 12DM–15DM ($6–$7.50) Fri–Sat (includes 1 drink). Sun–Thurs 9pm–5am, Fri–Sat 9pm–6am. U-Bahn: Uhlandstrasse.

Everyone from Paul McCartney to Sylvester Stallone has danced here. This club accommodates some 1,000 dancers nightly on its huge dance floor. Top DJs play the latest international hits. The light effects and superstereo are impressive. There's a nightly happy hour.

Café Keese. Bismarckstrasse 108. ☎ **030/3-12-91-11.** No cover, but a drink minimum of 10DM ($5) Fri and Sun, 14DM ($7) Sat. U-Bahn: Ernst-Reuther-Platz.

This dance club caters to a more traditional clientele. Here women can ask the men to dance, and the management even reserves the right to kick out any male patron who turns down a request. The orchestra plays a lot of slow music and the place is often jammed, especially on Saturday night. The Keese sees itself as something of a matrimonial bureau, and is always announcing statistics about the number of people who met on its premises and got married. Formal attire is requested. Open Tuesday to Thursday 8pm to 3am, Friday and Saturday 8pm to 4am, Sunday and Monday 4pm to 1am.

Chip. In the Berlin Hilton, Mohrenstrasse 30. ☎ **030/2-02-30.** Cover 10DM ($5) U-Bahn: Stadtmitte.

Chip is an unusual and appealingly glossy dance club. It features a high-tech battery of accessories—laserlike lights, video clips, and a fog machine that adds a surreal mist to the crowded dance floor. Open Wednesday to Saturday 9pm to 4am.

Life Is a Cabaret in Berlin

Cabaret life in between-the-wars Berlin was a legend that inspired writers that included Christopher Isherwood, among many others. These emporiums of *schmaltz* have been reborn in the former East Berlin—though the satire might be a bit less biting than it was during the Weimar Republic. Today's cabaret shows might remind you of Broadway blockbusters, without much of the intimacy of the smoky and trenchant cellar revues of the 1930s. But for access to talent that includes multilingual comedians and singers, jugglers, acrobats, musicians, plenty of coyly expressed sexuality, and lots of costume changes, consider an evening at the **Friedrichstadt-Palast,** Friedrichstrasse 107 (☎ **030/ 23-26-23-26;** U-Bahn/S-Bahn: Friedrichstrasse). Although showtimes might vary with whatever revue is featured at the time of your visit, they tend to begin Tuesday to Saturday at 8pm, with additional performances every Saturday and Sunday at 4pm. The most visible and well-publicized competitor is **Winter Garten Variété,** Potsdamer Strasse 96 (☎ **030/230-88-230;** U-Bahn/S-Bahn: Potsdamer Platz)). Shows, which are less high-tech than at the richly computer-ized Friedrichstadt-Palast, are usually presented Monday to Friday at 8pm, Saturday at 6 and 10pm, and Sunday at 6pm. Ticket prices are roughly equivalent at both venues, costing 69DM to 95DM ($34.50 to $47.50), depending on the performance and the seat.

Clärchen's Ballhaus. Auguststrasse 24–25. ☎ **030/2-82-92-95.** Cover 8DM ($4). U-Bahn: Rosenthaler Platz; S-Bahn: Oranienburger Strasse.

This place has been around since 1913, and it's schmaltzy enough to remind sentimental newcomers of the nostalgic old days. A renewed interest in ballroom danc-ing has kept it going. Live music from a dance band is the norm, with recorded music to fill in when the band takes a break. On Wednesday, women are encouraged to ask men to the dance floor. Open Tuesday, Wednesday, Friday, and Saturday 8:30pm to around 3am.

Far Out. Kurfürstendamm 156. ☎ **030/320-00-717.** Cover 8DM–12DM ($4–$6). U-Bahn: Adenauerplatz.

Large and artfully drab, this industrial-looking disco plays danceable rock from the '70s to the '90s for hundreds of high-energy dancers. You'll see lots of students and artists, many dressed up in artfully bizarre clothing. The place only really comes alive after midnight. Open Tuesday to Sunday 10am to between 4 and 6am, depending on the crowd.

Metropole. Nollendorfplatz 5, Schöneberg. ☎ **030/21-73-680.** Cover 20DM–25DM ($10–$12.50). U-Bahn: Nollendorfplatz.

On the outside, this club—originally built as a theatre around 1906—boasts one of the great proto–art deco facades of Berlin. Inside, you'll find a replica of a temple that might have been excavated in ancient Egypt, but with accessories that might have been designed for an early Hollywood stage set by Busby Berkeley. Most of the patrons are in their 20s, dancing the night away every Friday and Saturday 9:30pm till dawn. Don't confuse this place with the Kit Kat Club, an independent, more notorious venue which occupies the building's cellar (see "Gay & Lesbian Berlin," below).

The Love Parade

The **Love Parade** is the techno bash to end all bashes. On the second weekend of July, around 600,000 (mostly) young people converge in the Center of Berlin for 48 decidedly hedonistic hours. What began in 1988 as a DJ's birthday party with about 150 friends has grown into an immense corporate event that wreaks havoc on the rest of the city's usually impeccable organization (particularly the public transportation system).

The Center of Berlin becomes awash with litter and good-natured debauchery. Because of the frenzied jiggling, gyrating, and very noisy good times, anyone wanting an even remotely peaceful weekend should follow the little old ladies and rock fans on the fast train out of town. The event starts off on Saturday afternoon, when a booming caravan of floats carries the best DJs in Europe from Ernst-Reuter-Platz to the Brandenburg Gate. If you want to see the procession, come early and grab as high a view as possible.

Everything imaginable is imbibed in high quantities, and every year serious worries are voiced over the deluge of urine in the Tiergarten, site of the evening celebrations. The entire city, in fact, transforms itself into a huge party. The BVG (public transport system) offers a 10DM ($5) "no limit" ticket to speed you from one rave to another. Traveling revelers should note that club prices skyrocket during the weekend.

Lots of fuss and bother or a really good time? It all depends on your point of view. This is a must for anybody with a love of synthesizers and a lot of steam to let off. The Love Parade has become an international fixture to rival Mardi Gras around the world.

SO36. Oranienstrasse 190, Kreuzberg. ☎ **030/61-40-13-06.** Cover 10DM ($5). U-Bahn: Prinzenstrasse.

The lines begin to form here about 30 minutes before the place even opens, but they move quickly as Berliner hipsters get into the spirit of one of the city's more witty and unconventional clubs. Its name derives from the postal code SO36 that applied to this district before World War II. Inside, two very large rooms, a stage, an ongoing rush of danceable music, and a scene that combines a senior prom in the high school gym with some of the more bizarre aspects of Berlin after Dark. Lots of women come here, both gay and straight, and a higher percentage of heterosexual men than you might have expected along this strip of bars in Kreuzberg. If you're lucky enough to be in town for the once-per-month Turkish drag night, you'll find one of the most amusing transvestite shows in Berlin, where Fatima the belly dancer is likely to be male, beguiling, and well versed in the satirical aspects of life in a Turkish harem. The club in open most nights, based on an evolving schedule, 10:30 to at least 4am.

Tresor. Leipzigerstrasse 8.I. ☎ **030/2-29-06-11.** Cover 5DM-25DM ($2.50-$12.50) Wed, 25DM ($12.50) Fri–Sun. U-Bahn: Mohrenstrasse.

One of Berlin's best techno venues, this club really packs them in. The building was once part of Globus Bank; downstairs there's a bunkerlike atmosphere, with prison-type metal bars and harsh acoustics. The spacious dance floor upstairs has lighter house sounds. There's a bar in the back. In summer, tables are placed outside, and food is served. The club is open from 10pm Wednesday and from 11pm Friday to Sunday. It's closed on other nights.

LIVE MUSIC

A Trane. Bleibtreustrasse 1. ☎ **030/3-13-25-50.** Cover 15DM–20DM ($7.50–$10). Music begins around 10pm. S-Bahn: Savignyplatz.

This small and smoky jazz house is an excellent choice for either beginning or ending an evening of bar-hopping in the neighborhood. It features musicians from all over the world. It's open Monday to Thursday 8pm to 4am, Friday and Saturday 9pm to 4am.

Knaack-Klub. Greifwalderstrasse 224. ☎ **030/4-42-70-60.** Cover 10DM–15DM ($5–$7.50). S-Bahn: Alexanderplatz.

This four-story club features a live-music venue, two floors of dancing, and a games floor. There are usually four live rock shows a week, with a fairly even split between German and international touring bands. Show days vary. There's dancing on Wednesday, Friday, and Saturday nights. Hours are Monday to Friday 10pm to 4am, Saturday and Sunday 10pm to 7am.

Oxymoron. In the courtyard of the complex at Rosenthaler Strasse 40–41. ☎ **030/ 283-91-88-6.** Cover 14DM–20DM ($7–$10) S-Bahn: Hackescher Markt.

This is a good example of Berlin's newest crop of hyper-trendy, high-visibility hang-outs where the food is served almost as an afterthought to an exhibitionistic/voyeuristic scene that can be a lot of fun and in some cases, intriguing. The setting is a high ceilinged room with old-fashioned proportions and enough battered kitsch to remind you of a turn-of-the-century coffeehouse in Franz-Josef's Vienna. Local wits refer to it as a *gesamtkunstwerk*—a self-obsessed, self-sustaining work of art that might have been appreciated by Wagner. Most nights after around 11pm, a slightly claustrophobic, much-used annex room—all black with ghostly flares of neon—opens for business as a disco, usually with a clientele that's about 75% hetero and 100% iconoclastic. If live bands appear at all, it will usually be on a Thursday. Open daily 11am to midnight.

Quasimodo. Kantstrasse 12A. ☎ **030/3-12-80-86.** Cover 20DM ($10). U-Bahn: Zoologischer Garten.

This is the top Berlin jazz club. Although many different styles of music are offered here, including rock and Latin, jazz is the focus. Local acts are featured on Tuesday and Wednesday, when admission is free. Summer visitors should check out the "Jazz in July" festival. The club is open Tuesday to Saturday 9pm to 2am, with shows beginning at 10pm.

Wild at Heart. Wienerstrasse 20. ☎ **030/6-11-70-10.** Cover 7DM ($4) for concerts only. U-Bahn: Görlitzer Bahnhof.

This club, with its kitschy knickknacks, colored lights, and wine-red walls, is dedicated to the rowdier side of rock. Hard-core punk, rock, and rockabilly bands from Germany and elsewhere are featured. Live performances take place Wednesday to Saturday nights. It's open Monday to Friday 8pm to 4am, Saturday and Sunday 8pm to 10am (yes, you may miss breakfast).

DRAG SHOWS

Chez Nous. Marburgerstrasse 14. ☎ **030/2-13-18-10.** Cover 60DM ($30), which includes first drink. U-Bahn: Wittenbergplatz.

The famous show at Chez Nous is played to an essentially straight crowd in a mock Louis XIV setting. Some of the world's best transvestite acts appear here, from a sultry, boa-draped star from Rio de Janeiro to a drag queen who looks like a gun moll from the 1940s. Shows are nightly at 8:30 and 11pm.

La Vie en Rose. Europa Center. ☎ **030/3-23-60-06.** Cover 35DM–60DM ($17.50–$30). U-Bahn: Zoologischer Garten.

This club offers a highly polished, Vegas-style revue to a straight clientele, often businessmen. This is where "Barbra," "Dolly," and "Judy" are likely to appear. The box office is open daily 10am to midnight. Shows start at 9pm Sunday to Thursday and at 10pm on Friday and Saturday.

GAY & LESBIAN BERLIN

Traditionally, lesbian and gay life centered around the **Nollendorfplatz** (U-Bahn: Nollendorfplatz), the so-called "Pink Village." There is a history of homosexuality here at the **Schwules Museum,** Mehringdamm 61 (☎ 030/693-11-72), open Wednesday to Sunday from 2 to 6pm. Admission is 7DM ($3.50) adults, 4DM ($2) students. The **State-Supported Spinnboden-Lesbenarchiv,** Anklamerstrasse 38 (☎ 030/448-58-48), caters to all sorts of lesbian cultural events. **Man-o-Meter,** Motzstrasse 5 (off Nollendorfplatz) (☎ 030/216-80-08), is a gay information Center.

Today, Motzstrasse is the location of many gay and lesbian bars. A trio of popular gay bars, **Tom's,** the **Prinz-Knecht,** and the **Knast Bar,** are sometimes referred to as "the Bermuda Triangle."

In the latter half of June, the **Lesbisch-schwules Stadtfest** (Lesbian Street Fair) takes place at Nollendorfplatz. This is topped in size, though not in exuberance, the last week in June by the **Christopher Street Day** parade, when 200,000 people congregate to have fun and drop inhibitions.

Begine Café-und-Kulturzentrum für Frauen. Potsdamerstrasse 139. ☎ **030/ 215-43-25.** No cover. Mon–Sat 5pm–1am, Sun noon–midnight. U-Bahn: Bulowstrasse.

This is a Center for feminists and one of Berlin's best places for women to meet other women. It has a changing array of art exhibitions, and features poetry readings, German-language discussions, lectures, and other social events. Call in advance for the schedule. The premises are occasionally transformed into a disco.

Connection Disco. Fuggerstrasse 31–33. ☎ **030/218-1432.** Cover 12DM ($6). Fri–Sat 11pm–4am. U-Bahn: Wittenbergplatz.

Other discos occasionally challenge its entrenched grip on gay nightlife in Berlin, but somehow Connections continues to endure as an after-dark staple. It's very large, with two floors and a network of independently operated shops and specialty bars. Come here to dance to techno and trance music, but know in advance that this place is proud of the darkened labyrinth of cellar rooms it maintains for trysts—management cites them as the largest network of back rooms in Berlin.

Kit Kat Klub. in the basement of the Metropole, Nollendorfplatz 5, Schöneberg. ☎ **030/ 21-73-680.** Cover 20DM–25DM ($10–$12.50). U-Bahn: Nollendorfplatz.

In Liza Minnelli's cinema version of *Cabaret,* Sally Bowles was an entertainer at the Kit Kat Club. Today's incarnation of that fictional club presents far more than dominatrix-style singers with hearts of gold. You'll check most of your clothes at the door (retain your shoes), and enter a ultra-permissive lounge, bar, and disco where Mr. or Ms. Right will probably show you all their charms on the first date. Tuesday, Wednesday, Friday, and Saturday, are the venue for heterosexuals; Thursday and Sunday are all-gay and all-male. On those nights, clients must enter between 9 and 11pm, after which the doors are locked to newcomers and the partying continues till much later.

Hafen Bar. Motzstrasse 19. ☎ **030/214-11-18.** U-Bahn: Viktoria-Luise-Platz.

One of the most consistently popular, and most consistently attitude-free, of the gay bars in the Bermuda Triangle is Hafen, whose aura has been compared to a very hip, and relatively permissive kneipe. Locals praise it for a "high flirtation" quotient, foreign journalists find the dialogues amusing and spontaneous, and overall, it provides a good introduction to Gay Berlin before toddling off to more controversial, and raunchier, bars nearby. It's open daily 8pm to 5am.

Knast Ba. Fuggerstrasse 34. ☎ **030/2-18-10-26.** Daily 9pm–dawn. U-Bahn: Wittenbergplatz.

Dark and amiably battered, this is one of the two or three bars in Berlin most frequently cited for a macho-looking crowd that appreciates the allure of leather, rubber, and anything that even begins to resemble a uniform.

Kumpelnest 3000. Lützowstrasse 23. ☎ **030/2-61-69-18.** U-Bahn: Kurfürstenstrasse.

Gay or straight, you're welcome here. All that's asked is that you enjoy a kinky good time in what used to be a brothel. This crowded and chaotic place is really a bar now, but there's also dancing to disco classics. Berliners often show up here for early morning fun after they've exhausted the action at the other hot spots. Open daily 5pm to 5am, even later on weekends.

Lenz die Bar. Eisenacherstrasse 3. ☎ **030/217-7820.** U-Bahn: Viktoria-Luise-Platz.

It's convivial, it attracts lots of neighborhood acquaintances, and at its best it can be a lot of fun. Caipirinas are one of the enduringly popular drinks. Priced at 12DM ($6) each, they bring a bit of Brazilian samba to foggy Berlin on a cold dark night. It's open nightly 7pm to 4am.

Prinzknecht. Fuggerstrasse 33. ☎ **030/23-62-74-44.** U-Bahn: Viktoria-Luise-Platz.

It's large, brick-lined, and mobbed with ordinary guys who just happen to be gay, and who just happen to be involved in computers, media, the building trades, and show business. The combination can be unpretentious and a lot of fun, especially when frothy pink Hemingways are bought by friends for friends, and when the stories start getting raunchy. If you want a place that manages to be both high class and earthy, within walking distance of lots of other gay options, this might be appropriate. It's open daily 3pm to 3am.

Schwuz. Mehringdamm 61, Berlin-Kreuzberg. ☎ **030/693-7590.** Cover 10DM ($5) U-Bahn: Mehringdamm.

If you hadn't been warned in advance, you might not even know that this was a nightclub, hidden as it is behind the conventional-looking facade of the Café Sundström. You'll descend into a battered-looking warren of basement rooms, outfitted in a surreal combination of glossy stainless steel that alternates with structural beams and cinderblock. The mostly gay, mostly male, and mostly under 35-year-old crowd comes here to dance the night away, every day 11pm till dawn or around 4am, whichever comes first. There are two separate dance floors, one with cutting edge, the other with more traditional dance music.

Tom's Bar. Motzstrasse 19. ☎ **030/2-13-45-70.** Daily 10pm–6am. U-Bahn: Nollendorfplatz.

Tom's becomes crowded after 11pm with young gay men. Most of the clients show up here in rugged-looking T-shirts, flannel, jeans, and/or black leather. Upstairs, the porno action is merely on the screen; downstairs it's real. Monday nights feature two-for-one drinks. There's a cover charge for special occasions only.

THE BAR & CAFE SCENE
BEER GARDENS & WINE CELLARS

Historischer Weinkeller. Alt-Pichelsdorf 32 (about a mile west of the Olympia-Stadion). ☎ **030/3-61-80-56.** Reservations required. U-Bahn: Olympia-Stadion.

This squat and unpretentious inn might be the site of one of your more interesting evenings in Berlin. The setting is a highly atmospheric vaulted cellar. In winter the staff performs the medieval ceremony of "burning the punch," during which a sugar cone is lighted in your punch. As it burns, you're supposed to make a wish. The ritual takes place three times a week on Wednesday, Friday, and Saturday between 11 and midnight. The punch, a kind of hot spiced wine, costs 12DM ($6) per glass. You can also order beer or one of more than 100 German wines, as well as full meals that cost 26DM to 42DM ($13 to $21). (If you plan to dine, make reservations in advance.) During summer months, an outdoor rustic beer garden is open. Open daily noon to midnight.

Joe's Beer Haus. Hardenbergstrasse 29 (opposite the Kaiser Wilhelm Memorial Church). ☎ **030/2-62-10-20.** U-Bahn: Zoologischer Garten.

This cozy pub in the city Center is attractively decorated with traditional Teutonic accessories. Even in winter, when you're snug and warm inside, you get the feeling you're sitting out under the chestnut trees. The kitchen offers good plain German food, including Bavarian specialties, and some Italian dishes. Open Monday to Saturday 11am to 4am and Sunday 11am to 1am; the best time to come here is 7pm to midnight.

Loretta Im Garten (Pupasch). Lietzenburgerstrasse 89. ☎ **030/8-82-33-54.** U-Bahn: Uhlandstrasse.

This surprisingly rustic indoor/outdoor beer garden is large, sometimes rowdy, and very German. It's outfitted with durable wooden banquettes, battered accessories, a large outdoor area, and a children's play area with its own Ferris wheel. Menu items include platters of sausage with sauerkraut and potatoes, spareribs, and stuffed baked potatoes. There's no live music; this a place for talk, gossip, and beer drinking. Many locals also come here for lunch. Open only April to early October, daily 11am to 3am.

THE BEST BARS

Bar am Lützowplatz. Lützowplatz 7. ☎ **030/26-26-807.** U-Bahn: Nollendorferplatz.

Many hip locals cite this as their favorite bar, partly because it manages to be beautiful, chic, breezy, and artsy, and partly because it provides a concentrated kind of conviviality within a neighborhood that otherwise is prosperous but just a bit staid. Known as one the longest and narrowest bars in Berlin, it presents a flattering and almost reverential portrait of Mao-Tse-Tung as its visual focal point, the humor of which cannot be lost on the devoted capitalists and *bons vivants* who come here to see, be seen, and flirt. It's open daily 5pm till 4am.

Greenwich Bar—aka Cookie's. Gipsstrasse 5. No phone. U-Bahn: Weinmeisterstrasse.

Its decor evokes the body of the Michelin Guide's animated tire, because of the foam-padded bands of florescent green Naugahyde that surround the room. That, along with built-in rows of bubbling aquariums and the refusal of management to post a sign identifying the location of this very in spot, create an iconoclastic setting where about 30% of the clients are openly gay and the remainder mysteriously undefined. It's open daily 6pm to 6am, serving stiff, party-colored drinks and martinis priced at from 10DM ($5) each. Recorded music plays, usually focusing on soul, drum and bass, and house music.

Harry's New York Bar. In the Grand Hotel Esplanade, Lützowufer 15. ☎ **030/25-47-88-21.** U-Bahn: Nollendorfplatz, Wittenbergplatz, or Kurfürstenstrasse.

Harry's is an aggressively stylized bar with minimalist decor, pop art, and photographs of all the American presidents. It's modeled after the famous watering hole, Harry's New York Bar, in Paris. Its drink menu is a monument to the oral traditions of the IBF (International Bar Flies) Society, and includes such favorites as "Mizner's Dream" (created in 1962 for the Boca Raton Hotel Club in Florida) and the 1964 classic, "The Petrifier" (ingredients unlisted), for two. The menu lists almost 200 drinks, as well as a limited selection of food. Open daily noon to 2am.

Kurvenstar. 1 Grossepraesidentumstrasse. ☎ **030/28-59-97-10.** U-Bahn: Hackescher Markt.

One of the most quirky and famous offbeat bars in Hackescher Höfe celebrates an artfully tacky decor that elevates the worst of the decorative and plasticized excesses of the 1970s into an art form of the highest degree of kitsch. Come here for ideas on how to recycle everything you might have stashed within your attic. Also visit for a drink, priced at around 12DM ($6), a dialogue, perhaps a snack, but not a full meal.

Newton Bar. Gendarmenmarkt. ☎ **030/20-61-29-99.** U-Bahn: Stadtmitte.

There have been more reviews about Berlin's Newton Bar than virtually any other watering hole in town. You might be rejected at the door by a bouncer who disapproves of your sense of style. Here's what you'll get if you're admitted: a high-ceilinged, well-proportioned room that evokes 1960s modernism at its best, and a deeply engrained sense of the well-heeled and socially conscious *bourgeoisie* looking for like-minded people. It's condemned for its sense of *chicki-miki* (self-conscious chic) by clients of counterculture bars in less expensive neighborhoods. But regardless of how you feel, you can't help but be intrigued by a huge black-and-white mural that sweeps an entire runway of naked fashion models across your field of vision, and service rituals inspired by Old Prussia. Love it or hate it, it's hard to ignore the Newton Bar. It's open daily 5pm till at least 2am.

Lore.Berlin. Neue Schönhauser Strasse 20. ☎ **030/28-04-51-34.** U-Bahn: Rosenthaler Platz.

This is the bar most often cited by hipsters as a watering hole that combines cutting-edge design, fabulous dance music, and a stimulating mix of clients from all branches of Berlin society. The setting is a long and narrow, eerily backlit bar area where theatrical lighting makes almost everyone look attractive. Most clients remain at the bar, talking, flirting, and gossiping about the new Berlin, except for the high energy danceaholics. These migrate to a blackened semi-cellar, where the hulking remains of what was originally built in the 19th century as a coal-fired heating station add visual interest and an oblique reference to kink. Even the washrooms and washbasins here are worth a comment, designed like poured-concrete reinterpretations of ancient Roman aqueducts.

Roses. Oranienstrasse 187. Kreuzberg. No phone. U-Bahn: Prinzenstrasse.

It might have been known 30 years ago as a storefront selling food supplies to the neighborhood's *hausfrauen,* but it's very different from that today. You'll find a claustrophobic pair of rooms whose level of kitsch has been elevated to an art form, flickering candles, lavish graffiti, a Jamaican gastarbeiter selling cookies reputed to have been baked with hashish, and gay and straight clients who seem very, very hip to whatever is happening in Berlin's *nacht-szene.* It's open nightly 6pm till at least 4am.

Times Bar. In the Savoy Hotel, Fasanenstrasse 9–10. ☎ **030/31-10-30.** U-Bahn: Zoologischer Garten.

The cozy and intimate Times Bar has a quiet charm reminiscent of a wood-paneled private library in someone's home. The bar is dedicated to the *Times* (of London), whose latest edition is often displayed in the window. Guests sit in leather-upholstered chairs and read English-language newspapers. Menu items range from lobster soup to ice cream. Open daily 11am to 3am.

FINDING A *KNEIPE*

A *Kneipe* is a cozy rendezvous place, the equivalent of a Londoner's local pub. The typical Berliner has a favorite Kneipe for relaxing after work and visiting with sympathetic friends. There are hundreds in Berlin. Here's a handful to get you started.

Gaststätte Hoeck (Wilhelm Hoeck). Wilmersdorferstrasse 149. ☎ **030/3-41-81-74.** U-Bahn: Bismarckstrasse.

The oldest Kneipe in Charlottenburg (1892) still sports original wood panels with inlaid glass on the walls. It also has a brightly illuminated facade jammed with local beer slogans. You (and half of the neighborhood) can have a drink in the very rowdy, sometimes raucous bar area, where (among other oddities) a clown may be playing the harmonica. The separate dining room serves traditional food. More than a dozen kinds of beer are offered (if in doubt, just ask for our favorite, Pilsner Urquell), as well as wine by the glass. Main courses cost 10DM to 20DM ($5 to $10); hot food is served Monday to Saturday 11am to 11pm. Regular hours, however, are 8am to midnight.

Lutter und Wegner 1811. Schlüstrasse 55. ☎ **030/8-81-34-40.** S-Bahn: Savignyplatz.

This place was named after a gastronomic and social landmark, Lutter und Wegner, a hangout for actors in the 19th century. You can have a drink in the stand-up bar, or make reservations in advance to dine. Try the local specialty, Königsberger Klopse, with potatoes and a fresh salad. The wide selection of drinks ranges from single-malt Scottish whiskies to Italian grappas. Main courses range from 29DM to 39DM ($14.50 to $19.50). The restaurant is open daily 6pm to midnight; the bar is open daily 6pm to 1:30am or even later, depending on business. In summer, you can sit on a terrace and observe the passing parade.

CAFE LIFE

At its mid-19th-century zenith, Berlin was famous for its cafes. Max Krell, an editor, once wrote: "Cafes were our homeland. They were the stock exchange of ideas, site of intellectual transactions, futures' market of poetic and artistic glory and defeat." They've changed with the times, but cafes are still going strong in Berlin—particularly, these days, in what used to be East Berlin. In the heart of the old East German capital is a complex of about 100 bars, shops, and restaurants, called *Die Hackenschen Höfe* (S-Bahn: Hackescher Markt). This stylish mini-mall attracts hip counter-culture denizens who wander between galleries, boutiques, and fashionable cafes. It has become one of the most prominent places in the city to go drinking.

Café Adlon. Kurfürstendamm 69. ☎ **030/8-83-76-82.** U-Bahn: Adenauerplatz.

At the turn of the century, Café Adlon's imposing neoclassical decor, overstuffed sofas, and formal waiters made it one of the most prestigious spots in the neighborhood. The clientele is a bit less formal today, and the whole place is somewhat tattered around the edges, but the cafe still offers charming summertime vistas from its sidewalk tables.

Inside, there's a collection of Berlin kitsch. Open Sunday to Thursday 8am to 11pm and Friday and Saturday 8am to midnight.

Cafe Aedes. Rosenthaler Strasse 40–41. ☎ **030/285-82-75.** U-Bahn: Weinmeisterstrasse.

Tucked away within what were once small 19th-century factories, this is a trendy and convivial cafe with a counterculture clientele that's very very hip to the changing face of Berlin and its cultural scene. The decor includes lots of shimmering glass and free-form concrete, and the clientele includes a mixed collection of merchants, artists, performers, writers, and business persons. Whisky with soda costs 11DM ($5.50), platters of simple food range from 9.50DM to 17DM ($4.75 to $8.50). Beef consomme, salmon steaks with mango sauce, pasta with tuna and fresh tomatoes, and all vegetarian salads are what its all about—that and ongoing dialogues. Open daily 10am to midnight.

Café/Bistro Leysieffer. Kurfürstendamm 218. ☎ **030/8-85-74-80.** U-Bahn: Kurfürstendamm.

This cafe opened in the early 1980s in what used to be the Chinese embassy. Some of the embassy's ornate moldings and lighting fixtures are still in place; a pair of gilded lions still guards the entrance. On the street level is a pastry and candy shop, but you can climb the flight of stairs to a marble-and-wood-sheathed cafe with a balcony overlooking the busy Ku'damm. The elegant breakfast menu here features Parma ham, smoked salmon, freshly baked baguettes, French butter, and, to round it off, champagne. Meals range from 18DM to 26DM ($9 to $13). Open daily 10am to 7pm.

Café Silberstein. Oranienburger Strasse 27. ☎ **030/2-81-20-95.** S-Bahn: Oranienburger Tor.

From the outside, this place looks like an art gallery, but once inside, you'll see that it's an artsy cafe, one of Berlin's trendiest, with sushi, ambient music, and an ultrahip clientele. This is one of the best places to enjoy "new Berlin" in the formerly grim eastern sector. Open Monday to Friday 9pm to 4am and Saturday and Sunday noon to 5am.

Cafe Wintergarten in Literaturhaus Berlin. Fasanenstrasse 23. ☎ **030/882-54-14.** U-Bahn: Hohenzollernplatz or Spichernstrasse.

Set within a Tuscan-style brick villa that was built in 1885 one block south of the Ku'-damm, a few steps from the Käthe-Kollwitz-Museum, this cafe is part of a private foundation that's devoted to the promotion—through lectures and research—of German literature. In addition to a prestigious and respectable bookshop that fills the building's basement, it contains lecture halls, offices that have links to Germany's academic community, and exhibition space for temporary exhibitions that cost from 5DM to 8DM ($2.50 to $4) to see. The best way to unlock the secrets of this place is by heading for the cafe and restaurant, whose tables fill two old-fashioned Berliner-style rooms and spill into a much sought after garden during clement weather. If you re hungry, the cheerful, old-Berliner style staff will serve platters of noodles with cheese, rigatoni with beef strips, Argentinian steaks with herbs and parslied potatoes, and cucumber and tuna salads. Open daily 9:30am to 1am.

A CASINO

Spielbank Berlin. Marlene Dietrich Platz 7 (Potsdamer Platz). ☎ **030/255-990.** Cover 10DM ($5). U-Bahn: Potsdamer Platz.

It's brassy, it sparkles with lots of chrome, and the staff is about as jaded as any you'll find in a city that's legendary for its jaded citizens. The setting is a high-ceilinged, scarlet affair that might remind you of an airport. The basement is devoted to slot machines; the upper floors (Casino Royale) to a battery of more sophisticated gambling devices that include roulette and baccarat. Men must wear a necktie for access to the Casino Royale, but not to the basement-level slot machines. The cover charge of 10DM ($5) is refunded in the form of a casino chip. There are no maximum bets—the amount you lose, or can bet on any one play, depends on your credit rating with the casino. The slot machines are accessible daily 11:30am to 3am; the rest of the complex is available for bets daily 2pm to 3am. This is the only casino in Berlin: It's only competition is a simple and rather small facility within the Forum Hotel, on Alexanderplatz.

10 A Side Trip: Potsdam & Its Palaces

24km (15 miles) SW of Berlin, 140km (87 miles) NE of Leipzig, 148km (92 miles) NE of Magdeburg

The best day trip from Berlin is to the baroque town of Potsdam on the Havel River. It's often been called Germany's Versailles. The town has many historic sights, as well as parks and a beautiful chain of lakes formed by the river. It was beautifully planned, with large parks and many green areas. The palaces and gardens of **Sans Souci Park,** which lies to the west of Potsdam's historic core, are the major attractions here. A mile northwest of Sans Souci is the **Neuer Garten** on the Heiliger See, which contains the **Schloss Cecilienhof.**

From the beginning of the 18th century, Potsdam was a residence and garrison town of the Prussian kings. Soviet propagandists called it a "former cradle of Prussian militarism and reactionary forces." World attention focused on Potsdam July 17 to August 2, 1945, when the Potsdam Conference helped shape postwar Europe.

ESSENTIALS

GETTING THERE By Train Potsdam Hauptbahnhof is on the major Deutsche Bundesbahn rail lines, with 29 daily connections to the rail stations in Berlin (23 min. to Bahnhof Zoo and 54 min. to Ostbahnhof). There are also 14 trains daily to and from Hannover (3 to $3^1/2$ hr.), and 15 daily trains to and from Nürnberg (6 to $6^1/2$ hr.). For rail information and schedules, call ☎ **1805/ 996633.**

Potsdam can also be reached by S-Bahn Lines S3, S4, and S7 from Berlin, connecting at Wannsee station with Lines R1, R3, and R4. Travel time on these lines from Berlin to Potsdam is 30 minutes. For more information, call **BVG Berlin** (☎ **030/19-449**).

By Bus Verkehrsverbund Potsdam provides regional bus service with frequent connections between Berlin and Potsdam at Wannsee station (bus 133) in Berlin. For travel information and schedules, call **BVG Berlin** (☎ **030/ 19-449**).

By Car Access is via the E30 Autobahn east and west or the E53 north and south. Allow about 30 minutes to drive here from Berlin.

VISITOR INFORMATION Contact **Potsdam-Information,** Friedrich Strasse 5 (☎ **0331/27-55-80**), open April to October, Monday to Friday 9am to 8pm, Saturday 10am to 6pm, and Sunday 10am to 4pm; November to March, Monday to Friday 10am to 6pm and Saturday and Sunday 10am to 2pm.

GETTING AROUND By Public Transportation Ask at the tourist office about a **Potsdam billet,** costing 8.50DM ($4.25) and good for 24 hours on the city's public transportation. In Potsdam, **bus A1,** leaving from the rail station, will deliver you to the Potsdam palaces. Call ☎ **0331/2-80-03-09** for more information.

By Boat Since the area around Potsdam is surrounded by water, boat tours in fair weather are a popular diversion. Call **Weisse Flotte Potsdam** at ☎ **0331/29-15-27** for more information.

By Bicycle You can rent a bicycle from **City Rad Potsdam,** at the Potsdam Hauptbahnhof (☎ **0331/619052**), but you can't ride your bike on the grounds of Sans Souci Park. The rental shop is open May to October, Monday to Friday 9am to 7pm, Saturday and Sunday 9am to 8pm. Bicycles rent for 20DM ($10) per day.

EXPLORING THE PARKS & PALACES

A British air raid on April 14, 1945, destroyed much of the old city center, but the major attraction, Sans Souci Park and its palaces, survived.

✪ **Sans Souci Palace.** Zur historischen Mühle. ☎ **0331/96-94-202.** Daily 8am–8pm. Tram: 94 or 96. Bus: 614, 631, or 632 to reach the sights in the park.

Sans Souci Park, with its palaces and gardens, was the work of many architects and sculptors. The park covers an area of about a square mile. Its premier attraction is the palace of Frederick I ("the Great"), **Sans Souci,** meaning "free from care." Frederick was one of the most liberal and farsighted of the Prussian monarchs. He was a great general, but he liked best to think of himself as an enlightened patron of the arts. Here he could get away from his duties, indulge his intellectual interests, and entertain his friend Voltaire. The style of the buildings he had constructed is called

"Potsdam rococo," and is primarily the achievement of Georg Wenzeslaus von Knobelsdorff.

Sans Souci (or Sanssouci) Palace, with its terraces and gardens, was inaugurated in 1747. The long one-story building is crowned by a dome and flanked by two round pavilions. The elliptically shaped Marble Hall is the largest in the palace, but the music salon is the supreme example of the rococo style. A small bust of Voltaire commemorates Voltaire's sojourns here. The palace is open April to October, Tuesday to Sunday 9am to 5pm; November to January, Tuesday to Sunday 9am to 3pm; and February and March, Tuesday to Sunday 9am to 4pm; closed Monday. Admission is 10DM ($5) for adults and 5DM ($2.50) for children and students.

Bildergalerie (Picture Gallery), Östlicher Lustgarten (☎ 0331/9694181), was built between 1755 and 1763. Its facade is similar to that of Sans Souci Palace, and the interior is one of the most flamboyant in Germany. The collection of some 125 paintings features works by Italian Renaissance and baroque artists along with Dutch and Flemish masters. Concerts of the Potsdam Park Festival take place here. The Bildergalerie is open the same hours as Sans Souci Palace. Admission is 4DM ($2) for adults and 2DM ($1) for children.

West of the palace is the **Orangerie** (☎ 0331/969-4280), built between 1851 and 1864. It was based on Italian Renaissance designs. Its purpose was to shelter southern plants during the cold months. In the central core is the Raphael Hall, which holds 47 copies of that master's paintings. In addition, you can visit five lavishly decorated salons. Admission is 6DM ($3) for adults and 3DM ($1.50) for children. The Orangerie is open mid-May to mid-October, Friday to Wednesday 10am to 5pm.

The largest building in the park is the extravagant **Neues Palais** (☎ 0331/9694255), built between 1763 and 1769, at the end of the Seven Years' War. Crowning the Center is a dome. The rococo rooms, filled with paintings and antiques, were used by the royal family. The most notable chamber is the Hall of Shells, with its fossils and semiprecious stones. At the palace theater, concerts take place every year April to November. The Neues Palais has the same hours as the Sans Souci, except that it's open Monday and closed Friday. It charges 8DM ($4) for adults and 4DM ($2) for children.

Schloss Charlottenhof. South of Okonomieweg. ☎ 0331/9-69-42-28. Admission 8DM ($4) adults, 4DM ($2) children. Mid-May to mid-Oct, Tues–Sun 9am–5pm. Tram: 1 or 4.

This palace was built between 1826 and 1829 by Karl Friedrich Schinkel, Germany's greatest master of neoclassical architecture. He also designed most of the furniture inside. The schloss now closes in winter. The nearby **Roman Baths** are on the north of the artificial lake known as *Maschinenteich* (machine pond). These baths, constructed between 1829 and 1835, were built strictly for the romantic love of antiquity and have no practical purpose.

Neuer Garten. On Heiliger See, about a mile northwest of Sans Souci. ☎ 0331/2-31-41. Free admission. Same hours as Sans Souci. Bus: 695.

On Heiliger See, or "holy lake," in the northern part of Potsdam, lies the Neuer Garten. The nephew and successor to Frederick the Great, Frederick William II, had these gardens laid out.

Schloss Cecilienhof. In Neuer Garten. ☎ 0331/9-69-42-44. Admission 8DM ($4) adults, 6DM ($3) students with guided tour (2DM less without), free for children under 6. Tues–Sun 9am–12:30pm and 5–7pm. The guided tour only offered May 15–Oct 15. Bus: 695.

This palace was completed in the style of an English country house. Kaiser Wilhelm II had it built between 1913 and 1917 for Crown Prince Wilhelm. The palace was occupied as a royal residence until March 1945, when the crown prince and his family fled to the West. In addition to the regular guided tour, offered in summer, there's a tour of the private rooms of Crown Prince Wilhelm and Princess Cecilie on the upper story. The tour takes place at 11am and 2pm and costs 3DM ($1.50) adults and 2DM ($1) students and children. Note that you can lunch here and spend the night here.

Cecilienhof was the headquarters of the 1945 Potsdam Conference, attended by the heads of the allied powers, including Truman, Stalin, and Churchill. You can visit the studies of the various delegations and see the large round table, made in Moscow, where the actual agreement was signed.

WHERE TO STAY

Arkona Hotel Voltaire. Friedrich-Ebert-Strasse 88, 14467 Potsdam. ☎ **0331/2-31-70.** Fax 0331/2-31-71-00. www.hotelvoltaire.potsdam.de. E-mail: hotelvoltaire@potsdam.de. 143 units. MINIBAR TV TEL. 234DM–274DM ($117–$137) double; from 375DM ($187.50) suite. AE, DC, MC, V. Parking 20DM ($10). Tram: 92.

This hotel, the best in Potsdam, is a radical renovation of the Brühlsche Palace, formerly a dour and crumbling relic built in 1732. Only the palace's baroque facade has been retained. The site belongs to the small Arkona chain. Rooms are scattered over three floors and, in almost every case, overlook the quiet, pleasant garden in back. All rooms have safes.

Dining/Diversions: On the premises is a well-run restaurant, Hofgarten.

Amenities: Concierge, room service, hair dryers, dry cleaning, laundry, newspaper delivery, baby-sitting, secretarial services, valet parking, courtesy car, bike rental, children's programs.

WHERE TO DINE

✪ **Juliette.** Jägerstrasse 39. ☎ **0331/2701-791.** Reservations required. Main courses 34DM–39DM ($17–$19.50). AE, V. Daily noon–11pm. Tram 94 or 96. FRENCH.

At last, Potsdam has a world-class restaurant. The cozy and intimate Juliette lies in the Center of the restored Holländisches Viertel (Dutch Quarter), 3 blocks north of the Altar Markt. You'll feel at home the moment you enter this restored old house, with its blazing fireplace, low ceilings, and tiny little windows. There is no more romantic choice in the city. Most of the excellent waiters are from France. Menu items include saddle of boar in cranberry sauce, fresh grilled fish, and some wonderful chicken dishes. All the desserts are freshly made on-site.

Villa Kellerman. Mangerstrasse 34–36. ☎ **0331/29-15-72.** Reservations recommended. Main courses 18DM–35DM ($9–$17.50); fixed-price menu 80DM ($40). AE, DC, MC, V. Fri–Sun noon–midnight, Tues–Thurs 6pm–midnight. S-Bahn: Potsdam Stadt. Bus: 92 or 93. ITALIAN.

One of the most talked-about restaurants in Potsdam is in an 1878 villa, once occupied by author Bernhardt Kellerman. The Italian cuisine here attracts a diverse clientele from finance and the arts. Your meal might include marinated carpaccio of sea wolf; ravioli stuffed with cheese, spinach, and herbs; John Dory in butter-and-caper sauce; and an array of veal and beef dishes. The wine list is mostly Italian.

4 Saxony & Thuringia

To go to the regions of the former East Germany today can still be an adventure in travel. Once difficult to visit, famous cities are being restored and are inviting visitors from the west. These include: Dresden, destroyed during World War II and poignantly restored at least in part; Leipzig, where Johann Sebastian Bach spent most of his musical life as cantor (choirmaster) of St. Thomas Church; Meissen, famous for exquisite porcelain; Potsdam, once the residence of the Prussian kings; and Weimar, still glowing from its 1999 designation as European City of Culture. In addition, unspoiled scenery and medieval towns like Quedlinburg invite you to wander off the beaten track.

Since reunification, many visitors have come from around the world to explore the new political landscape and to honor the memory of the intellectual giants who once made East Germany their home—Goethe, Luther, Bach, Schiller, and Brecht, among others. Hotels are being built and tourist facilities developed. But the traveler should still take care in this rapidly changing terrain. The state of politics here is sometimes erratic and unpredictable, and the economy is weaker than in western Germany. The fears and frustrations of the population have given rise to small neo-Nazi groups. Some of them have been known to assault nonwhite foreigners and members of certain religious groups (notably Muslims), embarrassing the millions of other tolerant and liberal Germans.

Eastern Germany today is a region in transition. Its long isolation also means that you'll find here some of Germany's most unspoiled countryside and untouched villages, where rural traditions that have disappeared from most of western Europe still linger. A visit can provide you with unforgettable new experiences and stories you can tell your grandchildren.

Getting around eastern Germany is easier than it has ever been. Some 1,600km (1,000 miles) of Autobahns and about 11,000km (7,000 miles) of secondary highways cut across the region. Train schedules are a bit chaotic, as the German government incorporates the former East German system into its vast national network. Since 1991, long-distance bus service has linked Berlin with Dresden and Leipzig. Service is still not frequent, however, as buses exist mainly to supplement the rail network.

1　Weimar

260km (162 miles) SW of Berlin, 22km (14 miles) E of Erfurt

Weimar, a beautiful 1,000-year-old town on the edge of the Thuringian Forest, is an important destination for those interested in German history and culture. Unlike many cities in the former East Germany, Weimar still retains much of its old flavor. Many of its important historical monuments were spared from the bombings of World War II. Its atmospheric, narrow, winding streets, lined with houses with high-pitched gabled roofs, seem left over from the Middle Ages. A 19th-century writer called Weimar "one of the most walkable towns of Europe," and so it remains today.

Weimar's history as a cultural center is centuries old. Lucas Cranach the Elder worked here in the 16th century. From 1708 to 1717, Bach was court organist. In 1775, the great Goethe came to reside at the court of Dowager Duchess Anna Amalia and her son, Charles Augustus II, and he attracted such notables as Herder and Schiller.

Later in the 19th century, Franz Liszt was musical director of the National Theater; under his auspices, Wagner's *Lohengrin* had its first performance. It was also at Weimar that the German national assembly met in February 1919, in the aftermath of World War I, to draw up the constitution for what was to be called the Weimar Republic.

ESSENTIALS

GETTING THERE　By Train　Weimar Hauptbahnhof is on the major Deutsche Bundesbahn rail lines, which link Erfurt and Leipzig with Dresden. There are frequent daily connections in both directions. Trains from Berlin travel via Leipzig. For rail information and schedules, call ☎ **1805/996633.**

By Bus　Regional buses to all parts of the city and the surrounding area are run by **Verkehrsgesellschaft Weimar** (☎ **03643/2-42-00**).

By Car　Access is via the E40 Autobahn east and west.

VISITOR INFORMATION　Head first for Weimar's tourist agency, the **Tourist-Information Weimar,** Am Markt 10 (☎ **03643/2-40-00**). The office is open April to October, Monday to Friday 10am to 6pm and Saturday and Sunday 10am to 4pm; November to March, Tuesday to Friday 9am to 6pm and Saturday 9am to 1pm.

EXPLORING THE TOWN

Weimar enjoys a scenic location on the Ilm River, set against the backdrop of the Ettersberg and Vogtland hills. The city has many popular sights, but perhaps the best thing to do here is simply to wander about on foot. A walk at night through the old streets that once felt the footsteps of Goethe, Bach, Wagner, and Schiller is particularly rewarding.

The town's main square, called the **Marktplatz,** or market square, retains the old flavor of the city. Instead of breakfast at your hotel, visit one of the bakeries near the square and compose your own breakfast, the way many locals do. The daily produce market still takes place on the Marktplatz. The painter Lucas Cranach the Elder lived here during his last year, from 1552 to 1553; you can view the richly decorated **Lucas Cranach the Elder House.**

For a midday break from sightseeing, we suggest a visit to Park an der Ilm or **Goethe Park,** flanking the river. Goethe himself actually landscaped this park. It sports numerous 18th-century pavilions, and is the best place in Weimar for a picnic.

If you've had a little too much Schiller and Goethe, flee the inner city and escape to **Baushaus Universität** on Marienstrasse, just across the footpath in front of the Bauhaus building. Here you can meet Weimar students, nearly all of whom speak English.

In the evening, head for one of the smoky beer halls near **Herderplatz,** keeping in mind that Nietzsche, who spent the last 3 years of his life here, discovered them long before you.

✪ **Goethe Nationalmuseum.** Am Frauenplan 1. ☎ **03643/54-53-20.** Admission 8DM ($4) adults, 5DM ($2.50) students, 2.50DM ($1.25) children. Mar–Oct, Tues–Sun 9am–4pm; Oct 26–Mar 14, Tues–Sun 10am–4pm. Bus: 1, 4, 6, 8, or 71.

Weimar's principal attraction is the house where Johann Wolfgang von Goethe (1749–1832) lived from 1782 to 1832. It's a typical example of a baroque German nobleman's house. There are 14 exhibition rooms, some pretty much as Goethe and his wife, Christiane Vulpius, left them. The library contains more than 5,000 volumes.

The writer's mineral collection is here also, as well as much original art. Although Goethe's reputation rests today on his writing, he had wide-ranging interests. You can see evidence of his interest in science (he was an early advocate of the belief in the common origin of all animal life, for example). He died in Weimar on March 22, 1832.

Goethes Gartenhaus. Im Park an der Ilm. ☎ **03643/54-53-75.** Admission 4DM ($2) adults, 3DM ($1.50) students and senior citizens, 1.50DM (75¢) children. Mar 15–Oct 25, Wed–Mon 9am–6pm; Oct 26–Mar 14, Wed–Mon 10am–4pm. Bus: 1, 4, 6, 8, or 71.

In a park on the Ilm River stands a plain cottage with a high-pitched roof. Goethe selected this house as his first residence when he came to Weimar. Even after he moved to other quarters, he still came here in summer to find peace and tranquility. He described the park around him as "infinitely beautiful," and so it remains today.

✪ **Schillerhaus.** Schillerstrasse 9. ☎ **03643/54-53-50.** Admission 5DM ($2.50) adults, 3DM ($1.50) children. Mar 15–Oct 25, Wed–Mon 9am–6pm. Bus: 1, 4, 6, 8, or 71.

After his friend Goethe, Friedrich von Schiller (1759–1805) is the greatest name in German literature. He lived here with his family from 1802 to 1805, and wrote his last works here, including *Wilhelm Tell.* The attic rooms have been furnished as they were in Schiller's day.

Liszt House. Marienstrasse 17. ☎ **03643/54-53-88.** Admission 4DM ($2) adults, 3DM ($1.50) students, 1.50DM (75¢) children. Jan 7–Mar 14, 9am–4pm; Mar 15–May 9, 9am–6pm; May 10–Aug 29, 9am–7pm; Aug 30–Oct 24, 9am–6pm; Oct 25–Dec 31, 9am–4pm. Closed daily 1–2pm. Bus: 4, 6, 8, or 71.

Franz Liszt (1811–86), the Hungarian composer and pianist, spent the last period of his life here. You'll find several mementos, both personal and musical, from the composer's life, including letters exchanged between Liszt and his son-in-law, as well as the piano at which he played and taught his pupils. The house was once the home for the royal gardeners of Weimar.

Kunstsammlungen zu Weimar. Burgplatz 4. ☎ **03643/54-60.** Admission 6DM ($3) adults, 3DM ($1.50) children. Self-parking 2DM ($1) hourly. Apr–Oct, Tues–Sun 10am–6pm; Nov–Mar, Tues–Sun 10am–4:30pm. Bus: 5.

This structure was begun under the guidance of Goethe in 1789 and completed in 1803. The previous castle had burned down in 1774; only a tower survived. In one of the wings is a series of galleries dedicated not only to Schiller and Goethe but also to two other famous names associated with Weimar: Johann Gottfried Herder (1744–1803), the German critic and philosopher who was a pioneer of the *Sturm und Drang* ("Storm and Stress") literary movement, and Christoph Martin Wieland (1733–1813), the poet and critic who wrote the satirical romance *The Republic of Fools.* The museum has a shop, which is open April to October, 10am to 6pm.

   The ground floor displays works by Lucas Cranach the Elder. On some of the upper floors you can see exhibits from Walter Gropius's Bauhaus school, which started in Weimar. The primary aim of this movement was to unify arts and crafts within the context of architecture. Its appeal derived from the changing sensibilities of the Industrial Age, as well as from the need for inexpensive construction techniques in an era of rising costs and exploding demand for housing. Followers around the globe may have been impressed, but not the good people of Weimar. They "tolerated" Gropius's school until 1925, and then bombarded it in the press, until it finally moved to Dessau. There it stayed until the Nazis closed it in 1933, claiming it was a center of "Communist intellectualism."

Wittumspalais. Am Palais 3. ☎ **03643/54-53-77.** Admission 6DM ($3) adults, 4DM ($2) students and senior citizens, 2DM ($1) children. Mar 15–Oct 25, Tues–Sun 9am–6pm; Oct 26–Mar 14, Tues–Sun 10am–4pm. Bus: 4, 6, or 8.

If you follow Rittergasse to the end, you will come upon the 1767 Wittumspalais, once the residence of Dowager Duchess Anna Amalia, who presided over the German Enlightenment, which brought a stark rationalism to literature and the arts. The old ducal dower house is devoted to mementos of the movement.

Stadtkirche St. Peter and Paul. Herderplatz 8 (follow Vorwerksgasse). ☎ **03643/ 85-15-18.** Free admission. Apr–Oct, Mon–Sat 10am–noon and 2–4pm, Sun 11am–noon and–3pm; Nov–Mar, Mon–Sat 11am–noon and 2–3pm, Sun 2–3pm. Bus: 1 or 7.

The origins of this church date from the founding of Weimar itself. The present building consists of three naves designed in a late Gothic style. Its most precious treasure is an altar painting begun by Lucas Cranach the Elder in the last year of his life and completed by his son.

Schloss Belvedere (Château of Belvedere). Belvederer Allee. ☎ **03643/54-61-62.** Admission 5DM ($2.50) adults, 3DM ($1.50) children. Apr–Oct, Tues–Sun 10am–6pm; closed Nov–Mar. Bus: 12. From Weimar, follow the Belvedereschlossallee south for 3km (2 miles).

The baroque Schloss Belvedere was a favorite retreat of Anna Amalia and the "enlightened" Weimar set. It has an orangerie, along with the open-air theater and an English-style park. Inside the château are displays of dainty rococo art and a collection of historical coaches.

Schloss Tiefurt. On the outskirts of Weimar in the village of Tiefurt. ☎ **03643/85-06-66.** Admission 6DM ($3) adults, 4DM ($2) students and senior citizens, 2DM ($1) children. Mar 25–Oct 28, Tues–Sun 9am–6pm; off-season, Tues–Sun 10am–4pm. Bus: 3 from Goetheplatz; Tiefurt is the last stop. Go east along Tiefurter Allee.

This was formerly the site of another summer retreat of Duchess Anna Amalia. Guests today can wander through its pavilions and gardens. Coming here is a good excursion on a lovely day if you have extra time.

MORE SIGHTS

In the **cemetery,** south of the town center, Am Posseckschen Garten, you can see the controversial **Denkmal der März Gefallenen,** a monument to the revolutionaries whose slaughter in 1919 so affected Gropius and his Bauhaus followers. But most interesting today is the **Goethe-Schiller Mausoleum,** once the family vault of the Weimar dynasty, where Goethe and Schiller, friends in life, lie side by side in death. It was built in 1825–26 according to plans drawn up by Coudray, who consulted Goethe on the design and construction. Schiller was entombed here in 1827 and Goethe in 1832, both in oak coffins. Visiting hours are daily 9am to 1pm and 2 to 5pm. Admission is free. A Russian-style **chapel** is on the south side of the mausoleum. It was built in 1859 for Maria Pavlovna, daughter-in-law of Duke Carl August.

BUCHENWALD   The Buchenwald bus (no. 6) from Weimar's Hauptbahnhof goes 6km (4 miles) northwest of Weimar to **Gedenkstätte Buchenwald** (☎ **03643/43-00**), the site of the concentration camp. It is estimated that a quarter of a million Jews, Slavs, Gypsies, homosexuals, political prisoners, prisoners of war, and others were confined here from 1937 until the camp's liberation by the U.S. Army in 1945. Buchenwald was officially a work camp, so many fewer people were killed here than at Auschwitz. Nonetheless, 56,000 people died in this camp, and many, many thousands of others were sent on from here to the death camps in the east.

Goethe Gets a Touch-Up

The news out of Weimar is weird but true: Someone's been fiddling with Goethe. Around 30 years ago, the city's most famous corpse suffered the indignity of being dug up, loaded onto a cart, and pulled off to the nearby Goethe Museum. Why? Well, in the fall of 1970, shortly before the dirty deed was done, local authorities discovered that Goethe's sarcophagus had a broken lock. When they took a look inside, they saw that his corpse was in a bad state of decomposition. Weimar was an important weapon in East Germany's propaganda war against the cultural decadence of West Germany. Communist higher-ups decided that something had better be done soon or the great *Kulturstadt* (city of culture) would be shamed by its mistreatment of the great scribe's remains.

So the national poet and creator of *Faust* was removed from his comfortable resting place and brought to the museum, where the corpse's remaining fragments of flesh were removed by means of a process called "maceration." A special preserving agent was then applied to the bones to strengthen them. The laurel wreath around Goethe's head was likewise doused and strengthened.

Unfortunately, all did not run smoothly. The shroud Goethe was wearing was sent off for examination but, typically, got tangled up in bureaucratic red tape and didn't arrive back in Weimar in time for his reburial. It has since been kept hidden in the Schiller Museum (talk about dirty linen). The report outlining this skullduggery was only made public in 1999.

Furthermore, atrocities practiced in Buchenwald have made its very name synonymous with human perversity.

A memorial with a cluster of "larger-than-life" people, representing victims of fascism, was created by Prof. Fritz Cremer to honor the people from 32 nations who lost their lives here.

Buchenwald's sad history continued when Soviet occupation forces used the site as an internment camp from 1945 to 1951. It's believed that they sent thousands of prisoners here to die. All this was kept quiet until the winter of 1989. Before that time, the Soviets had attempted to exploit the Buchenwald museum as a showcase illustrating "the suffering of Soviet soldiers and the German Communists." The museum now reflects both the Soviet and the Nazi past of the camp.

You can visit Buchenwald May to September, Tuesday to Sunday 9:45am to 6pm; October to April, Tuesday to Sunday 8:45am to 5pm. Admission is free.

SHOPPING

A visit to Weimar's antique stores offers a chance to buy porcelain, silver, crystal, and furniture that survived the devastation of World War II. The most interesting shops include **Antikitäten am Palais,** Schillerstrasse 22 (☎ **03643/59625**), and its immediate neighbor, **Kaiser Antikitäten,** Schillerstrasse 22 (same phone). Also appealing are **Antikitäten am Schloss,** Obereschlossgasse 2 (☎ **03643/51-29-93**), **Goethe-Antiquariat,** Kaufenstrasse 7 (☎ **03643/40-25-67**), selling books only; and **Thiersch Antikitäten,** Bräuhausgasse 15 (☎ **03643/40-25-40**).

WHERE TO STAY
EXPENSIVE

✪ **Kempinski Hotel Elephant Weimar.** Am Markt 19, 99423 Weimar. ☎ **03643/80-20.** Fax 03643/80-26-10. www.weimar.de/kempinski. E-mail: reservation.wei@kempinski.com.

102 units. MINIBAR TV TEL. 310DM–390DM ($155–$195) double; 480DM–750DM ($240–$375) suite. AE, DC, MC, V. Free parking. Bus: 10, 11 or 71.

The Elephant is Weimar's most famous hotel, although it's actually inferior to the Hilton (see below). Many celebrities have stayed at this hotel, including Tolstoy and Bach; the most notorious guest was Adolf Hitler. The Elephant became best known in Germany through Thomas Mann's novel *Lotte in Weimar* (published in English as *The Beloved Returns*). The elegant facade of this building (ca. 1696) is set off by a beautifully weathered terra-cotta roof, a series of elongated bay windows stretching from the second to the third floors, and, best of all, a frontage onto the old marketplace, which contains a dried-up fountain dedicated to Neptune. An art-deco decor and bold color schemes make the rooms dramatically appealing. (The bedside reading lamps are a bit dim, however.)

Dining/Diversions: The hotel maintains two restaurants, the more formal Anna Amalia and the Elephantenkeller (see "Where to Dine," below).

Amenities: Concierge, room service, dry cleaning, laundry service, twice-daily maid service, baby-sitting, secretarial services, conference rooms; a health club is located nearby.

Hilton Weimar. Belvederer Allee 25, 99425 Weimar. ☎ **800/445-8667** in the U.S. and Canada, or 03643/72-20. Fax 03643/72-27-41. www.hilton.com. E-mail: hilton.weimar@t-online.de. 306 units. A/C MINIBAR TV TEL. 330DM–410DM ($165–$205) double; from 685DM ($342.50) suite. AE, DC, MC, V. Parking 18DM–22DM ($9–$11). Bus: 1.

Ironically, credit for the excellence of the hotel's construction and the lavishness of its materials is due to the former East German government, which designed and built this hotel a few months before reunification. Now run by Hilton, it stands beside Goethe Park, a swath of greenery with posh residences and embassies left over from the Weimar Republic. The lobby is dramatic, with sun-flooded skylights and glass walls. Rooms are small but comfortable. Two floors are rented to nonsmokers, and two rooms are suitable for those with disabilities.

Dining/Diversions: The Kolonnaden Bar services the fine Restaurant Esplanade/Trattoria Esplanade. The Biergarten is also popular.

Amenities: 24-hour room service, hair dryers, concierge (who can arrange local sightseeing tours), baby-sitters, massage, impressive indoor pool, two saunas, cosmetic salon, health club.

MODERATE

Amalienhof. Amalienstrasse 2, 99423 Weimar. ☎ **03643/54-90.** Fax 03643/54-91-10. www.vch.de/amalienhof.weimar E-mail: amalienhof.weimar@t-online.de. 31 units. 180DM–200DM ($90–$100) double; 250DM ($125) suite. Rates include buffet breakfast. AE, MC, V. Free parking. Bus: 1.

This hotel was originally constructed in 1826 in neoclassical style. Today, its small, modern rooms are comfortably furnished and well maintained. The hotel has a great location, lying directly south of Goethe National Museum, within an easy walk of the town's historic core and major attractions. The breakfast buffet, the only meal served here, is decent.

Russischer Hof. Goetheplatz 2, 99423 Weimar. ☎ **03643/77-40.** Fax 03643/77-48-40. 124 units. TV TEL. 190DM–320DM ($95–$160) double. Rates include buffet breakfast. AE, DC, MC, V. Parking 10DM–15DM ($5–$7.50). Bus: 11 or 71.

Russischer Hof was built in 1805 by Russian aristocrats for their visits to the Weimar court. It sports a dark green and white facade and opens onto an important square in the center of town. Inside, the pastel-colored public areas are elegant and intimate. Rooms are in a somewhat lackluster modern annex behind the hotel.

INEXPENSIVE

Thüringen. Brennerstrasse 42, 99423 Weimar. ☎ **03643/903-675.** Fax 03643/903-676. 36 units. 150DM ($75) double. Rates include buffet breakfast. AE, MC, V. Bus: 1 and 7.

This affordable hotel in the center of town dates from 1897 but has been completely renovated and restored in modern style. The small rooms are clean and simply but adequately furnished. The focal point of the public areas is a glassed-in winter garden. The hotel is known for its *gutbürgerlich* (home-style) cookery, which one reader described as "just like my Saxon mother used to cook."

WHERE TO DINE

Kempinski Hotel Elephant Weimar. Am Markt 19. ☎ **03643/80-26-39.** Reservations recommended. Main courses 36DM–41DM ($18–$20.50); 3-course fixed-price lunch 58DM ($29); 5-course fixed-price dinner 97DM ($48.50). AE, DC, MC, V. Anna Amalia 6:30–10:30pm daily, and noon–3pm on weekends only in winter and daily in summer. Elephantenkeller Mon–Sat 10am–3am, Sun 12:30–3pm. Bus: 10, 11 or 71. GERMAN/INTERNATIONAL.

There are two restaurants in this previously recommended hotel. The more formal, **Anna Amalia,** is modern, skylit, and airy, with spacious tables, a garden terrace, and good service. Its German and international dishes are among the very best in the city. The chefs have an unerring sense of flavor and proportion, as well as a fertile imagination. They use only the finest of ingredients available at the local markets. Fillet Stroganoff, pork medallions, and sauerbraten are among the menu items. Goethe, Schiller, Bach, Liszt, and Wagner all wined and dined here.

You can reach the historic **Elephantenkeller** (Elephant Cellar) by a flight of stone steps at a separate entrance. It's decorated in a rustic style, with square travertine columns. An autumn specialty is *Zwiebelmarkt* salads, made from onions from the famous October onion market, a tradition dating from 1653.

Ratskeller. In the Rathaus, Markt 10. ☎ **03643/85-05-73.** Reservations recommended. Main courses 16DM–25DM ($8–$12.50). AE, MC, V. Daily 11am–midnight. Bus: 7 or 71. THURINGIAN.

A flight of stairs leads into a pair of dining rooms. The first is vaulted and white, the second more modern, paneled, and with a prominent bar. Everything is clean, correct, and proper. You might begin with goose liver on toast, followed with schnitzel, goulash with mixed salad, or pork cutlets prepared four different ways. These dishes aren't dazzling, but they're very satisfying. The venison, when in season, is excellent, and the wild boar and duck in red-wine sauce is reason enough for a meal here.

Weissen Schwan. Am Frauenplan (in the center of the town near Goethe House). ☎ **03643/20-25-21.** Reservations recommended. Main courses 15DM–30DM ($7.50–$15); fixed-price menus 35DM–100DM ($17.50–$50). AE, DC, MC, V. Sun and Tues–Thurs 11:30am–11pm, Fri–Sat noon–midnight. Bus: 7 or 71. THURINGIAN/INTERNATIONAL.

This leading restaurant specializes in regional cuisine, using fresh produce and the best of the local beef, game, and poultry. It's in a building that dates from the early 16th century. The library is still preserved. The atmosphere is mellow. Along with Thuringian specialties, somewhat standard international dishes are also offered.

WEIMAR AFTER DARK

A good national theater, live music venues, and dance clubs provide a variety of choices for nightly entertainment. The city's bars and outdoor cafes are good places to drink and talk. Just walk down Schillerstrasse or along the Theaterplatz. All of the bars and cafes in this area carry free copies of *Schlagseite* and *Boulevard*, local entertainment

The Thuringian Forest: Germany's Green Heart

"There is indeed no forest on all the earth as beautiful as the Thuringian," wrote the Danish novelist Martin Anderson Nexö in his tale "The Doll." Trekkers and nature lovers have long extolled the scenic beauties of this region, which has often been called "the green heart of Germany." The *Thüringer Wald* was the former stamping ground of such philosophers and artists as Goethe, Schiller, Martin Luther, Ludwig Bechstein, and Bach.

The mountains within the forest, though not nearly as tall as the German Alps, are geological highlights. The highest peaks, around 985m (3,230 feet), are composed of gneiss, porphyry, and granite; the foothills are made of softer strata of sandstone and sedimentary limestone.

The scenic, 160km (100-mile), northwest-to-southeast ramble known as the "Thuringian High Road" was one of the most popular destinations anywhere for East German schoolchildren and campers before reunification. You can take a lowland driving version by following route 88 between Eisenach and Ilmenau, a city that Goethe loved.

Just as attractive as the region's scenic beauty are the dozens of unspoiled, charming medieval villages that pepper the landscape. **Dornburg** has a series of three palaces, perched high above the River Saale. **Altenburg,** directly south of Leipzig, is the home of a hilltop castle. Finally, **Arnstadt,** founded in 704, is the oldest town in the Thuringian Forest. It lies just beyond Erfurt. Today, the town's medieval walkways and buildings are being restored to their former glory.

---

papers. *Takt* is another good resource; you can save 5DM ($2.50) by picking it up in the tourist office (see above), the only place where it's free.

Weimar's main performance venue, reopened in 1999, is the **Deutsches National-altheater,** Theaterplatz (☎ 03643/75-53-34), where Franz Liszt and Richard Strauss once conducted. Call the box office or the tourist office for information about schedules. Tickets cost 14DM to 40DM ($7 to $20).

C-Keller Galerie, Markt 21 (☎ 03643/50-27-55), combines an art gallery with a cafe that serves beer, wine, tea, and light meals. It's a popular place to unwind. The art gallery has works for sale by local, national, and European artists. The cafe is open daily noon to midnight. Its most visible competitor is **Galerie C-1,** Karl-August-Allee 1 (☎ 03643/50-23-01), which presents good food, fresh from the nearby marketplace, along with an oft-changing exhibition of modern paintings. **Cranach Galerie,** Cranach Haus, Marktplatz 12 (☎ 03643/903768) is a more formal gallery with a wider range of works. It's open Tuesday to Friday 10am to 10pm.

The most popular and animated disco in Weimar isn't exactly cutting edge—it's more like Hannover than Hamburg or Berlin. But if you're interested in hearing a medley of disco favorites from the '70s and '80s, head for **Bistro Corona-Sthröter,** Goethe-Platz 5 (☎ 03643/515308). It's open daily 9pm to midnight. Admission costs 5DM ($2.50) per person.

A three-story medieval tower, **Studentclub Kasseturm,** Goetheplatz (☎ 03643/904323), has a beer hall on the first floor, live music on the second, and dancing on the third. As the name suggests, students flock to this place. Cover ranges from 5DM ($2.50) to as much as 25DM ($12.50), if there's a particularly well-known band. There's no cover on Monday, Tuesday, and Thursday. The club opens Monday to Saturday at 8pm, with no set closing time.

The most popular place in Weimar for punk and alternative rock is **Haus für Socio-Kultur,** Gerberstrasse 3 (☎ **03643/51-27-14**), a large, loud rock club (or a pub, depending on the evening) with a graffiti-art exterior. Hours are daily 8pm to 3am. There's no cover charge.

SIDE TRIPS FROM WEIMAR
ERFURT
The small, 1,254-year-old city of Erfurt, on the Gera River, is one of the most visited cities of eastern Germany, because it still exudes the spirit of a medieval market town. Erfurt is filled with historic houses, bridges, winding cobblestone alleys, and church spires reaching toward the skyline, as well as decorative and colorful Renaissance and baroque era facades. The city emerged from World War II relatively unscathed, and remains one of the best places to see what yesterday's Germany looked like. Nearly everything of interest is concentrated in the Altstadt (Old Town) area. It's well worth your time to take 2 or 3 hours to walk around this city of "flowers and towers."

Why flowers? Erfurt is a center of the German horticultural trade. It's also Europe's largest vegetable seed producer. One of Europe's biggest horticultural shows, the *Internationale Gartenbauaustellung,* is held here in the Cyriaksburg Park every year from the end of March to September.

GETTING THERE   You can reach Erfurt after a 24km (15-mile) train ride from the Weimar Hauptbahnhof; there are frequent connections. For rail information and schedules, call ☎ **1805/996633.** Access by car is via the E40 Autobahn and State Highway 4. After arriving, head for the **Erfurt Tourist-Information** at Kräerbrücke (☎ **0361/6-6400**). It's open Monday to Friday 10am to 6pm, Saturday 10am to 4pm, and Sunday 10am to 1pm.

Exploring the City
Well-preserved patrician mansions built in both the Gothic and Renaissance style are the town's dominant feature. Many of the narrow streets are lined with old half-timbered houses. One of Erfurt's curiosities is the **Krämerbrücke** (Shopkeepers' Bridge), which has spanned the Gera since the 14th century. It has houses on both sides, nearly three dozen in all, and is filled with book stalls, cafes, and antiques shops. You'll certainly want to spend some time here browsing.

The ecclesiastical center is the **Domberg,** where two Catholic churches stand side by side, their 15th-century walls almost closing in on each other. The **Dom (cathedral)** (☎ **0361/6461-265**), on Domplatz, was begun in the 12th century and later rebuilt in the 14th century in the Gothic style. Its stained-glass windows above the choir date from 1370 to 1420 and are unusual in Germany for depicting scenes of everyday life. The interior of the cathedral is richly baroque, but it also has some notable works from 1160: a Romanesque altar of the Virgin and the statue-candelabra known as "the Wolfram." Note also the 13th-century tombstone of the count of Gleichen and his two wives. One version of a local legend says that the second woman wasn't his wife at all, but a Saracen beauty from the Holy Land who had saved his life under mysterious circumstances. The Dom is open May to October, Monday to Friday 9 to 11:30am and 12:30 to 5pm, Saturday 9 to 11:30am and 12:30 to 4:30pm, and Sunday 2 to 4pm; November to April, Monday to Saturday 10 to 11:30am and 12:30 to 4pm, and Sunday 2 to 4pm.

Its neighbor is the Gothic **Church of St. Severi** (☎ **0361/6-46-12-56**), a "hall type" church with 5 naves. Don't miss seeing its extraordinary font, a masterpiece of intricately carved sandstone, rising practically to the roof. You might also look for a notable sarcophagus of the saint (ca. 1365) in the southernmost aisle. St. Severi is

TIMBUKTU   KALAMAZOO

AT&T Direct® Service

The easy way to call home from anywhere.

Global
connection
with the AT&T
Network

AT&T
direct
service

For the easy way to call home, take the attached wallet guide.

linked to the Dom by a 70-step open staircase. It's open May to October, Monday to Friday 9am to noon and 1:30 to 5pm, Saturday 9 to 11:30am and 12:30 to 4:30pm, and Sunday 2 to 4pm; November to April, Monday to Saturday 10 to noon and 1:30 to 4pm, and on Sunday 2 to 4pm. Admission is free.

The most beautiful churches are the Romanesque **Peterskirche,** dating from the 12th and 14th centuries, and the 13th-century **Predigerkirche,** of the Order of Mendicant Friars. There are also three early Medieval churches: **Agidienkirche, Michaeliskirche,** and **Allerheiligengeistkirche.** The tourist office (see above) will give you a map pinpointing all the locations. Most can be reached on foot.

Where to Stay & Dine

Dorint Hotel. Meienbergstrasse 26–27, 99084 Erfurt. ☎ **0361/5-94-90.** Fax 0361/5-94-91-00. www.dorint.de. E-mail: infoerfurt@dorint.com. 142 units. MINIBAR TV TEL. 215DM–305DM ($107.50–$152.50) double; 320DM–380DM ($160–$190) suite. AE, DC, MC, V. Parking 16DM ($8).

Erfurt's newest hotel, in the heart of town, was built as a sophisticated enlargement of an inn (*Gasthaus*) from the 1300s. The medieval part—meticulously conserved and restored—faces onto a side street, the Futterstrasse. Otherwise, the hotel is modern, restrained, and tasteful. Most rooms correspond to middle-to-upscale chain-hotel standards. An additional 13 retain the wood paneling and architectural quirks of their original medieval construction, and are more interesting. On the premises you'll find a Jacuzzi, steam room, sauna, and solarium. The in-house restaurant, Rebstock, the nerve center of the hotel's medieval section, is cozy and appealing. Lunch and dinner are served here daily. Meals range from 36DM to 63DM ($18 to $31.50).

Radisson SAS Hotel Erfurt. Halfway between the station and the town center, Juri-Gagarin-Ring 127, 99084 Erfurt. ☎ **0361/5-51-00.** Fax 0361/551-02-10. www.radisson.com. E-mail: angela.weisheit@radissonSAS.com. 317 units. MINIBAR TV TEL. 210DM–265DM ($105–$132.50) double, 275DM–300DM ($137.50–$150) suite. Rates include buffet breakfast. AE, DC, MC, V. Parking 15DM ($7.50).

The Radisson SAS Hotel Erfurt is one of the town's better addresses. Its modern rooms are comfortable but a bit cramped. Baths are very compact and have inadequate shelf space. The hotel restaurant offers Thuringian specialties as well as international dishes. A wide selection of wines is available.

EISENACH

This town lies on the northwestern slopes of the Thuringian Forest, at the confluence of the Nesse and Horsel Rivers, 48km (30 miles) west of Erfurt. Eisenach, once a center of the East German auto industry, is not particularly charming, but it does have one of the region's finest castles, and a few sights associated with Luther and Bach, who was born here. Its ancient market square is ringed by half-timbered houses.

GETTING THERE   Many trains from Erfurt (see above) arrive every day. For rail information and schedules, call ☎ **03691/1805/996633.** Access by car is via the A4 Autobahn east and west. For tourist information, contact **Eisenach-Information,** Markt 3 (☎ **03691/79230**), open Monday to Friday 9am to 6pm and Saturday 10am to 2pm. Here you can pick up a map with the locations of all the tourist sites.

Exploring the Town

Eisenach is best known as the site of ✪ **Schloss Wartburg,** Schlossberg 2 (☎ **03691/ 7-70-73;** bus 3), reached only after a rigorous climb up a 180m (600-foot) hill. Hitler called Wartburg Castle "the most German of German castles" and engaged in a battle with local authorities to take down its cross and replace it with a swastika. This ancient castle belonged to the landgraves of Thuringia and once hosted the medieval Minnesinger poets, immortalized by Wagner in *Tannhäuser*. This was also where Martin Luther hid upon his return from the Diet of Worms in 1521, so he could complete his translation of the Bible—he is said to have "fought the Devil with ink" at Wartburg. The castle has now been turned into a regional museum. It's open April to October daily 8:30am to 4:30pm, November to March daily 9am to 3:30pm. Admission to the palace, museum, and Luther's room is 11DM ($5.50) for adults, 8DM ($4) senior citizens, 6DM ($3) for students and children.

Eisenach is also the birthplace of Johann Sebastian Bach (1685–1750). **Bachhaus,** Am Frauenplan 21 (☎ 03691/20-37-14; Bus: 3), contains many mementos of the Bach family, along with a collection of musical instruments. It's open April to September, Monday noon to 6:45pm and Tuesday to Sunday 9am to 6:45pm; October to March, Monday 1 to 5:45pm and Tuesday to Sunday 9am to 5:45pm. Admission is 5DM ($2.50) for adults, 4DM ($2) for students and children.

You can also visit the **Lutherhaus,** home of the Cotta family, Lutherplatz 8 (☎ 03691/2-98-30; Bus: 1 or 5). Martin Luther stayed here as a schoolboy. It's open daily 9am to 5pm. Admission is 5DM ($2.50) for adults and 2DM ($1) for children and students.

Where to Stay & Dine

Arkona Hotel Thüringer Hof. Near the railway station, Karlsplatz 11, 99817 Eisenach. ☎ **03691/280.** Fax 03691/281-900. E-mail: 03691280-7@t-online.de. 127 units. MINIBAR TV TEL. 195DM–235DM ($97.50–$117.50) double; 350DM ($175) suite. AE, DC, MC, V. Parking 12DM–18DM ($6–$9). Bus: 3.

This hotel was originally a very glamorous inn in the early 19th century. Today it's a part of the Arkona chain. It boasts six floors of well-designed but small rooms. Baths are compact. On the premises are a bar and a well-managed and cozy restaurant, the Wintergarten. The hotel is located near almost every site of historic interest in town.

Romantik Hotel Kaiserhof. Wartburger Allee 2, 99817 Eisenach. ☎ **03691/21-35-13.** Fax 03691/20-36-53. www.romantikhotels.com. E-mail: kaiserhof@romentik.de. 64 units. MINIBAR TV TEL. 170DM–280DM ($85–$140) double. Rates include buffet breakfast. AE, DC, MC, V. Free parking. Bus: 3.

Romantik Hotel Kaiserhof is the best in town. Rooms are furnished in traditional style, but with modern conveniences, such as hair dryers. You can dine either in the Turmschanke, which serves a substantial regional cuisine, or in the Zwinger. There's also a gift shop.

2 Leipzig

164km (102 miles) SW of Berlin, 111km (68 miles) NW of Dresden, 126km (78 miles) NE of Erfurt

If you have limited time and have to choose between Dresden and Leipzig, make it Dresden. But if you can work Leipzig into your itinerary, you'll be richly rewarded.

More than any other city in former East Germany (except Berlin, of course), Leipzig brings you into the Germany of today. This once-dreary city is taking on a new life and vitality; a visit here can be absolutely invigorating. Glassy skyscrapers and glitzy nightlife add a cosmopolitan flavor you don't encounter in much of the rest of the region. The approximately 20,000 students who study in the area, as did Nietzsche, Goethe, and Leibniz, help add a spark. One resident put it this way: "Our grunge and metal bands are just as good as those of Berlin, and our cafes just as super cool."

ATTRACTIONS ●

Altes Rathaus **8**
Auerbachs Keller **11**
Bach-Museum **14**
Bose Haus **12**
Deutsche Bücherei **17**
Königshaus **10**
Museum der Bildenden Künste **16**
Museum in der Rundken Ecke **7**
Musikinstrumenten-Museum **18**
Nasch Markt **9**
Neues Rathaus **15**

Neus Opernhaus **19**
Nikolaikirche **21**
Schillerhaus **1**
Thomaskirche **13**
University of Leipzig **20**
Zoologischer Garten Leipzig **2**

ACCOMMODATIONS ■

Holiday Inn Garden Court **5**
Inter-Continental Leipzig **4**
Kempinski Hotel Fürstenhof **6**
Zum Goldener Adler **3**

Leipzig is also famous for more traditional music. Johann Sebastian Bach is closely associated with Leipzig; Mozart and Mendelssohn performed here; and Wagner was born here in 1813.

Because of its strategic value as a rail center, both the RAF and the U.S. Air Force bombed the city heavily in World War II, but it's been rebuilt, more or less successfully. It still has some narrow streets and houses from the 16th and 17th centuries, as well as some Jugendstil (art nouveau) flair. And Leipzig is once again a major rail terminus. From its Hauptbahnhof—with 26 platforms, the largest in Europe—lines radiate to all the chief German cities and to the rest of the continent.

ESSENTIALS

GETTING THERE By Plane The **Leipzig-Halle International Airport** lies 11km (7 miles) northwest of the city center. About 50 airlines link Leipzig with major German cities, such as Munich and Frankfurt, and also some continental destinations. For **Airport Information,** call ☎ **0341/2241156.** A bus runs between the airport and the Leipzig Hauptbahnhof every 30 minutes, Monday to Friday 4am to 8pm and Saturday and Sunday 4:30am to 8pm (trip time: 40 min.). The fare is 10DM ($5). Taxis are also available, meeting all arriving planes, but the 25- to 30-minute ride to the city center will cost 50DM ($25) and up.

By Train The **Leipzig Hauptbahnhof,** Willy-Brandt-Platz, lies on the major Deutsche Bundesbahn rail line, with frequent connections to German cities. 17 trains arrive daily from Berlin (trip time: 2 hr. 10 min. to 2 hr. 50 min.); 23 trains from Dresden (1 hr. 35 min. to 2 hr.); and 15 trains from Frankfurt (5 hr.). For information and schedules, call ☎ **1805/99-66-33.** The **Hauptbahnhof** has recently been restored and contains many cafes, shops, and restaurants; it's one of the most happening places in Leipzig.

By Bus Long-distance bus service to such cities as Berlin is provided by **Leipzieger Verkehrsbetriebe.** Buses depart from the east side of the main rail station. For information and schedules, call ☎ **0341/29-17-77.**

By Car Access is via the Halle–Dresden Autobahn east and west or the E51 Autobahn north and south.

VISITOR INFORMATION Contact the **Tourist-Information** office at Richard Wagner Strasse 1 (☎ **0341/7104260**), Monday to Friday 9am to 7pm; Saturday 9:30am to 4pm and Sunday 9:30am to 2pm. The office can supply a map pinpointing the major sights. This place becomes a beehive of activity at the time of the annual trade fairs.

SPECIAL EVENTS Upon arrival, be sure to drop in at the tourist office and see if any festivals are taking place. In late June, for example, during the **Leipziger Jazztage,** the churches, the student clubs, and the opera house fill with music. In early June, the city stages its official **Street Music Festival,** when musicians—some good, some surprisingly good, many awful—play in the area of the Markt, the parks, and other outdoor venues. Sometime during the second week of June, the **Leipziger Stadtfest** turns Sachsenplatz and Grimaische Strasse into one big carnival.

GETTING AROUND A public transit system of trams, light railways, and buses provides frequent service to all parts of the city. An S-Bahn (light railway) serves the suburbs, arriving and leaving from the Hauptbahnhof in the center of Leipzig.

EXPLORING THE CITY

Goethe, who was a student at Leipzig, called the city *klein Paris* (miniature Paris). We wouldn't go quite that far, but Leipzig definitely has its charms. One of the best things to do is to explore the handsomely restored art nouveau **Arkaden (arcades)** that thread through the historic core of the city center. "Mädler Mall" is Leipzig's finest arcade. This is the site of the famous **Auerbachs Keller** (see "Where to Dine," below), the setting for one of the scenes of Goethe's *Faust.* A bronze group of characters from Faust, sculpted in 1913, beckon you down a stone staircase into the cellar restaurant. Nearby is a lovely art nouveau coffee shop called **Mephisto,** decorated appropriately in devilish reds and blacks. All through the Mädlerpassage you can find boutiques as chic and sophisticated as those in Berlin.

A gateway leads to **Nasch Markt,** which occupies the space behind the Altes Rathaus. If you walk around the front of the Altes Rathaus, you'll find yourself within Am Markt, the city's best-known square, at the edge of which stands the **Königshaus.** Originally built in the late 1700s on the site of an even older building, the Königshaus at one time functioned as the city's official guest house for VIPs; it housed both Napoléon and Richard Wagner during their sojourns here.

Neues Rathaus on Burgplatz was erected on the site of the old Pleissenburg, the citadel where Martin Luther held a momentous disputation in 1519. The best place in Leipzig to go people-watching is on **Peterstrasse,** below Markt.

THE TOP ATTRACTIONS

✪ **Thomaskirche (St. Thomas Church).** Thomaskirchhof 18 (just off Marktplatz). ☎ 0341/9-60-28-55. Free admission. Apr–Oct daily 8am–6pm, Nov–Mar daily 9am–5pm. Tram: 4, 6, 8, 10, 11, or 13.

Leipzig's most famous resident, Johann Sebastian Bach (1685–1750) was cantor here from 1723 until his death. He spent his most creative years as choirmaster at this church, and is buried just in front of the altar. Both Mozart and Mendelssohn performed in the Thomaskirche as well, and Richard Wagner was christened here in 1813. The church was built on the site of a 13th-century monastery, and was heavily restored after World War II. Its high-pitched roof dates from 1496. The city's Thomaner Choir presents concerts every Sunday morning and Friday evening, when it's in residence—the choir is often on tour.

Altes Rathaus. Markt 1. ☎ **0341/96-51-30.** Admission 5DM ($2.50) adults, 2.50DM ($1.25) children. Tues 2–8pm, Wed–Sun 10am–6pm. Tram: 4 or 6.

The 16th-century Town Hall stands on the 12th-century Renaissance Markt. Allied bombs rained down on the building, but it has been carefully restored. Inside, you'll find the Stadtgeschichtliches Museum, chronicling the city's history, both cultural and political.

Bach-Museum. Thomaskirchhof 16. ☎ **0341/964-4135.** Admission 6DM ($3) adults, 4DM ($2) children, 12DM ($6) family ticket. Daily 10am–5pm. Guided tours at 11am and 3pm. Tram: 4, 6, 8, 10, 11, or 13.

The reconstructed Bose House stands in the shadow of the Thomaskirche. It was once the home of the Bach family and now contains the largest Bach archives in Germany. Many mementos of the composer are also found here.

Museum der Bildenden Künste. Grimmaische Strasse 1–7. ☎ **0341/21-69-90.** Admission 8DM ($4) adults, 5DM ($2.50) children. Tues and Thurs–Sun 10am–6pm, Wed 1–10pm. Tram: 4, 6, 8, 10, 11, 13, 15, or 20.

The 2,500 paintings and sculptures in this museum include works by Dürer, Rubens, Rembrandt, Rodin, and van Eyck. The building was constructed in 1888 as the home of the Supreme Court of the Reich and became a museum in 1952. One section displays exhibits relating the story of Georgi Dimitroff, once head of the Communist

Singing Through the Centuries: The St. Thomas Boys' Choir

In recent times while the Vienna Boys' Choir enjoyed worldwide fame, Leipzig's St. Thomas Choir (Thomasknabenchor) languished in obscurity in the eastern zone. Now all that is changing. Any musical expert can tell you that the Leipzig choir has plenty of talent, and as it tours more widely in Europe, its fame will no doubt grow.

The choir has been here since the 13th century. The boys sang on every occasion in the Middle Ages—city celebrations, the installation of bishops, and even executions. Today, the setting for this venerable musical force is the **Thomaskirche (St. Thomas Church).** Choirboys still follow an almost medieval regime within a distinctive subculture that's a world unto itself. Each newcomer is assigned a "mentor" from among the trusted older members of the choir, and all members are required to eat, sleep, study, and rehearse according to a semi-monastic regimen. The most famous member was none other than Johann Sebastian Bach. He wrote his great cantatas for this choir and was cantor (choirmaster) for 27 years.

party in Bulgaria. Hitler accused Dimitroff and other Communist leaders of responsibility for the Reichstag fire. Hermann Göring himself interrogated Dimitroff, but the trial in Leipzig resulted in an acquittal. In the carefully preserved courtroom, tapes of the Reichstag trial are played (in German).

Museum in der Runden Ecke. Dittrichring 24 (north of Thomaskirche). ☎ **0341/ 96-12-44-3.** Free admission. Wed–Sun 2–6pm. Tram: 1, 2, 4, 6, 15, 17, 21, or 24 to Goerderlerring or Thomaskirche.

This museum, one of Leipzig's newest, could hardly have been imagined a few years ago. The building was the headquarters of the dreaded Stasi, the East German Ministry for State Security. One exhibition, called "The Power and Banality of the East German Secret Police," documents the meticulous and paranoid methods by which the police monitored every exchange of information in the country. They constantly seized private letters and listened in on phone conversations—at times monitoring up to 2,000 calls at once. The exhibition also traces the steps local people took to throw off the Communist regime and end Stasi terror. On the nights of December 4 and 5, 1989, local citizens seized the building. Leipzig is called *Heldenstadt,* or "city of heroes," for its role in toppling the government of East Germany.

Musikinstrumenten-Museum (Museum of Musical Instruments). University of Leipzig, Täubschenweg 2C. ☎ **0341/214-2120.** Admission 5DM ($2.50) adults, 2DM ($1) children. Tues–Sat 10am–5pm, Sun 10am–2pm. Tram: 4, 6, 15, or 20.

This museum exhibits musical instruments, chiefly Italian, German, and French treasures of the 16th to the 19th centuries. Occasionally performances are given, when the historical instruments are played.

Schillerhaus. Menckestrasse 42, Gohlis. ☎ **0341/5-66-21-70.** Admission 4DM ($2) adults, 1DM (50¢) children. Oct–Apr, Tues–Wed and Fri 10am–5pm, Thurs 10am–4pm, Sat 11am–5pm; May–Sept, Tues–Sun 11am–6pm. Tram: 6, 20 or 24.

In this small farmhouse in Gohlis, a suburb about 20 minutes from the center of Leipzig, Friedrich von Schiller (1759–1805), the greatest name after Goethe in

German literature, wrote his "Ode to Joy" in 1785. Beethoven incorporated the poem into the great final movement of his Ninth Symphony.

Zoologischer Garten Leipzig. Pfaffendorfer-Strasse 29. ☎ **0341/5-93-35-00.** Admission 11DM ($5.50) adults, 5DM ($2.50) children and students. Nov–Mar daily 9am–5pm; Apr and Oct daily 9am–6pm; May–Sept daily 9am–7pm. Tram: 20 or 24.

This zoo breeds animals to help conserve endangered species. It was founded in 1878 and is internationally known for the breeding of carnivores. The biggest aquarium in eastern Germany outside Berlin is also here.

MORE SIGHTS & ACTIVITIES

The German Museum of Books and Scripts, the **Deutsche Bücherei,** Deutscher Platz 1 (☎ **0341/2-27-12-23;** tram 21), is the central archive of German literature. You can visit it free, but only with special permission, Monday to Saturday 9am to 4pm. The archive was established in 1912 to showcase the fine art of German printing and bookbinding. It's said to possess every item of German literature ever published. It also has a copy of *Iskra*, the Bolshevik newspaper that Lenin came here to print secretly in 1900.

Contrary to popular belief, Thomaskirche isn't the oldest church in Leipzig. That distinction belongs to **Nikolaikirche,** on Nikolaistrasse, erected in 1165. Many works by Bach, including the *St. John Passion*, were first performed here.

If the weather is fair, head for the **Leipzig University Tower,** near Nikolaikirche. This metal and glass tower overlooks street performers who take over on summer weekends. It's the greatest free show in Leipzig. (Well, not exactly free—the performers will pass the hat at the end of their acts.) Just beware of the skateboard warriors, who make walking about a bit perilous. The **Universität Leipzig,** founded in 1409, has contributed greatly to the cultural growth of the city. The East German government rechristened it Karl Marx University, but the old name was restored in 1990. **Augustusplatz** is the ideal center to rub elbows with the thousands of students who study here.

To escape the fumes and noise of the city, head for such "green lungs" as **Johanna-park** on Karl-Tauchnitz-Strasse, or one of the wildly overgrown cemeteries by the **Völkerschlachdenkmai.** On hot days, the fountains in **Sachensplatz** often become a spectacle of pasty white skin splashing about.

SHOPPING   Leipzig has emerged as the art-buying capital of the former East Germany. Galleries hold rich inventories of paintings and sculpture by artists whose works were once unknown to western consumers. **Galerie für Zeitgenössiche Kunst,** Karl-Tauchnitz-Strasse 11 (☎ **0341/140-810**) displays international art, showing about 14 exhibitions a year. It charges 5DM ($2.50) for adults, 3DM ($1.50) for students and children (free for those 10 and under). Other good galleries include **ARTCO Galerie für Zeitgenössische Kunst,** Ferdinand-Rhode-Strasse 14 (☎ **0341/ 960-38-51**); **Galerie Eigen Art,** Barfussgassch 2–8 (☎ **0341/960-78-86**); and **Galerie Michael Beck,** Gottschedstrasse 12 (☎ **0341/862-25-50**).

If you're looking for examples of the antique furniture and art objects that many Leipziegers have dragged down from their attics since reunification, head for any of the dozen or so antiques dealers conducting business within the town's core. Antiques shops catering to walk-in clients include **Musik-Antiquariat,** Thomaskirchhof 15 (☎ **0341/960-48-63**), which is devoted entirely to musical instruments; **H. Beier,** Nikolaistrasse 55 (☎ 0341/960-1038); and **Zentralantiquariat Leipzig GmbH,** at Talstrasse 29 (☎ **0341/216-170**).

WHERE TO STAY

Holiday Inn Garden Court. Rudolf-Breitscheid-Strasse 3 (opposite the main station), 04105 Leipzig. ☎ **0341/1-25-10.** Fax 0341/12-51-10-0. www.holiday-inn.com. E-mail: hileifzig@aol.com. 121 units. A/C MINIBAR TV TEL. 159DM–320DM ($79.50–$160) double; 200DM–270DM ($100–$135) suite. Rates include buffet breakfast. AE, CB, DC, MC, V. Parking 15DM ($7.50). Tram: 11, 15, 16, or 28.

Although this hotel is a top choice, it still ranks below the Inter-Continental. Rooms are brightly decorated and well-furnished. Each has a safe, satellite TV, and VCR. No-smoking rooms are available. The public areas are brightly decorated with original and limited-edition prints by Peter Kuckei, a fascinating and internationally acclaimed artist.

Dining/Diversions: The hotel has one of the best restaurants in the area, with a chef who vows he "will not tolerate monotony." He offers a richly varied cuisine, with a focus on local delicacies and produce.

Amenities: Room service, hair dryers, laundry, baby-sitting; health club with sauna, steam bath, and workout equipment.

Inter-Continental Leipzig. Gerberstrasse 15 (5 min. from Altes Rathaus), 04105 Leipzig. ☎ **800/327-0200** in the U.S. and Canada, or 0341/98-80. Fax 0341/9-88-12-29. www.hotel-interconti-leipzig.de. E-mail: leipzig@interconti.com. 447 units. MINIBAR TV TEL. 168DM–370DM ($84–$185) double; from 450DM ($225) suite. Special offers on weekends. AE, CB, DC, MC, V. Parking 20DM ($10). Tram: 4 or 6.

This silver-and-concrete high-rise, the city's tallest building, stands today as one of the finest hotels in Leipzig. It's much improved in the last few years, and now receives guests from all over the world. The lobby is spacious and elegant. Rooms are comfortably furnished.

Dining/Diversions: The Brühl Restaurant, which contains a piano bar and wine cellar, offers breakfast and à la carte dining in the evening. Low-priced Saxon dishes are served in the Bierstube. The Yamato Restaurant features sushi, sashimi, and teppanyaki. The hotel also has a casino, lobby bar, and cafe lounge.

Amenities: 24-hour room service, hair dryers, same-day laundry, massage, hair-dresser, florist, health club with indoor pool, solarium, sauna, fitness machines, two bowling lanes, car-rental desk, business center, beauty salon.

✪ Kempinski Hotel Fürstenhof. Tröndlinring 8, 04105 Leipzig. ☎ **800/426-3135** in the U.S., or 0341/14-00. Fax 0341/1-40-37-00. E-mail: reservationlpz@kempinski.com. 92 units. A/C MINIBAR TV TEL. 390DM–520DM ($195–$260) double; from 670DM ($335) suite. AE, DC, MC, V. Parking 35DM ($17.50). Tram: 15.

This hotel, located in a historic 18th-century building, is the best in Leipzig. Its interior has been redecorated to reflect the building's original, almost-forgotten neoclassical theme. A corps of English and Swedish designers have outfitted the rooms in a modern interpretation of neoclassical style. The ballroom (the Serpentinensaal) and a monumental staircase date from the 19th century.

Dining/Diversions: The hotel maintains a good restaurant that serves full breakfast, lunch, and dinner.

Amenities: Concierge, room service, hair dryers, dry cleaning, laundry service, twice-daily maid service, baby-sitting, rock-ringed swimming pool, secretarial services, health club with Jacuzzi and sauna, conference rooms, business center.

Zum Goldener Adler. Portitzer Strasse 10 (in the Sellerhausen district), 04318 Leipzig. ☎ **0341/24-40-00.** Fax 0341/2440084. 20 units. TV TEL. 140DM ($70) double; Fri–Sun 160DM ($80) double. MC, V. Tram: 6.

This is a good bet for unpretentious, cost-conscious lodging. The hotel is about a mile northeast of Leipzig's center, easily reached by tram or taxi. Rooms are small but reasonably comfortable and offer a simple but appealing decor. There's a bar and an unpretentious, sometimes moderately rowdy bistro that specializes in beer, burgers, steaks, wursts, and pastas.

WHERE TO DINE

Apels Garten. Kolonnadenstrasse 2. ☎ **0341/9-60-77-77.** Reservations recommended. Main courses 16DM–30DM ($8–$15); fixed-price menus 33DM–42DM ($16.50–$21). AE, MC, V. Mon–Sat 11:30am–midnight, Sun 11:30am–3:30pm. Tram: 4, 6, 8, 10, 11, or 13. GERMAN.

Its name commemorates the site of a 400-year-old garden, no longer in existence. Today you'll find a modern mid-1980s building with a conservatively decorated street-level restaurant known for its home-style German food. Specialties include wild-duck soup with homemade noodles, roast goose with potatoes and vegetables, grilled wurst with potatoes and red cabbage, and sauerbraten with onions and red cabbage. The cuisine is more robust than refined, but it's very filling.

✪ **Auerbachs Keller.** Mädler Passage (off the market square, close to the Altes Rathaus), Grimmaischestrasse 2–4. ☎ **0341/21-61-00.** Reservations recommended. Historic Rooms, main courses 30DM–40DM ($15–$20); fixed-price menu 65DM–120DM ($32.50–$60). Big Room, main courses 25DM–36DM ($12.50–$18). AE, MC, V. Historic Rooms Mon–Sat 6pm–midnight. Big Room daily 11:30am–midnight. Tram: 4 or 6. GERMAN/INTERNATIONAL.

Many visitors to Leipzig eat at their hotels. However, we suggest that you escape for at least 1 night to dine at the famous Auerbachs Keller, the restaurant and tavern where Goethe staged the debate between Faust and Mephistopheles in his play *Faust.* The cellar dates from 1530 and has a series of 16th-century murals representing the *Faust* legend. The chefs prepare mainly regional cuisine of Saxony, along with a selection of international dishes. Some of the most tempting offerings are fillet of veal, beef, or saddle of lamb, prepared with special sauces and served with seasonal vegetables. The menu changes every 2 months. You can also order from a fine selection of wines and beers. Guests have a choice of the Historic Rooms (dinner only) or the Big Room, which has a different menu.

Between 11:30am and 6pm, Monday to Saturday, visitors can see the Historic Rooms for a charge of 1.50DM (75¢).

Paulaner Palais. Klostergasse 3–5. ☎ **0341/2-11-31-15.** Reservations recommended, especially Mon–Fri. Main courses 17DM–30DM ($8.50–$15). AE, DC, MC, V. Daily 11am–midnight. Tram: 4 or 6. GERMAN/BAVARIAN/AUSTRIAN.

This large restaurant is on the street level of a fine rococo 18th-century building. One section is decorated like a typical Bavarian inn; others are dedicated to the style of Meissen (known for porcelain), Leipzig itself, and Sans Souci (known for rococo extravagance). More seats are in a summer courtyard. A continental cuisine is served. Although there's an excessive emphasis on boiled meats such as *Tafelspitz* (beef) and heavy sauces, the place remains an enduring local favorite. Wiener schnitzel and braised veal shank are two of the chef's other specialties. Foaming mugs of only one kind of beer are served: Paulaner Bier, brewed in Munich, the hometown of the owner.

LEIPZIG AFTER DARK

Leipzig's active nightlife offers something for everyone. The area around the Markt is full of bars, cafes, and other entertainment options; it's a good place to kick off your search for a nightspot.

THE PERFORMING ARTS   The **Leipzieger Oper** is one of Germany's most acclaimed opera companies. Its home is the **Neues Opernhaus,** Augustusplatz 8 (☎ **0341/126-12-61;** tram: 4, 5, 12, 13, or 15), opposite Das Gewandhaus (see below). The box office is open Monday to Friday 10am to 8pm, and Saturday 10am to 4pm. Tickets are 18DM to 60DM ($9 to $30), with students getting up to one-third off, depending on the performance. The smaller **Kellertheater** (☎ **0341/1261261**) presents small ensemble progressive performances of all types. Call the box office for information. Tickets are 15DM to 30DM ($7.50 to $15).

The home of the famous ✪ **Gewandhaus Orchestra** is a modern concert hall built in 1981, **Das Gewandhaus** (☎ **0341/1-27-02-80;** tram: 4, 5, 12, 13, or 15), which faces the Neues Opernhaus across Augustusplatz. Founded in 1781, the orchestra saw some of its greatest days under the baton of Felix Mendelssohn, who died in Leipzig in 1847. Other notable conductors have included Wilhelm Furtwängler, Bruno Walter, and Kurt Masur. Concerts, ballets, organ recitals, and other events are staged here. Tickets are 20DM to 65DM ($10 to $32.50).

The main theater is the **Schauspielhaus,** Bosestrasse 1 (☎ **0341/12680;** tram 1, 2, 4, 6, 15, 17, 21, or 24), home to several arts companies which jointly stage an eclectic mix of theatrical and musical productions. Tickets cost from 20DM to 50DM ($10 to $25), and are half-price for students. The box office is open weekdays 10am to 6pm, Saturday 10am to 1pm, and 1 hour before show time.

BARS   On the street level of the Auerbachskeller is the **Mephisto Bar,** Mädlerpassage (☎ **0341/216100;** tram: 4 or 6), which honors Goethe and the Faust legend. It is also happens to be the hippest bar and cafe in Leipzig, and the best seat for people-watching in the historic core. Within a decor whose colors (black, red, orange, and green) emulate the fires of hell, you can sit at cramped tables, stand amid the crowd of trendies, and sip cocktails, beer, or wine, or order simple platters such as Camembert with grapes, soups, salads, or pâtés with toast. The most popular cocktail is the "Mephisto Feuer" (Satan's fire), made from a combination of schnapps, orange juice, and sekt. There's live music presented, without a cover charge, usually Thursday to Saturday, beginning around 8pm. Open daily 1pm to midnight.

Another favorite Leipzig watering hole is the **Letterman Bar,** Gottsched Strasse 1 (☎ **0341/961-1293;** tram: 5 or 16), which is laid back and appealingly but discreetly permissive.

DANCE CLUBS   **Tanzpalast,** Bosestrasse 1 (☎ **0341/960-05-96;** tram 1, 2, 4, 6, 16, 17, 21, or 24), features three discos and seven bars. On the terrace, steaks and barbecue are served. There's live music Wednesday and Friday. It opens nightly at 11pm and might close anytime between from 4 to 10am. Cover is 5DM ($2.50). Leipzig's newest and trendiest disco is **Distillery,** Kurt Eisner Strasse, at the corner of Löszniger Strasse (☎ **0341/ 963-0718;** bus: 89; tram: 5 or 16). The cutting-edge scene here resembles Berlin or Hamburg more than staid eastern Germany. It's open Friday 11pm to 6am and Saturday 11pm to 9am. Cover is 8DM ($4) on Friday and 10DM to 15DM ($5 to $7.50) on Saturday.

LIVE MUSIC   Built against the old city wall, **Moritzbastei,** Universitätsstrasse 9 (☎ **0341/702590;** tram: 4, 6, 15, or 20), is an all-in-one complex that houses three music halls, a pub with six bars, and a cafe. It's popular with students. On Wednesday, Friday, and Saturday evenings, DJs play African, heavy metal, and rock mixed with contemporary dance music 8pm to 5am; cover is 5DM to 11DM ($2.50 to $5.50). Other nights, live bands play jazz and blues; cover ranges from 10DM to 25DM ($5 to $12.50). During the summer, foreign movies are shown on the roof for 10DM ($5). Open 10am to midnight, or to 5am on dance nights.

For more blues, jazz, and the occasional presentation of German-language satire and cabaret, head to **Pfeffermühle,** Thomaskirchhof 16 (☎ **0341/960-31-96;** tram: 4, 6, 8, 10, 11, or 13), on Monday night, when the bands start up at 10pm. Other nights, people gather to drink and talk. The courtyard here is very popular during warm weather.

GAY BARS & CLUBS   The friendly, ultracool bar **RosaLinde,** Lindenauer Markt 22 (☎ **0341/484-15-11;** tram: 5, 13, 15, 17, or 27), is the central focus of gay Leipzig. It's open nightly at 8pm. Come here for a drink and to find out what's happening around town. An equally worthy and popular gay hangout is **Blaue Trude,** Katharinenstrasse 17 (☎ **0341/212-6679;** tram: 1, 2, 3, 4, 6, 8, 15, 17, 21, 24, 27 or 31), which functions as a bar every night 8pm to 2am, and as a gay (mostly male) disco every Wednesday to Saturday from around 10pm to 5am. Entrance is free.

VARIETY   The best cabaret in town, **Gohglmohsch,** Markt 9 (☎ **0341/ 9-61-51-11;** tram: 4 or 6), presents a nightly German-language show of satire and music that can get quite bawdy and extremely critical of the modern German state and the foibles of the bourgeoisie. The cafe here is open daily 5pm to 3am; the show starts at 8pm. (Its tongue-in-cheek name, incidentally, translates from a medieval Saxon dialect as "Rubbish.") Tickets cost 25DM ($12.50), but students get discounts of around 17DM ($8.50), depending on the show. **Schaubühne Lindenfels,** Karl Heine-Strasse 50 (☎ **0341/ 484620;** tram: 1, 2, 4, 6, 15, 17, 21, or 24), offers alternative theater and cinema in a laid-back cafe-bar complex. Open daily 10am to 1am. Nightly movies cost 7DM to 9DM ($3.50 to $4.50). Theater productions are 12DM to 20DM ($6 to $10) and run Thursday to Saturday and sometimes Sunday. Call for information.

SIDE TRIPS FROM LEIPZIG
LUTHERSTADT WITTENBERG

This is the city associated with **Martin Luther** (1483–1546), leader of the German Reformation. It attracts pilgrims from all over the world. Wittenberg's other famous son was humanist Philipp Melanchthon (1497–1560), a Protestant reformer and scholar and a friend of Luther's and later of Calvin's. Both are honored with statues in front of the Rathaus. Wittenberg is a handsome enough city, but a stop here isn't a must unless you're particularly interested in Luther.

Wittenberg lies 68km (42 miles) northeast of Leipzig and 100km (62 miles) southwest of Berlin. Access by car is via the A9 Autobahn north and south, Route 187 east, and Highway 2 north and south. The Wittenberg Bahnhof is on the major Deutsche Bundesbahn rail line (Halle–Berlin), with frequent connections. It's an hour by train from Leipzig. For travel information, contact **Wittenberg-Information,** Schloss-strasse 2 (☎ **03491/ 49-86-10**), open Monday to Friday 9am to 6pm, Saturday 10am to 2pm, and Sunday 11am to 3pm.

Both Luther and Melanchthon are buried in the **Schlosskirche,** Friedrichstrasse 1a (☎ **03491/40-25-85**), which dates from the 15th century but was rebuilt in the 19th. It was on the Schlosskirche doors that Luther nailed his "Ninety-Five Theses" in 1517. The bronze doors were added in 1858 and bear the Latin text of the theses. The church is open November to April, Tuesday to Saturday 10am to 5pm, and Sunday 11:30am to 5pm; May to October, it's open Monday 2 to 5pm, Tuesday to Saturday 10am to 5pm, and Sunday 11:30am to 5pm. Services are held Sunday at 10am and Wednesday at noon. There's an organ concert every Tuesday at 2:30pm. Admission is free; a guided tour costs 2DM ($1).

Part of an Augustinian monastery in which Luther lived has been turned into the **Lutherhalle Wittenberg,** Collegienstrasse 54 (☎ **03491/420-30**). The parish church here, where Luther preached, dates from the 14th century. An oak tree marks the spot outside the Elster gate where Luther publicly burned his papal bull of excommunication in 1520. It's open November to March, Tuesday to Sunday 10am to 5pm; April to October, Tuesday to Sunday 9am to 6pm. Admission is 7DM ($3.50) for adults, 4DM ($2) for students, 2DM ($1) for children 7 to 18, and free for children 6 and under.

You can also visit the **Stadtkirche,** Kirchplatz (☎ **03491/40-44-15**), where Luther did the majority of his preaching. It's called the "Mother Church of the Reformation." Sections date to the 13th century, making it the oldest structure in Wittenberg. The altar is by Lucas Cranach the Elder, who was once Bürgermeister of Wittenberg and a friend to Luther. It's open Monday to Saturday 9am to noon and 2 to 5pm and Sunday 11am to noon and 2 to 5pm. Admission is free.

Where to Stay & Dine

Park Inn. Neustrasse 7–10, 06886 Wittenberg. ☎ **0049/46-10.** Fax 0049/46-12-00. E-mail: plwittenberg@parkhtls.com. 171 units. MINIBAR TV TEL. 185DM–300DM ($92.50–$150) double. Rates include buffet breakfast. AE, CB, DC, DISC, MC, V. Parking 13DM ($6.50).

This is one of the best hotels in town, located in the historic city center on a pedestrian mall. It's often filled in summer with pilgrims coming to pay their respects to Martin Luther. Rooms are comfortable but a bit lackluster, with modern furnishings, compact baths, and rather thin towels. The hotel restaurant serves both regional and international dishes, and there's also a bar.

QUEDLINBURG

In 1994, UNESCO cited Quedlinburg as "an extraordinary example of a medieval European city," and added it to its list of World Heritage Sites.

Quedlinburg, which survived World War II intact, is nestled at the foot of a rock pinnacle, and crowned by a castle and an abbey church. It has origins going back to a Saxon settlement in the early 10th century. Here you'll see an architectural masterpiece, the church of St. Servatius, as well as a well-preserved castle and cobbled lanes with half-timbered houses dating from the 16th and 17th centuries.

There are three trains a day from Leipzig (travel time: 3 hr.). Call ☎ **1805/ 99-66-33** for information and schedules. Access by car is along B6. For tourist information, contact **Quedlinburg-Information,** Markt 2 (☎ **03946/90-56-24**), open May to September, Monday to Friday 9am to 8pm, Saturday and Sunday 9am to 6pm; October, March, and April, Monday to Friday 9am to 6pm, Saturday and Sunday 10am to 3pm; November to February, Monday to Friday 9am to 5pm, Saturday and Sunday 10am to 3pm.

Begin your tour in the **Altstadt (Old Town),** site of the **Markt (Marketplace).** The **Rathaus,** in the Renaissance style of the 1600s, was originally built in 1310. The statue (ca. 1420) on the left of the facade is of Roland, Charlemagne's knight. The buildings on the other three sides of the Markt are from the 1600s and 1700s. Branching off the square are small cobblestone lanes right out of the Middle Ages. The area around Breitstrasse has several colorful alleyways.

Take the ramp up to the castle to the broad terrace that offers a panoramic view of the medieval town. Here, on the site of the original 9th-century church, stands Quedlinburg's major attraction, the **Stiftskirche St. Servatius,** Schlossberg 1 (☎ **03946/709-900**), one of the architectural masterpieces of the Romanesque era. The church was started in 1070 but wasn't consecrated until 1129. Craftsmen from northern Italy were imported to create the friezes and capitals above the central nave. Three aisles with diagonal rib vaulting divide the crypt beneath the chancel. The aisles are adorned with frescoes depicting scenes from the Bible.

The church is filled with treasures, including a treasury (Domschatz) with manuscripts from as far back as the 10th century. In 1990, a number of ecclesiastical artifacts that had disappeared after the war turned up in Texas, when the heirs of a U.S. Army officer tried to sell them. The purloined treasures have been returned and are now on permanent display. The church is open May to October, Tuesday to Saturday 10am to 6pm; off-season, Tuesday to Saturday 10am to 4pm and on Sunday noon to 4pm. Admission is 6DM ($3) for adults and 4DM ($2) for children.

Burgberg Schloss, Schlossberg 1 (☎ 03946/27-30), crowning the hill (Schlossberg), was once part of an abbey. A Saxon stronghold in the 10th century, the castle was expanded from the late 16th to the mid–17th centuries. The castle complex includes the Schlossmuseum, which displays 16th- and 17th-century Italian and Flemish paintings as well as exhibits on the history of the town. A Princes' Hall from the mid-1700s and the throne room can also be visited. The castle is open May to September, Tuesday to Sunday 10am to 6pm; off-season, Tuesday to Sunday 10am to 5pm. Admission is 5DM ($2.50) for adults and 3DM ($1.50) for children.

Where to Stay

✪ **Romantik Hotel Am Brühl.** Billungstrasse 11, 06484 Quedlinburg. ☎ 03946/9-61-80. Fax 03946/9-61-82-46. www.hotelambruehl.de. E-mail: hotelambruehl@online.de. 47 units. MINIBAR TV TEL. 190DM–210DM ($95–$105) double; 290DM ($145) suite. Rates include buffet breakfast. AE, DC, V. Free parking.

This romantic and tranquil hotel is run by the Schmidt family. Rooms come in a variety of shapes and sizes. All are well furnished with first-rate mattresses and fine linens; some open onto castle views. Virtually all major attractions are within walking distance. The hotel offers good dining facilities. There's a sauna and a solarium on the premises.

Romantik Hotel Theophano. Markt 13–14 (on the marketplace), 06484 Quedlinburg. ☎ 03946/9-63-00. Fax 03946/96-30-36. www.hoteltheophano. E-mail: theophan@t-online.de. 22 units. TV TEL. 180DM–250DM ($90–$125) double; 290DM ($145) suite. Rates include buffet breakfast. AE, MC, V. Parking 12DM ($6).

Two old guild houses, each about 350 years old, were completely renovated and combined into one hotel. The small rooms are brightly furnished, individually decorated, and often outfitted with antiques. Some have canopied beds. The location is central for sightseeing. The hotel's Weinstube is open Monday to Saturday 6pm to midnight, serving a regional cuisine. In summer, guests can sit in the courtyard.

Zum Goldenen Sonne. Steinweg 11 (a 5-min. walk from the railway station), 06484 Quedlinburg. ☎ 03946/9-62-50. Fax 03946/96-25-30. www.Hotel-QLB.de. E-mail: Info@Hotel-QLB.de. 27 units. MINIBAR TV TEL. 140DM–170DM ($70–$85) double. Rates include buffet breakfast. AE, MC, V. Parking 5DM ($2.50).

This hotel, which dates from 1671, is a good traditional choice. It stands near the Mathildenbrunne, a landmark fountain. The building's wood-beam construction is typical of this part of Germany. The small rooms are cozily furnished in rustic style. The restaurant serves international and regional cuisine, daily from 11am. In summer, the beer garden is popular with locals and visitors alike.

Where to Dine

Ratskeller. Markt 1 (in the Rathaus). ☎ 03946/27-68. Reservations recommended. Main courses 18DM–32DM ($9–$16); fixed-price menu 22DM–36DM ($11–$18). AE, DC, MC, V. Thurs–Tues 11:30am–10:30pm. Closed Jan. GERMAN/INTERNATIONAL.

This longtime favorite is within walking distance of the railway station. Wine buffs should order the rare Saxon wine. The food is hearty and regional. Many of the meat and game specialties are served with wine sauerkraut and dumplings. In season, venison is likely to be on the menu.

3 Dresden

198km (123 miles) S of Berlin, 111km (69 miles) SE of Leipzig

Dresden, once known as "Florence on the Elbe," was celebrated throughout Europe for its architecture and art treasures. Then came the night of February 13, 1945, when Allied bombers rained down phosphorus and high-explosive bombs on the city, which had no military targets. By morning, the Dresden of legend was but a memory. No one knows for sure how many people died, but the number is certainly in the tens of thousands, and perhaps more. If you're interested in the subject, you might want to read Kurt Vonnegut's novel *Slaughterhouse Five.*

Today Dresden is undergoing a rapid and dramatic restoration, and is once again a major sightseeing destination. For example, its once-fabled *Schloss* (castle), for decades only a few blackened walls, is scheduled to be completely rebuilt by the year 2003. Dresden also boasts beautiful churches and palaces, as well as many world-class museums—among the finest in all of Germany.

City officials want the entire city rebuilt by the year 2006 in time for Dresden's 800th anniversary. Even though that dream is a long way from being realized, much has already been accomplished. Thankfully, the work has proceeded along sensible lines, and has none of the unreal, theme-park feeling that some restorations produce. Wherever you go you will not be allowed to forget the Allied bombings of February 1945, which destroyed about three-quarters of the Altstadt.

Regrettably, the city has recently become a center for neo-Nazi skinheads, who occasionally single out foreigners as targets of attack. Be especially careful walking the streets at night. The area north of the Elbe has seen the most violence.

ESSENTIALS

GETTING THERE **By Plane** The **Dresden-Klotsche** airport lies 10km (6 miles) north of the city center. The airport is served by Lufthansa and most international carriers, with regularly scheduled flights from 11 German cities and other major European cities. For flight information, call ☎ **0351/8813360.** A shuttle bus, **Airport Liner** (☎ **0351/2-51-82-43**), runs from the airport to the city center (trip time: 20 min.); one-way fare is 8DM ($4). To go from the airport to the center of Dresden by taxi costs 30DM ($15).

By Train Dresden has two main rail stations, the **Hauptbahnhof,** on Wiener Platz, and the **Dresden-Neustadt,** at Schlesischer Park. Trams 3 and 11 connect the two. The city is served by the Deutsche Bundesbahn rail line, with frequent connections to major and regional cities. From Berlin, 15 trains arrive daily (trip time: 2 to 2$^1/_2$ hours); 12 trains pull in from Frankfurt (trip time: 7 to 8 hours). For rail information and schedules, call ☎ **1805/99-66-33.**

By Car Access is via the E40 Autobahn from the west or the E5 Autobahn from the north (Rostock, Berlin) or from the south.

VISITOR INFORMATION Before tackling museum-filled Dresden, head first to the **Information-Center,** Pragerstrasse 10 (☎ **0351/49-19-20**). It's open April to October, Monday to Friday 10am to 8pm, Saturday 9am to 4pm, and Sunday 10am to 2pm; November to March, Monday to Friday 10am to 6pm, Saturday 9am to 4pm, and Sunday 10am to 2pm. Here you can book your accommodations and purchase a map of Dresden, information booklets in English, and tickets for theater, opera, and concerts.

The **Central Post Office,** Hauptpostamt, Königbrückerstrasse 21–29 (☎ **0351/ 819-13-70**), is in Dresden-Neustadt and is open Monday to Friday 8am to 6pm and Saturday 8am to noon.

Dresden

ATTRACTIONS ●
Albertinum **18**
Altmarkt **5**
Alstadt **3**
Frauenkirche **19**
Gemäldegalerie Alte Meister (Zwinger) **9**
Grosser Garten **2**
Historical Museum (Zwinger) **9**
Katholische Hofkirche **8**
Kreuzkirche **4**
Porcelain Museum (Zwinger) **9**
Royal Palace (Schloss) **7**
Semper Opera House **10**
Stadtmuseum Dresden **20**
Zwinger palace complex **9**

ACCOMMODATIONS ■
Bülow Residenz **14**
Hilton Dresden **17**
Hotel am Terrassenufer **16**
Hotel Coventry **1**
Kempinski Hotel Taschenbergpalais **6**
Martha Hospiz **13**
Seidler Art'otel **11**
Villa Emma **15**
Westin Bellevue **12**

GETTING AROUND   By Public Transportation   If you plan to see more than the historic core of Dresden, you might use the bus and tram lines. A ride of four stops or fewer costs 2.20DM ($1.10), or you can purchase a 24-hour pass for 12DM ($6). Maps and tickets are sold at Fahrkarten dispensers outside the main rail station. After midnight, service is curtailed, although most major lines still operate every hour. Dresden's S-Bahn reaches the suburbs.

By Funicular   There are two funiculars in Dresden. The **Standseilbahn** links the suburb of Loschwitz to a hillside residential area, Weiber Hirsch. The **Schwebebahn** links Loschwitz with Oberloschwitz, and takes passengers to the viewing site at Loschwitzhöhe, which gives you an excellent view of the city. This funicular was the first of its kind in the world, built in 1898–1900.

By Ferry   Five ferries service Dresden. One is a vehicular ferry across the River Elbe between Dresden–Kleinzschachwitz and the Pillnitz Castle. Call **Sächsischer Dampfschiffahrt** at ☎ **0351/86-60-90** for more information.

SEEING THE SIGHTS

The amount of restoration going on here is tremendous. At present, and for years to come, expect to see some of the major sights of Dresden behind scaffolding. Despite the reconstruction, there are still many ruins of the war left, most notably the baroque **Frauenkirche (Church of Our Lady),** at Neumarkt, built between 1726 and 1743 and once known throughout Europe for its cupola. The East German government deliberately let the blackened hulk remain, as a reminder of the horrors of modern warfare. But today the church is slowly being rebuilt.

The restored **Katholische Hofkirche (Catholic Court Church),** Schlossplatz (☎ **0351/49-51-133**), is the biggest church in Saxony. It was built by the son of August the Strong, Frederick Augustus II, who ruled from 1733 to 1763. The church's facade has 38 biblical and historical figures in the high baroque style. Inside, you can see the crypt with the tombs of 49 rulers of Saxony and a box allegedly containing the heart of August the Strong. On the main floor you can see a beautiful stone pulpit by the royal sculptor, Balthasar Permoser (1651–1732), one of the leading sculptors of his time in Saxony. There's also an 18th-century church organ. Admission is free. This church, also known as the Cathedral of St. Trinitas, is open Monday to Saturday 9am to 5pm, Saturday 10am to 5pm, and Sunday noon to 5pm.

The **Kreuzkirche (Church of the Cross)** stands at the Altmarkt, or old market square. This church is the home of the Kreuzchor, the famous boys' choir of Dresden. Its architecture is a combination of baroque and art nouveau. The present building is from the late 18th century, although a church on this spot stood here as early as the 13th century. You can also view the reconstructed **Rathaus (town hall)** and the 18th-century **Landhaus** at the Altmarkt, which today contains a minor museum, **Museum für Geschichte der Stadt Dresden** (☎ **0351/498660**), displaying the artifacts of Dresden over the centuries. The museum is open Saturday to Thursday 10am to 6pm; on Wednesday May to September, it's open until 8pm. It charges 4DM ($2) for adults, 3DM ($1.50) ages 6 to 15 (free 5 and under).

Of Dresden's many parks and gardens, the best and most popular is the **Grosser Garten,** to the southeast of the Altstadt. This park, which was mapped out in 1676, contains a zoo and a botanical garden. In the center is a *Lustschloss* (pleasure palace) built in 1670.

THE MAJOR MUSEUMS

✪ **Zwinger.** Theaterplatz 1. ☎ **0351/4-91-46-19.** Gemäldegalerie Alte Meister 7DM ($3.50) adults, 4DM ($2) children and senior citizens; Rüstkammer 3DM ($1.50) adults, 2DM

Wallpavillon

Marhematisch–
Physikalischer Salon

Nymphenbad

Zoological
Museum

Julian–Grimau–Allee

graben

Picture
Gallery

Theaterplatz

Kronentor

Zwinger-

Historical
Museum

Porcelain
Collection

Glockenspielpavillon

($1) children and senior citizens; Porzellansammlung 3DM ($1.50) adults, 2DM ($1) children and senior citizens. You may visit all museums for 12DM ($6) adults, 7DM ($3.50) for children and senior citizens. Tues–Sun 10am–6pm. Porzellansammlung closed Thurs also. Tram: 1, 2, 4, 7, 8, 11, 12, 14; bus: 82, 94 to Postplatz.

Augustus the Strong, elector of Saxony (he was also king of Poland), built this baroque masterpiece, modeled after Versailles, in 1719. Here he staged tournaments and kept his dozens of concubines. His physique was called Herculean, his temperament Rabelaisian, but he also had a great love for the arts. Today this complex of baroque buildings holds a collection of museums.

The Zwinger was initially conceived by M. D. Pöppelmann (1662–1736) as the forecourt of the castle. In the center of the large quadrangle are formal gardens, fountains, and promenades, forming a deep curving bay enclosed by pavilions. Notable are the Wallpavilion in the center of the semicircular arched gallery in the west end, and the *Nyphenbad* (Bath of Nymphs) with its graceful fountains and mythological figures by Balthasar Permoser, who helped Pöppelmann in the construction of the Zwinger. On the northeast side is a Renaissance-style building, added in 1846 by Gottfried Semper (1803–79). Semper's two-story pavilions are linked by one-story galleries. The architectural critic, Sir Nikolaus Pevsner, once wrote: "What exultation in these rocking curves, and yet what grace! It is joyful but never vulgar; vigorous, boisterous perhaps, but never crude."

The most important museum in the complex is the **Gemäldegalerie Alte Meister,** which has its entrance at Theaterplatz 1. This gallery, one of the best on the

A Cruise on the Elbe

You can take a cruise on the historic River Elbe from central moorings below the Brühl Terrace. **Sächsischer Dampfschiffahrt** (☎ 0351/86-60-90) offers a 4¹/₂-hour cruise along the Elbe from Dresden to the border of the Czech Republic. These trips take you through some of the finest river scenery in eastern Germany, including an area known as "Swiss Saxony," one of Germany's most popular natural wonders. It's a land of table-shaped outcrops, isolated pillars, deep gorges, and sheer sandstone cliffs. The upper reaches of the Elbe flow in wide curves through these fantastically shaped rock formations. April to October, departures are twice daily. The round-trip cost is 32DM ($16) per person.

Even if you don't make a river trip, it's exciting to watch the boats lower their funnels to pass under the bridges. The *Blaues Wunder* (Blue Wonder), one of Dresden's most celebrated bridges, is a beautiful expression of the bridge-building genius that flourished here at the turn of the century.

---

continent, has as its showpiece Raphael's *Sistine Madonna*. You'll also find Giorgione's *Sleeping Venus*, Antonello da Messina's *The Martyrdom of St. Sebastian*, Titian's *Tribute Money*, and many famous works by Veronese, Tintoretto, Correggio, and Annibale Carracci. You'll also see Flemish, Dutch, and German paintings by van Dyck, Vermeer, Dürer, and Rembrandt, among others. The Rubens collection includes his spectacular *Neptune*, full of rearing horses, and an exquisite *St. Jerome*.

The **Rüstkammer (Historical Museum)** displays a collection of weaponry from the 15th to 18th centuries.

✪ **Albertinum.** Brühl Terrace. ☎ **0351/4-91-4619.** Admission 7DM ($3.50) adults, 4DM ($2) children and students. Fri–Wed 10am–6pm. Tram: 1, 3, 5, 7, or 8 to Rathenau Platz.

This imposing imperial structure houses one of Germany's great galleries. It's named for the Saxon King Albert, who between 1884 and 1887 converted this former royal arsenal into a home for a vast collection of art and precious jewelry. The most famous exhibition is the extraordinary **Grünes Gewölbe (Green Vaults),** a dazzling collection of 16th- to 18th-century treasures: rococo chests, ivory carvings, jewelry, intricately designed mirrors, and priceless porcelain. Many pieces were created by the craftspeople of local guilds; others were acquired from the far corners of the earth.

On the remaining two floors is the **Gemäldegalerie Neue Meister,** a collection of 19th- and 20th-century art, from Corot to Otto Dix. We are especially fond of the desolate and haunting landscapes of Caspar David Friedrich, the German Romantic artist. Impressionists and post-impressionists are well represented, including Gauguin, Degas, Manet, Monet, Corinth, Liebermann, Klimt, and van Gogh. Antifascist artists, whose works were either destroyed or banned in the Nazi era, are also on display.

Stadtmuseum Dresden. Wilsdruffer Strasse 2. ☎ **0351/49-86-60.** Admission 4DM ($2) adults, 2DM ($1) children. Sat–Thurs 10am–6pm. Tram: 3 or 5.

This museum contains a rich display of Dresden's history. Especially fascinating are the photographs of the controversial 1945 Allied bombings. Most Germans view the air raids as pointless destruction; one British historian claims they were "Churchill's revenge for the Nazi bombing of Coventry."

BUS TOURS

Responding to the flood of visitors coming to see the city's historic core, **Stadtrundfahrt Dresden,** Königstrasse 6 (☎ 0351/899-5650), has organized a flotilla of red and white buses that feature—via pre-recorded descriptions and headsets—running commentary in eight languages. Every day April to October 9:30am to 5pm, buses depart at 30-minute intervals, and November to March at 60-minute intervals, for circular tours of the city that incorporate overviews of all the major monuments. Visitors can hop on or off the bus at any of 12 points along the way, and they can even postpone some of the stops until the following day. The point of origin of each tour begins at the Schlossplatz, adjacent to the Augustusbrücke. Additional stopovers include the Zwinger, the Grünes Gewölbe, the Frauenkirche, and many of the parks, gardens, and architectural highlights of the city. The price is 29DM ($14.50) per adult. It's free for children under 15.

SHOPPING

Perhaps because of Dresden's destruction in the final days of World War II, there's an emphasis here on collecting the high-quality antiques that remain. You'll find many antiques dealers in the city. Most of the inventory has been culled from homes and estate sales in the relatively unscathed surrounding hamlets. Some of the most appealing shops line either side of a lane called **Am Goldenen Reiter,** accessible via Hauptstrasse 17–19. Here, look for a roster of handcrafted goods and gift items. If you're seeking antiques and artwork, pay a visit to **Antikitäten und Kunst,** Obergraben 19 (☎ **0351/801-4331**), and its similarly named competitor, **Kunst und Antikitäten,** Görlitzerstrasse 39 (☎ **0351/804-5658**). An especially convenient antique gallery is **Antikitäten,** on the lobby level of the Kempinski Hotel Taschenbergpalais, Am Taschenberg (☎ **0351/490-1519**).

The oldest manufacturer of porcelain in Dresden is **Wehsener Porzellan,** 5km (3 miles) southeast of the center at Donaustrasse 72 (☎ **0351/470-73-40;** tram: 13; bus: 72 or 76). Its hand-painted objects are the most charming and interesting in Dresden. Anything you buy can be shipped. You can also take a free tour of the studios and factory.

And don't overlook the city's role as a purveyor of modern painting and sculpture. Two of the most interesting art galleries are **Galerie Gebrüder Lehmann,** Gorlitzerstrasse 16 (☎ **0351/801-1783**), and **Galerie am Blauen Wünder,** Pillnitzer Landstrasse 2 (☎ **0351/268-40-20**).

Weihnachtsland am Zwinger, Kleine Brüdergasse 5 (☎ **0351/862-1230**), is the best-stocked and most interesting gift shop in Dresden, with a year-round emphasis on Christmas, New Year's, and Easter ornaments that are handmade in the nearby Erzgebirge region. Look for pieces of delicate Plauener Spitze lace that's designed to hang on hooks affixed by suction cups to the glass of your windows—it's easy to transport and some pieces of it can be acquired for less than 10DM ($5). There are also elaborately detailed Easter eggs, carved wooden figurines in the shape of either soldiers or angels, and framed still lifes and landscapes made from assemblages of dried flowers.

WHERE TO STAY

Since reunification and the amazing increase in tourism, Dresden's hotel prices have soared, as has the demand for rooms. Even so-called "budget" hotels can command 250DM ($142.50) a night for a double.

VERY EXPENSIVE

✪ **Kempinski Hotel Taschenbergpalais.** Taschenberg 3, 01067 Dresden. ☎ **0351/4-91-20.** Fax 0351/4-91-28-12. www.kempinski-dresden.de. E-mail: reservations@kempinski-dresden.de. 213 units. A/C MINIBAR TV TEL. 390DM–540DM ($195–$270) double; from 630DM ($315) suite. AE, DC, MC, V. Parking 25DM ($12.50). Tram: 5 or 8.

Few hotels of post-reunification Germany have sparked as much pride among local citizens as this one. Its history dates from the early 18th century, when the elector of Saxony built a baroque castle for his favorite mistress, the Countess Cosel, who for mysterious reasons was later banished from his court. For 250 years, the palace was the pride of Dresden, a site visited almost as much as the Zwinger. But Allied bombing raids left it a smoldering ruin. Only the surreal remains of a massive marble staircase survived.

In 1993, a Frankfurt-based real-estate developer spent $175 million on transforming the ruin into Dresden's finest hotel, restoring the five-story baroque, sculpture-dotted facade to its original opulence. Rooms are the most opulent in town. Those on the west and north sides overlook the Zwinger or the Opera. Baths are quite opulent as well, with heated floors, heated racks of plush towels, robes, hair dryers, and both tubs and shower stalls. Today, a tiny ruined portion of the structure has been artfully retained as a reminder of the bombs of 1945.

Dining/Diversions: A restaurant, the Intermezzo, overlooks the hotel's garden-style courtyard. It serves some of the finest meals in Dresden. There's also a piano bar.

Amenities: Health club with swimming pool and sauna, concierge, 24-hour room service, twice-daily maid service; dry cleaning, laundry, in-room massage, baby-sitting, and secretarial services are all available at an additional charge.

EXPENSIVE

✪ **Bülow Residenz.** Rähnitzgasse 19 (near the Opera), 01097 Dresden. ☎ **0351/8-00-30.** Fax 0351/8-00-31-00. www.Buelow-residenz.de. E-mail: info@www.Buelow-Residenz.de. 30 units. MINIBAR TV TEL. 390DM–480DM ($195–$240) double; 490DM–680DM ($245–$340) suite. AE, DC, MC, V. Parking 15DM ($7.50). Tram: 6, 7, 8, or 9.

This hotel, with a restored facade from the 1700s, has been a success since its opening in the early '90s. The formal lounge, with its plush seating, sets the tone. A garden patio is the perfect place to be on a summer day. Individually decorated rooms are unusually spacious, compared to most in Dresden. Oversize beds and contemporary redwood furnishings make for a restful ambience. Baths have hair dryers.

Dining/Diversions: The hotel restaurant, Caroussel, serves exceptional meals, specializing in regional, British, and various international dishes.

Amenities: Concierge, dry cleaning, laundry, twice-daily maid service, and baby-sitting.

✪ **Hilton Dresden.** An der Frauenkirche 5, 01067 Dresden. ☎ **800/445-8667** in the U.S. and Canada, or 0351/8-64-20. Fax 0351/8-64-27-25. www.hilton.com. E-mail: Dresden-Hilton@t-online.de. 333 units. MINIBAR TV TEL. 410DM–445DM ($205–$222.50) double; 780DM–900DM ($390–$450) suite. AE, DC, MC, V. Parking 25DM ($12.50). Tram: 3, 5, 7, 8, or 12.

This hotel is one of the best in the region. Its conservative mansard-roofed facade blends harmoniously with the baroque buildings on the nearby Neumarkt. A glassed-in passageway connects the hotel to a 19th-century building, the Sekundo-genitur, which contains two restaurants and an array of banqueting and conference rooms. Rooms are mid-sized and short on style, but well maintained. Baths are small, and have hair dryers. Double-glazed windows cut down on the noise. The rooms facing the Frauenkirche are the best.

Dining/Diversions: There are 11 restaurants and cafes. The Rossini is recommended in "Where to Dine," below; others include a bistro, a Bierclub, a Viennese coffeehouse, and a Saxon-style wine cellar.

Amenities: Concierge (to arrange city tours), room service (6am to midnight), laundry, baby-sitting, fitness club (with pool, whirlpool, sauna, and solarium).

✪ **Villa Emma.** Stechgrundstrasse 2, 01324 Dresden. ☎ **0351/26-48-10.** Fax 0351/2-64-81-18. www.prima-hotels.com/gdresden.htm. 21 units. TV TEL. 380DM–450DM ($190–$225) double. Rates include buffet breakfast. AE, DC, MC, V. Free parking. Tram: 11.

This special boutique hotel is the best place for those who don't want to stay at the big chain hotels. It lies 9km (5¹/₂ miles) east of the city center in a forest park of oak, beach, and birch, ideal for walking or jogging. In many ways it has more grace and charm than the highly rated Bülow Residenz. The house is styled with art deco touches. The sunny, spacious rooms are extremely luxurious, with custom-made furnishings and even some original stained-glass windows. Baths have massaging showerheads. Amenities include room service, dry cleaning, laundry service, and a sauna. There's also a good restaurant on the premises.

Westin Bellevue. Grosse Meissner Strasse 15, 01097 Dresden. ☎ **0351/8050.** Fax 0351/8051609. www.westin.com. 339 units. MINIBAR TV TEL. 280DM–450DM ($140–$225) double; from 550DM ($275) suite. Rates include breakfast. AE, DC, MC, V. Parking 20DM ($10). Tram: 4 or 5.

The Bellevue stands by the most attractive part of the Elbe. If you look out the hotel's windows or from its terraces to the opposite riverbank, you'll know you're in the spot where Canaletto painted his magnificent scenes. The ornate walls of a pair of courtyards that survived the 1945 bombings have been integrated into the structure and are now a protected monument. Some rooms overlook the courtyards; others in modern wings that often open onto the Elbe. Whether you stay in the old part or in the new, you'll find well-appointed, air-conditioned rooms. Baths, however, are far from grand, with inadequate towels. All rooms offer better views than those of the Hilton.

Dining/Diversions: Five eating places offer a variety of cuisines, together with consistently good service. Guests can enjoy drinks in the foyer bar.

Amenities: Room service, laundry, baby-sitting, shopping arcade, fitness club with indoor pool, solarium, "bronzarium," and saunas.

MODERATE

Hotel Coventry. Hülsestrasse 1, 01237, Dresden-Altreick. ☎ **0351/28260.** Fax 0351/281-6310. 53 units. MINIBAR TV TEL. 150DM–210DM ($75–$105) double; 235DM–290DM ($117.50–$145) suite. Rates include breakfast. AE, MC, V. Take the train from the Alstadt Hauptbahnhof for 3km (2 miles) southwest to the suburb of Altreick, or take trams 9 or 13 to the Hülsestrasse stop.

This inviting new four-story hotel is in the suburb of Altreick, about a 20-minute drive south of the city center. The location may seem far flung, but it's an easy trip to the center, and many visitors prefer the tranquility of the place. Rooms are comfortable, cozy, and artfully decorated with a soothing, modern simplicity. Many open onto balconies. The in-house restaurant, Coventry Gardens, is a real gem. There's also a piano bar.

Hotel am Terrassenufer. Terrassenufer 12. 01069 Dresden. ☎ **0351/440-95-00.** Fax 0351/440-96-00. www.hotel-terrassenufer.de. E-mail:hotel-terrassenufer.de. 195 units. MINIBAR TV TEL. 220DM–260DM ($110–$130) double. AE, DC, MC, V. Tram: 1, 3, or 5.

Comfortable and reasonably priced, this hotel was built in the 1960s as a student dormitory. In the 1990s, it was renovated and enlarged into the streamlined 12-story hotel you see today. Set on the riverbank, a short walk from Dresden's historic core, it offers large, airy, big-windowed rooms with lots of sunlight. On the premsies is a circle-shaped greenhouse, home of the Pavilion restaurant. It's open daily noon to 11pm. There's also a small bar in the lobby that gets busy around 6pm every day.

Martha Hospiz. Nieritzstrasse 11, 01097 Dresden-Neustadt. ☎ **0351/8-17-60.** Fax 0351/8176222. www.vch.de/martha.hospiz.dresden. 50 units. TV TEL. 190DM–230DM

($95–$115) double. Rates include buffet breakfast. AE, MC, V. Free parking. Tram: 3, 5, 7, 8, 10, or 11.

This simple but comfortable four-story hotel is a quiet 5-minute walk from the commercial heart of modern Dresden. It's a great value. The conservatively modern rooms are spotlessly maintained. Baths are a bit small but neatly organized. The hotel contains few amenities other than its rustic restaurant, Kartoffelkeller.

✪ **Seidler Art'otel.** Ostra-Allee 33, 01067 Dresden. ☎ **0351/4-92-20.** Fax 0351/ 4-92-27-77. www.artotel.de. E-mail: dresden@artotel.de. 174 units. MINIBAR TV TEL. 295DM– 335DM ($147.50–$167.50) double. Rates include buffet breakfast. AE, DC, MC, V. Parking 15DM ($7.50). Tram: 8, 9, 11, or 26.

The six floors of this dramatic postmodern hotel are the most self-consciously "arty" of any hotel in Dresden. They were designed by Denis Santachiara, whose work has been heralded in Munich, Milan, New York, and Paris. One floor is an art gallery that focuses on striking contemporary paintings and sculpture by German artists. Rooms are warmer and more comfortable than you might expect. There's a sauna on the premises, but only a limited roster of exercise equipment. The staff is very conscious of cutting-edge trends in German cities. The hotel's bar and restaurant is called The Factory, plus there is an Italian restaurant called Tomato.

WHERE TO DINE
EXPENSIVE

✪ **Fischgalerie.** Maxstrasse 2 (a 10-min. walk from both the Zwinger and the Kempinski Hotel). ☎ **0351/4-90-35-06.** Reservations recommended. Main courses 26DM–49.50DM ($13–$24.75). AE, MC, V. Tues–Fri noon–3pm, and Tues–Sat 6–11pm. Tram: 8, 9, or 26. SEAFOOD.

This is the best seafood restaurant in town. Its culinary pizzazz stems directly from the chef's experience in upscale restaurants in Berlin and other cities. The interior, with its dramatic lighting, minimalist design, and blue-black color scheme, will remind you of a sophisticated enclave in Milan. There's a small aperitif bar near the entrance, and a theatrical-looking open-view kitchen. Menus change every week, depending on the season, availability of ingredients, and the inspiration of the chef. Fresh seafood dishes might include salmon with fresh spinach and champagne sauce; grilled fillet of zander with red risotto; a combination of scampi with John Dory, served with tomato-flavored *spaghettini*, and crepes stuffed with diced crabmeat. As an appetizer you might try the fresh oysters from Brittany, or marinated herring served with coarsely textured black bread. On Wednesday and Friday nights, there's an assortment of very fresh sushi. Live jazz is presented on the 2nd and 4th Tuesday of each month.

Rossini. In the Dresden Hilton, An der Frauenkirche 5. ☎ **0351/8-64-28-55.** Main courses 32DM–44DM ($16–$22). AE, DC, MC, V. Daily noon–3pm and 6–11:30pm. Tram: 3, 5, 7, 8, or 12. ITALIAN.

Rossini offers Italian cuisine in a stylish setting, one floor above the lobby of the Dresden Hilton. Menu items might include chicken-liver pâté in marsala wine, a buffet of Sicilian antipasti, carpaccio of swordfish marinated in marsala vinaigrette, Sicilian-style fish soup, or grilled lamb with anchovy sauce. Dessert might be cassata made with ricotta cheese and candied fruit, or a *granita* (sorbet) of oranges and lemons floating on white wine.

MODERATE

Brauhaus am Waldschlösschen. Am Brauhaus 8B, in the Neustadt district, 5km (3 miles) northeast of the city center. ☎ **0351/811-990.** Reservations required. Main courses 9DM–27DM ($4.50–$13.50). AE, DC, MC, V. Daily 11am–1am. Tram: 11, 52; bus: 92. GERMAN.

This is a newly built replica of the old-fashioned beer halls and beer gardens that played such an important role in Dresden's past. Around 250 diners and drinkers can cram into a series of dining rooms, and another 800 can be accommodated within the sprawling garden (open April to October). Expect heaping platters of such time-tested Teutonic favorites as roast pork shank, sautéed fish with parsley and onions, schnitzels, soups, wursts, and roasts. Live music, usually from a jazzy pianist, is presented every evening 6 to 10pm, and on Saturday and Sunday, a full oompah band plays music throughout the afternoon. Beer (Waldschlösschen) is brewed on the premises, and comes in several degrees of darkness.

Italianisches Dörfchen. Theaterplatz. ☎ **0351/498160.** Reservations not necessary. Main courses 26DM–34DM ($13–$17). AE, DC, MC, V. Daily 10am–midnight. Tram: 1, 2, 4, 7, 8, 11, 12, 14, or 17. ITALIAN/INTERNATIONAL

Italianisches Dörfchen is a stately looking neoclassical building that was erected in 1911 on the site of the cluster of cottages ("the Italian Village") that once housed the mostly Italian crews of laborers building the nearby monuments of the Saxon kings. Today, it contains a quartet of restaurants, each of which has a different theme. The best way to decide which of them you'll patronize involves wandering through the formal premises of the building inspecting them. Choices include the **Biersaal,** whose painted ceiling evokes the 18th century, the neoclassical **Weinzimmer,** a formal, rather uncomfortable and fussy-looking room outfitted in red, the **Bellotto,** an upscale Italian eatery on the top floor, and the **Café,** a graceful-looking antique room whose windows overlook the river. Prices in all four areas are about the same, although if you're interested just in coffee, tea, a drink, and/or pastries, you'd be best-advised to head directly for the cafe.

Kügelgen Haus Restaurant. Hauptstrasse 13. ☎ **0351/80-44-760.** Reservations recommended. Main courses 20DM–29DM ($10–$14.50). AE, DC, MC, V. Daily 11am–midnight. SAXON/GERMAN.

This restaurant is in the vaulted cellar of a museum devoted to the paintings of three members of the von Kügelgen family, whose portraits and landscapes were important in Germany's romantic age. The kitchen serves up ample portions of such rib-sticking fare as pork cutlets with braised mushrooms and onions, Zigeuner-steak with mushrooms and roast potatoes, and platters of wurst with potatoes and salad. The dining complex also includes a cafe and a little beer bar.

The museum is often ignored by visitors, but the collection upstairs is an interesting diversion. Admission is 5DM ($2.50); it's open Wednesday to Sunday 10am to 5pm.

INEXPENSIVE

Ayers Rock. Münzgasse 8. ☎ **0351/490-1188.** Reservations not necessary. Main courses 12DM–23DM ($6–$11.50). AE, DC, MC, V. Daily 11am–2am. Tram: 1, 2, 4, 14. AUSTRALIAN.

The success of this likable Australian restaurant is proof of the growing sophistication of Dresden. It was named and modeled after the geological oddity in central Australia that deeply impressed the owner during one of his holidays. Lighthearted and breezy, the place serves 170 kinds of cocktails, priced from 7.80DM to 14DM ($3.90 to $7) each, as well as some brands of German and Aussie beer on tap. Menu items are inspired by what's cooking Down Under, and include a savory version of lamb with green-bean stew; grilled veal shank; fresh asparagus with strips of chicken breast; and roebuck steak with mushrooms and glass noodles. After 8:30pm, the bar area gets crowded with those who are young at heart and available.

Café Schinkelwache. Sophienstrasse am Theaterplatz. ☎ **0351/490-39-09.** Reservations recommended. Pastries 2DM–9.50DM ($1–$4.75); platters 9.60–14.50DM ($4.80–$7.25). No credit cards. Daily 10am–midnight. Tram: 1, 2, 4, 7, 8, 11, 12, 14, or 17. CONTINENTAL.

Designed like a miniature Ionic-style temple, and one of the architectural gems of Dresden, this sandstone structure was built in 1832 by noted architect Karl Friedrich Schinkel to house soldiers and guards. In 1995, it was rebuilt and reconfigured into the café you'll see today. Its interior is more cozy and small-scale than you'd imagine from a view of its stately-looking facade. During clement weather, tables and parasols spill onto the terrace surrounding the building. You can order just about anything you want here, since choices include pastries, meal-sized salads, soups, cold platters, toasts, and at least two full-fledged dishes of the day. Wine, beer, and coffee are the preferred drinks.

Sophienkeller im Taschenbergpalais. Taschenberg 3. ☎ **0351/497-260.** Reservations recommended. Main courses 18.50DM–27DM ($9.25–$13.50). AE, DC, MC, V. Daily 11am–1pm. Tram: 5 or 8. GERMAN.

The food here approximates the hearty medieval feasts you might have expected in the Royal Saxon Court, albeit in a more sanitized version. Your happiness in these deep but bustling cellars depends on where you happen to sit. Four distinct areas are available, but the ones we prefer, and the ones that are the most authentically historic, are the Grosses and Kleines Zunfi Gewölbe, where flickering candles, set beneath vaulted ceilings, provide most of the illumination. Waitresses in traditional dirndls haul steaming platters of grilled rabbit with thyme, or perhaps fillet of salmon in puff pastry with a white wine and shrimp sauce. A culinary specialty here is "August's Hunting Trophy," comprised of roasted medallions of venison, wild boar, and roebuck, served with asparagus and dumplings. It's a bit theme-ish, especially in its emphasis on 18th-century costumes, but the food is hearty and flavorful and the ambience can be very romantic.

DRESDEN AFTER DARK

Dresden is Saxony's cultural center. There's always a variety of options for nightlife here, whether you're looking for drama, classical concerts, punk-rock shows, dancing, or just a good place to drink.

THE PERFORMING ARTS   Between the Elbe River and the Zwinger, on the western side of Theaterplatz, stands the ✪ **Semper Opera House,** Theaterplatz 2 (☎ **0351/491-17-05;** tram: 1, 2, 4, 7, 8, 11, 12, 14, or 17). Both Wagner and Weber conducted here. The building was designed by Gottfried Semper, the same architect who mapped out the famous picture gallery in the Zwinger. Restorers have brought the Renaissance-style two-tiered facade and the interior of the building back to life. Careful attention was paid to the replacement of Semper's original paintings and decorations. More importantly, the fine acoustics for which the opera house was known have been reestablished. Good seats can be had for 9DM to 120DM ($4.50 to $60). The opera company takes a vacation mid-July to September.

The **Dresden Philharmonic** appears at the **Kulturpalast,** in the Altmarkt (☎ **0351/48-660;** tram: 3 or 5). Tickets cost 18DM to 38DM ($9 to $19). Concerts are also performed in summer in the courtyards of the Zwinger.

For musical theater, come to the **Staats Operette,** Pirnaer Landstrasse 131, about 5m (3 miles) southeast of the city center (☎ **0351/07-99-29;** tram: 14), which mainly performs works from the 19th and early 20th centuries. The box office is open Sunday 1 hour before the show, Monday 11am to 4pm, Tuesday to Friday 11am to 7pm, and Saturday 4 to 7pm. Tickets cost 10DM to 35DM ($5 to $17.50).

The classical stage for drama in the city is **Schauspielhaus,** Postplatz (☎ 0351/ **491-350;** tram: 1, 2, 4, 7, 8, 11, 12, or 14), where dramas by Goethe, Schiller, and Shakespeare (in German) are performed. Performances usually start at 7:30pm. The box office is open Monday to Friday 10am to 6:30pm, and Saturday and Sunday 10am to 3pm. Tickets are 18DM to 35DM ($9 to $17.50). The Schauspielhaus box office also handles tickets and inquiries for the **Residenzteater im Schloss,** Schlossplatz (☎ **0351/49-13-50;** tram: 1, 4, or 11), a small theater focusing on modern drama and small ensemble pieces. The cost is 20DM to 30DM ($10 to $15). Both theaters are closed during August.

For a family theater experience, check out **Theater Junge Generation,** Meissner Landstrasse 4 (☎ **0351/42-91-20;** tram: 1; bus: 94), which interprets Shakespeare and fairy tales in a way that both kids and parents can enjoy. The box office is open Monday to Saturday 10am to 4pm, and 1 hour before performances. Ticket prices are 17DM to 50DM ($8.50 to $25). In summer, some members of the troupe bring their acts outdoors, usually to the courtyard in front of the Staffhof, an imposing building originally intended as a stable.

Tickets for classical concerts, dance, and opera are available from the tourist office or the **Schinkelwache** box office, Theaterplatz (☎ **0351/49-11-705;** tram: 1, 2, 4, 7, 8, 11, 12, 14, or 17), a historic building that was originally a guardhouse for the nearby castle.

BARS   A small, low-key bar, **Café Hieronymous,** Louisenstrasse 10 (☎ 0351/ **8-01-17-39;** tram: 7 or 8), is the place to go if you don't want to deal with intrusive music or patrons. Open daily 7pm to 2am. **Die 100,** Alaunstrasse 100 (☎ **0351/801-3957;** tram: 7, 8, or 11), is a cheap and trendy drinking place, set in a cellar under a vaulted arch. It's popular with students and artists. Open daily 5pm to 3am.

At **Planwirtschaft,** Louisenstrasse 20 (☎ **0351/801-3187;** tram: 7 or 8), an upstairs cafe is open 8am to 1am, but at the downstairs bar, you can drink until 3am on weekends. It doesn't look like much, but **Raskolnikoff,** Böhmische Strasse 34 (☎ **0351/804-5706;** tram: 3, 5, 7, 8, or 11), is a hip dive with sand-covered floors. Artists, intellectuals, and wanna-bes tend to congregate here. Open Sunday to Thursday 11am to 2am and Saturday 7pm to 2am.

At **Kleine Busmann's Brazil,** Kleine Brüdergasse 1 (☎ **0351/862-12-00;** tram: 1, 2, 4, or 11), you're likely to experience culture shock when you cross the street between the Zwinger and this Brazilian bar and restaurant where the music is hot and the food is spicy. Platters of food—roasted fillet of pork is a specialty—are priced at 17DM to 28DM ($8.50 to $14), although some specialty items, such as roasted rattlesnake, cost up to 79DM ($39.50). Most clients, however, opt just for a drink at the serpentine-shaped bar. Live music begins every night around 9pm. Open daily 11am to 2am.

At **Las Tapas,** Münzgasse 4 (☎ **0351/496-01-08;** tram: 1, 2, 4, or 14), within a stone-floored room modeled after an Iberian tasca, you'll find small tables and a stand-up bar area, where up to 40 kinds of Spanish-style marinated mushrooms, sausages, serrano hams, salted almonds, baked artichokes, and prawns in bacon are displayed behind glass. Priced at 3DM to 11DM ($1.50 to $5.50), they go well with beer or the Spanish wines sold here. More substantial platters, priced at 17DM to 25DM ($8.50 to $12.50), include lamb tenderloins with eggplant, and spits of marinated pork tenderloin served with sherry sauce. Open daily 11am to between 1 and 2am, depending on business.

GAY BARS & CLUBS   Although limited, Dresden has its share of gay nightlife options. Foremost among them are **Roses,** Jordanstrasse 32 (☎ **0351/80-26-210;**

tram: 7 or 8); and **Queens,** Görlitzerstrasse 3 (☎ **0351/803-1650;** tram: 7 or 8), both of which cater to a youngish or young-at-heart crowd of gay men and to a lesser extent, women, from many miles around Dresden. The town's only leather bar is **Bunker,** Bischofsweg (no phone; tram: 7 or 8).

CLUBS   A dance club with room for everyone is **DownTown and Groove Station,** Katherinenstrasse 11–13 (☎ **0351/802-88-01;** tram: 7 or 8). Monday is gay and lesbian night, and on Sunday there's dinner and dancing. Open daily 9pm "until everybody leaves." Cover is 8DM ($4).

Four nights of live music are balanced by three nights of dancing at **Studentklub Barenzwinger,** Bruhlisseher Garten 1 (☎ **0351/4-95-14-09;** tram: 1, 2, 4, or 5), a club built into a tunnel under the street. But even the discos here, held on Wednesday, Friday, and Saturday, tend to favor big-beat sounds like reggae and heavy metal. The club is open 8pm to midnight on Tuesday and Thursday, 3am on Wednesday (if the evening goes well), 1 or 2am on Friday, and 3 or 4am on Saturday. On Sunday it holds a bierabend (beer evening), and on Monday there's a concert or movie. Cover is 10DM to 20DM ($5 to $10) for bands and 5DM to 8DM ($2.50 to $4) for the disco.

JAZZ   **Projekttheater Dresden,** Louisenstrasse 47 (☎ **0351/804-30-41;** tram: 7 or 8), a publicly funded organization, usually, but not always, gives a live jazz performance at 9pm Tuesday to Sunday, and also maintains separate areas for the presentation of avant-garde films, lectures, and art exhibitions. Don't expect a nightclub-style cabaret, as no drinks are served. Tickets, available at the box office 1 hour before show time, are 20DM ($10). Call to see if there is a performance scheduled. All types of jazz bands hit the stage at **Tonne,** Am Brauhaus 3 (☎ **0351/802-6017;** tram: 7 or 8), on Friday and Saturday nights, when the music starts at 9pm. Check on other nights for infrequent shows. The club is open daily 8pm to 2am. Tickets are 15DM to 20DM ($7.50 to $10).

VARIETY   You'll find a wide variety of concert, theater, and dance performances at **Scheune,** Alaunstrasse 36 (☎ **0351/804-55-32;** tram: 7, 8, or 11), which also serves drinks and Indian food. It's open Monday to Friday 4pm to 2am, Saturday and Sunday 11am to 2pm. Cover is 10DM to 20DM ($5 to $10). A busy and often aggressively promoted cultural complex, **Reisa Efau,** Adlergasse 14 (☎ **0351/866-02-11;** tram: 1), provides several options. It has two rooms where punk and other music shows are held at 9pm for a 5DM ($2.50) cover. A movie theater charges 5DM ($2.50) for screenings held Thursday at 9pm in the summer and Sunday at 8pm in the winter. The bar on-site is open daily 8pm to 2am. Finally, gallery space here often hosts one-artist shows; viewing hours are Monday to Thursday 10am to 6pm, Friday 5 to 9pm, and Saturday 2 to 6pm.

Finally, for an insight into Germany's newest crop of political satirists, head for the irreverent premises of **Herkules Keule,** Sternplatz 1 (☎ **0351/492-5555;** tram: 1, 2, 4, 8, or 11). Although it was well known during the heyday of the former DDR, its sometimes scathing pronouncements have reached their sharpest and most shrill since reunification. Come here if your knowledge of German is extremely good, and only if you're prepared from caustic, sometimes bitchy humor that touches on everything from politics to human sexuality. Shows are presented Monday to Friday at 7:30pm and Saturday at 6 and 9pm. Admission is 20DM to 30DM ($10 to $15), depending on the night of the week.

A SIDE TRIP TO THE SPREEWALD & SORB COUNTRY

A fascinating side trip, about an hour's drive north of Dresden, is to the history-rich Sorb country of Spreewald (Forest of the Spree), nearly 260km^2 (100 square miles) of woodland, pastures, and canals. The flat, water-soaked landscape has an eerie beauty, and legends abound about spirits that inhabit the thick forests. Over a period of at least a thousand years, the people of the region channeled the marshlands into a network of canals, streams, lakes, and irrigation channels, building their houses, barns, and chapels on the high points of otherwise swampy ground. Ethnologists consider this area a distinctive human adaptation to an unlikely landscape, and botanists appreciate the wide diversity of bird and animal life that flourishes in the lush and fertile terrain.

The area is inhabited by the Sorbs, descendants of Slavic tribes who settled here in the 6th century. They speak a language similar to Czech and Polish. The Sorbs were targeted by the Nazis, who outlawed their language and killed many of them. It's estimated that there are still 100,000 Sorbs living in Germany, 30,000 of whom inhabit the Spreewald. They grow vegetables and fruit in a protected landscape, using labor-intensive methods even today.

The Spreewald is at its most appealing in early spring and autumn, when the crowds of sightseers depart and a spooky chill descends with the fog over these primeval forests and shallow medieval canals. To get here from Dresden, take Autobahn 13 north until you come to either the first turnoff, to Lübbenau, or the second turnoff, 10km (6 miles) farther, to Lübben. From either hamlet, drive toward the port (*Hafen*). From there, tour companies will take you through the canals via a shallow-draft boat propelled by a long pole, like a Venetian gondola. The guide is often a woman in traditional dress. Several waterside cafes along the canals serve food and drink.

Boat tours cost about 12DM ($6) for 3 hours. Your best bet is simply to wander down to the piers near the hamlet's center and hop aboard the next departure. Few people speak English. The boat tour companies operate only April to early October, with departures scheduled every day between 9am and 4pm. The companies include **Kahnfahrhafen Flottes Rudel,** Eisenbahnstrasse 3 (☎ 03546/8269), in Lübben; and, in Lübbenau, **Kahn Fahr GmbH,** Dammstrasse (☎ 03542/2225).

If you're interested in paddling around the Spreewald on your own, head for **Bootsverleih Gebauer,** Lindenstrasse, Lübben (☎ 03546/7194), where canoes can be rented for around 20DM ($10) an hour. *Note:* The tourist office in Lübben, the main point of departure for most Spreewald cruises, is on Ernst von Houwald Damm 16 (☎ 03546/3090). The tourist office in Lübbenau, a secondary point of departure, is at Am Weg 15 (☎ 03542/3668).

4 Meissen

23km (14 miles) NW of Dresden, 174km (108 miles) S of Berlin, 85km (53 miles) E of Leipzig

This "city of porcelain" is most often visited on a day trip from Dresden, although since reunification it now has suitable accommodations for those who'd like to spend the night and get acquainted with the area.

Meissen lies on both banks of the Elbe, with the Altstadt on the left bank. It's a very old town, dating from A.D. 929. Since 1710, Meissen has been known around the world as the center for the manufacture of Dresden china. The early makers of this so-called "white gold" were virtually held prisoner here, because the princes who ruled the city wanted to keep their secrets to themselves. Today, shoppers can find here the greatest selection of porcelain in all Germany. However, not wanting to undercut their distributors in such cities as Munich or Berlin, Meissen porcelain manufacturers keep their prices about the same as elsewhere.

| **Wine in Meissen** |

The terraces of the nearby vineyards in the Elbe Valley produce fine wines, for which Meissen has been known for 1,000 years. Look for the hard-to-obtain Meissner Domhert.

ESSENTIALS

GETTING THERE   By Train   Meissen Bahnhof is on the Deutsche Bundesbahn rail line, with frequent connections to Dresden and other major and regional cities. For rail information, call ☎ **1-94-19.**

By Bus   Regional buses connecting Dresden with Meissen are operated by **Verkehrs-gesellschaft Meissen.** Consult the tourist office in Meissen for a schedule of connections, or ask at the tourist office in Dresden.

By Car   Access is via the E40 Autobahn from Dresden or the E49 from Leipzig.

By Boat   If you're in Dresden in summer, you can go to Meissen by boat in about an hour and enjoy the scenery along the Elbe. The **Sächsischer Dampfschiffahrt** (☎ **0351/86-60-90**) leaves on Saturday and Sunday at 9:30am from Dresden's Brühl Terrace, the fortified embankment on the other side of the Hofkirche.

VISITOR INFORMATION   Contact **Tourist-Information Meissen,** Markt 3 (☎ **03521/45-44-70**), November to March, Monday to Friday 10am to 5pm and Saturday 10am to 3pm (closed Saturday in January); April to October, Monday to Friday 10am to 6pm, Saturday and Sunday 10am to 3pm.

EXPLORING THE TOWN

Towering over the town is the Gothic-style **Dom,** Domplatz 7 (☎ **03521/ 45-24-90**), one of the smallest cathedrals in Germany, built between 1260 and 1450. Until the year 1400, the bishops of the diocese of Meissen had their seat next to the cathedral. Later, Saxon rulers were buried here, the first in 1428. Inside are works of art, including a painting by Lucas Cranach the Elder, along with rare Meissen porcelain. The cathedral has been Protestant since the 16th century. It's open April to October daily 9am to 6pm (until 4pm November to March). Admission is 3.50DM ($1.75).

Sharing the castle quarter with the cathedral is **Albrechtsburg Castle,** Domplatz 1 (☎ **03521/47-070**), where the first Meissen porcelain was made. Construction of the castle began in 1471 and went on intermittently until 1525. From 1710 to 1864 it was the site of the Meissen Porcelain Manufactory. It's open daily 10am to 6pm; closed January 8 to January 16. Admission is 6DM ($3) for adults, 3DM ($1.50) for children 6 to 16, and free for children 5 and under. Guided tours cost 8DM ($4) for adults and 5DM ($2.50) for children.

But the prime attraction in town is the ✪ **Porzellan-Manufaktur,** Talstrasse 9 (☎ **03521/46-87-00**). At this factory, you can see how the centuries-old process of making Meissen china is still carried on, using the same traditional designs. Guided tours depart at 30-minute intervals every Monday to Friday 9am to 4:30pm, and cost 6DM ($3) per person. On the premises you can visit the **Porcelain Museum,** with 3,000 pieces, plus the workshop. Admission is 9DM ($4.50) for adults and 6DM ($3) for students.

The original factory was established back in 1710, not long after Johann Friedrich Böttger first succeeded in producing fine red stoneware in 1707 and then, in 1708, European white hard-paste porcelain. Böttger, then an apprentice pharmacist, had taken up alchemy and claimed to be able to make gold. When the Elector Augustus the Strong heard about this, he had Böttger put behind bars and ordered him to prove his claim. Böttger labored for many years, eventually producing "white gold," or porcelain. It wasn't long before Meissen porcelain was sought after in every great palace of Germany. The two most famous designers responsible for the classic Meissen motifs were Johann Gregorious Höroldt (1720–55), who produced the renowned blue onion pattern, and Johann Joachim Kändler (1706–75) who created figurines, giant animals, and elegant table services.

SHOPPING   At **Porzellan-Manufaktur** (see above), you can purchase recently crafted, hand-painted porcelain, which the outfit can ship home for you. The staff are experts at packing fragile objects. However, don't expect prices here to be much cheaper than in other German cities. If you're looking for 18th- or 19th-century porcelain (and can afford it), or for antique furniture, bibelots, and artworks, head for **Meissener Antikitäten,** Holweg 4 (☎ **03521/45-37-52**).

WHERE TO STAY

Parkhotel Pannonia Meissen. Hafenstrasse 27 (on the Elbe, directly across the water from the castle), 01662 Meissen. ☎ **03521/7-22-50.** Fax 03521/72-29-04. www.pannonia-hotels.com. E-mail: h1699@accor-hotels.com. 97 units. TV TEL. 197DM–272DM ($98.50–$136) double; 252DM–312DM ($126–$156) suite. Rates include buffet breakfast. AE, DC, MC, V. Parking 10DM ($5).

For decades, Meissen didn't have a suitable hotel, but this art nouveau villa filled the void in the early '90s. You can request a room in the original villa, although most accommodations are in the more sterile modern annexes. A suite on the top floor under the eaves is perfect for romantic couples. Most rooms open onto panoramic vistas.

Dining/Diversions: Both regional specialties and international dishes are served in the dining room. Even if you're not a guest, consider having a meal here. Lunch is served daily noon to 2pm and dinner daily 6 to 10pm. The hotel is also the site of frequent chamber-music concerts in the evening.

Amenities: Room service, laundry, baby-sitting, fitness room, sauna, solarium, whirlpool.

WHERE TO DINE

✪ **Vincenz Richter.** An der Frauenkirche 12 (uphill from Meissen's Marktplatz). ☎ **03521/45-32-85.** Reservations recommended. Main courses 22DM–28DM ($11–$14). AE, DC, MC, V. Tues–Fri 11am–4pm, Sat 11am–midnight, Sun noon–5pm. SAXON.

This charming, hearty, and traditional restaurant is in a vine-sheathed 1523 building. It has a hardworking, devoted staff and a cozy setting of Germanic charm. The bar stocks an impressive inventory of local wines, while the kitchens serve ample portions of well-flavored Saxon food.

5 Franconia & the German Danube

The Renaissance swept across all of Germany, but it concentrated its full force on that part of northern Bavaria that had once been a Frankish kingdom. Franconia today holds many of Germany's greatest medieval and Renaissance treasures. Its hillsides are still dotted with well-preserved medieval castles, monasteries, and churches. From the region's feudal cities sprang some of Germany's most significant artists—Albrecht Dürer, Lucas Cranach, Veit Stoss, Adam Krafft, and many others. Today Franconia draws music lovers from all over the world to its annual **Mozart Festival** in Würzburg and **Wagner Festival** in Bayreuth.

Franconia owes much of its beauty to the limestone range along the southern edge of the province. Between these hills and the edge of the Bavarian Forest is the upper **Danube,** which begins about 30km (20 miles) from Regensburg. The Danube gradually builds force from the smaller streams flowing out of the Alps and Swabian Jura, and by the time it reaches the Austrian border, at Passau, it's large enough to carry commercial ships and barges. Although not as important to the German economy as the Rhine, the Danube was responsible for the growth of several influential towns.

Franconia's countryside is equally compelling, especially the forest called **Frankenwald.** This scenic region stretches from the Bohemian Forest on the border of the Czech Republic in the east to the fringes of Frankfurt in the west. The most beautiful part is called Frankisches Schweiz, the "Switzerland of Franconia." It's bounded by Bamberg on the west, Bayreuth in the east, and Kulmbach in the north.

OUTDOORS IN FRANCONIA   The best **hiking** is found in the northern stretches of the province. Even the Germans themselves, who rush to the Bavarian Alps, often overlook hiking possibilities in this region. It's estimated that there are some 25,000 hiking trails in Franconia. Local tourist officials can provide details of the best hikes in their region. The most trails are found in the largest park in Germany, **Altmühltal Nature Park,** and in the Frankenwald. If you're a serious hiker, consider contacting **Fremdenver-kehrsverbund Franken,** Fürther Strasse 21, D-904 29 Nürnberg (☎ **0911/26-42-02**) for complete information about the hiking trails of Franconia.

Franconia can also be explored by **bike.** At all train stations in the area, you can rent a bike for 12DM ($6) per day or for half-price if you have a valid train ticket. Local tourist offices can supply information on

the best biking routes. The **Danube Bicycle Path** cuts right through Regensburg; cyclists can ride along its 650km (400 miles) from the river's source to Passau. The Regensburg tourist office (see below) is the most helpful source to contact to organize a biking trip. You can even go as far as Vienna. There's also the **Five Rivers Bicycle Path,** a circular route through the valleys of the Danube, Naab, and Vils that takes 3 to 5 days to complete. This path links Regensburg with Amberg and Nürnberg. Maps and further information about these cycling tours can be obtained from the local tourist information offices.

EXPLORING THE REGION BY CAR

Because of its location, **Ulm** is best explored while visiting Augsburg (see chapter 6, "The Romantic Road"). To see the real heart of Franconia, we suggest the following driving route.

Day 1   The traditional start of the Franconia tour is **Bayreuth** (pronounced By-roit), the city of Wagner. It was here that the great musician finally settled, building the Festspielhaus, a theater appropriate for his grand-scale operas. Ever since 1876, hordes of opera buffs from around the world have poured in for the annual Wagner festival, but the cultural scene in Bayreuth makes it a fascinating place to visit at any time of the year.

Day 2   Take B22 64km (40 miles) west of Bayreuth to **Bamberg,** one of Germany's great historic cities. The monumental center, where you'll want to spend the most time, is actually a small island in the river. Be sure to check out the cathedral, transitional Gothic in style, and the Diocesan Museum.

Day 3   From Bamberg, take the A73 Autobahn 61km (38 miles) south to **Nürnberg,** an easy trip that will leave you time for a full day of sightseeing. Here you can take in the German National Museum, the Albrecht Dürer House, the Kaiserburg, or the St.-Sebaldus-Kirche, consecrated in 1273.

Day 4   From Nürnberg, take the E56 for 100km (62 miles) to **Regensburg.** One of the best-preserved cities in Germany, Regensburg has an old quarter that requires half a day to explore. See St. Peter's Cathedral, the Altes Rathaus, and St. Ulrich's Diocesan Museum.

Day 5   For a final look at life along the Danube, continue on E56 to **Passau,** 117km (73 miles) southeast of Regensburg. This frontier town, located on the Austrian border, lies at the junction of the Danube, the Ilz, and the Inn Rivers. Spend the day exploring its old town and patrician houses.

1 Bayreuth

230km (143 miles) N of Munich, 64km (40 miles) E of Bamberg, 92km (57 miles) NE of Nürnberg

Bayreuth lies in a wide valley on the upper basin of the Roter Main River. In the town's early years, the counts of Andechs-Meranien gave it the protection of a fortified castle. In the Middle Ages, Bayreuth became the property of the Hohenzollerns and grew into one of the leading centers of this part of Germany. It's now the capital of the district of upper Franconia.

Bayreuth is forever associated with the memory of **Richard Wagner** (1813–83). The town is worth a visit for its baroque and rococo architectural treasures even if you're not interested in its favorite son, but most people come here because it's the annual home of the Wagner opera festival, and the premier location for Wagnerian performance in the world. Bayreuth is Valhalla to Wagner enthusiasts.

Wagner's "endless melody" is said to pervade Bayreuth even to this day. The composer's early successes attracted the attention of Ludwig II, king of Bavaria. With the king's support, Wagner opened his first **Festspielhaus** in an old residence in Bayreuth in 1876; later he built and designed a new Festspielhaus, especially suited for his own operas. Wagner not only composed the music for his music dramas but also wrote the librettos and even designed the stage sets. *Tristan and Isolde* remains perhaps his most daring opera; his best known is the four-opera *Ring of the Niebelungs*.

ESSENTIALS

GETTING THERE   By Plane   Lufthansa (☎ **800/645-3880**) offers three daily scheduled flights from Frankfurt Airport to Bayreuth.

By Train   The **Bayreuth Hauptbahnhof** is on the main Nürnberg–Pegnitz–Bayreuth and the Bayreuth–Weiden rail lines, with good connections. Express trains arrive from Nürnberg every hour. For rail information and schedules, call ☎ **1-94-19.**

By Bus   Long-distance bus service to Berlin and Munich is provided by **Bayern Express** and **P. Kuhn Berlin GmbH.** For information, call the **Deutsches Reisebüro** in Bayreuth (☎ **0921/88-50**). Local and regional buses in the area are run by **OVF Omnibusverkehr Franken GmbH** in Bayreuth (☎ **01805/996633**).

By Car   Access by car is via the A9 Autobahn from the north and south.

VISITOR INFORMATION   Contact **Tourist-Information,** Luitpoldplatz 9 (☎ **0921/8-85-88**), Monday to Friday 9am to 6pm and Saturday 9:30am to 1pm.

GETTING AROUND   Many streets within the historic core of Bayreuth are exclusively reserved for pedestrians, and that, coupled with the city's small size, make walking between points of interest both easy and efficient. The centerpiece of the old town is the Marktplatz, from which buses 1, 7, 8, 9, and 16 make frequent runs to and from Bayreuth's modern neighborhoods around the Hauptbahnhof. One-way bus fare is 2.70DM ($1.35). Most able-bodied visitors opt to walk.

THE BAYREUTHER FESTSPIELE

The town's claim to fame is that it's the site of the Richard Wagner opera festival, which takes place between mid-July and the end of August. If you arrive in Bayreuth then, you may think that the whole town has turned out to pay homage to the great composer, who built his opera house here, lived here, and was buried here following his death in Venice.

Visitors should know that tickets to the festival operas are almost impossible to obtain (there's a 5-year waiting list) but can sometimes be booked as part of a package tour (see chapter 2). Tickets cost 80DM to 300DM ($40 to $150).

Warning: During the 5 weeks of the festival, hoteliers raise their rates quite a bit. Always firmly establish the rate before booking a room, and make reservations far in advance.

SEEING THE SIGHTS

Festspielhaus. Am Festspielhügel. ☎ **0921/7-87-80.** Guided tour only, 3DM ($1.50). Tours offered in German only; English leaflets are available. Apr–Sept Tues–Sun at 10 and 10:45am, and 2:15 and 3pm. Oct and Dec–Mar Tues–Sun at 10 and 10:45am. Tours might not be given during rehearsals and at festival time. Bus: 2.

The operas of Wagner are dispensed like a musical Eucharist to Wagnerian pilgrims at the Festspielhaus, at the northern edge of town. The theater, designed by the composer himself, is not a beautiful building, but it's an ideal Wagnerian facility, with a huge stage capable of swallowing up Valhalla, and excellent, beautifully balanced acoustics

A Woman of Culture

The Margravine Wilhelmine (1709–58) was Frederick the Great's sister and a life-long friend of Voltaire. She was also one of the most cultivated women of the 18th century. Wilhelmine was in line for the Prussian throne, but instead married the Margrave Friedrich of Brandenburg-Bayreuth, although shortly thereafter decided he was rather dull. ("Margrave" and "Margravine" are titles of nobility similar to Marquess.) She turned her attention to culture and ushered in the most brilliant period in Bayreuth's history, bringing in composers, decorators, writers, and artists. Wilhelmine personally spearheaded a movement that became known as "Bayreuth rococo." This style of architecture, characterized by garlands and flowers, differed markedly from the more rustic French rococo, which was in vogue at the time.

throughout the auditorium. Because of the design, the orchestra never overwhelms the singers. The festival was opened here in 1876 with the epic Ring cycle. When the composer died in Venice, his wife, Cosima, took over. In the post–World War II era, Wagner's grandsons, Wolfgang and Wieland, have produced the operas, with exciting avant-garde staging and the best musicians and singers from all over the world.

Franz-Liszt-Museum. Wahnfriedstrasse 9. ☎ **0921/7-57-28-18.** Admission 3DM ($1.50) Sept–June. Daily 10am–noon and 2–5pm, July–Aug daily 10am–5pm. Bus: 2 to Villa Wahnfried.

Wagner's father-in-law was Franz Liszt (1811–86), the great Hungarian-born composer and piano virtuoso who revolutionized piano playing. His daughter, Cosima, married Wagner. Liszt is buried in the Bayreuth cemetery. The museum, which opened on October 22, 1993 (Liszt's birthday), shows the room where the composer died. It also displays memorabilia related to his life and work.

Markgräfliches Opernhaus. Opernstrasse. ☎ **0921/759-69-22.** Guided tours (in German only) 4DM ($2) adults, 2DM ($1) children. Apr–Sept Tues–Sun 10am-5pm; Oct–Mar Tues–Sun 10am-3pm. Bus: 2.

This is the only authentic baroque theater in Germany. It's still in its fine original condition. Behind its weathered wooden doors is a world of gilded canopies and columns, ornate sconces, and chandeliers. The house was built under the auspices of the Margravine Wilhelmine, who was known for her taste and her cultivation of the arts; her name has been given to a special baroque style called *Wilhelmian*. Her brother, Frederick the Great, formally opened the theater in 1748. Up until that time, operas (notably those of Telemann) had been performed in the court theater.

Today, the opera house, which seats only 520, is used for Bayreuth's "second" festival: the **Franconian Weeks' Festival,** usually held late in May. Concerts are also given during the summer.

Neues Schloss (New Palace). Ludwigstrasse (1 block from the Markgräfliches Opernhaus). ☎ **0921/759-69-21.** Guided tours (in German, with English leaflets available) 5DM ($2.50) adults, free for children. Tours given Apr–Sept, Tues–Sun 10am–noon and 1:30–4:30pm; Oct–Mar, Tues–Sun 10am–noon and 1:30–3pm. Bus: 2.

The well-preserved Neues Schloss in the center of town also shows the influence and enlightened taste of the talented and cultured Wilhelmine (1709–58). This baroque palace dates from the mid-18th century. The apartments of Wilhelmine and her husband, Margrave Friedrich, are decorated in a late-rococo style with period furnishings.

Richard-Wagner-Museum (Wahnfried). Richard-Wagner-Strasse 48 (south of the town center). ☎ **0921/7-57-28-16.** Admission 4DM ($2), 5DM ($2.50) at festival time. Apr–Oct daily 9am–5pm (to 8pm Tues and Thurs). Nov–Mar daily 10am–5pm (to 8pm Thurs). Bus: 2.

Wagner lived here from 1874, and the house remained in his family until 1966. Only the front of the original Wahnfried—which means "illusory peace"—remains intact. On display is a wide range of Wagner memorabilia, including manuscripts, pianos, furnishings, artifacts, and even a death mask. If you walk to the end of the garden, fronting the rotunda, you'll see the graves of the composer and his wife.

Altes Schloss Ermitage (Hermitage). On Rte. 22, 5km (3 miles) northeast of Bayreuth toward Weiden. ☎ **0921/75-96-90.** Gardens free; palace 5DM ($2.50) adults, free for children. Gardens daily 24 hours. Palace Apr–Sept, Tues–Sun 9–11:30am and 1–4:30pm; Oct–Mar, Tues–Sun 10–11:30am and 1–2:30pm. Bus: 22 (runs every 20 min. during the day).

The margraves of Bayreuth also had a pleasure palace outside the city, reached via a road lined with chestnut trees that were planted in honor of Frederick the Great. Georg Wilhelm built it in 1718 as a retreat. The structure looks as if it had been hewn out of a rock, but the interior felt the touch of Margravine Wilhelmine. Seek out the Japanese salon and the rococo music room. The castle is set in a park, full of formal as well as English-style gardens. In them, you can see the New Palace of the Hermitage, built around 1750. Its columns are covered with polychrome pebbles in mosaic style, a unique structural element in German architecture. A part of the palace becomes a cafe in summer, and sometimes hosts painting exhibitions.

WHERE TO STAY
EXPENSIVE

Bayerischer Hof. Bahnhofstrasse 14 (in front of the train station), 95444 Bayreuth. ☎ **0921/7-86-00.** Fax 0921/7-86-05-60. www.bayerischer-hof.de. E-mail: 100332.1776@ compuserve.com. 56 units. MINIBAR TV TEL. 210DM–270DM ($105–$135) double; 486DM–666DM ($243–$333) suite. Rates include buffet breakfast. AE, DC, MC, V. Parking 10DM ($5).

Bayerischer Hof, near the Hauptbahnhof, is equaled only by the Hotel Königshof in style and amenities. This hotel combines contemporary and traditional furnishings. Some rooms have French pieces; others are Nordic and modern in design.

Dining/Diversions: Each of the hotel's three dining areas has a distinctive character, though the menu is the same (see "Where to Dine," below). Entertainment is sometimes provided in the Lounge Bar, which is open from 6pm to midnight.

Amenities: Room service, laundry, baby-sitting, indoor pool, sauna, sundeck, conference rooms.

MODERATE

Goldener Anker. Opernstrasse 6 (next door to the Markgräfliches Opernhaus), 95444 Bayreuth. ☎ **0921/6-50-51.** Fax 0921/6-55-00. 35 units. TEL. 200DM–250DM ($100–$125) double; from 350DM ($175) suite. Rates include continental breakfast. AE, DC, MC, V. Closed Dec 20–Jan 10. Parking 15DM ($7.50). Bus: 2.

Goldener Anker is extremely popular locally, although it doesn't have the amenities, services, and style of the Bayerischer Hof. It has hosted distinguished composers, singers, and conductors for more than 200 years. The framed photographs on the time-seasoned oak-paneled walls are museum treasures. The guest book includes signatures of notables like Richard Strauss, Arturo Toscanini, Fritz Kreisler, Bruno Walter, William Saroyan, Lauritz Melchior, and Patrice Chereau. Furnishings include fine antiques and Oriental rugs. Rooms are individually designed.

INEXPENSIVE

Brauerei-Gasthof Goldener Löwe. Kulmbacher Strasse 30, 95445 Bayreuth. ☎ **0921/ 74-60-60.** Fax 0921/4-77-77. 11 units. TEL. 130DM–140DM ($65–$70) double. Rates include continental breakfast. AE, DC, MC, V. Free parking. Bus: 2.

This is an unpretentious, well-managed inn, the town's best affordable choice. The facade is set off by window boxes loaded with flame-red geraniums. Rooms have a Bavarian theme of checker-patterned down comforters and light-grained pinewood trim. Rooms and baths are small but comfortable. The atmosphere is informal and homelike. The smiling staff is very hospitable. In the tavern bar you can drink beer or perhaps join in a game of cards before heading for the dining room for a selection of *Klössen* (Franconian dumplings).

Hotel-Gasthof Spiegelmühle. Kulmbacher Strasse 28, 9445 Bayreuth. ☎ **0921/4-10-91.** Fax 0921/4-73-20. 13 units. TV TEL. 129DM–139DM ($64.50–$69.50) double. Rates include continental breakfast. AE, DC, MC, V. Free parking. Bus: 6.

This high-ceilinged building, which dates from 1555 and was once a working mill, has been transformed into a modest and unassuming, although clean and comfortable hotel. In spite of its lack of pretensions, well-known conductors and singers often stay here during the festival. Many of the rooms are small but quite adequate. Do not count on anybody speaking English. There's a bar, plus a breakfast room and a Bierstube/Biergarten, serving good traditional Bavarian and international food.

WHERE TO DINE
EXPENSIVE

✪ **Schloss Tiergarten.** Oberthiergartener Strasse 36, 6km (4 miles) south of Bayreuth center, 95406 Bayreuth. ☎ **09209/98-40.** Fax 09209/9-84-13. Reservations recommended. Main courses 35DM–48DM ($17.50–$24); fixed-price menus 109DM ($54.50). AE, DC, MC, V. Daily noon–2pm, 6–10pm. Bus: 11. CONTINENTAL.

This building with a hexagonal baroque tower was constructed as a private hunting lodge. There are two dining rooms, the Kamin (meaning "fireplace") and the Venezian-ischersalon. The cuisine is in the culinary traditions of France, Italy, and Germany. Menu items might include lobster risotto with basil, stuffed halibut with caviar sauce and kohlrabi noodles, and terrine of sweetbreads. There's an impressive wine list.

The establishment is also a cozy hotel with eight large rooms boasting all the modern accoutrements. Doubles run 220DM to 290DM ($110 to $145), including breakfast.

MODERATE

Bayerischer Hof. Bahnhofstrasse 14 (in front of the train station). ☎ **0921/7-86-00.** Reservations recommended. Main courses 20DM–40DM ($10–$20). AE, DC, MC, V. Daily 7am–1am. FRENCH.

This previously recommended hotel has a selection of restaurants offering both French and Franconian cooking. The Hans-Sachs-Stube, an air-conditioned replica of an old inn, has walls covered with pictures of famous opera singers who have performed in Bayreuth or dined here. The food is superbly precise and refined, combining inventive French dishes with the best of Franconian taste. You can also dine at the hotel's bistro, Spanische Stube, or at Gendarmerie, the main à la carte restaurant. Each dining room has a different decor, although the seasonally adjusted menu is the same in all three.

INEXPENSIVE

Braunbierhaus. Kanzleistrasse 15. ☎ **0921/6-96-77.** Main courses 10DM-23DM ($5–$11.50). AE, DC, MC, V. Mon–Sat 11:30am–2pm and 5:30–10:30pm, Sun 11:30am–2pm. Bus: 3. FRANCONIAN.

The oldest house in Bayreuth, Braunbierhaus was built in 1430, with foundations that date from the 13th century. It offers inexpensive and down-to-earth food as well as its own beer. The specialty of the kitchen is a *Holzfäller* steak ("woodcutter's steak") served with hash-brown potatoes and a fresh salad. Portions are large, appetites are hearty, and the special house beer is consumed in mass quantities. No one puts on airs here.

2 Bamberg

238km (148 miles) NW of Munich, 61km (38 miles) NW of Nürnberg, 97km (60 miles) NE of Würzburg

This little city is one of the gems of Franconia, although visitors often pass it by. Bamberg is set in the rolling Franconian hills where the Regnitz River flows into the Main. It's loaded with attractions, including numerous architectural treasures, and suffered very little damage in World War II.

In the Middle Ages Bamberg was a powerful ecclesiastical center. Originally, it was two towns divided by the river: the ecclesiastical town of the prince-bishopric, of which it was the capital for 800 years, and the secular town of the burghers. Bamberg's architecture reflects over 1,000 years of building, with styles ranging from Romanesque to Gothic, Renaissance to baroque, up to the eclecticism of the 19th century. There are narrow cobblestone streets, ornate mansions and palaces, and impressive churches.

Today, Bamberg and beer go together like barley and hops. The town has been called "a beer drinker's Eden." The average Bamberger drinks 50 gallons of beer a year, making the rest of the German people look like teetotalers by comparison. There are more breweries here than in Munich. Beer lovers come from afar for Rauchbier, a smoked beer first brewed in 1536.

ESSENTIALS

GETTING THERE   By Train   The **Bamberg Bahnhof** is on the Stuttgart–Hof and the Berlin–Munich rail lines, with frequent connections in both directions. Most visitors arrive from Nürnberg (see below) in just 1 hour. For information and schedules, call ☎ **01805/99-66-33.**

By Bus   Bamberg has bus links with Bayreuth five times daily. The trip takes 1 hour 40 minutes and costs 15DM ($7.50) one-way. Contact **Omnibus Verkehr Franken** (☎ **09561/76009**).

By Car   Access by car is via the B22 from Würzburg or the A73 from Nürnberg.

VISITOR INFORMATION   Contact the **Bamberg Tourist Information Office,** Geyerswörthstrasse 3 (☎ **0951/87-11-61**). Office hours are Monday to Friday 9am to 6pm, Saturday to 3pm, and Sunday 10am to 2pm, May to October.

GETTING AROUND   A well-run network of buses fan out from the Zentralomnibusbahnhof on Promenadestrasse, next to the railway station,. A single ride costs 1.80DM (90¢) with a 5-ride ticket going for 5DM ($2.50). For more information, head to I Punkt in the railway station, open Monday to Friday 7am to 7pm, and Saturday 9am to 2pm. Bus maps and tickets can be purchased at the station or from machines at stops along the route.

EXPLORING THE CITY

The center square is dominated by the **Alte Hofhaltung,** the Renaissance imperial and episcopal palace, with a courtyard surrounded by late-Gothic framework buildings. Inside the palace are the remains of the original *diet* (assembly) hall, built in the 11th century. Elaborately decorated and furnished, the palace is noted for its frescoed Kaisersaal and its Chinesisches Kabinet, the latter covered with walls of marquetry. Don't miss the rose garden.

Among other places of interest is the **Altes Rathaus,** the strangest town hall in Germany. Determined not to play favorites between the ecclesiastical and secular sections of the city, the town authorities built this Gothic structure on its own little island in the middle of the Regnitz River, halfway between the two factions—a true middle-of-the-road (or river) political stand. From the island, you get the best view of the old fishers' houses along the banks in the section called "Little Venice."

E. T. A. Hoffmann Haus. Schillerplatz 26. ☎ **0951/20-31-22.** Admission 2DM ($1) adults, 1DM (50¢) children. May–Oct Tues–Fri 4–6pm, Sat–Sun 10am–noon. Bus: 10.

This was the home of the writer and poet from 1809 to 1813. The little narrow-fronted house is filled with mementos and memorabilia of the man whose strange tales formed the basis of Jacques Offenbach's famous opera *The Tales of Hoffmann.*

Kaiserdom (Imperial Cathedral). Domplatz. ☎ **0951/50-23-30.** Admission free. Apr–Oct daily 9am–6pm; Nov–Mar daily 9am–5pm. Diözesanmuseum 4DM ($2) adults, 2DM ($1) students, 1DM (50¢) children over 15, free for children under 15. Diözesanmuseum Tues–Sun 9am–5pm. Bus 10.

This cathedral on a hillside was begun in 1215 in Romanesque and early-Gothic style. It has a double chancel, the eastern one raised on a terrace to compensate for the slope. The massive towers at the four corners of the church dominate Bamberg's skyline. The interior contains some fine religious art. Best known is the 13th-century equestrian statue, the **Bamberger Reiter,** which represents the idealized Christian king of the Middle Ages. Among the many tombs is that of Emperor Heinrich II, who erected the original cathedral; sculptor Tilman Riemenschneider labored more than a decade over this masterpiece of a tomb, as well as the one devoted to the emperor's wife, Kunigunde (who was suspected of adultery, commemorated in a scene on the tomb). In the west chancel is the only papal tomb north of the Alps, containing the remains of Pope Clement II, who died in 1047. The rich cathedral treasury may be seen in the adjoining **Diözesanmuseum.**

✪ **Neue Residenz.** Domplatz. ☎ **0951/5-63-51.** Admission 5DM ($2.50) adults, 4DM ($2) children. Apr–Oct daily 9am–noon and 1:30–5pm; Nov–Mar daily 9am–noon and 1:30–4pm. Bus: 10.

Opposite the Alte Hofhaltung is the 17th-century Neue Residenz, the much larger palace of the prince-bishops, showing both Renaissance and baroque influences. This was the site of one of the most famous unsolved mysteries in Germany. In 1815, a corpse found beneath the windows of the palace turned out to be the body of Marshal Berthier, Napoléon's chief of staff, who retired here after Napoléon was exiled to Elba. No one knows if Berthier was murdered or committed suicide.

Upstairs, you can view works by German masters, including the Master of the Life of the Virgin and Hans Baldung Grien (don't miss his *The Great Flood*). On the second floor are the former **Imperial Apartments,** with Gobelin tapestries, baroque furnishings, and parquet floors. Notable is the **Emperors' Hall,** with allegorical frescoes and portraits of who was who yesterday.

SHOPPING   The primary shopping district in Bamberg is around the cathedral, where you will find stores of all kinds, including more than a dozen antiques shops and numerous galleries. An antiques store that has it all, **Sebok,** Untere Königstrasse 21 (☎ **0951/20-25-93**), offers paintings, books, furniture, fine jewelry, silver, glass, toys, watches, clocks, and more. Auctions are held every 2 months, with the summer auction falling in July. **Manger,** Grüner Markt 7 (☎ **0951/2-34-54**), is a kitschy souvenir shop. If you're interested in local ceramics, go to **Topferladen,** Untere Brücke 1 (☎ **0951/5-69-13**), where you'll find candleholders, cups, dinnerware, vases, and garden statuary.

WHERE TO STAY

EXPENSIVE

Bamberger Hof Bellevue. Schönleinsplatz 4, 96047 Bamberg. ☎ **0951/9-85-50.** Fax 0951/98-55-62. www.bambergerhof.de. E-mail: bbghof.wrb@sskba.de. 50 units. MINIBAR TV TEL. 220DM–320DM ($110–$160) double; 850DM ($425) suite. Rates include buffet breakfast. AE, DC, MC, V. Parking 15DM ($7.50). Bus: 8 or 12.

This hotel plays a bit of second fiddle to the Residenzschloss Bamberg (see below), but the service and accommodations of both are roughly on a par. A great old palace of stone, crowned by a tower and facing a little park, it's the choice for soaking up the mellow atmosphere of yesteryear. Try to book one of the large rooms with sitting areas.

Dining: The Bamberger Hof, the hotel's first-class restaurant, serves international cuisine with attentive service.

Amenities: Concierge, hair dryers, room service, laundry, dry cleaning service.

✪ **Residenzschloss Bamberg.** Untere Sandstrasse 32, 96049 Bamberg. ☎ **0951/6-09-10.** Fax 0951/6-09-17-01. www.hotel-residenzschloss.de. E-mail: info@hotel-residenzschloss.de. 185 units. MINIBAR TV TEL. 295DM–335DM ($147.50–$167.50) double; 500DM–590DM ($250–$295) suite. Rates include buffet breakfast. AE, DC, MC, V. Bus: 8.

This elegant hotel is on a bank of the Regnitz, near the Altstadt and across from the Bamberg Symphony Orchestra building. This is the preferred choice in town, a blend of old and new. The building, with its ocher-colored baroque walls, was constructed by the local archbishop in 1787 as a hospital. Today, the original hospital chapel continues to host local weddings. A less-glamorous modern annex is connected to the main building by a glass-sided breezeway. Baths are a bit small but tidily kept. The hotel is popular with conventioneers.

Dining: The hotel's most elegant restaurant, the Fürstbischof von Erthal, is open for dinner only, 6 to 10pm, and serves a menu of *Neuer Küche* (new cuisine) dishes. Buffet breakfasts and lunches are served in the garden-inspired decor of the Orangerie.

Amenities: Steam bath, sauna, solarium, exercise bikes, weight-lifting equipment.

MODERATE

Barock Hotel am Dom. Vorderer Bach 4, 96049 Bamberg. ☎ **0951/5-40-31.** Fax 0951/5-40-21. 19 units. MINIBAR TV TEL. 155DM–175DM ($77.50–$87.50) double. Rates include buffet breakfast. AE, CB, DC, MC, V. Closed Feb 1–Mar 1. Bus: 8 or 12.

Barock Hotel am Dom offers you some of the same style, tradition, and romance of the pacesetters above, but at a better price. The owners of this symmetrical building have retained every detail of the original ornamented facade and renovated key areas of the interior. The result is a winning combination of baroque elements in a well-lit modernized building. Rooms are attractively furnished, although a bit cramped. Reservations are important. The rates include a nourishing breakfast (the only meal available) of wurst and cheese, served in the most unusual breakfast room in Bamberg—the old cellar, where tables are set up under the plastered stone vaulting.

Hotel Brudermühle. Schranne 1, 96049 Bamberg. ☎ **0951/95-52-20.** Fax 0951/9-55-22-55. www.brudermuehle.de. E-mail: info@brudermuehle.de. 16 units. TV TEL. 185DM ($92.50) double; 195DM–215DM ($97.50–$107.50) apt. Rates include continental breakfast. DC, MC, V. Bus: 8 or 12.

The Hotel Brudermühle is a traditional German city inn without pretense or glamour. Reasonable rates, good local cookery, and a hospitable, family-style welcome make this a worthwhile choice for those who like no-frills functionality. Rooms are tiny, but housekeeping is good. The functional modern furnishings are less interesting than the views of the old town from the windows. The building was constructed in 1314 as a mill powered by the Regnitz River. The hotel couldn't be more centrally located, within a few blocks of the cathedral.

National. Luitpoldstrasse 37, 96052 Bamberg. ☎ **0951/2-41-12.** Fax 0951/2-24-36. www.ringhotels.de. E-mail: hotelnational@t-online.de. 44 units. MINIBAR TV TEL. 145DM-169DM ($72.50-$84.50) double; 200DM-220DM ($100-$110) suite. Rates include buffet breakfast. AE, CB, DC, MC, V. Parking 9DM ($4.50). Bus: 5.

The National is still a favorite, though it no longer enjoys the renown it used to. Modernization has removed some of its quaint charm, and it lacks the style of the Romantik Hotel-Weinhaus Messerschmitt (see below), but the price is right, the food is good, and the rooms are first rate. With its black mansard roof, iron balconies, baroque and classical detailing, and opulent public rooms, the hotel is attractive, if small. It has well-maintained and traditionally furnished rooms, a bar, and a formal restaurant that serves good continental and Franconian specialties. Room service, laundry, and dry cleaning are available.

✪ Romantik Hotel-Weinhaus Messerschmitt. Langestrasse 41, 96047 Bamberg. ☎ **0951/ 2-78-66.** Fax 0951/26-14-1. www.hotel-messerschmitt.de. E-mail: Hotel-Messerschmitt@ t-online.de. 17 units. MINIBAR TV TEL. 255DM ($127.50) double; 265DM ($132.50) triple. Rates include buffet breakfast. AE, DC, MC, V. Parking 8DM ($4). Take any bus going to Central Station.

This old hotel, beloved by traditionalists, is Bamberg's most romantic choice. The building dates from 1422, making it one of the oldest in the area. The present exterior is 18th century, a gabled expanse of pale blue and yellow with baroque-style window frames. Inside, paneling, ceramic ovens, and antiques make a mellow decor. Many of the beds have meticulously crafted headboards. The owner and his staff do everything to be helpful. The exceptional kitchen serves both Franconian and international dishes. Locals love the platter of eels in dill sauce; the gastronomically timid might settle for the local duck instead.

INEXPENSIVE

Hotel Garni Graupner. Langestrasse 5, 96047 Bamberg. ☎ **0951/98-04-00.** Fax 0951/98-04-040. E-mail: www.hotel-grupner@t-online.de. 30 units, 26 with bathroom. TEL. 85DM ($42.50) double without bathroom, 110DM-130DM ($55-$65) double with bath; 150DM-165DM ($75-82.50) junior suite. Rates include continental breakfast. AE, MC, V. Parking 12DM ($6). Bus: 1, 2, 4, 5, 8, or 16.

Much renovated, rebuilt, and overhauled over the years, this hotel has accepted overnight guests since the 14th century. It's your best bet if you can't afford the properties outlined above. You can usually get a room here, perhaps with a view over the Altstadt, and it will be clean and decent, although short on charm. If the main hotel is full, guests are directed to the lackluster 1960s annex, about 8 blocks away across the canal. It offers 10 modern rooms for the same price charged in the main hotel, each with private bath. Locals frequent the big-windowed cafe and pastry shop on the ground floor, open daily 7am to 7pm. The same family also owns a rose-garden cafe, a stone's throw from the cathedral.

WHERE TO DINE

Historischer Brauereiausschank Schlenkerla. Dominikanerstrasse 6. ☎ **0951/5-60-60.** Main courses 12DM-18DM ($6-$9). No credit cards. Wed-Mon 9:30am-midnight. Closed Jan 7-21. Bus: 8 or 12. FRANCONIAN.

Diners congregate here much as they did in 1678, when the place was a brewery. The decor is rustic, with long wooden tables and smallish chairs. The price is right, and the cozy, *gemütlich* atmosphere is genuine. Wholesome and unpretentious Franconian fare is served here. You can sample such local dishes as *Bierbrauervesper* (smoked meat and sour-milk cheese) and *Rauchschinken* (smoked ham). Patrons wash down these dishes with a hearty malt, Rauchbier, which has an intense smoky aroma and flavor.

Romantik Restaurant-Weinhaus Messerschmitt. Langestrasse 41. ☎ **0951/2-78-66.** Main courses 27DM–42DM ($13.50–$21). AE, DC, MC, V. Daily 11am–2pm and 6–10pm. Buses 1, 2. FRANCONIAN/INTERNATIONAL.

You can dine better here, and in a more refined atmosphere, than anywhere else in town. This pleasant restaurant is more than 160 years old. The cuisine is presented simply but is remarkably well crafted. Menu items depend on shopping. Freshwater fish are kept in an aquarium. Game is another specialty. Veal and lamb dishes are prepared with exquisite care. Some of the offerings, such as eels in dill sauce, may be a bit too regional for you, but the Franconian duck is an exquisite choice.

BAMBERG AFTER DARK

Sinfonie an der Regnitz, Mussstrasse 7 (☎ **0951/9-64-71-00**) is home to the Bamberg Symphony Orchestra from September 11 to July 17. From the last week in June to mid-July there's a summer festival with weekend symphonic concerts. Tickets are 35DM to 60DM ($17.50 to $30).

    Hofburg Repertory Theater performs at the **E.T.A. Hoffman Theater,** Schillerplatz 5 (☎ **0951/87-14-33;** box office 0951/87-14-31). Its season runs from September to July 24. The productions range from 18th-, 19th-, and 20th-century classics to contemporary musicals. The box office is open daily 10am to 1pm and 1 hour prior to show time (also 4 to 6pm on Wednesday). In June and July, the company moves outdoors, performing a series of German-language drama within the courtyard of the Alte Hofaltung (see above). Tickets for both indoor and outdoor performances are 18DM to 35DM ($9 to $17.50), but students with a valid ID card pay half price. For more information about these and other cultural events in Bamberg, contact the Tourist Information Office (see "Visitor Information," above).

    A young crowd gathers at **Jazzclub,** Obere Sandstrasse 18 (☎ **0951/5-37-40**), to listen to punk, gothic, and alternative music on Tuesday and Thursday nights from 9pm to 1am, when the cover is 5DM ($2.50). Mid-September to April, the club opens its cellar for live jazz on Friday and Saturday 9pm to 2am, when the cover is 10DM to 50DM ($5 to $25), depending on the group.

3 Nürnberg (Nuremberg)

169km (105 miles) NW of Munich, 225km (140 miles) SE of Frankfurt, 204km (127 miles) NE of Stuttgart

When this city celebrated its 900th birthday in 1950, the scars of World War II were still fresh. Nürnberg was once the ideal of medieval splendor, but that legacy was lost in the ashes of war. With the exception of Dresden, no other German city suffered such devastation in a single air raid. On the night of January 2, 1945, 525 British Lancaster bombers rained fire and destruction on this city, the ideological center of the Third Reich.

    Nürnberg today has regained its vitality. Now it's a symbol of postwar prosperity. The largest city in Franconia, Nürnberg is swarming with people, both longtime residents and *Gastarbeiter* (foreign workers), who have flooded the city in recent years—many from the old Soviet bloc countries to the east. For most of the year the city is thronged with visitors, too. It's a notable industrial center, still associated with its traditional gingerbread products and handmade toys. The first pocket watches, the Nürnberg eggs, were made here in the 16th century.

Centuries of art and architecture made Nürnberg a treasure. During the 15th and 16th centuries, Nürnberg enjoyed a cultural flowering that made it the center of the **German Renaissance,** bringing together Italian Renaissance and German Gothic traditions. In the artists' workshops were found such great talents as Veit Stoss, Peter Vischer, Adam Krafft, Michael Wolgemut, and above all, Albrecht Dürer. Koberger set up his printing press here, and Regiomontanus built an astronomical observatory. Here, too, flourished the guilds of the Meistersingers, composed of prosperous artisans; Wagner made their most famous member, Hans Sachs, the hero of his opera *Die Meistersinger von Nürnberg.*

Many of Nürnberg's most important buildings, including some of the finest churches in Germany, have been restored or reconstructed. The old part of the city, the **Altstadt,** lies mainly within a pedestrian zone. Today's visitors can see the ruins of the ramparts that once surrounded the city in addition to more modern sites, such as the **Justice Palace,** where the War Crimes Tribunal sat in 1946.

Visitors can also see the **Zeppelinfeld arena,** the huge amphitheater where, from 1927 to 1935, Hitler staged those dramatic Nazi rallies that were immortalized by Leni Riefenstahl in *Triumph des Willens* (*Triumph of the Will*). Hitler's architect, Albert Speer, constructed what has been called a "concrete mecca," whose grounds today have been turned into a park with apartment blocks, a trade fair, and a concert hall. Speer's Congress Hall, larger than the Colosseum in Rome, has become a recording studio and warehouse.

ESSENTIALS

GETTING THERE   By Plane   Nürnberg Flughafen is 6km (4 miles) north of the city center. Despite its relatively small size (it's only the ninth busiest in Germany), this airport is served by 14 airlines in scheduled flights to dozens of destinations throughout Europe. These are supplemented by charter flights. For information and schedules, call ☎ **0911/9-37-00.**

By Train   The **Nürnberg Hauptbahnhof** lies on several major German rail lines, with frequent connections to big cities and many smaller regional towns. Travel time to Frankfurt is 2 hours 8 minutes; to Berlin, 6 hours; and to Munich, 1 hour 40 minutes. For information and schedules, call ☎ **01 805/99-66-33.**

By Bus   Long-distance bus service from such cities as Munich and Frankfurt is provided by Europabus Lines 183 and 189E of Deutsche Touring GmbH, operating out of Frankfurt. For information in Nürnberg, call **Reisebüro Olcay** (☎ **0911/ 22-69-92**). Regional bus service with frequent connections to neighboring towns is offered by **OVF Omnibusverkehr Franken GmbH,** Kopernikusplatz 14 in Nürnberg (☎ **0911/4-39-06-66**).

By Boat   The Main–Danube Canal links the Rhine, the Main, and the Danube. For information about riverboat connections, call the **Hafenver-Waltung Nürnberg** (☎ **0911/64-29-40**).

By Car   From Munich, take the A9 Autobahn north; from Frankfurt, head southeast along the A3 Autobahn; from Berlin, take the A9 Autobahn south.

VISITOR INFORMATION   Contact **Tourist Information,** in the Hauptbahnhof (☎ **0911/2-33-61-32**), Monday to Saturday 9am to 7pm. An additional branch in the **Rathaus** (☎ **0911/2-33-61-35**) is open Monday to Saturday 9am to 6pm and also Sundays in May 10am to 1pm and 2 to 4pm.

Nürnberg

ATTRACTIONS
Albrecht Dürer House **18**
Beautiful Fountain **13**
Germanisches National
   Museum **5**
Handwerkerhof **3**
Hauptmarkt **11**
Helig-Geist-Spital **10**
Kaiserburg **19**

Lochgäfangis **12**
Rathaus **12**
St. Lorenz-Kirche **9**
St. Sebaldus-Kirche **14**
Spielzeugmuseum/
   Toy Museum **15**

ACCOMMODATIONS
Atrium Hotel **1**

Burghotel-Grosses
   Haus **16**
City Hotel **8**
Deutscher Kaiser **7**
Drei Linden **20**
Dürer-Hotel **17**
Le Meridien Grand Hotel **2**
Maritim **4**
Weinhaus Steichele **6**

GETTING AROUND   Nürnberg has its own subway system that consists of an east-west and a north-south line that intersect at the Hauptbahnhof. Depending on the distance you travel, one-way fares cost from 2.50DM to 3.30DM ($1.25 to $1.65). Principal stops within Nürnberg's medieval core include Lorenzkirche and Weisser Turm. For more information, call ☎ **0911/27-07-99.** Be alert to the benefits of walking between two points at opposite ends of the old town, the Hauptbahnhof (main railway station) and the Kaiserburg (the base of the city's medieval castle), a 30-minute trek that will lead you through the heart of the city's medieval core, past most of the historic monuments. To summon a taxi, call ☎ **0911/1-94-10.** Many hotels can arrange bike rentals; otherwise, contact **Fahrradkiste,** Knauerstrasse 9 (☎ **0911/2-87-90-64**). The best cycling paths are along the Pegnitz River.

EXPLORING THE CITY

You can easily spend a full day here seeing the sights. Begin at the central market square, **Hauptmarkt,** the most colorful place in Nürnberg, filled with kiosks stacked tall with fresh produce brought in from the countryside. Nearly all the city's attractions lie nearby within the **medieval fortifications,** parts of which still remain. Between the main wall (which has rampart walks) and the secondary wall once ran the waters of a protective moat. Set at the "corners" of the Altstadt are the massive stone towers, still intact, of the city gates. The remains of dozens of other gateway towers still exist along the ramparts. Crowning the northern periphery of the Altstadt is the **Kaiserburg.**

The best example of Nürnberg's aesthetic passion is the **Beautiful Fountain** on Marktplatz. This stone pyramid, 18m (60 feet) high, dates from 1396 and is adorned with 30 figures arranged in four tiers. Within it is enclosed the symbol of Nürnberg, the journeyman's ring.

At some point in your day wander over to **Handwerkerhof,** near the main train station. In this mall, you can see artisans creating the products for which Nürnberg has been known since the Middle Ages: glassware, pewter (often in the form of beer mugs), intricate wood carvings, and toys. Naturally, this mall is busiest at Christmastime.

If you're interested in a famous landmark of World War II, visit the **Justizgebäude,** Fürtherstrasse 22 (U-Bahn: Bärenschanze), where the "Judgment of Nürnberg" took place. Here in room 600, the surviving leaders of the Third Reich stood trial in October of 1946 for crimes against humanity. Afterwards, 10 were hanged. The building still serves as a courthouse, and you'll have to ask the guard at the door if you can enter.

✪ **Albrecht Dürer House.** Am Tiergartnertor, Albrecht-Dürer-Strasse 39. ☎ **0911/ 2-31-25-68.** Admission 8DM ($4) adults, 2.50DM ($1.25) students and children 6–15, free for children 5 and under. Mar–Oct, Tues–Sun 10am–5pm (Thurs until 8pm); Nov–Feb, Tues–Fri 1–5pm, Sat–Sun 10am–5pm. Tram 4. Bus: 36.

The town's most popular shrine is the Albrecht Dürer House, just a short walk up the cobblestoned Bergstrasse from the Dürer Monument and St. Sebald Church. Typical of the half-timbered burghers' houses of the 15th century, the structure is the only completely preserved Gothic house in Nürnberg. The first floors are sandstone, surmounted by two half-timbered stories and a gabled roof with a view of the town below. Exhibits inside the house are devoted to Dürer's life and works. Many of the rooms are furnished with important historical pieces and contain original etchings and woodcuts, plus copies of Dürer's paintings.

✪ **Germanisches Nationalmuseum (Germanic National Museum).** Kartäusergasse 1 (near the Hauptbahnhof). ☎ **0911/1-33-10.** Admission 8DM ($4) adults, 6DM ($3) children. Tues and Thurs–Sun 10am–5pm, Wed 10am–9pm. U-Bahn: Opernhaus.

The largest museum of German art and culture is just inside the south section of the medieval city walls. It covers the entire spectrum of German craftsmanship and fine arts from their beginnings to the 20th century. The prehistoric and early historical section contains finds from the Stone Age and from the burial sites of the Merovingians. The extensive painting and sculpture sections include works by Albrecht Dürer and Veit Stoss, a sculptor and wood-carver known for his "nervous" angular forms and realism. The boundless variety and richness of German handcrafts is fully evident in this museum. There's also an important library and archive here.

Kaiserburg. Burgstrasse. ☎ **0911/22-57-26.** Admission (including all parts of the castle) 9DM ($4.50) adults, 8DM ($4) students, free for children 15 and under. Apr–Sept daily 9am–5pm; Oct–Mar daily 9:30am–4pm. Bus: 36 or 46.

The Burg looms above the city from its hilltop at the northern edge of the Altstadt. From 1050 to 1571, it was the official residence of the German kings and emperors, including Frederick Barbarossa, the zealous crusader who entertained the emperor of Byzantium and the sultan of Tyre within its walls. The castle is divided into three complexes: the Kaiserburg (Imperial Castle), the Burgraves' Castle, and the Municipal Buildings of the Free City.

The oldest portion is the **Pentagonal Tower** (1050). It probably dates from the previous palace of the Salian kings, over which the Burgraves' Castle was constructed. Although the **Burgraves' Castle** has been in ruins since it was destroyed by fire in

Albrecht Dürer & the German Renaissance

If Dürer's father had had his way, his son would have become a goldsmith. Fortunately, that didn't happen. Albrecht Dürer (1471–1528) began his artistic career as apprentice to Michael Wolgemut, then the leading artist in Nürnberg, in 1486. There he learned to excel in woodcutting and engraving. Almost everyone is familiar with the sketch he made of praying hands—it's been reproduced so often it's become a greeting-card cliché.

Dürer was not content to stay at home in Nürnberg. Beginning in 1490, he embarked on a series of travels that eventually took him to Italy, where he came into contact with the artists of the Renaissance. On his return to Nürnberg, he brought their ideas back with him. Dürer was thus largely responsible for pulling art north of the Alps out of the medieval world and into the new era.

Dürer was one of the first major world masters to paint an acknowledged self-portrait. In fact, he painted three of them, and his very first known drawing is a sketch of himself at the age of 13. These paintings show clearly how he saw the artist's role, and the importance of his own mission. The last self-portrait (in the Alte Pinokothek in Munich), shows Dürer in an almost Christlike stance, representing the artist as an elevated figure concerned with the expression of universal ideas. Other important paintings of his include the portrait of *Charlemagne* at the Germanisches Nationalmuseum in Nürnberg, and his *Four Apostles,* commissioned for the Nürnberg Rathaus.

A restless man, Dürer was always probing into the world about him; he produced several theoretical works on art, on architecture, and on the science of proportion. Even more interesting, at one point he invented a mechanical device for drawing a picture that was a first step toward the principle of the photographic camera.

1420, the remains offer the visitor an interesting look into the layout of a feudal castle. The watchmen and guards used the heavy ramparts with the parapet walks and secret passages to protect the burgraves and the emperors, who lived in the inner core of the castle complex.

The **Kaiserburg,** grouped around the inner court within the ramparts of the Burgraves' Castle, was the residence of the kings and emperors of Germany. Most of the buildings were constructed during the 12th century, centered around the once magnificent Palas built by Konrad III in 1138. The great Knights' Hall on the ground floor and the Imperial Hall on the floor above look much as they did when King Frederick III rebuilt them in the 15th century, with heavy oak beams and painted ceilings. The rooms are decorated with period Gothic furnishings. Adjoining the Palas is the Imperial Chapel—actually two chapels, one above the other in cross section but united at the center by an open bay. Thus, the emperor could worship with his court in the upper chapel to the same liturgy as the lesser members of his retinue in the lower chapel.

The third set of buildings, outside the Burgraves' Castle, was erected by the council of Nürnberg in the 14th and 15th centuries when it took over the responsibility of protecting the emperor. This section includes the imperial stables (now a youth hostel), the massive bastions of the fortress, the Tiefer Brunnen (Deep Well), and the castle gardens. Even more impressive than the fortress is the view of the roofs and towers of Nürnberg from its terraces.

The complex also includes the new **Kaiserburg Museum** (☎ **0911/13-310**), which contains antique weaponry, armor, and paintings, and explains the history of the castle.

Lochgefängnis. Rathausplatz. ☎ **0911/233-60.** Admission 4DM ($2) adults, 2DM ($1) children. Tues–Sun 10am–4pm. Closed Jan–Mar and Oct–Nov. Bus: 36, 46, or 47.

Under the Altes Rathaus is a medieval prison with its original cells and torture chamber, a gruesome attraction. Opposite the torture chamber lie the remnants of a room that once hid the city council's treasures and important documents during wars and emergencies. An underground passage from the dungeons to the outside world existed from 1543 until 1945, when bombing rendered it impassable.

St.-Lorenz-Kirche. Lorenzer Platz 10. ☎ **0911/20-92-87.** Free admission. Mon–Sat 9am–5pm, Sun 2–4pm. U-Bahn: Lorenzkirche.

Across the Pegnitz River is the largest and stateliest church in Nürnberg. Begun in 1270, it took more than 200 years to complete, but the final result is one of Gothic purity, inside and out. The twin towers flank the west portal. The portal's sculptures depict the theme of redemption, from Adam and Eve through the Last Judgment. Upon entering the church, note the color and detail in the stained-glass rosette above the portal. Much of the church's stained and painted glass dates from the 15th century. The interior is marked by pillars that soar upward to become lost in the vaulting shafts above the nave. Each pillar is adorned with sculptures carrying on the theme introduced at the entrance. The oldest of these is *Mary with Child,* created around 1285. The continuing theme of the sculptures urges you toward the single east choir, the last portion of the church to be completed (1477). *The Angelic Salutation* (1519), carved in linden wood by Veit Stoss, is suspended from the roof of the church just behind the Madonna Chandelier. To the left of the altar is the Gothic Tabernacle, hewn from stone by Adam Krafft (1496), its upthrusting turret repeating the vertical emphasis of the church. Above the high altar is another masterpiece by Stoss, a carved crucifix. The painted panels at the beginning of the choir are by Michael Wolgemut, Dürer's teacher.

Spielzeugmuseum (Toy Museum). Karlstrasse 13–15. ☎ **0911/2-31-31-64.** Admission 8DM ($4) adults, 4DM ($2) children. Tues and Thurs–Sun 10am–5pm, Wed 10am–9pm. Bus: 36.

Nürnberg is a major toy center, so it's only fitting that the city devote a museum to this industry. Toys, both hand- and machine-made, fill three floors. Some date from medieval times. The collection of old dollhouses is vastly amusing, as is a mechanical Ferris wheel. You'll often see adults here (even without children).

✪ **St.-Sebaldus-Kirche.** Sebalderplatz. ☎ **0911/22-56-13.** Free admission. Mar–May daily 9:30am–6pm; June–Oct daily 9:30am–8pm; Nov–Feb daily 9am–4pm. Sunday services at 8:30 and 10am. U-Bahn: Lorenzkirche.

Consecrated in 1273, this church is a fine example of 13th-century transition from Romanesque to German Gothic styles. The nave and west choir are late Romanesque, with a narrow chancel containing a simple altar and an ancient bronze baptismal font. The larger east choir, consecrated in 1379, is pure Gothic and contains the church's most important treasures. Between the two east pillars is a huge 16th-century crucifixion group dominated by a life-size crucifix by Veit Stoss. Just behind the altar is the elaborate shrine of St. Sebald, whose remains are encased in a monument cast in brass by Peter Vischer in 1519. It's supported by an array of snails and dolphins and adorned with a host of statuettes. The nave of the church also holds several important works of art, including 14th-century statues of St. Catherine and St. Sebald and the *Madonna with a Halo* (1440).

SHOPPING

Located near the railway station in the center of the city, **Handwerkerhof** (U-Bahn: Hauptbahnhof) is a crafts mall in a medieval castle setting, where Franconian artisans create and sell a wide range of handicrafts. It's open March 20 to December 23, weekdays 10am to 6:30pm and Saturdays 10am to 4pm. In December, it opens Sundays 10am to 6:30pm.

Obletter, Königstrasse 2 (☎ 0911/2-14-99-90; U-Bahn: Lorenzkirche), near the town center, has been the largest store for children's toys and playthings in Nürnberg for 20 years. Toys, many of them computerized, cover two floors (street level and cellar) of a building near the town center. For policy reasons, you'll find few of the war games that you'd expect in an equivalent Stateside store, a credit to the establishment's enlightened management. Be warned: Some of the devices, although intended for use by children and teens, might even appeal to adults.

Hofman, Rathaus Platz 7 (☎ 0911/20-48-48 U-Bahn: Lorenzkirche), is devoted entirely to tin figures. The owner paints his historic soldiers, Christmas decorations, and other objects while manning the store.

At **Kistner,** Weinmarkt 6 (☎ 0911/20-34-82; U-Bahn: Lorenzkirche), you can step back in time. This wonderful store is full of antique books, prints, and engravings, including some by Dürer, Rembrandt, and other masters. The owner, Herr Kistner, is an expert in the field.

Villeroy & Boch, Königstrasse 13 (☎ 911/22-31-82 U-Bahn: Lorenzkirche), sells sets of china, crystal ware, and porcelain trinkets that make good souvenirs.

The largest department store in the city, **Karstadt,** Königstrasse 14 (☎ 0911/21-30; U-Bahn: Lorenzkirche), carries clothing, housewares, and other home furnishings.

If you're hungry, stop by **Lebkuchen Frauenholz,** Bergstrasse 1 (☎ 0911/24-34-64; U-Bahn: Lorenzkirche), a bakery that sells fresh gingerbread and honey packed in a container that looks like a half-timbered 18th-century German building.

Adding variety to prudence, **Condomi,** Ludwigstrasse 57 (☎ 0911/23-27-84; U-Bahn: Weisser Turm), sells condoms in various colors, textures, flavors, and scents. It also has postcards and T-shirts.

WHERE TO STAY
EXPENSIVE

Atrium Hotel. Münchenerstrasse 25 (5 min. drive from the city center), 90478 Nürnberg. ☎ 0911/4-74-80. Fax 0911/4-74-84-20. www.hotel-net.de/atrium. E-mail: atrium.nbg@ t-online.de. 200 units. MINIBAR TV TEL. 200DM–368DM ($100–$184) double; from 590DM ($295) suite. Rates include buffet breakfast. Children under 12 stay free in parents' room. AE, DC, MC, V. Parking 18DM ($9). Tram: 9. Bus: 36.

The Atrium is not as grand as Le Meridien Grand Hotel or even the Maritim, but it's close to the top of the heap. This hotel is one of the most modern in town; it looks like a four-story collection of concrete cubes set up on stilts. Inside, it's flooded with natural light, with many windows offering views of the landscaped park around it. Rooms and baths are spacious. Three rooms are specially designed for travelers with disabilities. The hotel is directly connected to the Meistersingerhalle, where concerts and conventions take place.

Dining/Diversions: An attractive and formal restaurant, the Parkrestaurant Meistersingerhalle specializes in continental and Franconian food. The Rôtisserie Médoc features international grill specialties. The Terrace Restaurant is open May to September, weather permitting. There's also a dignified bar called Henry's.

Amenities: Room service, laundry, dry cleaning, indoor pool.

Le Meridien Grand Hotel. Bahnhofstrasse 1–3 (across from the Hauptbahnhof), 90402 Nürnberg. ☎ **800/367-8340** in the U.S., or 0911/2-32-20. Fax 0911/2-32-24-44. www.lemeridien-hotels.com. E-mail: LeMeridien@grand-hotel.de. 182 units. A/C MINIBAR TV TEL. 360DM–420DM ($180–$210) double; from 600DM ($300) suite. AE, DC, MC, V. Parking 20DM ($10). U-Bahn: Hauptbahnhof.

This old-world palace is the best place to stay in Nürnberg; it's superior to its rival, the Maritim. The Grand is a solid, six-story blockbuster built "when hotels were really hotels"—that is, before World War I. Rooms are the finest and most spacious in town. Many have a private sitting area. Smoke-free rooms are available, and a trained staff is always there to assist you.

Dining/Diversions: The hotel restaurant, Brasserie, offers formal dining, with a cuisine both Franconian and international. It's a worthy choice for dining even if you're not staying here. A cozy pub, Opus, serves wine and beer, local specialties, and light snacks.

Amenities: Room service, laundry, dry cleaning, sauna, health club, solarium.

Maritim. Frauentorgraben 11, 90443 Nürnberg. ☎ **0911/2-36-30.** Fax 0911/2-36-38-36. www.maritim.de. E-mail: mglerschmann.nur@maritime.de. 315 units. A/C MINIBAR TV TEL. 288DM–472DM ($144–$236) double; 680DM ($340) suite. AE, DC, MC, V. Parking 22DM ($11). U-Bahn: Hauptbahnhof.

Maritim attracts those who prefer modern convenience to old-world charm. It used to be the city's most stylish hotel, until the Meridien chain upgraded the Grand. Rooms are good-sized—although not as spacious as the Grand's—with large beds and many extra amenities. Try an upper-floor room for a panoramic view over Nürnberg's medieval fortifications and busy traffic artery.

Dining/Diversions: The hotel's restaurant, the Nürnberger Stuben, serves local and international cuisine. Live piano music is played nightly in the elegant hotel bar, Nürnberger Treff.

Amenities: Room service, laundry, dry cleaning, indoor pool, solarium, sauna, steam bath, newsstand.

MODERATE

Burghotel-Grosses Haus. Lammsgasse 3, 90403 Nürnberg. ☎ **0911/20-44-14.** Fax 0911/22-38-82. www.altstadthotels-nuernberg.de. E-mail: duerer-hotel@altstadthotels.com. 46 units. MINIBAR TV TEL. 175DM–291DM ($87.50-$145.50) double; 225DM–350DM ($112.50–$175) suite. Rates include continental breakfast. AE, DC, MC, V. Parking 15DM ($7.50). Tram: Tiergärtnertor. Bus: 36.

This reliable hotel provides good solid comfort for the travel-weary. Sure, it's a ways down the pecking order among local hotels, but its limited facilities remain a good value. This unusual hotel offers the luxury of a heated indoor pool opening onto a tile bar area furnished with plants, antiques, and bar stools; here you can sip your favorite drink and pretend you're in the Caribbean. Even better, your door will practically open into one of the most historic parts of the old city—you're right next to Dürer's house.

Dürer-Hotel. Neutormauer 32, 90403 Nürnberg. ☎ **0911/20-80-91.** Fax 0911/22-34-58. E-mail: duerer-hotel@altstadthotels.com. 107 units. MINIBAR TV TEL. 230DM–300DM ($115–$150) double. Rates include buffet breakfast. AE, DC, MC, V. Parking 13DM ($6.50). Tram: 4 or 9. Bus: 36 or 46.

The Dürer has steadily grown in prestige since it opened in the late '80s. It stands beside the birthplace of its namesake, right under the castle and near all the major sightseeing attractions. The ambience is one of cozy antique charm, combined with modern amenities. The Dürer offers the Bistro Bar, a fitness center, and a garage. The only meal served is breakfast, but you're a short walk from restaurants and cafes. Laundry service and dry cleaning are also available.

INEXPENSIVE

City Hotel. Königstrasse 25–27 (near St.-Lorenz-Kirche), 90402 Nürnberg. ☎ **0911/ 22-56-38.** Fax 0911/20-39-99. 20 units. TV TEL. 180DM ($90) double. Rates include continental breakfast. AE, DC, MC, V. Closed for 2 weeks after Christmas. Parking 14DM ($7). U-Bahn: Lorenzkirche.

This serviceable if unspectacular hotel provides good value. It occupies the third, fourth, and fifth floors of an old-fashioned building, on a wide pedestrian thoroughfare. Take a small elevator upstairs to the third-floor reception area, where the efficient owner will show you one of her simple, cramped, but immaculate rooms. The tiny baths have shower stalls.

Deutscher Kaiser. Königstrasse 55, 90402 Nürnberg. ☎ **0911/20-33-41.** Fax 0911/ 2-41-89-82. 51 units. TEL. 179DM–199DM ($89.50–$99.50) double. AE, DC, MC, V. U-Bahn: Hauptbahnhof.

This attractive, gray-stone, 19th-century building, with steep gables and a high-pitched roof studded with dormers, stands at the top of a pedestrian mall. Three Romanesque-style arches lead into the main lobby. The general effect is one of comfort in immaculate surroundings. Rooms are small but have comfortable beds. Baths are cramped. This hotel is crowded during December and February, when it's a popular off-season retreat for German visitors. The breakfast room is rather simple, yet fresh and clean. In the basement is a cafe-restaurant.

Drei Linden. Aussere-Suizbacher-Strasse 3, 90489 Nürnberg. ☎ **0911/53-32-33.** Fax 0911/55-40-47. 28 units. MINIBAR TV TEL. 180DM ($90) double. Rates include buffet breakfast. AE, MC, V. Parking 15DM ($7.50). Tram: 8. Bus: 45.

This old-fashioned renovated guest house first opened in 1877. Today it provides small but comfortable rooms with tiny baths. Its restaurant has a good reputation and is often frequented by locals.

Weinhaus Steichele. Knorrstrasse 2–8 (near Jakobsplatz), 90402 Nürnberg. ☎ **0911/ 20-22-80.** Fax 0911/22-19-14. 58 units. TV TEL. 180DM–200DM ($90–$100) double. Rates include buffet breakfast. AE, DC, MC, V. Parking 15DM ($7.50). U-Bahn: Weisser Turm.

This small and charming hostelry retains its old-fashioned allure. It's located on a tranquil street, but not far from the bustling activity of the train station, just outside the city wall. The building is a beautifully balanced and handcrafted structure of heavy stone blocks with a curved sloping roofline. Any overflow of guests spills into a modern annex next door that blends harmoniously with the older building. Rooms are decorated in a rustic Bavarian style.

WHERE TO DINE
EXPENSIVE

✪ **Essigbrätlein.** Weinmarkt 3. ☎ **0911/22-51-31.** Reservations required. Main courses 34DM–43DM ($17–$21.50); fixed-price lunch 68DM ($34) for 3 courses, 78DM ($39) for 4 courses; fixed-price dinner 112DM ($56). AE, DC, MC, V. Tues–Fri noon–1:30pm; Tues–Sat 7–9:30pm. Closed Jan 1–15 and 2 weeks in Aug (dates vary). U-Bahn: Karstadt. FRANCONIAN/ CONTINENTAL.

This is now the outstanding dining choice of Nürnberg, dwarfing all other competition. The city's most ancient restaurant, dating from 1550, was originally a meeting place of wine merchants. Its upscale Franconian and continental cuisine is reason enough to go to the city in the first place. The cuisine is so inventive and refreshing, with many nouvelle recipes, that we'd view this as worth a detour. The chef firmly believes in market-fresh ingredients. Look for an ever-changing menu based on seasonal availability, but count on much care going into the preparation of each dish. The traditional specialty is roast loin of the beef (what the name of the restaurant means in German). If Dürer were alive today, he'd definitely make this elegant tavern his choice for dining.

Goldenes Posthorn. Glöckleingasse 2. ☎ **0911/22-51-53.** Reservations required. Main courses 12DM–36DM ($6–$18); fixed-price meals 28DM ($14) at lunch, 38DM–75DM ($19–$37.50) at dinner. AE, DC, MC, V. Mon–Sat noon–2:30pm and 6–11:30pm. U-Bahn: Lorenzkirche. FRANCONIAN.

Goldenes Posthorn claims to be in the oldest house in Germany. Among its mementos are a drinking glass used by Albrecht Dürer and a playing card belonging to Hans Sachs from about 1560. Although the restaurant's glory days—it was once celebrated as among the finest in Germany—are long gone, no other place can match its antique atmosphere. Its modern Franconian cuisine features such old-fashioned but satisfying dishes as quail stuffed with goose liver and nuts, venison in red wine with plums, fresh carp (in winter), and wurst with a mixture of onions and vinegar. Two special fixed-price dinners are offered, a four-course house menu and a five-course Franconian menu. There are also fine wines dating from 1889.

MODERATE

Heilig-Geist-Spital. Spitalgasse 16. ☎ **0911/22-17-61.** Main courses 12DM–30DM ($6–$15); 3-course fixed-price menu 23DM–40DM ($11.50–$20). AE, DC, MC, V. Daily 11:30am–midnight. Bus: 46 or 47. FRANCONIAN.

You wouldn't want to get much more Franconian than this. Heilig-Geist-Spital, Nürnberg's largest historical wine house, in business for 650 years, is entered through an arcade above the river. The main dishes are typical Franconian fare, hearty and filling. Carp is a specialty, as is pork knuckle—we're sure no one has altered this recipe since the days of Dürer himself. In season, you can order leg of venison with noodles and berries. The wine list is abundant and excellent, with more than 100 vintages.

Weinhaus Steichele. Knorrstrasse 2. ☎ **0911/20-22-80.** Main courses 12DM–40DM ($6–$20). AE, DC, V. Mon–Sat 11am–midnight. U-Bahn: Weisser Turm. FRANCONIAN/ BAVARIAN.

Steichele's walls are covered with polished copper pots, antique display cases lit from within, and hanging chandeliers carved into double-tailed sea monsters and other mythical beasts. The specialties here are a delight, and the wine list is superb. Try roast shoulder of pork with potato balls and sauerkraut, or *Husarenspiess,* with onions, ham, paprika, cucumbers, hot sauce, French fries, and salad. Surely if former patron Hermann Hesse himself returned today, he would notice no major alteration in the cuisine. Amid all the change going on in Nürnberg, this place still respects older times.

INEXPENSIVE

Bratwurst-Häusle. Rathausplatz 1 (opposite the Rathaus). ☎ **0911/22-76-95.** Main courses 9.80DM–16.50DM ($4.90–$8.25). AE, MC, V. Mon–Sat 10am–10:30pm. U-Bahn: Lorenzkirche. FRANCONIAN.

This is the most famous bratwurst eatery in the city. You might make it a luncheon stopover as you explore historic Nürnberg. Prices are kept at a 1970s level, but portions are as large as ever. In winter, you'll find an open hearth to warm you; in summer, this is a refreshingly cool retreat from the heat. Fixed-price menus also include Franconian specialties; most diners, especially the large student clientele, prefer simply a platter of bratwurst and beer.

Historische Bratwurst-Glöcklein. Im Handwerkerhof. ☎ **0911/22-76-25.** Reservations recommended. Main courses 9.80DM–14.40DM ($4.90–$7.20); fixed menu 23DM–39DM

($11.50–$19.50). No credit cards. Mon–Sat 10:30am–9pm. U-Bahn: Hauptbahnhof. FRANCONIAN.

If you want to try bratwurst in all its variations, this place is for you. Nürnbergers refer to it as their Bratwurst-Lokale, and it's the only serious rival to Bratwurst-Häusle (see above). The kitchen prepares a bratwurst as a main course, with traditional side dishes, all served on tin plates. Since beer goes perfectly with wurst, you'll enjoy sampling some of the brews on tap while admiring the craftsmanship of the room, which dates from the Middle Ages. Ham hocks are a specialty. Be careful that you don't spend your entire afternoon on the sun terrace—it's that tempting.

NÜRNBERG AFTER DARK

A theater complex offering quality productions of drama and opera, the **Städtische Bühnen,** Richard-Wagner-Platz 2–10 (☎ **0911/2-31-38-08;** U-Bahn: Opernhaus), houses the Kammerspiele, Opernhaus, and Schauspielhaus. The box office is open Monday to Friday 9am to 6pm; tickets are 11DM to 89DM ($5.50 to $44.50). Students get 25% off, and the general public can check on discounted seats at the box office 1 hour before each performance.

Touring cabaret acts play at the **Loni-Ubler-Haus,** Marthastrasse 60 (☎ **0911/ 54-11-56;** U-Bahn: Hauptbahnhof), on Saturday and Sunday at 8pm. The box office is open Tuesday to Friday 9am to 11pm, and tickets are 15DM to 90DM ($7.50 to $45). The city's premier outdoor venue, **St. Katarina,** is located in the ruins of the Katharinenkirche, Katherinenkloster 1 at Peter-Vischer-Strasse (U-bahn: Lorenzkirche). It hosts concerts by an eclectic mix of international musical acts. Call the box office (☎ **0911/2-31-25-30**), Monday to Thursday 10am to 1pm and Friday 10am to noon, for recorded show listings and ticket information.

A garden house glowing in blue light marks the rear entrance to **Starclub,** Maxtorgraben 33 (☎ **0911/55-16-82;** U-Bahn: Rathenauplatz), the "House of 11 Beers." Brews start at 4.20DM ($2.10), accompanied by baguette sandwiches 5DM ($2.50) and other cheap snacks. Students come around for backgammon and darts or animated conversation on the patio out front. It's open daily 11am to 1am. An artists' hangout, **Triebhaus,** Karl-Griolenberger-Strasse 28 (☎ **0911/22-30-41;** U-Bahn: Weisser Turm), opens early for big breakfasts that run 6.50DM to 29DM ($3.25 to $14.50), and offers soup, salad, and sandwich specials from 6.50DM to 12.50DM ($3.25 to $6.25) throughout the day. At night it dims the lights and keeps serving drinks. It's open Sunday to Wednesday 8am to 1am, and Thursday to Saturday until 2am. Food is served until 10:30pm and breakfast is served all day.

Another low-key arts scene, **Café Ruhestörung,** Tetzelgasse 21 (☎ **0911/ 22-19-21;** U-Bahn: Lorenzkirche or Rathenauplatz), offers some of the best people-watching in the city. Just sit on the patio and order a drink or a sandwich and watch the world waltz past. Draft beers are 4.50DM to 5.50DM ($2.25 to $2.75). Open Monday to Friday 7:30am to 1am and Saturday and Sunday 9:30am to 1am.

Forum, Regensburgerstrasse 334 (☎ **0911/4-08-97-44;** S-Bahn: Frankenstadion; bus: 44), is a two-story club split between indie rock and house dancing on Fridays, and techno raves and live bands on Saturday. Admission is 10DM to 15DM ($5 to $7.50). At **Mach I,** Kaiserstrasse 1–9 (☎ **0911/203030;** U-bahn: Lorenzkirche), Thursday and Friday move from disco to hip-hop, warming up for Saturday's big house party. Cover is 8DM ($4) on Thursday, 10DM ($5) on Friday, and 15DM ($7.50) on Saturday. It's open Thursday and Friday 10pm to 4am, and Saturday 10pm to 5am.

A popular gay bistro, **Cartoon,** An der Sparkgasse 6 (☎ **0911/22-71-70;** U-bahn: Lorenzkirche), serves beer, wine, and light meals Monday to Saturday noon to midnight, and Sunday 2pm to 11pm. For later hours, hit the dance clubs, all of which have both gay and straight clientele.

4 Regensburg

122km (76 miles) NE of Munich, 100km (62 miles) SE of Nürnberg, 114km (71 miles) NW of Passau

Regensburg is one of Germany's best-preserved cities, relatively undamaged by World War II bombings. Despite this, it remains relatively obscure to many foreign visitors. Even if you don't have time to explore the city's museums or the interiors of its many historical monuments, try to take in the view of the Danube from one of its bridges, especially at sunset.

Regensburg started as a Celtic settlement called Radespona, around 500 B.C. The Romans later took it over, renamed it Castra Regina, and made it their center of power on the upper Danube. From the 7th century, the town was the center from which Christianity spread over southern Germany. The architecture of Regensburg testifies to its long history and past grandeur, which reached its peak by the beginning of the Gothic era. Its buildings and towers offer an unspoiled glimpse into history, and many of its ancient structures are still in active use today. The best example is the **Stone Bridge,** built in 1146 on 16 huge arches, in continuous service for more than 800 years.

ESSENTIALS

GETTING THERE   By Train   The **Regensburg Hauptbahnhof** is on major rail lines, including Passau–Regensburg–Nürnberg and Munich–Landshut–Regensburg, with frequent connections in all directions. From Munich, 20 trains arrive daily (trip time: $1^1/_2$ hr.), and from Frankfurt, 10 trains daily (trip time: $3^1/_4$ hr.). The trip from Nürnberg takes only an hour; from Passau (see below), $1^1/_2$ hours. For rail information and schedules, call ☎ **01805/99-66-33.**

By Bus   Regional buses service the nearby towns. Call ☎ **0941/58-50-00** for information. For bus runs to such cities as Munich or Nürnberg, service is provided by **Firma Watzinger** in Bad Albach (☎ **09405/12-01**).

By Car   Access by car is via the A3 Autobahn from east and west and the A93 from north and south.

VISITOR INFORMATION   Contact **Tourist-Information,** Altes Rathaus (☎ **0941/5-07-44-10**). Hours are Monday to Friday 8:30am to 6pm, Saturday 9am to 4pm, and Sunday 9:30am to 4pm.

GETTING AROUND   You can walk around the center of Regensburg covering the highlights. To get from the Hauptbahnhof to the town's medieval core (Altstadt) take any of the bright yellow *Altstadt Buses* that line up along Maximilianstrasse, next to the station. One-way fare is 1 DM (50¢). Buses run at 6-minute intervals every Monday to Friday 8:30am to 8:30pm. There's no service on Saturday and Sunday. If you wish to go farther afield, you'll find an adequate system of bus routes fanning out from the railway station. A single ride costs 3.50DM ($1.75), and buses run 6am to midnight daily. A list of bus routes is available at the railway station at the Presse & Buch kiosk.

SEEING THE SIGHTS

Regensburg is a city of churches; it was once the focal point from which Christianity spread throughout Germany and even into Central Europe via the Danube. The most majestic of these churches is the towering **Dom St. Peter's,** Domplatz (☎ **0941/ 5-97-1002;** bus: 1, 2, or 3), which was begun in the 13th century on the site of an earlier Carolingian church. Because it was constructed with easily eroded limestone and green sandstone, this French Gothic edifice is constantly being restored. The massive spires of the two western towers, added in the mid-19th century, were almost completely replaced in 1955 with a more durable material. The well-preserved stained-glass windows in the choir (14th century) and south transept (13th century) are impressive. Most of the pillar sculptures in the aisles of the nave were made in the cathedral workshop in the mid-14th century. The two little sculptures in the niches on opposite sides of the main entrance are called *The Devil* and *The Devil's Grandmother* by the townsfolk. The cathedral is home to a famous boys' choir, the Dompatzen, which performs every Sunday morning at 9am mass. The performance is open to all. From May to October, the cathedral is open Monday to Saturday 8am to 6pm and Sunday noon to 6pm; November to April, Monday to Saturday 8am to 4pm and Sunday noon to 4pm. Admission is free.

You can also visit the cathedral treasures at the **Domschatzmuseum,** Krauter-markt 3 (☎ **0941/51-068;** bus: 1, 2, or 3), which displays goldsmiths' work and splendid textiles from the 11th to 20th centuries. Entrance is through a portal in the north aisle of the cathedral. It's open April to October, Tuesday to Saturday 10am to 5pm and Sunday noon to 5pm; December to March, generally only Friday and Saturday 10am to 4pm and Sunday noon to 4pm; closed in November. The charge is 3DM ($1.50) for adults and 1.50DM (75¢) for children. You can also buy a combination ticket to the Domschatzmuseum and the Diozesanmuseum St. Ulrich (see below) that costs 5DM ($2.50) for adults and 7DM ($3.50) for a family. (Admission to the cloister isn't included with this ticket.)

The permanent collection of the **Diozesanmuseum St. Ulrich** is on exhibit in the former Church of St. Ulrich, an early Gothic building to the side of the cathedral, Domplatz 2 (☎ **0941/5-10-68;** bus: 1, 2, 6, or 11). Sculptures, paintings, and goldsmiths' work form a representative selection of religious art in the diocese from the 11th to the 20th centuries. Of particular interest are various works on loan from the monastic foundations of the diocese. The museum is open April to October, Tuesday to Sunday 10am to 5pm. Admission costs 3DM ($1.50) for adults and 1.50DM (75¢) for children, under 6 free.

Crossing the cathedral garden, you enter the **cloister** with its Romanesque All Saints' Chapel and St. Stephen's Church. The ancient frescoes on the walls of the chapel depict liturgical scenes from All Saints' Day. The 11th-century church of St. Stephen contains an altar made of a hollowed limestone rock with openings connecting to early Christian tombs. You can only visit the cloister and St. Stephen's Church on one of the guided tours, which are given from May to October Monday to Saturday at 10am, 11am, and 2pm, Sunday and holidays at noon and 2pm; November to April Monday to Saturday at 11am and Sunday and holidays at noon. The charge is 4DM ($2) adults, 2DM ($1) students and children, free for children under 6.

Of all the remnants of Roman occupation of Regensburg, the ancient **Porta Praetoria** behind the cathedral is the most impressive, with its huge stones piled in the form of an arched gateway. Through the grille beside the eastern tower you can see the original level of the Roman street, nearly 3m (10 feet) below—which is why you often have to step down into the churches of Regensburg.

Of the four **Museen de Stadt Regensburg,** the most important is **Kunst- und Kulturgeschichtliche Sammlungen,** Dachauplatz 2–4 (☎ **0941/5-07-24-48;** bus: 1, 2, or 3). This is not only the main museum of the city, but also one of the most notable in east Bavaria. Its displays show major developments in the history of the region from the earliest days up to the present. You'll see relics of the Roman period, such as a stone tablet marking the establishment of a garrison at Regensburg in the 2nd century. There's also a stone altar to the Roman god Mercury, as well as several Christian tombstones. The museum is open Tuesday to Sunday 10am to 4pm. Admission is 4DM ($2) for adults and 2DM ($1) for children.

No town hall in Germany has been preserved better than Regensburg's **Altes Rathaus,** Rathaus Platz (☎ **0941/5-07-44-11;** bus 1, 2, or 3). This Gothic structure, begun in the 13th century, contains a Reichssaal (Imperial Diet Hall), where the Perpetual Diet sat from 1663 to 1806. In the basement of the Rathaus are the dungeons, with the torture chamber preserved in its original setting. The Altes Rathaus is open daily. Guided tours in German are conducted Monday to Saturday every 30 minutes 9:30am to noon and 2 to 4pm; Sunday and holidays, every 30 minutes 10am to noon. Tours in English are offered May to September, Monday to Saturday at 3:15pm only. The cost is 5DM ($2.50) for adults and 2.50DM ($1.25) for children.

A SIDE TRIP TO WALHALLA

An interesting excursion is to **Walhalla** (☎ **0941/96-16-80**), which lies on the steep northern bank of the Danube. This Greek-like temple was constructed between 1830 and 1842 on orders of Ludwig of Bavaria. It honors great Germans, most of them in the arts. The attraction itself isn't that spectacular—most visitors come for the view and the lovely ride down the river. Walhalla is open April to September daily 9am to 5:45pm, October daily 9am to 4:45pm, and November to March daily 10 to 11:45am and 1 to 4:45pm. There's a boat to Walhalla from Regensburg April to October daily at 10:30am and 2pm, with an additional departure May to September, Tuesday to Sunday at noon. The ride takes 45 minutes and costs 11DM ($5.50) each way for adults, and 5DM ($2.50) for children. For information about departures, call **Regensburger Personen Schiffahrt,** Werftstrasse 8 (☎ **0941/553-59**).

WHERE TO STAY
EXPENSIVE

Parkhotel Maximilian. Maximilianstrasse 28, 93047 Regensburg. ☎ **0941/5-68-53.** Fax 0941/5-29-42. www.maximilian-hotel.de. E-mail: pmaximilia@aol.com. 52 units. MINIBAR TV TEL. 278DM–298DM ($139–$149) double; 400DM ($200) suite. Rates include breakfast. AE, DC, MC, V. Parking 18DM ($9). Bus: 1, 2, 3, or 6.

The next best thing to staying in one of Mad King Ludwig's palaces is to check into the Parkhotel Maximilian, an exquisitely renovated neo-rococo building. Its facade and public areas have been classified a public monument. The main salon, with a ceiling supported by columns of polished red stone, continues the theme of 18th-century opulence coupled with 20th-century convenience. Rooms are attractively furnished.

Dining: The indoor day cafe is a Bavarian fantasy in soft colors, crystal chandeliers, and elaborate plaster detailing. There's also a German restaurant offering hearty Bavarian dishes.

Amenities: Room service, laundry, dry cleaning.

MODERATE

Bischofshof am Dom. Krautermarkt 3, 93047 Regensburg. ☎ **0941/5-84-60.** Fax 0941/58-46-146. www.hotel-bischofshof.de. E-mail: info@hotel-bischofshof.de. 54 units. TV TEL. 225DM–250DM ($112.50–$125) double; 325DM ($162.50) suite. AE, DC, MC, V. Parking 12DM ($6). Bus: 1.

This hotel was constructed as an ecclesiastical academy by the bishops of Regensburg in 1810. Today it blends 19th-century monastic with modern secular. Many of the units have hosted princes and even emperors. Rooms are attractively furnished; some have minibars. Baths are a bit small but well maintained. Part of the hotel takes in a piece of a Roman gateway. Behind the building is one of Regensburg's most popular sun terraces. Hotel restaurants offer French, Bavarian, and international dishes. There's *gutbürgerlich* (home-cooked) cuisine at lunch, and a gourmet menu for dinner. Guests can also sit in the hotel's Weinstube, or in one of the 350 seats in the beer garden. The beer comes from a brewery dating from 1649.

Karmeliten. Dachauplatz 1, 93047 Regensburg. ☎ **0941/5-43-08.** Fax 0941/56-17-51. 80 units. TV TEL. 180DM–220DM ($90–$110) double; from 230DM ($115) suite. Rates include buffet breakfast. AE, DC, MC, V. Parking 10DM ($5). Closed Dec 20–Jan 20. Bus: 1, 2, or 3.

In spite of its 130 years of tradition, the Karmeliten has a young, modern look. It's set on a square about 3 blocks from the river and a 4-minute walk from the Dom, reached via an open-air fruit-and-vegetable market. The whole place has a homelike atmosphere. Rooms and baths are a bit cramped. The restaurant, open 24 hours, serves good Spanish and German specialties.

INEXPENSIVE

Straubinger Hof. Adolf-Schmetzer-Strasse 33 (a 15-min. walk east of the cathedral), 93055 Regensburg. ☎ **0941/60030.** Fax 0941/79-48-26. www.germanguide.de./baxern/100117.htm. 60 units. 160DM–180DM ($80–$90) double. Rates include breakfast. AE, DC, MC, V. Bus: 1. Free parking.

This attractive, unpretentious hotel is little publicized, but bargain-hunters should seek it out. The small rooms are simple but satisfactory, with lots of sunlight. Most contain a minibar, TV, and phone. Baths are tiny and towels are rather thin. Inexpensive and satisfying lunches and dinners, both German and regional, are served in the dining room.

WHERE TO DINE

You can satisfy your sweet tooth by stopping by **Princess Konditorei,** Rathaus Platz 2 (☎ **0941/5-76-71;** bus 1, 2, or 3), which has a tempting array of homemade pastries and candies.

Gänsbauer. Keplerstrasse 10. ☎ **0941/5-78-58.** Reservations recommended. Main courses 20DM–34DM ($10–$17); fixed-price dinner from 45DM–100DM ($22.50–$50). AE, DC, MC, V. Daily 6pm–1am. Bus: Fischmarkt. BAVARIAN/INTERNATIONAL.

For elegant dining, call for a table at Gänsbauer, one of the best restaurants in the city. The setting is mellow and old-fashioned, but the cuisine is strictly *neue Küche— cuisine moderne* with a continental influence. Well-known Bavarian dishes are given a lighter touch. Only the freshest ingredients are used. Our recently sampled baby turbot in a Pernod sauce was superb in every way. The desserts are often exotic. The restaurant occupies a 500-year-old building with an open space where you can sit in fair weather. The street in front is a pedestrian zone, and there are tables here in summer.

✪ Historisches Eck. Watmarkt 6. ☎ **0941/5-89-20.** Reservations required. Main courses 39DM–45DM ($19.50–$22.50); fixed-price dinners 90DM–120DM ($45–$60); fixed-price lunch 55DM ($27.50). AE, DC, MC, V. Tues–Sat 11:30am–1:30pm (last order) and 6:30–9:30pm (last order). Bus: 1, 2, 3, or 6. GERMAN.

This is the most elegant and charming restaurant in town, located midway between the cathedral and the town hall (Rathaus), and convenient to virtually every historic monument. It occupies what was originally a chapel built around 1250, and retains today the high vaulted ceilings and solid ornamentation of its original construction.

Try the roast pigeon with chives, asparagus, and Bohemian-style noodles, or fish (*waller*) from the Danube served on a bed of hot sprouts. The menu has such refreshing change-of-pace fare as sliced tongue of veal with ratatouille, or—only for the adventurous—a well-flavored ragout of freshwater fish with eels, served with a beet-flavored cream-and-red-wine sauce. The wine list is the finest in the region. Your welcome here will be remarkably warm.

Ratskeller. Rathausplatz 1 (5 min. from the Dom). ☎ **0941/5-17-77.** Reservations recommended. Main courses 18DM–38DM ($9–$19); fixed-price lunch 22DM–30DM ($11–$15). AE, DC, MC V. Tues–Sun 10:30am–3pm; Tues–Sat 5:30pm–midnight. Bus: 1, 2, 3, or 6. FRANCONIAN.

Traditional and unspoiled—that describes the Ratskeller. Here you'll get some of the best meals for your money in Regensburg. This comfortable establishment consists of two dining rooms with vaulted ceilings, paneled walls, and painted crests. The Germanic cuisine is good, with other internationally inspired offerings that add variety and flair. The best buy is the fixed-price luncheon. The Franconian soups are good and hearty. You can also try schnitzel cordon bleu or, for an exotic touch, an Indonesian *nasi-goreng*.

REGENSBURG AFTER DARK

The town's cultural center, **Alte Mälzerei,** Galgenberger Strasse 20 (☎ **0941/ 7-57-49;** bus: 6), hosts concerts and theater productions, as well as a rundown bar and beer garden which serves cheap drinks 6pm to 1am daily. In the same complex, **Cartoon,** Galgenberger Strasse 20 (☎ **0941/7-57-38;** bus: 6), has live reggae, blues, and rock bands on the main floor and a disco in the cellar. The club opens daily at 11am (2pm on weekends), and begins its entertainment at 8pm. Nighttime cover is 20DM to 30DM ($10 to $15). Closing hours vary. The only late-night bar in town, **Wunderbar,** Keplerstrasse 11 (☎ **0941/5-31-30;** bus: Altstadtbus), serves drinks until 3am, 7 nights a week.

Südhaus Dance Theatre, Untere Bachgasse 8 (☎ **0941/5-19-46;** bus: Altstadt-bus), is the best of the local dance clubs. Easy to spot, its entrance is marked by a statuary angel holding a lit bar sign. It's open Tuesday and Thursday 11pm to 3am, Friday and Saturday 11pm to 4am. On Thursday, it's the town's best lesbian and gay rendezvous. Admission is 50DM ($25) Tuesday and 6DM ($3) other nights. Somewhat more fashionable, and a bit more pretentious is **Scala,** Gesandtenstrasse 6 (☎ **0941/ 5-22-93;** bus: Altstadtbus), where the dance floor is hemmed in by three bars. This club attracts an under-35 crowd. It's open Wednesday to Sunday 11pm to 3am (until 4am Friday and Saturday). Admission is 3DM to 7DM ($1.50 to $3.50).

If the weather's right when you reach Regensburg, head for the town's oldest inn, the **Goldene Ente,** Badstrasse 32 (☎ **0941/8-54-55;** bus: 12), which has a beer garden at the end of Eisernen Steg Brücke (along the Danube). Under the chestnut trees, you can sample spareribs, Würstchen, grilled schnitzel, and, of course, that famous brew. Beer prices range from 4.30DM to 4.80DM ($2.15 to $2.40).

5 Passau

191km (119 miles) E of Munich, 117km (73 miles) SE of Regensburg

For years, Passau languished in a lost corner of West Germany. But since reunification, the beauty and nostalgia of this old city has been appreciated more and more. With its romantic river setting and stately streets, Passau is a city of great harmony. It's located at the confluence of the Danube and two of its tributaries, the Ilz and Inn Rivers. Passau's bustling port is worth a visit in itself.

ESSENTIALS

GETTING THERE   By Train   Since Passau is a German border station, **Inter-City** trains stop here, with frequent daily arrivals from such cities as Nürnberg, Munich, and Vienna. The other major rail links include Frankfurt–Nürnberg–Passau–Vienna and Nürnberg–Regensburg–Passau, with frequent connections. Trip time from Nürnberg is 2 hours; from Frankfurt, 4¹/₂ hours; from Munich, 1 hour; from Regensburg, 1 hour; and from Vienna, 3¹/₄ hours. For rail information and schedules, call ☎ **01805/99-66-33.**

By Bus   There are no long-distance buses serving Passau. However, buses service the outskirts of the city. For a recorded list of schedules (in German), call ☎ **0851/ 7-34-35.**

By Car   Access is by the A3 Autobahn from the north or south.

VISITOR INFORMATION   For information, contact the **Tourist Information Office,** Bahnhof 36 (☎ **0851/95-59-80**). April to October, hours are Monday to Friday 9am to 6pm, Saturday and Sunday 10am to 2pm; November to March, Monday to Thursday 9am to 5pm and Friday 8:30am to 4pm.

GETTING AROUND   A local bus, called **City-Bus,** runs through Passau from the Rathaus (Town Hall) to the Hauptbahnhof (train station) every 15 minutes. It connects all the places recommended below. Call the tourist office for schedule information.

CRUISING THE DANUBE

One reason for visiting this Dreiflüssestadt (town of three rivers) on the Austrian frontier is to take one of the numerous boat tours along the Danube and its tributaries, the Inn and the Ilz. Trips range from a 45-minute three-river tour to a steamer cruise downriver to Vienna. The cruises depart from Fritz-Schäffer Promenade. Many passengers prefer to go by boat, then take a train back.

You might also be tempted to board one of the passenger ferries that make runs (May to October only) every day from Passau downstream to the Austrian city of Linz. The trips take 5 hours each way, cost 35DM ($17.50) per person, and depart from the city's riverfront piers at 9am and at 1:10pm.

If you're interested in gaining even greater insights into life along the Danube, you can continue by train from Linz to Vienna, buying a ferryboat, train, and hotel package priced at a reasonable 249DM ($124.50) per person, which will include round-trip transit by boat and train to Vienna, via Linz, from Passau, and 1 night's stay at a four-star hotel in Vienna. For information about either the day trip to Linz or the overnight sojourn in Vienna, contact the **Donau-Schiffahrt Line** through its local representative, Würm & Koeck, Höllgasse 26, 94032 Passau (☎ **0851/929-292**).

SEEING THE SIGHTS

The **Altstadt** is built on a rocky spur of land formed by the confluence of the Inn and the Danube. To best appreciate its setting, cross the Danube to the **Veste Oberhaus,** St. Georg Berg 125, a medieval episcopal fortress towering over the town and the river. Note how arches join many of the houses, giving them a unity of appearance. As you view the town, you can sense that the architecture here is more closely allied to northern Italy and the Tyrolean Alps than to cities to the north. Veste Oberhaus houses a museum of regional history (☎ **0851/4933512**), going back to medieval times. It's open March to January, Tuesday to Thursday 9am to 5pm, Friday 9am to 7pm, Saturday and Sunday 10am to 5pm. Admission is 7DM ($3.50) for adults and 4DM ($2) for children. Take the shuttle bus to the castle.

Dominating the town are the twin towers of the **Dom (St. Stephen's Cathedral)**, Domplatz 9 (☎ **0851/39-33-74;** bus: City-Bus). The original Gothic plan is still obvious in spite of its 17th-century reconstruction in grand baroque style. Its most unusual feature is the octagonal dome over the intersection of the nave and transept. The interior of the cathedral is mainly Italian baroque—almost gaudy, with its many decorations and paintings. Of particular interest is the choir, which remains from the Gothic period. A newer addition is a huge organ, said to be the largest church organ in the world, built in 1928 and placed in an 18th-century casing. Concerts are given May to October Monday to Saturday at noon, costing 4DM ($2) for adults and 3DM ($1.50) for children and students, and also at 7:30pm on Thursday, costing 10DM ($5) for adults, 5DM ($2.50) for children. The Dom is open Monday to Saturday 8 to 11am and 12:30 to 6pm. Admission is free.

Below the cathedral, on the bank of the Danube, is the **Marktplatz** and the 13th-century **Rathaus,** with a facade decorated with painted murals depicting the history of the town. Inside, the huge knights' hall contains two large 19th-century frescoes illustrating incidents from the legend of the Niebelungen. The Town Hall has a Glockenspiel in its tower that plays at 10:30am, 2pm, and 7:25pm; on Saturday there's an additional performance at 3pm.

Next to the Rathaus, the **Glasmuseum (Glass Museum),** Rathausplatz (☎ **0851/ 3-50-71;** bus: City-Bus), features an impressive array of glassware from the 1700s to the 1930s, collected from Bavaria, Austria, Bohemia, and other parts of Europe. In all, there are 30,000 items on display, including the world's largest collection of Bohemian glass. The Biedermeier period of 1840 and the Jugendstil period of 1910 are particularly emphasized. The museum is open April to September, daily 10am to 4pm; October to March, daily 1 to 4pm. Admission is 5DM ($2.50) for adults, 3DM ($1.50) for students and older children, and free for children under 12.

WHERE TO STAY
EXPENSIVE

Holiday Inn. Bahnhofstrasse 24 (across from the Hauptbahnhof), 94032 Passau. ☎ **0851/ 5-90-00.** Fax 0851/5-90-05-29. E-mail: holiday-inn-passau@t-online.de. 131 units. A/C TV TEL. 180DM–330DM ($90–$165) double; 400DM ($200) suite. AE, DC, MC, V. Parking 20DM ($10). Bus: City-Bus.

The Holiday Inn is rather sterile, but it's the best hotel in Passau. It's been integrated into the city's largest shopping center. Rooms all have up-to-date amenities and tiny baths.

Dining/Diversions: There's a good restaurant, Batavia, serving both international and regional specialties, and an intimate bar, the Amadeo.

Amenities: Room service, laundry, health club, swimming pool, sauna, solarium.

MODERATE

Passauer Wolf. Rindermarkt 6, 94032 Passau. ☎ **0851/9-31-51-10.** Fax 0851/9-31-51-50. 40 units. MINIBAR TV TEL. 185DM–280DM ($92.50–$140) double. Rates include breakfast. AE, DC, MC, V. Parking 18DM ($9). Bus: City-Bus.

This hotel on the banks of the Danube has an elegant baroque facade. It isn't as up-to-date as the Holiday Inn but has better food and more character. Rooms are modern and comfortable. Service is efficient. Room service and laundry service are available.

The hotel's **Passauer Wolf Restaurant** is one of the most distinguished in town; you may want to dine here even if you're not a guest. It serves classic dishes and regional specialties. It's open Monday to Friday noon to 2pm and 6 to 10pm, and Saturday 6 to 10pm only.

Weisser Hase. Ludwigstrasse 23 (off Ludwigsplatz, halfway between the Dom and the Hauptbahnhof), 94032 Passau. ☎ **0851/9-21-10.** Fax 0851/9-21-11-00. www.weisserhase. de. E-mail: info@weisser-hase.de. 108 units. TV TEL. 200DM–280DM ($100–$140) double. Rates include buffet breakfast. AE, DC, MC, V. Parking 15DM ($7.50). Bus: City-Bus.

Weisser Hase straddles the peninsula between the Danube and the Inn Rivers, in the heart of Passau. Some prefer this hotel to the more highly rated Passauer Wolf, because it provides more value for your money. Rooms have modern furnishings. There's a Weinstube with Bavarian-Austrian decor—carved wood and provincial chairs. The sauna is free to guests.

INEXPENSIVE

✪ **Altstadt-Hotel Laubenwirt.** Bäugasse 23–29, 94032 Passau. ☎ **0851/33-70.** Fax 0851/33-71-00. www.alstadt-hotel.de. E-mail: info@alstadt-hotel.de. 57 units. TV TEL. 145DM–250DM ($72.50–$125) double. Rates include buffet breakfast. AE, DC, MC, V. Parking 10DM ($5) in underground garage. Bus: City-Bus.

The waters of the Danube, the Ilz, and the Inn converge at a point just a few steps from the foundations of this hotel. You'd stay here just for the view, but it's also a very well-run hotel for a good price. Many guests who could afford the Holiday Inn seek out this little charmer for its ambience. Rooms are comfortably furnished in traditional style; some overlook the confluence of the rivers. The in-house pub is a popular gathering spot for locals. The hotel also has a good restaurant, the Donaustuben, which has a fresh catch of fish delivered to the chef daily. In summer, guests can enjoy breakfast or other meals on the terrace.

Hotel König. Untere Donaulande 1, 94032 Passau. ☎ **0851/38-50.** Fax 0851/38-54-60. 41 units. TV TEL. 160DM–220DM ($80–$110) double. AE, V. Parking 10DM ($5). Bus: City-Bus.

This hotel is located at the edge of a spit of land separating the Danube and Inn Rivers. It stands behind massive stucco-covered buttresses and a salmon-colored facade. Despite its fortresslike appearance, it has an interior that's comfortably up-to-date. Each of the well-scrubbed rooms has pinewood accents. The best ones open onto views of the Danube or the Inn, although the location isn't as scenic as that of the Altstadt-Hotel Laubenwirt (see above). A sauna and solarium are available.

WHERE TO DINE

For another dining option, head to the **Passauer Wolf** hotel (see above), which has one of the better restaurants in town.

Heilig-Geist-Stift-Schenke. Heiliggeistgasse. ☎ **0851/26-07.** Reservations recommended. Main courses 14DM–35DM ($7–$17.50). AE, DC, MC, V. Thurs–Tues 11am–1am. Closed Jan. Bus: City-Bus. BAVARIAN/AUSTRIAN.

Each year we hope for the opening of a first-class restaurant in Passau, but until that great day comes, this little inn born in 1358 remains the top choice in town, with its hearty, stick-to-the-ribs fare. In summer, you can sit in a beautiful wine garden under chestnut trees. Indoors, the dining room has an open fireplace, decorated with old tools used to press grapes. The restaurant has its own vineyard, and you can order its wines under the label "Grüner Veltliner." The ancient kitchen serves up many good, low-cost regional dishes, including boiled rump steak Austrian-style and roast suckling pig. *Passauer Schlosserbaum* is a dessert specialty (the waiter will explain). Bavarian, Austrian, and international dishes are featured.

PASSAU AFTER DARK

Combining quality drama with a dramatic setting, the **Stadttheater Company** is housed in the **Stadttheater Passau,** Gottfried-Schäffer-Strasse (☎ **0851/9-29-19-10**), a beautiful baroque opera house built by the local prince-bishops. Call for performance schedules and ticket prices. Summertime brings drama, pantomime, opera, jazz, and classical concerts to town, scheduled as part of the **Europäische Wochen (European Weeks) Festival,** which runs June to early August. Call ☎ **0851/ 560960** for information; for schedules, tickets, or reservations, contact the **Kartenzentrale der Europäischen Wochen Passau,** Dr.-Hans-Kapfinger-Strasse 22 (☎ **0851/752020;** fax 0851/7560207).

Home to Passau's popular cabaret company, **Theater im SchaarfrichterHaus,** Milchgasse 2 (☎ **0851/3-59-00**), is open September to July. It also hosts a series of jazz concerts throughout the year. Contact the theater for schedules, prices, and ticket availability.

Café Innsteg, Innstrasse 15 (☎ **0851/5-12-57**), housed in a bungalow hanging over the Inn River, offers the town's most scenic setting in which to relax with a drink. Like every other cafe-bar in town, it's open from midmorning until 1am. **Café Kowalski,** Obere Sandstrasse 1 (☎ **0851/24-87**), is less dramatic but also has balcony views of the river. Underground, across the river, **Joe's Garage,** Lederergasse 38 (☎ **0851/3-19-99**), is a friendly student dive named after a Frank Zappa album.

6 Ulm

97km (60 miles) SE of Stuttgart, 138km (86 miles) W of Munich

Visit Ulm for its architectural heritage and its history—not for great shopping, nightlife, or even an exciting local life. Ulm is a bit sleepy, smug, and satisfied with its monuments, especially its undeniably magnificent cathedral. The town is situated at a strategic spot on the Danube. Ulm's importance as a commercial river port has made it a prosperous city ever since the Middle Ages. Today, Ulm is a center of scientific and technological research, as befits the birthplace of Albert Einstein, who started life here in 1879. The old, narrow alleyways of the Altstadt lead to a modern city of riverbank promenades, beer gardens, spacious squares, and pedestrian zones.

ESSENTIALS

GETTING THERE By Train The **Ulm Hauptbahnhof** is on several major and regional rail lines, with frequent connections in all directions. More than 40 trains per day arrive from Munich (trip time: 45 min.) and some 50 or more from Stuttgart (67 min.). Daily trains also arrive from Cologne (4 hr. 6 min.). From Frankfurt (2 hr. 20 min.), you can take an ICE (InterCity-Express), the fastest and most comfortable way to travel by rail. For rail information and schedules, call ☎ **01805/996633.**

By Bus There are no buses from major cities; local buses service only satellite towns—mostly bedroom communities of Ulm.

By Car Access by car is via the A8 Autobahn east and west or the A7 north and south. It takes about 1¹/₂ hours to drive to Ulm from Munich and about 3 hours to drive from Frankfurt.

VISITOR INFORMATION Tourist-Information, Münsterplatz (☎ **0731/ 1-61-28-30**), is open Monday to Friday 9am to 5pm and Saturday 9am to 1pm.

GETTING AROUND Ulm's only tram line runs east–west, interconnecting the suburban convention center (Messe) with the main railway station (Hauptbahnhof) and Söflingen. Ulm's historic core (Altstadt) lies within an easy walk from the Hauptbahnhof. Buses 3, 7, and 8 radiate from the station to the suburbs. Buses and trams run at intervals of between 10 and 30 minutes, depending on the time of day and day of the week, and cost from 2.30DM to 3.50DM ($1.15 to $1.75), depending on the distance you travel.

SEEING THE SIGHTS

If you approach the town from the Stuttgart–Munich Autobahn, you'll miss the best view. So sometime during your visit, you should cross the Danube into Neu Ulm for a look at the gables and turrets of the Altstadt, which line the north bank of the river. Here is the **Fisher's Quarter,** with its little medieval houses and tree-shaded squares. Nearby are the elaborate Renaissance patrician houses and the Gothic Renaissance **Rathaus.**

✪ **Ulm Münster.** Münsterplatz 1. ☎ **0731/15-11-37.** Münster free; tower 5DM ($2.50) adults, 3DM ($1.50) children. Nov–Feb daily 9am–4:45pm; Mar daily 9am–5:45pm; Apr and Sept daily 8am–6:45pm; May–June daily 8am–6:45pm; July–Aug daily 8am–7:45pm; Oct daily 8am–5:45pm. Buy tickets an hour before the climb. Bus: 2, 7, or 9.

Before you even get close to the city, you'll see the towering Ulm Münster on the sky-line. Its 162m (530-foot) steeple is the tallest of any cathedral in the world, and the Ulm Münster itself is second only to Cologne Cathedral in size. Without the pews, the nave of the church could hold nearly 20,000 people, more than twice the population of Ulm at the time the cathedral was begun in 1377. When Ulm joined the Protestant movement in 1531, work on the building was suspended, not to be continued until 1844; it was completed in 1890. Miraculously, the cathedral escaped serious damage during World War II.

The exterior is almost pure German Gothic, even though bricks were often used in the walls along with the more typical stone blocks. The unusual feature of the Münster is that its architects placed as much emphasis on horizontal lines as on the vertical. Before entering, stop to admire the main porch whose three massive arches lead to two 15th-century doors. This section dates from the 14th and 15th centuries and contains a wealth of statues and reliefs.

The five aisles of the cathedral lead directly from the hall below the tower through the nave to the east chancel. The conspicuous absence of a transept heightens the emphasis on the chancel and also increases the length of the nave. Huge pillars towering into steep arches enclose each of the five aisles. The ceiling is swept into net-vaults so high that any of Germany's church steeples could sit comfortably beneath them. The nave is so large that, even with pews, it can accommodate more than 11,000 people at one service.

You can climb the tower as far as the third gallery (768 steps), where you can look out on the town and surrounding countryside over the Danube plain as far as the Alps.

Rathaus. Marktplatz 1. ☎ **0731/16-10.** Free admission. Mon–Fri 8am–6pm. Bus: 2, 5, or 6.

The Rathaus was built in 1370 as a warehouse but has served as the town hall since 1419. It contains some ornate murals dating from the mid-16th century. On the south gable hang coats of arms of cities and countries with which Ulm is linked by commerce. On the east gable is an astronomical clock from 1520. Above the interior staircase is a reproduction of the flying machine constructed by A. L. Berblinger, called "the tailor of Ulm." In 1811, he was one of the first people to make a serious attempt at flight.

Ulmer Museum. Marktplatz 9 (near the cathedral). ☎ **0731/16-14-330.** Admission 5DM ($2.50) adults, 3DM ($1.50) children. Tues–Wed and Fri–Sun 11am–5pm, Thurs 11am–8pm. Bus: 2, 5, or 6.

The Ulm Museum contains an important collection of arts and crafts produced in Ulm and upper Swabia from medieval times onward. There are also successive exhibitions of both ancient and modern art and artifacts, ranging from the region's prehistory up to the 20th century, with works by Klee, Kandinsky, and Picasso.

Farther up the Danube: Sigmaringen

Schloss Sigmaringen (☎ 07571/729-110), one of the most impressive castles in Germany, lies about 97km (60 miles) southwest of Ulm, dramatically situated on a rock above the Danube. Inside, the rooms are filled with period furniture, porcelain objects, and works of art. The castle also holds displays of the 15th- and 16th-century paintings and one of the biggest private collections of arms in Europe. Schloss Sigmaringen is open November and February to April, daily 9:30 to 4:30pm; May to October, daily 9am to 4:45pm; December and January, only by private arrangements. To get to Sigmaringen from Ulm, take a train on the Ulm–Frieberg line, or drive southwest on the B311 and then west on the B32. From the north, take the B313. There are also trains from Stuttgart.

WHERE TO STAY

Neu-Ulm Mövenpick Hotel. Silcherstrasse 40, 89231 Neu Ulm. ☎ **0731/8-01-10.** Fax 0731/8-59-67. www.movenpick-neu-ulm.com. E-mail: hotel.neu.ulm@moevenpick.com. 135 units. MINIBAR TV TEL. 240DM–285DM ($120–$142.50) double; 260DM–390DM ($130–$195) suite. AE, DC, MC, V. Parking 8DM–12DM ($4–$6). Bus: 2, 3, or 7.

This hotel beside the Danube contains rather bland, but well-maintained, rooms. Many feature views of the river. On the premises you'll fine a cafe, a pub, and a Swiss-inspired restaurant with a salad buffet. The English-speaking staff is helpful. Room service and laundry service are available.

Ulmer Spatz. Münsterplatz 27 (just beside the cathedral), 89073 Ulm. ☎ **0731/6-80-81.** Fax 0731/6-02-19-25. 35 units. TV TEL. 150DM–160DM ($75–$80) double. Rates include continental buffet breakfast. AE, MC, V. Bus: 2, 3, or 4.

The Ulmer Spatz is a corner stucco hotel-and-restaurant combination, with most of its simply furnished rooms overlooking the cathedral tower. This is an exceedingly modest but clean and comfortable place. Its chief recommendation is its location in the center of Ulm. Rooms are a bit cramped. The little Weinstube serves tasty Franconian meals in a mellow setting.

WHERE TO DINE

Zum Pflugmerzler. Pfluggasse 6. ☎ **0731/6-80-61.** Reservations recommended. Main courses 18DM–38DM ($9–$19). No credit cards. Mon–Fri 11am–2pm and 6–11pm, Sat 11am–3pm. Closed last 2 weeks in July and 1st 2 weeks in Aug. Bus: 2, 3, or 4. GERMAN/INTERNATIONAL.

This intimate restaurant is a winning choice for stick-to-the-ribs fare. Since it's open later than most restaurants in Ulm, it's a good place for a late-night supper in an old-world setting. The kitchen turns out home-style Swabian, Bavarian, and international meat and fish dishes. A specialty is Swabian *Fischmaultasche,* which looks like large ravioli, usually stuffed with a spinach-and-ricotta mixture. *Tafelspitz,* the famed boiled beef dish, is served with either a horseradish sauce or a green-herb sauce.

ULM AFTER DARK

The two best beer halls in town are **Barfusser,** Lautenberg 1 (☎ **0731/6-02-11-10**), a brew pub that also makes its own pretzels; and **Erstes Ulmer Weizenbierhaus,** Kronengasse 12 (☎ **0731/6-24-96**), which serves more than 20 varieties of Weizenbier and also has a menu of Franconian dishes that range in price from 5.50DM to 12.80DM ($2.75 to $6.40).

The aptly named Romantic Road, or *Romantische Strasse,* is one of Germany's most popular tourist routes. The road stretches for 290km (180 miles) between Würzburg in the north and Füssen in the foothills of the Bavarian Alps. Strung along the way is a series of medieval villages and 2,000-year-old towns. Frankfurt and Munich are convenient gateways for exploring the road by car, coach, or rail.

Another way to tour the route is by **bicycle.** Cyclists can begin at Würzburg and follow the bike path along the Main River. Tourist offices along the road provide cycling maps and other helpful information. Campgrounds are generally 10 to 20km (6 to 12 miles) apart. Bikes can be rented at any train station along the Romantic Road for 12DM ($6), or 6DM ($3) with a valid train ticket.

The Romantic Road is more than just a scenic route—it's also a powerful marketing organization composed of 26 municipalities, each of which would love to welcome you for a visit. The Romantic Road Association will provide information on sights and attractions and mail information packs in English. Contact the **Romantische Strasse Arbeitsgemeinschaft,** Marktplatz, 91550 Dinkelsbühl (☎ **09851/ 9-02-71**).

THE TOWNS OF THE ROMANTIC ROAD   Every town on the road has its special charms and attractions—and its drawbacks. **Rothenburg,** for example, is a perfect museum town but is overwhelmed with tourists. **Dinkelsbühl** is less perfect—it doesn't do as good a job of transporting you into the past—but at least it has an integrity of its own, independent of tourists. **Nördlingen** is less romantic even than Dinkelsbühl, but is more real. **Augsburg** is Bavaria's third largest city (after Munich and Nürnberg) but still has a rich medieval past. **Würzburg,** traditionally the first town on the route, is the bustling center of the Franconian wine region and home to one of Germany's greatest palaces.

BUS TOURS OF THE ROMANTIC ROAD   Green-and-white buses make three runs a day among all the member towns. April to October, a deluxe motor coach equipped with reclining seats and toilets departs from Frankfurt every morning at 8am, making stops on the main squares of 26 towns en route, eventually pulling into Füssen at 8:40pm. One-way transit between Frankfurt and Füssen costs 129DM ($64.50), but you can get off the bus and reboard it later at any town en route. Buses also run the other way, from Füssen to Frankfurt,

The Romantic Road

following more or less the same schedule. Make advance reservations by phoning **Deutsche Touring GmbH** (☎ **069/79-03-256**), Am Römerhof 17, Frankfurt.

1 Würzburg

280km (174 miles) NW of Munich, 119km (74 miles) SE of Frankfurt, 109km (68 miles) NW of Nürnberg

For Germans, the south begins at Würzburg, one of the loveliest baroque cities in the country. Würzburg is the best starting point for the Romantic Road. This city on the Main is young and lively (and often crowded in summer), and has a population of some 50,000 students, who give it a German version of *joie de vivre*. It's also a center of the Franconian wine region.

Würzburg remained faithful to the Roman Catholic Church throughout the Reformation. It's has been called "the town of Madonnas" because of the more than 100 statues of its patron saint that adorn the house fronts. The best known of these statues is the baroque *Patrona Franconiae*, also known as the "Weeping Madonna," which stands among other Franconian saints along the buttresses of the 15th-century Alte Mainbrücke, Germany's second-oldest stone bridge.

On March 16, 1945, Würzburg was shattered by a bombing raid. In a miraculous rebuilding program, nearly every major structure has been restored.

ESSENTIALS

GETTING THERE   By Train   The **Würzburg Hauptbahnhof** lies on several major and regional rail lines, with frequent connections to all major German cities. From Frankfurt, 30 trains arrive per day (trip time: 1¹/₂ hr.); from Munich, 20 trains (2¹/₂ hr.); from Nürnberg, 30 trains (1 hr. 10 min.); and several trains from Berlin (5 hr. 50 min.). For rail information and schedules, call ☎ **01805/99-66-33.**

By Bus   For bus service along the Romantic Road, see "Bus Tours of the Romantic Road," above.

By Car   Access is via the A7 Autobahn from the north and south or the A3 Autobahn from the east and west. The A81 Autobahn has links from the southwest.

VISITOR INFORMATION   Contact the **Tourist Information Office,** Pavillon vor dem Hauptbahnhof (☎ **0931/37-24-36**). It's open Monday to Saturday 10am to 6pm.

GETTING AROUND   The quickest and most efficient means for covering the central core of Würzburg is by tram (streetcar). A single fare is 2.30DM ($1.15), or else you can purchase a ticket good for 24 hours at any station for 7.20DM ($3.60). The same fare applies to buses, which also serve the city. For information about routes and schedules, call ☎ **0931/361352.**

SEEING THE SIGHTS

In spring and summer, the liveliest place in town is the **Markt** (**central marketplace**). Here street performers entertain and vendors hawk their wares, ranging from fresh fruit to souvenir trinkets. You can also stroll down the traffic-free **Schönbornstrasse,** with its modern boutiques and cafes. The wine merchants here will sell you a Bocksbeutel, the emerald-green, narrow-necked wine bottle that's native to the region. It's said that the shape came about because wine-drinking monks found it the easiest to hide under their robes.

Mainfränkisches Fortress (Festung Marienburg). ☎ **0931/4-30-16.** Admission 3.50DM ($1.75) adults, free for children under 14. Admission including the Fürstenbaumuseum 6DM ($3) adults, free for children under 14. Apr–Oct, Tues–Sun 10am–5pm; Nov–Mar, Tues–Sun 10am–4pm. Bus: 9.

Marienberg Fortress, located across from the Altstadt, over the stone bridge, was the residence of the local prince-bishops from 1253 to 1720. Although portions of the stronghold have been restored, the combination of age and wartime destruction has taken a serious toll on its thick walls and once-impenetrable ramparts. But what remains is worth a visit. The 8th-century **Marienkirche,** one of the oldest churches in Germany, stands within its walls.

In the former arsenal and Echter bulwark, to the right of the first courtyard, is the **Mainfränkisches Museum** (☎ **0931/4-30-16**), housed here since 1946. It's the historical museum of the former Bishopric of Würzburg and Dukedom of Franconia as well as the provincial museum of lower Franconia. On display is a collection of important sculptures by the great flamboyant Gothic master, Tilmann Riemenschneider (1460–1531), called "the master of Würzburg." The sculptor came to live here in 1483 and was the town's mayor in 1520 and 1521. Never a totally decorative artist, Riemenschneider concentrated on the reality of people's appearance, highlighting their hands, faces, and clothing. The museum also displays paintings by Tiepolo and sandstone figures from the rococo gardens of the prince-bishops' summer palace. A tribute to one of the few industries of the city, wine making, is paid in the press house, which contains historic casks and carved cask bases and a large collection of glasses and goblets. Admission is 5DM ($2.50) adults, 3DM ($1.50) students; children 14 and under are free. Open Tuesday to Sunday 10am to 5pm.

Fürstenbaumuseum (☎ **0931/4-38-38**) is situated in the restored princes' wing of the fortress. Here the visitor gets a glimpse of the living quarters and living conditions of the prince-bishops up to 1718. The urban-history section offers a stroll through 1,200 eventful years of Würzburg's history, including an exhibit relating to the discovery of X-rays by Wilhelm Conrad Röntgen in 1895. A model of the town shows its appearance in 1525, and another shows the destruction after the bombing of 1945.

✪ **The Residenz (Schloss und Gartenverwaltung Würzburg).** Residenzplatz 2, Tor B. ☎ **0931/355-1712.** Admission 8DM ($4) adults, 6DM ($3) students, free for children under 15 and seniors. Apr–Oct, Tues–Sun 9am–6pm; Nov–Mar, Tues–Sun 10am–4pm. Tram: 1 or 5.

The Residenz of Würzburg is the last and finest of a long line of baroque castles built in Bavaria in the 17th and 18th centuries. This great horseshoe-shaped edifice was begun in 1720 to satisfy Prince-Bishop Johann Philipp Franz von Schönborn's passion for elegance and splendor. Its design was the joint effort of the best Viennese, French, and German architects working under the leadership of an architect of genius, Balthasar Neumann (1687–1753). Both an architect and an engineer, Neumann was known for his technical virtuosity and the harmony of his compositions. He stands today as one of the towering figures of baroque architecture. This castle shows a unity of purpose and design unusual in structures of such size.

At the center of the castle is the masterful Treppenhaus (staircase). The high, rounded ceiling above is decorated with a huge fresco by Tiepolo. At its center, Apollo is seen ascending to the zenith of the vault. The surrounding themes represent the four corners of the world, the seasons, and signs of the zodiac. The painting appears to be overflowing onto the walls of the upper hall.

The other important attraction in the Residenz is the court chapel, in the southwest section. Neumann placed the window arches at oblique angles to coordinate the windows with the oval sections, thus creating a muted effect. The rectangular room is divided into five oval sections, three with domed ceilings. Colored marble columns define the sections, their gilded capitals enriching the ceiling frescoes by Johann Rudolf Byss. At the side altars, Tiepolo painted two important works: *The Fall of the Angels* on the left and *The Assumption of the Virgin* on the right.

During the summer, a **Mozart festival** is held in the upper halls. For information, call ☎ **0931/35-51-70.**

Dom St. Kilian. Domstrasse (at the end of Schönbornstrasse). ☎ **0931/5-36-91.** Free admission. Easter–Oct, Mon–Sat 10am–5pm, Sun 1–6pm; Nov–Easter, Mon–Sat 10am–noon and 2–5pm, Sun 12:30–1:30pm and 2:30–6pm.

This cathedral, begun in 1045, is the fourth-largest Romanesque church in Germany. The interior was adorned with high-baroque stucco work, done after 1700. The imposing row of bishops' tombs begins with that of Gottfried von Spitzenberg (ca. 1190), who was one of the first prince-bishops to rule over the town. Look for three sandstone tombstones by Riemenschneider, constructed between 1502 and 1506. The Dom is dedicated to St. Kilian, an Irish missionary to Franconia in the 7th century.

A DAY TRIP FROM WÜRZBURG

The most interesting excursion in the area is to the **Schloss Veitshöchheim,** Hofgarten 1 (☎ **0931/91-582**), about 8km (5 miles) away. You can take a Main River excursion (about 30 min.) to this delightful summer retreat of the 17th- and

18th-century prince-bishops. The palace here contains rococo and Empire furniture. But it is the fantastic rococo park that makes the trip worthwhile. Take time to wander among the fine and sometimes comical statues along shaded walks and avenues bordered by lime trees. The park is open daily 7am to dusk. The palace can be visited April to October, Tuesday to Sunday 9am to noon and 1 to 5pm. Admission to the park is free, but a visit to the palace costs 3DM ($1.50) for adults, 2DM ($1) for children and seniors, free for children under 15.

WHERE TO STAY
EXPENSIVE

Hotel Maritim. Pleichertorstrasse 5, 97070 Würzburg. ☎ **0931/3-05-30.** Fax 0931/3-05-39-00. 287 units. A/C MINIBAR TV TEL. 259DM–391DM ($129.50–$195.50) double; 450DM–550DM ($225–$275) suite. Rates include buffet breakfast. AE, DC, MC, V. Parking 24DM ($12). Tram: 1 or 5.

Nothing in Würzburg can match this hotel for comfort and style, not even the closest contender, Rebstock (see below). The Maritim has views over the Main River and is linked to the city convention center. Its modern and imposing yellow facade is topped by a baroque-style mansard roof. Rooms are good-sized and comfortable, with hair dryers.

Dining/Diversions: A Weinstube and a cafe are on the premises, but the Palais is the place for gourmets. Shining crystal and an amber glow from the lamps combine to create the most elegant restaurant in town. Dinner is served nightly Tuesday to Saturday. The refined continental menu changes frequently, but typical dishes are rabbit fillet with figs, marinated salmon with coriander, and breast of goose in orange-and-mustard sauce. Reservations are necessary. The hotel also has a large terrace and bar.

Amenities: Room service, laundry, dry cleaning, sauna, solarium, and indoor pool.

Hotel Rebstock. Neubaustrasse 7, 97070 Würzburg. ☎ **800/528-1234** in the U.S., or 0931/3-09-30. Fax 0931/3-09-31-00. www.rebstock.com. E-mail: rebstock@rebstock.com. 72 units. MINIBAR TV TEL. 284DM–360DM ($142–$180) double; 360DM–400DM ($180–$200) suite. Rates include buffet breakfast. AE, DC, MC, V. Closed Jan 4–25. Parking 18DM ($9). Tram: 1, 3, or 5.

The impressive Rebstock is housed in a palace that dates from 1408. It's not as stylish as the Maritim, but it appeals to those nostalgic for a taste of old Germany. Through a classical doorway, you enter a wide foyer with carved wooden doors and an old Spanish sea chest. The interior is tasteful. Rooms are equipped with hair dryers; 30 are air-conditioned. A winter garden with a fountain, chimney, and bar replaces an old courtyard.

Dining/Diversions: Gourmet cuisine is served in the main parquet-floor restaurant. The Fränkische Weinstube has oak beams, stark-white walls, and a gilded baroque painting along with a carved Madonna. Guests gather to drink local wine.

Amenities: Room service, laundry, health club, dry cleaning; car-rental and bicycle-rental facilities are also available.

Walfisch. Am Pleidenturm 5, 97070 Würzburg. ☎ **0931/3-52-00.** Fax 0931/3-52-05-00. www.hotel-walfisch.com. E-mail: walfisch@hotel-walfisch.com. 41 units. MINIBAR TV TEL. 225DM–285DM ($112.50–$142.50) double. Rates include breakfast. AE, DC, MC, V. Parking 15DM ($7.50). Tram: 1, 3, or 5.

From the windows of this inn's modernized rooms, you can gaze across the Main as far as Marienberg Castle, high on the opposite hill. Walfisch is a good third choice after the Maritim and Rebstock. Rooms range from small to medium; most are air-conditioned. Furnishings are typically Franconian: heavy draperies, provincial cupboards, and flowery fabrics.

Dining/Diversions: The highlight of staying here is ordering your breakfast while overlooking the banks of the Main. In the timbered but modern dining room, generous portions of traditional German food are served. The Weinstube serves a good selection of wine.

Amenities: Room service.

MODERATE

Franziskaner. Franziskanerplatz 2, 97070 Würzburg. ☎ **0931/3-56-30.** Fax 0931/3-56-33-33. E-mail: hotel-franziskaner@t-online.de. 47 units. TV TEL. 190DM–240DM ($95–$120) double. Rates include buffet breakfast. AE, DC, MC, V. Tram: 1.

For homespun cleanliness, this hotel is a winner—and the price is right, too. You'll receive a hearty welcome from the staff. The lobby has attractive black panels surrounded with natural wood; the breakfast room has fine large windows looking out to the greenery beyond. Rooms are well furnished; 40 have TV. The hotel itself serves only breakfast, but an on-site restaurant under separate management offers Franconian specialties.

Gasthof Greifenstein. Hafnergasse 1 (just off the Marienkapelle and its food market), 97070 Würzburg. ☎ **0931/3-51-70.** Fax 0931/5-70-57. E-mail: info@greifenstein.heu.de. 40 units. A/C MINIBAR TV TEL. 200DM–240DM ($100–$120) double; 450DM ($225) suite. Rates include continental breakfast. AE, DC, MC, V. Parking 10DM ($5). Tram: 1.

The 300-year-old Greifenstein, which was recently renovated, has been faithfully restored to its original design. It's a true tavern, abounding in village atmosphere. The upper-floor rooms have a private entrance and are calm and quiet; they have views over a pedestrian walkway in back. Some are quite small and cramped, but all are reasonably comfortable, clean, and cozy. The economical restaurant offers hearty German cuisine.

Hotel und Weinrestaurant Schloss Steinburg. Auf dem Steinberg, 97080 Würzburg. ☎ **0931/9-70-20.** Fax 0931/9-71-21. 50 units. MINIBAR TV TEL. 190DM–260DM ($95–$130) double. Rates include buffet breakfast. AE, CB, DC, MC, V. Free parking and a garage for 10DM ($5). Take Rte. 27 3km (2 miles) toward Fulda.

This turreted castle and its outbuildings sprawl high on a hill overlooking Würzburg. The castle foundations date from the 13th century, but what you see was largely rebuilt around 1900. It's a good choice for motorists, offering a tranquil setting and reasonable rates. From the sun terrace, guests can view the Main River, the acres of vineyards surrounding the property, and the web of rail lines that carry cargo far into the distance. Rooms have a country nostalgia. Each comes with a hair dryer. The hotel has an indoor pool and a sauna.

INEXPENSIVE

Schönleber. Theaterstrasse 5, 97070 Würzburg. ☎ **0931/1-20-68.** Fax 0931/1-60-12. 34 units, 27 with bathroom. TV TEL. 110DM ($55) double without bath, 120DM–170DM ($60– $85) double with bath. Rates include buffet breakfast. AE, DC, MC, V. Closed Dec 22– Jan 6. Parking 16DM ($8). Tram: 1, 2, 3, or 5.

You'll find the salmon-colored facade of this family hotel in the central part of historic Würzburg. The ground floor is rented to boutiques that monopolize the two enormous arched windows facing the sidewalk. The upper floors offer smallish but comfortable rooms. Baths are very cramped and have rather thin towels. The staff is friendly and helpful.

St. Josef. Semmelstrasse 28, 97070 Würzburg. Tel **0931/30-86-80.** Fax 0931/3-08-68-60. E-mail: hotel.et.josef@online.de. 35 units. MINIBAR TV TEL. 147DM–167DM ($73.50–$83.50) double. Rates include buffet breakfast. AE, DC, MC, V. Parking 12DM ($6). Tram: 1, 2, 3, or 5.

St. Josef is the best inexpensive accommodation in the Altstadt. Its owner has been successful in bringing it up-to-date. Rooms, though small, are pleasantly furnished and well maintained. Breakfast is the only meal offered, but there are many Weinstuben and restaurants in the area. Fresh flowers add a personalized touch to this well-run establishment.

WHERE TO DINE

Try the local specialty, *Zwiebelkuchen,* which is like a quiche Lorraine, and also look for a fish specialty, *Meerfischle.* White Franconian wine goes well with the local sausage.

Backöfele. Ursulinergasse 2. ☎ **0931/5-90-59.** Reservations recommended. Main courses 14DM–50DM ($7–$25). MC, V. Mon–Sat 11:30am–1am, Sun 11:30am–midnight. Tram: 1 or 4. FRANCONIAN.

Since this place is a short walk from both the Residenz and the Rathaus, you'll probably eat here at least once while you're in Würzburg. Even the locals don't really know whether to call it a beer hall, a wine cellar, or a restaurant. Regardless, the place serves well-prepared traditional food in copious quantities.

Ratskeller Würzburg. Langgasse 1 (near the Alte Mainbrücke). ☎ **0931/1-30-21.** Reservations required Sat–Sun. Main courses 13DM–38DM ($6.50–$19). AE, DC, MC, V. Daily 11:30am–2:30pm and 5:30pm–midnight. Tram: 1, 2, 3, or 5. FRANCONIAN/FRENCH.

This 500-year-old Ratskeller, part of the Rathaus, is not only an interesting place to visit, but also serves tasty Franconian fare at reasonable prices. Country cookery is an art here, as you'll discover if you order the boiled breast of beef with horseradish sauce and noodles. The English-speaking host will help you with menu selections. Game is featured in season. The place also specializes in local beer and Franconian white wines.

✪ **Weinhaus Zum Stachel.** Gressengasse 1. ☎ **0931/5-27-70.** Reservations required. Main courses 17.50DM–35DM ($8.75–$17.50); fixed-price menu 55DM ($27.50). MC. Daily 11am–1am. Tram: 1, 3, 4, or 5. FRANCONIAN.

No other wine house in Würzburg is as old as this one, which dates to 1413. Seats and walls have been burnished by the homespun clothing of many hundreds of drinkers and diners during the past 500 years. The portions are generous. Try veal cordon bleu, a tender pepper steak aromatically flavored with cognac, or the more prosaic rump steak with onions. Some dishes, such as chateaubriand, are so elaborate that they're prepared only for two. The chef is proudest of his freshwater fish prepared according to old family recipes. In summer, you can dine in a vine-draped outdoor courtyard. Wines are from the restaurant's own vineyards.

Weinstuben Juliusspital. Juliuspromenade 19. ☎ **0931/5-40-80.** Reservations required. Main courses 17DM–25DM ($8.50–$12.50). No credit cards. Thurs–Tues 10am–midnight. Tram 1, 3, or 5. FRANCONIAN.

One of the best known of Würzburg's Franconian wine taverns, the Juliusspital is decorated with traditional paneling and a beamed ceiling. It's distinguished by its wide range of regional dishes. The restaurant is a top address for wine connoisseurs, with an array of characteristic Franconian vintages.

Wein- und Fischhaus Schiffbäuerin. Katzengasse 7. ☎ **0931/4-24-87.** Reservations recommended. Main courses 26DM–48DM ($13–$24). No credit cards. Tues–Sun 11am–2:30pm; Tues–Sat 6–10pm. Closed Jan 1–8, and mid-July to mid-Aug. Tram: 3 or 4. SEAFOOD.

One of the best dining spots in the region is this combined wine-house/fish restaurant, across the river in an old half-timbered building on a narrow street, about 1 minute from the old bridge. The house specializes in freshwater fish, such as pike, carp, char, tench, trout, wels, and eel. Most of these dishes are priced per 100 grams (3.5 oz.). Soup specialties are fish, snail, lobster, and French onion.

WÜRZBURG AFTER DARK

Much of Würzburg's nightlife takes place in its numerous Weinstuben, many of which have an interesting character. For music and cultural happenings, scan the flyers posted in the *Studentenhaus* on Am Exerzierplatz at Münzstrasse.

A one-stop entertainment complex, **Autonomes Kulturzentrum Würzburg,** Frankfurter Strasse 87 (☎ **0931/41-78-00;** tram: 2 or 5), houses a bar and beer garden and offers a disco Thursday to Saturday with a cover charge of 10DM to 15DM ($5 to $7.50). On Tuesday and Wednesday it hosts concerts, with tickets costing 25DM ($12.50). The complex is open Monday to Wednesday 6pm to 7am, Thursday to Saturday 6pm to 3am, Sunday 3pm to 1am. Call for listings and ticket information.

The city's oldest jazz cellar, **Omnibus,** Theaterstrasse 10 (☎ **0931/5-61-21;** bus: 14 or 20), has been packing it in for live acts for nearly 3 decades. This is also where people come to drink and play chess. It's open Monday to Thursday 8pm to 1am and Friday and Saturday 9pm to 2am. Cover for performances ranges from 15 to 20DM ($7.50 to $10). A place for a cheap meal or a drink, **Standard,** Oberthurstrasse 11a (☎ **0931/5-11-40;** bus: 14 or 20), is open daily 10am to 1am. It occasionally has a live band on the weekend. **Kult Stattkneipe,** Landwehrstrasse 10 (☎ **0931/5-31-43;** tram: 1, 3, or 5), keeps the stereo cranking. It's open 9am to 1am Monday to Friday, and 10am to 1am on weekends.

2 Miltenberg

29km (18 miles) S of Mespelbrunn, 71km (44 miles) W of Würzburg

This riverside town, along with Amorbach (see below), is located to the west of the traditional route of the Romantic Road, but it's very popular and well worth a visit. Miltenberg is sleepy, traditional, and full of half-timbered buildings. If you're looking for a medieval town, but want to avoid the tour-bus hordes that overrun places like Rothenburg (see below), Miltenberg is for you.

The town, which is still enclosed within its walls and gate towers, is attractively situated under a steep wooded hill crowned by a castle. Its municipal charter dates from 1237, but the place was actually settled centuries earlier by the Romans. The best way to appreciate Miltenburg's charm is on a fast drive-through, with a pedestrian detour through its charming **Marktplatz.** Here, on steeply sloping terrain centered around a Renaissance-era red sandstone fountain and a wealth of flowers, you'll find a phalanx of half-timbered houses, and one of the oldest inns in Germany, the **Haus zum Reisen.**

ESSENTIALS

GETTING THERE By Train   Three or four trains per day arrive from Würzburg, 90 minutes away, and about a dozen come every day from the important railway junction of Aschaffenburg, 45 minutes away. For railway information, call ☎ **06021/19419** in Aschaffenburg or ☎ **01805/996633.**

By Car   From the north, take Route B469 into town (it's signposted). From Würzburg, take the A3 west and then minor roads.

VISITOR INFORMATION   The **tourist office,** Engelplatz 69 (☎ **09371/ 40-41-19**), offers pamphlets describing brief walking tours through the town. It's open Monday to Friday 9am to 5:30pm.

SEEING THE SIGHTS

Park your car in the first convenient parking lot and walk into the center of town—don't attempt to drive. Other than the above-mentioned Marktplatz, the main attraction in town is **Schloss Miltenburg.** (Be warned in advance that this castle is sometimes rather confusingly identified simply as "Miltenburg.") Don't expect a rich tour of a medieval-looking interior, as all but a fraction of the castle's inside (a cafe) has been closed for a long-standing series of renovations. You can visit the courtyard, however, and climb to the top of a watchtower for a sweeping view over the surrounding forest. The courtyard, the tower, and the cafe that's associated with the site are open only April to October, Tuesday to Sunday 11am to 5:30pm. Admission costs 3DM ($1.50) per adult, 1.20DM (60¢) for children under 12.

Beer-lovers might want to take a guided tour through one of the town's breweries, such as **Brauhaus Faust,** Hauptstrasse 219 (☎ **09371/97130**), or **Kalt-Loch Brauerei,** Hauptstrasse 201 (☎ **09371/2283**). These tours, given in German, take you through the full range of the hops-gathering and brewing processes and include several mugs' worth of tasting. The cost is 8DM ($4) per participant. If you like tasting more than touring, just sit down at any restaurant or pub in town—they all serve ample quantities of these breweries' products. A particularly good cafe is the **Café Bauer,** Hauptstrasse 41 (☎ **09371/2384**).

During your exploration of Miltenburg, don't overlook the oldest and most historic bar in town, a 500-year-old hangout that locals refer to simply as **Weinhaus,** Marktplatz 185 (☎ **09371/5500**). Here, every evening between 5pm and midnight, you can order any of the local vintages, at a per-glass price of 6DM to 10DM ($3 to $5).

WHERE TO STAY & DINE

✪ **Haus zum Riesen.** Hauptstrasse 99. ☎ **09371/67238.** Fax 09371/67176. 15 units. TV TEL. 130DM–190DM ($65–$95) double; 220DM ($110) suite. Rates include breakfast. No credit cards.

This awesomely historic hotel is permeated with a polite sense of modern management. Its origins date back to 1190, just before it hosted Frederick Barbarossa during his expeditions in this part of Germany. During the Thirty Years' War, it housed VIPs from both sides, depending on who was in control at the moment. Today, this hotel is the most evocative in town, graced with charmingly old-fashioned rooms, usually with beamed ceilings.

However, the place is probably more famous as a restaurant than as a hotel. Inside the old dining room, you can order such medieval-sounding dishes as roasted bear steak (the bear is imported from Russia), as well as a dish that we've seen in no other restaurant in Germany, *Ochsenfetzen* ("Torn-apart ox"). This delicacy, which has been the subject of many articles in culinary reviews and is based on authentic medieval scholarship, uses brisket of beef marinated for 2 weeks in marinades that change every 2 days. A hearty red wine is the best accompaniment for this age-old dish. Main courses cost from 17DM to 37DM ($8.50 to $18.50) at lunchtime, and from 18DM to 50DM ($9 to $25) at dinner. Meals are served Wednesday to Monday 11am to 9pm, and Tuesday 11am to 6pm.

Hotel Altes Bannhaus. Hauptstrasse 211, 63897 Miltenberg. ☎ **09371/3061.** Fax 09371/68754. 10 units. MINIBAR TV TEL. 174DM–184DM ($87–$92) double. AE, MC, V.

This medieval hotel is set on the main street of town, behind a severely dignified stone facade that's graced with an elaborate iron bracket. The place treads the fine line between authentically historical and merely dowdy. Overall, however, its vaulted stone cellars and massive masonry are charming. Rooms are more angular and modern looking than the authentically antique public areas. Each has functional furniture, small windows, and vestiges of the early 1960s. The restaurant is open daily for lunch and dinner.

3 Amorbach

11km (7 miles) S of Miltenberg, 92km (57 miles) SW of Würzburg.

This little town shouldn't take up too much of your time, but it does offer a few rewarding sights, notably the Abtai Kirch of St. Maria, and it also contains one of the finest hotels in the region. As you wander about Amorbach's center, note the way that local homeowners have dotted many of the half-timbered facades with flower boxes.

ESSENTIALS

GETTING THERE   By Train or Bus   Three or four trains arrive every day from Würzburg (trip time: 90 min.), and 12 arrive from Aschaffenburg (trip time: 45 min.). For railway information, call ☎ **06021/19419** in Aschaffenburg or ☎ **01805/996633.**

BY CAR   From Miltenberg, follow route 469 south for 11km (7 miles).

VISITOR INFORMATION   The Stadt Verkehrsarnt, at the Rathaus, Marktplatz 1 (☎ **09373/20940**), is open Monday to Friday 9am to 5:30pm.

SEEING THE SIGHTS

Much of the fun of a visit to Amorbach lies simply in wandering through the streets of the old town, where half-timbered medieval buildings, some of them a bit artfully askew, still evoke old Germany.

The town's most important monument is the **Abtai Kirche St. Maria,** Kirchplatz (☎ **09373/971545**). This impressive church underwent at least a half-dozen enlargements and alterations between the 8th and the 18th centuries, but it still manages to retain a degree of charm and cohesiveness. The interior is a mass of ornate baroque stucco, centering around one of the most impressive baroque-era organs in Germany. Entrance is free, but a guided tour, conducted in German, costs 4.50DM ($2.25) per person. It's open daily 9:30am to noon and 1:30pm till between 4 and 6pm, depending on the season and schedule of religious services and maintenance.

A small museum called **Sammlung Berger** (The Berger Collection), Wolkmannstrasse 2 (☎ **09373/618**), holds around 17,000 teapots, many from the U.S. and Britain. Part of the funding of this museum comes from a local teapot manufacturer, whose wares are for sale in the museum shop. Entrance is free. It's open only April to October, Tuesday to Sunday 1 to 6pm.

The ruined remains of **Wildenberg Castle,** Odenwald (☎ **09373/20940**), lie 5km (3 miles) southeast of Amorbach. Originally built a thousand years ago, it's now little more than a jumble of impressive medieval-looking rock piles. The restored watchtower, however, can be climbed every Sunday, 10am to 5pm, for a fee of 2.50DM ($1.25). The view over the Odenwald Forest is excellent.

WHERE TO STAY & DINE

✪ **Der Schafhof Amorbach.** Odenwald. ☎ **09373/97330.** Fax 09373/4120. E-mail: Der.Schafhof.Amorbach@t-online.de. 22 units. MINIBAR TV TEL. 660DM–720DM ($330–$360) double; 800DM ($400) suite. Prices reduced on selected midwinter weekends to 450DM–490DM ($22–$245) double and 650DM ($325) suite. Rates include breakfast. AE, DC, MC, V. From Amorbach, follow the N47 (the Niebelungenstrasse) west for 5km (3 miles).

The most reliable and carefully manicured hotel in the district lies within what was originally a Benedictine monastery (around 1450) and rebuilt in 1721 in a country-baroque style. The more historic rooms lie within the former abbey; more modern, better-equipped units are within a well-built modern annex. Our favorite lie under the eaves of the main building, and are crisscrossed with a labyrinth of hand-hewn ceiling beams. All rooms are stylishly and comfortably outfitted in a plush but conservative style.

Dining/Diversions: Two good restaurants serve both lunch and dinner. The Benedicter Stube, located within what was originally the monastery's winepress, is open daily except Wednesday and Thursday. The more formal Aptstube, within the masonry walls of the building's oldest section, serves more upscale cuisine at both lunch and dinner; it's open daily except Monday and Tuesday.

4 Bad Mergentheim

47km (29 miles) S of Würzburg, 106km (66 miles) NE of Stuttgart

Most of this spa town's fame derives from its role during and after the Renaissance as the home, beginning in 1525, of the Teutonic Knights, one of the most durable orders of feudal knights. From their base in Bad Mergentheim, they received tributes and pledges of allegiance from as far away as Lithuania. The knights' way of life ended abruptly in 1809, when Napoléon forcibly disbanded the order, consequently threatening the very existence of the town.

But Bad Mergentheim's fortunes were reversed in 1826, when a shepherd discovered rich mineral springs a short walk north of the town center during the time when Germany's spas were expanding at a rapid pace. The water turned out to be the strongest sodium sulfate water in all of Europe; it was said to have health-giving properties, especially in the treatment of digestive disorders. With the knights gone, the little town had discovered the key to its future prosperity.

ESSENTIALS

GETTING THERE   By Train or Bus   Access by train is easier and more convenient than by bus. From Würzburg, trains arrive almost every hour (trip time: 40 min.). From Stuttgart, they arrive at intervals of 90 to 120 minutes (trip time: 90 min.). For information about **railway schedules,** call ☎ **0931/19419** (Würzburg Railway station), or ☎ **01805/996633.** For bus service along the Romantic Road, see "Bus Tours of the Romantic Road," at the beginning of this chapter.

By Car   From Würzburg, head south along Route 19.

VISITOR INFORMATION   The Tourist Office, called **Kultur und Verkehrsamt,** is at Marktplatz 3 (☎ **07931/571-31**). It's open Monday to Friday 8:30am to 5:30pm, Saturday 10am to noon.

SEEING THE SIGHTS

The best way to see the town is to wander through its historically evocative streets, most of which radiate outward from the meticulously restored **Marktplatz.** Schloss Park leads to the spa establishments on the right bank of the Tauber. The Kursaal is a pump room with both a visitors' center and bathing facilities.

The most impressive structure in town, noted for its relatively large size, is the somewhat sterile and barren-looking **Munster Kirche Sankt Johannes,** Ledermarkt 12 (☎ 07931/1250), which was begun around 1250 and completed several centuries later. It's open daily 9am to dusk; entrance is free. More interesting is the medieval castle that once served as the Teutonic Knights' home base, the **Deutschordenschloss,** site of the **Deutschordensmuseum,** Schloss 16 (☎ 07931/52212). Inside, you'll find a sweeping retrospective of chivalry's preconceptions and preoccupations, with all the requisite displays of suits of armor and weapons. Surprisingly, this medieval order of knights has been restored today, and now serves as a religious and charitable organization. Note the corner towers in the inner courtyard, which are furnished with Renaissance spiral staircases. In the 18th century the castle park was landscaped in the English manner. The building is open Tuesday to Sunday 10am to 5pm, charging an entrance of 6DM ($3), and an additional 9DM ($4.50) for a German-language guided tour.

A second-tier attraction that's a lot less worthwhile than a promenade through the town itself is the **Wildpark Bad** (Bad Mergentheim Game Preserve; ☎ 07931/41344), 5km (3 miles) east of the town center. It contains wild animals both in cages and roaming within natural environments. Mid-March to October, it's open daily 9am to 6pm; November to mid-March, only Saturday and Sunday 10am to 5pm. Entrance costs 11DM ($5.50) for adults, 6DM ($3) for children.

WHERE TO STAY & DINE

Haus Bundschu. Cronbergstrasse 15, 97980 Bad Mergentheim. ☎ **07931/9330.** Fax 07931/933-633. www.hotel-bundschu.de. E-mail: info@hotel-bundschu.de. 33 units. MINIBAR TV TEL. 170DM–190DM ($85–$95). Rates include breakfast. AE, DC, MC, V.

Stylish, understated, and cozy, this hotel was built about 15 years ago in a style that incorporated a masonry-covered courtyard, lots of exposed wood, and touches of Romantic Road nostalgia. It lies within a 5-minute walk of the town center. Rooms are sunny, thanks to big windows, and well maintained. The hotel contains an excellent restaurant, where set-price menus cost 40DM to 75DM ($20 to $37.50).

✪ **Hotel Victoria.** Poststrasse 2–4, 97980 Bad Mergentheim. ☎ **07931/593-0.** Fax 07931/593-500. www.hotel-victoria.de. E-mail: Hotel-victoria@t-online.de. 78 units. MINIBAR TV TEL. 218DM–286DM ($109–143) double; 314DM;423DM ($157;$211.50) suite. Half board 45DM ($22.50) extra per person. AE, DC, MC, V. Parking 16DM ($8) per day.

The best hotel in town occupies a stately, five-story, ocher-colored building. Inside, the color scheme is an oft-repeated and very pleasing combination of champagne, beige, yellow, and black. Rooms are modern and plush, with lots of concealed, very elegant lighting and supremely comfortable mattresses. The in-house restaurant prepares succulent, sometimes splendid food. A full range of massage and health programs is available.

AN EXCURSION TO STUPPACH

The agrarian village of **Stuppach** (population 500), located 11km (7 miles) southeast of Bad Mergentheim, is the site of one of the region's most important artistic treasures, the **Stuppacher Madonna** by Matthias Grünewald (ca. 1475–1528). This dark, brooding work is firmly opposed to the lighter motifs of such contemporaneous artists as Dürer. It's the artistic centerpiece of the village's only church, the **Fahrkirche Maria Krönung,** Kirchplatz (☎ 07931/2615), which can be visited, without charge, daily 9am to dusk.

5 Weikersheim

10km (6 miles) E of Bad Mergentheim, 40km (25 miles) S of Würzburg

The architecture of this riverside town is consistently 18th century; it's one of the most stylistically unified towns on the Romantic Road. Weikersheim also boasts one of the mightiest castles on the Romantic Road.

ESSENTIALS

GETTING THERE   By Train or Bus   Trains pull into Weikersheim from Würzburg at intervals of 60 to 120 minutes throughout the day (trip time: 40 min.). From Stuttgart, they arrive at intervals of 90 to 120 minutes (trip time: 90 min.). For information about railway schedules, call the station at ☎ **0931/8315.** For bus service along the Romantic Road, see "Bus Tours of the Romantic Road," at the beginning of this chapter.

By Car   Take the B232 from Bad Mergentheim.

VISITOR INFORMATION   The **Tourist Office** at Marktplatz 7 (☎ **07934/ 10255**) is open Monday to Friday 9:30am to 5pm.

SEEING THE SIGHTS

During its formative years, the very existence of the town was dependent on its castle, **Schloss Weikersheim,** Schlossstrasse (☎ **07934/8364**). It was begun in 1586 and completed a century later in a severely dignified style that had nothing to do with the baroque style then popular in other parts of Germany. When Count Ludwig II re-established Weikersheim as his family's main residence, he ordered that the old moated castle be replaced with a magnificent new Renaissance palace.

You can visit the castle's interior for 4DM ($2) per person, daily 9am to noon and 1 to 5pm. Its architectural and decorative highlight is the **Rittersaal (Knight's Hall),** which was completed in 1603 and shows the transition between the baroque and the earlier Renaissance style. This is the most sumptuous banqueting hall ever built in Germany. Note the bas-reliefs of game animals lining the walls. The entrance doorway is carved with a scene of a battle against the Turks. The gigantic chimneypiece is adorned with an allegory illustrating the motto, "God gives luck." Also, allow some time to wander through the well-preserved **gardens,** with their chestnut trees and formal clipped hedges offset by the fiery color of flower arrangements.

To one side of the castle is the **Marktplatz,** a semi-circular market square that opens onto sweeping vistas. It was laid out in the early 18th century.

WHERE TO STAY & DINE

Flair Hotel Laurentius. Marktplatz 5, 97990 Weikersheim. ☎ **07934/91080.** Fax 07934/910818. 11 units. TV TEL. 165DM-175DM ($82.50-$87.50) double. AE, DC, MC, V.

The most appealing hotel in town is an old-fashioned monument to the art of hospitality. It's an ideal stopover along the Romantic Road, either for a meal or an overnight stay. Its vaulted, street-level area is the site of a cozy restaurant and wine bar, where menus range from 44DM to 110DM ($22 to $55). Upstairs, a series of high-ceilinged rooms contain a pleasing, unpretentious mix of good reproductions and genuine antiques. Baths are quirkily old-fashioned, but not without charm. There's also a sauna on the hotel's premises.

6 Creglingen

19km (12 miles) E of Weikersheim, 40km (25 miles) S of Würzburg

The history of Creglingen goes back more than 4,000 years. Originally, it was an important Celtic stronghold. Later on, around the year 1000, it was mentioned in written sources as a wine-growing site. By 1349, the town had gained the right to call itself a "city." Around the same time, Creglingen became an important pilgrimage site, thanks to the legend of a local farmer who claimed to have seen Jesus and a phalanx of angels plowing his fields.

Today, Creglingen is one of the quietest hamlets along the Romantic Road, with a tiny but colorful inner core of buildings that evoke Germany of long ago, and a charming but substandard set of accommodations, usually in local farmhouses. The surrounding countryside is called "The Lord God's Little Land"—locals believed that it resembled the Garden of Eden. You might think so too if you explore the local streams and lakes, where anglers fish for pike, carp, trout, eel, or perch.

ESSENTIALS

GETTING THERE   By Train or Bus   Rail connections from Würzburg arrive about once every 2 hours, pulling into the hamlet of Steinach, about 12 miles from Creglingen. At the station, an employee will call a local taxi to carry you the rest of the way into Creglingen. For railway information, call the information service for the local train lines at ☎ **07951/19419.** For bus service along the Romantic Road, see "Bus Tours of the Romantic Road," at the beginning of this chapter.

By Car   Follow the signs west from Weikersheim.

VISITOR INFORMATION   Tourist information is available at Bad Mergentheimer Strasse 14 (☎ **07933/631**), open Monday to Friday 9am to 5:30pm.

SEEING THE SIGHTS

Creglingen is home of one of the most quirky museums in Germany, the **Fingerhutmuseum (Thimble Museum),** Herrgottstal (☎ **07933/370**). Here, sociologists have accumulated the largest collection of thimbles in Europe. Some of them are bone rings dating from prehistoric times; others are made of brass that was smelted in Creglingen during the Middle Ages. It's open daily April to October 9am to 6pm; the rest of the year, Tuesday to Sunday 10am to noon, and 1 to 4pm. Admission is 2DM ($1).

More stately is the **Feuerwehrmuseum (Fire-Brigade Museum),** in the Schloss Waldmannshofen, in the nearby hamlet of Waldmannshofen (for information, call either the tourist office or ☎ **09355/674**). Inside, you'll find a collection of implements and tools used since medieval times to fight the scourge of fire. It's open only Easter to late October, daily 10am to noon and 2 to 4pm. Entrance is free.

The most important local attraction is the **Herrgottskirche (Chapel of our Lord).** For information, contact the tourist office (☎ **07933/631**), which is set 3km (2 miles) south of Creglingen within the Gerrgottstal Valley. It's clearly posted from the village center. The chapel was built by the counts of Hohenlohe around 1525. Its enormous altarpiece, a 19m-(33-foot-) tall structure showing the ascension of Mary, was decorated in the 16th century by master craftsman Tilman Riemenschneider and members of his workshop. All the artist's sensitivity is translated into the expression of the Virgin. The work, Riemenschneider's masterpiece, is set in a filigree shrine specially constructed to catch the day's changing light effects. The chapel can be visited daily April to October, 9:15 to 5:30pm; November to March, 1 to 4pm. Admission is 2DM ($1).

WHERE TO STAY

Accommodations are not plentiful in Creglingen; most visitors are merely passing through. However, there is one truly offbeat choice.

Heuhotel Ferienbauernhof. Weidenhof 1, 97993 Creglingen. ☎ **07933/378.** Fax 07933/ 7515. E-mail: terren@heuhotel.online.de. 6 units with shower and toilet; 25 sleeping places in a hayloft with communal baths. 40DM ($20) double, with breakfast included; 28DM ($14) per person for a sleeping site in the hayloft, with a cold supper included. No credit cards. From Creglingen, drive 10km (6 miles), following the signs to the hamlet of Weidenhof.

Don't expect plush comforts here; the allure of this place derives from its close links to nature and its age-old sense of Teutonic virtue. It lies within a solid-looking German farmhouse owned by the Stahl family. The six spartan rooms each have a thin but passably comfortable mattress and a stripped-down bath. More folkloric is the establishment's barn, where a hayloft provides a soft, sweet-smelling bed for clients who enjoy as close a contact with nature as possible. Don't expect privacy, as the only barriers between the sleeping sites are burlap bags, sewn together and stretched on ropes as a kind of privacy screen. Your comfort here is enhanced by the warm welcome from the owners.

7 Rothenburg ob der Tauber

117km (73 miles) NE of Stuttgart, 51km (32 miles) SE of Würzburg

If you have time for only one town on the Romantic Road, make it Rothenburg. Admittedly, if you arrive at Rothenburg's Bahnhof, at the northeast corner of town, you may find it hard to believe that this is the best-preserved medieval city in Europe. Contemporary life and industry have made an impact, and as you leave the station you'll first see factories and office buildings. But don't be discouraged. Inside those undamaged 13th-century city walls is a medieval town seemingly untouched by the passage of time.

The only drawback to this gem of a city is that it suffers from serious over-crowding, especially in summer. (The Rothenburg locals go so far as to put bumper stickers on their cars proclaiming in German, "I'm not a tourist—I actually live here.") Ironically, Rothenburg for centuries was impoverished and forgotten. It was first mentioned in written records in 804 as Rotinbure, a settlement above ("ob" in German) the Tauber River. The town grew to be a free imperial city, reaching its apex of prosperity under Burgermeister Heinrich Toppler in the 14th century.

ESSENTIALS

GETTING THERE   By Plane   The nearest regional airport is Nürnberg (see chapter 5); from there it's a 2-hour train ride to Rothenburg.

By Train   You can reach Rothenburg via a daily train from Frankfurt (trip time: 3 hr.), from Hamburg (trip time: 5¹/₂ hr.), or from Berlin (trip time: 7 hr.). Rothenburg lies on the Steinach–Rothenburg rail line, with frequent connections to all major German cities, including Nürnberg and Stuttgart. For information, call ☎ **01805/996633.**

By Bus   For bus service along the Romantic Road, see "Bus Tours of the Romantic Road," at the beginning of this chapter. Regular long-distance buses (Lines EH 190 and 190A) service Rothenburg from Frankfurt, Würzburg, Augsburg, and Munich, as well as Füssen. For information and reservations, call ☎ **069/79-03-50** in Frankfurt. Regional bus service is provided by **OVF Omnibusverkehr Franken GmbH,** Kopernikusplatz 14, 90459 Nürnberg (☎ **0911/4-39-06-66**).

By Car Access by car is via the minor road south from Creglingen, or the A7 Autobahn on the Würzburg-Ulm run.

VISITOR INFORMATION Contact **Stadt Verkehrsamt,** Rathaus (☎ **09861/ 4-04-92**). November to April, it's open Monday to Friday 9am to 12:30pm and 1 to 5pm and Saturday 10am to 7pm; May to October, it's open Monday to Friday 9am to 6pm and Saturday 10am to 3pm.

SPECIAL EVENTS The cultural event of the year is the **Meistertrunk festival,** held the second weekend of September; it celebrates the entire history of the town, with more than 1,000 participants in costume. Concerts, historical exhibitions, a parade, and a play about the Burgermeister Nusch's wager (see the Reichsstadtmuseum listing, below) are the festival's highlights. The play is also staged in July and October. For details, contact the visitor information office (☎ **09861/4-04-92**).

EXPLORING THE TOWN

For an excellent view, take a walk on the town walls. The wall tour, from the massive 16th-century Spitaltor (at the end of the Spitalgasse) to the Klingentor, takes about a half hour.

If you want to escape the tourist hordes, you can rent a bike at **Hermann Kat's,** Galgengasse 33 (☎ **09861/6111**), or at **Rad und Tat,** Bensenstrasse 17 (☎ **09861/ 87984**), for about 20DM ($10) per day. Get a map from the tourist office and head out along the Tauber River. Of course, it's best if you bring a picnic lunch to enjoy in some romantic spot on the water.

✪ **Rathaus.** Marktplatz. ☎ **09861/4-04-92.** Rathaus free; tower 1DM (50¢) adults, 50pf (25¢) children. Rathaus Mon–Fri 8am–6pm. Tower Apr–Oct daily 9am–12pm and 1–5pm; Nov–Mar usually closed although occasionally open on weekends.

Rothenburg's town hall consists of an older Gothic section from 1240 and a newer Renaissance structure facing the square. From the 50m (165-foot) tower of the Gothic hall you get an overview of the town below. The tower was first used as a sentry's lookout, but after a fire destroyed the Gothic hall's twin (where the Renaissance hall now stands) in 1501, it became a lookout for fire. Guards had to ring the bell every quarter hour to prove that they were awake and on the job.

The new Rathaus, built in 1572 to replace the portion destroyed in the fire, is decorated with intricate friezes, an oriel extending the building's full height, and a large stone portico opening onto the square. The octagonal tower at the center of the side facing the square contains a grand staircase leading to the upper hall. On the main floor is the large courtroom.

✪ **St.-Jakobskirche (Church of St. James).** Klostergasse 15. ☎ **09861/404-92.** Admission 2.50DM ($1.25) adults, 1DM (50¢) children. Apr–Oct, Mon–Fri 9am–5:30pm, Sun 7:30am–5:30pm; Dec daily 10am–5pm; Nov and Jan–Mar, 10am–noon and 2–4pm.

The choir of this vertical Gothic church dates from 1336. In the west gallery is the Altar of the Holy Blood, a masterpiece by the famous Würzburg sculptor Tilman Riemenschneider (ca. 1460–1531). The Rothenburg Council commissioned the work, which was executed between 1499 and 1505, to provide a worthy setting for the Reliquary of the Holy Blood. This relic, venerated in the Middle Ages, is contained in a rock-crystal capsule set in the reliquary cross (ca. 1270) in the center of the shrine. The scene on the altar beneath *The Last Supper* immediately makes a strong impact on the viewer. Christ is giving Judas the morsel of bread, marking him as the traitor. The apostle John is leaning on Christ's bosom. The altar wings show (left) the entry of Christ into Jerusalem and (right) Christ praying in the Garden of Gethsemane. The altar casing is the work of Erhard Harschner, Rothenburg's master craftsman. The fine painted-glass windows in the choir date from the late-Gothic period. To the left is the tabernacle (1390–1400), which was recognized as a place of sanctuary for condemned criminals.

Reichsstadtmuseum. Klosterhof 5. ☎ **09861/404-58.** Admission 6DM ($3) adults, 4DM ($2) children. Apr–Oct daily 10am–5pm; Nov–Mar daily 1–4pm.

The historical collection of Rothenburg is housed in this 13th-century Dominican nunnery. The cloisters are well preserved, and you can visit the convent hall, kitchen, and apothecary. The museum collection includes period furniture and art from Rothenburg's more prosperous periods, including the original glazed elector's tankard, and a new section of archaeological objects from prehistoric times up to the Middle Ages. Among the artistic exhibits is the 1494 *Rothenburg Passion* series, 12 pictures by

Martinus Schwartz that depict scenes from the suffering of Christ. You can also see the works of English painter Arthur Wasse (1854–1930), whose romantic pictures manage to capture the many moods of the city. Finally, there's a Jewish section, with gravestones from the Middle Ages and some cult objects.

But perhaps the most interesting object on display is an enormous tankard that holds 3^1/$_2$ liters—more than 6 pints. You'll find echoes of its story all over the city. In 1631, during the Thirty Years' War, the Protestant city of Rothenburg was captured by General Tilly, commander of the armies of the Catholic League. He promised to spare the town from destruction if one of the town burghers could drink down the huge tankard full of wine in one draught. Burgermeister Nusch accepted the challenge and succeeded, thus saving Rothenburg. Look for the clock on the Marktplatz with mechanical figures representing this event.

Kriminal Museum. Burggasse 3. ☎ **09861/53-59.** Admission 6DM ($3) adults, 3DM ($1.50) children under 13. Apr–Oct daily 9:30am–6pm; Nov and Jan–Feb daily 2–4pm; Dec and Mar daily 10am–4pm.

The only museum of its kind in Europe, the Kriminal Museum is housed in a structure built in 1395 for the Order of the Johanniter, who cared for the sick. The building was redone in 1718 in the baroque style; it's the only example of baroque architecture in town. The museum's four floors provide an insight into the life, laws, and punishments of medieval days. You'll see chastity belts, shame masks, a shame flute for bad musicians, and a cage for bakers who baked bread too small or too light.

SHOPPING

Kunstwerke Friese, Grüner Markt (☎ **09861/71-66**), specializes in cuckoo clocks, and also carries Hummel figurines, pewter beer steins, music boxes, and dolls. It's Christmas every day at **Weihnachtsdorf (Christmas Village),** in the market square, which is filled with shops carrying everything from clothing and accessories to cuckoo clocks, but the real attractions are locally made toys and Christmas ornaments. If you collect teddy bears, you'll love **Teddyland,** Herrengasse 10 (☎ **09861/89-04**), which stocks more than 5,000 of them. Bear images are printed on everything from T-shirts to bags and watches.

WHERE TO STAY
EXPENSIVE

✪ **Burg Hotel.** Klostergasse 1–3, 91541 Rothenburg ob der Tauber ☎ **09861/9-48-90.** Fax 09861/ 94-89-40. www.burghotel.rothenburg.de. E-mail: burghotel.rothenburg@ online.de. 19 units. MINIBAR TV TEL. 180DM–300DM ($90–150) double; from 270DM– 320DM ($135–$160) suite. Rates include buffet breakfast. AE, DC, MC, V. Parking 10DM ($5).

Although it ranks beneath the Bären and the Eisenhut (see below), this inn is full of German charm. It lies at the end of a cul-de-sac in an old-fashioned timbered house that overlooks the Tauber Valley—just the kind of place Red Riding Hood might have visited to see Grandma. Parking is in a historic garage—the barn of a former Dominican monastery. Rooms are spread across three floors (no elevator). There are many extras, such as private safes and spacious baths with large mirrors and hair dryers. Any room is likely to please, but for the best views, ask for number 7, 12, or 25. The inn also boasts state-of-the-art housekeeping.

Dining: The hotel is classified as a "garni" inn, meaning it serves breakfast only, but there are many fine dining spots within a few minutes' walk (see below).

Amenities: Since this is really just a glorified B&B, it does not have many amenities, though it does offer bike rentals.

✪ **Eisenhut (Iron Helmet).** Herrengasse 3–5 (across from the Rathaus), 91541 Rothenburg ob der Tauber. ☎ **09861/70-50.** Fax 09861/7-05-45. www.eisenhut.com. E-mail: hotel@eisenhut.rothenburg.de. 78 units. MINIBAR TV TEL. 300DM–395DM ($150–$197.50) double; 540DM–650DM ($270–$325) suite. AE, DC, MC, V. Parking 15DM ($7.50).

Eisenhut is the most celebrated inn on the Romantic Road and the finest small hotel in Germany. It's also the most expensive hotel in town, but it's worth the money. Even though some other properties, such as the Bären (see below), have style and tradition, none can match the Eisenhut. If this hotel has a problem, it might be its very popularity. The staff appears forever overworked. The hotel is composed of four medieval patrician houses joined together. Rooms range from medium to spacious, and all are individualized. Yours may contain hand-carved and monumental pieces or have a 1940s Hollywood touch with a tufted satin headboard. All are enhanced by bedside controls, hair dryers, private safes, spacious baths, and ample closet space.

Dining/Diversions: There's a three-story, galleried dining hall, as well as a multi-tiered flagstone terrace on the Tauber. Meals are served à la carte from noon to 2pm and from 6:30 to 9:30pm. There's also a piano bar and a Bavarian beer garden.

Amenities: Room service, dry cleaning, laundry service, baby-sitting, secretarial services, concierge, jogging track, and nature trails. Bicycle rentals are available for 20DM ($10) per day.

Goldener Hirsch. Untere Schmiedgasse 16–25 (off Wenggasse), 91541 Rothenburg ob der Tauber ☎ **09861/70-80.** Fax 09861/70-81-00. www.goldenerhirsch.rothenburg.de. 72 units. MINIBAR (in some) TEL. 190DM–320DM ($95–$160) double. Rates include breakfast. AE, DC, MC, V. Parking 5DM ($2.50).

This is one of the leading inns of Rothenburg, in the same class as the Burg and Bären (see below). It looks a bit more austere than some of the other inns, and lacks a certain coziness. Nevertheless, it's extremely pleasant and well maintained. Because of its popularity, this hotel annexed another house across the street. In spite of the age of the building, the rooms are very modern, with built-in furniture, evoking Scandinavia more than Bavaria. Try for one of the older units, which are larger and furnished in a more Bavarian motif. Baths are tiny and lack adequate shelf space; only the most superior rooms have hair dryers.

Dining/Diversions: The Blue Terrace offers a panoramic view of the Tauber Valley, or you can have dinner in the wood-paneled, cozy Ratsherrenstube. The hotel also maintains a bar.

Amenities: Room service, baby-sitting, and concierge.

Hotel Bären. Hofbronnengasse 9 (directly south of the Rathaus), 91541 Rothenburg ob der Tauber ☎ **09861/9-51-880.** Fax 09861/951-88-60. 35 units. MINIBAR TV TEL. 250DM–330DM ($125–$165) double. Rates include buffet breakfast. AE, MC, V. Parking 10DM ($5).

Dating from 1577, this is one of the oldest inns along the Romantic Road. Only the Eisenhut is a better choice than this. Although modernized by the Müller family, it still has 15-inch oak beams and ornate wainscoting. A major improvement was to reduce the number of rooms and enlarge the rest. Each is styled differently; all have good mattresses and fine bed linen that make for a good night's sleep.

Dining: The owner is a gifted chef who offers excellent food. Three dining rooms with varied cuisine serve both Bavarian and international dishes. (See Restaurant Bärenwirt in "Where to Dine," below.)

Amenities: Concierge.

MODERATE

Hotel Reichs-Küchenmeister. Kircheplatz 8 (near St.-Jakobskirche), 91541 Rothenburg ob der Tauber ☎ **09861/97-00.** Fax 09861/869-65/87-04-09. www.reichskuechenmeister. rothenburg.de. E-mail: hotel@reichskuechenmeister.rothenburg.de. 53 units. TV TEL. 140DM–280DM ($70–$140) double; 250DM ($125) suite for 2, 360DM ($180) for 5. Rates include buffet breakfast. AE, CB, DC, DISC, MC, V. Parking 8DM ($4) lot, 12DM ($6) garage.

We like this hotel a lot. It's one of the town's oldest structures and was salvaged from a World War II firestorm through a massive, thoroughly sensitive restoration. It's both stylish and well equipped. Rooms are furnished with regional wooden furniture; some contain minibars. Baths are a bit small, but maintenance is tidy. Facilities include a Finnish sauna, whirlpool, solarium, and Turkish bath; use of the sauna costs 15DM ($7.50) extra. Seventeen rooms are available in the annex across the street. For its restaurant, see "Where to Dine," below.

INEXPENSIVE

Bayerischer Hof. Ansbacherstrasse 21, 91541 Rothenburg ob der Tauber ☎ **09861/ 60-63.** Fax 09861/8-65-61. 9 units. TV TEL. 120DM–150DM ($60–$75) double. Rates include breakfast. AE, MC, V. Closed Jan. Free parking.

This little B&B doesn't even try to compete with the grand inns of the town. The Bayerischer Hof stands midway between the Bahnhof and the medieval walled city. Petra and Harald Schellhaas welcome guests to their recently renovated, clean, and well-furnished accommodations. The exterior looks somewhat sterile, but inside the hotel is full of cozy Bavarian touches, like the traditional painted furniture. Beds are comfortable, though mattresses are a bit thin. Rooms and baths are small, but the housekeeping is excellent and the staff is most hospitable. The food is very good.

Zum Greifen. Obere Schmiedgasse 5 (off Marktplatz), 91541 Rothenburg ob der Tauber ☎ **09861/22-81.** Fax 09861/8-63-74. 21 units, 15 with shower or bath. 74DM ($37) double without bath, 135DM ($67.50) double with shower or bath. Rates include buffet breakfast. AE, MC, V. Closed Aug 22–Sept 2 and Dec 22–Feb 7.

Don't expect glamour and glitz here—just home-style warmth and comfort. Located in a patrician 1374 house, this hotel stands next door to the prestigious Baumeisterhaus restaurant (see "Where to Dine," below). Rooms are simple but cozy and comfortable. The staff is willing to help in any way. You can order your morning coffee in the garden amid roses and geraniums. The dining room is closed Monday.

WHERE TO DINE
EXPENSIVE

✪ **Louvre.** Klingengasse 15. ☎ **09861/87809.** Reservations required. Main courses 39DM–48DM ($19.50–$24); fixed-price menu 57DM–145DM ($28.50–$72.50). Daily 6–11pm. NEW GERMAN.

At long last, Michelin has recognized that Rothenburg serves some of the best cuisine in this part of Germany. It has finally awarded a star to the Louvre. Chef Berhard Reiser is a man of multiple talents, and he has brought a lighter touch to the kitchens of Rothenburg with his *Neuer Küche* (new cuisine) style of cookery. While most Rothenburg chefs stick to the tried-and-true dishes, Herr Reiser is limited only by the availability of produce. His appetizers are dazzling, especially the goose liver terrine with huckleberries and white port or his consommé of crayfish with ravioli. For a main course, try the perfectly cooked halibut with a potato sauce or else the roulade of guinea fowl with herb-infused cabbage and white-flour dumplings. The elegant cuisine is served against a mainly black decor with high-tech lighting and paintings on display. The wine list, for the most part, is good and fairly priced.

⭐ **Restaurant Bärenwirt.** In the Hotel Bären, Hofbronnengasse 9. ☎ **09861/9-44-10.** Reservations recommended. Main courses 19DM–50DM ($9.50–$25). AE, MC, V. Daily 11:30am–2pm and 6–9pm. FRANCONIAN/INTERNATIONAL.

The *VIF Gourmet Journal* has cited the "Bear" as one of the finest restaurants in all of Germany. The decor is elegantly subdued and the service impeccable. The food and wine served here have never been better. On occasion, the chef is known to serve a historical menu from the Middle Ages—highly appropriate for a hotel (see above) that has been around since 1577. Menu changes are based on the season and the chef's inspiration.

MODERATE

Baumeisterhaus. Obere Schmiedgasse 3 (right off Marktplatz). ☎ 09861/9-47-00. Reservations required for courtyard tables. Main courses 25DM–65DM ($12.50–$32.50). AE, DC, MC, V. Daily 11:30am–2pm and 6–9pm. FRANCONIAN.

The Baumeisterhaus is housed in an ancient patrician residence, built in 1596. It contains Rothenburg's most beautiful courtyard (which only guests can visit). The patio has colorful murals, serenely draped by vines. Frankly, although the menu is good, the romantic setting is the main attraction here. One of the chef's best dishes is sauerbraten (braised beef marinated in vinegar and served with spätzle, small flour dumplings). The food, for the most part, is the rib-sticking fare beloved by Bavarians, including roast suckling pig with potato dumplings or roast pork shoulder. Apple strudel is everybody's favorite dessert.

Ratsstube. Marktplatz 6. ☎ 09861/92411. Reservations recommended. Main courses 18DM–35DM ($9–$17.50). MC, V. Mon–Sat 9am–11pm, Sun noon–6pm. Closed Jan 7–Mar 1. FRANCONIAN.

The Ratsstube enjoys a location right on the market square, one of the most photographed spots in Germany. It's a bustling center of activity throughout the day, beginning when practically every Rothenburger stops by for a cup of morning coffee. Inside, a true tavern atmosphere prevails, with hardwood chairs and tables, vaulted ceilings, and pierced copper lanterns. On the à la carte menu are many Franconian dishes, including sauerbraten and venison, both served with fresh vegetables and potatoes. For dessert, you can order homemade Italian ice cream and espresso. This place is a longtime favorite of those who prefer typical Franconian cookery without a lot of fuss and bother. If you arrive at 9am, you can order an American breakfast.

Reichs-Küchenmeister. Kircheplatz 8 (near St. Jakobskirche). ☎ 09861/97-00. Reservations required. Main courses 20DM–35DM ($10–$17.50). AE, MC, V. Daily 11:30am–2pm and 6–9:30pm. FRANCONIAN.

The food served here is perfect for cold days. Liver-dumpling or goulash soup, sauerbraten, or pork tenderloin are typical dishes. We recently discovered that the chef makes one of the best Wiener schnitzels in town. White herring and boiled salmon are usually available. The restaurant has a typical Weinstube decor, along with a garden terrace and a Konditorei (cake shop). The service is warm and efficient.

ROTHENBURG AFTER DARK

Count Picasso among those who have enjoyed the show at the **Figurentheater,** am Burgtor at Herrengasse 38 (☎ 09861/73-54 or 09861/33-33). Puppet shows are presented year-round Monday to Saturday at 8pm, and June 15 to September, also at 3pm. The evening shows cost 15DM ($7.50) for adults and 12DM ($6) for students. Matinee tickets are 10DM ($5) for adults, with children and student tickets costing 7 and 8DM ($4) respectively.

The most idyllic place to go in the evening is **Unter den Linden** (☎ 09861/ **59-09**), at Detwang. This is a cafe-bar on the River Tauber. You reach it by going under the arch at St. Jakobskirche and following Klingengasse through the town gate, heading down a path to Detwang. The cafe is open April to October daily 10am to 10pm, but it reduces its hours in winter, depending on weather conditions. If you'd like to sample some local wine, try **Zur Hölle,** Burggasse 8 (☎ 09861/42-29), a mellow place in the town's oldest house. A wide assortment of Franconian and international wines is offered at 7DM ($3.50) and 10DM ($5) per glass.

8 Dinkelsbühl

93km (58 miles) SW of Nürnberg, 14km (71 miles) NE of Stuttgart, 105km (65 miles) SE of Würzburg

Still surrounded by its medieval walls and towers, Dinkelsbühl is straight out of a Brothers Grimm story, even down to the gingerbread, which is one of the town's main products. Behind the 10th-century walls, the town retains its quiet, provincial attitude in spite of the many visitors who come here. The cobblestone streets are lined with fine 16th-century houses, many with carvings and paintings depicting biblical and mythological themes.

ESSENTIALS

GETTING THERE By Train The nearest train station is in Ansbach, which has several trains daily from Munich, Nürnberg, and Stuttgart. From Ansbach, Dinkelsbühl can be reached by bus. Train rides from Munich or Frankfurt take about 2¹/₂ to 3 hours, depending on the connection. For rail information, call ☎ 01805/ 996633.

By Bus For bus service along the Romantic Road, see "Bus Tours of the Romantic Road," at the beginning of this chapter. Regional buses link Dinkelsbühl with local towns. There are three to five buses a day to Rothenburg and five to six buses a day to Nördlingen.

By Car Access is via the A7 Autobahn or Route 25.

VISITOR INFORMATION Contact **Stadt Verkehrsamt,** Marktplatz (☎ 09851/ **9-02-40**), open Easter to October, Monday to Friday 9am to noon and 2 to 6pm, Saturday 10am to 1pm and 2 to 4pm, and Sunday and holidays 10am to 7pm; November to March, Monday to Friday 9am to noon and 2 to 5pm, and Saturday 10am to 1pm.

SPECIAL EVENTS This dreamy village awakens once a year for the **Kinderzeche (Children's Festival),** held from July 14 to 23. This festival commemorates the saving of the village by its children in 1632. According to the story, the children pleaded with conquering Swedish troops to leave their town without pillaging and destroying it— and got their wish. The pageant includes concerts given by the local boys' band dressed in historic military costumes.

EXPLORING THE TOWN

Dinkelsbühl is a lively, wonderfully preserved medieval town, full of narrow, cobblestone streets. You might begin your explorations at the 14th-century gateway, **Rothenburger Tor,** and then head down the wide Martin Luther Strasse to the market square. Along the way you can take in the town's fine collection of early Renaissance burghers' houses. Dinkelbühl's main attraction is the late-Gothic **Georgenkirche,** on Marktplatz, built between 1448 and 1499. The church contains a carved Holy Cross Altar and pillar sculptures, many from the 15th century. The best evening activity here is to take a walk around the ramparts. There's even a night watchman making the rounds about town, as in medieval times.

WHERE TO STAY & DINE

✪ **Blauer Hecht.** Schweinemarkt 1, 91150 Dinkelsbühl. ☎ **09851/58-10.** Fax 09851/58-11-70. 44 units. TV TEL. 150DM–180DM ($75–$90) double. Rates include continental breakfast. AE, DC, MC, V. Closed Jan. Parking 15DM ($7.50).

This up-to-date inn is the best in town. The elegant ochre building dates from the 17th century and has three hand-built stories of stucco, stone, and tile. Although it's centrally located, rooms are tranquil. Most are medium in size, although there are some small singles. Amenities include a small fitness center with a sauna, solarium, and indoor pool. The hotel restaurant serves a good regional cuisine. Meals range from 35DM to 65DM ($17.50 to $32.50).

Deutsches Haus. Weinmarkt 3, 91550 Dinkelsbühl. ☎ **09851/60-58.** Fax 09851/79-11. E-mail: deutsches.haus@online.de. 15 units. TV TEL. 165DM–210DM ($82.50-$105) double; 240DM ($120) triple. Rates include continental breakfast. AE, DC, MC, V. Closed Dec 23–Jan 6. Parking 15DM ($7.50).

The facade of Deutsches Haus, which dates from 1440, is rich in painted designs and festive wood carvings. A niche on the second floor of the arched entrance houses a 17th-century Madonna. Each room in this casually run hotel is different—you may find yourself in one with a ceramic stove or in another with a Biedermeier desk. For the tradition-minded, there are no finer rooms in town. Cozy comfort is the rule here.

Even if you don't stay here, you may want to dine in the **Altdeutsches Restaurant,** one of the finest in Dinkelsbühl. It's intimate and convivial, and serves Franconian and regional specialties daily 11:30am to 2pm and 6 to 9:30pm. Meals cost from 15DM to 30DM ($7.50 to $15) for main courses and 32DM to 60DM ($16 to $30) for menus. In the afternoon, many visitors drop in for coffee and freshly baked pastries.

✪ **Eisenkrug.** Dr. Martin-Luther-Strasse 1, 91550 Dinkelsbühl. ☎ **09851/57700.** Fax 09851/577070. E-mail: eisenkrug.h@online.de. 20 units. MINIBAR TV TEL. 140DM-160DM ($70-$80) double. Rates include continental breakfast. AE, DC, MC, V.

The sienna walls of this centrally located hotel were originally built in 1620. Today the Eisenkrug's forest-green shutters are familiar to everyone in town; many celebrate family occasions at the hotel restaurant. There's even a cafe with alfresco tables in warm weather. The stylish rooms are wallpapered with flowery prints and filled with engaging old furniture. An additional nine rooms are in an equally fine guest house nearby, where doubles cost 125DM to 135DM ($62.50 to $67.50). All rooms in the newer wing are rather standardized and modern looking. The older rooms offer more charm, although some tend to be smaller. Some of the beds are canopied. Baths range from small to spacious.

Zum kleinen Obristen serves a gourmet international cuisine. The chef takes an indigenous Franconian-Swabian approach, with many innovative touches. The superior wine cellar has some really unusual vintages. À la carte meals cost 22DM to 45DM ($11 to $22.50). The restaurant is open noon to 2pm and 7 to 11pm; closed Monday and Tuesday evenings.

9 Nördlingen

130km (81 miles) NW of Munich, 95km (59 miles) SW of Nürnberg

Nördlingen is one of the most irresistible medieval towns along the Romantic Road. It's still encircled by well-preserved fortifications from the 14th and 15th centuries. Things are rather tranquil around Nördlingen today; nonetheless, the town still employs sentries to sound the reassuring message, *So G'sell so* (all is well), as they did in the Middle Ages.

The area wasn't always so peaceful. The town sits in a gigantic crater called the Ries. Once thought to be the crater of an extinct volcano, it is now known that the Ries was created by a meteorite at least half a mile in diameter. It struck the ground some 15 million years ago at more than 100,000 miles per hour. Debris was hurled as far as Slovakia, and all plant and animal life within a radius of 100 miles was destroyed. Today the Ries is the best preserved and most scientifically researched meteorite crater on earth. The American astronauts from *Apollo 14* and *Apollo 17* did their field training in the Ries in 1970. Contact the **Rieskrater-Museum** (see below) for tours of the crater.

ESSENTIALS

GETTING THERE   By Plane   The nearest major airport is in Nürnberg; from there you can make either bus or rail connections to Nördlingen.

By Train   Nördlingen lies on the main Nördlingen-Aalen-Stuttgart line, with frequent connections in all directions. Call ☎ **0185/996633** for schedules and more information. Nördlingen can be reached from Stuttgart in 2 hours, from Nürnberg in 2 hours, and from Augsburg in 1 hour.

By Bus   For bus service along the Romantic Road, see "Bus Tours of the Romantic Road," at the beginning of this chapter.

By Car   Access by car is via the A7 Autobahn north and south and Route 29 from the east. From Dinkelsbühl, take Route 25 south.

VISITOR INFORMATION   Contact the **Verkehrsamt**, Marktplatz 2 (☎ **09081/ 841-15**), open Easter to October, Monday to Thursday 9am to 6pm, Friday 9am to 4:30pm, and Saturday 9:30am to 7pm; November to Easter, Monday to Thursday 9am to 5pm and Friday 9am to 3:30pm.

EXPLORING THE TOWN

You can walk around the town on the covered parapet on top of the perfectly preserved walls. Along the way, you'll pass 11 towers and five fortified gates. At the center of the circular Altstadt, within the walls, is **Rübenmarkt.** If you stand in this square on market day, you'll be swept into a world of the past—the country people here have preserved many traditional customs and costumes, which, along with the ancient houses, evoke a living medieval city. Around the square stand a number of buildings, including the Gothic **Rathaus.** An antiquities collection is displayed in the **Stadtmuseum,** Vordere Gerbergasse 1 (☎ **09081/2738230**), open Tuesday to Sunday 1:30 to 4:30pm; closed November to February. Admission is 5DM ($2.50) for adults and 1.50DM (75¢) for children, students, travelers with disabilities, and seniors.

St. Georgskirche, on the square's northern side, is the town's most interesting sight and one of its oldest buildings. This Gothic Hall Church is from the 15th century. Plaques and epitaphs commemorating the town's more illustrious 16th- and 17th-century residents decorate the fan-vaulted interior. Although the original Gothic altarpiece by Friedrich Herlin (1462) is now in the Reichsstadtmuseum in Rothenburg, a portion of it, depicting the Crucifixion by Nikolaus Gerhart van Leydeu, remains in the church. Above the high altar today stands a more elaborate baroque altarpiece. The church's most prominent feature, however, is the 90m (295-foot) French Gothic tower, called the "Daniel." At night, the town watchman calls out from the steeple, his voice ringing through the streets. The tower is accessible daily October to March 9am to 5:30pm and April to October 9am to 8pm. Admission to the tower is 3DM ($1.50) for adults and 2DM ($1) for students and children. It's free to visit the church, which is open Easter to October, Monday to Friday 9:30am to 12:30pm and 2 to 5pm, and Saturday and Sunday 9:30am to 5pm.

Rieskrater-Museum, Eugene Shoemaker Platz 7 (☎ 09081/2738220), documents the impact of the stone meteorite that crashed into the earth here on the Alb plateau, nearly 15 million years ago. Hours are Tuesday to Sunday 10am to noon and 1:30 to 4:30pm. Admission is 5DM ($2.50) for adults and 2.50DM ($1.25) for children and students.

WHERE TO STAY

Astron Hotel Klösterle. Am Klösterle 1, 86720 Nördlingen. ☎ **09081/8-80-54.** Fax 09081/2-27-40. www.astron-hotels.de. 98 units. MINIBAR TV TEL. 202DM–256DM ($101–$128) double. Rates include continental breakfast. AE, DC, MC, V. Parking 15DM ($7.50).

The accommodations here are the best and most luxurious in town. This historic, white-sided, red-roofed building was originally constructed as a monastery in the 1200s. Since then, its ziggurat-shaped gables and steep roof have been an essential part of Nördlingen's medieval center. The hotel offers elevator access, a cozy bar (the Tarantelstube), and a hardworking, polite staff. Under the sloping eaves of its top floor are a sauna, a fitness center, and a series of conference rooms. Rooms have dark-wood fixtures, lots of electronic extras, and larger-than-expected baths. The restaurant, richly paneled with dark-grained wood and filled with modern art, serves lunch daily 11:30am to 2pm and dinner 6 to 10pm.

Kaiser Hotel Sonne. Marktplatz 3, 86720 Nördlingen. ☎ **09081/50-67.** Fax 09081/2-39-99. E-mail: kaiserhof-hotel-sonne@T-online.de. 43 units (35 with baths). MINIBAR TV TEL. 150DM ($75) double without bath, 230DM ($115) double with bath. Rates include breakfast. AE, MC, V. Free parking.

The Sonne is in a bull's-eye position next to the cathedral and the Rathaus. It has a heady atmosphere from having entertained so many illustrious personalities since it opened as an inn in 1405. Among its guests have been emperors, kings, and princes, including Frederick III, Maximilian I, and Charles V, the great poet Goethe, and, in more recent times, American astronauts. Many of the rooms contain hand-painted four-poster beds. In the hotel's restaurant, you can order main courses such as rump-steak Mirabeau and caloric German desserts. It's all quite casual; the waitresses even urge you to finish all the food on your plate.

WHERE TO DINE

Meyers-Keller. Marienhöhe 8. ☎ **09081/44-93.** Reservations required. Main courses 26DM–40DM ($13–$20); fixed price menu 45DM–139DM ($22.50–$69.50). AE, MC, V. Tues 5–11pm and Wed–Sun 11am–2pm and 5–11pm. Closed last 2 weeks of Feb. Local bus to Markplatz. FRENCH.

The conservative, modern decor here seems a suitable setting for the restrained Neuer Küche style of the talented chef and owner, Joachim Kaiser. The cuisine changes according to the availability of ingredients and the inspiration of the chef; typical selections are likely to include roulade of sea wolf, salmon with baby spinach and wild rice, and John Dory with champagne-flavored tomato sauce. There's also an impressive array of European wines, many reasonably priced. The chef is adroit with both rustic and refined cuisine.

Meyers-Keller also has a cheaper section, featuring local cuisine, with a combination of Bavarian, Swabian, and Franconian specialties. Here you can order main courses for 9DM to 20DM ($4.50 to $10), with a fixed-price menu costing 40DM ($20). There's also a small bar on site, where light meals range from 6DM to 15DM ($3 to $7.50).

10 Donauwörth

40km (25 miles) N of Augsburg, 11km (7 miles) S of Harburg, 95km (59 miles) NW of Munich.

Visitors come to Donauwörth for its architecture and sense of history, rather than for specific attractions. The town is located on what was the last navigable point on the Danube, which led to its becoming a key stop on the trade route between Augsburg and Nürnberg. Its attempted capture by the Imperial party in 1608 led directly to the division of Germany into warring Protestant and Catholic military alliances, leading to the Thirty Years' War.

The oldest part of town sits on an island in the middle of the stream, access to which is via the oldest surviving gate in town, the **Riederstor,** which funnels traffic along the island's most historic and evocative street, the **Reichsstrasse.** Donauwörth was badly damaged in World War II bombing raids in 1945, but it has been carefully restored. Part of the town's fortifications survived.

ESSENTIALS

GETTING THERE   By Train   Trains arrive from Augsburg at 30-minute intervals throughout the day (trip time: 35 to 45 min.). Trains also come hourly from Munich (trip time: 90 min.). For railway information call ☎ **0906/5040** in Donauwörth or **01805/996633.**

By Bus   For bus service along the Romantic Road, see "Bus Tours of the Romantic Road," at the beginning of this chapter.

By Car   From Augsburg, follow Route 2 north. From Nördlingen, take Route 25.

VISITOR INFORMATION   Tourist information is at Rathausgasse 1 (☎ **0906/ 7891-51**), open Monday to Friday 9am to 5:30pm.

EXPLORING THE TOWN

The town is dominated by the Heiligeskreuz or Holy Cross Church, a large 1720 baroque building with concave interior galleries. It's an outstanding example of the distinctive churches built and decorated by the craftsmen of Wessobrunn.

The site that draws the greatest numbers of visitors is the **Käthe-Kruse-Puppen-Museum,** Pflegstrasse 21A (☎ **0906/789185**). Inside, you'll find a small-scale collection of the dolls and dollhouses that were designed by master artisan Käthe-Kruse, whose most prolific period during the 1950s and 1960s has been called a high point in the history of doll making. May to September, it's open Tuesday to Sunday 11am to 5pm; October to April, Tuesday to Sunday 2 to 5pm. Entrance costs 4.50DM ($2.25) for adults, half-price for children under 12.

WHERE TO STAY & DINE

Posthotel Traube. Kapellstrasse 14–16, 86609 Donauwörth. ☎ **0906/706-440.** Fax 0906/706-5180. E-mail: info@posthoteltraube.de. 42 units. 136DM–150DM ($68–$75) double; 185DM ($92.50) suite. AE, DC, MC, V.

This hotel has a history going back to the 1600s and a guest list that included Goethe and Mozart. Despite its modern conveniences, there's still the definite sense of old Mittel Europa here, thanks to a somewhat creaky staff and a no-nonsense approach to innkeeping. Rooms are nostalgically outfitted with engravings and prints of old-fashioned Germany. On the premises is a worthy, solid-looking restaurant serving conservative and traditional German food items every day at lunch and dinner, with set menus priced 30DM to 35DM ($15 to $17.50).

11 Augsburg

68km (42 miles) NW of Munich, 80km (50 miles) E of Ulm, 160km (100 miles) SE of Stuttgart

Augsburg's 2,000 years of history have made it one of southern Germany's major sightseeing attractions. It's the Romantic Road's largest town and serves also as a gateway to the Alps and the south.

Augsburg was founded under Emperor Tiberius in 15 B.C., though little remains from the early Roman period. The wealth of art and architecture from the Renaissance, on the other hand, is staggering. Over the years, Augsburg has hosted many distinguished visitors and boasts an array of famous native sons, including painters Hans Holbein the Elder and the Younger and playwright Bertolt Brecht. In 1518, Martin Luther was summoned to Augsburg to recant his 95 theses before a papal emissary. Today, Augsburg, with a population of about 250,000, is an important industrial center and Bavaria's third largest city, after Munich and Nürnberg.

ESSENTIALS

GETTING THERE   By Train   Ninety **Euro** and **Inter-City** trains arrive here daily from all the important German cities. For railway information, call ☎ **01805/ 996633.** Sixty trains per day arrive from Munich (trip time: 30 to 50 min.) and 35 from Frankfurt (trip time: 3 to 4¹/₂ hr.).

By Bus   For bus service along the Romantic Road, see "Bus Tours of the Romantic Road," at the beginning of this chapter.

By Car   Access is via the A8 Autobahn east and west. From Donauwörth, take Route 2 south.

VISITOR INFORMATION   Contact **Tourist-Information,** Rathaus Platz and Bahnhafstrasse 7 (☎ **0821/50-20-70**), open October 15 to May, Monday to Friday 9am to 5pm and Saturday 10am to 1pm; May to October 14, Monday to Friday 9am to 6pm, Saturday 10am to 4pm, and Sunday 10am to 7pm.

GETTING AROUND   The public transportation system in Augsburg consists of four tram lines and 31 bus lines. It operates from 5am to midnight daily and is provided by **Verkehr gemeinschaft Augsburg Vga** (☎ **0821/3245888**). **Augsburger Verkehrsverbund AVV** (☎ **0821/15-70-07**) provides the service for transport outside the city.

SEEING THE SIGHTS

Extending southward from the Rathaus is the wide **Maximilianstrasse,** lined with shops and old burghers' houses and studded with fountains by the Renaissance Dutch sculptor Adrien de Vries.

✪ **The Fuggerei.** At the end of Vorderer Lech. ☎ **0821/31-98-810.** Museum 1DM (50¢) adults, 70 pf (35¢) students and children. Museum Mar–Dec daily 9am–6pm. Tram: 1.

During the 15th and 16th centuries, Augsburg became one of Europe's wealthiest communities, mainly because of its textile industry and the political and financial

Augsburg map showing streets and landmarks including Mozarthaus, Oblatterwallturm, Bert Brecht Str., Riederstr., Fünfgratturm, Auf dem Kreuz, Frauentorstr., Jesuitengasse, Unt. Graben, Gänsbühl, Dom St. Maria, Hoher Weg, Spenglergl., Mauerberg, Paracelsusstr., Unt. Jakobermauer, Rauwoffst., Lechhauser Str., Hofgarten, Obstmarkt, Ludwigstr., Mittl. Graben, Lauteriech, Jakobertor, Stadttheater, Grottenau, Karlstr., Leonhardsberg, Pilgerhausstr., Jakoberstr., Kappenec, Jakoberwallturm, Perlachturm, Rathaus, Fuggerei, Stadtarchiv, Annastr., Maxim-Mus., Alte Silberschmiede, Ob. Graben, Vogelmauer, Vogeltor, Jakoberwallstr., Fuggerstr., Winterg., Zeugg., Rom. Mus., Katharinengasse, Maximilianstr., Schaezler-Palais, Hallstr., Am Schwall, Forster Str., Kapuzinerg., Backergasse, Schäfflerhof, Beethovenstr., Armenhausg., Provinostr., Schießgrabenstr., Konrad-Adenauer-Allee, Ulrichspl., Weite Gass, Schwibbogen pl., To Kongresshalle, Kitzenmark, Church of St. Ulrich & St. Afra, Kirchgasse, Prinzstr., Rembolostr., Stettenstr. Pl., Hl. Geist-Spital, Rotes Tor. Scale: 0 – 1/8 mi, 0 – 1/8 km. Legend: Church †

clout of its two banking families, the Welsers and the Fuggers. The Welsers have long since faded away. But the founders of the powerful Fugger family have established themselves permanently by an unusual legacy, the Fuggerei, set up in 1519 by Jakob Fugger the Rich to house poorer Augsburgers. It's Europe's oldest welfare housing.

The basic features, laid down in 1521, are still in force today. The nominal rent of 1.72DM ($1.05) per annum (formerly one Rheinish guilder) has not changed in more than 450 years. The only obligation is that tenants pray daily for the souls of their founders. The Fuggerei is a miniature, self-contained town with its own gates, which are shut from 10pm to 5am and guarded by a night watchman. Franz Mozart, a master mason fallen on hard times—great-grandfather of Wolfgang Amadeus Mozart— once lived at Mittlere Gasse 14.

The Fugger Foundation owns the Fuggerei. A house at Mittlere Gasse 13, next to the one once occupied by Mozart's ancestor, is now the Fuggerei's museum. The rough 16th- and 17th-century furniture, wood-paneled ceilings and walls, and cast-iron stove, as well as other objects of everyday life, show what it was like to live here in earlier times.

Dom St. Maria. Hoher Weg. ☎ **0821/3-16-63-53.** Free admission. Mon–Sat 7am–6pm, Sun noon–6pm. Tram: 2.

The cathedral of Augsburg has the distinction of containing the oldest stained-glass windows in the world. These Romanesque windows, dating from the 12th century, are in the south transept, and depict Old Testament prophets in a severe but colorful style. They are younger than the cathedral itself, which was begun in 944, and partially Gothicized in the 14th century. The 11th-century bronze doors, leading into the three-aisle nave, are adorned with bas-reliefs of a mixture of biblical and mythological characters. The cathedral's interior, restored in 1934, contains side altars with altarpieces by Hans Holbein the Elder and Christoph Amberger. You'll find the ruins of the original basilica in the crypt beneath the west chancel.

The cathedral stands on the edge of the park, which also fronts the Episcopal Palace, where the basic creed of the Lutheran Reformation was presented at the Diet of Augsburg in 1530.

Rathaus. Am Rathausplatz 2. ☎ **0821/50-20.** Admission 3DM ($1.50) adults, 1DM (50¢) children 7–14, free for children 6 and under. Daily 10am–6pm. Tram: 1 or 2.

In 1805 and 1809, Napoléon visited the Rathaus, built by Elias Holl in 1620. Regrettably, the building was also visited by an air raid in 1944, leaving it a mere shell of what had once been a palatial eight-story monument to the glory of the Renaissance. Its celebrated "golden chamber" was left in shambles. But now, after a costly restoration, the Rathaus can again be visited by the public, on walking tours that offer a view of the "golden chamber" as well as other rooms. Tours take place May to October 18 daily at 2pm, costing 12DM ($6) for adults and 9DM ($4.50) for children.

Church of St. Ulrich and St. Afra. Ulrichplatz 19. ☎ **0821/34-55-60.** Free admission. Daily 9am–6pm. Tram: 1, 2, or 4.

Near the southern end of Maximilianstrasse is the Hercules Fountain, and behind it, the most attractive ecclesiastical compound in Augsburg. The churches of St. Ulrich and St. Afra were constructed between 1476 and 1500 on the site of a Roman temple. As a tribute to the 1555 Peace of Augsburg, which recognized two denominations, one Roman Catholic and the other Lutheran, these two separate churches—Catholic St. Afra and Protestant St. Ulrich—stand next to each other. The churches are mainly 15th-century Gothic with baroque overlays. St. Afra is the most elaborate, with a magnificent altar and finely carved baroque railings bordering the entrance. St. Ulrich is the former monastery assembly hall, taken over by the Lutherans. The shared crypt contains the tombs of the two namesake saints. The lance and saddle of St. Ulrich are displayed in the sacristy.

Schaezlerpalais. Maximilianstrasse 46 (facing the Hercules Fountain). ☎ **0821/3244102.** Admission 4.50DM ($2.25) adults, 2DM ($1) children and students. Wed–Sun 10am–4pm. Tram 1.

The Schaezlerpalais, a 60-room mansion constructed between 1765 and 1770, contains an amazing art collection. Most of the works in the collection are by German artists of the Renaissance and baroque periods, including Hans Holbein the Elder and Hans Burgkmair. One of the most famous paintings is Albrecht Dürer's portrait of Jakob Fugger the Rich. Rubens, Veronese, Tiepolo, and others are also represented. The palace-gallery also contains a rococo ballroom, with gilded and mirrored wall panels and a ceiling fresco, *The Four Continents.* Here, on April 28, 1770, Marie Antoinette danced the night away.

WHERE TO STAY
EXPENSIVE

✪ **Steigenberger Drei Mohren.** Maximilianstrasse 40, 86150 Augsburg. ☎ **800/ 223-5652** in the U.S. and Canada, or 0821/5-03-60. Fax 0821/15-78-64. www.steigenberger.de. E-mail: dm023@aol.com. 107 units. MINIBAR TV TEL. 299DM–379DM ($149.50–$189.50) double; from 550DM ($275) suite. Rates include buffet breakfast. AE, DC, MC, V. Parking 22DM ($11). Tram: 1.

The original "Three Moors," dating from 1723, was one of the most renowned hotels in Germany before its destruction in a 1944 air raid. In 1956, it was reconstructed in a modern style in four- and five-story buildings. It remains the premier hotel in town in spite of increasing competition from Romantik Hotel Augsburger Hof. The drawing room contains a slatted natural-wood ceiling and wall, along with a room-wide mural of Old Augsburg. Rooms are comfortable and inviting, with thick carpets, double-glazed windows, private safes, hair dryers, and trouser presses. They vary in size and appointments, however, ranging from small economy specials to spacious and luxurious suites.

Dining: The formal dining room offers international cuisine. On the breakfast terrace, umbrellas and garden chairs overlook flower beds and three free-form fountains.

Amenities: Room service, laundry, dry cleaning; staff can arrange golf nearby. Within walking distance is the Original Art Nouveau Baths, with massage facilities, steam bath, sauna, and solarium.

MODERATE

Dom Hotel. Frauentorstrasse 8, 86152 Augsburg. ☎ **0821/34-39-30.** Fax 0821/ 34-39-32-00. www.domhotel-augsburg.de. E-mail: info@domhotel-augsburg.de. 43 units. TV TEL. 150DM–210DM ($75–$105) double. Rates include buffet breakfast. AE, DC, MC, V. Free parking; 8DM ($4) garage. Tram: 2.

The Dom Hotel lacks the decorative flair of the Steigenberger Drei Mohren, but it does have an indoor pool. That, combined with the moderate rates, makes this one of the most appealing choices in town. The 15th-century half-timbered structure rises imposingly beside Augsburg's famous cathedral. You don't get a lot of style here but you do get comfort. Rooms on most floors are medium in size and nicely appointed, although we prefer the smaller attic accommodations, where you can rest under a beam ceiling and enjoy a panoramic sweep of the rooftops of the city. Breakfast is the only meal served; during warm weather it can be enjoyed in a garden beside the town's medieval fortifications.

Hotel Am Rathaus. Am Hinteren Perlachberg 1, 86150 Augsburg. ☎ **0821/34-64-90.** Fax 0821/346-4-999. www.hps-hotels.de. E-mail: rathaus@hps.hotels.de. 32 units. MINIBAR TV TEL. 240DM ($120) double. Rates include buffet breakfast. AE, DC, MC, V. Parking 12DM ($6). Tram: 1.

This contemporary hotel's location is its best asset—it's adjacent to the back of Augsburg's famous town hall. It may be short on style, but it offers good value. The lobby is traditional, with Oriental carpets and comfortable chairs. Rooms are accented with darkly stained wood and range in size from small to medium. The breakfast buffet is well stocked. There's no restaurant or bar on the premises.

Romantik Hotel Augsburger Hof. Auf dem Kreuz 2, 86152 Augsburg. ☎ **0821/ 34-30-50.** Fax 0821/3430555. 36 units. MINIBAR TV TEL. 140DM–250DM ($70–$125) double. Rates include buffet breakfast. AE, DC, MC, V. Parking 10DM ($5). Tram: 2.

This hotel was originally built in 1767 in a solid, thick-walled design with exposed beams and timbers. It's a favorite for its romantic and traditional atmosphere, its good location in the town center, and its excellent food. Rooms are completely up to date but not as romantic as the hotel's name suggests. They range from small to spacious. Some baths seem crowded in as an afterthought, but each is beautifully maintained and contains a hair dryer. Rooms overlooking the tranquil inner courtyard are more expensive than ones facing the street. The on-site restaurant serves German and international food.

INEXPENSIVE

Hotel Garni Weinberger. Bismarckstrasse 55, 86391 Stadtbergen, about 3km (2 miles) west of town center, along Augsburgerstrasse. ☎ **0821/24-39-10.** Fax 0821/43-88-31. 31 units. 150DM ($75) double. Rates include buffet breakfast. No credit cards. Closed Aug 15–30. Free parking. Tram: 2.

The Weinberger is one of the best budget accommodations in the area. Rooms are small but well kept. The private baths are rather cramped. Corridor baths are adequate and tidy. Many of the patrons are Germans, who know a good bargain. The hotel's cafe is one of the most popular in the area for snacks.

WHERE TO DINE

Die Ecke. Elias-Holl-Platz 2. ☎ **0821/51-06-00.** Reservations required. Main courses 24DM–45DM ($12–$22.50); fixed-price dinner 69DM ($34.50) for 4 courses, 98DM ($49) for 6 courses. AE, CB, MC, V. Daily 11:30am–2:30pm and 5:30pm–1am. Tram: 2. FRENCH/SWABIAN.

This restaurant's guests have included Hans Holbein the Elder, Wolfgang Amadeus Mozart, and, in more contemporary times, Rudolf Diesel of engine fame, and Bertolt Brecht. The Weinstube ambience belies the skilled cuisine of the chef—the elegant fare here is rivaled only by the Oblinger. Breast of duckling might be preceded by a pâté or pheasant. The fillet of sole in Riesling is a classic, and venison dishes in season, a specialty, are the best in town.

Fuggerei Stube. Jakoberstrasse 26. ☎ **0821/3-08-70.** Reservations recommended. Main courses 20DM-30DM ($10-$15); set-price menu 40DM ($20). AE, MC, V. Tues–Sun 11:30am–2pm; Tues–Sat 6:30pm–1:30am. Tram: 1. GERMAN/SWABIAN.

This affordable restaurant can fit 60 persons at a time into its large, *gemütlich* dining room. Expect generous portions of well-prepared food such as sauerbraten, pork schnitzel, game, and fish dishes. The beer foaming out of the taps here is Storchenbräu; most visitors find that it goes wonderfully with the conservative German specialties that are this establishment's forte.

✪ **Oblinger.** Pfäarrle 14 (near the cathedral). ☎ **0821/3-45-83-92.** Reservations required. Main courses 20DM–40DM ($10–$20). AE, DC, MC, V. Tues–Sun 11:30am–2pm; Tues–Sat 6–11pm. Closed Aug 1–19. Tram: 2. CONTINENTAL/SEAFOOD.

Oblinger is the best in Augsburg's center. It's a charming, intimate, 20-seat restaurant offering a changing array of seasonal specialties. The surroundings are unpretentious, the waiters are attentive, and the cuisine has real personality. Recently we enjoyed the goose-liver terrine with mushrooms and cabbage, and then an equally well-prepared sole roulade with crepes. The turbot with chanterelles or the stuffed Bresse pigeon are excellent as well. There's also a superb selection of more than 350 varieties of wine.

Welser Kuche. Maximilianstrasse 83. ☎ **0821/961-10.** Reservations required. Feasts 60DM ($30) Thurs only, 75DM ($37.50) for 6 courses, and 85DM ($42.50) for 8 courses, without drinks. AE, DC, MC, V. Dinner seatings are daily at 8pm. Located close to the rail station. Tram: 2. SWABIAN.

Come to the Welser Kuche for a medieval feast on wooden tables. The traditional menu is served nightly by *knechte* and *mägde* (knaves and wenches) in 16th-century costumes. Fixed-price menus, called "Welser Feast," are eaten with a dagger and your fingers for cutlery. Stone walls, knotty-pine paneling, and stucco arches frame the wooden tables. Recipes here are from a cookbook, discovered in 1970, that belonged to Philippine Welser (b. 1527), Baroness of Zinnenburg and wife of Habsburg archduke Ferdinand II. It takes about 3 hours to eat a meal here. Sometimes parties of two or four can be seated at the last minute, but reservations should be made as far in advance as possible. To reserve by phone, call ☎ **08231/9-61-10** or fax 08231/96-11-28. The reservations office is open Monday to Friday 8am to 6pm and Saturday 8am to noon.

AUGSBURG AFTER DARK

Kongresshalle, Güggingerstrasse 10 (☎ **0821/3-24-23-48;** information line 0931/5-86-86; tram: 1), presents concerts by the local ballet and opera companies and the chamber and symphony orchestras. Call for schedules, prices, and reservations. It's closed in August. The internationally renowned **Mozart Festival** is held in Augsburg every September. Contact the Tourist-Information office (see above) for details. In the courtyard of the Fugger Palace, the city hosts a **musical theater** production each June and July. Tickets run 22DM to 67DM ($11 to $33.50). Information and reservations are available by calling ☎ **0821/3-66-04** Tuesday to Sunday 11:30am to 1pm and Tuesday to Friday 4:30 to 6pm.

Maximilianstrasse, the main shopping street, continues to be the focus of nightlife after the shops close, with its many cafes. **Brauereigasthaus Drei Königinnen,** Meister-Veits-Gässchen 32 (☎ **0821/15-84-05;** tram: 2 or 4), doubles as an art gallery, has a pleasant beer garden that's open until 11pm, and has a main bar that closes at 7am. Another garden/bar combo that keeps the same hours is **Thorbräukeller,** Heilig-Kreuz-Strasse 20 (☎ **0821/51-19-91;** tram: 2 or 4). **Liliom,** Unterer Graben 1 (☎ **0821/51-40-84;** tram: 2 or 4), is equipped with a good stereo system to go with drinks and conversation; here, too, local artwork is often available for purchase. The bar is open Monday to Thursday 7pm to 7am and Friday to Sunday 6pm to 1am.

12 Füssen

92km (57 miles) S of Augsburg, 119km (74 miles) SW of Munich

Füssen is situated in the foothills of the Bavarian Alps, at the end of the Romantic Road. The town is mainly a base for those going on to the castles at Neuschwanstein and Hohenschwangau, but it also has a number of attractive buildings, including a 15th-century castle once used by the bishops of Augsburg as a summer palace. In addition, Füssen is ideally located for excursions into the surrounding countryside.

ESSENTIALS

GETTING THERE   By Plane   The nearest major airport is in Munich.

By Train   Trains from Munich and Augsburg arrive frequently throughout the day. For information, call ☎ **01805/99-66-33.** Train time from Munich is 2¹/₂ hours; from Frankfurt, 6 to 7 hours.

By Bus   For bus service along the Romantic Road, see "Bus Tours of the Romantic Road," at the beginning of this chapter. Regional service is provided by **RVA Regionalverkehr Schwäben Allgau GmbH** in Füssen (☎ **08362/3-77-71**). This company runs at least 14 buses a day to the royal castles (see below). A one-way ticket costs 2.50DM ($1.50).

By Car   Access by car is via the A7 Autobahn from the north and also the B17 from Augsburg.

VISITOR INFORMATION   Contact the **Kurverwaltung,** Kaiser-Maximilian-Platz 1 (☎ **08362/93-85-0**). Hours vary but are usually in summer Monday to Friday 8:30am to 6:30pm and Saturday 9am to 2:30pm; and in winter, Monday to Friday 9am to 5pm and Saturday 10am to 1pm.

EXPLORING THE TOWN

Füssen's main attraction is the **Hohes Schloss,** Magnusplatz (☎ **08362/90-31-64**), one of the finest late-Gothic castles in Bavaria. It was once the summer residence of the prince-bishops of Augsburg. Inside you can visit the Rittersaal or "Knight's Hall," known for its stunning coffered ceiling. There's also a collection of Swabian art work from the 1400s to the 1700s. The castle is open Tuesday to Sunday 11am to 4:30pm, and charges 4DM ($2) for admission.

Immediately below the castle lies the 8th-century **St. Mangkirche** and its **abbey** (☎ **08362/48-44**), which was founded by the Benedictines and grew up on the site where St. Magnus died in 750. In the 18th century it was reconstructed in the baroque style, and in 1803 it was secularized. Free tours of the abbey are given July to September on Tuesday and Thursday at 4pm and on Saturday at 10:30am; May, June, and October on Tuesday at 4pm and Saturday at 9:30am; and January to April on Saturday at 10:30am.

Within the abbey complex, signs point the way to the **Chapel of St. Anne,** where you can view the macabre *Totentanz* or "dance of death," painted by an unknown local artist in the early 15th century. It has a certain bizarre fascination. The chapel is open April to October Tuesday to Sunday 9am to 6pm. Admission is free. Nearby is the **Museum of Füssen** (Heimatmuseum; ☎ 08362/90-31-45), which displays artifacts relating to the history and culture of the region, including a collection of musical instruments. It keeps the same hours as the chapel, and charges 5DM ($2.50) to enter.

The principal shopping spot in town is the **Reichenstrasse,** which was known in Roman times as the Via Claudia. This cobblestone street is flanked with houses from the Middle Ages, most of which have towering gables.

A ROCOCO MASTERPIECE

From Füssen, you can take a fascinating side trip to the ✪ **Wieskirche** (☎ 08862/ 501), one of the most extravagant rococo buildings in the world, a masterpiece by Dominikus Zimmermann. The Wieskirche is a noted pilgrimage church, drawing visitors from all over the globe. It's located on the slopes of the Ammergau Alps between Ammer and Lech, in an alpine meadow just off the Romantic Road near Steingaden, where there is a visitor information office (☎ 08862/200). The staff at the office can give you a map and confirm that the church is open.

With the help of his brother, Johann Baptist, Zimmermann worked on this church from 1746 to 1754. The ceiling is richly frescoed. It's amazing that so much decoration could be crowded into so small a place. The great Zimmermann was so enchanted with his creation that he constructed a small home in the vicinity and spent the last decade of his life here. A bus heading for the church leaves Füssen Monday to Friday at regular intervals (less often on the weekend). Visitors should check the timetable at the station for bus information or ask at the Füssen tourist office (see above). The trip takes 1 hour and costs 10DM ($5) round-trip.

WHERE TO STAY

Fürstenhof. Kemptenerstrasse 23, 87629 Füssen. ☎ **08362/70-06.** Fax 08362/3-90-48. 15 units. TV TEL. 110DM–130DM ($55–$65) double. Rates include continental buffet breakfast. AE, MC, V. Free parking.

This hotel offers small but well-furnished and well-maintained rooms. The ceilings are of massive exposed paneling, with full-grained beams set into modern stucco. Breakfast is the only meal served.

Hotel Christine. Weidachstrasse 31, 87629 Füssen (5-min. ride from the train station). ☎ **08362/72-29.** Fax 08362/94-05-54. 13 units. TV TEL. 160DM–250DM ($80–$125) double. Rates include continental breakfast. No credit cards. Closed Jan 15–Feb 15. Free parking.

The Christine is one of the best local choices. The staff spends the long winter months refurbishing the rooms so they'll be fresh and sparkling for spring visitors. Breakfast, the only meal served, is presented on beautiful regional china as classical music plays in the background. A Bavarian charm pervades the hotel, and the small- to medium-sized rooms are very cozy, though hardly fit for King Ludwig were he to return. Baths are a bit cramped.

Hotel-Schlossgasthof Zum Hechten. Ritterstrasse 6, 87629 Füssen, directly below the castle. ☎ **08362/9-16-00.** Fax 08362/91-60-99. www.hotel-hechten.com. E-mail: hotel.hechten@t-online.de. 35 units, 25 with shower or bath. 100DM ($60) double without shower or bath. 150DM ($75) double with shower or bath. Rates include buffet breakfast. AE, MC, V. Free parking outside.

The family owners have maintained this impeccable guesthouse for generations. Today it has some of the area's most comfortable lodgings. You'll open your window in spring to a flower box of geraniums. Rooms are small to medium, and baths are spotless but a bit cramped. The family's hospitality is boundless. There are two restaurants (one a buffet dining room), where typical Swabian and Bavarian cuisine are served, with plenty of dishes for vegetarians as well.

Seegasthof Weissensee. An der B-310, 87629 Füssen-Weissensee, 6km (4 miles) from central Füssen on B310. ☎ **08362/9-17-80.** Fax 08362/91-78-88. 19 units. MINIBAR TEL. 130DM ($65) double. Rates include breakfast. No credit cards. Free parking.

The paneled rooms at this hotel have sliding-glass doors opening onto a balcony overlooking the lake. Breakfast is an appetizing and generous meal of cheese, cold cuts, bread, pastry, eggs, and beverages. The fish that your obliging hosts serve you for dinner might have been caught in the ice-blue waters of the nearby lake, whose far shore you can see from the dining room. Owners take extra care for the comfort of their guests. Rooms and baths are a bit small.

Steig Mühle. Alte Steige 3, 87629 Füssen-Weissensee. ☎ 08362/91-76-0. Fax 08362/31-48. E-mail: pension-steigmuehle@t-online.de. 13 units. TV TEL. 105DM–115DM ($52.50–$57.50) double. Rates include buffet breakfast. No credit cards. Free outside parking, 4.50DM ($2.25) in garage. Mid-Nov to mid-Dec. From Füssen, take Rte. 310 toward Kempten, a 5-min. drive.

Owners and hosts Gunter and Hedwig Buhmann like things to be cozy—their chalet-like guest house is almost a cliché of Bavarian charm. Rooms open onto a view of the lake or mountains, and many have their own balconies. They're furnished in a neat, functional style and kept immaculately clean. There aren't a lot of frills here, but the place offers one of the best values in the area.

WHERE TO DINE

Fischerhütte. Uferstrasse 16, Hopfen am See (3 miles northwest of Füssen). ☎ 08362/9-19-70. Reservations recommended. Main courses 20DM–45DM ($10–$22.50). AE, MC, V. Daily 11:30am–2pm and 6–9:30pm. Closed Tues in Jan–Mar. SEAFOOD.

This restaurant is at the edge of the lake, within sight of dramatic mountain scenery. There are four gracefully paneled, old-fashioned dining rooms, along with a terrace in summer. As its name (Fisherman's Cottage) suggests, the establishment specializes in seafood. Menu items read like an international atlas: one-half of an entire Alaskan salmon (for two); North Atlantic lobster; a garlicky version of French bouillabaisse; fresh alpine trout, prepared pan-fried or with aromatic herbs in the style of Provence; and grilled halibut. A limited array of meat dishes is also offered, as well as succulent desserts. In summer, a beer garden serves simple Bavarian specialties.

Zum Schwanen. Brotmarkt 4. ☎ **08362/61-74.** Reservations required. Main courses 12DM–32DM ($6–$16). AE. Tues–Sun 11:30am–2pm; Tues–Sat 5:30–9pm. SWABIAN/BAVARIAN.

A conservative yet flavorful blend of Swabian and Bavarian specialties is served to the loyal clients of this small, attractively old-fashioned restaurant. Specialties include homemade sausage, roast pork, lamb, and venison. Service is always helpful and attentive, and you get good value here, along with generous portions.

13 Neuschwanstein & Hohenschwangau

3km (2 miles) E of Füssen, 116km (72 miles) SW of Munich

Just east of Füssen are the two "Royal Castles" of Hohenschwangau and Neuschwanstein, among the finest in Germany. Hohenschwangau, the more sedate of the two, was built by Maximilian II in 1836; Neuschwanstein was the brainchild of his son, "Mad" King Ludwig II. The extravagant Ludwig was responsible for two other architectural flights of fancy besides Neuschwanstein: Linderhof, near Oberammergau, and Herrenchiemsee, on an island in Chiemsee (see chapter 8). Ludwig died under mysterious circumstances in 1886 (see box below).

After you've fought the crowds to get into these royal castles (in summer, the lines to get in can seem endless), you can spend the remaining time hiking around the surrounding alpine peaks and valleys for what might be some of the most memorable walks of your life. For one of the grandest panoramas in all of the Alps (in any country), hike up to the ✪ **Marienbrücke** (the trail is signposted), which spans the Pöllat Gorge behind Neuschwanstein Castle. If you're properly dressed and have stout boots, continue uphill from the gorge for another hour for the most splendid view possible of Mad King Ludwig's fantasy castle.

ESSENTIALS

GETTING THERE   By Bus   Ten buses a day arrive from Füssen (see above).

By Car   Head east from Füssen along the B17.

VISITOR INFORMATION   Information about the castles and the region in general is available at the **Kurverwaltung,** Rathaus, Münchenerstrasse 2, in Schwangau (☎ **08362/8-19-80**), open Monday to Friday 8am to 5pm.

VISITING THE ROYAL CASTLES

Be prepared for very long lines (sometimes up to an incredible 4 or 5 hours) at the castles in the summer, especially in August. On some days, 25,000 people visit.

✪ HOHENSCHWANGAU

Not as glamorous or spectacular as Neuschwanstein (see below), the neo-Gothic **Hohenschwangau Castle** nevertheless has a much richer history. The original structure dates from the days of the 12th-century knights of Schwangau. When the knights

The Fairy-Tale King

Ludwig II, often called "Mad" King Ludwig (although some Bavarians hate that label), was born in Munich in 1845, the son of Maximilian II. Only 18 years old when he was crowned king of Bavaria, handsome Ludwig initially attended to affairs of state, but he soon grew bored and turned to less subtle pursuits. Ludwig was a loner who never married. As time went on, he became more and more obsessed with acting out his grand and extravagant fantasies.

At the baroque palace of **Nymphenburg,** the summer residence of the Bavarian rulers, you can still see in the Marstall Royal Stables the richly decorated coaches and sleighs in which young Ludwig loved to travel, often at night, with his spectacular entourage. His crown jewels can be admired in the treasury in the Königsbau wing of the **Residenz** palace, in the heart of Munich (see chapter 7).

Ludwig had a long association with Richard Wagner and was both a great fan and a benefactor of the composer. The king had Wagner's operas performed for his own pleasure and watched them in royal and solitary splendor. At Linderhof, the first romantic palace that he built, he went so far as to reconstruct the Venus grotto from the Munich opera stage design for *Tannhäuser.*

Ludwig's architectural creations are legendary. To construct his own Versailles, he chose one of Germany's most beautiful lakes, Chiemsee. He called the palace **Herrenchiemsee** in homage to Louis XIV, the Sun King. Today, visitors can enjoy the castle's Versailles-style Hall of Mirrors and its exquisite gardens (see chapter 8). **Linderhof,** in the Graswang Valley near Oberammergau, was a smaller creation but became his favorite castle; it was the only one completed by the time of his death (see chapter 8).

Nestled in a crag high above the little town of Hohenswangen is the most famous of the royal designer's efforts, the multiturreted Disney-like **Neuschwanstein.** From a distance, the castle appears more dreamlike than real. It's the most photographed castle in Germany. The king's study, bedroom, and living room sport frescoes of scenes from Wagner's operas *Tristan and Isolde* and *Lohengrin* (see below).

Finally, Ludwig's excesses became too much, and he was declared insane in 1886 when he was 41 years old. Three days later, he was found drowned in Lake Starnberg on the outskirts of Munich. He may have committed suicide, or he may have been murdered. A memorial chapel lies on the bank of the lake. Ludwig is buried along with other royals in the crypt beneath the choir of St. Michael's Church.

faded away, the castle began to fade too, helped along by the Napoleonic Wars. When Ludwig II's father, Crown Prince Maximilian (later Maximilian II), saw the castle in 1832, he purchased it and in 4 years had it completely restored. Ludwig II spent the first 17 years of his life here and later received Richard Wagner in its chambers.

The rooms of Hohenschwangau are styled and furnished in a much heavier Gothic mode than those in Neuschwanstein. Many are typical of the halls of knights' castles of the Middle Ages in both England and Germany. There's no doubt that the style greatly influenced young Ludwig and encouraged the fanciful boyhood dreams that formed his later tastes and character. Hohenschwangau, unlike Neuschwanstein, has a comfortable look about it, looking more like an actual home than just a museum.

Among the most attractive chambers is the **Hall of the Swan Knight,** named for the wall paintings depicting the saga of Lohengrin. Note the Gothic grillwork on the ceiling, with the open spaces studded with stars.

Hohenschwangau, Alpseestrasse (☎ 08362/8-11-27), is open March 15 to October 15, daily 8:30am to 5:30pm; October 16 to March 14, daily 9:30am to 4:30pm. Admission is 12DM ($6) for adults and 9DM ($4.50) for students and children 6 to 15; children 5 and under enter free. There are several parking lots that serve both castles.

✪ NEUSCHWANSTEIN

Neuschwanstein was King Ludwig II's fairy-tale castle (see the front cover of this book). Construction lasted 17 years until the king's death, when all work stopped, leaving a part of the interior uncompleted. From 1884 to 1886, Ludwig lived in these rooms on and off for a total of only about 6 months.

The doorway off to the left side of the vestibule leads to the king's apartments. The **study,** like most of the rooms, is decorated with wall paintings showing scenes from Nordic legends. The theme of the study is the Tannhäuser saga. The only fabric in the room is hand-embroidered silk, used in curtains and chair coverings, all designed with the gold-and-silver Bavarian coat of arms.

From the vestibule, you enter the **throne room** through the doorway at the opposite end. This hall, designed in Byzantine style by J. Hofmann, was never completed. The floor is a mosaic design, depicting the animals of the world. The columns in the main hall are the deep copper red of porphyry. The circular apse where the king's throne was to have stood is reached by a stairway of white Carrara marble. The walls and ceiling are decorated with paintings of Christ in heaven looking down on the 12 apostles and six canonized kings of Europe.

The **king's bedroom** is the most richly carved in the entire castle—it took $4^{1}/_{2}$ years to complete this room alone. The walls are decorated with panels carved to look like Gothic windows, as well as with a mural depicting the legend of Tristan and Isolde. In the center is a large wooden pillar completely encircled with gilded brass sconces. The ornate bed is on a raised platform with an elaborately carved canopy. Through the balcony window you can see the 46m (150-foot) waterfall in the Pollat Gorge, with the mountains in the distance.

The fourth floor of the castle is almost entirely given over to the **Singer's Hall,** the pride of Ludwig II and all of Bavaria. Modeled after the hall at Wartburg, where the legendary song contest of Tannhäuser supposedly took place, the Singer's Hall is decorated with marble columns and elaborately painted designs interspersed with frescoes depicting the life of Parsifal.

The castle, located at Neuschwansteinstrasse 20 (☎ 08362/8-10-35), can be visited year-round. In September, visitors have the additional treat of hearing Wagnerian concerts along with other music in the Singer's Hall. For information and reservations, contact the tourist office, **Verkehrsamt,** at the Rathaus in Schwangau (☎ 08362/8-19-80). Tickets go on sale in early June, and sell out rather quickly. The castle can only be visited on one of the guided tours, which are given year-round, except November 1, December 24, 25, and 31, January 1, and Shrove Tuesday. April to October, tours are given 9am to 5:30pm; November to March, 10am to 4pm. Admission is 12DM ($6) for adults, 9DM ($4.50) for children and students, free for children 15 and under.

Reaching Neuschwanstein involves a steep half-mile climb from the parking lot at Hohenschwangau Castle (see above). This can be a 25-minute walk for the athletic, an eternity for those less so. To cut down on the climb, you can take a bus to Marienbrücke, a bridge that crosses over the Pollat Gorge at a height of 93m (305 feet). From that vantage point, you, like Ludwig, can stand and meditate on the glories of the castle and its panoramic surroundings. If you want to photograph the castle, don't wait until you reach the top, where you'll be too close for a good shot. It costs 3.50DM ($1.75) for the bus ride up to the bridge or 2DM ($1) if you'd like to take the bus back down the hill. From Marienbrücke, it's a 10-minute walk to Neuschwanstein castle. This footpath is very steep.

The most traditional way to reach Neuschwanstein is by horse-drawn carriage; this costs 8DM ($4) for the ascent and 4DM ($2) for the descent. Some readers have complained about the rides being overcrowded and not at all accessible for visitors with disabilities.

WHERE TO STAY & DINE NEARBY

Hotel Lisl and Jägerhaus. Neuschwansteinstrasse 1–3, 87645 Hohenschwangau. ☎ **08362/88-70.** Fax 08362/8-11-07. www.lisl.de. E-mail: info@lisl.de. 47 units. TV TEL. 272DM–372DM ($136–$186) double; 390DM–470DM ($195–$235) suite. AE, DC, MC, V. Free parking.

This graciously styled villa, with an annex across the street, provides views as well as comfort. Both houses sit in a narrow valley, surrounded by their own gardens. Most rooms have a view of at least one of the two royal castles; some superior rooms open onto views of both. We prefer the rooms in the main building to the more sterile annex. Two pleasant dining rooms in the main house serve good meals.

Hotel Müller Hohenschwangau. Alpseestrasse 16, 87645 Hohenschwangau. ☎ **08362/ 8-19-90.** Fax 08362/81-99-13. www.hotel-mueller.de. E-mail: info@hotel-mueller.de. 44 units. TV TEL. 240DM–300DM ($120–$150) double; 350DM–450DM ($175–$225) suite. Rates include buffet breakfast. AE, DC, MC, V. Closed Jan 1–Feb. Free parking. Füssen bus.

The location of this hospitable inn, near the foundations of Neuschwanstein Castle, makes it very alluring. Rooms are comfortable, inviting, and have a bit of Bavarian charm. On the premises, you'll find a well-maintained restaurant lined with burnished pinewood and a more formal evening restaurant with views over a verdantly planted sun terrace. Nature lovers especially enjoy hiking the short distance to nearby Hohenschwangau Castle.

7 Munich

The people of Munich never need much of a reason for celebrating. If you arrive here in late September, you'll find them in the middle of the **Oktoberfest,** which draws more than seven million people every fall and lasts for 16 days, ending on the first Sunday in October. Although Oktoberfest, when beer flows as freely as water, is the most famous of Munich's festivals, the city is actually less inhibited during the more interesting pre-Lenten **Fasching** (see chapter 2). Even the most reserved Germans get caught up in this whirl of colorful parades, masked balls, and revelry.

Munich is a lively place all year—fairs and holidays seem to follow one on top of the other. But this is no "oompah" town. Here you'll find an elegant and tasteful city with sophisticated clubs and restaurants, wonderful theaters, fine concert halls, and fabulous museums. According to various polls, it's also the Germans' first choice as a place to live.

1 Orientation

Munich is just slightly smaller than Berlin or Hamburg. You can explore the heart of Munich on foot, but many attractions are in the environs, so you'll have to rely on a car or public transportation.

ARRIVING

BY PLANE   About 29km (18 miles) northeast of central Munich at Erdinger Moos, the **Franz Josef Strauss International Airport** (☎ 089/97-52-13-13), inaugurated in 1992, is among the most modern, best-equipped, and most efficient airports in the world. A second terminal was begun in 2000 and should be completed by 2003. The airport handles more than 400 flights a day, serving at least 65 cities worldwide. Passengers can fly nonstop from New York, Miami, Chicago, and Toronto.

S-Bahn (☎ 089/55-75-75) trains connect the airport with the Hauptbahnhof (main railroad station) in downtown Munich. Departures are every 20 minutes for the 40-minute trip. The fare is 14DM ($7); Eurailpass holders ride free. A taxi into the center costs about 120DM ($60). Airport buses, such as those operated by Lufthansa, also run between the airport and the center.

BY TRAIN   Munich's main rail station, the **Hauptbahnhof,** on Bahnhofplatz near the city center, is one of Europe's largest. It contains a hotel, restaurants, shopping, car parking, and banking facilities. All major German cities are connected to this station. Some 20 daily trains connect Munich to Frankfurt (trip time: 3¾ hr.), and 23 to Berlin (trip time: 8 hr.). For information about long-distance trains, call ☎ **01805/99-66-33.**

The rail station is connected with the **S-Bahn** rapid-transit system, a 418km (260-mile) network of tracks, providing service to various city districts and outlying suburbs. For S-Bahn information, call ☎ **089/55-75-75.** The **U-Bahn** (subway) system serving Munich is also centered at the rail station. In addition, buses fan out in all directions.

BY BUS Munich has long-distance bus service from many German and European cities. Depending on their point of origin. buses depart from the section of the Haupt-bahnhof called the West-Wing Starnberger Bahnhof, or from the Deutsche Touring Terminal on Arnulfstrasse 3, about a block away. For information about connections, tariffs, and schedules, call Deutsche Touring GmbH at ☎ **089/54-58-70-11**). Regional service to towns and villages within Bavaria can be arranged through Oberbayern Autobus, Heidemann-Strasse 220 (☎ **089/32-30-40**), or DER, Landshuher Allée (☎ **089/120-4242**).

VISITOR INFORMATION

The main tourist office, **Fremdenverkehrsamt,** at the Hauptbahnhof, Bahnhofplatz 2 (☎ **089/2-33-03-00**), is found at the south exit opening onto Bayerstrasse. It offers a free map of Munich and will also reserve rooms (see "Where to Stay," later in this chapter). Its hours are Monday to Saturday 10am to 8pm and Sunday 10am to 6pm.

CITY LAYOUT

Munich's **Hauptbahnhof,** or rail station, lies just west of the town center and opens onto Bahnhofplatz. From there you can take Schützenstrasse to one of the major centers of Munich, **Karlsplatz** (nicknamed *Stachus*). Many tram lines converge on this square. From Karlsplatz, you can continue east along the pedestrians-only Neuhauser-strasse and Kaufingerstrasse until you reach **Marienplatz,** which is located deep in the **Altstadt (old town)** of Munich.

From Marienplatz you can head north on Dienerstrasse, which will lead you to Residenzstrasse and finally to **Max-Joseph-Platz,** a landmark square, with the Nationaltheater and the former royal palace, the Residenz. East of this square runs **Maximilianstrasse,** the most fashionable shopping and restaurant street of Munich, containing the prestigious Kempinski Hotel Vier Jahreszeiten München. Between Marienplatz and the Nationaltheater is the **Platzl** quarter, where you'll want to head for nighttime diversions; here you'll find some of the finest (and also some of the worst) restaurants in Munich, along with the landmark Hofbräuhaus, the most famous beer hall in Europe.

North of the old town is **Schwabing,** a former bohemian section whose main street is Leopoldstrasse. The large, sprawling municipal park grounds, the **Englischer Garten,** are due east of Schwabing.

FINDING AN ADDRESS/MAPS In the Altstadt, "hidden" squares may make finding an address difficult; therefore, you may need a detailed street map, not the more general maps handed out free by the tourist office and many hotels. The best ones are published by Falk, and they're available at nearly all bookstores and at many newsstands. These pocket-size maps are easy to carry and contain a detailed street index at the end.

Munich Neighborhoods

9
To Airport
11
2R

Church ✝
S-Bahn Ⓢ
U-Bahn Ⓤ

Luitpold-
park

Leopoldstr.

Englisher

Schleißheimerstr.

Schwabing

Garten

Ⓤ

Arabellapark

Museum
Quarter

Bogenhausen

Ludwigstr.

Königsplatz
Odeonsplatz
Hofgarten
Residenz
Max-Joseph-Platz
Maximilianstr.
Marien-
platz
Kaufingerstr.
Platzl

Prinzregentstr.

Isar

Karlsplatz
(Stachus)
Neuhauserstr.
Altstadt

Residenz Str.

Lehel

Maximilians-
brücke

12

Senglinger
Tor Platz

Isatorplatz
Gärtner-
platz
Ludwigsbrücke
Gasteig

Ⓢ

Ⓢ

Ⓢ

304

Ⓢ

Haidhausen

Frühlings-
anlagen

Ⓢ

Ⓤ

Flaucher

Ⓤ

Ⓢ

2R

Hellabrun
Tierpark (Zoo)

13

8

Neighborhoods in Brief

Altstadt   This is the historic part of Munich, the site of the original medieval city. The Alstadt is bounded by the Sendlinger Tor ("Tor" means gate) and Odeonsplatz to the north and the south, and by the Isar Tor and Karlstor to the east and west. The hub is **Marienplatz,** with its Rathaus (Town Hall) and its Glockenspiel performance. You can walk across the district in about 15 minutes.

Schwabing   This is a large northern section. After 1945 it became known as the bohemian district of Munich, similar to Greenwich Village in New York. **Leopoldstrasse** makes almost a straight axis through its center. The Englischer Garten forms its eastern border, the Studentenstadt is to its north, and Olympiapark and Josephplatz mark its western border.

Olympiapark   Host to rock and pop concerts on weekends, this residential and recreational area was the site of the 1972 Olympics, which is remembered for the terrorist attack by the Arab "Black September" group against Israeli athletes.

Museum Quarter   Between the Altstadt and Schwabing is the museum district, containing such great museums as the **Alte Pinakothek** (see "Seeing the Sights," later in this chapter). Bordered by Briennerstrasse and Theresienstrasse, it covers only 2 blocks, but it can take days to explore in depth if you visit all the state-owned museums.

Nymphenburg   Take the U-Bahn to Rotkreuzplatz, then tram 12 to reach the Nymphenburg district, about 8km (5 miles) northwest of the city center, site of the summer palace of the Wittelsbach dynasty and the famous porcelain manufacturer (see "Seeing the Sights," later in this chapter).

2 Getting Around

The best way to explore Munich is by walking. In fact, because of the vast pedestrian zone in the center, many of the major attractions can only be reached on foot. Pick up a good map and set out.

BY PUBLIC TRANSPORTATION

The city's underground rapid-transit system, the **U-Bahn** or Untergrundbahn network, is modern and relatively noise-free. The above-ground **S-Bahn,** or Stadtbahn, services suburban locations. At the transport hub, Marienplatz, U-Bahn and S-Bahn rails cross each other.

The same ticket entitles you to ride both the U-Bahn and the S-Bahn, as well as **trams** (streetcars) and **buses.** The U-Bahn is the system you will probably use most frequently. You're allowed to use your Eurailpass on S-Bahn journeys, as it's a state-owned railway. Otherwise, you must purchase a single-trip ticket or a strip ticket for several journeys at one of the blue vending machines positioned at the entryways to the stations.

If you're making only one trip, a **single ticket** will average 3.60DM ($1.80), although it can reach as high as 14DM ($7) to an outlying area. A more economical option is the **strip ticket,** called *Streifenkarte* in German. It's good for several rides and sells for 15DM ($7.50). A trip within the metropolitan area costs you two strips, which are valid for 2 hours. In that time, you may interrupt your trip and transfer as you like to any public transportation, as long as you travel in one continuous direction. When you reverse your direction, you must cancel two strips again. Children 6 to 14 use the red *Kinderstreifenkarte,* costing 6DM ($3) for five strips; for a trip within

Munich U-Bahn & S-Bahn

the metropolitan area, they cancel only one strip. Children over the age of 15 pay adult fares. A **day ticket** for 9DM ($4.50), called a *Tageskarte*, is also a good investment if you plan to stay within the city limits. If you'd like to branch out to Greater Munich—that is, within an 80km (50-mile) radius—you can purchase a day card for 18DM ($9). For public transport information, dial ☎ **089/21-03-30.**

BY TAXI

Cabs begin at 5DM ($2.50), plus an additional 2.20DM ($1.10) per kilometer. Call ☎ **089/21-610** for a radio-dispatched taxi.

BY CAR

It's usually cheaper to rent a car before leaving for Germany (see "Getting Around," in chapter 2), though you can also rent one here. Major car-rental companies have easy-to-spot offices at the airport.

If you're already in Munich and plan on making excursions into the Bavarian countryside, it's often more convenient to rent a car in the city center instead of trekking out to the airport. Car-rental companies are listed under *Autovermietung* in the yellow pages of the Munich phone book. Companies include **Avis,** Nymphenburger Strasse 61 (☎ **089/12-60-00-20**), and **Sixt/Budget Autovermietung,** Einsteinstrasse 106 (☎ **089/418-0050**), with another branch (☎ **089/55-02-447**) at Munich's railway station.

Because of heavy traffic, don't attempt to see Munich itself by car. And beware if your hotel doesn't have parking. Parking garages tend to be expensive, often 25DM to 45DM ($12.50 to $22.50) per night.

BY BICYCLE

The tourist office sells a pamphlet for 50pf (25¢) called *Radl-Touren für unsere Gäste;* it outlines itineraries for touring Munich by bicycle. One of the most convenient places to rent a bike is **Aktiv-Rad,** Hans-Sachs-Strasse 7 (☎ **089/26-65-06;** U-Bahn: Frauenhoferstrasse). It's open Monday to Friday 10am to 1pm and 2 to 6:30pm, Saturday 10am to 1pm. Depending on the bike, rentals cost from 18DM to 39DM ($9 to $19.50) per 24-hour period.

Fast Facts: Munich

American Express　American Express, Promenadeplatz 6 (☎ **089/29-09-00;** tram: 19), is open for mail pickup and check cashing Monday to Friday 9am to 6pm and Saturday 9:30am to 12:30pm. There are no ATM machines at American Express, but across the street, at Deutsche Bank, Promenadeplatz 1, there are several available 24 hours.

Bookstores　Try **Anglia English Bookshop,** Schellingstrasse 3 (☎ **089/ 28-36-42;** U-bahn: Universität), in the Schwabing district, which sells English-language titles and travel books. It's open Monday to Friday 9am to 6:30pm and Saturday 10am to 2:30pm.

Business Hours　Most **banks** are open Monday to Friday 8:30am to 12:30pm and 1:30 to 3:30pm (many stay open to 5:30pm on Thursday). Most **businesses** and **stores** are open Monday to Friday 9am to 6pm (many stay open to 8 or 9pm on Thursday) and Saturday 9am to 2pm. On *langer Samstag* (the first Saturday of the month) stores remain open until 6pm.

Consulates　See "Embassies & Consulates" in "Fast Facts: Germany," in chapter 2.

Currency Exchange   You can usually get a better rate at a bank than at your hotel. On Saturday and Sunday or at night, you can exchange money at the rail station exchange, in Bahnhofplatz; it's open daily 6am to 11:30pm.

Dentists   For an English-speaking dentist, go to Klinik und Poliklinik für Kieferchirurgie der Universität München, Lindwurmstrasse 2A (☎ 089/51-60-29-11; U-Bahn: Goetheplatz), the dental clinic for the university. It deals with emergency cases and is always open.

Doctors   The American, British, and Canadian consulates as well as every hotel keep a list of recommended English-speaking physicians.

Drugstores   For an international drugstore where English is spoken, try International Ludwig's Apotheke, Neuhauserstrasse 11 (☎ 089/2-60-30-21; U-bahn/S-Bahn: Marienplatz), in the pedestrian shopping zone. It's open Monday to Friday 9am to 8pm, and Saturday 9am to 4pm.

E-mail   Head for the **Times Square Online Bistro** in the Hauptbahnhof, Bayerstrasse side (☎ 089/55-08-8000). They have 16 computer work stations, a bistro, and bar, and are open daily 6am to 1am.

Emergencies   For emergency **medical aid,** or for the police, call **110.** For the fire department, call **112.**

Fax   Head for any of the many hole-in-the-wall kiosks labeled Deutsche Telecom. These include locations on the Marienplatz and in the Hauptbahnhof. Deutsche telecom phone cards are available in denominations of 12DM to 50DM ($6 to $25). You can use these to operate self-service fax machines.

Laundry/Dry Cleaning   A good dry-cleaning establishment is **Paradies Reinigung,** Octtingenstrasse 29 (☎ 089/22-34-65). Look in the Yellow Pages under either *Wascherei* or *Waschsalon* for a coin-operated laundry near your hotel.

Post Office   The **Postamt München** (main post office) is across from the Hauptbahnhof, at Bahnhofplatz 1 (☎ 089/599-0870). If you want to have your mail sent to you, have it addressed Poste Restante, Postamt München, Bahnhofplatz 1, 80074 München, for general delivery. Take along your passport to reclaim any mail. The office is open Monday to Friday 7am to 8pm, Saturday 8am to 4pm, and Sunday 9am to 3pm. There are no fax, phone, or telex facilities available in the post office.

Radio   Bayern 2 at 88.4 FM presents news in English, French, and Italian from Monday to Friday at 8:50am. You can also listen to the Voice of America at 1197 AM.

Rest Rooms   Use the word *toilette* (pronounced twa-*leht*-tah). Rest rooms may be labeled WC, or "H" (for *Herren,* men) and "F" (for *Frauen,* women). In the center of Munich are several clean, safe, and well-kept public facilities.

Safety   Munich, like all big cities, has its share of crime, especially pickpocketing and purse- and camera-snatching. Most robberies occur in the much-frequented tourist areas, such as Marienplatz and the Hauptbahnhof, which is particularly dangerous at night. Many tourists lose their valuables when they carelessly leave clothing unprotected as they join the nude sunbathers in the Englischer Garten.

Television   There are two national TV channels, ARD (Channel 1) and ZDF (Channel 2). Sometimes these stations show films in the original language (most often English). The more expensive hotels often have cable TV, with such channels as CNN.

3 Where to Stay

There are many rooms available in Munich, though most are costly. Bargains are few and hard to find—but they do exist.

Fremdenverkehrsamt (main tourist office), Bahnhofplatz 2 at the Hauptbahnhof (☎ 089/2-33-03-00), open daily 10am to 8pm, is especially good if you arrive in Munich without a hotel reservation. Here, Bavarian personnel (most speak English), with some 35,000 listings in their files, will help you find a place to stay. Tell them what you can afford. They'll book you a room and even give you a map with instructions on how to reach it. Keep your receipt. If you don't like the room, go back to the tourist office, and they'll book you another at no extra charge. Reservations are free but a deposit equal to 10% of the total value of your stay will be collected in advance. For direct access to the hotel booking department, call ☎ **089/233-30-123**, or fax 089/233-300-30.

IN CENTRAL MUNICH
VERY EXPENSIVE

✪ **Bayerischer Hof & Palais Montgelas.** Promenadeplatz 2–6, 80333 München. ☎ **800/223-6800** in the U.S., or 089/2-12-00. Fax 089/2-12-09-06. www.bayerischerhof.de. E-mail: hbh@compuserve.com. 396 units. MINIBAR TV TEL. 430DM–650DM ($215–$325) double; from 790DM ($395) suite. AE, DC, MC, V. Parking 34DM ($17). Tram: 19.

The Bayerischer Hof hotel and the 17th-century Palais Montgelas combine to form a Bavarian version of New York's Waldorf-Astoria. This establishment has been beneficiary of zillions of marks worth of improvements and is now better than ever, a rival even of the front-ranking Kempinski Hotel Vier Jahreszeiten (see below). It's been a favorite ever since King Ludwig I used to come here to take a bath (the royal palace didn't have bathtubs back then). Rooms range from medium to extremely spacious. The decor ranges from Bavarian provincial to British country house chintz. Many beds are four-posters. The large baths have a private phone and plenty of shelf space. Palais Montgelas has 20 of the most upscale rooms as well as conference and banqueting rooms.

Dining/Diversions: The major dining room, the Garden Restaurant, evokes the grandeur of a small palace, with an ornate ceiling, crystal chandeliers, and French provincial chairs (see "Where to Dine," below). Generous drinks and charcoal specialties from the rotisserie are served in the clublike bar. There's also the Kleine Komödie Theater, a Trader Vic's, and the best nightclub in Munich (see "Munich After Dark," below).

Amenities: Room service, laundry, baby-sitting, rooftop pool and garden with bricked sun terrace, sauna, massage rooms, shopping mall with boutiques and salons.

✪ **Hotel Palace.** Trogerstrasse 21. D-81675 München. ☎ **800/223-5652** for toll-free reservations in the US and Canada, or 089/41971-0. Fax 089/41971-819. 72 units. A/C MINIBAR TV TEL. 460DM–510DM ($230–$255) double; 570DM–2,000DM ($285–$1,000) suite. AE, DC, MC, V. U-Bahn: Prinzregentumplatz.

It's tasteful, it's restrained, it's perfectly mannered, and it's very, very aware of how prestigious a stay here can really be. One of Munich's newest hotels, it's sought out by

---

Dialing Germany

Remember that the phone numbers in this book contain an initial 0 in the German city code. That 0 is only used within Germany. Omit it when calling from abroad.

ⓘ Family-Friendly Hotels

Gästehaus Englischer Garten *(see p. 265)*   This ivy-covered villa oasis of calm and tranquility provides old-fashioned family atmosphere.

Hotel Jedermann *(see p. 264)*   Families on a budget like this hotel, which supplies cribs or cots.

performers at the nearby theaters and concert halls as a peaceful and nurturing address in Bogenhausen, a stylish residential neighborhood east of Munich's medieval core. Originally built in 1986 as an office building, it was later transformed into a hotel. Public areas are streamlined and contemporary, graced with elaborate hyper-modern balustrades on travertine-sheathed staircases. Rooms are immaculate and upscale.

Dining/Diversions: The Palace Restaurant is an all-white room with slipcover-sheathed chairs and a reputation for chic clients eating chic food. Its bar—an undeniably glam hangout—is useful for spotting musicians who have included Anna Sophie Mutter (who lives a few buildings away), Loren Maazel, James Levine, and Zubin Mehta.

Amenities: 24-hour srvice, a health club with its own exercise equipment, sauna, and steam room, a concierge who can arrange virtually anything.

✪ **Kempinski Hotel Vier Jahreszeiten München.** Maximilianstrasse 17, 80539 München. ☎ **800/426-3135** in the U.S., or 089/2-12-50. Fax 089/21-25-20-00. www.kempinski-vierjahreszeiten.de. E-mail: reservation.hvj@kempinski.com. 364 units. A/C MINIBAR TV TEL. 520DM–820DM ($260–$410) double; from 990DM ($495) suite. AE, DC, MC, V. Parking 30DM ($15). Tram: 19.

This grand hotel is not only the most elegant in Munich, but it's also Germany's most famous and distinctive, and among the finest in the world. Its tradition stretches back to 1858. Rooms and suites—which have hosted royalty, heads of state, and famed personalities from all over the world—combine the charm of days gone by with modern amenities. The antique-style beds feature fine linen on sumptuous mattresses. The large baths are equipped with all sorts of special treats, including luxurious robes. The windows opening onto Maximilianstrasse are double-glazed.

Dining/Diversions: The Restaurant Vier Jahreszeiten (open daily) is recommended in "Where to Dine," below. In the Jahreszeiten Bar, piano music plays nightly during the cocktail hour, and an international trio performs until 2am.

Amenities: Room service, laundry service, baby-sitting, massages; indoor pool and sauna, solarium, sun terrace.

✪ **Rafael.** Neuturmstrasse 1, 80331 München. ☎ **089/29-09-80.** Fax 089/22-25-39. www.hotelrafael.com. E-mail: info@hotelrafael.com. 73 units. A/C MINIBAR TV TEL. 680DM–750DM ($340–$375) double; from 980DM ($490) suite. AE, DC, MC, V. Parking 36DM ($18). U-Bahn/S-Bahn: Marienplatz. Tram: 19.

One of Munich's smaller hotels is also one of its most posh. Only the Kempinski Hotel Vier Jahreszeiten München and the Bayerischer Hof (see above) outclass this sophisticated and luxurious winner. The stylish and elegant wedge-shaped building combines neo-Renaissance, neoclassical, and Biedermeier touches. It's located within sight of the Frauenkirche at Marienplatz. A marble staircase sweeps upward to the very comfortable rooms, each with specially crafted furniture or original antiques. Baths are well appointed.

Dining: The culinary showplace is Mark's Restaurant, an intimate place with 75 seats and a piano bar. Its setting is elegant, featuring rose-colored damask table-cloths and Wedgwood china along with Beard silver. Chef Holgar Stromberg cooks up a dazzlingly creative Italian cuisine, flavored with accents from Asia.

Amenities: Concierge, 24-hour room service, laundry, baby-sitting, valet parking. The service staff is among the most professional in southern Germany. The hotel also maintains a rooftop pool (May to October) with a view over the historic district and boutiques.

EXPENSIVE

Eden-Hotel-Wolff. Arnulfstrasse 4–8 (opposite the train station), 80335 München. ☎ **089/55-11-50.** Fax 089/55-11-55-55. www.ehw.de. E-mail: sales@ehw.de. 211 units. MINIBAR TV TEL. 290DM–480DM ($145–$240) double; 400DM–600DM ($200–$300) suite. 1 child up to age 6 stays free in parents' room. Rates include buffet breakfast. AE, DC, MC, V. Parking 25DM ($12.50). U-Bahn/S-Bahn: Hauptbahnhof.

If you must stay in the train station area, this is your best bet, despite the fact that it's often booked by groups. The stone-clad Eden-Hotel-Wolff misleads with its sedate exterior. The interior is richly traditional, with chandeliers and dark-wood paneling. A few of the rooms are small, but most are spacious, and all are tastefully furnished in a decor that runs the gamut from extremely modern to rustic. Baths are large. Private safes, hair dryers, and double-glazed windows are added features. Some units are hypo-allergenic, with special beds and a private ventilation system.

Dining/Diversions: The theme in the main dining room, Zirbelstube, is Bavarian—there's a natural pine ceiling, gleaming brass lantern sconces, and thick stone arches. Excellent Bavarian dishes and a savory international cuisine are the fare. On a cold night, the bar with a fireplace is a snug, cozy retreat.

Amenities: Concierge, baby-sitting, dry cleaning, laundry, secretarial services and conference rooms; bicycle and car rentals are available at the hotel tour desk.

Hotel Opera. St-Anna Strasse 10, 80538 München. ☎ **089/22-55-33.** Fax 089/ 21-04-09-77. www.deutschland-hotel.de. E-mail: reception@hotel-opera.de. 25 units. TV TEL. 320DM–360DM ($160–$180) double; 500DM ($250) suite. Rates include breakfast. AE, MC, V. Parking 45DM ($22.50) nearby. U-Bahn: Lehel.

This charming little gem (not to be confused with the Hotel an der Opera) is a recent discovery of ours. It's filled with comfort and an authentic Bavarian atmosphere so lacking in many postwar Munich hotels. Each room is beautifully and individually decorated, often with antiques from the countryside. Some contain French doors leading to small balconies. Those at the rear on the third and fourth floors are more tranquil, although they're slightly smaller than those fronting the street. Baths are relatively small but well-maintained. The location is desirable, too, only a 12-minute walk from the chic Maximilianstrasse, with some of the city's major attractions virtually at your doorstep.

Dining: The hotel serves breakfast only but does operate a 24-hour bar. Many good restaurants lie within walking distance.

Amenities: Jacuzzi, concierge, 24-hour room service, dry cleaning, laundry, roof garden, garden terrace.

Platzl. Sparkassenstrasse 10, 80331 München. ☎ **089/23-70-30.** Fax 089/23-70-38-00. www.platzl.de. E-mail: info@platzl.de. 167 units. MINIBAR TV TEL. 322DM–442DM ($161–$221) double. Rates include buffet breakfast. AE, DC, MC, V. Parking 20DM ($10). U-Bahn: U3 or U6 to Marienplatz.

This restored hotel, owned by the Ayinger brewery, is centrally located in the historic Altstadt, opposite the world-famous Hofbräuhaus and close to Marienplatz. It's the beer-drinker's favorite—more beer is consumed in and around this hotel than at any other place in Europe. It's one of the best choices in Munich for a real taste of home-style German hospitality. Many rooms are quite small and are decorated in a rustic Bavarian motif.

Dining: The hotel's restaurant, Pfistermühle, serves Bavarian cuisine.

Amenities: 24-hour room service, laundry, dry cleaning, sauna and Jacuzzi, conference rooms for business travelers, boutique.

MODERATE

Advokat Hotel. Baaderstrasse 1, 80469 München. ☎ **089/21-63-10.** Fax 089/21-63-190. www.hotel-advokat.de. E-mail: info@hotel-advokat.de. 50 units. MINIBAR TV TEL. 260DM–320DM ($130–$160) double; 320DM–420DM ($160–$210) suite. S-Bahn: Isartor.

This hotel occupies a six-story apartment house originally constructed in the 1930s. Its stripped-down, streamlined interior borrows in discreet ways from Bauhaus and minimalist models. One Munich critic said the rooms look as if Philippe Starck had gone on a shopping binge at Ikea. The result is an aggressively simple, clean-lined, and artfully Spartan hotel with very few amenities and facilities. The German government gives it three stars. The Advokat lies around the corner from its more upscale neighbor, the Hotel Admiral, with which it shares management, but whose rooms cost 50DM ($28.50) more, double occupancy, per category. There's no restaurant on the premises and no particular amenities to speak of other than a cozy in-house bar. But the prices are reasonable, and the staff is helpful.

An der Oper. Falkenturmstrasse 11 (just off Maximilianstrasse, near Marienplatz), 80331 München. ☎ **089/2-90-02-70.** Fax 089/29-00-27-29. 68 units. MINIBAR TV TEL. 270DM–340DM ($135–$170) double. Rates include buffet breakfast. AE, MC, V. Parking 25DM ($12.50) nearby. Tram: 19.

This five-floor hotel, built in 1969, is superbly located for sightseeing or shopping in the traffic-free malls, and it's just steps from the Bavarian National Theater. In spite of its basic decor, there are touches of elegance. Rooms, which range from small to medium, have double-glazed windows, a small sitting area with armchairs, and a table for those who want breakfast in their rooms.

Hotel Exquisit. Pettenkoferstrasse 4, D-80336 München. ☎ **089/55-19-900.** Fax 089/55-199-499. www.augustiner-restaurant.com. 50 units. MINIBAR TV TEL. 180DM–340DM ($90–$170) double. Rates include breakfast. AE, DC, MC, V. U-Bahn: Sendlinger Tor.

One of the most appealing hotels in the Sendlinger Tor neighborhood lies behind a wine-colored facade on a quiet residential street that seems far removed from the heavy traffic and bustle of the nearby theater district. Built in 1988, it has a paneled lobby whose focal point is a bar that gets busy around 6 or 7pm. Staff is unusually pleasant, offering a genuine welcome and ushering you up to rooms that are spacious and comfortably furnished. About half overlook an ivy-draped garden, others look over the street. Baths are efficient.

Hotel Olympic. Hans Sachs Strasse 4, D-80469 München. ☎ **089/231-89-0.** Fax 089/231-89-199. 38 units. MINIBAR TV TEL. 215DM–280DM ($107.50–$140) double; 650DM–1200DM ($325–$600) suite. Rates include breakfast. AE, DC, MC, V. U-Bahn: Sendlinger Tor.

Built as a private villa around 1900, this hotel represents one of Munich's most appealing conversions of an antique building into a hip and attractive hotel. The lobby occupies a high-ceilinged, Victorian vestibule that retains many of the original details. Breakfast is served in a very large, graciously proportioned dining room where memories of the grand bourgeoisie of the Industrial Revolution still seem to permeate the woodwork. Rooms are minimalist and all white, much more modern than the ground-floor reception areas, but comfortable and well-engineered. The hotel has earned an increasing number of gay clients recently, thanks to its location within a neighborhood that's loaded with gay bars and hangouts.

Königswache. Steinheilstrasse 7, 80333 München. ☎ **089/5-42-75-70.** Fax 089/ 5-23-21-14. E-mail: koenigswache@t-online.de. 40 units. MINIBAR TV TEL. 169DM–265DM ($84.50–$132.50) double. Rates include buffet breakfast. AE, MC, V. Parking garage (reservation required) 12DM ($6). U-Bahn: Theresienstrasse.

Built in 1962, the Königswache has much to recommend it, in spite of its sterile facade. The location, about a 10-minute ride from the Hauptbahnhof and only 2 minutes from the technical university, is between Karlsplatz and Schwabing—a district safer at night than the railway-station area. The staff speaks English. Rooms are modern and comfortable. Baths are small.

Splendid. Maximilianstrasse 54, 80538 München. ☎ **089/29-66-06.** Fax 089/2-91-31-76. 36 units, 30 with bathroom. TV TEL. 140DM–205DM ($70–$102.50) double without bathroom, 210DM–320DM ($105–$160) double with bathroom; 270DM–500DM ($135–$250) suite. AE, DC, DISC, MC, V. U-Bahn: Lehel. Tram: 17 or 19.

The Splendid is one of the most attractive old-world hotels in Munich. Antiques, Oriental rugs, and chandeliers decorate the public areas. Rooms have the aura of a country home. Most are decorated in a style known as "Bavarian baroque," although two recently remodeled ones are in the Louis XVI style. You can order breakfast—the only meal served—in your room, or have it on a trellised patio. Room prices are scaled according to size, furnishings, and time of year, with the highest prices charged at fair and festival times. Room service is provided.

INEXPENSIVE

Am Markt. Heiliggeistrasse 6, 80331 München. ☎ **089/22-50-14.** Fax 089/22-40-17. 32 units, 13 with bathroom. TV TEL. 116DM ($58) double without bath, 160DM ($80) double with bath. Rates include continental breakfast. No credit cards. Parking 12DM ($6). S-Bahn: Marienplatz.

This popular, though not luxurious, Bavarian hotel stands in the heart of the older section. Owner Harald Herrler has maintained a nostalgic decor in the lobby and dining room. Behind his reception desk is a wall of photographs of friends or former guests, including the late Viennese chanteuse Greta Keller. As Mr. Herrler points out, when you have breakfast here, you're likely to find yourself surrounded by opera and concert artists; the hotel is close to where they perform. Rooms are quite small but trim, modern, and neat. Mattresses are well worn but still comfortable. All units, even those without private baths, have sinks with hot and cold running water.

Hotel Bristol München. Pettenkoferstrasse 2, D-80336 München. ☎ **089/54-82-22-0.** Fax 089/59-14-51. www.bristol-muc.com. E-mail: hotel@bristol-muc.com. 57 units. MINIBAR TV TEL. 169DM ($84.50) double. Rates rise to 280DM ($140) during trade fairs. AE, MC, V. U-Bahn: Sendlinger Tor.

Built around 1960, in a four-story format that includes a boxy-looking facade and a tiny reception area, this is an easy-to-live-in hotel with a kindly management. Quieter rooms in back overlook a sheltered courtyard. Each has a tiny balcony, and efficient but comfortable furnishings. There's no restaurant on-site, but the desk staff maintains good dialogues with several worthwhile restaurants within the neighborhood.

Hotel Jedermann. Bayerstrasse 95, 80335 München. ☎ **089/54-32-40.** Fax 089/ 54-32-4111. www.hotel-jedermann.de. E-mail: hotel-jedermann@cube.net. 55 units, 34 with shower and toilet. TV TEL. 95DM–140DM ($47.50–$70) double without bath; 140DM–260DM

($70–$130) double with shower and toilet; 120DM–160DM ($60–$80) triple without bath; 180DM–280DM ($90–$140) triple with shower and toilet. Rates include buffet breakfast. MC, V. Parking 10DM ($5). 10-min. walk from Hauptbahnhof (turn right on Bayerstrasse from south exit).

This pleasant, cozy spot has been deftly run by the Jenke family since 1961. Its central location and good value make it a desirable choice, especially for families (cribs or cots are available). The old-fashioned Bavarian rooms are generally small, but cozy and comfortable. Most have private safes. A generous breakfast buffet is served in a charming room.

Hotel Utzelmann. Pettenkoferstrasse 6, 80336 München. ☎ **089/59-48-89.** Fax 089/59-62-28. 11 units (3 with shower and toilet, 4 with shower but no toilet). 95DM ($47.50) double without bath; 115DM ($57.50) double with shower but no toilet, 150DM ($75) double with shower and toilet. Rates include breakfast. No credit cards. U-Bahn: Sendlinger Tor.

Old-fashioned and respectable, this bed-and-breakfast is an antique oddity within a neighborhood filled with more conventional hotels and apartment buildings. Other than a tiny reception area (on the street level), it occupies two floors of an ocher-colored stucco building whose rooms are high-ceilinged, with the large, old-fashioned dimensions of 19th-century parlors. Biggest of the lot is room no. 4. Expect a combination of simple, Formica-covered furniture mingled with older, more valuable pieces, and a sense of thrift and discretion. The biggest inconvenience for occupants of rooms without showers involves a trek to the ground floor whenever you want to bathe. Otherwise, toilets are all on the same floor as the rooms themselves. Breakfast is the only meal served.

Pension Westfalia. Mozartstrasse 23, 80336 München. ☎ **089/53-03-77.** Fax 089/5-43-91-20. http://home.t-online.de/home/pension-westfalia/. E-mail: pension-westfalia@t-online.de. 19 units, 11 with bath. TV TEL. 90DM–95DM ($45–$47.50) double without bath, 125DM–135DM ($62.50–$67.50) double with bath. Rates include buffet breakfast. No credit cards. U-Bahn: Goetheplatz. Bus: 58.

This four-story town house, originally built in 1895, near Goetheplatz is one of Munich's best pensions. It faces the meadow where the annual Oktoberfest takes place. Rooms are rather functional, and short on extras, but well maintained. Owner Peter Deiritz speaks English. Parking is free on the street, when available.

Uhland Garni. Uhlandstrasse 1, 80336 München. ☎ **089/54-33-50.** Fax 089/54-33-52-50. www.hotel-uhland.de. E-mail: hotel-uhland@compuserve.com. 25 units. MINIBAR TV TEL. 150DM–305DM ($75–$152.50) double. Rates include buffet breakfast. AE, DC, MC, V. Free parking. Bus: 58.

Located in a residential area, just a 10-minute walk from the Hauptbahnhof, the Uhland could easily become your home in Munich. It offers friendly, personal service. The stately town mansion, built in art nouveau style, stands in its own small garden. Rooms are soundproof, snug, traditional, and cozy. Baths contain hair dryers. Only breakfast is served.

IN SCHWABING

✪ **Gästehaus Englischer Garten.** Liebergesellstrasse 8, 80802 München-Schwabing. ☎ **089/3-83-94-10.** Fax 089/38-39-41-33. 25 units, 19 with bath. MINIBAR TV TEL. 140DM–150DM ($70–$75) double without bath, 158DM–212DM ($79–$106) double with bath. AE, MC, V. Parking 10DM ($5). U-Bahn: Münchener Freiheit.

This oasis of charm and tranquility, close to the Englischer Garten, is one of our preferred stopovers in Munich. The decor of the small to medium rooms has been called "Bavarian grandmotherly"; furnishings include genuine antiques, old-fashioned but

Munich Accommodations & Dining

ACCOMMODATIONS ■

Advocat Hotel **52**
Am Markt **41**
An der Oper **29**
Bayerischer Hof & Palais
  Montgelas **12**
Eden-Hotel-Wolff **16**
Gästehaus Englischer
  Garten **5**
Hotel Bristol München **48**
Hotel Exquisit **47**
Hotel Jedermann **17**
Hotel Olympic **49**
Hotel Opera **26**
Hotel Palace **55**
Hotel Utzelmann **46**
Kempinski Hotel Vier
  Jahreszeiten München **28**
Königswache **2**
München City Hilton **53**
Pension Westfalia **59**
Platzl **36**
Preysing **54**
Rafael **37**
Splendid **27**
Uhland Garni **44**

DINING ◆

Alois Dallmayr **31**
Andescher am Dom **23**
Asam Schlössel **56**
Austernkeller **38**
Bamberger Haus **7**
Bar-Restaurant Morizz **58**
Biergarten
  Chinesischer Turm **54**
Boettner's **30**
Buon Gusto **37**
Café Glockenspiel **39**
Café Luitpold **10**
Der Katzlmacher **5**
Deutsche Eiche
  (German Oak) **51**
Donisl **33**
Galleria **40**
Garden Restaurant **14**
Gästhaus Glockenbach **60**
Gaststätte zum
  Flaucher **56**
Hirschgarten **1**
Hundskugel **21**
Hunsiger's Pacific **13**
Käfer Am Hofgarten **9**
Käfer-Schänke **8**
Kay's Bistro **50**
Locanda Picolit **4**
Mark's Restaurant **36**
Nürnberger Bratwurst
  Glockl am Dom **22**
Planet Hollywood **35**
Prinz Myshkin **34**
Ratskeller München **32**
Restaurant Königshof **19**
Restaurant Lenbach **15**
Restaurant Vier
  Jahreszeiten **25**
Sausalito's **11**
Spago **3**
Spatenhaus **24**
Straubinger Hof **43**
Sushi & Soul **57**
Tantris **5**

Times Square Online Bistro **18**
Weinbauer **5**
Weinhaus Neuner **20**
Weisses Brauhaus **41**
Zum Alten Markt **42**
Zum Burgerhaus **45**

✝ Church
ⓘ Information
✉ Post Office
--○-- S-Bahn
--☐-- U-Bahn

Blütenstrasse
Adalbertstrasse
Schackstrasse
Schellingstrasse
Türkenstrasse
Amalienstrasse
University
Prof.-Huberplatz
Veterinärstr.
Königinstrasse
Theresienstrasse
Ludwigstrasse
Kaulbachstrasse
Königin strasse
ENGLISCHER GARTEN
Türkenstrasse
Schoenfeldstrasse
Von-der-Tann Strasse
Prinzregentenstrasse
Lerchenfeld strasse
Oettingenstrasse
Oskar -von -Miller- Ring
Brienerstrasse
Galeriestrasse
Theater-museum
K. Scharnagl -Ring
Unsöldstrasse
Wagmüllerstr.
Odeons-platz
HOFGARTEN
Hofgartenstrasse
Christophstrasse
Liebigstrasse
Reitmorstrasse
Isar
Promenade-platz
Karl-Faulhaber-Strasse
Theatinerstrasse
Residenz strasse
Residenz
Cuvilliés Theater
Marstall-strasse
St.-Anna-Pfarrstr.
St.-Anna-strasse
Thierschstrasse
Sternstrasse
Widenmayerstrasse
Frauen-platz
Max-Joseph-Platz
Nationaltheater
Bürkleinstr.
Liebigstrasse
Kaufingerstrasse
Weinstrasse
Pfister-strasse
Am Kosttor-Platz
Museum für Völkerkunde
Maximilianstrasse
Maximilians-brücke
Diener-strasse
Judisches Museum München
Knöbelstrasse
Marien-platz
Im Tal
Th.-Wimmer-Ring
Isartor-platz
Steinsdorfstrasse
Westenriederstrasse
Viktualienmarkt
Frauenstrasse
Kanalstrasse
Thierschstrasse
Isar
Blumenstrasse
Rumfordstr.
Zweibrücken strasse
Innere Weiner Strasse
Cornelliusstrasse
Müllerstr.
Baader-platz
Morassistrasse
Ludwigs-brücke
Kellerstrasse
Gärtner-platz
Reichenbachstrasse
Baaderstrasse
Erhardtstrasse
Rosenheimerstrasse
Klenzestrasse
Fraunhofer
Deutsches Museum
Zeplinstrasse
Lilienstrasse
Hochstrasse
Isar

0   1/5 Mi
0   0.2 Km

exceedingly comfortable beds, and Oriental rugs. Baths are small and not one of the hotel's stronger features, but their maintenance is first rate. Fifteen units are across the street in an annex; these are small apartments, each with a bath and a tiny kitchenette. Try for room 10, 20, 30, or 90. In fair weather, breakfast is served in a rear garden.

IN HAIDHAUSEN

München City Hilton. Rosenheimerstrasse 15, 81667 München. ☎ **800/455-8667** in the U.S. and Canada, or 089/4-80-40. Fax 089/48-04-48-04. www.hilton.com. E-mail: munich-city@hilton.com. 499 units. A/C MINIBAR TV TEL. 415DM–580DM ($207.50–$290) double; from 700DM ($350) suite. AE, DC, MC, V. Parking 26DM ($13). S-Bahn: Rosenheimer Platz.

The München City Hilton lies beside the Deutsches Museum and the performing arts center, Gasteig. This low-rise hotel, designed with red brick, shimmering glass, and geometric windows, is reminiscent of a Mondrian painting. Munich's historic center is an invigorating 25-minute walk across the river. Rooms contain modern adaptations of Biedermeier furniture and plush carpeting. The well-stocked baths contain hair dryers, luxurious robes, and large, sumptuous towels.

Dining/Diversions: The Hilton offers good drinking and dining facilities, including Zum Gasteig, a Bavarian restaurant decorated in typical style; Löwen-Schanke, a Bavarian pub; and Café Metropolitan, where you can order a leisurely breakfast or afternoon tea.

Amenities: 24-hour room service, laundry, dry cleaning, baby-sitting; flower shop, newsstand.

Preysing. Preysingstrasse 1, 81667 München. ☎ **089/45-84-50.** Fax 089/45-84-54-44. 76 units. A/C MINIBAR TV TEL. 340DM ($170) double; 450DM–650DM ($225–$325) suite. Rates include breakfast. AE, DC, MC, V. Parking 21DM ($10.50). Tram: 18.

If you want a quiet location and don't mind a hotel on the outskirts, consider the Preysing, located across the Isar near the Deutsches Museum. (A short tram ride will whisk you into the center of the city.) When you first view the building, a seven-story modern structure, you may feel we've misled you. However, if you've gone this far, venture inside for a pleasant surprise. The hotel's style is agreeable, with dozens of little extras to provide homelike comfort. Fresh flowers are everywhere, and the furnishings have been carefully selected. Fresh fruit is supplied daily. The spacious baths have hair dryers and deluxe toiletries. The staff is one of the most thoughtful in Munich.

Dining: Only breakfast is served.

Amenities: Room service, laundry, baby-sitting, indoor pool, sauna, solarium, whirlpool.

4 Where to Dine

Munich is one of the very few European cities that has more than one "three-star" restaurant. This is the place to practice *Edelfresswelle* ("high-class gluttony"). The classic local dish, traditionally consumed before noon, is *Weisswurste*, herb-flavored white-veal sausages blanched in water. Sophisticated international cuisine is popular throughout the city, too.

IN CENTRAL MUNICH
VERY EXPENSIVE

✪ **Boettner's.** Pfisterstrasse 9. ☎ **089/22-12-10.** Reservations required. Main courses 48DM–68DM ($24–$34). AE, DC, MC, V. Summer Mon–Sat 11:30am–3pm and 6–10pm. Sept–May Mon–Sat 11:30am–10pm. U-Bahn: Marienplatz. INTERNATIONAL.

Cafe Culture

You can follow the German custom of dining on coffee and cake in the afternoon at one of Munich's fine cafes. The famous **Café Luitpold,** Briennerstrasse 11 (☎ 089/ 29-28-65; U-Bahn: Odeonsplatz), open since 1888, attracted such notables as Ibsen, Kandinsky, and Johann Strauss the Younger. It's open Monday to Friday 9am to 8pm and Saturday 8:30am to 7pm. From **Café Glockenspiel** on the Marienplatz (☎ 089/ 26-42-56; U-Bahn/S-Bahn: Marienplatz), you can watch the miniature tournament staged each day by the mechanical clock on the Rathaus facade. It's open daily 10 to 1am. Two famous purveyors of fine chocolate and pastry are **Confiserie Reber,** Herzogspitalstrasse 9 (☎ 089/26-52-31; U-Bahn/S-Bahn: Karlsplatz/Stachus), and **Confiserie Kreutzkann,** Maffeistrasse 4 (☎ 089/29-32-77; U-Bahn/S-Bahn: Marienplatz), which has a cafe on the premises that's open 8:30am to 7pm.

Long featured in this guide, Boettner's—in business since 1901 when it first opened as a tea and oyster shop—has moved to a new location where it has kept its old devotees but gained new and younger fans. The restaurant today is housed in Orlandohaus, a Renaissance structure in the very heart of Munich. Culinary fans from yesterday will recognize its wood-paneled interior which was dismantled and also moved to the site. If anything, the cookery seems better than ever—at least it's lighter and more refined. Try the lobster stew in a cream sauce and almost any dish with white truffles. Pike balls appear delectably in a Chablis herb sauce, and succulent lamb or venison also appears enticingly in a woodsy morel sauce. Desserts are as sumptuous as ever. The French influence is very evident, as are many traditional Bavarian recipes.

✪ **Garden Restaurant.** In the Bayerischer Hof Hotel, Promenadeplatz 2–6. ☎ **089/ 21200.** Reservations recommended. Main courses 40DM–60DM ($20–$30); fixed-price lunch 59DM–98DM ($29.50–$49); fixed-price dinners 69DM–98DM ($34.50–$49). AE, DC, MC, V. Daily noon–3pm and 6–11:30pm. Tram: 19. MEDITERRANEAN/INTERNATIONAL.

This showcase restaurant within one of the showcase hotels of Munich looks like a miniature pastel-colored palace. It's set in a solemnly hushed room filled with blooming plants off the otherwise bustling hotel lobby. Upscale food is served to a cosmopolitan crowd. Menu items are about as cultivated and esoteric as you can find in Munich. Examples include thin noodles with strips of quail and mushroom sauce, a bouquet of salad greens "land and sea" accented with lobster meat and calves' liver, a soup of exotic mushrooms in puff pastry, and fillet of beef stuffed with goose liver and fresh mushrooms. Despite the elaborate menu, one of the most sought after dishes is fillet of Dover sole in lemon-butter sauce, served simply but flavorfully with fresh spinach and boiled potatoes. Desserts are appropriately lavish, and wine choices are among the most varied in Munich.

Restaurant Königshof. In the Hotel Königshof, Karlsplatz 25 (Am Stachus). ☎ **089/ 55-13-60.** Reservations required. Main courses 48DM–62DM ($24–$31); fixed-price menu 144DM–184DM ($72–$92). AE, DC, MC, V. Daily noon–2:30pm and 6:30–10pm. U-Bahn/ S-Bahn: Karlsplatz/Stachus. Tram: 19. INTERNATIONAL.

The Geisel family has made major renovations to the dining room, with its oyster-white panels of oak, polished bronze chandeliers, silver candelabra, and porcelain. The waiters are polite and skilled. The chefs here are highly inventive. They like extremely fresh ingredients, and the food here reflects this passion. If available, try the foie gras with sauternes, loin of lamb with fine herbs, curried breast of duck, lobster with vanilla butter, or sea bass supreme.

Tipping

If a restaurant bill says *Bedienung,* that means a service charge has already been added, so just round up to the nearest mark.

Restaurant Vier Jahreszeiten. In the Kempinski Hotel Vier Jahreszeiten München, Maximilianstrasse 17. ☎ **089/2-12-50.** Reservations required. Main courses 35DM–59DM ($17.50–$29.50); 5-course fixed-price menu 110DM ($55). AE, DC, MC, V. Daily noon–1:30pm. Tram: 19. INTERNATIONAL.

Restaurant Vier Jahreszeiten is in a quiet and elegant location within walking distance of the opera house. The atmosphere is dignified and refined, the service extremely competent, and the food prepared along classic French lines with many imaginative variations, including Asian influences. The menu changes every 4 to 6 weeks, but appetizers are likely to include mushroom soufflé served with artichoke-cream sauce, freshly made vegetable soup flavored with pesto, or turbot encased in basil-flavored crust. For a main course, try breast of Bresse chicken with scampi, flavored with a ginger sauce; or roast medaillons of venison with cherry-pepper sauce. Another specialty is blanquette of veal and lobster. Desserts include strawberries Walterspiel, or, for two, tangerine soufflé served with foamy vanilla sauce.

EXPENSIVE

Austernkeller. Stollbergstrasse 11. ☎ **089/29-87-87.** Reservations required. Main courses 33DM–49DM ($16.50–$24.50). AE, DC, MC, V. Daily 5–11:30pm. Closed Dec 23–26. U-Bahn: Isartor. SEAFOOD.

This "oyster cellar" is a delight to both visitors and locals. You get the largest selection of oysters in town, from raw oysters to elaborate preparations such as oysters Rockefeller. A delectable dish to start is the shellfish platter with fresh oysters, mussels, clams, scampi, and sea snails. Or you might begin with a richly stocked fish soup or cold hors d'oeuvre. French meat specialties are also offered, but the focus is seafood—everything from lobster thermidor to shrimp grilled in the shell. The decor is elegant and refined, and the service is attentive.

Galleria. Ledererstrasse 2 at Sparkassenstrasse. ☎ **089/29-79-95.** Reservations recommended. Main courses 30DM–42DM ($15–$21); fixed-price dinner 79DM–89DM ($39.50–$44.50). AE, DC, MC, V. Mon–Sat noon–3pm and 6–11pm. Closed Aug 10–30. U-Bahn/S-Bahn: Marienplatz. ITALIAN.

This is one of the most appealing of the several Italian restaurants in Munich's center, and the one that takes the greatest risks with experimental Italian cuisine. It provides gracious service and a roster of dishes that change with the availability of ingredients and the inspiration of the chefs. Examples are poached sea wolf with fresh vegetables in fennel sauce; an aromatic guinea fowl scented with lavender; homemade spaghetti with white, Italian truffles; herb-flavored risotto with chunks of lobster and braised radicchio (the best we've had in Munich); and roasted soft-shell crabs with a light onion sauce. Dessert might include a smooth zabaglione served with pears marinated in port wine.

Kay's Bistro. Utzschneiderstrasse 1. ☎ **089/2-60-35-84.** Reservations required. Main courses 32DM–46DM ($16–$23). AE, MC. Daily 7pm–3am. U-Bahn/S-Bahn: Marienplatz. INTERNATIONAL.

It's fun, media-hip, and schmaltzy, with a clientele that's either blatantly gay or very, very tolerant. Every month or so, the decor is redefined, based on glittering themes

A Map Note

For the location of restaurants in this section, see the "Munich Accommodations & Dining" map on pp. 266–267.

that have included Carnival in Rio, Grace and the Grand Prix of Monaco, Chinatown, "Hooray for Hollywood," and—when we happened to drop in—New York City. The accessories change almost as often as the cuisine, and might include shopping bags from Bloomingdale's; plastic replicas of the Statue of Liberty, and the kinds of campy and scattered paraphernalia you might find in a messy NYC apartment. Even the background music is carefully calibrated to go with the theme of the moment. The place is fun, campy, and favored by celebrities who have included disco diva Gloria Gaynor. Cuisine is light, urbane, and flavorful, and sometimes named after pop icons, such as Indian-style chicken breast "Diana Vreeland." Drinks include, among others, Louisiana milk punch and an almost psychedelic Velvet Underground.

Marks Restaurant. In the Hotel Rafael, Neuturmstrasse 1. ☎ **089/290980.** Reservations recommended. Fixed-price lunch in Mark's Corner 53DM ($26.50); fixed-price dinner in Mark's Restaurant 116DM–149DM ($58–$74.50); main courses in Mark's Restaurant 38DM–60DM ($19–$30). AE, DC, MC, V. Daily noon–2pm and 7–11pm. U-Bahn/S-Bahn: Marienplatz. CONTINENTAL.

This restaurant, in the prestigious Hotel Rafael, is appropriately elegant with impeccably trained staff. Lunch is served in a small, cozy enclave off the lobby, Mark's Corner, and is usually limited to a set price menu favored by business people. Dinners are swankier and more elaborate; they're served one floor above street level in a formal dining room that overlooks a monumental staircase and the lobby below. On Sunday and Monday night only, the formal dining room is closed, and dinner is served in Mark's Corner. Menu items change according to the season and the inspiration of the chef. Many dishes are somewhat experimental but still succeed beautifully. Examples include fillet of beef with a ragout of artichokes and potatoes and deep-fried baby garlic buds; sea wolf with green lentils, bacon, and goose liver; fillet of pike perch pan fried in soy sauce and served with root vegetables; and fillet of beef with horseradish, served with dumplings and Savoy cabbage.

MODERATE

✪ **Alois Dallmayr.** Dienerstrasse 14–15. ☎ **089/2-13-51-00.** Reservations required. Main courses 29.50DM–75DM ($14.75–$37.50); fixed-price menus 49.50DM ($24.75) for 3 courses, 68DM ($34) for 4 courses. AE, DC, MC, V. Mon–Wed 9:30am–7pm, Thurs–Fri 9:30am–8pm, Sat 9am–4pm. Tram: 19. CONTINENTAL.

Alois Dallmayr, which traces its history back to 1700, is the most famous delicatessen in Germany. After looking at its tempting array of delicacies from around the globe, you'll think you're lost in a millionaire's supermarket. Dallmayr has been a purveyor to many royal courts. Here you'll find Munich's most elegant consumers. The upstairs dining room serves a subtle German version of continental cuisine, owing a heavy debt to France. The food array is dazzling, ranging from the best herring and sausages we've ever tasted to such rare treats as perfectly vine-ripened tomatoes flown in from Morocco and papayas from Brazil. The famous French poulet de Bresse, beloved of gourmets, is also shipped in. The smoked fish is a taste sensation, and the soups are superbly flavored, especially the one made with shrimp. If you're dining alone, you might prefer to sit at the counter instead of a table. This bustling restaurant is crowded at lunchtime.

Buon Gusto (Talamonti). Hochbruckenstrasse 3. ☎ **089/296-383.** Reservations recommended. Main courses 18DM–36DM ($9–$18). AE, MC V. Mon–Sat noon–11pm. U-Bahn/ S-Bahn: Marienplatz. TUSCAN/ITALIAN.

Devotees claim that this is the finest Italian restaurant in Munich. Its interior features two dining areas: a simple, rustic-looking bistro overlooking an open kitchen, and a more formal dining room. Menu items and prices are identical in both areas. Owned and managed by an extended family, the Talamontis, whose members are likely not to speak English, the site emphasizes fresh ingredients, strong and savory flavors, and food items inspired by the Italian provinces of the Marches and Tuscany. Delectable examples include ravioli stuffed with mushrooms and herbs, roasted lamb with potatoes, lots of different forms of scallopini, and fresh fish served simply, with oil or butter and lemon. The various risottos are especially flavorful. During Oktoberfest and trade fairs, the place is mobbed.

✪ **Hunsiger's Pacific.** Maximilliansplatz 5 (entrance is on the Max-Joseph-Strasse). ☎ 089/5502-9741. Main courses 35DM–50DM ($17.50–$25); fixed-price 2-course lunch 22DM ($11). AE, DC, MC, V. Mon–Fri noon–2:30pm, daily 6–10:30pm. Closed Sun May–Sept. U-Bahn/S-Bahn: Karlsplatz/Stachus. CONTINENTAL/ASIAN.

This restaurant offers great value on excellent food. The menu is the creative statement of one of the city's most innovative young chefs, Werner Hunsiger. Fish is the premier item here—often flown in from Pacific waters just hours after it's caught. Preparation is based on classic French-inspired methods, but many of the innovative flavors come from Malaysia (coconut milk), Japan (wasabi), Thailand (lemongrass), and India (curry). You could begin with a tuna carpaccio with sliced plum, fresh ginger, and lime. Main courses include a succulent version of bouillabaisse with aïoli, which you might follow with cold melon soup garnished with a dollop of tarragon-flavored granita. Fried monkfish in the Malaysian style and turbot in chili and ginger sauce are evocative of Hawaii.

Käfer Am Hofgarten. Odeonsplatz 6–7. ☎ **089/290-7530.** Reservations recommended. Main courses 20DM–42DM ($10–$21). AE, V. Mon–Thurs 11am–1am, Fri 11am–3am, Sat 9:30am–3am, Sun 9:30am–1am. U-Bahn: Odeonsplatz. ITALIAN/FRENCH.

This likable and stylish bistro and bar is set midway between the imposing bulk of the Residenz and the Bavarian Ministry of Finance. It's a replica of something you might find in Paris or Lyon. There are outdoor terraces in front and back. Staff members are attentive and polite. A live pianist bashes out cabaret and jazz tunes every night. Tables are spaced close to one another, which enhances the sense of intimacy, though your conversation is likely to be overheard by your immediate neighbors. Menu items change daily according to the season and the inspiration of the chefs, but might include carpaccio of beef with olive oil and aromatic herbs; pressed fillet of duck prepared with braised cabbage, apples, *Rösti*, and noodles; pastas with seafood; succulent and very fresh salads; and seasonal rabbit braised with a medley of fresh root vegetables.

Nürnberger Bratwurst Glöckl am Dom. Frauenplatz 9. ☎ **089/29-52-64.** Reservations recommended. Main courses 14DM–30DM ($7–$15). No credit cards. Daily 9am–1am. U-Bahn/S-Bahn: Marienplatz. BAVARIAN.

This place, a short walk from Marienplatz, facing the cathedral, is the coziest and warmest of Munich's local restaurants. You sit in chairs that look as if they were made by a Black Forest wood-carver. Upstairs is a dining room decorated with reproductions of Dürer prints. The restaurant has a strict policy of shared tables. The plates are tin. The homesick Nürnberger comes here just for one dish: Nürnberger Schweinwurstl mit Kraut (those delectable little sausages). Last food orders are at midnight.

Planet Hollywood. Platzl 1. ☎ **089/2903-0500.** Reservations accepted only Mon-Wed and Sun. Main courses 15DM–35DM ($7.50–$17.50). AE, MC, V. Daily 11:30am–midnight. Bar Mon–Thurs 11:30am–1am, Fri–Sun 11:30am–3am. S-Bahn: Marienplatz or Isartor. AMERICAN.

This is the Munich branch of the financially troubled Planet Hollywood. Memorabilia associated with *Titanic* and seemingly every film made by Bruce Willis or Sly Stallone surrounds visitors. Cocktails are served in a commodious bar area. You can eventually gravitate into either the main dining room, or a satellite room that immortalizes the achievements of Hollywood's favorite Teuton, Arnold Schwarzenegger. The staff will be quick to tell you that he once lived in Munich. Menu items are firmly grounded in American pop culture, and include burgers (with several vegetarian versions), New York strip steaks, chili, club sandwiches, tacos, and ice-cream sundaes. For a memorable dessert, try the "famous" *Apfelstrudel*, reputedly made according to a recipe perfected by Arnold's mother. You can have a good time here, even if you find the venue very similar to everything you left America to forget.

Ratskeller München. Im Rathaus, Marienplatz 8. ☎ **089/2-19-98-90.** Reservations required. Main courses 16.50DM–35DM ($8.25–$17.50). AE, MC, V. Daily 10am–midnight. U-Bahn/S-Bahn: Marienplatz. BAVARIAN.

Throughout Germany you'll find Ratskellers, traditional cellar restaurants in Rathaus (city hall) basements, serving good inexpensive food and wine. Munich is proud of its Ratskeller. The decor is typical: dark wood and carved chairs. The most interesting tables are in the semiprivate dining nooks in the rear, under the vaulted painted ceilings. Bavarian music adds to the ambience. The menu, generally a showcase of regional fare, also includes some international dishes, many of them vegetarian, which is unusual for a Ratskeller. Recently the chef added an array of grilled food that's lighter than the usual heavy fare offered in many German ratskellers.

Restaurant Lenbach. Ottostrasse 6. ☎ **089/549-1300.** Reservations recommended for dinner. In restaurant, main courses 24DM–120DM ($12–$60); in cafe-bistro, main courses 9DM–28DM ($4.50–$14). AE, DC, MC, V. Restaurant Mon-Sat 6pm–midnight, cafe-bistro daily 11am–midnight; bar Mon-Sat 3pm-3am. U-Bahn/S-Bahn: Karlsplatz/Stachus. EUROPEAN/MEDITERRANEAN.

One of the most appealing restaurants in Munich occupies the grandiose premises of a 19th-century palace (Bernheimerpalais am Lenbachplatz). The decorative theme revolves around the Seven Deadly Sins, albeit with a decidedly stylish, and highly permissive, twist. Adultery is represented by a provocative large-scale pre-Raphaelite painting behind the bar. The theme within the ultracomfortable drinking lounge is

ⓕ Family-Friendly Restaurants

Tower Restaurant, Olympiapark *(see p. 292)*   For a panoramic view of the Alps as well as the Olympic grounds, take your kids here to dine and, later, out onto one of the observation platforms.

Nürnberger Bratwurst Glöckl am Dom *(see p. 272)*   Hot dogs will never taste the same again after your child has tried one of those delectable little sausages from Nürnberg.

Café Glockenspiel   Your kids can down delectable Bavarian pastries while enjoying the miniature "tournament" staged each day near the clock on the Rathaus facade.

Sloth. Even the toilet is accessorized with jailhouse bars and manacles, to represent Wrath. Other "sins" await your own discovery. Food items seem less important than the decor, but are likely to include a "seven sins" platter that contains foie gras, lobster, carpaccio of beef, and mozzarella tarts; lamb loin "Lenbach style" served with a gratin of potatoes and zucchini; salmon-trout *en papillote;* and heaping platters of fresh shellfish.

Spatenhaus. Residenzstrasse 12. ☎ **089/2-90-70-60.** Reservations recommended. Main courses 25DM–43.90DM ($12.50–$21.95). AE, MC, V. Daily 9:30am–12:30am. U-Bahn: Odeonsplatz or Marienplatz. BAVARIAN/INTERNATIONAL.

The Spatenhaus, one of Munich's best-known beer restaurants, has wide windows overlooking the opera house on Max-Joseph-Platz. You can sit in an intimate, semi-private dining nook or at a big table. Spatenhaus has old traditions, typical Bavarian food, and generous portions at reasonable prices. If you want to know what all this fabled Bavarian gluttony is all about, order the "Bavarian plate," which is loaded down with various meats, including pork and sausages. (After that, you'll have to go to a spa.) Of course, to be loyal, you should order the restaurant's own beer, Spaten-Franziskaner-Bier, with your meal.

Weinhaus Neuner. Herzogspitalstrasse 8. ☎ **089/2-60-39-54.** Reservations recommended. Main courses 24DM–38DM ($12–$16). Fixed-price lunch 24DM–35DM ($12–$17.50), fixed-price dinner 69DM ($34.50). AE, MC, V. Mon–Sat 12:30–2pm and 5:30–10pm. U-Bahn/S-Bahn: Karlsplatz/Stachus. BAVARIAN.

This is an *Ältestes Weinhaus Münchens,* one of the city's landmark taverns. It dates from the late 15th century and is the only building in Munich that has its original Tyrolean vaults. The place brims with warmth and charm. Once young priests were educated here, but after Napoléon brought secularization, it became a wine tavern and a rendezvous for artists, writers, and composers, including Richard Wagner. The casual Weinstube is the less-formal section and has lots of local atmosphere. The restaurant section is elegant, with candles and flowers. The chef happily marries nouvelle cuisine and regional specialties.

Zum Alten Markt. Am Viktualienmarkt, Dreifaltigkeitsplatz 3. ☎ **089/29-99-95.** Reservations recommended. Main courses 20DM–38DM ($10–$19). No credit cards. Mon–Sat 11am–10:30pm. U-Bahn/S-Bahn: Marienplatz. Bus: 52. BAVARIAN/INTERNATIONAL.

Snug and cozy, Zum Alten Markt serves beautifully presented fresh cuisine at a good price. Located on a tiny square just off Munich's large outdoor food market, the restaurant has a mellow charm and a welcoming host, Josef Lehner. The interior decor, with its intricately coffered wooden ceiling, came from a 400-year-old Tyrolean castle. In summer, tables are set up outside. Fish and fresh vegetables come from the nearby market. You might begin with a tasty homemade soup, such as cream of carrot, or perhaps black-truffle tortellini in cream sauce with young onions and tomatoes. The chef makes a great *Tafelspitz* (boiled-beef). You can also order classic dishes such as roast duck with apple sauce or a savory roast suckling pig.

INEXPENSIVE

Andechser am Dom. Weinstrasse 7a. ☎ **089/29-84-81.** Reservations recommended. Main courses 17DM–22DM ($8.50–$11). AE, DC, MC, V. Daily 10am–midnight. U-Bahn/S-Bahn: Marienplatz. GERMAN.

This restaurant and beer hall is set on two floors of a postwar building adjacent to the back side of the Frauenkirche. It serves large amounts of a beer brewed in a monastery near Munich (Andechser), as well as generous portions of German food. No one will mind if you order a snack, a full meal, or just a beer. Menu items are often accompanied with German-style potato salad and green salad and include such dishes as veal schnitzels, steaks, turkey croquettes, roasted lamb, fish, and several kinds of sausages that taste best with tangy mustard. In good weather, tables are set up both on the building's roof and on the sidewalk in front, both of which overlook the back of one of the city's finest churches.

Bar-Restaurant Morizz. Klenzestrasse 43. ☎ **089/201-6776.** Reservations recommended. Main courses 17DM–31DM ($8.50–$15.50). MC. Sun–Thurs 7pm–12:30am, Fri–Sat 7pm–1:30am. U-Bahn: Fraunhoferstrasse. CONTINENTAL/THAI/INTERNATIONAL.

This is *the* hip gay restaurant of Munich. As estimated by the staff, it has a 70% gay male clientele; lesbian women and gay-friendly straights make up the rest of the clients. Part of the space is devoted to a sprawling, attractive bar, where red leather chairs, mirrors, and an impeccably trained staff evoke a 1920s Paris hotel bar. You can enjoy at least 40 single malt whiskies, a half dozen single-barrel bourbons, and a wide array of unusual wines. The adjacent dining room offers an appealing combination of international and continental food, prepared by a central-European staff whose interpretation of Thai cuisine is especially enjoyable. Try the *vorspeisen-teller* of mixed Thai specialties; some fans find the lemongrass almost addictive. Other choices include veal preparations, fresh fish, pastas, and salads (including one garnished with strips of confit of duckling).

Deutsche Eiche (German Oak). Reichenbachstrasse 13. ☎ **089/231-1660.** Reservations not necessary. Main courses 11.50DM–25DM ($5.75–$12.50). AE, MC, V. Daily 8am–midnight. U-Bahn: Fraunhoferstrasse. GERMAN.

The building was constructed in 1864, and there's been a restaurant with a mostly gay, or at least arts-oriented, clientele since its very debut. In the 1970s, Fassbinder, the noteworthy film director, hung out here a lot, usually dressed entirely in chains and leather. Late in the 1990s, the place was renovated into a less evocative, more streamlined-looking beerhall, still with a healthy percentage of gay clients, and with direct access to a 26-room hotel and one of the busiest gay saunas in Munich. Accommodations in the hotel are relatively affordable at 170DM to 190DM ($85 to $95) for a double. Each has TV and telephone and an all-white, efficient-looking collection of furnishings. But we primarily recommend the place as a restaurant and bar hangout. Simple beerhall-style food includes chili with French bread; vegetarian strudel; roasted pork with potato dumplings; pork schnitzel with french fries; wienerschnitzels, pork Cordon Bleu, and grilled turkey steak with fresh mushrooms.

Donisl. Weinstrasse 1. ☎ **089/22-01-84.** Reservations recommended. Main courses all 12DM ($6). AE, DC, MC, V. Daily 9am–midnight. U-Bahn/S-Bahn: Marienplatz. BAVARIAN/INTERNATIONAL.

Donisl is Munich's oldest beer hall, dating from 1715. Readers have praised this Munich-style restaurant as *gemütlich,* with its relaxed and comfortable atmosphere, although the seating capacity is about 550. In summer you can enjoy the hum and bustle of the Marienplatz by dining in the garden area out front. The restaurant has two levels, the second of which is a gallery. English is spoken. The standard menu offers traditional Bavarian food as well as a weekly changing specials menu. A specialty is *Weisswürste,* the little white sausage that has been a decades-long tradition of this place. The chef also prepares a good duck. Select beers from Munich's own Hacker-Pschorr Brewery top the evening. A zither player at noon and an accordion player in the evening entertain diners.

Hundskugel. Hotterstrasse 18. ☎ **089/26-42-72.** Reservations required. Main courses 15DM–35DM ($7.50–$17.50). No credit cards. Daily 10am–midnight. U-Bahn/S-Bahn: Marienplatz. BAVARIAN.

The city's oldest tavern dates from 1440, and apparently serves the same food it did back then. Why mess with success? Perhaps half the residents of Munich at one time or another have made their way here. The cookery is honest Bavarian with no pretensions. Although the chef makes a specialty of *Spanferkel* (roast suckling pig with potato noodles), you might prefer *Tafelspitz* (boiled beef) in dill sauce or roast veal stuffed with goose liver. To begin, try one of the hearty soups, made fresh daily.

Prinz Myshkin. Hackenstrasse 2. ☎ **089/26-55-96.** Reservations recommended. Main courses 16DM–30DM ($8–$15). AE, MC, V. Daily 11am–1am. U-Bahn/S-Bahn: Marienplatz. VEGETARIAN.

This popular vegetarian restaurant near the Marienplatz offers freshly made salads, some macrobiotic selections, Indian and Thai vegetarian dishes, as well as vegetarian *involtini* (stuffed roll ups) and casseroles, soups, and zesty pizzas, many of which are excellent. Wine and beer are sold as well. Smaller portions of many items are available for 8.50DM ($4.25).

Straubinger Hof. Blumenstrasse 5. ☎ **089/2-60-84-44.** Reservations recommended. Main courses 18DM–28DM ($9–$14). AE, V. Mon–Fri 9am–9:30pm, Sat 9am–3pm. U-Bahn/S-Bahn: Marienplatz. BAVARIAN.

Consistently crowded, this restaurant in the Altstadt is a well-managed, unpretentious, traditional place sponsored by the brewers of Paulaner beer. No one will mind if you stop in just for a brew in the morning and afternoon, although during peak lunch and dinner hours, it's good form to order at least a small plate of cheese or wurst, or a steaming platter of *Tafelspitz* (boiled beef with horseradish) or roasted knuckle of pork. The food here caters to nostalgia—you may see the term *Grossmutter Art* ("in the style of grandmother") on the menu. The restaurant is close to the Viktualienmarkt, guaranteeing, at least in theory, ultrafresh produce. Portions are ample and prices are reasonable. In summer, seating spills out onto the pavement. For a traditional Bavarian dessert, try the old-fashioned house specialty, *Apfelschmarrn.*

Sushi & Soul. Klenzestrasse 71. ☎ **089/20-10-992.** Reservations recommended. Main courses 25DM–28DM ($12.50–$14). No credit cards. Daily 6pm–1am. U-Bahn: Fraunhoferstrasse. JAPANESE.

Huge windows open onto a quiet residential street. Expect big airy spaces, flickering candles, and a minimalist decor whose main ornamentation derives from a hip and stylish crowd of good-looking singles and couples. The menu is based on sushi, salads, and hot Japanese food. Fresh ingredients go into the tasty fare, which is a refreshing change of pace from the typical Bavarian diet.

Times Square Online Bistro. Bayerstrasse 10 A (in the Hauptbahnhof). ☎ **089/550-8800.** Reservations not necessary. Breakfasts 11.80DM–16.80DM ($5.90–$8.40); snacks 5.50DM–12.90DM ($2.75–$6.45); main courses 10.80DM–23.90DM ($5.40–$11.95). AE, DC, MC, V. Sun–Thurs 6am to 1am; Fri–Sat 6am–midnight. U-Bahn/S-Bahn: Hauptbahnhof. CONTINENTAL.

Food is well-prepared here, and its salads are especially humongous—very fresh medleys of exotic-looking greens loaded with vitamins. But the place has a gimmick that many computer-literate travelers especially appreciate: There are banks of online computers lining one side, which you can rent for 4.50DM ($2.25) per quarter hour. The setting is high-ceilinged, sunny, and very large; there's a bar in the middle, and a section for conventional (non-computerized) dining, where you can order items that include Zurich-style pork cutlets; baked camembert; tagliatelle; and spinach strudel.

Weisses Bräuhaus. Tal 7. ☎ **089/29-98-75.** Reservations recommended, especially for the back room. Main courses 20DM–32DM ($10–$16). No credit cards. Daily 8am–midnight. U-Bahn/S-Bahn: Marienplatz. BAVARIAN/RHENISH.

Weisses Bräuhaus is big, bustling, and Bavarian with a vengeance. Not for the pretentious, this informal place does what it's been doing for centuries: serve home-brewed beer. At one time the famous salt-trade route between Salzburg and Augsburg passed by its door, and salt traders were very thirsty. The front room, with smoke-blackened dark-wood paneling and stained glass, is for drinking and informal eating; the back room has white tablecloths and black-outfitted waiters. You can sample typical Bavarian dishes: smoked fillet of trout, rich potato soup, roast pork with homemade potato dumplings and cabbage salad, or Viennese veal goulash with mushrooms and cream sauce. You'll have to share your table, but that's part of the fun.

Zum Burgerhaus. Pettenkoferstrasse 5. ☎ **089/59-79-09.** Reservations recommended. Main courses 24DM–31DM ($12–$15.50). AE, MC, V. Mon–Sat 11am–2:30pm and 6–10:45pm. U-Bahn: Sendlinger Tor. GERMAN.

Set behind Sendlingertorplatz, behind an antique, ocher-colored facade, this is a well-managed restaurant serving flavorful food to a loyal neighborhood clientele. Within several dining rooms outfitted with paneling and Bavarian memorabilia, you can order such good-tasting menu items as mixed whitefish with braised herbs; fillet of pike perch in olive oil with spinach and saffron sauce; and medallions of venison with juniperberries and noodles.

NEAR THE SÜDBAHNHOF

✪ **Gästhaus Glockenbach.** Kapuzinerstrasse 29, corner of Maistrasse. ☎ **089/53-40-43.** Reservations recommended. Main courses 45DM–55DM ($22.50–$27.50); fixed-price menus 50DM ($25) lunch, 170DM ($85) dinner. AE, MC, V. Tues–Sat noon–2pm (last order); Tues–Sat 7–10pm (last order). Closed 1 week at Christmas. U-Bahn: Goetheplatz. MODERN CONTINENTAL.

This unpretentious restaurant is capable of holding its own against more expensive, more *grand bourgeois* establishments, such as Tantris (see below). The setting is a 200-year-old building close to the Glockenbach, a tributary of the nearby Isar. The dignified country-baroque interior is accented with vivid modern paintings and the most elegant table settings in town. Cuisine changes with the season. You'll find imaginative preparations of venison and pheasant in autumn, lamb and veal dishes in springtime, and shellfish whenever in season. Ultrafresh vegetables and exotica are imported from local farms and from sophisticated purveyors worldwide. Wines are mostly from Italy, France, and Austria.

NEAR THE ISAR, SOUTH OF CENTER

Asam Schlössl. 45 Maria-Einsiedel-Strasse. ☎ **089/7-23-63-73.** Main courses 12.50DM–38.50DM ($6.25–$19.25). AE, DC, MC, V. Daily 11am–1am. U-Bahn: Thalkirchen. BAVARIAN/INTERNATIONAL.

This Augustiner brewery restaurant offers a relaxed, relatively informal hideaway amid the congestion of Munich. The building was built as a private villa in 1724. Some of the original castlelike design remains, though the structure has been expanded and renovated over the years. All brews offered are products of Augustiner, including both pale and dark versions of Weissebier, beer fermented from wheat. Menu items include such typical Bavarian fare as beef braised in red wine (*Böffla-mott*) with *Semmelknödel*

Beer Gardens

If you're in Munich anytime between the first sunny spring day and the last fading light of a Bavarian-style autumn, you should head for one of the city's celebrated beer gardens (*Biergartens*). Traditionally, beer gardens were simply tables placed under chestnut trees planted above the storage cellars to keep beer cool in summer. (Lids on beer steins, incidentally, were meant to keep out flies.) It's estimated that today Munich has at least 400 beer gardens and cellars. Food, drink, and atmosphere are much the same in all of them.

Bamberger Haus, Brunnerstrasse 2 (☎ **089/3-08-89-66;** U-Bahn: Scheidplatz), located northwest of Schwabing at the edge of Luitpold Park, is named after a city noted for mass consumption of beer. The street-level restaurant serves Bavarian and international specialties: well-seasoned soups, grilled steak, veal, pork, and sausages. If you only want to drink, you might visit the rowdier and less-expensive beer hall in the cellar. Main courses in the restaurant range from 16DM to 38DM ($8 to $19). A large beer costs 5.10DM ($2.55). The restaurant is open daily 11am to 10pm, the beer hall daily 11am to 1am. American Express, MasterCard, and Visa are accepted.

Englischer Garten, the park lying between the Isar River and Schwabing, is home to several beer gardens. Our favorite is ✪ **Biergarten Chinesischer Turm,** Englischer Garten 3 (☎ **089/3-83-87-20;** U-Bahn: Giselastrasse). It's the largest and most popular of its kind in Europe, taking its name from its location at the foot of an easy-to-find pagoda-like tower. Beer and Bavarian food, and plenty of it, are what you get here. A large glass or mug of beer (ask for *ein mass Bier*), enough to bathe in, costs 11DM ($5.50). It will likely be slammed down, still foaming, by a server carrying 12 other tall steins. The

(bread dumplings), and a dish beloved by emperor Franz Josef of Austria, *gesottener Tafelspitz mit frischen Kren,* a savory form of the familiar boiled beef with horseradish.

IN SCHWABING

This district, which was called "bohemian" in the 1940s, overflows with restaurants. Many of them are awful, but there are several good ones, some of which attract a youthful clientele. The evening is the best time for a visit.

VERY EXPENSIVE

✪ **Tantris.** Johann-Fichte-Strasse 7, Schwabing. ☎ **089/36-19-59-0.** Reservations required. Fixed-price 5-course lunch 158DM ($79); fixed-price dinner 198DM ($99) for 5 courses, 225DM ($112.50) for 8 courses; special 5-course dinner Tues–Thurs (including wine) 235DM ($117.50). AE, DC, MC, V. Tues–Sat noon–3pm and 6:30pm–1am. Closed public holidays and annual holidays in Jan and May. U-Bahn: Dietlindenstrasse. FRENCH/INTERNATIONAL.

Tantris serves Munich's finest cuisine. Chef Hans Haas was voted the top chef in Germany in 1994, and, if anything, he has refined and sharpened his culinary technique since. The setting is unlikely: a drab commercial area, with bare concrete walls and a garish decor. But once inside, you're transported by the fine service and excellent food that's a treat for the eye as well as the palate. The choice of dishes is wisely limited, and the cooking is subtle and original. You might begin with a terrine of smoked fish served with green cucumber sauce, then follow with classic roast duck on mustard-seed sauce, or perhaps a delightful concoction of lobster medallions on black noodles.

food is cheap—a simple meal begins at 16DM ($8). Homemade dumplings are a specialty, as are all kinds of tasty sausages. You can also get a first-rate *Schweinbraten* (a braised loin of pork served with potato dumpling and rich brown gravy), which is Bavaria's answer to the better-known sauerbraten of the north. Huge baskets of pretzels are passed around, and they're eaten with *Radi*, the large, tasty white radishes famous from these parts. Oompah bands often play, adding to the festive atmosphere. The place is open every day May to October 11am to 10pm or midnight, but November to April, its hours depend on the weather and the number of guests.

If you're going to the zoo, you might want to stop at the nearby **Gaststätte zum Flaucher,** Isarauen 8 (☎ **089/7-23-26-77;** Bus: 52), for fun and food. Gaststätte is mellow and traditional, with tables set in a tree-shaded garden over-looking the river. Here you can order the local specialty, *Leberkäse*, a large loaf of sausage eaten with freshly baked pretzels and plenty of mustard. Beer costs from 5.10DM ($2.55) for a half-liter mug. Main courses cost from 9.50DM to 16DM ($4.75 to $8). May to October it's open daily 10am to midnight; November to April, only Friday, Saturday, and Sunday 10am to 8pm.

Hirschgarten, Hirschgartenstrasse 1, in Nymphenburg Park, near the palace (☎ **089/17-25-91;** S-Bahn: Laim; tram 17 to Romanplatz), is the largest open-air restaurant in Munich, capable of seating more than 8,000 beer drinkers and merrymakers. Full meals cost 10DM to 28DM ($5 to $14). A 1-liter stein of Augustiner beer goes for 4.95DM ($2.50). It's open daily 10am to midnight. MasterCard is accepted. For information on Munich's other favorite drinking spots, beer halls, see "Munich After Dark," below.

MODERATE

✪ **Der Katzlmacher.** Kaulbacherstrasse 48. ☎ **089/348129.** Reservations recommended. Main courses 35DM–48DM ($17.50–$24); fixed-price dinners 75DM–85DM ($37.50–$42.50). MC, V. Tues–Sat noon–2:30pm and 6:30pm–11pm. U-Bahn: Universität. ITALIAN.

Few Italian restaurants would have had the nerve to adopt as their name a pejorative German term referring to Italians. This one did, however, and its sense of humor has helped make it beloved by loyal local fans. The setting is a postwar building near the university, whose dining rooms are evocative of an elegant and rustic mountain lodge high in the Italian Alps. Stylish and theatrical, and filled with well-dressed, prosperous-looking clients, it contains lavishly carved paneling, masses of artfully arranged flowers, and huge amounts of charm. The cooking is based on the culinary traditions of the Marches, Friuli, and Emilia-Romagna, all known for their fine cuisines and agrarian bounty. The owner is Claudio Zanuttigh, who supervises menu specialties that might include calzone stuffed with spinach and pine nuts, carpaccio of duck breast, a commendable grilled swordfish with red wine vinaigrette, eel with champagne sauce, and a succulent version of *fritto misto del pesce* based on whatever is in season.

✪ **Locanda Picolit.** Siegfriedstrasse 11. ☎ **089/396447.** Reservations recommended. Main courses 29DM–38DM ($14.50–$19); fixed-price menu 69DM ($34.50). AE, DC, V. Tues–Fri noon–2:30pm and Tues–Sun 5–11pm. U-Bahn: Münchner Freiheit. ITALIAN.

If you come here in the summer and sit on the outdoor terrace with a view over a garden, it's easy to believe that you've suddenly been transported to the Mediterranean world. The interior is full of streamlined furnishings and dramatic, oversized modern paintings. Menu items come from all over Italy, but the favorites are those from the owner's native Friuli, near Venice. There's a lavish use of in-season asparagus, arugula, shellfish, rabbit, wild mushrooms, and venison in such alluring preparations as ravioli stuffed with lobster, tagliatelle, rotini, linguini with braised radicchio and shellfish, and, when available, *saltimbocca* (veal with ham).

Spago. Neureutherstrasse 15 at Arcisstrasse. ☎ **089/271-2406.** Reservations recommended. Main courses 28DM–38DM ($14–$19); fixed-price lunch 39DM ($19.50); fixed-price dinner 68DM ($34). AE, DC, V. Mon–Sat 11:30am–2:30pm and 6–11pm. U-Bahn: Josephsplatz or Universität. ITALIAN.

Less self-conscious and self-promotional than its Los Angeles namesake, this amiable multilingual Italian restaurant still offers lots of Italian pizzazz as well as good, upscale Italian food. Some of the dishes are tagliatelle with porcini mushrooms, braised breast of chicken stuffed with herbs and spinach, ravioli with artichoke hearts or with potatoes and chanterelles, an especially delectable fish baked with herbs in a salt crust and wild mushrooms sautéed with herbs and arugula, a perfectly prepared suckling lamb with mint and balsamic vinegar, and an array of desserts as beautiful as they are tasty.

INEXPENSIVE

Sausalito's. Türkenstrasse 50. ☎ **089/28-15-94.** Reservations not necessary. Main courses 16DM–23DM ($8–$11.50). AE, MC, V. Daily 5pm–1am. U-Bahn: Universität. MEXICAN.

Imagine a sprawling labyrinth of rooms whose layout and lighting suggests a German beerhall. Then imagine that instead of boozy, middle-aged clients swilling beer, it's loaded with young, nubile, and sexually active students from the nearby university. Add to that a heady blend of tequila-based parti-colored drinks and tacos, and you'll have the equivalent of Spring Break in Daytona Beach with a German accent. Come here to drink, dialogue, mingle, and to chow down on fajitas, enchiladas, quesadillas, steaks, burritos, and burgers.

Weinbauer. Fendstrasse 5. ☎ **089/39-81-55.** Reservations recommended. Main courses 13.50DM–25DM ($6.75–$12.50). No credit cards. Mon–Fri 11am–midnight, Sat 3pm–midnight. U-Bahn: Münchner Freiheit. BAVARIAN.

Just off Leopoldstrasse is this small, relatively untrammeled and affordable restaurant. The decor evokes a small-town dining room in the Alps. The food is reliable but hardly spectacular. Menu items include Wiener schnitzel, Nürnberger wurst'l with sauerkraut, sirloin steak with an herb-butter sauce, goulash soup, and *Blutwurst* and *Leberwurst* platters. Any of these might be washed down with a half liter of draft beer.

IN BOGENHAUSEN

Käfer-Schänke. Prinzregenstrasse 73. ☎ **089/4-168-247.** Reservations required. Main courses 34DM–55DM ($17–$27.50); fixed-price lunch 48DM ($24). AE, DC, MC, V. Mon–Sat 11:30am–midnight. Closed holidays. U-Bahn: Prinzregentenplatz. Bus: 55. GERMAN/INTERNATIONAL.

This is a great spot for casual dining with elegant style, in a setting that evokes a chalet. It's located on the second floor of a famous gourmet shop called Käfer. The cuisine roams the world for inspiration—from Lombardy to Asia. You select your hors d'oeuvres from the most dazzling display in Munich. Often Käfer-Schänke devotes a week to a particular country's cuisine. On one visit, we enjoyed the classic soup (sea bass with fennel) of the French Riviera. The salads have what one reviewer called "rococo splendor." From a cold table, you can choose smoked salmon or smoked eel. Venison, quail, and guinea hen are also regularly featured.

5 Seeing the Sights

Munich is stocked with so many treasures that any visitor who plans to "do" the city in a day or two will not only miss out on many major sights but will also fail to grasp the city's spirit and absorb its special flavor. There are, however, a few vital highlights.

THE TOP ATTRACTIONS
THE CITY CENTER

Marienplatz is the heart of the Altstadt, or Old City. On its north side is the **Neues Rathaus (New City Hall),** built in 19th-century Gothic style. Each day at 11am and also at noon and 5pm in the summer, the Glockenspiel on the facade performs a miniature tournament, with enameled copper figures moving in and out of the archways. You may wish to climb the 55 steps to the top of the Rauthaus's tower (an elevator is also available) for a good view of the city center. The **Altes Rathaus (Old City Hall),** with its plain Gothic tower, is to the right. It was reconstructed in the 15th century, after being destroyed by fire.

South of the square you can see the oldest church in Munich, **St. Peter's.** The **Viktualienmarkt,** just off Marienplatz and around the corner from St. Peter's church, has been a gathering place since 1807. Here, people gossip, browse, and snack, as well as buy fresh country produce, wines, meats, and cheese.

To the north lies **Odeonsplatz,** Munich's most beautiful square. The **Residenz (Royal Palace)** is just to the east, and the **Theatinerkirche** is to the south. Adjoining the Residenz is the restored **Nationaltheater,** home of the acclaimed Bavarian State Opera and Bavarian National Ballet.

Running west from Odeonsplatz is the wide shopping avenue, Briennerstrasse, leading to **Königsplatz.** Flanking this large Grecian square are three classical buildings constructed by Ludwig I—the **Propyläen,** the **Glyptothek,** and the **Antikensammlungen.** The busy Ludwigstrasse runs north from Odeonsplatz to the section of Munich known as **Schwabing.** This is the Greenwich Village or Latin Quarter of Munich, proud of its artistic and literary heritage. Ibsen and Rilke lived here, as well as members of the Blue Rider group, which influenced abstract art in the early 20th

---

⭐ Frommer's Favorite Munich Experiences

A Morning at the Deutsches Museum. It would take a month to see all of the largest technological museum in the world, but a morning will at least whet your appetite. Everything is here: the first automobile by Benz (1886), the original V-2 rocket (Hitler's secret weapon), the first diesel engine, and plenty of buttons to push.

An Afternoon at Nymphenburg Palace. The Wittelsbach family considered this the best place to be on a hot afternoon—and so might you. The grounds of Germany's largest baroque palace are filled with lakes, waterfalls, and pavilions.

A Night at the Opera (Cuvilliés Theater). It's the most beautiful rococo theater in the world: a small, elaborately gilded tier-boxed structure from the mid–18th century.

A Day in the Beer Gardens. Münchners gather on weekends in summer to down high *masse* of beer and watch the world go by, especially at Chinesischer Turm in the Englischer Garten.

Munich Attractions

Alte Pinakothek **2**
Altes Rathaus **17**
Antikensammlungen **5**
Asamkirche **9**
Bayerisches
  Nationalmuseum **26**
Cuvilliés Theater **23**
Deutsches Museum **13**
Deutsches Theater **8**
Englischer Garten **27**
Frauenkirche **19**
Glyptothek **4**
Haus der Kunst
  (Staatsgalerie
  Moderner Kunst) **25**
Hofgarten **24**
Isartor **14**
Karlstor **6**
Marienplatz **16**
Mathäuskirche **10**
Michaelskirche **7**
Münchner
  Stadtmuseum **11**
Nationaltheater **20**
Neue Pinakothek **1**
Neues Rathaus **18**
Peterskirche **15**
Residenz **21**
Städtische Galerie
  im Lenbachhaus **3**
Theatinerkirche **22**
University **28**
Viktualienmarkt **12**

NYMPHENBURG
Amalienburg **33**
Badenburg **34**
Magdalenenkiause **30**
Marstallmuseum **32**
Pagodenburg **29**
Schloss **31**

‡ Church
(i) Information
✉ Post Office
–O– U-Bahn
–□– S-Bahn

To Olympiapark

← To Nymphenburg
  (see inset)

NYMPHENBURG

29
30
Kleiner See
Nymphenburger Kanal
Schloss
31
Schlosspark
32
Grosser See
33
34
Zuccalistrasse
Richildenstrasse
Hirschgartenstr.

Schackstrasse
Blütenstrasse
Adalbertstrasse
Türkenstrasse
Schellingstrasse
University
Prof.-Veterinärstr.
Huberplatz
28
Ludwigstrasse
Amalienstrasse
Theresienstrasse
Türkenstrasse
Kaulbachstrasse
Königin strasse
Schoenfeldstrasse
Englischer Garten
Oskar-von-Miller- Ring
Von-der-Tann Strasse
Briennerstrasse
27
Galeriestrasse
Theater-museum
Prinzregentenstrasse
25
Lerchenfeld strasse
Oettingenstrasse
Odeons-platz
Hofgarten
24
Unsöldstrasse
26
23
Hofgartenstrasse
Karl-Faulhaber-Strasse
Christophstrasse
K. Scharnagl -Ring
Promenade-platz
Theatinerstrasse
Residenz-strasse
Residenz
St.-Anna-Pfarrstr.
Liebigstrasse
Wagmüllerstr.
Reitmorstrasse
22
21
Marstallstrasse
Thierschstrasse
Sternstrasse
Widenmayerstrasse
Isar
Frauen-platz
Max Joseph-Platz
20
Am Kosttor-Platz
Bürkleinstr.
Pfisterstrasse
Museum für Völkerkunde
Maximilianstrasse
Maximilians-brücke
19
Weinstrasse
18
Dienerstrasse
Judisches Museum München
Knöbelstrasse
Kaufingerstrasse
17
Marien-platz
16
Im Tal
Th.-Wimmer-Ring
15
11
Isartor-platz
12
Westenriederstrasse
14
Kanalstrasse
Frauenstrasse
Zweibrücken strasse
Thierschstrasse
Steinsdorfstrasse
Cornelius strasse
Blumenstrasse
Rumfordstr.
Morassistrasse
Isar
Müllerstr.
Ludwigs-brücke
Innere Weiner Strasse
Baader-platz
Gärtner-platz
Klenzestrasse
Reichenbachstrasse
Baaderstrasse
Erhardtstrasse
Deutsches Museum
Zepplinstrasse
Lilienstrasse
Hochstrasse
Rosenheimerstrasse
Kellerstrasse
Fraunhofer
13
Isar

0   1/5 Mi
0   0.2 Km
N

283

century. Today Schwabing's sidewalk tables are filled with young people from all over the world.

Isartor (Isar Gate) is one of the most-photographed Munich landmarks. It's located east of Marienplatz at Isartorplatz. This is the only tower left from the fortified wall that once encircled Munich. The other major gate of Munich is the **Karlstor,** once known as Neuhauser Tor, lying northeast of Karlsplatz (also called Stachus) at the end of Neuhauserstrasse. It formed part of the town's second circuit of walls, dating from the 1500s. The Karlstor lost its main tower (built 1302) in an 1857 explosion.

MUSEUMS & PALACES

✪ **Alte Pinakothek.** Barerstrasse 27. ☎ **089/23-80-52-16.** Admission 7DM ($3.50) adults, 4DM ($2) students, free for children 14 and under. Daily 10am–5pm (until 8pm Thurs). U-Bahn: Königsplatz. Tram: 27. Bus: 53.

This is one of the most significant art museums in the world. The nearly 900 paintings on display in this huge neoclassical building represent the greatest European artists of the 14th through the 18th centuries. Begun as a small court collection by the royal Wittelsbach family in the early 1500s, the artistic treasure trove grew and grew. There are only two floors with exhibits, but the museum is immense; we do not recommend that you try to cover it all in one day. Pick up a floorplan to guide you through the dozens of rooms.

The following are a few highlights. The landscape painter *par excellence* of the Danube school, Albrecht Altdorfer, is represented by no fewer than six monumental works. Works of Albrecht Dürer include his final, and greatest, *Self-Portrait* (1500). Here the artist has portrayed himself with almost Christ-like solemnity. Also displayed is Dürer's last great painting, a two-paneled work called *The Four Apostles* (1526). Works by Lucas Cranach include his *Venus.*

Several galleries are given over to Dutch and Flemish masters. There are more Rubens here than in any other museum in Europe. Roger van der Weyden's *St. Columbia Altarpiece* (1460–62) measures nearly 3m (10 feet) across, a triumph of his subtle linear style. Rembrandts and Van Dycks are also displayed. French, Spanish, and Italian artists can be found in both the larger galleries and the small rooms lining the outer wall. Note Raphael's *Holy Family* and Leonardo's *Madonna.*

✪ **Residenz.** Max-Joseph-Platz 3. ☎ **089/29-06-71.** Museum and Treasury 8DM ($4) adults, 6DM ($3) students and seniors; Old Residenz Theater 4DM ($2) adults, 2.50DM ($1.25) students; free for children 15 and under. Combined ticket 14DM ($7) adults, 9DM ($4.50) students and children. Museum and Treasury Tues–Sun 10am–4:30pm (last tickets sold at 4pm); Theater daily 10am–4pm. U-Bahn: Odeonsplatz.

When one of the Bavarian royals said that he was going to the castle, he could have meant any number of places, especially if he was Ludwig II. But if he said that he was going home, he could only be referring to the Residenz. This enormous palace, with a history almost as long as that of the Wittelsbach family, was the official residence of the rulers of Bavaria from 1385 to 1918. Added to and rebuilt over the centuries, the complex is a conglomerate of various styles. Depending on how you approach the Residenz, you might first see a German Renaissance hall (the western facade), a Palladian palace (on the north), or a Florentine Renaissance palace (on the south facing Max-Joseph-Platz).

The Residenz has been completely restored since its almost total destruction in World War II and now houses the Residenz Museum, a concert hall, the Cuvilliés Theater, and the Residenz Treasury. The **Residenz Museum** (☎ **089/29-06-71**) comprises the southwestern section of the palace, some 120 rooms of art and furnishings collected by centuries of Wittelsbachs.

The Residenz

Ground Floor

State Collection of Egyptian Art

Four-shaft Room

Court Garden Wing

Hofgartenstrasse

④ Entrance Hall

Festival Hall Building

Bavarian Academy

Stone Room Wing

Imperial Courtyard

Trier Wing

of Science

Battle Room Wing

Apothecaries' Courtyard

③

Hercules Chest

Ladies' Floor

Coin

Collection

Tower Building

Fountain

Foyer

Old Residenz Theater

Old Residenz

Residenzstraße

② ⑥ Chapel Courtyard

Foyer Courtyard ⑤

Apothecaries' Wing

Antler Corridor

Wittelsbach

Cabinet Garden

Vestment Rooms

Grotto Courtyard

Fountain

Ancestoral Gallery

Antiquarium

Courtyard

Ruins of All Saints Church

Royal Building Courtyard

Kitchen Courtyard

Marstallplatz

Nibelungen Rooms ①

Treasury

New Residenz Theater

Royal Building
Max-Joseph-Platz

Upper Floor

Theater Floor

Imperial Hall

New Hercules Room

Theatiner Corridor

Stone Room

Trier Room

Trier Corridor

Charlotte Corridor

Charlottentrakt

Kurfürst's Rooms Wing

Papal Rooms

Rich Rooms

Ludwig I's Rooms

Porcelain Gallery

Battle Rooms

1 Entrance to Residenz Museum
2 Entrance to Chapel Court
3 Entrance to Imperial Court
4 Entrance to Hercules Room
5 Entrance to Old Residenz Theater
  (Cuvilliés Theater)
6 Entrance to Max Joseph Room

285

The **Ancestral Gallery** is designed like a hall of mirrors, except that instead of mirrors, there are portraits of the Wittelsbach family, set into gilded, carved paneling. The largest room in the museum section is the **Antiquarium,** possibly the finest example of interior Renaissance secular styling in Germany. Frescoes adorn nearly every inch of space on the walls and ceilings. The room is broken into sections by pilasters and niches, each with its own bust of a Roman emperor or a Greek hero. The central attraction is the two-story chimneypiece of red stucco and marble, completed in 1600. It's adorned with Tuscan pillars and the coat of arms of the dukes of Bavaria.

On the second floor of the palace, directly over the Antiquarium, is an enormous collection of Far Eastern porcelain. Note also the fine assemblage of Oriental rugs in the long, narrow **Porcelain Gallery.**

If you have time to view only one item in the **Schatzkammer (Treasury),** make it the 16th-century Renaissance statue of *St. George Slaying the Dragon.* This equestrian statue is made of gold, but you can barely see the precious metal for the thousands of diamonds, rubies, emeralds, sapphires, and semiprecious stones embedded in it. Both the Residenz Museum and the Schatzkammer are entered from Max-Joseph-Platz on the south side of the palace.

From the Brunnenhof, you can visit the **Alte Residenztheater** or **Cuvilliés Theater.** This is Germany's most outstanding example of a rococo tier-boxed theater. Directly over the huge center box, where the royal family sat, is a crest in white and gold topped by a jewel-bedecked crown of Bavaria held in place by a group of cherubs in flight. Court architect François de Cuvilliés designed the theater in the mid–18th century (see box under "Munich After Dark," below). During World War II the interior was dismantled and stored. After the war, it was reassembled in the reconstructed building. In summer, this theater is the scene of frequent concert and opera performances. Mozart's *Idomeneo* was first performed here in 1781.

To the north of the Residenz, the Italianate **Hofgarten,** or Court Garden, is one of the special "green lungs" of Munich. The garden was laid out between 1613 and 1617. It's enclosed on two sides by arcades; in the center is the Hofgarten temple, a 12-sided pavilion dating from 1615.

✪ **Bayerisches Nationalmuseum (Bavarian National Museum).** Prinzregentenstrasse 3. ☎ **089/21-12-401.** Admission 6DM ($3) adults, 3.50DM ($1.75) students and seniors, free for children under 15, free for all Sun. Tues–Sun 9:30am–5pm. U-Bahn: Lehel. Tram: 17. Bus: 53.

In 1855, King Maximilian II began an institution to preserve Bavaria's historic and artistic treasures. The collection grew so rapidly that it had to be moved to larger quarters several times over the past 100 years. Its current building, near the Haus der Kunst, contains three vast floors of sculpture, painting, folk art, ceramics, furniture, and textiles, as well as clocks and scientific instruments.

After entering the museum, turn right into the first large gallery, the **Wessobrunn Room,** devoted to early church art from the 5th through the 13th centuries. Some of the museum's oldest and most valuable works are here, including ancient and medieval ivories. The most famous is the Munich ivory from about A.D. 400. At the crossing to the adjoining room is the stone figure, the *Virgin with the Rose Bush,* from Straubing (ca. 1300), one of the few old Bavarian pieces of church art influenced by the spirit of mysticism.

The **Riemenschneider Room** is devoted to the works of the great sculptor Tilman Riemenschneider (1460–1531) and his contemporaries. Characteristic of the sculptor's works is the natural, unpainted wood of his carvings and statuary. Note especially the *12 Apostles from the Marienkapelle in Würzburg* (1510), the central group of the high altar in the parish church of Münnerstadt (1490–92), and the figure of St. Sebastian (1490).

The second floor contains a fine collection of stained and painted glass—an art in which medieval Germany excelled. Other rooms include baroque ivory carvings, Meissen porcelain, and ceramics. Also on display are famous collections of 16th- to 18th-century arms and armor, and the collection of antique clocks, some dating from the 16th century.

✪ **Deutsches Museum (German Museum of Masterpieces of Science and Technology).** Museumsinsel 1 (on an island in the Isar River). ☎ **089/21-791.** Admission 10DM ($5) adults, 7DM ($3.50) seniors, 4DM ($2) students, 3DM ($1.50) children 6–12, free for children 5 and under. Daily 9am–5pm (closes at 2pm the 2nd Wed in Dec). Closed major holidays. S-Bahn: Isartor. Tram: 18.

This is the largest technological museum in the world. Its huge collection of priceless artifacts and historic originals includes the first electric dynamo (Siemens, 1866), the first automobile (Benz, 1886), the first diesel engine (1897), and the laboratory bench at which the atom was first split (Hahn, Strassmann, 1938). There are hundreds of buttons to push, levers to crank, and gears to turn, as well as a knowledgeable, English-speaking staff to answer questions and demonstrate how steam engines, pumps, or historical musical instruments work.

Among the most popular displays are those on mining, with a series of model coal, salt, and iron mines, as well as the electrical power hall, with high-voltage displays that actually produce lightning. There are also exhibits on transportation, printing, photography, and textiles, and halls devoted to air-and-space and high-tech themes. Activities include glassblowing and paper-making demonstrations. The astronomy exhibition is the largest in Europe. A good restaurant and a museum shop are on the premises.

✪ **Schloss Nymphenburg.** Schloss Nymphenburg 1, 8km (5 miles) northwest of the city center. ☎ **089/17-90-86-68.** Admission to castle 7DM ($3.50), free for children under 15. Admission to all attractions 15DM ($7.50), free for children under 15. Nov–Mar daily 10am–4pm; Apr–Oct daily 9am–6pm. Parking beside the Marstallmuseum. U-Bahn: Rotkreuz-platz, then tram 17 toward Amalienburgstrasse. Bus: 41.

In summer, the Wittelsbachs would pack up their bags and head for their country house, Schloss Nymphenburg. A more complete, more sophisticated palace than the Residenz, it was begun in 1664 by Elector Ferdinand Maria in Italian-villa style and took more than 150 years to complete. The final palace plan was created mainly by Elector Max Emanuel, who in 1702 decided to enlarge the villa by adding four large pavilions connected by arcaded passageways. Gradually the French style took over, and today the facade is a subdued baroque.

The palace interior is less subtle, however. Upon entering the main building, you're in the **great hall,** decorated in rococo colors and stuccos. The frescoes by Zimmermann (1756) depict incidents from mythology, especially those dealing with Flora, goddess of nymphs, for whom the palace was named. Concerts are still presented here in summer.

From the main building, turn left and head for the **arcaded gallery** connecting the northern pavilions. The first room in the arcade is the Great Gallery of Beauties, painted in 1710. More provocative, however, is Ludwig I's Gallery of Beauties in the south pavilion. Paintings by J. Stieler (1827 to 1850) include the *Schöne Münchnerin* (*Lovely Munich Girl*) and a portrait of Lola Montez, the dancer whose affair with Ludwig caused a scandal.

To the south of the palace buildings, in the rectangular block of low structures that once housed the court stables, is the **Marstallmuseum.** In the first hall, look for the glass coronation coach of Elector Karl Albrecht, built in Paris in 1740. From the same

Deutsches Museum

Second Floor

Ceramics · Glass · Technical Toys · Paper

Glass-blowing

Writing & Printing

Aeronautics

Special Exhibition

Textile Technology · Photography

First Floor

New Energy Techniques

Physics

Optics

Fraunhofer Room

Brander Room

Hall of Fame

Sailing Wherry

Aeronautics

History of Museum

Industrial Chemistry · Chemistry

Atomic & Nuclear Physics

Musical Instruments

Telecommunications

Ground Floor

Oil & Natural Gas · Surface Mining · Metallurgy · Welding & Soldering

Machine Tools

Turbines · Mineral Resources · Power Machinery

Rescue Cruiser

Entrance Hall

Marine Navigation

Wind Mill

Courtyard

Electrical Power

Museum Shop · Hydraulic Engineering · Roads & Bridges

Vehicle Engineering

Railways

Tunneling Tower

Model Railways · Mountain Railways

Basement

Oil & Gas · Mining

Ore Dressing

Marine Navigation · Power Machinery · Modern Mining

Motor Vehicles

Hydraulic Engineering

Motor Vehicles

period comes the hunting sleigh of Electress Amalia, with the statue of Diana, goddess of the hunt; even the sleigh's runners are decorated with shellwork and hunting trophies.

The coaches and sleighs of Ludwig II are displayed in the **third hall.** His constant longing for the grandeur of the past is reflected in his ornately designed state coach, which was meant for his marriage to Duchess Sophie of Bavaria, a royal wedding that never took place. The fairy-tale coach wasn't wasted, however, since Ludwig often used it to ride through the countryside to one of his many castles, creating quite a picture. The coach is completely gilded, inside and out. In winter the king would use his state sleigh, nearly as elaborate as the Cinderella coach.

Nymphenburg's park stretches for 200ha (500 acres). A canal runs through it from the pool at the foot of the staircase to the cascade at the far end of the English-style gardens. A number of delightful pavilions are in the park: the Amalienburg, Electress Amalia's hunting lodge; the Badenburg Pavilion, a bathing pavilion near the lake of the same name; the Pagodenburg, decorated in chinoiserie style; and the Magdalenenklause (Hermitage), meant to be a retreat for prayer and solitude.

✪ **Staatsgalerie Moderner Kunst (State Gallery of Modern Art).** Haus der Kunst, Prinzregentenstrasse 1. ☎ **089/21-12-71-37.** Staatsgalerie, 6DM ($3) adults, 3.50DM ($1.75) students and seniors. Daily 10am–5pm (until 8pm on Friday). Closed some holidays. U-Bahn: Odeonsplatz. Bus: 53.

Munich's State Gallery of Modern Art is housed in the west wing of the massive Haus der Kunst, which was constructed in 1937. It contains a comprehensive collection of 20th-century art and sculpture. The largest section is devoted to modern German art. You'll see paintings by Klee, Marc, Kirchner, and Beckmann, and by Italian stars such as Marino Marini and Renato Guttoso, as well as works of American abstract expressionism, minimalist art, and more.

The east wing of the **Haus der Kunst,** Prinzregentenstrasse 1 (☎ **089/211-270**), is entered separately and requires a separate ticket. It's devoted to changing exhibitions, which often feature exciting new artists. Traveling exhibitions of worldwide importance stop here. Admission is 12DM ($6) for adults, and 8DM ($4) for children 6 to 18; children 5 and under free. Open daily 10am to 10pm and Friday to Monday 10am to 6pm.

MORE ATTRACTIONS
MUSEUMS
Antikensammlungen (Museum of Antiquities). Königsplatz 1. ☎ **089/59-83-59.** Admission 6DM ($3) adults. Joint ticket to the Museum of Antiquities and the Glyptothek 10DM ($5) adults, free for children under 14, free for everyone on Sun. Tues and Thurs–Sun 10am–5pm, Wed 10am–8pm. U-Bahn: Königsplatz.

This collection grew around the vase collection of Ludwig I, who had fantasies of transforming Munich into a second Athens. It was originally called the Museum Antiker Kleinkunst (Museum of Small Works of Ancient Art). Many pieces are small in size but not in value or artistic significance.

The museum's five main-floor halls house more than 650 Greek vases. The oldest, the pre-Mycenaean "goddess from Aegina" (3000 B.C.), carved from a mussel shell, is in room I. The upper level of the Central Hall is devoted to large Greek vases discovered in Sicily and to Etruscan art. On the lower level is the collection of Greek, Roman, and Etruscan jewelry. (Note the similarities with today's design fashions.) Also on this level are rooms devoted to ancient colored glass, Etruscan bronzes, and Greek terra-cottas.

Glyptothek. Königsplatz 3. ☎ **089/28-61-00.** Admission 6DM ($3) adults, 3.50DM ($1.75) seniors, 1DM (50¢) children. Joint ticket to the Museum of Antiquities and the Glyptothek 10DM ($5) adults, free for children under 14. Tues–Wed and Fri–Sun 10am–5pm, Thurs 10am–8pm. U-Bahn: U2 to Königsplatz.

The ideal neighbor for the Museum of Antiquities, the Glyptothek supplements the pottery and smaller pieces of the main museum with the country's largest collection of ancient Greek and Roman sculpture. Included are the famous pediments from the temple of Aegina, two marvelous statues of *kouroi* (youths) from the 6th century B.C., the colossal figure of a *Sleeping Satyr* from the Hellenistic period, and a splendid collection of Roman portraits.

Münchner Stadtmuseum (Municipal Museum). St. Jacobs-Platz 1. ☎ **089/233-22370.** Admission 8DM ($4) adults, 5DM ($2.50) students and children 6-15 (free 5 and under). Tues–Sun 10am–6pm. U-Bahn/S-Bahn: Marienplatz.

Munich's Municipal Museum offers insight into the city's history and people's daily lives. A wooden model shows Munich in 1572. Special exhibitions about popular arts and traditions are presented frequently. The museum's most important exhibit is its Moorish Dancers (*Moriskentanzer*) on the ground floor. These 10 figures, each 60cm (2 feet) high, carved in wood, and painted in bright colors by Erasmus Grasser in 1480, are among the best examples of secular Gothic art in Germany. The second-floor photo museum traces the early history of the camera back to 1839. Daily at 6 and 9pm, the film museum shows two different films from its extensive archives. The historical collection of musical instruments on the fourth floor is one of the greatest of its kind in the world. The main courtyard has a cafeteria.

Neue Pinakothek. Barerstrasse 29 (across Theresienstrasse from the Alte Pinakothek). ☎ **089/23-80-51-95.** Admission 7DM ($3.50) adults, 4DM ($2) students and seniors. Tues–Sun 10am–5pm (until 8pm on Wed). U-Bahn: Königsplatz. Tram: 27. Bus: 53.

This museum offers a survey of 18th- and 19th-century art, including paintings by Gainsborough, Goya, David, Manet, van Gogh, and Monet. Among the more popular German artists represented are Wilhelm Leibl and Gustav Klimt. Note particularly the genre works by Carl Spitzweg, whose paintings poke gentle fun at everyday life in Munich.

✪ **Stadtische Galerie im Lenbachhaus.** Luisenstrasse 33. ☎ **089/23-33-20-00.** Admission 8DM ($4) adults, 4DM ($2) students and children 6–12, free for children 5 and under. Tues–Sun 10am–6pm. U-Bahn: Königsplatz.

This gallery is in the ancient gold-colored villa of portrait painter Franz von Lenbach (1836–1904). It's devoted both to his work and that of other artists. Enter through the gardens. You'll first be greeted by a large collection of early pieces by Paul Klee (1879–1940). There's also an outstanding group of works by Kandinsky, leader of the Blue Rider movement in the early 20th century, and many 19th- and 20th-century paintings throughout the villa. The enclosed patio is pleasant for a coffee break.

CHURCHES

Munich has many beautiful churches in addition to those listed below. Visitors should not miss the **Asamkirche**, on Sendlinger Strasse (☎ 089/260-93-57; U-Bahn/S-Bahn: Marienplatz), a beautiful rococo church built between 1733 and 1746 and dedicated to St. John of Nepomuk. The **Michaelskirche**, or St. Michael's Church, Neuhauserstrasse 52 (☎ 089/231-7060; U-Bahn/S-Bahn: Marienplatz), is the largest Renaissance church north of the Alps. It was built by Duke William the Pious from 1583 to 1597. Lastly, the **Matthäuskirche**, or St. Matthew's Church, Nussbaumstrasse 1 (U-Bahn: Sendlinger Tor), is a modern Evangelical cathedral completed in 1955.

✪ **Frauenkirche (Cathedral of Our Lady).** Frauenplatz 12. ☎ **089/29-00-82-0.** Free admission. Sat–Thurs 7am–7pm, Fri 7am–6pm. U-Bahn/S-Bahn: Marienplatz.

When the smoke cleared from the 1945 bombings, only a fragile shell remained of Munich's largest church. Workmen and architects who restored the 15th-century Gothic cathedral used whatever remains they could find in the rubble, along with modern innovations. The overall effect of the rebuilt Frauenkirche is strikingly simple, yet dignified. The twin towers with their onion domes, which remained intact, have been the city's landmark since 1525. Instead of the typical flying buttresses, huge props on the inside, which separate the side chapels, support the edifice. Twenty-two simple octagonal pillars support the Gothic vaulting over the nave and chancel.

Entering the main doors, your first impression is that there are no windows (most of them are hidden by the enormous pillars). According to legend, the devil laughed at the notion of hidden windows and stamped in glee at the stupidity of the architect— you can still see the strange footlike mark called "the devil's step" in the entrance hall. In the chapel directly behind the high altar is the cathedral's most interesting painting: Jan Polack's *The Protecting Cloak* (1510), showing the Virgin holding out her majestic robes to shelter all humankind. The collection of tiny figures beneath the cloak includes everyone from the Pope to peasants.

Peterskirche (St. Peter's Church). Rindermarkt 1 (near the Rathaus). ☎ **089/ 2-60-48-28.** Church free; tower 2.50DM ($1.25) adults, 1.50DM (75¢) students, 50pf (25¢) children. Apr–Oct daily 8am–7pm (or even longer); Nov–Mar daily 8am–6pm. U-Bahn/ S-Bahn: Marienplatz.

Munich's oldest church (1180), known locally as Old Peter, has turned over a new leaf, and it's a gold one at that. The white-and-gray interior has been decorated with gilded baroque accents and trompe l'oeil medallions. It contains a series of murals by Johann Baptist Zimmermann, but nothing tops the attraction of the bizarre relic in the second chapel on the left: the gilt-covered and gem-studded skeleton of St. Mundita. From its resting place on a cushion, it stares at you with two false eyes in its skull. Jewels cover the mouth of its rotten teeth, quite a contrast to the fresh roses usually kept in front of the black-and-silver coffin. The church also has a tall steeple, which you can climb, though it lacks an elevator. Colored circles on the lower platform tell you whether the climb is worthwhile: If the circle is white, you can see as far as the Alps.

Theatinerkirche. Theatinerstrasse 22. ☎ **089/21-06-96-0.** Free admission. Church daily 6am–7:30pm; crypt May–Nov 1, Mon–Fri 10am–1pm and 2–4:30pm, Sat 10am–3pm. U-Bahn: Odeonsplatz.

Named for a small group of Roman Catholic clergy (the Theatines), this church, dedicated to Saint Kajetan, is Munich's finest example of Italian baroque. Two Italian architects, Barelli and Zucalli, began building it in 1662. François de Cuvilliés the Elder added the facade a century later, and his son finally completed the structure in 1768. Fluted columns that line the center aisle support the arched ceiling of the nave. Above the transept, dividing the nave from the choir, the ceiling breaks into an open dome, with an ornate gallery decorated with large but graceful statues. Nothing detracts from the whiteness of the interior except the dark wooden pews and the canopied pulpit. Since 1954 the church has been under the care of the Dominican Friars.

PARKS & ZOOS

Munich's city park, the 18th-century **Englischer Garten,** borders Schwabing on the east and extends almost to the Isar River. This is one of the largest and most beautiful city parks in Germany. It was the brainchild of Sir Benjamin Thompson, the English scientist who spent most of his life in the service of the Bavarian government. You can wander for hours along the walks and among the trees, flowers, and sunbathers. Nude sunbathing is permitted in certain areas of the park (some claim these areas are Munich's most popular tourist attraction). For a break, stop for tea on the plaza near the Chinese pagoda, or have a beer at the nearby beer garden. You might also take along a picnic put together at the elegant shop of **Alois Dallmayr,** or less expensive fare from **Hertie,** across from the Hauptbahnhof, from **Kaufhof** at Marienplatz, or from Munich's famous open-air market, the **Viktualienmarkt.**

Hellabrunn Zoo stands in Tierpark Hellabrunn, about 6km (4 miles) south of the city center, at Tierparkstrasse 30 (☎ **089/62-50-80;** U-Bahn: Thalkirchen; bus: 52). It's one of the largest zoos in the world, with hundreds of animals roaming in a natural habitat. A walk through the attractive park is recommended even if you're not a zoo buff. There's a big children's zoo, as well as a large aviary. You can visit the zoo daily 8am to 6pm (in winter, 9am to 5pm); admission is 12DM ($6) for adults, 9DM ($4.50) for students and seniors, 6DM ($3) for children ages 4 to 14, and free for children 3 and under.

THE OLYMPIC GROUNDS

Olympiapark (☎ **089/30-67-24-14;** U-Bahn: Olympiazentrum), site of the 1972 Olympic Games, occupies 300ha (740 acres) at the city's northern edge. More than 15,000 workers from 18 countries transformed the site into a park of nearly 5,000 trees, 43km (27 miles) of roads, 32 bridges, and a lake. Olympiapark has its own railway station, U-Bahn line, mayor, post office, churches, and elementary school. The planners even broke the city skyline by adding a 293m (960-foot) television tower in the center of the park.

The area's showpiece is a huge stadium, capable of seating 69,300 spectators, and topped by the largest roof in the world—nearly 67,000m² (80,000 square yards) of tinted acrylic glass. The supports for the stadium are anchored by two huge blocks, each capable of resisting 4,000 tons under stress. The roof serves the additional purpose of collecting rainwater and draining it into the nearby Olympic lake.

Olympia Tower, Olympiapark (☎ **089/30-67-27-50**), is open daily 9am to midnight. A ticket for a ride up the tower (on the speediest elevator on the continent, no less) costs 5DM ($2.85) for adults and 2.50DM ($1.25) for children under 15. An exclusive dining spot in the tower is the **Tower Restaurant** (☎ **089/30668585**), which features a selection of international and German dishes. Food is served daily 11am to 5:30pm and 6:30pm to midnight. A complete dinner costs 65DM to 78DM ($32.50 to $39). Before or after dinner, you'll want to take in the extraordinary view, which reaches to the Alps. Four observation platforms look out over Olympiapark. The Tower Restaurant revolves around its axis in 60 minutes, giving guests who linger a changing vista of Munich. American Express, Diners Club, MasterCard, and Visa are accepted.

At the base of the tower is the **Restaurant Olympiasee,** Spiridon-Louis-Ring 7 (☎ **089/30-67-28-08**), serving genuine Bavarian specialties, with meals costing 10DM ($5) and up. Food is served daily 9:30am to 7pm (9pm in summer). The restaurant is popular in summer because of its terrace. No credit cards are accepted.

Near Olympiapark, you can visit the **BMW Museum,** Petuelring 130 (☎ **089/ 38-22-33-07;** U-Bahn: Petuelring or Olympiazentrum), where the history of the automobile is stunningly displayed in an atmosphere created by Oscar-winner Rolf Zehetbauer, a "film architect." The exhibition "Horizons in Time," housed in a demisphere of modern architecture, takes you into the future and back to the past. You can view 24 video films and 10 slide shows (an especially interesting one shows how people of yesterday imagined the future). Many of the exhibits are in English. The museum is open daily 9am to 5pm, charging 5.50DM ($2.75) for adults and 4DM ($2) for children. While here, you might also ask about BMW factory tours.

ESPECIALLY FOR KIDS

Of all the museums in Munich, kids will like best the **Deutsches Museum,** Museumsinsel 1 (☎ **089/2-17-91;** S-Bahn: Isartor; tram: 18), which has many "hands-on" exhibits. For details, see "The Top Attractions," above.

On the third floor of the **Münchner Stadtmuseum,** St. Jakobsplatz 1 (☎ **089/ 23-32-23-70;** U-Bahn/S-Bahn: Marienplatz), is an array of marionettes and hand puppets from around the world. Another special department is devoted to fairground art, including carousel animals, shooting galleries, roller-coaster models, and wax and museum figures. The main exhibit contains the oldest-known carousel horses, dating from 1820. For hours and admission fees, see "More Attractions," above.

Spielzeugmuseum, in the Altes Rathaus, Marienplatz 15 (☎ **089/29-40-01;** U-Bahn/S-Bahn: Marienplatz), is a historical toy collection. It's open daily 10am to 5:30pm. Admission is 5DM ($2.50) for adults, 1DM (50¢) for children, and 10DM ($5) for a family.

For a truly charming experience, go to the **Münchener Marionetten Theater,** Blumenstrasse 32 (☎ **089/26-57-12;** U-Bahn/S-Bahn: Marienplatz), which was established in 1858. It stages marionette productions of operas by Mozart and other composers every Wednesday, Thursday, Saturday, and Sunday at 3pm, and every Saturday at 8pm. At matinees adults pay 9DM ($4.50) entrance; children 7DM ($3.50). At evening shows tickets for both adults and children go for 16DM ($8). Matinees tend to be more animated and crowded than evening shows, and are particularly well-suited for younger children ages 4 and up.

Bavaria Film Studio, Bavariafilmplatz 7, Geiselgasteig (☎ **089/64-99-23-04;** tram: 25 to Bavariafilmplatz), is Europe's largest filmmaking center—Munich's version of Hollywood. Visitors can watch such spine-tingling thrillers as *Adventure in the Devil's Mine* and *Cosmic Pinball.* The 30-minute Bavaria Action Show features a stunt team demonstrating fist fights and fire stunts, tumbling down staircases, and even taking a 28m-(92-foot-) high plunge. Guided 1 1/2-hour tours (some in English) are given March to October, daily 9am to 4pm (off-season 10am to 3pm). Admission is 17DM ($8.50) for adults, 15DM ($7.50) for students and senior citizens, 12DM ($6) for children ages 4 to 14, and free for children 3 and under.

Hellabrunn Zoo has a large children's zoo, where kids can pet the animals. For details, see "More Attractions," above.

6 Organized Tours

BY BUS

Blue buses that give sightseeing tours in both German and English leave from the square in front of the Hauptbahnhof, at Hertie's, year-round. Tickets are sold on the bus; no advance booking is necessary. A 1-hour tour, costing 19DM ($9.50) for adults and 10DM ($5) for children 6 to 12, leaves daily May to October at 10am, 11:30am, 1pm, 2:30pm, and 4pm; November to April, daily at 10am and 2:30pm.

A 2 1/2-hour tour, including the Olympic Tower, costs 33DM ($16.50) for adults and 17DM ($8.50) for children. Departures are May to October at 10am and 2:30pm and November to April at 10am and 2:30pm.

A second 2 1/2-hour tour, costing 33DM ($16.50) for adults and 17DM ($8.50) for children, visits the famous Neue Pinakothek (painting gallery), the Frauenkirche, and the chiming clocks at Marienplatz. It departs Tuesday to Sunday at 10am.

A third 2¹/₂-hour tour, costing 33DM ($16.50) for adults and 17DM ($8.50) for children, visits Nymphenburg Palace and the Schatzkammer. It departs daily at 2:30pm.

If you'd like to go farther afield and visit major attractions in the environs (such as Berchtesgaden or Ludwig II's castles), contact **Panorama Tours.** The office is at Arnulfstrasse 8 (☎ **089/54-90-75-60**), to the north of the Hauptbahnhof. Hours are Monday to Friday 7:30am to 6pm, Saturday 7:30am to 1pm, and Sunday and holidays 7:30 to 10am.

BY BIKE

Pedal pushers will want to try Mike Lasher's popular **Mike's Bike Tour,** St. Bonifatiusstrasse 2 (☎ **089/6-51-42-75**). His bike-rental services include maps and locks, child and infant seats, and helmets at no extra charge. English and bilingual tours of central Munich run from March through November at 11:30am and 4pm daily (call to confirm). Customers love Mike's charm. Participants meet under the tower of the old town hall, a gray building on the east end of Marienplatz. Mike, the consummate guide, will be here—whistle in mouth—letting everyone know who he is. The tour veers from the bike paths only long enough for a lunch stop at a beer garden. Fear not, fainthearted: the bikes are new and the rides are easy, with plenty of time for historical explanations, photo opportunities, and question-and-answer sessions. Bike rentals for tours without a guide (Mike will supply a map) are 30DM ($15) for the day; full-day guided tours begin at 50DM ($25).

7 Sports & Outdoor Pursuits

BEACHES, POOLS & WATER SPORTS

On hot weekends, much of Munich embarks for nearby lakes, the **Ammersee** and the **Starnbergersee,** where bathing facilities are clearly marked. You can also swim at **Maria-Einsiedel,** in the frigid, snow-fed waters of the Isar River. The city has several public swimming pools as well. The largest of these includes the giant competition-size pool in the Olympiapark, the **Olympia-Schwimmhalle** (☎ **089/30-67-22-90;** U-Bahn: Olympiazentrum). Admission is 14DM ($7.40). Information on both sailing and windsurfing is available from the **Bayerischer Segler-Verbund,** Georg-Brauchle-Ring 93 (☎ **089/15-70-23-66**).

FITNESS CENTERS & HEALTH CLUBS

Several of Munich's larger hotels have installed their own state-of-the-art exercise equipment. There also are gyms and health clubs scattered throughout the city, and many sell temporary passes to newcomers. For information, ask your hotel receptionist or contact the **Bayerischer Landes-sportverbund,** Georg-Brauchle-Ring 93 (☎ **089/15-70-20**).

ICE-SKATING

During winter's coldest months, a lake in the Englischer Garten freezes over and is opened to ice-skaters. Also blocked off for skaters is a section of the Nymphenburger Canal, near the palace. Be alert to the GEFAHR (danger) signs that are posted whenever temperatures rise and the ice becomes too thin. The indoor rink is the **Olympic Icestadium** in the Olympiapark, Spiridon-Louis-Ring 3 (☎ **089/30-67-21-50;** U-Bahn: Olympiazentrum).

JOGGING

Regardless of the season, the most lushly landscaped place in Munich is the **Englischer Garten** (U-Bahn: Münchner Freiheit), which has a 11km (7-mile) circumference and an array of dirt and asphalt tracks. Also appropriate are the grounds of the **Olympiapark** (U-Bahn: Olympiazentrum), or the park surrounding **Schloss Nymphenburg** (U-Bahn: Rotkreuzplatz, then tram 17 toward Amalienburgstrasse; bus: 41). More convenient to the center of the city's commercial district is a jog along the embankments of the Isar River.

RAFTING

Raft trips on the Isar River are conducted between the town of Wolfratshausen and Munich early May to late September. Be advised that a raft may contain up to 60 other passengers. If you still want to try it, call **Franz and Sebastian Seitner,** Heideweg 9, 82515 Wolfratshausen (☎ **08171/1-83-20**).

ROWING

Rowboats add to the charm of the lakes in the **Englischer Garten.** There's a kiosk at the edge of the Kleinhesseloher See where you can rent them. There are also rowboat rentals on the southern bank of the **Olympiasee,** in the Olympiapark.

SKIING

Because of the proximity of the Bavarian and Austrian Alps, many Munich residents are avid skiers. For information on resorts and getaway snow-related activities, contact the **Bayerischer Segler-Verbund,** Georg-Brauchle-Ring 93, 80992 München (☎ **089/ 15-70-23-66**).

SPECTATOR SPORTS

Munich loves soccer and has one of Europe's outstanding teams, **Bayern München,** which plays at the Olympic Stadium in Olympiapark. If you want to attend a match, call ☎ **089/54-81—81-81**.

TENNIS

At least 200 indoor and outdoor tennis courts are scattered around greater Munich. Many can be booked in advance by calling **089/54-81-81-81**. For information on Munich's many tennis tournaments and competitions, contact the **Bayerischer Tennis Verbund,** Georg-Brauchle-Ring 93, 80992 München (☎ **089/15-70-23-66**).

8 Shopping

The most interesting shops are concentrated on Munich's pedestrians-only street, between Karlsplatz and Marienplatz. Store hours in Munich are generally Monday to Friday 9 or 9:30am to 6pm and Saturday 9 or 9:30am to 1 or 2pm.

ANTIQUES

Philographikon Galerie Rauhut. Maximilianstrasse 15. ☎ **089/22-50-82.** U-Bahn/ S-Bahn: Marienplatz.

This important gallery, set midway between the Hotel Vier Jahreszeiten and the National Opera House, represents one of the most celebrated success stories of Munich's art world. In 1978, Mr. Rauhut, a television producer, transformed his hobby of collecting rare engravings and manuscripts into a career by establishing this shop. Here you'll find one of the most comprehensive collections of antique art in

Munich. Prices range from 50DM ($25) for a 19th-century steel engraving, to tens of thousands of deutschmarks for pre-Gutenberg illuminated manuscripts. Other curiosities include antique maps; English, French, and German botanical prints; and a series of rare prints by a Swiss-born engraver, Karl Bodmer, whose depictions in the 1820s of native American Indians are increasingly valuable on both sides of the Atlantic.

Squirrel. Schellingstrasse 54. ☎ **089/2-72-09-29.** U-Bahn: Universität.

This unusual shop, established 20 years ago by its charming owners, Urban Geissel and his wife, Gisela, houses a collection of luggage made by English and French purveyors for the aristocrats of the Jazz Age. There are examples from such English makers as Finnegan's and Harrods. Although they tend to be heavy, they're still serviceable and richly imbued with the nostalgia of the great days of oceangoing travel.

ART

Galerie für Angewandte Kunst München. Pacellistrasse 8. ☎ **089/2-90-14-70.** U-Bahn: Karlsplatz.

This is one of Germany's largest, most visible, and most historic art galleries, established in the 1840s as a showcase for local artists. The complex contains an upscale art gallery and a sales outlet, the Ladengeschäft, where attractive crafts are sold at prices that begin at 40DM ($20). Works by more than 400 artists are displayed and sold here. Examples include sculpture in all kinds of media, crafts, textiles, and woven objects.

BOOKS

Hugendubel. Marienplatz 22. ☎ **01803/484-484.** U-Bahn/S-Bahn: Marienplatz.

Not only is this Munich's biggest bookstore, but it also enjoys the most central location. It sells a number of English-language titles, both fiction and nonfiction, and also offers travel books and helpful maps.

CHINA, SILVER & GLASS

Kunstring Meissen. Briennerstrasse 4. ☎ **089/28-15-32.** U-Bahn: Odeonsplatz.

During the coldest days of the Cold War, this was Munich's exclusive distributor of Meissen and Dresden china, manufactured behind the Iron Curtain in East Germany. With reunification, Kunstring's exclusive access became a thing of the past. Despite that, the shop still contains one of Munich's largest inventories of the elegant porcelain.

✪ **Rosenthal.** Dienerstrasse 17. ☎ **089/22-26-17.** U-Bahn/S-Bahn: Marienplatz.

Rosenthal, established in 1879 in the Bavarian town of Selb near the Czech border, is one of the three or four most prestigious names in German porcelain. Much (though not all) of the line today focuses on contemporary design, an approach that separates it from the more traditional ways of Nymphenburg, Sevrès, or Limoges. The manufacturer pre-establishes prices for Rosenthal patterns and maintains them rigidly, so there are no price breaks at this factory outlet. You will, however, find the widest array of Rosenthal patterns available in Germany. In addition to porcelain, the line includes furniture, glass, and cutlery.

CRAFTS

Bayerischer Kunstgewerbeverein (Bavarian Association of Artisans). Pacellistrasse 6–8. ☎ **089/2-90-14-70.** U-Bahn: Karlsplatz.

At this showcase for Bavarian artisans, you'll find excellent handcrafts: ceramics, glasses, jewelry, wood carvings, pewter, and seasonal Christmas decorations.

✪ **Ludwig Mory.** Marienplatz 8. ☎ **089/22-45-42.** U-Bahn/S-Bahn: Marienplatz.

This shop, located near the cathedral, is the most famous purveyor of Bavarian beer steins in Munich, in business since the 1830s. After seeing it, you'll never want to drink Budweiser from a can again. The steins range from 100DM ($50) for an honest but unpretentious souvenir to much more for a richly decorative work of art that might round off a private collection.

Otto Kellnberger Holzhandlung. Heiliggeistrasse 8. ☎ **089/22-64-79.** U-Bahn/S-Bahn: Marienplatz.

This small but choice emporium of traditional wood carvings evokes remote alpine Bavaria. Its inventory features all the folkloric charm and much of the folkloric kitsch you might find in remote Oberammergau.

Prinoth. Guido Schneblestrasse 9A. ☎ **089/56-03-78.** U-Bahn: Laimerplatz.

Most of the wood carvings sold here are produced in small workshops in the folklore-rich Italian South Tyrol. The selection is wide-ranging, and since the shop is 6km (3½ miles) west of Munich's tourist zones, prices are reasonable compared to those of shops closer to the Marienplatz.

✪ **Wallach.** Residenzstrasse 3. ☎ **089/22-08-71.** U-Bahn/S-Bahn: Marienplatz.

We consider Wallach the finest place in Germany for handcrafts, both new and antique, as well as folk art. Shop here for a memorable object to remind you of your trip. You'll find antique churns, old hand-painted wooden boxes and trays, milking stools, painted porcelain clocks, dirndls, leather pants, wooden wall clocks, doilies, napkins, towels, and more.

DEPARTMENT STORES

Hertie. Bahnhofplatz 7. ☎ **089/5-51-20.** U-Bahn/S-Bahn: Hauptbahnhof.

This is our favorite department store in Munich, a sprawling four-story-plus basement emporium of all aspects of the German version of the good life. A fixture near the main railway station since the turn of the century, it has survived wars and revolutions with predictable mercantile style.

Kaufhof. Marienplatz. ☎ **089/23-18-51.** U-Bahn/S-Bahn: Marienplatz.

This is one of the largest department stores in town. You can wander freely among displays that are art forms in their own right. The inventory includes virtually everything, from men's, women's, and children's clothing to housewares, and much more.

Ludwig Beck am Rathauseck. Am Marienplatz 11. ☎ **089/23-69-10.** U-Bahn/S-Bahn: Marienplatz.

Most merchandise here is intended for local residents; however, visitors will also be interested in this four-floor shopping bazaar, which sells handmade crafts from all over Germany, both old and new. Items include decorative pottery and dishes, etched-glass beer steins and vases, painted wall plaques, decorative flower arrangements, unusual kitchenware, fashions, textiles, and much more.

ENGRAVINGS & POSTCARDS

Philatelie und Ansichtskarten. Bahnhofplatz 2. ☎ **089/59-67-57.** U-Bahn: Bahnhofplatz.

It doesn't really look like a shop at all, but rather like a dusty storeroom at a museum. It's the rendezvous for academics and collectors from throughout Germany, who phone in special requests for antique engravings and postcards that depict specific settings, personalities, and places. Merchandise, each piece carefully inventoried and stored in cardboard boxes arranged by subject, ranges from the sober to the schmaltzy.

FASHION

Bogner Haus. Residenzstrasse 15. ☎ **089/2-90-70-40.** U-Bahn/S-Bahn: Marienplatz.

Before you head for the slopes, shop here for the latest in ski clothing and styles. Willy Bogner, the filmmaker and Olympic downhill racer, sells this flamboyant attire. The store also sells more formal clothing for men and women.

✪ **Dirndl-Ecke.** Am Platzl 1/Sparkassenstrasse 10. ☎ **089/22-01-63.** U-Bahn/S-Bahn: Marienplatz.

One block up from the famed Hofbräuhaus, this shop gets our unreserved recommendation. It's a stylish place specializing in high-grade dirndls, feathered alpine hats, and all clothing associated with the alpine regions. Everything sold is of fine quality—there's no tourist junk. Other merchandise includes needlework hats, beaded belts, and pleated shirts for men. Be sure to see the stylish capes, the silver jewelry in old Bavarian style, the leather shoes, and the linen-and-cotton combinations, such as skirts with blouses and jackets. Bavarian clothing for children is also available.

Exatmo. Franz-Josef-Strasse 35. ☎ **089/33-57-61.** U-Bahn: Giselastrasse.

Only a district like Schwabing could sustain a business like this, one of the most unusual clothiers in Munich. It operates from a showroom complete with mock-medieval murals. Among the racks of clothing are garments inspired by the puffy sleeves and dramatic flair of 17th-century fashions. The store purchases old pieces of linen, such as bed sheets from army surplus inventories across Europe, for reconfiguration into jackets, vests, and ruffled shirts that hang beautifully. Elizabethans would have loved these styles. A second branch, located across from the Hofbräuhaus, is at Platzl-Pfisterstrasse 11 (☎ **089/29161531;** U-Bahn/S-Bahn: Marienplatz).

Frankonia. Maximiliansplatz 10. ☎ **089/2-90-00-20.** Tram: 19.

This store, established in 1907, has Munich's most prestigious collection of traditional Bavarian dress (called *Tracht*). If you see yourself dressed hunter style, or in traditional alpine garb, this place can outfit you well. There's a fine collection of wool cardigan jackets with silvery buttons.

Furore. Franz-Josef-Strasse 41. ☎ **089/34-39-71.** U-Bahn: Giselastrasse.

If you're shopping for fashionable undergarments (brassieres, *bustiers,* slips), and if you've been working out at the gym and look fabulous, this is the place for you. The designs are tasteful, in some cases filmy and subtly erotic, in silk, cotton, and synthetics. There's also a loungewear collection.

Loden-Frey. Maffeistrasse 7–9. ☎ **089/21039-0.** U-Bahn/S-Bahn: Marienplatz.

You can see the twin domes of the Frauenkirche above the soaring glass-enclosed atrium of this shop's showroom. Go here for the world's largest selection of loden clothing and traditional costumes, as well as for international fashions from top European designers such as Armani, Valentino, and Ungaro.

Maendler. Theatinerstrasse 7. ☎ **089/2-91-33-22.** U-Bahn: Odeonsplatz.

This store is divided into a series of boutiques well known to virtually every well-dressed woman in Bavaria. You'll find the creative vision of Joop, New York New York, and Jil Sander here. Looking for that special something for your dinner with the mayor or the president of Germany? Ask to see formal eveningwear by Jean-Paul Gaultier. For something more experimental and daring, head for the branch called

Rosy Maendler, Maximiliansplatz 12 (same phone; tram: 19), where you'll find a more youthful version of the same store.

Red/Green of Scandinavia. Kaufingerstrasse 9. ☎ **089/2-60-64-89.** U-Bahn/S-Bahn: Marienplatz.

This shop near the Marienplatz sells men's and women's relaxed, casual clothing, appropriate for wearing on a private yacht or the local golf links. Most of the inventory comes from Denmark, and since everything was designed to withstand the blustery winds and the clear sunlight of the Baltic, they're study enough for any activity.

FOOD
✪ **Dallmayr.** Dienerstrasse 14–15. ☎ **089/2-13-50.** Tram: 19.

What Fortnum & Mason is to London, the venerable firm of Dallmayr is to Munich. Gastronomes as far away as Hamburg and Berlin telephone orders for exotica not readily available anywhere else. Dallmayr's list of prestigious clients reads like a who's who of German industry and letters. Wander freely among racks of foodstuffs, some of which are too delicate to survive shipment abroad, others of which can be shipped anywhere.

JEWELRY & WATCHES
Carl Jagemann's. Residenzstrasse 3. ☎ **089/22-54-93.** U-Bahn/S-Bahn: Marienplatz.

Its reputation for quality and honesty goes back to 1864, as does some (but not all) of the merchandise it sells. It's one of the Altstadt's largest purveyors of new and antique timepieces of all types, from wristwatches to fine reproduction grandfather clocks. There's also a collection of new and antique jewelry.

Hemmerle. Maximilianstrasse 14. ☎ **089/24-22-60-0.** U-Bahn/S-Bahn: Marienplatz.

This is *the* place for jewelry. The original founders of this conservative shop made their fortune designing bejeweled fantasies for the Royal Bavarian Court of Ludwig II. All pieces are limited editions, designed and made in-house by Bavarian craftspeople. The company also designs its own wristwatch, the Hemmerle.

MUSIC
Hieber Musikhaus. In the Rathaus, Landschaftstrasse. ☎ **089/29-00-80-40.** U-Bahn/S-Bahn: Marienplatz.

This is the largest music store in Munich, and with a history going back to 1884, it's also one of the oldest. Its stock of librettos for operas by Wagner, Mozart, Puccini, and Verdi are among the most extensive anywhere.

PORCELAIN
✪ **Porzellan-Manufaktur-Nymphenburg.** Nordliches Schlossrondell 8. ☎ **089/1-79-19-70.** Bus: 41.

At Nymphenburg, about 8km (5 miles) northwest of the heart of Munich, you'll find one of Germany's most famous porcelain factories, on the grounds of Schloss Nymphenburg. You can visit its exhibition and sales rooms, Monday to Friday 8:30am to 5pm. Shipments can be arranged if you make purchases. There's also a more central branch in Munich's center at Odeonsplatz 1 (☎ **089/28-24-28;** U-Bahn: Odeonsplatz).

TOYS
Münchner Poupenstuben und Zinnfiguren Kabinette. Maxburgstrasse 4. ☎ **089/29-37-97.** U-Bahn: Karlsplatz.

This is Germany's oldest miniature pewter foundry, dating from 1796. Many Germans visit Munich every December to purchase traditional Christmas decorations of a type once sold to Maximilian I, king of Bavaria. Managed by matriarchs of the same family, this store is one of the best sources in Germany for miniature houses, furniture, birdcages, and people, all cunningly crafted from pewter or carved wood. Some of the figures are made from 150-year-old molds that are collector's items in their own right. Anything in this place would make a great gift not only for a child but also for an adult with a nostalgic bent.

Obletter's. Karlsplatz 11. ☎ **089/55089510.** U-Bahn: Karlsplatz.

Established in the 1880s, this is one of the largest emporiums of children's toys in Munich. The two floors of inventory contain everything from folkloric dolls to computer games.

WINE

Geisel's Vinothek. Schützenstrasse 11. ☎ **089/55-13-71-40.** U-Bahn/S-Bahn: Hauptbahnhof.

Other than Dallmayr (see "Food," above), which has a much larger scale, this is the most sophisticated wine shop in Munich. Its inventory includes wines from Germany, Austria, Italy, and France, with bottles starting at 15DM ($7.50). The shop also doubles as a restaurant.

9 Munich After Dark

To find out what's happening in the Bavarian capital, go to the tourist office on Platform 12 at the Hauptbahnhof (☎ 089/2-33-03-00) and request a copy of *Monatsprogramm,* costing 2.50DM ($1.40). It contains a complete cultural guide, telling you not only what's being presented—including concerts, opera, special exhibits, and museum hours—but also how to purchase tickets.

THE PERFORMING ARTS

Nowhere else in Europe, other than London and Paris, will you find so many musical and theatrical events. And the good news is that seats don't cost a fortune—so count on indulging yourself and going to several performances. You'll get good tickets for anything from 15DM to 75DM ($7.50 to $37.50).

If you speak German, you'll find at least 20 theaters offering plays of every description: classic, comic, experimental, contemporary—take your pick. The best way to find out what current productions might interest you is to go to a theater-ticket agency. Head for **WOM (World of Music),** Kaufingerstrasse 15 (☎ 089/2601-9100; S-Bahn: Marienplatz). WOM's leading competitors include **München Tickets** (☎ 089/54-81-81-81) and **Hieber am Dom** (☎ 089/2900-8014), both of which deal in tickets to basically the same cultural, entertainment, and sporting events within Bavaria, with access to the same computer database. Unfortunately, the use of a credit card for payment, both at WOM and at its competitors, carries a surcharge of at least 20DM ($10) per order. Be advised that for some sporting events (such as soccer) and musical events (including most of the operas subsidized by the city of Munich), where season tickets and long-term subscriptions reduce availability, you'll have to go to the venue's box office, as organizers tend not to cooperate with outside ticket agencies.

✪ **Altes Residenztheater (Cuvilliés Theater).** Residenzstrasse 1. ☎ **089/2185-1940,** or 089/21-85-19-20 for ticket information. Opera tickets 30DM–255DM ($15–$127.50); play tickets 20DM–80DM ($10–$40). U-Bahn: Odeonplatz.

François Cuvilliés

In the 17th and 18th centuries, Bavaria's rulers were determined to rival Rome itself. They adorned their city with churches, abbeys, and monuments. In the cutthroat competition for commissions that followed, an unlikely candidate emerged for the role of Munich's most brilliant master of the rococo style.

François Cuvilliés (1695–1768) was a dwarf born in Belgium. Like many of his peers, he became first a page boy and later court jester to Max Emanuel, elector of Bavaria. When the elector was exiled, François accompanied him, and in St-Cloud near Paris, he absorbed his patron's interest in the aesthetics of French baroque architecture. Ambitious and witty, he won Max Emanuel's friendship and support. When the elector was reinstated with pomp and ceremony as ruler of Bavaria, François became a draftsman for the court's chief architect.

Cuvilliés proved himself so talented that in 1720 Max Emanuel sent him for a 4-year apprenticeship to one of the leading architects of Paris, Jacques-François Blondel. After his return to Munich, his work soon eclipsed that of his master. By 1745, the former jester had been elevated to the title of chief architect to the Bavarian court.

His commissions between 1726 and his death in 1768 include some of southern Germany's most important rococo monuments, such as the interior of the **Amalienburg Pavilion** in the park of Nymphenburg Palace and the facade of the **Theatinerkirche.** His most famous creation is the remarkable **Altes Residenztheater,** familiarly called by his name. All his work is notable for a flamboyant sinuousness.

Cuvilliés' son, François Cuvilliés the Younger (1731–77), also became an architect, although he never achieved the greatness of his father. Most notably, he put the finishing touches on the facade of the **Theatinerkirche,** which his father had left unfinished at his death.

An attraction in itself (see "Residenz" in "The Top Attractions," above), this is also an important performance venue. The **Bavarian State Opera** (☎ 089/21-85-19-19) and the **Bayerisches Staatsschauspiel** (☎ 089/2185-1920), perform smaller works here, in keeping with the tiny theater's more intimate character. Box-office hours are the same as those for the Nationaltheater (see "Bayerischen Staatsoper," below).

✪ **Bayerischen Staatsoper.** Performing in the Nationaltheater, Max-Joseph-Platz 2. ☎ **089/2185-1920.** Tickets 12DM–285DM ($6–$142.50), including standing room. U-Bahn/S-Bahn: Marienplatz.

The **Bavarian State Opera** is one of the world's great companies. The Bavarians give their hearts and souls to opera. Productions here are beautifully mounted and presented, and the company's roster includes some of the world's greatest singers. Hard-to-get tickets may be purchased at the box office Monday to Friday 10am to 6pm and Saturday 10am to 1pm, plus 1 hour before each performance. The Nationaltheater is also the home of the **Bavarian State Ballet.**

Bayerisches Staatsschauspiel (State Theater). Max-Joseph-Platz. ☎ **089/21-85-19-40.** Tickets 20DM–65DM ($10–$32.50). U-Bahn/S-Bahn: Marienplatz.

This repertory company is known for its performances of the classics: Shakespeare as well as Goethe and Schiller, and others. The box office, around the corner on

Maximilianstrasse, is open Monday to Friday 10am to 6pm, Saturday 10am to 1pm, and 1 hour before performances.

Deutsches Theater. Schwanthalerstrasse 13. ☎ **089/55-23-44-44.** Tickets 29DM–30DM ($14.50–$15); higher for special events. U-Bahn/S-Bahn: Karlsplatz/Stachus.

Musicals are popular here, but operettas, ballets, and international shows are performed as well. During Carnival in January and February, the theater becomes a ballroom—the costume balls and official black-tie festivities here are famous throughout Europe.

Münchner Kammerspiele. Maximilianstrasse 26–28. ☎ **089/233-3700.** Tickets 10.50DM–47.50DM ($5.25–$23.75). U-Bahn: Marienplatz. S-Bahn: Isartor. Tram: 19.

Contemporary plays as well as classics are performed here. The season runs early October to July. You can reserve tickets by phone Monday to Friday 10am to 6pm, but you must pick them up at least 2 days before a performance. The box office is open Monday to Friday 10am to 6pm and on Saturday 10am to 1pm, plus 1 hour before performances. There's also a second, smaller theater called **Werkraum,** Hildegardstrasse 1 (same phone as above), where new works are presented.

✪ **Münchner Philharmoniker (Munich Philharmonic Orchestra).** Performing in the Gasteig Kulturzentrum in the Haidhausen district, Rosenheimerstrasse 5. ☎ **089/ 54-81-81-81.** Tickets 18.50DM–92DM ($9.25–$46). S-Bahn: Rosenheimerplatz. Tram: 18 to Gasteig. Bus: 51.

This famous orchestra was founded in 1893. Its music director is James Levine, and its home is the Gasteig Cultural Center, where it performs in Philharmonic Hall. The center also shelters the Richard Strauss Conservatory and the Munich Municipal Library, and has five performance halls. You can purchase tickets at the ground-level Glashalle, Monday to Friday 10am to 8pm and Saturday 10am to 4pm. The Philharmonic season runs mid-September to July.

BEER HALLS

The Bierhalle is a traditional Munich institution, offering food, entertainment, and, of course, beer. It is said that Müncheners consume more beer than anyone else in Germany. Bernd Boehle once wrote: "If a man really belongs to Munich he drinks beer at all times of the day, at breakfast, at midday, at teatime; and in the evening, of course, he just never stops." A liter of beer will generally set you back about 10DM ($5). For information on outdoor beer gardens, see the "Beer Gardens" box, above.

Augustinerbräu. Neuhäuserstrasse 27. ☎ **089/23-18-32-57.** U-Bahn/S-Bahn: Karlsplatz/ Stachus. Tram: 19.

This beer hall's dark-wood panels and carved-plaster ceilings make the place look older than it is. It's been around for less than a century, but beer was first brewed on this spot in 1328 (or so they claim). The long menu changes daily, and the cuisine is not for dieters: It's hearty, heavy, and starchy, but that's what customers want. Open daily 9am to midnight.

✪ **Hofbräuhaus am Platzl.** Am Platzl 9. ☎ **089/22-16-76.** U-Bahn/S-Bahn: Marienplatz.

The state-owned Hofbräuhaus is the world's most famous beer hall. Visitors with only 1 night in Munich usually come here. The present Hofbräuhaus was built in 1897, but the tradition of a beer house on this spot dates from 1589. This one was the setting for the notorious meeting where Hitler took control of the tiny German Workers' Party in 1920. Fistfights erupted as the Nazis attacked their Bavarian enemies, right here in the beer palace.

Today, 4,500 beer drinkers can crowd in here. Several rooms, including a top-floor room for dancing, are spread over three floors. With its brass band (which starts playing at 11am), the ground-floor Schwemme is what you always expected of a beer hall—eternal Oktoberfest. In the second-floor restaurant, strolling musicians entertain, and dirndl-clad servers offer mugs of beer between sing-alongs. Every night the Hofbräuhaus presents a typical Bavarian show in its Fest-Hall 8pm to midnight. Admission is 9DM ($4.50). The hall is open daily 9am to midnight.

Max Emanuel Brauerei. Adalbertstrasse 33. ☎ **089/2-71-51-58.** Cover 10DM ($5) Wed, 13DM ($6.50) Fri–Sat. U-Bahn: Universität.

Löwenbräu turned this brewery into a beer hall in the 1920s. It still serves steins of beer and platters of filling German grub. On Wednesday and Friday the second floor plays host to a popular salsa disco. Open daily 11am to 1am.

Türkenhof. Türkenstrasse 78. ☎ **089/2-80-02-35.** U-Bahn: Universität.

This beer hall is not the stereotypical schmaltzy old-Bavaria tourist trap. Here you'll find cosmopolitan cuisine made by a Greek co-owner and lively, intelligent conversation flowing among the student patrons. It's a big, fun bar created out of a 150-year-old butcher shop. There are five varieties of Augustiner beer available on tap. Open Sunday to Thursday 11am to 1am; Friday and Saturday 11am to 3am.

Waldwirtschaft Grosshesselöhe. George-Kalb-Strasse 3. ☎ **089/74994030.** S-Bahn to Isartal Bahnhof. Tram: 7.

This popular summertime rendezvous, located above the Isar River near the zoo, has seats for some 2,000 drinkers. Music ranging from Dixieland to English jazz to Polish is played throughout the week. Entrance is free and you bring your own food. Open daily 11am to 11pm (they have to close early because neighborhood residents complain).

NIGHTCLUBS

Bayerischer Hof Night Club. In the Hotel Bayerischer Hof, Promenadeplatz 2–6. ☎ **089/2-12-09-94.** Cover 18DM ($9) Fri–Sat after 10pm; higher for special events. No cover for hotel guests. Tram: 19.

Here in the extensive cellars of the Bayerischer Hof hotel (see "Where to Stay," above) you'll find some of Munich's most sophisticated entertainment. Within one very large room is a piano bar where a musician plays every night 7 and 10pm. Behind a partition that disappears after 10pm is a bandstand for live orchestras, which play to a crowd of dancing patrons every night 10pm to 3 or 4am, depending on business. Entrance to the piano bar is free, but there's a cover charge to the nightclub Friday and Saturday nights. Drinks begin at 15.50DM ($7.75). The club and bar are open daily 7pm to 3 or 4am. Daily happy hour is 7pm to 8:30pm, with drinks starting at 9.50DM ($4.75).

Feierwerk. Hansastrasse 39–41. ☎ **089/7-69-36-00.** Cover 10DM–20DM ($5–$10). U-Bahn: Heimeranplatz.

Whether it's independent theater or rock 'n' roll, the multiple stages inside this complex have hosted it. Entertainment ranges from the commercially viable to the truly underground. In the summer, this already-roomy complex expands outside into circus tents. Open daily 9pm to 4am.

Kunstpark Ost. Grafingerstrasse 6. ☎ **089/49-00-27-30.** Cover 8DM–12DM ($4–$6). S-Bahn: Ostbahnhof.

Set within the sprawling premises of what used to be a factory, this is Munich's newest complex of bars, restaurants, and dance clubs. People tend to move randomly from venue to venue, without any particular loyalty to one or the other. Your best bet is to show up sometime after 8pm, when all the bars will be functioning. The discos don't get going until at least 10:30pm.

Nachtwerk. Landesbergerstrasse 185. ☎ **089/5-78-38-00.** Cover 10DM–13DM ($5–$6.50). S-Bahn: Donnersbergerbrücke.

This dance club in a huge factory warehouse also books bands. It's a festive place, not nearly as pretentious as other, more "exclusive" discos. Patrons even dance to rock music. The club is open Thursday 10pm to 4am and Friday and Saturday 10:30pm to 4am.

Night Flight. Franz Josef Strauss Airport, Wartungsallee 9. ☎ **089/97-59-79-99.** Cover 6DM ($3) Tues–Thurs 10pm–2am, 10DM–15DM ($5–$7.50) Fri–Sat. S-Bahn: Flughafen.

This nightclub is located in the midst of enormous airfield hangars; it's designed to highlight the visual effect of airplane departures and arrivals. To get here you'll have to drive 40km (25 miles) north of the city or take a 30-minute ride on the S-Bahn. There are three bars, a dance floor, and a restaurant. Frenetic dancing to techno music is the main attraction. In summer, dancers cool off and catch their breath on an outdoor terrace, where the main sport is watching the airport.

Oklahoma. Schäftlarnstrasse 156. ☎ **089/7-23-43-27.** Cover 10DM–20DM ($5–$10). U-Bahn: Talkirchen.

File under surreal. German and European bands decked out in cowboy hats and boots struggle with the nuances of an extremely foreign musical form. Even when the results are dead-on mimicry, there's something strange about watching German "cowboys" line dance or lean on the bar while guzzling Spaten. Cover is usually at the low end of the scale, rising when English and American acts hit the stage. Depending on your mood, this place can be a lot of fun. Pull on your jeans and come on in Tuesday to Saturday 7pm to 1am.

Parkcafé. Sophienstrasse 7. ☎ **089/59-83-13.** Cover 10DM ($5.70). U-Bahn: Lebachplatz.

Who'd ever guess this home to chic freaks was a Nazi hangout in the 1930s? The place contains five lively bars, two of them outfitted like the inside of a ship plus a strident color scheme using oranges and reds, among other colors. Many nights are themed, ranging from "Black Beat" music on Wednesdays to "gay Sundays." It's open Wednesday to Sunday 10pm to 4am. It's also open the first Tuesday of every month 11pm to 4am.

Rattlesnake Saloon. Schneeglöckchenstrasse 91. ☎ **089/1-50-40-35.** Cover 5DM–12DM ($2.50–$6). S-Bahn: Fasanerie.

Same owner, same concept as Oklahoma (see above)—the difference is the rib-eye steaks, barbecued pork, chili, and other southern U.S. dishes available to hungry country-music fans. If you never learned line dancing at home, you can give it a chance here under the watchful eye of a Teutonic instructor. Open Wednesday to Sunday 7pm to 1am. The location is 5km (3 miles) north of the Marienplatz.

JAZZ

Jazzclub Unterfahrt. Einsteinstrasse 42. ☎ **089/448-2794.** Cover 12DM–25DM ($6–$12.50). U-Bahn: Max-Weber-Platz.

This is Munich's leading jazz club, attracting artists from throughout Europe and North America. Reaching it requires wandering down a labyrinth of underground cement-sided corridors that might remind you of a bomb shelter during the Cold War. Once inside, the space opens to reveal flickering candles, a convivial bar, high ceilings, and clusters of smallish tables facing a stage and whatever singers and musicians happen to be emoting at the time. Off to one corner is an art gallery. The bar here opens daily at 7pm; live music is daily 9pm to midnight or 1am.

Mister B's. Herzog-Heinrichstrasse 38. ☎ **089/53-49-01.** Cover 8DM–10DM ($4–$5). U-Bahn: Goetheplatz.

This small, dark club hosts a slightly older, mellower crowd than the rock and dance clubs. Blues, jazz, and rhythm-and-blues combos take the stage Thursday to Saturday. Open Tuesday to Sunday 8pm to 3am.

Schwabinger Podium. Wagnerstrasse 1. ☎ **089/39-94-82.** Cover: free to 10pm, depending on the venue. U-Bahn: Münchner Freiheit.

This club offers varying nightly entertainment. Oldies and rock 'n' roll dominate some evenings. Open Sunday to Thursday 8pm to 1am and Friday and Saturday 8pm to 3am.

THE BAR & CAFE SCENE

Alter Simpl. Türkenstrasse 57. ☎ **089/2-72-30-83.** Tram: 18. Bus: 53.

Once a literary cafe, Alter Simpl takes its name from a satirical revue of 1903. Today it attracts a wide segment of locals. The real fun of the place occurs after 11pm, when the iconoclastic artistic ferment begins to resemble Berlin more than Bavaria. Open daily 11am to 3am, later on weekends.

Café Extrablatt. Leopoldstrasse 7, Schwabing. ☎ **089/33-33-33.** U-Bahn: Universität.

Owner Michael Grater is a prominent Munich newspaper columnist who has created a sprawling, smoke-filled sanctuary for writers, artists, and counterculture observers. Inside, it's decorated with celebrity photos and features a spacious well-designed bar, but the sidewalk tables are preferable during warm weather. Regulars convene here to converse and keep tabs on who's doing what, where. Open Monday to Thursday 7am to midnight, Friday and Saturday 9am to 1am, and Sunday 9am to midnight.

Café Puck. Türkenstrasse 33. ☎ **089/2-80-22-80.** U-Bahn: Universität.

A dark-paneled retreat for students, artists, and workers, this cafe plays a variety of roles for its diverse crowd. It's a bar to students; a restaurant to the locals, who like the daily menu of German, American, Chinese, and Mexican dishes; and a hangover cure for artists and young people who creep in after mid-day for a big American breakfast. There's usually plenty of conversation and someone who wants to practice English, and there are always German- and English-language newspapers.

Haus der 111 Biere. Franzstrasse 3. ☎ **089/33-12-48.** U-Bahn: Münchener Freiheit.

This unassuming corner bar is the type of small, dark place that adds character to any urban neighborhood. Among the beer selections is the strongest brew in the world: EKU Doppelbock Kulminator, a 22-proof oddity. Open Sunday to Thursday 5pm to 1am and Friday and Saturday 5pm to 3am.

Havana Club. Herrnstrasse 30. ☎ **089/29-18-84.** S-Bahn: Isartor.

This is not the spicy Cuban club you might expect. Employees may tell you about the bar's brush with fame, when Gloria Estefan made an appearance here, but its day-to-day function is as a lively singles bar fueled by rum-based cocktails. Open Monday to Wednesday 6pm to 1am and Thursday to Saturday 7pm to 2am.

Master's Home. Frauenstrasse 11 (close to the Marienplatz). ☎ **089/22-99-09.** S-Bahn: Marienplatz or Isartor

This is one of the historic core's most animated and convivial bars. It seems to attract a wider range of clients than most other watering holes in Munich. The setting is the ground floor of an imposing 19th-century building, within a large room outfitted with antiques and warm colors. The style evokes an Edwardian-era club in London. The premises also contain a restaurant, where fixed-price seven-course Italian-inspired meals cost 75DM ($37.50). Open nightly 6:30pm to 3am, with the last order accepted in the kitchen at 1:30am.

Nachtcafé. Maximiliansplatz 5. ☎ **089/59-59-00.** Tram: 19.

It hums, it thrives, and it captures everyone's nocturnal imagination. No other nightspot in Munich attracts such an array of soccer stars, film celebrities, literary figures, and, as one employee put it, "ordinary people, but only the most sympathetically crazy ones." Waves of patrons appear at different times of the evening: at 11pm, when live shows here begin; at 2am, when the restaurants close; and at 4am, when die-hard revelers seek a final drink in the predawn hours. There's no cover charge. The decor is updated 1950s; the music is jazz, blues, and soul. Open daily 9pm to 6am.

O'Reilly's Irish Pub. Maximilianstrasse 29. ☎ **089/29-33-11.** U-Bahn/S-Bahn: Marienplatz.

The all-Irish staff lends an air of authenticity to this pub, located in a historic vaulted cellar close to the Hotel Vier Jahreszeiten. Besides the obligatory Irish and German beers, you can also find good brews from England and the Czech Republic, as well as decent Irish stew, steaks, burgers, and mixed grills. Live Gaelic music is performed at irregular intervals throughout the month. Open Monday to Thursday 4pm to 1am, Friday to Sunday 2pm to 3am.

Pusser's. Falkenturmstrasse 9. ☎ **089/22-05-00.** U-Bahn/S-Bahn: Marienplatz.

This is the only European franchise of a small, well-run chain of restaurant-bars based in Tortola, British Virgin Islands. Its nostalgic decor celebrates the British navy of the 18th and 19th centuries. The specialties are Caribbean-inspired dishes and rum-based drinks. The cellar houses a piano bar. Open Monday to Saturday 5pm to 3am, Sunday 6pm to 3am.

Schultz. Barerstrasse 47. ☎ **089/2-71-47-11.** U-Bahn: Universität.

Schultz is a New York-style bar in Schwabing. It's popular with theater people, who crowd in as they do at Schumann's (see below) for smoke-filled chatter. The food is uncomplicated, and the decor, as they say here, is "unobvious and understated." Open daily 5pm to 1am.

Schumann's. Maximilianstrasse 36. ☎ **089/22-90-60.** Tram: 19.

Located on Munich's most desirable shopping street, Schumann's doesn't have to waste any money on decor. The local *beau monde* keep it fully fashionable. In cold weather, guests retreat inside, but in summer, they prefer the terrace that spills out onto the street. Schumann's is known as a "thinking man's bar." Author Charles Schumann wanted a bar that would be an artistic, literary, and communicative social focus. Popular with the film, advertising, and publishing worlds, his place is said to have contributed to a remarkable renaissance of bar culture in the city. Open Monday to Friday 5pm to 3am, Sunday 6pm to 3am. Oddly enough, it's closed on Saturday.

Shamrock. Trautenwolfstrasse 6. ☎ **089/33-10-81.** U-Bahn: Giselastrasse.

At this beer-lover's bar, you can compare the great brews of Germany with the best of the Irish exports. There's free entertainment every night at 9pm, when a mixed bag of

Irish, rock, country, folk, funk, or blues musicians take to the stage. Located near the university, Shamrock gets a fair share of the student crowd. Open Monday to Thursday 5pm to 1am, Friday 5pm to 3am, and Saturday and Sunday 2pm to 3am.

Tomate Sports. Siegesstrasse 19. ☎ **089/34-83-93.** U-Bahn: Münchener Freiheit.

Why is this bar named after a fruit? That's the only mystery about the place, which upon entrance, is immediately recognizable as a traditional sports bar, with a big-screen television broadcasting an overdose of athletics throughout the evening. Besides the soccer and rugby you might expect, the regulars also watch U.S. events, so stop in if you're a homesick American sports fan. The Paulaner brewery owns and operates this bar. Open Wednesday to Friday 7:30pm to 3am, Saturday 5:30pm to 3am, and Sunday to Tuesday 7:30pm to 1am.

GAY CLUBS

Munich's gay and lesbian scene is centered around the blocks between the Viktualien-markt and Gärtnerplatz, particularly on Hans-Sachs-Strasse.

Bau. Müllerstrasse 41. ☎ **089/269-208.** U-Bahn: Sendlinger Tor.

Macho and swaggering, this gay bar encourages leather, denim, and as many uniforms as can be crammed onto the bodies that ring its street-level bar. Dimly lit and international, it's not as scary as it might look at first. Don't be surprised if you spot several New York City cop uniforms on either level. It's open nightly 8:30pm to 3am.

Moritzz. Klenzestrasse 43. ☎ **089/2-01-67-76.** U-Bahn: Frauenhoferstrasse.

This is a stylish gay bar ringed with mirrors. Relax with drinks or food in red leather armchairs clustered around marble-topped tables. The eclectic menu includes well-prepared Thai dishes. Full meals, served until midnight, average 50DM ($25). Open Sunday to Thursday 7pm to 2am and Friday and Saturday 7pm to 3am.

Nil. Hans-Sach-Strasse 2. ☎ **089/26-55-45.** U-Bahn: Sendlinger Tor.

It's fun, it's convivial, and it has a clientele that's somewhat younger than the one at Teddy-Bar, just across the street (see below). In addition to fit and youthful German men hanging with one another at the octagon-shaped bar, you're likely to see faded stars (including Barbara Valentine, hailed during the 1960s as Germany's answer to Brigitte Bardot) from German stage and screen, sipping drinks with their men friends, reflecting on the glory days of their youth. Most of the clients come here to drink and mingle, but if you're hungry, platters of food are well-prepared and relatively inexpensive at 9.50DM to 18.50DM ($4.75 to $9.25).

Ochsen Garten. Müllerstrasse 47. ☎ **089/26-64-46.** U-Bahn: Sendlinger Tor.

Although it's a lot smaller and more cramped than most of its competitors, this is the leading leather bar in Munich, site of most of the city's leather S&M conventions, and a hangout for regular guys who appreciate their sense of machismo. It's at its most crowded Thursday, Friday, and Saturday nights; on other nights it's likely to be virtually empty. It's open nightly 10pm to 3am.

Teddy-Bar. Hans-Sachs-Strasse 1. ☎ **089/260-33-59.** U-Bahn: Sendlinger Tor.

Gay and neighborly, and ringed with varnished pine and a collection of teddy bears, this is a congenial bar patronized by gay men over 30. It's relatively easy to strike up a dialogue here, and if you're hungry, there are platters of Bavarian and German food. It's open nightly 6pm to 3am.

10 Side Trips from Munich

The **Bavarian Alps** are within easy reach (see chapter 8), or you can head for **Neuschwanstein** (see chapter 6) to see Ludwig II's fairy-tale castle.

DACHAU

In 1933, what had once been a quiet little artists' community just 16km (10 miles) from Munich became a tragic symbol of the Nazi era. Shortly after Hitler became chancellor, Himmler and the SS set up the first German concentration camp on the grounds of a former ammunition factory. The files show that more than 206,000 prisoners arrived here between 1933 and 1945, but the exact number of people imprisoned is unknown.

Upon entering the camp, **KZ-Gedenkstätte Dachau,** Alte-Roemar-Strasse 75 (☎ **08131/17-41**), you are faced by three memorial chapels—Catholic, Protestant, and Jewish—built in the early 1960s. Immediately behind the Catholic chapel is the "Lagerstrasse," the main camp road lined with poplar trees, once flanked by 32 barracks, each housing 208 prisoners. Two barracks have been rebuilt to give visitors insight into the conditions the prisoners endured.

The museum is housed in the large building that once contained the kitchen, laundry, and shower baths. Photographs and documents show the rise of the Nazi regime and the SS; other exhibits show the persecution of Jews and other prisoners. Every effort has been made to present the facts. The tour of Dachau is a truly moving experience.

You can get to the camp by taking the frequent S-Bahn train S2 from the Hauptbahnhof to Dachau (direction: Petershausen), then bus 724 or 726 to the camp. The camp is open Tuesday to Sunday 9am to 5pm; admission is free. The English version of a documentary film, *KZ-Dachau,* is shown at 11:30am, 2pm, and 3:30pm. All documents are translated in the catalog, which is available at the museum entrance.

The Bavarian Alps 8

If you walk into a rustic alpine inn along the German-Austrian frontier and ask the innkeeper if he or she is German, you'll most likely get the indignant response, "Of course not! I'm Bavarian." Some older inhabitants of the region can still remember when Bavaria was a kingdom with its own prerogatives, even while a part of the German Reich (1871–1918).

The huge province of Bavaria includes not only the Alps but also Franconia, Lake Constance, and the capital city of Munich. In this chapter, we'll explore the mountainous region along the Austrian frontier, a world unto itself. The hospitality of this area is famous, and the picture of the plump, rosy-cheeked innkeeper with a constant smile is no myth. Many travelers think of the Alps as a winter vacationland, but you'll find that nearly all the Bavarian resorts and villages boast year-round attractions.

Munich is the major driving gateway, with Autobahns leading directly to the Bavarian Alps. If you're beginning your tour in Garmisch-Partenkirchen in the west, you should fly into Munich. However, if your destination is Berchtesgaden in the eastern Alps, the nearest airport is Salzburg, Austria.

OUTDOORS IN THE BAVARIAN ALPS The Bavarian Alps are both a winter wonderland and a summer playground. The **skiing** here is the best in Germany. A regular winter snowfall in January and February usually measures from 30 to 50cm (12 to 20 inches). This leaves about 2m (6 feet) of snow in the areas served by ski lifts. The great **Zugspitzplatt** snowfield can be reached in spring or autumn by a rack railway. The Zugspitze, at 2,960m (9,720 feet) above sea level, is the tallest mountain peak in Germany. Ski slopes begin at a height of 2,650m (8,700 feet).

The second great ski district in the Alps is **Berchtesgadener Land,** with alpine skiing centered on Jenner, Rossfeld, Götschen, and Hochschwarzeck. Snow conditions are consistently good until March. Visitors will find a cross-country skiing center, many miles of tracks kept in first-class condition, natural toboggan runs, one artificial ice run for toboggan and skibob runs, and artificial ice-skating and curling rinks.

In summer, **alpine hiking** is a major attraction—climbing mountains, enjoying nature, and watching animals in the forest. Hikers are able at times to observe endangered species firsthand. One of the best areas for hiking is the 1,240m (4,060-foot) **Eckbauer,** lying on the southern fringe of Partenkirchen (the tourist office at Garmisch-Partenkirchen will supply maps and details). Many visitors come to the Alps in summer just to hike through **Berchtesgaden National Park,** bordering the Austrian province of Salzburg. The 2,466m (8,091-foot) Watzmann Mountain, the Königssee (Germany's cleanest, clearest lake), and parts of the Jenner—the pride of Berchtesgaden's four ski areas—are within the boundaries of the park, which has well-mapped trails cut through protected areas, leading the hiker through spectacular natural beauty. For information about hiking in the park, contact **Nationalparkhaus,** Franziskanerpl 7, 83471 Berchtesgaden (☎ **08652/64343**).

From Garmisch-Partenkirchen, serious hikers can embark on full-day or overnight alpine treks, following clearly marked footpaths and staying in isolated mountain huts. Some huts are staffed and serve meals. For the truly remote unsupervised huts, you'll be provided with information on how to gain access. For information, inquire at the local tourist office or write to the government-subsidized **German Alpine Association,** Von-Kaahr-Strasse 2–4, 80997 München (☎ **089/14-00-30;** fax 089/ 140-03-11) which will also direct you to a privately owned tour operator, the **Summit Club,** an outfit devoted to the organization of high-altitude expeditions throughout Europe and the world.

If you're a true outdoors-person, you'll briefly savor the somewhat touristy facilities of Garmisch-Partenkirchen, and then use it as a base for explorations of the rugged Berchtesgaden National Park. You can also stay at one of the inns in Mittenwald or Oberammergau and take advantage of a wide roster of outdoor diversions there. Any of the outfitters below will provide directions and link-ups with their sports programs from wherever you decide to stay. Street maps of Berchtesgaden and its environs are usually available for free from the **Kurdirektion** (tourist office), Königsseer Strasse, Berchtesgaden (☎ **08652/967-0**), and more intricately detailed maps of the surrounding alpine topography are available for a fee.

Another summer activity is **ballooning,** which, weather permitting, can be arranged through **Outdoor Club Berchtesgaden,** Ludwig-Ganghofer-Strasse 20^1/$_2$ (☎ **08652/50-01**).

Anglers will find plenty of **fishing** opportunities (especially salmon, pike perch, and trout) at Lake Hintersee and the rivers Ramsauer Ache and Königsseer Ache. To acquire a fishing permit, contact the **Kurdirektion** (tourist office; see above) at Berchtesgaden, which will direct you to any of four different authorities, based on where you want to fish. For fishing specifically within the Hintersee, contact tourist officials in Ramsau at ☎ **08657/9889920.**

Despite the obvious dangers, **hang gliding** or **paragliding** from the vertiginous slopes of Mount Jenner can be thrilling. To arrange it, contact **Summit Club** (see above).

You can also practice your **kayaking** or **white-water rafting** techniques on one of the area's many rivers (water level permitting), such as the Ramsauer, Königisser, Bischofswiesener, and Berchtesgadener Aches. For information and options, contact the above-mentioned **Outdoor Club Berchtesgaden.**

If you would like to go **swimming** in an alpine lake—not to everyone's body temperature—there are many *"lidos"* found in the Bavarian Forest.

Of course, there's plenty to do outdoors during the winter as well, including some of the greatest **alpine** and **cross-country skiing** in all of Europe. Call the local "Snow-Telefon" at ☎ **08652/967-297** for current snow conditions. There's also skating between October and February at the world-class ice-skating rink in Berchtesgaden. Less reliable, but more picturesque, is skating on the surface of the Hintersee Lake,

once it's sufficiently frozen. A particularly cozy way to spend an hour on a winter's night is to huddle with a companion in the back of a **horse-drawn sled.** Rides can be arranged in Garmisch through Brandtner, GMbH, at the **Café Waldstein,** Königseer Fussweg 17 (☎ **08652/2427**). The cost is around 90DM ($45) per hour.

EXPLORING THE REGION BY CAR

Acclaimed as one of the most scenic drives in all of Europe, the ✪ **Deutsche Alpen-strasse (German Alpine Road)** stretches for some 480km (300 miles) between Berchtesgaden in the east and Lindau on Lake Constance in the west (see chapter 9). The road goes through mountains, lakes, forests, and "castles in the sky." We prefer to take the drive in early spring or early autumn. In winter, mountain passes are often shut down, and even those highways that remain open can be dangerous.

Day 1　After your stopover in Munich (see chapter 7), head south along Autobahn A8 (drive in the right lane if you want to avoid the hysterical speeders on the left). Turn south on Route B20 for **Berchtesgaden,** 158km (98 miles) southeast of Munich. After settling in and having lunch, take an afternoon excursion to **Obersalzberg** and **Kehlstein** (you can go by bus).

Day 2　While still based in Berchtesgaden, explore the **Königssee,** to the south (about 2 hr. by boat). This long, narrow lake, famed for its steep banks and dark waters, is one of Europe's most dramatic and romantic sights. In the afternoon, drive west along the alpine road and then north on Route B20 some 20km (12 miles) to **Bad Reichenhall.** This is one of Germany's most famous spas. Return to Berchtesgaden for the night.

Day 3　Get back on Autobahn A8 toward Munich but turn off at **Prien,** 85km (53 miles) southeast of Munich. The premier attraction here is the Neues Schloss, a fantastic castle begun by Ludwig II in 1878 on the island of Herrenchiemsee. You can find food and lodging at Prien.

Day 4　Get back on the Autobahn to Munich, but take a cross-country route (472) toward Bad Tölz, which is one of Bavaria's leading spas, although it lacks any major attractions. Continue west from Bad Tölz along 472 to the town of Bichl, at which point you head south along Route 11 until you reach Benediktbeuern, a distance of 14km (9 miles) from Bad Tölz. Here you'll find **Benediktbeuern,** the most ancient Benedictine monastery in upper Bavaria. Records trace it back to the year 739. After a look, continue 6km (4 miles) south along Route 11 to **Kochel am See,** with its alpine vistas. Follow Route 11 south to the express highway, Route 2, which you then follow 32km (20 miles) to **Mittenwald** on the Austrian frontier. Plan an overnight stay.

Day 5　You'll want to spend as much time as possible in **Mittenwald.** Goethe called it a "living picture book"—we think it looks like part of *The Sound of Music* film set. It's also a major center for violin making. Give it at least a morning before driving northwest for 20km (12 miles) on Route 2 to **Garmisch-Partenkirchen,** two towns combined. After checking in, head for the major attraction, the **Zugspitze,** the highest peak in German territory. Wear warm clothing. This could be the highlight of your trip to Bavaria.

Day 6　Leaving Garmisch-Partenkirchen, head north on Route 2 for 20km (12 miles) toward **Oberammergau.** Along the way, you'll pass **Kloster Ettal,** founded in 1330. Its original 10-sided church is a stunning example of the Bavarian rococo style. Some 10km (6 miles) to the west is **Schloss Linderhof,** one of "Mad King" Ludwig's royal residences, built between 1874 and 1878 on the grounds of his hunting lodge. These two attractions will take up most of your day, but you'll still arrive in the little old wood-carver's village of Oberammergau, 11km (7 miles) northeast of Linderhof, in time to wander about. Later, enjoy a hearty Bavarian dinner before turning in to your alpine bed.

1 Berchtesgaden

158km (98 miles) SE of Munich, 18km (11 miles) SE of Bad Reichenhall, 23km (14 miles) S of Salzburg

Ever since Ludwig I of Bavaria chose this resort as a favorite hideaway, the tourist business in Berchtesgaden has been booming. The village is situated below the many summits of Watzmann Mountain—2,713m (8,901 ft.) at its highest point. According to legend, the mountain peaks were once a royal family who were so evil that God punished them by turning them into rocks.

Berchtesgaden is a quiet old alpine village with ancient winding streets and a medieval marketplace and castle square. Its name is often linked with Hitler and the Nazi hierarchy, but this impression is erroneous. Hitler's playground was actually at Obersalzberg, on a wooded plateau about half a mile up the mountain.

ESSENTIALS

GETTING THERE   By Air   The nearest airport is **Salzburg Airport** (☎ **0662/ 8580**). It has regularly scheduled air service to Frankfurt, Amsterdam, Brussels, Berlin, Dresden, Düsselddorf, Hamburg, London, Paris, and Zurich. Major airlines serving the Salzburg airport are Austrian Airlines (☎ **0662/85-45-11**), Lauda Air (☎ **0662/ 85-63-64**), Air France (☎ **0662/17-89**). Lufthansa (☎ **0662/809-080**), and Tyrolean (☎ **0662/85-45-33**). From Salzburg you can take a 1-hour train ride to Berchtesgaden, although you'll have to change trains at Freilassing.

By Train   The **Berchtesgaden Bahnhof** lies on the Munich–Freilassing rail line. Twelve trains a day arrive from Munich (trip time: $1^1/2$ hr.). For rail information and schedules, call ☎ **01805/99-66-33**. Berchtesgaden has three mountain rail lines— the Obersalzbergbahn, Jennerbahn, and Hirscheckbahn—going to the mountain plateaus around the resorts. For more information, contact **Berchtesgadener Bergbahn AG** (☎ **08652/9-58-10**) and **Obersalzbergbahn AG** (☎ **08652/ 25-61**).

By Bus   Regional bus service to alpine villages and towns around Berchtesgaden is offered by **RVO Regionalverkehr Oberbayern** at Berchtesgaden (☎ **08652/54-73**).

By Car   Access by car is via the A8 Autobahn from Munich in the north or Route 20 from the south. The drive from Munich takes about 2 hours.

VISITOR INFORMATION   Contact the **Kurdirektion,** Königsseerstrasse 2 (☎ **08652/967-0**). It's open Monday to Friday 8am to 5pm and Saturday 9am to noon.

SEEING THE SIGHTS

The Stiftskirche (Abbey Church), dating from 1122, is adjacent to the Königliches Schloss Berchtesgaden. The church is mainly Romanesque, with Gothic additions. One of its ancient twin steeples was destroyed by lightning and rebuilt in 1866. The interior contains many fine works of art; the high altar has a painting by Zott dating from 1669. In the vestry is a small silver altar donated by Empress Maria Theresa of Austria.

Schlossplatz, partially enclosed by the castle and Stiftskirche, is the most attractive plaza in town. On the opposite side of the square from the church is a 16th-century arcade that leads to **Marktplatz,** with typical alpine houses and a wooden fountain from 1677 (restored by Ludwig I in 1860). Some of Berchtesgaden's oldest inns and houses border this square. Extending from Marktplatz is the **Nonntal,** lined with more old houses, some built into Lockstein Mountain, which towers above the town.

A minor but interesting museum, **Heimatmuseum,** Schloss Aldelsheim, Schroffen-bergallee 6 (☎ **08652/44-10**), is devoted to alpine wood carving. The craft here pre-dates the more fabled wood carving at Oberammergau. Some of the best examples in Germany are on display in this museum. Entry is allowed only as part of a guided tour offered Monday to Friday at 10am and again at 3pm for a charge of 3DM ($1.50).

Königliches Schloss Berchtesgaden. Schlossplatz 2. ☎ **08652/20-85.** Admission 7DM ($3.50) adults, 3DM ($1.50) children 6–16, free for children 5 and under. Easter–Sept, Sun–Fri 10am–1pm and 2–5pm; Oct–Easter, Mon–Fri 10am–1pm and 2–5pm. Bus: 9539.

In the Middle Ages, Berchtesgaden grew up around a powerful Augustinian monastery. Its monks introduced the art of wood carving, for which the town is still noted. When the town became part of Bavaria in 1809, the abbey was secularized and eventually converted to a palace for the royal Wittelsbach family. Now it is a museum, mostly devoted to the royal collection of sacred art, including wood sculptures by the famed artists Veit Stoss and Tilman Riemenschneider. There's also a gallery of 19th-century art, a collection of Italian furniture from the 16th century, and a display of 17th- and 18th-century pistols and guns.

Salzbergwerk Berchtesgaden. Bergwerkstrasse 83. ☎ **08652/6-00-20.** Admission 21DM ($10.50) adults, 11DM ($5.50) children. May 1–Oct 15 daily 9am–5pm; Oct 16–Apr 30, Mon–Sat 12:30–3:30pm. Bus: 9539.

These salt mines at the eastern edge of town were once owned by the Augustinian monastery. Operations began here in 1517. The deposits are more than 300m (990 feet) thick and are still processed today from four galleries or "hills." Visitors are first given protective miner's clothing. Older children will especially enjoy the guided tours that begin with a ride into the mine on a small wagon-like train. After nearly a half-mile journey, visitors leave the train and explore the rest of the mine, sliding down a miner's slide, and riding on the salt lake in a ferry. The highlight of the tour is the "chapel," a grotto containing unusually shaped salt formations illuminated for an eerie effect. The 1$\frac{1}{2}$-hour tour can be taken any time of the year, in any weather.

WHERE TO STAY

Hotel Fischer. Königsseerstrasse 51, 83471 Berchtesgaden, a short uphill walk from the rail-way station. ☎ **08652/95-50.** Fax 08652/6-48-73. www.hotel-fischer.de. E-mail: info@hotel-fischer.de. 40 units. TV TEL. 170DM–252DM ($85–$126) double. Rates include buffet breakfast. V. Closed Nov to mid-Dec and mid-Mar to Apr 10. Parking 6DM ($3).

This hotel overlooking the town was built in the late 1970s in the Bavarian style. It may be the best choice in town. Fronted with dark-stained wooden balconies against a cream-colored facade, it rambles pleasantly along the hillside. Rooms are cozy and traditional, each with a regional theme. On the premises are an indoor swimming pool, a sauna, a solarium, and an alpine-style restaurant and bar.

Hotel Krone. Am Rad 5, 83471 Berchtesgaden. ☎ **08652/94600.** Fax 08652/946010. 21 units. TV TEL. 110DM–150DM ($55–$75) double; from 160DM ($80) suite. MC. Closed: Nov 1–Dec 20.

One of the most appealing bargains in Berchtesgaden is this well-built chalet-inspired hotel. Operated by live-in managers, the Grafe family, and permeated with a sense of alpine thrift and good cheer, it offers cozy rooms sheathed with varnished pine. Each has a balcony or terrace, a comfortable mattress, and a compact bath. The dining room, and its adjacent bar, charges only 18DM ($10.25) per person extra for half board, a price so low that it virtually guarantees that most guests will take at least one of their daily meals here.

Vier Jahreszeiten. Maximilianstrasse 20, 83471 Berchtesgaden. ☎ **08652/95-20.** Fax 08652/50-29. www.berchtesgaden.com/vier-jahreszeiten. E-mail: millers-hotel@online.de. 59 units. TEL. 165DM–260DM ($82.50–$130) double. Rates include buffet breakfast. AE, DC, MC, V. Free outdoor parking; 10DM ($5) in garage.

Vier Jahreszeiten is an old inn with modern extensions in the heart of the village. The inn has been remodeled and improved over the years and now offers a good level of comfort to its guests, almost rivaling the Fischer. Some of the newer units, with tiny sitting rooms and balconies, resemble suites; most have minibars and TVs. In addition to the colorful and distinguished Hubertusstube (see "Where to Dine," below), there's a terrace for summer dining and viewing. The hotel also offers an indoor pool, a sauna, and a solarium.

Watzmann. Franziskanerplatz 2, 83471 Berchtesgaden. ☎ **08652/2005.** Fax 08652/5174. 38 units, 30 with shower. 33DM–69DM ($16.50–$34.50) double without shower, 59DM–72DM ($29.50–$36) double with shower. AE, DC, MC, V. Closed Nov 1–Dec 25. Free parking.

This is a good bet for an affordable choice. The Watzmann is located opposite the church on the main square. It has a large outdoor terrace and a cozy Bavarian-inspired decor, with turn-of-the-century artifacts, huge carved wooden pillars, oak ceilings, and wrought-iron chandeliers. Everyone seems to stop here for a beer, coffee, or lunch. Rooms are small but well maintained. Those with baths have shower stalls; for those without, corridor baths are adequate (you rarely have to wait in line).

WHERE TO DINE

Hubertusstube. In the Hotel Vier Jahreszeiten, Maximilianstrasse 20. ☎ **08652/9520.** Reservations recommended. Main courses 18DM–40DM ($9–$20). AE, DC, MC, V. Daily 11am–2pm and 6pm–midnight. GERMAN.

You'll get an undeniable sense of Bavarian *gemütlichkeit* in this richly paneled restaurant, where a trio of old-fashioned dining rooms, each with a century-old history of hospitality, offers well-prepared food and a view of the alps. Menu items include rich servings of such game dishes as roasted venison with red wine sauce, as well as perfectly prepared pepper steaks, roasted pork shank, and salmon-trout. Service is traditional and very polite.

Panorama Restaurant. In the Alpenhotel Kronprinz, Am Brandholz. ☎ **08652/60-70.** Reservations recommended. Lunch main courses 18DM–35DM ($9–$17.50); dinner main courses 12DM–35DM ($6–$17.50). AE, DC, MC, V. Daily noon–3pm and 6–11pm. GERMAN/INTERNATIONAL.

The decor includes lots of blond birchwood paneling and touches of pale blue, but virtually no one notices it because the windows encompass a sweeping view of Obersalzburg and the nearby mountains. Good-tasting menu items within the pair of dining rooms include braised trout with almonds; pepper steak; goulash or *leberknoedelsuppe;* veal or pork schnitzels; and a savory version of the traditional rib-sticker, *schweinshaxen* (port shank).

SIDE TRIPS TO KÖNIGSSEE & OBERSALZBERG
✪ KÖNIGSSEE

This is the "jewel in the necklace" of Berchtesgaden. The waters of this scenic lake appear to be dark-green because of the steep mountains that jut upward from its shores. Low-lying land on the lake's northern edge contains a parking lot and a few charming inns and bathing facilities, but the rest of the lake is enclosed by mountains, making it impossible to walk along the shoreline. The only way to explore the waters, unless you're like one of the mountain goats you may see above, is by boat. Electric motorboats—no noisy gas-powered launches allowed—carry passengers on tours around the lake throughout the summer and occasionally even in winter.

The favorite spot on Königssee is the tiny flat peninsula on the western bank, the site of a basilica as early as the 12th century. Today the Catholic **Chapel of St. Bartholomew** is still used for services (except in winter). The clergy must arrive by boat, since there's no other way to approach the peninsula. The adjacent buildings include a fisher's house and a restaurant, which was once a favored hunting lodge of the Bavarian kings. Here you can sample trout and salmon caught in the crisp, clean waters. At the southern end of the lake you come to the Salet-Alm, where the tour boats make a short stop near a thundering waterfall. If you follow the footpath up the hillside, you'll reach the summer pastures used by the cattle of Berchtesgaden. Just over the hill is **Lake Obersee,** part of Königssee until an avalanche separated them 8 centuries ago. If you prefer a shorter trip, you can take the boat as far as St. Bartholomew and back.

To reach Königssee from Berchtesgaden by car, follow the signs south from the town 5km (3 miles). It's also a pleasant hour's walk or a short ride by electric train or bus from the center of town.

For information about boat excursions, call **Schiffahrt Königssee** at ☎ **08652/ 96-36-18.** An entire tour of Königssee requires about 2 hours. There are boats in summer every 15 minutes, so getting off one boat and climbing aboard another is easy if you want to break up the tour. During the summer, the first boat departs every morning at 7:15am and the last boat leaves at 5:30pm. In winter, boats leave about every 45 minutes. The important stops are at Salet and St. Batholomä. A round-trip fare for a lake tour is 22.50DM ($11.25) for adults and half fare for children.

✪ OBERSALZBERG

The drive from Berchtesgaden to Obersalzberg at 1,000m (3,300 feet) is one of Bavaria's most scenic routes. Obersalzberg was where Hitler settled down in a rented cottage after his prison term while he completed *Mein Kampf.* After he came to power in 1933, he bought Haus Wachenfeld and had it remodeled into his residence, the **Berghof.** Obersalzberg became the center for holiday living for Nazis such as Martin Bormann and Hermann Göring.

Today, you can walk around the ruins of Hitler's Berghof. This was where the famous 1938 meeting took place between Hitler and British Prime Minister Neville Chamberlain. The result was the Munich Agreement, which Chamberlain so mistakenly declared would bring "peace in our time." The Berghof was destroyed in 1952 by Bavarian government authorities at the request of the U.S. Army—the Americans did not want a monument to Hitler. One of the only fully remaining structures from the Nazi compound is a guesthouse called the General Walker Hotel that was used by U.S. troops stationed in Europe.

Hitler built the bunkers and air-raid shelter in 1943. Three thousand laborers completed the work in 9 months, connecting all the major buildings of the Obersalzberg area to the underground rooms. Many readers have expressed their disappointment when reaching this site, apparently thinking they would tour Hitler's sumptuously decorated private apartments. The only structures open to visitors are a part of Hitler's air raid shelter system and prison cells used by the Reichssicherheitsdienst (state security police), which were considered a last refuge for Hitler and other high officials. Wear good walking shoes and be prepared to run into some VERBOTEN! signs.

A major point of interest is the **Kehlstein,** or **Eagle's Nest,** which can be reached only by a thrilling bus ride up a 7km-(4¹/₂-mile-) long mountain road, blasted out of solid rock. This outstanding feat of engineering was begun in 1937 under the leadership of Bormann, who intended it as a 50th-birthday gift for Hitler. The Eagle's Nest was not, as the name may suggest, a military installation. It was a site for relaxation and was not popular with Hitler, who rarely visited it.

To reach the spot, you must enter a tunnel and take a 120m (400-foot) elevator ride through a shaft in the Kehlstein Mountain to its summit. The building, with solid granite walls and huge picture windows, houses a mountain restaurant, the Kehlsteinhaus, which is open mid-May to mid-October. You can enjoy the panoramic view and explore the rooms of the original teahouse, which include Eva Braun's living room. Below you'll have a view of the Obersalzberg area. Nearby is the site of Martin Bormann's house and the SS barracks. To the north you can see as far as Salzburg, Austria; below the mountain to the west is Berchtesgaden, with its rivers dwindling off into threads in the distance.

For information about trips to Obersalzberg and Kehlstein, call ☎ 08652/54-73. Local RVO buses based in Berchtesgaden run from the Berchtesgaden Post Office to Obersalzberg-Hintereck. The round-trip journey costs 5.80DM ($2.90). Entrance to the bunker and prison cells is 5DM ($2.50); they're open daily 9am to 5pm. From Obersalzberg (the Hintereck parking lot), the Kehlstein line operates daily mid-May to mid-October; during that time full catering services are offered at Kehlsteinhaus. The bus to Kehlstein and elevator ride through the rock costs 20DM ($10). If you're up to it, instead of taking the elevator, you can walk the final stretch to the Eagle's Nest from the summit parking lot in about 30 minutes. The Kehlstein road is closed to private vehicles.

Guided tours in English are offered by the American-run **Berchtesgaden Mini Bus Tours,** Königsseerstrasse 2 (☎ **08652/6-49-71**). Tours, including Obersalzberg, Eagle's Nest, and the Bunker System as an afternoon history package, are conducted daily mid-May to mid-October, starting at the Berchtesgaden tourist office. The service also takes visitors to sights such as the Salt Mines and the Königssee. A 3¹/₂-hour tour costs 55DM ($27.50) adults, 13DM ($6.50) under 25, free 6 and under. There's a tour information and ticket booth at the Berchtesgaden tourist office, across the street from the train station. One of the most popular tours offered is the "Sound of Music" tour to nearby Salzburg.

Obersalzberg is also becoming an important health resort; the ruins of Bormann's Gusthof Farm are now the Skytop Lodge, a popular golfing center in summer and a ski site in winter.

Where to Stay

Hotel zum Türken. 83471 Berchtesgaden-Obersalzberg. ☎ **08652/24-28.** Fax 08652/47-10. 17 units, 13 with shower or bath. 130DM ($65) double without shower or bath, 210DM ($105) double with shower or bath. Rates include continental breakfast. AE, DC, MC, V. Closed Tues. Free parking. Obersalzberg bus from Berchtesgaden.

The Hotel zum Türken, located in Obersalzberg, is legendary. It's designed in the alpine style and has terraces (for hotel guests only) with views. On its facade is a large painted sign of "The Turk"—legend has it that the first owner was a veteran of the Turkish war. In the 1930s, anti-Nazi remarks led to trouble for the proprietor, Herr Schuster, who was arrested. Afterward Bormann used the building as a Gestapo headquarters; it then fell victim to air raids and looting in April 1945. Herr Schuster's daughter, Therese Partner, was able to buy the ruin from the German government in 1949. The small-to-medium-sized rooms are well maintained. They don't have private phones, but there is an international pay phone in the main hallway. There's also a self-service bar on the ground floor.

2 Bad Reichenhall

135km (84 miles) SE of Munich, 20km (12 miles) SE of Salzburg

The best German spas can call themselves *Staatsbad,* and Bad Reichenhall bears that title with pride. This old salt town is the most important curative spa in the Bavarian Alps. Mountain chains surround it, protecting it from the winds. Its brine springs, with a salt content as high as 24%, are the most powerful saline springs in Europe, and the town has been a source of salt for more than 2,400 years. The combination of the waters and the pure air has made Bad Reichenhall a recognized spa for centuries.

In 1848 King Maximilian of Bavaria stayed here, popularizing Bad Reichenhall as a fashionable resort. Today, visitors come from all over the world to take the waters, which supposedly treat asthma and other respiratory ailments. Treatment sessions take place almost exclusively in the morning at seven resort institutes, the therapy ranging from simply drinking the water to pneumatotherapy—even electronic lungs for the most serious cases. Although Bad Reichenhall takes the medical side of the cure seriously, spa authorities encourage visitors to enjoy its many attractions as well.

ESSENTIALS

GETTING THERE   By Air   The nearest airport is Salzburg (see Berchtesgaden above for data about airport arrivals). From Salzburg it's a 20-minute train ride into Bad Reichenhall, with trains leaving every hour throughout the day, with a change in Freilassing. There are also frequent bus and rail connections to and from Berchtesgaden, either trip taking about 45 minutes. Buses or trains leave every hour from Berchtesgaden heading for Bad Reichenhall.

By Train   Bad Reichenhall is connected to the airport at Munich (see chapter 7) by frequent train service through Rosenheim. The trip takes about $2^1/_2$ hours. For information and schedules, call ☎ **01805/99-66-33.**

By Bus   Regional bus service to and from Bad Reichenhall is provided by Regionalverkehr Oberbayers Betrieb (☎ **08652/54-73** for information). From the spa, you can take a bus to various beautiful spots in the Bavarian Alps, including Berchtesgaden.

By Car   Access is by the A8 Autobahn, from Munich in the north and Salzburg in the south. Exit on Federal Highway 21 into Bad Reichenhall.

VISITOR INFORMATION   For tourist information, go to the **Kur- und Verkehrsverein im Kurgastzentrum,** Wittelsbacherstrasse 15 (☎ **08651/60-63-03**). It's open Monday to Friday 9am to 5pm and Saturday 9am to 2pm.

SIGHTS & ACTIVITIES

The ideal climate permits a complete spectrum of outdoor events, from excursions into the mountains for skiing or hiking to tennis tournaments. Gardeners and botanists will enjoy the spa gardens; the sheltered location of the town amid the lofty Alps permits the growth of several varieties of tropical plants, giving the gardens a lush, exotic appearance. There's also a wide choice of indoor activities, from symphony concerts to folklore presentations to gambling in the casino.

The great fire of 1834 destroyed much of the town, but many impressive churches survived. An outstanding example is **St. Zeno,** a 12th-century Gothic church showing a later baroque influence. Its most remarkable feature is its painted interior, centering on the carved altarpiece of the *Coronation of the Virgin.*

Bad Reichenhaller Saltmuseum, Alte Saline Reichenhall (☎ **08651/7-00-25-1**), just a short walk from the Kurgarten, is the home of the ancient industry responsible for the growth and prosperity of Bad Reichenhall from Celtic times to the present.

Parts of the old plant still stand today, but most of it was reconstructed in the mid-19th century by Ludwig I of Bavaria. The large pumps and huge marble caverns are impressive. Tours are offered May 1 to October 31, daily 10am to noon and 2 to 4pm; November to May 10, Tuesday and Thursday 2 to 4pm. Admission is 8.50DM ($4.25) for adults and 4.50DM ($2.25) for children; a combination ticket for the Saltmuseum and the Salzberwerk Berchtesgaden (see above) is 25DM ($12.50) adults and 13DM ($6.50) children.

SHOPPING

Shops here are predictably upscale, rather limited in scope, and conservative. The town's only department store, **Kaufhaus Huhasz,** Ludwigstrasse 23 (☎ **08651/ 9-73-80**), stocks some traditional items. About 90% of the resort's shops are in a pedestrian-only zone, which is centered around the **Ludwigstrasse** and the **Salzburgerstrasse.** Since 1856, **Josef Mack Co.,** Ludwigstrasse 36 (☎ **08651/7-82-80**), has been the region's best place for medicinal herbs, many of which are grown in the Bavarian Alps.

WHERE TO STAY

Hotel Bayerischer Hof. Bahnhofplatz 14, 83426 Bad Reichenhall. ☎ **08651/60-90.** Fax 08651/60-91-11. 64 units. MINIBAR TV TEL. 140DM–220DM ($70–$110) double. Rates include buffet breakfast. AE, DC, MC, V. Parking 8DM ($4).

This modern and inviting hotel is in the center of the spa on Main Street. It has a surprising number of facilities for a small place, although it's hardly in the same league as the Steigenberger or the Parkhotel Luisenbad. Rooms are furnished in a well-maintained, functional modern style. The staff is well trained. The hotel is equipped with a roof-garden indoor pool with Finnish sauna, a solarium, a bowling alley, and a salon for massage and cosmetic treatments. In addition to the main restaurant, there's a cafe with live music and a nightclub with international acts. The reception desk is helpful in arranging excursions to Obersalzburg, Berchtesgadener Land, and Salzburg. Guests can also rent bikes. If you visit in winter, the staff will arrange cross-country and downhill skiing.

Parkhotel Luisenbad. Ludwigstrasse 33, 83435 Bad Reichenhall. ☎ **08651/60-40.** Fax 08651/6-29-28. www.parkhotel.de. E-mail: Luisenbad@parkhotel.de. 89 units. MINIBAR TV TEL. 254DM–344DM ($127–$172) double; 244DM–394DM ($122–$197) suite. Rates include continental breakfast. DC, MC, V. Parking 2DM–10DM ($1–$5).

A world unto itself, Parkhotel Luisenbad is an 1860s hotel with a new wing in a garden setting. It's a good second choice to the Steigenberger, especially if you like traditional hotels. Its best feature is the indoor pool with a glass wall, bringing the outdoors inside. Rooms range from medium to spacious. The more modern ones are handsome, with bold colors and tasteful furnishings, but many guests prefer the older, more traditional rooms. Baths are well maintained, with hair dryers and deluxe toiletries.

Dining: The lobby and the Restaurant die Holzstube (see "Where to Dine," below) have been renovated in a classic provincial style and decorated in warm colors, making the hotel more attractive than ever.

Amenities: Thermal baths, inhalations, massages, mud baths, Finnish sauna, Jacuzzi, room service, laundry service, dry cleaning.

Salzburger Hof. Mozartstrasse 7, 83435 Bad Reichenhall. ☎ **08651/9-76-90.** Fax 08651/ 97-69-99. 25 units. TV TEL. 130DM–160DM ($65–$80) double. Rates include continental breakfast. AE, MC, V. Parking 5DM ($2.50).

This three-story hotel is one of the best buys in town. Its public areas are filled with old Bavarian charm. Best of all are the compact rooms, most of which contain streamlined sofas, beds with built-in headboards, and armchairs around a breakfast table; all open onto tiny balconies. Price depends on the view.

✪ **Steigenberger Axelmannstein.** Salzburger Strasse 2–6, 83435 Bad Reichenhall. ☎ **800/223-5652** in the U.S. and Canada, or 08651/77-70. Fax 08651/59-32. www. bad-reichenhall.steigenberger.de. E-mail: bad-reichenhall@steigenberger.de. 159 units. MINIBAR TV TEL. 355DM–475DM ($177.50–$237.50) double; 590DM–990DM ($295–$495) suite. Rates include buffet breakfast. AE, DC, V. Parking 10DM ($5).

This first-class hotel, set in its own 3ha (7¹/₂-acre) garden, is the best in town for traditional charm and spa conveniences, far superior to its closest rival, the Parkhotel Luisenbad. Public areas are traditionally furnished with antiques and reproductions. Rooms are well furnished and generally spacious. Many have views of the encircling Bavarian Alps. Baths are medium in size, and come with hair dryers and deluxe toiletries.

Dining/Diversions: The Parkrestaurant, opening onto a garden, attracts many nonresidents, as does the cozy Axel-Stüberl, with regional dishes. The wood-paneled Axel-Bar features live entertainment daily.

Amenities: Cure department, sauna, solarium, fitness center, cosmetic studio, hairdresser, indoor pool, tennis court, room service, laundry service, and dry cleaning.

WHERE TO DINE

Restaurant die Holzstube. In the Parkhotel Luisenbad, Ludwigstrasse 33. ☎ **08651/ 60-40.** Reservations recommended. Main courses 20DM–30DM ($10–$15). AE, DC, MC, V. Daily noon–2pm and 6:30–9pm. GERMAN/ITALIAN/INTERNATIONAL.

The old-fashioned tradition and service here attract many regular patrons. This a place where you can watch the flowers bloom and enjoy a world-class cuisine (with many diet-conscious selections). You might try one of the kitchen's own original recipes: for example, marinated and roasted medallions of venison Königin Luise, served with bacon, chanterelles, and whortleberries.

✪ **Schweizer Stuben.** Kirchberg Schlössl, Thumseestrasse 11, Kirchberg. ☎ **08651/ 27-60.** Reservations required. Main courses 29DM–44DM ($14.50–$22); fixed-price meals 39DM ($19.50) at lunch, 72DM–92DM ($36–$46) at dinner. AE, DC, MC, V. Thurs–Tues 11am–3pm and 6pm–midnight. INTERNATIONAL.

No restaurant, even those in the luxury hotels, can hold a candle to this place for cuisine. It's located southwest of town in the center of the suburb of Kirchberg. The kitchen prepares light international dishes, along with specialties from Bavaria and the Berchtesgaden region. The decor is appropriately rustic. The chef seems to have a bent for updating contemporary classics. The fixed-price menu at lunch is an especially good value.

BAD REICHENHALL AFTER DARK

Most guests on the nighttime circuit head for the **Bad Reichenhall Casino,** Wittelsbacherstrasse 17 (☎ **08651/40-91**), which offers roulette, American roulette, blackjack, and 50 types of slot machines. You must show your passport if you plan to do any gaming. It's open daily 3pm to 3am; admission is 5DM ($2.50). Men must wear jackets and ties. The **theater,** also located here at the Kurgastzentrum, site of the casino, is a setting for operas, operettas, plays, ballets, musicals, symphonies, folkloric evenings, and chamber musical recitals. The tourism office (see "Visitor Information," above) keeps a complete list of events and ticket prices. When weather permits, performances are staged in an open-air pavilion. Tickets are 40DM to 63DM ($20 to $31.50).

If you want to hang out with the locals, go to the **Axel Bar,** a woodsy bar in the Steigenberger Axelmannstein Hotel, Salzburgerstrasse 2–6 (☎ **08651/77-70**). Here you can dance to rather sedate disco music interspersed with folk tunes. There's also the **Tiffany Bar** at the Hotel Bayerischer Hof, Bahnhofplatz 14 (☎ **08651/24-80**), where folks sometimes dance to live music but mostly just drink. The Bayerischer Hof's nightclub hosts international acts. Good old-fashioned Bavarian suds is the order of the evening at everybody's favorite beer hall, **Burgerbräu,** Rathausplatz (☎ **08651/60-89**).

3 Chiemsee

Prien am Chiemsee: 85km (53 miles) SE of Munich, 22km (14 miles) E of Rosenheim, 64km (40 miles) W of Salzburg

Chiemsee, known as the "Bavarian Sea," is one of the most beautiful lakes in the Bavarian Alps. It's surrounded by a serene landscape. In the south, the mountains reach almost to the water. Resorts line the shores of this large lake, but the main attraction is its two islands, **Frauenchiemsee** and **Herrenchiemsee,** where Ludwig II built his palace, Neues Schloss.

ESSENTIALS

GETTING THERE   By Train   Prien Bahnhof is on the major Munich–Rosenheim–Freilassing–Salzburg rail line, with frequent connections in all directions. Ten trains arrive daily from Munich (trip time: 1 hr.). For information, call ☎ 01805/99-66-33.

By Bus   Regional bus service in the area is offered by **RVO Regionalverkehr Oberbayern,** Betrieb Rosenheim (☎ **08031/6-20-06** for schedules and information).

By Car   Access by car is via the A8 Autobahn from Munich.

VISITOR INFORMATION   Contact the **Kur- und Verkehrsamt,** Alte Rathausstrasse 11, in Prien am Chiemsee (☎ **08051/6-90-50**). It's open Monday to Friday 8:30am to 6pm and Saturday 9am to noon.

GETTING AROUND   By Steamer   From the liveliest resort, Prien, on the lake's west shore, you can reach either Frauenchiemsee or Herrenchiemsee via lake steamers that make regular trips throughout the year. The round-trip fare to Herrenchiemsee is 14DM ($7), 16DM ($8) to Fraueninchiemsee. The steamers, operated by **Chiemsee-Schiffahrt Ludwig Fessler** (☎ **08051/60-90**), make round-trips covering the entire lake. Connections can also be made from Gstadt, Seebruck, Chieming, Übersee/Feldwies, and Bernau/Felden. Large boats leave Prien/Stock for Herrenchiemsee May to September, daily, about every 20 minutes 9am to 5pm. The last return is at 7:25pm.

By Bus   There's also bus service from the harbor to the DB station in Prien (Chiemsee-Schiffahrt) and around the lake by RVO.

EXPLORING THE ISLANDS
FRAUENCHIEMSEE

Frauenchiemsee (or Fraueninsel) is the smaller of the lake's two major islands. On its sandy shore stands a fishing village that holds an elaborate festival at Corpus Christi (usually in late May). Fishing boats are covered with flowers and streamers, fishers are outfitted in Bavarian garb, and young women of the village dress as brides. As the boats circle the island, they stop at each corner for the singing of the Gospels. The island is also the home of a Benedictine convent, Frauenchiemsee Abbey, founded in 782, which makes it the oldest in Germany. The convent is known for a liqueur called Kloster Likör—it's supposed to be an "agreeable stomach elixir."

You can walk around the island in about 30 minutes to enjoy panoramic views of the lake. **Torhalle** (☎ **08054/72-56**), a summer-only art gallery, is installed in the ancient hall that used to be the gatehouse of the Frauenwörth convent. Admission is 4DM ($2) for adults and 1.50DM (75¢) for children.

HERRENCHIEMSEE

Herrenchiemsee (or Herreninsel) is home to the fantastic ✪ **Neues Schloss,** Herrenchiemsee 3 (☎ **08051/30-69**), begun by Ludwig II in 1878 (see "The Fairy-Tale King," in chapter 6). Never completed due to the king's death in 1886, the castle was to have been a replica of Versailles, which Ludwig admired. When work was halted in 1886, only the center of the enormous palace had been completed. Nonetheless, the palace and its formal gardens, surrounded by woodlands of beech and fir, remain one of the grandest and most fascinating of Ludwig's constructions.

The palace **entrance** is lit by a huge skylight over the sumptuously decorated stair-case. Frescoes depicting the four states of existence alternate with Greek and Roman statues in niches on the staircase and in the gallery above. The vestibule is adorned with a pair of enameled peacocks, Louis XIV's favorite bird.

The **Great Hall of Mirrors** is unquestionably the most splendid room in the palace and the most authentic replica of Versailles. The 17 door panels contain enormous mirrors reflecting the 33 crystal chandeliers and the 44 gilded candelabra. The vaulted ceiling is covered with 25 paintings depicting the life of Louis XIV.

Practically every inch of the **state bedroom** has been gilded. On the dais, instead of a throne, stands the richly decorated bed, its purple-velvet draperies weighing more than 135kg (300 pounds). Separating the dais from the rest of the room is a carved wooden balustrade covered with gold leaf. On the ceiling, a huge fresco depicts the descent of Apollo, surrounded by the other gods of Olympus. The sun god's features bear a strong resemblance to those of Louis XIV.

The **dining room** is a popular attraction for visitors because of the so-called "little table that sets itself." A mechanism in the floor permitted the table to go down to the room below to be cleared and re-laid between courses. Over the table hangs an exquisite chandelier of Meissen porcelain, the largest in the world and the single most valuable item in the palace.

You can visit Herrenchiemsee at any time of the year. April to September, tours are given daily 9am to 5pm; off-season, daily 10am to 4pm. Admission (in addition to the round-trip boat fare) is 8DM ($4) for adults, 5DM ($2.50) for students, and free for children under 16.

WHERE TO STAY & DINE

Bayerischer Hof. Bernauerstrasse 3, 83209 Prien am Chiemsee. ☎ **08051/60-30.** Fax 08051/6-29-17. E-mail: Hotel-bayerischer-hof@t-online.de. 46 units. TV TEL. 160DM–180DM ($80–$90) double. Rates include buffet breakfast. AE, MC, V. Closed Nov and last week of Jan. Parking 10DM ($5).

The Estermann family will welcome you to the Bayerischer Hof. The rustic decor creates the illusion that this relatively severe modern hotel is older than it is. Of particular note is the painted ceiling in the dining room. The rest of the hotel is more streamlined—modern, efficient, and quite appealing, although the Yachthotel Chiemsee outside of town has more style and flair. Nonetheless, the rooms are very comfortable.

Yachthotel Chiemsee. Harrasser Strasse 49, 83209 Prien am Chiemsee. ☎ **08051/69-60.** Fax 08051/51-71. www.yachthotel.de. E-mail: info@xachthotel.de. MINIBAR TV TEL. 255DM–320DM ($127.50–$160) double; 340DM–470DM ($170–$235) suite. Rates include buffet breakfast. AE, DC, MC, V. Free parking.

The best place to stay on the lake is the Yachthotel Chiemsee, on the western shore of the "Bavarian Sea." This hotel offers attractively furnished rooms, all with balconies or terraces opening onto the water. Lakeside rooms are equipped with two double beds and a pull-out sofa for groups of four or more. Most rooms are fairly spacious.

Dining/Diversions: A choice of restaurants—complete with a lakeside terrace and a marina—awaits you. The most elegant room, with an excellent view, is the Seepavillon. The Seerestaurant is slightly more rustic but still has an elegant flair, and the Zirbelstüberl goes alpine-Bavarian all the way. The menu is the same in all three.

Amenities: Room service (7am to midnight), laundry, baby-sitting, sailing (a two-masted yacht with a skipper is available May to September), rowing, squash, tennis, riding, golf (nearby), horse-drawn carriage trips, spa department, beauty-care center, sauna, solarium, health and fitness center, outdoor whirlpool, indoor pool, hair dryers.

4 Bad Wiessee

53km (33 miles) S of Munich, 18km (11 miles) SE of Bad Tölz

If you've always believed that the best medicine is the worst tasting, you should feel right at home in Bad Wiessee—the mineral springs of this popular spa on the Tegernsee are saturated with iodine and sulfur. However, the other attractions of this small town more than make up for this healthful discomfort. The spa, with a huge lake at its feet and towering Alps rising behind it, is a year-round resort. In summer, swimming and boating are popular; in winter, you can ski on the slopes or skate on the lake.

The springs are used for the treatment of many diseases, including rheumatism and heart and respiratory conditions. In spite of its tiny size, Bad Wiessee is advanced in its medicinal facilities, as well as in its accommodations and restaurants.

The main season begins in May and ends in October. During these busy times, you should definitely make a reservation. Many hotels close in winter, so be warned if you're an off-season visitor. In recent years the town has become increasingly popular with vacationers from Munich.

From Bad Wiessee, any number of tours are possible, including visits to Munich, Chiemsee, and the castles of Neuschwanstein, Herrenchiemsee, and Linderhof (see chapter 6). You can also visit Salzburg and Innsbruck in Austria. The tourism office (see below) will supply details.

ESSENTIALS

GETTING THERE   By Train   Travelers arriving by train disembark at Gmund, 3km (2 miles) away. At the railway station there, a flotilla of buses (9 to 11 per day) meet every major train, with easy connections on to Bad Wiessee. For rail information, call ☎ **01805/99-66-33.**

By Bus   3 to 5 buses depart every day for Bad Wiessee from Munich's Hauptbahnhof, with additional stops along the Zweibrückestrasse, adjacent to Munich's Deutsches Museum (trip time: 90 minutes). Round-trip transport costs 21DM ($10.50) per person. For bus information, call ☎ **08022/86-03-20.**

By Car   Access from either Munich or Salzburg is via the A8 Autobahn. Take the Holzkirchen exit heading toward Bad Wiessee and follow the signs.

VISITOR INFORMATION   For information, go to the **Kuramt,** Adrian-Stoop-Strasse 20 (☎ **08022/8-60-30**). May to October, the tourism office's hours are Monday to Friday 8am to 6pm and Saturday and Sunday 9am to noon. In the off-season, hours are Monday to Friday 8am to noon and 2 to 5pm.

SIGHTS & ACTIVITIES

Bad Wiesse offers plenty of activities, apart from its health treatments. In summer, there's sailing or windsurfing on the lake, or mountain biking and hiking. A drive up the **Wallberg Road** winds through the Moorsalm pasture to an altitude of 1,000m (3,300 feet). There's also plenty of golf and tennis. In winter, experienced alpine skiers are drawn to the Wallberg, and there are many cross-country trails as well. Wintertime hiking is also a possibility, as about 100km (60 miles) of paths are cleared of snow. The less athletic can enjoy horse-drawn sleigh rides. Finally, you can also take a **mountain cable car,** which travels 1,550m (5,100 feet) high.

The town of Bad Wiesse has an old-world charm. It's best explored via the old-fashioned steam train or by taking a carriage ride. During the annual lake festivals in summer, locals don traditional clothing and parade through the town. Worth the trip is the nearby **Tegernsee Ducal palace,** which contains the former monastery of St. Quinn, founded in A.D. 746.

SHOPPING

You'll find traditional Bavarian souvenirs, loden coats, and lederhosen here. For a full selection of traditional Bavarian clothes, go to **Friedl Mandel,** Lindenplatz (☎ **08022/8-14-58**). If you want to acquire one-of-a-kind wood carvings, either religious or secular, head for the studio of **Franz Trinkl,** Dr. Scheid Strasse 9A (☎ **08022/87-49**), where you'll find a charming and idiosyncratic collection of artfully carved figurines.

WHERE TO STAY & DINE
EXPENSIVE

Hotel Lederer am See. Bodenschneidstrasse 9–11, 83707 Bad Wiessee. ☎ **08022/82-90.** Fax 08022/82-92-61. www.lederer.com. E-mail: hotel@lederer.com. 114 units. TV TEL. 160DM–360DM ($80–$180) double. AE, DC, MC, V. Closed Oct–Feb. Free parking.

This spa and holiday hotel is the most distinguished choice in town. From the balcony of your room, you'll look out onto the Tegernsee and the Lower Bavarian Alps. The atmosphere is pleasant, with good service and attractive, well-maintained rooms, ranging in size from medium to spacious. The hotel stands in a large park, and there's an indoor pool for swimming as well as a meadow for sunbathing.

Dining/Diversions: The hotel restaurant turns out an international cuisine of good standard. Sometimes there's a barbecue on the terrace facing the lake, followed by entertainment or dancing in the nightclub.

Amenities: The hotel has its own medical staff and "beauty farm," including a sauna, solarium, and indoor pool. Other amenities include tennis courts, beauty salon, concierge, room service, and dry cleaning and laundry service.

MODERATE

Kurhotel Rex. Münchnerstrasse 25, 83707 Bad Wiessee. ☎ **08022/8-62-00.** Fax 08022/862-01-00. 58 units. TV TEL. 194DM–234DM ($97–$117) double; 264DM ($132) suite. No credit cards. Closed Nov 1–Apr 5. Free parking.

A modern hotel with much charm and character, Kurhotel Rex is set against a backdrop of the Lower Bavarian Alps. It's an ideal choice for a vacation by the lake.

The decorator tried to make the place as warm and inviting as possible. The well-maintained rooms are furnished in Bavarian style. The hotel has good food and caters to special dieters, and its Bierstuberl is a lively gathering place.

Landhaus Hotel Sapplfeld. Im Sapplfeld 8, 83707 Bad Wiessee. ☎ **08022/9-84-70.** Fax 08022/8-35-60. www.silence.de/hotels/sapplfeld. 16 units. TV TEL. 208DM–280DM ($104–$140) double. Rates include buffet breakfast. MC, V. Free parking. Garage 20DM ($10).

This typical Bavarian inn, with geranium-filled balconies and a roof overhang, is a real alpine resort, where people come to have a good time. It attracts scenery lovers in summer, and skiers in winter. Rooms range from small to medium in size and are completely modern; each has a balcony. The hotel has a sauna where, as is usual for Germany, men and women are segregated.

Park Hotel Resi von der Post. Zilcherstrasse 14, 83707 Bad Wiessee. ☎ **08022/9-86-50.** Fax 08022/98-65-65. 30 units. TV TEL. 188DM ($94) double; from 218DM ($109) suite. Rates include buffet breakfast. AE, DC, MC, V. Free parking.

This enduring favorite has been around much longer than many of its fast-rising competitors. It has been considerably modernized, and now has well-furnished, traditional rooms. Baths are a bit cramped. The atmosphere in the hotel's restaurant is often bustling, as diners who live nearby fill the place; many show up in Bavarian dress. Ask for the special cheese of the Tegernsee district, *Miesbacher.* Make reservations early for this hotel; it's usually booked up for the year by summer.

INEXPENSIVE

Kurhotel Edelweiss. Münchnerstrasse 21, 83707 Bad Wiessee, a quarter-mile north of the center. ☎ **08022/8-60-90.** Fax 08022/8-38-83. www.bad-wiessee.de/edelweiss. E-mail: hoteledelweiss-hocht@online.de. 40 units. TV TEL. 130DM–160DM ($65–$80) double. Rates include continental breakfast. No credit cards. Free parking.

This chalet/guest house is ornamented with wooden balconies and painted detailing. Rooms are functionally but comfortably furnished. Additional but less-desirable units are available in the motel-like outbuildings beside the main structure. The modern public areas are suffused with a certain German kitsch. The Bavarian-style restaurant is open for hotel guests only.

Wiesseer Hof. Sanktjohanserstrasse 46, 83707 Bad Wiessee. ☎ **08022/86-70.** Fax 08022/86-71-65. www.wiesseerhof.com. 60 units. TV TEL. 160DM–200DM ($80–$100) double. Rates include buffet breakfast. MC, V. Free parking.

This modern, but still traditional, four-story hotel looks like an overgrown chalet. Rooms are snug and cozy in the alpine tradition, with such amenities as private safes and hair dryers. Most have balconies, festooned in summer with boxes of geraniums, with views over a lawn dotted with greenery. The stuccoed wooden walls of the public areas create a *gemütlich* warmth. The kitchen features many good Bavarian specialties.

5 Mittenwald

106km (66 miles) S of Munich, 18km (11 miles) SE of Garmisch-Partenkirchen, 37km (23 miles) NW of Innsbruck

The year-round resort of Mittenwald, which lies in a pass in the Karwendel Range, seems straight out of *The Sound of Music.* Especially noteworthy and photogenic are the painted Bavarian houses with overhanging eaves. On the square stands a monument to Mathias Klotz, who introduced violin making to Mittenwald in 1684. The town is now a major international center for this highly specialized craft.

ESSENTIALS

GETTING THERE By Train Hourly train service runs on the express rail line between Munich and Innsbruck, Austria. From Munich, trip time is 1½ to 2 hours; from Frankfurt, 5 to 6 hours. Call ☎ **01805/99-66-33** for information.

By Bus Regional bus service from Garmisch-Partenkirchen and nearby towns is frequently provided by **RVO Regionalverkehr Oberbayern** at Garmisch (☎ **08821/ 94-82-74** for schedules and information).

By Car Access by car is via the A95 Autobahn from Munich.

VISITOR INFORMATION Contact the **Kurverwaltung und Verkehrsamt,** Dammkarstrasse 3 (☎ **08823/3-39-81**). It's open Monday to Friday 8am to noon and 1 to 5pm, and Saturday and Sunday 10am to noon.

SIGHTS & ACTIVITIES

The town's museum, which contains a workshop, has exhibits that trace the history of violins and other stringed instruments, from their invention through various stages of their evolution. The **Geigenbau- und Heimatmuseum,** Ballenhausgasse 3 (☎ **08823/25-11**), is open Monday to Friday 10am to noon and 2 to 5pm, and on Saturday and Sunday 10am to noon. Admission is 3DM ($1.50) for adults and 1DM (50¢) for students and children. The museum is closed November 1 to December 22.

In the surrounding countryside, the scenery of the Wetterstein and Karwendel ranges constantly changes. Some 130km (80 miles) of hiking paths wind up and down the mountains around the village. You can hike through the hills on your own, take part in mountain-climbing expeditions, or take horse-and-carriage trips and motorcoach tours from Mittenwald to nearby villages. In the evening in the various inns, there's typical Bavarian entertainment, often consisting of folk dancing and singing, zither playing, and yodeling. Concerts during the summer are held in the music pavilion. Mittenwald also has good spa facilities, in large gardens landscaped with tree-lined streams and trout pools. In winter the town is a skiing center.

SHOPPING

The classical stringed instruments crafted here have been sought after by professional musicians for centuries. Prices may be steep for the amateur violinist, but a visit to **Geigenbau Leonhardt,** Mühlenweg 53A (☎ **08823/80-10**), is educational and interesting even if you're just browsing.

If you've ever had the desire to traipse about in a dirndl, embroidered blouse, or lederhosen, head for **Trachtenstubön,** Obermarkt 35 (☎ **08823/85-55**).

WHERE TO STAY

Alpenrose. Obermarkt 1, 82481 Mittenwald. ☎ **08823/92700.** Fax 08823/3720. E-mail: alpenrose.mittenwald@t-online.de. 18 units. MINIBAR TV TEL. 128DM–185DM ($64–$92.50) double; 192DM ($96) suite. Rates include buffet breakfast. AE, DC, DISC, MC, V. Free parking.

This particularly inviting hotel is located in the village center at the foot of a rugged mountain. The facade is covered with decorative designs and window boxes. The inn's basic 14th-century structure was once part of a monastery. Rooms are divided between the Alpenrose (the former monastery) and its annex, the Bichlerhof. Try to stay in the main building, where rooms have a great deal of charm, with finely woven fabrics, old-fashioned farmhouse cupboards, and dark wood paneling. Baths in both buildings are a bit cramped. The tavern room, overlooking the street, has many ingratiating features, including handmade chairs, flagstone floors, and a square tile stove in the center. In the Josefikeller, beer is served in giant steins, and musicians play in the evening. The dining room provides excellent meals, including Bavarian specialties.

Gästehaus Sonnenbichl. Klausnerweg 32, 82481 Mittenwald. ☎ **08823/9-22-30.** Fax 08823/58-14. www.sonnenbichl.de. 20 units. MINIBAR TV TEL. 114DM–160DM ($65–$91.20) double. Rates include buffet breakfast. No credit cards. Closed Nov 1–Dec 15.

One of the more modest inns in town, this chalet nevertheless offers good value and comfort. It has a view of the village set against a backdrop of the Alps. The small but exceedingly well-kept rooms are freshly decorated in vivid natural colors. Reserve well in advance. Breakfast is the only meal served.

Hotel Post. Obermarkt 9, 82481 Mittenwald. ☎ **08823/10-94.** Fax 08823/10-96. www.posthotel-mittenwald.de. E-mail: posthotel-mittenwald@onlinehome.de. 80 units. MINIBAR TV TEL. 190DM–260DM ($95–$130) double; 280DM–320DM ($140–$160) suite. Rates include buffet breakfast. No credit cards. Parking free outside or 8DM ($4) inside.

The Post provides Mittenwald's finest lodging. It's the most seasoned and established chalet hotel in the village, dating from 1632, when stagecoaches carrying mail and passengers across the Bavarian Alps stopped here to refuel. A delightful breakfast is served on the sun terrace, with a view of the Alps. On a cool day, enjoy a beer in the snug lounge/bar, which has an open fireplace. For a night of hearty Bavarian specialties, head for the wine tavern or the Poststüberl. Beds here are among the most comfortable in town, with duvets and beautiful linen. The maids are especially helpful. Amenities include an indoor pool, massage facilities, exercise room, and sauna.

WHERE TO DINE

Restaurant Arnspitze. Innsbruckerstrasse 68. ☎ **08823/24-25.** Main courses 28.50DM–42.50DM ($14.25–$21.25); fixed-price meal 43DM ($21.50) at lunch, 83DM ($41.50) at dinner. AE. Wed 6–9pm, Thurs–Mon noon–2pm and 6–9pm. BAVARIAN.

This traditionally decorated restaurant, housed in a modern chalet hotel on the outskirts of town, is the finest in Mittenwald. The cuisine is solid, satisfying, and wholesome. You might order sole with homemade noodles or veal steak in creamy smooth sauce, then finish with one of the freshly made desserts. There's an excellent fixed-price lunch.

6 Garmisch-Partenkirchen

97km (60 miles) SW of Munich, 117km (73 miles) SE of Augsburg, 60km (37 miles) NW of Innsbruck

The twin villages of Garmisch and Partenkirchen make up Germany's top alpine resort. In spite of their urban flair, the towns maintain the charm of an ancient village, especially Partenkirchen. Even today, you occasionally see country folk in traditional dress, and you may be held up in traffic while the cattle are led from their mountain-grazing grounds down through the streets of town.

ESSENTIALS

GETTING THERE   By Train   The **Garmisch-Partenkirchen Bahnhof** lies on the major Munich–Weilheim–Garmisch–Mittenwald–Innsbruck rail line, with frequent connections in all directions. Twenty trains per day arrive from Munich (trip time: 1 hr. 22 min.). For information and schedules, call ☎ **01805/996633.** Mountain rail service to several plateaus and the Zugspitze is offered by the **Bayerische Zugspitzbahn** at Garmisch (☎ **08821/79-70**).

By Bus   Both long-distance and regional buses through the Bavarian Alps are provided by **RVO Regionalverkehr Oberbayern** in Garmisch-Partenkirchen (☎ **08821/ 94-82-74**).

By Car   Access is via the A95 Autobahn from Munich; exit at Eschenlohe.

Hiking in the Bavarian Alps

Hiking is Bavaria's favorite pastime. Locals believe firmly in the emotional and spiritual benefits of walking and hill climbing and tend to hit the trails the moment the snows melt.

The tourist office in Garmisch-Partenkirchen will point you to hiking trails of varying degrees of difficulty, all with clearly designated signs. The office also offers a brochure outlining the half-dozen best trails. You don't have to be an Olympic athlete to enjoy them. Most hikes will take an energetic 4 to 5 hours, but some of them are shorter and easy enough for children.

An easily accessibly destination is the 1,240m (4,060-foot) **Eckbauer** peak that lies on the southern fringe of Partenkirchen. The easy trails on its lower slopes are recommended for first-time alpine hikers. You can even take a chairlift to the top, where, in the real Bavarian style, the Bergasthof will serve you a glass of buttermilk. In less than an hour you can descend on relatively easy trails through a forest. The cable car stretching from Garmisch to the top of the Eckbauer departs year-round from the Eckbauerbahn (☎ **08821/7970**), adjacent to the ski stadium in Garmisch. Round-trip costs 19DM ($9.50) for adults, 12DM ($6) for children, and 44DM ($22) for two adults and a child.

More demanding are the slopes of the rugged ✪ **Alpspitz** region, which begins about a mile southwest of Garmisch. The area is interlaced with wildflowers, unusual geology, alpine meadows, and a network of cable cars and hiking trails spread over a terrain ranging in altitude between 1,400m (4,600) and 1,920m (6,300 feet). The highest trails are around the summit of the Alpspitz at 2,603m (8,541 feet).

One of the most appealing ways to gain a high-altitude panorama over this region is to take a triangular trip up the Alpspitz. Begin your journey at the Kreuzeckbahn/Alpspitzbahn cable car terminus, a mile south of Garmisch. The cable car will carry you uphill along the Kreuzeckbahn for a 4-minute ride across a jagged landscape to the lowest station of the Hochalm cable car. Here the Hochalmbahn will carry you uphill for another 4 minutes to the top of the Osterfelderkopf, 1,920m (6,300 feet) above sea level. Cable cars for both stages of this trip depart at 30-minute intervals daily 8:15am to 5:15pm. After your visit to the Osterfelderkopf summit, you can return to Garmisch via a different route, a direct downhill descent via the Alpspitzbahn, a 10-minute ride above jagged

VISITOR INFORMATION   Contact the **Verkehrsamt,** Richard-Strauss-Platz (☎ **08821/18-06**). It's open Monday to Saturday 8am to 6pm and Sunday and holidays 10am to noon.

GETTING AROUND   An unnumbered municipal bus services the town, depositing passengers at Marienplatz or the Bahnhof, from which you can walk to all centrally located hotels. This free bus runs every 15 minutes.

EXPLORING THE AREA

Garmisch-Partenkirchen is a center for winter sports, summer hiking, and mountain climbing. The symbol of the city's growth and modernity is the **Olympic Ice Stadium,** built for the 1936 Winter Olympics and capable of holding nearly 12,000 people. On the slopes at the edge of town is the **Ski Stadium,** with two ski jumps and gorges, soaring cliffs, and grassy meadows. At the points where the cable car lines intersect, you might want to embark on short, high-altitude hikes to observe the unique alpine flora and fauna. Snacks are served at cafes and restaurants at major points on the itinerary.

Round-trip passage along this three-tiered alpine itinerary costs 42DM ($21) for adults and 25DM ($12.50) for children 5 to 16; it's free for children 4 and under. These fares and times of departure can fluctuate. For the latest details, call either the information service for the above-mentioned cable cars (☎ **08821/7970**) or check with the Garmisch **Verkehrsamt** (tourist office) on Richard-Strauss-Platz (☎ **08821/18-06**).

From Garmisch-Partenkirchen, many other peaks of the Witterstein range are accessible as well, via the 10 funiculars ascending from the borders of the town. From the top of the 1,780m (5,850-foot) **Wank** to the east, you get the best view of the plateau on which the villages of Garmisch and Partenkirchen sit. This summit is also a favorite with the patrons of Garmisch's spa facilities because the plentiful sunshine makes it ideal for the *Liegekur* (deck-chair cure).

Another interesting hike is through the **Partnachklamm Gorge,** a canyon with a roaring stream at the bottom and sheer cliff walls rising on either side of the hiking trail. Take the Graseck Seilbahn from its departure point at the bottom of the gorge, less than a half mile south of Garmisch's ski stadium, and get off at the first station, which is adjacent to a cozy hotel, the **Forsthaus Graseck** (☎ **08821/5-40-06**). You might want to get a meal or drink here first. Afterward descend on foot along narrow paths by the sides of the stream, as it cascades downhill. The path crosses the gorge and returns you to the point where you entered. Many readers have found this one of their most memorable adventures in Bavaria. The experience of walking along a rocky ledge just above a rushing river and often behind small waterfalls, while looking up at 365m (1,200 feet) of rocky cliffs, is truly awesome (and sometimes wet).

From its departure point to the Forsthaus, the 3-minute cable car ride costs 5DM ($2.50) per person each way. For information about the Seilbahn, contact Forsthaus Graseck (☎ **08821/5-40-06**). The cable car operates at 20-minute intervals 8am to 8pm, 11pm on weekends.

a slalom course. In 1936, more than 100,000 people watched the events in this stadium. Today it's still an integral part of winter life in Garmisch—the World Cup Ski Jump is held here every New Year.

The town and its environs offer some of the most panoramic views and colorful buildings in Bavaria. The pilgrimage **Chapel of St. Anton,** on a pinewood path at the edge of Partenkirchen, is all pink and silver, inside and out. Its graceful lines are characteristic of the 18th century, when it was built. The **Philosopher's Walk,** in the park surrounding the chapel, is a delightful spot to wander, just to enjoy the views of the mountains around the low-lying town.

This area has always attracted German romantics, including "Mad" King Ludwig (see the box, "The Fairy-Tale King," in chapter 6). Perhaps with Wagner's music ringing in his ears, the king ordered the construction of a hunting lodge here in the style of a Swiss chalet, but commanded that the interior look like something out of *The Arabian Nights*. The lodge, **Jagdschloss Schachen,** is still here. It can only be reached after an arduous climb. The tourist office will supply details. Mid-June to mid-September, tours at 11am and 2pm often leave from the Olympic Ski Stadium heading for the lodge, but check before you go.

TO THE TOP OF THE ZUGSPITZE

From Garmisch-Partenkirchen, you can see the tallest mountain in Germany, the ✪ **Zugspitze,** 2,960m (9,720 feet) above sea level. Ski slopes begin at a height of 2,650m (8,700 feet). For a panoramic view of both the Bavarian and the Tyrolean (Austrian) Alps, go all the way to the summit. The Zugspitze peak can be reached in one of two different ways from the center of Garmisch. The first begins with a trip on the cog railway, the Zugspitzbahn, which departs from back of the Garmisch's main railway station daily every hour 8:35am to 2:35pm. The train travels uphill, past lichen-covered boulders and coursing streams, to a high-altitude plateau, the Zugspitzplatte, where views sweep out over all Bavaria. At the Zugspitzplatte, you'll transfer onto a cable car, the Gletscher Sielbahn, for a 4-minute ride uphill to the top of the Zugspitze. There, far-reaching panoramas, a cafe and restaurant, a gift shop, and many alpine trails await. Total travel time for this itinerary is about 55 minutes, but you may want to linger at the first stop, the Zugspitzplatte, before going on up.

The other way to get to the summit is to take the Zugspitzbahn for a briefer trip, disembarking 14km (9 miles) southwest of Garmisch at the lower station of the Eibsee Sielbahn (Eibsee Cable Car), next to a clear alpine lake. The cable car will carry you from there directly to the summit of the Zugspitze, for a total transit time of about 38 minutes. The Eibsee Sielbahn makes its run at least every half hour 8:30am to 4:30pm (5:30pm in July and August).

Round-trip tickets allow you to ascend one way and descend the other, in order to enjoy the widest range of spectacular views. April to October, round-trip fares are 79DM ($39.50) for adults, 69DM ($34.50) for seniors, 55DM ($27.50) for teenagers ages 16 and 17, and 47DM ($23.50) for children ages 5 to 15. Group fare for two adults and a child costs 175DM ($87.50). In winter, round-trip fares are reduced to 64DM ($32) for adults, 46DM ($23) for those ages 16 and 17, and 39DM ($19.50) for children ages 5 to 15. For more information, contact the Bayerlsche Zugspitzbahn, Olympiastrasse 27, Garmisch-Partenkirchen (☎ **08821/7-97-0;** or 08821/79-97-97 for a recorded message).

SHOPPING

Your best bets are in the traffic-reduced Ludwigstrasse in Partenkirchen and in the almost traffic-free zone from Richard-Strauss-Platz to Marienplatz in Garmisch. A vast array of stores sell boots, boutique items, clothing, jewelry, art, antiques, and more. If you like traditional Bavarian dress but don't want to spend a lot of money, head for **Loisachtaler,** Burgstrasse 20 (☎ **08821/ 5-23-90**). Here, Petra Ostler has assembled the area's finest collection of secondhand clothing. Take your pick: a jaegermeister loden coat, an alpine hat with pheasant feathers, or a cast-off dirndl. They all look like new.

WHERE TO STAY
EXPENSIVE

Grand Hotel Sonnenbichl. Burgstrasse 97, 82467 Garmisch-Partenkirchen. ☎ **08821/ 70-20.** Fax 08821/70-21-31. www.sonnenbichl.de. E-mail: grand-hotel-sonnenbichl@ t-online.de. 93 units. MINIBAR TV TEL. 250DM–350DM ($125–$175) double; 700DM–980DM ($350–$490) suite. Rates include buffet breakfast. AE, DC, MC, V. Free parking. Take Rte. 23 toward Oberammergau.

The most upscale hotel in the area is on the hillside overlooking Garmisch-Partenkirchen, 1.5km (1 mile) from the city center and 3km (2 miles) from the Bahnhof. It has excellent views of the Wetterstein mountain range and the Zugspitze (from front rooms only; rear rooms open onto a rock wall). Some of the spacious rooms are showing a bit of wear and tear; a few lack a complete bathtub. The decor is generally art nouveau.

Dining/Diversions: The hotel serves excellent food. You can have light, modern cuisine in the elegant gourmet restaurant, the Blauer Salon, or Bavarian specialties in the Zirbelstube. Afternoon coffee and fresh homemade cake are served in the lobby or on the sunny terrace. Drinks are available in the Peacock Bar.

Amenities: Room service, laundry, dry cleaning, pool, sauna, solarium, fitness and massage rooms.

MODERATE

✪ **Posthotel Partenkirchen.** Ludwigstrasse 49, 82467 Garmisch-Partenkirchen. ☎ **08821/93630.** Fax 08821/93-63-2222. 59 units. MINIBAR TV TEL. 250DM–280DM ($125–$140) double; 290DM–480DM ($145–$240) suite. Rates include continental breakfast. AE, DC, MC, V. Free parking.

The Posthotel Partenkirchen, which was founded in 1542, has emerged as one of the town's most prestigious hotels. In recent years, it has even surpassed its major rival, the Reindl's Partenkirchner Hof. Here you'll experience Old-World living and personalized service. The U-shaped rooms are stylish, with antiques and elaborately carved furnishings. The sunny balconies overlook a garden and offer a view of the Alps. Rooms are generally medium in size, though some are quite spacious.

Dining/Diversions: The restaurant here is unusually fine (see "Where to Dine," below). In the rustic Weinlokal Barbarossa, there are nooks for quiet before- or after-dinner drinks.

Amenities: Room service (7am to 11pm), laundry, golf, tennis, swimming, mountain climbing, skiing, cycling, hiking, horseback riding, paragliding.

Reindl's Partenkirchner Hof. Bahnhofstrasse 15, 82467 Garmisch-Partenkirchen. ☎ **08821/ 5-80-25.** Fax 08821/73401. www.garmisch-partenkirchen.com/Reindl. E-mail: reindl@oberland. net. 88 units. MINIBAR TV TEL. 200DM–310DM ($100–$155) double; 320DM–650DM ($160–$325) suite. AE, DC, MC, V. Closed Nov 9–Dec 15. Parking 12DM ($6).

Reindl's opened in 1911, and from the beginning it attracted a devoted following. Owners Bruni and Karl Reindl maintain a high level of luxury and hospitality in this special Bavarian retreat. The annexes, the Wetterstein and the House Alpspitz, have balconies, and the main four-story building has wraparound verandas, giving each room an unobstructed view of the mountains and town. Rooms are among the most attractive in town. The best are the suites opening onto panoramic views of mountains or the garden. Fine wool carpeting and rustic pine furniture add to the allure.

Dining: The Reindl's restaurant is well respected (see "Where to Dine," below).

Amenities: Room service, laundry, covered pool, sauna, sun room, health club, open terrace for snacks, two attractive gardens.

✪ **Romantik-Hotel Clausing's Posthotel.** Marienplatz 12, 82467 Garmisch-Partenkirchen. ☎ **08821/70-90.** Fax 08821/70-92-05. www.clausings-posthotel.de. E-mail: info@ clausings-posthotel.de. 45 units. MINIBAR TV TEL. 180DM–300DM ($90–$150) double; from 400DM ($200) suite. Rates include buffet breakfast. AE, DC, MC, V.

The history and identity of Garmisch are bound up in events that took place at this hotel in the heart of town. It began as a tavern in 1512. During the Thirty Years' War, it sheltered refugees from besieged Munich. In 1891, it was bought by the Berlin beer baron who invented Berliner Weissen, which quickly became one of the most popular brands in Garmisch. Nowadays, the upgraded hotel retains its sense of

Gemütlichkeit. Rooms range from spacious to rather small and cozy, successfully mingling Bavarian antique charm with modern comforts. Baths are beautifully kept. The most glamorous restaurant here is the Stüberl, a paneled enclave of warmth and carefully presented cuisine. The Verandah offers simple platters, drinks, and glassed-in comfort in winter, and open-air access to the bustling Marienplatz in summer. Live music is presented at the Post-Hörnd'l every evening year-round between 6pm and midnight.

INEXPENSIVE

Gasthof Fraundorfer. Ludwigstrasse 24, 82467 Garmisch-Partenkirchen. ☎ **08821/ 21-76.** Fax 08821/9-27-99. www.gasthof-fraundorfer.de. E-mail: fravendorfer@gap. baynet.de. 30 units. TV TEL. 134DM–174DM ($67–$87) double; 194DM–325DM ($97–$162.50) family room for 2–5 people. Rates include buffet breakfast. AE, MC, V. Free parking.

The family-owned Gasthof Fraundorfer is located on Partenkirchen's main street, just a 5-minute walk from the old church. Its original style has not been updated, so it retains the character of bygone days. There are three floors under a sloping roof, with a facade brightly decorated with murals depicting a family feast. You'll be in the midst of village-centered activities, near interesting shops and restaurants. Rooms are furnished with traditional alpine styling, some with four-poster beds, all with firm mattresses. Some larger units are virtual apartments, suitable for up to five guests. Baths are compact with shower stalls. Owners Josef and Barbel Fraundorfer are proud of their country-style meals. There's Bavarian yodeling and dancing Wednesday to Monday nights. Dinner reservations are advised. The owners also operate the Gästehaus Barbara in back, with 20 more beds, including a *Himmelbett* ("heaven bed"). A double in their new house costs 150DM ($75).

Haus Lilly. Zugspitzstrasse 20a (15-min. walk from the Bahnhof), 82467 Garmisch-Partenkirchen. ☎ **08821/5-26-00.** 8 units. 103DM ($51.50) double; 153DM ($76.50) triple or quad. Rates include buffet breakfast. No credit cards. Free parking.

Many visitors appreciate this spotlessly clean guest house. It wins prizes for its copious breakfasts and the personality of its smiling owner, Maria Lechner, whose English is limited but whose hospitality is universal. Each small room comes with a comfortable bed fitted with a good mattress and includes free access to a kitchen, so in-house meal preparation is an option. Baths are small and have shower stalls. Breakfast is a combination of cold cuts, rolls, cheese, eggs, pastries, and coffee, tea, or chocolate.

Hotel Hilleprandt. Riffelstrasse 17 (near the Zugspitze Bahnhof and the Olympic Ice Stadium), 82467 Garmisch-Partenkirchen. ☎ **08821/28-61.** Fax 08821/7-45-48. www.hotel-hilleprandt.de. E-mail: hotelhilleprandt@t-online.de. 18 units. TV TEL. 142DM–178DM ($71–$89) double; 196DM ($98) suite. Rates include buffet breakfast. MC, V. Free parking.

This cozy, tranquil chalet is a good budget choice. Its wooden balconies, attractive garden, and backdrop of forest-covered mountains give the impression of an old-time alpine building. However, a complete renovation has brought streamlined modern comfort. Rooms are small but comfortable. Each has a private balcony. Guests enjoy a fitness room, a sauna, and a pleasant breakfast room.

WHERE TO DINE
EXPENSIVE

Posthotel Partenkirchen. Ludwigstrasse 49, Partenkirchen. ☎ **08821/93630.** Reservations required. Main courses 25DM–41DM ($12.50–$20.50). AE, DC, MC, V. Daily noon–2pm and 6–9:30pm. CONTINENTAL.

The restaurant at the Posthotel Partenkirchen is renowned for its distinguished continental cuisine—in fact, its reputation has spread throughout Bavaria. The interior dining rooms are rustic, with a mellow, old-fashioned atmosphere. You could imagine Dürer having a meal here. Everything seems comfortably subdued, including the diners. Perhaps your best choice is to order one of the fixed-price menus, which change daily. The à la carte menu is extensive, featuring game in the autumn. Other main dishes include schnitzel cordon bleu and mixed grill St. James. The Wiener schnitzel served with a large salad is the best we've had in the resort.

✪ **Reindl's Restaurant.** In the Partenkirchner Hof, Bahnhofstrasse 15. ☎ **08821/ 5-80-25.** Reservations required. Main courses 38DM–50DM ($19–$25). AE, DC, MC, V. Daily noon–2:30pm and 6:30–11pm. Closed Nov 10–Dec 15. CONTINENTAL.

One of the best places to eat in Partenkirchen is Reindl's, a first-class restaurant in every sense of the word. The seasonal menu offers *cuisine moderne* as well as regional Bavarian dishes. As a good opening to a fine repast, we suggest the scampi salad Walterspiel with fresh peaches, lemon, and tarragon, or homemade goose-liver pâté with Riesling jelly. For a main dish, try *coq au Riesling* (chicken in wine) with noodles or veal roasted with *Steinpilzen,* a special mushroom from the Bavarian mountains. For dessert, try either the Grand Marnier sabayon with strawberry and vanilla ice cream or something more spectacular: a Salzburger Nockerl for two.

MODERATE

Alpenhof. Am Kurpark 10. ☎ **08821/5-90-55.** Reservations recommended. Main courses 18DM–42DM ($9–$21); fixed-price lunch 25DM–30DM ($12.50–$15). DC, MC, V. Daily 11:30am–2pm and 5:30–9:30pm. Closed 3 weeks in Nov. BAVARIAN.

Alpenhof is widely regarded as the finest restaurant in Garmisch besides the hotel dining rooms at the Posthotel Partenkirchen and Reindl's Partenkirchner Hof. The cuisine here is neatly grounded in tradition. Renate and Josef Huber offer a variety of Bavarian specialties, as well as trout "any way you want," salmon grilled with mousseline sauce, and ragout of venison. For dessert, try a soufflé with exotic fruits. An exceptional fixed-price meal for 28.50DM ($16.25)—the best for value at the resort—is presented daily. In summer, try for an outside table; in winter, retreat to the cozy interior, which is flooded with sunlight from a greenhouse.

INEXPENSIVE

Flösserstuben. Schmiedstrasse 2. ☎ **08821/28-88.** Reservations recommended. Main courses 12DM–32.50DM ($6–$16.25). AE, MC. Daily 11:30am–2:30pm and 5–10pm (or as late as 1:30am, depending on business). GREEK/BAVARIAN/INTERNATIONAL.

Regardless of the season, a bit of the Bavarian Alps always seems to flower in this intimate restaurant, close to the town center. On most evenings, the weathered beams above the dining tables reverberate with laughter and good cheer. You can select a seat at a colorful wooden table or on an ox yoke-inspired stool in front of the spliced saplings that decorate the bar. Moussaka and souvlaki, Hungarian goulashes, sauerbraten, and all kinds of Bavarian dishes are abundantly available.

Riessersee. Reiss 6 (2 miles from the center of town). ☎ **08821/9-54-40.** Main courses 12DM–36DM ($6–$18). Daily 8am–9pm. AE, MC, V. BAVARIAN.

This cafe-restaurant is located on the shores of a small lake with emerald-green water. Stop in here after you explore the Zugspitze. It's the ideal place for a leisurely lunch or afternoon coffee with cakes, ice cream, and chocolates. You may like the place so much you'll stick around for one of the Bavarian dinner dishes. Caviar and lobster are available on occasion, and excellent veal dishes are served all the time.

GARMISCH-PARTENKIRCHEN AFTER DARK

You can test your luck at the town's casino, **Spielbank Garmisch-Partenkirchen,** Am Kurpark 74 (☎ **08821/530-99**). Admission costs 5DM ($2.50) per person, and presentation of a passport is required. The casino is open daily 3pm to 2am. Beginning at 7pm, men must wear jackets and ties. Friday and Saturday, games of seven-card stud poker are arranged (book in advance).

If you'd like to meet the locals at night, head for one of the taverns for a beer. All major hotels have bars, but for a change of pace go to the **Irish Pub,** Rathausplatz 8 (☎ **08221/7-87-98**), and order a Guinness. This pub, in the center of town, attracts one of the most convivial crowds in the area.

Many hotels have dance floors that keep the music pumping into the wee hours, but for dancing of a different sort, check out the summer program of **Bavarian folk music and dancing,** held every Saturday night mid-May to September in the Bayernhalle, Brauhausstrasse 19. During the same season Saturday to Thursday, **classical concerts** are held at the Garmisch park bandstand. On Friday, these live shows move to the Partenkirchen bandstand. Check with the local tourist office (see above) for details about these programs as well as a 5-day **Johann Strauss Festival** held in June.

7 Oberammergau

95km (59 miles) SW of Munich, 20km (12 miles) N of Garmisch-Partenkirchen

In the summer of 2000, Oberammergau staged its famous Passion Play, which is performed only 1 year out of 10. Surely the world's longest-running show, it began in 1634 when the town's citizens took a vow to give dramatic thanks after they were spared from the devastating plague of 1633. The town is packed to the gills all summer for this major event.

However, a visit to Oberammergau is ideal at any time, even without the performance. The town is in a wide valley surrounded by forests, green meadows, and mountains. It offers first-class hotels and cozy inns, and has long been known for the skill of its wood-carvers. Numerous hiking trails lead through the nearby mountains to hikers' inns. You can also simply go up to the mountaintops on the Laber cable railway or the Kolben chairlift.

Oberammergau also offers opportunities for tennis buffs, minigolf players, cyclists, swimmers, hang-gliding enthusiasts, and canoeists. The recreation center, Wellenberg, with open-air pools, fountains, sauna, solarium, and restaurant, is one of the Alps' most beautiful. The surrounding Ammer Valley is a treasure trove for explorers. And Oberammergau is often used as a base for visiting Linderhof Castle, the Benedictine monastery at Ettal, or the fairy-tale Neuschwanstein and Hohenschwangau castles (see chapter 6).

ESSENTIALS

GETTING THERE By Train The **Oberammergau Bahnhof** is on the Murnau–Bad Kohlgrum–Oberammergau rail line, with frequent connections in all directions. Through Murnau, all major German cities can be reached. Daily trains arrive from Munich in 2 hours and from Frankfurt in 7 hours. For rail information and schedules, call ☎ **01805/996633.**

By Bus Regional bus service to nearby towns is offered by **RVO Regionalverkehr Oberbayern** in Garmisch-Partenkirchen (☎ **08821/94-82-74**). An unnumbered bus goes back and forth between Oberammergau and Garmisch-Partenkirchen.

By Car   Many visitors drive here, the trip taking 1¹/₂ hours from Munich and 5¹/₂ hours from Frankfurt. Take the A95 Munich–Garmisch-Partenkirchen Autobahn and exit at Eschenlohe.

VISITOR INFORMATION   Contact the **Verkehrsbüro,** Eugen-Papst-Strasse 9A (☎ **08822/9-23-10**). It's open Monday to Friday 8:30am to 6pm and on Saturday 8:30am to 1pm.

EXPLORING THE TOWN

Oberammergau has much to offer besides the play. Consider taking an excursion to either the **Berg Laber,** which rises to the east of the town, or **Berg Kolber,** to the west. Berg Laber, slightly more dramatic, is accessible via a cable-gondola (☎ **08822/4770**) that operates year-round 9am to 11:30am and 1 to 5 or 5:30pm. The 10-minute ascent costs 20DM ($10) per person. The top of Berg Kolber is accessible via a two-passenger chairlift (☎ **08822/4760**) that operates year-round 9 to 11:45 am and 1 to 4:30 or 4:45pm. The cost is 10DM ($5) round-trip.

Aside from the actors, Oberammergau's most respected citizens are **wood-carvers,** many of whom have been trained in the village wood-carver's school. In the **Pilatushaus,** Ludwig-Thoma-Strasse (☎ **08822/16-82**), you can watch local carvers, as well as painters, sculptors, and potters, as they work. Mid-May to October, their hours are Tuesday to Friday 1:30 to 6pm. You'll see many examples of their art throughout the town, on the painted cottages and inns and in the churchyard.

Heimatmuseum, Dorfstrasse 8 (☎ **08822/9-41-36**), has a notable collection of Christmas crèches, all hand carved and painted, from the 18th through the 20th century. It's open May 20 to October 15, Tuesday to Saturday 2 to 6pm; off-season, Saturday only 2 to 6pm. Admission is 4DM ($2) for adults, 2DM ($1) for students, and 1DM (50¢) for children under 14.

When strolling through the village, note the frescoed houses named after fairy-tale characters, such as the "Hansel and Gretel House" and "Little Red Riding Hood House."

WHERE TO STAY & DINE

The cost of accommodation in Oberammergau includes a universally imposed *kurtaxe* (special tax) of 2.50DM ($1.25). This entitles visitors to a card providing small discounts at local attractions.

MODERATE

Hotel Restaurant Böld. König-Ludwig-Strasse 10, 82487 Oberammergau. ☎ **08822/ 91-20.** Fax 08822/71-02. www.hotel-boeld.de. E-mail: hotel-boeld@t-online.de. 57 units. MINIBAR TV TEL. 174DM–234DM ($87–$117) double. Rates include buffet breakfast. AE, DC, MC, V. Free outdoor parking; 10DM ($5) in garage.

This well-designed chalet hotel has steadily improved in quality and now is among the town's premier choices, in a neck-to-neck race with Parkhotel Sonnenhof. It lies only a stone's throw from the river. Rooms are well furnished; most have balconies. A sauna, solarium, and whirlpool are offered for guests' relaxation. The restaurant features both international and regional cuisine. In the bar, you'll find a tranquil atmosphere and attentive service.

Parkhotel Sonnenhof. König-Ludwig-Strasse 12, 82487 Oberammergau. ☎ **08822/ 91-30.** Fax 08822/30-47. E-mail: sonnenhof.oberammergau@t-online.de. 65 units. TV TEL. 190DM–210DM ($95–$105) double; 200DM–230DM ($100–$115) suite. Rates include buffet breakfast. AE, CB, DC, MC, V.

Shopping for Wood Carvings

The region's wood carvings are among the most sought after in the Germanic world, and many an example has graced the mantelpieces and whatnot shelves of homes around the globe. Most subjects are religious, deriving directly from 14th-century originals; however, to cater to the demands of modern visitors, there's been an increased emphasis lately on secular subjects, such as drinking or hunting scenes. Competition is fierce for sales of these woodcarvings, many of which are made in hamlets and farmhouses throughout the region. Know before you buy that even some of the most expensive "handmade" pieces might have been roughed in by machine prior to being finished off by hand.

The **Holzschittschule (Wood Carving School)** has conditions of study that might remind you of the severity of the medieval guilds. Students who labor over a particular sculpture are required to turn it in to the school, where it's either placed on permanent exhibition or sold during the school's once-a-year sell-off, usually over a 2-day period in July.

Josef Albl, Devrientweg 1 (☎ **08822/64-33**), a taciturn but prestigious wood-carver, specializes in bas-reliefs, some of which are complicated and highly detailed. His subjects are both religious and secular, including hunting scenes. Some of the simple pieces sell for as little as 10DM ($5.70), although commissioned pieces can stretch into the tens of thousands of dollars.

Tony Baur, Dorfstrasse 27 (☎ **08822/8-21**), has the most sophisticated inventory of wood carvings. The shop employs a small cadre of carvers who usually work from their homes to create works inspired by medieval originals. The outgoing and personable sales staff is quick to admit that the forms of many of the pieces are roughed in by machine, but most of the intricate work is completed by hand. Pieces are crafted from maple, pine, or linden (basswood). Prices start at 20DM ($10) and go up to 10,000DM ($5,000). Carvings are in their natural grain, stained, or poly-chromed (some of the most charming), and in some instances, partially gilded.

Peter Zwink, Schnitzlergasse 4 (☎ **08822/8-57**), is the place to go for clocks. If you have your heart set on buying a cuckoo clock, you'll probably find one to your liking here, even though, as the staff will point out, the cuckoo clock belongs to the Schwarzwald (see chapter 10). The more simple carved, handmade clocks are battery-run and cost 120DM ($60). More sophisticated clocks with mechanical movement and sound start at 600DM ($300). Look for mantel clocks and floor clocks carved in baroque designs. Some need to be wound only once a year, a tradition that some families carry out as part of their New Year's Day rituals.

Short on charm and alpine rusticity, this modern hotel still has a lot going for it. It's placed far enough away from the summer crowds to offer guests peace and tranquility, but it's still within walking distance of the center. The hotel overlooks the Ammer River and a beautiful Pfarrkirche (parish church). Rooms are well-maintained, filled with first-class comforts, and have balconies with an alpine vista, often of Oberammergau's mountain, the Kobel. Facilities here are more extensive than at most hotels in the area, including an indoor pool, sauna, and even a bowling alley. There's also a children's playroom. Two restaurants offer many international dishes, although the Bavarian specialties are the better choices.

Schlosshotel Linderhof. Linderhof 14 (near the palace), 82488 Ettal. ☎ **08822/7-90.** Fax 08822/43-47. 29 units. MINIBAR TV TEL. 150DM–166DM ($75–$83) double. Rates include breakfast. AE, CB, DC, MC, V.

This hotel is designed with gables, shutters, and half-timbering in the style of a Bavarian chalet. The famous palace is only about 350m (400 yards) away. Rooms are dignified and high-ceilinged, with tasteful hints of 19th-century gentility but with modern conveniences, such as hair dryers. The cozy restaurant is responsible for much of the hotel's business. It features an array of fixed-price menus, focusing on such standard food as pork schnitzel with mixed salad and cream-of-tomato soup. You can dine on a stone terrace accented with parasols and potted flowers. The restaurant is open daily 8am to 8pm.

Turmwirt. Ettalerstrasse 2, 82487 Oberammergau, 5 min. from the town center. ☎ **08822/9-26-00.** Fax 08822/14-37. www.minotel.com. E-mail: turmwirt@t-online.de. 22 units. MINIBAR TV TEL. 150DM–190DM ($75–$95) double. Rates include buffet breakfast. AE, DC, MC, V. Free parking.

A cozy Bavarian-style hotel, the Turmwirt offers small, snug rooms, many with private balconies opening onto mountain views. The present building was constructed in 1889 and has been altered and renovated many times. It's an intricately painted green-shuttered country house with a well-maintained homelike interior. The owners are three generations of the Glas family, who often present Bavarian folk evenings.

Wolf Restaurant-Hotel. Dorfstrasse 1, 82487 Oberammergau. ☎ **08822/30-71.** Fax 08822/10-96. E-mail: hotel.wolf@gap.baynet.de. 32 units. TV TEL. 130DM–190DM ($65–$95) double. Rates include buffet breakfast. AE, DC, MC, V.

An overgrown Bavarian chalet, Wolf Restaurant-Hotel is at the heart of village life. Its facade, like others in the area, has an encircling balcony, heavy timbering, and window boxes spilling cascades of geraniums. Inside, it retains some local flavor, although concessions to modernity have been made, such as an elevator. Facilities include a sauna, solarium, and outdoor pool. Rooms range from small to medium. Five are singles. Dining here can be both economical and gracious. The Hafner Stub'n is a rustic place for beer drinking as well as enjoying light meals. There's always a freshly made soup of the day. Main courses, such as Wiener schnitzel or roast pork with dumplings and cabbage, are generous.

INEXPENSIVE

Alte Post. Dorfstrasse 19, 82487 Oberammergau. ☎ **08822/91-00.** Fax 08822/91-01-00. www.ogau.com. E-mail: altepost@ogan.de. 32 units. TV TEL. 120DM–160DM ($60–$80) double. Rates include continental breakfast. AE, DC, MC, V. Closed Oct 25–Dec 19. Free parking.

Alte Post is a provincial inn located in the village center, built in chalet style. It has a wide overhanging roof, green-shuttered windows painted with decorative trim, a large crucifix on the facade, and tables set on a sidewalk under a long awning. It's the village's social hub. The interior has a storybook charm, with a ceiling-high green ceramic stove, alpine chairs, and shelves of pewter plates. The rustic rooms range in size from cozy to spacious and have wood-beamed ceilings and wide beds with giant posts; most have views. The main dining room is also rustic, with a collection of hunting memorabilia. The restaurant serves excellent Bavarian dishes. There's also an intimate drinking bar.

Hotel Café-Restaurant Friedenshöhe. König-Ludwig-Strasse 31, 82487 Oberammergau. ☎ **08822/35-98.** Fax 08822/43-45. www.neuschwanstein-country.net. 17 units. TEL. 120DM–180DM ($60–$90) double. Rates include buffet breakfast. AE, DC, MC, V. Closed Nov–Dec 14.

This villa enjoys a beautiful location. It's one of the town's best bargains, although for quality it's not in the same league as the Böld or the Parkhotel Sonnenhof. It once hosted Thomas Mann. Rooms range from rather small singles to spacious doubles. They're furnished in tasteful modern style and are well maintained. TVs are available on request. Opt for one of the corner rooms if possible (they're bigger). Baths tend to be too small. The restaurant serves quality Bavarian and international cuisine. There's a choice of four dining rooms, including an indoor terrace with a panoramic view and an outdoor terrace.

Hotel Schilcherhof. Bahnhofstrasse 17, 82487 Oberammergau. ☎ **08822/47-40.** Fax 08822/37-93. 26 units. 110DM–160DM ($55–$80) double. Rates include continental breakfast. AE, V. Closed Nov 15–Christmas. Free parking.

An enlarged chalet with surrounding gardens, the Schilcherhof has a modern wing with snug, good-value rooms. In summer, the terrace overflows with beer and festive living. Nearby is the Ammer River, which flows through the village. Although the house is built in the old style, with wooden front balconies and tiers of flower boxes, it has a fresh look.

SIDE TRIPS FROM OBERAMMERGAU

✪ **SCHLOSS LINDERHOF**   Until the late 19th century, a modest hunting lodge, owned by the Bavarian royal family, stood on a large piece of land 13km (8 miles) west of the village. But in 1869, "Mad" King Ludwig struck again, this time creating a French rococo palace in the Ammergau Mountains. This is his most successful creation. Unlike his palace at Chiemsee (see above), Schloss Linderhof was not meant to copy any other structure. And unlike the Neuschwanstein palace (see chapter 6), its concentration of fanciful projects and designs was not limited to the palace interior. In fact, the gardens and smaller buildings at Linderhof are, if anything, more elaborate than the two-story main structure.

The most interesting rooms are on the second floor, where ceilings are much higher because of the unusual roof plan. Ascending the winged staircase of Carrara marble, you'll find yourself at the **West Gobelin Room** (music room), with carved and gilded paneling and richly colored tapestries. This room leads directly into the **Hall of Mirrors,** where the mirrors are set in white-and-gold panels, decorated with gilded woodcarvings. The hall's ceiling is festooned with frescoes depicting mythological scenes.

The **king's bedchamber** is the largest room in the palace and overlooks the Fountain of Neptune and the cascades in the gardens. In the tradition of Louis XIV, who often received visitors in his bedchamber, the king's bed is closed off by a carved and gilded balustrade.

In the popular style of the previous century, Ludwig laid out the **gardens** in formal parterres with geometrical shapes, baroque sculptures, and elegant fountains. The front of the palace opens onto a large pool where, from a gilded statue in its center, a jet of water sprays 32m (105 feet) into the air.

The park also contains several other small but exotic buildings, including the **Moorish Kiosk,** where Ludwig often spent hours smoking chibouk and dreaming of himself as an Oriental prince. The unique magic grotto is built of artificial rock, with stalagmites and stalactites dividing the cave-like room into three chambers. In the main chamber, an artificial lake is illuminated from below; in Ludwig's time it had a current produced by 24-dynamo engines. A gilded shell-shaped boat is tied to a platform called the Lorelei Rock.

Schloss Linderhof, 82488 Ettal-Linderhof (☎ **08822/35-12**), is open to the public throughout the year, and makes a good day trip from Munich, as well as from

Oberammergau. It's open April to September daily 9am to 5:30pm; October to March, the grotto and Moorish Kiosk are closed, but the castle is open daily 9:30am to noon and 1 to 4pm. Admission in the summer is 10DM ($5) for adults, 7DM ($3.50) for students, and free for children 14 and under. In winter, admission is 7DM ($3.50) for adults, 4DM ($2) for students, and free for children 14 and under.

Buses run between Oberammergau and Schloss Linderhof seven times per day, beginning at 9am; the last bus leaves Linderhof at 5:35pm. Round-trip fare is 9.20DM ($4.60). Motorists from Oberammergau should follow the signs to Ettal, about 5km (3 miles) away, then go another 5km (3 miles) to Draswang, and from there follow the signs to Schloss Linderhof.

✪ **KLOSTER ETTAL**   Kloster Ettal, on Kaiser-Ludwig-Platz at Ettal (☎ **08822/ 7-40**), lies in a lovely valley sheltered by the steep hills of the Ammergau. This abbey was founded by Duke Ludwig the Bavarian in 1330. Monks, knights, and their ladies shared the honor of guarding its statue of the Virgin, attributed to Giovanni Pisano. In the 18th century, the golden age of the abbey, there were about 70,000 pilgrims here every year.

The church of Our Lady, within the abbey, is one of the finest examples of Bavarian rococo architecture in existence. The impressive baroque facade was built from a plan based on the designs of Enrico Zuccali. Around the polygonal core of the church is a two-story gallery. Visitors stand under a vast dome, admiring the fresco painted by John Jacob Zeiller in the summers of 1751 and 1752.

The abbey stands 3km (2 miles) south of Oberammergau, along the road to Garmisch-Partenkirchen. Admission is free, and it's open daily 8am to 8pm in summer, 6pm in winter. Buses from Oberammergau leave from the Rathaus and the Bahnhof once per hour during the day, with round-trip fare 5DM ($2.50). Call ☎ **8821/94-82-74** for information.

9 Lake Constance (Bodensee)

Mild climate and plentiful sunshine make Lake Constance (*Bodensee* in German) a top vacation spot for lovers of sun and sand, as well as for sightseers and spa-hoppers. The hillsides that slope to the water's edge are covered with vineyards and orchards and dotted with colorful hamlets and busy tourist centers. A network of cruise ships and ferries links every major center around the lake. Even though the 260km (162-mile) shoreline of Lake Constance is shared by three nations—Austria, Germany, and Switzerland—the area around the lake is united in a common cultural and historical heritage.

Lake Constance is actually divided into three lakes, although the name is frequently applied only to the largest of these, the Obersee. The western end of the Obersee separates into two distinct branches: One, the Überlingersee, is a long fjord; the other, the Untersee, is more irregular, jutting in and out of marshland and low-lying woodland. The two branches are connected by a narrow channel—which is actually the upper Rhine.

Lake Constance offers a wealth of **activities,** including swimming, sailing, windsurfing, diving, and rowing. Local tourist offices will connect you with various outfitters. You can swim either in the cold waters of the lake itself, or in one of the heated lakeside pools. The Eichwald Lido at Lindau boasts a half-mile-long "beach," with plenty of lawns for sunbathing German-style. The other popular place for lakeside swimming at a heated pool is the Jakob Lido at Constance.

One of the best ways to see the lake is to cycle around it. **Bicycles** can be rented at all the major train stations, including Lindau and Konstanz. Car ferries allow bikes on board.

Sailing on Lake Constance is a major attraction. Some boatyards and sailing schools rent boats; you'll be asked to show some proof of proficiency (a certification from a sailing school, for example). On a more casual level, rowboats and motorboats can be rented at all major hotels along the lake.

From Munich, motorists should take the B12, via Landsberg and Kempten, to reach the lake. Drivers from Frankfurt head south along the A81 Autobahn to Memmingen, transferring to B18. The nearest international airport to Lake Constance is at Zürich, 79km (49 miles) southwest of the town of Konstanz. The Munich airport is about 225km (140 miles) north of the lake.

Ferry - - -

AUSTRIA

SWITZERLAND

Bregenz

Lindau

Deutsche Alpenstrasse

B18

B308

Wasserburg

Kressbronn

Langenargen

Bodensee

Staad

Rorschach

Arbon

Romanshorn

Wangen

32

Weingarten

Ravensburg

Tettnang

B30

467

Friedrichhafen

Immerstaad

B31

Eriskirch

Markdorf

B33

Meersburg

Überlingen

B31

Mainau

Konstanz

Überlinger See

B33

Zellersee

Gnadensee

Untersee

Radolfzell

Reichenau

B34

1 Lindau

179km (111 miles) SW of Munich, 32km (20 miles) S of Ravensburg

Lindau dates from the end of the 9th century. It was a free imperial town of the Holy Roman Empire from the Middle Ages to 1804, when it became a part of Bavaria. For centuries, it was a center of trade between Bavaria and Switzerland.

Its unique setting on an island at the eastern end of Lake Constance made Lindau a prime tourist attraction. Today this garden city is under landmark protection, and has outgrown its boundaries and spread to the shores of the mainland. It now caters to the tourist's every whim, from bathing to baccarat. Lindau is a charming city. You can wander at will through the maze of winding narrow streets lined with houses that have stood the test of time. At the harbor stand two **lighthouses:** one, Mangturm, was built in the 1200s, the other in 1856. Each tower is some 37m (120 feet) tall and can be climbed by the hearty, along narrow spiral staircases. The reward is a panoramic vista of the Alps, both Swiss and Austrian. Another interesting building is the 15th-century **Rathaus.**

ESSENTIALS

GETTING THERE   Lindau is connected to the mainland by a road bridge and a causeway for walkers and trains. It's a transportation link between the western part of Lake Constance and the towns of Austria and Switzerland, which lie directly across the water. Regional flights come in to the Friedrichshafen airport (see below). The nearest major airport is Zürich.

By Train   The Lindau Bahnhof is on the major Basel–Singen–Radolfzell–Lindau and Lindau–Kissleg–Memmingen–Buchloe rail lines, with frequent connections in all directions. Call ☎ 01805/996633 for information and schedules.

By Bus   Regional bus service along Lake Constance is offered by **RAB Regionalverkehr Alb-Bodensee GmbH** in Friedrichshafen (☎ 07541/30130).

By Ferry   Five to seven ferries per day (depending on the season) link Lindau with Konstanz. Before reaching Lindau, boats stop at Meersburg, Mainau, and Friedrichshafen; the entire trip takes 3 hours. Call the tourist office for information and schedules.

By Car   Access by car from Munich is via Autobahn A96 and B31.

VISITOR INFORMATION   **Tourist-Information** is at Ludwigstrasse 68 (☎ 08382/26-00-30). April to September 5, the office is open Monday to Saturday 9am to 7pm; in winter, Monday to Friday 9am to noon and 2 to 5pm.

SEEING THE SIGHTS

A tour of this *Ferieninsel* (Holiday Island) begins with the **old harbor,** seen from the lakeside promenade. The **Mangturm,** the old lighthouse, stands on the promenade as a reminder of the heavy fortifications that once surrounded the city. It also marks the point where Lindau was once divided into two islands. The entrance to the harbor is marked by the 33m (108-foot) **New Lighthouse** and the **Bavarian Lion,** standing guard as yachts and commercial ships pass by below. From the promenade, you can gaze out past these monuments over the water to the Alps on the opposite side of the lake.

Hauptstrasse, in the center of the town, is the main street of the Altstadt. The most easily recognizable building here is the **Altes Rathaus,** erected in 1422. The stepped gables are typical of the period, but the building's facade also combines many later styles of architecture. The interior, once used as a council hall, is the town library. Frescoes represent scenes from a session of the 1496 Imperial Diet.

Just north of Hauptstrasse is the town's most familiar landmark, the round **Diebsturm (Thieves' Tower)**, with its turreted roof. Next to it is the oldest building in Lindau, the 11th-century **St. Peter's Church,** which houses a war memorial chapel. In the church is a group of frescoes by Hans Holbein the Elder.

Returning to Hauptstrasse, which cuts through the exact center of the island, follow the street eastward to the **Haus zum Cavazzen,** Am Marktplatz (☎ **08382/ 94-40-73**), the handsomest patrician house on Lake Constance. It now houses the municipal art collection. Included are exhibits of sculpture and painting from the Gothic, Renaissance, and baroque periods. Some of the rooms are furnished with period pieces showing how wealthy citizens lived in the 18th and 19th centuries. Among the rarities is a collection of mechanical musical instruments. This attraction can be visited by guided tour only, April to October, Tuesday to Sunday 10am to noon and 2 to 5pm. Admission is 5DM ($2.50) adults, 7DM ($3.50) students and children; children under 10 enter free.

Passing across Am Marktplatz and by the Collegiate Church and St. Stephen's Church, both baroque, you come to the strange pile of rocks known as **Heathen's Wall,** dating from Roman times. Beyond this is the **Stadtgarten (Town Garden),** which, although peaceful during the day, livens up at night when the wheels of the town's casino begin to spin.

OUTDOOR PURSUITS

For 15DM ($7.50) you can rent a bike from the train station (☎ **08382/2-12-61**) and go cycling along the lake. Bikes can be rented Monday to Friday 9am to 7pm and 2:30 to 6pm, and Saturday 9:30am to 7pm. Lindenhofpark is the most scenic area (it's also ideal for a picnic).

The town has three lakeside beaches, all open in summer Monday to Friday 10:30am to 7:30pm and Saturday and Sunday 10am to 8pm. The biggest beach is **Eichwald,** about a half-hour walk away to the right along Uferweg, facing the harbor, or take bus 1 or 2 to Anheggerstrasse, then bus 3 to Karmelbuckel. Once here, admission is 5DM ($2.50) for adults, 3DM ($1.50) for children. Another, smaller beach, attracting families, is **Römerbad;** it charges 5DM ($2.50) for adults or 3DM ($1.50) for children. To reach the final beach, **Lindenhofbad,** take bus 1 or 2 to Anheggerstrasse, then bus 4 to Alwind. Admission is 4DM ($2) for adults and 3DM ($1.50) for children.

You can rent windsurfers at **Kreitmeir,** In der Grub 17 (☎ **08382/23330**) for 15DM ($7.50) per hour. At the little dock next to Lindau's rail bridge, you can rent a paddleboat for 14DM ($7), a motorboat for 45DM ($22.50), or an electric boat for 35DM ($17.50) from **Bootsvermietung Hodrius** (☎ **08382/42-85**).

SHOPPING

Michael Zeller is known throughout Bavaria for staging a twice-yearly **Internationale-Bodensee-Kunstauktion** (art auction) here in the spring and fall (dates vary). There's a much smaller auction in December. His year-round store, **Michael Zeller,** 3 Bindergasse (☎ **08382/9-30-20**), offers Lindau's best selection of watercolors, engravings, and prints, along with jewelry and porcelain, and even some furniture. For the town's best selection of pottery, head for **Angelika Ochsenreiter,** Ludwigstrasse 29 (☎ **08382/ 2-38-67**), which has teapots, cups, dishes, and animal figures.

WHERE TO STAY

EXPENSIVE

Hotel Bayerischer Hof. Seepromenade, 88131 Lindau. ☎ **800/223-5652** in the U.S. and Canada, or 08382/91-50. Fax 08382/91-55-91. www.bayerischerhof-lindau.de. E-mail: bayerischerhof-lindau@t-online.de. 100 units. MINIBAR TV TEL. 265DM–530DM

($132.50–$265) double; 750DM–790DM ($375–$395) suite. Accommodation is free for children under 10. Rates include buffet breakfast. AE, CB, DC, MC, V. Parking 12DM–18DM ($6–$9).

This Old-World hotel clearly outdistances all others in Lindau. It opens onto the lakeside promenade and looks almost like a hotel on the Mediterranean. The atmosphere and service here are first rate. The large rooms are the finest in Lindau, each well furnished with traditional styling. Most have good views; the less desirable units overlook a narrow thoroughfare.

Dining/Diversions: The cuisine is the best in town. The formal dining room has wide-screened windows with views of the lake. There's also a lounge and a bar.

Amenities: Room service, hair dryers, laundry and dry cleaning service, twice-daily maid service, massage, baby-sitting, secretarial services, sundeck, conference rooms, business center, and health club with sauna. A beauty salon and boutiques are nearby.

Hotel Reutemann und Seegarten. Seepromenade, 88131 Lindau. ☎ **08382/91-50.** Fax 08382/91-55-91. www.bayerischerhof-lindau.de. E-mail: bayerischerhof-lindau@at-online.de. 64 units. MINIBAR TV TEL. 210DM–370DM ($105–$185) double. Children under 10 free. Rates include buffet breakfast. AE, CB, DC, MC, V. Parking 12DM–18DM ($6–$9).

Located next to its parent, the superior Bayerischer Hof, this hotel consists of two villas. The Reutemann has large rooms and baths with heated towel racks and huge tubs. The Seegarten, built like a Bavarian villa, with little flower-filled balconies and trailing vines, has spacious and handsome rooms, especially those with lake views (which cost more, naturally). Both villas have their own waterfront gardens with furniture for sunbathing.

Dining/Diversions: The romantic Zum Lieben Augustin tavern (closed in winter) is shared with the Bayerischer Hof. It serves good regional and international dishes, along with lots of beer and wine.

Amenities: Concierge, hair dryers, room service, dry cleaning and laundry service, in-room massage, baby-sitting, secretarial services, fitness center with sauna, business center and conference rooms; a beauty salon and boutiques are nearby.

MODERATE

Hotel-Garni Brugger. Bei der Heidenmauer 11, 88131 Lindau. ☎ **08382/9-34-10.** Fax 08382/41-33. www.lindau-magazin.de/hotel-brugger. 23 units. MINIBAR TV TEL. 152DM–250DM ($76–$125) double. Additional bed 40DM ($20) extra. Rates include continental breakfast. AE, DC, MC, V. Parking 12DM ($6).

This modest, charming little hotel is the best affordable choice in Lindau. It's pleasingly proportioned, with a gabled attic and French doors that open onto the balconies in the back. The small rooms are up-to-date, furnished in a functional modern style, with lots of light. The latest innovation is a winter garden filled with potted plants. The location is an easy walk from the lake and casino.

Insel-Hotel. Maximilianstrasse 42 (a quarter-mile from the lake), 88131 Lindau. ☎ **08382/ 260-160.** Fax 08382/260-1666. 28 units. MINIBAR TV TEL. 184DM–194DM ($92–$97) double. Rates include continental breakfast. AE, CB, DC, MC, V. Parking 18DM ($9).

Although not as stylish as its closest competitor (above), the Insel is still a good buy for the area. Its small but comfortable rooms are furnished with modern pieces. The breakfast room opens onto Maximilianstrasse, a pedestrian zone. A small selection of snacks can be ordered daily 10am to 7pm.

WHERE TO DINE

✪ **Hoyerberg Schlüssle.** Hoyerbergstrasse 64, at Lindau-Aeschach. ☎ **08382/2-52-95.** Reservations required in the restaurant; not required in the cafe. Main courses 49DM–64DM

($24.50–$32); fixed-price menu 100DM ($50). AE, DC, MC, V. Restaurant Tues–Sat noon–2pm and 6–10:30pm; cafe Tues–Sat 2–5pm. Closed Jan 15–Feb 28. CONTINENTAL.

The Hoyerberg Schlüssle is the only restaurant on the lake that can rival the superb Seehotel Siber at Konstanz (see below). The inner room is beautifully decorated, with a view of the mountains and lake. You can also dine on the two terraces. Continental delicacies include cream of scampi soup, Bodensee pike perch stuffed with champagne-flavored herbs, and Allgäuer saddle of venison with small flour dumplings and French beans. Meals here are memorable; the chef has great flair and style— and doesn't oversauce.

Villino. Hoyren (a half-mile east of Lindau's center), Hoyerberg 34, 88131 Lindau. ☎ **08382/934512.** Fax 08382/93450. Reservations recommended. Main courses 54DM–56DM ($27–$28); set-price 5-course menu 128DM ($64). MC, V. Tues–Sun 6–10:30pm. ITALIAN.

Set in the suburb of Hoyren, this hotel is better known for its excellent Italian restaurant than for its bedrooms. Only dinner is served, within a comfortable room decorated in high-tech Milanese style. The elegant menu items include pesto-laced spaghetti, Sicilian-style fish soup, a heaping platter of scampi served with stuffed squid and fresh tomatoes, anglerfish and lobster fried with cardamom, and a particularly succulent version of leg of lamb with garlic sauce.

If you're too stuffed to move on after your meal, the establishment maintains 10 rooms, priced at 220DM to 360DM ($110 to $180) each, plus six suites at 400DM ($200) each. Each unit has a private balcony, minibar, TV, and telephone. Rates include breakfast, and parking is free.

Zum Sünfzen. Maximilianstrasse 1. ☎ **08382/58-65.** Reservations recommended. Main dishes 18DM–70DM ($9–$35). AE, DC, MC, V. Daily 9:30am–11pm. GERMAN/BAVARIAN.

Owned by the same family that runs the Insel-Hotel, this is an old, all-wood house/ restaurant serving good food at reasonable prices. Dishes range from roast pork with vegetables to fillet of venison. Fresh fish from Lake Constance is a specialty. The food is the type you might be served in a middle-class private home along the lake.

LINDAU AFTER DARK

Lindau's casino, Oskar-Groll-Anlage 6 (☎ 08382/50-51), offers slot machines from noon to 2am and blackjack and roulette from 7pm to 2am. The bet ceiling is 12,000DM ($6,000) for roulette. Admission is 5DM ($2.50), and a passport is required as proof of age. Men should wear a jacket and tie.

SIDE TRIPS FROM LINDAU

WASSERBURG The town of Wasserburg, which means "water castle," lies 6km (4 miles) west of Lindau. You can wander the traffic-free town's narrow streets, taking in the crooked little medieval houses. Its **fortress,** which stands on a promontory on a loop of the Inn River, is an enchanting discovery. It was sold to the Hapsburgs when its owner, the Fuggers of Augsburg, accumulated serious debts. Eventually the Bavarian government took over.

Head first for the center of the town, Marienplatz, where you can see the tall stepped gables of the Town Hall or **Rathaus.** Guided tours of the second floor Ratssaal are given Tuesday to Friday at 10am, 11am, 2pm, 3pm, and 4pm, and Saturday and Sunday at 10am and 11am. Tours cost 2DM ($1). The hall is richly adorned with painted panels and carved woodwork. The most interesting church, **St. Jakob,** can be seen on the Kirchplatz. The nave is a masterpiece by the Gothic architect Hans von Burghausen. In the 15th century a chancel and tower were added. If the church is open, you can seek out its elaborate late Renaissance pulpit, another architectural masterpiece.

LANGENARGEN　This town, which lies 8km (5 miles) west of Wasserburg, is celebrated for its **Montfort Castle,** Untere Seestrasse 5, named for its original founders, the counts of Montfort-Werdenberg. When King Wilhelm I of Württemberg took over, he reconstructed it in a faux-Moorish style. If you climb its tower, you'll be rewarded with a panoramic view of the lake. Hours are Easter to October only 10am to noon and 9am to 5pm; admission is 2DM ($1) adults, 1DM (50¢) children.

　　Langenargen Stadtmuseum (City Museum), Marktplatz 20 (☎ 07543-3410), is worth a visit if you're interested in some of the slightly more obscure (but still talented) 20th-century painters. Notable is a series of works by Hans Purrmann (1880–1966), a great admirer of Henri Matisse. Purrmann lived at Langenargen from 1915 until 1935. The Nazis denounced his art as "decadent" and prevented it from being seen publicly in Germany. The museum is open April to October Tuesday to Sunday 10am to noon and 2:30 to 5pm. Admission is 3DM ($1.50).

2 Friedrichshafen

22km (13 1/2 miles) W of Lindau; 20km (12 miles) S of Ravensburg

Friedrichshafen is set at the northeastern corner of the Bodensee, near the lake's widest point. This mostly modern city was almost completely rebuilt after the devastation of World War II. It's graced with one of the longest waterfront exposures of any town along the lake. Besides that, the town's highlights are two interesting museums and the dome-capped **Schlosskirche,** the premier reminder of Friedrichshafen's baroque past.

ESSENTIALS

GETTING THERE　By Air　The **Friedrichshafen** airport (☎ 07541/28401) lies 5km (3 miles) north of town. Flights come in from Zürich, Frankfurt, Düsseldorf, and Berlin. The nearest major airport is Zürich, 100km (62 miles) away.

By Train　Friedrichshafen is the largest railway junction along the northern edge of the Bodensee and serves as a major transfer point for rail passengers going on to other cities and resorts along the lake. The town has two railway stations, the **Stadtbahnhof,** in the center, and the **Hafenbahnhof,** along the Seestrasse, about three-quarters of a mile away. Both of these stations are interconnected by buses 1, 2, 3, 4, 5, 6, and 7. Trains arrive from Ulm and Stuttgart at intervals of 1 to 2 hours throughout the day. For information and schedules, call ☎ **01805/99-66-33.**

By Bus　Regional bus service along Lake Constance is provided by **RAB Regionalverkehr Alb-Bodensee GmbH** in Friedrichshafen (☎ **07541/30130** for more information).

By Car　Friedrichshafen is easily reached from both Stuttgart and Munich. From Stuttgart, follow Autobahn 8 east to the city of Ulm, then turn south onto Route 30 directly into Friedrichshafen. From Munich follow Autobahn 96 west/southwest to Lindau, then head west on Route 31 along Lake Constance to Friedrichshafen.

By Boat　April to October, about eight lake steamers travel between Friedrichshafen and Lindau, Bregenz (Austria), and Konstanz. For departure times and details, call ☎ **07541/201389.** A ferry runs year-round between Friedrichshafen and Romanshorn, Switzerland (trip time: 40 min.) and costs 9.40DM ($4.70) for adults and 5DM ($2.50) for children.

VISITOR INFORMATION   The city's **Tourist Information Office** is at Bahnhof-platz 2 (☎ **07541/30010**). May to September, it's open Monday to Friday 9am to 5pm, Saturday 10am to 2pm. October to April, it's open Monday to Thursday 9am to noon and 2 to 5pm, and Friday 9am to 1pm.

EXPLORING THE TOWN

The best thing to do in town is to stroll the lake-fronting **Seepromenade,** with its sweeping view that extends on clear days all the way to the Swiss Alps. Cycling along the broad Seestrasse is also a delight. A kiosk within the Stadtbahnhof rents bikes for 10DM to 15DM ($5 to $7.50) a day. Contact the tourist office for details.

The town's architectural highlight is the 17th-century **Schlosskirche,** Schlossstrasse 33 (☎ **07541/21422**). The palatial ecclesiastical buildings that were once part of the church's monastery were converted in the 1800s into a palace for the kings of Württemberg. Today, they're privately owned and can't be entered, but the church itself is well worth a visit. It's open only Easter to October, daily 9am to 6pm.

Zeppelin-Museum (☎ **07541/38010**), in the Hafenbahnhof, Seestrasse 22, is a tribute to Count Ferdinand von Zeppelin. This native of Konstanz invented and tested the aircraft that bore his name around 1900. Within the museum's premises you'll find a re-creation of the giant and historic zeppelin called the *Hindenburg,* which exploded in a catastrophic fire in New Jersey in 1937, possibly due to sabotage. In addition to memorabilia associated with zeppelins and their inventor, the museum also contains a full-scale replica of the passenger cabins aboard the famous blimp. May to October, it's open Tuesday to Sunday 10am to 6pm; November to April, Tuesday to Sunday 10am to 5pm. Admission is 12DM ($6) for adults and 6DM ($3) for children 16 and under. There's a gift shop as well.

Of interest to students of educational techniques is Friederichshafen's **Schulemuseum,** Friedrichstrasse 14 (☎ **07541/32622**), which traces the development of education between 1850 (when classes were taught by monks and nuns) and 1930 (when education was the responsibility of the German state). The museum lies near the Schlosskirche in the historic heart of town. Look for the reconstructions of schoolrooms from various periods in the 19th and 20th centuries. April to October, the museum is open daily 10am to 5pm; November to March, Tuesday to Sunday 2 to 5pm. Admission costs 2DM ($1) for adults and 1DM (50¢) for children.

WHERE TO STAY

Hotel Buchhorner Hof. Friedrichstrasse 33, 88045, Friedrichshafen. ☎ **07541/20-50.** Fax 07541/3-26-63. www.ehi.com/travel/ehi/germany. E-mail: info@buchorn.de. 96 units. MINIBAR TV TEL. 170DM–259DM ($85–$129.50) double; 260DM–350DM ($130–$175) suite. AE, DC, MC, V. Parking 12DM ($6).

This charming four-star lakeside hotel provides a compromise between the luxurious, modern comfort of larger hotels and the traditional hospitality of smaller inns. It's housed in the oldest building in town. Rooms are well furnished. The restaurant serves adequate fare at lunch and dinner, and the bar is a cozy retreat. The fitness center has a sauna, a steam room, a Turkish bath, whirlpools, and a solarium. There's also a bicycle-rental desk.

Hotel City-Krone. Schanzstrasse 7, 88045, Friedrichshafen. ☎ **07541/70-50.** Fax 07541/70-51-00. www.Hotel-City-Krone.de. E-mail: citykrone@t-online.de. 86 units. MINIBAR TV TEL. 212DM–272DM ($106–$136) double. Rates include breakfast. AE, DC, MC, V. Free parking.

This modern building in a lakeside setting isn't very traditional or charming, but it's comfortable and fun. Rooms are adequately furnished. The restaurant, Old City, and the bar, Ulf's Nightcafé, are the brightest stars here. Old City turns out reasonable fare of regional specialties and international dishes, and Ulf's Nightcafé gives you an excellent opportunity to mix and mingle with locals, both young and old, who frequent the bar at night. Ask the hotel desk about excursions by bike, train, ship, or foot. Amenities include a sauna, solarium, and swimming pool.

Hotel Goldenes-Rad. Karlstrasse 43, 88045, Friedrichshafen. ☎ **800/528-1234** or 07541/28-50. Fax 07541/28-52-85. E-mail: goldenese-rad@t-online.de. 70 units. MINIBAR TV TEL. 179DM–259DM ($89.50–$129.50) double; 350DM ($175) suite. Rates include buffet breakfast. AE, DC, MC, V. Parking 8DM ($4).

Located in the pedestrian center in the middle of town, this traditional hotel is a short walk from Lake Constance, the ferry, and the new Zeppelin Museum. Rooms are comfortable and modern, with hair dryers, cosmetic mirrors, and safes. The restaurant serves a light cuisine, with many fresh fish specialties and fixed-price menus that change daily. Amenities, surprising for a hotel in this price range, include a gym, sauna, and solarium; massages and bike rentals are also available. The location is not very car-friendly; however, the hotel does have its own parking lot nearby. The English-speaking staff is courteous and helpful.

Seehotel Friedrichshafen. Bahnhofplatz 2 (near the railway station), 88045 Friedrichshafen. ☎ **07541/30-30.** Fax 07541/30-31-00. 132 units. MINIBAR TV TEL. 220DM–265DM ($110–$132.50) double; 335DM ($167.50) suite. Rates include buffet breakfast. AE, DC, MC, V. Parking free outside; 10DM ($5) inside.

This is one of the newest and most appealing hotels in town. It's right beside the Seepromenade. The small rooms are sensibly, even stylishly, decorated. Some have air-conditioning; most have views of the water. There's a bar and a restaurant. The staff is sensitive and well trained.

WHERE TO DINE

Hotel-Restaurant Maier. Poststrasse 1–3, Fischbach, 88048 Friedrichshafen, 6km (4 miles) west of Friedrichshafen. ☎ **07541/40-40.** Reservations recommended. Main courses 20DM–50DM ($10–$25). AE, DC, MC, V. Daily 11am–2pm and 6–10pm. INTERNATIONAL/ GERMAN.

Set at the center of the hamlet of Fischbach, at the edge of the lake, this establishment is better known for its restaurant than for its bedrooms. Local diners appreciate the generous, well-prepared portions, the attentive service, and the sweeping views over the lake. One dining room is contemporary and modern; the other a re-creation of a traditional *stube* in the mountains. Menu items include marinated herring, venison in red wine sauce with mushrooms, salmon-trout or pike perch from the nearby Bodensee, schnitzels, goulash soup, and elaborate pastries for dessert.

The establishment also contains 50 rooms, each with minibar, TV, and telephone. Doubles cost 165DM to 230DM ($82.50 to $115) and include breakfast and free parking.

Restaurant Kurgarten. Olgastrasse 20. ☎ **07541/3-20-33.** Reservations not necessary. Main courses 20DM–30DM ($10–$15). MC, V. Daily 10am–midnight. INTERNATIONAL.

Depending on the time of day, this place might look like a cafe, a bar, or a restaurant. It has a beautiful view over its own garden and the lake. There's a wide range of tasty menu items. Vegetarian choices include mushrooms stuffed with spinach and zucchini stuffed with ratatouille. Other good options include an Argentine beefsteak with herb butter and grilled scampi on rice with slices of local vegetables and salad.

3 Meersburg

190km (118 miles) S of Stuttgart, 143km (89 miles) SE of Freiburg

Like the towns of Italy's lake district, this village on the northern shore of Lake Constance cascades in terraces down the hillside to the water. The heart of Meersburg is a pedestrian area. You can drive into town as far as the Neues Schloss; then you must leave your car and explore on foot. In the center, the streets become narrow promenades and steps wander up and down the hillside. From the dock, both large and small boats set out for trips on the water. Many water sports are offered here. One charming little feature of Meersburg is the presence of a town watchman who still makes nightly rounds, keeping alive an ancient tradition.

ESSENTIALS

GETTING THERE   By Plane   Regional flights come in to the Friedrichshafen airport, 20km (12 miles) from Meersburg. The nearest international airport is at Zürich, 80km (49 miles) away.

By Train   The nearest rail station is in **Überlingen,** 14km (9 miles) away, on the Basel–Singen–Radolfzell–Lindau rail line, with frequent connections in all directions. Call ☎ **01805/996633** for more information. From Überlingen station, buses depart for Meersburg at 30-minute intervals every day 6:15am to 9:45pm, charging 7DM ($3.50) each way. Buses are marked either "Meersburg" or "Friedrichshafen" but always bear number "7395" on the front.

By Bus   Buses arrive about every 30 minutes throughout the day from Friedrichshafen. Regional bus service along Lake Constance is provided by **RAB Regionalverkehr Alb-Bodensee GmbH** in Friedrichshafen (call ☎ **07541/30130** for information).

By Ferry   Regular ferry service goes to the town of Konstanz.

By Car   Access by car is via the A7 Autobahn from the north or Highways 31 and 33. You can drive from Munich in about 3 hours; from Frankfurt in about 4^1/$_2$ hours; and from Stuttgart in about 2 hours.

VISITOR INFORMATION   For tourist information, contact the **Kur- und Verkehrsamt,** Kirchstrasse 4 (☎ **07532/43-11-11**). May to October it's open Monday to Friday 8am to 6:30pm and Saturday 10am to 2pm. November to May it's open Monday to Friday 9am to noon and 2:30 to 5pm.

SPECIAL EVENTS   The surrounding vineyards produce excellent wine, and on the second weekend in September wine makers around the lake come to Meersburg for the **Lake Constance Wine Festival.**

EXPLORING THE TOWN

After you enter the town through the ancient **Obertor (Upper Gate),** you'll be on Marktplatz. Here lies the 16th-century **Rathaus,** which contains a typical German Ratskeller. Leading off from this is **Steigstrasse,** the most interesting artery, passing between rows of half-timbered houses whose arcades serve as covered walkways above the street.

Nearby, at Schlossplatz, is the ✪ **Altes Schloss** (☎ **07532/80000**), which dates from 628 and is the oldest intact German castle. All the relics of a warring age are here—clubs, flails, armor, helmets, and axes—along with 30 fully furnished rooms, decorated with pieces from the various epochs. The bishops of Konstanz lived in this castle until the 18th century, when they moved to the Neues Schloss (see below). The baron of Lassberg, an admirer of medieval romance, then took over, and invited Annette von Droste-Hülshoff (1797–1848), his sister-in-law and Germany's leading female poet, to come as well. She had the castle turned into a setting for artists and writers. You can visit her luxuriously furnished chambers, as well as the murky dungeons and the castle museum with its medieval jousting equipment. The castle is open March to October, daily 9am to 6:30pm; November to February, daily 10am to 6pm. Admission is 9DM ($4.50) for adults, 8DM ($4) students, and 6DM ($3) for children. Next to the castle is the **Castle Mill** (1620), with a 9m (28-foot) wooden waterwheel, the oldest of its kind in Germany.

You go from the medieval to the baroque when you enter the **Neues Schloss,** Schlossplatz (☎ 07532/414071), which faces the Altes Schloss. The leading architect of the 18th century, Balthasar Neumann, was responsible for some of the castle's design. Ceiling paintings and frescoes were done by prominent artists and craftsmen. Elegant stucco moldings grace the ceilings and walls. The Spiegelsaal, or Hall of Mirrors, is the setting for an international music festival in summer. On the top floor is the **Dornier Museum,** which traces the history of Germany's aircraft and aerospace industries. Admission is 5DM ($2.50) for adults and 4DM ($2) for children and students. It's open March to November, daily 10am to 6pm.

On the promenade below stands the **Great House,** which dates from 1505. It now holds ticket offices for the railway and steamer lines on Lake Constance. Regular ferry service to Konstanz leaves from the dock on the outskirts of town.

OUTDOOR PURSUITS

Rock-strewn beaches lie west of the town center; here you can go swimming or just soak up the sun for free. But you'll find the amenities better at the **Beheiztes Freibad,** Uferpromenade (☎ 07532/41-40-60), east of the harbor. Here you can lie on the grass on a strip of sand adjacent to the lake, or immerse yourself in any of three outdoor swimming pools. There's also a sauna on the premises, plus refreshment stands. Entrance to the compound costs 6DM ($3) for adults, 4DM ($2) for students, 3DM ($1.50) for children; free for children under 4.

If you'd like to cycle along the lakefront promenades, head first to **Sport Pfan,** Unterstadtstrasse 7 (☎ 07532/48873). You can rent one of the shop's 10 bicycles for 15DM ($7.50) a day. It operates only April to October.

WHERE TO STAY

Gasthof zum Bären. Marktplatz 11, 88709 Meersburg. ☎ **07532/4-32-20.** Fax 07532/43-22-44. www.meersburg.de/baeren. E-mail: gasthofzumbaeren@t-online.de. 20 units. TV TEL. 120DM–185DM ($60–$92.50) double. Rates include continental breakfast. No credit cards. Closed mid-Nov to mid-Mar. Parking 8DM ($4).

A Taste of Honey

Just 10km (6 miles) from Meersburg is the famous **Wallfahrtskirche** (☎ 07556/9-20-30) at Birnau, 5km (3 miles) southeast of Überlingen. This pilgrimage basilica, which dates from the mid-18th century, was built in rococo style, with rose, blue, and beige marble predominating. A celebrated statuette here is called the *Honigschlecker,* or "honey-taster"—it shows a baby sucking a finger as he's yanked out of a nest of bees. It's to the right of the St. Bernard altarpiece. The church is open daily 7am to 7pm. Admission is free.

This picture-book hotel in the heart of town offers the best value in Meersburg. There's an ornately decorated corner tower, purple wisteria covers most of the facade, window boxes overflow with red geraniums. The hotel was constructed in 1605 on the foundations of a building from 1250 (the cellar of the original Bären is still here). The small rooms are attractive, snug, and cozily furnished. The innkeepers speak English. The inn has two good restaurants, serving both regional and international food, including vegetarian dishes. Fish from Lake Constance is a specialty.

Seehotel zur Munz. Seestrasse 7, 88709 Meersburg. ☎ **07532/43590.** Fax 07532/77-85. 11 units. TV TEL. 150DM–190DM ($75–$95) double. Rates include buffet breakfast. AE, MC, V. Parking 10DM ($5) covered; 6DM ($3) uncovered.

If you're not looking for glamour or a romantic atmosphere, and want to save some marks, consider checking in here. Only a pedestrian walkway and an iron railing separate this hotel from the tree-lined lakefront. The ambience within lets you forget urban bustle. The Seehotel zur Munz is the simplest of our recommendations, but it's clean, decent, and comfortable in every way.

Strandhotel Wilder Mann. Bismarckplatz 2, 88709 Meersburg. ☎ **07532/90-11.** Fax 07532/90-14. 33 units. TV TEL. 190DM–275DM ($95–$137.50) double; 350DM ($175) suite. Rates include buffet breakfast. AE, MC, V. Parking 10DM ($5).

This baroque country hotel is just beyond a stone embankment at the edge of the lake. The building's facade is the backdrop for a painted illustration of a traditional folk figure, called *der wilde Mann*. Here he's contemplating whether to have a stag or a unicorn for supper. The small rooms are comfortable and cozily furnished. There's a good view from the lakeside terrace at the restaurant. The hotel is open year-round, though the restaurant is closed from late October to early April.

Weinstube Löwen. Marktplatz 2, 88709 Meersburg. ☎ **07532/4-30-40.** Fax 07532/ 43-04-10. www.hotel-loewen-meersburg.de. E-mail: hotel-loewen-meersburg@t-online.de. 21 units. TV TEL. 150DM–220DM ($75–$110) double. Rates include buffet breakfast. AE, MC, V. Parking 8DM ($4).

Weinstube Löwen is an old, charming inn on the market square. Its facade has green shutters, geranium-filled window boxes, and vines reaching the upper windows under the steep roof. The Fischer family has updated its interior while keeping a homelike ambience. All but a few rooms have been modernized in a streamlined functional style. They are, however, a bit cramped. The wood-paneled Weinstube, with a white ceramic corner stove, serves good food and drink. Consider a meal here even if you're not a guest.

WHERE TO DINE

Winzerstube zum Becher. Höllgasse 4, near the Altes Schloss. ☎ **07532/90-09.** Reservations required. Main courses 20DM–45DM ($10–$22.50); fixed-price meals 37DM–58DM ($18.50–$29) at lunch, 65DM–100DM ($32.50–$50) at dinner. AE, DC, V. Tues–Sun noon–2pm and 6–10pm; drinks, snacks, and lunch Tues–Sun 11am–2pm and 5pm–midnight. Closed mid-Dec to mid-Jan. REGIONAL/GERMAN.

Year after year this little independently run restaurant manages to serve better food than any hotel in town. If you've come to Germany with images of a handcrafted Weinstube that radiates warmth, then you should dine here. A pea-green tile oven tucked away in a corner provides heat in winter. The chairs are not that comfortable, but the rest of the flowered, paneled, and happily cluttered room provides a cozy atmosphere. The specialty of the chef is onion-flavored Swabian *Rostbraten* with spätzle, along with a host of other specialties, including fresh fish from Lake

Constance. A superb fixed-price dinner cuts down on the cost. The restaurant also offers drinks (mostly wine) and snacks.

MEERSBURG AFTER DARK

Spiegelsaal (Hall of Mirrors), in the Neues Schloss at Schlossplatz (☎ 07532/ 431111), is the splendid backdrop for an annual international chamber-music festival. It takes place every Saturday from the last week in June to the first week in September. You might hear, for example, two baroque ensembles, a string quartet, and a pianist playing the works of Schumann. Tickets run from 24DM to 28DM ($12 to $14). Call ☎ 07532/43-11-11 for information.

The **Konstanz Stadttheater,** the oldest theater in Germany, dating from 1609, moves to its summer theater in Meersburg during July and August. For more details about the Meersburg program offerings, call ☎ 07532/43-11-10.

4 Konstanz (Constance)

179km (111 miles) S of Stuttgart, 76km (47 miles) NE of Zürich

Crowded against the shores of Lake Constance by the borders of Switzerland, the medieval town of Konstanz had nowhere to grow but northward across the river. Today this resort city lies on both banks of the Rhine, as the river begins its long journey to the North Sea. Its strategic position made Konstanz the most important city on the lake. Nowadays tourists come to enjoy the shops, the largest beach in the area, and the magical beauty of nearby **Mainau Island.**

Konstanz's history is long and distinguished. Early Celtic dwellings here were possibly fortified by the Romans under Claudius in A.D. 41. In the 3rd century, the fort was seized by the Germanic tribes, who later became Christianized and founded a bishop's see around A.D. 580. In the 12th century, Emperor Frederick I Barbarossa came here to make peace with the Lombard states. Many years later, after the defeat of the Protestant league, which it had supported, Konstanz was ceded to Austria. It remained part of Austria until 1805, when it was returned to Germany. Although Konstanz never regained the political status it had held in the early part of the 16th century, it is today still the economic and cultural center of the district.

ESSENTIALS

GETTING THERE   By Train   Konstanz is on the main Konstanz–Singen–Villingen–Offenburg rail line, the Schwarzwaldbahn, with frequent connections to the major cities of Germany. For information, call ☎ 01805/99-66-33.

By Bus   Regional bus service around Konstanz is provided by **SBG Südbaden Bus GmbH** at Radolfzell (☎ 07732/9-94-70). **RAB Friedrichshafen** (☎ 07541/ 2-20-77) offers service along the lake going east.

By Boat   Ferry service and lake cruises operate between Konstanz, Mainau Island, Meersburg, Lindau, and Bregenz. The operator is **Bodensee-Schiffsbetriebe,** Hafenstrasse 6 (☎ 07531/28-13-89 for schedules and information).

By Car   Access by car is via the B33.

VISITOR INFORMATION   Contact **Tourist-Information,** Bahnhofplatz 13 (☎ 07531/13-30-30). April to October, the office is open Monday to Friday 9am to 8pm, Saturday 9am to 4pm, and Sunday 10am to 1pm; November to March, Monday to Friday 9am to noon and 2 to 6pm; it's also open the first four Saturdays of December 9am to 4pm.

SEEING THE SIGHTS

The best way to see Konstanz is from the water. The **shoreline** is fascinating, with little inlets that weave in and out around ancient buildings and city gardens. Several pleasure ships offer tours along the city shoreline and across the lake to Meersburg and several other destinations. Contact **Bodensee-Schiffsbetriebe,** Hafenstrasse 6 (☎ 07531/28-13-89). Car ferries from Konstanz to Meersburg leave every 15 minutes during daylight hours. Service is limited to two ferries per hour 8:30 to 11pm, and one ferry per hour 12:05 to 5:30am. Saturdays, Sundays, and holidays, service may also be curtailed. For information, contact **Stadtwerke Konstanz** (☎ 07531/ 80-33-66).

During the summer, outdoor concerts are presented in the **city gardens.** Below the gardens is the **Council Building,** where the Council of Constance met. The building was originally constructed as a storehouse in 1388, but came to be used for meetings during its early years. The hall was restored in 1911 and decorated with murals depicting the history of the town. On the harbor in front is an obelisk erected in memory of Count Ferdinand Zeppelin, the citizen of Konstanz who invented the dirigible in the late 19th century.

The towers of the Romanesque **basilica** rise behind the city garden. Begun in 1052, this church took centuries to complete. The neo-Gothic spire was added only in 1856. During the Council of Constance, the members of the synod met here. From the top tower, a view opens onto the lake and the city.

MAINAU ISLAND   The unusual, almost tropical island of Mainau, lies 6km (4 miles) north of Konstanz, in the arm of the Bodensee known as the Überlingersee. Here palms and orange trees grow and fragrant flowers bloom year-round, practically in the shadow of the snow-covered Alps. In the center of this botanical oasis is an ancient castle, once a residence of the Knights of the Teutonic Order, now owned by Swedish Count Lennart Bernadotte. Only the island's gardens and parks can be visited by the public. They're open daily March to October 7am to 10pm; in winter, 9am to 5pm.

There are four restaurants on the island, but no overnight accommodations. You can reach Mainau either by tour boat from Konstanz or by walking across the small footbridge connecting the island to the mainland, north of the city. Admission is 17DM ($8.50) for adults, 9DM ($4.50) for students, and 5.50DM ($2.75) for children. For more information, call ☎ **07531/3030.**

OUTDOOR PURSUITS   **Strandbad horn,** Eichhornstrasse 89 (☎ **07531/6-35-50**), at the tip of the peninsula, is the largest and most popular beach in the area. You can rent windsurfers for 10DM ($5) per hour. There's also a nude section. From the town center, bus 5 runs here about every 30 minutes.

If you'd like to go biking along the lake, visit **Velotours,** Mainaustrasse 34 (☎ **07531/9-82-80**), where rentals cost from 20DM ($10) per day. Open March to October daily 9am to 5:30pm. Rowboats and paddleboats can be rented at **Am Gondelhafen** (☎ **07531/2-18-81**); they cost 15DM to 18DM ($7.50 to $9) per hour. Open April to October daily 10am to dusk.

SHOPPING

The best way to explore the shopping options in this cosmopolitan town is to walk down the main commercial artery, **Hussenstrasse.** Among the best stores are **Jacqueline,** Hussenstrasse 29 (☎ **07531/2-29-90**), known for its stylish garments for women over 35; and its immediate neighbor, **Petra,** Hussenstrasse 29 (☎ **07531/2-36-86**), whose upscale garments are more youthful and sexy. Men can look for tuned-in fashion, both formal and sporty, at **Pierre,** Hussenstrasse 3 (☎ 07531/2-21-50); and **Holzherr,** Rossgartenstrasse 32 (☎ 07531/128730). For knit shirts, shorts, and tennis garb, try **La Coste,** Hussenpassage 5 (☎ 07531/2-77-02).

WHERE TO STAY

Buchner Hof. Buchnerstrasse 6, 78464 Konstanz, in Petershausen, across the Rhine from Konstanz. ☎ **07531/8-10-20.** Fax 07531/81-02-40. E-mail: Hotel-Buchner-Hof-Konstanz@ t-online.de. 15 units. TV TEL. 140DM–180DM ($70–$90) double; 210DM ($105) suite. Rates include continental breakfast. AE, DC, MC. Closed Dec 23–Jan 7. Free outdoor parking; 10DM ($5) in garage.

Though located in Petershausen, this hotel is just a short walk from most points of interest. The pleasantly furnished rooms range from small to medium. Baths are tiny. There's also a sauna and solarium. The hotel is named after composer Hans Buchner, who became organist at the town cathedral in 1510 and was one of the first musicians to arrange and catalog the wealth of Gregorian chants found in the region.

Mago Hotel. Bahnhofplatz 4, 78462 Konstanz, a 2-min. walk from the station. ☎ **07531/ 2-70-01.** Fax 07531/2-70-03. 34 units. MINIBAR TV TEL. 170DM–210DM ($85–$105) double; 220DM–280DM ($110–$140) suite. Rates include buffet breakfast. MC, V. Parking 10DM ($5) in garage.

The Mago is a small hotel with personal service and helpful owners. It was recently much improved. All the small rooms have ceiling fans and TVs with six English-language channels, including CNN and British SKY. Most rooms open to the lake. Only breakfast is served.

✪ **Steigenberger Insel Hotel.** Auf der Insel 1, 78462 Konstanz. ☎ **800/223-5652** in the U.S. and Canada, or 07531/12-50. Fax 07531/2-64-02. www.SRShotels.com. E-mail: steigenberger.inselhotel@t-online.de. 115 units. MINIBAR TV TEL. 330DM–410DM ($165–$205) double; 540DM–670DM ($270–$335) suite. Rates include buffet breakfast. AE, DC, MC, V. Parking 10DM ($5).

The Insel started life as a Dominican monastery in the 13th century; now it's the single finest place to stay along the German side of the lake. It has a prime location— on an island, with its own lakeside gardens and dock. The white step-gabled building holds an inner Romanesque cloister. Most of the spacious doubles have a living-room look, with sofas, armchairs, and coffee tables.

Dining/Diversions: The formal Seerestaurant offers an international cuisine. The less-formal Dominikaner Stube specializes in regional cookery. At twilight, guests gather at the intimate, club-like Zeppelin Bar, where the walls are cluttered with framed letters and documents. (The man who pioneered the zeppelin also turned this abbey into a hotel.)

Amenities: Hair dryers, room service, laundry, dry cleaning, baby-sitting, sauna, plus lake facilities for swimming.

WHERE TO DINE

Casino Restaurant am See. Seestrasse 21. ☎ **07531/81-57-65.** Reservations required. Jacket and tie required for men. Main courses 32DM–53DM ($16–$26.50). AE, DC, MC, V. Daily 6pm–midnight. INTERNATIONAL.

If you happen to lose at roulette on one of your casino outings in Konstanz, you can revive your spirits (and drink a few, too) on the lakeside terrace of this casino restau-rant. The view is lovely, and the food first rate. The restaurant offers a good choice of dishes; try the fresh fish or saddle of lamb. The food is backed up by a good wine cellar.

✪ **Seehotel Siber.** Seestrasse 25, 78464 Konstanz. ☎ **07531/6-30-44.** Fax 07531/ 6-48-13. www.integra.fr/relaischateaux/siber. E-mail: seehotel.siber@t-online-de. Reservations required. Main courses 56DM–70DM ($28–$35); fixed-price menus 85DM–150DM ($42.50–$75) at lunch, 120DM–185DM ($60–$92.50) at dinner. AE, DC, MC, V. Daily noon–2pm and 6–10pm. CONTINENTAL.

This outstanding restaurant, in an art-nouveau villa near the casino overlooking the lake, is the best not only in Konstanz but along the entire lake. Bertold Siber, one of the leading chefs in Germany, is in charge. The menu features a conservative version of *cuisine moderne.* Offerings change daily. Your meal might begin with lobster terrine with butter and red basil or freshly caught lake trout with an array of seasonings. Try either the roast Barbary goose with Beaujolais sauce or the stuffed turbot with lobster, if they're available. Most guests opt for one of two fixed-price dinners, although à la carte meals are also offered.

The Seehotel Siber is also a Relais & Châteaux hotel, renting handsomely furnished rooms in a building adjacent to the restaurant. The 11 double rooms cost 270DM to 390DM ($135 to $195), and the one suite goes for 590DM ($295).

NEARBY DINING

Schwedenschenke. Mainau Island. ☎ **07531/30-31-56.** Reservations recommended. Main courses 16DM–28DM ($8–$14) for lunch; 32DM–40DM ($16–$20) for dinner. AE, DC, MC, V. Daily 11am–9:30pm. Bus: 4 from the center of Konstanz. REGIONAL/SWEDISH.

Visitors sometimes make a pilgrimage to Mainau Island in Lake Constance for a meal in this old-fashioned restaurant. The chef's specialty is assorted lake fish, including perch, pike perch, and trout. You can also try Hungarian goulash, Swedish meatballs in cream sauce, and *Tafelspitz* (boiled beef with horseradish sauce). Pike perch fillets are served in a spicy sauce of tomatoes, capers, shallots, and mushrooms.

KONSTANZ AFTER DARK

Classical music offerings throughout the year are numerous. The concert season of the **Bodensee Symphony Orchestra** (☎ 07531/59-46-14), runs September to April, and a **summer music festival** is held mid-June to mid-July. There's also an **outdoor music festival** on the Island of Mainau for 3 days in July. Contact the visitor information office (see above) for tickets, schedules, and venues. In May, the **Bodensee Festival** (☎ 07541/72071) offers a mix of classical concerts and theatrical productions, presented at various locations around the shores of the lake. Tickets are 15DM to 75DM ($7.50 to $37.50).

Plays have been staged at the **Stadttheater Konstanz,** Konzilstrasse 11 (☎ 07531/ 130021), Germany's oldest active theater, since 1609. It has its own repertory company. In July and August, the company moves to its summer theater in Meersburg (see "Meersburg," above). Ticket prices depend on the production.

In the main room of the **Konstanz Casino,** Seestrasse 21 (☎ 07531/81-57-65), you try your luck at blackjack, seven-card stud poker, or roulette. Slot machines are located in a side room. Entry into the casino requires a passport as proof of age, and there's a cover of 5DM ($2.50). Men are required to wear jackets and ties. The casino is open daily 2pm to 2am, 3am Friday and Saturday. A restaurant on the premises (see "Where to Dine," above) offers continental cuisine from 6 to 11pm.

Those in the party mood should go next door to **Siber,** Seestrasse 19 (☎ 07531/6-30-46), which offers drinking and dancing for 15DM to 20DM ($7.50 to $10) 10pm to 3am daily except Tuesday. On weekends, the DJs at **Theatercafé,** Konzilstrasse 3 (☎ 07531/2-02-43), mix hip-hop and house late into the night.

Latin beats play Monday, Friday, and Saturday nights at **Rheinterrasse,** Spanierstrasse 5 (☎ 07531/5-60-93). Good Dixieland jazz and country are found at **Hafenhalle,** Hafenstrasse 10 (☎ 07531/2-11-26), every Sunday. Call for details.

For a good pub, head to **Brauhaus J. Albrecht,** Konradigasse 2 (☎ 07531/2-11-26), which has been brewing its own beer for more than 475 years. **Seekuh,** Konzilstrasse 1 (☎ 07531/2-72-32), books winter shows to heat up the night. It's open daily 6pm to 1am weekdays and 7pm to 2am weekends. In the summer, the beer garden is a popular hangout.

Two **music festivals** featuring contemporary rock, jazz, and cabaret music are also held during the summer. An international menagerie of bands descends on the town June 23 to July 4 for a series of concerts held in huge tents. Ticket prices are 20DM to 47DM ($10 to $23.50), but there are a few free shows, too. Throngs of revelers flood the town on July 17 for the annual **Rock Am See festival,** where a 65DM ($32.50) ticket buys you admission to an all-day event that draws international stars. For schedules, call the festival office at ☎ 07531/9-08-80.

5 Reichenau

10km (6¹/₂ miles) NW of Konstanz

Set within the more southerly of the two arms that stretch westward from the Bodensee, Reichenau is a small historic island that was only recently connected to the mainland by a causeway. By the end of the 800s, it was the site of three separate monasteries, the oldest of which had been established in 724. Later Reichenau became a political force within the Holy Roman Empire. Today, much of the island is devoted to the cultivation of vegetables and salad greens, and consequently has a sedate, unflashy aura, much prized by escapists looking for a quiet getaway.

ESSENTIALS

GETTING THERE   By Train   Reichenau's railway station lies midway between the much larger railway junctions of Radolfzell (to the west) and Konstanz (to the east). Trains from throughout Germany and Switzerland make frequent stops at both those cities, from which passengers heading to Reichenau can transfer onto a small railway line that makes runs at hourly intervals on to Bahnhof Reichenau. Buses from Bahnhof Reichenau to Insel Reichenau (the city's historic core), take 10 minutes each way. For information call ☎ 01805/99-66-33.

By Bus   Bus service to Reichenau is limited and inconvenient. For information, call **SBG GmbH** (☎ 07732/19449).

By Car   From Konstanz, motorists should take Route 33 east to Reichenau.

By Boat   For information about the ferryboats that ply the waters between Reichenau and the German lakeside hamlet of Allensbach, call ☎ 07533/6361.

VISITOR INFORMATION   The tourist office is the **Verkehrsbüro,** Mittelzell, Ergat 5 (☎ 07534/92070). May to September, it's open Monday to Friday 8:30am to noon and 2 to 6pm, Saturday 9am to noon; October and April, Monday to Friday 8:30am to noon and 2 to 5pm; November to March, Monday to Friday 8:30am to noon.

EXPLORING THE TOWN

The island is divided into three separate villages (Oberzell, Mittelzell, and Niederzell), each of which is centered around the remains of a medieval monastery. The most impressive of these is the **Münster St. Maria and Markus** Burgstrasse (☎ 07534/276), in

Mittelzell. Originally founded in 725, it became one of the most important centers of learning in the Carolingian era. It reached its peak around 1,000, when it was the home of about 700 monks. The structure is beautiful in its simplicity. Entrance is free, but a visit to the treasury costs 2DM ($1). The church is open daily, year-round, 9am to 6pm; its treasury is open only May to October, Monday to Saturday 11am to noon and 3 to 4pm. While you're in the vicinity, notice the **Krautergarten (Herb Garden),** in the shadow of the cathedral on the Hermann Contractus Strasse. It emulates the herb and vegetable gardens maintained by monks in the Middle Ages.

The hamlet of Niederzell is home to **Stiftskirche St. Peter and St. Paul,** Eginostrasse (no phone). If it's not open at the time of your arrival, the tourist office will call someone to unlock the gates for you. In 1990, during restorations of the church's apse, a series of Romanesque frescoes were uncovered and are now on view.

The nearby hamlet of Oberzell is the site of the **Stiftskirche St. George,** Seestrasse (no phone). Rising abruptly from a cabbage field, it has a severely dignified, very simple facade, and a series of charmingly naive medieval frescoes inside. It's open daily 9am to 6pm. Admission is free.

A final site worth a stop is the **Heimatmuseum,** in the Stadthaus, Ergat 7, in Mittelzell (no phone). This is a showcase for the handcrafts and folklore that developed on Reichenau and the surrounding region. It's open May to October Tuesday to Sunday 3 to 5pm. Entrance costs 3DM ($1.50) adults, 1DM (50¢) children.

SHOPPING

For a sampling of the many wines produced within the Bodensee region, head for **Winzer Vereins,** Munsterplatz (☎ **07534/293**), where you'll be able to see rack upon rack of local vintages. You can even get a single glass to decide if you want to buy a whole bottle.

WHERE TO STAY

Seehotel Seeschau. An der Schiffslände, 78479 Reichenau. ☎ **07534/257.** Fax 07534/ 72-64. www.seeschau.mdo.de. 23 units. MINIBAR TV TEL. 230DM–350DM ($115–$175) double; 450DM–520DM ($225–$260) suite for 2. AE, DC, MC, V. Free parking.

This comfortable, well-maintained hotel is set directly beside the lake. It features good-sized rooms with upscale reproductions of antique furniture and, in many cases, views over the lake. There's a good restaurant and a bar. This hotel is especially appealing in the midsummer, when the flowers around its windows burst into bloom.

Strandhotel Löchnerhaus. Schiffslände 12, 78478 Reichenau. ☎ **07534/80-30.** Fax 07534/582. www.strandhotel-reichenau.mdo.de. E-mail: loechnerhaus-respo@kermit. mbo.de. 42 units. MINIBAR TV TEL. 220DM–280DM ($110–$140) double. Rates include breakfast. AE, DC, MC, V. Closed Jan–Feb. Parking 15DM ($7.50).

This is a good, well-managed hotel, just a stone's throw from the lakefront. It's set within a pleasant garden, and offers well-maintained rooms, many of which have private verandas or terraces and lake views. There's a restaurant (see below). Amenities include boats for rent and a private beach.

WHERE TO DINE

Restaurant Strandhotel Löchnerhaus. Schiffslände 12. ☎ **07534/80-30.** Reservations recommended. Main courses 32DM–45DM ($16–$22.50). AE, DC, MC, V. Daily 11am–9pm. Closed Jan–Feb. GERMAN/INTERNATIONAL.

This restaurant, with its hardworking, kindly staff, is the traditional favorite of many locals. The 1950s-style dining room has lake views. Menu items include sea bass cooked either in Riesling sauce or in a potato crust, whitefish from the Bodensee, rack of lamb with horseradish and mint, grilled meats such as steak, and a savory version of goulash.

6 Überlingen

40km (25 miles) N of Konstanz; 46km (28¹/₂ miles) E of Ravensburg, 24km (15 miles) W of Friedrichshafen

Locals call the town of Überlingen, founded in the 1200s, a German version of Nice because of its sunny weather and lakeside location. It's also one of the best preserved medieval sites along the Bodensee.

ESSENTIALS

GETTING THERE By Train Rail passengers are funneled through nearby Friedrichshafen, from where a smaller rail line goes through Überlingen to Radolfzell. Trains run in either direction along that line at hourly intervals throughout the day. Überlingen's railway station lies on the extreme western edge of town. For rail information call ☎ **01805/99-66-33.**

By Bus Regional bus service along Lake Constance is provided by **RAB Regionalverkehr Alb-Bodensee GmbH** in Friedrichshafen (call ☎ **07541/30130** for more information).

By Car Überlingen is off Route 31, just northwest of Konstanz. From Stuttgart via Ulm, take Route 30 south then Route 31 west at Friedrichshafen. From Munich follow Autobahn 96 west/southwest to Lindau, then Route 31 west to Friedrichshafen and Überlingen.

By Boat April to October, 8 to 10 ferryboats a day carry passengers to Überlingen from Konstanz (trip time: 1 hr. 20 min.) for 14DM ($7) each way. For information call the **Weiss Flote,** an armada of lake steamers maintained by the Bodensee Schiffsbetriebe GmbH (☎ **07531/281398**). No cars are carried on any of these ferries.

VISITOR INFORMATION Tourist information is available at Ergat 5 (☎ **07534/9-20-70**). May to October, the office is open Monday to Friday 9am to 6pm, Saturday 9am to 1pm, and Sunday 2am to 5pm; November to April, Monday to Friday 9am to 1pm and 2 to 5pm.

EXPLORING THE TOWN

The most important of the city monuments is the **Münster,** a surprisingly large medieval structure that required 200 years to build. The larger of its two towers functioned during war as a military watchtower and was later capped with an eight-sided Renaissance lantern. The severely dignified exterior is offset by an elaborate and intricate Gothic interior. Take special notice of the main altar piece, carved in the early 1600s by Jorg Zurn. The cathedral is open daily 8am to 6pm.

On the opposite side of the square is Überlingen's **Rathaus,** built in the late 1400s. Most of its interior is devoted to municipal offices, except for the Ratsaal, whose vaulted ceiling and lavishly paneled walls make it the most beautiful public room in town. Notice the coats of arms representing various factions of the Holy Roman Empire. Open Monday to Friday 9am to noon and 2:30 to 5pm, Saturday 9am to noon. Entrance is free.

The city maintains a **Museum of Folklore (Heimatmuseum)** within one of its most prized buildings, the Reichlin-von-Meldlegg Haus, Krummeberggasse 30 (☎ **07551/991-079**). This building artfully emulates the style of the Florentine Renaissance. Inside you can also visit both a chapel and a lavishly ornate rococo ballroom. The building and its museum are open Tuesday to Saturday 9am to 12:30pm and Sunday 10am to 3pm. Admission is 4DM ($2) adults and 3DM ($1.50) children.

Also look for the **Franziskanerkirche,** Spitalgasse. Especially striking about this church is the contrast between its severely dignified exterior and its lavishly baroque interior. Open daily 8am to noon and 2 to 5pm.

The townspeople of Überlingen took great care to ornament the medieval fortifications that protected them from outside invaders. The best preserved of these walls is the **Stadtmauer,** which in recent times was landscaped into a graceful ramble lined with trees and shrubbery. It's part of the encircling walls that flank the north and east side of town.

Along Überlingen's waterfront promenade (Seepromenade), which offers a view of the faraway Swiss Alps, are two of the largest old buildings in town. One of these is the **Greth,** originally a market and storage vault for corn. Today it houses the city's tourist office. Immediately next door is the fanciful Gothic-era **Zeughaus,** Seepromenade (call tourist office for information). It contains a collection of medieval armor and weapons. It's open only Easter to October, Monday to Saturday 10:30am to noon. Admission is 5DM ($2.50).

Überlingen is also the site of one of the best known medical clinics on the Bodensee. The **Buchinger Clinic,** Willhelmbeckstrasse 27 (☎ **07551/8070**) is expensive, aristocratic, and exclusive. Good spa treatments are available within two of the town's hotels, the Kur und Gasthaus Routher and the Gasthaus Seepark.

WHERE TO STAY & DINE

Landgasthof Adler. Hauptstrasse 44, Lippertsreute, 8862 Überlingen, 10km (6 miles) north of the center. ☎ **07553/8-25-50.** Fax 07553/82-55-70. www.landgasthofzumadler.de. E-mail: landgasthof-adler-voegele@t-online.de. 17 units. TV TEL. 110DM–160DM ($55–$80) double. Rates include breakfast. MC. Restaurant Fri–Tues 11:30am–2pm; Fri–Wed 5pm–midnight. Closed Nov. Free parking.

Set within the confines of a bucolic hamlet (Lippertsreute), this hotel and restaurant occupies two antique buildings, the older of which was built 300 years ago. Rooms are cozy, unpretentious, and appealingly (and artfully) rustic.

The restaurant is well known to locals. It serves heaping, well-prepared portions of time-tested Swabian dishes such as *Spanferkel* (roast suckling pig), *Zweibelrostbraten,* and Bodensee whitefish prepared with white wine sauce. Main courses are 12DM to 40DM ($6 to $20) each.

✪ **Parkhotel St. Leonhard.** Obere St. Leonhard-Strasse 71, 8862 Überlingen, 1.5km (1 mile) north of the center. ☎ **07551/80-81-00.** Fax 07551/80-85-31. www.parkhotel-sankt-leonhard.de. E-mail: info@parkhotel-sankt-leonhard.de. 145 units. MINIBAR TV TEL. 258DM–290DM ($129–$145) double; 360DM–410DM ($216–$246) suite. Rates include breakfast. AE, MC, V. Restaurant open daily 11:30am–2pm and 5:30–11pm. Free parking.

Set on a hilltop, this hotel provides rest and recuperation to urban visitors. The woodsy-looking chalet is flanked by more angular, modern annexes. Rooms are good-sized, modern, conservative, comfortable, and well designed. The hotel has its own swimming pool, sauna and exercise room, two restaurants (one of which is a folkloric Weinstube) and a bar. The more formal restaurant serves meals priced at 45DM to 72DM ($22.50 to $36).

7 Ravensburg

20km (12 miles) N of Friedrichshafen, 32km (20 miles) N of Lindau

Ravensburg isn't on Lake Constance, but it's nearby and makes a good side trip. The town boasts one of the most impeccably preserved medieval cores in the region. During the 1400s, the linen trade made Ravensburg into one of the richest in Germany, but economic stagnation set in during the 1600s as a result of the Thirty Years' War. Today this quiet town is a tourist's delight.

ESSENTIALS

GETTING THERE   By Train   Most passengers change trains in nearby Ulm. From there, trains depart at hourly intervals for Friedrichshafen, stopping en route in Ravensburg (trip time: 1 hr.). For information call ☎ **01805/99-66-33.**

By Bus   Most bus routes into Ravensburg start at nearby villages and hamlets. For information, call **0751/2766.**

By Car   From Stuttgart, follow Autobahn 8 east to the city of Ulm, then turn south onto Route 30 directly into Ravensburg. From along Lake Constance, you can take routes B33, B30, or 467 north to Ravensburg.

VISITOR INFORMATION   Head to the **Stadtverkehrsamt,** Kirchestrasse 16 (☎ **0751/82324**). It's open Monday 8am to noon, Tuesday to Friday 8am to 5:30pm, and Saturday 9am to noon.

EXPLORING THE TOWN

You'll appreciate that cars are banned from the narrow labyrinth of alleyways within Ravensburg's historic core. Two of the most evocative streets are **Untere Breite Strasse** and **Charlottenstrasse,** both of which lie near the town's central square. Lining the Marienplatz are the late-Gothic **Rathaus;** the 14th-century **Kornhaus,** once one of the largest corn exchanges in the region and now the town's library; and the **Waaghaus,** originally built in the 1400s as a warehouse for municipal supplies and now a bank. Look also for the old city **watchtower** and the Renaissance-era **Lederhaus,** the town's post office.

Also on the Marienplatz is the **Karmeliteenklosterkirche.** It was originally a monastery in the 14th century and later housed a mercantile association devoted to the promotion of the linen trade. The complex's church can be visited every day 8am to 6pm. Nearby, at the corner of Kirkstrasse and the Herrenstrasse, is the **Liebfrauenkirche,** the parish church of Ravensburg. Deceptively simple on the outside, the 14th-century structure has been radically but authentically reconstructed on the inside. Look for remnants of original stained glass and a heavy sobriety reminiscent of the Middle Ages.

Part of Ravensburg's allure derives from its well-preserved network of medieval fortifications, studded with defensive towers. The most visible of these is the 52m (170-foot) **Mehlsack Tower,** which has been adopted as the municipal symbol of Ravensburg itself. You can climb to its heights by means of 240 heavily worn circular steps, but only on the third Sunday of every month mid-March to mid-October 10am and noon. Entrance is free. Two other defensive towers can be spotted from the Marienplatz. These are the **Obertor,** the oldest gate in the city walls, accessible via Marktstrasse, and the **Günerturm** (Green Tower), covered with moss-colored ceramic tiles, many of which date from the 14th century. Neither the Günerturm nor the Obertor can be visited.

Ravensburg's only noteworthy museum is its **Heimatmuseum,** devoted to local folklore and handcrafts. It lies within the Folkshaus, Charlottenstrasse 36 (for information contact the tourist office) and is open Tuesday to Saturday 3 to 5pm. Admission is 3DM ($1.50).

WHERE TO STAY

Hotel-Gasthof Obertor. Markstrasse 67, 88212 Ravensburg. ☎ **0751/3-66-70.** Fax 0751/3-66-72-00. www.hotelobertor.de. E-mail: hotelobertor@t-online.de. 32 units. TV TEL. 170DM–210DM ($102–$126) double. Rates include breakfast. AE, DC, MC, V. Free parking.

This hotel was built in the 12th century as a farmhouse and is almost as old as the town. It has a lovely garden terrace in front and a park in the back. Rooms vary greatly in size and in personality, so you may want to take a peek at a couple before deciding which to take. Turn-of-the-century antiques abound, mostly made of cherry wood—typical of the Bodensee area. The restaurant has a fine view of the grounds and serves mostly Swabian/regional cuisine. It's open for lunch and dinner. The hotel also offers a small gym with sauna, whirlpool, and solarium.

✪ **Romantikhotel Waldhorn.** Marienplatz 15, 88212 Ravensburg. ☎ **07151/36120.** Fax 07151/3612-100. www.waldhorn.de. E-mail: bouley@waldhorn.de. 35 units. MINIBAR TV TEL. 210DM–280DM ($105–$140) double; 235DM–350DM ($117.50–$175) suite. Rates include breakfast. AE, DC, MC, V. Parking 15DM ($7.50).

The most appealing hotel in Ravensburg occupies a late-18th-century building and a more modern annex. Because both buildings lie within the town's all-pedestrian zone, it's easy to get a sense of the relaxed local lifestyle. Rooms are comfortable and cozy, and the staff is very charming. The hotel is known for its two restaurants. The Rebleuterhaus, a simple and likable Weinstube, serves Swabian specialties such as large ravioli stuffed with meat and spinach and spätzle, a thick local pasta; the fixed-price menu is 69DM ($34.50), and it's open daily 5pm to 7am. The more expensive, and much more glamorous, of the two restaurants is recommended below.

WHERE TO DINE

✪ **Romantikhotel Waldhorn.** Marienplatz 15. ☎ **0751/36120.** Reservations recommended. Main courses 44DM–60DM ($22–$30). Set menu 169DM ($84.50). AE, DC, MC, V. Tues–Sat 11:30am–2pm and 6–7pm. MODERN INTERNATIONAL.

This sophisticated restaurant is directed by celebrity chef Marcel Bouley. The stylish, gracefully antique dining room has massive ceiling beams. The Asian-influenced cuisine is among the most subtle, celebrated, and exotic in Germany. Menu items combine eastern and western culinary traditions with verve and zest and change according to the seasons and the inspiration of the much-applauded chef. Your meal might include medallions of lamb with miso, lemon, and mint tempura or lobster ravioli with braised sweetbreads, brown butter sauce, caviar, and rosettes of zucchini.

A SIDE TRIP TO WEINGARTEN

An important archaeological excavation is located within the agrarian hamlet of Weingarten, a sleepy village 5km (3 miles) north of Ravensburg. To reach the village, take bus 1 or 2 from Marienplatz. In the 1950s, teams of archaeologists discovered one of the richest troves of German graves in the country. Artifacts from the dig lie in the free **Alamannen Museum,** located in Kornhaus, Karlstrasse 28 (☎ **0751/40-51-25**). It's open Wednesday, Saturday, and Sunday 3 to 5pm; closed February and November.

Weingarten is also home to the largest baroque church in Germany, the **Weingarten Basilica** (☎ **0751/430-71**), which rises to about 60m (200 feet). It was established in 1056 by the wife of a prominent official in the Guelph dynasty. Inside is one of the holiest relics in Germany, a mystical vial, which, according to legend, contains several drops of Christ's blood. The relic was entrusted to the convent by the sister-in-law of William the Conqueror, the Guelph queen Juditha. Another highlight of the church is the organ, one of the largest in the country; its installation required 13 years, beginning in 1737. Also noteworthy are the ceiling frescoes by Cosmas Damian Asam, one of the leaders of the Baroque School. The church is open daily 8am to 6pm.

Finally, if you can manage to schedule your visit for the Friday after Ascension (the Thursday 40 days after Easter), you can witness a massive **procession** of pilgrims, at the head of which are more than 2,000 horsemen. The breeding of horses for this procession is a matter of quiet pride among local farmers.

For further information on Weingarten, call the **tourist office** at ☎ **0751/ 40-51-25.**

10 The Black Forest (Schwarzwald)

The Black Forest covers a triangular section roughly 145km (90 miles) long and 40km (25 miles) wide in southwestern Germany. The pine- and birch-studded mountains here are alive with fairy-tale villages, well-equipped spas, and modern ski resorts. The peaks in the southern part of the forest reach as high as 1,525m (5,000 feet) and are excellent for skiing in winter and hiking or mountain climbing in summer. The little lakes of Titisee and Schluchsee are popular for boating, swimming, and ice-skating. Fish abound in the streams and lakes.

GETTING TO THE BLACK FOREST   International airports serving the area are located in Stuttgart (see chapter 11) and the Swiss city of Basel. Basel lies only 70km (44 miles) from Freiburg in Breisgau, the "capital" of the Black Forest. Trains run north and south through the Rhine Valley, with fast, frequent service to such Black Forest towns as Freiburg and Baden-Baden. Motorists should take the A5 Autobahn, which runs the length of the Schwarzwald. From Lake Constance (see chapter 9), continue along Route 13 for about 64km (40 miles) until you reach the Black Forest.

Exploring the Region by Car   The roads through the forest are excellent, especially the **Schwarzwald Hochstrasse** (Black Forest High Road or Ridgeway, Route B500), which runs almost the entire length of the region, from Baden-Baden to Freudenstadt, then resumes at Triberg and goes on to Waldshut on the Rhine. While taking this scenic road, you'll have many opportunities to park your car and explore the countryside or to turn off on one of the side roads leading to hospitable villages, ancient castles, and rolling farmlands.

1 Freiburg im Breisgau

208km (129 miles) SW of Stuttgart, 70km (44 miles) N of Basel (Switzerland), 280km (174 miles) S of Frankfurt

This scenic and interesting city, the largest in the Black Forest region, is often overlooked because of its out-of-the-way location. When approached from the Rhine plain on the west, Freiburg is silhouetted against towering mountain peaks, which are only an hour from the town by funicular or car.

Because of its remarkable climate, Freiburg is a year-round attraction and sports center. The city lies in the path of warm air currents that come up from the Mediterranean through the Burgundy Gap. In

early spring, the town is usually bursting into bloom while the surrounding mountain peaks are still covered with snow. In the autumn, the smell of new wine fills the narrow streets even as snow is already falling on the nearby peaks.

ESSENTIALS

GETTING THERE   By Train   Frequent trains connect Freiburg to major airports in Basel (Switzerland) and Stuttgart. Daily trains also go to Freiburg from Frankfurt (trip time: 2 hr.), and Hamburg (trip time: 8 hr.), as well as Berlin and Zürich, Switzerland. For information, call ☎ **01805/99-66-33.**

By Bus   Long-distance bus service is provided by the **Südbaden Bus GmbH,** Central Bus Station, Freiburg (☎ **0761/3-61-72**), which has service from Freiburg to the EuroAirport Basel-Mulhouse, and **EuroRegioBus** (☎ **0761/3-61-72**), which has a bus between Freiburg and the French cities of Mulhouse and Colmar.

By Car   Access by car is via the A5 Autobahn north and south.

VISITOR INFORMATION   For tourist information, contact **Freiburg Information,** Rotteckring 14 (☎ **0761/3-88-18-80**). The office is open June to August, Monday to Saturday 9am to 8pm and Sunday 10am to noon, and other months, Monday to Friday 9am to 6pm and Saturday 9am to 2pm.

GETTING AROUND   Freiburg is well-serviced by buses and trams, the latter running in the inner city. A one-way fare costs 3.50DM ($1.75), although you can buy a day pass for 8DM ($4), and two people can buy a day pass for 10DM ($5). For schedules and information, or to buy passes, go to Plus-Punkt, Salzstrasse 3 (☎ **0761/451-1500**) in the Altstadt. Hours are Monday to Friday 8am to 7pm and Saturday 8am to 2pm. Most of the city's public transportation network is shut down between 12:30am and 5:30am.

SEEING THE SIGHTS

Freiburg Cathedral. Münsterplatz. ☎ **0761/31-099.** Cathedral free; 3.50DM ($1.75) adults, 1.50DM (75¢) children, and free for children under 15 to climb the tower. Cathedral Mon–Sat 10am–6pm, Sun 1–6pm. Tower May–Oct Mon–Sat 9:30–5pm, Sun 1–5pm; Nov–Apr, Wed–Sat 9:30am–5pm. Tram: 4, 5, or 6.

This cathedral is one of the great masterpieces of Gothic art in Germany. Its unique spire is of filigree stonework; the steeple sits on an octagonal belfry, which holds a historic 5-ton bell dating from 1258. Although begun in 1200 in the Romanesque style, by the time it was completed in 1620 the builders had incorporated various Gothic styles.

Upon entering by the south door, you'll be in the transept facing an early 16th-century sculpture of the adoration of the Christ child by the Magi. If you turn left into the nave, you'll see at the far end of the aisle, by the entrance to the tower, a fine 13th-century statue of the Virgin flanked by two adoring angels. The high altar has an altarpiece built between 1512 and 1516 by Hans Baldung Grien. Resting against one of the Renaissance pillars along the aisle is a carved 16th-century pulpit, with stairs winding around the curve of the column. The figures below the stairs are likenesses of the townspeople, including the sculptor.

In the aisles are 14th-century stained-glass windows. The oldest stained glass, dating from the 13th century, is in the small round windows of the south transept. Some pieces, however, have been removed to the Augustiner Museum and replaced by more recent panels.

Augustiner Museum. Augustinerplatz. ☎ **0761/2-01-25-31.** Admission 4DM ($2) adults, 2DM ($1) students, free for children 17 and under. Tues–Sun 10am–5pm. Guided tours Wed at 12:30pm, Sun at 11am. Tram: 1.

The Augustiner Museum is housed in the former church and monastery of the Order of St. Augustine. It contains the town's finest collection of art, including religious art spanning more than 1,000 years. Among the treasures are some of the cathedral's original stained-glass windows, as well as the most important of its medieval gold and silver treasures, brought here for safekeeping. Among the best works in the collection are *The Snow Miracle* by Mathias Grünewald and works by Hans Baldung Grien, who was a pupil of Albrecht Dürer. There's also a rich collection of fine late-Gothic wooden sculpture, as well as art nouveau glass objects.

Museum für Neue Kunst. Marienstrasse 10A. ☎ **0761/2-01-25-81.** Free admission. Tues–Sun 10am–5pm. Tram: 1, 4, 5, or 6.

This modern art collection was formerly housed in the Augustiner Museum. Painting and sculpture, beginning with examples of German expressionism, Neue Sachlichkeit, and other classic modern works, especially by artists of southwest Germany, are displayed here.

MORE SIGHTS IN THE ALTSTADT   In Münsterplatz, across from the cathedral, is the **Kaufhaus,** the most colorful building in Freiburg. This Gothic structure, with oriel windows at each end, was originally an ancient emporium, to which a balcony was added in 1550. Above the massive supporting arches, the facade is decorated with the statues of four emperors of the Habsburg dynasty, all but one of whom visited Freiburg during their reigns. The red-painted building is still used as the town's official reception hall.

The **Rathaus,** on the attractive Rathausplatz just west of Münsterplatz, became a happy marriage of two 16th-century merchants' houses when an arcade was built between them in 1900. The Renaissance houses are in good condition. The most remarkable of the decorations on the oriel windows and facades is the relief *The Maiden and the Unicorn.*

WHERE TO STAY
EXPENSIVE

Colombi Hotel. Rotteckring 16, 79098 Freiburg. ☎ **0761/2-10-60.** Fax 0761/3-14-10. www.colombi.de. E-mail: colombi.freiburg@t-online.de. 135 units. MINIBAR TV TEL. 410DM–450DM ($205–$225) double; from 520DM ($260) suite. AE, DC, MC, V. Parking 20DM ($10). Tram: 10, 11, or 12.

This is the most luxurious hotel in town. Snow-white walls and angular lines make the Colombi easy to spot in the downtown area. Despite its central location, it's quiet and peaceful. Many business conferences take place here, but the Colombi caters to independent travelers as well. Rooms are well furnished and appointed; the suites are especially luxurious.

Dining: The on-site restaurant (see "Where to Dine," below) is the finest in Freiburg.

Amenities: Concierge, room service, newspaper delivery, beauty parlor, sauna, pool, laundry, hair dyers, and dry cleaning.

MODERATE

Central-Hotel. Wasserstrasse 6, 79098 Freiburg. ☎ **0761/3-19-70.** Fax 0761/3-19-71-00. www.central-freiburg.de. E-mail: central.hotel@t-online.de. 49 units. MINIBAR TV TEL. 195DM–250DM ($97.50–$125) double. Rates include buffet breakfast. AE, CB, DC, MC, V. Parking 15DM ($7.50). Tram: 5 or 6.

Near the pedestrian zone and the cathedral is the modern Central-Hotel, designed with skylights, marble floors, and pleasantly furnished rooms and lobby. Rooms are standard but still quite comfortable. Although maybe a bit bland compared to some other hotels reviewed here, this is a decent choice at a good price. A buffet breakfast with a wide choice of dishes is included in the rate. Drinks are offered in a cozy corner bar.

Park Hotel Post. Eisenbahnstrasse 35, 79098 Freiburg. ☎ **0761/38-54-80.** Fax 0761/3-16-80. www.park-hotel-post.de. E-mail: park-hotel-post-freiburg@t-online.de. 41 units. MINIBAR TV TEL. 219DM–299DM ($109.50–$149.50) double. Rates include buffet breakfast. AE, MC, V. Parking 14.50DM ($7.25). Tram: 10, 11, or 12.

This baroque hotel, with an elaborate zinc cap on its octagonal turret, is centrally located, within walking distance of the major attractions and the rail station. This has been one of the leading hotels in town for a long time, although its services, amenities, and style don't match the Colombi. Rooms come in a variety of shapes and sizes, are attractively furnished and well kept, and are among the most comfortable in town. Breakfast is the only meal served.

Victoria. Eisenbahnstrasse 54, 79098 Freiburg, 135m (450 ft.) from the Hauptbahnhof. ☎ **0761/20-73-40.** Fax 0761/20-73-44-44. www.hotel-victoria.de. E-mail: hotel.victoria@ t-online.de. 63 units. MINIBAR TV TEL. 209DM–259DM ($104.50–$129.50) double. Rates include buffet breakfast. AE, DC, MC, V. Parking 6DM–16DM ($3–$8).

The Victoria is peaceful, thanks to its location fronting Colombi Park. The facade is a symmetrical 19th-century rectangle, with big windows and a wrought-iron balcony above the front door. The public rooms are lavishly paneled. Guest rooms are small but pleasantly furnished. Some are reserved for nonsmokers. Many rooms contain antiques. The hotel also has a cocktail bar, a coffee shop, and an Italian restaurant.

Zum Roten Bären. Oberlinden 12, 79098 Freiburg. ☎ **0761/38-78-70.** Fax 0761/3-87-87-17. www.roter-baeren.de. E-mail: info@roter-baeren.de. 25 units. TV TEL. 195DM–350DM ($97.50–$175) double. Rates include buffet breakfast. AE, DC, MC, V. Parking 15DM ($7.50). Tram: 1.

This is one of the oldest buildings in Freiburg, with parts dating from 1120. It's said to be the oldest inn in Germany. A modern wing blends in pleasantly. The interior is delightfully decorated, emphasizing original construction elements along with scattered pieces of antique furniture. Rooms are well styled and furnished, some with minibars. Try for one in the older section; they have more tradition and atmosphere. The fine restaurant serves traditional food and wine. In summer, you can stop by for a glass of wine or beer on the Weinstube's terrace.

INEXPENSIVE

Rappen. Münsterplatz 13, 79098 Freiburg. ☎ **0761/3-13-53.** Fax 0761/38-22-52. www.hotelrappen.de. 20 units, 16 with bath. MINIBAR TV TEL. 100DM–120DM ($50–$60) double without bath, 130DM–190DM ($65–$95) double with bath. Rates include buffet breakfast. AE, DC, MC, V. All trams stop 18m (60 feet) behind the hotel.

This charming inn in the pedestrians-only Altstadt has a lot more cozy Black Forest ambience than such nearby competitors as the Central. It's marked with a wrought-iron hanging sign, little dormer windows in its steep roof, window boxes, and shutters. Rooms are small and simply but comfortably furnished; the most desirable have views of the cathedral. There are three dining rooms, all with beamed ceilings, leaded-glass windows, and coach lanterns. The cuisine is notable for local dishes, including a goulash of venison.

WHERE TO DINE
EXPENSIVE

✪ **Eichhalde.** Stadtstrasse 91. ☎ **0761/5-48-17.** Reservations required. Main courses 45DM–52DM ($22.50–$26); fixed-price menu 46DM ($23) for 3 courses, 90DM–120DM ($45–$60) for 4 and 5 courses. MC. Sun–Mon and Wed–Fri noon–2pm; Wed–Mon 6:30–10pm. Tram: 14. FRENCH/GERMAN.

This notable French bistro lies in the Herden district, a long walk from the center. It gets a lot of neighborhood patronage. Fixed-price lunches and dinners are available. The bill of fare is likely to include goose-liver terrine with port aspic, sea bass in thyme sauce, and turbot salad with mustard sauce. The chef has steadily built up a good local reputation, and the food here is always reliable and well prepared.

✪ **Hans-Thoma-Stube/Colombi Restaurant.** In the Colombi Hotel, Rotteckring 16. ☎ **0761/2-10-60.** Reservations required. Main courses 49DM–65DM ($24.50–$32.50); 3-course business lunch 44DM–59DM ($22–$29.50); fixed-price dinner 98DM ($49) for 4 courses, 158DM ($79) for 7 courses. AE, DC, MC, V. Daily noon–3pm and 6pm–midnight. Tram: 10, 11, or 12. REGIONAL/FRENCH.

This is justifiably the most acclaimed restaurant in the area. Gracious and skillful service, along with a sumptuous setting, ensure a memorable meal. Choice ingredients, masterly preparation, and creative presentation delight both the eye and the palate. The chef prepares a light modern cuisine, although many regional dishes are also offered. The menu is ever changing, based on the seasons, but might include a terrine of turbot, chanterelles over fillet of venison, or an array of Atlantic fish dishes perfectly prepared and impeccably served. There are two 18th-century–style dining rooms.

Weinstube zur Traube. Schusterstrasse 17. ☎ **0761/3-21-90.** Reservations required. Main courses 38DM–49DM ($19–$24.50); fixed-price menus 76DM–110DM ($38–$55). AE, V. Tues–Sat noon–3pm and 6–10pm. Closed last 2 weeks in Aug. Tram: 10, 11, or 12. FRENCH/SWABIAN.

This 600-year-old Weinstube is the coziest choice in town for tavern dining. The pewter and earthenware dinner services decorating the walls are art objects in their own right, and the ceramic stove is more than 300 years old. The food here is regional and well prepared, emphasizing game, meat, and fish. Try the pike roulade with crab sauce. Fresh ingredients get a lot of respect around here and are deftly handled by the kitchen staff. There's also a fine wine list.

MODERATE

Oberkirchs Weinstuben. Münsterplatz 22, 79098 Freiburg. ☎ **0761/202-68-68.** Fax 0761/202-68-69. Reservations recommended. Main courses 26DM–40DM ($13–$20). AE, MC, V. Mon–Sat noon–2pm and 6:30–9:15pm. Closed Jan. Tram: 1, 4, or 5. GERMAN.

The innkeeper provides excellent regional cooking and comfortable rooms in this traditional Freiburg establishment. The setting, on a colorful square, is pure picture-postcard. The main Weinstube is old, with a monumental ceiling-high ceramic stove made with ornate decorative tiles. You get good old-fashioned food here—tasty soups, meat dishes, poultry—and plenty of everything. In season, you might try young pheasant. In the rear is a modern complex fronting an open patio with a fish pond.

The Weinstube also has 25 excellent rooms, all with private baths or showers. Doubles cost 230DM to 300DM ($115 to $150), with continental breakfast included.

Wolfshöhle. Konviktstrasse 8. ☎ **0761/3-03-03.** Reservations recommended. Main courses 29DM–39DM ($14.50–$19.50); fixed-price menus 40DM–82DM ($20–$41). AE, DC, MC, V. Summer, Mon–Sat 11am–midnight; off-season, Mon–Sat noon–2pm and 6pm–midnight. Tram: 10, 11, or 12. ITALIAN.

Wolfshöhle's warmly paneled ambience might remind you of a cozy inn high in the mountains on the border between Italy and the German-speaking world. The cuisine is sophisticated but fortifying. Choices include veal scaloppini with lemon and fillet of veal delicately seasoned, well-prepared lamb dishes, and calves' liver. You might begin with a hearty soup, or select an appetizer such as veal with tuna, the antipasto of the day, or two different versions of carpaccio.

An Excursion to the Upper Black Forest

From Freiburg you can make a 145km (90-mile) one-day circuit through one of the most scenic parts of the Black Forest, returning in time for dinner. Along the way, you'll pass a trio of the highest summits in the Black Forest, and pass two of the region's most beautiful lakes.

Head immediately south to **Schauinsland** along a narrow twisting road. At the car park you can climb some 100 steps to the belvedere tower for a panoramic view of the area.

Continuing south, you reach **Belchen** mountain, which rises to a height of 1,115m (4,640 feet). From where the road ends, you can walk to the summit in about 20 minutes. On a clear day, you can look out from the observation platform here and take in a panoramic sweep of the Rhine plain, plus a view of the Alps from Säntis to Mont Blanc.

Upon leaving, continue east to the hamlet of Todtnau, where visitors can walk up a footpath to **The Falls of Todtnau,** about a mile away. Back at Todtnau, continue east along Route 317 to Feldberg. Here a chairlift takes visitors to the 1,450m (4,750-ft.) **Seebuck** peak, which is crowned by the Bismarck monument and offers another sweeping panoramic view of the Black Forest.

Back on the road again, follow Route 317 east until it becomes Route 500 heading south to **Schluchsee,** one of the loveliest lakes of the area and the most important body of water in the Black Forest.

After a visit here, head north along Route 500 to the hamlet of **Lenzkirch,** from which you'll have a view of Lake Titisee. The road then continues to the resort of **Titisee** itself (see below). After a visit you can return to Freiburg by heading west along Route 31.

FREIBURG AFTER DARK

An impressive entertainment complex, the **Konzerthaus** hosts a variety of events, ranging from classic music to theater to pop concerts. In June and July, huge tents are raised to house the annual **Zeltmusik festival,** which emphasizes jazz but includes other musical styles as well. Summer also brings a series of **chamber-music concerts** to the Kaufhaus, in Münsterplatz, and a program of **organ recitals** to the Freiburg Cathedral. Information about all venues and events listed above, including program schedules and ticket sales, is available from **Freiburg Information** (see above).

The city also has a thriving bar and club scene that goes on into the wee hours. Two clubs in one, **Crash,** Schnewlinstrasse 3 (☎ 0761/3-24-75; tram: 1, 4, 5, or 6), serves drinks and plays punk, house, and funk as background music to the lively banter of patrons; in the basement, **Drifler's Club** plays house and techno for dancers. Crash is open Wednesday to Saturday 10pm until 3:30am, and Drifler's Thursday to Saturday midnight to 4am. There is no cover at either club. **Club Parabel,** Universitätstrasse 3 (☎ 0761/3-06-34; tram: 1, 4, 5, or 6), plays everything from pop to techno. It's open Thursday 11pm to 3am and Friday and Saturday 11pm to 4am, and also on nights before holidays. The 10DM ($5) cover includes the price of your first drink.

Jazz Haus, Schnewlinstrasse 2 (☎ 0761/3-49-73; tram: 1, 4, 5, or 6), hosts pop, folk, blues, and jazz shows by international, regional, and local bands. The club is open nightly 8pm until 1am, with a cover of 15DM to 30DM ($7.50 to $15). Occasionally bands play jazz or rock at **Le Cher,** Niemensstrasse 8 (☎ 0761/3-28-00; tram: 1, 4, 5, or 6), but usually it's a place just to drink and talk. It's open Monday to

Saturday 11am to 1am and Sunday 3pm to 1am. Until 8pm, the **Café Atlantik,** Schwabentorring 7 (☎ **0761/3-30-33;** tram: 1), serves up spaghetti platters for 8.50DM ($4.25), but later on, it's mainly a place to drink and listen to the occasional band. Open daily 11am to 1am.

   Hausbrauerei Feierling, Gerberau 46 (☎ **0761/2-66-78;** tram: 1 or 2), is a brewery-pub, with a beer garden across the street. It's open daily 11am to midnight. Those who want a darker, smoky bar, should head to the local Irish pub, the **Isle of Innisfree,** Augustinaplatz 2 (☎ **0761/22984;** tram: 1, 4, 5, or 6), which sometimes has live music. **Cafe Brasil,** Wannerstrasse 21 (☎ **0761/28-98-88;** tram: 1, 5, or 6) has a tropical feel. It's open daily 10am to 7am.

2 Badenweiler

35km (22 miles) S of Freiburg, 240km (150 miles) W of Stuttgart

Badenweiler is one of the smallest, and one of the most charming, spa towns in the Black Forest. It's also known as the site of the best-preserved Roman baths north of the Alps. Town authorities here are intent on keeping their community spotless, squeaky-clean, and steeped in Black Forest myth and legend. Badenweiler is located halfway between Freiburg and Basel, near the Swiss border.

ESSENTIALS
GETTING THERE   By Train   There's no railway station in Badenweiler, so rail passengers should first go to Freiburg, then switch onto any of the dozen-or-so daily trains that carry them to the town of Müllheim. From there, it's easiest to take any of the taxis lined up at the railway station for the 4km- (2¹/₂-mile-) eastward trip to Badenweiler. There's also a bus (marked "Badenweiler") from Müllheim; it's timed to coincide with the arrival of trains.

By Bus   Unless you're coming into Badenweiler from one of the nearby communities, bus travel is not convenient.

By Car   From the A5 Autobahn, which runs north to south between Karlsruhe and Basel, exit at the Müllheim/Badenweiler exit, then follow the signs to Badenweiler.

VISITOR INFORMATION   Head for **Kur-Touristik,** Ernst-Eisenlohr-Strasse 4 (☎ **07632/7-21-10**), which is open Monday to Friday 8:30am to noon and 3 to 5pm and Saturday 8:30am to noon.

WHAT TO SEE & DO
The springs that pour water into the spa facilities here are very little changed since Roman days, a fact that the local resort, the **Cassiopeia Therme,** Kurpark (☎ **07632/7990**), won't let you forget. It offers mud packs, massage, sauna, and steam bath treatments. The well-preserved Roman baths, originally built in A.D. 75, still stand today within the Kurpark, or spa gardens. Tours of the ancient Roman baths, complete with descriptions of how the Romans actually bathed, are given Tuesday at 5pm and Sunday at 11:15am. Tours cost 2DM ($1). For information, contact the spa directly. The baths are open daily 9am to 10pm. The cost is Monday to Friday 19DM ($9.50) adults, 12DM ($6) children; Saturday, Sunday, and holidays 16DM ($8) adults, 9DM ($4.50) children; 38DM ($19) two adults and up to 3 children under age 18; an evening card for Monday to Friday after 7pm is 10DM ($5) for everyone.

   In addition to spa treatment, the town offers a wide range of hiking trails through the Black Forest, the most interesting of which is a trek to the **Schloss Bürgeln,** 7846 Schliengen (☎ **07626/237**), 20km (12 miles) south of Badenweiler. It's also accessible by car (follow the signs from Badenweiler's center). Schloss Bürgeln was built in

1764 by order of the abbot of St. Blasein. It offers a commanding view of the surrounding countryside; on a clear day, you can see Basel, the Vosges of France, and the bend in the Rhine as it flows into Switzerland. Especially noteworthy are the verdant gardens around the castle. The castle can only be visited March to November, on guided tours given every day except Tuesday, at 11am, 2pm, 3pm, 4pm, and 5pm. If there are classical concerts there is no 5pm tour. Adults pay 5DM ($2.50), children under 12, 2DM ($1).

One of the highlights of Badenweiler's cultural scene is the four-times-per-year concert series conducted inside the town's most prestigious hotel, the Römerbad (see below), in March, June, September, and November. All tickets cost 50DM to 60DM ($25 to $30) and are sold exclusively by the hotel itself, often as part of overnight packages.

WHERE TO STAY

Hotel Ritter. Friedrichstrasse 2, 79410 Badenweiler, a 10-min. walk west from the center. ☎ **07632/83-10.** Fax 07632/831299. www.hotelritter.de. E-mail: hotelritter@t-online. 75 units. TV TEL. 288DM–368DM ($144–$184) double; 382DM–400DM ($191–$200) suite. Rates include breakfast. Half board is included for 2 or more nights; otherwise it costs 25DM ($12.50) per person. AE, MC, V.

Informal and personal, this hotel is composed of a trio of buildings. The oldest and most traditional looking is a 150-year-old chalet that contains the cheapest of the accommodations. Newer and somewhat more comfortable lodgings lie within a pair of relatively new annexes. Rooms are cozy, simple, modern, and clean. On the premises, there's a bar and a restaurant, plus an indoor swimming pool, with a glass door overlooking a forest and the carefully maintained lawns.

✪ **Hotel Römerbad.** Schlossplatz 1, 79410 Badenweiler. ☎ **07632/7-00.** Fax 07632/70200. www.hotel-roemerbad.de. E-mail: info@hotel-roemerbad.de. 110 units. TV TEL. 335DM–445DM ($167.50–$222.50) double; 435DM–495DM ($217.50–$247.50) suite. Rates include breakfast. AE, DC, MC, V. Parking 8DM ($4).

This is the best, most elaborate, and most historic spa and hotel in town, attracting urbanites in need of R&R from throughout Germany. The staff is steeped in an Old-World sense of courtliness. The clientele has included Nietzsche, Thomas Mann, and Andy Warhol. The domes, mansard roofs, and balconies of this bone-white structure inspire a comparison to an elaborate wedding cake. Inside, the place combines an opera-house grandeur with antiques, ornate ceiling medallions, and touches of gilt. Rooms are traditionally furnished, often spacious, and beautifully maintained, with sumptuous beds.

The Römerbad is also known for its seasonal presentations of concerts. The hotel's concert hall, built in the early 1800s as a shelter for horses and carriages, is sought out by music lovers throughout the country. A series of classical or jazz concerts, each performed over a period of about 4 days, is presented three or four times a year. For information, contact the hotel directly.

Dining/Diversions: The Römerbad Restaurant is formal, elegant, and courtly. There's also a paneled bar evocative of a private club.

Amenities: Room service (7am to 10:30pm), massage, concierge, indoor and outdoor swimming pools (linked with a waterfall that re-creates an alpine stream), two tennis courts, small concert hall, easy access to a nine-hole golf course.

✪ **Hotel Schwarzmatt.** Schwarzmattstrasse 6, 79410 Badenweiler, a short walk east of the town center. ☎ **07632/8-20-10.** Fax 07632/820120. 41 units. TV TEL. 396DM–446DM ($198–$223) double; 540DM ($270) suite. Rates include breakfast. No credit cards. Indoor parking 12DM ($6); outdoor parking free.

Although it ranks behind the Römerbad, this hotel is a consistently popular choice, thanks to its reasonable prices, lack of pretension, and hardworking, English-speaking staff. The modern, three-story building is adorned with flower boxes along its balconies, and flanked by verdant evergreens. The comfortable rooms range from medium to large, all have a VCR and safe, plus elegant beds and immaculate baths. There's a well-managed restaurant within an airy, well-lit room on the ground floor (see "Where to Dine," below), a beauty parlor, massage facilities, and an indoor swimming pool.

Romantik Hotel zur Sonne. Moltkestrasse 4, 79410 Badenweiler. ☎ **07632/75-08-0.** Fax 07632/75-08-65. www.zur-Sonne.de. E-mail: hotel@zur-sonne.de. 55 units. MINIBAR TV TEL. 170DM–200DM ($85–$100) double. Rates include breakfast. Half board 30DM ($15) per person. AE, CB, DC, MC, V. Parking 8DM ($4) for garage.

Comfortable and cozy, this hotel occupies a rambling chalet that was built in stages beginning around 350 years ago. Rooms come in a variety of shapes and sizes and are attractively furnished, with traditional Black Forest motifs and the views of a quiet street near the center of the resort. All are exceedingly comfortable and well maintained. On the premises is a well-managed restaurant, recommended below.

WHERE TO DINE

Romantik Hotel zur Sonne. Moltkestrasse 4. ☎ **07632/75-08-0.** Reservations recommended. Main courses 27DM–45DM ($13.50–$22.50); fixed-price menus 60DM–110DM ($30–$55). AE, DC, MC, V. Daily noon–2pm and 6–9pm. ITALIAN/GERMAN.

This hotel is more famous among locals for its Italian and German cuisine than for its rooms. The Weinstube decor includes old paneling and timbers. Menu items feature a savory mixture of German and Italian cuisine, including braised guinea fowl with arugula, carpaccio of veal with arugula and shaved Parmesan cheese, lobster cocktail, and ravioli stuffed either with lobster and sage, or with ham and ricotta, according to your tastes. In springtime, an entire menu category is devoted exclusively to variations on asparagus.

Schwarzmatt. In the Hotel Schwarzmatt, Schwarzmattstrasse 6. ☎ **07632/8-20-10.** Reservations not necessary. Main courses 39DM–48DM ($19.50–$24); fixed-price menus 85DM–98DM ($42.50–$49). AE, MC, V. Daily noon–2pm and 7–10pm. REGIONAL/ INTERNATIONAL.

There's nothing about this restaurant that's homey or traditional. Instead, you'll find an airy, high-ceilinged, modern decor with views out over the garden. The well-prepared food consists of specialties of the Black Forest, as well as such international dishes as steaks, pastas, salads, and casseroles. The menu is ever changing but always good. The kitchen staff is skillful, and the service professional. Every afternoon from 3 to 5pm there's a buffet with an impressive assortment of regional and international cakes and other treats served with coffee.

3 Titisee

53km (33 miles) E of Freiburg, 160km (99 miles) W of Stuttgart

Titisee is the quintessential German retreat, favored by thousands for its ability to soothe, relax, and refresh the spirit and body. This small lakeside resort, which can be traversed on foot within about 12 minutes, offers access to all the natural bounty of the Schwarzwald. Well-marked hiking trails lead up the hillsides. Motorized vehicles are forbidden on the lake, for the sake of swimmers and general tranquility. Nearby rises the Feldberg, at 1,525m (5,000 feet) the highest point in the Black Forest.

Titisee has a year-round population of 2,000, although on busy summer days when visitors come in from nearby cities such as Freiburg, the population can easily swell to three times that amount. More facilities are available at the more workaday community of Neustadt, about 6km (4 miles) away.

ESSENTIALS

GETTING THERE   By Train   From Freiburg, trains arrive at intervals of every 30 minutes (trip time: 45 min.). The Titisee rail station is on Parkstrasse (☎ **07651/ 8298**). For information call ☎ **01805/996633.**

By Bus   Bus connections into Titisee are mostly limited to rural hamlets within the surrounding Schwarzwald. For information, call the local bus company, **Südbaden Bus GmbH,** at ☎ **07651/5120.**

By Car   Titisee is set near the junction of highway B31 and B317. It's clearly marked from each of the larger towns that surround it. Driving time from Freiburg is 45 to 60 minutes, depending on traffic; from Stuttgart the trip takes 90 minutes.

VISITOR INFORMATION   Contact the tourist office at Strandbadstrasse 4 (☎ **07651/98040**). May to October, it's open Monday to Friday 8am to noon and 1:30 to 5:30pm, Saturday 10am to noon and 3 to 5pm, and Sunday 10am to noon. November to April, it's open Monday to Friday only. There's another tourist office in nearby Neustadt, at Sebastian-Kneipp-Anlage (☎ **07651/20-62-50**), maintaining the same hours.

WHAT TO SEE & DO

The cold, clear waters of Lake Titisee are among the most sought after in the region. The town's premier bathing spot is **Schwimmbad Titisee,** Strandbadstrasse (☎ **07651/8272**), which combines the chlorinated waters of the town's largest swimming pool with immediate access to a sandy beach adjacent to the lake, complete with cabanas, showers, and refreshment stands. Entrance to the complex costs 6DM ($3) adults, 3.50DM ($1.75) children and students. It's open daily May to September 15, 9am to 7pm.

Except for a handful of medium-sized steamers that slowly circumnavigate the lake (see below), local ordinances allow only rowboats, foot-operated paddleboats, and electric (not gas-operated) motorboats on the water's surface, a rule that keeps noise, pollution, and rowdiness to a minimum. You can rent rowboats and paddleboats for 13DM to 15DM ($6.50 to $7.50) per hour; electric motorboats that putt-putt demurely across the lake rent for 14DM to 19DM ($7 to $9.50) per hour. About a half-dozen purveyors of these rental craft line the edges of the Seestrasse, the town's main lakefront promenade; the two best are **Drubba** (☎ **07651/981200**), and **Schweizer-Winterhalder** (☎ **07651/8214**).

Schweizer-Winterhalder also operates **lake steamers,** which provide a more comfortable excursion. June to September, they depart during the day at hourly intervals from the company's pier. Trips last about 40 minutes and are priced at 6DM ($3) per person. Don't expect museums or monuments at this outdoorsy resort. Spa clients within Titisee head for the facilities within the **Hotel Brügger,** Am See, Strandbadstrasse 14 (☎ **07651/ 8010**), which are open to residents of other hotels. In nearby Neustadt, the **Kneipp-Kur,** in the Kurpark (☎ **07651/1270**), offers an equivalent spa facility, which offers treatments for cardiac and vascular disorders, rheumatism, and intestinal diseases.

Shoppers and boaters head to the stores that line the lakefront **Seestrasse.** In the early evening, a Bavarian-style marching band promenades along the lakefront, its members stopping at various hotels en route.

WHERE TO STAY

Brugger am See. Strandbadstrasse 14, 79822 Titisee. ☎ **07651/80-10.** Fax 07651/82-38. www.hotel-brugger.de. E-mail: hotel.brugger@t-online.de. 65 units. TV TEL. 190DM–320DM ($95–$160) double. Rates include breakfast. Half board 38DM ($19) per person. MC, V. Free parking.

This is one of the leading spa hotels around the waterfront. Its allure lies in its relaxation and beauty treatments. The building is a modified chalet, with balconies and an all-window dining room. Rooms are contemporary and mostly good-sized, with exceedingly comfortable furnishings. The restaurant serves classic German fare typical of the region, along with fresh fish from the lake. In addition to cure baths and other spa-related facilities, the hotel also maintains an indoor pool and a salon.

Hotel Rauchfang. Bärenhofweg 2, 79822 Titisee. ☎ **07651/8-25-50.** Fax 07651/8-81-86. www.hotel-rauchfang.de. E-mail: hotel-rauchfang@gmx.de. 17 units. TV TEL. 159DM–179DM ($79.50–$89.50) double. Prices include breakfast. Half board 26DM ($13) per person. AE, MC, V. Free parking.

Rauchfang is one of the best values among pension-hotels in the upper Black Forest region. It's an authentic reproduction of a chalet-style building. The interiors of the public areas are covered in pine. Although the rooms appear somewhat stark and small, the beds are comfortable; you'll probably spend a very pleasant evening here. Guests can enjoy the indoor pool, sauna, and steam-room, as well as the miles of forest walks stretching in all directions.

Parkhotel Waldeck. Parkstrasse 6, 78922 Titisee. ☎ **07651/80-90.** Fax 07651/8-09-99. www.parkhotel@waldeck.de. E-mail: parkhotel.waldeck@t-online.de. 53 units. MINIBAR TV TEL. 152DM–238DM ($76–$119) double; 220DM–330DM ($110–$165) suite for 2. Rates include buffet breakfast. Half board 31DM ($15.50) per person. AE, DC, MC, V. Parking in garage 8DM ($4).

This hotel is extremely popular, and for good reason—it offers tremendous value and numerous amenities. A richly decorated interior with Oriental rugs, hexagonal floor tiles, and a beamed and paneled wooden ceiling greets you, along with the bright faces of the helpful staff. The exterior is sheltered against a pine-covered hillock. The small rooms are colorful and comfortable—however, you may not spend a lot of time in them. You can swim in the indoor pool, go for a hike on the miles of nearby forest trails, or just relax in the Jacuzzi. There are two dining rooms and two bars.

✪ **Trescher's Schwarzwaldhotel am See.** Seestrasse 10, 79822 Titisee-Neustadt. ☎ **07651/805-0.** Fax 07651/8116. www.schwarzwaldhotel-trescher.de. E-mail: trescher@mail.swapcom.net. 101 units. MINIBAR TV TEL. 260DM–390DM ($130–$195) double; 390DM–420DM ($195–$210) suite. AE, CB, DC, MC, V. Closed Nov 1–Dec 15. Parking 20DM ($10).

This sprawling hotel, right in the center of the resort, is the most comprehensive in Titisee. It's composed of three massive annexes, each bordering a flower-filled courtyard constructed on a platform built directly into the waters of the lake. The spacious rooms are graceful and conservatively decorated.

Dining/Diversions: Two bars and three restaurants are on the premises, the most formal of which is the Terrasse (see "Where to Dine," below).

Amenities: The hotel has one of the most appealing indoor swimming pools along the Titisee, as well as facilities for boating, fishing, and tennis. A concierge can arrange virtually anything. There's also room service, laundry, dry cleaning, and hair dryers in the rooms.

WHERE TO DINE

Trescher's Schwarzwaldhotel am See. Seestrasse 10. ☎ **07651/805-0.** Reservations required. Main courses 29DM–49DM ($14.50–$24.50); fixed-price lunch 42DM–65DM ($21–$32.50). AE, CB, DC, MC, V. Daily 7am–11pm. Closed Nov 7–Dec 20. INTERNATIONAL/BLACK FOREST.

The formal dining room in this hotel (recommended above), with picture windows opening onto the lake, is the finest choice for cuisine at Titisee. Diners here enjoy refined service and sublime cuisine. Many of the chef's specialties are regional. Appetizers include melon with Black Forest ham and carpaccio of beef with Parmesan. As for main courses, the Black Forest trout is delectably broiled and served with parsley potatoes, and there's also a hunter's plate, Black Forest style, with spätzle (dumplings). A good authentic regional choice is the boiled calf's head and tongue, served in an onion–red wine sauce. For dessert, try the Black Forest cherry bombé.

NEARBY PLACES TO STAY & DINE

Just 5km (3 miles) west of Titisee, or 32km (20 miles) east of Freiburg, lies **Hinterzarten,** one of the major pockets of posh within the Black Forest. You may want to retreat here instead of Titisee itself, as Hinterzarten is more tranquil and luxurious. In the center of town stands St. Oswald's, a church constructed in 1146.

✪ Park Hotel Adler. Adlerplatz 3, 79856 Hinterzarten. ☎ **07652/1270.** Fax 07652/127-717. 90 units. MINIBAR TV TEL. 270DM–450DM ($135–$225) double; 450DM–620DM ($225–$310) junior suite; 500DM–960DM ($250–$480) suite. Rates include buffet breakfast. AE, DC, MC, V. Parking 10DM ($5).

This is one of the great inns of the Black Forest. Chic and country estate-ish, the inn suggests luxury at every turn, with a wealth of leisure facilities. It's located in the middle of a lovely 4ha (10-acre) park. Rooms are sumptuously appointed and beautifully maintained, many are quite spacious. Beds are so comfortable you won't want to get out of them, and the beautiful baths are filled with amenities. The hotel's family ownership dates from 1446.

Dining/Diversions: This world-famous hotel has seven different restaurants. Each serves a high-quality cuisine based on the freshest ingredients. An orchestra accompanies dinner in the main 17th-century dining room, and later moves into the bar to play for dancing.

Amenities: Indoor pool, sauna, tennis courts, driving range, Jacuzzi, sauna, beauty salon, hairdresser, open-air tennis courts, bike rentals, golf courses nearby, concierge, room service, baby-sitting, laundry, dry cleaning.

Hotel Reppert. Adlerweg 21–23, 79856 Hinterzarten. ☎ **07652/1208-0.** Fax 07652/1208-11. www.reppert.de. E-mail: hotel@reppert.de. 43 units. MINIBAR TV TEL. 290DM–436DM ($145–$218) double; 382DM–450DM ($191–$225) suite. Rates include buffet breakfast. Half board 25DM–42DM ($12.50–$21) per person. AE, DC, MC, V. Closed Nov 24–Dec 12. Garage parking 15DM ($7.50).

Although not rated as highly as the Park Hotel Adler, this is a good second choice, a luxurious and traditional four-star hotel in a sunny and central location in a church meadow fronting the village pond. Its many rooms open onto balconies, each shaded by an umbrella. A rich, warm ambience inhabits the comfortable, well-furnished rooms. The traditional lobby is filled with antiques.

Dining: The hotel's restaurants are among the finest in the area for atmosphere, efficient service, and cuisine.

Amenities: Concierge, room service, baby-sitting, faxes, hair dryers, laundry and dry cleaning. The thermae is a unique pool and sauna combined; it was once voted best in the nation. Other facilities include swimming pool, two Jacuzzis, aromatherapy rooms, sauna, steam bath, massage, bike rentals, tennis, riding, water sports, and a hotel program that features guided walks.

4 Triberg

138km (86 miles) SW of Stuttgart, 48km (30 miles) NE of Freiburg

Triberg, deep in the heart of the Black Forest, is home to the highest waterfall in the country. It also claims to be the birthplace of the cuckoo clock. If you're looking for an interesting traditional timepiece, this is the place to find it. You'll also find many little shops selling wood carvings, music boxes, and other traditional crafts.

ESSENTIALS
GETTING THERE   By Plane   The nearest major airport is at Stuttgart, 2¹⁄₂ hours away by train.

By Train   Trains arrive daily from Munich (trip time: 4¹⁄₂ hr.) and from Frankfurt (trip time: 3 hr.). The **Triberg Bahnhof** is on the Konstanz–Singen–Villingen–Offenburg Schwarzwaldbahn rail line, with frequent connections in all directions. Call ☎ **01805/99-66-33** for schedules and information.

By Bus   Regional bus service in the Black Forest area is provided by **SBG Südbaden Bus GmbH** in Villingen (☎ **07721/9-28-521**).

By Car   Access is via the A5 Autobahn north and south; exit at Offenburg and then follow the signs along Route 33 south.

VISITOR INFORMATION   For tourist information, contact the **Kurverwaltung, Kurhaus** (☎ **07722/95-32-30**), open year-round Monday to Friday 9am to 5pm and May to October also Saturday 10am to noon.

EXPLORING THE AREA
The waterfall, called the **Gutach Falls,** is exceptional, but be prepared to walk an hour or so to reach it. The falls drop some 160m (530 feet), spilling down in seven stages. To get there, you park your car in a designated area near the Gutach Bridge (in the town center) and then walk along a marked trail. It's open daily 9am to 6pm in summer, and costs 2.50DM ($1.25) adults, 1DM (50¢) children. At the bottom of the falls is a year-round cafe/restaurant serving the famed Black Forest cake for which, by then, you'll have worked up an appetite.

    Schwarzwald-Museum of Triberg, Wallfahrstrasse 4 (☎ **07722/44-34**), brings the olden days of the Black Forest vividly to life, with displays of dresses, handcrafts, furnishings, bird music boxes, and, of course, clocks and clock making. You can also

---

Stop for Clocks

You may want to make a stop along the B33 between Triberg and Hornberg at the **Haus der 1000 Uhren (House of 1,000 Clocks),** An der Bundesstrasse 33, 78098 Triberg-Gemmelsbach (☎ **07722/96300**). You'll recognize the shop immediately because of the giant cuckoo clock and waterwheel in front. A painter of clock faces, Josef Weisser, launched the business in 1824; today his great-great-grandson owns the place. The shop is open Monday to Saturday 9am to 5pm. It ships to the United States and Canada and takes all major credit cards. There's another branch in the center of Triberg, near the entrance to the waterfall.

Wunderhiking in the Black Forest

You can see the loveliest parts of the Black Forest by hiking the ancient trail of the cuckoo-clock traders. Really. The market trail follows the route of the traders who, centuries ago, carried the famous Black Forest clocks across Europe. Along the village-to-village journey, you'll pass through deep, fragrant pinewoods and sunny pastures where farmhouses are set scenically on hillsides.

The circle trail starts at Triberg, with its waterfalls. An arrangement with a series of hotels along the trail, beginning with the **Parkhotel Wehrle** (see below), allows you to hike with only a small rucksack; vans haul your luggage on to the next hotel. You can hike anywhere from 1 to 2 to 10 days and more if you have the time (but most hikers have their fill long before this). Distances for a day's hike between hotels can be anywhere from 20 to 27km (12 to 17 miles).

Clearly marked signs guide you across this easy trail, and the Parkhotel Wehrle provides detailed road descriptions and a road map, with instructions in English, to set you on your way. Restaurants and farmhouses offering food and refreshment are not far apart, and the area is quite safe, even for a woman walking alone.

see the famed Schwarzwaldbahn railway, which really works, a mineral exhibit of the area, and Europe's largest barrel organ collection. The museum is open May to October, daily 9am to 6pm; November to April, Monday to Friday 9am to 6pm and Saturday and Sunday 10am to 5pm. Admission is 7DM ($3.50) for adults, 4DM ($2) for students, and 3DM ($1.50) for children.

One of the most beautiful churches in the Black Forest, the **Wallfahrtkirche Maria in der Tannen (Church of Our Lady of the Fir Trees),** is within easy reach. Built in the early 18th century, it has superb baroque furnishings, including a remarkable pulpit.

After a visit to the church, drive to the **Freilchtmuseum Schwarzwälder** in Gutach (☎ **07831/2-30**), which contains original Black Forest homes as many as 4 centuries old. In summer, guides demonstrate weaving on some of the looms and other skills. The museum is open April to October, daily 8:30am to 6pm. Admission is 8DM ($4) for adults and 4DM ($2) for children and students. From the A5, turn off at the Offenburg exit and follow B33 toward Gengenbach, Hausach, and Triberg; at Hausach, turn right to Gutach.

A 16km (10-mile) drive south of Triberg is the **Deutsches Uhrenmuseum (German Clock Museum),** Gerwigstrasse 11, in Furtwangen (☎ 07723/92-01-17). It's open daily November to April 10am to 5pm and May to October 9am to 6pm. Admission is 5DM ($2.50) for adults and 3DM ($1.50) for children. This museum presents a history of timepieces, including displays of a wide variety of Black Forest clocks, some from the early 18th century. Many are elaborate and complicated. Look for the mechanical music automata and the cuckoo clocks.

WHERE TO STAY

Romantik Parkhotel Wehrle. Gartenstrasse 24 (1 mile from the train station), 78098 Triberg. ☎ **07722/86-02-0.** Fax 07722/86-02-90. E-mail: parkhotel.wherle@t-online.de. 52 units. TV TEL. 195DM–420DM ($97.50–$210) double; from 420DM ($210) suite. Rates include buffet breakfast. AE, DC, MC, V. Free parking outdoors; 10DM ($5) in garage.

Built in the early 1600s, Parkhotel Wehrle was acquired around 1730 by the family that has owned it ever since. Its lemon-yellow walls and gabled mansard roof occupy one of the most prominent street corners in town. The main house offers an Old-World atmosphere, but forest-loving vacationers often request accommodation near the woods in a separate chalet, where a pool and breeze-filled balconies create a modern sylvan retreat. The good-sized rooms are beautifully furnished and individually decorated, sometimes with antiques. Some rooms have minibars; all have hair dryers. The restaurant is the finest in the area (see "Where to Dine," below). Amenities include indoor and outdoor pools, sauna, fitness room, room service, and laundry.

Römischer Kaiser. Sommerauerstrasse 35 (just over a mile outside Triberg), 78098 Triberg-Nussbach. ☎ **07722/44-18.** Fax 07722/44-01. 26 units. TV, TEL. 112DM–122DM ($56–$61) double. Rates include continental breakfast. AE, DC, MC, V. Closed Nov 15–Dec 7. Free parking.

This comfortable, charmingly preserved hotel has been owned by several generations of the same family since 1840. The exterior has lots of exposed wood. Rooms come in a wide range of shapes and sizes, but all are pleasant and well maintained. Baths are roomy.

The very popular restaurant here serves fresh fish throughout the year. Menu items include lake trout served with watercress mousse, and wild salmon with lobster-cream sauce and fresh asparagus. The food is not on par with that served at the more glamorous Parkhotel Wehrle, but it's satisfying in every way, and your bill will be a lot cheaper.

WHERE TO DINE

✪ **Parkhotel Wehrle.** Marktplatz. ☎ **07722/8-60-20.** Reservations required. Main courses 34DM–54DM ($17–$27); fixed-price meals 56DM ($28) lunch, 68DM–118DM ($34–$59) dinner. AE, DC, MC, V. Daily noon–2pm and 6–10pm. CONTINENTAL.

People come from great distances to eat at this fine, famous restaurant. Meals here are accompanied by the ticking of a stately grandfather clock; meanwhile, the clientele relaxes in the comfort of cane-bottomed French-style armchairs. The cuisine is intelligent and imaginative, with a focus on natural flavors. Even simple dishes have a certain flair. Try the trout or saddle of venison with juniper berry cream sauce and spätzle. A traditional dessert is apples baked with pine honey and flambéed with Kirschwasser. Some of the game specialties are prepared for two.

5 Freudenstadt

92km (57 miles) N of Freiburg

One of the most important transportation hubs in the northern tier of the Black Forest is Freudenstadt, a riverside town known for clear air, streaming sunshine, and a sense of cleanliness and conservatism. Originally founded in 1599 by Duke Friedrich I of Württemberg, Freudenstadt provided a home at the time for Protestants fleeing religious persecution within Carinthia, in southern Austria. French troops set most of the town ablaze in the closing days of World War II, but it was completely rebuilt, more or less to the original plans, before 1950.

ESSENTIALS

GETTING THERE   By Train   Trains from Frankfurt arrive at hourly intervals throughout the day (trip time: $3^1/_2$ hr.). There are also 10 trains per day from Munich (trip time: $4^1/_2$ hr.). Freudenstadt has two railway stations, the **Stadtbahnhof** (☎ **07441/4554** for information), in the center of town, and the **Hauptbahnhof** (☎ **07441/2015** for information), about a mile south of the center. Most trains stop at both. For information, call ☎ **01805/99-66-33.**

By Bus   Bus travel tends to be convenient only for those coming from surrounding hamlets. Buses stop at both the Bahnhofplatz and the Marktplatz. For information, call ☎ **07441/1555.**

By Car   Driving from Stuttgart, following the B28, takes about ¼ hour; from Karlsruhe via the B462, about ½ hour.

VISITOR INFORMATION   The **Tourist Information Office** is at Am Promenadeplatz 1 (☎ **07441/86-47-10**). It's open year-round Monday to Friday 9am to 6pm, Saturday 10am to 1pm.

EXPLORING THE TOWN

Freudenstadt's appeal lies not so much in the town itself, as in its ideal location in the midst of the best hiking and camping country in the Black Forest. Trails wind for hundreds of miles through the nearby hills. In winter the snow-covered paths are great for skiing.

Unlike many German towns, Freudenstadt has no castle overshadowing it, but it certainly does have an enormous castle square. This plot of land, the largest marketplace in Germany, was laid out in the 16th century for a castle that was never built. History's loss is today's gain. The market square that greets the visitor to Freudenstadt is a maze of lawns and concrete, broken by patches of flowers and kiosks. The buildings surrounding the square are mainly postwar, since the air raids and fires of World War II almost completely destroyed the city. A few of the old Renaissance structures on the square have been reconstructed, up to their neat little archways and gabled roofs.

The town takes pride in its **Stadtkirche,** Marktplatz (☎ **07441/6087**), dating from the 17th century. The unusual L-shaped architecture of the church brings the two main aisles together at right angles. Over the entrance stand identical towers, topped with rounded domes and narrow spires. The church's most important treasure is the 12th-century reading desk, supported by carved and painted likenesses of the Evangelists. The church is open daily 10am to 5pm. Entrance is free.

Regrettably, Freudenstadt doesn't have any other museums or attractions worth mentioning, with the exception of a small regional folk and crafts museum, the **Heimatmuseum,** in the Stadthaus, Marktplatz (☎ **07441/6177**). It's open Monday 3 to 6pm, Tuesday and Wednesday 9 to 11am and 3 to 6pm, Thursday 9 to 11am and 3 to 7pm, Friday 3 to 6pm, and Sunday 10am to noon; closed on Saturday. Entrance is free.

WHERE TO STAY

Hotel Baren. 33 Langestrasse (near the Marktplatz), 72250 Freudenstadt. ☎ **07441/ 27-29.** Fax 07441/2887. 24 units. TV TEL. 150DM–180DM ($75–$90) double. MC, V. Free parking.

This establishment is best known for its well-managed restaurant (see "Where to Dine," below), but it's also an eminently respectable hotel. The cozy interior, lined with old panels and capped with heavy ceiling beams, might remind you of the inside of a prosperous local farmhouse. Rooms are cozy, traditionally decorated, and well maintained. The staff is charming and polite, managing to convey a nostalgic sense of traditional Germany.

Hotel Hohenried im Rosengarten. Zeppelinstrasse 5 (about a mile south of Freudenstadt's center), 72250 Freudenstadt. ☎ **07441/24-14.** Fax 07441/25-59. E-mail: hotelhohenried@ gmx.de. 27 units. TV TEL. 180DM–190DM ($90–$95) double; 220DM ($110) suite. AE, DC, MC, V. Bus 14.

This three-story hotel is designed like a modern version of an alpine chalet. The garden contains more than 2,000 well-tended rose bushes. Views from the windows of the comfortable and contemporary-looking rooms overlook a golf course and stately trees. In summertime, the balconies are adorned with geranium-filled flower boxes. The hotel also has a pleasant restaurant that charges from 20DM to 30DM ($11.40 to $17.10) for main courses at lunch and dinner. On the premises are an indoor pool, a sauna, and a solarium. The staff is polite and English-speaking.

Luz Posthotel. Stuttgarterstrasse 5, 72250 Freudenstadt. ☎ **07441/8970.** Fax 07441/84533. 52 units. TV TEL. 140DM ($70) double; 180DM ($90) suite. Rates include breakfast. AE, DC, MC, V. Free parking.

This hotel, built in 1809, was almost demolished during World War II and then was reconstructed along more modern lines shortly thereafter. Since then, strands of climbing ivy have added to a more antique-looking appearance. Today, this comfortable, contemporary, four-story hotel combines touches of Black Forest nostalgia with a smooth, conservatively modern decor. Many of the civic-minded organizations of Freudenstadt (including the Lion's Cub and the Rotarians) meet within this hotel's restaurants at regular intervals. Rooms are medium-sized, clean, tastefully modern, and comfortable. On the premises, you'll find a bar, a woodsy-looking *stube*, and a modern, international-looking dining room, the Restaurant Posthotel.

WHERE TO DINE

✪ **Hotel Baren.** 33 Langestrasse. ☎ **07441/27-29.** Reservations recommended. Main courses 16DM–30DM ($8–$15); fixed-menus 30DM–40DM ($15–$20). MC, V. Sun–Thurs 11am–3:30pm and 6–10pm, Fri 11am–3:30pm. SWABIAN/GERMAN.

This is an attractive, pleasingly proportioned 200-year-old inn. The warmly decorated, richly beamed and paneled interior will soothe urban hearts. The well-prepared cuisine emphasizes fresh Atlantic and Mediterranean fish. Look for fillet of monkfish with garlic and parsley, fillets of sole with a Riesling sauce, spicy fish soup redolent with saffron and garlic, savory game dishes, and beer and wine from every part of Germany.

Jägerstüble. Marktplatz 12. ☎ **07441/23-87.** Reservations recommended. Main courses 16DM–40DM ($8–$20). MC, V. Tues–Sat 11am–2pm and Tues–Sun 7–9pm. SWABIAN/ GERMAN.

Like most of the buildings around it, this is an excellent re-creation of a medieval house that was severely damaged during World War II. Inside, foaming mugs of beer and hardworking waitresses in folkloric costumes contribute to an unpretentious re-creation of the Germany of another era. The hearty and savory dishes include *Eisbein* (veal shank) with sauerkraut, farmer's omelets, venison steak prepared with garlic and red wine, and goulash of venison.

WHERE TO STAY NEARBY

If you want to experience the Schwarzwald at its most isolated and remote, consider a stay at either of the following two hotels, which are positioned south and north of the hamlet of Baiersbronn, respectively. Baiersbronn lies 6km (4 miles) northwest of Freudenstadt. Trains arrive in Baiersbronn about once an hour from Stuttgart and Karlsruhe, stopping in Baiersbronn before continuing south for another 6km (4 miles) to Freudenstadt. Local buses (marked "Baiersbronn") depart from the Marktplatz in Freudenstadt for Baiersbronn, but there are only about four a day, and they won't take you anywhere near either of the two hotels. For the short distance involved, it's a lot more convenient to take any of the taxis lined up in Freudenstadt's Marktplatz.

✪ **Hotel Bareiss.** Gärtenbühlweg 14, 072270 Baiersbronn/Mitteltal. ☎ **07442/470.** Fax 07442/47320. E-mail: hotelbareiss@t-online.de. 100 units. MINIBAR TV TEL. 448DM–662DM ($224–$331) double; 550DM–844DM ($275–$422) apt; from 740DM ($370) suite. Rates include breakfast. AE, DC, MC, V. Garage parking 9DM ($4.50). From the center of Baiersbronn, follow signs pointing to Hotel Bareiss for 10km (6 miles), heading south.

This five-star resort hotel is equivalent in most ways to the Hotel Traube Tonbach (see below), but it's a bit less formal and a lot less stiff. It provides a soothing, carefully orchestrated, well-manicured environment, where peace, quiet, and access to the surrounding forest are fiercely guarded. You'll find lots of urban refugees on site, recuperating from stressful careers. Rooms are spacious, carefully maintained, conservatively modern, and very comfortable. All have views over the forest.

Dining: The formal dining room is reserved exclusively for guests. There are also three other restaurants. The Restaurant Bareiss serves sublime French food at dinner only, every day except Monday and Tuesday. The cuisine here is among the finest in Germany, although the Schwarzwaldstube in the Hotel Traube Tonbach is even better. The hotel's middle-bracket choice is the cozy-looking Kaminstube, offering German and Alsatian food. There's also a budget-conscious Bierstube on the premises, featuring Black Forest and international food.

Amenities: On the premises are an indoor/outdoor swimming pool; a tennis court; a health club with an exercise room, sauna, whirlpool, and massage facilities; a "beauty farm" with massage, skin, and hairstyling facilities; a concierge; and facilities for bicycle rentals. Services include room service, dry cleaning, and laundry.

✪ **Hotel Traube Tonbach.** Ortsteil Tonbach, Tonbacherstrasse 237, 07442 Baiersbronn. ☎ **07442/4920.** Fax 07442/492-692. www.traube-tonbach.de. E-mail: info@traube.tonbach.de. 175 units. MINIBAR TV TEL. 350DM–524DM ($175–$262) double; 736DM–1,000DM ($368–$500) suite. Rates include breakfast and parking. Half board 45DM ($22.50) per person. AE, DC, MC, V. Parking 7DM–14DM ($3.50–$7).

In 1957, this establishment was massively enlarged into the stately looking, many-balconied resort you see today, and immediately attracted one of the grandest resort clienteles in Germany. Set closer to Baiersbronn (only about a mile north of town) than its competitor, the Bareiss (see above), the Traube Tonbach prides itself on its conservatism, its strictly enforced sense of peace and quiet, and the glamour of its very upscale clientele. Rooms are good-sized, solid, well built, quiet, and very, very comfortable. Service is good. You'll find a safe and secure sense of well-upholstered, well-managed grandeur throughout. Ask the staff for advice on nearby hiking trails.

Dining: The resort contains three recommended restaurants, the most formal of which, the Schwarzwald Stube, is one of the best in all of Germany. Less formidably grand are the Köhlertube, serving German and international food, and a congenial Bierstube, the Bauernstube, specializing in Swabian food.

Amenities: Three separate swimming pools, sauna, whirlpool, beauty salon, exercise facilities, massage, indoor bowling alley, tennis courts, concierge, room service, laundry, dry cleaning.

6 Calw

20km (12¹/₂ miles) S of Pforzheim, 66km (41 miles) N of Freudenstadt

Many residents of other parts of Germany call Calw the most appealingly folkloric town in the Black Forest. Hermann Hesse, who was born here in 1877, described Calw as "the most beautiful place I know."

ESSENTIALS

GETTING THERE   By Train   Trains arrive at Calw's Bahnhof at hourly intervals from both Stuttgart and Karlsruhe. Both cities are about an hour away. For railway information, call ☎ **01805/99-66-33.**

By Bus   Buses that travel between Horb, Nagold, and Pforzheim make stops at Calw's Bahnhofplatz. For information, call ☎ **07051/968850.**

By Car   Calw lies midway between Pforzheim and Nagold, along Highway B463. From the A8 Autobahn, exit at the signs indicating Calw.

VISITOR INFORMATION   The **Tourist Information office** in Calw is at Markt-brücke 7 (☎ **07051/96-88-10**). It's open Monday to Friday 9am to 12:30pm and 2 to 5pm (to 6:30pm Thursday), and also Saturday April to October 9:30am to 12:30pm.

EXPLORING THE TOWN

Calw's allure derives from its impressive and meticulously maintained roster of late 17th- and early 18th-century houses, whose half-timbered facades add an undeniable charm to such sites as the Marktplatz. The town's most prominent bridge, the 14th-century **Nikolausbrücke,** in the center, merits a stroll in admiration of its carefully chiseled masonry.

The birthplace of Hermann Hesse, the **Hesse Haus,** Marktplatz 30 (☎ 07051/7522), is a literary shrine for scholars and fans. Entrance is 5DM ($2.50) adults, 3DM ($1.50) children and students. The only other formal attraction in town is a free small-scale folklore museum called **Palais Vischer,** Bischofstrasse 10 (same phone as Hesse Haus).

The environs of Calw also merit some attention if you have the time. Of exceptional interest is the hamlet of **Zavelstein,** which is signposted in Calw. Follow the road south for 5km (3 miles). A drive to this little hamlet is especially interesting in late March and April, when the meadows blossom with edelweiss and crocuses. You might want to continue south in the direction of Talmühle-Seitzental, where you'll see a sign pointing along a twisting road leading to **Neubulach** (☎ 07053/969-51-0). Until it closed in the mid-1920s, this was one of the most active silver mines in the Black Forest. Long after it was abandoned, the medical profession learned that its dust-free interior was beneficial in the treatment of asthma. A therapy center is located inside. The mine's ancient shafts can be visited on guided tours given daily April to November 10am to noon and 2 to 4pm, costing 4DM ($2) for adults and 2DM ($1) for children.

WHERE TO STAY

Hotel Kloster Hirsau. Ortsteil Hirsau, Wildbacher Strasse 2, 75365 Calw. ☎ 07051/9-67-40. Fax 07051/96740. www.hotel-kloster-hirsau.de. E-mail: info@kloster-hirsau.de. 43 units. MINIBAR TV TEL. 145DM–225DM ($72.50–$112.50) double. Rates include breakfast. Half board 35DM ($17.50) per person. AE, DC, MC, V. Free parking; parking in garage 5DM ($2.50).

Parts of the foundation of this historic hotel date from 1092, when the site functioned as a monastery that was noted for housing overnight visitors. Today the establishment retains its medieval touches and antique charm. The good-sized rooms have lots of Schwarzwald-inspired features, including pinewood trim and reproductions of traditional furniture. The oldest are numbers 114 to 235. The hotel also offers a beauty salon, sauna, and swimming pool.

WHERE TO DINE

Ratstube. Marktplatz 12, 75365 Calw. ☎ **07051/9-20-50.** Reservations recommended. Main courses 22DM–32DM ($11–$16). Daily noon–2:30pm and 5:30–9:30pm. AE, DC, MC, V. SWABIAN/INTERNATIONAL.

This is the most popular and reliable restaurant in town. The interior is a labyrinth of masonry-sided rooms. The well-prepared, but not particularly innovative dishes include *Zwiebelrostbraten,* fillet of sole in wine sauce; stingray in black butter sauce; trout with almonds or meunière-style; and an array of sausages served with cabbage and roasted potatoes. Service is competent.

The inn also rents the best rooms within the town center. A double costs 165DM ($82.50).

Restaurant Klosterschanke. Wildbader Strasse 2. ☎ **07051/96740.** Reservations recommended. Main courses 43DM–46DM ($21.50–$23); fixed-price menus 55DM–98DM ($27.50–$49). DC, V. Lunch noon–2pm; Kafe mit Kuchen (coffee and cakes) 2–5pm; dinner 6–11pm. SWABIAN/INTERNATIONAL.

Cozy and historically authentic, this restaurant occupies a trio of dining rooms whose beamed and/or vaulted ceilings in some cases are hundreds of years old. Menu items include fresh house-marinated sardines; rack of lamb with white beans; *Zwiebelrostbraten;* monkfish braised in olive oil with herbs; and several kinds of schnitzel. Although cuisine here never reaches the sublime, it's always fresh and competently prepared.

7 Pforzheim

35km (22 miles) S of Karlsruhe, 53km (33 miles) SW of Stuttgart

Set at the northern edge of the Black Forest, at the junction of three rivers (the Würm, the Enz, and the Nagold), Pforzheim is one of the Schwarzwald's largest settlements. It was founded by the Romans as a fortified camp, and developed into an important mercantile center during the Middle Ages. Key industries have traditionally included the crafting of jewelry and clock making. Although it was severely damaged by bombs during World War II, Pforzheim is a worthwhile site for an overnight stay between forays into the Black Forest.

ESSENTIALS

GETTING THERE   By Train   Trains pull into Pforzheim at least once an hour from Munich (trip time: 3 hr.), Frankfurt (trip time: 2 hr.), and Stuttgart (trip time: 1½ hr.). The railway station lies within an 8-minute walk of the center. For information, call ☎ **01805/99-66-33.**

By Bus   Bus travel to Pforzheim is a lot less practical than rail travel. The bus stop is at Leopoldsplatz, in the town center.

By Car   Pforzheim lies beside the high-speed A-8 Autobahn that stretches between Munich and Karlsruhe. Transit from Stuttgart takes between 75 and 90 minutes, from Munich around 2½ hours, and from Frankfurt around 2 hours.

VISITOR INFORMATION   Head to **Stadinformation,** Marktplatz 1 (☎ **07231/ 1454560**), open Monday to Friday 9am to 6pm.

EXPLORING THE TOWN

Much of Pforzheim was demolished by Allied bombs during World War II. Of the limited number of buildings that have been restored to their former grandeur, the **Sankt Michaelerskirche (St. Michael's Church),** Schlossberg 10 (☎ **07231/ 102484**), is the most dramatic. It was built in stages between the 1200s and 1400s, and combines aspects of both Romanesque and Gothic architecture. It's open daily 8:30am to 6pm. A fine example of a more modern church is the **Stadtkirche,** on Melanchthonstrasse (no phone), in the town center across from the Parkhotel. Rebuilt from the town's rubble during the 1950s, this is a symbol of Pforzheim's rebirth from the devastation of World War II.

For insights into the role that clock-making has always played in Pforzheim, head for the city's **Technisches Museum,** Bleichstrasse 81 (☎ **07231/392869**), where souvenirs and mementos of the clock-making trade commemorate humankind's painstaking efforts to organize time. On the premises is a reconstruction of a clock-making studio from the early 1800s. The museum is open every Wednesday 9am to noon and 3 to 6pm, and every 2nd and 4th Sunday 10am to 5pm. Admission is free, although donations are appreciated.

The equally nostalgic **Schmuckmuseum,** Jahnstrasse 42 (☎ **07231/392-126**), is devoted to Pforzheim's jewelry-making trade. Its collection includes ornaments from the 3rd century B.C. to modern times, and is one of the most unusual anywhere. The museum is open Tuesday to Sunday 10am to 5pm. Admission is 5DM ($2.50).

If you're passionate about botany or gardening, you might enjoy a visit to the **Alpengarten (Alpine Garden),** Auf dem Berg 6 (☎ **07231/70590**), in which about 100,000 varieties of high-altitude plants are grown in a natural-looking milieu. It's set adjacent to the banks of the Würm River, about 3km (2 miles) south of Pforzheim's center, and is open April to November, daily 8am to 7pm. Admission costs 4DM ($2). To reach it from Pforzheim, follow the signs pointing to Würm.

WHERE TO STAY

Hotel Royal. Wilhelmbeckerstrasse 3A (less than a mile north of the center), 75179 Pforzheim. ☎ **07231/14250.** Fax 07231/142599. 43 units. MINIBAR TV TEL. 185DM–195DM ($92.50–$97.50) double. Rates include breakfast and free parking. AE, DC, V. Bus: 29.

Equivalent in most ways to the Parkhotel (see below), the Royal's only drawback is its location on the outskirts of town. It was built in 1995 in a two-story, modern format. Rooms are small to medium-sized, contemporary, sunny, comfortable, clean, and utterly without pretension. On the premises are a bar and a restaurant, Etagen. The staff is polite and well trained.

Parkhotel. Deimlingerstrasse 36, 75175 Pforzheim. ☎ **07231/1610.** Fax 07231/161690. E-mail: parkhotelpforzheim@s-direktnet.de. 144 units. A/C MINIBAR TV TEL. 205DM–265DM ($102.50–$132.50) double. Rates include breakfast. AE, CB, DC, DISC, MC, V.

Set in the center of town, the four-story, contemporary Parkhotel is the meeting place for most of the civic and charitable organizations in Pforzheim. Inside, you'll find a streamlined, tasteful decor with lots of exposed wood and stone. On the premises, there's a sauna, Jacuzzi, fitness center, bar, and two restaurants, the less pretentious of which is recommended below. Rooms are good-sized, airy, contemporary, soothing, and comfortable.

WHERE TO DINE

Parkrestaurant. In the Parkhotel, Deimlingerstrasse 36. ☎ **07231/1610.** Reservations not necessary. Main courses 31DM–40DM ($15.50–$20); fixed-price menus 75DM–105DM ($37.50–$52.50). AE, DC, DISC, MC, V. Open daily noon–3pm and 6–11:30pm. GERMAN.

This well-managed restaurant offers solid home-style cuisine, a view over the Stadt Theater and the banks of the Enz River, and a polite, well-trained staff. We prefer this place to the Galarestaurant, its more upscale sibling within the same hotel. Menu items include schnitzels, stews, roulades and grills, soups, salads, and hearty, regional desserts layered with chocolate and whipped cream.

A MEDIEVAL EXCURSION FROM PFORZHEIM

One of the Schwarzwald's most evocative sights lies 18km (11 miles) to the northeast of Pforzheim, within the agrarian hamlet of Maulbronn. **Kloster Maulbronn** (☎ **07043/17-52-480**) has been called the best-preserved medieval monastery north of the Alps. Most of its more than 30 stone-sided buildings were constructed between 1150 and 1390, within an encircling wall that protected the monks and their allies from outside attackers. The most visible of the buildings is the compound's church, which combines aspects of Romanesque and Gothic architecture, and which influenced the design of later structures throughout central and northern Europe. Look for the complicated irrigation system, still intact, which distributed water to key elements within the compound. Most visitors arrive by car or taxi from the center of Pforzheim, although there's also a bus that departs for Maulbronn from Pforzheim's Leopoldplatz at 50-minute intervals throughout the day. The monastery is open March to October, daily 9am to 5:30pm; November to February, Tuesday to Sunday 9:30am to 5pm. Admission is 8DM ($4) adults, 4DM ($2) children and students.

8 Baden-Baden

111km (69 miles) W of Stuttgart, 111km (69 miles) NE of Freiburg, 174km (108 miles) S of Frankfurt

Baden-Baden, where the bath-conscious Roman emperor Caracalla once came to ease his arthritic aches, was rediscovered in the 19th century by the nobility of Europe. Swanky clients such as Queen Victoria, Kaiser Wilhelm I, Napoléon III, Berlioz, Brahms, and Dostoyevsky helped make Baden-Baden the most elegant and sophisticated playground in Germany. Tolstoy set a scene in *Anna Karenina* here, though he gave the town a different name. Today the clientele may have changed, but Baden-Baden still evokes an aura of 19th-century privilege, combined with the most up-to-date facilities. More recent clients have included everybody from Barbra Streisand to Yasser Arafat.

Baden-Baden is the ideal choice for sports and outdoor enthusiasts. Golf, tennis, and horseback riding are all popular here. Lovers of horse racing will enjoy the international racing season each August at Iffezheim Track. The surrounding countryside is good for hiking and mountain climbing. During the winter, Baden-Baden is a convenient center for skiing. After a day on the slopes, you can return to a soothing swim in a thermal pool and a night out at the casino.

ESSENTIALS

GETTING THERE **By Train** Baden-Baden is on major rail lines connecting Frankfurt and Basel, and Stuttgart and Munich. There are 20 trains daily from Stuttgart (trip time: 1 hr. 15 min.); 25 from Munich (trip time: 4 hr. 10 min.), and 45 from Frankfurt (trip time: 3 hr.). For information, call ☎ **01805/99-66-33.** The railway station is at Baden-Oos, north of town; regrettably, it's an expensive 20-minute taxi ride from the town center.

By Bus Long-distance bus service is provided to Freudenstadt and Tübingen (Line 1070), operated by **Deutsche Touring GmbH** (☎ **0721/30804** for information).

By Car Access to Baden-Baden is via the A5 Autobahn north and south or the A8 Autobahn east and west. The drive south from Frankfurt takes 2 hours; from Munich, about 4 hours.

VISITOR INFORMATION For information, contact **Tourist-Information,** Schwarzwaldstrasse 7 (☎ **07221/27-52-00**), daily 9am to 7pm.

GETTING AROUND   Baden-Baden is serviced by a network of buses whose routes coincide at the Leopoldplatz, in the center. Bus 201, which runs at ten-minute intervals, interconnects most of the important sites with the railway station, about 5km (3 miles) from the center. One-way fare is 3.50DM ($1.75), and a day pass, good for 24 hours of unlimited public transport for two adults and two children, costs 8 DM ($4).

TAKING THE WATERS

The center of Baden-Baden activity is **Lichtentaler Allee,** the park promenade along the bank of the Oosbach River (affectionately called the Oos—pronounced ohs), which runs through the center of town. As you stroll along this walk, you'll be amazed at the variety not only of exotic shrubs and trees but also of the rhododendrons, azaleas, and roses. At the north end of the park, on the banks of the stream, are the buildings of the **Kurgarten,** including the classical Kurhaus, used as an entertainment complex.

Your hotel can give you full information on the facilities available at both the Friedrichsbad and the Caracalla, which are in the heart of the Altstadt.

Caracalla-Therme. Römerplatz 1. ☎ **07221/27-59-40.** Admission 25DM ($12.50) for 3 hours, 29DM ($14.50) for 4 hours. Daily 8am–10pm. Bus: 1.

Caracalla-Therme has been made more pleasing visually by the addition of a round colonnaded extension with splashing and cascading pools. You can decide on your own bath system here. Medicinal treatment includes mud baths, massages, and whirlpools. The slightly radioactive water, rich in sodium chloride, comes from artesian wells 1,800m (6,000 feet) under the Florentiner Mountain. Its temperature is around 70°C (160°F). Bathers usually begin in cooler pools, working up to the warm water. The baths also have a sauna area, with foot baths and sun baths; sauna temperatures go from 85°C to 90°C (185°F to 200°F). You must wear bathing suits in the pools, but everyone goes nude in the saunas. Also offered are group water gymnastics. There's a bar and a cafeteria.

Friedrichsbad. Römerplatz 1. ☎ **07221/27-59-20.** Admission 36DM ($18) without soap-brush massage, 48DM ($24) with soap-brush massage. Mon–Sat 9am–10pm, Sun 9am–8pm (last admission always 7pm).

Friedrichsbad, also known as the Old Baths, was built from 1869 to 1877 at the behest of Grand Duke Friedrich von Baden. Following the Roman-Irish method, it takes about 2 hours to have the complete bath program, which involves a shower, two saunas 55°C to 70°C (130°F to 160°F), a brush massage soaping, thermal steam baths, and three freshwater baths ranging from warm to 15°C (60°F). After a 30-minute period of rest and relaxation you're supposed to feel rejuvenated. Other types of therapy, including massage, electrotherapy, and hydrotherapy, are also offered. Massages are 33DM ($16.50) for 20 minutes and 66DM ($33) for 40 minutes.

Pump Room (Trinkhalle). Kaiserallee 3. ☎ **07221/9070.** Free admission. Apr–Oct daily 10am–5:30pm. Bus: 1.

The spa gardens contain the Pump Room (*Trinkhalle*), where visitors can sip the water. The loggia of the hall is decorated with frescoes depicting Black Forest legends. The springs of Baden-Baden have been recognized for more than 2,000 years, and their composition is almost the same today as when the Romans built their baths here in the 3rd century.

THE CASINO

Spielbank. Kaiserallee 1. ☎ **07221/2-10-60.** Bus: 1.

The Spielbank, open year-round, is the oldest casino in Germany, popular for more than 200 years. Dostoyevsky is said to have written *The Gambler* after he lost his shirt, and almost his mind, at the tables here. The various casino rooms were designed in the style of an elegant French château. Jackets and ties for men are mandatory, as is eveningwear for women. To enter the casino during gambling hours, you must possess a valid passport or identification card and be at least 21 years old.

The historic gaming rooms may be viewed daily 10am to noon on a tour costing 6DM ($3). For those who want to gamble later, a full day's ticket is available for 10DM ($5). The minimum stake is 10DM ($5), but visitors are not obligated to play. Hours are daily 2pm to 2am (3am Friday and Saturday). Admission is 5DM ($2.50) Sunday to Thursday, rising to 10DM ($5) Friday and Saturday.

SPORTS & OUTDOOR PURSUITS

For an entirely new perspective on the area, go hot-air ballooning. **Balloon 2000** offers rides between the Black Forest and the Vosges. Contact pilot Jean-Marc Culas (☎ 07223/6-00-02) for details. A 2-hour, champagne breakfast trip over the Rhine Valley goes for 500DM ($250) per person.

For a more up-close and personal experience, rock climbing at all levels and altitudes can be enjoyed on the Battert rocks directly over the city. For a climber's guide, contact the **German Alpine Club,** Rathausplatz 7 (☎ 07221/1-72-00). You can also walk the 8km (5-mile) nature trail from the Strouzda chapel via Friesenberg to Fremersberg.

Horse races are another diversion. **The International Club,** Lichtentaler Allee 8 (☎ 07221/2-11-20), invites all comers to "Spring Meeting" May 27 to June 4 and to "Grand Week" August 25 to September 3. Those not content to watch can ride on a 1km (0.62-mile) track, provided by **Equestrian Hall,** Gunzenbachstrasse 4A (☎ 07221/949625) from 25DM ($12.50) per hour. Instruction is also available.

Many other outdoor sports are offered as well. The local 18-hole course in Fremersberg is one of the most scenic in Europe; contact the **Baden-Baden Golf Club** at ☎ 07221/2-35-79. For tennis, contact either **TH 365,** Rheinstrasse (☎ 07221/6-78-08), which serves up two indoor courts under a retractable roof, or **Red-White Tennis Club** at Lichtentaler Allee 5 (☎ 07221/2-41-41), which offers 10 outdoor courts. Swimmers can take a dip in the indoor and outdoor **swimming pools** in Bertholdbad at Ludwig-Wilhelm-Strasse 24 (☎ 07221/93-26-11), at a cost of 4.50DM ($2.25) for adults and 3DM ($1.50) for students per day. There's also swimming at **Sandweier Beach** (☎ 07221/5-14-33), at the converted gravel pit at Kühlsee, mid-May to mid-September.

SHOPPING

A flower-flanked pedestrian zone includes **Sophienstrasse** and **Gernsbacher Strasse.** These streets are lined with upscale boutiques, among the most expensive in Germany. Women's clothing by one of Germany's most emulated designers is available at **Escada Boutique,** Sophienstrasse 18 (☎ 07221/39-04-48). Another shop, **Münchner Moden,** Lichtentalerstrasse 13 (☎ 07221/3-10-90), carries women's designs in loden-colored wool during autumn and winter, and offers Austrian and Bavarian silks, linens, and cottons during warmer months. The best men's store, **Herrenkommode,** Sophienstrasse 16 (☎ 07221/2-92-92), is a bit more international, focusing on Giorgio Armani and Renee Lazard.

Leather goods by Gold Pfiel and other manufacturers are sold at **Inka,** Sophienstrasse 26 (☎ 07221/2-39-55), where the inventory includes luggage, wallets, and handbags. Cuckoo clocks, puppets, and other locally produced items can be found at **Boulevard,** Lichtentaler Strasse 21 (☎ 07221/2-44-95). An intriguing antiques store is **Peter Liebman,** Sophienstrasse 13 (☎ 07221/3-13-33), which specializes in baroque furniture from the 18th century and Biedermeier furniture from the 19th century, plus a wide array of other German antiques from silver to lamps.

Among the beeswax- and honey-based products available at **Schwarzwald Bienen-Honig-Haus,** Langestrasse 38 (☎ **07221/3-14-53**), are candles, cosmetics, candies, schnapps, and wine. Several varieties of bottled honey are sold as well. A multitude of libations are available by the bottle at **Schulmeister,** Maria Victoria Strasse 13-A (☎ **07221/2-41-70**), but especially tasty are the house cherry or raspberry *eau de vie,* clear brandies. A 400-year-old wine tavern and shop, **Nägelsförster Hof,** Nägelsförst 1 (☎ **07221/3-55-50**), conducts daily wine tastings of the vintages available for purchase.

WHERE TO STAY
VERY EXPENSIVE

✪ **Brenner's Park Hotel & Spa.** An der Lichtentaler Allee, 76530 Baden-Baden. ☎ **07221/90-00.** Fax 07221/3-87-72. www.brenners-park.de. E-mail: info@brenners-park.de. 100 units. MINIBAR TV TEL. 546DM–980DM ($273–$490); 1,200DM–2,650DM ($600–$1,325) suite. AE, DC, MC, V. Parking 28DM ($14). Bus: 1.

This sumptuously furnished hotel is one of the finest in the world, far outdistancing the two Steigenberger properties (see below). It lies in a large private park facing the River Oos and Lichtentaler Allee. The spa facilities here, Baden-Baden's best, are a major draw. Some of its international habitués wouldn't dare let a year go by without making an appearance at this glamorous place. Rooms and suites are the last word in luxurious appointments. Beds are sumptuous and baths are state of the art.

Dining/Diversions: A pianist plays every afternoon in the lounge and in the evening at the Oleander Piano Bar. There's gourmet dining in the main restaurant, Park, and in the Schwarzwald-Stube.

Amenities: Room service, laundry, dry cleaning, hair dryer in room, pool, sauna, solarium, massage-and-fitness studio, beauty spa, modern facilities for diagnosis and therapeutics. The staff includes an expert team of beauticians and masseurs. Golf, tennis, riding, climbing, and walking on marked paths and promenades can be arranged.

EXPENSIVE

✪ **Der Kleine Prinz (The Little Prince).** Lichtentalerstrasse 36, 76530 Baden-Baden. ☎ **07221/34-66-00.** Fax 07221/34-660-59. www.derkleineprinz.de. E-mail: info@derkleineprinz.de. 40 units. A/C MINIBAR TV TEL. 195DM–350DM ($97.50–$175) double; 295DM–450DM ($147.50–$225) suite. Rates include buffet breakfast. AE, CB, DC, MC, V. Parking 15DM ($7.50).

This small hotel is located in a century-old baroque building in the central pedestrian zone, a short walk from the casino and the thermal baths. Two elegant city mansions were combined to form the most personalized, cozy, and intimate nest at the spa. Norbert Rademacher, who owns the hotel with his wife, has had 25 years experience in the United States as director at the Waldorf-Astoria and the New York Hilton. He and his wife have totally renovated and upgraded the hotel. Each of the good-sized rooms has its own special feature: an open fireplace, a tower, a balcony, or a whirlpool bathtub. Some have air-conditioning. Personalized service adds to the attractiveness of this intimate, immaculate hotel.

Dining/Diversions: The small ground-floor restaurant is an elegant place for a four-course dinner; you can have drinks at the adjacent lobby bar.

Amenities: Concierge, room service, dry cleaning and laundry service, twice-daily maid service, baby-sitting, secretarial services, business center, and conference rooms. A health club, tennis, and racquetball courts are nearby.

✪ **Hotel Belle Epoque.** Maria-Viktoria-Strasse 2b, 76530 Baden-Baden. ☎ **07221/300-66-0.** Fax 07221/300-66-6. www.hotelbelleepoque.de. E-mail: info@hotelbelleepoque.de. 16 units. A/C TV TEL. 295DM–475DM ($147.50–$237.50) double; 495DM–675DM ($247.50–$337.50) suite. Rates include buffet breakfast. AE, DC, MC, V. Bus: 201.

One of the newest and also the most charming hotels has opened here, and it's operated by the same people who run the romantic Der Kleine Prinz (see above). Constructed as a private home in 1870, this gem lives up to its namesake. Each room is different, medium in size, and luxuriously furnished with swag draperies and lace curtains, and either antiques or reproductions. The Rademacher family welcomes you, and will, if possible, give you the style of furnishings you request—Empire, Louis XV, Louis XVI, Biedermeier, Victorian, Louis Philippe, whatever.

Privahotel Quisisana. Bismarckstrasse 21 (an 8-min. walk from the town center), 76530 Baden-Baden. ☎ **07221/36-90.** Fax 07221/36-92-69. 69 units. TV TEL. 340DM–420DM ($170–$210) double; 440DM–520DM ($220–$260) suite. Rates include continental breakfast. AE, MC, V. Free parking. Bus: 216.

Although Brenner's Park Hotel and even the Steigenberger properties are far superior, this runner-up is more tranquil. It's set in a spacious park, 8 minutes away from the town center on foot. Some of the most up-to-date health facilities in the Black Forest are here. You can spend an early morning in group calisthenics, for example, followed by treatments with any one of a dozen skin- and muscle-toning techniques. One of the more unusual facilities is the tepidarium, where a room is warmed to body temperature as you sit and listen to meditation music. Rooms are beautiful, well kept, spacious, and well appointed, furnished with both traditional and modern styling.

Dining: The elegant restaurant serves excellent international and regional cuisine from the world-class kitchens.

Amenities: Room service, laundry, dry cleaning, swimming pool, sauna, "beauty farm," various medical treatments.

Steigenberger Badischer Hof. Langestrasse 47, 76530 Baden-Baden. ☎ **800/223-5652** in the U.S. and Canada, or 07221/93-40. Fax 07221/93-44-70. www.steigenberger.com. E-mail: badischer-hof@steigenberger.com. 139 units. MINIBAR TV TEL. 310DM–450DM ($155–$225) double; 550DM–850DM ($275–$425) suite. Rates include buffet breakfast. AE, DC, MC, V. Parking 20DM ($10). Bus: 201.

A Baden-Baden landmark, this famed traditional hotel isn't quite as highly rated as Brenner's, but it's neck-and-neck with its sibling, the Europäischer Hof (see above). Badischer Hof is on a busy street in the center of town, but in the back you'll find an elegant garden with a wide balustraded terrace, flowerbeds, and a lawn around a stone fountain. The hotel began its career in 1809 as a social center for famous personalities, who came here for "the season." The four-story-high colonnaded hallway, with its great staircase and encircling balustraded balconies, is the hotel's most distinguishing feature. The well-furnished rooms are priced according to size and view. Many have private balconies. Each is elegantly appointed with tasteful fabrics and comfortable beds. Those in the monastery building have thermal water piped into the baths.

Dining: Dining is in the Park Restaurant, where a first-class international cuisine is served. Vegetarian food and regional specialties are also featured.

Amenities: Room service, hair dryer in room, laundry, dry cleaning, swimming pool, thermal spring pool, open-air thermal pool, sauna, beauty and health center, medical baths, physiotherapy.

Steigenberger Europäischer Hof. Kaiserallee 2 (opposite the Kurgarten and the casino), 76530 Baden-Baden. ☎ **800/223-5652** in the U.S. and Canada, or 07221/93-30. Fax 07221/93-37-12. 145 units. MINIBAR TV TEL. 308DM–454DM ($154–$227) double; 555DM–2,000DM ($277.50–$1,000)suite. Rates include buffet breakfast. AE, DC, MC, V. Parking 30DM ($17.10). Bus: 201.

This is the liveliest and most social of the centrally located hotels, with a far more bustling atmosphere than Brenner's or the other Steigenberger (see above). The elegant Europäischer Hof is adjacent to the Oos River, which runs at the edge of the Kurpark.

The hotel consists of a pair of joined structures that were built back when spacious living facilities were more affordable. Its colonnaded central hallway is stunning. Many suites and rooms open onto balconies. The staff is a bit too formal but highly efficient.

Dining: In the restaurant, formal Old-World service combines with a sweeping view of the park.

Amenities: Room service, laundry, dry cleaning; a hairdresser and beauty parlor are also on site.

MODERATE

Bad-Hotel zum Hirsch. Hirschstrasse 1, 76530 Baden-Baden. ☎ **800/223-5652** in the U.S. and Canada, or 07221/93-90. Fax 07221/3-81-48. 58 units. 250DM–290DM ($125–$145) double. Rates include buffet breakfast. AE, CB, DC, DISC, MC, V. Parking 22DM ($11). Bus: 201.

This beautiful old-fashioned hotel is a tranquil compound of several buildings. Its antique furnishings make it a living museum of fine period pieces. The formal dining room is dominated by crystal chandeliers and paneled walls; the Blauer Salon is equally attractive, with blue-velvet provincial armchairs and classic draperies. The interesting old-style rooms are individually furnished, as if in a country home; some offer minibars and TVs. All have piped-in thermal water.

The restaurant is reserved for guests. In summer, you can drink coffee on the wisteria-shaded terrace. Amenities include a newsstand, dry cleaning, laundry, sauna, beauty salon, social program, hair dryers in room, and adapter plugs.

Haus Reichert. Sophienstrasse 4, 76530 Baden-Baden. ☎ **07221/2-41-91.** Fax 07221/2-95-34. www.hotelhausreichert.de. 26 units. MINIBAR TV TEL. 236DM–336DM ($118–$168) double. Rates include continental breakfast. AE, DC, MC, V. Parking 10DM ($5). Bus: 201.

The five-floor 19th-century Haus Reichert is an inviting place to stay in a central location, not far from the casino. Rooms are good-sized, high-ceilinged, and comfortable, although practically none of the original furniture or detailing has survived the many renovations. Most are priced at the lower end of the scale. There is limited room service confined to drinks and snacks. Exercise equipment, a pool, a sauna, and a beauty farm are at your disposal.

INEXPENSIVE

Hotel am Markt. Marktplatz 18, 76530 Baden-Baden. ☎ **07221/27-04-0.** Fax 07221/27-04-44. 27 units, 12 with bathroom or shower. 115DM ($57.50) double without bathroom or shower, 150DM ($75) double with bathroom or shower. Rates include continental breakfast. AE, MC, V. Bus: 201.

Hotel am Markt, on the old marketplace, is far removed from the grander social life of Baden-Baden and its deluxe palace hotels. But though it may be at the bottom of the pecking order, it's number one in town for economy. The location is first rate, with the quiet interrupted only by chimes from the church across the square. A tiny terrace cafe in front has petunia-filled window boxes. There's no lounge to speak of, but there's a tavern dining room with a relaxed and informal atmosphere. Innkeeper Herr Bogner offers small, simply furnished comfortable rooms. A restaurant is open for house guests 6 to 9pm daily.

WHERE TO DINE

Münchner Löwenbräu. Gernsbacher Strasse 9 (in the Altstadt). ☎ **07221/2-23-11.** Main courses 15DM–32DM ($7.50–$16). AE, DC, V. Daily 10am–11pm. Bus: 201. GERMAN/BAVARIAN.

Baden-Baden has many fine restaurants dispensing haute cuisine, but this isn't one of them—the food here is simple and affordable. The terrace is beneath a copse of clipped and pruned linden trees, and the indoor dining room, with its curved glass walls, is up a flight of stone steps at the rear. Many kinds of German sausage are offered, along with Bavarian specialties and a wide selection of cheeses. Regional devotees order pork knuckles fresh from "the pork-knuckle grill." Regulars often ask for the "Löwenbräu platter of bites," which is a hearty plate with everything from black pudding to sliced pork. For dessert, we'd suggest the apple fritters. The restaurant also has a popular beer garden.

Park-Restaurant. In Brenner's Park Hotel, Schillerstrasse 6 (at the corner of Lichtentaler Allee). ☎ **07221/90-00.** Reservations required. Main courses 46DM–65DM ($23–$32.50). AE, DC, MC, V. Daily 7–11am, noon–2pm, and 7:30–9:30pm. Bus: 201. INTERNATIONAL/ RHINELAND.

Park-Restaurant serves the best food in the center of Baden-Baden, although its cuisine is not quite as refined as that of Zum Alde Gott (see below) on the outskirts. This is one of the renowned spa dining rooms of Europe, and the cuisine and service are definitely worth the high price. The emphasis is on French (Alsatian) dishes, along with regional Badish and Rhine Valley foods. Specialties include pâté of quail and goose liver and roast saddle of venison or lamb noisettes with tarragon sauce. For dessert, try an ice-cream soufflé. No matter who's in charge of the kitchen here, the same superb standards are always maintained.

Stahlbad. Augustaplatz 2. ☎ **07221/2-45-69.** Reservations required. Main courses 29DM–55DM ($14.50–$27.50). AE, DC, MC, V. Tues–Sun noon–2pm and 6–10pm. Bus: 201. CONTINENTAL.

Stahlbad is a luxury restaurant with an elegant decor. Although its food may not be as good as the Brenner's Park Hotel's, it's the most tranquil and charming choice in the center of town, mainly because of its garden terrace. The owner, Frau Uschi Mönch, welcomes you in the dining room. The decor and atmosphere evoke a tavern, with prints, copper vessels, antique pewter plates, mugs, and engravings. Continental specialties are pepper steak and venison steak (in hunting season), fresh fish, and lobster thermidor (very expensive). The homemade fettuccine Alfredo with white truffles (in season) is as good as any you'll have in Rome.

DINING AT NEUWEIER

It's traditional for Baden-Baden's visitors to dine at the satellite resort of Neuweier, 10km (6 miles) southwest via Fremersbergstrasse. Here are two suggestions:

Schloss Neuweier. Mauberbergstrasse 21. ☎ **07223/96-14-99.** Reservations required. Main courses 42DM–54DM ($21–$27); 3-course fixed-price lunch 85DM ($42.50); 3- or 4-course gourmet dinner menu 85DM ($42.50); 5-course menu 125DM ($62.50). AE, MC. Wed–Mon noon–2pm and 6:30–9:30pm. Bus: 6. INTERNATIONAL.

Schloss Neuweier is a small 12th-century castle entirely surrounded by defensive water fortifications and vineyards belonging to the estate. Its restaurant is not large but offers impeccable service in a decor of tile walls hung with portraits of former inhabitants. The house proudly serves local wines, including an excellent Riesling, and practices international cookery with flair. Try the brisket with horseradish sauce or the baked ray. The kitchen is consistent, and dishes are well prepared.

✪ Zum Alde Gott. Weinstrasse 10. ☎ **07223/55-13.** Reservations required. Main courses 49DM–55DM ($24.50–$27.50). AE, DC, MC, V. Fri–Wed noon–3pm and 6:30pm–midnight. Bus: 6. BADISCHE.

Here's where the true gourmand comes to dine. In this attractive and very old wine cellar, Wilfried Serr, the most distinguished chef in the Baden-Baden area, mixes his palette of flavors with astounding skill and imagination. Wild game in season is a fine art here. Try also the Black Forest trout or the sea bass. There are only 12 tables, in soft green and white, and the ambience is bright and cheerful. An added bonus is an open-air terrace.

BADEN-BADEN AFTER DARK

A busy annual schedule of concert, dance, and dramatic performances entertains locals and visitors alike. The centerpiece for most of the resort's cultural activities is the oft-photographed **Kurhaus**, Kaiserallee 1 (☎ **07221/353207**). Originally built in the 1870s as the focal point of the resort, the Kurhaus does not, as its name implies, contain spa facilities, but is rather a catch-all entertainment complex. In the same building is Baden-Baden's casino, the **Spielbank** (see "The Casino," above).

The **Theater am Goetheplatz,** Goetheplatz (☎ **07221/93-27-00**), is a well-maintained and beautiful baroque-style theater that presents opera, ballet, and drama productions. It opened auspiciously with the world premiere of the Berlioz opera *Beatrice et Benedict* in 1862. A month-long celebration of music is held during the summer, when the **Musikalischer Sommer Festival** brings a series of concerts to venues scattered throughout the town. For dates, schedule, and ticket information, contact the **Philharmonic Orchestra of Baden-Baden** at Schloss Solms, 76530 Baden-Baden (☎ **07221/93-27-00**), or the tourist information office (see "Visitor Information," above).

Bars in the resort hotels often have low-key entertainment. Try the **Jockey Bar,** in the lobby of the Steigenberger Badischer Hof (tel **07221/93-4484**), or the **Oleander Bar** in Brenner's Park Hotel, Lichtentaler Allee (☎ **07221/9000**).

11

Heidelberg, Stuttgart & the Neckar Valley

Ancient castle ruins in the midst of thick woodlands, quiet university towns, busy manufacturing centers—you'll find all these in the countryside of southwestern Germany. The area extends along the Neckar River from Heidelberg past medieval towns and modern cities as far as Tübingen. The Neckar flows between the Black Forest and the Schwäbische Alb. Although the river is open to commercial shipping vessels as far as Stuttgart, much of the valley has remained unspoiled. The castles that rise around every bend in the river were once home to the German royal families of Hohenstaufen and Hohenzollern. Some of these ruins were the summer palaces of kings and emperors. Today, castles and country palaces sometimes offer bed and board to travelers.

1 Heidelberg

120km (75 miles) NW of Stuttgart, 20km (12 miles) SE of Mannheim, 88km (55 miles) S of Frankfurt

Summertime in Heidelberg, according to the song from *The Student Prince,* is a time for music and romance. Today, it's also a time when droves of visitors invade this beautiful city. Heidelberg is one of the few German cities that was not leveled by air raids in World War II, and therefore still has original buildings from the later Middle Ages and early Renaissance. Modern Heidelberg is centered around Bismarckplatz at the foot of the Theodore-Heuss-Brücke; in this part of the city, you'll find many of the best hotels and restaurants. The tall buildings and shopping plazas here contrast with the Altstadt nearby. Across the Neckar are sports grounds, a zoo, and a large botanical garden.

Heidelberg is, above all, a university town, and has been since 1386. Students make up much of the population. The colorful atmosphere that university life imparts to the town is felt especially in the old student quarter, with its narrow streets and lively inns. This oldest university in Germany is officially named **Ruprecht-Karl-University,** honoring both its founder, Elector Ruprecht I of the Palatinate, as well as the man who, in 1803, made it the leading university in the state of Baden, Margrave Karl Friedrich. The school was founded after the Great Schism of 1378, when conflicting claims to the papacy created unrest, and German teachers and students fled the Sorbonne in Paris.

The university grew rapidly. At first monastic in character, it changed in the 16th century with the appointment of a married rector. The so-called Old University was built in the early 18th century; the New University was constructed nearby from 1930 to 1932. Funds for this structure came from American sources, including Henry Ford. Today, lecture halls, institutes, seminar buildings, and clinics are scattered all over town, but a new university quarter has been developed on the plain in the Neuenheim district, with multistory buildings and a modern cancer-research center.

ESSENTIALS

GETTING THERE **By Plane** The nearest major airport is Frankfurt (see chapter 12), with a direct bus link to Heidelberg. The shuttle bus between Frankfurt and Heidelberg costs 45DM ($22.50) per person. Call ☎ **06221/77-00-77** for shuttle information.

By Train Heidelberg's **Hauptbahnhof** is an important railroad station, lying on the Mannheim line, with frequent service to both regional towns and major cities. From Frankfurt, 40 trains arrive per day (trip time: 1 hr.); from Stuttgart, 30 trains (trip time: 45 min.). Travel time to and from Munich is about $3^1/2$ hours. For information, call ☎ **01805/996633.**

By Bus Regional bus service is provided by **BRN Busverkehr Rhein-Neckar** at Heidelberg (☎ **06221/606220**).

By Car Motorists should take the A5 Autobahn from the north or south.

VISITOR INFORMATION Contact **Tourist-Information,** Pavillon am Hauptbahnhof (☎ **06221/1-94-33**). It's open Monday to Saturday 9am to 7pm and Sunday 10am to 6pm. Here visitors can purchase a Heidelberg Card, which provides discounts on attractions and free use of public transportation. It costs 19DM ($9.50) for an adult and two children for up to 2 days.

GETTING AROUND Heidelberg is crisscrossed with a network of trams and buses, many of which intersect at the Bismarckplatz in the town center. Bus 41 and 42 travel at frequent intervals between the railway station and the Universitätsplatz. The Altstadt stretches on either side of the Hauptstrasse between the Bismarckplatz and the Universitätsplatz. Bus or tram fares cost 3.50DM ($1.75) for a single ride, although a 24-hour pass, valid for up to five persons traveling within a group, costs 10.50DM ($5.25).

EXPLORING THE TOWN

✪ **TOURING HEIDELBERG CASTLE** You can reach the huge red-sandstone Heidelberg Castle (☎ **06221/53-84-0**), set amid woodlands and terraced gardens, by several routes. Either take a 2-minute cable-car ride, or drive up the winding Neue Schlosstrasse past the old houses perched on the hillside, or walk. Walking is the most rewarding approach because of the constantly changing scenic view of the town and surrounding countryside. You can take the more gradual slope from the Klingentor, or make the shorter walk up the steep Burgweg from Kornmarkt. The cable car leaves from the platform near the Kornmarkt, and costs 4DM ($2) round-trip for adults and 2DM ($1) for children.

The castle is a dignified ruin today, but even in its deteriorated state, it's one of the finest Gothic-Renaissance castles in Germany. Entering the walls at the main gate, you first come upon the huge **Gun Park** to your left, from which you can gaze down upon Heidelberg and the Neckar Valley. Straight ahead is the **Thick Tower,** or what remains of it after its 8m (25-foot) walls were blown up by the French in the late 17th

Exploring on Two Wheels

Unique in Germany, the **Neckar Valley Cycle Path** allows you to ride all the way from the source of the Neckar in Villingen-Schwenningen to the confluence of the Rhine at Mannheim. The path is marked with a signpost showing a green bicycle and a red wheel mark. The route follows the river the whole way, though many cyclists go only as far as Heidelberg. Along the way, you'll pass castles, manor houses, vineyards, country inns, and such old towns as Rottweil and Esslingen. Most German cyclists average about 48km (30 miles) per day on the trail.

Suggested stopovers along the way are Sulz, Tübingen, and Heilbronn. In the town of Neckarsulm, you can make a stop to visit the **German Bicycle Museum,** housed in Deutschorden Castle. It's close to the cycle path. Here you can see the original "dandy horse," the first bicycle, invented in 1819.

century. Leaving the Gun Park via Elizabeth's Gate (erected by Friedrich V in 1615 for his Scottish wife, Elizabeth Stuart, daughter of James I), you come to the Bridge House and the bridge crossing the site of the former moat.

Along the north side of the courtyard stretches the stern **palace of Friedrich IV,** erected 1601 to 1607. The palace is less damaged than other parts of the castle, and its rooms have been almost completely restored, including the gallery of princes and kings of the German empire from the time of Charlemagne. The palace's terrace, the Altan, offers a panoramic view of the plain of the Neckar. The ancient bell tower, at the northeast end of the Altan, dates from the early 1500s.

At the west end of the terrace, in the cellars of the castle, is the **Wine Vat Building,** built in the late 16th century and worth a visit for a look at the Great Cask, symbol of the abundant and exuberant life of the Rhineland-Palatinate. This huge barrel-like monstrosity, built in 1751, is capable of holding more than 208,000l (55,000 gallons) of wine.

To the east, connecting the palace of Friedrich IV to the **Ottheinrich Building,** itself an outstanding example of German Renaissance architecture, is the **Hall of Mirrors Building,** constructed in 1549—a Renaissance masterpiece. Only the shell of the original building remains, enough to give you an idea of its former glory, with its arcades and steep gables decorated with cherubs and sirens.

Next to Ottheinrich's palace is the Chemist's Tower, housing the **Pharmaceutical Museum** (☎ 06221/25880). This museum shows a chemist's shop with utensils and laboratory equipment from the 18th and 19th centuries. It's open daily 10am to 5pm, and admission is 4DM ($2) for adults and 2DM ($1) for children.

A 1-hour guided tour of the castle costs 4DM ($2) for adults and 2DM ($1) for children. Tours are frequent, especially in summer. Admission to the grounds is free; admission to the entrance courtyard and Great Cask is 4DM ($2) for adults, 2DM ($1) for children. Open daily 8am to 6pm.

EXPLORING THE ALTSTADT   All the important sights of Heidelberg lie on or near the south bank of the Neckar. You should cross to the other side of the river (via the 18th-century Karl Theodore Bridge) for the best overall view. **Philosophenweg (Philosopher's Way),** halfway up the hill on the north bank, offers an especially good vista.

In the town itself, a tour of the main attractions begins with **Marktplatz** in front of the Rathaus. On market days the square is filled with stalls of fresh flowers, fish, and vegetables. At the opposite end of the square is the late-Gothic **Heiliggeistkirche,** built around 1400, the largest Gothic church in the Palatinate. For nearly 300 years, the church was the burial place of the electors, but most of the graves were destroyed in the French invasion late in the 17th century. In 1706, a wall was erected to divide the church between Roman Catholics and Protestants. The wall has since been removed and the church restored to its original plan. Around the corner is the famous old mansion **Zum Ritter,** recommended in the hotel listings below.

Kurpfälzisches Museum (Museum of the Palatinate). Hauptstrasse 97. ☎ **06221/ 58-34-00.** Admission 5DM ($2.50) adults, 3DM ($1.50) students, 1.50DM (75¢) children 17 and under. Tues and Thurs–Sun 10am–5pm, Wed 10am–9pm. Bus: 11,12, 35 or 42.

This museum is housed in a baroque palace. It contains a large collection of painting and sculpture from 6 centuries. Notable is the Riemenschneider Altar from Windsheim (1509), showing Christ and the 12 Apostles. There's also an archaeological collection with a cast of the jawbone of the 500,000-year-old Heidelberg Man and a section on the history of the Palatinate. The restaurant is a good lunch stop (see "Where to Dine," below).

Studentenkarzer (Student Jail). Augustinergasse 2. ☎ **06221/54-23-34.** Admission 1.50DM (75¢) adults, 1DM (50¢) students and children 14 and under. Apr–Oct, Tues–Fri 10am–4pm. Bus: 10, 12, or 35.

The walls and even the ceilings of the prison are covered with graffiti and drawings, including portraits and silhouettes. The last prisoners were held here in 1914. Ring the caretaker's bell (same address) for admission.

SHOPPING

The main shopping street is the traffic-free **Hauptstrasse,** which is filled with stores selling glass, crystal, handcrafts, and other items. Heidelberg is also known for its markets, including the one held on Wednesday and Sunday mornings at Marktplatz, and another held Tuesday and Friday mornings at Friedrich-Ebert-Platz. A giant flea market sprawls along Guteramtsstrasse near the Customs office one Saturday a month, but there isn't a designated week within which it falls.

In a city of this size, there are lots of stores to choose from. **Michael Kienscherff,** Hauptstrasse 177 (☎ **06221/2-42-55;** tram: 1 or 5), offers a wide assortment of handcrafts from all over Germany: music boxes, nativity scenes, nutcrackers, and glass and crystal ornaments. The two branches of **Gätschenberger,** Hauptstrasse 6 and 42 (☎ **06221/1-44-80;** tram: 1 or 5), share a telephone, but no. 42 is known for its array of fine linens and embroideries for bed, bath, and table, whereas no. 6 sells men's and women's undergarments. An oddly named toy store, **Muckels Maus,** Plöck 71 (☎ **06221/2-38-86;** tram: 1 or 5), is the place to find beautifully handcrafted puppets, including replicas of characters from the operas of Mozart, antique-looking and ultramodern dolls, and wooden blocks and figures.

Other shops of interest include **Unholtz,** Hauptstrasse 160 (☎ **06221/2-09-64;** tram: 1 or 5), which carries Solingen cutlery, tableware, and scissors; and **Spiess & Walther,** Friedrich-Ebert-Anlage 23a (☎ **06221/2-22-33;** bus: 11 or 33), which features exclusive designs in contemporary furniture, antiques, and textiles. For all things leather, stop by **Leder-Meid,** Hauptstrasse 88 (☎ **06221/2-25-70;** tram: 1 or 5), which sells the crafts of German and other manufacturers. **Tischer,** Hauptstrasse 73 (☎ **06221/1-48-00;** tram: 1 or 5), carries quality cooking items.

If you want more variety under one roof, go to either of Heidelberg's two best department stores, **Kaufhof,** Hauptstrasse 22–32 (☎ **06221/50-40;** tram: 1 or 5), or **Horten,** Bergheimerstrasse 7 (☎ **06221/91-60;** tram: 1 or 5).

Heidelberg

ATTRACTIONS ●
Alte Brücke **17**
Heidelberg Castle **2**
Heiliggeistkirche **7**
Kornmarkt **3**
Kurpfälzisches Museum **11**
Marktplatz **6**
Old University **10**
Rathaus **4**
Studentenkarzer **9**

ACCOMMODATIONS ■
Alt Heidelberg **13**
Der Europäusцge Hof-Hotel
  Europa **14**
Heidelberg Renaissance
  Hotel **16**
Hotel Anlage **12**
Hotel Hirschgasse **18**
Hotel Vier Jahreszeiten **8**
Hotel Zum Ritter St. Georg **5**
Nekar-Hotel Heidelberg **15**
Parkhotel Atlantic **1**

397

Boating in the Neckar

Heidelberg is a good point from which to explore the romantic Neckar Valley. From April to early October, you can take a boat tour along the river as far as Neckarsteinach and back. There are usually four or five round-trips daily, and you need not return on the same boat. Boats are operated by the **Rhein-Neckar-Fahrgastschiffahrt GmbH,** Stadthalle, Heidelberg (☎ **06221/2-01-81**). Trips between Heidelberg and Neckarsteinach cost 16DM ($9.60) round-trip, and those between Heidelberg and Hirschhorn (which operate June 17 to September 30) cost 22DM ($13.20) round-trip. You can order drinks or snacks on the boat. Some of the people who take visitors on this pleasant trip are descended from the Neckar fishers who helped Mark Twain when he rafted down from Hirschhorn. The same families have been working the Neckar since the early 1600s.

WHERE TO STAY
EXPENSIVE

✪ **Der Europäische Hof-Hotel Europa.** Friedrich-Ebert-Anlage 1, 69117 Heidelberg. ☎ **800/223-4541,** 800/223-6800 in the U.S. and Canada, or 06221/5150. Fax 06221/51-55-06. www.europaeischerhof.com. E-mail: reservations@europaeischerhof.com. 118 units. A/C MINIBAR TV TEL. 360DM–550DM ($180–$275) double; 590DM–950DM ($295–$475) suite. AE, DC, MC, V. Parking 25DM ($12.50). Tram: Bismarckplatz.

This glamour hotel is by far the best in Heidelberg. It fronts the city park in the heart of town, within walking distance of the castle and the university. Its interior is like that of a gracious home, with antiques, crystal chandeliers, and Oriental rugs. Some rooms and several suites face a quiet inside garden; front rooms in the oldest section tend to be noisy (from traffic). Each room has a hair dryer, room safe, and trouser press. Most are air-conditioned. Nineteen have whirlpool tubs.

Dining/Diversions: Meals are served in the Louis XVI restaurant, the Garden Room, or the finely paneled Kurfürstenstube (see "Where to Dine," below). Before dinner, guests congregate around the curved bar in the wood-paneled lounge. In summer, meals are served on the open terrace with a view of the water fountains.

Amenities: Room service, laundry, dry cleaning, shopping arcade.

✪ **Hotel Hirschgasse.** Hirschgasse 3, 69100 Heidelberg. ☎ **06221/45-40.** Fax 06221/45-41-11. www.hirschgasse.de. E-mail: hirschgasse@compuserve.com. 20 units. MINIBAR TV TEL. 295DM ($147.50) junior suite for 2; 350DM–450DM ($175–$225) senior suite for 2; 450DM–550DM ($225–$275) salon suite for 2. AE, DC, MC, V. Free parking. Bus: 34.

This historic country home-style hotel, nestled on the hillside of a historic lane adjoining Philosopher's Way, is tops in Heidelberg for its tranquil and romantic setting. It dates from 1472 and has lodged such impressive figures as Mark Twain and Bismarck. Rooms are all suites decorated in Laura Ashley designs. Each has a salon, hair dryer, and Jacuzzi. For American guests, there's cable-TV news from home.

Dining/Diversions: Regional, traditional, and modern cuisine is offered in Le Gourmet, which since 1472 has been attracting diners from Europe and abroad. The Mensurstube keeps alive the atmosphere of the old student fraternities (see "Where to Dine," below).

Amenities: Room service, laundry, baby-sitting, terrace garden; horseback riding and golf can be arranged.

✪ **Hotel Zum Ritter St. Georg.** Hauptstrasse 178, 69117 Heidelberg. ☎ **06221/13-50.** Fax 06221/13-52-30. www.ritter-heidelberg.de. E-mail: info@ritter-heidelberg.de. 40 units. MINIBAR TV TEL. 285DM–385DM ($142.50–$192.50) double; 440DM–550DM ($220–$275) suite. Rates include buffet breakfast. AE, DC, MC, V. Bus: 10, 11, or 12.

A glorious old inn right out of the German Renaissance, the Zum Ritter is a well-preserved rarity, although it's inferior to the Hirschgasse (see above) in comfort and antique charm. Built in 1592 by Frenchman Charles Bèlier, it's now listed among the major sight-seeing attractions of this university town. There are no public lounges. Many rooms are somewhat cramped, but beds are most comfortable and the baths have been renewed.

Dining: The hotel's restaurant (see "Where to Dine," below), which serves an eclectic fare of German and international dishes, actually outshines the accommodations.

Amenities: Dry cleaning, laundry service, conference rooms; a shopping arcade is within walking distance.

MODERATE

Alt Heidelberg. Rohrbacher 29, 69115 Heidelberg. ☎ **800/528-1234** in the U.S. and Canada, or 06221/91-50. Fax 06221/16-42-72. E-mail: info@altheidelberg.bestwestern.de. 79 units. MINIBAR TV TEL. 258DM ($129) double; 308DM ($154) triple. Rates include buffet breakfast. AE, DC, MC, V. Parking 15DM ($7.50). Tram: 1. Bus: 41, 42.

This five-story hotel is set on a street corner in the commercial center of Heidelberg's old town. The interior is streamlined and a bit sterile. Rooms are individually decorated and windows are double-glazed. The bar has occasional live piano music. A well-managed restaurant, the Graimberg, serves French and German cuisine.

Heidelberg Renaissance Hotel. Vanerowstrasse 16, 69115 Heidelberg. ☎ **06221/90-80.** Fax 06221/90-86-08. www.marriott.com. 251 units. A/C MINIBAR TV TEL. 225DM–260DM ($112.50–$130) double; 340DM ($170) junior suite; 440DM ($220) suite. AE, DC, MC, V. Parking 20DM ($10). Tram: 1, 4, or 5

This hotel sits on the banks of the Neckar, just a few minutes from the Altstadt and the main train station. Although it doesn't have the flair and traditional style of Der Europäische Hof, it's far superior to its nearest rival, Holiday Inn Crowne Plaza at Kurfürstenanlage 1. The exit from the Autobahn is only minutes away, making it convenient for motorists. Rooms are comfortably furnished and newly renovated, many with views over the river or the hills beyond. As a special service, the hotel operates a Lufthansa check-in counter, and a Lufthansa airport bus operates between the Frankfurt International Airport and the hotel 18 times per day.

Dining/Diversions: The elegant Globetrotter Restaurant, with a terrace on the Neckar, features international dining, popular buffet lunches, and Sunday brunch. The Pub Pinte serves not only draft beer but also regional dishes, and the lobby bar offers snacks and drinks.

Amenities: Room service, laundry, dry cleaning, health club, indoor swimming pool, sauna, solarium, massage, gift shop, business center.

Neckar-Hotel Heidelberg. Bismarckstrasse 19, 69115 Heidelberg. ☎ **06221/905-150.** Fax 06221/9051510. 35 units. TV TEL. 180DM–240DM ($90–$120) double. Rates include continental breakfast. AE, MC, V. Closed Dec 20–Jan 7. Free parking. Bus: 10, 12, or 35.

If the Parkhotel Atlantic and Alt Heidelberg are full, this hotel is a good bet in this price range. It enjoys an enviable position on the Neckar River near the center of the university town. There's a superb view of the Odenwald Forest. The facilities are substantial, and the spacious rooms are fitted with modern furnishings. Breakfast is the only meal served.

✪ Parkhotel Atlantic. Schloss-Wolfsbrunnen-Weg 23, 69117 Heidelberg. ☎ **06221/60-42-0.** Fax 06221/60-42-60. 24 units. MINIBAR TV TEL. 180DM–220DM ($90–$110) double. Rates include buffet breakfast. AE, DC, MC, V. Free parking. Bus: 11, 12, 33. Head east from the Hauptbahnhof, along Kurfürstenanlage going through the tunnel, and take the 2nd right, bringing you to Heidelberg Castle; continue straight beyond the castle to the hotel.

This grand hotel on the wooded outskirts of Heidelberg, near the castle, offers modern comfort in annexes built around the core of an older villa. Visitors are assured calm and comfort, and can take advantage of the many woodland trails extending through the Neckar Valley. This hotel's setting makes it the best in its price range; hotels in the city center, unless soundproofed, get a lot of traffic noise. Rooms are decorated in 1965-ish modern style but are quite comfortable, though not large.

INEXPENSIVE

Hotel Anlage. Friedrich-Ebert-Anlage 32, 69117 Heidelberg. ☎ **06221/2-64-25.** Fax 06221/16-44-26. 20 units. TV TEL. 145DM–185DM ($72.50–$92.50) double. Rates include continental breakfast. AE, DC, MC, V. Parking 9DM ($4.50). Bus: 11, 12, or 33.

Hotel Anlage is one of Heidelberg's best affordable hotels, located in the heart of the city, on the street leading up to the castle. It occupies one wing of a lavishly built, late-19th-century palace. Rooms are cozy and have cable TV (with English programs). The pleasant restaurant is reserved for guests.

Hotel Vier Jahreszeiten. Haspelgasse 2 (near the Alte Brücke), 69117 Heidelberg. ☎ **06221/2-41-64.** Fax 06221/16-31-10. www.4-jahreszeiten.de. E-mail: info@ 4-jahreszeiten.de. 22 units, 19 with bath. TV TEL. 130DM ($65) double without bath, 195DM–225DM ($97.50–$112.50) double with bath. Rates include continental breakfast. AE, DC, MC, V. Closed Dec 24–Jan 10. Parking 15DM ($7.50). Bus: 33, 34.

This hotel is a worthy choice for any of the "four seasons." It's located near the starting point for many interesting walks. Several famous student inns and the castle are also nearby. The hotel has been improved over the years, and the small rooms are comfortable, if rather plain. Mattresses and towels are a bit thin, but the price and the location are hard to beat.

WHERE TO DINE
EXPENSIVE

✪ **Kurfürstenstube.** In Der Europäische Hof-Hotel Europa, Friedrich-Ebert-Anlage 1. ☎ **06221/51-50.** Reservations required. Main courses 49DM–58DM ($24.50–$29); fixed-price meals from 82DM ($41). AE, DC, MC, V. Daily noon–3:30pm and 6:30–11:30pm. Tram: Bismarckplatz. FRENCH.

The best dining spot in Heidelberg is in the ground-floor wing of this deluxe hotel. The wood-paneled grill room is attractively decorated with provincial furnishings. The menu is in English, but the cuisine is mainly French, with both fixed-price and à la carte meals. Only the highest quality seasonal ingredients are used. Perhaps the menu will feature roast John Dory with garlic-flavored cream sauce and braised peppers and tomatoes, or saddle of Limousin lamb with a coating of herbs, essence of basil, green beans, and pesto-flavored polenta. The chef never oversauces or overseasons. For a spectacular finish, try the crepes flambée with bananas and maple sauce. The wine list is the most impressive in town.

Simplicissimus. Ingrimstrasse 16. ☎ **06221/18-33-36.** Reservations required. Main courses 35DM–39DM ($17.50–$19.50); fixed-price menu 88DM ($44). AE, MC, V. Wed–Mon 6–11pm. Closed 1 week in Mar and 1st 3 weeks in Aug. Bus: 11, 12, 33, 35, 41. FRENCH.

This elegant spot is ideal for a gourmet rendezvous. Johann Lummer, one of the finest chefs in Heidelberg, prepares a *cuisine moderne* with consummate skill. His restaurant in the Altstadt is decorated simply but with taste and style, with white paneling, globe lights, and touches of crimson. *Gourmet* magazine said that Herr Lummer "paints with food," and we agree. Not only are his dishes delectable to the taste buds, but their presentation is equally pleasing. The menu varies but is likely to include fresh mushrooms in cream sauce with homemade noodles, or crayfish with fresh melon and herb-flavored cream sauce.

Zum Ritter St. Georg. Hauptstrasse 178. ☎ **06221/1-35-0.** Reservations recommended. Main courses 18DM–65DM ($9–$32.50); fixed-price menus 38DM–58DM ($19–$29). AE, DC, MC, V. Daily noon–2pm and 6–10pm. Bus: 10, 11, or 12. GERMAN/INTERNATIONAL.

Zum Ritter is popular with both students and professors, who know that they can get not only good German cooking here but also the wonderful Dortmunder Actien-Brauerei beer. It's located in one of Heidelberg's most famous Renaissance buildings. You dine either in the first-class Great Hall (the Rittersaal) or in the smaller Councillors' Chamber. We like the elegant larger room, with its sepia ceilings, wainscoting, and Oriental rugs. The house specialty is saddle of Odenwald venison for two (in season); when this dish is offered, locals flock here. A good beginning might be game soup St. Hubertus with brandy foam, and crêpes suzette is a fine dessert.

✪ **Zur Herrenmühle.** Hauptstrasse 237–239. ☎ **06221/60-29-09.** Reservations recommended. Main courses 47DM–55DM ($23.50–$27.50); fixed-price menus 95DM–110DM ($47.50–$55). AE, DC, MC, V. Mon–Sat 5:30pm–midnight. Bus: 33. FRENCH/INTERNATIONAL.

This family-owned restaurant is in a 17th-century house, with thick walls and antique paneling. The sophisticated maître d' adds both glamour and an appropriate theatricality. The succulent classical cuisine is based on fresh ingredients. Try the rack of lamb with herbs and homemade green noodles, or the roast roebuck with a vinegar-and-honey sauce. The desserts make better use of fresh fruit than any other place in town; try the sorbet flavored with blood oranges and served with a parfait of mandarin oranges. The service here is equaled only at the Kurfürstenstube.

MODERATE

Kurpfälzisches Museum Restaurant. Hauptstrasse 97. ☎ **06221/2-40-50.** Reservations required. Main courses 17.50DM–40DM ($8.75–$20). AE, DC, MC, V. Daily Noon–2:30pm and 6–10pm. Bus: 1, 35, 97. GERMAN.

This quiet culinary oasis at the museum makes an interesting stopover for lunch. The baroque palace setting is sometimes more interesting than the food. You can order such dishes as rump steak Madagascar with green pepper while you enjoy the view of the little garden and splashing fountain. The food is satisfying, though hardly a challenge to the chefs at Kurfürstenstube or Simplicissimus.

✪ **Mensurstube.** In the Hotel Hirschgasse, Hirschgasse 3. ☎ **06221/45-40.** Reservations recommended. Main courses 25DM–35DM ($12.50–$17.50). DC, MC, V. Daily noon–2pm and 6–10pm. Bus: 34. GERMAN/REGIONAL.

No other place in Heidelberg captures bygone days quite like this one. In this rustic and cozy spot, you sit at tables more than 2 centuries old—you can still see where Bismarck and many others carved their names. Swords hang from the ceiling—in the past, when dueling was the regular sport of the student fraternities, many duels were fought in what is now the dining room. Traditional recipes are served; the menu is limited but all the ingredients are fresh. Potato soup is a good starter, followed by homemade noodles, oxtail, and lamb shank. *Rinderfilet* (fillet of beef) is often served with bone marrow and a red-wine sauce with potatoes gratin. Almost everything is best accompanied by fresh-draft Pils.

INEXPENSIVE

Konditorei-Café Schafheutle. Hauptstrasse 94. ☎ **06221/1-46-80.** Main courses 15DM–18DM ($7.50–$9). V. Mon–Fri 9:30am–7pm, Sat 9am–6pm. Closed holidays. Bus: 10 or 12. PASTRIES/GERMAN.

Rain need never ruin your summer outing in this partially roofed cafe garden. You can order light meals, and there's also a large choice of pastries. Service is attentive. This is a good choice for afternoon coffee or for a quick bite as you're dashing up to Heidelberg Castle.

HEIDELBERG AFTER DARK

Nights here are alive with the youthful enthusiasm of Heidelberg's students. Early evenings often start in the bars along Hauptstrasse; then late nights get rolling in the clubs around Marktplatz.

THE PERFORMING ARTS   The main performance stage is **Theater der Stadt,** Friedrichstrasse 5 (☎ **06221/58-35-02;** bus: 41 or 42), where nightly entertainment includes plays, opera, and dance productions. For five weeks beginning in late July, the **Schlossfest-Spiele** festival brings opera, classical music, jazz, and theater to venues around the area, including Heidelberg Castle. Contact ☎ **06274/583-52** for tickets.

HISTORIC STUDENT DRINKING CLUBS   Heidelberg's most famous and revered student tavern, ✪ **Zum Roten Ochsen (Red Ox Inn),** Hauptstrasse 217 (☎ **06221/2-09-77;** bus: 33), opened in 1703. For six generations it has been in the Spengel family, who have welcomed everybody from Bismarck to Mark Twain. It seems that every student who has attended the university has left his or her mark (or initials) on the walls. The series of rooms, where revelers sit at long oak tables under smoke-blackened ceilings, is arranged in horseshoe fashion; the U part has a pianist who sets the musical pace. As the evening progresses, the songs become louder and louder. Motherly looking waitresses bring in huge steins of beer and plates of food. A mug of beer costs 4.50DM ($2.25) and up. Meals go from 21DM to 39DM ($10.50 to $19.50). The place is open daily 11:30am to 2pm and 5 to 11pm (sometimes to midnight). Closed mid-December to mid-January.

Next door is **Zum Sepp'l,** Hauptstrasse 213 (☎ **06221/2-30-85;** bus: 41 or 42), the second most famous drinking club in Heidelberg. It's also filled with photographs and carved initials of former students, along with memorabilia that range from old Berlin street signs to Alabama license plates. The building itself dates from 1634. Meals cost 15DM to 30DM ($7.50 to $15). A mug of beer goes for 5.80DM ($2.90). There's live piano music daily from 8pm to midnight. When the university is closed, the activity here dies down considerably. It's open daily from 10am to 1am.

BARS & CAFES   Students also like to drink beer at **Reichsapfel,** Unterestrasse 35 (☎ **06221/2-79-50;** bus: 41 or 42), a popular hangout for more than 300 years. It sells nothing but beer. Open daily 6pm to 1am. **Max Bar,** Marktplatz 5 (☎ **06221/2-44-19;** bus: 11 or 33), is another beer-drinker's bar, but you can also get a baguette or croissant to soak up some of the alcohol. There's indoor and patio seating. Open daily 8pm to 1am. When you tire of beer and want a more spirited drink, wander over to **Sonder Bar,** Unterestrasse 13 (☎ **06221/2-52-00;** bus: 41 or 42), which stocks more than 150 brands of whisky, 10 kinds of vodka, and sundry other potions, besides its 11 types of beers. Open daily 7pm to 1am.

Catch up on the latest news and trends at **Café Journal,** Hauptstrasse 162 (☎ **06221/16-17-12;** bus: 41 or 42), where drinkers linger over beer while scanning newspapers and magazines from all over Europe and the United States. Open daily 8am to 1am. **Hard Rock Cafe,** Hauptstrasse 142 (☎ **06221/2-28-19;** bus: 41 or

42), has a branch here, open 10am to 1am. A popular bar with a mixed gay crowd, **Mata Hari,** Oberbadgasse 10 (☎ **06221/18-18-08;** bus: 11 or 33), is a mellow place to meet and drink. Open 11pm and 3am nightly.

LIVE MUSIC & CLUBS   The **Schwimmbad Musik Club,** Tiergartenstrasse 13 (☎ **06221/47-02-01;** bus: 33), which features trendsetting local and international bands, is open Wednesday and Thursday 8pm to 3am, Friday and Saturday 8pm to 4am. Cover is 7DM to 20DM ($3.50 to $10), depending on the act. At **Dr. Flotte,** Hauptstrasse 130 (☎ **06221/2-05-69;** bus: 41 or 42), jazz bands appear on Sunday September to May, 4 to 7pm. A variety of music is featured at other times. Open daily 11am to 1am (Friday and Saturday to 3am).

Named after a barbecue sauce from Texas, **Ziegler-Bräu/Billy Blue's,** Bergheimer Strasse 1B (☎ **06221/2-53-33;** tram: 1 or 5), serves up barbecue in the front room while local and international bands kick out soul, funk, and blues in the back Wednesday to Saturday nights. Open daily 5pm to 3am; cover is 6DM ($3) on Wednesday or 5DM on weekends (otherwise free).

Known as one of the oldest jazz clubs in Germany, **Cave 54** Krämergasse 2 (☎ **06221/278-40;** bus: 11 or 33), is a perennial favorite. It offers live jazz every Sunday, with other nights devoted to soul, funk, and reggae. Open daily 10pm to 3am, cover is 5DM ($2.50) on Tuesday night and 12DM ($6) on Sunday (otherwise free).

2 Hirschhorn, Eberbach & Heilbrunn

From April to early October, you can take a boat tour in the Neckar Valley as far as Neckarsteinach and back (see "Boating in the Neckar" above). You can also see the many attractions along the banks of the Neckar by car, driving eastward along the right bank of the river.

HIRSCHHORN

This medieval town, 26km (16 miles) east of Heidelberg, is known as the gem of the Neckar Valley. It obtained municipal rights in 1391. Overlooking the town and the river from a fortified promontory is the 18th-century **Hirschhorn Castle.** The castle defenses are from the 14th century, and wall paintings from that period can be seen in the chapel. The castle is now a hotel and restaurant (see below). For a view of the sharp bend of the Neckar below the town, climb to the top of the tower.

GETTING THERE   Access by car is via Route 45 east from Heidelberg. Hirschhorn lies on the Neckarelz–Heidelberg rail line with frequent local service between the two towns. For information, call ☎ **01805/99-66-33.**

WHERE TO STAY & DINE

Schloss-Hotel. Auf Burg Hirschhorn (on Route B37), 69434 Hirschhorn. ☎ **06272/13-73.** Fax 06272/32-67. E-mail: t@online.schlosshotel.hirschhorn.de. 25 units. MINIBAR TV TEL. 180DM–243DM ($90–$121.50) double; 243DM ($121.50) suite. Rates include continental breakfast. AE, DC, MC, V. Closed mid-Dec through Jan. Free parking.

This hotel offers rooms in a hilltop castle looming over the center of town. Rooms have river views and collections of good antiques. Some are in a guesthouse annex, but those in the castle have more space, style, and tradition. Central heating and an elevator have been installed. The restaurant serves traditional dishes to nonresidents, but you have to phone in advance. Specialties include various kinds of game, smoked trout, and home-baked bread. Food service is daily 8 to 10am, noon to 2pm, and 6 to 9:30pm. Meals begin at 80DM ($40).

EBERBACH

The Imperial City of Eberbach, established in 1227, is 11km (7 miles) farther along the Neckar. Its castle, which dates all the way from 1190, was mostly destroyed in the 15th century, but its ivy-covered ruins attract many visitors today. The old Pfarrhof, the medieval center of the town, is within the city walls. Eberbach is proud to be the city where Queen Victoria was conceived; the event is commemorated by a plaque outside her parents' home, Haus Thalheim.

GETTING THERE   Routes 37 and 45 connect to the A5 Autobahn heading north and south or the A6 going east and west. From Heidelberg, head east along Route 37. Eberbach lies on the Neckarelz–Heidelberg rail line, with frequent service. Call ☎ **01805/99-66-33** for information.

VISITOR INFORMATION   Contact the **Kurverwaltung,** Im Kuzentrum, Kellerei-strasse 32 (☎ **06271/48-99**), Monday to Friday 8am to noon and 2 to 5:30pm; May 15 to October 15, also Saturday 8:30am to noon.

WHERE TO STAY & DINE

Hotel zum Karpfen. Am Alten Markt 1–4, 69412 Eberbach. ☎ **06271/7-10-15.** Fax 06271/71010. 68 units. 150DM–180DM ($75–$90) double; 230DM ($115) suite. Rates include buffet breakfast. AE, MC, V. Free parking.

This is the best and most colorful hotel in town. On its facade are authentic *sgraffiti* (scratched-on paintings) depicting the story of Eberbach. The building is more than 2 centuries old. The small rooms are well-maintained and furnished, most with phones and about half with TVs. The Old-World restaurant serves well-prepared meals daily 7am to noon.

HEILBRONN

Heilbronn is today a major commercial and cultural center. It was made an Imperial City by Emperor Karl IV in 1371; however, documents show that a Villa Heilbrunna existed here in A.D. 741. The town owes its name to a holy spring (Heiligbronn) that bubbled up from beneath the high altar at **St. Killian's Church,** the city's most important monument. The old city was largely destroyed in World War II, but the church has been rebuilt in its original Gothic and High Renaissance style. The church's 64m (210-foot) tower is the earliest example of Renaissance architecture in Germany. Inside are excellent original wood carvings, preserved during the war, including an elaborate choir and altar.

Opposite the church is the **Rathaus,** also reconstructed, a combination of Gothic and Renaissance architecture. On its balcony is an astronomical clock dating back to 1580. It was designed by the best-known horologist of the time, Isaak Habrecht, who created the famous clock inside the cathedral at Strasbourg, France.

Heilbronn is the largest producer of wine in the Neckar Valley, growing mainly Trollinger and Riesling grapes. The 220ha (550 acres) of vineyards around the town yield about 5 million liters of wine annually. Every September, a large arena around the Rathaus is converted into a **"wine village."** At various booths you can sample the vintage, often at bargain prices. Merriment and music fill the air. Local food is sold as well, including *Zwiebelkuchen* (onion cake) and *Dicker Hund,* which has been compared to a "pork hamburger" (don't order it rare).

Perhaps to compensate for all the wine and beer drinking, the town definitely believes in keeping fit. Some 4,000ha (10,000 acres) of wooded parkland surround the city, accessible by footpaths and nature trails.

GETTING THERE   Access by car is via the A6 Autobahn east and west and the A81 north and south. From Heidelberg, drive south along Route 45, then take A6 east. Heilbronn lies on the major Stuttgart–Würzburg rail line with frequent service. Call ☎ **01805/99-66-33** for information. Bus service to Stuttgart is provided by **Regional Bus Stuttgart GmbH** at Heilbronn (☎ **07131/6-24-50** for more information). For local transport information, call Heilbronner Verkehrbund at ☎ **07131/78560.**

TOURIST INFORMATION   Contact the **Stadtisches Verkehrsamt,** Rathaus, Marktplatz 7 (☎ **07131/56-22-70**), Monday to Friday 9am to 4pm and Saturday 9am to 7pm.

WHERE TO DINE

Ratskeller. Im Rathaus, Marktplatz 7. ☎ **07131/8-46-28.** Reservations recommended. Main courses 14.80DM–36DM ($7.40–$18). AE, MC, V. Mon–Sat 11am–1am. Closed 10 days in Sept. GERMAN/SWABIAN.

This is your best bet for dining in Heilbronn. It's an authentic Ratskeller, unlike so many others, but it's been given the modern treatment, with upholstered banquettes and wrought-iron grillwork. The rib-sticking fare here is solid and reliable. Main dishes include goulash, pepper steak with French fries and salad, and grilled sole. Fish specialties and vegetarian meals are also featured. There's an impressive wine list, although many diners consider the "wine of the cellar" (house wine) perfectly adequate.

3 Stuttgart

203km (126 miles) SE of Frankfurt, 222km (138 miles) NW of Munich, 126km (78 miles) SE of Heidelberg

Unlike many large, prosperous industrial centers, Stuttgart is not a city of concrete—on the contrary, two-thirds of the land inside the city limits is devoted to parks, gardens, and woodland. Yet Stuttgart is one of Germany's largest manufacturing cities, the home of Mercedes and Porsche, Zeiss optical equipment, and many other industrial concerns. It's also the site of international trade fairs and congresses.

As a cultural center, it's without peer in southwestern Germany. The Stuttgart Ballet is known throughout the world; its State Opera and Philharmonic Orchestra are also highly regarded. In addition, Stuttgart boasts an abundance of theater groups, cultural festivals, and museums, and is also the largest wine-growing city in Germany.

The name "Stuttgart" comes from a stud farm owned by one of the dukes of Swabia, son of Emperor Otto the Great; a horse can be seen today in the city's coat of arms. By 1427, Stuttgart had become the capital and residence of the counts of Württemberg. The city grew and prospered under the reign of Kaiser Wilhelm I (1816–64). At the turn of the 20th century it had a population of 175,000. By the beginning of World War I, Stuttgart had reached out to embrace several districts, notably ancient Cannstatt, so that its landmass extended as far as the Neckar River.

In World War II, 53 bombing attacks leveled 60% of Stuttgart's buildings. Not one of its landmarks or historic structures came through intact. After the war, Stuttgart became the capital of the newly formed state of Baden-Württemberg (many still prefer to call it "Swabia"). Stuttgart's population today is about 580,000.

ESSENTIALS

GETTING THERE   By Plane   The **Stuttgart Echterdingen Airport** (☎ **0711/ 948-33-88**) is 14km (9 miles) south of the city near Echterdingen. The airport has connections with most major German and European cities. Trip time from Frankfurt is 50 minutes; from Hamburg or Berlin, 1¼ hours. The commuter train to Stuttgart's main rail station leaves from below the arrival level of Terminal 1. Trains depart every 20 minutes, taking 27 minutes to reach the heart of Stuttgart. A one-way fare is 4.60DM ($2.30). A taxi to the center of the city costs from 40DM ($20).

By Train   Stuttgart has rail links to all major German cities, with frequent connections. The train station is directly north of the historic area. Forty-five daily trains run from Munich (trip time: 2 to 3 hr.), and 30 trains run from Frankfurt (trip time: 1½ to 2 hr.). For information, call ☎ **01805/ 99-66-33.**

By Bus   Long-distance bus service from several major German cities, including Frankfurt, is provided by Europabus Line 1012. Call **Deutsche Touring GmbH** in Stuttgart (☎ **0711/2265881**) or in Frankfurt (☎ **069/7-90-35-0**) for information.

By Car   Access by car is via the A8 Autobahn east and west or the A81 north and south.

VISITOR INFORMATION   Information about transportation, sightseeing, and hotels is available at the **Touristik-Zentrum,** Königstrasse 1A (☎ **0711/ 2-22-82-40**), which is open Monday to Friday 9:30am to 8:30pm and Saturday 9:30am to 6pm. Sunday hours are 11am to 6pm, May to October, and 1 to 6pm, November to April.

GETTING AROUND   Stuttgart has a streamlined bus and streetcar system, as well as a modern U-Bahn, with more lines planned for the future. A 3-day pass, called a *Tageskarte,* costs 20DM ($10). It allows visitors to travel on all city transportation facilities. For information, call ☎ **0711/19449.**

EXPLORING THE CITY

Many of the most remarkable structures in today's Stuttgart are of advanced design, created by such architects as Ludwig Mies van der Rohe, Walter Gropius, Hans Scharoun, and Le Corbusier. The **Liederhalle,** Schloss-Strasse, constructed in 1956 of concrete, glass, and glazed brick, is fascinating inside and out. The hall contains three auditoriums.

The town's older section is clustered around **Schillerplatz** and the statue of the great German poet and dramatist, Schiller. **Neues Schloss,** on Schlossplatz, can be visited only by group tour. It was originally constructed between 1746 and 1807 and rebuilt beginning in 1958. Today it houses state government rooms. The modern **Rathaus** faces the old Marktplatz, where flowers, fruit, and vegetables are sold in open stalls.

For the best view of Stuttgart, climb to the top of the 512m (1,680-foot) **Birkenkopf,** west of the city. The hill was created from the debris of Stuttgart dumped here after World War II. After the 20-minute walk to the top, you'll be rewarded by a view of the city and the surrounding Swabian Hills, covered with vineyards and woods.

A free organized walking tour through historical Stuttgart leaves from the inner courtyard of the Altes Schloss on Schillerplatz on Saturday at 10am, lasting until about 5pm. There's also a bus tour, starting at 1pm and continuing until 3:30pm, which winds its way through the city. The cost is 32DM ($16) for adults and 25DM ($12.50) for children, if they need a seat. For tickets, contact the tourist office (☎ **0711/ 2-22-82-40**).

Fernsehturm (Television Tower). Jahnstrasse 120, Stuttgart-Degerloch, south of the city, just off B3. ☎ **0711/232597.** Admission 5DM ($2.50) adults, 3DM ($1.50) children. Daily 9am–10:30pm. Tram: 15.

This 217m (712-foot) tower, capped with a red-and-white transmitter, soars above a forested hillock south of Stuttgart. It was designed and built in 1956 using radically

Stuttgart

GERMANY

● Stuttgart

ATTRACTIONS ●

Altes Schloss **10**
Liederhalle **1**
Neues Schloss **11**
Rathaus **12**
Staatsgalerie
   (State Gallery
   of Stuttgart) **8**
Staatstheater **9**

ACCOMMODATIONS ■

City Hotel **13**
Hotel Ruff **2**
Hotel am Schlossgarten **7**
Hotel Wörtz-Zur
   Weinsteige **14**
Mack und Pflieger **5**
Park Hotel Stuttgart **6**
Rieker **3**
Steigenberger Hotel
   Graf Zeppelin **4**

Church ✝
Information ⓘ
Post Office

innovative applications of aluminum and pre-stressed reinforced concrete, and served as a prototype for larger towers in Toronto and Moscow. You'll find a restaurant at the tower's base, and a cafe, bar, restaurant, observation platform, and information about the tower's construction at the top of a 150m (492-foot) elevator. Food is served daily 10am to 11pm. Look outside for the mobile platforms used by window washers. Views from the top are panoramic.

Altes Schloss and Württembergisches Landesmuseum. Schillerplatz 6. ☎ 0711/2-79-34-00. Admission 5DM ($2.50) adults, 3DM ($1.50) children. Tues 10am–1pm, Wed–Sun 10am–5pm. U-Bahn: Schlossplatz.

One of Stuttgart's oldest standing structures, this huge ducal palace was originally a moated castle built in the 13th century and was later redone in the 16th century in Renaissance style. Now it houses the Württembergisches Landesmuseum, which traces the art and culture of Swabia from the Stone Age to the present. The most valuable items include a survey of European glass through the ages, the ducal art chamber, and the crown jewels. The museum also houses a large collection of Swabian sculptures; an exhibition of clocks, coins, and musical instruments; the famous treasures of the tomb of the Celtic prince of Hochdorf (ca. A.D. 530); and a large collection from the Merovingian period in the early Middle Ages.

✪ Staatsgalerie (State Gallery of Stuttgart). Konrad-Adenauer-Strasse 30–32. ☎ 0711/2-12-40-50. Admission 9DM ($4.50) adults, free for children 13 and under; special exhibitions 15DM ($7.50) adults, 8DM ($4) students and children. Free admission Wed. Wed and Fri–Sun 10am–6pm, Tues and Thurs 10am–9pm. Open to midnight the first Saturday of each month. U-Bahn: Staatsgalerie.

The city's finest art museum exhibits works spanning some 550 years. However, the best collection is from the 19th and 20th centuries, especially the works of the German expressionists–Kirchner, Barlach, and Beckmann–as well as representatives of the Bauhaus school and Blue Rider group, such as Klee and Feininger. There are also good examples of French art of the 19th and 20th centuries and of the European and American postwar avant-garde.

Mercedes-Benz Museum. Mercedesstrasse 136, Stuttgart-Cannstatt. ☎ 0711/1-72-25-78. Free admission. Tues–Sun 9am–5pm. S-Bahn: 1 to Gottlieb-Daimler-Stadion; then walk to the entrance of the plant, where you'll be taken on a special bus to the museum.

This museum honors the oldest automobile factory in the world and the invention of the motorcar by Carl Benz and Gottlieb Daimler. Nearly 75 historical vehicles are shown, including a Daimler Reitwagen from 1885, the first motor bicycle. You can also see the Daimler company's first Mercedes of 1902. Race cars on display date from 1899, and include the Blitzen-Benz, the Silver Arrow, the Sauber Mercedes, the Indy car, and some vehicles built especially to achieve speed records.

SHOPPING

Home to clothing designers Hugo Boss and Ulli Knecht, Stuttgart has its fair share of boutiques that range from interesting to elegant. **Klett Passage,** located across from the train station, is an underground mall full of upscale shops. If you follow the Königstrasse from the station for about half a mile, you'll likely find anything you want in one of the retail stores that line the street. There are boutiques along the Calwer Strasse, especially in the gleaming chrome-and-glass arcade, **Calwer Passage.** Bargains galore can be found at the Saturday morning **flea market** held on the Karlsplatz between the old castle and the new palace, where clothes, books, furniture, household items, art, and just about anything else is likely to turn up.

The latest styles for men can be found at **Holy's,** Königstrasse 54A (☎ **0711/ 22-29-44-4;** S-Bahn: Hauptbahnhof), which carries the work of local heroes Boss and Knecht as well as other leading international designers, from Prada to Dolce Gabbana. North of the city, **Salamander,** Stammheimerstrasse 10, Kornwestheim (☎ **07154/ 1-50**), has a factory outlet selling shoes for the whole family in styles ranging from fun and functional to more conservative.

Gunter Krauss, Kronprinzstrasse 21 (☎ **0711/29-73-95;** S-Bahn: Stadtmitte), has won numerous design awards for its interior of white marble, mirrors, and gilded fixtures; it houses an impressive array of designer jewelry. In business since 1723, **Tritschler,** Am Marktplatz (☎ **0711/29-15-82;** U-Bahn: Charlottenplatz), stocks glass, porcelain, and fine china as well as cutlery and decorative housewares. **Pavillon,** Eberhardstrasse 31–33 (☎ **0711/24-31-34;** U-Bahn: Rathaus), specializes in silver from the 19th and 20th centuries, and also sells glass, crystal, Meissen porcelain, and a few paintings.

Hans Rehn, Buchsenstrasse 25–31 (☎ **0711/2-26-23-61;** S-Bahn: Stadtmitte), sells German-made pens and stationery, leather wallets, and other small well-made items. A fantasyland of playthings, **Kurtz,** Am Marktplatz 10 (☎ **0711/23-85-20;** U-Bahn: Charlottenplatz), sells puzzles, games, dolls, and toys for children of all ages. The city's largest bookstore, **Wittwer,** Königstrasse 30 (☎ **0711/2-50-70;** S-Bahn: Hauptbahnhof), carries many books in English and has tables placed throughout the store so you can comfortably scan potential purchases. For a bit of everything, head to the city's largest department store, **Breuninger,** Marktstrasse 3 (☎ **0711/21-10;** U-Bahn: Charlottenplatz), where glass elevators whisk you through several floors of housewares, furnishings, and fashion. Take a break for chocolate or gingerbread at **Susi,** Königstrasse 1 (☎ **0711/2-26-41-15;** S-Bahn: Hauptbahnhof), and you'll feel well rewarded no matter how the shopping is going.

WHERE TO STAY

No matter when you come to Stuttgart, you'll probably find an international trade fair in progress, from the January glass-and-ceramics exposition to the December book exhibition. (Stuttgart is also southern Germany's most important publishing center.) Good accommodations may be difficult to find at almost any time, so you should reserve in advance.

EXPENSIVE

Hotel am Schlossgarten. Schillerstrasse 23, 70173 Stuttgart, on the Hauptbahnhof square. ☎ **0711/2-02-60.** Fax 0711/2-02-68-88. E-mail: ssschlossgarten@t-online.de. 116 units. MINIBAR TV TEL. 430DM–510DM ($215–$255) double; from 540DM ($270) suite. AE, DC, MC, V. Parking 21DM ($10.50). U-Bahn: Hauptbahnhof.

This tasteful 10-floor hotel isn't splashy, but it offers very good conveniences and comfort. Rooms are good-sized and well furnished, with satellite TVs, hair dryers, and feather comforters.

Dining/Diversions: The bar is warm and cozy, but even more intimate is the Zirbelstube, with knotty-pine walls and birch armchairs. More formal and elegant is the Restaurant Schlossgarten. Both serve the same menu of German and Swabian dishes.

Amenities: Room service, laundry, dry cleaning, Jacuzzi, sauna, terrace garden, conference facilities.

✪ **Steigenberger Hotel Graf Zeppelin.** Arnulf-Klett-Platz 7, 70173 Stuttgart. ☎ **800/223-5652** in the U.S. and Canada, or 0711/2-04-80. Fax 0711/2-04-85-42. www.steigenberger.com. 195 units. A/C MINIBAR TV TEL. 380DM–460DM ($190–$230) double; 660DM–760DM ($330–$380) suite. AE, DC, MC, V. Parking 25DM ($12.50). U-Bahn: Hauptbahnhof.

This is the best hotel for those who come to wheel and deal with Stuttgart business-people. Although situated right at the train station, it's not only attractive but also dignified and stylish, once you get by its plain postwar exterior. The spacious soundproof rooms are colorfully decorated.

Dining/Diversions: Guests congregate in the Zeppelin-Bar. Restaurant Graf Zeppelin features a lunch buffet, the Zeppelin-Stüble serves Swabian dishes, the Maukenescht is the wine bar, and the ZEPP 7 bistro-cafe has a fish menu only. The Gourmet Restaurant has the best and most expensive cuisine.

Amenities: Room service, laundry, dry cleaning, hair dryer in room, Jacuzzi, men-only beauty salon, sauna, indoor pool with wood-paneled waterside lounge.

MODERATE

City Hotel. Uhlandstrasse 18, 70182 Stuttgart, directly west of Charlottenplatz. ☎ **0711/ 21-08-10.** Fax 0711/2-36-97-72. 31 units. MINIBAR TV TEL. 185DM–220DM ($92.50–$110) double. Rates include buffet breakfast. AE, DC, MC, V. Free parking. U-Bahn: Olgaeck.

The City is a renovated bed-and-breakfast-type hotel, within walking distance of the sights in the city center. It offers pleasantly furnished but hardly spectacular rooms equipped with private showers (no tubs), radios, hair dryers, and direct-dial telephones. The generous breakfast buffet, the only meal served, is offered in a sunny winter garden.

Hotel Ruff. Friedhofstrasse 21, 70191 Stuttgart. ☎ **0711/2-58-70.** Fax 0711/2-58-87-404. E-mail: rema-ruff@t-online.de. 90 units. MINIBAR TV TEL. 200DM–390DM ($100–$195) double. Rates include buffet breakfast. AE, DC, MC, V. Parking 15DM ($7.50). U-Bahn: Turlenstrasse/ Burgerhospital.

This hotel, although not as centrally located as the City Hotel, has a lot more style and better rooms. Other side benefits are an attractively tiled indoor pool with a sauna and a manicured garden where a waiter will take your drink order. Rooms are well maintained and inviting, and a good value for the price. Most are medium in size, although some are quite small. The attractive dining room serves both Swabian and international food.

Park Hotel Stuttgart. Villastrasse 21, 70190 Stuttgart. ☎ **0711/2-80-10.** Fax 0711/2-86-43-53. www.parkhotel-stuttgart.de. 69 units. MINIBAR TV TEL. 240DM ($120) double; 260DM ($130) suite. Rates include buffet breakfast. AE, DC, MC, V. Parking 12DM ($6). Tram: 1, 2, or 14.

If you're looking for a first-class accommodation in a secluded and quiet area, this is your place. It's outside the center in the gardens of the Villa Berg, within walking distance of a mineral-water pool surrounded by a park. Rooms are good-sized, well designed, and have a decidedly personal air. Amenities include hair dryers, room service, laundry, and dry cleaning services. There are two on-site restaurants. The Villa Berg serves a German/international menu in a colorful setting. The less-formal and less expensive Radio-Stüble offers Swabian dishes.

INEXPENSIVE

Hotel Wörtz-Zur Weinsteige. Hohenheimerstrasse 28–30, 70184 Stuttgart. ☎ **0711/ 2-36-70-00.** Fax 0711/2-36-70-07. www.hotel-woertz.de. E-mail: hotelwoertz@t-online.de. 25 units, 22 with bath or shower. TV TEL. 130DM ($65) double without bath or shower, 160DM–300DM ($80–$150) double with bath or shower. Rates include buffet breakfast. AE, DC, MC, V. Parking 10DM ($5). S-Bahn: Dobelstrasse.

The amber lights of a Weinstube welcome visitors to this local favorite in Stuttgart, which has the best rooms and the best food of all local hotels in this price range. The small rooms are paneled and sometimes have massive hand-carved armoires; all are soundproof. The Weinstube evokes the feeling of a remote corner of Swabia—it's perfect for relaxing after a long trip. The hotel is known for its garden terrace. See our recommendation of the restaurant in "Where to Dine," below.

Rieker. Friedrichstrasse 3, 70174 Stuttgart. ☎ **0711/22-13-11.** Fax 0711/29-38-94. www.hotel-rieker.de. E-mail: info@hotel-Rieker.de. 63 units. TV TEL. 198DM–258DM ($99–$129) double. Rates include breakfast. AE, DC, MC, V. Parking 15DM ($7.50). U-Bahn: Hauptbahnhof.

This well-furnished hotel offers a convenient location and a certain charm. Its public areas have lots of comfortably upholstered armchairs and Oriental rugs scattered over parquet or terrazzo floors. Some of the virtually soundproof rooms are designed with sleeping alcoves and draw curtains. It's only a 1-minute walk from Stuttgart's Municipal Air Terminal, where buses leave frequently for Echterdingen Airport. Amenities include a concierge, hair dryers, dry cleaning, laundry service, a car-rental desk, and a tour desk.

Mack und Pflieger. Kriegerstrasse 7–11, 70191 Stuttgart, an 8-min. walk from the Hauptbahnhof. ☎ **0711/29-19-27.** Fax 0711/29-34-89. 40 units, 25 with bath or shower. TV TEL. 170DM–240DM ($85–$120) double with bath or shower. Rates include buffet breakfast. AE, DC, MC, V. Free parking. U-Bahn: Hauptbahnhof.

This hotel, behind an uninspired modern facade, is actually two in one. Hotel Mack and Hotel Pflieger stand close to each other and are under the same management. Check in at the Mack, since there's always someone there at the reception desk. Homelike and cozy, the hotel offers up-to-date rooms that are small and basic but still quite adequate. The least expensive are singles without bath or shower.

WHERE TO DINE
EXPENSIVE

✪ **Délice.** Hauptstätter Strasse 61. ☎ **0711/6-40-32-22.** Reservations recommended. Main courses 47DM–63DM ($23.50–$31.50); fixed-price menu 130DM ($65). Mon–Fri 6:30pm–midnight. No credit cards. Closed 2 weeks in June. U-Bahn: Österreichischer Platz. AUSTRIAN/INTERNATIONAL.

A 200-year-old vaulted ceiling arches over the tables of this sophisticated cellar-level restaurant. This icon of *neue Küche* is a showcase for the cuisine of Vienna-born Friedrich Gutscher, whose alchemy in the kitchen can be observed from some of the tables. The menu changes virtually every week. Starters might include a summer version of cream of cucumber soup, or its midwinter counterpart, consommé of pigeon with truffles. A succulent main course might be a fillet of Brittany sea wolf marinated in lemon juice and olive oil and served with a salad of warm asparagus and exotic mushrooms. A nougat truffle, or a traditional Austrian treat called *Topfenknoedel* (a cottage cheese dumpling) are excellent desserts. The wine list is almost overwhelming, with selections from virtually every wine-producing region in Europe.

MODERATE

Alte Kanzlei. Schillerplatz 5A. ☎ **0711/29-44-57.** Reservations recommended. Main courses 15DM–36DM ($7.50–$18). AE, DC, MC, V. Daily 11am–11pm. U-Bahn: Schlossplatz. SWABIAN/INTERNATIONAL.

This popular folkloric restaurant is in the section of the old castle (Altes Schloss) originally built in 1533. One of the most popular Swabian specialties is *Maultaschen,* the Stuttgart version of ravioli, stuffed with ham or spinach. Equally popular is *Stuttgarter Ratsherrenteller,* fillet of pork and beef served with *spätzle* (dumplings), fresh vegetables, and mushroom gravy. To accompany your meal, ask for the local Pils beer or some of the region's fine wines, such as the pale rosé known as Tuniberg or one of the full-bodied red wines made from the Trollinger grape.

Zeppelin-Stüble. In the Steigenberger Hotel Graf Zeppelin, Arnulf-Klett-Platz 7. ☎ **0711/ 20-48-184.** Fax 0711/2048-542. Reservations recommended. Main courses 16.80DM–36DM ($8.40–$18); fixed-price menus 49DM–77DM ($24.50–$38.50). AE, DC, MC, V. Mon–Fri 11:30am–2:30pm and 6–11:30pm. U-Bahn: Hauptbahnhof. SWABIAN.

In this elegantly appointed restaurant furnished with Swabian antiques, each dish is individually prepared from fresh ingredients, according to the season. Swabian specialties like *Rostbraten* (roast beef) and *Maultaschen* (Stuttgart's version of ravioli) are offered. Although many restaurants in Stuttgart have abandoned true Swabian cuisine for more international fare, the chefs here still turn out the old-fashioned specialties preferred by locals. The kitchen does an excellent *Schwäbischer* sauerbraten with spätzle and salad.

Zur Weinsteige. In the Hotel Wörtz, Hohenheimerstrasse 30. ☎ **0711/2-36-70-00.** Fax 0711/2367007. Reservations recommended. Main courses 15DM–46DM ($7.50–$23); business lunch 18DM ($9); fixed-price menus 46DM–160DM ($23–$80). AE, CB, DC, MC, V. Tues–Sat noon–2pm and 6–10pm. Closed holidays, 3 weeks in Jan, and 3 weeks in Aug. S-Bahn: Dobelstrasse. INTERNATIONAL.

The interior of this place is a celebration of German handcrafts. Everything looks handmade, from the hand-blown leaded glass in the small-paned windows to the carved columns and tables and chairs. International cuisine, with numerous Swabian specialties, is offered. In summer, you'll be tempted to sit among the grapevines stretching over the sun terrace. Also worth seeing is the wine cellar, well stocked with the best regional wines and a good selection of German and international wines. You can even buy wine directly from the hotel's vineyards. Next to the cellar is a room for sitting and tasting.

STUTTGART AFTER DARK

Listings of the various cultural events as well as tickets are available from the tourist office (see above). The magazine *Lift,* available at newsstands, lists all the happenings around Stuttgart.

THE PERFORMING ARTS Staatstheater, Oberer Schlossgarten (☎ 0711/ 20-20-90; S-Bahn: Hauptbahnhof), is the leading cultural venue in Stuttgart. The theater consists of a Grosses Haus for opera and ballet, a Kleines Haus for theater, and the Kammer-theater, which puts on experimental works. This is home to the world-class **Stuttgart Ballet,** established by the American choreographer John Cranko in the 1960s, and now led by Reid Anderson. It also houses the respected **Staatsoper (State Opera).** Tickets are 16DM to 140DM ($8 to $70), and can be purchased at the Staatstheater box office. Closed August and September.

Classical and other concerts may be heard in the three halls of the **Liederhalle,** Schloss-Strasse (☎ 0711/2167110; U-Bahn: Liederhalle/Berlinerplatz), which is home to the **Stuttgarter Philharmoniker,** under the baton of Jörg Peter Weigle, and the **Radio Symphony Orchestra.** Tickets for all concerts are on sale at **SKS Russ,** Charlottenplatz 17 (☎ 0711/1635321; U-Bahn: Charlottenplatz). Prices are 15DM to 40DM ($7.50 to $20).

THE BAR, CAFE & CLUB SCENE You might start your evening with a drink at **Amadeus,** Charlottenplatz 17 (☎ 0711/29-26-78; U-Bahn: Charlottenplatz), where students and locals gather. It's open 11am to 2am Monday and Tuesday, 11am to 3am Wednesday and Thursday, and 11am to 4am Friday and Saturday. For a trendier locale, head to **Palast der Republik,** Friedrichstrasse 27 (☎ 0711/2-26-48-87;

U-Bahn: Keplerstrasse), a 100-year-old bar that attracts an artsier crowd. DJs play funk and soul. It's open Monday to Wednesday 11am to 2am, and Thursday to Saturday 11am to 3am.

Café Stella, Hauptstätter Strasse 57 (☎ **0711/6-40-25-83;** U-Bahn: Österreichischerplatz), hosts local jazz bands on the first Monday of the month. It's open Monday to Thursday 9am until 1am.

Gay men dance at **King's Club,** Calverstrasse 21 (☎ **0711/2-26-45-58;** S-Bahn: Stadtmitte), until Sunday, when they're booted for a women-only night. The club is open Wednesday to Sunday 10pm to 6am, with a 10DM ($5) cover Friday and a 15DM ($7.50) cover Saturday, including two drinks. **Laura's Club,** Rotebühlplatz 4 (☎ **0711/29-01-60;** S-Bahn: Stadtmitte), is a lesbian and gay bar with a dance floor. It's open Thursday to Sunday 10pm to 5am. There's no cover.

4 Tübingen

47km (29 miles) S of Stuttgart, 153km (95 miles) NE of Freiburg

Though it's often compared to Heidelberg, this quiet old university town on the upper Neckar has a look and personality all its own. Gabled medieval houses are crowded against the ancient town wall at the bank of the river. In summer, the only movement that disturbs this peaceful picture is from the students, who pole gondola-like boats up and down the river. This far upstream, the Neckar is too shallow for commercial vessels, so Tübingen has been spared the industrial look of a trading community.

Progress has not passed the city by, however. In spite of its medieval aspect, it has a new residential and science suburb in the shadow of the Schoenbuch Forest north of the city, with medical facilities, research institutes, and lecture halls affiliated with the university. The buildings of the old university, founded in 1477, are located north of the botanical gardens. The humanist Melanchthon taught here in the 16th century, and later on Schiller, Hegel, and Hölderlin were students.

ESSENTIALS

GETTING THERE   By Air   The nearest major airport, at Stuttgart (see above), has good connections to Tübingen, including a direct bus link.

By Train   The Stuttgart–Tübingen rail line offers frequent service. Tübingen also has good rail ties to other major cities in Germany, including Frankfurt (trip time: $3^1/2$ hr.), Berlin (trip time: 11 hr.), and Hamburg (trip time: $8^1/2$ hr.). For information, call ☎ **01805/99-66-33.**

By Bus   Long-distance buses link Tübingen with major German cities, like Stuttgart. For information, call **Deutsche Touring GmbH** in Frankfurt (☎ **069/23-07-35**) or in Stuttgart (☎ **0711/226588**).

By Car   Access is via Route 27 west from the A8 Autobahn running east and west or Route 28 east from the A81 Autobahn running north and south.

VISITOR INFORMATION   Contact the **Verkehrsverein,** An der Eberhardsbrücke (☎ **07071/9-13-60**), open Monday to Friday 9am to 7pm and Saturday 9am to 5pm.

SEEING THE SIGHTS

An unusual feature of Tübingen is an artificial island in the Neckar. Through it runs a promenade, known as **Platanenallee,** always alive with summer strollers who cross over to the island via the wide Eberhardsbrücke. From there, you get a panoramic view of the town, with its willows and houses reflected in the river. Towering above the other buildings is the Renaissance castle, which is now used by the university. It's worth climbing up to the castle for the dramatic view from the terraces.

The narrow streets of the Altstadt wind up and down the hillside, but they all seem to lead to **Marktplatz,** where festive markets are held on Monday, Wednesday, and Friday. You'll feel as if you're stepping into the past when you come upon the scene of country people selling fruit and vegetables in the open square. In the center of all this activity stands the softly murmuring Renaissance fountain of the god Neptune. Facing the square is the **Rathaus,** which dates from the 15th century but also has more recent additions, including the 19th-century painted designs on the facade.

On a hillside above Marktplatz is **Stiftskirche,** Holzmarkt, the former church of the Stift, an Augustinian monastery. The monastery became a Protestant seminary in 1548, and its church became the Collegiate Church. Worth seeing inside are the tombs of the dukes of Württemberg in the chancel and the 15th-century French Gothic pulpit and rood screen. The church is open daily 9am to 5pm. You can climb the tower (entrance on the left of the chancel) for a panoramic view. The chancel and tower are open April to November daily 10:30am to 5pm. Admission to the tower is 3DM ($1.50) for adults and 2DM ($1) for children.

Hölderlinturm, Bursagasse 6 (☎ **07071/2-20-40**), lies at the end of a walk by the Neckar River. This was the home of the lyric poet, Friedrich Hölderlin, who resided here with the Zimmer family from the onset of his mental illness at age 36 until his death in 1843. Hölderlin is not well known outside Germany, but we highly recommend that you read a few of his poems in translation. Most tours of the museum are in German, but you can request one in English; otherwise you won't understand many of the exhibits. The house is open Tuesday to Friday 10am to noon and 3 to 5pm; Saturday and Sunday 2 to 5pm. Admission is 3DM ($1.50) adults, 2DM ($1) children and students.

WHERE TO STAY

Hotel am Bad. Am Freibad 2, 72072 Tübingen. ☎ **07071/79740.** Fax 07071/7-53-36. 35 units. MINIBAR TV TEL. 154DM–176DM ($77–$88) double. Rates include buffet breakfast. AE, MC, V. Closed Dec 10–Jan 10. Free outdoor parking; 7DM ($3.50) in garage.

This hotel, located in the center of one of Tübingen's well-maintained public parks, offers woodland calm not far from the city center. Its rambling rose-colored exterior complements the masses of red flowers on the sun terrace. Rooms are modest and a bit small but still comfortable. The hotel has one bar and one restaurant, specializing in Bavarian food. There's also an Olympic-size pool practically at its back door.

Krone Hotel. Uhlandstrasse, 72072 Tübingen. ☎ **07071/1-33-10.** Fax 07071/13-31-32. www.krone-tuebingen.de. E-mail: info@krone-tuebingen.de. 50 units. TV TEL. 200DM–310DM ($100–$155) double; from 310DM–370DM ($155–$185) suite. Rates include buffet breakfast. AE, DC, MC, V. Closed Dec 23–31. Free parking.

The town's most prestigious hotel is located right off the river, in the heart of Tübingen. It's traditional and conservative, with a homelike atmosphere. The decor includes a liberal use of antiques or good reproductions. Rooms are personalized; many are decoratively tiled.

The owners, Karl and Erika Schlagenhauff, provide some of the best meals in town (recommended even if you're not staying here). There are three dining rooms: the formal dining salon; the Uhlandstube, with an old tavern atmosphere; and a country-style room—all served by one kitchen. The menu is international; typical dishes include fillet of sole in butter, Wiener schnitzel, and tournedos Rossini. Service is daily noon to 2:15pm and 6 to 10:30pm.

WHERE TO DINE

In addition to the restaurants below, the **Krone Hotel** (see above) is a good dining spot.

Restaurant Museum. Wilhelmstrasse. ☎ **07071/2-28-28.** Reservations recommended. Main courses 18DM–42DM ($9–$21). AE, MC, V. Daily 11:30am–2:30pm; Tues–Sun 6:30pm–11:30pm. INTERNATIONAL/SWABIAN.

This is one of Tübingen's foremost restaurants. It's a pleasant place to dine on international specialties, such as Marseille snail soup, or regional dishes, such as Swabian medallions of veal. The lunches here are considered by many locals (including students) to be not only the best in town but also the best value.

Restaurant Rosenau. Beim Neuen Botanischen Garten. ☎ **07071/6-88-66.** Reservations recommended. Main courses 29DM–42DM ($14.50–$21). AE, DC, MC, V. Tues–Sun 11am–midnight. GERMAN/SWABIAN.

This restaurant, near the botanical gardens, has the finest food in the town center, though it's not as good as at the Gasthof Waldhorn (see below), on the outskirts. Landgasthof Rosenau is like a roadhouse with a cafe annex. The owner serves superb Swabian specialties along with modern cuisine. The typical regional fare is listed under the gutbürgerlich selections. Try the tasty and filling Swabian hot pot with spätzle (dumplings) and fresh mushrooms. From the section of the menu "reserved for gourmets," you might choose a delectable veal steak with morels. Desserts are often elaborate concoctions. In fair weather, guests can order drinks out in the sun.

NEARBY DINING

✪ **Gasthof Waldhorn.** Schönbuchstrasse 49, 6km (4 miles) from the town center. ☎ **07071/6-12-70.** Reservations required. Main courses 47DM–58DM ($23.50–$29); business lunch 98DM ($49); fixed price dinners 95DM–160DM ($47.50–$80). AE. Wed–Sun noon–2:30pm and 6:30pm–midnight. Closed Aug 18–30. GERMAN/FRENCH.

The finest restaurant in the area is not in Tübingen but on its outskirts, at Tübingen-Bebenhausen. It's decorated like a farmhouse. Herr and Frau Schilling offer a light German and French cuisine based on regional ingredients, backed up by an impressive wine list (with many half bottles). This restaurant truly deserves its star. The chef combines inventiveness with a solid technique. The menu changes daily but is likely to include trout terrine and wild venison with forest mushrooms, along with whatever vegetable is in season. The dessert specialty is a soft cream concoction flavored with rose hips. Behind the house is a garden with five tables for summer dining.

TÜBINGEN AFTER DARK

Student-inspired nightlife makes this old town very young at heart. Just head into the Marktplatz at night and follow the sound of revelry. You can order a beer and read the comics hanging on the walls of **Marktschenke,** Am Markt 11 (☎ 07071/2-20-35), then join the students spilling outside into the square. Daily hours are 9am to 1am. Or you might start your evening in the ancient **Boulanger,** Collegiumsgasse 2 (☎ 07071/2-33-45), where you could offer to pick up Hegel's bar tab, which has gone unpaid for more than 200 years. A riverside retreat, **Neckarmüller,** Gartenstrasse 4 (☎ 07071/2-78-48), has a barroom, but more inviting in nice weather are the picnic tables on the banks of the river. It's open daily 11am to 1am. Also on the Neckar, **Ammerschlag,** Ammergasse 13 (☎ 07071/5-15-91), has live music one Sunday a month, ranging from blues to rap. Hours are daily 3pm until 1am.

Located next to the Stiftskirche steps, **Tangente-Night** (☎ 07071/2-30-07) is a place to dance to techno, acid jazz, and house at night. It's open daily 11am until 3am.

Dancing is also top priority at **Zentrum Zoo,** Schleifmuhleweg 86 (☎ **07071/ 9-44-80**), open Tuesday and Thursday to Saturday 9pm until 2am; Sunday 8:30pm to 1am. Cover is 6DM ($3).

5 Schwäbisch Hall

97km (60 miles) NE of Stuttgart, 138km (86 miles) W of Nürnberg

Technically, this medieval town is not in the Neckar Valley; however, if you skip it in your travels through this region, you'll have missed one of the treasures of south-western Germany. Schwäbisch Hall is located in the heart of the forests of the Schwäbische Alb, where it clings to the steep banks of the Kocher River, a tributary of the Neckar. The houses of the Altstadt are set on terraces built into the hillside; from the opposite bank they appear to be arranged in steps, overlooking the old wooden river bridges.

ESSENTIALS

GETTING THERE **By Train** Trains run daily from Stuttgart and Nürnberg into the Bahnhof Schwäbisch Hall. For information call ☎ **01805/99-66-33.**

By Bus Regional bus service in the area is offered by **Stuttgart GmbH** (☎ **07131/ 6-24-50**) for schedules and information.

By Car Access is via the A6 Autobahn running east and west, or Route 14 from the east and Route 19 from the north.

VISITOR INFORMATION The **Verkehrsverein** is at Am Markt 9 (☎ **0791/ 75-12-46**). Open October to April, Monday to Friday 9am to 5pm; May to September, Monday to Friday 9am to 6pm and Saturday 10am to 3pm.

SEEING THE SIGHTS

Marktplatz is perhaps the most attractive market square in all of Germany. Flanking the sloping square are fine half-timbered patrician houses, and at the lower end stands the baroque Rathaus. In the center of the square is a 16th-century Gothic fountain adorned with statues of St. Michael with St. George and Samson. The Marktplatz is the scene of festive occasions, such as the annual Kuchenfest, celebrating the ancient salt industry that grew around the salt springs in Schwäbisch Hall.

On the north side of Marktplatz, facing the Rathaus, are 54 large, imposing, deli-cately curved stone steps leading to **Michaelskirche.** This cathedral is a 15th-century Gothic Hallenkirche with a 12th-century tower. Many pews date from the 15th cen-tury, as does St. Michael's altarpiece in the side chapel. The church is open Monday 2 to 5pm, Tuesday to Saturday 9am to noon and 2 to 5pm, and Sunday 11am to noon and 2 to 5pm.

WHERE TO STAY & DINE

Der Adelshof. Am Markt 12 (on Marktplatz), 74523 Schwäbisch Hall. ☎ **0791/7-58-90.** Fax 0791/60-36. www.interamerica.com. E-mail: hotel.adelshof@t-online.de. 47 units. TV TEL. 205DM ($102.50) double; 480DM ($240) suite. Rates include breakfast. AE, DC, MC, V. Free parking.

The Adelshof is in an attractive stone building, much of it dating from 1400. Its advantage is its location, right in the center of town. Rooms are clean and comfort-able, if a bit small. The hotel also contains a small fitness room, with sauna and solar-ium available for an extra charge. Downstairs, the restaurant, open Tuesday to Sunday evenings, serves some of the best food in town. The recently refurbished, 500-year-old Kellerbar has become one of the town's most popular bars; it's open daily 7pm to 3am.

Hotel Hohenlohe. Am Weilertor 14, 74523 Schwäbisch Hall. ☎ **0791/7-58-70.** Fax 0791/75-87-84. www.ringhotels.de. E-mail: hotelhohenlohe@t-online.de. 113 units. MINIBAR TV TEL. 218DM–268DM ($130.80–$160.80) double; 298DM–470DM ($149–$235) suite. Rates include buffet breakfast. AE, DC, MC, V. Parking 10DM ($5) inside and free outside.

The Hohenlohe is on the left bank of the Kocher River, in the historic Freie Reichsstadt district opposite the town center. Rooms are pleasant and compact, with bright color accents. Many have good views. Breakfast is served on an open-view roof deck. The restaurant offers regional meals; a cafeteria and a bar are also on the premises. Other facilities include two indoor pools and a saltwater outdoor pool, a sauna, a solarium, a bowling alley, and a massage parlor.

A NEARBY PLACE TO STAY & DINE

✪ **Wald und Schlosshotel Friedrichsruhe.** 74639 Friedrichsruhe-Zweiflingen. ☎ **07941/ 6-08-70.** Fax 07941/6-14-68. www.friedrichsruhe.de. E-mail: schlosshotelfriedrichsruhe@ t-online.de. 45 units. TEL. 295DM–420DM ($147.50–$210) double; 490DM–690DM ($245– $345) suite. Rates include continental breakfast. AE, CB, DC, MC, V. Parking 15DM ($7.50). Take a train from Schwäbisch Hall to Öhringen; then take either a taxi, or a bus marked ZWEIFLINGEN.

This hotel is about 27km (17 miles) from Schwäbisch Hall on the Hohenlohe plateau, about 6km (4 miles) north of the little village of Öhringen. One of the hotel's three buildings was constructed between 1712 and 1719 as a three-story hunting lodge. A second building, added in 1953, about a 3-minute walk from the original lodge, was designed to look old, but inside rooms are modern, with up-to-date conveniences, such as hair dryers. Some have a TV and minibar. There are saunas, a heated indoor pool, a jogging track, an outdoor pool, and tennis courts.

This establishment's restaurant facilities are excellent. The more formal choice is The Restaurant, where red walls, white damask napery, and brass chandeliers provide the setting for elegant cuisine. À la carte meals begin at around 50DM ($25). Less formal (and less expensive) is the richly atmospheric Jägerstube, with a regional decor of mounted antlers, carved-back chairs, and an old porcelain stove.

12 Frankfurt

The thriving industrial metropolis of Frankfurt, Germany's fifth-largest city, may well be your first glimpse of Germany. Most international flights land here at Frankfurt's huge airport, and its massive 19th-century railway station is the busiest in Europe.

Frankfurt is a heavily industrial city, with more than 2,450 factories operating around the ford (*Furt*) on the Main River, where the Frankish tribes once settled. As the home of the Bundesbank, Germany's central bank, Frankfurt is also the country's financial center. It's been a major banking city ever since the Rothschilds opened their first bank here in 1798. Frankfurt also has a leading stock exchange.

Frankfurt's international trade fairs in spring and autumn bring some 1.2 million visitors to the city and its *Messengelände* (fairgrounds), often causing a logjam at hotels. Fairs include the Motor Show, the Textile Fair, the Chemical Industries Fair, and the Cookery Fair. But the best known is the International Book Fair, which draws some 5,500 publishers from nearly 100 countries and is the most important meeting place in the world for the acquisition and sale of book rights and translations.

1 Orientation

ARRIVING

BY PLANE **Flughafen Frankfurt/Main** (☎ **069/69-01**) lies 11km (7 miles) from the city center at the Frankfurter Kreuz, the intersection of two major expressways, A3 and A5. This airport, continental Europe's busiest, serves more than 240 destinations in about 110 countries worldwide, including many American cities. It's Germany's major international gateway. All important German airports can be reached via Frankfurt. Flying time from Frankfurt to Berlin and Hamburg is 70 minutes, and to Munich, 60 minutes.

At the Airport Train Station beneath Terminal 1, you can connect to German InterCity trains and S-Bahn commuter trains to Frankfurt and nearby cities. Terminal 2 is linked to Terminal 1 by a people-mover system, Sky Line, which provides quick transfers (the airport's standard connection time is 45 min. maximum).

Train information is available at the **German DB Travel Center** (☎ **01805/99-66-33**). **S-Bahn** line S-8 between the airport and Frankfurt center runs every 10 minutes and deposits passengers at the main rail station in 11 to 15 minutes. A one-way ticket costs 5.80DM ($2.90); tickets should be purchased before boarding.

BY TRAIN   Frankfurt's main rail station, the **Hauptbahnhof,** the busiest in Europe, is the arrival point for some 1,600 trains per day carrying about 255,000 passengers. A train arrives from most major cities of Germany every hour until 8pm. Many other European cities also have direct rail links with Frankfurt. For travel information, ticket reservations, and seat information, call **Deutsche Bahn** (☎ **01805/99-66-33**).

BY BUS   Frankfurt has long-distance bus service to about 800 German and European cities. Buses depart from the south side of the Hauptbahnhof. For information, contact **Deutsche Touring,** Am Römerhof 17 (☎ **069/230735**).

BY CAR   The A3 and A5 Autobahns intersect at Frankfurt. The A3 comes in from the Netherlands, Cologne, and Bonn, and continues east and south to Würzburg, Nürnberg, and Munich. The A5 comes from the northeast (Hannover, Bad Hersfeld) and continues south to Heidelberg, Mannheim, and Basel (Switzerland). From the west, the A60 connects with the A66, which leads to Frankfurt and the inner city, hooking up with the A3. Road signs and directions are frequently posted.

VISITOR INFORMATION

The **tourist office** is in two locations: the Hauptbahnhof, opposite the main entrance (☎ **069/21-23-88-49**), and in Römer (☎ **069/21-23-87-08**). Both branches open Monday to Friday 8am to 9pm and on the weekends 9am to 6pm. **Amerika Haus** is an American cultural institute at Staufenstrasse 1 (☎ **069/9-71-44-80**).

CITY LAYOUT

The Hauptbahnhof, at the western edge of the center of town, opens onto a large street called **Am Hauptbahnhof.** As you walk out of the station, Düsseldorferstrasse will be on your left and Baselerstrasse on your right, heading south toward the Main River. You have a choice of three streets heading east to the center of the **Altstadt** (old town): Taunusstrasse, Kaiserstrasse, and Münchner Strasse. Münchner Strasse leads directly into **Theaterplatz,** with its opera house. Taunusstrasse leads to three of the major Altstadt squares in the southern part of the city: **Goetheplatz, Rathenauplatz,** and (most important) the **Hauptwache,** with its U-Bahn connections. In this section of Frankfurt, along Kaiserstrasse, some of the best shops are found; major attractions, including Goethe-Haus, are also nearby.

The **Main River** flows slightly south of the Altstadt. Many bridges, including the Alte Brücke and the Obermainbrücke, cross this important waterway. On the south bank of the Main is a popular district, **Alt-Sachsenhausen,** center of the apple-wine taverns (more about them later). For other major attractions, you'll have to branch out, heading east to the Frankfurt Zoo or northwest to the Palmengarten (both easily reached by public transportation).

STREET MAPS   Arm yourself with a detailed street map, not the general overview handed out by the tourist office. Maps are sold at most bookstores and news kiosks. See "Bookstores" in "Fast Facts: Frankfurt," below.

2 Getting Around

BY PUBLIC TRANSPORTATION

Frankfurt is linked by a network of fast, modern subways, trams, and buses, all of which are administered by the **RMV (Rhein-Main Verkehrsverbund),** Mannheimer Strasse 15 (☎ **069/27-30-70**). All methods of public transport can be used within their respective fare zones at a single price, which includes transfers between any of them. Tickets are purchased at green, coin-operated automatic machines (*Fahrscheine*) that are lined up adjacent to each of the points of departure. The machines accept all

Frankfurt

Miquel allee — MIQ./ADICKESALLEE — Adickes allee

Franz Rücker allee

Grüneburg Park

Hansa alle

Eysseneckstraße — Cron-stettenstr

Holzhousenstr.

HOLZHAUSENSTRAßE

Leipziger Str.

Falkstrasse

1

Miquel allee

Bremer Straße

Wolfgangstr.

Baustraße

Grüneburgweg

Fürstenbergerstr.

5

Wolfsgangstr.

6

7

Grüneburgweg

GRÜNEBURGWEG

3

Siesmayer str.

Feldburgstr.

Freidburgstr.

2

University

Senckenbergani

Bockenheimer Landstraße

West End

8

Staufenstr.

Gärtnerweg

ESCHENHEIMER TOR

Schumannstr.

Beethovenstr.

4

Rothschild's Park

9

Bockenheimer Anl.

13

Mendelssohnstr.

12

10

Lindenstr.

Bockenheimer

16

17

Hochstr.

18

11

Arndtstr.

Guiollett str.

HAUPTWACHE

14

TAUNUSANLANGE

15

Gr. Bockenheimerstr.

19

Junhof str.

Haupt-Güterbahnhof

Neue Mainzer

20

Berliner str.

21

22

Westendstraße

Untermainbr.

THEATERPLATZ

HAUPTBAHNHOF

Taunus str.

Kaiserstr.

Munchen str.

23

Mainzer Land str.

30

29

Leuschner str.

24

26

25

Schweizer Pl.

31

Untermain kai

Main

27

Oppenheimer

Gutleut straße

Schaumainkai

28

Friedensbrücke

Gutleutveritel

Kennedy allee

Güterbahnhof

32

S-Bahn ——
U-Bahn Station

33

34

ATTRACTIONS ●
Alte Oper **16**
Deutsches
 Architekturmuseum **26**
Deutsches Filmmuseum **24**
Dom St. Bartholomäus **42**
Goethe-Haus **20**
Liebieghaus **28**
Museum für
 Kunsthandwerk **23**
Museum für Moderne
 Kunst **40**
Palmengarten **3**
Römer **22**
Städel Gallery **27**

ACCOMMODATIONS ■
Admiral **37**
Am Zoo **36**
An Der Messe **13**
Arabella Sheraton Grand
 Hotel **38**
Continental **31**
Diana **10**
Falk Hotel **1**
Frankfurt Savoy Hotel **29**
Hotel Hessischer Hof **14**
Hotel Palmenhof **4**
Hotel Robert Mayer **2**
Hotel Westend **12**
Hotelschiff Peter Schlott **32**
Kempinski Hotel Gravenbruch
 Frankfurt **48**
Le Meridien Parkhotel **30**
Mozart **6**
Steigenberger Frankfurter
 Hof **21**

DINING ◆
Altes Zollhaus **35**
Avocado Bistro **17**
Bistrot 77 **33**
Café Laumer **9**
Churrasco **43**
Die Gans in
 Sachsenhausen **34**
Erno's Bistro **8**
Gargantua **5**
Germania **47**
Humperdinck **7**
Jaspers **46**
Jewel of India **11**
Mövenpick am
 Opernplatz **15**
Peninsula **39**
Steinernes Haus **41**
Weinhaus Brückenkeller **44**
Zum Bitburger **18**
Zum Gemalten Haus **25**
Zum Grauen Bock **45**
Zur Hauptwache **19**

denominations of coins, and bills up to 50DM, but be alert that any change you receive will be in coins, so try to use the smallest bills possible. A 24-hour ticket, good for unlimited travel inside Frankfurt's central zone, costs 8DM ($4) for adults and 5DM ($2.50) for children. Zone charts and additional information in six languages are displayed on all the automatic machines. Except for bus travel (where you have the additional option of paying the driver directly for your passage), be sure to buy your ticket before you board any of the public transport conveyances of Frankfurt. If you're caught traveling without the proper ticket, you may be fined 60DM ($30).

If you want to simplify the ticket-buying process, both for public transport and museum admissions within Frankfurt, consider the purchase of a **Frankfurter Tageskarte (Frankfurt Card)** from either of the city's tourist offices. These cards allow unlimited travel anywhere within the greater Frankfurt area, plus transport on the shuttle bus going to and from the airport, plus half-price admission to any of the city's museums. The cost is 10DM ($5) for a 1-day card and 15DM ($7.50) for a 2-day card. For more information, contact the tourist office.

BY TAXI

There's no surcharge for calling for a taxi; dial ☎ **069/54-50-11, 069/23-00-33,** or **069/25-00-01.** Otherwise, you can get a cab either by standing at any of the city's hundreds of clearly designated taxi stands, or by hailing one with an illuminated dome light. Taxis charge by the trip and by the carload, without surcharge for pieces of luggage. Some are suitable for carrying up to six passengers, others for a maximum of only four. Regardless of their size, the initial fee you'll pay for a Frankfurt taxi is 3.80DM ($1.90); additional kilometers cost 2.15DM to 2.55DM ($1.10 to $1.30) each, depending on the time of day. The most expensive rates are charged on holidays between the hours of 10pm and 6am; the least expensive are charged between 10am and 4pm.

BY RENTAL CAR

The big rental companies each maintain offices at the airport and at central locations throughout Frankfurt. The most reliable are **Avis,** whose downtown branch is at Schmidtstrasse 39 or inside the Hauptbahnhof (☎ **069/27-99-7010**); and **Hertz,** whose offices are in the Hauptbahnhof (☎ **069/23-04-84**), and on the Hanauer Landstrasse 117 (☎ **069/44-90-90**). Also recommended is **Europcar,** which maintains offices at the Hauptbahnhof (☎ **069/242-9810**) and downtown at Am Industriehof 3–5 (☎ **069/970-6410**).

Fast Facts: Frankfurt

American Express   Centrally located at Kaiserstrasse 8 (☎ **069/2-10-50;** U-Bahn/S-Bahn: Hauptwache), the American Express offices are open Monday to Friday 9:30am to 6pm and on Saturday 9:30am to 12:30pm. Unless you have an American Express card or traveler's checks, you'll be charged 2DM ($1) for using their mail service.

Bookstores   The best English-language bookstore is **British Bookshop,** Börsenstrasse 17 (☎ **069/28-04-92;** U-Bahn/S-Bahn: Hauptwache). It's open Monday to Friday 9:30am to 7pm and Saturday 9:30am to 4pm. Many English-language editions are also for sale at **Sussmann's Presse und Buch,** Zeil 127 (☎ **069/1-31-07-51;** U-Bahn/S-Bahn: Hauptwache), open Monday to

Wednesday and Friday 9am to 7pm, Thursday 9am to 8pm, and Saturday 9am to 4pm.

Consulates   See "Fast Facts: Germany," in chapter 2, for a list of consulates in Frankfurt.

Currency Exchange   Go to the Hauptbahnhof's **Reise-Bank AG** kiosk (☎ **069/24-27-85-91** or **069/24-27-85-92**), which is open daily 7:30am to 10pm. The same bank maintains two separate branches within the Frankfurt airport. The smaller branch (☎ **069/69-07-20-71**) is open daily 7am to 7pm; the larger (☎ **069/69-03-50-61**) is open daily 6am to 11pm.

Dentist   For an English-speaking dentist, call ☎ **069/19292** to arrange an appointment.

Doctor   For an English-speaking doctor, call ☎ **069/19292** to arrange an appointment.

Drugstores   For information about pharmacies open near you, call ☎ **069/ 19292.**

Emergencies   Dial ☎ **110** for the police; ☎ **112** for a fire, first aid, and ambulance; ☎ **069/1-92-92** for emergency medical service; and ☎ **6-60-72-71** for emergency dental service.

Internet Access   Head for **Euro-Net,** Willy-Brandt-Platz/Euro-Tower (☎ **069/242-9370;** U-Bahn: Willy-Brandt-Platz), a cybercafe with computers and Internet access, as well as five chic bars and a kitchen serving everything from Spanish-style tapas to sushi until 1am each morning.

Laundry   Try **SB Wasch Center,** Grosse Seestrasse 46 (☎ **069/77-35-80;** U-Bahn: Leipzigerstrasse), open daily 6:30am to 10pm.

Luggage Storage/Lockers   Lockers can be rented and luggage stored at the Hauptbahnhof.

Post Office   The central post office is at Zeil 108–110 (60001 Frankfurt) near the Hauptwache (☎ **069/21-11:** U-Bahn/S-Bahn: Hauptwache). It's open Monday to Friday 9am to 6pm and Saturday 9am to 1pm. Go there to pick up general delivery mail (*Poste Restante*). There's also a post office at the Hauptbahnhof 60036 Frankfurt (☎ **069/2-42-42-70**), open Monday to Friday 6:30am to 9pm, Saturday 8am to 6pm, and Sunday and holidays 11am to 6pm.

Rest Rooms   There are many decent public facilities in central Frankfurt, especially in the Altstadt.

Safety   Frankfurt is a relatively safe city, but you should still stay alert at all times. Stay out of the area around the Hauptbahnhof at night, as muggings are frequent.

Taxis   See "Getting Around," earlier in this chapter.

Telegrams/Telex/Fax   You can send all of these at the **post office** at the Hauptbahnhof (☎ **069/2-42-42-70**). See above for hours.

3 Where to Stay

Frankfurt is notorious for room shortages during busy trade fairs. If you have the bad luck to arrive when one of them is scheduled, you might find all the more central hotels fully booked. To find an available room, either tourist office will charge you 5DM ($2.50) for a room-finding service.

IN THE CENTER
VERY EXPENSIVE

Arabella Sheraton Grand Hotel. Konrad-Adenauer-Strasse 7, 60313 Frankfurt. ☎ **800/ 325-3535** in the U.S. and Canada, or 069/2-98-10. Fax 069/2-98-18-10. www.luxurycollection. de. E-mail: sales.grand-hotel-frankfurt@arabellasheraton.de. 78 units. A/C MINIBAR TV TEL. 525DM–840DM ($262.50–$420) double; from 950DM ($475) suite. AE, DC, MC, V. Parking 34DM ($17). U-Bahn: Konstablerwache.

This hotel in the heart of the shopping district is one of the most modern and glamorous in Frankfurt, though it's not as stylish as either the Steigenberger Frankfurter Hof or the Hessischer Hof. It's designed in the international big-city style, and is a favorite of business travelers. The hotel has an atrium lobby. Rooms are large and often outfitted with art deco-inspired furniture. Baths are luxurious.

Dining/Diversions: The hotel boasts one of the best Chinese restaurants in Frankfurt (Dynasty) and operates two Japanese restaurants (Sushi bar and Teppen Yaki). There's also a rustic German restaurant offering regional specialties, as well as a bar and a cafe. For the main restaurant, Peninsula, see "Where to Dine," below.

Amenities: 24-hour room service, laundry, baby-sitting, fitness center, sauna, solarium, pool.

✪ Hotel Hessischer Hof. Friedrich-Ebert-Anlage 40, 60325 Frankfurt. ☎ **800/223-6800** in the U.S. and Canada, or 069/7-54-00. Fax 069/75-40-29-24. www.hessischer-hof.de. E-mail: info@heissischer.hof.de. 117 units. A/C MINIBAR TV TEL. 555DM–645DM ($277.50–$322.50) double; from 705DM ($352.50) suite. Children 12 and under stay free in parents' room. AE, DC, MC, V. Parking 25DM ($12.50). S-Bahn: Platz der Republik.

A private and traditional place with an elegant atmosphere, this hotel has first-class style and amenities all the way. It's topped only by the Steigenberger Frankfurter Hof. The hotel is located opposite the trade-fair building. The relatively modest postwar exterior doesn't prepare you for the spacious and glamorous interior. Many rooms are furnished with antiques. Baths are equipped with perfumed soap, luxurious robes, and a hair dryer. The staff follows the old European custom of having guests leave their shoes outside the bedroom door at night, to be returned shined the next morning.

Dining/Diversions: Sèvres-Restaurant offers both traditional and modern cuisine. Its walls are decorated with original Sèvres porcelain. Jimmy's Bar is an elegant rendezvous spot in Frankfurt.

Amenities: Room service, daily laundry, baby-sitting, fitness equipment.

Le Meridien Parkhotel. Wiesenhüttenplatz 28–38 (near the Hauptbahnhof), 60329 Frankfurt. ☎ **800/225-5843** in the U.S. and Canada, or 069/2-69-70. Fax 069/2-69-78-84. www.forte-hotels.com. E-mail: GM1275@forte-hotels.com. 296 units. A/C MINIBAR TV TEL. 455DM–875DM ($227.50–$437.50) double; 875DM–1,005DM ($437.50–$502.50) suite. AE, DC, MC, V. Parking 30DM ($15). U-Bahn/S-Bahn: Hauptbahnhof.

We prefer this hotel over its bigger, more impersonal competitors: the Frankfurt Intercontinental and the Frankfurt Marriott. Le Meridien Parkhotel provides not only warmth but also personal attention for its guests, mainly from the world of commerce. The hotel has been built in two sections—an ornately decorated, recently renovated 1905 building and a sleek but duller 1970s wing. In the older part, rooms have a luxurious atmosphere and are individually designed. The newer section's decor is modern. All rooms and suites are in the five-star category. Baths are well maintained, have robes, hair dryers, and deluxe vanity items.

Dining/Diversions: Le Park Restaurant offers excellent German regional and international cuisine. The Casablanca Bar has piano music and a lively atmosphere; it attracts both foreign visitors and locals.

ⓘ Family-Friendly Hotels

Admiral *(see p. 427)*   This family favorite near the zoo has rooms that are simply furnished but comfortable—and the price is right.

Am Zoo *(see p. 426)*   This clean, well-furnished, and comfortable hotel is just across from the zoo entrance in a quiet, safe neighborhood.

Le Meridien Parkhotel *(see p. 424)*   Children under 16 stay free in their parents' room at this pricey chain hotel located across from a city park.

Amenities: Room service, laundry, dry cleaning, baby-sitting, overnight shoe shine, sauna, solarium, business center, shopping boutique.

✪ **Steigenberger Frankfurter Hof.** Am Kaiserplatz, 60311 Frankfurt. ☎ **800/223-5652** in the U.S. and Canada, or 069/2-15-02. Fax 069/21-59-00. www.steigenberger.com. 332 units. AC MINIBAR TV TEL. 420DM–620DM ($210–$310) double; 720DM–770DM ($360–$385) suite. AE, DC, MC, V. Parking 35DM ($17.50). U-Bahn/S-Bahn: Hauptwache.

This grand hotel, run by the Steigenberger chain, is the number-one choice of traditionalists. Its position in the center of the city is ideal for vacationers and businesspeople alike; it's just a few short blocks from the Hauptbahnhof, near the sights of the Altstadt. Its art collection, featuring Gobelin tapestries, is outstanding. In spite of its size, it offers both well-maintained comfort and a personalized atmosphere. Rooms and suites are furnished in a restrained and dignified modern style. Baths include hair dryers and luxurious robes.

Dining/Diversions: There are a few choices for dining: a Japanese restaurant; the thatch-roofed Hofgarten Restaurant; and the cozy Kaiserbrunnen, which offers light meals, wines, and champagne in a Biedermeier decor. The hotel's Lipizzaner Bar is one of the most elegant in the city. But the best spot in the hotel is the provincial-style Frankfurter Stubb. A pianist plays at teatime in the lobby lounge.

Amenities: 24-hour room service, same-day laundry and valet service, dry cleaning, shoe-shine service, baby-sitting, full business-services center, shopping arcade with hairdresser and beauty parlor, wine and gourmet boutique.

EXPENSIVE

An Der Messe. Westendstrasse 104, 60325 Frankfurt. ☎ **800/221-6509** in the U.S., or 069/74-79-79. Fax 069/74-83-49. E-mail: hotel-am-zoo@t-online.de. 46 units. MINIBAR TV TEL. 280DM–500DM ($140–$250) double. Rates include breakfast. AE, DC, MC, V. Underground garage parking 20DM ($10). Tram: 16 or 19.

This quiet charmer is the choice of seasoned and discriminating visitors to Frankfurt. It's a 5-minute walk from the university, the Hauptbahnhof, the banking district, and the fairgrounds. The staff does much to make guests feel comfortable. Rooms are large and stylishly furnished; many have an Asian motif. Baths are luxurious and have hair dryers. A half-dozen singles are rented, but they're hard to come by unless you reserve well in advance.

Dining: Breakfast, the only meal offered, is served in a light, airy room.

Amenities: Concierge, room service, dry cleaning, laundry service, baby-sitting, car rental and tour desk.

Frankfurt Savoy Hotel. Wiesenhüttenstrasse 42 (near the Hauptbahnhof), 60329 Frankfurt. ☎ **069/27-39-60.** Fax 069/27-39-67-95. www.savoyhotel.de. E-mail: info@t.savoyhotel.de. 144 units. MINIBAR TV TEL. 285DM–390DM ($142.50–$195) double. Rates include buffet breakfast. AE, DC, MC, V. Parking available in multi-story car park nearby for 25DM ($12.50). U-Bahn/S-Bahn: Hauptbahnhof.

This hotel offers first-class comfort and a lighthearted ambience. Swedish furnishings are used throughout. The good-sized rooms contain trouser presses and hair dryers.

Dining: The Rhapsody offers a continental menu with many international dishes.

Amenities: Fitness club with an indoor pool, a dry or steam sauna, and a solarium; room service, concierge, dry cleaning, laundry.

Hotel Palmenhof. Bockenheimer Landstrasse 89–91, 60325 Frankfurt. ☎ **069/753-0060.** Fax 069/753-00666. E-mail: hotel.palmenhof@t-online.de. 46 units. MINIBAR TV TEL. Mon–Thurs 290DM–320DM ($145–$160) double; 455DM–495DM ($227.50–$247.50) suite. Fri–Sun 175DM ($87.50) double; 255DM–305DM ($127.50–$152.50) suite. Rates include breakfast. Parking 18DM ($9). AE, DC, MC, V. U-Bahn: Westend.

This hotel, just a short walk from Frankfurt's Botanical Gardens, is set in a much-renovated, five-story art nouveau building, some of whose original architectural details have been carefully preserved. Rooms are high-ceilinged and relatively spacious, with art nouveau furnishings.

Dining/Diversions: In the hotel's basement is a cozy-looking restaurant, Bastei, that's open Monday to Friday for lunch and dinner. Set-price menus cost from 25DM to 60DM ($30).

Amenities: Room service, hair dryer in room, concierge, dry cleaning/laundry.

MODERATE

Am Zoo. Alfred-Brehm-Platz 6 (across from the zoo entrance), 60316 Frankfurt. ☎ **069/94-99-30.** Fax 069/94-99-31-99. E-mail: hotelamzoo@t-online.de. 85 units. TEL. 199DM ($99.50) double. Rates include continental breakfast. AE, DC, MC, V. Closed Dec 20–Jan 5. Parking behind the hotel 7.50DM ($3.75). Tram: 11, 14, or 16.

This modern hotel is bland on the outside, but welcoming on the inside. Rooms are well maintained, with simple but comfortable modern pieces; 80 contain minibars and TVs. The street-level breakfast room is the hotel's most charming feature, with linen-covered tables and stained-glass windows.

Continental. Baselerstrasse 56, 60329 Frankfurt. ☎ **069/23-03-41.** Fax 069/23-29-14. E-mail: hotelconti@t.aol.com. 84 units. TV TEL. 185DM–398DM ($92.50–$199) double. Rates include buffet breakfast. AE, DC, MC, V. Parking 25DM ($12.50). U-Bahn/S-Bahn: Hauptbahnhof.

The Continental, the choice of many businesspeople, is a leader among middle-bracket hotels near the Hauptbahnhof. Founded in 1889, it enjoyed its heyday in the belle epoque era. Rooms are modern and comfortable, though the baths are small. Around the corner are lively bars, but serenity prevails inside. The windows have been soundproofed to keep out traffic noise. The hotel has a pleasant restaurant, Conti, with an international cuisine.

Hotel Robert Mayer. Robert-Mayer-Strasse 44, 60486 Frankfurt. ☎ **069/970910.** Fax 069/97091010. www.frankfurt.de/hotel-robert-mayer. 11 units. TV TEL. 230DM–350DM ($115–$175) double. Rates include breakfast. AE, DC, MC, V. U-Bahn: Bockenheimer Warte.

This is one of the most artfully decorated hotels in town. It's within walking distance of the trade fair complex. Though the building dates from 1905, rooms date from 1994, when the manager hired 11 lesser-known artists to each impose his or her vision on one of the rooms. You might find a thought-provoking jumble of furniture inspired by Frank Lloyd Wright, or an anonymous Milanese postmodernist set adjacent to pop art. Creature comforts, however, remain high. There's no restaurant on the premises, but many dining options lie within a short walk.

Hotel Westend. Westendstrasse 15, 60325 Frankfurt. ☎ **069/746-702.** Fax 069/745-396. 20 units. MINIBAR TV TEL. Mon–Thurs 230DM–290DM ($115–$145) double; Fri–Sun 180DM

($90) double; 320DM–390DM ($160–$195) doubles during trade fairs. AE, MC, V. Free parking. U-Bahn: Hauptbahnhof.

This small hotel, built in the late 19th century, is a winner, thanks to its courtly staff and its carefully polished roster of French and German antiques. There's no restaurant on the premises, but few of the clients, many of whom seem involved in some kind of media, seem to mind—dozens of dining options lie within a short walk.

✪ **Mozart.** Parkstrasse 17 (near the Alte Oper), 60322 Frankfurt. ☎ **069/55-08-31.** Fax 069/1568061. 35 units. MINIBAR TV TEL. 220DM ($110) double; 270DM ($135) during trade fairs. Rates include buffet breakfast. AE, DC, MC, V. Closed Dec 24–Jan 1. U-Bahn: Holzhausen-strasse. Bus: 36.

Perhaps the best small hotel in Frankfurt, the Mozart stands on the periphery of the Palmengarten, right off the busy Fürstenbergerstrasse. Everything inside—walls, furniture, bed coverings—is white or pink. Rooms are small but comfortable. The breakfast room, with its crystal chandeliers and Louis XV-style chairs, could pass for an 18th-century salon. The staff is polite and helpful.

INEXPENSIVE

Admiral. Hölderlinstrasse 25, 60136 Frankfurt. ☎ **069/44-80-21.** Fax 069/43-94-02. www.hotel-admiral.com. E-mail: hoteladmiral@ad.com. 48 units. MINIBAR TV TEL. 160DM–220DM ($80–$110) double. Rates include breakfast. AE, DC, MC, V. Parking 10DM ($5). U-Bahn: Zoologischer Garten (Zoo).

The Admiral is a favorite with families, who like its location near the zoo, a short haul from the center of Frankfurt. Rooms are plainly but comfortably furnished, with a Scandinavian-style decor. Baths are small but adequate. Only breakfast is served.

Diana. Westendstrasse 83, 60325 Frankfurt. ☎ **069/74-70-07.** Fax 069/74-70-79. 26 units. TV TEL. 175DM ($87.50) double; 225DM ($112.50) triple. Rates include continental breakfast. AE, DC, MC, V. Parking 8DM ($4). U-Bahn: Westend. Bus: 17.

Spotless and homey, the Diana is a leader in its price class. It's a copy of a private villa, with a drawing room and an intimate breakfast salon. It's located in the Westend district on a pleasant residential street. The small rooms are rather lackluster but comfortable and clean. The towels are rather thin.

Falk Hotel. Falkstrasse 38A, 60487 Frankfurt. ☎ **069/70-80-94.** Fax 069/70-80-17. www.hotel-falk.de. 32 units. MINIBAR TV TEL. 160DM–480DM ($80–$240) double. Rates include buffet breakfast. AE, DC, MC, V. Free parking. U-Bahn: Leipzigerstrasse.

The Falk may be stark outside, but it's still a good choice. It's located on a small quiet side street in the center of the city, near the exhibition center, the main railway station, and the university. This hotel is bright and modern but has enough traditional touches to lend warmth and coziness. The small, uncluttered rooms are spotlessly maintained.

Hotelschiff Peter Schlott. Mainberg, 65929 Frankfurt. ☎ **069/300-4643.** Fax 069/307-671. www.hotel-schiff-schlott.de. 19 units (all with washbasins, 10 with showers, none with toilets). 110DM–120DM ($55–$60) double without shower, 120DM–150DM ($60–$75) double with shower. Rates include breakfast. AE, DC, MC, V. S-Bahn: Höchst.

This 1950s riverboat, now permanently moored at the Frankfurt suburb of Höchst, has some of the smallest, but most evocative, rooms in the area. The style evokes life at sea: Everything is tiny and cramped; mattresses are a bit thin; and towels are small and not particularly plush. But the unusual nature of the accommodations help soften any disagreeability, and the waters of the Main lap soothingly beneath your portholes. On the premises is a cozy, small-scale restaurant that's open daily for both lunch and dinner. You'll have to exercise caution on this ship's narrow and steep staircases. If you have enormous amounts of luggage, consider a stay in a more conventional hotel.

IN GRAVENBRUCH

✪ **Kempinski Hotel Gravenbruch Frankfurt.** Frankfurt/Neu-Isenburg, 63263. ☎ **800/ 426-3135** in the U.S. and Canada, or 06102/50-50. Fax 06102/50-59-00. www.kempinski-frankfurt.com. E-mail: hgk@mail.pop-frankfurt.com. 283 units. A/C MINIBAR TV TEL. 458DM–588DM ($229–$294) double; 745DM–2,450DM ($372.50–$1,225) suite. AE, DC, MC, V. Free parking. Free transfers to/from the airport every half hour 7am–9pm. From the airport, it's a 20-min. taxi ride via A3 and B459 across Gravenbruch.

This place in the suburbs, only 15 minutes from the Frankfurt airport, is recommended for guests wanting to escape the bustle of a commercial setting. Here you'll find luxury combined with rural charm. The hotel is set back from Route B459 on 15ha (37 acres) of parkland, complete with a lake. The structure was built on the foundation and old walls of a former manor house dating from 1568. More modern residential wings are positioned along the lakeshore, but some touches of the old country-mansion character remain, including the large atrium-style courtyards. Rooms are attractive and baths well maintained.

Dining/Diversions: Many in-the-know Frankfurters journey here just to sample the cuisine. The elegant and formal Restaurant Forsthaus opens onto a view of the park. The Forsthaus-Schänke has a stone-slab floor, as well as draft beer from a barrel; it's housed in what in the 16th century were horse stables. The lobby bar offers dancing to music from international entertainers.

Amenities: Room service, laundry facilities, baby-sitting, heated indoor and outdoor pools, fitness center, sauna, solarium, tennis courts, boutiques, hairdressing salon, beauty and fitness farm, massage service, hair dryers, golf and horseback riding available nearby.

4 Where to Dine

As in most German cities, the cafe here is an important institution, where people read newspapers, enjoy a beer or coffee and cake, and watch the passing parade. Try **Café Laumer** at Bockenheimer Landstrasse 67, in an enviable location between the Palmengarten and the Alte Oper, where habitués often have their favorite marble-topped table. The 250-year-old **Zur Hauptwache** is the cafe nearly everybody finds without any guidance. It's located in the heart of the Frankfurt pedestrian zone on an der Hauptwache. Sample the special beer, Römer Pilsner.

At some point in your visit, head across the Main River to the Alt-Sachsenhausen district to eat a meal and drink **apple wine,** Frankfurt's specialty.

IN THE CENTER
EXPENSIVE

Avocado Bistro. Hochstrasse 27. ☎ **069/292-867.** Reservations recommended. Main courses 38DM–44DM ($19–$22). AE, MC, V. Mon–Sat noon–2:30pm and 6–10:30pm. U-bahn: Opernplatz. FRENCH/GERMAN.

This upscale bistro has lots of fresh flowers and a battalion of formally dressed waitstaff providing impeccable service. Overall the setting is romantic and charming—it's a suitable venue for either a seduction or a sales pitch. Menu items might include such well-prepared dishes as quail breast with zucchini flowers, green beans, and a crabmeat-enhanced vinaigrette; carpaccio of tuna with soya; and fillet of pike with green asparagus and salmon-flavored caviar.

Gargantua. Liebigstrasse 47. ☎ **069/720718.** Reservations recommended. Main courses 42DM–55DM ($21–$27.50); fixed-price lunches 49DM–120DM ($24.50–$60); fixed-price

A Map Note

For the location of the restaurants in this section, see the "Frankfurt" map on pp. 420–421.

---

dinners 95DM–120DM ($47.50–$60). AE, DC, MC, V. Mon–Sat noon–1:30pm and 6:30–9:30pm. U-Bahn: Westend. GERMAN/FRENCH.

This well-managed, much-talked-about restaurant has a dining room and an outside garden, which can accommodate 30. The owner (Klaus Trebes) writes a well-known weekly food column in the *Frankfurter Allgemeinerzeitung*. Menu items include roasted sea bass with an infusion of clams and artichoke hearts, blackened tuna, venison in port sauce, and anglerfish with a saffron-flavored cream sauce. Overall, this place is stylish, warm, and creative, with generous portions and an undeniable culinary zeal.

Peninsula. In the Arabella Sheraton Grand Hotel, Konrad-Adenauer-Strasse 7. ☎ 069/2-98-11-72. Reservations recommended. Main courses 32DM–42DM ($16–$21); fixed-price menus 46DM–65DM ($23–$32.50). AE, DC, MC, V. Mon–Fri noon–2:30pm; daily 6:30–10:30pm. U-Bahn: Konstablerwache. MEDITERRANEAN.

One of Frankfurt's most stylish and elegant restaurants lies just above the lobby level of this previously recommended five-star hotel. Mirrors and polished cherry wood adorn the dining room, a favorite of the city's industrial and financial moguls. The chefs call their style *cuisine vitale,* stressing healthful and succulent preparations of fresh ingredients, artfully presented. Examples include a liaison of salmon and John Dory with rice in chervil sauce, and a "composition of seafood" featuring several fish and shellfish, served with leaf spinach and two sauces. The dessert menu is appropriately elegant; a particular favorite is the Irish-coffee tart.

✪ Weinhaus Brückenkeller. Schützenstrasse 6. ☎ 069/29-80-07-0. Reservations required. Main courses 45DM–58DM ($22.50–$29). AE, DC, MC, V. Mon–Sat 6:30–11pm. Closed Dec 20–Jan 8. U-Bahn Konstablerwache. GERMAN/INTERNATIONAL.

Weinhaus Brückenkeller, in the heart of the Altstadt, is one of Frankfurt's leading restaurants and a favorite spot of well-heeled North American visitors. Tables are candlelit, and strolling musicians encourage singing. Here the age of Bismarck lives again. Franconian carvings adorn the alcoves, and huge wooden barrels are decorated with scenes from Goethe's *Faust.* The food is light and subtle. A typical meal might begin with cream of sorrel soup or more substantial roast goose liver with green beans, followed by saddle of venison or young lamb. For a perfect finish, you might order a soufflé of strawberries with vanilla sauce. The *Tafelspitz* (boiled beef) is the best in town. The evening meal includes homemade sourdough bread. The wine cellar holds an excellent collection of German wines, including the best from the Rhineland. Personal attention and efficient service are hallmarks.

MODERATE

Jewel of India. Wilhelm-Hauff Strasse 5. ☎ 069/752375. Reservations recommended. Main courses 16DM–70DM ($8–$35); fixed-menus 40DM–80DM ($20–$40). AE, MC, V. Sun–Fri 11:30am–2:30pm; daily 5:30–11:30pm. U-Bahn: Westend or Messe. INDIAN.

The decor here includes ornate carvings around the windows and black and white paintings accented with semi-precious gemstones. The main draw, however, is the savory Indian cuisine, which includes lots of vegetarian choices, as well as tandoori chicken in a saffron-yogurt marinade, and slow-cooked lamb with cumin and coriander.

Steinernes Haus. Braubachstrasse 35 (around the corner from the Rathaus). ☎ **069/28-34-91.** Main courses 20DM–52.50DM ($10–$26.25); daily platters 15DM–20DM ($7.50–$10). V. Daily 11am–11pm. Tram: 11. GERMAN.

The 500-year-old Steinernes Haus, in the historic heart of Frankfurt, was restored simply and unpretentiously after the war. Locals come here for the good German beer, along with hearty rib-sticking fare. The daily main-dish specialty includes salad and potatoes. Other choices include a selection of sausages, beef fillet, and such popular German dishes as *Zigeunerhackbraten* (spicy meat loaf) and *Frankfurter Rippchen* (smoked pork). The best choice is a fillet steak cooked on a hot plate right at your table.

INEXPENSIVE

Churrasco. Domplatz 6. ☎ **069/28-48-04.** Reservations recommended. Main courses 16DM–26DM ($8–$13). AE, DC, MC, V. Daily 11am–11:30pm. U-Bahn: Römer. ARGENTINE.

Churrasco is where Frankfurters go for succulent Argentinean beefsteak, the best cuts in town. A red sign with a steer marks this dimly lit tavern. Menu items include delicious fillet or T-bone steaks and several styles of grilled salmon and jumbo shrimp. Lower-priced orders of rump steak are also available. All cuts are charcoal grilled to your specifications. Rounding out the menu are fresh salads and a limited list of desserts.

Mövenpick am Opernplatz. Opernplatz 2. ☎ **069/2-06-80.** Reservations recommended. Main courses 15.90DM–36DM ($7.95–$18). AE, DC, MC, V. Mon–Sat 8am–11pm, Sun 11am–11pm. U-Bahn: Hausen. SWISS/FRENCH.

This busy member of a Swiss-owned restaurant chain is clean, efficient, and bustling, partly because of its location in the commercial heart of Frankfurt, and partly because of a well-maintained setting, good value, and reasonable prices. Within the busy premises you'll find three different areas: a simulation of an outdoor terrace, an informal spot with leather banquettes and a look like a French bistro, and an area that pays homage to the art deco heyday of Hollywood. Try the antipasti buffet, a lavish display containing salads, marinated fish and vegetables, guacamole, small tarts, and an herb-laden roster of Italian dishes; a small platter is 15DM ($7.50), a large is 20DM ($10). There's also a large selection of salads and pastas, roast rib of Angus beef with horseradish cream sauce, scampi in bordelaise sauce, and more. Everything is competently prepared, but not exactly exciting.

Zum Bitburger. Hochstrasse 54 (near the Alte Oper). ☎ **069/28-03-02.** Reservations required. Main courses 16.50DM–35DM ($8.25–$17.50). AE, DC, MC, V. Mon–Fri 11:30am–1am. Closed July 16–25. U-Bahn: Alte Oper. CONTINENTAL.

This brewery-operated restaurant has a long and proud tradition. Waiters somehow manage to slip through the crowds with mugs of beer and hearty platters of food. The standard but well-prepared dishes include grilled rump steak, goulash, and sausages with red cabbage and home-fried potatoes. You can begin with the soup of the day, and there's always a fresh seasonal salad. The kitchen serves hot food until midnight.

IN ALT-SACHSENHAUSEN

Alt-Sachsenhausen has been called the most Frankfurt-ish neighborhood in the city, but now that the main street, Schweizerstrasse, is filled with bistros, cafes, and boutiques catering to tourists, some of the old character is gone. Nonetheless, it remains an interesting place, especially for its many apple-wine taverns.

Bistrot 77. Ziegelhüttenweg 1 (less than a mile from the city center), Frankfurt-Sachsenhausen. ☎ **069/61-40-40.** Reservations required. Main courses 38DM–52DM ($19–$26); fixed-price meals 60DM ($30); "menu surprise" 150DM ($75). AE, MC, V. Mon–Fri noon–2pm; Mon–Sat 7–10pm. Closed Dec 24–Jan 6. Bus: 62. Tram: 16. FRENCH/ALSATIAN.

⊕ Family-Friendly Restaurants

Churrasco *(see p. 430)*   Kids delight in the atmosphere of the pampas at this Argentine restaurant. Children's portions are available.

Zum Gemalten Haus *(see p. 432)*   You can dine early at this apple-wine tavern, where children will discover some of the biggest and tastiest franks they've ever eaten.

Bistrot 77 is one of the most chic of Frankfurt's restaurants. The overall impression is one of light and glass, with a black-and-white tile floor and an airy latticework ceiling. In summer, tables are set on the terrace. Dominique and Guy Mosbach, two French citizens, have made a name for themselves with their contemporary cuisine, a frequently changing array of imaginatively prepared fish and meat dishes, along with intriguing appetizers and desserts.

Die Gans in Sachsenhausen. Schweizerstrasse 76. ☎ **069/62-26-25.** Reservations recommended. Main courses 29DM–40DM ($14.50–$20); fixed-price menus 44DM–68DM ($22–$34). AE, DC, MC, V. Mon–Sat 6–11pm. Closed Dec 23–Jan 5. U-Bahn: Schweizer Platz. CONTINENTAL/GAME.

Stylish, sophisticated, and relatively casual, this is a refreshing tribute to the combined cuisines of Europe, with a special emphasis on the game dishes that have always been dear to Frankfurt residents. In the intimate, bistro-like dining room, you'll be offered a choice of such dishes as zesty fish soup with strips of smoked salmon; mousse of smoked ham; venison and rabbit; North Atlantic lobster; fish ravioli with spinach sauce; and a perfectly cooked roast rack of lamb with Provençale herbs.

Jaspers. Schifferstrasse 8 (near Affentorplatz), Sachsenhausen. ☎ **069/614-117.** Reservations recommended. Main courses 18DM–38DM ($9–$19); fixed-price menu 32DM ($16). AE, DC, MC, V. Mon–Sat 6pm–1am. Train 16 or 17. CONTINENTAL.

This stylish, international bistro is lined with mirrors and art nouveau accessories, with vague references to the bistros of Lyon. The food is more Germanic than French, but still has some Mediterranean overtones. You might try the fish soup, or the snails prepared in calvados and served over a bed of spinach, or the excellent Wiener schnitzel. The roasted lamb is especially succulent as well.

THE APPLE-WINE TAVERNS (APFELWEINSTUBEN)

In these taverns you drink local apple wine (like hard cider), which many locals enjoy and many foreigners consider a cousin to vinegar. Our verdict: It's an acquired taste. Tradition says that you won't like the apple wine until you've had three big steins. After that, what does taste matter? Other apple-wine taverns, besides those listed below, include **Mutter Ernst,** Alte Rothofstrasse 12 (☎ **069/28-38-22**), and **Apfelwein-wirtschaft Wagner,** Schweizerstrasse 71 (☎ **069/61-25-65**).

Germania. Textorstrasse 16, Sachsenhausen. ☎ **069/613-336.** Reservations not accepted. Main courses 8.80DM–25DM ($4.40–$12.50). No credit cards. Daily noon–2pm and 5–10pm. Train 16 or 17. GERMAN.

Those searching for local authenticity will thrill to the coziness and warmth of this old-fashioned apple wine house, where hearty portions and genuine earthiness are a way of life. Don't even think about ordering beer here, as it simply isn't served. The drink of choice is tart and pungent apple wine, served at 2.80DM ($1.60) per glass. You'll consume it elbow-to-elbow with fellow diners at long trestle tables, probably amid lots of cigarette smoke and conviviality. Menu items include a roster of sausages, as well as herb-enriched pork ribs (*Rippchen mit Kraut*) and a salty version of cheese with onions (*Handkäse mit Musik*) that invariably inspires you to order more drink. Friday night brings fresh fish, especially catfish and whiting, usually served with parsley butter sauce.

Zum Gemalten Haus. Schweizerstrasse 67. ☎ **069/61-45-59.** Reservations recommended. Main courses 12DM–25DM ($6–$12.50). No credit cards. Wed–Sun 10am–midnight. Tram: 16. HESSIAN.

Chances are you'll share a table here with other patrons, perhaps in the garden if the weather is fair. The kitchen provides ample portions of good Hessian cooking. If you're in a group, try the "Frankfurter Platte," which usually includes liver pâté, blood sausage, the chef's special Frankfurter Wurst, sauerkraut, and perhaps knockwurst with sauerkraut or potato salad. The *Eisbein*, or pork knuckle with mashed potatoes, washed down with apple wine, is the cook's specialty. The apple wine is homemade.

Zum Grauen Bock. Grosse Rittergasse 30–45. ☎ **069/61-80-26.** Reservations recommended. Main courses 16DM–42DM ($8–$21); 3-course fixed-price menu 25DM–38DM ($12.50–$19). AE, MC, V. Mon–Sat 5pm–1am. U-Bahn: Lokalbahnhof. GERMAN.

Sometimes the communal singing here is so robust that it's necessary to slide back the roof on a summer night. An accordionist goes from table to table, involving everyone in the singing. Featured on the menu is cheese with vinegar, oil, and onions (*Handkas mit Musik*), but you may want to leave the subtle pleasures of this dish to the locals. Instead, try a German specialty, the huge pork shank with sauerkraut and boiled potatoes (*Schweinshaxen*). A good beginning is the liver dumpling soup or the goulash soup.

IN WESTEND

Erno's Bistro. Liebigstrasse 15 (between the Alte Oper and the Palmengarten). ☎ **069/72-19-97.** Reservations required. Main courses 48DM–56DM ($24–$28); business menu 50DM ($25); fixed-price menu 125DM ($62.50); special dinner with wine 175DM ($87.50). AE, DC, MC, V. Mon–Fri noon–2pm and 7–10pm. Closed mid-June to mid-July. U-Bahn: Westend. FRENCH.

Erno's, a chic midtown rendezvous, draws everybody from visiting film stars to bank executives. This small place with an English-speaking staff offers fine service, plus a commendable cuisine that seems to improve year after year. The kitchen serves only fish brought fresh by air from European waters. The chef offers both *cuisine moderne* and what is known as *cuisine formidable*. The most exciting (and expensive) appetizer is a version of foie gras. For a main course, we'd suggest the grilled brill, whose flesh is very delicate and light, served with a rare type of mushroom. Another excellent choice is fillet of venison coated with truffles and served with a smooth and creamy savoy cabbage.

✪ **Humperdinck.** Grüneburgweg 95 (near the Palmengarten). ☎ **069/722-122.** Reservations required. Main courses 38DM–79DM ($19–$39.50). AE, DC, V. Mon–Fri noon–3pm; Mon–Sat 6:30pm–1am. Closed July–Aug 3. U-Bahn : Grünebergweg. INTERNATIONAL.

If you can afford it, there's no better table waiting for you in Frankfurt today. The setting at this elegant *Neuer Kuche* restaurant is classical, refined, and dignified. Dress as you would to a wedding. The place is named after Engelbert Humperdinck, composer of the opera *Hänsel und Gretel,* who once lived at this fashionable address in the western sector of Frankfurt. Patron Alfred Friedrich is clearly a master chef, familiar with cuisines worldwide but thoroughly determined to make his own culinary statement. There is a short à la carte menu, but the set meals are clearly the showcase of the evening. You might see on the menu scampi in truffle sauce with fresh truffles, a rich herb soup with butter croutons, a salmon Schnitzel with vegetable risotto, or even couscous.

IN HEILIGENSTOCK

Altes Zollhaus. Friedberger Landstrasse 531, in Heiligenstock (4 1/2 miles north of Frankfurt). ☎ **069/472-707.** Reservations recommended. Main courses 28DM–38DM ($14–$19); fixed-menus 55DM ($27.50). AE, DC, MC, V. Tues–Sun 6–10:30pm. Bus: 30 to Heiligenstock. GERMAN.

This restaurant is set within a 235-year-old half-timbered structure that was originally a tollhouse. Within its timbered and nostalgically antique-looking premises, you can enjoy relatively formal meals whose ingredients change with the seasons. Between October and February, expect a rich assortment of game dishes, especially venison and pheasant, usually cooked with wine sauce and herbs. In spring, look for different combinations of asparagus dishes, including an "asparagus cocktail" garnished with strips of ham and vinaigrette sauce. During warm weather, additional seating is set up within the garden.

5 Seeing the Sights

When bombs rained on Frankfurt in 1944, nearly all the old half-timbered buildings were leveled. In what might have been a record reconstruction, however, residents of Frankfurt rebuilt their city into a fine mélange of modern and traditional architecture and faithfully restored some of their most prized old buildings as well.

THE ALTSTADT

The Altstadt (U-Bahn/S-Bahn: Hauptwache) centers around three Gothic buildings with stepped gables, known collectively as the **Römer,** Römerberg (☎ **069/ 21-23-48-14**). These houses were originally built between 1288 and 1305 and bought by the city a century later for use as the Rathaus. The second floor of the center house is the **Imperial Hall (Kaisersaal),** lined with the romanticized portraits of 52 emperors; 13 of them celebrated their coronation banquets here. You can visit this hall daily 10am to 1pm and 2 to 5pm. An hourly tour costing 3DM ($1.80) is obligatory. Tickets can be purchased at the entrance to the Römer.

The elaborate facade of the Römer, with its ornate balcony and statues of four emperors, overlooks **Römerberg Square.** On festive occasions in days gone by, the square was the scene of oxen roasts that featured flowing wine. Today, unfortunately, the Fountain of Justitia pours forth only water, but oxen are still roasted on special occasions.

The dominant feature of the Altstadt is the 15th-century red-sandstone tower of the **Dom St. Bartholomäus,** Domplatz 14 (☎ **069/29703236**), in whose chapel the emperors of the Holy Roman Empire were elected and crowned for nearly 300 years. In the cloister of the church is the **Dom Museum** (☎ **069/28-92-29**), which exhibits robes of the imperial electors. It's open Tuesday to Friday 10am to 5pm and Saturday and Sunday 11am to 5pm. Admission is 2DM ($1) for adults and 1DM (50¢) for children.

Alte Nikolaikirche (Old Nicholas Church), Römerberg (☎ **069/292449**), is a historic church across from the Rathaus. Originally, it was a court chapel; after the 15th century it served as the church for the city fathers. Today, it's home to the Lutheran St. Paul's congregation. Inside are ancient gravestones as well as a copy of a medieval sculpture, Schmerzensmann, dating from 1370. Outside are Gothic sandstone sculptures portraying St. Nicholas. The 40-bell Glockenspiel plays at 9:05am,

---

A Map Note

For the location of the attractions in this section, see the "Frankfurt" map on pp. 420–421.

12:05pm, and 5:05pm; a church hymn and a German folk song are played. A number of materials in English, including a church guide and a free walking map, are available at the information table in the church. A musical vespers service (English-German) is held each Wednesday in summer 5:30 to 6:30pm, with tea, cookies, and conversation afterward to the accompaniment of the organ. The church is open daily 10am to 8pm (in winter 6pm). An American pastor on staff is available to answer questions and give free tours, including a trip to the roof gallery, and to help travelers needing advice or those in emergency situations. Contact the church office across from the church.

At the northern edge of the Altstadt is An der Hauptwache, named for the old guard house (Hauptwache) which stands upon it. This square is the heart of modern Frankfurt. Underneath is the Hauptwache U-Bahn station with a modern shopping promenade.

MUSEUMS

✪ **Goethe-Haus.** Grosser Hirschgraben 23–25. ☎ **069/13-88-00.** Admission 7DM ($3.50) adults, 3DM ($1.50) students, 2DM ($1) children. Apr–Sept, Mon–Fri 9am–6pm; Sat, Sun, and holidays 10am–4pm. Oct–Mar, Mon–Fri 9am–4pm; Sat, Sun, and holidays 10am–4pm. U-Bahn/S-Bahn: Hauptwache.

This house, where Johann Wolfgang von Goethe (1749–1832) was born, has been a shrine for Goethe enthusiasts since it opened to the public in 1863. One observer wrote that the postwar restoration was carried out "with loving care and damn-the-expense craftsmanship." The house is decorated in various styles, all reflecting the fashion trends of the 18th century: neoclassical, baroque, and rococo. You can view the library, where Goethe's father worked and often watched the street for the return of his son. A portrait of the severe-looking gentleman hangs behind the door of his wife's room.

On the second floor is an unusual astronomical clock built around 1749 and repaired in 1949 to run for another 200 years. One room contains a picture gallery with paintings collected by Goethe's father. These works, mainly by contemporary Frankfurt artists, influenced Goethe's artistic views for a great part of his life. The poet's rooms contain one of his most important childhood possessions, a puppet theater, which played a significant role in his novel *Wilhelm Meister*.

Annexed to the house is the **Frankfurter Goethe-Museum.** This museum contains a library of 120,000 volumes and a collection of about 30,000 manuscripts, as well as 16,000 graphic artworks and 400 paintings associated with Goethe and his works.

✪ **Liebieghaus.** Schaumainkai 71. ☎ **069/21-23-86-17.** Admission 5DM ($2.50) adults, 2.50DM ($1.25) seniors, students, and children. Tues and Thurs–Sun 10am–5pm, Wed 10am–8pm. Tram: 16 to Otto-Hahn-Platz.

This sculpture museum stands alongside the Bargello in Florence as one of the most important in Europe. The building is an 1896 villa. Its collection includes objects from ancient Egypt, classical Greece and Rome, and medieval and renaissance Europe. Highlights include a small 8th-century B.C bronze horse, and Roman copies of the *Torso* of Polycletus, Praxiteles's *Satyr*, and Myron's *Athena*. Although the most ancient artifacts generate the most excitement, the medieval section is also fascinating. Look for the *Virgin and Child* created in Trier in the 11th century, the head of Bärbel von Ottenheim (attributed to van Leyden in 1462), the Riemenschneider *Madonna*, Andrea della Robbia's altarpiece of the Assumption, and the 16th-century *Black Venus with Mirror.*

✪ **Städel Gallery.** Schaumainkai 63 (on the south bank of the Main). ☎ **069/6-05-09-80.** Admission 10DM ($5) adults, 8DM ($4) children 6–16, 3DM ($1.80) children 5 and under; free for everyone Tues and Thurs–Sun 10am–5pm, Wed 10am–8pm. U-Bahn: Schweizer Platz.

This is Frankfurt's most important art gallery, containing a fine collection of most European schools of painting. The first floor features French impressionists such as Renoir and Monet, along with German painters of the 19th and 20th centuries. Note in particular Kirchner's *Nude Woman with Hat.* Also on the first floor is Tischbein's portrait of Goethe in the Campagna in Italy. But if you're short on time, go directly to the second floor to view the outstanding collection of Flemish primitives, 17th-century Dutch artists, and 16th-century German masters such as Dürer, Grünewald, Memling, Elsheimer, and many others. One of the most impressive paintings is Jan van Eyck's *Madonna* (1433). Lucas Cranach is represented by a large winged altarpiece and his rather impish nude Venus. Recent acquisitions include Jean Antoine Watteau's *L'Ile de Cythére* (1709). In the Department of Modern Art are works by Bacon, Dubuffet, Tapiès, and Yves Klein.

Deutsches Filmmuseum (German Film Museum). Schaumainkai 41, at the corner of Schweizerstrasse. ☎ **069/21-23-88-30.** Admission 5DM ($2.50) adults, 3DM ($1.50) students, 2.50DM ($1.25) children; film screenings 8DM ($4) adults, 6DM ($3) students and children. Tues, Thurs, Fri, and Sun 10am–5pm, Wed 10am–8pm, Sat 2–8pm. U-Bahn: Schweizer Platz.

This is the finest film museum in Germany. Old films from the collection are shown continuously on the second floor. The rooms downstairs chronicle the history of the filmmaking industry. Exhibits include Emile Reynaud's 1882 Praxinoscope, Edison's Kinetoscope from 1889, and a copy of the Lumière brothers' Cinematograph from 1895. There are also models illustrating how special effects are shot, including those in *King Kong.*

Deutsches Architekturmuseum. Schaumainkai 43. ☎ **069/21-23-88-44.** Admission 8DM ($4) adults, free for children. Tues and Thurs–Sun 10am–5pm, Wed 10am–8pm. U-Bahn: Schweizer Platz.

Like the film museum, this is the best of its kind in Germany. Exhibits trace the saga of architecture from the Sumerians to today's most modern statements. The displays are arranged in what has been called "a house within a house," that is, a series of intimate galleries encased in a villa. The permanent collection consists of some two-dozen commissioned large-scale models, but these are not always on view, since floor space is often needed for temporary exhibitions.

Museum für Kunsthandwerk. Schaumainkai 17. ☎ **069/21-23-40-37.** Admission 8DM ($4) adults, 4DM ($2) students and children over 5. Tues and Thurs–Sun 10am–5pm, Wed 10am–8pm. U-Bahn: Schweizer Platz.

More than 30,000 objects, ranging across Europe and Asia, are exhibited at the Museum of Applied Arts. Two buildings house the collection: a 19th-century villa and 1985 structure designed by New York architect Richard Meier. The museum has an outstanding collection of German rococo furnishings (called *Mainzer Meistermöbel*) created in Mainz. The glassware is a highlight, with some Venetian pieces from the 15th century. On the second floor, the Far East and Islamic department has a rich collection of Persian carpets and faïence dating from the 9th century. One of Germany's finest porcelain collections is here as well.

Museum für Moderne Kunst. Domstrasse 10 (in the center of the Innenstadt, near Römerberg). ☎ **069/21-23-04-47.** Admission 10DM ($5) adults, 5DM ($2.50) for students and children; free for everyone Tues and Thurs–Sun 10am–5pm, Wed 10am–8pm. U-Bahn: Rümer. Tram: 11 to Domstrasse.

This museum opened in 1991 in a building created by Hans Hollein, the Viennese architect. The structure is designed like a boat, but in spite of its somewhat bizarre shape, the gallery has a bright, spacious air. (Some unkind critics have claimed that the dazzling architecture is more interesting than the exhibits.) Major artists since the 1950s are displayed here, including Roy Lichtenstein (see his *Brush-stroke*) and George Segal, with his *Jazz Combo.* Modern German artists include George Flintzer, Inge Rambow, August Sambe, Gerhard Richter, and others.

THE PALMENGARTEN

The **Palmengarten,** Siesmayerstrasse 61 (☎ **069/21-23-39-39;** U-Bahn: Westend; bus: 36), is a park and a botanical garden. During the last decade, the gardens have been renewed and the conservatories and historic greenhouses completely reconstructed. You can admire a perennial garden, an expanded rock garden, and a beautiful rose garden. The 1869 palm house is now surrounded by a huge gallery that serves as an exhibition hall for flower shows and other botanical exhibitions. In recent years new conservatories have been added: The Tropicarium is a complex for tropical vegetation; the Subantarctic House displays plants from southern Chile, Argentina, and New Zealand; and the Entrance Conservatory houses insectivorous plants and bromeliads. Collections of orchids, palms, succulents, water lilies, and many others are also on display.

Admission to the botanical garden is 7DM ($3.50) for adults and 3DM ($1.50) for children, or 15DM ($7.50) for a family ticket. It's open daily March to September 9am to 6pm, October and February 9am to 5pm, and November to January 9am to 4pm. In the park area, there's a small lake where people can row boats. In summer, concerts are given in the band shell; evening events include open-air dancing, jazz, and fountain illumination. There are some facilities for food.

ESPECIALLY FOR KIDS

Children love the **Palmengarten** (see above). Take along a picnic (**Hertie,** at An der Zeil 390, has a good deli), and then rent a rowboat and take the kids on an excursion. Another option is the **Senckenberg Museum of Natural History,** Senckenberganlage 25 (☎ **069/7-54-20;** U-Bahn: Bockenheimerwarte), which has an interesting collection of fossils, including dinosaur bones. Admission is 7DM ($3.50) for adults, 3DM ($1.50) for students and children over 3, and free for children 2 and under. Open daily 9am to 5pm. Children will also enjoy the circus performances at the **Tiger Palast,** Heiligkreuzgasse 16–20 (☎ **069/9200-2250;** U-Bahn: Konstablerwache), which include jugglers, acrobats, and magic acts.

Another interesting possibility is **Struwwelpeter Museum,** Schirm am Römerberg (☎ **069/28-13-33;** U-Bahn: Römer), which is dedicated to memorabilia associated with one of Germany's most famous children's books, *Struwwelpeter* (*Slovenly Peter*). The story was written and illustrated by a local doctor, Heinrich Hoffman (1798–1874), who opened the first hospital for neurology in Frankfurt. His Slovenly Peter character gained popularity in the United States after Mark Twain translated Hoffman's work. On the premises is a museum shop selling posters, postcards, and actual copies of the Struwwelpeter books translated into many different languages. The museum is open Tuesday to Sunday 11am to 5pm; July and August, it remains open on Wednesday till 8pm. Entrance is free. The kindly staff members are strictly volunteer.

✪ **Zoologischer Garten.** Alfred-Brehm-Platz 16. ☎ **069/21-23-37-35.** Admission 11DM ($5.50) adults, 5DM ($2.50) children 6–17, free for children 5 and under. Oct–Mar daily 9am–5pm; Apr–Sept daily 9am–7pm. U-Bahn: Zoologischer Garten (Zoo).

This zoo is intent on education as well as entertainment, and proves interesting for both young and old. Most animals are in enclosures resembling their native habitats. One of the best examples is the African Veldt Enclosure, landscaped with hills and bushes; antelopes and ostriches roam freely. In the Exotarium, fish and various reptiles live under special climatic conditions. Penguins swim and dive in an artificially cooled polar landscape. There's also an aviary where you can watch birds preparing unusual nests. The building for small mammals, with its nocturnal section, is one of the largest and most diversified of its kind in the world.

6 Sports & Outdoor Pursuits

BICYCLING
Bicycles can be rented from **Holger's Rad-Laden,** Eschersheimer Landstrasse 470 (☎ **069/522004;** U-Bahn/S-Bahn: Weisserstein), for 15DM ($9) per day.

FITNESS CENTERS & HEALTH CLUBS
Many major hotels in Frankfurt maintain health clubs, but if yours doesn't, consider a day ticket to one of the semiprivate health clubs such as **Sport Fabrik,** Ginnheimer-strasse 47 (☎ **069/970-7210;** U-Bahn/S-Bahn: Ginnheim), or **Sportschule Petrescu,** Bleichstrasse 55–57 (☎ **069/29-59-06;** U-Bahn/S-Bahn: Hauptwache). Both offer roughly equivalent arrays of exercise machines, free weights, saunas, and massage facilities. A day pass ranges from 40DM to 110DM ($20 to $55), depending on what facilities you want to use.

GOLF
Golf Anlage im Frankfurter Waldstadion, Morfelder Landstrasse 362, 60528 Frankfurt (☎ **069/67-80-4114**), located within the city limits, is open to all. This course has nine holes, plus a floodlit driving range. Open daily 9am to 9pm.

ICE-SKATING
Between November and April, you can skate at the **Eissporthalle,** am Bornheimer Hang 4, Ratsweg (☎ **069/21-23-08-25;** U-Bahn/S-Bahn: Eissporthalle). Open Monday to Friday 9am to 9pm, Saturday 10am to 9pm, and Sunday 10am to 8pm. Admission is 8DM ($4) for adults and 6DM ($3) for children.

JOGGING
A good jogging route is along the quays of the River Main, using both sides of the river and the bridges to create a loop. Another choice is the centrally located Gruneberg Park, whose walkways are suitable for jogging.

TENNIS
Few of the tennis courts in Frankfurt allow non-members to play. A noteworthy exception is the **Tennisplata Eissporthall,** Am Bornheimer hang, 60486 Frankfurt (☎ **069/41-91-41;** U-Bahn/S-Bahn: Eissporthalle), which has a half-dozen courts. They're open April to October daily 7am to sundown. The cost is 20DM ($10) per hour.

7 Shopping

When it comes to shopping, Frankfurt has everything. The specialty shops here are so much like those back in the States that most visitors from America will feel right at home. Shops in the central area are open Monday to Friday 9am to 6:30pm and Saturday 9am to 2pm (to 4 or 6pm on the first Saturday of the month).

THE SHOPPING SCENE

In Frankfurt, the shopping scene is divided into different regions. On the **Zeil,** a pedestrian zone between the Hauptwache and Konstablerwache, you'll find department stores, clothing shops, shoe stores, and furniture outlets. Once one of the most famous shopping streets on the Continent, the Zeil was destroyed in the war and hasn't regained its former prestige, though it still has the highest sales of any shopping area in Germany. In the 14th century, it was a cattle-round-up market. Nearby is the **Kleinmarkthalle,** a covered market with international grocery products.

The **Hauptwache,** in the center of Frankfurt, has two shopping areas, one above and one below ground. Groceries, book dealers, flowers, clothing, tobacco, photo supplies, recordings, and sporting equipment abound. In the Hauptwache-Passage are restaurants, travel agencies, and banks.

Schillerstrasse, another pedestrian zone, lies between Hauptwache and Eschenheimer Turm, near the stock exchange. Walking from Schillerstrasse northeast toward Eschenheimer Tor, you'll pass many elegant boutiques and specialty shops.

Southwest of the Hauptwache is the Alte Oper. You can reach it by taking either the **Goethestrasse,** with its exclusive stores, evocative of Paris or Milan, or the parallel **Grosse Bockenheimerstrasse,** traditionally nicknamed Fressgasse. Most wine dealers, delis, and butcher shops here look back on a long and venerable past. At **Opernplatz** you'll find a variety of restaurants and cafes.

West of the Hauptwache is Rossmarkt, leading to **Kaiserstrasse.** It passes the BFG skyscraper, which has three floors of exclusive retail stores, boutiques, and restaurants and directly connects the downtown area to the Hauptbahnhof. Kaiserstrasse is also known for its large selection of stores selling clothing, audio and photography equipment, and stainless-steel ware. The heart of the fur trade in Frankfurt is **Düsseldorfer Strasse,** opposite the Hauptbahnhof. Most book dealers are located around the Hauptwache and **Goetheplatz.** Antiques, old books, etchings, and paintings on **Braubachstrasse** can be found near the Römer, at the Dom, and on Fahrgasse.

Art and antiques are the domain of **Alt-Sachsenhausen,** an appealing and original neighborhood. The famous **Frankfurt Flea Market** takes place here every Saturday 8am to 2pm along the Main River on the Sachsenhausen side. To get there, walk from the Römer toward the river and cross the Eisener Steg bridge.

DEPARTMENT STORES & MALLS   The 45 shops of the **Zeil Galerie,** Zeil 112–114 (☎ **069/92-07-340;** U-Bahn/S-Bahn: Hauptwache), sell everything imaginable. The three best department stores in the city are **Kaufhof,** Zeil 116 (☎ **069/ 2-19-10**); **Hertie,** Zeil 90 (☎ **069/92-90-50**); and Japanese-transplant **Mitsukoshi,** Kaiserstrasse 13 (☎ **069/9218870;** U-Bahn/S-Bahn: Hauptwache), all of which carry the wide variety expected in such establishments.

FOOD & WINE   Konditorei Lochner, Karl-Becher-Gasse 10 (☎ **069/ 9-20-73-20;** U-Bahn/S-Bahn: Alte Oper), specializes in marzipan cookies and creamy Frankfurter Kranz cake, and also has a coffee bar. A small bakery-cafe, **Laumer,** Bockenheimer Landstrasse 74 (☎ **069/72-79-12;** U-Bahn/S-Bahn: Bockenheimer Warte), sells a wide variety of sweets and has a popular cafe. Regional wines, including those produced by the city's own vineyards, are available at **Weingutes,** Limpurger Gasse 2 (☎ **069/21-23-36-80;** U-Bahn/S-Bahn: Römer).

JEWELRY   Expensive but worth it, the jewelry found at **Friedrich,** Goethestrasse 9 (☎ **069/28-43-53;** U-Bahn/S-Bahn: Alte Oper), is the product of Cristoph and Stephan Friedrich, two of Germany's best designers. The brothers work with gold, platinum, silver, and assorted gemstones. One of the best centers of elegant jewelry is **Gerhard Wempe,** An der Hauptwache 7 (☎ **069/29-17-77;** U-Bahn/S-Bahn: Hauptwache). Items start at nearly 1,000DM ($600). The shop also carries about 46 brands of watches.

LEATHER GOODS   Fink Exklusiv Schuhe, Goethestrasse 9 (☎ **069/28-99-04;** U-Bahn/S-Bahn: Alte Oper), carries leather clothing and shoes for both men and women.

PORCELAIN, CHINA & CRYSTAL   The porcelain dinnerware, crystal, and glassware at **Rosenthal,** Goethestrasse 1 (☎ **069/28-85-90;** U-Bahn/S-Bahn: Alte Oper), are designed exclusively for the shop, and include classic and original contemporary patterns. Great deals can be found at the factory outlet **Höchster Porzellan Manufaktur,** Berliner Strasse 60, at the Kornmarkt in suburban Höchst (☎ **069/29-52-99;** U-Bahn/S-Bahn: Römer). This is Germany's second oldest porcelain manufacturer after Meissen. Among the items found in the shop are dinnerware, candleholders, vases, figurines, and Austrian glassware.

  Lorey, Schillerstrasse 16 (☎ **069/29-99-50;** U-Bahn/S-Bahn: Hauptwache), carries one of the city's best selections of Hummel and Meissen figurines, plus porcelain and china, housewares, crystal, and accessories.

TOYS & CHILDREN'S BOOKS   The best places for children's toys in Frankfurt are the three department stores listed above and **Behle Spiel & Ferienzeit,** Grosse Friedberger Strasse 7–11 (☎ **069/92-00-850;** U-Bahn/S-Bahn: Konstablerwache).

8 Frankfurt After Dark

For details of what's happening in Frankfurt, you can pick up copies of *Journal Frankfurt* at newsstands throughout the city. Also listing events are *Fritz* and *Strandgut,* both free and available at the tourist office.

  To purchase tickets for many major cultural events, go to the tourist office at the Hauptbahnhof. The department store **Hertie,** Zeil 90 (☎ **069/294848**), also has a theater ticket office, which is open during regular store hours.

THE PERFORMING ARTS

Theater der Stadt Frankfurt, Untermainanlage 11 (☎ **069/21237999;** U-Bahn: Willy-Brandt-Platz), has three stages. One belongs to the **Frankfurt Municipal Opera,** whose productions have received worldwide recognition in recent years. Two stages are devoted to drama. If your German is adequate, you might want to see a performance of **Städtische Bühnen/Schauspiel** (☎ **069/21-23-79-99**), a forum for classic German plays as well as modern drama. A variety theater, **Kunstlerhaus Mouson Turm,** Waldschmidtstrasse 4 (☎ **069/4058-9520;** U-Bahn/S-Bahn: Merianplatz), hosts plays, classical music concerts, and dance programs almost every night of the week. Tickets run 20DM to 40DM ($10 to $20).

Alte Oper. Opernplatz. ☎ **069/1-34-04-00.** Tickets 30DM–200DM ($15–$100). Box office Mon–Fri 8:30am–8:30pm, Sat 9:30am–2pm. U-Bahn: Alte Oper.

The old opera house is still the pride of Frankfurt, even though opera is no longer presented here. This building was reopened in 1981, following its reconstruction after

World War II bombings. The original structure had been officially opened in 1880 by Kaiser Wilhelm I. At that time it was hailed as one of the most beautiful theaters in Europe. Today the Alte Oper is the site of frequent symphonic and choral concerts.

✪ **Oper Frankfurt/Ballet Frankfurt.** Willy-Brandt-Platz (between the Hauptbahnhof and the Innenstadt). ☎ **069/21-23-79-99.** Opera and ballet 20DM–210DM ($10–$105). Box office Mon–Fri 8am–8pm, Sat 8am–6pm. U-Bahn: Willy-Brandt-Platz.

This is Frankfurt's premier showcase for world-class opera and ballet. Acclaimed for its dramatic artistry, the **Frankfurt Opera** is under the charge of conductor Sylvain Cambreling. The world renown **Frankfurt Ballet** is directed by William Forsythe.

English Theater. Kaiserstrasse 52 (near the Hauptbahnhof). ☎ **069/24-23-16-20.** Plays 43DM–50DM ($21.50–$25); reduced student price 20DM ($10); musicals 65DM ($32.50); reduced student price 40DM ($20). On Tues and Sun prices are 8DM ($4) less. Box office daily 10am–7pm. S-Bahn: Hauptbahnhof.

This English-language theater was founded by the actress Judith Rosenbauer, who is still its artistic director. It began in a Sachsenhausen backyard, but was later moved to this location, compliments of the city of Frankfurt. The art deco auditorium, which seats 230, has an adjoining cafe. Musicals, comedies, dramas, and thrillers are produced. During the season (September to July), performances are Tuesday to Saturday at 8pm and Sunday and Wednesday at 6pm.

THE CLUB & BAR SCENE

In a 16-square-block area in front of the Hauptbahnhof, you'll find a rowdy kind of entertainment: what the Germans call *erotische spiele.* Doormen will practically pull you inside to view porno movies, sex shows, sex shops, even discos teeming with prostitutes. *Warning:* This area can be dangerous—don't come here alone.

For less lurid activities in a safer environment, head to the live-music clubs, discos, bars, and cafes across the Main River in the **Sachsenhausen** district. Most gay bars and clubs are located in a small area between Bleichstrasse and Zeil.

DANCE CLUBS

Cooky's. Am Salzhaus 4. ☎ **069/28-76-62.** Cover Sun and Tues–Thurs 11DM ($5.50), Fri–Sat 14DM ($7). U-Bahn/S-Bahn: Hauptwache.

Tuesday to Sunday, DJs at Cooky's mix a dance soundtrack of hip-hop and house music. Hours are Tuesday, Thursday, and Sunday 11pm to 4am, Friday and Saturday 10pm to 6am.

Dorian Gray. O Level of Section C in the Frankfurt airport. ☎ **069/69-02-21-21.** Cover 15DM–20DM ($7.50–$10). U-Bahn/S-Bahn: Flughafen.

This popular disco and continental bistro can be reached from the heart of the city in about 15 minutes aboard an S-train, which departs from Hauptbahnhof every 20 minutes. Its well-appointed lounges and club room draw an elegant well-dressed crowd. Open Sunday, Wednesday, and Thursday 9pm to 4am, Friday and Saturday 10pm to 6am.

Nacht Leben. Kurt-Schumacher-Strasse 45. ☎ **069/2-06-50.** Cover 8DM–10DM ($4–$5). U-Bahn/S-Bahn: Konstablerwache.

This club has a cafe-bar upstairs and a disco downstairs. Here you can either have drinks and conversation, or dance to the throbbing beat of hip-hop, funk, soul, and house. The club occasionally books a live band. Open Monday to Wednesday 11:30am to 2am, Thursday to Saturday 11:30am to 4am.

LIVE MUSIC

An Sibin. Wallstrasse 9. ☎ **069/6-03-21-59.** U-Bahn/S-Bahn: Hauptwache.

This Irish cellar pub is decorated with pushcarts, wagons, and antique instruments. There's a band on most nights; the music is Irish-only on Tuesday. You'll find Guinness on tap, English and Irish pub grub, and a friendly barkeep who'll teach you a few phrases in Gaelic. Open Monday to Thursday 7pm to 2am, Friday and Saturday 7pm to 3am.

Der Jazzkeller. Kleine Bockenheimer 18A, near Goethestrasse. ☎ **069/28-85-37.** Concerts 12DM–40DM ($6–$20), disco 9DM ($4.50). U-Bahn/S-Bahn: Alte Oper.

This basement club, established in 1952, is one of the most famous and atmospheric jazz clubs in Germany. Its reputation is as solid as the 200-year-old redbrick walls that surround it. The place has played host to such jazz luminaries as Louis Armstrong, Dizzy Gillespie, and Gerry Mulligan. Wednesday and Friday, patrons dance to the club's "Cool Music Mix." Thursday and Saturday, live music is presented. Open Tuesday to Sunday 9pm to 3am.

Dreikönigskeller. Färberstrasse 71. ☎ **069/62-92-73.** U-Bahn/S-Bahn: Schweizerplatz.

This tiny place features live performances of any and every pop musical style from the 1940s through the contemporary music scene. It opens daily at 8pm.

Jazz-Kneipe. Berliner Strasse 70. ☎ **069/28-71-73.** Cover 5DM–20DM ($2.50–$10). U-Bahn/S-Bahn: Römer.

A venue for soloists, duos, and small ensembles, Jazz-Kneipe hosts solo piano or piano/guitar or piano/bass duos Sunday to Wednesday. On Friday and Saturday, trios and quartets perform jazz or blues. Open daily 8pm to 4am.

Sinkkasten. Brönnerstrasse 9. ☎ **069/28-03-85.** Disco 8DM ($4), concerts 12DM–40DM ($6–$20). U-Bahn/S-Bahn: Konstablerwache.

At this live-music institution, regulars show up regardless of who's playing. Rock, reggae, blues, pop, jazz, and African music bands might be found here, except on Thursday, Saturday and late Friday, when the club turns disco. Come early to beat the crowd or risk being turned away. Open Sunday to Thursday 9pm to 2am, Friday and Saturday 9pm to 3am.

BARS, CAFES & TAVERNS

Jimmy's, in the Hotel Hessischer Hof, Friedrich-Ebert-Anlage 40 (☎ **069/75400;** S-Bahn: Platz der Republik), is a luxurious candlelit bar with a whisper of background music. It's a relaxing place to unwind, but it's not cheap—drinks start at 23DM ($11.50) and beers at 11DM ($5.50). One of the best-known beer halls in Frankfurt, **Maier Gustl's Bayrisch Zell,** in the Hauptbahnhof, Münchner Strasse 57 (☎ **069/ 23-20-92;** S-Bahn: Hauptbahnhof), is a timbered re-creation of a mountain chalet. It has two dance floors, which hold nearly 1,000 people. After hoisting a few steins of brew, exuberant patrons dance to a Bavarian brass band and a modern show band that alternate sets every 30 minutes. Some of the tables have table-to-table telephones, a slightly sleazy nod to the surrounding red-light district. Meals include *Eisbein mit sauerkraut* (leg of pork), the most expensive dish on the menu at 19DM ($9.50). Beers, available in different sizes and brands, run from 8DM to 12DM ($6).

Lovers of apple wine should head to **Mutter Ernst,** Alte Rothofstrasse 12 (☎ **069/ 28-38-22;** U-Bahn/S-Bahn: Alte Oper), open daily 9am to 10pm (to 5am Saturday), and **Apfelweinwirtschaft Wagner,** Schweizerstrasse 71 (☎ **069/61-25-65;** U-Bahn/ S-Bahn: Schweizerplatz), open daily 11am to midnight, where you can order traditional German dishes to accompany your beverage.

Club Voltaire, Kleine Hochstrasse 5 (☎ **069/29-24-08;** U-Bahn/S-Bahn: Alte Oper), is a place for impromptu poetry readings. You can listen or join in. Full meals at 10DM to 15DM ($7.50) draw as many students as the poetry and drinking.

GAY CLUBS

Blue Angel. Bronnerstrasse 17. ☎ **069/28-27-72.** Cover 10DM ($6). U-Bahn/S-Bahn: Konstablerwache.

This club was named after gay icon Marlene Dietrich's first movie hit. The DJs keep you guessing by mixing dance styles. The revelry often picks up steam late in the night, so hours generally extend into the early morning. Open daily 10pm, usually to 4 or 5am.

Harvey's Cafe Bar. Bornheimer Landstrasse 64. ☎ **069/49-73-03.** U-Bahn/S-Bahn: Hauptwache.

This indoor/outdoor bistro sometimes has live disco bands on the weekend. It's a popular place for a gay date. Open daily 9am to 1am (to 2am Friday and Saturday).

Lucky's Manhattan. Schäfergasse 27. ☎ **069/28-49-19.** U-Bahn/S-Bahn: Konstablerwache.

Best described as a gay cafe and bar wrapped into one, Lucky's also has aspects of a conservative tearoom. Most folks come here to drink beer or apple wine, or perhaps to nibble on a limited array of toasts and crepes. It's a worthwhile place to begin, but not to end, an evening on the town. Open daily noon to 2am.

Mr. Dorian's Club. Alte Gasse 34. ☎ **069/29-45-06.** U-Bahn/S-Bahn: Konstablerwache.

This small but not particularly crowded place caters to a clientele of gay men in their 30s and 40s. Regulars come to talk and have a leisurely drink. Open Sunday to Thursday 6pm to 2am, Friday to Saturday 6pm to 3am.

The Stall. Stiftstrasse 22. ☎ **069/29-18-80.** U-Bahn/S-Bahn: Konstablerwache.

This is the most visible and crowded leather bar in Frankfurt. It attracts a woodsy, macho-looking set that's been a part of the local gay scene for years. Open Sunday to Thursday 9pm to 4am, Friday and Saturday 9pm to 6am.

9 Side Trips from Frankfurt

Picturesque Aschaffenburg and some of the leading spas of Germany lie on the doorstep of Frankfurt. Another good side trip is to Mainz (see chapter 13).

ASCHAFFENBURG

40km (25 miles) SE of Frankfurt, 77km (48 miles) NW of Würzburg

Aschaffenburg was originally a Roman settlement on the right bank of the Main River, and later became an important town in the Middle Ages. In recent years, it's grown industrially, but even with 250 garment manufacturers, the town has remained peaceful and provincial. Its many parks and shady lanes make it a fitting gateway to the streams and woodlands of the Spessart Hills. Weekly fairs are held on the square, where fishers along the banks of the Main sell seafood straight from their buckets. Many traditional shops are in a pedestrian zone, with lamps, fountains, and flowers.

ESSENTIALS

GETTING THERE   By Train   The **Aschaffenburg Bahnhof** is on the major Nürnberg–Würzburg–Frankfurt line, and on the regional Maintal Aschaffenburg–Mittenburg–Wertheim line, with frequent connections in all directions. From

Frankfurt, 45 trains arrive daily (trip time: 30 to 45 min.). For information, call ☎ **01805/99-66-33.**

By Bus   There is no direct bus service between Frankfurt and Aschaffenburg.

By Car   Access by car is via the A3 Autobahn east and west.

VISITOR INFORMATION   Contact **Tourist-Information,** Schlossplatz 1 (☎ **06021/39-58-00**). It's open Monday to Friday 9am to 5pm and Saturday 10am to 1pm.

GETTING AROUND   Aschaffenburg and the immediate region around it are served by a network of green-painted buses whose junction point is the city's main railway station (*Hauptbahnhof*). Since many of the streets within the city's historic core are reserved for pedestrians, many sightseers take bus 1, 4, 5, or 8 between the Hauptbahnhof and the Stadthalle (Town Hall), immediately adjacent to the *Altstadt*. Buses run daily 5:30am to 9pm. Rides within the central zone cost 2DM ($1) per person each way. For information, call the city tourist office (☎ **06021/ 39-58-00**).

SEEING THE SIGHTS

The best park in Aschaffenburg is **Schönbusch Park,** Kleine Schönbuschallee 1 (☎ **06021/386-570;** bus: 4), located 3km (2 miles) across the Main. It's a marvel of planning, using the natural surroundings as a setting for formal 18th-century gardens, shady lanes, temples, and gazebos. At the edge of the mirror-smooth lake is a small neoclassical castle, really a country house, once used by the electors of Mainz. The house is open April to October, Tuesday to Sunday 10am to 12:30pm and 2:30 to 5pm. Admission is 5DM ($2.50) for adults, 4DM ($2) for students, and free for children under 15. In summer, it's possible to rent a small boat to go on the lake. There's also a cafe-restaurant open daily 8am to 8pm.

The most impressive castle in Aschaffenburg is the huge Renaissance **Schloss Johannisburg,** Schlossplatz 4 (☎ **06021/386-570;** bus: 1, 2, or 8), reflected in the waters of the Main. Erected from 1605 to 1614, it became the residence of the rulers of the town, the prince-electors of Mainz. The red sandstone castle is almost perfectly symmetrical, with four massive lantern towers surrounding an inner courtyard. April to October, the castle is open 9am to noon and 1 to 5pm, Tuesday to Sunday; off-season, Tuesday to Sunday 11am to 4pm. Admission is 5DM ($2.50) for adults and 4DM ($2) for children 14 and under. While here you might visit the Schlossweinstuben (see "Where to Dine," below). From the castle gardens you can reach the **Pompeianum,** built by Bavaria's King Ludwig I as a replica of the Castor and Pollux palace discovered among the ruins of Pompeii. The Pompeianum is open mid-March to mid-October, Tuesday to Sunday 10am to noon and 2:30 to 5pm. Admission is 4DM ($2) for adults, 3DM ($1.50) for students, and free for children.

Stiftskirche St. Peter and St. Alexander, Stiftsgasse 5 (☎ **06021/2-24-20;** bus: 1, 4, or 10), has stood on its hill overlooking the town for 1,000 years. Its architecture has changed over the centuries, however, as it was remodeled and reconstructed, and today it stands as a combination of Romanesque, Gothic, and baroque. Its most precious treasure is the painted retable *The Lamentation of Christ,* by Mathias Grünewald. The interior is decorated with several paintings of the school of Lucas Cranach, as well as a marble-alabaster pulpit by Hans Juncker. One of the oldest pieces is a Roman-style crucifix from 980. Adjacent to the north side of the church is a Romanesque cloister from the 13th century. The church is open Wednesday to Monday 10am to 1pm and 2 to 5pm. Admission is 3DM ($1.50) adults and 2DM ($1) children and students.

WHERE TO STAY

Aschaffenburger Hof. Frohsinnstrasse 11, 63739 Aschaffenburg. ☎ **06021/386810.** Fax 06021/2-72-98. 60 units. TV TEL. 148DM–198DM ($74–$99) double. Rates include breakfast. AE, DC, V. Parking 8DM ($4). Bus: 1, 3, 4, 6, or 10.

This establishment is housed in a tall yellow building with a single balcony on each floor. The small rooms, although no style-setters, are pleasantly furnished. Each has a small refrigerator. Try for one overlooking the courtyard. The restaurant is locally popular for its fresh, modern cuisine that includes some vegetarian dishes. The hotel offers room service, dry cleaning, and laundry service.

Hotel Dalberg. Pfaffengasse 12-14. D-63739 Aschaffenburg.☎ **06021/3560.** Fax 06021/21-98-94. 26 units. MINIBAR TV TEL. 215DM ($107.50) double. AE, MC, V. Bus: 1 or 4.

Newly built in 1994, this hotel occupies a prominent site that's within a five-minute walk from Aschaffenburg's historic core and its pedestrian zone. Rising behind an all-white, four-story facade, it offers cozy, well-designed rooms. On the premises you'll find a rustic-looking Weinstube serving regional cuisine and a bar.

Hotel Post. Goldbacherstrasse 19, 63739 Aschaffenburg. ☎ **06021/33-40.** Fax 06021/1-34-83. www.post-ab.de. E-mail: info@t.post.ab.de. 69 units. MINIBAR TV TEL. 195DM–220DM ($97.50–$110) double. Rates include breakfast. AE, DC, MC, V. Parking 8DM ($4). Bus: 1, 3, 4, 6, or 10.

This is the town's premier hotel, offering greater comfort than its nearest rival, Aschaffenburger Hof (see above). Close to the heart of town, it was built in 1919, and completely renovated in 2000. Rooms are well maintained and decorated in traditional style. The dining room is a stylized version of an old posting inn; it includes an original mail coach, timbered walls and ceiling, and lead-glass windows. Reasonably priced and very good Franconian meals are served here. The hotel offers room service and laundry service, and has a sauna, indoor swimming pool, and solarium.

Syndikus. Löherstrasse 35, 63739 Aschaffenburg (a few blocks from the cathedral). ☎ **06021/2-35-88.** Fax 06021/2-92-80. www.aburg.net. E-mail: syndikus35@ad.com. 27 units. TV TEL. 140DM ($70) double; 160DM–220DM ($80–$110) suite. Rates include breakfast. AE, CB, DC, DISC V. Parking 6DM ($3). Bus: 3 or 6.

An unpretentious three-story facade greets visitors to this hotel. The bar area is rustically decorated with timbered ceilings and wheel chandeliers. All rooms are well maintained and have up-to-date furnishings. Although the hotel is open year-round, its restaurant is closed in August.

WHERE TO DINE

Schlossweinstueben. Schloss Johannisburg. ☎ **06021/1-24-40.** Reservations recommended. Main courses 10DM–38DM ($5–$19). No credit cards. Tues–Fri 11am–11pm, Sat–Sun 10am–midnight. Bus: 1, 3, or 4. FRANCONIAN/BAVARIAN.

One of the most alluring corners of this historic castle is its popular wine cellar. Here you'll find a wide variety of German wines to complement the conservative but well-prepared menu items. A meal might begin with liver-dumpling soup, then follow with a game specialty (depending on the season). The selection of very fresh fish is likely to include trout and pike. There is no pretension to this cuisine—it's just good, hearty, rib-sticking fare.

WIESBADEN

40km (25 miles) W of Frankfurt, 151km (94 miles) SE of Bonn

This sheltered valley, between the Rhine and the Taunus Mountains, has held a spa since Roman times. Today Wiesbaden competes with Baden-Baden for the title of

Germany's most fashionable resort. Its success is based partly on its 26 hot springs, with temperatures of 47°C to 66°C (117°F to 150°F), and partly on its proximity to Frankfurt's transportation centers, which gives the spa a distinctly international flavor.

Wiesbaden is also a major cultural center. Every spring it plays host to the International May Festival of music, dance, and drama. The major concert halls are in the **Kurhaus,** a lively, multi-roomed structure centered around a cupola-crowned hall. In addition to concerts, the complex hosts plays and ballets, plus a variety of social gatherings, such as international conferences, congresses, exhibitions, and trade fairs. It also holds a casino, a lively restaurant, and an outdoor cafe.

For the more active visitors, Wiesbaden offers horseback riding, a golf course, swimming, tennis, and hiking. The streets of the city are enjoyable for strolling, as is the **Kurpark,** which has a lake surrounded by old shade trees. It's especially beautiful at night, when the lights of the spa are reflected in the water and the huge fountains are lit. The park stretches for half a mile northward along the Kuranlagen, ending in a fancy residential quarter, the Sonnenberg. People-watching on the **Wilhelmstrasse** is another favorite pastime.

ESSENTIALS

GETTING THERE   By Train   Trains run between Frankfurt airport and Wiesbaden about every hour, leaving from the airport's lower level (trip time: 30 min.). Tickets can be purchased at machines in the station area or at the airport's railway ticket counter. There's also frequent train service from the center of Frankfurt on S-Bahn S-1 and S-9 (trip time: 30 to 40 min.). For information, call ☎ **01805/996633.**

By Bus   Deutsche Touring GmbH in Frankfurt (☎ **069/7903261**) operates frequent service to Wiesbaden (Line T81 or T82).

By Car   Wiesbaden lies at a major crossroads, with access via the A3 Autobahn from the north and south, connecting with the A66 Autobahn from the west and east. Travel time by car from Frankfurt (Route 66) is about 20 to 30 minutes, depending on traffic. From the Frankfurt airport to Wiesbaden by car is about 20 minutes.

VISITOR INFORMATION   The **Verkehrsbüro,** Marktstrasse 6 (☎ **0611/1-72-97-80**), is open Monday to Friday 9am to 6pm and Saturday 9am to 3pm. Closed on Sundays.

GETTING AROUND   The Hauptbahnhof is the junction point for most of the city's bus lines. Buses are blue-sided, and charge 2.50DM ($1.25) to 3.50DM ($1.75) for rides to most points in town, depending on distance. Buses run daily 5am to midnight. Kirchgasse is one of the most prominent streets in the pedestrian zone, but the closest point to catch a bus is in front of the Stadtteater.

SHOPPING   The shopping scene here is prosperous, squeaky-clean, and in the eyes of some, a bit smug. The resort's major shopping artery is **Wilhelmstrasse.** Wiesbaden is also a center for antiques, although we find them too pricey. **Taunusstrasse** is lined with antique shops.

WHERE TO STAY

Zur Rose (see "Where to Dine," below) also rents inexpensive rooms.

Very Expensive

✪ **Hotel Nassauer Hof.** Kaiser-Friedrich-Platz 3–4, 65183 Wiesbaden. ☎ **800/223-6800** in the U.S., or 0611/13-30. Fax 0611/13-36-32. www.nassauer-hof.de. E-mail: rezeption@ t.nassauer.hof.de. 198 units. A/C MINIBAR TV TEL. 435DM–580DM ($217.50–$290) double; 680DM–2,500DM ($340–$1,250) suite. AE, DC, MC, V. Parking 25DM ($12.50). Bus: 5, 18, or 25.

The superluxurious Nassauer Hof, often referred to as the "grande dame" of Wiesbaden, is among the most appealing in town. It's an old favorite with up-to-date conveniences. The spacious rooms feature soundproof windows, elegant furnishings, and comfortable mattresses; some have air-conditioning. Baths contain deluxe beauty products, hair dryers, and robes. The hotel stands in the city center, within walking distance of the Kurhaus, Spielbank, theaters, and the shopping area.

Dining/Diversions: The cozy Nassauer Hof Bar has an open fireplace and piano entertainment. Guests usually have an aperitif here before dinner. The bright, sunny Orangerie offers a refined German cuisine at lunch and dinner. The more expensive Ente Restaurant boasts the finest cuisine in Wiesbaden (see "Where to Dine," below). Other choices include the Entenkeller, a wine and beer cellar with a lighter menu, and the Bistro & Gourmet Boutique, open for both lunch and dinner.

Amenities: 24-hour room service, laundry, baby-sitting, Lancaster Beauty Spa, indoor thermal swimming pool, sauna, solarium, fitness room.

Expensive

Hotel Klee am Park. Parkstrasse 4, 65189 Wiesbaden. ☎ **0611/9-00-10.** Fax 0611/9-00-1310. www.klee-am-park.de. Email: hotel-klee-am-park@t-online.de. 54 units. MINIBAR TV TEL. 245DM–320DM ($122.50–$160) double. AE, DC, MC, V. Free parking. Bus: 2 or 8.

This hotel is highly recommended for those who might find the older, more luxurious Nassauer Hof a bit too monumental. Klee am Park is a square, modern hotel in a tranquil setting, surrounded by its own informal gardens. The theater, casino, and shopping area are nearby. Rooms have French doors opening onto balconies; some have sitting areas large enough for entertaining.

Dining/Diversions: Guests will find a cafe and restaurant where French cuisine is served, plus a comfortable English-style bar. The hotel's kitchen is known for its excellent and novel fare. Alfresco dining on the summer terrace is an added treat.

Amenities: Concierge, room service, hair dryers, laundry, dry cleaning.

Ramada Hotel Wiesbaden. Abraham-Lincoln-Strasse 17, 65189 Wiesbaden. ☎ **800/ 854-7854** in the U.S. and Canada, or 0611/79-70. Fax 0611/76-13-72. www.ramada.com. E-mail: rene.mooren@t.marrid.com. 205 units. A/C MINIBAR TV TEL. Mon–Thurs 180DM–271DM ($90–$135.50) double; Fri–Sun 165DM–185DM ($82.50–$92.50) double (rate includes breakfast); 290DM–350DM ($145–$175) suite. AE, DC, MC, V. Free parking. Bus: 5, 18, or 25.

Lots of businesspeople stay at the Ramada instead of staying in Frankfurt, as it's only 20 minutes from the Frankfurt airport. It's also a good center for visitors to Wiesbaden, within a 5-minute walk of the Kurhaus and the elegant boutiques and old cafes of the pedestrian zone. Rooms are modern and comfortably furnished. The small baths are well maintained.

Dining/Diversions: The restaurant, Abrahams, offers a variety of regional and international dishes. Try a glass of Rhine wine or draft beer in the rustic bar or a snack on the terrace bordering the indoor pool.

Amenities: Pool, sauna, fitness room, solarium, baby-sitting, and laundry service.

Moderate

✪ Admiral Hotel. Geisbergstrasse 8, 65193 Wiesbaden (a 5-min. walk from the Kurhaus). ☎ **0611/5-86-60.** Fax 0611/52-10-53. Email: hoteladmiral@t.rol.com. 28 units. TV TEL. 215DM ($107.50) double. Rates include buffet breakfast. AE, DC, MC, V. Parking 15DM ($7.50). Bus: 1 or 8.

The centrally located Admiral is a favorite of traditionalists and one of the best values in Wiesbaden. Readers constantly praise the owners for their hospitality. Rooms are furnished in a charmingly old-fashioned way, often with brass beds. Baths are small yet clean and contain hair dryers. The hotel offers health food. The owners are a retired U.S. Army officer and his German-born wife.

Hotel am Landeschaus. Mortitzstrasse 51, 65185 Wiesbaden (within walking distance of the railroad station). ☎ **0611/99-66-60.** Fax 0611/99-66-66. 20 units. TV TEL. 180DM ($90) double. Rates include buffet breakfast. AE, MC, V. Closed Dec 22–Jan 5. Parking 8DM ($4). Bus: 10, 14, or 16.

This hotel in central Wiesbaden is one of the spa's best reasonably priced hotels. It's completely modern, but also warm, cozy, and inviting. Rooms are well kept, with small, clean baths. Guests can enjoy drinks in a rustic ale tavern.

Inexpensive
Hotel Klemm. Kapellenstrasse 9, 65193 Wiesbaden (near the Kurhaus). ☎ **0611/58-20.** Fax 0611/58-22-22. www.info-wiesbaden.de. 60 units. TV TEL. 170DM–230DM ($85–$115) double. Rates include breakfast. AE, DC, MC, V. Bus: 1, 2, or 8.

This hotel occupies a late 19th-century Jugendstil villa with solid stone walls. Although the setting is well scrubbed and respectable, it has touches of genteel shabbiness that seem to go well with the nostalgia that permeates this part of Wiesbaden. This place enjoys many repeat visitors. Rooms are simple, but comfortable and clean. Only breakfast is served.

WHERE TO DINE
✪ **Ente Restaurant.** In the Hotel Nassauer Hof, Kaiser-Friedrich-Platz 3–4. ☎ **0611/ 133666.** Reservations required. Main courses 39DM–58DM ($19.50–$29); fixed-price dinner 105DM–165DM ($52.50–$82.50). AE, DC, MC, V. Restaurant and bistro daily noon–2:30pm and 6pm–midnight. Bus: 5, 18, or 25. CONTINENTAL.

This restaurant has the best food in town. The innovative chef makes sure the meals are as pleasing to the eye as they are to the palate. Cuisine is light and modern. Specialties change from week to week. Typical offerings include parfait of duck livers, a whole roast duck for two, roast medallions of venison with chanterelles, and clams in puff pastry. Desserts alone are reason to visit, especially the lemon soufflé with strawberries and the mountain-honey ice cream. Ente also has one of the best wine lists in Europe. Many are moderate in price. A boutique, delicatessen, wine cellar, and bistro are attached.

✪ **Käfer's.** In the Kurhaus, Kurhausplatz 1. ☎ **0611/53-62-00.** Reservations recommended. Main courses 26DM–50DM ($13–$25). AE, DC, MC, V. Daily 11:30am–2am. Bus: 1, 2, or 8. INTERNATIONAL.

Käfer's directs two restaurants within one of the stately and prestigious Kurhaus. The more appealing of the two is Käfer's Bistro, a replica of the kind of bustling, upscale, well-run bistro you might find in Lyon or Paris. In an adjoining room is the airier, quieter, and more self-consciously formal Casino Restaurant. The menu and prices are the same as in the bistro, but the atmosphere is calmer and frankly a bit more stuffy. Men are required to wear a jacket and tie. Menu items change every 2 weeks. Examples might include smoked salmon served with a *Rösti* pancake, crème fraîche, and chives; Canadian lobster with yogurt-flavored cocktail sauce and lemon; penne pasta with pesto sauce and grilled giant prawns; vegetarian dishes; and in springtime, asparagus with filet mignon, bacon, or salmon steak. Dessert might be a mousse flavored with three kinds of chocolate.

Zur Rose. Bremthaler Strasse 1 (east of the town center), 65207 Naurod. ☎ **06127/ 40-06-06.** Reservations recommended. Main courses 36DM–48DM ($18–$24); fixed-price menus 55DM–79DM ($27.50–$39.50). AE, DC, MC, V. Daily 11am–midnight. Bus: 21, 22, or 23. FRENCH/GERMAN.

This nearly two-hundred-year-old restaurant, located in a half-timbered building, offers a cozy, nostalgic decor, with a ceramic-tile oven, rose-colored lace tablecloths, and candlelight. You can enjoy freshly baked rolls as you peruse the menu. Begin with cucumber-cream soup with dill-flavored shrimp, then try the Barbarie duck breast with goose-liver sauce. Smoked salmon, trout, and other fresh fish and shrimp are also regularly featured. For dessert, try puff pastry filled with fresh fruits or poppy-seed mousse with rum-marinated fruits.

Zur Rose also rents 10 rooms, each with shower, TV, and phone. The charge for a double is 135DM ($67.50), including breakfast.

WIESBADEN AFTER DARK

"Rien ne va plus" is the call when the ball starts to roll on the gaming tables at the **Spielbank Wiesbaden,** Im Kurhaus, Kurhausplatz 1 (☎ **0611/53-61-00;** bus: 1, 8, or 16). The casino is open daily 3pm to 3am and admission is 5DM ($2.50). Roulette, blackjack, and poker are the featured games. It's located at the end of Wilhelmstrasse, one of the most famous streets in Wiesbaden. To enter, you must present a passport or an identification card. Men must wear jackets and ties.

Music and **theater** flourish in Wiesbaden throughout the year. For information on performances during your visit, check at the Wiesbaden tourist office (see "Visitor Information," above). For information about any of the conference and cultural facilities in the **Kurhaus** compound, Kurhaus Platz 1, including the casino and theater, call ☎ **0611/17290.**

Hessisches Staatstheater, Christian-Zais-Strasse (☎ **0611/13-23-25;** bus: 1), built in 1894 by Emperor Wilhelm II, is one of the most beautiful theaters in Germany. It presents a program of operettas, musicals, ballets, and plays. The season lasts September 15 to June 30; tickets are 7DM to 70DM ($3.50 to $35).

An important event is the **International May Festival.** The festival features concerts, classical in-house drama productions, and a wide selection of guest performances by internationally renowned theaters. For information and tickets, call ☎ **0611/132325.**

The **Prak Café,** Wilhelmstrasse 36 (☎ **0611/3-93-21;** bus: 1), incorporates a cafe, brasserie, and disco. It's sprawling and often very busy. Much louder is **The Big Apple,** Kirchgasse 66 (☎ **0611/37-40-33;** bus: 4, 5, 14, or 15), where music that will remind you of New York City and Los Angeles is played to a crowd of enthusiastic dancers, mostly in their early 20s. For beer in an appealingly old-fashioned atmosphere, head for the **Ratskeller** (also known as the **Rathsbräu Keller,** Schlossplatz (☎ **0611/300023;** bus: 4), or the **Ratstube,** Matstrasse 8 (☎ **0611/37-25-08;** bus: 4, 5, 14, or 15).

BAD HOMBURG

16km (10 miles) N of Frankfurt, 45km (28 miles) NE of Wiesbaden

Bad Homburg is one of Germany's most attractive spas, still basking in the grandeur left over from turn-of-the-century Europe. The spa's saline springs are used to treat various disorders, especially heart and circulatory diseases. The town has been a popular watering spot since Roman times. Royalty from all over the world have visited. King Chulalongkorn of Siam (Thailand) was so impressed that he built a Buddhist temple in the Kurpark. Czar Nicholas I erected an onion-domed Russian chapel nearby. The name of the town was popularized by England's Edward VII when, as Prince of Wales, he visited the spa and introduced a new hat style, which he called the "homburg." The town became the gaming capital of Europe when the Blanc brothers opened the casino in 1841.

The spa park is a verdant, carefully landscaped oasis in the middle of an otherwise rather commercial-looking town. The actual spa facilities are in the **Kaiser Wilhelms**

Bad, im Kurpark (☎ **0611/17290**). They're open Monday to Friday 10am to 10pm, Saturday 10am to noon. The immaculately tended gardens in the surrounding Kurpark are filled with brooks, ponds, arbors, and seasonal flowers. The town center has a sprawling pedestrian-only district that offers many shops, restaurants, and cafes.

ESSENTIALS

GETTING THERE   By Train   There's rail service by S-Bahn (S-5) from the center of Frankfurt. Call ☎ **01805/996633** for information.

By Bus   The **Alpina-Airport-Express** is Bad Homburg's hourly, nonstop shuttle service to and from the Frankfurt airport (trip time: 30 min.).

By Car   Access by car from the north or south is via the A5 Autobahn, exiting at Bad Homburg.

VISITOR INFORMATION   For information, go to the **Verkehrsamt im Kurhaus,** Louisenstrasse 58 (☎ **06172/675110**). It's open Monday to Friday 8:30am to 6:30pm and Saturday 9am to 1pm.

GETTING AROUND   Public transport in Bad Homburg is provided by a network of green and white buses, whose main junction points are the Hauptbahnhof, a 10-minute walk southwest of the city center, and in front of the Kurhaus, in the city center. Buses, which run daily 5am to midnight, charge 2.20DM ($1.10) per ride. Visitors from Frankfurt usually opt to take the S-5 train, which runs from Frankfurt's main railway station to Bad Homburg for a cost of 6.10DM ($3.05) each way.

SIGHTS & ACTIVITIES

Bad Homburg Palace. Schlossverwaltung (a few blocks from the spa gardens). ☎ **06172/ 67-50.** Admission 7DM ($3.50) adults, 5DM ($2.50) children. Palace and formal gardens Mar–Oct Tues–Sun 10am–5pm; Nov–Feb Tues–Sun 10am–4pm. Bus: 1, 4, or 11.

This palace was the residence of the landgraves of Hesse-Homburg from its construction in 1680 until the mid–19th century. Its builder, Prince Frederick II von Homburg, preserved the White Tower from the medieval castle that stood on the site. In the late 19th century, the palace became a summer residence for Prussian kings and, later, German emperors. After World War I the state assumed ownership. The interior contains 18th-century furniture and paintings, including a bust of Prince Frederick II by Andreas Schluter, Germany's greatest baroque sculptor. The former "telephone room of the empress" includes *Cleopatra* by Pellegrini.

Taunus Therme. Seedammweg. ☎ **06172/4-06-40.** Admission Mon–Fri, 23DM ($11.50) for 2 hr., 31DM ($15.50) for 4 hr., 45DM ($22.50) for all day; Sat–Sun and holidays, 26DM ($13) for 2 hr., 35DM ($17.50) for 4 hr., 49DM ($24.50) for all day; daily, free for children 3 and under. Sun–Tues 9am–11pm, Wed and Fri–Sat 9am–midnight. Bus: 6.

A large, fascinating recreation area, Taunus Therme boasts several pools, a sauna, a solarium, and a health center, plus TVs, cinemas, and two restaurants.

WHERE TO STAY

Expensive

Maritim Kurhaus-Hotel. Kurpark, Ludwigstrasse, 61348 Bad Homburg. ☎ **06172/ 66-00.** Fax 06172/66-01-00. Email: reservierung@hom.de. 148 units. MINIBAR TV TEL. 269DM–316DM ($134.50–$158) double; 480DM–580DM ($240–$290) suite. AE, DC, MC, V. Parking 20DM ($10). Bus: 1, 2, 3, 4, 11, or 12.

This hotel near the spa facilities offers visitors plush rooms, many with tall bay windows. As sleek and up-to-date as this hotel is, it's still far outclassed by the Steigenberger

Bad Homburg. Double rooms feature king-size beds; singles have queen-size beds. All contain computer outlets. Some rooms have balconies or terraces, permitting wide-angle views over the greenery of the surrounding park. The luxurious baths contain hair dryers and plush towels. The second and fifth floors are reserved for nonsmokers.

Dining: Both international and regional fare are served at the Bürgerstube, which is open daily. Large buffet breakfasts are also offered.

Amenities: Big-windowed indoor pool, sauna, laundry service, room service from 6:30am to 11pm, baby-sitting, concierge.

✪ **Steigenberger Bad Homburg.** Kaiser-Friedrich-Promenade 69–75 (opposite the spa gardens and casino), 61345 Bad Homburg. ☎ **800/223-5652** in the U.S. and Canada, or 06172/18-10. Fax 06172/18-16-30. www.bad-homburg.steigenberger.de. Email: bad-homburg@steigenberger.de. 169 units. A/C MINIBAR TV TEL. 316DM–430DM ($158–$215) double; 495DM–695DM ($247.50–$347.50) suite. AE, DC, MC, V. Parking 22DM ($11). Bus: 1, 2, 3, 4, 11, or 12.

This is the resort's best and most prestigious hotel. Europe's high society used to stroll here in days of yore, and an ambience of luxury still prevails. Rooms are beautifully furnished, each with individually adjustable air-conditioning and extra-long beds. The spacious baths contain deluxe luxury items, hair dryers, and sumptuous robes. Fifty-three rooms are reserved for nonsmokers.

Dining: The elegant Parkside Restaurant offers creative contemporary cuisine. There's also the French-style Charly's Bistro.

Amenities: Sauna, steam bath, solarium, beauty center, baby-sitting, 24-hour room service, laundry, dry cleaning.

Moderate
✪ **Hardtwald Hotel.** Philosophenweg 31 (a 20-min. walk from the center of town), 61350 Bad Homburg. ☎ **06172/98-80.** Fax 06172/8-25-12. 42 units. MINIBAR TV TEL. 195DM–355DM ($97.50–$177.50) double. Rates include buffet breakfast. AE, DC, MC, V. Parking 15DM ($7.50). Bus: 3.

This hotel, which resembles a chalet set in a forest, is an ideal retreat near the spa gardens. In spring, flowers overflow from its window boxes. Its rooms overlook the forest. The chef in the excellent, flower-filled dining room uses only the freshest of ingredients to prepare his well-known international and German dishes. In summer, tables are set on the large patio. Next to the hotel is a stable where you can rent horses.

Parkhotel Bad Homburg. Kaiser-Friedrich-Promenade 53–55, Am Kurpark, 61348 Bad Homburg. ☎ **06172/80-10.** Fax 06172/80-14-00. www.Bad-Homburg.de. E-mail: Parkhotel.Bad-Homburg@t-online.de. 123 units. MINIBAR TV TEL. 270DM–358DM ($135–$179) double; 300DM–400DM ($150–$200) suite. Rates include buffet breakfast. AE, DC, MC, V. Parking 14DM ($7). Tram: 5.

This is your best bet for a moderately priced spa vacation. This hotel has an enviable location in the middle of the Kurpark's well-maintained gardens, near the thermal springs. Although its design is modern and angular, its edges are softened with window boxes. Rooms are conservatively furnished. Baths are well kept and contain hair dryers. On the premises are a bar and a sunny room for writing postcards. Restaurant Jade serves Chinese cuisine. Amenities at the hotel include sauna, health club, solarium, and room and laundry service.

Inexpensive
Haus Daheim. Elisabethenstrasse 42 (a short walk from the Kurhaus), 61348 Bad Homburg. ☎ **06172/67-73-50.** Fax 06172/677-35-500. 19 units. TEL. 185DM–265DM ($92.50–$132.50) double. Rates include buffet breakfast. AE, DC, MC, V. Parking 15DM ($7.50). Tram: 5.

When you're trying to save, head here. This hotel, in a light-blue corner building, is one of the finest small hotels in the town. The comfortable rooms have good beds with firm mattresses. This is an admittedly modest choice after the hotels reviewed above, but for value, it's hard to beat.

WHERE TO DINE

Casino-Restaurant. Im Kurpark. ☎ **06172/1-70-10.** Reservations required. Jacket and tie required for men. Main courses 18DM–46DM ($9–$23); fixed-price menus 50DM–55DM ($25–$27.50). AE, DC, V. Daily 6–10:30pm. Tram: 5. FRENCH/GERMAN.

Until a few years ago, this was the only restaurant in Germany that directly adjoined the gaming tables of a casino. It's one of the finest in town, although not in the same class as Sängers or Oberle's. The dining room is decorated in a formal, vaguely English style. It offers attentive service and a winning combination of light French and German cuisine. The frequently changing menu features seasonal specialties with the freshest of ingredients—head chef Gunther Schwanitz begins each workday at the local markets. Lobster is a universal favorite here, attracting diners from as far away as Frankfurt. Although the main kitchen service stops at 10:30pm, there's a reduced menu until 12:30am.

Oberle's Restaurant. Obergasse 1. ☎ **06172/2-46-62.** Reservations required. Main courses 39DM–52DM ($19.50–$26); fixed-price menus 79DM–110DM ($39.50–$55). AE, MC. Tues–Sat 6:30–11:30pm. Bus: 1, 2, 3, 4, 11, or 12. INTERNATIONAL.

This is the second-best restaurant in Bad Homburg. The kitchen staff prides itself on a superb cuisine. Try the goose-liver mousse, marinated and warmed fillets of salmon served in saffron-and-Pernod sauce, sweetbreads of veal in a sauce of white wine and mustard, or a deliciously caloric version of cream and wild-mushroom soup. The menu is changed according to the season, and only the freshest of ingredients are used. The decor is art nouveau and art deco. In summer, guests can order their meals on a sun terrace.

✪ **Sängers Restaurant.** Kaiser-Friedrich-Promenade 85 (next to the Steigenberger Bad Homburg). ☎ **06172/92-88-39.** Reservations required. Main courses 45DM–55DM ($22.50–$27.50); fixed-price meals 55DM ($27.50) at lunch, 98DM–165DM ($49–$82.50) at dinner. AE, MC, V. Tues–Fri noon–2pm; Mon–Sat 7–11pm. Closed 2 weeks in midsummer. Bus: 1, 4, 11, or 12. FRENCH.

Local food lovers and spa devotees crowd this restaurant to enjoy the highly personal and inventive cuisine, the best in the spa. The two elegant dining rooms are outfitted in the style of Louis XIV. Menu items might include carpaccio of turbot with Iranian caviar, goose-liver terrine served with brioche and gelatin of wild berries, a foam-capped version of celery soup with quail eggs, roast breast of duck on a bed of rhubarb, and a succulent array of desserts.

BAD HOMBURG AFTER DARK

Spielbank Im Kurpark (☎ 06172/1-70-10; tram: 5), called the "Mother of Monte Carlo," is the spa's major attraction. This casino opened way back in 1841 and helped make Bad Homburg famous. Roulette, blackjack, and baccarat are the games here. Passports are required for entrance, and men must wear jackets and ties. Admission is 5DM ($2.50); hours are daily 2:30pm to 3am.

The most active disco in town is the **Tennis Bar,** Kisseleffstrasse (☎ 06172/2-60-41; bus: 6), named for the municipal tennis courts in the nearby Kurpark. It offers both recorded and live rock music. If you thought you were too old to hang out in a disco, think again, as this one attracts clients ages 25 and over. It's open from 9pm

Tuesday to Saturday, with a varying cover. More traditional is the town's favorite beer hall and Weinstube, **Zum Wasser Weibehen,** Am Mühlberg 57 (☎ **06172/2-98-78;** bus: 1, 4, or 11). And about a mile east of the town center, you'll find another folkloric place, **Zum Ruppe Karl,** Hamburgerstrasse 6 (☎ **06172/4-24-84;** bus: 2 or 12.), whose home-style cuisine is enhanced with the establishment's homemade apple wine. The **Kurhaus** also contains a handful of bars, cafes, and shops that usually stay open late.

BAD NAUHEIM

35km (22 miles) N of Frankfurt, 64km (40 miles) NE of Wiesbaden

Like many spas throughout Germany, Bad Nauheim became popular in the early part of the 20th century, when the railroad became a convenient and inexpensive means of transportation. Still going strong today, this resort at the northern edge of the Taunus Mountains is a center for golf, tennis, and ice-skating, as well as the starting point for hiking up the 236m (773-foot) Joannisberg, which towers over the town.

The warm carbonic-acid springs of the spa are used to treat heart and circulatory disorders and rheumatic diseases. The Kurpark is attractive, well maintained, and filled with promenaders all summer long. The impressive bathhouse is the single largest complex of Jugendstil architecture in Germany. The Sprudelhof (fountain court), at the center, stretches from the Hauptbahnhof to the Kurpark and all the way to the Kurhaus. All the important sights, including the bathhouse complex, can be visited in half a day. The resort has a busy activity calendar, with concerts twice daily, along with operas, plays, dances, park illuminations, and fashion shows.

ESSENTIALS

GETTING THERE   By Train   Bad Nauheim can easily be reached from Frankfurt. Trains arrive at least once per hour (every 30 min. during rush hours) during the day (trip time: 30 min.). Service is on the Weatherman line between Frankfurt and Giessen. For information call ☎ **01805/99-66-33.**

By Car   Access is via the A5 Autobahn from the north and the south. Driving time from Frankfurt is about half an hour.

VISITOR INFORMATION   For information, go to the **Verkehrsverein,** Neue Kurolonnade (☎ **06032/21-20**). It's open Monday to Friday 9am to noon and 2 to 5pm, Saturday 9am to noon and 2 to 4pm, and Sunday 10am to noon.

WHERE TO STAY

Advena Hotel Rosenau. Steinfurther Strasse 1, 61231 Bad Nauheim (west of Grosser Teich, the town lake). ☎ **06032/9-64-60.** Fax 06032/964-6666. 54 units. A/C MINIBAR TV TEL. 180DM–248DM ($90–$124) double. Rates include continental breakfast. AE, DC, MC, V. Closed Dec 27–Jan 8. Free parking.

This is one of the better choices at the resort, though it's not nearly as good as the Parkhotel am Kurhaus. The Rosenau is an updated version of a German manor house, with white walls and a red-tiled hip roof. Inside, the decor is one of light-toned wood and pastel colors. Rooms are modern and attractive, with such amenities as electric trouser presses. On the premises there's both a good bistro and the fine Rosengarten restaurant (see "Where to Dine," below), plus a small pool.

Hotel Gaudesberger. Hauptstrasse 6, 61231 Bad Nauheim. ☎ and fax **06032/25-08.** 8 units, none with bath. TEL. 90DM ($45) double. Rates include continental breakfast. AE, DC, MC, V. Closed Jan 15–Feb 15.

This centrally located hotel is known mainly for its restaurant (see "Where to Dine," below). Rooms are simply furnished. The place is plain and decent, not grand in any way. The staff speaks no English.

Elvis in Bad Nauheim

Many famous guests have visited this spa, including Otto von Bismarck (1859) and Richard Strauss (1927). Franklin D. Roosevelt spent about 2 years here with his family when he was a small child. Locals believe that Bad Nauheim was spared destruction during World War II, even though a Nazi radio transmitter was installed here, because President Roosevelt had fond memories of the place.

Real fame came to the spa when a private named Elvis Presley arrived and found a home off-base, right next to the Kurhaus. The singer was stationed in nearby Friedberg/Hessen at Ray Barracks Kaserne from October 1958 to March 1960, and his presence had an electrifying effect on the German youth scene. It was here that Elvis fell in love with Priscilla, "my little girl." She was 14 at the time, and when she first drove up to the plain, old-fashioned villa where he lived, the street was full of German girls, waiting by the sign AUTOGRAPHS BETWEEN 7 AND 8PM ONLY. After that first meeting, she saw him once more, and when he returned to the States he vowed to send for her.

Elvis wasn't the only famous American to visit. It was the habit of newspaper magnate William Randolph Hearst to come here every year with his mistress, Marion Davies, and a dozen or so of her women friends—Hearst would have the women chauffeured around the countryside in style. He firmly believed Bad Nauheim's physicians were the answer to his minor heart problem. Here he had his notorious meeting with Mussolini in 1931 ("a marvelous man") and from here he flew to Berlin to meet Hitler in 1934. He claimed that he had done "much good" in advising Hitler to drop his persecution of the Jews, but afterwards he spent most of his life trying to live down his image as a supporter of the Nazi cause.

Parkhotel am Kurhaus. Nordlicher Park 16, 61231 Bad Nauheim. ☎ **06032/30-30.** Fax 06032/30-34-19. E-mail: info@parkhotel-badnauheim-bestwestern.de. 159 units. MINIBAR TV TEL. 261DM–366DM ($130.50–$183) double; 380DM–480DM ($190–$240) suite. Rates include continental breakfast. AE, DC, MC, V. Parking 12DM ($6).

This modern hotel is the finest in town, with better amenities than the Rosenau. It's located in the middle of the park that rings the resort's thermal springs. Its public areas are filled with green plants and arching windows. Rooms, with big sliding glass windows and balconies, provide calm, quiet, and conservative comfort. Baths are luxurious and contain deluxe luxury items and hair dryers. There are two restaurants and a cafe, in addition to a Bierstube, wine tavern, and bar. Special diets and vegetarian menus are offered. Amenities include room service, laundry, and baby-sitting. Nonsmoking rooms are available on the third floor.

WHERE TO DINE

Restaurant Gaudesberger. In the Hotel Gaudesberger, Hauptstrasse 6. ☎ **06032/25-08.** Reservations recommended. Main courses 16DM–30DM ($8–$15). AE, DC, MC, V. Thurs–Tues 11:30am–2pm and 5:30–9pm. INTERNATIONAL.

A large menu of well-prepared dishes is offered here in comfortable but simple surroundings. You can stick to the tried-and-true choices, such as chateaubriand with béarnaise sauce or herring fillet in dill sauce, or you can dip into the other specialties, such as pork in curry-cream sauce, ox tongue in Madeira sauce, or trout and salmon prepared in at least four different ways. Ingredients are fresh and everything is prepared home-style. The staff is cooperative and courteous.

Rosengarten. In the Hotel Rosenau, Steinfurther Strasse 1. ☎ **06032/9-64-60.** Main courses 26DM–42DM ($13–$21); fixed-price buffet lunch 36DM ($18). AE, DC, MC, V. Tues–Sun noon–2pm and 6–10pm. Closed Dec 27–Jan 30. INTERNATIONAL.

This restaurant is known as one of the best in town. It serves a fixed-price lunch plus à la carte evening meals. The flavorful dishes might include cream of tomato and young-vegetable soup, roast breast of young hen, and fillet of salmon with fresh herbs, plus several different pork and game dishes, depending on the season. The cookery is not innovative, but we are impressed with its honesty and freshness. There are no pretensions here.

The Rhineland 13

Few rivers of the world can claim such an important role in the growth of a nation as the Rhine. The Rhine rises in Switzerland and ultimately flows through the Netherlands in its progress to the sea, but most of its 1,370km (850 miles) snake through the mountains and plains of Germany. For more than 2,000 years, it has been a chief trade route, its deep waters enabling modern seagoing vessels to travel downstream from the North Sea as far as Cologne.

From earliest times, the Rhine has also been a main road for religious, intellectual, and artistic ideas. It has been called a "triumphal avenue of the muses," and a trip along its banks today reveals endless treasures. Legend and history wait around every bend of the river.

From Mainz north to Koblenz, the winding river cuts through steep vine-covered hillsides dotted with towns whose names are synonymous with fine German wine. Here you'll find the dramatic Lorelei, the legendary rock from which a siren lured men to their doom. The saga of *The Nibelungenlied,* the best known of the Rhine legends, is associated with the topography from the Siebengebirge (the Seven Mountains) near Bonn, where Siegfried slew the dragon, to the city of Worms, where Brünnhilde plotted against the dragon-slayer.

The Rhine is also the home of many of Germany's largest and most modern cities. **Cologne** (Köln) and **Düsseldorf** vie for trade and tourism. Cologne is also a common starting point for boat tours of the river.

Roadways along the Rhine tend to be heavily trafficked, so allow adequate time. Highways, not Autobahns, hug both the left and right banks of the river, and at many points you'll come across car-ferries that can take you across. The most scenic stretch for driving is the mid-Rhine, between Koblenz and Mainz. EuroCity and InterCity trains connect all the major cities, including Cologne, Düsseldorf, Bonn, and Mainz. Rail service also extends as far north as Hamburg and as far south as Munich.

EXPLORING THE REGION BY CAR

Day 1 If you're beginning in the south, your gateway to the Rhine can be the city of **Speyer,** one of the oldest Rhine cities, 93km (58 miles) south of Mainz. A morning visit to its Kaiserdom (imperial cathedral) will suffice. You can then continue north on Route 9 to **Worms,** the ancient city where Siegfried began his legendary

The Rhineland

adventures, as recorded in *The Nibelungenlied*. Worms contains St. Peter's Cathedral, one of the purest Romanesque basilicas in the Rhine valley. Stay overnight here.

Day 2 After Worms, continue north along Route 9 to **Mainz.** There's a lot to see in this 2,000-year-old former Roman city, including the Museum Gutenberg, devoted to the man who invented movable type here in 1440. With its many attractions and good food and wine, Mainz deserves a full day.

Day 3 Take Route B455 toward Wiesbaden. The highway will run into A66, the Autobahn. Go to the western extension of A66, which then changes its name to B42. Continue along this route for some 35km (22 miles) to **Rüdesheim** for the night. For dinner, head for one of the wine taverns in the area, preferably along the tiny alley of Drosselgasse. Here you'll not only learn about the history of wine making, you'll also get to taste the best selection of Rhine wines in the area.

Day 4 In the morning, take a side detour north on Route 42 to Assmannshausen via the Niederwald Monument, which commemorates the unification of Germany under Bismarck. Explore the wine town of **Assmannshausen** in the morning. This town produces a red wine called *Spätburgunder,* which you may want to sample at a tavern for lunch.

If you return to Rüdesheim, you can take the car-ferry to Bingen, crossing to the more scenic left bank and continuing along Route 9. Bingen merits only a passing stopover, but outside the town, the highway is celebrated for its scenery, its romantic old castles, and its Rhineland landmarks. This stretch is so filled with castles that you'll despair of ever visiting them all. Keep on B9 for its entire length, some 64km (40 miles) to **Koblenz,** where, after the busy day you've had, you'll want to stay overnight.

Day 5   Since Koblenz was bombed almost out of existence in World War II, you may want to pass on after breakfast, getting back on Route B9 and following the signs to **Bonn,** some 63km (39 miles) to the northwest. Everyone talks about how dull Bonn is, but there's still quite a bit to see here, including Beethoven's House. You can also visit a spa called **Bad Godesberg,** southeast of Bonn, where you might spend the night or at least enjoy a meal.

Day 6   From Bonn, and only if you have an extra day, you can continue west toward France for an overnight stay in **Aachen,** an ancient city lying at the frontiers of Belgium, Germany, and the Netherlands. Aachen is inseparably linked with Charlemagne. Visit its Dom, Rathaus, and Couven Museum.

Day 7   Retrace your route west, toward Bonn. Get on the A3 Autobahn north and continue for some 27km (17 miles) to **Cologne** (Köln), which may well be the highlight of your Rhineland motor trip.

Day 8   After Cologne, it's just 40km (25 miles) north on A57 to the city of fashion and industry, **Düsseldorf.**

1 Speyer

93km (58 miles) S of Mainz, 21km (13 miles) SW of Heidelberg

One of the oldest Rhine cities, Speyer celebrated its two-thousandth jubilee in 1990. It became a significant religious center early on. The Diet of Speyer, in 1529, united the followers of Luther in a protest against the Church of Rome.

ESSENTIALS

GETTING THERE   By Train   Trains reach Speyer only by connections at Heidelberg and Mannheim. The trip from Frankfurt takes 2 hours; from Munich, 5 to 6 hours. Call ☎ **01805/99-66-33** for schedules.

By Bus   About one bus per hour arrives from Heidelberg. Regional service is provided by **BRN Busverkehr Rhein-Neckar GmbH** at Ludwigshafen (☎ **06231/51-21-22**).

By Car   You can drive from Frankfurt in about an hour, from Munich in about 4 hours. Access is by the A61 Autobahn east and west connecting with Route 9 south.

VISITOR INFORMATION   For information, go to the **Verkehrsamt,** Maximilianstrasse 11 (☎ **06232/14-23-92**). Open year-round Monday to Friday 9am to 5pm; May to October, also open Saturday 10am to 4pm and Sunday 11am to 3pm; in the off-season, also open Saturday 10am to noon.

GETTING AROUND   A blue-and-white "City Shuttle" (bus) runs from the Speyer Hauptbahnhof through the town to Festplatz near the cathedral, east of the Altstadt. It connects most major hotels and restaurants. The bus comes every 10 minutes, and the service runs daily 7am to 7pm. The trip costs 1DM (50¢).

Cruising the Rhine

The best way to get a really intimate look at the river valley that helped shape the history of Europe is to travel its waters by ship. A wide range of cruises is available from several shipping lines. These range from a 800km (500-mile) tour on a luxury yacht to 1-day cruises to historical and artistic sites.

The premier carrier is **KD River Cruises of Europe,** Frankenwerft 15, 50667 Köln 1 (☎ **0221/25-83-01-1**). This company has been running cruises since early in the 19th century; today it owns a fleet of more than 25 vessels. Its river tours, elegant but nonglitzy, are on compact but comfortable ships equipped with open-air pools, dining rooms, bars, and highly competent multilingual staffs. Although a traditional band might play over dinner, the main entertainment comes from chatting with fellow passengers and taking in the sweeping views of the landscape.

Depending on your tastes and schedule, you can book anything from a short day tour from Cologne, to a longer tour that might take 5 days of leisurely cruising. Our favorite excursion from Cologne is a trip past many of the Rhine's most evocative ruins and landscapes, to Mainz. This tour is offered April to October, every day via a hydrofoil (*Tragflugelboot*) that departs from Cologne at 9am, arriving in Mainz at 1:15pm. We suggest that you spend the night at any of our recommended hotels in Mainz, but if you want to return to Cologne the same day, another hydrofoil departs from Mainz at 2:30pm, arriving in Cologne at 6:05pm. The round-trip cost is 250DM ($125) per adult, and 60DM ($30) for accompanying children under 14.

A longer option is a 6-day cruise between Amsterdam and Basel, priced at 1,500DM to 2,200DM ($750 to $1,100) per person, double occupancy, all-inclusive. Shorter, 4-day cruises between Strasbourg and Cologne cost 750DM to 1,150DM ($375 to $575), per person, double occupancy. During the longer river tours, ships dock at cities of historical or cultural interest. For an additional surcharge, you can participate in motorcoach or walking tours of the city where you're docking.

Day cruises don't stop for very long, but passengers can still often embark or disembark at such historic towns as Bonn, Linz, Bräubach, St. Goarshausen, and Rüdesheim. On day excursions, children up to age 4 and holders of Eurailpasses travel free, and children ages 4 to 13 pay 5DM ($2.50). Tickets for day excursions cannot be reserved and should be bought directly on the pier before departure. Arrangements for cruises of 2 nights or more can be booked through the company's U.S.-based sales representative. For more information in the U.S., contact **KD River Cruises of Europe** (represented in North America by JFO Cruise Service), 2500 Westchester Ave., Purchase, NY 10577 (☎ **800/346-6525**); or 323 Geary St., San Francisco, CA 94102 (☎ **800/858-8587**).

THE IMPERIAL CATHEDRAL

Nothing brings back the medieval German empire as much as the ✪ **Kaiserdom (Imperial Cathedral)** in Speyer (☎ **06232/10-22-98**), the greatest building of its time. This cathedral, consecrated in the early 11th century, is the largest Romanesque edifice in Germany. Having weathered damage by fires, wars, and restorations, the cathedral was finally restored to its original shape from 1957 to 1961. When you enter the church through the single west door set in a stepped arch, you're immediately caught up in the vastness of its proportions; the whole length of the nave and east chancel opens up before you, lit by the muted daylight from above. The church contains the royal tombs of four emperors, three empresses, and four German kings, as well as a row of bishops' tombs. Open April to October, Monday to Saturday 9am to 7pm and Sunday 1:30 to 6pm; November to March, Monday to Friday 9am to 5pm, Saturday 9am to 4pm, and Sunday 1:30 to 4:30pm.

WHERE TO STAY

Am Wartturm. Landwehrstrasse 28, 67346 Speyer. ☎ **06232/6-43-30.** Fax 06232/64-33-21. 17 units. TEL. 130DM–180DM ($65–$90) double. Rates include breakfast. No credit cards. Free parking.

In this modern but modest little guest house, the Heck family rent simply furnished, comfortable, but rather small units. They also operate a plain but good restaurant, open for lunch and dinner. Service is polite and attentive. When the weather is cooperative, you can enjoy breakfast, lunch, or dinner in the hotel's garden, whose centerpiece is a small goldfish pond.

Rhein-Hotel Luxhof. At the Rhine Bridge, just outside the town, 68766 Hockenheim. ☎ **06205/30-30.** Fax 06205/3-03-25. E-mail: luxhof@t-online.de. 45 units. TV TEL. 160DM–180DM ($80–$90) double. Rates include buffet breakfast. AE, DC, MC, V. Free parking.

This hotel has an unusual character. It's modern in style, but somehow the spirit of a rambling country inn has been retained. The blandly decorated rooms are well designed and compact, often featuring small sitting areas that open onto tiny balconies. The dining rooms are charming and colorful, and the hotel has a sauna, a solarium, and other fitness facilities.

WHERE TO DINE

Backmulde. Karmeliterstrasse 11–13. ☎ **06232/7-15-77.** Reservations required. Main courses 38DM–48DM ($19–$24); fixed-price dinner 72DM–110DM ($36–$55). AE, DC, MC, V. Tues–Sat 11am–1:30pm and 7pm–midnight. Closed 3 weeks from the end of Aug to mid-Sept. FRENCH/SEAFOOD.

Backmulde is owned by Gunter Schmidt, who has researched the centuries-old recipes of the Rhineland-Palatinate, added a modern touch, and come up with a combination that has made this Speyer's most important restaurant. You can savor such unusual delicacies as gratiné of oysters in champagne sabayon, quail stuffed with well-seasoned sweetbreads, and a meltingly tender roast lamb with freshly picked spinach.

2 Worms

45km (28 miles) S of Mainz, 43km (27 miles) SW of Darmstadt

This ancient city traces its beginnings from the earliest civilizations. Before the Romans settled here, Germanic peoples had made Worms their capital. Here, Siegfried began his legendary adventures, recorded in *The Nibelungenlied*. Later on, the town's most famous visitor, Martin Luther, arrived under less than desirable circumstances. He was "invited" to appear before the Imperial Diet at Worms, and after refusing to retract his grievances against the Church of Rome, Holy Roman Emperor Charles V declared him an outlaw. Now that Worms is mainly Protestant, a huge monument to Luther and other giants of the Reformation has been erected.

Worms also makes an excellent base for a tour of the Deutsche Weinstrasse, or German Wine Road, an 80km (50-mile) route through local wine towns (see below).

ESSENTIALS

GETTING THERE   By Plane   The nearest airport is at Frankfurt (see chapter 12), 69km (43 miles) away.

By Train   Worms enjoys good rail connections to major German cities. It lies on the main Mainz–Mannheim line, with frequent service. For rail information and schedules, call ☎ **01805/99-66-33.**

By Bus   Regional bus service for the area is provided by **BRN Busverkehr Rhein-Neckar GmbH** (☎ **06241/1077028**) in Worms.

By Car   From Mainz (see section 3, below), continue south along Route 9.

VISITOR INFORMATION   For tourist information, go to the **Verkehrsverein,** Neumarkt 14 (☎ **06241/2-50-45**). It's open year-round Monday to Friday 9am to 6pm; April to October, also open Saturday 9am to noon.

GETTING AROUND   A network of cream-colored buses traverse most neighborhoods of the town and its suburbs. The city's main junction point is the Hauptbahnhof. Buses run 6am to midnight, and charge 2.80DM ($1.40) and 5DM ($2.50), paid directly to the driver.

SEEING THE SIGHTS

Towering physically and historically above all the other ancient buildings of the city is the majestic ✪ **Dom St. Peter,** Lutherring 9 (☎ **06241/61-15;** bus: 2). This basilica is a fine example of High Romanesque style. The east choir, with a flat facade and semicircular interior, is the oldest section, dating from 1132. It was designed as the sanctuary, where the clergy performed the rites of divine service. The chancel glows with the gold and marble of the pillared enclosure of the baroque high altar by the famous 18th-century architect Balthasar Neumann. This opulent work was so large that there was no place for a proper transept. In Gothic times the choir stalls stood in the apse, but later they were built into the transept. The interior has a quiet elegance, with little decoration other than the rosette window and several memorial slabs and monuments. Well worth seeing is the highly decorated 14th-century side chapel of St. Nicholas, with its Gothic baptismal font and new stained-glass windows. The cathedral is open for visitors April to October, daily 8am to 6pm; in winter, daily 9am to 5pm.

North of the Altstadt is the restored **old Jewish quarter** (Bus: 2). Before World War II, Worms had one of the oldest Jewish communities in Germany. The **synagogue,** Hintere Judengasse 6 (☎ **06241/853-4701**), which dated from the 11th century, was destroyed in 1938. It has been rebuilt, using some of the original masonry. Inside, you'll find the **Raschi-Haus Museum** (same phone), containing memorabilia from the original synagogue and references to the Holocaust. Both the synagogue and its museum are open daily May to October, 10am to noon and 2 to 6pm; November to April, 10am to noon and 2 to 5pm. Admission is 3DM ($1.50). A staff member inside will point you in the direction of the **Jewish cemetery (Judenfriedhof),** off the Lutherring, one of the oldest and largest in Europe, with hundreds of tombstones, some of them more than 900 years old.

WHERE TO STAY

Central Hotel Worms. Kämmererstrasse 5, 67547 Worms. ☎ **06241/6-45-70.** Fax 06241/2-74-39. E-mail: central.hotel@t-indis.de. 19 units. TV TEL. 145DM–165DM ($72.50–$82.50) double. Rates include buffet breakfast. AE, DC, DISC, MC, V. Closed Dec 22–Jan 22. Parking 8DM ($4). Bus: 2 or 4.

This is one of the best small hotels in the city, although it's a modest and unassuming choice. Innkeeper Alexandra Hill rents comfortably furnished but rather small rooms.

The reception staff speaks English, and the hotel has an ideal central location, within walking distance of all major historic monuments.

Dom-Hotel. Am Obermarkt 10, 67547 Worms (about a block from the cathedral). ☎ **06241/69-13.** Fax 06241/2-35-15. www.dom-hotel.de. E-mail: dom-hotel@t-online.de. 62 units. A/C MINIBAR TV TEL. 160DM–220DM ($80–$110) double; 230DM ($115) suite. Rates include buffet breakfast. AE, DC, MC, V. Free parking. Bus: 2.

This is an ideal choice for the in-and-out traveler. Recently renovated, the all-purpose hotel is a postwar structure built in a complex of shops and boutiques. Rooms are a little bandboxy and functionally furnished, but each is well maintained. The guest lounge is a good place to relax. In the wood-paneled dining room, a breakfast buffet is offered, and later in the day, French cuisine is served.

Hotel Nibelungen. Martinsgasse 16, 67547 Worms. ☎ **06241/92-02-50.** Fax 06241/92-02-55-05. 46 units. MINIBAR TV TEL. 160DM–210DM ($80–$105) double. Rates include buffet breakfast. AE, MC, V. Parking 5DM ($2.50). Bus: 2.

The most modern place to stay in Worms is the Nibelungen, in the center of town. It offers up-to-date comfort behind a rather sterile facade. The well-furnished rooms are the best in town and are generally spacious, although devoid of any particular Rhinelander flavor. Breakfast is the only meal served.

WHERE TO DINE

Le Bistro Léger. Siegfriedstrasse 2. ☎ **06241/4-62-77.** Reservations recommended. Main courses 18.50DM–35DM ($9.25–$17.50). MC. Mon–Sat noon–2pm and 6–11pm. Bus: 2. RHINELAND.

The nostalgically decorated Le Bistro Léger offers a regional cuisine at reasonable prices. An outdoor terrace is a favorite in warm weather. Fresh ingredients go into the food. You might try veal cutlets prepared in the style of the Rhineland, fish fillet, or oysters (in season). The well-chosen wine list is mostly German.

Rôtisserie Dubs. Kirchstrasse 6, at Rheindurkheim, take Rte. 9 north for 8km (5 miles). ☎ **06242/20-23.** Reservations required. Main courses 38DM–49DM ($19–$24.50); fixed-price menu 65DM–125DM ($32.50–$62.50). No credit cards. Fri–Mon 6–10pm; Sun–Mon 11:30am–2pm. CONTINENTAL.

The prices are a bit steep for the area, but you're paying for imaginative cookery and quality ingredients. Despite rustic ceiling beams and the massive stonework of the fire-place, Rôtisserie Dubs has a feeling of elegant airiness. The light continental cuisine adds to that impression. After traveling through France, owner Wolfgang Dubs decided to feature such dishes as salmon in champagne marinade and delicately seasoned pike-and-cabbage soup. His steak in snail sauce is worth the trip outside of town (it may not sound appealing but is quite sublime). Regrettably, at this writing, this highly appealing restaurant is open only 2 days a week at lunch, and only 4 days a week for dinner.

WORMS AFTER DARK

The city's most important showcase for music, classical drama (in German only), and opera is the circa 1962 **Städtisches Spiel und Festhaus,** Rathenaustrasse 4 (☎ **06241/22525;** bus: 2). For information about coming events, either contact the theater directly, or call **Theater-Kasse,** Rathenaustrasse 4 (☎ **06241/225-25**), for a list of upcoming events and ticket availability.

Don't expect raucous nightlife in Worms. Our best advice, if you want a drink within cozy circumstances in the town center, is to head for the **Judengasse** (Bus: 2), a street with a denser collection of nightlife options than any other in town. One of the most appealing is the **Altstadt Bar,** Judengasse 17 (☎ **06241/222-16**), which opens for business every day at 3pm, carrying on into the wee hours.

A DRIVING TOUR OF THE GERMAN WINE ROAD

Germany's oldest designated tourist route, the **Deutsche Weinstrasse,** runs south for 80km (50 miles) from Bockenheim, a small town 14km (8¹/₂ miles) west of Worms, to Schweigen-Rechtenbach on the frontier with France. This is a land of old castles (most in ruins) and venerable vineyards. Most of the wines produced here are whites, with special emphasis on clear, aromatic Rieslings and Weissburgunders. The area also abounds in old Rhineland-Palatinate inns and wine taverns, serving hearty local specialties such as "white cheese."

Armed with a good map, available at the Worms tourist office, you can set out to explore the area beginning in the north at **Bockenheim.** From Bockenheim, follow Route 271 directly south to Grünstadt, where signs point the way to the village of **Neuleiningen,** 10km (6 miles) away. The locals here are known rather unflatteringly as *Geesbocke* or "billy goats," a reference to their longtime poverty—goats (supposedly) were the only livestock they could afford. Today they bear the label with a certain pride. While here, sample the local fare at **Alte Pfarrey,** Untergasse 54, Oberstadt (☎ 06359/86066), where set-price menus cost 42DM ($21) at lunch or 120DM ($60) at dinner. Closed Monday and Tuesday for lunch but open for dinner.

From here, Highway 271 leads south to Kallstadt, a distance of 10km (6 miles), where our next stopover at **Bad Dürkheim** is signposted. This is a main target along the wine road heading south. Here you can view the remains of the **Monastery of Limburg,** once one of the most significant Romanesque structures in the country. The best restaurant is **Weinrefugium,** Schlachthausstrasse 1A (☎ 06322/6-89-74), which charges 35DM ($17.50) for a set-price menu of regional food. Closed Monday.

Route A37 en route to Kaiserslautern, west of Bad Dürkheim, leads to **Frankenstein Schloss,** a castle from the Middle Ages (now in ruins). Local legend claims it was this Schloss that inspired Mary Shelley's classic monster.

A journey 8km (5 miles) south along 271 leads to the **Deidesheim,** the medieval seat of the bishops of Speyer. The grounds that surround their former Schloss, now a picturesque ruin, have been turned into a lovely park. Some of the wine road's most charming half-timbered buildings are found on the main square, Marktplatz.

The most elegant hotel in the neighborhood is the very stylish **Deidesheimer Hof,** Marktplatz 1 (☎ 06326/96870), where doubles cost 240DM to 285DM ($120 to $142.50). Inside are two restaurants, the **Schwarzer Hahn,** where set-price menus go from 149DM to 185DM ($74.50 to $92.50), and the more artfully rustic **St.-Urban,** which charges 105DM ($52.50) for a set-price menu.

From Deidesheim, continue along Route 271 for another 15 minutes, following the signs to **Neustadt-an-der-Weinstrasse,** the largest town on the Weinstrasse, lying at the foot of the Haardt hills. Pass quickly through its ugly suburbs to reach the heart of the old town, with its narrow, often crooked streets. There are some 2,000ha (5,000 acres) of vineyards within the town limits, and the main streets are lined with taverns and wine shops. Neustadt's most appealing restaurant is **Gerberhaus,** Hintergasse 6 (☎ 06321/88700). Main courses cost 11DM to 18DM ($5.50 to $9). Closed Monday and Tuesday.

From Neustadt, you can drive 5km (3 miles) south to historic **Schloss Hambach** (☎ 06321/30-881), half a mile outside the village of Hambach. It's open March to November daily 9am to 6pm; admission is 9DM ($4.50).

A 8km (5-mile) drive south takes you into the sleepy hamlet of St. Martin, which for our money is the loveliest village along the wine road, filled with antique houses draped with flowering vines. A castle here, whose nostalgic ruins still tower over St. Martin, happens to have the best food and lodging along the wine road. Its name is **St. Martiner Castell,** Maikammer Strasse 2 (☎ 06323/95-10), and its 26 rooms rent for around 164DM ($82) double occupancy, with breakfast included. In its restaurant, set-price menus are 65DM to 90DM ($32.50 to $45).

Yet another 5km (3 miles) south (the road is signposted) takes you to **Gleisweiler,** a wine-producing hamlet known as the warmest village in Germany. Fig trees flourish in its rich soil and almost subtropical climate.

From Gleisweiler, it's 13km (8 miles) south along Route B38 to **Annweiler,** site of **Burg Trifels,** the Rhineland's most fabled castle, set imperiously on a jagged crag. In 1193, Richard the Lionhearted was captured and imprisoned here until he was bailed out with a huge ransom. From the panoramic peak, you can also view the ruins of Scharfenberg Castle and Anebos Castle to the south. Burg Trifels (☎ **06346/8470**) is open daily January to March and October to November 9am to 5pm; April to September 9am to 6pm; closed in December.

In Annweiler, if you opt to remain for the night, check out the facilities at **Zum Goldenen Lamm,** Ramberg, 7697 Annweiler (☎ **06345/8286**). Rooms cost 90DM ($45) each, with breakfast included. On the premises is a loud and sometimes rowdy, but very good, restaurant, which charges 20DM ($10) for a set-price meal.

The B38 leads next to **Klingenmünster,** a journey of only 8km (5 miles) south. From here, a sign points the way to the ruins of **Burg Landeck,** reached after a 30- to 40-minute stroll through a chestnut tree forest. At the end, the castle ruins stand at one of the most scenic spots along the wine road, with views extending as far as the Black Forest.

From here, B38 goes yet another 8km (5 miles) to reach **Bad Bergzabern,** a picturesque spa, without equal for its old half-timbered houses. The most appealing restaurant here is **Zum Engel,** Königstrasse 45 (☎ **06343/4933**), with set-price meals at 20DM to 38DM ($10 to $19). Closed Monday night.

From Bad Bergzabern, a 10km (6-mile) drive along Highway B38 (the final lap of your journey) will deliver you to **Schweigen-Rechtenbach,** a village at the French frontier. In the summer of 1935, local vintners constructed a gargantuan stone arch, the **German Wine Gate (Deutsches Weintor),** marking the southern end of this oft-traveled tourist route. From a gallery atop the gate, you can view miles of vineyards and even see a panorama of the Vosges in France. Visitors can cross the border, some 230m (250 yards) from the arch, to sample the vintages on the French side as well, as there are no border formalities here. You can follow a trail known as the *Weinlehrpfad* (wine inspection path), going on for a mile until you reach the vineyards at the hamlet of Sonenberg. This is one of the most rewarding walks along the wine route.

In Schweigen-Rechtenbach, one of the best values for lodging is found in the town center at **Am Deutschen Weintor,** Bacchusstrasse 1 (☎ **06342/7335**), which charges 90DM to 130DM ($45 to $65) for a double room, breakfast included. We suggest getting a meal at the **Hotel Schweigenhof,** Hauptstrasse 2, 76889 Schweigen-Rechtenbach (☎ **06342/244**), which charges 25DM to 90DM ($12.50 to $45) for a fixed-price lunch or dinner.

3 Mainz

13km (8 miles) S of Wiesbaden, 82km (51 miles) NW of Mannheim, 40km (25 miles) SW of Frankfurt

Mainz is located on the left bank of the Rhine, across from the Rhine's intersection with the Main River. It is thought that there may have been wine-producing vines in the area even before the coming of the Romans in 38 B.C., although it was from that time that the regions of the Rheingau and Rheinhessen became widely known for fine viticulture.

At the beginning of the Christian era, the settlement on the Rhine's left bank and the Roman fortifications opposite were connected by a bridge. In the 8th century, the town became a primary archbishopric. Over the centuries, church politics and a series of wars shuffled control of the city back and forth between the French (who called it "Mayence") and various German factions. Mainz never became the great commerce center that its location would seem to merit. However, today it's a bustling city, with a prosperous trade in wine and other businesses.

Most visitors will be interested in the relatively compact **Altstadt,** which has been restored with taste and care. The heart of the old town is the Marktplatz, which is dominated by the cathedral.

ESSENTIALS

GETTING THERE   By Plane   The nearest airport is at Frankfurt (see chapter 12). There is direct rail service from the airport (S-14 train) via Wiesbaden to Mainz. For information, call the Mainz Railway Station at ☎ **06131/15107553.**

By Train   From Frankfurt, an express train takes 25 minutes to reach Mainz, while the S-Bahn arrives in 40 minutes. There are also trains leaving Mainz for Heidelberg and Koblenz (trip time: 1 hr.) or Cologne (trip time: 2 hr.). Daily trains to and from Munich take about 4^1/$_2$ hours. For more rail information, call ☎ **01805/996633.**

By Bus   Regional bus service is provided by **ORN Omnibusverkehr Rhein-Nahe GmbH,** at Mainz (☎ **06131/67-10-26**).

By Car   Access by car to Mainz is via the A60 east and west, and the A63 south and A643 north.

VISITOR INFORMATION   Go to **Touristik Centrale,** Brückenturm am Rathaus (☎ **06131/28-62-10**). Open Monday to Friday 9am to 6pm and Saturday 9am to 1pm.

GETTING AROUND   Trams and buses fan out across the city from the Hauptbahnhof from 5am till around midnight. Fares are 2.10DM ($1.05) to 3.70DM ($1.85).

SPECIAL EVENTS   The most celebrated merrymaking in festive Mainz is the All Fools capers at **Carnival** each spring, on the Monday before Ash Wednesday. This festival is broadcast throughout Germany like the Macy's parade. Each year in June, the **Gutenberg Festival** sponsors a cultural season as a living memorial to the city's favorite son, the inventor of the movable-type printing press. There's also an annual **Wine Fair** in August and September. For information, contact the tourist office at ☎ **06131/286210.**

EXPLORING THE TOWN

✪ Dom und Diözesan Museum. Domstrasse 3. ☎ **06131/223727** or 06131/253344. Cathedral free; Diocesan Museum 5DM ($2.50) adults, 2.50DM ($1.25) children (charge applies to special exhibitions only). Cathedral Apr–Sept, Mon–Fri 9am–6:30pm, Sat 9am–4pm, Sun 12:45–3pm; Oct–Mar, Mon–Fri 9am–5pm, Sat 9am–4pm, Sun 12:45–3pm. Museum Mon–Wed and Fri 10am–4pm, Thurs 10am–5pm, Sat 10am–2pm. Bus: 1, 7, 13, 17, or 23.

Above the roofs of the half-timbered houses in the Altstadt rise the six towers of St. Martin's Cathedral, the most important Catholic cathedral in the country after Cologne's. It dates from A.D. 975 but was continually rebuilt and restored, reaching its present form mainly from the 13th and 14th centuries. Below the largest dome, a combination of Romanesque and baroque styles, is the transept, separating the west chancel from the nave and smaller east chancel. Many of the supporting pillars along the aisles of the nave are decorated with carved and painted statues of French and German saints.

A collection of religious art is housed in the cathedral's Diocesan Museum. In it are exhibitions of reliquaries and medieval sculpture, including works by the Master of Naumburg. In the 1,000-year-old cathedral crypt is a contemporary gold reliquary of the saints of Mainz. Among the most impressive furnishings in the sanctuary are rococo choir stalls and an early 14th-century pewter baptismal font.

✪ **Gutenberg Museum.** Liebfrauenplatz 5 (opposite the east towers of the cathedral). ☎ **06131/1226-40-44.** Admission 5DM ($2.50) adults; 2.50DM ($1.25) children 6–18, seniors, and students; free for children 5 and under. Tues–Sat 10am–6pm, Sun 10am–1pm. Free admission Sun and holidays. Closed Jan. Bus: 1, 7, 13, 17, or 19.

This museum is a unique memorial to the city's most famous son. In the rebuilt Gutenberg workshop, visitors can trace the history of printing, beginning with Johannes Gutenberg's hand press, on which he printed his 42-line-per-page Bible from 1452 to 1455. The collections cover the entire spectrum of the graphic arts in all countries, past and present, as well as printing, illustration, and binding. Two Gutenberg Bibles are the most popular exhibits.

Landesmuseum Mainz (Provincial Museum of the Central Rhineland). Grosse Bleiche 49–51. ☎ **06131/285-70.** Admission 5DM ($2.50) adults, 2.50DM ($1.25) children under 18; free admission Sat. Tues 10am–8pm, Wed–Sun 10am–5pm. Bus: 6, 15, or 23.

It's worth a visit here to get a pictorial history of Mainz and the middle Rhineland ranging from prehistoric times to the present. The **Lapidarium** shows one of the most important collections of Roman monuments in Europe. The most impressive exhibits are the Roman tombstones of soldiers and civilians of the 1st century A.D., and the towering Column of Jupiter, erected in Mainz at the time of Nero, around A.D. 65 to 68. There's a true-to-life replica of the column in front of the Parliament building.

SHOPPING

The city's most active shopping area is **Am Brand,** a short boulevard near the cathedral that's lined with shops on either side (bus: 1 or 54). One of the town's best clothing emporiums is **Peek & Kloppenburg,** Brand 38 (☎ **06131/23-27-61**), which sells clothing for men, women, and children, in styles ranging from very formal to chic and casual. For German designer fashions, head to **Sinn,** Am Brand 41 (☎ **06131/27-30**), which carries men's and women's clothing, and **Leininger,** Ludwigstrasse 11 (☎ **06131/28-88-20; bus: 54**), which sells outfits for women and children.

Whatever you can't find along the Am Brand will almost certainly be available among the vast inventories of Mainz's two most visible department stores, **Kaufhof,** Schusterstrasse 41 (☎ **06131/2541; bus: 54**), and **Lang,** Am Schillerplatz 8 (☎ **06131/231549; bus: 54**). To find a treasure trove of secondhand goods, shop the **Krempelmarkt flea market,** held along the banks of the Rhine on the first Saturday of each month, February to October (Bus: 54).

Many of Mainz's hotels, restaurants, and banks take an interest in modern art. You might also want to visit the city's most prestigious modern art gallery, **Galerie H. G. Lautner,** Augustinerstrasse 52 (☎ **06131/22-57-36; bus: 54**). Another place, **Galerie Kreiter-Kuhnt,** Badergasse 22 (☎ **06131/22-98-36; bus: 9**), is appealing to aficionados of middle Europe's contemporary art scene, as is **Atelier 9,** Heidelberger Fassgasse 18 (☎ **06131/23-26-42; bus: 9**).

WHERE TO STAY
EXPENSIVE

Atrium Hotel Mainz. Flugplatzstrasse 44, 55126 Mainz-Finthen. ☎ **06131/49-10.** Fax 06131/49-11-28. www.atrium-mainz.de. E-mail: info@atrium-mainz.de. 104 units. MINIBAR TV TEL. 270DM–380DM ($135–$190) double. AE, DC, MC, V. Free parking in the parking lot on the grounds; 15DM ($7.50) per night in the 24-car indoor garage. Bus: 16. Take the A60 and exit at the turnoff for Mainz-Finthen; drive through Finthen; the hotel is the last building on the right.

This modern hotel lies in the midst of orchards in the Rhine Valley. It's convenient to the nearby cities of Frankfurt and Wiesbaden, and only 15 minutes from the Frankfurt airport. The atmosphere is inviting. The bar has an open fireplace, and the atrium garden has a brook, pond, and exotic plants. Rooms are among the finest and most spacious in town (although not on the level of the Hilton's), with lots of amenities such as hair dryers and personal safes.

Dining/Diversions: There's a French restaurant and a bistro-bar, serving both regional specialties and international dishes.

Amenities: Concierge, room service, laundry, dry cleaning service, and a wide range of sports facilities, including an indoor pool, sauna, steam bath, fitness center, and tennis court.

✪ **Hilton International.** Rheinstrasse 68, 55116 Mainz (a 5-min. walk from the cathedral). ☎ **800/445-8667** in the U.S. and Canada, or 06131/24-50. Fax 06131/24-55-89. www.hilton.com. E-mail: sales-mainz@hilton.com. 434 units. A/C MINIBAR TV TEL. 485DM ($242.50) double; from 775DM ($387.50) suite. AE, DC, MC, V. Parking 30DM ($15). Bus: 7, 13, 17, 34, or 37.

The Hilton, renovated in 1998, is the most imaginatively designed and strikingly modern hotel along the Rhine Valley. It occupies two desirable plots of land near the center of town. Its twin sections are sheathed in reflective mirrors and soaring spans of steel and are connected by a glass-sided covered walkway above the traffic below. There are enough bars, restaurants, and health-club facilities to keep you busy for a week. The labyrinthine interior has sun-flooded atriums with live plants, piano bars made of polished mahogany and brass, and acres of marble flooring. The spacious rooms have lots of amenities and are the most artfully decorated in the region. Baths are also roomy.

Dining: The Brasserie is a fine dining place, as is the rustic, French-inspired Römische Weinstube.

Amenities: Room service, laundry, dry cleaning, hairdresser, sauna, supervised health and exercise club.

MODERATE

Hammer. Bahnhofplatz 6, 55116 Mainz. ☎ **06131/96-52-80.** Fax 06131/96-52-88-8. www.hotel-hammer.com. E-mail: info@hotel-hammer.com. 40 units. MINIBAR TV TEL. 168DM–230DM ($84–$115) double. Rates include buffet breakfast. AE, DC, MC, V. Parking 15DM ($7.50). Bus: 16 or 23.

The Hammer has a bright, inviting lobby and modern furnishings. Rooms are good size and come with hair dryers. The staff is excellent and very helpful. There's also a sauna, solarium, and fitness center.

Hotel Mainzer Hof. Kaiserstrasse 98, 55116 Mainz (a 10-min. walk from the Hauptbahnhof). ☎ **06131/28-89-90.** Fax 06131/22-82-55. www.info-mainz.de/hotel-mainzer-hof. 93 units. MINIBAR TV TEL. 190DM–290DM ($95–$145) double. Rates include buffet breakfast. AE, DC, MC, V. Parking 8DM ($4). Bus: 9.

Mainzer Hof is six floors of modernity directly on the Rhine, almost at the point where some of the boats dock. This hotel is a clean-cut, convenient stopover. The medium-sized rooms are well furnished and maintained and have hair dryers. In the basement is an Italian specialty restaurant; on the sixth floor is the restaurant Panorama Salon, reserved for groups. There's an inviting atmosphere in the lobby bar. Room service, laundry, and dry cleaning are provided.

WHERE TO DINE

✪ **Drei Lilien.** Ballplatz 2. ☎ **06131/22-50-68.** Reservations required. Main courses 28DM–42DM ($14–$21); fixed-price menu 55DM–80DM ($27.50–$40). AE, DC, V. Tues–Sat noon–2pm and 6:30–10pm. Bus: 15 to Schillerplatz. FRENCH.

Drei Lilien is an excellent place to have a French meal. The chef, H. J. Stuihmillers, practices a form of *cuisine moderne* that he has dubbed *cuisine du marché*, or "market fresh." Everything is cooked with imagination and the freshest seasonal ingredients. The decor of this wood-beamed, chandeliered place could be called "graciously rustic." Linens are impeccable, and the service is deferential. Try grilled steak with wild trumpet mushrooms in cognac sauce with grape leaves, or delicately poached baby turbot in champagne sauce.

Geberts Weinstuben. Frauenlobstrasse 94. ☎ **06131/61-16-19.** Reservations required. Main courses 25DM–40DM ($12.50–$20). AE, DC, MC, V. Mon–Fri 11:30am–2pm; Mon–Fri and Sun 6–10pm. Closed mid-July to mid-Aug. Bus: 7 or 21. PALATINATE.

This traditional Weinstube is housed in one of the oldest buildings in Mainz, with a decor that's almost spartan. But decor is not the reason people come here, and they come in great numbers. Once seated, you're treated to a traditional meal of game, fish, or regional specialties such as goose à l'orange. The menu is robust Palatinate fare.

Langolo. Augustinerstrasse 8. ☎ **06131/23-17-37.** Reservations not necessary. Pizzas and pastas 10DM–16.50DM ($5–$8.25); meat platters 18.50DM–18.80DM ($9.25–$9.40). No credit cards. Daily 11am–midnight. Bus: 6, 15, or 23. ITALIAN.

This informal Italian-inspired trattoria is known for its congenial staff and its excellent pizza and pasta. You can also order freshly made salads with shrimp or prosciutto, and meat dishes, consisting of escalopes of either pork or veal. Reasonable prices and a full bar generally keep this place packed.

Weinstube Lösch. Jakobsbergstrasse 9. ☎ **06131/22-03-83.** Reservations recommended. Main courses 16DM–40DM ($8–$20). No credit cards. Daily 5:30pm–1am. Bus: 6, 23. RHINELAND.

This old-fashioned Weinstube in the heart of the Altstadt has been popular for generations, and is rich in tradition. Meals feature both hot and cold dishes, plus lots of Rhine wine. The menu offers regional dishes and interesting salads. The pork schnitzel with mushrooms is particularly savory. There are only 12 tables, but they seat 85 guests. Six additional tables are placed out front in summer on the pedestrian mall.

MAINZ AFTER DARK

The cultural center of the city is **Frankfurter Hof,** Augustinerstrasse 55 (☎ **06131/ 22-04-38;** bus: 54), which stages concerts of classical music, jazz, folk, and pop. The center also hosts an annual tent festival featuring an eclectic mix of international performers. Tickets to all events cost between 10DM and 70DM ($5 and $35). Call for scheduled shows, festival dates and performers, and ticket information.

Although you can buy tickets at the offices of any of the theaters and entertainment venues in Mainz, a more convenient way is to contact the **Ticket Service,** which is a division of the town's tourist office at Brückenturm am Rathaus, 55116 Mainz (☎ **06131/28-62-10;** bus: 54). A privately funded competitor of the city's Ticket Service is **Kartenhaus,** Schillerstrasse 11 (☎ **06131/22-87-29;** bus: 54).

In terms of its nightlife, Mainz is sleepy enough to compel many residents to head to Cologne or Düsseldorf after dark. But if you don't want to get too quickly out of town, consider dancing the night away at the **Disco Kuz,** Winterhaven 12 (☎ **06131/28-68-60;** bus: 61), where good music and attractive people drink, dance, and talk. It's open nightly 10pm till at least 2am, charges an 8DM ($4) cover, and attracts a crowd aged 20 to around 35. A somewhat snobbier, smaller, and much more formal, nearby competitor is **L'Escalier,** Winterhaven 19 (☎ **06131/23-43-11;** bus: 61). It's outfitted in a style that evokes a semiprivate club in London. Open nightly after 10:30pm; 10DM ($5) cover. **Chapeau Claque,** Kleine Landgasse 4 (☎ **06131/ 223-111;** bus: 9), is a gay bar that's open nightly 5pm to 4am.

4 The Rheingau

Legend says that when God was looking for a place to set up Paradise, the sunny slopes between the Taunus Mountains and the Rhine nearly won the prize. Today the Rheingau is the kingdom of another god, Bacchus. Nearly every town and village from Wiesbaden to Assmannshausen, no matter how small, is a major wine producer. The names suddenly seem familiar—Bingen, Johannisberg, Rüdesheim, Oestrich—because we have seen them on the labels of many favorite wines.

The Rheingau is also rich in old churches and castles, as well as landmarks. The **Niederwald Monument,** on a hill halfway between Rüdesheim and Assmannshausen—it can be reached by cable car from either town—is a huge statue of Germania, erected by Bismarck in 1883 to commemorate the unification of Germany. Below it, on a small island at the bend of the Rhine, is the **Mäuseturm (Mouse Tower),** where, according to legend, the greedy archbishop of Mainz was devoured by a swarm of hungry mice. But the real attraction of the Rheingau is the cheerful character of the wine villages and their people. Rüdesheim and Assmannshausen are the most visited towns. Assmannshausen is actually part of Rüdesheim—its center lies 5km (3 miles) to the northwest of Rüdesheim's center on the Rhine River.

ESSENTIALS
GETTING THERE By Plane   The nearest airport is at Frankfurt (see chapter 12), 48km (30 miles) away.

By Train   The main rail station at Rüdesheim is on the Wiesbaden–Koblenz line, with frequent service to regional towns and connections to all major cities. For rail information and schedules, call ☎ **01805/99-66-33.** Train service from Frankfurt is via Wiesbaden and takes 1 hour.

By Bus   Bus service for the region is provided by **ORN Omnibusverkehr Rhein-Nahe GmbH,** in Wiesbaden (☎ **0611/97-75-822**).

By Car   Access by car is via the A61 Autobahn from the west and highway 42 connecting with the A671 from the west. From Frankfurt, motorists can take the A66 until they reach the junction with Route B42, which will be signposted and lead them right to Rüdesheim. Motorists heading from Koblenz on the west bank of the Rhine can use the A61 to Bingen, then follow the signs for the ferryboats that cross the river to Rüdesheim. For information on the ferry service, call ☎ **06721/1-41-40.** From Koblenz, you can also take B42 along the east bank of the river, which will lead directly into Rüdesheim. Route B42 links Rüdesheim with Assmannshausen.

VISITOR INFORMATION   For information about Rüdesheim and Assmannshausen (see below), go to the **Stadt Verkehrsamt,** Rheinstrasse 16 in Rüdesheim

(☎ **06722/19433**). It's open year-round Monday to Friday 8:30am to 6:30pm, and May to October also Saturday 10:30am to 5:30pm and Sunday 11:30am to 3:30pm.

RÜDESHEIM

With its old courtyards and winding alleyways lined with timbered houses, Rüdesheim is the epitome of a Rhine wine town. The vineyards around the village date back to the Roman emperor Probus. The full-bodied Riesling is produced here, as well as brandy and champagne (*sekt*). Rüdesheim is also the scene of the annual August wine festival, when the old taverns on the narrow and very touristy **Drossel-gasse** are crowded with visitors from all over the world. Drosselgasse has been called "the smallest but the happiest street in the world." April to November, you can listen to music and dance in these taverns daily noon to 1am.

To prove how seriously Rüdesheimers take their wine, they have opened a wine museum in Bromserburg Castle. The **Rheingau- und Weinmuseum,** Rheinstrasse 2 (☎ **06722/23-48**), charges 5DM ($2.50) for adults and 1DM (50¢) for children under 12, and is open mid-March to October daily 9am to 6pm. It traces the history of the grape and has an exhibition of wine presses, glasses, goblets, and drinking utensils from Roman times to the present.

WHERE TO STAY & DINE
Moderate
Hotel und Weinhaus Felsenkeller. Oberstrasse 39–41, 65385 Rüdesheim (in the center of the old town). ☎ **06722/9-42-50.** Fax 06722/4-72-02. www.ruedesheim-rhein.com. E-mail: felsenkeller@ruedesheim-rhein.com. 60 units. MINIBAR TV TEL. 148DM–212DM ($74–$106) double; 190DM–244DM ($95–$122) triple. Rates include buffet breakfast. AE, MC, V. Closed Nov–Easter. Garage parking 10DM ($5).

The beautifully carved timbers on the facade of this 1613 building suggest the traditional aura you'll find inside. A sampling of Rhine wine can be enjoyed in a room of vaulted ceilings and murals with vine leaves and pithy pieces of folk wisdom. In fair weather, guests can eat on the terrace. The small attractively modern and freshly painted rooms open onto views of the vineyards surrounding the house.

Breuer's Rüdesheimer Schloss. Steingasse 10. 65385 Rüdesheim. ☎ **06722/9-05-00.** Fax 06722/4-79-60. www.ruedesheimer-schloss.com. E-mail: ruedesheimer-schloss@ t-online.de. 21 units. MINIBAR TV TEL. 190DM–260DM ($95–$130) double. Rates include buffet and local champagne. AE, DC, MC, V. Closed Dec 22–Jan 5. Free outdoor parking; 15DM ($7.50) in garage.

This hotel is the first choice for staying and dining in town. The wine cellar dates from 1729. The Breuer family is noted for its wine cellars and plentiful food and drink. The medium-sized rooms are immaculately kept, and most are quite spacious, with radio, safe, hair dryer, and floor heating. The hotel staff will prepare for you a tailor-made package of excursions or perhaps a "gastronomic feast" and a musical evening on their premises.

Rüdesheimer Hof. Geisenheimerstrasse 1, 65385 Rüdesheim (a 10-min. walk from the Bahnhof). ☎ **06722/91-19-0.** Fax 06722/4-81-94. E-mail: ruedesheimer-hof@t-online.de. 42 units. 130DM–160DM ($65–$80) double. Rates include buffet breakfast. AE, DC, MC, V. Closed Dec to mid-Feb. Free parking.

This village inn, set back from the Rhine, boasts a side garden and terrace where wine tasters gather at rustic tables. Most of the units are roomy and comfortably furnished; 20 have TVs and 30 have telephones. The atmosphere is informal. If you stay here, you can sample the lifestyle of a Rhine village by mingling with the townspeople, eating the regional food, and drinking the Rheingau wines. If you're stopping by just to eat, you'll find meals priced 14DM to 32DM ($7 to $16) and up. Guests dine at cafe tables placed under a willow tree. Food is served daily 11:30am to 9:30pm.

Inexpensive

Gasthof Krancher. Eibinger-Oberstrasse 4 (a 10-min. hike uphill from the town center), 65385 Rüdesheim. ☎ **06722/27-62.** Fax 06722/4-78-70. 62 units. 100DM–120DM ($50–$60) double. Rates include buffet breakfast. V. Free parking.

Gasthof Krancher has been in the Krancher family for four generations. It's located next to the inn's own vineyards. Naturally, the Kranchers make their own wines, and they'll gladly show you the cellar where they store bottles that have won gold and silver medals. Everything is decorated in a regional motif. Rooms are a bit cramped but reasonably comfortable. None has a telephone, although 10 contain TVs. From your window you can look out on the vineyards. The cuisine is first class, as are the wines.

Hotel Rheinstein. Rheinstrasse 20, 65385 Rüdesheim (across from the riverside landing stage of the Cologne–Düsseldorf Anlegestelle). ☎ **06722/20-04.** Fax 06722/4-76-88. 40 units. TEL. 100DM ($50) double with shower; 140DM ($70) double with bath. Half board 65DM–75DM ($32.50–$37.50) per person. Rates include buffet breakfast. AE, DC, MC, V. Closed Dec–Mar.

The Rheinstein's elongated terrace facing the street is one of the most popular gathering places in Rüdesheim. Many locals drop in during the afternoon to enjoy the excellent cakes, all baked on the premises. Irene Gehrig offers small and well-kept rooms furnished with modern styling; some have TVs.

ASSMANNSHAUSEN

This old village at the northern edge of the Rheingau is built on the slopes of the east bank of the Rhine. Its half-timbered houses and vineyards seem precariously perched on the steep hillsides, and the view of the Rhine Valley from here is awe-inspiring. Assmannshausen is known for its fine burgundy-style wine. It lies 5km (3 miles) northwest of Rüdesheim and 60km (37 miles) west of Frankfurt.

WHERE TO STAY & DINE

Alte Bauernschanke-Nassauer Hof. Niederwaldstrasse 23, 65385 Rüdesheim-Assmannshausen (near the church, about ¹/₄ mile from the Rhine). ☎ **06722-4999-0.** Fax 06722/4-79-12. www.altebauernschaenke.de. E-mail: alte-bauernschanke@t-online.de. 52 units. TV TEL. 140DM–180DM ($70–$90) double; 250DM ($125) suite. Rates include buffet breakfast. AE, MC, V. Closed Dec–Mar.

The wine-grower owners have turned two of the oldest mansions in town into a hotel and restaurant. The interior decor is luxurious, the comfort fine, and the welcome hearty. Rooms are beautifully furnished in traditional style. The restaurant has live folk music every night. Try goulash soup, pepper steak with fresh green beans and French fries, and a bottle of the growers' red wine. The set price menu costs 30DM to 115DM ($15 to $57.50); the higher price is for a lavish, eight-course banquet.

Ewige Lampe und Haus Resi. Niederwaldstrasse 14, 65385 Rüdesheim-Assmannshausen. ☎ **06722/24-17.** Fax 06722/4-84-59. 24 units. 100DM–180DM ($50–$90) double. Rates include continental breakfast. No credit cards. Closed Jan 6–Feb 6. Free parking.

This hotel is within a few miles of historic vineyards, plus some woodland trails through Rhenish forest. You'll find a lot to do in this wine-producing center. Hosts Engelbert and Renate Uri will welcome you to their cozy, tastefully furnished guest house. Many of the medium-sized rooms have wooden ceilings, some have colorfully tiled baths, and all are impeccably clean. The fortifying breakfast is often served on a sun terrace under parasols. Meals are 25DM to 65DM ($12.50 to $32.50) per person.

✪ **Krone Assmannshausen.** Rheinuferstrasse 10, 65385 Rüdesheim-Assmannshausen. ☎ **06722/40-30.** Fax 06772/30-49. www.hotelkrone.com. E-mail: info@krone.as.de. 65 units. MINIBAR TV TEL. 250DM–320DM ($125–$160) double; 390DM ($195) junior suite; 590DM–780DM ($295–$390) suite. AE, DC, MC, V. Free parking.

This distinguished hotel offers the most luxurious accommodations in the entire Rüdesheim am Rhein district. It's on the banks of the Rhine, surrounded by lawns, gardens, and a pool. Its origins can be traced back 400 years. The inn is overscale, a great big gingerbread fantasy. A small second-floor lounge is virtually a museum, with framed letters and manuscripts of some of the famous people who have stayed here— Goethe, for one. There's a stack of about 40 autograph books dating from 1893 and signed by writers, painters, diplomats, and composers. You may stay in a medieval, a Renaissance, or a postwar building. The spacious rooms have an old-inn character, with traditional furnishings and compact baths.

Dining: Even if you're not overnighting, you should stop to sample some of the finest food served on the Rhine. Specialties are homemade pâtés, fresh salmon or eel from Lake Constance, and saddle of venison in season. For dessert, try the *Eisbecher Krone*. The owners, the Hufnagel family, known for the famous Assmannshauser Höllenberg Pinot Noir, maintain within the inn one of the finest cellars of Rhine wines in the world. Fixed-price menus cost 42DM to 78DM ($21 to $39) for lunch and 135DM ($67.50) for dinner.

Amenities: Room service (breakfast only), hair dryers, laundry, baby-sitting, pool, sauna.

5 Koblenz

88km (55 miles) SE of Cologne, 63km (39 miles) SE of Bonn, 100km (62 miles) NW of Frankfurt

Koblenz has stood at the confluence of the Rhine and the Mosel for more than 2,000 years. Its strategic location in the mid-Rhine region has made the city a vital link in the international river trade routes of Europe. The city is surrounded by vine-covered hills dotted with castles and fortresses. Koblenz is also the place where many cruises through the Rhine begin or end.

ESSENTIALS

GETTING THERE   By Plane   The nearest airports to Koblenz are Frankfurt (see chapter 12) and Cologne (see section 9 below).

By Train   The **Koblenz Hauptbahnhof** lies on a major rail line, with frequent connections to important German cities. For train information, prices, and schedules, call ☎ **01805/996633.** Thirty trains per day arrive from Frankfurt (trip time: 2 hr.) and 16 from Berlin (trip time: $8^{1}/_{2}$ hr.). Trains also arrive every 30 minutes from Cologne (trip time: 45 min. to 1 hr.).

By Bus   Rail is by far the best way to get to Koblenz, but information on bus service is available by calling ☎ **0261/303-88-23.**

By Car   Access by car to Koblenz is via the A48 Autobahn east and west, connecting with the A3 north to south.

VISITOR INFORMATION   For information about tours, boat trips on the Rhine, and bus and train connections, contact the **Koblenz Tourist Office,** Löhrstrasse 141 (☎ **0261/3-13-04**). It's open May to September, Monday to Friday 9am to 8pm, Saturday and Sunday 10am to 8pm; October and April Monday to Friday 9am to 6pm, Saturday and Sunday 10am to 6pm; November to March, Monday to Friday 9am to 5pm.

GETTING AROUND   The city is served by 10 main bus lines. Fare is 2.20DM ($1.10) to 4.80DM ($2.40), paid on the bus. A day pass, sold at the tourist office, costs 9DM ($4.50).

SEEING THE SIGHTS

Koblenz was heavily bombed during World War II, but many of the historic buildings have been restored. For the best overall view of the town, go to the point where the two rivers meet. This is called **Deutsches Eck** ("corner of Germany"). From the top of the base where a huge statue of Wilhelm I once stood, you can see the Altstadt and across the Rhine to the Ehrenbreitstein Fortress.

The focal point of the Altstadt is the **Liebfrauenkirche (Church of Our Lady),** a 13th-century Gothic basilica built on a Romanesque foundation, with twin towers topped by onion-shaped spires. The early 18th-century **Rathaus** was formerly a Jesuit college. In the courtyard behind the hall is a fountain dedicated to the youth of Koblenz called *The Spitting Boy* (*Das Schängelchen*), and that's just what he does. At the edge of the old town, near the Deutsches Eck, is Koblenz's oldest and most attractive church, **St. Castor's,** originally built in 836, though in its present form it dates mostly from the 12th century.

Festung Ehrenbreitstein (☎ 0261/970-30), across the Rhine from Koblenz, can be reached by chairlift. You can also drive there via the Pfaffendorfer Bridge just south of the Altstadt or take bus 8, 9, or 10 from the rail station. The fortress was constructed on a rock and towers 122m (400 feet) above the Rhine. The present walls were built in the 19th century. From the stone terrace, you get one of the best views along the Rhine; the panoramic vista includes not only Koblenz but also several castles on the river and many terraced vineyards. To reach the fortress, make the 2DM ($1) one-way passage across the river from the main Rhine dock. Ferries operate mid-April to late November, daily 9am to 5:15pm. The chairlift (*Sesselbahn*) operates May to September daily 9:30am to 6pm. Round-trip tickets cost 10DM ($5) for adults, 6DM ($3) for children under 14.

WHERE TO STAY
EXPENSIVE

Diehl's. Am Pfaffendorfer Tor 10, Ehrenbreitstein, 56077 Koblenz. ☎ **0261/9-70-70.** Fax 0261/9-70-72-13. www.eurohotel-online.com/diehl.koblenz.html. E-mail: info@diehls-hotel.de. 64 units. MINIBAR TV TEL. 160DM–280DM ($80–$140) double; 280DM–480DM ($140–$240) suite. Rates include buffet breakfast. DC, MC, V. Free parking. Bus: 7, 8, 9, or 10.

Diehl's is on the banks of the Rhine; all its public rooms, lounges, dining rooms, and guest rooms face the river directly. This old-style hotel lies below the Ehrenbreitstein fortress, linked by a little ferry boat to the center of town. The place often accommodates groups.

Dining: Elevators connect the hotel floors with the restaurant, Rheinterrasse, which features both Rhineland and international cuisine. The hotel is well known for the quality of its food, and its cellar is filled with some 30,000 bottles of wine from the Rhine and Mosel Valleys.

Amenities: Pool, sauna, Jacuzzi, jogging track, hair dryers, limited room service, laundry service, baby-sitting, and conference rooms.

Mercure. Julius-Wegeler-Strasse 6, 56068 Koblenz. ☎ **0261/13-60.** Fax 0261/1-36-11-99. www.mercure.com. 168 units. A/C MINIBAR TV TEL. 260DM ($130) double; 500DM ($250) suite. Rates include buffet breakfast. AE, DC, MC, V. Parking 20DM ($10). Bus: 9 or 10.

Glittering and stylish, the Mercure is easily the best hotel in town. It's perched on a hillock at the edge of the Rhine. Its streamlined architecture contrasts with the century-old trees and ancient stones of the medieval town surrounding it. Rooms are well-insulated against sound from the street and neighboring rooms; each has a VCR. One of the city's loveliest riverside promenades lies just a short walk away.

Dining/Diversions: The hotel has a restaurant that serves lunch and dinner and a separate breakfast room.

Amenities: Sauna, solarium, hot whirlpool, room service, laundry, dry cleaning, secretarial assistance.

MODERATE

Hotel Brenner. Rizzastrasse 20–22, 56068 Koblenz (near the Kurfürstl Schloss). ☎ **0261/ 91-57-80.** Fax 0261/3-62-78. www.eurohotel-online.com/brenner.koblenz.html. E-mail: brenner.koblenz@eurohotel-online.com. 24 units. MINIBAR TV TEL. 160DM–230DM ($80–$115) double. Rates include buffet breakfast. AE, DC, MC, V. Parking 12DM–15DM ($6–$7.50). Bus: 1 or 5 to Christuskirche.

This hotel is your best bet if you're seeking a good moderately priced choice. The small to medium-sized rooms are spotlessly maintained. Each bath has a hair dryer. The garden retreat is a good spot for getting back to nature.

Kleiner Riesen. Kaiserin-Augusta-Anlagen 18, 56068 Koblenz. ☎ **0261/3-20-77.** Fax 0261/16-07-25. 27 units. TV TEL. 150DM–180DM ($75–$90) double. Rates include buffet breakfast. AE, DC, MC, V. Parking 15DM ($7.50).

This is one of the few hotels in central Koblenz that sits directly on the banks of the Rhine. Its dining-room terrace and most of its rooms are close enough to view the boats as they go by. Within the city proper, only the Mercure is better. The Kleiner Riesen is a large, overgrown, informal chalet, with several lounges and comfortable rooms. It's away from town traffic, so it has a peaceful small-town quiet.

INEXPENSIVE

Hotel Scholz. Moselweisserstrasse 121, 56073 Koblenz (a 5-min. bus ride from the town center). ☎ **0261/94260.** Fax 0261/40-80-26. 62 units. TV TEL. 150DM ($75) double. Rates include buffet breakfast. AE, DC, MC, V. Closed Dec 20–Jan 7. Free parking. Bus: 6.

Scholz is a personally run family hotel. It offers sparsely furnished units that make for a reasonably priced overnight stopover. Rooms are small, as are the baths, but the beds are comfortable and the maintenance is good. Traditional German cuisine is served at the restaurant.

WHERE TO DINE

Gillstuga. In the Mercure, Julius-Wegeler-Strasse 6. ☎ **0261/13-60.** Reservations recommended. Main courses 18DM–46DM ($9–$23). AE, DC, MC, V. Daily 11:30am–midnight. Bus: 1 or 5. RHINELANDER/INTERNATIONAL.

Elegantly modern in both design and flavor, Gillstuga is one of the leading restaurants of Koblenz, though that's not saying much—Koblenz is a notoriously bad restaurant town. You dine on a wide flower-trimmed terrace in summer, with a partial view of the river, or inside in an ambience of pastel and polished wood. Dishes are well prepared, although rarely exciting. Start with smoked salmon in a mustard dill sauce or perhaps a smooth consommé of pink mushrooms. Fish dishes are excellent, especially the fried catfish with a lime sauce or perch Strindberg with onions and mustard. Strips of veal appear in a mushroom cream sauce with potato *Rösti* and a salad from the buffet.

Weinhaus Hubertus. Florinsmarkt 6 (across from the Old Rathaus). ☎ **0261/3-11-77.** Reservations recommended. Menus 13.50DM–25DM ($6.75–$12.50); glass of wine 4.30DM–7.80DM ($2.15–$3.90). MC, V. Wed–Mon 4pm–midnight. Bus: 1. GERMAN.

Weinhaus Hubertus looks like a timbered country inn. It's the oldest wine tavern in town, dating from 1696. The place offers German wines accompanied by a choice of homemade dishes—soups, sandwiches, and light platters, all designed to go well with the wines offered. The furnishings and the decor are family style, providing a home-like atmosphere. There's a choice here of 100 wines from all over Germany, 30 of these by the glass. In summer, you can enjoy the view of the Altstadt from the terrace.

KOBLENZ AFTER DARK

THE PERFORMING ARTS   The **Rheinische Philharmonie Orchestra** performs in the **Rhein-Mosel-Halle,** Julius-Wegeler-Strasse (☎ 0261/129-1652; bus: 9 or 10), which also hosts other performances. The symphony's season is September to June, and tickets cost 20DM to 100DM ($10 to $50). Call for listings, dates, and prices of other performances. The **Stadttheater (City Theater),** housed in the **Grosse-haus,** Dinehartplatz (☎ 0261/1292840 9am to noon; bus: 9 or 10), stages dramas, comedies, and musicals September to June. The box office is open daily 8am to noon and 1 to 4pm. Tickets are 35DM to 75DM ($17.50 to $37.50).

BARS   Three of our favorite bars in Koblenz are devoted to individual themes that local residents embrace with relish. The first is the arts-conscious (and devilish) **Mephisto,** Elzerhofstrasse 3 (☎ 0261/31735; bus: 1), the walls of which are covered with photographs of famous German actors dressed for the part of Mephistopheles in various productions of *Faust.* Open Sunday to Friday 7pm to 1am, and Saturday till 2am. Nearby is another establishment with an almost equivalent theme, the **Faustus Bar,** Elzerhofstrasse 11 (☎ 0261/17991; bus: 1), open 11am to 4pm and 6pm to 3am.

For a laugh or two as you drink, head for the **Blauer Biwel,** Entenpfuhl 9 (☎ 0261/35577; bus: 1), a bar where local stand-up comics sometime perform. Even if your German isn't up to the challenge, you might like the disco music they some-times play.

One of Koblenz's most counterculture pubs is **Klepsmühle,** Poststrasse 2A (☎ 0261/3-84-14). The music played here is mostly cutting-edge, with occasional touches of old-fashioned alpine evergreen music (yodeling and such). The pub-oriented clientele is mostly under age 40.

LIVE MUSIC   **Pflaumenbaum,** Friedrich-Ebert-Ring 32 (☎ 0261/30-90-70; bus: 9 or 10), is a smoke-filled, woodsy pub enhanced with live jazz, pop, and other types of music. Open daily 5pm to 4am. At **Irish Pub Koblenz,** Burgstrasse 7 (☎ 0261/ 17377; bus: 1), copious amounts of Guinness, Kilkenny, hard cider, and German beers are served as accompaniment to live music, everything from traditional Gaelic songs to progressive rock 'n' roll. Open Sunday to Thursday 1pm to 1am and Friday and Saturday 1pm to 2am.

DANCE CLUBS   Koblenz's largest nightlife complex lies 4km (2¹/₂ miles) north of the town center. **Extra,** August-Horch-Strasse 2 (☎ 0261/809-050; bus: 6045), includes a half-dozen movie theaters, and a scattering of bars and dance clubs that play everything from old-time mountain-style evergreen music to the cutting-edge. The best way to experience the complex is to wander through its hallways, popping into whatever place suits your fancy. Entrance to most of the bars is free; cover charge to some of the dance emporiums runs 5DM to 15DM ($2.50 to $7.50).

6 Bonn

72km (45 miles) S of Düsseldorf, 27km (17 miles) S of Cologne, 174km (108 miles) NW of Frankfurt

Until 1949, Bonn was a sleepy little university town, basking in its 2,000 years of history. Then suddenly it was shaken out of this quiet life and made capital of the Federal Republic of Germany. But in 1991, after the reunification of Germany, Berlin again became the official capital.

Although Bonn will continue to function as a smaller "second capital," no other cities stand to lose as much, especially in terms of prestige and political influence. Six of the major 15 departments of the German government, including the Defense Ministry, will remain here, although they will also have smaller offices in Berlin.

From the 13th through the 18th centuries, Bonn was the capital of the prince-electors of Cologne, who had the right to participate in the election of the emperor of the Holy Roman Empire. The city is also proud of its intellectual and musical history—Beethoven was born here; composer Robert Schumann and his wife, pianist Clara Schumann, lived here; and Karl Marx and Heinrich Heine studied in Bonn's university. Bonn's latest cultural addition is the "Museum Mile," which includes the **Bundeskunsthalle (Federal Art and Exhibition Hall)** and the **Kunstmuseum (Art Museum)**.

Bonn is also within sight of the **Siebenbirge (Seven Mountains),** a volcanic mountain range rising up on the eastern bank of the Rhine. The entire range is today a national park. The local wine produced on these slopes is known as Drachenblut (Dragon's Blood).

ESSENTIALS

GETTING THERE   By Plane   The nearest airport is **Flughafen Köln/Bonn** (see section 9, below). Buses from the airport to Bonn's main rail station run every 30 minutes daily 6am to 10:30pm.

By Train   The **Bonn Hauptbahnhof** is on a major rail line, with connections to most German cities. There are 12 trains daily to Berlin (trip time: 7 hr.), more than 30 trains to Frankfurt (trip time: 2 hr.), and service to Cologne every 15 minutes (trip time: 20 min.). For information, call ☎ **01805/996633.**

By Bus   Long-distance bus service goes to such cities as Munich, Stuttgart, Aachen, Brussels, and London. For information, call **Deutsches Touring GmbH** in Frankfurt (☎ **069/7-90-35-0**). Regional bus service to Bad Godesberg and nearby towns is provided by **Regionalverkehr Köln GmbH at Meckenheim** (☎ **02225/60-87**).

By Car   Access is by the A565 Autobahn connecting with the A3 Autobahn from the north or south.

VISITOR INFORMATION   Go to the **Bonn Tourist Office,** Cassius-Passage, Münsterstrasse 20 (☎ **0228/19433**), open Monday to Friday 9am to 6:30pm, Saturday 9am to 4pm, and Sunday 10am to 2pm.

GETTING AROUND   If you visit the Reisenzentrum under the Bonn railway station, you can pick up a free map outlining the city's transportation network. The office is open Monday to Saturday 5:30am to 10pm, and Sunday 6:30am to 10pm. Bus or underground tickets cost 2.20DM ($1.10) to 14.20DM ($7.10). From Automaten (ticket dispensers) you can purchase 4-ride tickets for 8DM ($4) to 12.80DM ($6.40), or day tickets for 9.50DM ($4.75) to 35DM ($17.50).

EXPLORING THE TOWN

Residents and tourist officials within Bonn show an extraordinary degree of civic and cultural pride whenever they discuss their city. Part of this manifests itself in walking tours that stress the 2,000 years of Bonn's history, with an emphasis on its role as a city of culture during the 19th century, and its changing role within Germany since reunification. April to October, 2-hour walking tours of Bonn are offered Saturday at 10:30am and 2pm, and Sunday at 10am. Between November and March, there's only one tour a week: Saturday at 2pm. Tours cost 22DM ($11) for adults and 11DM ($5.50) for students and children under 16. The meeting point for these tours is the Bonn Tourist Office (see above). Call ☎ **0228/19433** for reservations and advance confirmation.

The **government quarter,** along the west bank of the Rhine, is a complex of modern, rather nondescript white buildings. The two most impressive, both along Koblenzerstrasse, are the former residences of the president and chancellor. These empire-style villas are reminiscent of the older Bonn, before it became an international center of diplomatic activity. They are not open to the public. Running north along the Rhine from the government buildings is a tree- and flower-lined promenade, which ends at the **Alter Zoll.** This ruined ancient fortress makes a good viewing point from which visitors can see across the Rhine to the Siebengebirge and the old village of Beuel. These grounds have, in essence, become a city park.

✪ **Beethoven House.** Bonngasse 20 (in the old section of town, just north of the marketplace). ☎ **0228/9-81-75-25.** Admission 8DM ($4) adults, 6DM ($3) students and children. Guided tours by prior arrangement 15DM ($7.50). Apr–Sept, Mon–Sat 10am–5pm, Sun 11am–4pm; Nov–Mar, Mon–Sat 10am–6pm, Sun 11am–4pm. Tram: 61 or 62.

Beethoven House is Bonn's pride and joy. Beethoven was born in 1770 in the small house in back, which opens onto a little garden. On its second floor is the room where he was born, decorated only with a simple marble bust of the composer. Many of Beethoven's personal possessions are in the house, including manuscripts and musical instruments. In the Vienna Room, in the front of the house overlooking the street, is Beethoven's last piano. The instrument was custom-made, with a special sounding board to amplify sound so that the deaf composer could hear it.

Kunstmuseum Bonn. Friedrich-Ebert-Allee 2. ☎ **0228/77-62-60.** Admission 8DM ($4) adults, 4DM ($2) children. Tues–Sun 10am–6pm, Wed 10am–9pm. U-Bahn: Heussallee.

One of the major buildings along the new "Museum Mile," this triangular structure, flooded with light, contains one of the most important art collections along the Rhine. The highlight is 20th-century art, including works by Rhenish expressionists, most notably August Macke. There are also works by Kirchner, Schmidt-Rottluff, Campendonk, Ernst, Seehaus, and Thuar.

Haus der Geschichte der Bundesrepublik Deutschland. Willy-Brandt-Allee 14. ☎ **0228/9-16-50.** Free admission. Tues–Sun 9am–7pm. U-Bahn: Heussallee.

All the sweep and drama of Germany's modern history is brought to life in this museum, in artifacts, photographs, and other displays. Exhibits trace the history of Germany after 1945, up to the breakdown of law and order in the eastern sector that led to reunification. This museum is one of Bonn's most visited.

SHOPPING

Not surprisingly, you'll find lots of shops in town specializing in garments suitable for diplomacy and business. Most of the best are on the **Sternstrasse** (S-Bahn:

Hauptbahnhof), partly a pedestrian-only street for certain times of day. Fanning out from here, you'll find women's clothing at **Beatrix Moden,** Münsterplatz 26 (☎ **0228/63-46-96**); **Boecker,** Wenzelgasse 17 (☎ **0228/98-50-60**); and **La Belle,** Friedrichstrasse 51 (☎ **0228/63-74-75**).

Two notable shops sell antique German furniture. **Ehlers Antiquitäten,** Berliner Freiheit 28 (☎ **0228/65-72-88;** S-Bahn: Hauptbahnhof), specializes in 19th- and 20th-century pieces and also sells some English silver and glass. Eighteenth-century German and French furniture as well as Biedermeier is found at **Paul Schweitzer,** Loebestrasse 1 (☎ **0228/36-26-59;** S-Bahn: Godesberger Bahnhof), which also handles Oriental carpets, silver, French glass, and estate jewelry. A market called the **Flohmarkt,** at Rheinaue, Ludwig-Erhard-Strasse (Tram: 66), is where you'll find all manner of secondhand goods and collectibles. It's held the third Saturday of each month April to October.

WHERE TO STAY
VERY EXPENSIVE

Günnewig Bristol Hotel. Prinz-Albert-Strasse 2, 53113 Bonn (near Poppelsdorf Castle). ☎ **0228/2-69-80.** Fax 0228/2-69-82-22. www.guennewig.de. E-mail: bristol.bonn@ guennewig.de. 116 units. A/C MINIBAR TV TEL. 370DM–470DM ($185–$235) double; 570DM ($285) suite. Rates include American breakfast. AE, DC, MC, V. Parking 23DM ($11.50). Tram: 61 or 62.

This somewhat sterile, Cold War-era concrete-and-glass tower is still the best address in town. The good-sized rooms are the best in Bonn, with such extras as safes, trouser presses, and double-glazing on the windows, along with fashionable and well-equipped baths with hair dryers and robes. The staff is also the finest in town.

Dining/Diversions: The food is of a high standard without being exceptional. Diplomats patronize the Restaurant Majestic, the Hofkonditorei Bierhoff, and the Walliser Stuben. There's also a cozy lounge bar.

Amenities: Room service, laundry, dry cleaning, heated indoor pool, sauna, solarium.

EXPENSIVE

✪ **Dorint Hotel Venusberg.** An der Casselsruhe 1, 53127 Bonn, 2.5km (1^1/$_2$ miles) southwest of Bonn, via Trierer Strasse. ☎ **0228/28-80.** Fax 0228/28-82-88. www. dorint.com. E-mail: reservierkung.whjven@dorint.com. 85 units. MINIBAR TV TEL. 237DM– 494DM ($118.50– $247) double; from 744DM ($372) suite. Rates include continental breakfast. AE, DC, MC, V. Parking 14.50DM ($7.25).

The elegant and intimate hotel, built in a style evocative of a French country home, is surrounded by the beauty of the Venusberg nature reserve, part of the larger Kottenforst. About half the units offer private balconies overlooking the hills. There are six air-conditioned suites. Baths are well-accessorized.

Dining: The gourmet dining room has an outdoor terrace overlooking the seven nearby hills of local legends.

Amenities: Room service, laundry, dry cleaning, hair dryers, sauna, health club, massage facilities.

Hotel Domicil. Thomas-Mann-Strasse 24–26, 53111 Bonn (4 blocks north of the cathedral, near the Hauptbahnhof). ☎ **800/528-1234** in the U.S., or 0228/72-90-90. Fax 0228/ 69-12-07. www.bestwestern.com. E-mail: info@domicil.bonn.bestwestern.de. 42 units. MINI-BAR TV TEL. 280DM–420DM ($140–$210) double; 480DM ($240) suite. AE, DC, MC, V. Free parking. S-Bahn: Hauptbahnhof.

This modern and convenient hotel, like the Kaiser Karl (see below), is an oasis of charm and grace amid the rather sterile environment of Bonn. It's like an exclusive

London town house, and provides a viable alternative to the Günnewig Bristol. In the front, a glass-and-steel portico stretches over the sidewalk. The interior is one of the most elegant in the capital. The handsomely designed and spacious rooms range in style from belle epoque to Italian modern.

Dining/Diversions: You can enjoy a drink in the piano bar before heading for the Krull restaurant, where French and Italian meals are served. The hotel also has a night-club, the Joyce Evening Club.

Amenities: Room service, laundry, dry cleaning, sauna, car-rental facilities.

✪ **Kaiser Karl.** Vorgebirgstrasse 56, 53119 Bonn. ☎ **0228/98-55-70.** Fax 0228/ 98-55-777. 43 units. MINIBAR TV TEL. 290DM–390DM ($145–$195) double; 450DM– 850DM ($225–$425) suite. AE, DC, MC, V. Parking 20DM ($10). Bus: 624 or 634.

Kaiser Karl is one of Bonn's gems. Like the Domicil (see above), it has more style and atmosphere than other luxury leaders. Constructed in 1905 as a private town house, it was converted in 1983 into a stylish four-story hotel. The attractive decor includes lacquered Japanese screens, English antiques, Oriental carpets, Venetian mirrors, and Edwardian potted palms. Each beautifully furnished room has a safe.

Dining/Diversions: Breakfast is the only meal served. There's an elegant piano bar and a garden where you can order drinks.

Amenities: Room service, hair dryers, laundry, concierge, dry cleaning.

MODERATE

Sternhotel. Markt 8, 53111 Bonn (next to the Rathaus). ☎ **0228/7-26-70.** Fax 0228/7-26-71-25. www.sternhotel-bonn.de. E-mail: info@sternhotel-bonn.de. 89 units. MINI-BAR TV TEL. 155DM–295DM ($77.50–$147.50) double. Rates include buffet breakfast. AE, DC, MC, V. Parking 20DM ($10) garage. U-Bahn: Uni-Markt. Bus: 624, 625, or 626.

This is one of the best of Bonn's moderately priced hotels. It offers an informal, home-like atmosphere. Rooms are homelike. International meals are served in the dining room. The warmly decorated Bistro Miebach, under separate management, serves lunch and dinner.

INEXPENSIVE

Haus Hofgarten. Fritz-Tillmann-Strasse 7, 53113 Bonn (a 5-min. walk from the Hauptbahn-hof). ☎ **0228/22-34-72.** Fax 0228/21-39-02. 15 units. TV TEL. 125DM ($62.50) double without bathroom, 185DM ($92.50) double with bathroom. Rates include continental break-fast. AE, DC, MC, V. Parking 5DM ($2.50). Tram: 61 or 62.

A hard-working couple presides over this unique establishment, which offers the charm of another era. It's an excellent value for Bonn. A wide mahogany staircase leads to the cozy rooms, which are simply but comfortably furnished and very well kept. There's also a good-sized breakfast room.

Hotel Beethoven. Rheingasse 24–26, 53113 Bonn (across the street from the Stadttheater, a 10-min. walk from the Hauptbahnhof). ☎ **0228/63-14-11.** Fax 0228/69-16-29. www.hotel-beethoven-bonn.com. E-mail: hotel-beethoven@t-online.de. 59 units. TV TEL. 169DM–189DM ($84.50–$94.50) double. Rates include buffet breakfast. AE, DC, MC, V. Free parking. Tram: 62; Bus 638.

One of the Beethoven's wings faces the Rhine. The hotel's main attraction is a panoramic view of the river traffic from the high-ceilinged dining room, where first-class meals are served, supervised by the owner. Double-glazed windows prevent urban noises from disturbing the calm in the well-furnished rooms, which range from small to medium.

WHERE TO DINE
EXPENSIVE

Le Petit Poisson. Wilhelmstrasse 23A. ☎ **0228/63-38-83.** Reservations recommended. Main courses 50DM–55DM ($25–$27.50); fixed-price dinner 65DM–120DM ($32.50–$60). AE, DC, MC, V. Tues–Sat 6pm–midnight. Tram: 61 or 62. FRENCH/SEAFOOD.

The food here is the finest in the center of Bonn. All ingredients are fresh, and many dishes are temptingly light and contemporary. Try the cream of fish and mushroom soup. Savory meat and game dishes include venison in vermouth sauce. Many diplomats dine here.

Ristorante Grand'Italia. Bischofsplatz 1 (adjacent to the old market square). ☎ **0228/63-83-33.** Reservations recommended. Main courses 29DM–42DM ($14.50–$21); fixed-price menus 37.50DM–72.80DM ($18.75–$36.40). AE, DC, MC, V. Daily noon–3pm and 6–11:30pm. Tram: 62 or 66. ITALIAN/INTERNATIONAL.

This place is one of the most appealing Italian restaurants along the Rhine. Main courses might include a *filletto della casa* (fillet of beef prepared in a "special sauce" whose composition the chefs won't discuss), tagliorini with white truffles, and an autumnal version of roast pheasant. Also look for Roman-style *osso bucco* (veal shank layered with prosciutto), a succulent risotto Milanese, and such desserts as a velvety version of zabaglione.

MODERATE

Zur Lese. Adenauerallee 37. ☎ **0228/22-33-22.** Reservations recommended for lunch and dinner, not required for the afternoon cafe. Main courses 26DM–39DM ($13–$19.50); fixed-price meals 52DM–60DM ($26–$30); fixed-price, 3-course menu for lunch 39DM ($19.50). AE, DC, MC, V. Restaurant Tues–Sun 10am–11pm; cafe Tues–Sun 10am–11pm. GERMAN.

This restaurant's polite service and outdoor terrace with a sweeping view over the Rhine attract many local residents, especially in the afternoon, when visitors drop in for coffee, cakes, and glasses of wine after strolling in the nearby Hofgarten. Elegant, well-prepared lunches are also offered. Dinner is served in the cafe. A menu of German specialties (with English translations) includes pork with curry sauce and the chef's superb *Gulasch Lese.* You can also choose rainbow trout or lobster from the terrace aquarium. The food is home-style and hearty, with no pretense.

INEXPENSIVE

Em Höttche. Markt 4 (next to the Rathaus). ☎ **0228/69-00-09.** Reservations not accepted. Main courses 12DM–30DM ($6–$15). No credit cards. Daily 11am–1am. Tram: 47. Bus: 618. GERMAN.

Em Höttche has a long and colorful history, stretching all the way from 1389. It's fed thousands over the centuries with its rib-sticking fare—perhaps changing the recipes every 100 years or so. The interior has been restored, with carved-wood paneling, natural brick, old beamed ceilings, decoratively painted plaster, and curlicue chandeliers. Favorite dining spots are tables set inside the walk-in fireplace. On the à la carte list, you'll find specialties for two, including entrecôte. Fresh salmon is often available. Complement your meal with a carafe of local wine—the best buy in the house.

Im Bären. Acherstrasse 1–3 (5 min. from the Hauptbahnhof). ☎ **0228/63-32-00.** Reservations recommended. Main courses 10DM–35DM ($5–$17.50). No credit cards. Daily 9am–midnight. Tram: 61, 62, or 63. GERMAN.

This historic inn was first mentioned in documents dating from 1385. Today it occupies a prominent position in Bonn's pedestrian zone and is one of the best-known restaurants in town. Most diners head for tables on the street level, although there's a large additional room on the second floor. The food is hearty Rhinelander cuisine, including everything from simple wursts with potatoes to more elaborate steaks with béarnaise sauce and salad. Service is bustling, matter-of-fact, and efficient.

Im Stiefel. Bonngasse 30 (a few doors down from the Beethoven House). ☎ **0228/ 630805.** Reservations recommended. Main courses 15DM–35DM ($7.50–$17.50); fixed-price menus 20DM–60DM ($10–$30). AE, DC, MC, V. Mon–Sat 10am–1am. Tram: 61 or 62. RHINELAND.

This atmospheric restaurant is a local favorite. You dine at bare bleached tables in rooms with wood paneling and stained glass. There's a stand-up bar for mugs of beer. The short menu features down-home Rhineland dishes, including a local dish, *Hämmchen,* served with sauerkraut and mashed potatoes. A specialty is braised beef marinated in almond-raisin sauce.

BONN AFTER DARK

Once considered a dismal place to go out on the town, Bonn now has a thriving fine-arts community and a brisk nightlife. If you're in the area around the first Saturday in May, don't miss the spectacular annual fireworks display, visible for a distance of 26km (16 miles) south of the city.

THE PERFORMING ARTS   Bonn has always struggled with the perception that it can't compete with the larger arts communities in Hamburg and Berlin, and consequently it has compensated (or overcompensated) with an impressive roster of cultural events. One of the most visible is "La Scala of the Rhineland," the **Oper der Stadt Bonn,** Am Boselagerhof 1 (☎ **0228/77-36-67;** S-Bahn: Hauptbahnhof), where ballet and opera are performed at regular intervals mid-August to June. Box office hours are Monday to Friday 8am to 6pm, Saturday 9am to 4pm, and Sunday 10am to 2pm. Tickets are 25DM to 175DM ($12.50 to $87.50) each, depending on the event.

The **Bonn Symphony Orchestra** performs in Beethovenhalle, Wachsbleiche 26 (☎ **0228/7222100;** S-Bahn: Hauptbahnhof), September to June, with occasional free concerts given on Sunday mornings. Otherwise, tickets cost 20DM to 110DM ($10 to $55). On a more intimate scale, chamber music is sometimes presented within a small but charming concert hall within the **Beethoven House** (☎ **0228/981-7525** for details).

During the Bonner Summer Festival, mid-May to August, an international selection of dance and music groups perform, mostly for free, in open-air locations around the city. Contact ☎ **0228/19433** or 0228/774400 for details. In addition, the **Beethoven Festival,** a rekindling of both the nostalgia and the music associated with Bonn's greatest musical genius, takes place in September. Contact the visitor information center (see above) for information.

Bonn's **Theater-Kasse,** Mühlheimerplatz 1 (☎ **0228/773-6667;** S-Bahn: Hauptbahnhof), is a well-known and highly resourceful ticket agency associated with the city's tourist office. It has access to tickets for virtually every sporting, entertainment, and cultural venue in Bonn. Also call for information on performers, schedules, and prices.

DANCE CLUBS   A weekend-only club, **Sharon,** Oxfordstrasse 20–21 (no phone; S-Bahn: Hauptbahnhof), is straight out of the 1970s, with dancing to soul and funk under a spinning mirror ball and strobe lights. It's open 10pm to 5am, with a 10DM ($5) cover.

LIVE MUSIC & CABARET   Live jazz is featured Friday and Saturday 8pm to around 4am at **The Jazz Galerie,** Oxfordstrasse 24 (☎ **0228/63-93-24;** S-Bahn:

Hauptbahnhof). Cover is 12DM to 25DM ($6 to $12.50), depending on the band. The **Pantheon Theater,** Bundeskanzlerplatz (☎ **0228/21-25-21;** bus: 610), stages jazz and pop concerts, comedy shows, and political cabaret. Nearly every weekday there is a performance of some sort. Friday and Saturday, the facility becomes a disco. The box office is open Monday to Friday noon to 6:30pm.

BARS   Pawlow, Heerstrasse 64 (☎ **0228/65-36-03;** S-Bahn: Tanninbusche Sud), has an alfresco terrace. While here, don't let appearances intimidate you—a sometimes fierce-looking crowd with tattoos and body piercings is actually a bored intelligentsia at heart. Open daily 11am to 1am. **Bräuhaus Bönnsch,** Sterntorbrucke 4 (☎ **0228/ 65-06-10;** S-Bahn: Hauptbahnhof), serves the very smooth Bönnsch beer, as well as *Bönnsche Flammkuchen,* an old regional recipe for a sort of pizza topped with sour cream, onions, cheese, and meat. Open Sunday to Thursday 11:30am to 1am and Friday and Saturday 11:30am to 3am.

GAY BARS   The most crowded gay bar is **Boba's Bar,** Josefstrasse 17 (☎ **0228/ 65-06-85;** S-Bahn: Hauptbahnhof), near the railway station, adjacent to the Rhine. It welcomes a drinking (but not dancing) crowd in their 20s and 30s. It's open Sunday to Tuesday 9pm to 3am and Friday and Saturday 9pm to 5am. Another gay bar is **Charley,** Kölnstrasse at Theaterstrasse (☎ **0228/69-07-61;** S-Bahn: Hauptbahnhof), open Sunday to Thursday 9pm to 3am and Friday and Saturday 9pm to 5am. There's also **Le Copain,** Berliner Platz 5 (☎ **0228/63-99-35;** S-Bahn: Hauptbahnhof), which attracts a somewhat older clientele and is open 9pm to 2 or 3am.

7 Bad Godesberg

6km (4 miles) S of central Bonn

Part of greater Bonn, Bad Godesberg is one of the Rhine's oldest spa towns. It's located just opposite the legendary Siebengebirge (Seven Mountains), with a view of the crag, Drachenfels (Dragon's Rock), where Siegfried slew the dragon. Dragons are no longer found on the Rhine, but you can still see some ancient castle ruins on the hills. The most interesting is **Godesberg Castle,** built in the 13th century by the electors of Cologne (its ruins have been incorporated into a hotel, described below). From the promenade along the Rhine, you can watch a flow of boats and barges wending their way up and down the river.

Most of the spa's activity centers around the small but elegant 18th-century **Red-oute Palace.** Although the town is mainly a residential center, there is seemingly no end to the entertainment and cultural facilities here. Theaters, concerts, and social functions offer a constant whirl of events.

GETTING THERE   You can reach Bad Godesberg from Bonn by taking tram 16 or 63 from Bonn's central rail station. If you're driving from the center of Bonn, take the B9 (driving time: 20 min.). For information about the town, consult the Bonn Tourist Office (see above).

WHERE TO STAY

Günnewig Godesberg Castlehotel. Auf dem Godesberg 5, 53177 Bonn-Bad Godesberg. ☎ **0228/31-60-71.** Fax 0228/31-12-18. 13 units. TV TEL. 170DM ($85) double. Rates include continental breakfast. AE, DC, MC, V. Free parking. Tram: 16 or 63 from Bonn.

A winding road leads up to this hilltop castle ruin, now converted to a hotel that we highly recommend. Its tall tower and many of its rugged stone walls were erected in 1210 by the archbishop of Cologne and are still intact. A lounge built against one of the stone walls provides a sunny perch and a view of the spa and river. There's also a roof terrace, with tables for drinks. The small rooms are traditionally furnished and well maintained and have picture windows. The food in the restaurant is especially good.

WHERE TO DINE

✪ **Halbedel's Gasthaus.** Rheinallee 47. ☎ **0228/35-42-53.** Reservations recommended. Main courses 49DM–53DM ($24.50–$26.50); fixed-price menus 99DM–135DM ($49.50–$67.50). AE, MC. Tues–Sun 6–11pm (last order 10:30pm). Closed mid-July to mid-Aug. Tram: 16 or 610 from Bonn. CONTINENTAL.

Here, amid many nostalgic souvenirs and antique tables and chairs, the courtly owners will welcome you to their turn-of-the-century villa. The kitchen prides itself on using mostly German-grown produce. The chefs are true artists, using ingredients of superlative quality to create harmonious flavors and textures. Some of the dishes will be familiar; others are imaginative inventions. Menu choices might include wild mushroom soup, rack of lamb prepared French style, and a salad of dandelion greens and wild lettuce, followed by flavorful desserts.

Zur Korkeiche. Lyngsbergstrasse 104, 1km (^{1}/$_2$ mile) south of Bad Godesberg in the village of Lannesdorf. ☎ **0228/34-78-97.** Reservations recommended. Main courses 30DM–38DM ($15–$19); fixed-price menus 68DM–78DM ($34–$39). V. Tues–Sun 6pm–midnight. Closed 2 weeks in October and 2 weeks in April (dates vary). Bus: 14. CONTINENTAL.

Zur Korkeiche is a wine-and-sherry house. It's located in a well-maintained, 150-year-old half-timbered building. There are two stories of cozy comfort and tradition. The decor is rustic in a country-elegant way. The head chef prepares a light cuisine. Menu choices include a delicately seasoned smoked salmon in champagne sauce.

8 Aachen (Aix-la-Chapelle)

64km (40 miles) W of Cologne, 80km (50 miles) SW of Düsseldorf

The ancient Imperial City of Aachen (Aix-la-Chapelle), at the frontier where Germany, Belgium, and the Netherlands meet, is inseparably connected with Charlemagne. He selected this spot as the center of his vast Frankish empire. History is important at this spa town, but today there's also a youthful *joie de vivre* that attracts young people from all over the world. Visitors also come for the sulfurous hot springs or the magnificent cathedral, or to use Aachen as a launching pad for exploring the Benelux nations.

Aachen has an even longer history as a spa than as an imperial city. Roman legionnaires established a military bath here in the 1st century A.D. By the end of the 17th century, Aachen was known as the "Spa of Kings" because royalty from all over Europe came here to take the cure. In 1742 Frederick the Great visited, and in 1818 the "Congress of Monarchs" brought Czar Alexander from Russia. After World War II, the spa was rebuilt and today enjoys a mild reputation as a remedial center. Its springs are among the hottest in Europe. The treatment includes baths and the *Trinkkur* (drinking the water). The spa gardens are the center of resort activity, with attractive ponds, fountains, and shade trees.

Aachen can be visited as a sightseeing day trip from Cologne. However, those interested in using the spa facilities should stay at one of the hotels described below.

ESSENTIALS

GETTING THERE By Train The Hauptbahnhof at Aachen receives some 200 trains a day from all parts of Germany and from Paris, with easy connections from most major cities as well as nearby Cologne (trip time: 45 min.). Frankfurt is 3^1/$_2$ hours away, and Munich, 7 hours. For information, call ☎ **01805/996633.**

By Bus   It's best to take the train, but once you arrive in Aachen, regional bus service is provided by **BVR Busverkehr Rheinland GmbH** at Simmerath (☎ 02473/66-46 for schedules and information).

By Car   Access is by the A4 Autobahn east and west or the A44 north or south. Driving time from Cologne is 50 to 60 minutes, depending on traffic. Frankfurt is 3¹/₂ hours away by car; Munich, 6¹/₂ hours.

VISITOR INFORMATION   You'll find the **Tourist Office Aachen** on Friedrich-Wilhelm-Platz (☎ 0241/19433). Office hours are Monday to Friday 9am to 6pm and Saturday 9am to 2pm.

GETTING AROUND   Buses pull into the main railway station in the center of town at Peterskirchhof and Peterstrasse. Tickets are 2.30DM ($1.15) to 9.30DM ($4.65). A 24-hour pass, available at the bus station, offers unlimited travel within Aachen for 8DM ($4).

SEEING THE SIGHTS

Aachen's Altstadt is small enough to be covered on foot. Marktplatz, in the heart of town, is overshadowed by the Gothic Rathaus, which contains the city archives. From here, you can head down one of the most popular and busiest pedestrian precincts in the city, Krämerstrasse, which will lead to **Münsterplatz (Cathedral Square)** and the famous cathedral (see below), one of the masterpieces of architecture in the Western world. Past the cathedral you reach the Elisengarten, bordered on the south by the symbol of Bad Aachen, the Elisenbrunnen, a rotunda with a thermal drinking fountain. From Münsterplatz you can go through the great iron gate to the Fischmarkt, with old merchants' houses and the Fischpuddelchen fountain with spouting fish.

The **Wingerstberg Kurgarten** and the **Stadtgarten,** with its thermal bath and casino, lie to the northeast of town, and the **Hauptbahnhof** is on the southern ring, opening onto Römerstrasse.

✪ **Cathedral (Dom).** Klosterplatz 2. ☎ **0241/47-70-91-27.** Cathedral free; treasury 5DM ($2.50) adults, 3DM ($1.50) children. Mon 10am–12:30pm, Tues and Thurs–Sat 10am–5:30pm, Wed 10am–8:30pm, Sun 10am–5:30pm. Bus: 1, 11, or 21.

About A.D. 800 the emperor Charlemagne built the "octagon," the core of the Imperial Cathedral. Within stands the marble *Königsstuhl,* Charlemagne's throne, one of the most venerable monuments in Germany. (Visitors to the cathedral can view the throne of Charlemagne only with a guide; request one at the treasury or call ahead.) From 936 to 1531 the Holy Roman emperors were crowned here, until Frankfurt became the coronation city.

The cathedral is an unusual mixture of Carolingian (the well-preserved dome), Gothic (the choir, completed in 1414), and baroque (the Hungarian chapel), all united into a magnificent upward sweep of architecture. The treasury, in the adjoining house (entry: Klostergasse), is the most valuable and celebrated ecclesiastical treasure trove north of the Alps. But the cathedral itself holds its own share of wealth. The elaborate gold shrine (1215) in the chancel contains the relics of Charlemagne. The pulpit of Henry II (ca. 1002) is copper studded with precious gems.

Rathaus. Am Markt. ☎ **0241/4-32-73-10.** Admission 3DM ($1.50) adults, 1.50DM (75¢) children. Daily 10am–1pm and 2–5pm. Closed sometimes for official events. Bus: 4 or 11.

The 14th-century Rathaus was built on the original site of Charlemagne's palace. Part of the ancient palace structure can still be seen in the so-called Granus Tower at the east side of the hall. The richly decorated facade, facing the marketplace, is adorned with the statues of 50 German rulers, 31 of them crowned in Aachen. In the center, standing in relief, are the "Majestas Domini," the two most important men of their time in the Holy Roman Empire, Charlemagne and Pope Leo III.

On the second floor of the Rathaus is the double-naved and cross-beamed Imperial Hall, where coronation banquets took place from 1349 to 1531. Built as the successor to the Carolingian Royal Hall, today it contains exact replicas of the imperial crown jewels, true in size and material to the originals, presently in the Vienna Secular Treasury. On the walls are the Charlemagne frescoes, painted in the 19th century by Alfred Rethel, illustrating the victory of the Christian Franks over the Germanic heathens.

Couven Museum. Huhnermarkt 17. ☎ **0241/4-32-44-21.** Admission 2DM ($1) adults, 1DM (50¢) children. Tues–Wed and Fri–Sun 10am–5pm, Thurs 10am–1pm. Bus: 1, 11, or 21.

This gracefully designed villa gives you an insight into the decorative traditions of the late 18th and 19th centuries. It has one of the best collections of antique furnishings of any museum in the region. On the ground floor is a reproduction of a small-scale chocolate factory. You'll find treasures, some of them low-key and discreet, virtually everywhere you look.

Suermondt Ludwig Museum. Wilhelmstrasse 18. ☎ **0241/47-98-00.** Admission 6DM ($3) adults, 3DM ($1.50) children. Tues and Thurs–Fri 11am–7pm, Wed 11am–9pm, Sat–Sun 11am–5pm. Bus: 1, 11, or 21.

The impressive collection of medieval German sculpture, one of the finest in the land, includes a *Madonna in Robes* (1420) from the Swabian school and a *Virgin and Child* from the 14th-century Tournai school. The second landing has a good collection of primitive Flemish and German works, along with 17th-century Dutch and Flemish paintings. Look for works by Van Dyck and Jordaens. The museum also has modern works, especially from the 1920s and '30s.

WHERE TO STAY

Am Marschiertor. Wallstrasse 1–7, 52064 Aachen. ☎ **0241/3-19-41.** Fax 0241/3-19-44. www.vch.de/marschiertor.aachen. E-mail: hotel-marschiertor@t-online.de. 50 units. TV TEL. 160DM–195DM ($80–$97.50) double. Rates include buffet breakfast. AE, DC, MC, V. Parking 15DM ($7.50), opposite the hotel. Bus: 1, 11, or 21.

This charming hotel stands in the center of Aachen, not far from the Hauptbahnhof and next to the medieval town gate for which it's named. The hotel is quiet, with a courtyard and a view over the Altstadt and cathedral. The lobby and connecting hall are attractive, with antique furniture. The recently refurbished rooms have a cozy atmosphere, and each—generally medium in size—is well appointed and maintained.

Aquis Grana City Hotel. Büchel 32, 52016 Aachen. ☎ **0241/44-30.** Fax 0241/44-31-37. www.aachen-tourist.de. E-mail: aquishotel@t-aol.com. 99 units. MINIBAR TV TEL. 215DM–165DM ($107.50–$82.50) double; from 450DM ($225) suite. Children up to age 10 stay free in parents' room. Rates include buffet breakfast. AE, CB, DC, MC, V. Parking 10DM ($5). Bus: 1, 11, or 21.

Aquis Grana City Hotel is your best bet in the town center. The comfortable rooms offer all the modern amenities (including hair dryers) and range from spacious to medium. The staff is very alert to all your needs. Housekeeping rates an A+.

Dining/Diversions: The hotel has a good restaurant, featuring international and regional specialties. Favorite dishes include creamed soup with "herbs from Charlemagne's garden" and roast beef with home-fried potatoes. Low-calorie dishes are also served.

Amenities: There's a direct entrance from the hotel into the spa facilities. Room service, laundry, and dry cleaning can be arranged.

Hotel Benelux. Franzstrasse 21–23, 52064 Aachen (5-min. walk from the Hauptbahnhof). ☎ **0241/2-23-43.** Fax 0241/2-23-45. 30 units. TV TEL. 180DM–240DM ($90–$120) double. Rates include continental breakfast. AE, DC, MC, V. Parking 15DM ($7.50). Bus: 1, 11, or 21.

The warm and inviting Benelux is within walking distance of many major attractions. It's a small family-run hotel, tastefully decorated and personalized. Americans from the Southwest will feel at home in the lobby/reception area—it has probably the only cactus collection in Aachen. Rooms range from small to medium. On the premises is a Chinese/Mongolian restaurant. Other attractive features are a roof garden and a fitness room.

Hotel Brülls am Dom. Hühnemarkt, 52062 Aachen. ☎ **0241/31704.** Fax 0241/404-326. 10 units. TV TEL. 200DM ($100) double. No credit cards. Bus: 1, 11, or 21.

This is a solid, not particularly imaginative hotel that's ruled with a firm grip by the family who owns it. Set within a very short walk from the town center, it was built in the late 1950s in a modern, no-nonsense style consistent with postwar architecture in Germany. Rooms are cozy, clean, and small, with rustic furnishings that verge on kitsch.

WHERE TO DINE

La Bécasse. Hanbrucherstrasse 1 (just outside the Altstadt by the Westpark). ☎ **0241/7-44-44.** Reservations recommended. Main courses 43DM–60DM ($21.50–$30); fixed-price 6-course menu 105DM ($52.50). DC, MC, V. Daily 7–10:30pm; Tues–Fri noon–2:30pm. Bus: 15, 25, or 35. GERMAN/FRENCH.

This modern restaurant, full of greenery, serves a pleasing combination of light, modern French specialties and traditional German recipes. Although not in the same league as Gala (see below), La Bécasse is a discreetly classy place. Christof Lang, who realized early his "calling" of reproducing the fine foods of France, has been the owner since 1981. The food is imported every day from the wholesale markets at Rungis, outside Paris. Try his ragout of fish or his cassoulet.

Ratskeller. Am Markt (in the Rathaus). ☎ **0241/3-50-01.** Reservations recommended. In Postwagen Pub, platters 15DM–36DM ($7.50–$18); in Ratskeller Restaurant, main courses 18DM–43DM ($9–$21.50). AE, CB, DC, DISC, MC, V. Postwagen Pub daily 10am–11pm; Ratskeller Restaurant daily 11:30am–3pm and 6–10pm. Bus: 2, 11, or 25. WESTPHALIAN/GERMAN.

This is a charming, old-fashioned restaurant that's beloved by many senior citizens and office workers. The less-expensive venue is the Postwagen, a publike setting that serves platters and drinks in the afternoon. But we prefer the majesty of the brick-and-stone Ratskeller, where a sense of medievalism is enhanced by solid, conservative fare, such as sauerkraut with wurst; minestrone or potato soup; grilled steaks; fricassée of sole; and fresh berries and pastries for dessert.

Restaurant Elisenbrunnen. Friedrich-Wilhelm-Platz 14. ☎ **0241/297-72.** Reservations recommended. Main courses 22DM–48DM ($11–$24); fixed-price lunch 40DM ($20). AE, CB, DC, MC, V. Daily 11am–10pm. Bus 15, 25, 55. FISH/FRENCH/WESTPHALIAN.

This stately restaurant occupies the Elisenbrunnen Rotunda, built in 1838 to commemorate the visit of a local potentate, Queen Elisen. Today it shares the same site as the city tourist office. It specializes in regional dishes (such as Westphalian green cabbage with Mattwurst, or pork sausage); French specialties (choucroute garnie or chateaubriand with béarnaise sauce); and fresh fish. On warm days, you can dine on a large, well-maintained terrace in the shade of the Kaiserdom and the Rathaus.

✪ **Restaurant Gala.** Monheimsallee 44. ☎ **0241/15-30-13.** Reservations required. Main courses 35DM–49DM ($17.50–$24.50); fixed-price menu 55DM–150DM ($27.50–$75). AE, DC, V. Tues–Sat 7–10pm. Bus: 13. GERMAN.

The best dining place in Aachen is the elegant Restaurant Gala, which is loosely linked to one of the country's busier casinos. Light plays merrily through the crystal-draped decor onto the oak-paneled walls. Some of the paintings are Salvador Dalí originals. (The restaurant is named for his former wife.) The Gala can soothe the frayed nerves of the most inveterate gamblers. The kitchen turns out modern, lighter interpretations of regional food, including gamecock in calvados-and-mustard sauce or fillet of venison in blood sauce. Ingredients are trucked in daily from the Rungis markets near Paris. The wine list is encyclopedic; the French desserts are delectable.

AACHEN AFTER DARK

For information about what's happening in Aachen, pick up a copy of the booklet *Tourist-Information,* published and given away free by the tourist information office. Alternatively, you can buy a copy of a glossy-looking magazine, *Klenkes,* a monthly publication that's available in news kiosks around the city for 4DM ($2) each. For any local sports, entertainment, or cultural event, you can purchase tickets either from the establishment's ticket office or by contacting the tourist office's ticket booth (☎ **02451/180-2965**).

THE PERFORMING ARTS   Classical concerts are presented in the town's convention center, **Kongresszentrum Eurogress,** Mondheimsallee 52 (☎ **02451/151-011;** bus: 57), by the local symphony orchestra and by visiting chamber orchestras. The **Theater Aachen** (formerly known as the Stadtheater) Theaterplatz (☎ **02451/ 4784244;** bus: 33, 34, or 57) hosts opera, theater, and dance recitals. Ticket prices in both places are around 20DM to 170DM ($10 to $85). If you understand German and want to see experimental theater and plays by Bertolt Brecht, head for the small and rather cramped **Aachener Kultur und Theater Initiative,** Gasborn 9–11 (☎ **0241/2-74-58;** bus:166). Tickets are 30DM to 85DM ($15 to $42.50).

BARS & CAFES   There are at least a half-dozen bars in or around Aachen's Marktplatz. One of the most appealing is the **Martesa Keller,** Martesastrasse (☎ **0241/311-10;** bus: 13). This cozy, convivial, wood-paneled place offers live music, usually jazz, on most nights (usually Wednesday to Saturday, beginning around 8:30pm), and a bar open every night at 6pm. More youth-oriented is the **Café Kittel,** Pontstrasse 39 (☎ **0241/3-65-60;** bus: 13), which somewhat resembles a greenhouse; its menu concentrates on beer, wine, sandwiches, and quiche. Open Monday to Thursday 10am to 2am, Friday and Saturday 10am to 3pm, and Sunday 11am to 2am. The popular **Aoxomoxoa,** Reihstrasse 15 (☎ **0241/226-22;** bus: 57), has a different theme night to night; it's open nightly except Monday 5:30pm to 1am or later, depending on business.

DANCE CLUBS   Friday and Saturday nights, **Rotation,** Pontstrasse 135 (☎ **0241/ 4-88-74;** bus: 13), keeps the dance music cranking until 6am. Other nights, the music provides a background for drinking and socializing. Two things you won't find here are a cover and food. Open Sunday to Thursday 11am to 2am.

LIVE MUSIC   It's Irish in conception, but **Wild Rover,** Hirschgraben 13 (☎ **0241/3-54-53;** bus: 4 or 33), is a rock club first and foremost. The bands that take the stage nightly range from mainstream to punk. It's open daily 8pm to 2am, with a 6DM ($3) cover Sunday to Thursday, and a 4DM ($2) cover Friday and Saturday. A worthy competitor is the **Exil-Bar,** Schlosstrasse 2 (☎ **0241/51-23-45;** bus: 33, 34, or 57), where live music, including jazz and rock, is presented within a small, smoke-filled, and decidedly bohemian venue every night 6pm to 1am. A final nightlife venue is the **Domkeller,** Hof 1 (☎ **0241/3-42-65;** bus: 1, 11, or 21), which offers live blues or jazz on some nights, and lots of hubbub every night. Open Monday to Thursday 10am to 1am and to 2am Friday and Saturday.

9 Cologne

27km (17 miles) N of Bonn, 40km (25 miles) S of Düsseldorf, 188km (117 miles) NW of Frankfurt

Cologne (Köln), the largest city in the Rhineland, is so rich in antiquity that every time a new foundation is dug, the excavators come up with archaeological finds. Devastating though the World War II bombing was—nearly all the buildings of the Altstadt were damaged—reconstruction brought to light a period of Cologne's history that had been a mystery for centuries. Evidence showed that Cologne was as important and powerful during the early Christian era as it was during Roman times and the Middle Ages.

Cologne traces its beginnings to 38 B.C., when Roman legions set up camp here. As early as A.D. 50, the emperor Claudius gave it municipal rights as capital of a Roman province. In the early Christian era, a bishopric was founded here and a number of saints were martyred, including the patron of the city, St. Ursula. During the Middle Ages, as Cologne became a center for international trade, Romanesque and Gothic churches were built with prosperous merchants' gold. Today there is much to see from every period of the city's 2,000-year history—from the old Roman towers to the modern opera house. But Cologne is also a bustling modern city, with a lively population. It's increasingly becoming the fine-art capital of Germany.

ESSENTIALS

GETTING THERE By Plane Cologne and Bonn share the same airport, **Flughafen Köln/Bonn Konrad Adenauer,** 14km (9 miles) southeast of Cologne. Flights come from most major European cities. For complete information, call ☎ **02203/40-40-01.** Bus 170 from the airport to the center of Cologne operates every 30 minutes 6:05am to 7:35am, every 15 minutes to 8:35pm, and then every 30 minutes to 11:05pm. Travel time takes 20 minutes, and the fare is 8.70DM ($4.35) per person. A taxi, suitable for up to four passengers, costs from 60DM ($30).

By Train The **Cologne Hauptbahnhof** is in the heart of the city, next to the cathedral. For schedules, call ☎ **01805/996633.** This depot has frequent rail connections to all major German cities and many continental destinations. There are 17 trains per day from Berlin (trip time: 5$^1/_2$ hr.), 31 from Frankfurt (trip time: 2$^1/_2$ hr.), and 25 from Hamburg (trip time: 4$^1/_2$ hr.).

By Bus Cologne is linked to several major cities, including Frankfurt, by bus. For complete information and schedules, call **Deutsche Touring GmbH** (☎ **7-90-35-0**). Regional bus service to nearby cities such as Trier (see chapter 14) is provided by **Regionalverkehr Köln GmbH** at Euskirchen (☎ **02251/12-44-12**).

By Car Cologne is easily reached from major German cities. It's connected north and south by the A3 Autobahn and east and west by the A4 Autobahn.

VISITOR INFORMATION For tourist information, go to the **Köln Tourismus Office,** Unter Fettenhennen 19 (Am Dom) (☎ **0221/19433**), a few steps from the cathedral. November to April, it's open Monday to Saturday 8am to 9pm and Sunday 9:30am to 7pm; May to October, Monday to Saturday 8am to 10:30pm, Sunday 9:30am to 10:30pm.

GETTING AROUND   For 2.20DM to 14.20DM ($1.10 to $7.10) per single ride, depending on where you're going, you can purchase a ticket allowing you to travel on Cologne's excellent **bus, tram, U-Bahn,** and **S-Bahn** connections. A day ticket, the Kölner Tageskarte, which costs 9.50DM ($4.75), will allow you to travel throughout the city's transportation network for 4¹/₂ hours. For information about public transportation, call ☎ **0221/547-3333.**

For a taxi, call ☎ **0221/28-82** for a recorded message and then press 1 in reply. The meter will start at 3.60DM ($1.80) and rise 2.30DM ($1.15) per kilometer for rides between 6am and 10pm, and 2.50DM ($1.25) per kilometer for rides between 10pm and 6am.

EXPLORING THE CITY

One of the best panoramas over the ancient city of Cologne is available from within one of the cars of the Rhein-Seilbahn, the first and only cable car in Europe that was designed to span a major river. The Rhein-Seilbahn stretches between a point near the zoo, in the district of Cologne-Riehl, to the Rhein Park in Cologne-Deutz, a total of about 915m (3,000 feet). You get a good view of the busy river traffic along the Rhine. The cable car operates April to October, Monday to Friday 11am to 6pm, Saturday and Sunday 10am to 6pm. A one-way ticket costs 6.50DM ($3.25) for adults, 3.50DM ($1.75) for children; a round-trip ticket costs 9.50DM ($4.75) for adults, 5DM ($2.50) for children. For more information, call ☎ **0221/76-20-06.**

THE TOP ATTRACTIONS

✪ **Cologne Cathedral (Dom).** Domkloster. ☎ **0221/92584720.** Treasury and cathedral tower each 3DM ($1.50) adults, 1.50DM (75¢) children. Cathedral daily 7am–7pm, except during religious services. Cathedral tower daily 9am–5pm. Treasury Mon–Sat 9am–5pm, Sun and holidays 12:30–5pm. U-Bahn: Hauptbahnhof.

This majestic structure is one of the world's great cathedrals—the spiritual and geographical heart of the city. It's the largest Gothic cathedral in Germany. From the top of the south tower, you get panoramic views of the city and surrounding area.

Construction began in 1248, in order to house the relics of the three Magi brought to Cologne in 1164 by Archbishop Reinald von Dassel, chancellor to Frederick Barbarossa. After the completion of the chancel, south tower, and north-side aisles (around 1500), work was halted and not resumed until 1823. In 1880, the great enterprise was completed, and unlike many time-consuming constructions that change styles in midstream, the final result was in the Gothic style, true to the original plans.

For the best overall view of the cathedral, stand back from the south transept, where you can get an idea of its actual size and splendor. Note that there are no important horizontal lines—everything is vertical. The west side (front) is dominated by two towering spires, perfectly proportioned and joined by the narrow facade of the nave. The first two stories of the towers are square, gradually merging into the octagonal form of the top three stories and tapering off at the top with huge finials. There is no great rose window, so characteristic of Gothic architecture, between these spires—nothing detracts from the lofty vertical lines.

Entering through the west doors (main entrance), you are immediately caught up in the cathedral's grandeur. Although this portion of the church is somewhat bare, the clerestory and vaulting give a feeling of the size of the edifice. The towering windows on the south aisles include the Bavarian windows, donated by King Ludwig I of Bavaria in 1848. Like most windows in the nave, they are colored with pigments that have been burned on rather than stained. In the north aisles are the stained-glass Renaissance windows (1507–09).

Cologne

ATTRACTIONS ●
Cologne Cathedral (Dom) **8**
Gross St. Martin Church **18**
Kölner Philharmonie **10**
Museum für Angewandte
  Künst **16**
Oper der Stadt Köln **12**
Römisch-Germanische
  Museum **9**
St. Andreas Church **6**
St. Apostein Church **20**
St. Cecilia's Church
  (Cäcilienkirche) **21**

St. Georg Church **25**
St. Gereon Church **5**
St. Kunibert Church **1**
St. Maria im Kapitol Church **23**
St. Maria Lyskirchen **24**
St. Pantaleon Church **26**
St. Severin Church **27**
St. Ursula Church **3**
Schauspielhaus **19**
Schnütgen Museum **22**
Wallraf-Richartz Museum/
  Ludwig Museum **17**

ACCOMMODATIONS ■
Alstadt-Hotel **14**
Antik-Hotel Bristol **4**
Brandenberger Hof **2**
Das Kleine Stapelhäuschen **13**
Dom-Hotel Cologne **15**
Excelsior Hotel Ernst **7**
Hyatt Regency **11**

In the center of the transept is an elegant bronze-and-marble altar that can be seen from all parts of the cathedral. Behind the high altar, in the chancel, is *The Shrine of the Three Magi,* the most important and valuable object in the cathedral. It's designed in gold and silver in the form of a triple-naved basilica, and decorated with relief figures depicting the life of Christ, the Apostles, and various Old Testament prophets. Across the front of the chancel are two rows of choir stalls divided into richly carved partitions. The oak choir dates from 1310 and is the largest extant in Germany.

Surrounding the chancel are nine chapels, each containing important works of religious art. The Chapel of the Cross, beneath the organ loft, shelters the oldest full-size cross in the Occident, the painted, carved oak cross of Archbishop Gero (969–76). Directly across the chancel, behind the altar in Our Lady's Chapel, is the famous triptych masterpiece painted by Stephan Lochner (1400–51). When closed, the so-called *Altar of the City Patrons* shows the *Annunciation,* and when opened, it reveals the *Adoration of the Magi* in the center, flanked by St. Ursula, the patron saint of Cologne, and St. Gereon.

English-language tours are given Monday to Saturday at 10:30am and 2:30pm, and Sunday at 2:30pm. German-language tours are conducted Monday to Saturday at 11am, 12:30, 2, and 3:30pm, and every Sunday at 2 and 3:30pm. Tours last about an hour, and cost 7DM ($3.50) for adults, and 4DM ($2) for children and students.

Museum für Angewandte Kunst (Museum of Applied Art). An der Rechtsschule. ☎ **0221/22123860.** Admission 5DM ($2.50) adults, 2.50DM ($1.25) children 6–12, free for children 5 and under. Tues–Sun 11am–5pm, Wed 11am–8pm. U-Bahn: Hauptbahnhof.

This is a showcase for the arts and crafts of Germany dating from the Middle Ages, with the 20th century prominently featured. This museum is one of the best of its kind in Germany.

Römisch-Germanisches Museum (Roman-Germanic Museum). Roncalliplatz 4. ☎ **0221/244-38.** Admission 5DM ($2.50) adults, 2.50DM ($1.25) children, free for children 5 and under. Tues–Sun 10am–5pm. U-Bahn: Hauptbahnhof.

The most compelling treasure in this museum is the Dionysos-Mosaik, from the 3rd century A.D., discovered in 1941 when workers were digging an air-raid shelter. This elaborately decorated and colored mosaic was once the floor of an *oecus* (main room) of a large Roman villa. It depicts Dionysus, the Greek god of wine and dispeller of care. On the second floor of the museum is an unusual collection of Roman antiquities found in the Rhine Valley, including Roman glass from the 1st through 4th centuries, as well as pottery, marble busts, and jewelry.

Schnütgen Museum. Cäcilienstrasse 29. ☎ **0221/2-21-36-20.** Admission 5DM ($2.50) adults, 2.50DM ($1.25) children. Tues–Fri 10am–5pm and Sat–Sun 11am–5pm. U-Bahn: Neumarkt.

This is Cologne's best collection of religious art and sculpture. It's all displayed in an original setting, St. Cecilia's Church (*Cäcilienkirche*), which is a fine example of Rhenish-Romanic architecture. The works displayed include several medieval ivories, woodwork, and tapestries, including one showing rosy-cheeked Magi bringing gifts to the Christ child (1470). There are also many Madonnas, of all sizes and descriptions, carved in stone, wood, and metal.

Wallraf-Richartz Museum/Ludwig Museum. Bischofsgartenstrasse 1 (a short walk from Domplatz). ☎ **0221/221-22379.** Admission 10DM ($5) adults, 4DM ($2) children. Tues 10am–8pm, Wed–Fri 10am–6pm, Sat–Sun 11am–6pm. U-Bahn: Hauptbahnhof.

This is Cologne's oldest museum, begun in the 19th century with a collection of Gothic works by local artists, still one of the main attractions. The Wallraf-Richartz shows art from 1300 to 1900, and the Ludwig, art since 1900. Several well-known works from churches are exhibited as well, including the triptych of the *Madonna with the Vetch Flower* (1410). The painting collection represents nearly every period and school, from the Dutch and Flemish masters to the French impressionists to American art of the 1960s and '70s (the famous Ludwig Donation). Stephan Lochner's *Madonna in the Rose Garden* (1450) is a fine example of the German Gothic style. The museum also houses Germany's largest collection of works by Wilhelm Leibl as well as paintings by Max Ernst, Paul Klee, and Ernst Ludwig Kirchner.

CHURCHES

Cologne has 12 important Romanesque churches, all within the medieval city wall. Devastated during World War II, they have been almost completely restored and again recapture Cologne's rich early medieval heritage. **St. Panteleon,** Am Pantalonsberg 2 (U-Bahn: Poststrasse), built in 980, has the oldest cloister arcades remaining in Germany. **St. Gereon,** Gereonsdriesch 2–4 (U-Bahn: Christophestrasse), is elliptically shaped, with a decagon between its two towers. It contains the tomb of St. Gereon and other martyrs, and its crypt still has mosaics from the 11th century. **St. Severin,** Severinstrasse (U-Bahn: Severinstrasse), originated as a late 4th-century memorial chapel; the present church dates from the 13th to the 15th centuries.

The church of **St. Ursula** (1135), Ursulaplatz (U-Bahn: Hauptbahnhof), is on the site of a Roman graveyard. Legend has it that St. Ursula, patron saint of Cologne, was martyred in Cologne with her 11,000 virgin companions in about 451. **St. Maria im Kapitol,** Kasinostrasse 6 (U-Bahn: Heumarkt), is on the site where Plectrudis, wife of Pippin, built a church in the early 8th century. The cloverleaf choir of the present structure was modeled on that of the Church of the Nativity in Bethlehem. **St. Aposteln,** Neumarkt 30 (U-Bahn: Neumarkt), and **Gross St. Martin,** on the Rhine in the Altstadt (U-Bahn: Heumarkt), also have the cloverleaf choir design.

St. Georg, Am Waidmarkt (U-Bahn: Poststrasse), the only remaining Romanesque pillared basilica in the Rhineland, contains an impressive forked crucifix from the early 14th century. **St. Cecilia's (Cäcilienkirche),** Cäcilienstrasse 29 (U-Bahn: Neumarkt), is the site of the Schnütgen Museum for sacred art (see above). **St. Andreas,** near the cathedral (U-Bahn: Hauptbahnhof), contains a wealth of late Romanesque architectural sculpture. The remaining two Romanesque churches are on the Rhine: **St. Kunibert,** Kunibertskloster 2 (U-Bahn: Hauptbahnhof), and **St. Maria Lyskirchen,** Am Lyskirchen 12 (U-Bahn: Heumarkt), both of 13th-century origin.

SHOPPING

Shopping is not taken quite as seriously here as in Düsseldorf—with one exception. Increasingly, Cologne is emerging as the capital of contemporary art in Germany. The city is brimming with galleries.

ART GALLERIES We'll recommend the major ones to get you started, but there are many more. The gallery that launched Cologne as a European art mecca is **Galerie der Spiegel,** Richartstrasse 10 (☎ 0221/25-55-52; U-Bahn: Hauptbahnhof). Established amid the ruins of the wartime bombings in 1945, it was a focal point for the contemporary art that evolved from the shattered dreams of the postwar years. Since then, despite the volcanic changes that have rocked Germany, it has managed to hold its own against rising competition. You might want to walk along **St. Apernstrasse** (U-Bahn: Neumarkt), where many leading art galleries are located. **Galerie Greve,** Albertusstrasse 18 (☎ 0221/2-57-10-12; U-Bahn: Friesenplatz), changes its exhibits every season, specializing in international post-war avant-garde painting. Another excellent gallery for both modern and experimental art is **Galerie Werner,** Gertrudenstrasse 24 (☎ 0221/9-25-46-20; U-Bahn: Neumarkt), which sells contemporary European, particularly German, painters.

Cologne Water

The very word *cologne* has been a part of the common language since the introduction to the world many years ago of the scented water called *eau de cologne* (*Kölnisch Wasser*). **Eau de Cologne,** Glockengasse 4711 (☎ **0221/9-25-04-50;** U-Bahn: Neumarkt), sells the scented water first developed at this address by Italian chemist Giovanni Maria Farina in 1709. Originally employed to hide the stench of aristocrats who rarely bathed, cologne is now simply a sweet-smelling tradition and a cheap way to take home a little piece of Köln. The smallest 25 milliliter flacon costs a mere 7.95DM ($4).

OUTDOOR MARKETS   If you're interested in the kitschy artifacts that pour out of estate sales, with items that are slightly damaged, mismatched, or old-fashioned, be alert to the flea markets in Cologne's inner city. The most appealing are held within the **Alter Markt** (U-Bahn: Hauptbahnhof), at irregular intervals throughout the year, usually at least once a month. More regular are the outdoor food and vegetable markets, the largest of which is held on the **Wilhelmsplatz,** in the Nippes district (U-Bahn: Florastrasse), Saturdays 8am to at least 2pm.

WHERE TO STAY
VERY EXPENSIVE

✪ **Dom-Hotel Cologne.** Domkloster 2A, 50667 Köln 1. ☎ **800/225-5843** in the U.S., or 0221/2-02-40. Fax 0221/2-02-44-44. www.lemeridien-hotels.com. E-mail: gm1304@ forte-hotels.com. 123 units. MINIBAR TV TEL. 465DM–500DM ($232.50–$250) double. AE, DC, MC, V. Parking 30DM ($15). U-Bahn: Hauptbahnhof.

Few hotels in Germany have been so consistently awarded five stars or maintained such a standard of excellence. We prefer the Excelsior Hotel Ernst (see below), but there are many clients who will stay nowhere else but the Dom. The hotel's location, in the shadow of the cathedral, assures it a steady clientele. In summer the side portico overlooking the square is filled with cafe tables. Rooms have all modern conveniences and an interesting collection of period furniture. Try for one of the corner units, which are the most spacious and have the best views. To reach the hotel by car, drive into the square to the side of the Dom's flying buttresses.

    Dining: On the premises is a winter-garden bistro, the only dining facility.

    Amenities: 24-hour room service, laundry, dry cleaning, terrace garden, conference facilities.

✪ **Excelsior Hotel Ernst.** Domplatz, 50667 Köln. ☎ **0221/27-01.** Fax 0221/13-51-50. www.excelsiorhotelernst.de. E-mail: ehe@excelsiorhotelernst.de. 160 units. MINIBAR TV TEL. 490DM–695DM ($245–$347.50) double; from 1,200DM ($600) suite. Rates include continental breakfast. AE, DC, MC, V. Parking 35DM ($17.50). U-Bahn: Hauptbahnhof.

In spite of increased competition, notably from the Hyatt Regency, Cologne's long-time prestige hotel continues to hold its own as the premier address in Cologne. Founded in 1863, the hotel is known for its Empire-style lobby. The public areas contain old-master paintings, including an original work by Van Dyck. The breakfast room has a Gobelin tapestry. Rooms are spacious, with many amenities, including hair dryers and satellite TV. Most are air-conditioned.

    Dining/Diversions: The hotel has an outstanding restaurant, Hanse Stube (see "Where to Dine," below), and an intimate and cozy Piano Bar.

    Amenities: Concierge, room service, laundry, dry cleaning, massage, shoe shine, exclusive boutique, whirlpool, fitness area, Roman steam bath, hairdresser, barbershop.

✪ **Hyatt Regency.** Kennedy-ufer 2A, 50679 Köln-Deutz (across the Rhine from the Alstadt, a short walk from the train station). ☎ **800/228-12-34** in the U.S., or 0221/8281234. Fax 0221/828-13-70. 305 units. A/C MINIBAR TV TEL. 360DM–460DM ($180–$230) double; from 560DM–3,100DM ($280–$1,550) suite. AE, DC, MC, V. Parking 25DM ($12.50). Tram: 1 or 2.

This is the most spectacular and up-to-date hotel in Cologne. It's an architectural triumph: a mixture of reddish granite, huge expanses of glass, and a facade that combines art deco and neo-Aztec styles. The lobby is dramatic, with a 4m (12-foot) waterfall. Rooms are stylishly furnished and come with walk-in closets. Many have views of the Rhine and the cathedral on the other side. Baths have private phones, deep tubs with showers, robes, deluxe toiletries, and hair dryers. To get to the Alstadt from here, you can take the Hohenzollernbrücke, a bridge across the Rhine.

Dining/Diversions: Graugans offers a Germanic version of contemporary cuisine, and also has a wonderful Asian-influenced menu. You can also dine in the lobby cafe, with its excellent view of the Rhine and the Alstadt. The intimate bar connects to a garden terrace and serves a selection of international wines, as well as a local beer called Schael Sick.

Amenities: 24-hour room service, business center, laundry, dry cleaning, concierge, and fitness center with pool, sauna, steam room, massage facilities, solarium, and whirlpool.

EXPENSIVE

✪ **Antik-Hotel Bristol.** Kaiser-Wilhelm-Ring 48, 50672 Köln. ☎ **0221/12-01-95.** Fax 0221/13-14-95. www.koeln-hotels.de. E-mail: hotel@antik-hotel-bristol.com. 44 units. MINIBAR TV TEL. 195DM–380DM ($97.50–$190) double; 220DM–420DM ($110–$210) suite. Rates include buffet breakfast. AE, DC, MC, V. Closed Dec 23–Jan 2. Parking 25DM ($12.50). U-Bahn: Christophstrasse.

The Bristol is exceptional in that each of its rooms is furnished with genuine antiques, either regal or rustic. There's a different antique bed in almost every room, ranging from French baroque and rococo to something reminiscent of High Rhenish ecclesiastical art; the oldest four-poster dates from 1742. Baths include hair dryers and magnifying makeup mirrors. The Bristol stands in a little park, removed from traffic, with lots of greenery, flowers, and fountains, near an U-Bahn stop and within walking distance of the cathedral.

Dining: The hotel has the Bristol Bar for guests, but breakfast is the only meal served.

Amenities: Concierge, room service, dry cleaning, laundry service, in-room massage, twice-daily maid service, and baby-sitting.

MODERATE

Altstadt-Hotel. Salzgasse, 50667 Köln (2 min. from the Rhine boat-landing dock). ☎ **0221/2-57-78-51.** Fax 0221/2-57-78-53. 29 units. MINIBAR TV TEL. 150DM ($75) double; 250DM ($125) suite. Rates include buffet breakfast. AE, DC, MC, V. Closed Dec 20–Jan 6. Parking 20DM ($10). U-Bahn: Hauptbahnhof.

Guests have passed the word along to their friends, making this place a big success. Herr Olbrich learned about catering to international guests as a steward on the German-American Line. He has furnished his little hotel beguilingly. The restful rooms range from small to medium, are individually decorated, and come with a comfortable bed fitted with a good mattress. The small but well-kept baths mainly have shower stalls. There's a sauna on the premises. Advance reservations are recommended.

Das Kleine Stapelhäuschen. Fischmarkt 1–3, 50667 Köln. ☎ **0221/2-57-78-62.** Fax 0221/2-57-42-32. E-mail:stapelhaeschen@compuserve.com. 31 units, 10 with bath. TEL. 125DM ($62.50) double without bath, 210DM ($105) double with bath. Rates include buffet breakfast. AE, MC, V. U-Bahn: Heumarkt.

Stapelhäuschen was originally built in the 1100s near where fish were sold by Scottish Benedictine monks. The two tall, narrow town houses are on a corner of a historic square, and their ironwork announces the year of their construction: 1235. Inside you'll find a richly evocative decor and an occasional portrait of Irish-born St. Brigit. Rooms offer old-fashioned decor and clean, if slightly faded, furniture. On the premises is a good restaurant (see "Where to Dine," below).

INEXPENSIVE

Brandenburger Hof. Brandenburgerstrasse 2–4, 50668 Köln (behind the Hauptbahnhof). ☎ **0221/12-28-89.** Fax 0221/13-53-04. 45 units, 28 with bath. 90DM ($45) double without bath; 120DM ($60) double with bath; 105DM ($52.50) triple without bath; 125DM ($62.50) quad without bath. Rates include continental breakfast. No credit cards. Free parking. U-Bahn: Hauptbahnhof.

In this family-style hotel, all rooms are small, warm, and equipped with running water, and there's a well-kept bath on each floor. A full breakfast, including orange juice and eggs, is served in a cozy room or, in summer, in the garden. The hotel is about 3 blocks from the river and within walking distance of the cathedral.

WHERE TO DINE
VERY EXPENSIVE

✪ **Goldener Pflug.** Olpener Strasse 421, Merheim (on the outskirts of Cologne). ☎ **0221/ 89-55-09.** Reservations required. Main courses 28DM–49DM ($14–$24.50); fixed-price meal 49DM ($24.50) at lunch, 98DM–160DM ($49–$80) at dinner. AE, MC, V. Mon–Fri noon–3pm and 7–11pm, Sat 7–11pm. Tram: 1 to Merheim. FRENCH.

The Goldener Pflug is one of the top restaurants in Germany. The decor of this former tavern is simple, with a golden motif repeated in the walls, draperies, and upholstery. The chef, Herbert Schönberner, takes pleasure in serving demanding clients with jaded palates and sending them away satisfied. Top-quality ingredients are always used in his imaginative blend of classical repertoires. Try, for example, any of the truffled specialties, ranging from soups to a wide choice of delicately seasoned main courses. For dessert, the most exciting choices are apple cake flambé and soufflé à la Rothschild with strawberries.

Hanse Stube. On the ground floor of the Excelsior Hotel Ernst, Domplatz. ☎ **0221/27-01.** Reservations recommended. Main courses 50DM–60DM ($25–$30); 5-course fixed-price menu 120DM–160DM ($60–$80). AE, DC, MC, V. Daily noon–3pm and 6–11pm. U-Bahn: Hauptbahnhof. FRENCH.

One of Cologne's best restaurants, Hanse Stube offers top-drawer cuisine and service. The food here is better than that served in the dining room of the Dom Hotel. Prodigious talent and imagination go into shaping the cuisine. Of the chef's appetizers, none are better than a variation of salmon on truffled potato salad blended harmoniously with a Pommery mustard sauce. Unusual and tasty main courses include breast of guinea fowl stuffed with herbs or medaillons of venison with savoy cabbage and a sweet corn potato Rösti.

EXPENSIVE

Börsen Restaurant Maître. Unter Sachsenhausen 10–26 (near the stock exchange, a short walk from the cathedral). ☎ **0221/13-30-21.** Reservations recommended. Main courses 40DM–50DM ($20–$25); fixed-price menus 75DM–105DM ($37.50–$52.50). AE, DC, MC, V. Mon–Fri noon–2:30pm and Mon–Sat 6–11pm. U-Bahn: Hauptbahnhof. CONTINENTAL/ MEDITERRANEAN.

This busy place, which serves Cologne's financial community, offers not only good value but also a glimpse of everyday Cologne life, particularly at lunch. Seasonally adjusted fixed-price meals feature classic, conservative cookery made from fresh ingredients. The restaurant offers a choice of different dining areas. In the Börsen-Stube, which has the same hours as the main restaurant, main courses range from 25DM to 40DM ($12.50 to $20). The Börsen Schanke, open Monday to Friday 10am to 9:30pm, has meals starting at 15DM to 35DM ($7.50 to $17.50). There is a terrace for this beer restaurant, which serves local dishes.

Le Moissonnier. Krefelder Strasse 25 ☎ **0221/72-94-79.** Reservations recommended. Main courses 39DM–47DM ($19.50–$23.50); midday plat du jour 23DM ($11.50). No credit cards. Tues–Sat noon–1:45pm and 7–10:45pm. U-Bahn: Hansaring. FRENCH.

This charming brasserie is steeped in the aesthetic and culinary traditions of the early 20th century, with mirrors, cove moldings, dark paneling against ocher-colored walls, bentwood chairs, and tiled floors. Here you'll enjoy the carefully crafted cuisine of the restaurant's namesake, Vincent Moissonnier. Menu items change with the season and the inspiration of the chef but are likely to include risotto with almonds and truffle oil; carpaccio of turbot; and a house specialty that combines braised fillet of goose breast with tarragon and strips of goose liver served with prosciutto-studded mashed potatoes. Salads and fresh fish are all delicious, as are the sauerkraut and a Toulouse-inspired version of cassoulet loaded with pork, small sausages, and white beans.

MODERATE

Brauhaus im Walfisch. Salzgasse 13 (on a narrow street set back from the Rhine, near Heumarkt [Haymarket]). ☎ **0221/2-57-78-79.** Reservations required. Main courses 18DM–37DM ($9–$18.50). AE, DC, MC, V. Daily 11am–midnight. U-Bahn: Heumarkt. GERMAN/FRENCH.

Brauhaus im Walfisch isn't easy to find, but it's a good choice for atmospheric dining. This step-gabled inn with a black-and-white timbered facade dates from 1626. More important, it serves excellent food. There are many German specialties, often influenced by French cuisine. You might try the sole meunière or venison for two.

Das Kleine Stapelhäuschen. Fischmarkt 1–3 (a few minutes from the cathedral). ☎ **0221/ 2-57-78-62.** Reservations recommended. Main courses 20DM–40DM ($10–$20). AE, MC, V. Daily noon–11:30pm. Closed Dec 22–Jan 10. U-Bahn: Heumarkt. GERMAN.

This is one of the most popular wine taverns in Cologne. It's housed in an office building and opens on to the old fish-market square and the Rhine. The two-story dining room and service bar are antique in style. Provincial cabinets hold a varied wine collection. A wide cantilevered wooden staircase leads to mezzanine tables. Though wine is the main reason for coming here (it's that special), the cuisine is also excellent. A specialty is Rheinischer sauerbraten with almonds, raisins, and potato dumplings. Desserts are appropriately luscious.

Ratskeller. Rathausplatz 1 (in the Rathaus). ☎ **0221/2-57-69-29.** Reservations recommended. Main courses 25DM–38DM ($12.50–$19). AE, DC, MC, V. Mon–Sat noon–11pm, Sun 11am–3pm. U-Bahn: Heumarkt. GERMAN.

This busy and very traditional restaurant occupies a trio of dining rooms in the cellar of Cologne's landmark city hall. It welcomes the city's political, business, and journalistic communities during the lunch hour. Menu items are conservative German, particularly Rhenish, specialties, and include generous portions of sauerbraten, Schweinshaxen (roast leg of pork), and Kalbshaxen (roast leg of veal). Any of these might be preceded with steaming bowls of Leberknoedel soup or goulash, salads, and marinated herring in cream sauce with onions. During warm weather, tables spill out into a courtyard that's protected from the roar of traffic. Look for a lavish lunch buffet every Sunday, and a dinner buffet every Saturday. The price of each of those is 39DM ($22.25) per person.

Beer Taverns

Some of the best inexpensive places to eat (and drink) in Cologne are beer taverns. **Alt-Köln am Dom,** Trankgasse 7–9 (☎ **0221/13-74-71;** U-Bahn: Hauptbahnhof), is a re-creation of a group of old taverns, including one done in the Gothic style. You can come here for a beer or a good hot meal. The place seems like it could feed half the visitors to Cologne on any busy day. Some of the upper-floor tables provide box-seat views of the cathedral. On the face of the building is a mechanical clock; when it chimes the hours, a parade of figures emerges and disappears. The favorite main dishes include Wiener schnitzel, *Schweinshaxen* (pork knuckle), and a platter of sausage specialties with spicy mustard. Try also the braised beef Rhineland-style. Main courses cost 14DM to 30DM ($7 to $15). American Express, Diners Club, MasterCard, and Visa are accepted. It's open daily 11am to midnight (kitchen closes at 11:30pm).

Come to **Bräuhaus Sion,** Unter Taschenmacher 5 (☎ **0221/2-57-85-40;** U-Bahn: Heumarkt; tram: 5 or 7), if you want a traditional local Bräuhaus, where the beer is good, the wood paneling a little smoky with time and frequent polishing, and the food portions inexpensive and generous. The main courses are traditional and filling Westphalian fare, such as pigs' knuckles with sauerkraut and the inevitable bratwurst with savoy cabbage and fried potatoes. But the best traditional dish to order is *kölsch Kaviar* (blood sausage with onion rings). You can also ask for *halve Hahn,* which translates as "half rooster." On tap is the famed local beer, Kölsch, a light brew with an alcohol content of about 3%. It's served in *Stangen* (rods) about 7 inches tall. Main courses are 12DM to 32DM ($6 to $16). No credit cards are accepted. It's open daily 10am to 11:30pm, but closed Christmas Eve.

Früh am Dom, Am Hof 12–14 (☎ **0221/2-58-03-97;** U-Bahn: Hauptbahnhof), is the best all-around choice for economy and hearty portions. Well-cooked meals are served on scrubbed wooden tables, with a different German specialty offered every day of the week. The menu is in English. A favorite dish is a Cologne specialty of cured smoked knuckle of pork cooked in root-vegetable broth and served with sauerkraut and potato puree; apple puree and dumplings go well with this dish. Also sample a glass of Früh-Kölsch—a top-fermented brew with a dry, inimitable taste and a 1,000-year-old tradition. In summer, there's a beer garden. Meals cost 25DM to 60DM ($12.50 to $30). No credit cards are accepted. The tavern is open 8am to midnight; hot meals are served 11:30am to 11:30pm.

The venerable, beer-soaked **Haus Töller,** Weyerstrasse 96 (☎ **0221/ 2-40-91-87;** U-Bahn: Barbarossaplatz), a 15-minute walk south of the cathedral, has thrived as a brew house since 1876 by selling copious portions of two-fisted Teutonic food and foaming mugs of a local brew, Seon. No one will mind if you just want to spend a few hours drinking (the beer is very, very good), but if you want a meal, menu items include a local specialty, *Schinkenhempsel* (roast leg of pork), served with sauerkraut and roast potatoes. Main courses are 15DM to 26DM ($7.50 to $13); a mug of Seon will set you back 1DM (55¢). No credit cards are accepted. It's open Monday to Saturday 5pm to midnight.

COLOGNE AFTER DARK

One of Germany's major cultural centers, Cologne offers a variety of fine arts and nightlife options. Many clubs stay open into the early morning hours. You can pick up a copy of *Stadt Revue* for 4DM ($2.30) or *Kölner* for 4DM ($2) to find out what's happening in the city. If you're interested in attending a sports, entertainment-related, or cultural venue within Cologne, you can always head to the box office. More convenient, however, is the well-orchestrated services of **Köln-Ticket,** Roncalliplatz 4, next to the cathedral (☎ **0221/28-01;** U-Bahn: Hauptbahnhof).

THE PERFORMING ARTS

The most impressive grouping of theater space in Cologne is within the **Schauspielhaus,** Offenbachplatz (☎ **0221/8400;** U-Bahn: Neumarkt), the site of three theaters, each with its own agenda and schedule. Performances range from the avant-garde to the classic. **Der Keller,** Kleingedankstrasse 6 (☎ **0221/31-80-59;** U-Bahn: Ulrepsorte), hosts contemporary plays, usually in German, and dance performances. Tickets are 20DM to 45DM ($10 to $22.50) each; call either the number listed above or **Köln-Ticket** (☎ **0221/28-01**) for schedules and show times.

If your German is fluent and you're interested in absorbing some of the counterculture trends sweeping the country's literature and politics, you might be interested in the **Theater Kaiserhof,** Hohenzollenring (☎ **0221/139-2772;** U-Bahn: Rudolfplatz). Performances are sometimes comic, sometimes obscure, sometimes trenchant, sometimes grotesque, sometimes satirical, and often a combination of all of the above. Most shows begin at 8pm. Tickets cost 45DM to 95DM ($22.50 to $47.50).

Oper der Städt Köln. Offenbachplatz. ☎ **0221/22128400.** Tickets 22DM–110DM ($11–$55). AE, DC, MC, V. U-Bahn/S-Bahn: Neumarkt.

This is the leading opera house of the Rhineland, known for its exciting productions and innovative repertory of classical and contemporary works. Performances take place almost every evening except Tuesday, usually at 7:30pm. Dance programs are also presented. The box office is open 9am to 6pm Monday to Friday and Saturday 9am to 2pm.

Kölner Philharmonie. Bischofsgartenstrasse 1. ☎ **0221/28-01.** Tickets 15DM–250DM ($7.50–$125). U-Bahn: Hauptbahnhof.

This architectural showcase was completed during the late 1980s. The concert hall features a soaring roof, enviable acoustics, and some of the finest classical music along the country's western tier. The building is the home of two separate orchestras, the **Gürzenich Kölner Philharmoniker** and the **Westdeutscher Rundfunk Orchestra.** Pop and jazz programs are also presented. Performances are given almost every night at 8pm, except Monday.

THE CLUB & MUSIC SCENE

DANCE CLUBS   Live bands (Tuesday, Thursday, and Saturday) and DJs (Monday, Wednesday, Friday, and Sunday) play for dancers at **MTC,** Zulpicher Strasse 10 (☎ **0221/1-70-27-64;** U-Bahn: Zulpicherplatz), open 10pm to 3am. Cover is 6DM to 20DM ($3 to $10).

One of the city's most angular, dramatic, and surreal nightlife options is **E-Werk,** Schanzenstrasse 28 (☎ **0221/96-27-90;** U-Bahn: Keupstrasse), a combination of a disco and a large concert hall. It's housed within what used to be an electrical power plant. Recorded music alternates with live acts. The Backstreet Boys have played here. The place is open every Friday and Saturday night at 10pm.

JAZZ CLUBS   Klimperkasten (also known as **Papa Joe's Biersalon**), Alter Markt 50–52 (☎ **0221/258-2132;** U-Bahn: Hauptbahnhof), is a small and intimate jazz and piano bar open from 11am to 2am, with live music every night beginning around 8pm. The jazz is also hot at **Papa Joe's Jazzlokal,** Buttermarkt 37 (☎ **0221/257-7931;**

U-Bahn: Heumarkt). Sunday, when the music begins at 3:30pm and lasts until 1am, is the best day to come. The club is also open for live jazz Monday to Saturday 7pm to 2am. Surprisingly, there's never a cover.

LIVE-MUSIC CLUBS   Several times a week, usually at 8pm on Wednesday and Saturday, but with frequent exceptions, the **Underground,** Vogelsanger Strasse 200 (☎ **0221/542326;** U-Bahn: Venloerstrasse Gürtel), hosts rock groups that include relatively unknown local acts as well as high-profile bands. There's a disco on other nights. This place, in the words of a spokesperson, is "very alternative. If you're 40, you're probably too old to appreciate the music here." A food stand inside prepares pastas, burgers, and breakfast items for late-night (or early morning) hunger pangs. Cover is 12DM to 20DM ($6 to $10).

Prime Club (formerly known as Luxor), Luxemburgstrasse 40 (☎ **0221/924-460;** U-Bahn: Barbarossa Platz), offers some kind of live music most nights of the week, except Monday. You'll never know what to expect here. The management books unknown, inexperienced bands, some of whom show great promise.

A final contender in Cologne's live-music sweepstakes is **Kantine,** Kempenorstrasse 135 (☎ **0221/9726836;** U-Bahn: Lohsestrasse), whose musical style, hours, and free-form scheduling policies are similar to those at Prime Club. Kantine also has a beer garden.

BARS

A 110-year-old bar, **Päffgen Bräuhaus,** Friesenstrasse 64–66 (☎ **0221/13-54-61;** U-Bahn: Friesenplatz), serves its Kölsch brand of beer, along with regional cuisine. Seating is available indoors and out. Open daily 10am to midnight. **Altstadt Päffgen,** Heumarkt 62 (☎ **0221/2-57-77-65;** U-Bahn: Heumarkt), also serves the local brew with German dishes. Open Tuesday to Sunday noon to midnight. **Broadway,** Ehrenstrasse 11 (☎ **0221/25-52-14;** U-Bahn: Neumarkt) is a cafe and bar associated with an arts-conscious movie theater. It's decorated with playbills and memorabilia from theater productions of yesteryear. Drinks, coffee, tea, sandwiches, and simple platters of snack food are served. Open daily 10am to 1am.

A place where you might be tempted to hang out for an hour or two is the **Café Storchen,** Ursula Kloster 4–6 (☎ **0221/13-17-12;** U-Bahn: Hauptbahnhof), which has thrived as an appealingly battered, very informal bar and cafe since the early 1980s. It serves drinks, platters of uncomplicated food, and sandwiches, while patrons listen to recorded music, read newspapers, and play board games. Open Sunday to Friday 11am to 1am.

A somewhat different setting is **Museum Pub,** Zulpicher Platz 9 (☎ **0221/ 23-20-98;** U-Bahn: Zulpicherplatz), which sells foaming mugs of beer to thirsty students. Rock and punk music are usually blaring from the stereo. Some aspects of the place might remind you of student dives in the Latin Quarter of Paris. Open Sunday to Thursday 6pm to 1am, and Friday and Saturday 6pm till 3am.

Students who have rediscovered the styles of the 1960s and 1970s lounge about amid a decor of lava lamps, futuristic televisions, and other memorabilia at **Hallmackenreuthur,** Brusseler Platz 9 (☎ **0221/51-79-70;** U-Bahn: Rudolfplatz). This is a place to drink, eat a late breakfast (until 4pm), or have a plate of pasta (6 to 11pm). It's open daily 11am to 1am. A holdover from Cologne's leftist days is **Hotelux,** Rathenauplatz (☎ **0221/241136**). Both its food and scarlet decor are self-consciously Soviet. You can eat platters of Russian food, drink Russian beer or more than two dozen brands of Russian vodka, and sit within a garden whose greenery is thankfully apolitical. It's open daily 7pm to 1am.

GAY NIGHTLIFE

Cologne offers more diversions and distractions for gay men and women than any other city in the Rhineland. Head either to the Marienplatz area or the "Bermuda Triangle" (see below). A good gay bar for men and women near Marienplatz is **Quo Vadis Pub,** Pipinstrasse 7 (☎ **0221/258-1414;** U-Bahn: Heumarkt), which is open daily noon to midnight during the week and 11am to 1am on the weekend. Another gay bar in the Marienplatz area is the men-only leather bar called **Teddy Treff,** Stephansstrasse 1 (☎ **0221/248-310;** U-Bahn: Heumarkt), open daily 6pm till "late." **Chains,** Stephansstrasse 4 (☎ **0221/23-87-30;** U-Bahn: Neumarkt), is open 10pm to 2 or 3am. The most sophisticated rendezvous for gays and lesbians in Cologne today is called **Gloria,** Apostelnstrasse 11 (☎ **0221/254433;** U-Bahn: Neumarkt), which is generally packed with a cruisy crowd. If there's music playing, there's a cover of 10DM ($5). Open Sunday to Thursday 9am to 1am, Friday and Saturday 9am to 3am.

If you want to do as the Kölners do, consider a walk through what locals call **"the Bermuda Triangle"** formed by the locations of the four bar/clubs listed below. Visited as an ensemble, they provide plenty of insight into the lifestyle (and limitations) of the gay Rhineland. The first is **Schampanja,** Mauritiuswall 43 (☎ **0221/240-95-44** U-Bahn: Neumarkt), a small pub that sometimes books live bands (often punk). Nearby, along the same street, is **The Park,** Mauritiuswall 84 (☎ **0221/21-33-57** U-Bahn: Neumarkt), a cafe-style rendezvous point where table-hopping is a way of life. It's open daily 8am to 3am, but gay life is most visible in the late evening. A near-neighbor at the opposite end of the Bermuda Triangle is **Café Huber,** Schaafenstrasse 51 (☎ **0221/240-6530** U-Bahn: Zurticherplatz), where men drink, smoke, talk, and generally enjoy each other's company. It is open nightly 7pm till around 3am, depending on business.

Confused and don't know how to best approach the gay scene of Cologne? Pay a visit to **Checkpoint,** Pipinstrasse 7 (☎ **0221/925-76868;** U-Bahn: Zurticherplatz), a privately owned dispenser of information that performs some of its functions in cooperation with the city's official tourism authorities. It's open daily 5 to 9pm, and has a staff that's ready, willing, and able to tell you what's up in gay Cologne. They'll even sell you memorabilia.

The first weekend in July is devoted to the city's **Gay Pride Parade,** when as many as 500,000 spectators line the parade route for a glimpse of the floats and marchers. For specifics on the parade, contact Checkpoint (see above).

DRAG ACTS

Cologne isn't prudish when it comes to admiring the female figure, even if that figure isn't biologically female. For the most sophisticated drag acts in the Rhineland, head for the **Bar of the Hotel Timp,** Heumarkt 25 (☎ **0221/258-1409;** U-Bahn: Heumarkt). This tiny spot opens at 10am and presents drag acts every night from 1:30 to 4am (it stays open to 5 or 6am). The cover of 15DM ($7.50) gets you views of such camp heroines as the divine Marlene Dietrich, several European starlets, and even Leni Riefenstahl, the controversial *wünderkind* of German movies during the Hitler regime. Those who want a good table should get here early. The Hotel Timp's most appealing competitor is **Star-Treff,** Alte Wallgasse (☎ **0221/25-50-63;** U-Bahn: Friesenplatz), which offers at least one, and sometimes two, shows a night, usually beginning at 7:45pm and 10:45pm and stays open to 4am. Call in advance for the schedule. Cover is 15DM to 20DM ($7.50 to $10).

10 Düsseldorf

40km (25 miles) N of Köln, 230km (143 miles) NW of Frankfurt

Düsseldorf is a wealthy city—the richest in Germany. It's big and commercial, full of banks and industrial offices and skyscrapers, but also refreshingly clean. Düsseldorf got its start as a settlement on the right bank of the Rhine, but today it's spread out on both sides—the older part on the right and the modern, commercial, and industrial part on the left. The two sections are connected by five bridges, the most impressive being the Oberkassel. Parks and esplanades line the riverbanks. After 85% of the right bank was destroyed in World War II, the city could easily have grown into just another ugly manufacturing town, but Düsseldorf followed a modern trend in reconstruction, and today it's the most elegant metropolis in the Rhine Valley.

ESSENTIALS

GETTING THERE By Plane Düsseldorf International Airport, 6km (4 miles) north of the city, has regularly scheduled connections to 14 German, 47 European, and 132 international airports. Lufthansa connects New York to Düsseldorf with a daily nonstop flight, and also has service from Miami and Toronto. You can fly from Frankfurt to Düsseldorf on Lufthansa in just 45 minutes or from Munich or Berlin in an hour. For flight information, call ☎ **0211/421-22-23.** There are luggage-storage facilities at the airport.

The airport is linked to the **GermanRail** network. Transfer to the Düsseldorf main rail station is via S-Bahn 7, offering service daily 4:03am to 12:30am, with trains every 20 minutes (trip time: 12 min.). One-way fare is 3.20DM ($1.60). For information call ☎ **0211/3680596.** Regular airport buses also connect the airport with Bonn and Köln. A taxi ride to central Düsseldorf takes about 20 to 30 minutes, and costs from 30DM ($15), depending on traffic.

By Train The main train station, the **Düsseldorf Hauptbahnhof,** on Konrad-Adenauer-Platz in the southeastern sector, offers frequent connections to all major cities. The trip time to Frankfurt is about 2$^1/_2$ hours; to Munich, about 7 hours. For information, call ☎ **01805/996633.** Düsseldorf also has extensive regional rail links; for information on regional trains or trams, call ☎ **0211/5-82-28.** Luggage-storage facilities are available at the Hauptbahnhof.

By Bus Access to Düsseldorf is a lot easier by rail than by bus. The region's largest carriers are **Bandroch GmbH** (☎ **0211/353-862**) and **Adorf GmbH** (☎ **0211/ 320-771**), most of whose buses service small towns within the Rhineland that don't necessarily have railway stations of their own. Buses usually pull into Düsseldorf at the northern edge of the Bahnhofplatz.

By Car Access to Düsseldorf is by the A3 Autobahn north and south or the A46 east and west.

VISITOR INFORMATION For information, go to the **Verkehrsverein,** Konrad-Adenauer-Platz (☎ **0211/17-20-20** followed by 0 after the recorded message in German), opposite the railway station. It's open Monday to Saturday 8am to 8pm, and Sunday and national holidays 4 to 8pm. The office also has a hotel reservations service, which charges a one-time booking fee of 5DM ($2.50), along with a deposit that equals the price of the first night's accommodation. For the tourist office's room reservation services, call ☎ **0211/172-0226** Monday to Saturday 8am to 8pm, Sunday 4 to 8pm.

GETTING AROUND Düsseldorf is a big, sprawling city, so you'll probably want to rely on public transportation. The city and environs are served by a network

Düsseldorf

0 — 1/4 mi
0 — 1/4 km

Legend:
- Church †
- Information ⓘ
- Post Office ✉
- S-Bahn —

ATTRACTIONS ●
Deutsche Oper an Rhein **10**
Goethe-Museum Düsseldorf **6**
Heinrich-Heine-Institut **18**
Hofgarten **3**
Königsallee **17**
Kunst Halle Düsseldorf **7**
Kunstmuseum Düsseldorf **1**
Kunstsammlung
  Nordrhein-Westfalen **7**
Rathaus (Town Hall) **15**
St. Andreas Church **12**
St. Lambertus Church **13**

St. Rochus Church **2**
Schauspielhaus **9**
Schlossurm **14**
Thyssen-House **5**
Tonhalle (Düsseldorf
  Symphony Orchestra) **4**

ACCOMMODATIONS ■
Breidenbacher Hof **16**
Fürstenhof **19**
Hotel Grosser Kurfürst **8**
Steigenberger Park-Hotel **11**
Wurms Hotel **20**

● Düsseldorf
GERMANY

of **S-Bahn railways** that fan out to the suburbs, along with **buses** and **trams** (**Strassenbahn**) and a **U-Bahn** system. Ask at the tourist office (☎ **0211/17-20-20**) about purchasing a **Tagesnetzkarte,** a whole day visitor's ticket, for 11DM ($5.50).

Taxi meters begin at 4.90DM ($2.45), after which you'll be billed between 2.30DM and 2.50DM ($1.15 and $1.25) per kilometer, depending on the time of day. To call for a taxi in Düsseldorf, dial ☎ **0211/3-33-33.**

EXPLORING THE CITY

As in most German cities, there's an **Altstadt,** with a marketplace, a Gothic **Rathaus** (**Town Hall**), and a few old buildings and churches. Near the Rathaus on Burgplatz are two of the city's most famous landmarks, the twisted spire of **St. Lambertus Church** and the round **Schlossturm (Castle Tower),** both of 13th-century origin. A short walk to the east takes you to **St. Andreas Church,** one of the most important in Düsseldorf.

The Altstadt has been called "the longest bar in the world" because of the 200-plus bars and restaurants found here. The favorite drink here is a top-fermented Altbier (old beer), a dark, mellow brew that must be consumed soon after it's made.

A walk up **Königsallee,** called the "Kö" by Düsseldorfers, will give visitors a quick overview of the city and its residents. This street flanks an ornamental canal, shaded by trees and crossed by bridges. One bank is lined with office buildings, the other with elegant shops, cafes, and restaurants. Here you'll see women dressed in the very latest styles. Düsseldorf is the fashion center of Germany. It's known for its Fashion Weeks, which attract designers and buyers from all over Europe.

If you walk up the Kö toward the Trident Fountain at the northern end of the canal, you'll reach the **Hofgarten,** a huge rambling park. Here you can wander along the walks or sit and relax amid shade trees, gardens, fountains, and statues, almost forgetting you're in the very center of the city. Among the monuments is one to the poet Heinrich Heine. The Hofgarten is a good central point for seeing the city's major attractions—nearly all museums and cultural attractions are on its perimeter. Towering over the Hofgarten is Düsseldorf's most impressive skyscraper, the **Thyssen-House.** Residents call it the Dreischeibenhaus ("three-slice house"), because it actually looks like three huge monoliths sandwiched together. Northeast of the Hofgarten is **St. Rochus,** one of the city's finest modern churches.

Kunstsammlung Nordrhein-Westfalen. Grabbeplatz 5 (opposite the Kunsthalle). ☎ **0211/8-38-10.** Admission 12DM ($6) adults, 8DM ($4) children over 6 and students, free for children 5 and under. Tues–Sun 10am–6pm (until 8pm Fri). U-Bahn: Heinrich-Heine-Allee.

This architecturally impressive museum has an outstanding collection of modern art, including works by many major French, German, and American artists. There is an especially large collection of works by Julius Bissier, and also 16 works by Paul Klee— so many, in fact, that the Klee exhibition is rotated at regular intervals since all of it cannot be shown at the same time. Six temporary exhibitions of contemporary art are hosted in the large exhibition hall every year.

Goethe-Museum Düsseldorf. Schloss-Jägerhof (in the Jägerhof Castle at the Hofgarten), Jacobistrasse 2. ☎ **0211/8-99-62-62.** Admission 4DM ($2) adults, 2DM ($1) children. Tues–Fri and Sun 11am–5pm, Sat 1–5pm. Tram: 707. Bus: 722.

The Anton and Katharina Kippenberg Foundation sponsors this literary museum dedicated to Goethe's life and work. It emerged from the Kippenbergs' private collection of some 35,000 items, including autographs, books, busts, paintings, coins, medals, plaques, and china. About 1,000 pieces of the collection are shown in the permanent exhibition, including first drafts of well-known poems. The displays present a chronology of Goethe's life and work. There are also exhibits on various topics of the Goethe era.

Kunst Halle Düsseldorf. Grabbeplatz 4 (across from the Kunstsammlung Nordrhein-Westfalen). ☎ **0211/899-6240.** Entrance 12DM ($6) adults, 8DM ($4) for students and children over 10. Tues–Sat 11am–6pm (Friday till 9pm). U-Bahn: Heinrich-Heine-Allee.

The Kunst Hall Düsseldorf is devoted to contemporary art from the Rhineland and throughout Europe. No other museum in the city keeps up with changing trends in art as well as this one. Visiting exhibits of every shape and size, often bizarre, are displayed here. This museum should not be confused with the Kunstmuseum Düsseldorf.

Kunstmuseum Düsseldorf. Ehrenhof 5. ☎ **0211/8-99-24-60.** Admission 5DM ($2.50) adults, 2.50DM ($1.25) students and children. 10DM ($5) family ticket. Tues–Sun 11am–6pm. Tram: 701, 706, 711, or 715.

This is one of the largest and most comprehensive museums in the Rhineland. The painting collection includes works by Rubens, Caspar David Friedrich, and the Die Brücke and Der Blaue Reiter schools. The sculpture collection ranges from the late Middle Ages to the 20th century. There are also some 80,000 prints and drawings, as well as early Persian bronzes and ceramics, a glass collection, textiles from late antiquity to the present, and a design collection.

Heinrich-Heine-Institut. Bilkerstrasse 12–14. ☎ **0211/899-2902.** Admission 4DM ($2) adults, 2DM ($1) children and students, free for children under 10. Tues–Fri and Sun 11am–5pm, Sat 1–5pm. Tram: 704 or 707.

Heinrich Heine (1797–1856) was Germany's greatest lyric poet. More than 10,000 volumes, as well as the manuscript bequest of this Düsseldorf-born poet, are found here. Born into a Jewish family, Heine nominally converted to Christianity so that he could attend law school. He was the author of the famous *Die Lorelei,* and his poems were put to music by Schubert, Schumann, and Hugo Wolf. His work was prohibited during the Nazi era, during which *Die Lorelei* was officially attributed to an unknown author.

In the Altstadt, you visit the house where Heine was born. It's at Bölkerstrasse 53 and is marked by a plaque.

SHOPPING

Düsseldorf is a city of high fashion and high prices. Many chic Europeans visit the city just to shop for what's new and hot. The best and trendiest fashions are sold on the opulent east side of the Königsallee. The two largest concentrations of designer shops are found at the **Kö Galerie,** Königsallee 60, and the **Kö Center,** Königsallee 30. Each gallery has some 100 shops. Those not interested in dishing out big deutschmarks for designer duds should head for the more recently opened **Schadow Arcade,** off Schadowplatz, at the end of the Kö. Fashion here isn't so *haute,* but neither are the prices. Shoppers spend some one billion deutschmarks in the shops on Schadowstrasse annually—more than is spent on any other street in the country.

ANTIQUES   Düsseldorf's historic core contains a fine selection of antiques stores. **Monika Müser,** Schwanenmarkt (☎ **0211/327-346;** tram: 704 or 709), specializes in the intensely fashionable early 18th-century Biedermeier style. Antique silver, china, paintings, and other art objects are available from **Lothar Heubel,** Bastionstrasse 10 (☎ **0211/134-103;** U-Bahn: Heinrich-Heine-Allee), which also sells Asian and African antiques, including jewelry, ceramics, and Chinese items from the Han, Ming, and Tang dynasties, mixed in with a handful of antiques from Provence and the south of France.

DEPARTMENT STORES   **Carsch Haus,** Heinrich-Heine-Platz (☎ **0211/8-39-70;** U-Bahn: Heinrich-Heine-Allee), carries a good selection of fashions, as well as quality home furnishings, jewelry, and other items.

DESIGNER CLOTHING & ACCESSORIES   Designer shopping in Düsseldorf is limited only by your bank account. Two floors of men's casual clothing await you at **Fashonable,** Königsallee 58 (☎ **0211/32-75-66**). **Ritterskamp,** Trinkausstrasse 7 (☎ **0211/32-99-94**), also caters to both sexes, with designers such as Richard Tyler, Gianfranco Ferre, and Donna Karan. **Bogner Shop,** Königsallee 6–8 (☎ **0211/ 13-42-22**), carries functional sportswear that's meant for action on the golf course, tennis court, and ski slopes. The designers have their workshop on the second floor.

Chanel, Kö Center (☎ **0211/32-59-35**), offers the company's complete line of products, from clothing to cosmetics and fragrances. Also in Kö Center, German designer **Jil Sander** (☎ **0211/32-84-44**) has set up one of her many shops selling women's fashions. For strictly German fashions, check the racks of women's clothing and accessories at **MCM (Modern Creations Munich)**, Königsallee 68 (☎ **0211/32-23-50**).

Need shoes and accessories to go with your newly purchased outfits? Head for **Anena,** Kö Center (☎ **0211/32-73-03**), where one stop gives you access to the products of Calvin Klein, Jil Sander, Sonia Rykiel, Prada, Donna Karan, and other designers. Shoes and more shoes fill the racks at **Walter Steiger Schuhe,** Kö Galerie (☎ **0211/13-41-04**), the German designer of high-quality, high-fashion footwear. Choose from luggage, handbags, shoes, and other accessories at **Etienne Aigner,** Kö Galerie (☎ **0211/3-23-09-55**). In the boutique of **Louis Vuitton,** Kö Center (☎ **0211/32-32-30**), leather accessories, luggage, and handbags are sold.

DINNERWARE & KITCHEN ACCESSORIES   A diversity of items and styles can be found at **Georg Jensen,** Kö Galerie (☎ **0211/32-42-81**), the shop of the German designer who redefines silver flatware, bowls, candle sticks, coffee pots, and much more.

FURNITURE & DECORATIVE ACCESSORIES   One of Düsseldorf's largest purveyors of art-deco furniture and art objects is **Arts Decoratifs,** Hohestrasse 20 (☎ **0211/32-45-53;** U-Bahn: Heinrich-Heine-Allee). Look for lamps, vases, paperweights, and high quality, pre-war costume jewelry, some of which could make good souvenirs.

JEWELRY & WATCHES   Located in the heart of the designer shopping district, **Wempe Juwelier,** Königsallee 14 (☎ **0211/32-72-87**), is one of a chain of 23 shops scattered throughout Düsseldorf that carry Swiss watches and jewelry designs in gold, silver, and precious stones.

WHERE TO STAY
VERY EXPENSIVE

Breidenbacher Hof. Heinrich-Heine-Allee 36, 40213 Düsseldorf 1 (around the corner from Königsallee). ☎ **800/223-68-00** in the U.S., or 0211/1-30-30. Fax 0211/1-30-38-30. www.breidenbacherhof.de. E-mail: info@breidenbacherhof.de. 162 units. A/C MINIBAR TV TEL. 660DM–710DM ($330–$355) double; from 850DM ($425) suite. Rates include continental breakfast. AE, DC, MC, V. Parking 35DM ($17.50). U-Bahn: Heinrich-Heine-Allee. Tram: 76, 78, or 705.

This hotel is a citadel of luxury, refined taste, and understatement, imbued with elegance at every corner. Rooms are medium in size and are individually decorated in traditional styling, with elaborate beds. The spacious baths have makeup mirrors, scales, robes, and hair dryers. The service is grand, though a bit stuffy.

Dining/Diversions: The Bar Royal is a small and intimate meeting place, with leather chairs and soft piano music. Next door, the Grill Royal serves a traditional European cuisine and is one of the finest restaurants in Düsseldorf. The Breidenbacher Eck, an informal bistro, offers a full menu at lunch and dinner and snacks throughout the day until late at night. Trader Vic's is a Polynesian restaurant and bar.

Amenities: 24-hour room service, laundry, nearby health club, car-rental facilities.

Steigenberger Park-Hotel. Corneliusplatz 1, 40213 Düsseldorf 1 (at the beginning of Königsallee, next to the German Opera). ☎ **800/223-5652** in the U.S. and Canada, or 0211/1-38-10. Fax 0211/13-81-592. www.srs-worldhotels.com. E-mail: duesseldorf@ steigenberger.de. 134 units. MINIBAR TV TEL. 540DM–670DM ($270–$335) double; 1,250DM–1,950DM ($625–$975) suite. Rates include buffet breakfast. AE, DC, MC, V. Free parking. Tram: 78 or 79. Bus: 778.

This traditional deluxe German hotel is number two in the center, vastly surpassed by the Breidenbacher Hof. It has been completely modernized and re-equipped to meet modern demands. Its central location, overlooking the Hofgarten park, is virtually unbeatable, which may explain why it attracts so many conventions and groups. The Steigenberger maintains a high level of service in the Old-World style. All rooms, refitted to the latest standards, are cozy and comfortable. Baths have makeup mirrors, robes, and hair dryers.

Dining/Diversions: The French cuisine at the Menuett attracts gourmets from all over the world. Drinks are served in the Etoile Bar. In summer, you can have a leisurely meal in a terrace overlooking parks and gardens. There's also a little bistro.

Amenities: 24-hour room service, laundry, dry cleaning, shoe-shine service.

MODERATE

Fürstenhof. Fürstenplatz 3, 40215 Düsseldorf 1. ☎ **0211/38-64-60.** Fax 0211/37-90-62. 43 units. MINIBAR TV TEL. 195DM–380DM ($97.50–$190) double. Rates include buffet breakfast. AE, DC, MC, V. Closed Dec 24–Jan 2. Tram: 701, 707, or 708. Bus: 725.

This hotel is a good, safe choice in the center of town. It's modern, but not glaringly so. It opens onto a tree-filled square. Rooms are handsomely furnished, each ranging in size from medium to spacious. Nonsmoking rooms are available, and half the breakfast room is reserved for nonsmoking guests. There's a sauna and fitness room, and the buffet breakfast is one of the best in town.

Hotel Grosser Kurfürst. Kurfürstenstrasse 18, 40211 Düsseldorf. ☎ **0211/173370.** Fax 0211/16-25-97. 21 units. TV TEL. 155DM–330DM ($77.50–$165) double. Rates include continental breakfast. AE, MC, V. Closed Dec 22–Jan 4. Tram: 709 or 719.

Although this modern hotel has some expensive rooms, it's a bargain overall—at least by the pricey standards of Düsseldorf. Rooms are small and sparsely furnished, though well organized. Baths are also small and have somewhat thin towels. Breakfast is the only meal served, but several restaurants are nearby. Facilities include a sauna and a solarium.

INEXPENSIVE

Wurms Hotel. Scheurenstrasse 23, 40215 Düsseldorf (near Graf-Adolf-Strasse, about 4 blocks from the Hauptbahnhof). ☎ **0211/37-50-01.** Fax 0211/37-50-03. www.hotel-wurms.de. E-mail: hotel-wurms@t-online.de. 27 units, 24 with shower and toilet. TV TEL. 160DM–240DM ($80–$120) double with shower and toilet. Rates include buffet breakfast. AE, MC, V. Parking 15DM ($7.50). Tram: 734, 741, or 752. Bus: 835.

The Wurms Hotel, set in a five-story stucco building, is a good choice. The small rooms are done in dark wood offset by bright bedspreads and curtains. Baths are a bit plain but spotlessly maintained. A few rooms—rented only to singles—are without private baths. The buffet breakfast is the only meal served. The hotel is a short walk from the central landmark square, Graf-Adolf-Platz.

WHERE TO DINE
VERY EXPENSIVE

✪ **Im Schiffchen.** Kaiserswerther Markt 9 (on the outskirts of the city, at Kaiserswerth). ☎ **0211/40-10-50.** Reservations required. Main courses 64DM–99DM ($32–$49.50); fixed-priced menus 168DM–216DM ($84–$108). AE, DC, MC V. Tues–Sat 7–9:30pm. Tram: 79 to Klemensplatz. FRENCH/SEAFOOD.

The chefs at Im Schiffchen deliver a refined, brilliantly realized repertoire of the finest cuisine you'll find in any city along the Rhine. The ingredients that go into the meals are unimpeachably authentic—every tomato, every onion, every fish or piece of meat seems to have been thoroughly evaluated for quality before purchasing. The menu is ever-changing, based on seasonal variations, but you might find homemade goose-liver pâté with green peppercorns, a delectable Norwegian salmon in Vouvray sauce, or lobster cooked in chamomile tea. We could return again and again for the pike perch cooked aromatically in puff pastry. The desserts are luscious; try the granulated fruit mélange with almond cream.

✪ **Victorian Restaurant.** Königstrasse 3A. ☎ **0211/8-65-50-22.** Reservations required for the restaurant, recommended for the bistro. Main courses 52DM–70DM ($26–$35); fixed-price lunch 55DM–80DM ($27.50–$40); fixed-price menus 135DM ($67.50) and 165DM ($82.50). AE, DC, MC, V. Mon–Sat noon–3pm and 7–midnight. Tram: 709 or 719. Bus: 834. FRENCH/GERMAN.

This is the finest restaurant in the city center. The decor features sparkling crystal, black-leather banquettes, and masses of flowers. The food represents the best of both traditional and modern schools. Examples include heavenly deep-fried zucchini flowers stuffed with lobster mousse and flavored with a sauce of champagne vinegar and coriander, apple salad with slices of goose liver, and three-vegetable puree. The delectable desserts change with the inspiration of the pastry chef but might include terrine of oranges served with raspberry liqueur and fresh mint.

Nearby is the **Bistro im Victorian,** with a minimalist interior design. The kitchen area is wide open, so you can watch as the fresh ingredients are whipped into meals. Patrons can even discuss their food wishes with the chef himself. Meals in the Bistro begin at 40DM ($20).

EXPENSIVE

De' Medici. Amboss-Strasse 3 (on the outskirts, at Oberkassel). ☎ **0211/59-41-51.** Reservations required. Main courses 28DM–45DM ($14–$22.50). AE, DC, MC, V. Mon–Fri noon–2:30pm; Mon–Sat 6pm–midnight (last orders 10:30pm). U-Bahn: Amboss-Strasse. FRENCH/ITALIAN.

De' Medici is elegantly modern, serving two culinary traditions, French and Italian, which are blended harmoniously. The chefs make it their goal to create, startle, and amaze diners with zesty flavors. The oversize menu lists an array of tried-and-true dishes, with concessions to whatever was available in the market that day. The marinated sweetbreads over sautéed eggplant or medaillons of veal in puff pastry are both unusual and excellent.

Restaurant Savini. Stromstrasse 47, Unterbilk. ☎ **0211/39-39-31.** Reservations recommended. Main courses 37DM–49DM ($18.50–$24.50); fixed-price menus 49DM–98DM ($24.50–$49). AE, MC. Tues–Fri noon–3pm; Mon–Sat 7–11pm. Closed 3 weeks in July. Tram 704 or 709 to Unterbilk. ITALIAN/INTERNATIONAL.

If you don't mind the trip outside the center, this restaurant offers the finest Italian dining in Düsseldorf. The white-walled dining room has tastefully colored banquettes. The creative Italian cuisine uses produce that comes fresh from the market and is deftly handled in the kitchen. Menu items include carpaccio of beef with warm king prawns, black spaghetti with scallops, or sea bass with risotto of mushrooms. The restaurant also has one of the best Italian wine cellars in Germany.

Rheinturm—Top 180 Restaurant. Stromstrasse 20. ☎ **0211/84-85-80.** Reservations recommended. Main courses 33DM–50DM ($16.50–$25); fixed-price, 3-course lunch 55DM ($27.50); fixed-price 4-course dinner 64DM ($32). AE, DC, MC, V. Daily noon–2:30pm and 6:30–11:30pm. Tram: 704, 709, or 719. Bus: 725. INTERNATIONAL.

Most people come here for the view. This futuristic restaurant is set atop the spool-shaped summit of the city's tallest tower, affording a 360° panorama of Düsseldorf's buildings and parks. The competently prepared menu items include grills, game dishes, fish, and soups. Try the slices of smoked duck breast with creamy Savoy cabbage or rolls of salmon stuffed with turbot filling and served in Riesling-and-saffron sauce. Vegetarian courses are also featured. A trip to the tower's observation lookout costs 5.80DM ($2.90) for adults, 4.50DM ($2.25) for those 13 to 17, and 3DM ($1.50) for children 6 to 12. Kids 5 and under go free. The tower is open daily 10am to 11:30pm.

MODERATE

Zum Csikos. Andreastrasse 9. ☎ **0211/32-97-71.** Reservations recommended. Main courses 20DM–40DM ($10–$20). AE, DC, MC. Daily 6pm–2am. Closed July. U-Bahn: Opernhaus. HUNGARIAN.

When you tire of Germanic cookery, Zum Csikos makes a refreshing change of pace. The restaurant's name translates as "Hungarian cowboy." It's set on three levels of a narrow town house originally built in 1697. Candlelight gives the place (and the diners) a mellow glow. The home-style Hungarian food is well prepared, and the portions are hefty. The beef goulash is excellent, as is the chopped liver. The restaurant follows the Hungarian tradition of late-night closings.

✪ **Zum Schiffchen.** Hafenstrasse 5 (a block from the Rhine). ☎ **0211/13-24-21.** Reservations required. Main courses 16DM–39.50DM ($8–$19.75). AE, DC, MC, V. Mon–Sat noon–midnight. Tram: 705. RHINELAND.

If you want the most traditional and atmospheric place to dine, come here before anywhere else. Zum Schiffchen, in the heart of the Altstadt, is Düsseldorf's oldest restaurant. A golden model ship on top of the step-gabled building (which dates from 1628) reminds you of its location, near the river. The interior follows the tavern tradition of scrubbed wooden tables and rustic artifacts. Good, hefty portions of regional cuisine are the rule here. The menu is large, and the service by the blue-aproned waiters (called *Köbesse*) is rather hectic. Zum Schiffchen is the perfect place to sample Düsseldorf's local beer. Over the years, the restaurant has attracted a host of famous diners ranging from Napoléon and Heinrich Heine to Arthur Miller.

INEXPENSIVE

Im Alten Bierhaus. Alt-Niederkassel 75 (on the outskirts). ☎ **0211/55-12-72.** Reservations required. Main courses 14DM–18DM ($7–$9). No credit cards. Tues–Sat 3–11pm, Sun 11am–11pm. Closed 3 weeks in July (dates vary). Bus: 834. RHINELAND.

This place is actually more of a wine tavern than a restaurant. The building dates from 1641. Style connoisseurs will recognize it as typical of the Rhine's left bank (as opposed to the right). Traditional German specialties, many sautéed, are served here. The house specialty is *Speck-Pfannenkuchen,* a bacon pancake; a similar version is made with marmalade. On Sunday the beer drinkers pile in at 11am. The specialty of the house is a local dark and foamy brew called Altbier.

Zum Schlüssel. Gatzweilers beer hall, Bölkerstrasse 43–47. ☎ **0211/32-61-55.** Reservations recommended. Main courses 16DM–40DM ($8–$20). AE, DC, MC, V. Sun–Thurs 10am–midnight, Fri–Sat 10am–1am. U-Bahn: Heinrich-Heine-Allee. GERMAN.

This establishment is as Germanic as the Rhine. Zum Schlüssel is located on the original site of the famous Gatzweilers Alt brewery. The decor is that of a classic German Gasthaus, with the aura of a country inn. The service is courteous and swift. The food has both aroma and taste, and there's plenty of it; sample the *Eisbein* (pigs' knuckles) or a huge bowl of soup. Wash it all down with the house beer, Gatzweilers Alt.

DÜSSELDORF AFTER DARK

The place to go is the **Altstadt.** This half square mile of narrow streets and alleyways, between Königsallee and the Rhine River, is jam-packed with restaurants, discos, art galleries, boutiques, nightclubs, and some 200 song-filled beer taverns. Düsseldorfers refer to a night cruising the Altstadt as an *Altstadtbummel.*

THE PERFORMING ARTS   Classical music has long had an illustrious association with this city, once home to Brahms, Mendelssohn, and Schumann. Consequently, it's not surprising that both the **Düsseldörfer Sinfonie** and its home, **Tonhalle,** Ehrenhof 2 (box office ☎ **0211/8-99-61-23;** U-Bahn: Tonhalle), are world-famous. The Tonhalle is perhaps Germany's most successful modern concert hall after Berlin's Philharmonie. The highly regarded orchestra gives about a dozen concerts a year, with tickets running 36DM to 90DM ($18 and $45). **Deutsche Oper am Rhein,** Heinrich-Heine-Allee 16A (☎ **0211/8-90-82-11;** U-Bahn: Heinrich-Heine-Allee), is one of the city's renowned opera and ballet companies. Tickets are 20DM to 90DM ($10 and $45).

The city's dramatic venue, **Schauspielhaus,** Gustav-Gründgens-Platz (☎ **0211/ 36-99-11;** U-Bahn: Heinrich-Heine-Allee), is outstanding, known all over Germany. The production and acting here are first-rate. Performances (in German) take place September to June, and tickets cost 20DM to 80DM ($10 to $40).

BARS & BEER HALLS   The oldest brewery-bar in the city is **Bräuerei Schumacher,** Oststrasse 123 (☎ **0211/326004;** U-Bahn: Oststrasse), a popular establishment that serves only beer that's brewed by the company that owns it. It's open Sunday to Thursday 10am to midnight, Friday and Saturday 10am to 1am. The brewery **Bräuerei zum Uerige,** Berger Strasse 1 (☎ **0211/86-69-90;** U-Bahn: Heinrich-Heine-Allee), serves traditional German dishes along with its house brews. Open Sunday to Thursday 10am to midnight and Friday and Saturday 10am to 1am. Two other breweries, each serving beer brewed on the premises, are **Bräuerei im Suchschen,** Ratingerstrasse 28 (☎ **0211/137-470;** U-Bahn: Heinrich-Heine-Allee), and **Bräuerei zum Schlüssel,** Bölkerstrasse 43 (☎ **0211/326-155;** U-Bahn: Heinrich-Heine-Allee), both of which also offer platters of German food. Purists in Düsseldorf are quick to point out that the **Bräuerei zum Uel,** Rattingerstrasse 16 (☎ **0211/32-53-69;** U-Bahn: Heinrich-Heine-Allee), is not technically a brewery at all, because beer is not brewed on the premises. Nonetheless, students flock here for the house beers and international dishes. It's open Monday to Saturday 10am to 1am, and Sunday 11am to 1am.

Angel images fill every nook and cranny of **Engelchen** (German for "angel"), Kurzestrasse 15 (☎ **0211/32-73-56;** U-Bahn: Heinrich-Heine-Allee), where an alternative arts crowd gathers for conversation and coffee, beer, or mixed drinks. It's open Monday to Friday 9am to 2am and weekends 9am to 5am. **N.T. Pub,** Königsallee 27 (☎ **0211/138-000;** U-Bahn: Königsallee), is a conveniently located and convivial pub. It serves cafe-style platters and drinks every day 9am till after midnight.

DANCE CLUBS   Two hot dance spots, **Tor 3,** Ronsdorferstrasse 143 (☎ **0211/ 7-33-64-97**), and **Stahlwerk,** Ronsdorferstrasse 134 (☎ **0211/7-30-86-81**), face each other across the street (U-Bahn: Ronsdorferstrasse). Both intersperse recorded dance music with live acts from throughout Europe. Both draw a mixed, fashion-conscious crowd, are open Friday and Saturday from 10pm to about 5am, and charge a cover of 10DM to 35DM ($5 to $17.50).

JAZZ CLUBS   At the small and smoked-filled **Em Pootzke,** Mertensgasse 6 (☎ **0211/32-69-73;** U-Bahn: Heinrich-Heine-Allee), there's no cover and no food, just nightly live jazz and drinking 9pm to 1am.

LIVE-MUSIC CLUBS   A popular piano bar, **Bei Tino,** Königsallee 21 (☎ 0211/
32-64-63; U-Bahn: Königsallee), has music noon to 3am nightly; guests are often
allowed to play the piano. **McLaughlin's Irish Pub,** Kurzestrasse 11 (☎ 0211/
32-46-11; U-Bahn: Heinrich-Heine-Allee), serves Guinness and Murphy's with
stew and pies, and presents touring Irish bands on the weekend. It's open Sunday to
Thursday 11am to 1am, and Friday and Saturday 11am to 3am. Another pub with a
brogue, **Irish Pub Bei Fatties,** Hunsruckenstrasse 13 (☎ 0211/13-31-81; U-Bahn:
Heinrich-Heine-Allee), hosts live blues, rock, jazz, and Irish music on Friday and
Saturday. It's open Monday to Friday 2:30pm until 3am, Saturday 1pm to 3am and
Sunday noon to 3am.

GAY CLUBS   The centerpiece of gay life in Düsseldorf is the **Café Rosa Mond,**
Oberbilker Allee 310 (☎ 0211/77-52-42; U-Bahn: Oberbilke). It functions as a cafe,
a bar, and an organizer of gay-themed entertainment, which changes virtually every
night of the week. The staff can direct you to other gay-friendly venues. It's open
nightly 8pm to 3am or later.

14 The Mosel Valley

Those returning from Germany singing the praises of the Rhine as the most scenic German river have probably not yet toured the Mosel Valley. The Mosel meanders in a snakelike path through the mountains west of the Rhineland, passing town after town whose sole purpose seems to be to beautify the riverbanks. Nearly every village and hill has its own castle or fortress, often surrounded by vineyards.

The Mosel (*Moselle* in French) begins in the hills of France, but its most scenic portion is the last 193km (120 miles) before it enters the Rhine at Koblenz. Visitors to the area enjoy the lively landscapes, the legend-rich countryside, and, of course, the wines. Many of the rich and full-bodied Mosel wines are superior to those of the Rhine Valley.

If you enter Germany via France or Luxembourg, the Mosel route is a good way to begin your tour of the German countryside. You'll arrive first at the major city of **Trier** with its significant Roman ruins before weaving through the Hunsrück and Eifel mountains.

EXPLORING THE REGION BY CAR

The 125-mile drive along the Mosel between the Rhine city of Koblenz (see chapter 13) and the ancient city of Trier is one of the most rewarding in Germany. Although it's a relatively short distance, you should allow at least 3 days to fully enjoy the Mosel River Valley tour. Rustic country inns are scattered along both the left and right banks of the river.

Day 1 Leave **Koblenz** by crossing the Neue Moselbrücke (New Mosel Bridge) on the southern outskirts. Look for the sign pointing to Route 49 and follow the highway along the east bank of the Mosel. Some 16km (10 miles) south of Koblenz you come to **Winningen,** a village from the Middle Ages, set against a backdrop of vine-covered hills. Another 10km (6 miles) along the route stands **Alken,** a little wine town known for its Thurant Castle. Take the nearby bridge across the Mosel and continue on Route 49 heading south for 10km (6 miles) to **Moskelkern,** another wine village. Continue along for another 5km (3 miles) to where signs point the way to **Burg Eltz,** the most prominent and most visited castle along the Mosel (there's a picture of this castle on the 500DM banknote).

From Ries, it's another 6km (4 miles)—still on the left bank— to **Cochem,** a medieval wine town where you can find food and lodging. You can also take guided tours of its huge castle, Reichsburg Cochem.

The Mosel Valley

If you decide not to spend the night in Cochem, continue along the "wine road" with its panoramic scenery and towering promontories along the river—expect sharp curves in the highway. Vineyards cling to the rock-strewn hillsides. Route 49 goes along the left bank for 5km (3 miles) to the Ernest Brücke, where you can cross to the other side of the river. Follow the signposts for 5km (3 miles) to **Beilstein,** a market town of cobbled streets left over from the Middle Ages.

Day 2   After checking out Beilstein and its Metternich Castle, get back on Route 49, going for 6km (4 miles) to the bridge at Senheim. Here, we recommend that you cross the bridge to the left bank and go another 10km (6 miles) to **Alf,** a little village at the foot of Marienburg Palace, which dates from 1127. There are panoramic views of the Mosel and its vineyards here.

Then get on Route 53 and travel for another 8km (5 miles) to **Zell,** crossing back to the right bank of the river. To many, Zell is the loveliest of the Mosel wine towns, and you may want to linger. Zell is the headquarters of the producers of the fabled Schwarze Katze or "black cat" wine.

After Zell, go along Route 53 for some 18km (11 miles) to the old market town of **Traben-Trarbach,** the headquarters of the Mosel wine trade. After a look, continue south on Route 53 for 24km (15 miles) to **Bernkastel-Kues,** two wine villages on opposite sides of the river. A bridge connects the towns. Bernkastel exudes medieval charm. Visit any of its taverns for a glass of the local wine, Bernkasteler Doktor.

After Bernkastel-Kues (where you may decide to stop overnight), you can go for about another 65km (40 miles), passing some of the prettiest vineyard landscapes in

Germany, to **Trier,** a city dating from prehistoric times, where you can spend the night.

Day 3   You can easily devote an entire day or more to discovering Trier's charms—after all, "Trier stood for 1,300 years before Rome" (or so the local slogan goes). We recommend that you spend another night here, visiting its Roman monuments and strolling its ancient streets.

1   Cochem

92km (57 miles) NE of Trier, 51km (32 miles) SW of Koblenz

This medieval town, located in one of the best wine regions of the Mosel Valley, is crowded against the left bank of the river by a huge vineyard-covered hill. Because of its large number of inns, Cochem might be your best choice for an overnight stopover between Koblenz and Trier.

The town is a typical wine village, with tastings and festivals. But the biggest attraction is **Reichsburg Cochem** (☎ **02671/1787**), a huge castle at the top of the mound behind the town. The original 1027 structure was almost completely destroyed by Louis XIV's army in 1689. It has since been restored according to the original ground plans, and its medieval ramparts and turrets create a dramatic backdrop for the town. To reach the castle, follow the steep footpath from the center of town; the 15-minute walk is well worth it for the views of the town and the Mosel below. Although you can visit anytime, the interior of the castle is open daily mid-March to November 9am to 6pm. Guided tours are conducted at regular intervals. Admission is 7DM ($3.50) for adults and 3DM ($1.50) for children and students.

ESSENTIALS

GETTING THERE   By Train   The Cochem Bahnhof is on the Wasserbillig–Trier–Koblenz rail line, with frequent service between these connecting cities. For information, call ☎ **01805/99-66-33.**

By Bus   Regional bus service along the Mosel is provided by **RMV Rhein Mosel Verkehrsgesellschaft** (☎ **02671/8976**) and by **Moselbahn, GmbH** (☎ **0651/147750**).

By Car   Access is via the A48 Autobahn on the Koblenz–Trier express highway; exit either at Ulmen or at Kaisersesch.

By Boat   Boat rides on the Mosel River operate between Trier and Cochem. Contact **Mosel Personen Schiffahrt Gebrüder Kolb,** Briedern/Mosel (☎ **02673/1515**).

VISITOR INFORMATION   For tourist information, contact the **Verkehrsamt,** Endertplatz 1 (☎ **02671/60040**), open Monday to Friday 9am to 5pm and, May to October, also Saturday 10am to 3pm and Sunday 10am to noon.

SPECIAL EVENTS   During the first week of June, **Mosel-Wein-Woche** begins, celebrating the region's wines with tasting booths and a street fair. The similar **Weinfest** takes place in the last weekend of August. For information on either of these events, contact the tourist office (see above) or the **Weingut Winzerhof** (☎ **02671/72-97**) for details on dates, activities, and accommodations.

Thunderbird, It's Not

Mosel wines have the lowest alcoholic content (about 9%) of any white wine in the world. Because of this, they are best enjoyed in their youth.

SHOPPING   Die Geschenkidee Heimes, Herrenstrasse 13 (☎ **02671/9-11-22**), located on the town's main street, sells locally produced arts and crafts.

WHERE TO STAY

✪ **Alte Thorschenke.** Brückenstrasse 3, 56812 Cochem. ☎ **02671/70-59.** Fax 02671/42-02. 35 units. MINIBAR TV TEL. 165DM–225DM ($82.50–$112.50) double; 300DM ($150) suite. Rates include buffet breakfast. AE, DC, MC, V. Closed Jan 5–Mar 15. Parking 10DM ($5) in garage.

Both a hotel and a wine restaurant, the centrally located Alte Thorschenke is one of the oldest and best-known establishments along either side of the Mosel. The romantically conceived building, with its timbers and towers, was originally built in 1332. It became a hotel in 1960, when a modern wing was added. Most rooms are reached via a cantilevered wooden staircase that has creaked for centuries (there's also an elevator in the rear). Six rooms have four-poster beds. There's also a romantic Napoléon suite. Not to be ignored are meals in the tavern, accompanied by Mosel wine. In summer, guests often take their lunch at one of the sidewalk tables.

Guests of the hotel can visit the 500-year-old **castle of Baron von Landenberg,** in Eller, about 7km (4¹/₂ miles) from Cochem. Here, in the old cellars, you can taste the wines. To arrange a visit if you're not staying at the hotel, call ☎ **02675/2-77.**

Burg Hotel. Moselpromenade 23, 56812 Cochem. ☎ **02671/71-17.** Fax 02671/83-36. 43 units. TV. 110DM–200DM ($55–$100) double. Rates include buffet breakfast. AE, DC, MC, V. Free parking.

Parts of the ground floor of this cozy riverside hotel were built in the 1500s. Today, the feeling you'll get is one of solid, well-managed conservatism and discreet prosperity. Furnishings throughout are traditional and, in some cases, antique. Seven of the rooms—those priced 100DM to 120DM ($50 to $60)—are in a simple nearby annex. Rooms in the main house have more expansive balconies and more panoramic views of the river. The hotel offers an indoor pool, sauna, and solarium.

The two restaurants serve the same regional and international specialties. The more appealing is on the ground floor and holds a collection of antique weapons and artifacts. Set menus cost 15DM to 25DM ($7.50 to $12.50) at lunch and 15DM to 95DM ($7.50 to $47.50) at dinner. Typical dishes include specialties of the Mosel Valley. Naturally, a large selection of the best Mosel wine is available to accompany your meal.

Flair Hotel am Rosenhügel. Valwigerstrasse 57, 56812 Cochem-Cond. ☎ **02671/ 9-76-30.** Fax 02671/97-63-63. 23 units. TV TEL. 200DM ($100) double. Rates include buffet breakfast. MC, V. Closed Dec 15–Jan 3. Free parking.

The Rupp and Breslauer families are your hosts at this centrally located hotel, which has balconies and a sun terrace overlooking the Mosel. Rooms are modern, simple, and quite comfortable, though a bit small. Some offer panoramic views of the castle on the hill.

Lohspeicher. Obergasse 1, 56812 Cochem. ☎ **02671/39-76.** Fax 02671/17-72. 8 units. A/C TV TEL. 180DM ($90) double. Rates include continental breakfast. AE, MC, V. Closed Feb. Parking 10DM ($5).

A former warehouse, this generously proportioned 1832 building with hand-hewn beams has been renovated into a delightful and centrally located hotel and restaurant. Rooms, though generally a bit small, are comfortably furnished. In the restaurant, gourmet meals are presented at the best table in town (open Thursday to Tuesday noon to 11pm). Specialties include onion or snail soup, followed by all kinds of fish and game dishes. Try the fillet of venison with wild mushrooms in cream sauce.

WHERE TO DINE

Parkhotel Landenberg. Sehler Anlagen 1, 56812 Cochem-Sehl (about a mile from the Bahnhof). ☎ **02671/71-10.** Fax 02671/83-79. Reservations recommended. Main courses 21DM–52DM ($10.50–$26). AE, MC, V. Daily noon–2pm and 6–9pm. Closed Jan 5–Mar 15. GERMAN/INTERNATIONAL.

Parkhotel Landenberg offers a pleasing panoramic view over the Mosel. Delectable regional specialties include venison, wild boar, and fish—all best enjoyed with a good bottle of white Mosel wine from the hotel's own cellar.

Weissmühle im Enterttal. Endertstrasse 1. ☎ **02671/89-55.** Fax 02671/82-07. Reservations recommended. Main courses 26DM–39DM ($13–$19.50); fixed-menus 48DM–58DM ($24–$29). DC, MC, V. Daily noon–2pm and 6–9pm. From the center of Cochem, drive toward the Autobahn, following the signs for Koblenz/Trier; the inn is on the left of the road, 1.5km (1 mile) northwest of Cochem. GERMAN/FRENCH.

Set within Cochem's suburb of Enterttal, this respected restaurant is sought out by locals because of its fine cuisine. It offers a friendly welcome and a position in the middle of a little wine-producing village. You can dine within either the Müllerstube, a woodsy, antique-looking room that might remind you of an inn high in the Swiss Alps, or the brighter, sunnier, and larger Sommerrestaurant. A trademark dish is fresh trout from the small nearby lake, stuffed with herbs, baked, and kept warm beside your table by a hot stone.

A SIDE TRIP TO BURG ELTZ

The stately castle on the north bank of the Mosel is ✪ **Burg Eltz** (☎ **02672/ 95-05-00**), set above the village of Moselkern and surrounded by woodlands. It lies 29km (18 miles) northeast of Cochem and 29km (18 miles) southwest of Koblenz. Access is by the A48 and A61 Autobahns and Route 49. A parking lot, Antoniuskapelle, less than a mile from the castle, can be reached via Münstermaifeld. A bus runs to the castle every 5 minutes.

This is one of the few medieval castles in the region still intact. The original structure, built from the 12th to the 17th centuries, has been preserved in all its glory— the romance of the Middle Ages really comes alive here. The castle houses four separate residences, with original medieval furnishings, including some fine old paintings and tapestries. A treasury contains works by goldsmiths and silversmiths, armor, weapons, and other objects acquired by the family over the centuries. The castle is open daily April to November 1, 9:30am to 5:30pm. Admission is 9DM ($4.50) for adults and 6DM ($3) for children. If you want to fortify yourself before the trek back to town, stop at one of two small self-service restaurants in the castle.

2 Beilstein

11km (7 miles) E of Cochem, 111km (69 miles) W of Mainz

This unspoiled medieval wine town on the east bank of the Mosel has an unusual marketplace hewn right into the rocky hillside. Above the town stands the former cloister church and the ruins of the 12th-century **Metternich Castle.**

ESSENTIALS

GETTING THERE   By Train   The nearest rail station is at Cochem (see above).

By Bus   Service from Cochem and other points along the Mosel is available from **RMV Rhein Mosel Verkehrsgesellschaft** (☎ **02671/8976**) and from **Moselbahn, GmbH** (☎ **0651/147750**).

By Car Access by car is via the A48 Autobahn on the Koblenz–Trier run; exit at Kaisersesch.

VISITOR INFORMATION The nearest information office is at Cochem (see above).

WHERE TO STAY & DINE

Haus Burgfrieden. Im Muhlental 63, 56814 Beilstein (a 5-min. walk west of the town center). ☎ **02673/9-36-39.** Fax 02673/93-63-88. www.mosel.com. E-mail: f.von.metternich@ t-online.de. 72 units. TV TEL. 150DM ($75) double. Rates include buffet breakfast. No credit cards. Closed Nov–Mar. Free parking.

This hotel's simple but comfortable rooms are outfitted in an uncluttered modern style. They aren't very spacious, but the maintenance is good. On the premises is a dining room, where the chef offers an international menu specializing in game and fish. Meals range from 28DM to 63DM ($14 to $31.50). The food is wholesome and unpretentious.

Haus Lipmann. Marktplatz 3, 56814 Beilstein. ☎ **02673/15-73.** Fax 02673/15-21. 5 units. TV. 130DM–160DM ($65–$80) double. Rates include continental breakfast. No credit cards. Closed Nov 1–Apr 1. Free parking.

You can sample the wines that made Beilstein famous at its favorite inn, Haus Lipmann, in the town center. Time has been kind to this 1795 timbered building. The five guest rooms are located in its main house. They're all small, cozy, and very inviting, with tiny baths.

For six generations, the same family has tended the vast riverside vineyards that have won them acclaim. Try their Ellenzer Goldbäumchen or their Beilsteiner Schlossberg. The various places for drinking and dining are so tempting that it's difficult to choose one over the other. Most popular in summer, however, is the vine-covered terrace with a statue of Bacchus, overlooking the Mosel. Or try the antique-filled tavern or the wood-paneled Rittersaal, with its collection of old firearms and pewter. Candles are lit at night. In the cooler months, fires burn in the tall walk-in fireplace and the tiny open hearth, with its copper kettle on a crane. The Mosel eel in dill sauce is a classic choice, but especially delectable is the fresh wild trout. Meals cost 30DM to 55DM ($15 to $27.50); hours are daily noon to 2pm and 6 to 8pm. Activities get hectic at grape-harvest time.

3 Zell

69km (43 miles) NE of Trier, 105km (65 miles) W of Mainz, 35km (22 miles) S of Cochem

This old town, stretching along the east bank of the Mosel, is best known for its excellent wine, Schwarze Katze ("Black Cat"). The grape is king here, as you'll quickly realize if you visit during the annual autumn wine festival. Nearby, on the left bank of the Mosel, 8km (5 miles) from Zell and 32km (20 miles) from Cochem, stands the little wine village of **Alf.** The surroundings are idyllic, especially if you climb up to the Marienburg. From here, you get a fine view overlooking the Mosel and the vineyards of Zell.

ESSENTIALS

GETTING THERE By Train The nearest rail station is at Bullay, some 4km (2¹⁄₂ miles) away. For information, call ☎ **01805/99-66-33.**

By Bus Regional bus service is provided by **RMV Rhein Mosel Verkehrsgesellschaft GmbH** (☎ 02671/8976), and by **Moselbahn, GmbH** (☎ 0651/147750).

By Car   Access by car is via the A1 Autobahn north and south or Route 53 east and west.

VISITOR INFORMATION   Check with **Tourist-Information,** in the Rathaus, Balduinstrasse 44 (☎ **06542/7-01-22**), open Monday to Friday 9am to 5pm.

WHERE TO STAY & DINE

Weinhaus Mayer. Balduinstrasse 15, 56856 Zell. ☎ **06542/45-30** (Apr–Nov) or **06542/57-76** (Dec–Mar). Fax 06542/6-11-60. 30 units. MINIBAR TV TEL. 130DM–170DM ($65–$85) double. Rates include continental breakfast. V. Closed Dec–Mar. Free parking.

This five-story, rustic, balconied building in the center of town thrives as both a hotel and a wine house. It offers small, simply furnished rooms in the century-old main building. Some have a view of the Mosel. Less expensive rooms are in a less desirable annex on the same street. The in-house restaurant serves only dinner, daily 6 to 9pm; you might accompany your meal with one of the restaurant's bottles of Mosel Valley wines. Meals range from 15DM to 26DM ($7.50 to $13).

Zur Post. Schlossstrasse 21, 56856 Zell. ☎ **06542/42-17.** Fax 06542/4-16-93. 16 units. 130DM ($65) double. Rates include continental breakfast. AE, DC, MC, V. Closed Feb to mid-Mar. Free parking.

This beflowered hotel sits directly on the river. Its small rooms are carpeted, with French doors opening onto balconies. The owner takes pride in looking after her guests and ensuring their comfort. On the inviting sun terrace you can enjoy a glass of Mosel wine while watching the river traffic go by. Or you can sample the local wine in the warmly decorated Weinstube. Meals, served Tuesday to Sunday, cost 28DM to 50DM ($14 to $25).

4 Traben-Trarbach

60km (37 miles) NE of Trier, 103km (64 miles) W of Mainz, 18km (11 miles) SW of Zell

Thanks to their central location on the Mosel, halfway between Koblenz and Trier, the twin towns of Traben and Trarbach have become the wine capitals of the Mosel Valley. Their gardenlike promenades on both banks of the river are viewpoints for annual international speedboat and waterskiing competitions. The **July wine festival** attracts visitors from all over Europe to the old wine cellars and taverns of the towns.

Traben-Trarbach is also proud of its historic attractions. Above Trarbach, on the east bank of the river, are the remains of the 14th-century **Grevenburg Castle,** the scene of hard-fought battles to gain control of its strategic position. On the opposite bank, above Traben, are the ruins of **Mont Royal,** a late 17th-century fortress built by the invading Louis XIV. You can wander about these testimonials to faded grandeur at any time, without charge. Another attraction, just south of town, is the spa resort, **Bad Wildstein,** with its thermal springs.

ESSENTIALS

GETTING THERE   By Train   Rail passengers for Traben-Trarbach can arrive either at Trier or Bullay, then go the rest of the way by bus. Call ☎ **01805/99-66-33** for schedules and times.

By Bus   Regional bus service among the Mosel River towns is provided by **RMV Rhein Mosel Verkehrsgesellschaft** (☎ **06571/7141**) and by **Moselbahn, GmbH** (☎ **0651/147750**).

By Car   Access by car is via the A48 Autobahn (Trier–Koblenz); exit at Wittlich.

VISITOR INFORMATION   For tourist information, contact the **Kurverwaltung und Verkehrsamt,** Bahnstrasse 22, Traben (☎ **06541/83980**), open Monday to Friday 8am to noon and 1 to 5pm; May to October, also Saturday 1 to 4pm.

WHERE TO STAY & DINE

Hotel Moseltor. Moselstrasse 1, 56841 Traben-Trarbach. ☎ **06541/65-51.** Fax 06541/49-22. www.moseltor.de. E-mail: info@moseltor.de. 11 units. TV TEL. 135DM–200DM ($67.50–$100) double. Rates include continental breakfast. AE, DC, MC, V. Parking 12DM ($6) in garage.

You'll find this hotel on the outskirts of town at Im Otsteil Trarbach. Inside this masterpiece of 19th-century fieldstone masonry, a charming combination of new construction and antique elements creates a warm mixture of comfort and convenience. The inviting rooms have satellite TVs, hair dryers, private safes, and trouser presses.

Chef Ruth Bauer's reputation for light cuisine has spread so widely that German urbanites come here for gastronomic weekends. Bauer's restaurant is small, only 11 tables, with fixed-price meals costing 49DM to 67DM ($24.50 to $33.50). It's open Wednesday to Monday noon to 2pm and 6 to 9pm. The hotel is open year-round, but the restaurant is closed in February.

Rema Jugendstilhotel Bellevue. Am Moselufer, 56841 Traben-Trarbach. ☎ **06541/ 70-30.** Fax 06541/70-34-00. 50 units. MINIBAR TV TEL. 199DM–299DM ($99.50–$149.50) double. Rates include buffet breakfast. AE, DC, MC, V. Free outdoor parking; 10DM ($5) in garage.

This art-nouveau castle, right on the riverbank, is one of the finest hotels along the Mosel. It was designed in 1903 by the noted architect Bruno Moehring and features elaborate timberwork, a domed tower, a high-pitched roof, gables, and dormers. The cozy rooms are often furnished with antiques. Amenities include an indoor swimming pool and a sauna. The Clauss-Feist Restaurant is a romantic spot for both breakfast and dinner, with stained-glass windows and an old-German ambience. There's a cozy fireplace and intimate wood bar as well as an ivy-covered terrace for dining outside.

5 Bernkastel-Kues

48km (30 miles) NE of Trier, 113km (70 miles) W of Mainz

In a valley of wine towns, Bernkastel stands out as the most colorful. Its old Marktplatz is surrounded by half-timbered buildings dating from as early as 1608. In the center of the square stands the 17th-century **St. Michael's Fountain,** which flows with wine during the annual September wine festival. The ruined 11th-century **Landshut Castle** lies on a promontory above the town; it's worth a visit for the view. Like Traben-Trarbach, this town is split into twin villages on opposite banks of the Mosel.

ESSENTIALS

GETTING THERE   By Train   The nearest rail station is the Wittlich Hauptbahnhof, 20km (12¹/₂) miles west, with a bus or taxi connection to Bernkastel-Kues. For information, call ☎ **1-94-19.**

By Bus   Regional bus service along the Mosel River is provided by **RMV Rhein Mosel Verkehrsgesellschaft** (☎ **06571/7141**) and by **Moselbahn, GmbH** (☎ **0651/ 147750**).

By Car   Access by car is via the A48 Autobahn on the Koblenz–Trier run; exit at Wittlich.

VISITOR INFORMATION   Contact **Tourist-Information,** Gestade 5, in Bernkastel (☎ **06531/40-23-24**), open May to October, Monday to Friday 8:30am to 5pm and Saturday 10am to 4pm; November to April, Monday to Thursday 8:30am to 12:30pm and 1 to 5pm, and Friday 8:30am to 12:30pm and 1 to 3:30pm.

WHERE TO STAY & DINE

Doctor Weinstuben. Hebegasse 5, 54470 Bernkastel-Kues. ☎ **06531/96650**. Fax 06531/62-96. www.gastroline.de/doctor-weinstuben. E-mail: info@gastroline.de. 20 units. TV TEL. 150DM–190DM ($75–$95) double. AE, DC, MC, V. Free parking.

This intricately half-timbered building in the town center was constructed in 1652. Today it's the most visually interesting hotel in Bernkastel. Transformed into a tavern in 1830, it still has many of its original wood carvings. Its public areas are traditional, and the cozy but often too-small rooms are furnished in a simple, modern style.

The inn serves the best food in town, with meals beginning at 35DM ($19.95). Hours are daily noon to 2pm and 6 to 10pm. Many guests prefer to sample Mosel wine in the hotel's vine-covered courtyard. Look for the 100-year-old plant called "Blue Rain."

Römischer Kaiser. Markt 29, 54470 Bernkastel-Kues (on the riverside promenade). ☎ **06531/9-68-60**. Fax 06531/76-72. 38 units. TV TEL. 100DM–160DM ($50–$80) double. Rates include buffet breakfast. AE, DC, MC, V. Closed Feb.

The facade of this hotel has a view of the Mosel from many of the upper windows. The public areas are decorated almost like rooms in a private home, with paintings and Oriental rugs. Rooms are rather small but comfortable.

Many visitors come here just to sample the traditional cookery. Like any good restaurant along the Mosel, it features local wines. A separate menu lists all the things that anyone could possibly cook with prawns. The restaurant is open daily 11am to 9pm, with meals costing 25DM to 55DM ($12.50 to $27.50).

Zur Post. Gestade 17, 54470 Bernkastel-Kues. ☎ **06531/9-67-00**. Fax 06531/96-70-50. 42 units. MINIBAR TV TEL. 160DM–190DM ($80–$95) double. Rates include buffet breakfast. AE, DC, MC, V. Closed Jan. Free parking.

This centrally located hotel was once a stopover for horseback riders on the local postal routes. The well-maintained but small rooms have both traditional and modern furnishings. Baths are both tiny and tidy. Public areas include an elegantly crafted stairwell flanked by half-timbered walls and a paneled, beamed dining room. The restaurant serves excellent regional cookery daily noon to 2pm and 6 to 9pm. À la carte meals cost 42DM to 65DM ($21 to $32.50).

6 Trier (Treves)

124km (77 miles) SW of Koblenz, 143km (89 miles) SW of Bonn, 193km (120 miles) SW of Frankfurt

As the Romans spread over Europe, they established satellite capitals for ruling their distant colonies. Augusta Treverorum (Trier) was founded under Augustus in 16 B.C. It eventually became known as Roma Secunda—the second Rome. For nearly 5 centuries, well into the Christian era, Trier remained one of Europe's political, cultural, and ecclesiastical power centers.

But this city, Germany's oldest, actually dates back much farther. In 2000 B.C., according to legend, the Assyrians established a colony here, and archaeological findings indicate a pre-Roman Celtic civilization. The buildings and monuments still standing today, however, date from Roman and later periods.

Local Boy

Karl Marx was born and grew up in Trier; his birthplace is now a museum. As a young man, he traveled down the Mosel Valley and was so shocked by the exploitation of vineyard workers that he decided to write an article about their plight. Thus began his career.

Trier is an important gateway, lying only 10km (6 miles) from Luxembourg on the western frontier of Germany, where the Ruwer and Saar Rivers meet the Mosel. The city is rich not only in art and tradition, but also, because of its location, in wine—it's one of Germany's largest exporters.

ESSENTIALS

GETTING THERE   By Train   Trier Hauptbahnhof is on the Wasserbillig–Trier–Koblenz "Moselbahn" line and also the Trier–Saarbrücken line. Trier has frequent regional connections. There are 20 trains per day to Koblenz (trip time: 1 hr. 20 min.), 20 trains to Cologne (trip time: 2 hr. 25 min.), and 20 trains to Saarbrücken (trip time: 1 hr. 20 min.). For information, call ☎ **01805/99-66-33.**

By Bus   Buses between Trier and Bullay run along the Mosel River, leaving from the main station in Trier at Bussteig 3. Service is provided by **RMV Rhein Mosel Verkehrsgesellschaft** (☎ **02671/8976**) and by **Moselbahn, GmbH** (☎ **0651/147750**).

By Boat   Boat rides on the Mosel River operate between Trier and Cochem (see section 1). Contact **Mosel Personen Schiffahrt Gebrüder Kolb,** Briedern/Mosel (☎ **02673/1515**).

By Car   Access by car to Trier is via the A1 Autobahn north and south, the A48 east, and Route 51 from the north.

VISITOR INFORMATION   Contact **Tourist-Information,** An der Porta Nigra (☎ **0651/97-80-80**), open Monday to Saturday 9am to 6:30pm and Sunday 9am to 3:30pm.

GETTING AROUND   Most of Trier's attractions are within walking distance of each another, and few visitors need to take the bus. Bus tickets (purchased on the bus) cost 3DM ($1.50) within zone 1 (the city). For information, call ☎ **0651/71-72-73.**

SHOPPING   The richest selection of Mosel Valley products and crafts, especially objects involved with wine, is available from the **Welcome Shop,** Simeonstiftsplatz (☎ **0651/994-0540**). If you're interested in seeing the art of glassmaking, head for the glassmaking studio at the **Kunsthandwerkerhof,** Simeonstiftsplatz (☎ **0651/4-29-91**), where a small-scale team of glass artisans open their studio for observation, as well as offer their wares for sale.

SEEING THE SIGHTS

Every day May to October, the tourist office (see above) conducts a 2-hour **walking tour** that departs from the office at 1:30pm. The cost is 10DM ($5) per adult, 3DM ($1.50) for children 6 to 14.

EXPLORING THE ROMAN RUINS

When the last Roman prefect departed from Trier in about A.D. 400, he left behind a vast collection of monuments from the centuries of Roman domination. **Porta Nigra (Black Gate)** (☎ **0651/75424**) is the best-preserved Roman structure in Germany, the only survivor of the great wall that once surrounded Trier. The huge sandstone blocks, assembled without mortar, were held together with iron clamps—the marks can still be seen. From outside the gate, the structure appeared to be simply two arched entrances between rounded towers leading directly into the town, but intruders soon discovered that the arches opened into an inner courtyard where they were at the mercy of the town's defenders. During the Middle Ages, the Greek hermit Simeon, later canonized, chose the east tower as his retreat. After his death, the archbishop turned the gate into a huge double church. When Napoléon came this way, however, he ordered all the architectural changes to be removed and the original Roman core restored. Porta Nigra is open daily, April to October, 9am to 6pm; November and January to March, 9am to 5pm; and December, 10am to 4pm. Admission is 4DM ($2) for adults and 1.50DM (75¢) for children.

The Imperial Palace district, stretching along the site of the former medieval wall of the city, begins with the Roman building known today as the **Basilica,** Basilikaplatz (☎ **0651/72468**). Although much of the structure has been demolished, the huge hall that remains—believed to be the throne room—gives some idea of the grandeur of the original palace. The hall is 67m (220 feet) long, 27m (90 feet) wide, and 30m (98 feet) high. The two tiers of windows are arranged within high-rising arches in which fragments of the original wall paintings can be seen. Five large heating chambers outside the walls sent warm air through the hollow floor, in the unique method of Roman central heating. Today the Basilica serves as the main Protestant church in the city. It's open Monday to Saturday 9am to 6pm and Sunday 11am to 6pm. Admission is free.

Next to the Basilica stands the 17th-century **Kurfürstliches Palais (Electral Palace** (☎ **0651/94-94-218**), built in the German Renaissance style as a residence for the archbishop-electors, the town's governors. The palace cannot be entered because its interior is used for city offices, but the adjoining **Palace Gardens (Palastgarten),** full of ponds, flowers, and rococo statues, are always open and free.

The **Imperial Baths** (Kaiserthermen; (☎ **0651/44262**), at the south end of Palastgarten, were erected in the early 4th century by Constantine I. Of the huge complex, only the ruins of the hot baths remain. These were among the largest in the Roman empire, and although never completed, they were used in connection with the Imperial Palace. The older **Baths of St. Barbara** (Barbarathermen; ☎ **0651/762280**) are located on Südallee, near a Roman bridge. They're open daily 9am to 6pm, and admission to both is 4DM ($2).

The **Amphitheater,** Amphitheaterplatz (☎ **0651/73010**), is the oldest Roman construction in Trier, dating from A.D. 100. The stone seats, arranged in three circles separated by broad promenades, held at least 20,000 people. The ruins are open daily 9am to 6pm; admission is 4DM ($2).

A **collective ticket,** which grants admission to the amphitheater, the two sets of Roman baths, and the Porta Nigra, costs 9DM ($4.50) for adults, and 3DM ($1.50) for children under 18.

MORE SIGHTS & ACTIVITIES

Since medieval times, Trier has served as a warehouse and distribution center for thousands of liters of wine fermented in its underground cellars. At least 40 of these cellars lie beneath the streets of the city and surrounding suburbs and hamlets. The oldest and most venerable of these is **Vereinigte Hospitien,** Krahnen Ufer Strasse 19 (☎ **0651/94-50**), which only accepts visitors who phone in advance for a reservation. Be warned that if it's inconvenient for this outfit to receive you, they'll be quick to tell you. The quickest way to arrange a tour of this cellar, or any of its competitors, is to enlist the aid of the tourist office. The staff there knows which group of vintners is receptive to visits; they'll make suggestions as to the best spots for drop-ins.

✪ **Dom (St. Peter's Cathedral).** Domfriehof (north of the Palace Gardens and Basilica). ☎ **0651/7-58-01.** Cathedral free; Treasury 2DM ($1). Cathedral Apr–Oct, daily 6am–6pm, Nov–Mar, daily 6am–5:30pm. Treasury Apr–Oct, Mon–Sat 10am–5pm; Nov–Mar, Mon–Sat 10am–noon and 2–5:30pm.

From the outside, this cathedral, with its rough-hewn stonework, looks more like a fortress than a church. This is the third church to stand on the site of the former 4th-century palace of the Empress Helena, mother of Constantine. It was begun in 1035 in Romanesque style. The later Gothic and baroque additions only helped to pull the ecclesiastical architecture into a timeless unity. The interior combines baroque decoration with Gothic vaulting and archways. On the south aisle is a magnificent tympanum depicting Christ between the Virgin and St. Peter. The Treasury Museum contains many important works of art, including the 10th-century St. Andrew's Altar, an unusual portable altar made of wood and covered with gold and ivory.

✪ **Liebfrauenkirche.** Liebfrauenstrasse 2. ☎ **0651/75-801.** Free admission. Daily 8am–noon and 2–6pm.

This parish church, separated from the cathedral by a narrow passageway, is more pleasing aesthetically than its older neighbor. Begun in 1235, it was among the first examples of French Gothic architecture. The ground plan is in the shape of a Greek cross, creating a circular effect with all points equidistant from the central high altar. The structure is supported by 12 circular columns, rather than the typical open buttresses. The interior is bathed in sunlight, which streams through the high transoms. Although its restoration after the war changed some of the effect of the central construction, it's still unique among German churches.

Some of the church's more important works of art are now in the **Bischöfliches Museum,** Windstrasse 8 (☎ **0651/7-10-52-55**). The sepulcher of Bishop Karl von Metternich, who represented the archbishopric during the Thirty Years' War, is among the most interesting of those remaining. The museum is open Monday to Saturday 9am to 1pm and 2 to 5pm, Sunday 1 to 5pm; admission is 2DM ($1) for adults and 1DM (50¢) for children.

Karl-Marx-Haus. Brückenstrasse 10. ☎ **0651/4-30-11.** Admission 3DM ($1.50) adults, 2DM ($1) children. Apr–Oct, Mon 1–6pm, Tues–Sun 10am–6pm; Nov–Mar, Mon 3–6pm, Tues–Sun 10am–1pm and 3–6pm. Bus: 1, 2, 3, or 4.

This old burgher's house is where Karl Marx (1818–83) was born and where he lived until he finished school in 1835. The museum has exhibits on Marx's personal history, volumes of poetry, original letters, and photographs with personal dedications. There's also a collection of rare first editions and international editions of his works, as well as exhibits on the development of socialism in the 19th century. In the vicinity of the museum is a study center, **Studienzentrum Karl-Marx-Haus,** Johannestrasse 28 (same phone), for research on Marx and Engels.

✪ **Rheinisches Landesmuseum.** Weimarer Allee 1 (between the Imperial Baths and the Basilica, at the edge of the Palace Gardens). ☎ **0651/9-77-40.** Admission 7DM ($3.50) adults, 3DM ($1.50) children. Tues–Fri 9:30am–5pm, Sat–Sun 10:30am–5pm. Bus: 2, 6, 16, 26, or 30.

This is one of the outstanding museums of Roman antiquities north of the Alps. Numerous reliefs from funerary monuments show daily life in Roman times. The museum's most popular exhibit is the *Mosel Ship,* a sculpture of a wine-bearing vessel crowning a big burial monument of the 3rd century A.D. Also on display are many mosaics and frescoes, ceramics, glassware, a 2,700-year-old Egyptian casket complete with mummy, an outstanding numismatic collection, and prehistoric and medieval art and sculpture.

BOAT TOURS

Trier owes much of its majesty to the river that nurtured its medieval commerce. You can take a day cruise for a waterside view of its historic banks. Easter to October, boats depart daily at 9:15am from the city docks (Zurlauben) for a 4-hour trip along the river to **Bernkastel** (see above), passing vineyards, wine hamlets, historic churches, and semiruined fortresses en route. Participants spend 2 hours exploring Bernkastel before returning on the same boat to Trier, arriving back at 7:40pm. The cost is 44DM ($22) per person.

If you don't want to spend so much time on the river, you can take a shorter, hour-long excursion to the nearby historic hamlet of **Pfalzel.** Boats depart from Trier's docks daily Easter to October at 11am, 12:30pm, 2pm, 3:15pm, and 4:30pm. One-way costs 8DM ($4); round-trip is 10DM ($5). You can prolong your hour-long experience with a walk along the riverbanks in Pfalzel or can return almost immediately after your arrival on the next boat.

For information on either of these excursions, contact the tourist office (see above) or the boat operator **Gebrüder Kolb** (☎ 0651/2-63-17 in Trier, or 02673/15-15 at its corporate headquarters in the nearby town of Briedern).

WHERE TO STAY

EXPENSIVE

Dorint Porta Nigra. Porta-Nigra-Platz 1, 54292 Trier (across from the Roman ruins). ☎ **0651/2-70-10.** Fax 0651/2-70-11-70. www.dorint.de/trier. E-mail: infozgftri@dorint.com. 106 units. MINIBAR TV TEL. 250DM–310DM ($125–$155) double; 465DM ($232.50) suite. Rates include buffet breakfast. AE, DC, MC, V. Parking 16DM ($8). Bus: 3.

The six-story Dorint Porta Nigra combines style, comfort, and location, making it one of the two leading choices in Trier (the other is the Ramada, see below). Most rooms have sitting areas and ornately tiled baths. All were freshly renovated in 1999.

Dining/Diversions: Porta is the hotel's gourmet restaurant, and Forum is where breakfast and lunch are served. International and regional cuisine are featured in both. A cafe with an entire wall of glass provides a view of the Roman ruins. The hotel also has a casino offering roulette and blackjack.

Amenities: Room service, laundry, dry cleaning.

Ramada Hotel Trier. Kaiserstrasse 29, 54290 Trier. ☎ **800/854-7854** in the U.S., or 0651/9-49-50. Fax 0651/9-49-56-66. www.ramada-hotels.com/zqftr. E-mail: ramada.trier@marriott.com. 130 units. MINIBAR TV TEL. 182DM–196DM ($91–$98) double; 310DM–350DM ($155–$175) suite. AE, DC, MC, V. Parking 10DM ($5) outdoors; 20DM ($10) in garage. Bus: 1, 2, or 12.

This is the most important hotel built in Trier in many a year. It's located in the heart of the sightseeing zone, near the old Roman monuments. It may be too sleek and impersonal for some tastes, but it's serviceable in every way. Rooms are spacious, with streamlined modern furnishings. Some 42 have air-conditioning.

Dining: The Park Restaurant offers an international cuisine. In summer, you can dine on the terrace.

Amenities: Baby-sitting, laundry, room service, first-aid room.

MODERATE

Kessler. Brückenstrasse 23, 54290 Trier (next to the Karl-Marx-Haus). ☎ **0651/97-81-70.** Fax 0651/9-78-17-97. E-mail: Hotel-Kessler.Trier@t-online.de. 22 units. MINIBAR TV TEL.

140DM–250DM ($70–$125) double; 250DM–350DM ($125–$175) triple. Rates include buffet breakfast. AE, MC, V. Parking 5DM ($2.50) outside; 20DM ($10) in garage. Bus: 1, 2, 3, or 4.

The sunny Kessler is managed by Jörg Müller, who speaks English and does everything he can do to make your stay pleasant. Rooms are small but attractively maintained and furnished in a clean, modern style. Guests gather in the evening in the hotel's cozy bar. The breakfast is very good.

Petrisberg. Sickingenstrasse 11, 54296 Trier (a 10-min. walk from the Altstadt). ☎ **0651/ 46-40.** Fax 0651/4-64-50. www.freenet.de/HotelPetrisberg.de. 37 units. TV TEL. 170DM–190DM ($85–$95) double. Rates include buffet breakfast. MC, V. Free outdoor parking; 10DM ($5) in garage. Bus: 6.

Petrisberg is beautifully situated at a point where a forest, a vineyard, and a private park meet. Each room has a view of the greenery outside. The ground-floor Weinstube is the gathering place for many locals, particularly on weekends.

✪ **Römischer Kaiser.** Am Porta Nigra Platz 6, 54292 Trier. ☎ **0651/9-77-00.** Fax 0651/ 97-70-99. 43 units. MINIBAR TV TEL. 190DM–210DM ($95–$105) double. Rates include buffet breakfast. AE, DC, MC, V. Free parking. Bus: 1, 2, 3, or 4.

This hotel offers cozily furnished rooms in a prime location. Renovation in the mid-'90s restored the building to its original beauty as a 19th-century patrician house. The hotel's restaurant features an international cuisine, with both three-course and à la carte meals. Food is served daily noon to 10pm. Because of the hotel's location, visitors touring the area often drop in for a meal.

✪ **Villa Hügel.** Bernhardstrasse 14, 54295 Trier. ☎ **0651/3-30-66.** Fax 0651/3-79-58. 34 units. MINIBAR TV TEL. 170DM–250DM ($85–$125) double. Rates include buffet breakfast. AE, DC, MC, V. Free outdoor parking; 10DM ($5) in garage. Bus: 2 or 8.

This lovely, white, art nouveau villa, built in 1914, has more style and ambience than some of the more highly rated hotels, such as the Ramada. The windows overlook either a private garden with old trees or the city. Rooms are spacious and high-ceilinged. Four double rooms are so large that they're almost suites, making them favorites with families. You can order food and beverages on the two terraces. Facilities include a swimming pool and sauna.

INEXPENSIVE

Hotel Monopol. Bahnhofsplatz 7, 54292 Trier (across from the Hauptbahnhof). ☎ **0651/ 71-40-90.** Fax 0651/7-14-09-10. 35 units, 24 with shower or bath. 130DM ($65) double without shower or bath; 150DM ($75) double with shower or bath. Rates include buffet breakfast. No credit cards. Parking 5DM ($2.50). Bus: 1, 2, or 12.

If you're seeking inexpensive lodging, try the four-story Monopol. It's a completely updated, century-old hotel with a cooperative staff. Its rooms are both good-sized and well maintained, although completely sterile in decor. Rooms with shower or bath also contain a TV and telephone.

WHERE TO DINE

Palais Kesselstatt. Liebfrauenstrasse 10 (next to the cathedral). ☎ **0651/4-02-04.** Reservations recommended. Main dining room, main courses 27DM–42DM ($13.50–$21); fixed-price menus 55DM ($27.50); Weinstube platters 15.50DM–20DM ($7.75–$10); wine 3DM–9DM ($1.50–$4.50) per glass. AE, MC, V. Restaurant Tues–Sun 11:30am–2pm and 6–9:30pm. Weinstube, daily 10am–midnight. Bus: 1. GERMAN/INTERNATIONAL.

This is the most unusual and interesting restaurant in Trier. The pink-sided baroque building was originally the residence of the count of Kesselstatt. Inside, the three high-ceilinged dining rooms include the former chapel and the Kaminstube (chimney area), which has an enormous fireplace. Menu items are made with fresh ingredients and change with the seasons. They might include fresh greens with slices of duck breast in herb vinaigrette, consommé with strips of fillet steak, fillet of turbot with prawns in a vegetable sauce, and a dessert specialty of Bavarian cream with strawberry sorbet, served with fresh marinated strawberries.

The restaurant prides itself on stocking only Rieslings produced in nearby vineyards—an excellent selection. Anyone interested in sampling the region's legendary wines in a less-formal setting can head for the Weinstube. Here you can order glasses of wine, as well as simple platters of traditional German and international food.

✪ Pfeffermühle. Zurlaubener Ufer 76, Zurlauben. ☎ **0651/2-61-33.** Reservations required. Main courses 42DM–47DM ($21–$23.50); fixed-price menus 88DM–120DM ($44–$60). MC, V. Tues–Sat noon–2pm; Mon–Sat 6:30–9:30pm. Closed Dec 24–Jan 4. Bus: 5. FRENCH.

This is clearly the best restaurant in Trier. Siegberg and Angelika Walde use fresh ingredients and maintain a bright, well-decorated dining room with a river view. Their nouvelle French cuisine is delectable. Try the assorted fish, cooked à point, with homemade noodles, followed by petit fours. The list of Mosel wines is extensive. In summer, guests can enjoy their meals on a terrace.

Zum Domstein. Hauptmarkt 5. ☎ **0651/7-44-90.** Reservations recommended. Main courses 18DM–30DM ($9–$15); fixed-menus 45DM–54DM ($22.50–$27). MC, V. Daily 9am–midnight, with hot food served daily 11:30am–2pm and 6–9:30pm. Bus: 1, 2, or 12. RHINELAND.

Charming Zum Domstein is permeated with an old-time sense of bounty. It overlooks the flower stands and the fountain of Trier's central plaza. Ask for one of the wine tastings, which will get you either three glasses of wine (from the Mosel, the Ruwer, and the Saar) for a combined total of 8DM to 15DM ($4 to $7.50); or a half-dozen very small glasses showcasing separate regional vintages for a combined total of 11.50DM ($5.75). In addition, at least 10 regional whites and 6 regional and French reds are sold by the glass, while hundreds more, in bottles, are stored within the cellars.

The food here is as tempting as the wine; a typically savory offering is a platter of fillet of trout in a Riesling sauce or knuckle of lamb with vegetables. All the dishes are redolent with old-fashioned flavors; some are even said to have been enjoyed by the Romans, often with rich sauces. In winter, you'll want to find a spot near the huge tiled stove.

You might also want to look at the **Römischer Weinkeller,** originally built around A.D. 326. Original Roman artifacts, many connected with food and cooking, decorate the room. Dishes here are prepared according to recipes attributed to Marcus Gavius Apicius, said to have been the foremost chef at the court of the emperor Tiberius. Set menus in the cellar range from 27DM to 55DM ($13.50 to $27.50).

TRIER AFTER DARK

The cathedral hosts a series of free **organ recitals** in May, June, August, and September. Contact the tourist office (see above) for schedules.

TUFA (☎ **0651/718-24-12**) presents theater, established touring bands, and the occasional disco. Another student hangout, **Blaues Blut,** Pferdermarkt (☎ **0651/4-12-57**), features blue lights and tables covered in imported Turkish tile; outside, the terrace includes some of the only shade trees in the entire city (short-sighted architectural designers removed the rest). Open Monday to Saturday 9am to 2am and Sunday 10am to 2am. Thursday to Saturday there's dancing and DJs. A club with a beer garden, **Exhaus,** Zurmainer Strasse 114 (☎ **0651/2-51-91**), has both dancing and bands, usually Wednesday to Saturday. Days vary, but the hours are 8pm to 2am. Call to see what's scheduled. Cover is 5DM to 20DM ($2.50 to $10).

Jazz aficionados gather at **Milton's Playhouse,** Jakobstrasse 13 (☎ **0651/4-91-32**), open daily 10am to at least 1am. The aptly named **Irish Pub,** Jakobstrasse 10 (☎ **0651/4-95-39**), serves toasted sandwiches, along with Guinness and Harp. Many evenings you'll often find an Irish, English, or German band entertaining a rowdy drinking crowd.

The area's newest nightlife hotspot is **Riverside,** a complex of bars and restaurants on the city's outskirts, about a mile north of the town center. The most popular place here is **Disco Riverside,** Zur Mainer Strasse 173 (☎ **0651/2-10-06**), which draws a high-energy crowd of local dance enthusiasts Wednesday to Sunday, beginning around 10:30pm. Cover is 15DM ($7.50) and usually includes the first drink.

15 Bremen, Lower Saxony & North Hesse

The area between Frankfurt and Hamburg is Germany's most neglected tourist destination, yet it holds many discoveries. Some of Germany's best-preserved medieval towns, as well as some major spas, lie in the flatlands and rolling hills of Lower Saxony and North Hesse. The character of the area ranges widely, from the bustle of the port of Bremen to the isolation of the Lüneburg Heath.

Here you'll also find the beautiful Harz Mountains, perhaps the country's last stronghold of paganism, still a land of legends and fanciful names. It is said that the last bear was killed in the Harz in 1705, the last lynx in 1817, but there are still wildcats, badgers, deer, and foxes, as well as many limestone caves. The beech tree that grows in the Harz range has an unusual size and great beauty, and walnut trees abound.

1 Bremen

119km (74 miles) SW of Hamburg, 122km (76 miles) NW of Hannover

Bremen, Germany's oldest coastal city, is second only to Hamburg among German ports. As soon as you arrive at "this ancient town by the gray river," you see how closely Bremen is tied to the sea. The sights and smells of coffee, cacao, tropical fruit, lumber, and tobacco give the city an international flavor.

Bremen grew from a little fishing settlement on a sandy slope on the right bank of the river. It was already a significant port when it was made an episcopal see in 787. In the 11th century, under the progressive influence of Archbishop Adalbert, Bremen became known as the "Rome of the North." During the Middle Ages, it was one of the strongest members of the Hanseatic League, and in 1646 it became a free imperial city. It remains one of Europe's most important ports.

ESSENTIALS
GETTING THERE **By Plane** The **Bremen Flughaven** (☎ 0421/ 55950) lies only 3km (2 miles) southeast of the city center (take S-Bahn 5). It is used mainly as a commuter airport for flights within Germany.

By Train Bremen has excellent rail connections with leading German cities. Its **Hauptbahnhof** lies on major rail lines, including Hamburg–Bremen–Osnabrück–Münster and Hannover–Bremen–Bremerhaven. Thirty trains arrive daily from Hamburg (trip time:

0 40 mi
0 40 km

Deutsche
Bucht

76 A7
E45 76
Kiel
A23
76
Lübecker Bucht
E22 Rostock
A19
E55
A1 Lubeck
E47
A241
Wilhelms-
Haven
Bremer-
Haven
A27
A24 E26
Hamburg
25
A29
Bremen
A28
A1
E22
Lüneburg
Elbe
5
189
Oldenberg
A7
4
A27
Celle
A1
E37
214
Hannover
Wolfsburg
189
Weser
Bad
Oeynhausen
A2 217
A39
71
E8
E30
Hildesheim
E34
Hameln
A39
Braunschweig
A33
Detmold
Bad Pyrmont
Salzgitter
A2
1
Bodenwerder
83
Goslar
81
Elbe
Höxter
A7
Seesen
Saale
Bad
Karlshafen
E45 243
A9
E331 A44
Sababurg
Oberweser
A44
Göttingen
Nordhausen
Veckernagen
Münden
Kassel
A49
252
Homburg
4
253
Bad Wildungen
A7
Schwalmstadt
A4
Erfurt
Neustadt
E45
E40
Unstrut
A45
3
Alsfeld
E41
254
Grossenlüder
E49
Lauterbach
Fulda
89
Eisfeld
E51
A5
Gelnhausen
Steinau
A45
A66
279
E451
E41
Hanau
E45
Frankfurt
Aschaffenburg
Schweinfurt
Main
Mainz
A70 E48
Bayreuth
Würzburg
Bamburg

1 hr.), 35 trains from Hannover (trip time: 1 hr.), 13 trains from Berlin (trip time: 5 hr.), and 50 trains from Frankfurt (trip time: 4 hr. 15 min.). For information, call ☎ 01805/99-66-33.

By Bus   Rail travel to Bremen is far more efficient, but the city does have some bus links to other towns. Call ☎ 0421/5363288 for information. The bus station is in front of the railway station.

By Car   Access by car is via the A7 Autobahn east and west and the A27 north and south.

VISITOR INFORMATION   Contact the **Bremen Tourist Center,** Tourist-Information am Bahnhofsplatz (☎ 0421/308000). There's also a second branch at **Liebrauenkircher Hof,** near Markplatz. Both are open Monday to Wednesday 9:30am to 6:30pm, Thursday and Friday 9:30am to 8pm, and Saturday and Sunday 9:30am to 4pm.

GETTING AROUND   For information about public transportation within Bremen, call ☎ 0421/55-96-333. A single ticket, good for one trip on the city's network of buses and trams, costs 3.40DM ($1.70) to most destinations. For 8DM ($4), two adults and up to five children may ride all day on the network. The meter on local taxis begins at 3.60DM ($1.80).

EXPLORING THE CITY
ORGANIZED TOURS

Bremen has both bus and walking tours of its historic sites. **Bus tours,** conducted in both German and English, depart from the Hauptbahnhof daily at 10:30am. They cost 27.50DM ($13.75) for adults and 15DM ($7.50) for children under 12. **Walking tours** depart every day at 2pm, last 2 hours, and cost 10DM ($5). The combination of a morning bus tour with an afternoon walking tour offers a broadly comprehensive overview of Bremen. Tickets should be reserved in advance, then picked up at the tourist office (see "Visitor Information," above).

The city also sponsors **boat trips** around the harbor. They depart from the jetty in front of the Martinikirche every day March to October. You can reach the jetty from Marktplatz by walking southwest along Böttcherstrasse for about 3 minutes. Tours depart at 11:45am, 1:30pm, and 3:15pm. The cost is 15DM ($7.50) for adults and 8DM ($4) for children under 14. For more information, call the tourist office (see above).

THE TOP ATTRACTIONS

The main sights center around **Marktplatz,** the "parlor" of Bremen life for more than 1,000 years. The 9m (30-foot) statue (1404) of the city's protector, Roland, bears the "sword of justice" and a shield decorated with an imperial eagle. Local legend has it that as long as the statue stands in the Marketplace, Bremen will survive as a free city. During World War II, when this area was hard hit by Allied bombs, extensive measures were taken to protect the statue.

Across the square from the Rathaus stands another example of a happy merger of Gothic and Renaissance architecture, the **Schötting,** a 16th-century guild hall used by the chamber of commerce. Somewhat in contrast to these ancient masterpieces is the **Haus der Bürgerschaft,** home of Bremen's Parliament. The 1966 structure was scaled down to fit in with its surroundings. Even though the architecture is a maze of glass, concrete, and steel, it doesn't look entirely out of place.

Dom St. Petri (St. Peter's Cathedral). Sandstrasse 10–12. ☎ 0421/36-50-40. Cathedral free; museum 3DM ($1.50) adults, 2DM ($1) students, seniors, and children; tower 1DM

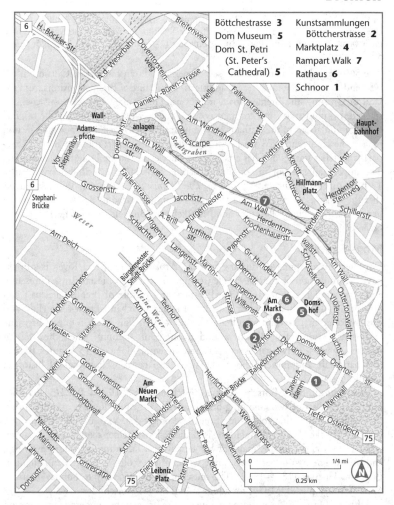

Böttchestrasse	**3**	Kunstsammlungen	
Dom Museum	**5**	Böttcherstrasse	**2**
Dom St. Petri		Marktplatz	**4**
(St. Peter's		Rampart Walk	**7**
Cathedral)	**5**	Rathaus	**6**
		Schnoor	**1**

(50¢). Cathedral Mon–Fri 10am–5pm, Sat 10am–2pm, Sun 2–5pm. Museum May–Oct, Mon–Fri 10am–5pm, Sat 10am–noon, Sun 2–5pm; Nov–Apr, Mon–Fri 11am–4pm, Sat 10am–noon, Sun 2–5pm. Cellar and tower May–Oct, Mon–Fri 10am–5pm, Sat 10am–noon; closed Nov–Apr and holidays. Bus: 30, 31, or 34.

St. Peter's, set back from the square, towers majestically over all other buildings in the Altstadt. Originally designed in 1043 as the archbishop's church, it was rebuilt in the 13th, 16th, and 19th centuries. There's a 12th-century bronze baptismal font in one of the Romanesque crypts. In the Bleikeller (Lead Cellar), there's a bizarre collection of mummified corpses of workers who fell from the roof during the construction. Their bodies were discovered in 1695.

You can also visit the **Dom Museum** (☎ **0421/365-04-11**), which displays artifacts found during the large-scale restoration of the cathedral, including medieval tombs and 15th-century wall paintings. Other exhibits include the remains of an early Romanesque building, and a collection of historic altar implements.

Rathaus. Marktplatz. ☎ **0421/36-10.** Admission 5DM ($2.50) adults, 2.50DM ($1.25) children. For tours, inquire at the tourist office (see "Visitor Information," above). Tours generally begin Mon–Sat 11am, noon, 3pm, 4pm; Sun 11am and noon. Tram: 1, 2, 3, or 5. Bus: 30, 31, or 34.

The 560-year-old Rathaus has seen several periods of transformation. Outside, at the west end, is one of the more recent additions, a sculpture of Bremen's visitors from the land of Grimm—the Bremen town musicians. The donkey, dog, cat, and cock are stacked, pyramid style, in a constant pose for the ever-present cameras. The original Gothic foundations of the Rathaus remain basically unchanged, but the upper section reflects the 17th-century Weser Renaissance style in the facade; the tall windows alternate with relief statues of Charlemagne and the electors of the Holy Roman Empire. The upper hall, part of the original structure, contains a beautifully carved early-17th-century oak staircase. A mural of *The Judgment of Solomon* (1537) reminds us that the hall was originally a council chamber and courtroom. Below the lower hall lies the historic wine cellar, the "good Ratskeller of Bremen" (see "Where to Dine," below).

MORE SIGHTS

Böttcherstrasse (tram: 4), running from Marktplatz to the Weser River, is a brick-paved reproduction of a medieval alley, complete with shops, restaurants, a museum, and galleries. The street was designed to present a picture of Bremen life, past and present. It was the brainchild of a wealthy Bremen merchant, Ludwig Roselius, and was dedicated in 1926 and rebuilt after World War II. This artery is one of Bremen's biggest attractions. Try to visit around noon, 3pm, or 6pm, when the Meissen bells strung between two gables set up a chorus of chimes for a full 15 minutes. Besides fine handcraft and pottery shops, the street also contains buildings of historical significance.

Kunstsammlungen Böttcherstrasse, Böttcherstrasse 8–10 (☎ **0421/33-65-066;** tram: 4), consists of two adjoining buildings. The Roselius House is a 16th-century merchant's home with a collection of medieval objets d'art and furniture. Next door, the Paula-Becker-Modersohn House is dedicated to Bremen's outstanding painter (1876–1907) and contains many of her best works, including paintings, drawings, and prints. The two upper floors house works of the sculptor, painter, and architect Bernhard Hoetger (1874–1949). The museum is open Tuesday to Sunday 11am to 6pm. Admission is 8DM ($4) for adults and 4DM ($2) for children.

Schnoor (Tram: 4, 5, or 6), the old quarter of Bremen, has undergone restoration by the custodian of ancient monuments. The cottages of this east-end district, once homes of simple fishermen, have been rented to artists and artisans in an effort to revive many old arts and crafts. Sightseers visit not only for the atmosphere but also for the unusual restaurants, shops, and art galleries.

Rampart Walk (Tram: 4, 5, or 6) is a peaceful green park where the ramparts protecting this Hanseatic city used to stand. Its gardens divide the Altstadt from the newer extensions of the city. The park is just a few short blocks from Marktplatz, along the canal (once Bremen's crown-shaped moat). Its major attraction is an ancient windmill that's stillfunctioning.

SHOPPING

Bremen has thrived on the salty air of business and commerce since it was founded. Today, you'll find lots of shopping options along two shopping streets, **Obernstrasse** and **Sögestrasse,** as well as dozens of boutique-inspired gift shops in the **Schnoor.** The city's cutest stuffed teddy bears, available in all sizes and degrees of fuzziness, are sold at **Bärenhaus,** Stabendanstrasse 9 (☎ 0421/32-64-03; tram: 4, 5, or 6), for prices that begin at 25DM ($12.50) for your garden-variety bear and can go much, much higher. Next door is **Rapunzel,** Schnoor 17 (same phone), an emporium for gift items, as well as T-shirts, souvenirs, books, and marionettes modeled after figures from the Brothers Grimm.

The best shop for women's fashions is **Roland Kleidung,** Sögestrasse 18–20 (☎ 0421/1-25-36; tram: 4, 5, or 6), although the town's largest department store, **Karstadt,** Obernstrasse 1 (☎ 0421/3-07-10; tram: 4, 5, or 6), also stocks an impressive selection of less expensive garments. Antiques, including some brass fixtures salvaged from old ships, are sold at **Antikitäten B&M,** Fedelhörn 19 (☎ 0421/328282; tram: 10). Two art galleries that contain sometimes riveting modern art are **Gallery Hubert,** Söge-strasse at Pelzstrasse 4 (☎ 0421/1-65-55-44; tram: 4, 5, or 6); and **Art Gallery,** Böttcherstrasse 8–20 (☎ 0421/33-88-20; tram: 4, 5, or 6), both of which represent artists from the region and throughout middle Europe.

Shoes are the best buy in Bremen, and **Leder-Koopman,** Georgstrasse 56 (☎ 0471/30-28-29; tram: 4, 5, or 6), is the best representative of the trade. The company has been making quality wallets, belts, bags, and other leather products for 100 years. Visit their shop to admire a level of craftsmanship that has become a rare commodity, and chances are you won't leave empty-handed. Bargain hunters swarm over the city's riverfront **flea markets.** The Weserflohmarkt is held at the Schlactel and Weser promenade every Saturday 8am to 5pm; on Sunday, the action shifts to Burgerweide 8am to 2pm.

WHERE TO STAY
VERY EXPENSIVE

✪ **Park Hotel Bremen.** Im Burgerpark, 28209 Bremen. ☎ **0421/3-40-80.** Fax 0421/3-40-86-02. www.parkhotel-bremen.de. E-mail: relax@park-hotel-bremen.de. 157 units. MINIBAR TV TEL. 525DM–610DM ($262.50–$305) double; 900DM ($450) suite. Rates include buffet breakfast. AE, DC, MC, V. Free parking in front of the hotel; 30DM ($15) in the garage. Tram: 5 or 6. Bus: 26.

This hotel is without question the most outstanding and charming in Bremen. It occupies an enviable site, in a park whose meandering lakes, exotic trees, and zoo are the pride of the city. It's also just a short ride from the center of town. The hotel's terra-cotta dome and evenly proportioned side wings were rebuilt in 1955 to emulate a turn-of-the-20th-century pleasure pavilion. Rooms are generally spacious and well appointed, with large windows overlooking the park.

Dining/Diversions: Among the dignified public rooms are a bar and three restaurants, one of which occupies an elegant terrace overlooking the lake. The gourmet Park Restaurant serves continental cuisine. There's also an informal bistro, Buten und Binnen.

Amenities: Room service, baby-sitting, laundry, dry cleaning, terrace and garden, jogging track, hair dryers; horseback riding is arranged, and free bicycles are provided.

MODERATE

Hotel Munte am Stadtwald. Parkallee 299, 28213 Bremen, in the Burgerpark, about 2.5km (1¹/₂ miles) from the center. ☎ **0421/2-20-20.** Fax 421/21-98-76. www.hotel-munte.de. E-mail: info@hotel-munte.de. 134 units. MINIBAR TV TEL. 195DM ($97.50) ground-floor double; 290DM ($145) upper-floor double. Rates include buffet breakfast. AE, DC, MC, V. Free outdoor parking; 8DM ($4) in garage. Bus: 22 or 23.

You'll think you're in the country at this brick hotel because it fronts directly on one of Bremen's biggest parks. Inside you'll find a wood-ceilinged pool area with a sauna, a steam room, a sympathetic Weinstube (called "The Fox"), and a sunny dining room with a panoramic view of the woods. The handsome rooms range from medium to spacious.

Hotel zur Post. Bahnhofsplatz 11, 28195 Bremen. ☎ **800/528-1234** in the U.S. and Canada, or 0421/3-05-90. Fax 0421/3-05-95-91. 194 units. MINIBAR TV TEL. 215DM–300DM ($107.50–$150) double; from 400DM ($200) suite. Rates include buffet breakfast. AE, DC, MC, V. Parking 19DM ($9.50). Tram: 1, 5, 6, or 10.

A longtime favorite, Hotel zur Post offers top-notch facilities and comfort, as well as Bremen's leading restaurant, L'Orchidée, and two other dining spots. Rooms are first rate and slightly larger than average. Laundry, dry cleaning, and room service are available, and the hotel also has a tropical fitness club, swimming pool, hairdresser, and beauty salon. It's an ideal choice for train passengers.

INEXPENSIVE

Hotel Mercure Columbus. Bahnhofsplatz 5–7, 28195 Bremen. ☎ **0421/3-01-20.** Fax 0421/1-53-69. www.hotels-bremen.de. E-mail: H0879@accor.hotels.com. 148 units. MINIBAR TV TEL. 203DM–246DM ($101.50–$123) double; 297DM ($148.50) suite. Rates include buffet breakfast. AE, DC, MC, V. Parking 12DM ($6). Tram: 1, 5, 6, or 10.

Mercure Columbus offers attractive and tasteful rooms. An elegant recent renovation has set a higher standard for this hotel, putting it on the same footing as Munte am Stadtwald or Hotel zur Post. Leisure facilities include a sauna with a relaxing room and a solarium; personal services include dry cleaning, laundry, and room service. The Hanseaten Bar is a popular rendezvous.

Residence. Hohenlohestrasse 42, 28209 Bremen. ☎ **0421/34-10-29.** Fax 0421/34-23-22. 30 units. MINIBAR TV TEL. 179DM–199DM ($89.50–$99.50) double. Rates include buffet breakfast. AE, DC, MC, V. Free outdoor parking; 12DM ($6) in garage. Tram: 1, 5, 6, or 10.

Residence advertises itself as an art deco hotel. The elegant public areas have high ceilings with polished crisscrossed timbers and chandeliers. On the premises you'll find a sunny breakfast room, as well as a Nordic sauna and a solarium. Rooms are comfortably furnished but small. There's also a 24-hour snack and drink service.

WHERE TO DINE

As a seaport, Bremen has developed its own style of cooking, concentrating much of its effort, naturally, on seafood from Scandinavia and the North Sea.

VERY EXPENSIVE

✪ **L'Orchidée.** In the Hotel zur Post, Bahnhofsplatz 11. ☎ **0421/3-05-90.** Reservations required. Main courses 49DM–58DM ($24.50–$29); fixed-price dinner 107DM ($53.50) for 5 courses, 147DM ($73.50) for 7 courses. AE, DC, MC, V. Tues–Sat 6:30–10pm. Closed 2 weeks at Easter and 4 weeks sometime in summer. Tram: 1, 5, 6, or 10. FRENCH/MODERN GERMAN.

L'Orchidée, on the 6th floor of the Hotel zur Post (see above), has an elegantly sophisticated gold, cream, and black decor to go with its candles, silverware, and fine porcelain. Year after year this hotel restaurant emerges at the top in Bremen. Veteran chefs watch over a well-trained kitchen crew, and the service is sophisticated and skillful. The dishes are simply delicious. Try the terrine of smoked eel and shrimps followed either by fillet of turbot with lobster or breast of pigeon in a red-wine sauce. The desserts are made fresh daily, and the wine list is extensive.

EXPENSIVE

Meierei im Burgerpark. Im Burgerpark. ☎ **0421/3-40-86-19.** Reservations required. Main courses 29DM–46DM ($14.50–$23). AE, DC, MC, V. Tues–Sun noon–2:30pm and 6:30–10pm. Tram: 6. CONTINENTAL.

This lovely restaurant in the center of a city park is managed by the Park Hotel (see above). Locals often combine a meal here with a promenade in the park. The restaurant occupies what was originally a local aristocrat's summer house, sheathed in lacy gingerbread and ringed with ornate verandas. It contains four dining rooms furnished in Hanseatic style. The food doesn't match the refined cuisine of the Park Restaurant, but we like the setting. Typical, and very good, dishes include fresh fish, consommé with scallops and saffron, fried breast of duck filled with herbs, sautéed squab with forest mushroom risotto, and medaillons of monkfish with orange butter and basil sauce. Coffee and pastries are served every afternoon.

✪ **Ratskeller.** Am Markt (in the Rathaus). ☎ **0421/32-16-76.** Reservations recommended. Main courses 30DM–40DM ($15–$20) in the Ratskeller Restaurant; 20DM–40DM ($10–$20) in the Ratskeller Bistro. Set menus 58.50DM–69DM ($29.25–$34.50) in the restaurant. Restaurant daily noon–2:30pm and 7–10:30pm; bistro daily 11am–midnight. AE, DC, MC, V. Tram: 1, 3, 5, 24, or 25. GERMAN/INTERNATIONAL.

This Ratskeller is one of Germany's most celebrated—and certainly one of the best. It's traditional for friends to gather in the evening over a good bottle of Mosel or Rhine wine (no beer is served). Appetizers include an assortment of smoked fish as well as creamy fish soup flavored with saffron; main courses often include fried pike perch in a basil sauce and chicken ragout Bremen-style (in a crayfish sauce with calves' sweetbreads, tongue, mushrooms, sausages, and a vegetable risotto). The outstanding wine list is one of the longest lists of German vintages in the world. Some of the decorative kegs have contained wine for nearly 200 years. There's also a less formal bistro, with a limited list of less expensive traditional dishes that include *Laubskaus* and simple platters of fresh fish.

MODERATE

Alte Gilde. Ansgaritorstrasse 24 (entrance on Hutfilterstrasse). ☎ **0421/17-17-12.** Reservations recommended. Main courses 18DM–26DM ($9–$13); fixed-price lunch 25DM–35DM ($12.50–$17.50); fixed-price dinner 27DM–40DM ($13.50–$20). AE, DC, MC, V. Mon–Sat 11am–3pm and 7–10:30pm. Tram: 2 or 3. Bus: 6, 25, or 26. CONTINENTAL.

Alte Gilde is located in one of the most ornately decorated houses in Bremen. In spite of the new building surrounding it, the 17th-century structure, with its gilt gargoyles and sea serpents, clings tenaciously to the past. The restaurant is in the vaulted cellar. The chef prepares many fresh fish dishes, as well as pork steak à la Kempinski, with poached eggs and béarnaise sauce—a lot of diners still go for this grandmotherly favorite.

✪ **Grashoff's Bistro.** Contrescarpe 80. ☎ **0421/1-47-40.** Reservations recommended. Main courses 40DM–45DM ($20–$22.50). DC, V. Mon–Fri 10am–6:30pm, Sat 10am–2pm. Tram: 4, 5, or 6. GERMAN.

This restaurant is well managed, charming, and concerned with quality and ambience. Its only real flaw is that it's never open for dinner—instead, it caters to mobs of office workers and shoppers at lunchtime. You'll get a distinct sense of the arts here, and a few memories of Paris as well, thanks to dozens of framed pictures hung edge-to-edge across the cream-colored, bistro-inspired walls. Menu items include a succulent version of spaghetti with lobster; flank steak in a pepper sauce; an oft-changing roster of fresh fish, such as turbot and fillet of sole; and desserts such as crème brûlée, fresh pastries, and tarts.

Pappagallo. Goetheplatz 4 (near the town center). ☎ **0421/32-79-63.** Reservations recommended. Main courses 31DM–40DM ($15.50–$20). DC, MC, V. Mon–Fri noon–2:30pm; Mon–Sat 6–11pm. Tram: 2 or 3. ITALIAN.

This is the best Italian restaurant in Bremen; it's a welcome break from a steady diet of north German cuisine. It occupies a Tuscan-style manor originally built by a local industrialist in 1842. Its interior is decorated in a radically modern style that might have been inspired by Milanese minimalism. The angularity is offset by succulent food prepared in sophisticated but time-tested ways. The menu changes every 2 weeks and reflects whatever is in season. Examples might include Sicily-inspired spaghetti Norma, rich with eggplant and mozzarella and herbs; spaghetti with fresh artichoke hearts and asparagus tips; risotto with scampi; and pasta with Parma ham and asparagus.

BREMEN AFTER DARK

Bremen nightlife offers a full range of activities. Many pubs and clubs, including those geared toward the gay community, are located in the **Ostertorsteinweg** district (Tram: 10).

THE PERFORMING ARTS   Classical concerts, opera, and dance performances by visiting companies are held in the **Theater am Goetheplatz** complex, Am Goetheplatz 1–3 (☎ **0421/365-3333;** tram: 2 or 3). Call for a list of scheduled performers, ticket prices, and available seating. One of its stages, Schauspielhaus (☎ **0421/ 3-65-30**), houses a theatrical company that occasionally performs in English. Tickets are 20DM to 45DM ($10 to $22.50) during the September-to-June season. Opera and other musical performances are scheduled in the **Musiktheater,** Am Goetheplatz (☎ **0421/3-65-33-33;** tram: 2 or 3), where tickets are 20DM to 60DM ($10 to $30). Experimental theater and modern dance can be found in the **Concordia,** Schwachauser Heerstrasse (☎ **0421/365-30;** tram: 1), where a seat costs 25DM to 45DM ($12.50 to $22.50). To attend productions of the Bremen Shakespeare Company, head for the **Theater am Leibnitzplatz,** Friedrich-Ebert-Strasse (☎ **0421/ 50-03-33;** tram: 6), where tickets are 25DM to 47DM ($12.50 to $23.50).

BARS   An early evening bar, **Achims Beck Haus,** Carl-Ronning-Strasse 1 (☎ **0421/ 1-55-55;** tram: 4, 5, or 6), is a gathering place for drinks and simple pub fare. Open Monday to Thursday 10am to 11pm and Friday and Saturday 10am to 2am. An art-scene hangout with a large street-front terrace and a sometimes rowdy clientele, **Litfass,** Ostertorsteinweg 22 (☎ **0421/70-32-92;** tram: 2 or 3), also has the longest bar in town. It serves breakfast, snacks, coffee, and beer. Open Sunday to Thursday 10am to 2am; Friday and Saturday 10am to 4am.

CASINO   Bremen's centrally located casino, **Bremer Spielbank,** 3 Boettcher Strasse 385 (☎ **0421/329-000;** tram: 4, 5, or 6), contains roulette and blackjack tables. Admission is 5DM ($2.85), and a passport is required, as are jackets and ties for men. Open daily 3pm to 3am.

DANCE CLUBS   The place to dance is **Delight,** Am Liebfrauenkirchhof 23 (☎ **0172/42-08-167;** tram: 4, 5, or 6), a basement club where the DJs play house and hip-hop. Weekends generally bring theme parties. The club opens at 10pm Wednesday and Thursday and 11pm Friday and Saturday; there's no set closing time. On weeknights, the cover is 10DM to 15DM ($5 to $7.50); on theme nights, it can be as much as 25DM ($12.50). The club is closed in August. In winter, **Modernes,** Neustadtwall 28 (☎ **0421/50-55-53;** tram: 1 or 8), is a movie house during the week, with dancing and live music on the weekend. The rest of the year, bands usually play 7pm to 11pm; afterwards, it's a dance club. Dancing costs 10DM ($5); admission to live music is 18DM to 40DM ($9 to $20). Twice monthly there's a free show.

GAY CLUBS   Much of the gay nightlife in and around Bremen is diverted into the clubs of nearby Hamburg, but there's still a few good spots. **Thealit,** Im Krummen Arm 1 (☎ **0421/70-16-32;** tram: 10), is the leading lesbian gathering place in town.

It offers platters of German and international food, priced around 17DM to 25DM ($8.50 to $12.50) every Monday to Saturday 6pm to 1am. Another gay bar of note, mostly for men, is **Rat und Tat**, Theodor-Körner-Strasse 1 (☎ **0421/70-00-08;** tram: 10).

LIVE MUSIC   For music in a bar setting, check out the band line-up at **Aladin's,** Hannoverschestrasse 11 (☎ **0421/43-51-50;** bus: 40), which also houses a two-room disco and a bar with rock 'n' roll memorabilia (it might remind you of a Hard Rock Cafe). Open Wednesday to Saturday 10pm to 7am; cover is 7DM ($3.50). **Moments,** Vordem Stein Tor 65 (☎ **0421/78007;** tram: 2, 3, or 10), hosts live rhythm and blues and jazz for a crowd of loyal regulars. Cover is 25DM to 35DM ($12.50 to $17.50) for most shows. The place functions as a disco on some nights; cover is then 10DM ($5.70). The **Club Kernerwahl,** Kernerwahl 1 (☎ **0421/70-58-52;** tram: 2, 3, or 10), also has live music. Both Moments and Kernerwahl are open Tuesday to Sunday 8pm till dawn.

VARIETY   Popular with children and adults, the ambitious puppet theater **Theatrium,** Bleicherstrasse 28 (☎ **0421/361-61-81;** tram: 2 or 3), produces entertaining interpretations of books, plays, and movies, ranging from classical works to Woody Allen. Tickets cost 18DM to 35DM ($9 to $17.50). In the same building, **Theater im Schnoor** (☎ **0421/32-60-54)** presents cabaret and underground theater productions, with tickets ranging from 15DM to 35DM ($7.50 to $17.50).

2 Lüneburg

124km (77 miles) NE of Hannover, 132km (82 miles) E of Bremen, 55km (34 miles) SE of Hamburg

Motorists driving south from Scandinavia through the Baltic port of Lübeck often find themselves on the Old Salt Road leading to the Hanseatic city of Lüneburg. This was the route over which the "white gold" of Lüneburg's salt mines was transported to the Scandinavian countries during the Middle Ages. Because of its heavy salt deposits, Lüneburg became a spa, which it remains today. In the **Kurpark** is a bathing house where visitors can take brine mud baths. In the **spa gardens,** there are indoor swimming pools, sauna baths, and tennis courts.

   Lüneburg is also the ideal starting point for excursions into the **Lüneburg Heath,** which is especially beautiful in late summer, when the heather is in bloom.

ESSENTIALS
GETTING THERE   By Train   The **Lüneburg Bahnhof** lies on two major rail lines, the Hamburg–Hannover line and the Lüneburg–Lübeck–Kiel–Flensburg line, with frequent connections. For information call ☎ **01805/99-66-33.**

By Bus   Long-distance bus service into Lüneberg is provided by **KVG GmbH** (☎ **04131/87-20-80)** or **VOG GmbH** (☎ **04131/88-07-0)**. The bus station is in front of the railway station.

By Car   Access is Route 4 from Hamburg.

VISITOR INFORMATION   Lüneburg Tourist Information is in the Rathaus Am Markt (☎ **04131/207-6620)**. It's open Monday to Friday 10am to 7pm (to 6pm November to April), and Saturday and Sunday 10am to 4pm.

EXPLORING THE AREA
Although most buildings in this 1,000-year-old city are from its most prosperous period, the 15th and 16th centuries, a total of seven centuries of architecture are represented here. The **Rathaus,** Am Markt, reached along Auf der Meere, is a perfect

example of several trends in architecture and design. You enter through a Gothic doorway into a Renaissance hall. The Great Council Room is the building's most outstanding feature, with sculptures and bas-reliefs by Albert von Soest (1566–84). Daily guided tours are conducted all year at 11am, 12:30pm, and 3pm. The cost is 6DM ($3) for adults and 4DM ($2) for children. For information, call ☎ 04131/30-92-30.

To understand Lüneberg's role as "the Salt City," visit the **Deutsches Salzmuseum,** Sülfmeisterstrasse 1 (☎ **04131/450-65**). Inside, a series of exhibits explore life in the Middle Ages and the role of salt in the region's economy and culture. Entrance is 6DM ($3) for adults, 4DM ($2) for children. Open May to September Monday to Friday 9am to 5pm, Saturday and Sunday 10am to 5pm. Off-season daily 10am to 5pm.

SHOPPING

The heath area is known for its craftspeople. Some of the best local arts and crafts are on sale at the tourist office (see above). The town's largest department store is **Karstadt,** Am Markt (☎ **04131/3040**). The main shopping streets are **Bäckerstrasse** and **Grapengiesserstrasse,** both lying in pedestrian zones. There's also an abundance of antiques stores, the best of which are **H. Beckhaus,** Am Markt 5 (☎ **04131/ 3-11-61**), and **Brüning,** Auf der Altstadt 16 (☎ **04131/40-23-03**).

WHERE TO STAY

Bremer Hof. Lünestrasse 13, 21335 Lüneburg (a 2-min. walk from Marktplatz). ☎ **04131/ 22-40.** Fax 04131/22-42-24. www.bremer-hof.de. E-mail: Hotel-Bremerhof@Luenecom.de. 53 units. 189DM–225DM ($94.50–$112.50) double. Rates include buffet breakfast. AE, DC, MC, V. Parking 8DM ($4). Bus: 3.

The logo of this hotel is an illustration of the animal musicians of Bremen, who, with their noise, frightened away robbers. The facade looks like something out of the 16th century. Rooms are modern and sunny, but a bit small. All but four have phones and TVs. The restaurant serves specialties of the Lüneburger Heide region. A bar and a 400-year-old wine cellar are open on weekends.

Hotel Bargenturm. Lambertiplatz, 21335 Lüneburg. ☎ **04131/72-90.** Fax 04131/72-94-99. www.Hotel-Bargenturm.de. E-mail: Keil@Hotel-Burgenturm.de. 40 units. MINIBAR TV TEL. 189DM ($94.50) double; 249DM ($124.50) junior suite. DC, MC, V. Parking 10DM ($5).

This three-story hotel at the edge of Lüneburg's historic center is one of the most modern in town. Its concrete walls and large expanses of glass make no concessions to the antique architecture of other parts of the city. Rooms are decorated with a no-nonsense comfortable modernity. The staff is multilingual and efficient. The restaurant, Luna, with its own bar area, serves Mediterranean food and wine.

Residenz-Ring Hotel. Münstermannskamp 10, 21335 Lüneburg. ☎ **04131/75-99-10.** Fax 04131/7-59-91-75. E-mail: info@residenzhotel.de. 35 units. MINIBAR TV TEL. 220DM–260DM ($110–$130) double. Rates include buffet breakfast. AE, DC, MC, V. Parking 8DM ($4). Bus: 1 or 6.

The rooms of this serviceable hotel are so separated from each other that you'll be reminded of an apartment building. Since the establishment is right inside the city's Kurpark, there's lots of shady greenery around. Rooms are functionally furnished and rather small but well maintained. Baths are a bit cramped. You'll find an inviting bar and an up-to-date restaurant, serving rather standard international and regional specialties.

WHERE TO DINE

Ratskeller. Am Markt 1 (on the market square). ☎ **04131/3-17-57.** Reservations recommended. Main courses 35DM–55DM ($17.50–$27.50); fixed-price, 4-course menus

The Lüneburg Heath

The Lüneburg Heath (in German, *Lüneburger Heide*) is one of the major attractions of northern Germany. The heath covers nearly 775km² (300 square miles) and includes many beautiful spots. The sandy soil is mainly covered with brush and heather, although there are a few oak and beech forests in the northern valleys. Toward late summer, the green of the heath flowers turns to purple; August and September are the most beautiful months. The best way to approach the heath is via the old town of Lüneburg, the area's transportation hub.

You'll find dramatic, windswept, and bleakly evocative scenery in the ✪ **Naturschützpark Lüneburger Heide,** a 260km² (100-square-mile) sanctuary for plants and wildlife. Its highest point is the Wilsederberg, a low-lying peak only 168m (550 feet) above sea level, accessible via a network of footpaths from the hamlet of Wilsede. This reserve, in the center of the heath, is a peaceful, pastoral scene of shepherds, sheep, and undulating hills. Strict laws enforce the maintenance of the thatch-roofed houses and rural atmosphere. One of the park's most charming hamlets is **Undeloh,** which has a good hotel, the **Heiderose,** Gästehaus Heideschmiede, Wilseder Strasse 13 (☎ **04189/311**), renting doubles for 160DM ($80), including breakfast. There are also a number of villages—listed on only the most detailed of maps—that post ZIMMER FREI (Room for Rent) signs. These accommodations might be on a heath farm or even a horse farm.

For information, contact **Fremdenverkehrsverbund Lüneburger Heide e.V.** Barkhausenstrasse 35, Lüneburg (☎ **04131/7-37-30**), the park's administrative headquarters, which can furnish maps and information on horseback riding and cycling. Open Monday to Friday 8am to 6pm. To reach the park from Lüneberg, drive 35km (22 miles) west, following the signs to Salzhausen. After you cross the bridge over the A7 Autobahn, follow the brown-and-white signs to the park. The tourist office (see above) compiles a list of places every summer where you can rent a bike.

25DM–60DM ($12.50–$30). AE, MC, V. Thurs–Tues 11am–10pm. Closed Jan 6–20. Bus: 3. GERMAN/CONTINENTAL.

This is a good choice for lunch, dinner, or in between. The Ratskeller serves satisfying but unspectacular meals in a town not known for its restaurants. The varied menu includes game and regional specialties, according to the season. You can always count on good home-style cooking in a pleasant setting, backed up by a fine wine list. Parts of the decor date from 1328.

LÜNEBURG AFTER DARK

Students make this a rowdier place with a later nightlife than most other small towns. Bars are located along the river on **Am Stintmarkt.** The most popular place to hang out, drink, and debate, is **Dialog,** Am Stintmarkt 12 (☎ **04131/39-11-39**), open daily noon to 2am. Dancers hit the **Garage,** Auf der Hude 72 (☎ **04131/3-58-79**), on Wednesday, Friday, and Saturday. DJs start mixing music at 10pm and stop at 5am. There's an 8DM ($4) cover.

Another important nightlife area is the **Schroederstrasse,** which is lined chock-a-block with bars and *nacht-cafés,* some of which provide live music. Locals like to duck in and out of as many bars as possible along this street during the course of an evening. Three of the best are **Max Bar,** Schroederstrasse 6 (☎ **04131/47-886**); **Café Central,** Schroederstrasse 1 (☎ **04131/40-50-99**); and **Lillienthal,** Schroederstrasse 8 (☎ **0413/40-11-44**).

3 Celle

45km (28 miles) NE of Hannover, 111km (69 miles) SE of Bremen, 117km (73 miles) S of Hamburg

The well-preserved town of Celle stands at the edge of a silent expanse of moorland, looking like something out of a picture book. Its ancient half-timbered houses were untouched by the war, and the legends carved on their beams seem to live on today. Most of the houses date from the 16th and 17th centuries—the oldest was built in 1526—but they're in such good condition that they could have been constructed in the 1900s.

ESSENTIALS

GETTING THERE   By Train   Celle Hauptbahnhof is on the Hamburg–Hannover rail line, with frequent connections to major German cities. Forty trains arrive daily from Hannover (trip time: 20 to 30 min.), and the same number pull in from Hamburg (trip time: 1 hr. 10 min. to 1 hr. 30 min.). For information, call ☎ **01805/99-66-33.**

By Bus   Long-distance bus connections, from cities such as Hannover, are provided by **Winkermann GmbH** (☎ **05143/98820**) and **Lempke & Koschick GmbH** (☎ **05143/46980**). Buses arrive in front of the main railway station.

By Car   Access by car is via the A7 Autobahn north and south, or Route 214.

VISITOR INFORMATION   Contact the **Verkehrsverein,** Markt 6 (☎ **05141/12-12**), open mid-November to March, Monday to Friday 9am to 5pm and Saturday 10am to 1pm; and April to mid-October, Monday to Friday 9am to 7pm and Saturday 10am to 4pm.

SEEING THE SIGHTS

Herzogschloss. West of the Altstadt. ☎ **05141/1-23-73.** Admission 5DM ($2.50) adults, 2.50DM ($1.25) children. Tours Apr–Oct, Tues–Sun at noon, 1, 2, 3, and 4pm; Nov–Mar, Tues–Sun at 11am and 3pm. Bus: 2, 3, or 4.

One of the landmarks of the town, the palace of the dukes of Brunswick and Lüneburg is a square Renaissance castle surrounded by a moat. There's a tower at each corner. The palace's bizarre 16th-century chapel was designed by Martin de Vos, with galleries and elaborate ornamentation. The pride of the castle, and of the town, is its baroque theater, the oldest in Germany (1674), still in regular use today. Call the tourist office (☎ **05141/12-12**) to arrange for a tour given by an English-speaking guide.

Bomann Museum. Schlossplatz 7. ☎ **05141/1-23-72.** Admission 4DM ($2) adults, 2DM ($1) children. Tues–Sun 10am–5pm. Bus: 2, 3, or 4.

For a picture of 16th- to 20th-century everyday life in Celle and the surrounding countryside, visit this fine regional museum. Included is a complete 16th-century farmhouse, as well as rooms from old cottages, period costumes, and Hannoverian uniforms from 1803 to 1866. In the portrait gallery of the Brunswick-Lüneburg dukes, you can see pictures of the electors, later kings of England and Hannover.

WHERE TO STAY

✪ **Fürstenhof Celle.** Hannoverschestrasse 55, 29221 Celle (at the edge of town). ☎ **05141/ 20-10.** Fax 05141/20-11-20. www.fuerstenhof.de. E-mail: reservation@fuerstenhof.de. 76 units. A/C MINIBAR TV TEL. 245DM–480DM ($122.50–$240) double; 420DM–950DM ($210–$475) suite. AE, DC, MC, V. Parking 12DM ($6). Bus: 3, 5, or 10.

This hotel, quite sophisticated for such a provincial town, is by far the best in Celle. It's a small-scale 17th-century manor house flanked by timbered wings. The brick court-yard in front of the salmon-colored mansion is shaded by a towering chestnut tree. The older and more traditional rooms are in the main house; more modern rooms are in an annex beyond the rear courtyard. Rooms range from medium to spacious.

Dining/Diversions: The elegant Restaurant Endtenfang, formal yet warm, is one of the best in Lower Saxony (see "Where to Dine," below). The barroom is in the ancient vaults of the mansion. The beer tavern, the Kutscherstube, built into the old coach house, is more formal, with old wooden tables and farm artifacts. There's also a bar, Die Bar im Unterhaus, that often offers dancing, and an Italian restaurant, Palio.

Amenities: Room service, laundry, baby-sitting, tile pool, sauna, beauty parlor, shops.

Hotel Celler Hof. Stechbahn 11, 29221 Celle. ☎ **05141/2-80-61.** Fax 05141/2-80-65. www.residenzhotels.de. E-mail: reservation@residenzhotels.de. 49 units. MINIBAR TV TEL. 170DM–310DM ($85–$155) double. Rates include buffet breakfast. AE, DC, MC, V. Parking 12DM ($6). Bus: 3, 5, or 10.

Celler Hof is on the street where tournaments were once held. The Old-World 1890 architecture of the hotel and its neighboring timbered houses renders the interior fur-nishings incongruously modern, although quite pleasing. Rooms, ranging from medium to spacious, have recently been renovated and are of a high standard. Many have a view of the castle. Guests can order lunch at the hotel's Stadtwache daily 11am to 3pm. No dinner is served, although there is a bar in the lobby.

Hotel Schifferkrug. Speicherstrasse 9, 29221 Celle. ☎ **05141/70-15.** Fax 05141/63-50. www.schifferkrug-celle.de. 12 units. TV TEL. 130DM–170DM ($65–$85) double. Rates include buffet breakfast. No credit cards. Free parking. Bus: 3, 5, or 10.

The brick-and-timber walls of this comfortable hotel have witnessed more than 3 centuries of innkeeping tradition. The small to medium-sized rooms have lace cur-tains and eiderdowns—old-fashioned comfort just like at Grandma's. There's a bar on the premises, along with a rustic Weinstube and a more formal restaurant serving conservative but tasty German food.

WHERE TO DINE

In addition to the restaurants below, you can stop in at **Café Kiess,** Grosserplan 16–17 (☎ **05141/22540**), which serves coffee, pastries, drinks, and platters of hearty German food with democratic, and rather conservative, aplomb every day 8am to 7pm. **Alex's Antik Café,** Schuhstrasse 6 (☎ **05141/21-75-40**), is open Tuesday to Saturday 8:30am to 6pm, and Sunday 9am to 6pm. The youth and arts cultures hang out here.

Historischer Ratskeller. Markt 14. ☎ **05141/2-90-99.** Reservations recommended. Main courses 14.80DM–36DM ($7.40–$18); fixed-price menus 45DM–65DM ($22.50–$32.50). AE, MC, V. Wed–Mon noon–3pm and 6–10pm. Bus: 3, 5, or 10. GERMAN.

Historischer Ratskeller is plusher than the typical Ratskeller and has better fare. Attentive waiters are constantly passing by, carrying silver platters heaped with spicy, flavorful German dishes, such as roast venison with juniper berries, pork schnitzels, and fillet steak with a cognac-cream sauce and peppercorns.

Restaurant Endtenfang. In the Fürstenhof Celle, Hannoverschestrasse 55. ☎ **05141/ 20-10.** Reservations recommended. Main courses 48DM–69DM ($24–$34.50). AE, DC, MC, V. Daily noon–2pm and 6:30–10pm. FRENCH.

Celle's most prestigious and stylish restaurant occupies an appealingly old-fashioned dining room on the street level of this previously recommended hotel. Service is efficient, helpful, and friendly. The menu focuses on game dishes, including two succulent versions of duck. (The word "Endtenfang," from an old regional dialect, means "the hunting reserve for duck-shooting.") Traditional adornments include a pepper-cream sauce, cabbage roulade, a potato and pear gratin, and fresh mushrooms, along with slices of red apples. Other main courses include halibut sautéed with fresh coriander and veal liver cooked with baby onions. The small dumplings that accompany many dishes are light and feathery. Desserts are quite imaginative, and the wine list is the finest in the area.

Ringhotel Celler Tor. Scheuener Strasse 2, 29229 Celle-Gross Hehlen, about 3km (2 miles) outside town. ☎ **05141/59-00.** Fax 05141/59-04-90. www.celler-tor-de. E-mail: info@celler-tor-de. Reservations recommended. Main courses 28.50DM–43.50DM ($14.25–$21.75); fixed-price menus 52DM–87DM ($26–$43.50). AE, DC, MC, V. Daily noon–3pm and 6–10pm. Bus: 8. GERMAN/INTERNATIONAL.

The Celler Tor is a cliché of German charm, with its gabled red-tile roof and banks of geraniums. When local residents want to celebrate a special occasion, they head here, knowing they can get a great selection of *gutbürgerlich* fare—that is, the food fondly remembered from childhood. In season, that means wild game, such as ragout of stag with mushrooms. You can also get good shrimp and rice dishes here.

The Celler Tor also rents 70 good rooms. A double costs 380DM to 496DM ($190 to $248), including buffet breakfast; eight suites are also available, at 550DM to 650DM ($275 to $325) each. Facilities include two pools, massage facilities, a sauna, a solarium, and a workout room.

4 Hannover

122km (76 miles) SE of Bremen, 151km (94 miles) S of Hamburg, 288km (179 miles) W of Berlin

In the summer of 2000, Hannover hosted Expo 2000, the first World Exposition of the new millennium, and the first to take place in Germany. Hannover is one of Germany's hubs of industry, transportation, and commerce. Its annual industrial trade fair is now the largest trade fair in the world, attracting producers and buyers from around the globe. Bombed into oblivion in World War II, Hannover was badly reconstructed. If you want half-timbered houses, head for Celle (see above). Nevertheless, Hannover does have some attractions, including one of the finest baroque gardens in the world.

ESSENTIALS

GETTING THERE   By Plane   Hannover is served by **Hannover-Langenhagen International Airport,** 10km (6 miles) north of the city center. Many international airlines fly here, as well as Lufthansa. Flying time between Hannover and Munich is 1 hour 10 minutes; between Frankfurt and Hannover, 50 minutes. For flight information, call ☎ **0511/9-77-12-23.** Shuttle buses run between the airport and the city every 20 minutes 5am to 11pm, depositing passengers at the Hauptbahnhof. The cost is 10DM ($5) each way.

By Train   Hannover lies at the junction of an important network of rail lines linking Scandinavia to Italy and Paris to Moscow. Some 500 trains per day pass through,

The House of Hannover

Every student of English history is aware of the role that Hannover played in the history of Great Britain. For more than 100 years, Britain was ruled by monarchs descended from the House of Hannover (or Hanover), who technically also ruled over the German city. The most notorious was George III, the occasionally insane king whose policies provoked the American Revolutionary War.

with frequent connections to major German and European cities. Nineteen trains arrive daily from Berlin (trip time: 3 hr. 50 min.), 40 trains from Frankfurt (trip time: 2 hr. 21 min. or 3 hr. 50 min., depending on the train), and 40 trains from Hamburg (trip time: 1 hr. 11 min. to 1 hr. 30 min.). For information, call ☎ 01805/99-66-33.

By Bus   Long-distance bus service to major German cities is offered by **Deutsche Touring Büro Hannover,** at the Hauptbahnhof (☎ 0511/32-94-19).

By Car   Access is via the A1 Autobahn north or south and from the A2 east and west.

VISITOR INFORMATION   Contact **Hannover Tourist Information,** located at Ernst-August-Platz 2 (☎ 0511/3-01-40). Here you can reserve hotel rooms (ask about special weekend packages), book sightseeing tours, obtain general information about the city, and purchase tickets for local events as well as for trains, trams, and buses. The office is open Monday to Friday 9am to 7pm and Saturday 9:30am to 3pm.

GETTING AROUND   The local public-transport system includes commuter trains, an extensive underground network, trams, and buses operated by several companies. Service is frequent and extensive. For information and schedules, contact **Regionalverkehr Hannover GmbH** (☎ 0511/9-90-01-30).

EXPLORING THE CITY

Market Church (Marktkirche), the Gothic brick basilica on Marktplatz, is one of Hannover's oldest structures, built in the mid–14th century. **Altes Rathaus,** facing the square, dates from 1425. It was badly damaged in the war, but has been restored and now houses the civic archives.

✪ **Herrenhäuser Garten (Royal Gardens of Herrenhäusen).** Herrenhäuser Strasse 4. ☎ **0511/30-14-22.** Admission 5DM ($2.50) adults, free for children. Apr–Sept daily 8am–7pm; Oct–Mar daily 8am–4:30pm. Waterworks display May–Sept Mon–Fri 11am–noon and 3–5pm, Sat–Sun and holidays 11am–noon and 2–5pm. U-Bahn: Herrenhäuser Gärten.

No matter where you go in Hannover, you won't be far from a park or garden. But make sure you don't miss this one, the only surviving example of Dutch/Low German early baroque-style gardening. Designers from France, the Netherlands, England, and Italy, as well as Germany, worked together to create this masterpiece of living art. **Grosse Garten,** from 1666, is the largest garden, consisting of a rectangle surrounded by a moat. Within the maze of walks and trees are examples of French baroque, rococo, and Low German rose and flower gardens. The Grosse Garten also contains one of the highest fountains in Europe, shooting jets of water 72m (236 feet) into the air, and the world's only existing baroque hedge-theater (1692), where plays by Shakespeare, Molière, and Brecht are still performed, along with ballets and jazz concerts. The smaller 17th-century **Berggarten,** across Herrenhäuser Strasse from the Grosse Garten, is a botanical garden with houses containing rare orchids and other tropical flowers.

Niedersächsisches Landesmuseum Hannover (Lower Saxony State Museum). Willy-Brandt-Allee (near the Maschpark). ☎ **0511/9-80-75.** Admission 6DM ($3). Tues–Wed and Fri–Sun 10am–5pm, Thurs 10am–7pm. Tram: 1, 2, 4, 5, 6, 7, 8, or 11. Bus: 132 or 267.

The Landesmuseum is one of the most important regional museums in Germany. There are exhibits on northern European biology and geology, ethnomedicine and ethnobotany, and on the history of Lower Saxony from the Paleolithic Age up to the Middle Ages. The aquarium shows a world of exotic fish, amphibians, and reptiles. In the newly created Kindermuseum, children can learn about prehistoric times with activities like grinding corn or working stone tools.

The museum's art gallery contains treasures spanning 7 centuries. A highlight is Meister Bertram von Minden's *Passion Altar* (1390–1400). You'll also see paintings by Rembrandt, Van Dyck, and Rubens (his *Madonna*), as well as the *Four Times of Day* series by Caspar David Friedrich.

Rathaus. Am Maschpark. ☎ **0511/1-68-53-33.** Elevator ride to dome 3DM ($1.50) adults, 2DM ($1) students and children. Rathaus Apr–Oct, Mon–Fri 9:30am–5:30pm, Sat–Sun 10am–5pm. U-Bahn: Markthalle. Tram: 3, 7, or 9. Bus: 22.

The "new" Rathaus is a large structure, built between 1901 and 1913. An inclined elevator—the only one in Europe other than the elevator at the Eiffel Tower—takes visitors up to the 10m (33-foot) dome. The building is attractive because of its location in the Maschpark, by a small lake. It's just a short distance from the extensive artificial Maschsee, frequented by Hannoverians for its beach, boats, and restaurants.

SHOPPING

Your first destination might be the **Galerie Luise,** a multilevel shopping mall at the corner of Luisenstrasse and Rathenaustrasse (Bus: 120), with upscale shops for clothing and home furnishings. **Der Herrenausstatter Hemdenstuhe,** Georgstrasse 42 (☎ 0511/36-38-04), and **Donna-Men,** Krämerstrasse 25 (☎ **0511/32-50-12**), are good choices for menswear. Donna-Men's counterpart for women's clothing is **Donna,** Lilienplatz 1 (☎ **0511/32-58-75;** U-Bahn: Markthalle). **Terner,** Luisenstrasse 9 (☎ **0511/36-39-31;** tram: 5), and **Joop,** Karmarsch Strasse 18 (☎ **0511/36-78-97-30;** bus:7), have three floors loaded with designer-inspired clothing for men, women, and children. If you want to duplicate the traditional look of rural, agrarian Germany, consider dropping into **Trachten Sander,** Seilwinderstrasse 3 (☎ **0511/36-36-55;** bus: 18), where dirndls, loden-colored coats, and jaunty-looking hats accessorized with pheasant feathers are all the rage.

Fine needlepoint, including material for curtains or upholstery, is available at **Bertold-Handarbeiten,** Grosse Parkhofstrasse 27 (☎ **0511/3-09-13-00;** U-Bahn: Markthalle). Souvenirs are sold at **Raachermantel,** Luisenstrasse 1 (☎ **0511/3-63-14-24;** tram: 5), which specializes in hand-carved figures, some inspired by German folklore and fairy tales. Also, one of the largest **flea markets** in all of Germany takes place every Saturday 7am to 4pm along Am Hohen Ufer (U-Bahn: Markthalle).

WHERE TO STAY

To escape the clutches of the city's pricey (and rather sterile) hotels, you might stay at a restaurant-hotel—either the Landhaus Ammann or the Georgenhof-Stern (see "Where to Dine," below).

EXPENSIVE

✪ **Forum Hotel Schweizerhof.** Hinuberstrasse 6, 30175 Hannover. ☎ **0511/3-49-50.** Fax 0511/3-49-51-23. www.forum-hotel-schweizerhof.de. E-mail: hannover@interconti.com. 203 units. MINIBAR TV TEL. 280DM–545DM ($140–$272.50) double; 895DM ($447.50) suite. Rates include buffet breakfast. AE, DC, MC, V. Parking 19.50DM ($9.75). Tram: 16.

This is one of the most imaginatively designed hotels in Hannover, with a lot more charm and atmosphere than other leading contenders. It sits on a quiet street in the central business district. Inside you'll find illuminated Plexiglas columns and sweeping expanses of russet-colored marble. The place serves an affluent clientele, often including visiting celebrities. Rooms are spacious and elegantly furnished; 85 are air-conditioned.

Dining: Schu's Restaurant is one of the most stylish in the city. Reservations are important. The hotel also offers the Gourmet's Buffet and the Zirbelstube, serving a regional cuisine.

Amenities: Room service, laundry, dry cleaning, airport pickup if arranged in advance, a terrace garden in summer.

✪ **Kastens Hotel Luisenhof.** Luisenstrasse 1–3, 30159 Hannover (near the Hauptbahnhof). ☎ **0511/3-04-40.** Fax 0511/3-04-48-07. E-mail: kastens-hotel-luisenhof@t-online.de. 165 units. MINIBAR TV TEL. 298DM–598DM ($149–$299) double; 550DM–950DM ($275–$475) suite. Rates include buffet breakfast. AE, DC, MC, V. Parking 15DM ($7.50). Tram: 16.

This is the leading hotel in town. Its stately glass-and-stone facade is just minutes from the Hauptbahnhof in the city center. A series of modernizations have enhanced comfort while maintaining conservative good taste. The carefully renovated rooms are spacious, stylishly furnished, and impeccably kept. The English-speaking staff welcomes overseas visitors.

Dining/Diversions: The lobby-level grill room serves superlative food; a few steps away, a cozy modern pub offers drinks and salads.

Amenities: Room service, hair dryers, laundry, dry cleaning.

MODERATE

Hotel Königshof. Königstrasse 12, 30175 Hannover. ☎ **0511/31-20-71.** Fax 0511/31-20-79. 82 units. TV TEL. 178DM–418DM ($89–$209) double. Discounts for children under 16 in parents' room. Rates include buffet breakfast. AE, DC, MC, V. Parking 10DM ($5). Bus: 20 or 39.

Both the skylights and the modernized crenellations on this hotel's mansard roof make it look like an updated feudal fortress. The hotel was built in 1984 above a glass-and-steel shopping arcade in the town center. Each plushly carpeted room has a couch that converts to a bed. Only breakfast is served at the hotel, but there's an Italian restaurant across the street.

Loccumer Hof. Kurt-Schumacher-Strasse 16 (near the Hauptbahnhof), 30159 Hannover. ☎ **0511/1-26-40.** Fax 0511/13-11-92. www.vch.de/loccumerhof.hannover. E-mail: Loccumerhof.hannover@vch.de. 87 units. MINIBAR TV TEL. 380DM–430DM ($190–$215) double. Higher rates during fairs. Rates include buffet breakfast. AE, DC, MC, V. Parking 10DM–13DM ($5–$6.50). Tram: 16.

This is one of the best economy finds in the city. The utilitarian rooms and baths are small. Service and frills are minimal. The standard fare in the hotel's dining room, however, is quite good.

WHERE TO DINE
VERY EXPENSIVE

✪ **Georgenhof-Stern Restaurant.** Herrenhauser Kirchweg 20, 30167 Hannover. ☎ **0511/70-22-44.** Fax 0511/70-85-59. Reservations required. Main courses 50DM–79DM ($25–$39.50); fixed-price meals 89DM–175DM ($44.50–$87.50). AE, DC, MC, V. Daily noon–2pm and 6–10pm. Tram: 4, 5, or 6. INTERNATIONAL.

This is Hannover's most famous restaurant, and it's well worth the price. It's in a country inn in a private park near the Herrenhäuser Gardens. International dishes of fresh seafood and game are featured. In summer, tables are set on the terrace, overlooking a garden and pond. The place also rents 14 clean and pleasant rooms, with traditional, handcrafted furniture. Doubles run 255DM to 525DM ($127.50 to $262.50); buffet breakfast is included.

✪ **Landhaus Ammann.** Hildesheimer Strasse 185. ☎ **0511/83-08-18.** Fax 0511/ 8-43-77-49. www.landhaus-ammann.de. E-mail: mail@landhaus-ammann. Reservations required. Main courses 45DM–65DM ($22.50–$32.50); fixed-price dinners 90DM–175DM ($45–$87.50); fixed-price lunch 90DM–175DM ($45–$87.50). Daily noon–2pm and 7–10pm. AE, DC, MC, V. Tram: 5. INTERNATIONAL.

This is the only restaurant in Hannover that serves better food and has a more luxurious atmosphere than the Georgenhof-Stern. Service is discreet and efficient, but never stuffy. The chefs turn out a distinguished cuisine, backed up by the city's finest wine cellar. The menu is adjusted seasonally to take advantage of fresh produce. Typical dishes include sea bass with caviar sauce.

The place also rents 15 beautifully furnished rooms; a double costs 320DM to 620DM ($160 to $310), including a buffet breakfast. The setting, near a park, is tranquil. Rooms, decorated in a traditional motif, have minibars, trouser presses, and hair dryers.

EXPENSIVE

Wichmann. Hildesheimer Strasse 230, at Hannover-Döhren. ☎ **0511/83-16-71.** Reservations required. Main courses 32DM–60DM ($16–$30); fixed-price dinner 125DM ($62.50) for 4 courses, 180DM ($90) for 7 courses. AE, MC, V. Mon–Sat noon–3pm and 6–11pm. Tram: 1 or 8. GERMAN.

This family-owned, white-walled, shuttered inn, with its slate walks and carefully tended flower beds, is on the eastern edge of Hannover. The garden serves as a pleasant setting for dining in the summer months. The place is an oasis of comfort. Cooking is German *gutbürgerlich*—wholesome and hearty. Try specialties such as fish terrine, rack of lamb, homemade noodles, and wine and cheese from all over Germany.

MODERATE

Altdeutsche Bierstube. Lärchenstrasse 4. ☎ **0511/34-49-21.** Reservations required. Main courses 18DM–40DM ($9–$20); fixed-price, 3-course menu 48DM ($24). AE, DC, MC, V. Mon–Fri noon–2pm; Mon–Sat 6pm–1am. Closed holidays. U-Bahn: Lister Platz. GERMAN.

With a decor that has changed little since its original construction around 1860, this old-fashioned Bierstube has remained stable and solid, despite the monumental changes that have transformed the society around it. The unpretentious food is hearty, wholesome, and filling, with the regular fare augmented by seasonal specialties. Three favorites include pork knuckles with sauerkraut, fillet of beef, and mixed grills.

Mövenpick Quartet. Georgstrasse 35. ☎ **0511/32-43-43.** Reservations recommended for the four restaurants, not for the cafe. Main courses 25DM–40DM ($12.50–$20); main courses in the vegetarian restaurant 14DM–28DM ($7–$14). AE, DC, MC, V. Restaurants daily 11:30am–midnight. Cafe daily 8am–midnight. Tram: 1, 2, 3, 4, or 5. INTERNATIONAL.

This is a well-managed, bustling restaurant complex whose four separate eating areas are managed by the Swiss-based chain, Mövenpick. The food is a smörgåsbord of international cuisines, including French (in **La Brasserie**); California (salads, seafood soups, and very fresh produce in **Opus 1**); Italian (in the self-service cafeteria, **Pick's**); and vegetarian (in **Grüneschnabel**). All sections, particularly the old-fashioned **Café Kröpcke**, have an elaborate array of high-calorie Central European pastries and desserts.

Steuerndieb. Steuerndieb 1, Hannover-Bothfeld, 30655 Hannover. ☎ **0511/90-99-60.** Reservations not required. Main courses 19DM–40DM ($9.50–$20); fixed-price menu

40DM–65DM ($20–$32.50) for 3 courses, 89DM ($44.50) for 7 courses. AE, DC, MC, V. Mon–Sat 9am–10pm, Sun 11am–6pm. Tram: 3 or 7. GERMAN.

In 1329, a stone-sided tower was erected about a mile east of central Hannover to guard the lumber produced in Eilenreide Forest. The tower's name, Steuerndieb, translates from the archaic German as "Stop, thieves!" Around 1850 a rustic restaurant was built on the site, and it has been known ever since for hearty and flavorful food. Many of the specialties are cooked over an open fire, and the restaurant offers a locally inspired menu that, unlike those of many other restaurants, features game year-round. Two popular dishes are venison with red cabbage, dumplings, and black-cherry sauce; and rabbit with black-pepper sauce and red cabbage.

The establishment also has a modern wing containing seven simple, white-walled rooms, each with private bath, TV, telephone, and view overlooking the forest. Doubles cost 250DM ($125), including a buffet breakfast.

HANNOVER AFTER DARK

Hannover Vorschau, a monthly newspaper devoted exclusively to the city's nightlife and cultural venues, is available for 3.50DM ($2) at news kiosks, but is usually given out free in the city's hotels.

THE PERFORMING ARTS The **Nieder Sächsische Stadtstheater Hannover GmbH,** Opernplatz 1 (☎ **0511/32-11-33,** or 0511/3-68-17-11 for tickets and information; U-Bahn: Kröpcke), built between 1845 and 1852, is the region's leading venue for ballet, concerts, and opera. Depending on the performance, tickets cost from 20DM to 75DM ($10 to $37.50) each. Less formal, with popular as well as classical offerings, is the **N. D. R. Symphoniker,** Rudolf Benigsen Ufer 22 (☎ **0511/9-88-29-90;** bus: 2 or 6), an ugly postwar building whose charm derives from what goes on inside. You can hear poetry readings, jazz and rock 'n' roll concerts, and chamber orchestras. Contact the theaters or the tourist office for schedules. Tickets cost 20DM to 50DM ($10 to $25).

BARS Oddly, many of Hannover's most appealing bars are Irish pubs. They include **The Irish Pub,** Brüderstrasse 4 (☎ **0511/1-45-89;** U-Bahn: Hauptbahnhof), which won a 1998 award as the best Irish Pub in Germany, and its most visible competitor, **The Irish Harp,** Schwarzer Bär (☎ **0511/44-70-70;** U-Bahn: Hauptbahnhof), which has a beer garden in good weather. Both establishments are open daily 5pm to 2am; serve both Guinness and Murphy's on tap, along with sandwiches, pies, fish-and-chips, and Irish stew; and occasionally book Irish music bands, for which there's a cover of 10DM to 12DM ($5 to $6).

Look for the tail of an airplane sticking out over the street to find the entrance to **Boomerang,** Engelbosteler Damm 45 (☎ **0511/169-45-69;** tram: 6). When you step inside, you'll find that the rest of the plane is still attached, suspended above the bar and dining area. Students and locals come here all day, and on Saturday there are restaurant parties and food sales to benefit local causes, from AIDS awareness to city-run children's gardens. Open Monday to Saturday, 10am to 1am; Sunday 10am to 2pm.

DANCE CLUBS The best place for mainstream dance is **Osho Disco,** Rauschplatz 7L (☎ **0511/34-22-17;** U-Bahn: Hauptbahnhof), a 14-year survivor of the club scene. It plays funk, house, and other dance music. It's open 10pm to "whenever," Wednesday to Sunday. Cover is 6DM to 10DM ($3 to $5). One of its leading competitors is **Palo Palo,** Rauschplatz 8A (☎ **051/33-10-73;** U-Bahn: Hauptbahnhof), where house, funk, blues, reggae, and old-fashioned Motown soul play every night 9:30pm till dawn, for a cover of 7DM to 10DM ($3.50 to $5) per person.

LIVE MUSIC   An alternative venue, **Café Glocksee,** Glockseestrasse 35 (☎ 0511/1-61-47-12; tram: 10), stages hard-core, punk, and techno shows. Thursday concerts start at 9pm; cover is 20DM ($10). On Friday and Saturday it's disco mania 11pm to 7am and again on Wednesday 6pm to 2am; cover is 5DM ($2.50).

GAY CLUBS   **Schwul Sau,** Schaufeldstrasse 38 (☎ 0511/7-00-05-25; tram: 6), hosts discos, theater performances, and private parties, attended by a crowd of gay and straight arts-conscious patrons. It's open Tuesday, Wednesday, and Friday 8pm to 3am, Saturday 9pm to at least 7am, and Sunday 3pm to 2am. Cover is 15DM to 20DM ($7.50 to $10) for parties or theater events, and 8DM ($4) for dancing. There's no cover Tuesday, Wednesday, or Sunday. A hip and happening dance spot, **Men's Factory,** Engelbosteler Damm 7 (☎ 0511/70-24-87; tram: 6), is open only on Friday, for a mixed dance night, and Saturday, for gay dance night. Friday cover is 15DM ($7.50); Saturday, it's 10DM ($5).

A CASINO   The **Spielbank,** Österstrasse 40 (☎ 0511/98-06-60; U-Bahn: Kröpcke), has an impressive roster of blackjack, roulette, and baccarat. It's set within a modern building, with none of the belle epoque trappings or decorations you might have hoped for, and contains both a bar and a restaurant. Men are required to wear jackets and ties, and women are requested to dress appropriately. Open daily 3pm to 3am. Admission costs 5DM ($2.50), and you must show your passport to enter.

5 Hameln

45km (28 miles) SW of Hannover, 48km (30 miles) W of Hildesheim

Hameln (Hamelin in English) has many, many interesting buildings and a history dating from the 11th century, but its main claim to fame is the folktale about the Pied Piper, which has been immortalized by the Brothers Grimm, Goethe, and Robert Browning, among others. According to legend, in 1284 the town was infested by rats. Soon after, there appeared a piper who offered, for a fee, to lure the vermin into the Weser River. The rat-catcher successfully performed the service, but the stingy denizens of Hameln refused to pay, claiming that he was a sorcerer. So the piper reappeared the next Sunday and played a tune that lured all the town's children, except one lame boy, into a mysterious door in a hill. The children and the Pied Piper were never heard from again.

There is some historical basis for the story. It appears that, several centuries ago, for some unknown reason, the children of Hameln did indeed leave the town. The story of the Pied Piper is retold every summer Sunday at noon in a special performance at the **Hochzeitshaus (Wedding House)** on Osterstrasse. In the town shops, you can buy rat figures made of every conceivable material, even candy.

ESSENTIALS

GETTING THERE   **By Plane**   The nearest major airport is Hannover-Langenhagen, 55km (34 miles) away.

By Train   The **Hameln Bahnhof** lies on the Hannover–Hameln–Altenbeken line, with frequent connections. Depending on the train, trip time from Hannover ranges from 45 to 55 minutes. For information, call ☎ 01805/99-66-33.

By Bus   Local and regional bus service to nearby towns and Hannover is available from **RVH Regional Verkehr** (☎ 05151/811414). Buses stop in front of the Hauptbahnhof.

By Car   It takes 3 hours to reach Hameln from Frankfurt and 6 to 7 hours from Munich. From Frankfurt, head northeast along the A5 Autobahn, then north on the

A7, and finally west on A27. From Munich, take the A9 Autobahn north to Nürnberg, the A3 west to Würzburg, then the A7 north toward Hannover, and finally A27
west to Hameln.

VISITOR INFORMATION   Contact the **Verkehrsverein,** Deisterallee (☎ **05151/
20-26-17**), open May to September, Monday to Friday 9am to 6pm, Saturday 9:30am
to 12:30pm and 2 to 4pm, and Sunday 9:30am to 12:30pm; October to April,
Monday to Friday 9am to 1pm and 2 to 5pm.

WHAT TO SEE & DO

Hameln's most interesting building is the Gothic **Münster,** at the end of Bäckerstrasse,
overlooking the Weser River. Other attractions include the **Rattenfängerhaus
(Rat-Catcher's House;** see "Where to Dine," below), on Osterstrasse, with frescoes
illustrating the Pied Piper legend, and the **Hochzeitshaus (Wedding House)** on
Osterstrasse, with its three attractive gables. The finest houses in the town are built
in what is known as Weser Renaissance style. You can admire these nicely sculpted
late-16th-century houses as you stroll along the pedestrians-only streets.

SHOPPING   There are lots of opportunities to buy folkloric art objects here. One
of the best bets for souvenir and gift hunting, **Renner,** Am Markt 6 (☎ **05151/
9-44-20**), has some genuinely charming objects. Antiques that might become part of
your family heirlooms are at **Antikitäten Bayer,** Bäckerstrasse 49 (☎ **05151/32-97**),
and **Antiqutiäten Franke,** Wendenstrasse 4 (☎ **05151/44388**). You also might
simply want to window-shop along the town's best shopping streets, the **Osterstrasse**
and the **Bäckerstrasse.**

NIGHTLIFE   The town's **Weserbergland Festhalle,** Rathausplatz (☎ **05151/
91-62-20**), hosts an array of concerts, opera and ballet performances, and theatrical
productions. Call the theater or the visitor information center (see above) for upcoming
events and ticket information. Tickets are 15DM to 45DM ($7.50 to $22.50).

WHERE TO STAY

Dorint Hotel Hameln. 164er Ring 3, 31785 Hameln. ☎ **05151/79-20.** Fax
05151/79-21-91. www.dorint.de/hameln. E-mail: Sabine.Lorenzen@dorint.com. 105 units.
MINIBAR TV TEL. 255DM–499DM ($127.50–$249.50) double. Rates include buffet breakfast.
AE, DC, MC, V. Parking 9DM ($4.50). Bus: 1 or 2.

This hotel stands in a park with lots of trees, but is within walking distance of the
heart of the Altstadt, at the northern edge of the Burgergarten. It rises like a modern
collection of building blocks, with oversize glass walls. Rooms are standard and
functional. Guests have access to a pool, sauna, solarium, and massage facilities.
There's also an international restaurant, Brochette, plus a beer pub called Alt Hamelin.

Hotel Zur Börse. Osterstrasse 41A, 31785 Hameln. ☎ **05151/70-80.** Fax 05151/2-54-85.
34 units. TV TEL. 189DM–340DM ($94.50–$170) double. Rates include buffet breakfast.
AE, DC, MC, V. Parking 7DM ($3.50). Bus: 1 or 2.

This balconied hotel within the walls of the Altstadt can be identified by the four
peaks of its modern roofline. The interior is refreshingly uncluttered. Rooms are
spacious and well maintained. The restaurant serves German cuisine.

Komfort-Hotel Garni Christinenhof. Alte Markstrasse 18, 31785 Hameln. ☎ **05151/
9-50-80.** Fax 05151/4-36-11. E-mail: hotelchristinenhof@t-online.de. 30 units. MINIBAR TV
TEL. 218DM–250DM ($109–$125) double. Rates include buffet breakfast. AE, MC, V. Closed
Dec 20–Jan 6. Free parking. Bus: 1 or 2.

The gabled windows of this half-timbered, 300-year-old building, overlook a cobblestoned street in the middle of the Altstadt. Despite the antique facade, much of the

hotel's interior is streamlined and modern, with many conveniences. There's a pool beneath the vaulted stone ceiling of the old cellar, plus a sauna, a solarium, and conference rooms. Rooms are well furnished, though small.

WHERE TO DINE

Klütturm. Auf dem Klütberg. ☎ **05151/6-16-44.** Reservations recommended. Main courses 25DM–40DM ($14.25–$22.80). AE, MC, V. Wed–Mon 11:30am–2:30pm and 6–10pm. Closed Jan–Feb 10. GERMAN/FRENCH.

Even the lovely decor here takes second place to the restaurant's panoramic view of the Altstadt. The cooking is traditional, with special care lavished on the dessert wagon, whose confections change every day. In season, the cook will prepare game dishes, and throughout the year you'll find an aromatically seasoned rack of baby lamb with fresh vegetables, a tender entrecôte of beef with escargots, and Barbary duckling with an orange-pepper sauce. Adjacent to the restaurant is a stone-sided tower, with 99 steps, built in the 1820s. It can be climbed, without charge, as part of your dining experience. From the top, panoramic views extend out over the surrounding landscapes.

Rattenfängerhaus. Osterstrasse 28. ☎ **05151/38-88.** Reservations recommended. Main courses 20DM–35DM ($10–$17.50). AE, DC, MC, V. Daily 11am–3pm and 6–11pm. Bus: 1 or 2. GERMAN.

Rattenfängerhaus (Rat-Catcher's House) dates from 1603. A meal here is practically like eating in a museum. The place is a little too touristy and crowded for some tastes, but it's an enduring favorite nonetheless. You can order traditional German dishes, including various kinds of schnitzels, roasted goose, or fillets of salmon with hollandaise sauce. Souvenirs of the Pied Piper are offered.

6 Bad Pyrmont

72km (45 miles) SW of Hannover, 48km (30 miles) SE of Bielefeld

This attractive spa has enjoyed a good reputation for more than 2,000 years. Its springs vary from the brine variety in the fields to the medicinal iron waters on the southern side of the valley of the Weser Hills. In the center of town you can drink a medicinal cocktail from the fountain at the Hyllige Born spring. Another popular pastime is taking mud baths. But Bad Pyrmont is a good place to vacation even if you don't come to take the waters. Horseback riding in the hills, hiking, tennis, and swimming, as well as concerts and shows, make the resort a lively place.

ESSENTIALS

GETTING THERE   By Train   The nearest airport is at Hannover, where there are good rail connections to Bad Pyrmont. There are frequent trains throughout the day on the Hannover–Paderborn main line. For information, call ☎ **01805/99-66-33.**

By Bus   Regional buses run between Hameln (see above) and Bad Pyrmont. The service is provided by **RVH Busline Hameln** (☎ 05151/1-20-15).

By Car   From Hannover, Route 217 leads southwest to Bad Pyrmont.

VISITOR INFORMATION   Go to **Kur- und Verkehrsverein,** Europaplatz 1 (☎ **05281/94-05-11**), open Monday to Friday 9am to 5pm and Saturday 10am to 12:30pm.

SHOPPING   There aren't many shops in this quiet town, but **Hildebrandt,** Hauptallee 3 (☎ **05281/60-99-25**), has an appealing collection of German handcrafts.

EXPLORING THE TOWN

The **Kurpark (Spa Park)** is among the most beautiful in Germany, with little temples, flowering trees, and even a palm garden, an unusual touch in this temperate climate. The concert house in the Kurpark has shows during the busy summer. At night, the central promenade is glamorously lit, giving the spa a festive air, while guests sit at sidewalk tables drinking beer.

After a stroll through town in the day, you can visit **Festung und Schloss Pyrmont,** Schloss Strasse (☎ **05281/94-92-48**), the town castle, built in 1792. It displays antiques and paintings. Open Tuesday to Sunday 10am to 5pm; admission is 3.50DM ($1.75).

WHERE TO STAY

Bad Pyrmonter Hof. Brunnenstrasse 32, 31812 Bad Pyrmont. ☎ **05281/94-10.** Fax 05281/94-12-00. 45 units. TV TEL. 140DM–180DM ($70–$90) double without bath, 160DM–200DM ($80–$100) double with bath. Rates include continental breakfast. AE, MC, V. Parking 6DM ($3).

This hotel is a good economical choice. It provides personal atmosphere and good service and has been considerably modernized. The small rooms are immaculate, restful, and suitably furnished. The restaurant is only open to guests.

Bergkurpark. Ockelstrasse 11, 31812 Bad Pyrmont. ☎ **05281/40-01.** Fax 05281/40-04. www.bergkurpark.de. E-mail: info@bergkurpark.de. 49 units. MINIBAR TV TEL. 190DM–380DM ($95–$190) double; 400DM ($200) suite. Rates include continental breakfast. AE, MC, V. Parking 6DM ($3). Bus: 3.

Bergkurpark is not the most distinguished hotel at Bad Pyrmont (that honor goes to the Steigenberger—see below), but it is the most glamorous architecturally. Its entry-way has a thatched roof covering a hewn stone and stucco facade with half-rounded picture windows—very dramatic. The hotel rents singles, twin-bedded rooms, and a few suites; all are very comfortable. Your room might be in a modern block with private terraces overlooking a park.

The hotel has its own park, a forest, a heated pool, and a terrace with sun parasols overlooking the garden. There are also exercise rooms and a sauna. Its restaurant serves the best food at the spa (see "Where to Dine," below). There's also an elegant cafe, Sans Souci, and the rustic Wilhelm-Busch-Stube, where beer, wine, and good food are served. Another bar is called Separée. Room service, laundry, and dry cleaning are provided.

Park-Hotel Rasmusen. Hauptallee 8, 31812 Bad Pyrmont. ☎ **05281/9-30-64.** Fax 05281/60-68-72. 12 units. TV TEL. 250DM ($125) double. Rates include continental breakfast. AE, MC, V. Closed Jan. Free parking in lot; 9DM ($4.50) in garage.

This gracefully renovated villa stands on a traffic-free promenade in the center of Bad Pyrmont. The spacious rooms are well furnished, with comfortable beds; many have balconies overlooking the promenade. The staff is pleasant. The tranquil dining room offers moderately priced local and international dishes. Trout and Dover sole are especially good choices. Main courses are 20DM to 35DM ($10 to $17.50), a very low price considering the quality of the food. In truffle season, the chef mingles truffles freely with such costly ingredients as caviar.

Steigenberger Bad Pyrmont. Heiligenangerstrasse 2–4, 31812 Bad Pyrmont (in the garden adjacent to the spa). ☎ **800/223-5652** in the U.S. and Canada, or 05281/15-02. Fax 05281/15-20-20. 154 units. MINIBAR TV TEL. 265DM–365DM ($132.50–$182.50) double; 460DM–805DM ($230–$402.50) suite. Rates include breakfast. AE, DC, MC, V. Parking 16DM ($8).

This venerable 19th-century monument is the premier hotel in the spa, drawing people from all over the world. It's the only hotel in town with direct (covered) access to the spa. The calm and quiet rooms have a conservative modern gloss. They're the most comfortable in town. This retreat is well suited to repairing the wear and tear of urban life. Nothing even comes near the Steigenberger for service and amenities.

Dining/Diversions: There's an elegantly formal restaurant, the Palmengarten, and two bars.

Amenities: Modern pool (independent from the spa) sauna, whirlpool, room service, laundry, dry cleaning, baby-sitting, concierge, hair dryers.

WHERE TO DINE
Restaurant Bergkurpark. In the Hotel Bergkurpark, Ockelstrasse 11. ☎ **05281/40-01.** Main courses 18DM–55DM ($9–$27.50); fixed-price lunch 30DM ($15). AE, MC, V. Daily 11:30am–2:30pm and 6:30–9pm. INTERNATIONAL.

This restaurant is part of one of the town's finest hotels (see above). In summer, diners like to eat on the beautiful terrace. Otherwise, food is served in an elegantly decorated restaurant with large, comfortable chairs. We were impressed by the size and cleanliness of the kitchen, which turns out a reliable array of international specialties, with an emphasis on fresh produce. Try the medallions of veal with cream morels, or salmon with a dill and morel sauce.

7 Goslar

90km (56 miles) SE of Hannover, 43km (27 miles) S of Braunschweig, 60km (37 miles) SE of Hildesheim

In spite of Goslar's growth, the old portion of the town looks just as it did hundreds of years ago. This ancient Hanseatic and imperial town at the foot of the Harz Mountains owed its early prosperity to the Harz silver mines, which were worked as early as 968. The 600-year-old streets are still in use today, as are the carved, half-timbered houses.

For hikers and other outdoor enthusiasts, Goslar is a good starting point for day trips and excursions into the **Harz Mountains,** where some of the area's best ski resorts and several spas are found. Bus tours into the Harz Mountains can be booked at the tourist office (see below).

The legends and folklore associated with the Harz Mountains are perhaps more intriguing than the mountains themselves. Walpurgis Eve (the famous Witches' Sabbath), is still celebrated each year on the night of April 30. The mountain on which the witches supposedly danced in olden times was the **Brocken,** whose granite top has been flattened by erosion. The area around the Brocken is now a national park.

ESSENTIALS
GETTING THERE   By Plane   The nearest major airport is in Hannover.

By Train   The **Goslar Bahnhof** is on the Hannover–Hildesheim–Goslar–Bad Harzburg rail line, with frequent connections. It takes about 1¹/₂ hours to get to Goslar from Hannover. For information, call ☎ **01805/99-66-33.**

By Bus   Long-distance bus service to Goslar is available through **Reisebüro Bokermann** (☎ 05321/25138). Regional bus service to all parts of the city and nearby towns is offered by **Regionalbus Braunschweig GmbH,** Geschaftstelle, Goslar (☎ **05321/34310**).

By Car   Access is via the A7 Autobahn north and south; exit at either Seesen or Rüden.

VISITOR INFORMATION   Contact the **Kur- und Fremdenverkehrs-gesellschaft,** Markt 7 (☎ 05321/7-80-60), open November to April, Monday to Friday 9am to 5pm and Saturday 9:30am to 2pm; May to October, Monday to Friday 9am to 6pm, Saturday 9:30am to 4pm, and Sunday 9:15am to 2:15pm.

SEEING THE SIGHTS

To best explore this 1,000-year-old town, park your car, put on a pair of comfortable shoes, and set out on foot through the Altstadt, which has more than 1,000 half-timbered buildings from the 15th to the 18th centuries. Don't miss any of the numerous attractions that await you. The impressive **Rathaus** on the Marktplatz was built in 1450. The portico, with Gothic cross-vaulting, opening on to the Marktplatz, was used by merchants for centuries. Above this is the citizens' meeting hall and the councilmen's meeting chamber, lavishly decorated in the early 1300s with a cycle of 55 paintings depicting biblical and heathen iconography and believed to incorporate the zinc miners returning home from the Rammelsberg mines.

Marktplatz, in front of the Rathaus, was for a long time the town's hub of activity. In the center of the large square is a 13th-century fountain with two bronze basins and the German imperial eagle at the top. Many visitors view the performance of the town's **Glockenspiel** here as the highlight of their visit. Every day at noon, 3pm, and 6pm (there's a smaller version of the spectacle at 9am), a procession of mechanized miners, representing the silver trade of long ago, traipses out of the innards of the clock tower.

The churches of Goslar provide a look into the architectural history of the area. Many of the oldest—five had already been built by 1200—have been expanded and altered from their original Romanesque style to their current Gothic appearance. The Romanesque **Marktkirche,** just behind the Rathaus, has 700-year-old stained-glass windows and a 16th-century bronze baptismal font. From Marktplatz, take Rosentorstrasse north to reach the 11th-century **Jakobikirche,** later transformed into a Gothic masterpiece, complete with baroque altars. The church contains a *Pietà* by Hans Witten (1520). Farther down the street, the **Neuwerkkirche,** in a garden, has retained its purely Romanesque basilica, and its well-preserved sanctuary contains a richly decorated choir and stucco reliefs. It was originally constructed as a Cistercian convent in the late 1100s.

The 12th-century **Frankenberg Kirche,** on Bergstrasse, was completely remodeled in the 1700s. Over the elaborate baroque pulpit and altars hangs the intricately carved Nun's Choir Gallery, bedecked with gilded saints and symbols.

One of the reminders that Goslar was once a free imperial and Hanseatic city is the **Breites Tor (Broad Gate),** a three-towered town gate with walls up to 4m (13 feet) thick. From here you can follow the old town fortifications to the **Kaiserpfalz,** Kaiserbleek 6 (☎ 05325/70-43-58), a Romanesque palace that was the ruling seat of the emperors in the 11th and 12th centuries. You can view the 19th-century murals that cover its walls and visit the Ulrichskapelle, where the heart of Heinrich III was placed inside a large sarcophagus. The site is open April to October, daily 10am to 5pm; off-season, daily 10am to 4pm. Admission is 3.50DM ($1.75) for adults and 2DM ($1) for children.

For a quick and less exhausting look at the history of Goslar, visit the **Goslarer Museum,** at the corner of Abzuchstrasse and Königstrasse (☎ 05321/433-94), which has displays of the architecture of the early town and several relics of the past. The museum also contains a large geological collection from the Harz Mountains. It's open April to October, Tuesday to Sunday 10am to 5pm; November to March, Tuesday to Sunday 10am to 4pm. Admission is 3DM ($1.50) for adults and 2DM ($1) for children.

Just outside Goslar, about a mile south of the town center (follow the signs), you can explore an ancient mine. As early as the 3rd century A.D., lead, zinc, copper, silver, tin, and a little gold were being mined here. The **Rammelsberger Bergbau-museum,** Bergtal 19 (☎ 05321/75-00), conducts guided tours at hourly intervals, on foot or on a small underground train. The museum is open daily 9am to 6pm. Walking tours cost 9DM ($4.50) for adults and 5DM ($2.85) for children; the train is 13.50DM ($6.75) for adults and 11.50DM ($5.75) for children. For more information, call either the museum or the tourist office in Goslar (☎ 05321/7-80-60).

WHERE TO STAY

Dorint-Harzhotel Kreuzeck. Am Kreuzeck 1–4, 38644 Goslar-Hahnenklee. ☎ 05325/7-40. Fax 05325/7-48-39. www.dorint.de. E-mail: info.ZETKRE@dorint.com. 112 units. MINIBAR TV TEL. 274DM–325DM ($137–$162.50) double. Rates include buffet breakfast. AE, DC, MC, V. Free outdoor parking; 8DM ($4) in garage. Bus: 2434 from Goslar. Take the A7 Autobahn and exit at Seesen.

About 14km (9 miles) from Goslar is a well-rated, comfortable hotel set on a small lake with beautiful mountain scenery. The hotel offers country hospitality and exceptional food, and you may want to drive here for a meal even if you can't stay. Rooms, which range from medium to spacious, are comfortable and tranquil, the best in the area. Numerous ski lifts are in the vicinity, as well as an 30km (18¹/₂-mile) cross-country ski course. Ice-skating rinks are also nearby, and guests can enjoy an old-fashioned ride in a horse-drawn sleigh. In summer, available activities include sailing, windsurfing, hiking, tennis, and cycling.

Goldene Krone. Breitestrasse 46, 38640 Goslar (near the Breites Tor). ☎ 05321/3-44-90. Fax 05321/34-49-50. www.touronline.de/harz/hotel/goldkrone. E-mail: Goldene-Kronegoslar@t-online.de. 26 units. TV TEL. 175DM ($87.50) double. Rates include buffet breakfast. AE, DC, MC, V. Free parking. Bus: A or B.

This 300-year-old, recently renovated village inn comes complete with a friendly innkeeper, Herr Dietmar Pflug, who attends to the rooms and the meals. If you enjoy local color, this is a real find. Rooms are small and simple but homelike and clean; they're a great value for the price. The food and drink are good and inexpensive.

Hotel Der Achtermann. Rosentorstrasse 20, 38640 Goslar. ☎ 05321/7000-0. Fax 05321/7000-999. www.der-achtermann.de. E-mail: info@der-achtermann.de. 152 units. TV TEL. 269DM–309DM ($134.50–$154.50) double. Rates include breakfast. AE, DC, MC, V.

This hotel is a bustling but somewhat dowdy three-star hotel whose amenities rival those of four-star hotels nearby. Just after World War II, one of the round-sided 500-year-old watchtowers in the city's wraparound fortifications was enlarged with a white-sided extension, thereby creating an intriguing but rather cumbersome-looking amalgam of old and new architecture. If you're looking for a place to stay within the city itself, this is your best bet. Rooms are well furnished and comfortable, except for a handful that are a bit too small (most, however, are spacious). There are several restaurants and cafes, many of which are especially popular at lunchtime with local workers.

Kaiserworth. Markt 3, 38640 Goslar. ☎ 05321/70-90. Fax 05321/2-11-14. www.harzart.de. E-mail: hotel@kaiserworth.de. 50 units. TV TEL. 189DM–260DM ($94.50–$130) double. Rates include buffet breakfast. AE, DC, MC, V. Parking 7DM ($3.50). Bus: A or B.

The Kaiserworth is a big, old-fashioned hotel, right in the heart of town. The building dates from 1494 and is a sightseeing attraction in itself. The exterior is Gothic, with an arched arcade across the front, topped by a turreted oriel window facing Marktplatz. The large rooms are designed for comfort; the corner rooms are big enough to be suites. Rooms 102, 106, 110, 202, and 206 offer the best views of the nearby Glockenspiel performance outside. The hotel has a sedate wood-paneled breakfast room and a vaulted dining room, Die Worth. Step through a 1,000-year-old cistern and you'll be in the cellar restaurant, the Dukatenkeller, with stone pillars and ecclesiastical chairs.

WHERE TO DINE

Die Worth. In the Kaiserworth, Markt 3. ☎ **05321/70-90.** Main courses 18DM–40DM ($9–$20); fixed-price lunch 28DM ($14). AE, DC, MC, V. Daily noon–2:30pm and 6–11pm. Bus: A or B. NORTH GERMAN.

This is the most rustic and also the most attractive dining room in Goslar. The restaurant is in a Gothic stone crypt with vaulted ceiling and arches, stained-glass windows, wrought-iron lanterns, and trestle tables. The food is good and the portions are hearty, although all the recipes are very familiar. In season, roast game is featured with wild mushrooms, mashed apples, and berries. Rump steak is always an excellent choice, as is the more unusual *Harzer blaubeer schmandschnitzel*, a local recipe that combines pork schnitzel with blueberry-flavored cream sauce.

Goldene Krone. Breitestrasse 46, 38640 Goslar (on the eastern edge of Goslar). ☎ **05321/ 3-44-90.** Fax 05321/34-49-50. Reservations recommended. Main courses 22DM–35DM ($11–$17.50); fixed-price meals 25DM–35DM ($12.50–$17.50) at lunch, 40DM ($20) at dinner. AE, MC, V. Daily 11:30am–2pm and 6–9pm. Bus: A or B. INTERNATIONAL/ NORTH GERMAN.

It seems like everyone in town knows about this historic Weinstube. The decor is rustic and cozy, and you'll feel at home with the polite service. In addition to the standard north German dishes, occasional international dishes appear on the changing seasonal menu.

The Goldene Krone also has 19 rooms for rent, all with showers, TVs, and phones. Doubles are 155DM to 195DM ($77.50 to $97.50).

8 Göttingen

132km (82 miles) S of Hannover, 47km (29 miles) NE of Kassel, 109km (68 miles) SW of Braunschweig

Heinrich Heine pronounced Göttingen "famed for its sausages and university." The university in this Gothic town is one of the oldest and most respected in Germany. It was established in 1737 by George II, king of England and elector of Hannover. In time, Göttingen became the most popular university town in Europe. The university suffered relatively little damage during World War II.

Medieval romanticism and lively student life make Göttingen worth a day's visit. By making a slight detour, you can explore the university town before dipping into the fairytale country of the upper Weser Valley. Göttingen is halfway between Bonn and Berlin.

ESSENTIALS

GETTING THERE   By Train   Göttingen has frequent daily rail connections from Munich (trip time: 6 hr.), from Frankfurt (2¹/₂ hr.), and from Hannover (1 hr.). It lies on the major Kassel–Bebra–Göttingen–Hannover line, with frequent connections in all directions. For information, call ☎ **01805/99-63-3.**

By Bus   Long-distance bus connection, from such cities as Hannover, is provided by **Winkermann GmbH** (☎ **05143/98820**) and **Lempke & Koschick GmbH** (☎ **05143/46980**). Buses arrive in front of the main railway station. Regional bus service to other parts of Lower Saxony is offered by **Regionalbus Braunsweig** (☎ **0551/5-06-84-22**).

By Car　Access is via the A7 Autobahn, which runs north to Hannover and Hamburg.

VISITOR INFORMATION　Contact **Tourist-Information,** Altes Rathaus, Markt 9 (☎ **0551/5-40-00**), open November to March, Monday to Friday 9:30am to 6pm and Saturday 10am to 1pm; April to October, Monday to Friday 9:30am to 6pm and Saturday and Sunday 10am to 4pm.

GETTING AROUND　A network of buses run throughout the city 6am to around 10:30pm. Their main junction point is at the corner of the Judenstrasse and Friedrich-strasse, at the edge of the Altstadt. Fare is 2.70DM ($1.35), with a four-ticket package priced at 9.80DM ($4.90).

SEEING THE SIGHTS

In the center of Göttingen, you can wander down narrow streets, looking at wide-eaved, half-timbered houses. Many of the facades are carved and painted, and some bear marble plaques noting the famous people who lived inside, such as the more than 40 Nobel Prize winners who temporarily made their home here.

Altes Rathaus (bus: 4, 8, 10, 11, or 14) was originally built for trade purposes around 1270, but it wasn't completed until 1443. Its highlights are the open arcade, the Gothic heating system, and the Great Hall, in which the people of Göttingen once received princes and dignitaries, held courts of law, and gave feasts. **Marktplatz,** in front of the Town Hall, is the most interesting section of Göttingen. Here, since 1910, stands the "most-kissed girl in the world," the smiling statue of the Ganseliesel on the market fountain. By tradition, every student who attains a degree must plant a kiss on the lips of the little goose-girl.

Stadtisches Museum, Ritterplan 7–8 (☎ **0551/4-00-28-45;** bus: 3, 8, or 9), chronicles the history and culture of southern Lower Saxony. The most interesting exhibits are in the Göttingen history wing on the second floor. Surprisingly, the museum takes an uncompromising look at the town's Nazi past—most German towns tend to conceal it. Everything is here, from Hitlerjugend memorabilia to pages ripped from the local Nazi-run newspaper. The museum is open Tuesday to Friday 10am to 5pm and Saturday and Sunday 10am to 1pm. Admission is 3DM ($1.50) for adults and 1DM (50¢) for children.

SHOPPING

The commercial heart of town is **Wenderstrasse** and **Grönestrasse,** both of which feature pedestrian malls during most of the shopping day. Here, you'll find an appealing roster of cafes and delicatessens selling sausages and cakes, as well as purveyors of the German-style good life. If you want souvenirs, the local tourist office (see above) sells T-shirts, cigarette lighters, beer mugs, and posters. Antiques are found at **Bohm,** Barfusserstrasse 12 (☎ **0551/5-78-86**). Junkier, dustier, less pretentious, and a lot less expensive is **Brocante,** Kurzestrasse 16 (no phone), where the accumulated treasures and debris of estate sales are displayed in an appealingly disorganized jumble. For the works of local and international painters and sculptors, try **Galerie Apex,** Burgstrasse 46 (☎ **0551/4-68-86**).

WHERE TO STAY

Central Hotel. Judenstrasse 12 (near the university), 37073 Göttingen. ☎ **0551/5-71-57.** Fax 0551/5-71-05. 38 units, 11 with bath. TEL. 130DM ($65) double without bath,

150DM–190DM ($75–$95) double with bath; 250DM ($125) suite. Rates include buffet breakfast. AE, DC, MC, V. Parking 8DM ($4). Bus: 4, 8, 10, 11, or 14.

Although this quiet hotel on a pedestrian walkway is centrally located, as its name indicates, its best feature is the imaginative care the designers have used to decorate the rooms. For example, one room is flamboyantly wallpapered and curtained in vivid yellow and white tones, and another seems to be covered in pink silk. Some have TVs.

Eden-Hotel. Reinhauser Landstrasse 22A, 37083 Göttingen (near the new Rathaus). ☎ **0551/7-60-07.** Fax 0551/7-67-61. www.eden-hotel.de. E-mail: info@eden-hotel.de. 100 units. MINIBAR TV TEL. 190DM–367DM ($95–$183.50) double. Rates include buffet breakfast. AE, MC, V. Parking 10DM ($5).

The centrally located Eden-Hotel offers comfortable rooms with private bath or shower, hair dryer, trouser press, and fax outlet. The hotel serves good Italian food in its restaurant, La Locanda, with meals costing 20DM to 38DM ($10 to $19). It recently opened a German restaurant as well. Service is polite and attentive. Laundry and pressing service are available. Facilities include a sauna, an indoor pool, and a solarium.

Gebhards Hotel. Goethe-Allee 22–23, 37073 Göttingen (in front of the Bahnhof). ☎ **0551/ 4-96-80.** Fax 0551/4-96-81-10. www.goettingen.de. E-mail: tourismus@goettingen.de. 60 units. MINIBAR TV TEL. 280DM–350DM ($140–$175) double; 390DM–450DM ($195–$225) suite. Rates include buffet breakfast. AE, DC, MC, V. Free parking. Bus: 4, 8, 10, 11, or 14.

Gebhards is the best hotel in town. It's housed in a grand building that evokes a Tuscan villa, with a modern balconied annex built onto the back. The renovated interior offers high-ceilinged public areas and a pleasant bar area. Rooms are well designed and furnished. The cheapest double has a toilet and shower; the most expensive is an apartment with a complete private bath.

The attached restaurant has hosted a king of Denmark and a few German presidents. The menu is likely to feature fresh fish and fresh fish terrines, turbot poached in cider, medallions of quail, and Swabian pork with apple compote. Meals are served daily noon to 2:30pm and 6pm to midnight.

WHERE TO DINE

Ratskeller. Markt 9. ☎ **0551/5-64-33.** Reservations recommended. Main courses 15DM–40DM ($7.50–$20). AE, DC, MC, V. Daily 11:30am–midnight. Closed Christmas Eve. Bus: 4, 8, 10, 11, or 14. NORTH GERMAN.

This 600-year-old restaurant lies in the historic cellar of the Altes Rathaus. This is the best place to eat in town, although Göttingen is not known for its restaurants. The menu is varied and extensive, with the longest list of soups and hors d'oeuvres in the region. The chef also prepares the best *Tafelspitz* (boiled beef) in the area. Specialties include Old German Farmer's Plate (chicken breast and pork steak with fried potatoes and roast onions) or fresh trout au bleu with parsley potatoes.

Zum Schwarzen Bären (The Black Bear). Kurzestrasse 12. ☎ **0551/5-82-84.** Reservations required. Main courses 15DM–59DM ($7.50–$29.50); fixed-price lunch 28DM ($14); fixed-price dinner 40DM ($20). AE, MC, V. Tues–Sun noon–2pm; Tues–Sat 6–10pm. Bus: 4, 8, 10, 11, or 14. NORTH GERMAN.

This fine restaurant is housed in a black-and-white timbered building (ca. 1500). It still has the original stained-glass leaded windows. Inside, the ambience is tavern style, with a ceramic stove in the corner and dining rooms with intimate booths. The innkeeper wisely recommends the brook trout from the Harz Mountains or *Bärenpfanne* (various fillets with spätzle).

GÖTTINGEN AFTER DARK

Pick up a copy of *Universitätsstadt Göttingen Informationsheft* for a complete rundown of entertainment listings.

THE PERFORMING ARTS   The local symphony orchestra and boys choir are very active, and an annual Handel music festival is held in June. Information on schedules, venues, and tickets is available by calling ☎ **0551/5-67-71** or by contacting the tourist office (see above). Tickets are 15DM to 30DM ($7.50 to $15).

For 100 years, the **Deutsches Theater,** Theaterplatz 11 (☎ **0551/4-96-90**), has been staging classical and contemporary drama. Its counterpart, the **Junges Theater,** Hospitalstrasse 6 (☎ **0551/49-50-15**), has produced experimental works for 40 years. Performances of both are held Tuesday to Sunday, with tickets costing 20DM to 30DM ($10 to $15) for adults and 15DM to 20DM ($7.50 to $10) for students. The box office is open Monday to Saturday 11am to 1pm and 6 to 8:30pm.

BARS   A small cafe with indoor and outdoor seating, **Schroeder's Kneipe,** Judenstrasse 29 (☎ **0551/5-56-47**), serves beer, wine, and coffee, as well as chocolate and other sweets. It also has pinball. Open daily 11am to 2am. One of the more offbeat social centers of Göttingen is **KAZ (Kommunikations Aktions-Zentrum),** Hospitalstrasse 6 (☎ **0551/5-30-62**), where everyone from senior citizens to anarchists meet for drinks in one of the two on-premises pubs. One also serves traditional German cuisine; the other offers sandwiches. Within the complex, political forums, local discussion groups, and cultural associations meet regularly. Opening hours change with the seasons and the scheduling of volunteers and group discussion leaders, but in most cases, the center is open Monday to Thursday, noon to 2am, Friday noon to 4pm, and Saturday 11am to 1am. A jazz soundtrack sets the mood at **Café Kadenz,** Judenstrasse 17 (☎ **0551/4-72-08**), where a mellow crowd meets for beer, wine, coffee, and perhaps a light meal or snack. Hours are Monday to Saturday 10am to 1am, Sunday 11am to midnight.

DANCE CLUBS   One of the oldest nightlife venues in Göttingen, **Die Oper,** Nikolaistrasse 1B (☎ **0551/48-79-98**), was built 150 years ago as a pub. It offers music and dancing for a crowd aged 20 to around 32. Open Wednesday, Thursday, Friday, and Saturday, 10pm to 3am; depending on business, it's often open Thursday night as well. Expect to pay a cover of 7DM ($3.50).

LIVE MUSIC   Performance jazz is only featured 1 night a week at the excellent **Blue Note,** Wilhelmsplatz 3 (☎ **0551/4-69-07**); on other nights, musicians explore blues, salsa, African, reggae, and other Caribbean forms. Open Sunday to Thursday 8pm to 2am; Friday and Saturday to 3am. Cover for most bands is 15DM to 35DM ($7.50 to $17.50). Popular with locals and students, **Irish Pub,** Muhlenstrasse 4A (☎ **0551/4-56-64**), hosts live music every night of the week, from local rockers to visiting Irish folk bands. The pub serves Guinness, Kilkenny, and hard cider. There's never a cover, and it's open nightly 6pm to 2am.

STUDENT TAVERNS   A visit to Göttingen is traditionally capped by going to one of the student taverns, such as the cramped but convivial **Zum Altdeutschen,** Prinzenstrasse 16 (☎ **0551/5-65-45**), open daily 4pm to 1am; or **Irish Pub,** Mühlenstrasse 4 (☎ **0551/456-64**), dispensing Guinness, open daily 6pm to 2am.

GAY CLUBS   Café Kabale, Geismarlandstrasse 19 (☎ **0551/48-58-30**), is where lesbians gather. It's open Monday to Friday 2pm to 2am, Saturday and Sunday 10am to 2am. **Café Protz** and **Faces,** Nikolaikirchhofstrasse 11 (☎ **0551/5-76-99**) offer a cafe and a bar setting, respectively, that are popular with gay men. Café Protz is open 9am to 2am daily; Faces, daily 5pm to 2am.

9 Bad Wildungen

43km (27 miles) SW of Kassel, 160km (100 miles) NE of Frankfurt am Main

Bad Wildungen is more than 700 years old. Its healing mineral springs have long attracted northern Europeans to the rolling hills and deep forests of the Waldeck region, southwest of Kassel. Thousands of annual visitors come here seeking treatment for kidney and gallbladder disorders, or simply for rest and relaxation and the numerous cultural activities.

ESSENTIALS

GETTING THERE **By Train** There's frequent service on the Kassel–Fritzlar line from Kassel. For information, call ☎ **01805/99-66-33.** The nearest airport is at Frankfurt am Main, 160km (100 miles) away.

By Bus Bus service in the region is provided by **B.K.W. GmbH** (☎ **05621/802810** for information).

By Car From Kassel, take Route 49 southwest, then go west on Route 253.

VISITOR INFORMATION For information, contact the **Kurverwaltung,** Langemarckstrasse 2 (☎ **05621/704113**), open Monday to Friday 8am to 4:30pm and Saturday 8am to noon.

SIGHTS & ACTIVITIES

Rising above the Altstadt is the massive tower of the 14th-century **Stadtkirche** (☎ **05621/40-11**), the most impressive (and oldest) structure in the town, with interesting Hallenkirch architecture. It was restored in 1995. The highlight of the church is its remarkable Niederwildungen Altarpiece, one of the best examples of early German painting. Painted in 1403 by Master Konrad von Soest, the wing-paneled altarpiece contains a large, dramatic scene of the crucifixion, flanked by six smaller scenes from the life of Christ. The work shows an obvious French influence in the use of delicate colors and figures, made even more vivid by the use of actual gold. The church is open daily 10:30am to noon and 2 to 5pm.

The **spa gardens** augment the town's natural wooded surroundings with carefully planted flowers from all parts of the world, as well as with several attractive buildings, including two band shells where outdoor concerts are frequently given. The grounds are dotted with lawn chairs. The modern horseshoe-shaped arcade houses the George-Viktor Spring, plus several exclusive shops and a small auditorium.

SHOPPING Bad Wildungen's shops carry fashion suitable for Germany's most sophisticated cities. Shops line either side of the Brunnenallee. One of the most appealing is **Manhenke,** Brunnenallee 28 (☎ **05621/960253**), which sells clothes and accessories for both men and women.

WHERE TO STAY

Hotel-Pension Die Hardtmühle. Im Urfftal 5-7, 34537 Bad Wildungen. ☎ **05626/ 99-90.** Fax 05626/7-43. 32 units. TEL. 130DM–170DM ($65–$85) double; 250DM ($125) apt for 4. Rates include buffet breakfast. AE, DC, MC, V. Free parking. 10km (6 miles) west of the town center; follow signs to Urfftal.

Don't check into this hotel if you're looking for lots of activities or anything approaching urban diversions. Come here instead for bucolic views of lazy cows grazing in nearby fields, an environment so pressure-free as to be almost somnolent, and access to outdoor pastimes. Accommodations are simple but comfortable, completely unpretentious, and suitable for catching up on the sleep you might have lost in more frenetic environments. Besides the double rooms, there's also one apartment, often rented by families. The family that runs the hotel doesn't speak much English, but this is still a great place for a getaway. There's a tennis court and an outdoor pool.

Maritim Badehotel. Dr.-Marc-Strasse 4 (at the entrance to the gardens, in the Kurpark), 34537 Bad Wildungen. ☎ **05621/79-99.** Fax 05621/79-97-99. www.maritim.de. E-mail: infowil@maritim.de. 230 units. MINIBAR TV TEL. 260DM–320DM ($130–$160) double; 380DM–900DM ($190–$450) suite. Rates include buffet breakfast. AE, DC, MC, V. Parking 15DM ($7.50).

The Maritim Badehotel is located in the center of the town's clinical and cultural activities. No hotel in Bad Wildungen comes close to this one for comfort, style, amenities, and facilities. This place evokes the grandeur of another era. Large and rambling, it branches out in two great wings from the circular domed entrance. The renovated rooms are large, comfortable, sunlit, and airy, all with views of the Waldeck woodlands and spa gardens.

Dining: The hotel's restaurant offers a rich cuisine for those not worried about calories. Special diets are also available, including vegetarian meals. Veal dishes are the specialty; the *Kalbsschnitzel* (veal scallops) cooked with herbs is a tasty choice.

Amenities: Large, heated indoor pool; therapeutic facilities, including carbon-dioxide baths, massages, and complete medical attention by a fine professional staff; room service; baby-sitting; concierge; dry cleaning; laundry; hair dryers.

Treff Hotel Quellenhof. Brunnenallee 54, 35437 Bad Wildungen (across the street from the Kurpark). ☎ **05621/80-70.** Fax 05621/80-75-00. 112 units. MINIBAR TV TEL. 226DM–268DM ($113–$134) double. AE, DC, MC, V.

This white-sided hotel has a mansard roof and art nouveau gables. Rooms are international in decor and carefully outfitted. There's a stylish restaurant (Park Restaurant; see "Where to Dine," below). There's also live music at Café Bistrot on Friday night and at the Moltemstoffel Bar on Saturday night. Facilities include a sauna, solarium, and whirlpool. The hotel also contains Bad Wildungen's only casino.

WHERE TO DINE

The hotel dining rooms enjoy a culinary monopoly in Bad Wildungen; there is no major independent restaurant.

Park Restaurant. In the Treff Hotel Quellenhof, Brunnenallee 54. ☎ **05621/80-70.** Reservations recommended. Main courses 14DM–45DM ($7–$22.50). AE, DC, MC, V. Daily 11am–2pm and 6–10pm. INTERNATIONAL.

Stylish, airy, and international, this is the showcase restaurant of the Treff Hotel (see above). Though it's a top place to dine, its prices are affordable. The immaculately clean interior is outfitted with lots of green plants. The staff is alert and well trained. Menu items include well-prepared salads, roasted meats, pastas, pastries, and such traditional German dishes as sauerbraten and *Rostbraten.*

BAD WILDUNGEN AFTER DARK

The tourist office keeps a list of special events, which are staged almost every week. Concerts and theater take place usually in the **Neues Kurhaus** in the town center or at the **Kursaal** in Reinhaltshausen, not far from Bad Wildungen. For tickets, call ☎ 05621/70-47-73.

Spielbank, Brunnenallee 54 (☎ **05621/96-00-56**), located in the Treff Hotel (see above), is the resort's only casino. It's minor league as Germany's casinos go. Open daily 2:30 to 10:30pm, with an entrance fee of 5DM ($2.50). Bring your passport.

Nighttime diversions in Bad Wildungen revolve around the **Brunnenallée** and its extension, the **Brunnenstrasse,** in the form of lively bars and cafes that stay open until around 2am. Some of the best include the **Warsteiner Ecke,** Brunnenstrasse 66 (☎ **05621/74172**); the **Ratskeller,** Marktplatz (☎ **05621/71855**); and **Hosenlantz,** Brunnenallée 32 (☎ **05621/92996**), a small, tucked-away bar with occasional live music. The most earthy and rowdy of the town's beer halls is **Bräuhaus,** Frankenberger-strasse 2 (☎ **05621/74150**), which is open Monday to Friday 6 to 11pm, Saturday noon to 11pm, and Sunday 8:30am to 4pm.

10 The Fairy-Tale Road

To tour the Fairy-Tale Road (Märchenstrasse) is to take a trip though the land made immortal by the Brothers Grimm. German folklore survived in rural areas at least until the mid–19th century, and much of its charm is still visible and nostalgically remembered today. The Grimm brothers were the earliest scholars of their country's folklore; they traveled to far-flung corners of Germany in the early 19th century to record the tales they heard. Their compendium, *Kinder- und Hausmärchen* (*Grimm's Fairy Tales*), is the world's second most frequently translated book, after the Bible.

Today you can follow the Fairy-Tale Road, a 595km (370-mile) route from Hanau, near Frankfurt, where the Brothers Grimm were born, to Bremen, where the "Town Musicians of Bremen" lived. The route goes through some of the prettiest medieval villages in the country, all listed on the German Tourist Office's maps of the road. In some towns, marionette shows (in German, but universal in appeal) are given in summer, and museums keep the legends alive, including the one in Ziegenhain in the Schwalm Valley, where costumes that might have been worn by Little Red Riding Hood and her grandmother are displayed.

DAY 1

Begin in **Hanau,** 20km (12¹/₂) miles east of Frankfurt on the River Main, where Jakob (1785–1863) and Wilhelm (1786–1859) Grimm were born. Appropriately, the Fairy-Tale Road starts at a monument to the story-telling brothers at Neustadter Marktplatz. The memorial, erected in 1898, is about all that will interest you in this traffic-clogged suburb of Frankfurt. Hanau was heavily bombed in World War II.

From Hanau, go along B43 about 20km (12 miles) northeast to **Gelnhausen,** where the remains of the imperial palace evoke memories of the emperor, Friedrich Barbarossa, and his lover, Beautiful Gela. Barbarossa constructed the castle here on an island in the 12th century.

Continue another 20km (12 miles) to **Steinau an der Strasse,** where the Grimm brothers spent their carefree youth. Visit the Amtshaus, the Renaissance palace, and see a performance at the fairy-tale puppet theater. Half-timbered buildings line cobblestone streets. The surrounding woods might have been the home of Snow White. In the center of the main square is a memorial fountain honoring the brothers.

Continue north on B40 following the directions to **Fulda,** noted for its baroque architecture, as exemplified by the bishops' palace on Schlossstrasse, overlooking the city. The prince-bishops were guardians of the tomb of St. Boniface, the apostle of Germany. Fulda's cathedral dates from 1704, and pilgrims still worship at the tomb of St. Boniface, in a crypt beneath the main altar. Consider staying overnight in Fulda.

Romantik Hotel Goldener Karpfen, Simpliziusbrunner 1 (☎ **0661/8-68-00;** fax 0661/8680100), in Fulda, was built in the baroque era, but the facade is of a later date. Try to arrive for afternoon tea in the hotel's elegant lounge. The place rents

50 cozy and comfortable rooms; a double goes for 300DM to 450DM ($150 to $225). The hotel also serves some of the best food in town. Meals range from 48DM to 90DM ($24 to $45).

DAY 2

Leave Fulda in the morning and take B254 into the Vogelsberg Mountains, going via Grossenlüder to **Lauterbach,** 24km (15 miles) northeast of Fulda. The town is known for its medieval half-timbered houses and its two castles, Eisenbach and Riedesel. In one of the Grimms' tales, the Little Scalawag loses his sock in Lauterbach. After your visit, follow Route 254 northwest to **Alsfeld,** a town of half-timbered houses and cobblestone streets. Its 1512 Altes Rathaus is a showpiece.

Follow the route along the Schwalm River, which the Germans call *Rotkäppchenland,* or Little Red Riding Hood country. Signs point to **Neustadt,** with its circular tower, from which Rapunzel might have let down her golden tresses. Continue north through Schwalmstadt for 29km (18 miles) to **Homberg.**

Krone Inn, Marktplatz (☎ **05681/93-07-73**), in Homberg, claims to be the oldest inn in Germany. The best of the hearty dishes is the Kronenplatte, which combines three kinds of meat with fresh vegetables, potato croquettes, and salad. Main courses cost from 15DM to 35DM ($7.50 to $17.50). Meals are served daily noon to 2pm and 6 to 9:30pm, but you can always stop in for a glass of wine or a foaming mug of beer. Credit cards are not accepted.

From Homberg, follow the signs for 39km (24 miles) north to **Kassel,** where you'll want to spend the night. The Waldeck Region and the Reinhards Forest around Kassel were the birthplace of many legends and tales about witches, sleeping princesses, strange beasts, and magic spells. These tales had a profound influence on the Grimm brothers, who lived in Kassel from 1798 to 1830. The **Bruder Grimm Museum,** at Schone Aussicht 2, contains letters, portraits, and mementos.

Schloss Hotel Wilhelmshöhe, Schlosspark 8 (☎ **0561/3-08-80;** 0561/3-08-8428), in Kassel, is not an old castle but a completely modern structure directly across the street from former imperial palaces. The 105-room hotel has many private terraces with views of the rolling castle park and its buildings, which were once a summer residence for the landgraves and electors of Hessen-Kassel. Later the area became the summer residence of Kaiser Wilhelm II. Doubles cost 280DM ($140), and meals begin at 45DM ($22.50).

DAY 3

Leaving Kassel, go along B3 for some 16km (10 miles) north to **Münden** (known more properly as Hannoversch-Münden). The Fulda and Werra Rivers meet here. In the town center are some 700 half-timbered houses built in many styles. Also in Münden is the tombstone of the much-maligned Doctor Eisenbart, who is remembered every year at a folk festival.

Jagshaus Heede, Hermannshager Strasse 81 (☎ **05541/23-95**), in Hann-Münden, is inside the town's nature preserve. The 18-room hotel is an enlarged former private house. There's a cafe-style sun terrace on the premises, as well as a children's playground. The dining room serves conservative German cuisine and offers generous portions; set-price meals cost 25DM to 45DM ($12.50 to $22.50); double rooms rent for 120DM ($60) each. AE, DC, MC, V.

From Münden you can detour from the Fairy-Tale Road, taking the Autobahn (E45) to Göttingen (see above), where you may want to spend the night.

DAY 4

Return to the Fairy-Tale Road by going back to Münden and then heading north on Route 80. About 10km (6 miles) north of Münden in the village of Veckerhagen, go left and follow the signs to Sababurg.

Right outside the village of Sababurg lies **Dornröschenschloss Sababurg,** Hofgeismar (☎ **05671/80-80**), a park and castle said to be the setting of the Sleeping Beauty legend. You'll almost start to believe the tale when you see the Italianate turrets of the castle. The park is said to be the oldest zoological garden in the world. The wilderness of ancient oak and beech trees, along with the tall ferns, adds to the fairy-tale atmosphere of the area. In the castle courtyard, where sweet-smelling briar roses still bloom, you half expect to see the prince coming to awaken Sleeping Beauty. The castle here has an excellent restaurant.

After viewing the castle, take the road back to the Weser Valley village of Oberweser and make a left turn onto B80 heading north. After some 13km (8 miles) you reach the spa of **Bad Karlshafen,** a resort noted for its baroque buildings.

Hotel Zum Schwan, Conradistrasse 3, Bad Karlshafen (☎ **05672/10-44;** 05672/1046), is an elegant 32-room spa hotel situated beside the main bathhouse, opposite the town pond. Built in 1765, it has the baroque facade of a palace, with an entrance terrace overlooking the river. Excellent meals are served here, with many regional dishes featured, costing 48DM ($24) and up. An attractively furnished double rents for 210DM ($105).

Continue on Route 80 north (which becomes Route 83) to **Höxter,** the eastern-most town in Westphalia. Among its many Renaissance and baroque buildings, the town's most visited attraction is Dechanei (the Deanery). You can take Corveyer Allee from Höxter for about 3km (2 miles) to Corvey, one of the oldest Benedictine abbeys in Germany, planned by Charlemagne and constructed by his son, Ludwig the Pious, in 822.

Follow the Weser River north for some 32km (20 miles) to the town of **Boden-werder,** the birthplace of Lügen Baron, known as the "Liar Baron" von Münchhausen. He's honored by the **Münchhausen Museum,** filled with mementos of his fanciful life.

After Bodenwerder, head northwest on Route 83 for Hameln (see above), where you'll want to spend the night.

DAY 5

After a night in Hameln, take Route 83 northwest to the Autobahn (E30) and continue west beyond Osnabruck until you connect with the E37 Autobahn heading northeast to **Bremen** (see above), the final stop of the trip.

16 Hamburg

Hamburg has many faces. A walk down the neon-lit Reeperbahn at night will revive those old memories of "Sin-City Europe." A ride around Alster Lake in the center city will reveal the elegance of its finest parks and buildings. A stroll along one of Hamburg's many canals will show you why this city has been called the "Venice of the North." Contrasts are evident wherever you look. Amid the steel-and-glass structures of the modern city is the old baroque Hauptkirche St. Michaelis. A Sunday-morning visit to the Altona fish market will give you a good look at early shoppers mingling with late-night partyers.

Hamburg has had to be flexible to recover from the many disasters of its 1,200-year history. This North Sea port was almost totally destroyed during World War II. But out of the rubble of the old, the industrious Hamburgers rebuilt a larger and more beautiful city, with huge parks, impressive buildings, and important cultural institutions. Hamburg is today the greenest city in Europe, with nearly 50% of its surface area marked with water, woodlands, farmland, and some 1,400 parks and gardens. Green is, in fact, the city's official color.

Hamburg, the second-largest city of Germany, lies on the Elbe River, 109km (68 miles) from the North Sea, 285km (177 miles) northwest of Berlin, 119km (74 miles) northeast of Bremen, and 150km (93 miles) north of Hannover.

1 Orientation

ARRIVING

BY PLANE   The **Airport Hamburg-Fuhlsbüttel,** Paul-Baumer-Platz 1–3, is 8km (5 miles) north of the city center. It's served by many scheduled airlines and charter companies, with regular flights to major German airports and many European and intercontinental destinations. **Lufthansa** (☎ **01803/80-38-03**) offers flights to Hamburg from most major German cities, and many national carriers fly into Hamburg, including Air France from Paris and British Airways from London. United Airlines, Delta, and Lufthansa offer direct flights from the United States. For flight information in Hamburg, call ☎ **040/507-50.**

An ultramodern terminal and passenger pier at the airport has a roof shaped like an enormous aircraft wing. This terminal contains an array of interesting shops and boutiques—even a branch of Harrods of London—as well as restaurants and other establishments.

The Hamburger Verkehrsverbund (HVV) **Air Express bus 110** runs every 10 minutes, linking the airport with the city's rapid-transit rail network (both U-Bahn and S-Bahn). A bus departs for the airport from the Hauptbahnhof every 20 minutes 5:40am to 9:20pm daily. Airport buses heading for the Hauptbahnhof leave daily 6:22am to 10:42pm. The one-way fare is 8.50DM ($4.25) for adults and 4DM ($2) for children under 12. A taxi from the airport to the city costs from 35DM ($17.50), with a trip time of 25 minutes.

BY TRAIN   There are two major rail stations, the centrally located **Hamburg Hauptbahnhof,** Hachmannplatz 10 (☎ **040/39-18-30-46**), and **Hamburg-Altona** (☎ **040/3918-2387**), in the western part of the city. Most trains arrive at the Hauptbahnhof, although trains from the north of Germany, including Westerland and Schleswig, pull into Altona. The two stations are connected by train and S-Bahn. Hamburg has frequent train connections with all major German cities, as well as frequent continental connections. From Berlin, 15 trains arrive daily (trip time: 2 hr. 30 min.), 37 from Bremen (trip time: 54 min. to 1 hr. 16 min.), and 33 from Hannover (trip time: 1 hr. 30 min.). For information, call ☎ **01805/996633.**

BY BUS   Because of Hamburg's location astride most of the rail lines of north Germany, the majority of passengers arrive by train. But if the bus appeals to you, call **Central Omnibus** (☎ **040/24-75-75**). From their headquarters across from the railway station, they'll supply information on fares and schedules for the buses that funnel passengers in from such other cities as Berlin, Hannover, Nürnberg, Munich, and Stockholm. Information about short-haul buses from surrounding towns and villages is available from **Hamburger Verkehrsverbund** (☎ **040/32880**).

BY FERRY   Ferry service links Harwich, England, and the St. Pauli Landungsbrücken in Hamburg (trip time: 20 hr.). For information, call **Scandinavian Seaways,** Van-der-Smissenstrasse (☎ **040/38-90-30**).

BY CAR   The A1 Autobahn reaches Hamburg from the south and west, the A7 from the north and south, the A23 from the northwest, and the A24 from the east. Road signs and directions to Hamburg are frequently posted.

VISITOR INFORMATION

For visitors to Hamburg, information is offered at several centers. **Tourist-Information,** Hauptbahnhof, Kirchenallee exit (☎ **040/30-05-12-01**), is open daily 7am to 11pm; and **Port Information,** St. Pauli Landungsbrücken (☎ **040/30-05-12-00**), is open daily 10am to 7pm. Hamburg also has a North American tourist representative, **Diversified Destinations International,** 38 West 32nd St., Suite 1210, New York, NY 10001 (☎ **212/967-3110**).

CITY LAYOUT

Hamburg is a showplace of modern architecture; historic structures stand side by side with towering steel-and-glass buildings. The 12km^2 (4^1/$_2$ square miles) of parks and gardens are a vital part of the city, as are the 57km^2 (22 square miles) of rivers and lakes. The city is not compact and can't be easily covered on foot. Many sections of interest are far apart; you'll have to depend on public transportation or taxis.

The **Alster** is the perfect starting point for a pleasurable exploration of Hamburg. This lake, rimmed by the city's most significant buildings, sparkles with the white sails of small boats and ripples with the movement of motor launches. The lake is divided by the Lombard and John F. Kennedy bridges into the **Binnenalster (Inner Alster)** and the larger **Aussenalster (Outer Alster).** The Binnenalster is flanked on the south and the west by the **Jungfernstieg,** one of Europe's best-known streets and Hamburg's most vital artery and shopping district. For landlubbers, the best view of the Alster is from this "maiden's path."

From the Hauptbahnhof, on the eastern fringe of the heart of town, in the vicinity of the Binnenalster, two major shopping streets fan out in a southwesterly direction, toward St. Petri Church and the Rathaus. They are **Spitalerstrasse** (reserved for pedestrians) and **Mönckebergstrasse,** paralleling it to the south. These streets contain some of the city's finest stores. Stay on Mönckebergstrasse to reach **Rathausmarkt,** which is dominated by the Rathaus, a Renaissance-style city hall palace.

The center of Hamburg offers fine opportunities for walking; for example, the eastern shoreline of the Binnenalster opens onto **Ballindamm,** which contains many elegant stores. At the foot of this lake is the Jungfernstieg, already mentioned; and along its western shoreline is yet another main artery, the Neuer Jungfernstieg. At the intersection of the Jungfernstieg and Neuer Jungfernstieg is one of the more fascinating streets of Hamburg, the **Colonnaden,** a colonnade of shops and cafes. In this neighborhood stands the Hamburgische Staatsoper, the famous modern opera house.

Neighborhoods in Brief

Central Hamburg   This is the commercial and shopping district of Hamburg, seat of many of its finest hotels and restaurants. The district centers around Binnenalster and the Rathaus (City Hall). Boat rides on the Alster lakes are a major attraction. Many historic buildings that withstood World War II stand here, including St. Petri, the oldest surviving structure.

The Harbor   The Port of Hamburg is the world's fifth-largest harbor, stretching for nearly 40km (25 miles) along the Elbe River. More than 1,500 ships from all over the world call each month. Since 1189, the stretch of water has been one of the busiest centers for trade on the Continent, making Hamburg one of Germany's wealthiest cities.

St. Pauli   This is the nightlife center of Hamburg, with lots of erotica. The district is split by its famous street, the Reeperbahn, neon-lit and dazzling, offering all sorts of nighttime pleasures—cafes, sex shows, bars, discos, and music halls.

Altona   Formerly a city in its own right, this western district is now integrated into Greater Hamburg. It was once populated mainly by Jews and Portuguese. Today it's the scene of Hamburg's famous Fischmarkt, which takes place at dawn every Sunday.

Pösseldorf   Northwest of Aussenalster, this is a tree-filled residential district, with many villas dating from the 1800s. Many exemplary Jugendstil buildings can be seen here. The district is largely occupied by upwardly mobile professionals, including a lot of media stars.

GETTING AROUND

A word to the wise: Park your car and use public transportation in this busy city. Practically all public transportation services in the Hamburg area—the **U-Bahn** (subway), **S-Bahn** (city rail), **A-Bahn** (commuter rail), buses, and harbor ferries—are run by **Hamburger Verkehrsverbund (HVV),** Steinstrasse 12. For information, call ☎ **040/32880.** Tickets are sold at Automats and railroad ticket counters.

BY PUBLIC TRANSPORTATION   Hamburg's **U-Bahn,** one of the best in Germany, serves the entire central area and connects with the **S-Bahn** surface trains in the suburbs. This network is the fastest means of getting around, but buses offer a good alternative. The advantage of surface travel, of course, is that you get to see more of the city.

Fares for both U-Bahn and bus are 2.50DM to 5DM ($1.25 to $7.50), depending on the distance. You buy your ticket from the driver or from vending machines at stops and stations. If you plan to make a day of it, you can purchase a **day ticket** for unlimited use of public transportation services for 8DM ($4).

There are also discount cards that offer free travel on all public transport in Hamburg, as well as free admission to 11 Hamburg museums and a 30% discount on city tours, guided tours of the port, and lake cruises. A 1-day card goes for 12.80DM ($6.40) for individuals or 24.50DM ($12.25) for families. A 3-day card costs 26.50DM ($13.25) for individuals and 43DM ($21.50) for families.

BY TAXI   Taxis are available at all hours; call ☎ **040/44-10-11** or 040/66-66-66. Taxi meters begin at 3DM ($1.50) and rise between 2.50DM ($1.25) and 3DM ($1.50) per kilometer after that, the cost of a trip from the airport to the city center depends on traffic.

Fast Facts: Hamburg

American Express   The Amex office in Hamburg is at Ballindamm 39 (☎ **040/ 30-90-80;** U-Bahn: Jungfernstieg) and is open Monday to Friday 9am to 5:30pm and Saturday 10am to 1pm.

Bookstores   Frensche, Landesbank Galerie, Spitalerstrasse 26C (☎ **040/ 32-75-85;** U-Bahn: Hauptbahnhof), is a good English-language bookstore with a large selection of books and tapes. It's open Monday to Wednesday 10am to 7pm; Thursday to Friday 10am to 7:30pm; Saturday 10am to 4pm.

Business Hours   Most **banks** are open Monday to Friday 8:30am to 12:30pm and 1:30 to 3:30pm (many until 5:30pm on Thursday). Most **businesses** and **stores** are open Monday to Friday 9am to 6pm and Saturday 9am to 2pm (4 or 6pm on the first Saturday of the month).

Car Rentals   We don't recommend that you rent a car for touring Hamburg, but an automobile is ideal for the environs. Rentals are available at **Avis,** Drehbahn 15–25 (☎ **040/34-16-51;** U-Bahn: Gansemarkt), or at **Hertz,** Kirchenallee 34-36 (☎ **040/2-80-12-01-03;** U-Bahn: Hauptbahnhof).

Consulates   See "Embassies & Consulates" in "Fast Facts: Germany," in chapter 2.

Currency Exchange   The most convenient place for recent arrivals to exchange foreign currency for deutschmarks is the **ReiseBank** at the Hauptbahnhof (☎ **040/32-34-83**), which is open daily 7:30am to 10pm. The same bank maintains a branch at the Altona Station (☎ **040/390-3770**), open Monday and Wednesday to Friday 7:30am to 7:30pm, and Tuesday and Saturday 9am to 2pm and 2:45 to 5pm. There's also a branch in Terminal 4 of Hamburg's airport (☎ **040/5075-3374**), open daily 6:30am to 10pm.

Doctor or Dentist   Ask at the British and American consulates or go to **Allgemeines Krankenhaus,** Lohmühlen Strasse 5, 20099 Hamburg (☎ **040/28-90-11;** U-Bahn: Stadthaus Brücke), where you'll find an English-speaking staff.

Drugstores   Pharmacies that stock foreign drugs include **Internationale Apotheke,** Ballindamm 39 (☎ **040/30-96-060;** U-Bahn: Jungfernstieg), open Monday to Friday 8am to 7pm and Saturday 9am to 3pm. **Roth's Alte Englische Apotheke,** Jungfernstieg 48 (☎ **040/34-39-06;** U-Bahn: Jungfernstieg), is open Monday to Friday 8:30am to 6:30pm and Saturday 9am to 2pm.

Hamburg Accommodations & Dining

ACCOMMODATIONS ■
Aussen Alster **16**
Europäischer Hof **22**
Garden Hotels Hamburg **12**
Hafen Hamburg **8**
Hamburg Marriott **24**
Hamburg Renaissance Hotel **25**
Hotel Abtei **11**
Hotel Lilienhof **23**
Kempinski Hotel Atlantic **18**
Maritim Hotel Reichshof **20**
Prem Hotel **14**
Radisson SAS Hotel Hamburg **5**
St. Raphael **21**
Steens Hotel **19**
Travel Charme Hotel
    Bellevue **15**
Vier Jahreszeiten **13**
Wedina Hotel **17**

DINING ◆
Alten Rathaus **28**
At Nati **2**
Cölln's Austernstuben **30**
Cuneo **7**
Eisenstein **32**
Fernsehturm Hamburg
    Restaurant **4**
Fischereihafen Restaurant **10**
Fischküche **31**
Il Ristorante **26**
Landhaus Scherrer **3**
Le Canard **1**
Nikolaikeller **29**
Old Commercial Room **9**
Ratsweinkeller Hamburg **27**
Restaurant Nil **6**

St.-Benedict-strasse
11
Fernsicht
Gellertstrasse
Bellevue
Sierichstrasse
Hans-Henny-Jahn-Weg
Osterbekstrasse
BARMBEK
Adolph-Schönfelder-Strasse
Weidestrasse
Herderstrasse
Beethovenstrasse
Hochallee strasse
Hallerstrasse
Mittelweg
Harvesthuder Weg
Alster-park
Bellevue
Herbert-Weichmann-Strasse
UHLENHORST
Winterhuder Weg
Hamburger Strasse
Oberaltenallee
5
Lerchenfeld Wartenau
Rothenbaumchaussee
ROTHERBAUM
12
Schöne Aussicht
Mundsburgerdamm
Mittelweg
Aussenalster
Schwanenwik
HOHENFELDE
Sechslingspforte
Mühlendamm
75
Lübecker-strasse
Alsterufer
13
14
15
An der Alster
16
Koppelstrasse
17
Wall-strasse
BORGFELDE
Th.-Heuss-Platz
Gustav-Mahler-Park
Wall
Kennedybrücke
Lombardsbrücke
18
19
Binnenalster
Ballindamm
Hachmannplatz
23
20
ST. GEORG
Hansaplatz
Steindamm
21
ABC-Strasse
24
Poststrasse
Jungfernstieg
22
Hauptbahnhof
Adenauerallee
Kurt-Schumacher-Allee
Spaldingstrasse
75
Heidenkampsweg
25 **26**
Rathaus Stock Exchange
Mönckebergstrasse
St. Petri Kirche
27
Speersort Steinstrasse
Mönckebergstrasse
Nordkanalstrasse
Hammerbrookstrasse
Mönckebergstrasse
Domstrasse
ALSTADT
30
Ost-West-Strasse
Dovenfleet
Oberbaum-brücke
Banksstrasse
Amsinckstrasse
Nagelsweg
28
29
Holzbr. Matten
Sande
Katharinen-strasse
31
Kajen
Brooktorkai

0   1/4 mi
0   1/4 km

Emergencies   Dial **110** for the police or an ambulance or emergency doctor or dentist; **112** for the fire brigade; and **01805/10-11-12** for the German Automobile Association (ADAC).

Laundry/Dry Cleaning   Your hotel reception desk can often recommend a laundry or dry cleaning place nearby. If not, try **Express Wasch-Center,** Friedrichstrasse 30 (☎ **040/3-19-14-34;** S-bahn: Reeperbahn), for both laundry and dry cleaning. Open Monday to Friday 9:30am to 10pm and Saturday 9:30am to 5pm.

Post Office   The post office at the Hauptbahnhof, Hachmannplatz 13 (☎ **040/ 3-25-51-60**), is convenient. You can make long-distance calls here far cheaper than at your hotel. Telegrams, telexes, and faxes can also be sent. It's open Monday to Friday 8am to 8pm, Saturday 8am to 6pm, and Sunday 10am to 4pm. A branch office located at the airport (☎ **040/5-00-04-85**) is open Monday to Friday 6:30am to 9pm, Saturday 8am to 6pm, and Sunday 10am to 6pm.

Rest Rooms   See "Fast Facts: Germany" in chapter 2. There are several decent public facilities in the center of Hamburg.

Safety   Hamburg, like all big cities of the world, has its share of crime. The major crimes that tourists encounter are pickpocketing and purse and camera snatching. Most robberies occur in the big tourist areas, such as the Reeperbahn and the area around the Hauptbahnhof, which can be dangerous at night, but much less so than in Frankfurt or Munich.

Telegrams/Telex/Fax   These can be sent from the post office at the Haupt-bahnhof, Hachmannplatz 13 (☎ **040/3-25-51-60**).

Transit Information   For U-Bahn and S-Bahn rail information, call the Hauptbahnhof, Hachmannplatz 10 (☎ **01805/996633**).

2 Where to Stay

Hamburg is an expensive city with an abundance of first-class hotels but a limited number of budget accommodations, especially in the center city. During a busy convention period, you may have trouble finding a room. A department within **Hamburg's Tourist Information Office (Tourismus Centrale),** Steinstrasse 7 (☎ **040/30-05-13-00;** fax 040/30-05-13-33), in the Hauptbahnhof, at Kirchenallee in the Wandelhalle, can book accommodations. Rooms from more than 200 hotels in all price categories are available. There's a fee of 6DM ($3) per reservation. You can use this agency on a last-minute basis, but no more than 7 days in advance of the time you'll need the room. Hotel-booking desks can also be found at the airport in Arrival Hall A.

NEAR THE HAUPTBAHNHOF
VERY EXPENSIVE

✪ **Kempinski Hotel Atlantic Hamburg.** An der Alster 72, 20099 Hamburg (near the Aussenalster). ☎ **800/426-3135** in the U.S., or 040/2-88-80. Fax 040/24-71-29. www.kempinski.atlantic.de. E-mail: hotel.atlantic@kempinski.com. 267 units. MINIBAR TV

A Map Note

To locate the hotels in this section, see the "Hamburg Accommodations & Dining" map on pp. 566–567.

TEL. 425DM–525DM ($212.50–$262.50) double; from 595DM ($297.50) suite. AE, DC, MC, V. Parking 30DM ($15). U-Bahn: Hauptbahnhof.

This sumptuous hotel, the Kempinski chain's flagship, is one of the two great hotels of the north. It's in a central location filled with trees and imposing villas and was one of the few buildings in the neighborhood to escape the bombs of World War II. Michael Jackson, Prince, and Madonna cast their votes for this hotel, but we still think Vier Jahreszeiten (see below) is number one. Most rooms are very spacious with high ceilings, private safes, and luxury mattresses. Some are air-conditioned. Baths are large, with hair dryers and robes.

Dining: The elegant Atrium Bar opens onto a neoclassical fountain; there's also a pub-style restaurant called Atlantic Mühle. The stylish Atlantic Restaurant is one of the finest in northern Germany, with some 55 cooks preparing modern haute cuisine that's matched by a superb wine list. Meals are served daily noon to 3pm and 6pm to midnight.

Amenities: Room service, laundry, dry cleaning, baby-sitting, sauna, solarium, Chanel Institut de Beauté, and a beautifully maintained chlorine-free indoor pool.

EXPENSIVE

Aussen Alster. Schmilinskystrasse 11, 20099 Hamburg (a 5-min. walk from the rail station and a 3-min. walk from the Alster). ☎ **040/24-15-57.** Fax 040/2-80-32-31. 27 units. TV TEL. 260DM–310DM ($130–$155) double. Rates include buffet breakfast. AE, DC, MC, V. Closed Dec 22–27. U-Bahn: Hauptbahnhof.

Small and exclusive, and on a quiet residential street, Aussen Alster attracts actors, advertising directors, executives, writers, and artists. Its stylish, ultramodern interior was designed by one of Germany's most famous architects. Hamburg film producer Klaus Feddermann and his partner, Burkhardt Stoelck, manage the place with panache. Rooms are medium-sized, white-walled, angular, and consciously simple. Everything is designed for style and comfort, from the luxurious beds to the immaculate baths with hair dryers.

Dining/Diversions: Have a drink in the hotel bar, where on cool nights a fireplace burns, and then enjoy the international restaurant, Schmilinsky, where Italian food is a specialty.

Amenities: Room service, laundry, garden (in back), sauna, solarium.

Europäischer Hof. Kirchenallee 45, 20099 Hamburg (across from the Hauptbahnhof). ☎ **040/24-82-48.** Fax 040/24-82-47-09. www.srs-worldhotels.com. 320 units. MINIBAR TV TEL. 250DM–440DM ($125–$220) double. Rates include buffet breakfast. AE, DC, MC, V. Parking 22DM ($11). U-Bahn: Hauptbahnhof.

Europäischer Hof is the largest privately owned hotel in Hamburg. It lacks the atmosphere of the Maritim Hotel Reichshof or the chic of Aussen Alster hotel, although it has its supporters, especially among business clients. The well-furnished and medium-sized rooms have soundproof windows; most have tiny art deco dressing rooms, fax ports, and fine carpets that make for a welcoming ambience.

Dining/Diversions: Two restaurants await visitors, the Chalet and the Burgerstube. A piano bar offers evening entertainment.

Amenities: 24-hour room service, laundry, dry cleaning, sauna, solarium, indoor pool, fitness room.

Maritim Hotel Reichshof. Kirchenallee 34–36, 20099 Hamburg (across from the Hauptbahnhof). ☎ **040/24-83-30.** Fax 040/24-83-38-88. www.maritim.de. E-mail: YvonneBredec/ HAM/Maritim@MARITIM. 303 units. MINIBAR TV TEL. 260DM–415DM ($130–$207.50) double; from 435DM ($217.50) suite. Rates include buffet breakfast. AE, DC, MC, V. Parking 20DM ($10). U-Bahn: Hauptbahnhof.

When the Reichshof was built in 1910, it was the largest hotel in Europe. In World War II it lost most of its upper floors, but the landmark art nouveau lobby remained

---

ⓘ Family-Friendly Hotels

Garden Hotels Hamburg *(see p. 573)*   For the family that can afford it, this traditional hotel in the western sector looks out onto the Outer Alster Lake. Here you'll find cozy comfort in a safe neighborhood.

Radisson SAS Hotel Hamburg *(see p. 573)*   Children will enjoy the setting and the surprising architecture.

Steens Hotel *(see p. 571)*   This simple but clean and safe hotel is great for a family on a budget.

---

intact. This hotel is a favorite with business travelers, so more than half its rooms are classified as singles. Rooms are medium to spacious, comfortable, and have double glazing; those on the top floor open onto good views of the city. Baths are small but with up-to-date plumbing.

Dining/Diversions: Tea is served in the lounge. The Piano Bar is open 5pm to 2am; live music begins at 9pm and continues past midnight. The Classic-Restaurant is excellent.

Amenities: Room service, laundry, dry cleaning, swimming pool, sauna.

✪   **Prem Hotel.** An der Alster 9, 20099 Hamburg. ☎ **040/24-83-40-40.** Fax 040/2-80-38-51. www.hotel-prem.de. E-mail: info@hotel-prem. 53 units. MINIBAR TV TEL. 340DM–395DM ($170–$197.50) double; 395DM–580DM ($197.50–$290) suite. AE, DC, MC, V. Free parking. Bus: 108.

This beautifully located mansion-hotel is called the "white house on the Alster." It attracts a well-heeled clientele. The glistening facade overlooks the lake, and the rear faces a quiet garden with umbrella-covered tables. The reception salons show off a personalized collection of French antiques and reproductions. Rooms, most furnished with Louis XV-style pieces, are well cared for with luxury mattresses. Garden-facing rooms are much quieter than those on the Alster. Half the baths are well equipped with big mirrors, marble tubs, and hair dryers. The rest are a bit cramped with shower stalls and fewer amenities.

Dining: You can enjoy breakfast in the white-and-gold rococo dining room jutting out into the garden. La Mer, the restaurant, is one of the finest in the city, famous for its imperial oysters and salmon roe. Service is formal, and the cuisine is both German and international.

Amenities: 24-hour room service, laundry, dry cleaning, sauna.

✪   **St. Raphael.** Adenauerallee 41, 20097 Hamburg. ☎ **800/528-1234** in the U.S. and Canada, or 040/24-82-00. Fax 040/24-82-03-33. www.bestwestern.com. E-mail: raphaelhotels@ t-online.de. 130 units. MINIBAR TV TEL. 258DM–318DM ($129–$159) double; 458DM ($229) suite. Rates include buffet breakfast. AE, DC, MC, V. Parking 10DM ($5). U-Bahn: Hauptbahnhof.

One of the gems of Hamburg, this Best Western hotel is a rival of the Prem, without the Prem's stuffiness. It's so special that it sometimes attracts the kind of clients who stay at the Vier Jahreszeiten or Kempinski. Rooms are beautifully appointed, with plush carpeting, soundproof windows, state-of-the-art baths, and many extras such as hair dryers and safes. The best are in the Raphael Royale wing, which has a private entrance in the rear.

Dining: A full-service restaurant offers everything from weekly specialties to weekly buffets. The Sunday champagne brunch is a popular affair.

Amenities: Room service, concierge, baby-sitting, dry cleaning, laundry. The hotel also has a rooftop fitness center, with a sauna, solarium, and Jacuzzi, plus a sweeping view of Hamburg.

Travel Charme Hotel Bellevue. An der Alster 14, 20099 Hamburg (facing the Alster, a short ride from the Hauptbahnhof). ☎ **040/28-44-40.** Fax 040/28-44-42-22. www.tc-hotels.de. E-mail: Bellevue@tc-hotels.de. 93 units. MINIBAR TV TEL. 205DM–300DM ($102.50–$150) double; 395DM ($197.50) suite. Rates include buffet breakfast. AE, DC, MC, V. Parking 15DM ($7.50). Bus: 108.

Many theatrical celebrities make this their Hamburg choice. Some larger rooms contain traditional furnishings, but the new singles are modern, often Scandinavian style. All have trouser presses and hair dryers. The front windows open onto the lake, but the back rooms are quieter.

Dining/Diversions: The ground-floor Alster Room serves as a breakfast room. Guests can enjoy international cuisine as well as regional specialties in the restaurant, Alster Charme, which is open for lunch. Another restaurant, Schifferstube, serves dinner. Live piano music is played several nights a week in the bar, after 6pm.

MODERATE

Steens Hotel. Holzdamm 43, 20099 Hamburg (near the Alster). ☎ **040/24-46-42.** Fax 040/2-80-35-93. E-mail: steenhotel@t-online.de. 11 units, 2 without bath. TV TEL. 170DM–180DM ($85–$90) double. Rates include continental breakfast. AE, MC, V. U-Bahn: Hauptbahnhof.

Despite its classy location, a short walk from the much more expensive Atlantic Hotel, this century-old house charges reasonable rates. Rooms are carefully maintained but short on style. Each has a private shower; all but two have a private toilet. Baths have hair dryers. Breakfast is the only meal served.

Wedina. Gurlittstrasse 23, 20099 Hamburg (near the lake, a 5-min. walk from the Hauptbahnhof). ☎ **040/24-30-11.** Fax 040/2-80-38-94. E-mail: wedina@aol.com. 42 units. TV TEL. 165DM–240DM ($82.50–$120) double. Rates include buffet breakfast. AE, DC, MC, V. Parking 15DM ($7.50). Bus: 108.

This recently remodeled 18th-century town house is a quiet retreat. Most rooms open onto a small, informal Tuscan-style garden. All are tastefully styled and range from small to medium, each with a good bed and a tidy bath with a hair dryer. The hotel is owned and run by an English-speaking family.

INEXPENSIVE

Hotel Lilienhof. Ernst-Merck-Strasse 4, 20099 Hamburg. ☎ **040/24-10-87.** Fax 040/2-80-18-15. 24 units, none with private bath. TV TEL. 120DM ($60) double without shower, 138DM ($69) double with shower. Rates include buffet breakfast. AE, DC, MC, V. U-Bahn: Hauptbahnhof.

This unpretentious five-story hotel is a good place to stay for convenience and the economy, but forget grand style. The simple, clean, and rather small rooms have double-insulated windows to keep out some noise from the heavy traffic on the street. The quieter rooms overlook the back of the hotel. None contain a toilet, but some have private showers, and adequate toilet facilities are scattered throughout the hallways.

IN BINNENALSTER & NEUSTADT
VERY EXPENSIVE

✪ **Vier Jahreszeiten.** Neuer Jungfernstieg 9–14, 20354 Hamburg (on the Binnenalster). ☎ **800/223-6800** in the U.S. and Canada, or 040/3-49-40. Fax 040/34-94-2600. www.hvj.de. E-mail: vier-jahreszeiten@hvj.de. 158 units. MINIBAR TV TEL. 495DM–625DM

($247.50–$312.50) double; from 1,050DM ($525) suite. AE, DC, MC, V. Parking 30DM ($15). U-Bahn: Hauptbahnhof.

This warm, mellow hotel is the finest in Germany and one of the best in the world. It was founded in 1897 by Friedrich Haerlin (today it's run by a Japanese company). Its position is ideal, right on the Binnenalster. Built in the baronial style, it evokes the grand Edwardian hotels. Antiques are used profusely throughout. Despite the large size, personal service is a hallmark. Although no two rooms are alike, they are all beautiful, with period furnishings, Oriental rugs, and all the modern amenities, including bedside controls and double glazing on the windows. This is a hotel for connoisseurs.

Dining/Diversions: The dining room, Haerlin, decked out with old tapestries, gold-framed mirrors, and four Dionysian porcelain cherubs, serves excellent international cuisine. There's also the informal Grill Room, where meats are roasted on spits along one wall. The tearoom, the two-level Condi (Hamburg's answer to Demel's of Vienna), is a favorite rendezvous point. There's also a cocktail bar, a wine shop, and a confectioner's shop selling the chef's own pastry.

Amenities: 24-hour room service, laundry, dry cleaning; horseback riding and golf can be arranged.

EXPENSIVE

Hamburg Marriott. ABC Strasse 52, 20354 Hamburg. ☎ **800/228-9290** in the U.S., or 040/35-05-0. Fax 040/35-05-17-77. www.marriott-hotels.com. 277 units. A/C MINIBAR TV TEL. 310DM–380DM ($155–$190) double; from 440DM ($220) suite. AE, DC, MC, V. Parking 25DM ($12.50). U-Bahn: Gänsemarkt.

This traditionally styled hotel is one of the finest in Hamburg. It was built on the site of the old Gänsemarkt, where geese were sold in the Middle Ages. The hotel is also near the Hanse Viertel shopping complex. The fashionable surrounding area is filled with boutiques, wine bars, shops, and restaurants. Rooms range from small to medium. The lower price is for standard rooms; the higher for studios. Lavish suites are also available. One hundred rooms are reserved for nonsmokers.

Dining/Diversions: Live music begins at 6pm in the lobby-level piano bar. The casual and moderately priced restaurant, American Place, features California wine and cuisine, plus food from New Orleans and Boston. All popular American holidays and events are celebrated here. Service is daily noon to 3pm and 5:30pm to midnight. A special theater menu is also available.

Amenities: Full concierge services, including baby-sitting and car rental; 24-hour room service; same-day laundry and dry cleaning (Monday to Friday). This is the only downtown hotel with a pool, sauna, whirlpool, and fitness center; it also has the Dominique Beauty Farm, ice machines on all floors, and fax and computer connections in each room.

Hamburg Renaissance Hotel. Grosse Bleichen, Hanse-Viertel, 20354 Hamburg. ☎ **800/228-9290** in the U.S. and Canada, or 040/34-91-80. Fax 040/34-91-89-19. www.renaissancehotels.com. 205 units. A/C MINIBAR TV TEL. 350DM–400DM ($175–$200) double; from 580DM ($290) suite. AE, DC, MC, V. Parking 25DM ($12.50). U-Bahn: Jungfernstieg.

A 19th-century building with 20th-century comfort, the nine-story Renaissance recently affiliated itself with Marriott but has kept its original name. From the sunken, antique-furnished lobby to the carpeted bar area, you'll be feted by the staff and serenaded by a resident pianist. Rooms range from well-appointed doubles to sumptuously upholstered suites. Most are quite spacious, with paired queen-sized beds fitted with luxury mattresses, plus large baths with robes, makeup mirrors, phones, and hair dryers. The hotel was constructed behind the facade of a historic building, and the entire complex was designed with connections to the Hanse Viertel Galerie Passage, Europe's longest shopping arcade.

Dining/Diversions: After drinks in the lounge bar, you can dine at the Brasserie Noblesse, which offers distinguished French and German cuisine.

Amenities: Room service, laundry, dry cleaning, massage, fitness area.

Radisson SAS Hotel Hamburg. Marseillerstrasse 2, 20355 Hamburg (in the Planten un Blomen Park). ☎ **040/3-50-20.** Fax 040/35-02-35-30. www.radisson.com/hamburgde. E-mail: res@hamza.rdsas.com. 560 units. A/C MINIBAR TV TEL. 270DM–430DM ($135–$215) double; from 550DM ($275) suite; business class 340DM–480DM ($170–$240) double. AE, DC, MC, V. Parking 19DM ($9.50). Bus: 102.

This 32-story high-rise hotel is of real architectural interest. It looks like a collection of narrow black lines banded together vertically. Although it's very professionally run and has many winning features, we'd rank it under the Hamburg Renaissance or the Marriott. The medium-sized rooms are beautifully appointed, many with paneled walls; all contain individually controlled air-conditioning, radios, trouser presses, and hair dryers. One floor is reserved for nonsmokers.

Dining/Diversions: Guests can order South Pacific-style dinners at Trader Vic's, or sample north German and Scandinavian cuisine in the rustic Vier-Landerstuben. For coffee, pastries, or drinks, the Park Bistro and Lobby Lounge are good choices; later, head for the 26th floor to enjoy a view over Hamburg and the harbor in the nightclub/bar, Top of Town.

Amenities: 24-hour room service, express laundry, baby-sitting; heated pool, sauna, solarium, fitness studio.

MODERATE

✪ **Hafen Hamburg.** Seewartenstrasse 9, 20459 Hamburg. ☎ **040/31-11-30.** Fax 040/31-11-3-755. www.hotel-hamburg.de. 230 units. TV TEL. 195DM–205DM ($97.50–$102.50) double. AE, DC, MC, V. Parking 12DM ($6). U-Bahn: Landungsbrücke.

This Hamburg landmark, constructed in the Wilhelmian style, offers panoramic views of the river and the harbor traffic. This hotel attracts the commercial traveler who's not on an expense account. The functionally furnished rooms are unusually spacious. If they're within your budget, book the more expensive harbor-view rooms. Each comes with a comfortable bed fitted with a fine mattress, plus a well-equipped private bath with plush towels and a hair dryer.

IN HARVESTEHUDE

Garden Hotels Hamburg. Magdalenenstrasse 60, 20148 Hamburg (a mile from the center). ☎ **040/41-40-40.** Fax 040/4-14-04-20. E-mail: garden@privat.eurochannel.net. 60 units. MINIBAR TV TEL. 280DM–440DM ($140–$220) double; from 550DM ($275) suite. AE, DC, MC, V. Parking 15DM ($7.50). U-Bahn: Hallerstrasse.

This hotel dates from 1791, and over the years it has entertained many luminaries, including King Christian VIII of Denmark in 1824. The location, however, isn't for everyone. It stands in the Hamburg-Harvestehude district on the western sector of the Outer Alster Lake, about a mile from the historic heart of town and some 10km (6 miles) from the airport. It attracts many visitors from the publishing industry. Modern art and well-chosen antiques add to the sophisticated comfort of the rooms. Most are generously sized, and the luxurious baths have hair dryers.

Dining/Diversions: The hotel, which serves breakfast only, has a bar adjoining the winter garden.

Amenities: 24-hour room service, laundry, dry cleaning, terrace garden, swimming pool, fitness area.

✪ **Hotel Abtei.** Abteistrasse 14, Harvestehude, 20149 Hamburg (5km/3 miles north of the center). ☎ **040/44-29-05.** Fax 040/44-98-20. E-mail: abtei@relaischateau.fr. 11 units. MINIBAR TV TEL. 350DM–500DM ($175–$250) double. AE, DC, MC, V. U-Bahn: Klosterstern.

This suburban hotel is small, choice, and engaging, with a discreet and well-trained staff. It occupies a 19th-century villa that was once an opulent private residence. The high-ceilinged rooms retain many aspects of a private home, including antique furniture and, in many cases, the building's original elaborate plasterwork and parquet floors. Each room contains its own stereo system. Every other year mattresses are renewed, and the beds are sumptuous. Baths are complete with hair dryers and robes. The hotel has a fine restaurant.

IN WINTERHUDE

✪ **Hanseatic Hotel.** Sierichstrasse 150, 22299 Hamburg-Winterhude. ☎ **040/48-57-72.** Fax 040/48-57-73. 12 units. TV TEL. 300DM–400DM ($150–$200) double. AE, MC, V. U-Bahn: Hudt Wackerstrasse. Alster ferry.

This hotel, on the banks of the Alster River, close to the Winterhude Market, is the smallest and most delightful place to stay in Hamburg. In summer, a little flower garden blooms in the front. The town house, painted a soothing white, was built around 1930. The interior evokes an English gentlemen's club, complete with prints of horses, chintz upholstery, and leather-bound books. Rooms, ranging from small to medium, are furnished in a one-of-a-kind manner, containing many antiques. Breakfast is the only meal served, but there's a bistro next door and other restaurants in the vicinity. Guests meet, mingle, and mix their own drinks at the complimentary bar.

IN NIENSTEDTEN

✪ **Louis C. Jacob.** Elbchaussee 401, 22609 Hamburg. ☎ **040/82-25-50.** Fax 040/82255444. www.hotel-jacob.de. E-mail: jacobrelaischateau.fr. 86 units. A/C MINIBAR TV TEL. 390DM–585DM ($195–$292.50) double; from 1,500DM ($750) suite. AE, DC, MC, V. Parking 24DM ($12). Lies 13km (8 miles) west via Elbchaussee.

Lying outside the city center along the Elbe, this tranquil deluxe hotel compares to the Vier Jahreszeiten and Kempinski Hotel Atlantic Hamburg. In summer you can sit out under linden trees 2 centuries old and enjoy views of the river traffic. Built in 1791 as a guesthouse, it has been brought up to stunning modernity after a major overhaul. The owners believe in spectacular luxury and coddling their guests. The hotel owns one of the biggest private art collections in the north of Germany. The medium to spacious rooms are elegantly appointed and decorated, with walk-in closets, private safes, data ports, luxury mattresses, and state-of-the-art baths, each with plush towels, toiletries, and a hair dryer.

Dining/Diversions: Even if you don't stay here, consider driving out for the modern French cuisine and a wine list finer than that of any other establishment in Hamburg (according to the *Wine Spectator*). The service is among the best in the city, and from the truffled scallops to the chocolate mousse cake, the food is impeccable.

Amenities: Room service, laundry/dry cleaning, concierge.

3 Where to Dine

Hamburg life is tied to the sea, and that includes the cuisine: lobster from Helgoland; shrimp from Büsum; turbot, plaice, and sole from the North Sea; and huge quantities of fresh oysters. Of course, there's also the traditional meat dish, hamburger steak, called *Stubenküchen,* and the favorite sailor's dish, *Labskaus,* made with beer, onions, cured meat, potatoes, herring, and pickle. The *Aalsuppe* (eel soup) is the best known of all Hamburg's typical dishes.

> ### ⓘ Family-Friendly Restaurants
>
> **Fernsehturm Hamburg Restaurant** *(see p. 577)*   It's family fun, as diners enjoy good food in a 900-foot revolving television tower.
>
> **Schulauer Fährhaus** *(see p. 581)*   This establishment stands at Wedel, the "welcome point" for ships arriving in the Hamburg harbor. Children will delight in watching the ships go by as they eat. Afterward, don't miss the downstairs museum of 200 little boats preserved in bottles.

IN BINNENALSTER & NEUSTADT

VERY EXPENSIVE

✪ **Cölln's Austernstuben.** Brodschrangen 1–5. ☎ **040/32-60-59.** Reservations recommended. Main courses 37DM–59DM ($18.50–$29.50). AE, DC, MC. Mon–Fri noon–3pm and 6–10pm, Sat 6–10pm. U-Bahn: Rathausmarkt. NORTH GERMAN/CONTINENTAL.

The food here is the best in central Hamburg. This "oyster-eating house" originally opened in 1761 as a waterfront fish house. It now occupies much larger quarters, filling seven dining rooms, and is one of the most stylish and best-liked restaurants in town. It serves oysters, of course, and many other dishes as well—try pheasant in puff pastry with white beans; minestrone studded with lobster meat and served with lobster-stuffed ravioli; schnitzels of salmon in balsamic-vinegar linden-flower sauce; or the breast of goose with wild mushrooms and pepper-flavored Bordeaux sauce.

EXPENSIVE

Fischküche. Kajen 12 (a 1-min. walk from the Elbe). ☎ **040/36-56-31.** Reservations recommended. Main courses 29.50DM–40DM ($14.75–$20). AE, DC, MC, V. Mon–Fri noon–3pm and 6–11pm. U-Bahn: Rödingsmarkt. SEAFOOD.

Breezy and unpretentious, this restaurant prides itself on specializing exclusively in fish. It's in a modern building, with a dining room brightly outfitted in bold colors and extravagant chandeliers. Menu items include a changing array of seafood, brought in fresh daily and priced with an eye for good value. Choices vary with the day's catch, but might include several different preparations of clear or creamy fish soup, marinated crabmeat salad, flounder with spaghetti and lemon-butter sauce, codfish with potatoes and onion, and fillet of monkfish in a mustard-herb sauce. It's hardly haute cuisine, but locals flock here for the robust specialties and no-nonsense service.

Il Ristorante. Grosse Bleichen 16. ☎ **040/34-33-35.** Reservations required. Main courses 30DM–45DM ($15–$22.50); fixed-price menu 59DM ($29.50) for 3 courses, 85DM ($42.50) for 5 courses. AE, DC, MC. Daily noon–11pm. U-Bahn: Jungfernstieg. ITALIAN/INTERNATIONAL.

The most fashionable Italian restaurant in Hamburg is located in the heart of town in a very modern building. The atmosphere is luxurious and formal; and only the freshest ingredients find their way into the kitchen. Even such simple dishes as carrot-and-celery soup have great flavor. After a taste of some well-chosen Italian wine, consider the perfectly prepared crayfish in a saffron sauce, or the marinated salmon with green asparagus mousse. Mellow balsamic vinegar and aromatic fresh herbs lend zest and flavor to many dishes. Impeccably trained waiters provide smooth service even if you aren't a familiar face.

MODERATE

✪ **Eisenstein.** Friedensallee 9. ☎ **040/3904-606.** Reservations recommended. Main courses 27DM–37DM ($13.50–$18.50); fixed-price lunch 23DM ($11.50); fixed-price dinners 49DM ($24.50). No credit cards. Daily noon–3pm and 6pm–midnight. U-Bahn: Altona Bahnhof. INTERNATIONAL.

Where to Stay

To locate the restaurants in this section, see the "Hamburg Accommodations & Dining" map on pp. 566–567.

The food available here is representative of the wide range of cultures that Hamburgers have been exposed to, thanks to the city's role as a great port. The menu lists specialties from Thailand, Japan (including sushi and sashimi), southern France, and Italy, as well as traditional and very fresh versions of the North German cuisine that Hamburg excels in, particularly fresh Atlantic Sea fish prepared virtually any way you want. The setting is a solid-looking, much-restored factory and former warehouse whose soaring, russet-colored brick walls envelop diners in a cozy womb against the sometimes gray weather outside. The clientele is artsy, hip, and stylish; the staff is cooperative, and the food is surprisingly flavorful, considering its diversity.

Ratsweinkeller Hamburg. Grosse Johannisstrasse 2. ☎ **040/36-41-53.** Reservations required. Main courses 20DM–60DM ($10–$30); fixed-price menus 26.50DM–120DM ($13.25–$60). AE, DC, MC, V. Mon–Sat 11am–10:30pm, Sun 11am–4pm. Closed holidays. U-Bahn: Rathausmarkt. HAMBURG/INTERNATIONAL.

The city takes pride in the distinguished Ratsweinkeller Hamburg, in business since 1896. The overall theme is suggested at the entrance, where you'll find a stone statue of Bacchus. The main dining hall has high vaulted ceilings, wood-paneled columns, and large stained-glass windows. The 26.50DM ($13.25) menu is one of the best values in town, and even more wallet-friendly are the large portions, which make appetizers unnecessary. One excellent dish is the halibut steak in curry sauce. The fresh sole *bonne femme* is heavenly and served in large portions; or try the Hamburg crab soup, the best in the city. Listen for the great-grandfather clock to chime the quarter hour, resounding throughout the chambers.

INEXPENSIVE

Alten Rathaus. Börsenbrücke 10 (in the Altstadt). ☎ **040/3751-89-07.** Reservations recommended. Main courses 28DM–32DM ($14–$16). AE, MC, V. Mon–Sat noon–3pm and 6–10pm. U-Bahn: Rathausmarkt. NORTH GERMAN.

This restaurant occupies a carefully preserved mid-19th-century building set close to the mouth of the Elbe, in the most historic part of the Altstadt. The upper floors are a preferred meeting place for civic associations, and a faithful clientele has been coming here for years. Surprisingly for Hamburg, no fish is served. Instead, the chefs prepare some of the town's best grilled meats, along with Argentine beef dishes and some savory chicken or turkey offerings. Scampi salad is a lunch favorite. Finish with the Tyrolean apple pie or vanilla ice cream in a hot strawberry sauce.

Nikolaikeller. Cremon 36. ☎ **040/36-61-13.** Reservations required. Main courses 19.50DM–34DM ($9.75–$17). AE, MC, V. Mon–Sat noon–10pm. Bus: 37. HAMBURG.

This is the type of food that brings Hamburg sailors in out of the fog to warm up. You can see the sprawling maritime facilities of Hamburg from the windows of this restaurant, which is often filled with a crowd of local businesspeople and workers. The Hamburg cuisine includes more than two dozen varieties of herring. You can also order goulash soup Altona-style; bacon pancakes topped with cranberries; fresh sole; or salmon. Ample quantities of local beer are provided in oversize mugs.

IN EIMSBÜTTEL

At Nati. Rutschbahn 11. ☎ **040/410-38-10.** Reservations not required. Main courses 24DM–40DM ($12–$20). AE, DC, MC, V. Mon–Thur noon–3pm and 5pm–midnight, Fri and Sun 11am–midnight, Sat 5pm–midnight. U-Bahn: Hauptbahnhof. TURKISH.

One of the best choices for a taste of authentic Turkish cuisine is this popular kebab restaurant, which has been offering delicious and very inexpensive meals from the central region of Anatolia for the last 22 years. The owner and chef, Ali Reza Kaya, has maintained a traditional kebab house atmosphere. The extensive menu includes various kebabs, lamb fillet with spinach, and scampi with garlic. On the desserts side the baklava and halvah are recommended, as are the traditional sweet lemon teas and, of course, the thick, strong Turkish coffee you can stand your spoon up in.

Fernsehturm Hamburg Restaurant. In the Heinrich-Hertz-Turm in Rotherbaum, Lagerstrasse 2–8. ☎ **040/43-80-24.** Reservations recommended. Main courses 24DM–48DM ($12–$24). AE, DC, MC, V. Daily noon–2:30pm and 5–11pm. S-Bahn: Sternschanze. U-Bahn: Messehallen. CONTINENTAL.

Fernsehturm, on the 14th floor of Hamburg's revolving 275m (900-foot) television tower, offers fine views and a cuisine that's just as good. Inside the tower are six sections, with separate decors inspired by New York, London, Paris, Copenhagen, Rome, and Hamburg. One of Hamburg's best-known chefs is in charge, and popular dishes include Argentine fillet steak and turbot in butter-and-champagne sauce. During the afternoon you can have coffee and cake for 12DM ($6). Visitors must purchase a 6.50DM ($3.25) ticket to ascend the tower.

IN ALTONA

✪ **Fischereihafen Restaurant.** Grosse Elbstrasse 143 (a 10-min. taxi ride from the wharf area of Landungsbrücken). ☎ **040/38-18-16.** Reservations required. Main courses 28DM–68DM ($14–$34); fixed-price 4-course menu 89DM ($44.50); "Hamburg menu" 65DM ($32.50). AE, DC, MC, V. Sun–Thurs 11:30am–10:30pm, Fri–Sat 11:30am–10pm. S-Bahn: Königstrasse. SEAFOOD.

Fischereihafen, established some 4 decades ago, is the best seafood restaurant in town, if you prefer true local fare rather than the internationally oriented cuisine of the pricey Cölln's Austernstuben. Every day, the staff buys only the freshest fish and shellfish at the Hamburg auction hall. The menu changes daily, depending on what seafood is available. The second floor is said to be full of "fish and VIPs"—the latter have included the likes of Helmut Kohl and Tina Turner. Appetizers include fillet of sole and lobster or a plate of fresh oysters, and the house special is turbot with salmon mousse dotted with truffles. Picture windows open onto a view of the Elbe.

✪ **Landhaus Scherrer.** Elbchaussee 130. ☎ **040/8-80-13-25.** Reservations required. Main courses 46DM–68DM ($23–$34); fixed-price menus 189DM ($94.50) and 198DM ($99). AE, DC, MC, V. Mon–Sat noon–2:30pm and 6:30–10:30pm. Bus 135. CONTINENTAL.

Once a brewery, the Landhaus is now a citadel of gastronomy on the Elbe at Altona. It has gained a reputation for correct service and imaginatively prepared cuisine. The chef's superbly precise, inventive cookery combines the flavors of the home region of northern Germany with those of lands farther afield. The result is an often stunning culinary achievement. Specialties are fresh seafood, as well as excellent meat. An unusual variation might be roast goose with rhubarb in cassis sauce. Dessert might be praline cream or one of 30 types of pastry loading down the sweets trolley. Because of its location in a country house surrounded by trees, this place is also popular for wedding receptions.

✪ **Le Canard.** Elbchaussee 139, Ottensen (southwest of Hamburg's center). ☎ **040/ 8-80-50-57.** Reservations required. Main courses 52DM–79DM ($26–$39.50); fixed-price menus 149DM–229DM ($74.50–$114.50). AE, DC, MC, V. Mon–Sat noon–2:30pm and 7–10:30pm. Bus 115. CONTINENTAL.

Le Canard is one of the best restaurants in Germany. Virtually every restaurant critic in the country has lauded the unusual *cuisine moderne* of its imaginative owner/chef, Josef Viehhauser. The unpretentious decor is made more alluring by the soft lighting. The lobster soup is the city's finest, and even the iced soup of potatoes—a kind of vichyssoise—comes graced with caviar. The crisp fried duck with a Bordeaux sauce is the best we've had in Hamburg, but we were especially drawn to an unusual concoction as an appetizer—a terrine of Roquefort with gazpacho jelly and olive bread. Pigeon with chanterelles is a delectable choice, or you can have your chanterelles with a perfectly sautéed turbot. The place isn't so trendy that they're afraid to serve an old-fashioned *Salzburger Nockerl* for dessert.

IN ST. PAULI

Cuneo. Davidstrasse 11. ☎ **040/31-25-80.** Reservations required. Main courses 18DM–40DM ($9–$20). MC, V. Mon–Sat 6:30pm–1:30am. Closed 2 weeks in July. U-Bahn: St. Pauli. ITALIAN.

Good Italian food at reasonable prices is what you'll find here. Behind an unprepossessing facade, unchanged since 1905, the place opens onto crowded rooms that look like an art director's concept of a Greenwich Village restaurant in the 1930s. Grilled fish is one of the best items on the menu, but you can also order pizza, carpaccio, spaghetti with pesto, gnocchi with Gorgonzola, and Venetian-style liver.

✪ **Old Commercial Room.** Englische Planke 10 (at the foot of St. Michaelis). ☎ **040/ 36-63-19.** Reservations required. Main courses 18.50DM–60DM ($9.25–$30); fixed-price menus 39DM–85DM ($19.50–$42.50). AE, DC, MC, V. Daily noon–midnight. Closed Dec 24. U-Bahn: St. Pauli. NORTH GERMAN.

The Old Commercial Room, founded in 1643, is so tied into Hamburg maritime life that many residents consider it the premier sailors' stopover. It's the best place in town for *Labskaus* (sailor's hash), prepared with devotion by the chef; if you order it, you're given a numbered certificate proclaiming you a genuine Labskaus-eater. You can also order many traditional north German dishes. The restaurant's name, along with that of the street, speaks of the historic mercantile links between Hamburg and England.

Restaurant Nil. Neuer Pferdemarkt 5. ☎ **040/4397-823.** Reservations recommended. Main courses 25DM–38DM ($12.50–$19); fixed menus 58DM–75DM ($29–$37.50). AE, DC, MC, V. Mon–Fri noon–2:30pm, Sun–Thurs 6–11pm, and Fri–Sat 6pm to midnight. U-Bahn: Feldstrasse. INTERNATIONAL.

Even though the name of this restaurant refers to Egypt's River Nile, don't imagine a decor influenced either by the desert or the Arab world. What you get is upscale French bistro, replete with mirrors, oiled mahogany, and polished brass. The name refers to the bounty provided by the Nile, as interpreted by North German tastes, and the cooking is superb. Clients derive from the worlds of publishing and the arts, with lots of cultural movers and shakers, many of whom have adopted this place as their preferred culinary hangout. Dishes include a carpaccio of beef with a black olive marinade and shiitake mushrooms; saltimbocca of calves' liver prepared with artichoke hearts; braised leg of turkey stuffed with sautéed leeks and served with noodles in an orange-flavored whisky sauce; and beef bourguignonne with braised shallots, mushrooms, and mashed potatoes.

4 Seeing the Sights

Before you tour the city, you can get a good overall view of Hamburg from the tower of the finest baroque church in northern Germany, ✪ **Hauptkirche St. Michaelis,** Krayenkamp 4C, Michaeliskirchplatz (☎ **040/3767-8100;** U-Bahn: Rüdingsmarkt or St. Pauli). Take the elevator or climb the 449 steps to enjoy the sweeping view from the top of the hammered-copper tower. The crypt is one of the largest in Europe, and contains the tombs of such famous citizens as the composer, Carl Philipp Emanuel Bach, and the church's builder, Ernst Georg Sonnin. There's also an audiovisual show that tells the history of the city. Hours are daily April to September, 9am to 6pm; October to March, 10am to 5pm. Entrance to the church is free, but to use the stairs or elevator costs 4.50DM ($2.25). A combined ticket for the tower, show, and crypt costs 9DM ($4.50).

The **Altstadt** actually has little left of the old architecture, but there are a few sights among the canals (fleets) that run through this section from the Alster to the Elbe. The largest of the old buildings is the **Rathaus,** Rathausplatz (☎ **040/36-81-24-70;** U-Bahn: Rathausmarkt), which is modern compared with many of Germany's town halls. This Renaissance-style structure was built in the late 19th century on a foundation of 3,780 pinewood piles. It has a sumptuous 647-room interior and can be visited on guided tours costing 3DM ($1.50). Tours in English are given Monday to Thursday, hourly 10:15am to 3:15pm; Friday to Sunday 10:15am to 1:15pm; no tours during official functions. The Rathaus's 49m (160-foot) clock tower overlooks Rathausmarkt and the **Alster Fleet,** the city's largest canal. A visit to the Rathaus can be combined with a stop at the 16th-century **Hamburg Stock Exchange,** Adolphsplatz 1 (☎ **040/3-61-30-20**), which is back-to-back with the Rathaus. Free guided tours are offered Tuesday and Thursday at 11am and noon.

A few blocks away is **St. Petri Kirche,** Mönckebergstrasse (☎ **040/32-57-400;** U-Bahn: Rathausmarkt), built in the 12th century and renovated in 1842. The lion-head knocker on the main door is the oldest piece of art in Hamburg, dating from 1342. The church is open Monday to Friday 10am to 6pm, Saturday 9am to 5pm, and Sunday 9am to noon and 1 to 5pm.

The nearby 14th-century Gothic **Jacobikirche,** Jakobikirchhof 22, entrance on Steinstrasse (☎ **040/32-77-44;** U-Bahn: Mönckebergstrasse), was damaged in World War II but has been restored. It contains several medieval altars, pictures, and sculptures, as well as one of the largest baroque organs in the world (Arp-Schnitger, 1693). The church is open Monday to Saturday 10am to 5pm, Sunday 10am to noon. Guided tours in English can be arranged.

Hamburg's tallest structure is the 275m (900-foot) **Heinrich-Hertz-Turm** (Television Tower), Lagerstrasse 2–8 (☎ **040/43-80-24;** U-Bahn: Sternschanze). Named after Heinrich Hertz, the Hamburg-born physicist whose work was instrumental in the harnessing of electricity, the tower was inaugurated in 1968 as an answer to a similar tower erected in East Berlin. Today, the structure still appeals, partly as a kitschy reminder of the Cold War and the Age of Sputnik, and partly for its panoramic view over Hamburg. You'll pay a one-time charge of 6.50DM ($3.25) for the elevator ride to the top. There, you'll find a self-service cafeteria and observation platform, open daily 10am to 6pm, and a more formal restaurant, Fernsehturm, that serves meals 11am to 11pm (see "Where to Dine," above). If you want a high-altitude tea, the site features two separate seatings of 1 hour each, at 3:30pm and 4:30pm. You'll get unlimited access to tea, coffee, and a buffet table laden with pastries, all for a price of 12DM ($6) per person, plus the cost of the elevator ride described above.

THE TOP ATTRACTIONS

✪ **Carl Hagenbeck's Tierpark.** Hagenbeckallee at Steilingen (in the northwest suburbs). ☎ **040/5-40-00-10.** Admission 21DM ($10.50) adults, 16DM ($8) children. Free for children under 6. Spring–fall daily 9am–6pm; winter daily 9am–5pm. U-Bahn: Hagenbeck's Tierpark.

The Tierpark's zoo, one of Europe's best, was founded in 1848 and today is home to about 2,100 animals. The unfenced paddocks and beautifully landscaped park are world famous. There are sea-lion and dolphin shows, rides on elephants and camels, a train ride through "fairyland," and a spacious children's playground. A restaurant serves well-prepared set menus priced at 18DM to 26DM ($9 to $13) 11:30am to closing time.

✪ **Kunsthalle.** Glockengiesser Wall. ☎ **040/24-86-26-12.** Admission 15DM ($7.50) adults, 12DM ($6) children, 21DM ($10.50) family pass. Tues–Wed and Fri–Sun 10am–6pm, Thurs 10am–9pm. U-Bahn: Hauptbahnhof.

This is the leading art museum in northern Germany. Outstanding is the altarpiece painted for the St. Petri Church in 1379 by Master Bertram, Hamburg's first painter known by name and a leading 14th-century German master. The 24 scenes on the wing panels depict the biblical story of humankind from creation to the flight into Egypt. Particularly interesting is the panel showing the creation of the animals, in which a primitive Christ-like figure is surrounded by creatures, from the fish of the sea to the fowl of the air. As a sardonic note, or possibly prophetic, one little fox is already chewing the neck of the lamb next to it. The museum also contains works by Master Francke, a Dominican monk. The altar of St. Thomas Becket (1424) is the first work to depict his murder in Canterbury cathedral.

   The museum collection also includes the distinctive visions of Philipp Otto Runge and Carl David Friedrich, German impressionists Max Liebermann and Lovis Corinth, and 20th-century artists Munch, Kirchner, Otto Dix, Beckmann, Kandinsky, and Paul Klee. In addition, the museum has an entire wing devoted to contemporary art.

Museum of Hamburg History (Museum für Hamburgische Geschichte). Holsten Wall 24. ☎ **040/42841-2380.** Admission 10DM ($5) adults, 5DM ($2.50) children, 18DM ($9) family ticket. Tues–Sat 10am–5pm, Sun 10am–6pm. U-Bahn: St. Pauli. Bus: 112.

In this museum you'll find a detailed portrait of Hamburg from the 8th through the 20th centuries. Scale models represent the changing face of the port, and reconstructions of various rooms—from the hall of a 17th-century merchant's house to an air-raid shelter from World War II—illustrate the different eras in Hamburg's history.

NEARBY ATTRACTIONS

At **Willkomm-Höft (Welcome Point),** every ship that passes this landscaped peninsula is welcomed in its own language, as well as in German, from sunrise to sunset (8am to 8pm in summer). The ships' national anthems are played as a salute. The station was founded in the late spring of 1952, at the point where a sailor first catches sight of the soaring cranes and slipways of the Port of Hamburg. As a vessel comes in, you'll see the Hamburg flag on a 40m (130-foot) mast lowered in salute. The ship replies by dipping its own flag. More than 50 arriving ships, and as many departing ones, pass Willkomm-Höft each day.

   The point can be reached by car from Hamburg via the Elbchaussee or Ostdorfer Landstrasse to Wedel in half an hour. You can also go to Wedel by S-Bahn; a bus will take you from the station to the point, or you can enjoy the 15-minute walk. In the summer, you can take a HADAG riverboat, leaving from St. Pauli Landungsbrücken, an hour's ferry ride.

In Wedel, you can have lunch at **Schulauer Fährhaus,** Parnastrasse 29 (☎ **04103/ 92-000;** S-Bahn: Wedel), attractively situated on the wide lower Elbe. The restaurant is run by the sons of Otto Friedrich Behnke, who founded Willkomm-Höft. It has large enclosed and open verandas, as well a spacious tea garden. Guests are welcomed for breakfast, lunch, tea, or dinner. Fish dishes are a specialty here, and the wine list is modest but interesting. The restaurant's own bakery turns out a tempting array of goodies. Main courses run 16DM to 34DM ($8 to $17). It's open daily from 9am to 10pm. MasterCard, Visa, and American Express are accepted.

In the cellars of the Schulauer Fährhaus is the **Buddelschiff-Museum** (☎ **04103/ 92000**), where more than 200 little vessels are carefully preserved in bottles. The museum is open March to October, daily 10am to 6pm; off-season, Wednesday, Saturday, and Sunday 10am to 6pm. Admission is 2.50DM ($1.25) for adults and free for children.

GARDENS & PARKS

The major zoo is the **Carl Hagenbeck's Tierpark** (see above), but Hamburg also has many other "green lungs."

Alsterpark lies on the northwest banks of Alster Lake, spread across 175 well-manicured acres. Beautiful shade trees and cultivated gardens greet you at every turn. From many places, you'll also have a panoramic view of the Hamburg skyline. Enter on Harvestehuderweg.

The **Hirschpark** (S-Bahn: Blankensee) is the deer park of Hamburg. Its main entrance is at Mühlenberg. The park is landscaped and has a game enclosure. You can visit the Hirschparkhaus for an old-fashioned tea with pastries.

Stadtpark (U-Bahn: Borgweg, in Winterhude), spread across some 182ha (450 acres) north of the center, has some 32km (20 miles) of footpaths and numerous recreational facilities. These include a planetarium, sunbathing areas (Hamburgers often prefer their sun sans attire), and open-air pools. Music concerts are often staged here in summer. For your own safety, avoid this place when darkness falls.

Finally, **Wallringpark** (☎ 040/24864723; U-Bahn: Stefansplatz), is actually a quartet of beautifully maintained parks and gardens, including the flower garden Planten und Blomen, the Alter Botanischer Garten, and the Kleine and Grosse (big and little) Wallanlagen parks, with many recreational facilities. A miniature railway connects all four. The entire complex is also a popular leisure park, with a roller-skating rink, playgrounds, greenhouses filled with tropical plants, restaurants, and an ice-skating rink in winter. A particular highlight is the illuminated-fountain concert, with classical or pop music, at the onset of darkness—10pm June to August, earlier as the summer wanes. The largest Japanese garden in Europe is in Planten und Blomen. Here, rock gardens, flowering plants, miniature trees, and winding pathways attract garden enthusiasts.

ESPECIALLY FOR KIDS

Although Hamburg is known for its X-rated entertainment, the city is actually a good place for a family vacation.

Carl Hagenbeck's Tierpark (☎ 040/54000147) is one of Europe's great zoos (see above), and many other parks in Hamburg have amusements for children—the **Wallringpark** has a roller-skating rink. Boat tours of the Alster and more lengthy tours of the Port of Hamburg will also delight kids.

Language is often not a problem for children, so they may enjoy the children's theater, **Theater für Kinder,** Max-Brauer-Allee 76 (☎ 040/38-25-38; U-Bahn: Altona). All tickets cost 43DM to 63DM ($21.50 to $31.50); call for show times.

BOAT TOURS

You can tour Hamburg by water, on both the Inner and the Outer Alster, experiencing all the charm of the Alsterpark, the villas, and the sailing boats set against the panorama of towers and church spires. **ATG-Alster-Touristik,** Am Anleger Jungfernstieg (☎ 040/ 3-57-42-40), has daily departures about every 30 minutes 10am to 6pm, with trips lasting 50 minutes. November to March, tours depart daily at 10:30am, noon, and 1:30pm. The ships leave from the Jungfernstieg quayside (U-Bahn: Jungfernstieg). Cassettes with a description of the tour in English, plus a brochure in four languages (including English), are available from the captain. Trips cost 16DM ($8) for adults and 8DM ($4) for children under 16.

HADAG Seetouristik und Fahrdienst AG, Bei den St. Pauli, Fischmarkt 28 (☎ 040/3-11-70-70), also conducts tours through the watery channels of Hamburg, in a comfortable heated pleasure boat. Tours are conducted in both German and English. They depart at hourly intervals every day April to October, 9am to 6pm, November to March, 10:30am to 3:30pm. Boats leave from the Landungsbrücken, Pier 3. The fare is 15DM ($7.50) for adults and 7.50DM ($3.75) for children under 14.

5 Sports & Outdoor Pursuits

BOATING

A paddle on the Aussenalster (Outer Alster Lake) can be one of the most relaxing and charming warm-weather activities in Hamburg. **H. Pieper** (☎ **040/24-75-78**), **Alfred Seebeck** (☎ **040/24-76-52**), and **Captain Prüsser** (☎ **040/31-31-40**) rent rowboats, paddleboats, one-occupant sailing dinghies, and small catamarans; prices begin at 20DM to 30DM ($10 to $15) per hour. Each of these boat rental outfits is open only April to late September, daily 10am to 8pm.

GOLF

Hamburg has many golf clubs, including **Golf Club auf der Wendlohe,** Oldesloer-strasse 251 (☎ **040/5-50-50-14**), and **Hamburger Golf-Club Falkenstein,** In de Bargen 59 (☎ **040/81-21-77**). Greens fees range from 75DM to 85DM ($37.50 to $42.50) for 18 holes.

JOGGING

Our personal favorite route, either for long promenades or jogging, is the pedestrian walkway that circumnavigates the Alster lakes. The total perimeter of the larger of the two lakes measures about 6km (4 miles); that of the more congested Binnenalster, about 1.5km (1 mile). Equally suitable for jogging and pedestrian rambles are the public parks flanking the northwestern edge of the inner city.

SPECTATOR SPORTS

For information about soccer matches and other spectator events, contact the **Hamburger Sportbund (Hamburg Sports Association),** Schäferkampsallee 1, 20357 Hamburg (☎ **040/41-90-80**).

SWIMMING

The rivers and lakes in Hamburg are being cleaned up, and there are many swimming pools. Two of the most popular are the **Alster-Schwimmhalle,** Ifflandstrasse 21 (☎ **040/22-30-12;** U-Bahn: Lohmühlenstrasse), and the **Holthusenbad,** Goernestrasse 21 (☎ **040/47-47-54;** U-Bahn: Eppendorfer Baum). The latter has the advantage of artificial waves, thermal baths, and steam baths. Alster-Schwimmhalle charges 14.50DM ($7.25) for all day; Holthusenbad, 14.50DM to 17.50DM ($7.25 to $8.75) for all day. Newest and biggest of all is the huge **Midsommerland Freibad,** Gotthelfweg (☎ **040/76-31-827;** S-Bahn: Harburg; bus: 142 or 143), in the suburb of Hamburg-Harburg. It's open daily May to September 8am to 10pm, charging 15DM ($7.50) for a full day's use.

TENNIS

Not surprisingly, the country that gave the world Steffi Graf and Boris Becker has no lack of tennis facilities. For names and addresses of tennis facilities, as well as information about upcoming tournaments, contact the **Deutscher Tennis Bund,** Haller-strasse 89 (☎ **040/4-11-78-0**).

6 Shopping

Hamburg is a city of merchants. In general, stores are open Monday to Friday 9am to 6:30pm (some till 8pm on Thursday) and on Saturday 9am to 2pm (until 4 or 6pm on *langer Samstag,* the first Saturday of the month). Unfortunately, the interesting shops are not concentrated in one location. Two of the oldest and most prestigious shopping streets, **Grosse Bleichen** and **Neuer Wall,** run parallel to the canals, connected transversely by Jungfernstieg and Ufer Strasse on the Binnenalster. Less expensive shopping streets are Spitalstrasse and Mönckebergstrasse.

Hamburg has nine major shopping malls. Even on the grayest, rainiest day in winter, you can shop in Hamburg in relative comfort. The glass-roofed **Hanse Viertel Galerie Passage** is some 200m (220 yards) long. There's a scattering of upscale cafes here, and even a stand-up seafood bar where glasses of beer or Sekt (sparkling wine) are served at tiny tables.

Mönckebergstrasse (U-Bahn: Hauptbahnhof), a street connecting the main station with the Rathaus, is the city's traditional shopping district, with big department stores such as **Karstadt,** Mönckebergstrasse 16 (☎ **040/30940**), part of a chain that carries many of the same brands and items as the other leading department stores, all competitively priced. The store is open Monday to Friday 9am to 8pm and Saturday 9am to 4pm. A thrifty alternative, **Kaufhof,** Mönckebergstrasse 3 (☎ **040/33-30-70**), carries less-expensive items than the surrounding department stores and also offers better deals on merchandise markdowns. Bargain hunters combing the store are apt to find good values. Hours are Monday to Friday 9:30am to 8pm and Saturday 9:30am to 4pm. More fashionable and upscale than any of the three mentioned above is **Alsterhaus,** Jungfernstieg 22 (☎ **040/359011**), which some New Yorkers have compared favorably to Bloomingdale's (same hours as Karstadt).

If you walk down Bergstrasse to the second part of the city center, you pass along **Jungfernstieg,** with tourist boats of the Alster Fleet on the right and a teeming shopping street on the other side. About a block farther along you come to the **Hamburger Hof,** the elegant entrance to one of the most attractive chains of shopping galleries in Europe. At the end of Jungfernstieg, you can cross Gänsemarkt to **Gänsemarkt Passage,** another shopping gallery, with stores on three levels.

An upmarket and youthfully fashionable shopping area is in **Eppendorf** (U-Bahn: Eppendorfer Baum), Hamburg's oldest village, first mentioned in written history in 1140. Many prosperous and avant-garde Hamburgers live in the stately 19th-century homes and apartments. The shopping district, from Klosterstern to Eppendorfer Markt, has exclusive boutiques selling fashions from Paris, Milan, and New York; colorful shops with odds and ends for your home; antiques shops; and places where you can not only make purchases but watch goldsmiths, hatmakers, potters, and weavers at work.

The Hamburg **Fischmarkt (fish market),** between Hexenberg and Grosse Elbstrasse (U-Bahn: Landungsbrücken), is held every Sunday from 5am in summer or 7am otherwise. Flowers, fruit, vegetables, plants, and pets are also for sale at this traditional market, in existence since 1703. It sometimes seems that the fish are just an afterthought nowadays. The nearby taverns are open to serve Fischmarkt visitors and vendors. **Seifarth and Company,** Robert-Koch Strasse 19 (☎ **040/5-24-00-27;** U-Bahn: Lattenkamp), is an upscale shop dealing in seafood, among other items. It smokes its own salmon, runs one of the leading mail-order caviar businesses in Europe, has one of the Continent's largest selections of tea, imports pâté and champagne from France, and stocks lobsters and Alaskan king crab. Everything can be shipped or ordered by mail.

One of the densest concentrations of antiques in Hamburg lies within the **Antik-Center,** Klosterwall 9–21 (☎ **040/32-62-85;** U-Bahn: Steinstrasse or Hauptbahnhof), a covered passageway loaded with more than 35 dealers and the accumulated loot of estate sales throughout England, Germany, and to a lesser degree, France. It's been compared to Portobello Road in London by aficionados of the trade who value the sheer volumes of objects that glint, sparkle, and evoke the values and aesthetics of other places and other times.

Jil Sander, Milchstrasse 8 (☎ **040/55-30-21-73;** U-Bahn: Damtor), is the best place to go for chic women's styling. Jil Sander burst upon Europe's fashion scene from her native city of Hamburg and has taken special efforts to make this three-floor store the flagship of her increasingly successful operation. Part of the success of her designs derives from their wearability—they are appropriate for the office, the boardroom, or cocktail hour. Another popular choice for women's fashions is **Escada Boutique,** Neuer Wall 32 (☎ **040/36-32-96;** U-Bahn: Hauptbahnhof), owned by the German design company of the same name. This store carries the firm's complete collection of women's sports, evening, business, and knit wear, plus accessories that include hats, bags, gloves, and shoes. A less-expensive division of Escada, **Laural Boutique,** Neuer Wall 41 (☎ **040/3-74-32-70;** U-Bahn: Hauptbahnhof), appeals to an active, younger clientele with alternative takes on casual day and elegant evening wear. If you think that hats have gone out of style, think again. **Monika Flac,** Bleichenhof Passage 35, off Grosse Bleichen (☎ **040/34-54-37;** U-Bahn: Hauptbahnhof), sells all kinds of hats, from serious garden party varieties festooned with cabbage roses to perky numbers that might have been favored by the late Jacqueline Onassis, as well as Homburgs and Stetson-style hats for men.

For high-fashion men's clothing, go to **Thomas-i-Punkt,** Gänsemarkt 24 (☎ **040/7-80-98-80;** U-Bahn: Hauptbahnhof), where you'll find suits, jackets, shirts, shoes, and belts carrying the exclusive Omen label. Ties, handkerchiefs, and other accessories are also available. Shoes, well made and fashionably styled, are sold to both men and women at **Prange Schuhhaus,** Jungfernstieg 38 (☎ **040/34-31-51;** U-Bahn: Jungfernstieg).

One of the city's leading hairdressers, for both men and women, is **Marlies Müller** at Tesdorpfstrasse 20 (☎ **040/4-44-00-40;** U-Bahn: Damtor). Besides hair styling and beauty treatments, a large perfume and cosmetic selection is also offered here.

Brahmfeld & Gutruf, Jungfernstieg 12 (☎ **040/34-61-03;** U-Bahn: Jungfern-stieg), is one of Germany's oldest jewelers, founded in 1743.

One of Hamburg's biggest selections of books, mostly in German but with lots of English-language texts as well, can be found at **Thalia Buchhandlung,** Spitalerstrasse 8 (☎ **040/3-02-07-01;** U-Bahn: Hauptbahnhof). A smaller branch of the same outfit, mostly with German-language titles, is at Hermannstrasse 18–20 (☎ 040-3-02-07-01; U-Bahn: Jungfernstieg).

Two stores of a nautical nature, **Binikowski,** Lokstedter Weg 68 (☎ **040/46-28-52;** U-Bahn: Eppendorfer Baum), established in 1955, is the place to find a *Buddelschiffe* (ship in a bottle), as well as ship models and clocks; while **Captain's Cabin,** St. Pauli Landungsbrücken (☎ **040/ 31-63-73;** S-bahn: Landungsbrücken), stocks ship models, telescopes, barometers, figureheads, lamps, nautical clothing for the whole family, prints, posters, and more.

Flags in all shapes and sizes fill **Gäth & Peine,** Luisenweg 109 (☎ **040/21-35-99;** U-Bahn: Burgstrasse), where just about every national ensign or known signal banner can be found.

If you've ever fancied yourself as someone who looks best in silk, you might pay a visit to Hamburg's **Haus des Osten,** Jungfernstieg 7 (☎ **040/34-36-80;** U-Bahn:

Jungfernsteig), which sells only silk clothing imported from Asia (usually China). There's an appealing collection of shirts and neckties for men, in all degrees of flamboyance and discretion. And for women, check out the kimonos, skirts, jumpers, undergarments, and scarves that fill the medium-sized premises of this well-stocked store.

7 Hamburg After Dark

To find out what's happening in Hamburg, pick up a copy of *Hamburger Vorschau* for 2.30DM ($1.15). Published once a month, it's available at various tourist offices, most hotels, and most newsstands.

THE PERFORMING ARTS

✪ **Hamburgische Staatsoper (Hamburg State Opera).** Damtorstrasse 28. ☎ **040/ 35-17-21.** Tickets 8DM–150DM ($4–$75). U-Bahn: Stefansplatz. U-Bahn: Damtor.

This modern opera house was built after the bombings of World War II. Its acoustics and technical facilities are among the most advanced in the world. The venue is the home of the **Hamburg State Opera,** and also the **Hamburg Ballet,** directed by Californian John Neumeier. For tickets, call the number listed above, or head for the ticket office at Grosstheaterstrasse 34.

Musikhalle. Johannes-Brahms-Platz. ☎ **040/34-69-20.** U-Bahn: Stefansplatz or Damtor.

This survivor of Germany's romantic age lies a few steps away from the Staatsoper, with which it shares some facilities and staff members. The building was painstakingly restored after World War II. It hosts concerts by the **Hamburg Symphony,** the **Hamburg Philharmonic,** the **NDR Symphony,** and the renowned **Monteverdi-Chor,** known for its interpretations of baroque and Renaissance music. Touring orchestras also perform here. In most cases, tickets don't exceed 60DM ($30). For tickets, call either the number listed above, or the number listed for the Staatsoper (see above).

THEATER   Hamburg is blessed with more than 40 theaters, but for most of these, a good knowledge of German is necessary. An exception, the **English Theatre of Hamburg,** Lerchenfeld 14 (☎ **040/2-27-70-89;** U-Bahn: Mundsburg), is the only English-speaking theater in the northern part of Germany. Tickets are 20DM to 47DM ($10 to $23.50). Performances are Monday to Saturday at 7:30pm; a matinee is presented on Tuesday and Friday at 11am.

If you understand German, try the ✪ **Deutsches Schauspielhaus,** Kirchenallee 39 (☎ **040/24-87-10;** U-Bahn: Hauptbahnhof). It's one of the outstanding theaters in the German-speaking world, performing both the classics and modern plays.

Other theaters are the cutting-edge **Thaliatheater,** Alstertor (☎ **040/32-81-44-44;** U-Bahn: Jungfernsteig), and the **Kammerspiele,** Hartungstrasse 9–11 (☎ **040/**

Ticket-Buying Tips

Tickets to sporting events, including soccer matches, are best acquired through the **Hamburger Sportbund (Handburg Sports Association),** Schäferkampsallee 1, 20357 Hamburg (☎ **040/419080). Theater-Kasse Reckewell,** Einkaufcentrum shopping mall on Osterfer Landstrasse (☎ **040/80-10-13),** can arrange virtually everything else. A third option for cultural (but not necessarily sporting) events in Hamburg is to contact Hamburg's Tourist Information Office **(Tourismus Centrale),** in the "Wendelhalle" of the city's main railway station (☎ **040/30-13-00).**

41-33-4444; U-Bahn: Hallerstrasse). Both stage a wide range of plays as well as musi-cal shows. A new production usually opens every month. Tickets at these theaters range from 20DM to 80DM ($10 to $40). Small ensemble performances such as *Evening with Marlene Dietrich* are the specialty of the **Schmidt Theater,** Spielbuden-platz 24 (☎ **040/31-77-880;** S-bahn: Reeperbahn). Its companion, **Schmidts Tivoli,** Spielbudenplatz 27–28 (same phone), hosts musicals and other popular performances. Tickets are 30DM to 100DM ($15 to $50). All of these are closed on Monday.

Two of Hamburg's busiest theaters are the **Neue Flora Theater,** Stresemannstrasse 159A (☎ **01805/4444;** U-Bahn: Altona), and the **Operettenhaus,** Spielbudenplatz 1 (same phone; S-bahn: Reeperbahn), which have enjoyed an unprecedented success with *Phantom of the Opera* (at the Neue Flora), and *Cats* (at the Operettenhaus). Performances have run within these theaters for 9 and 13 years, respectively, with only vague hints that they might be nearing the ends of their runs. The cost of seeing either of these shows is 119DM to 219DM ($59.50 to $109.50), depending on your seat and the night you attend.

Hansa Theater, Steindamm 17 (☎ **040/24-14-14;** U-Bahn: Hauptbahnhof), is a north German variety show that claims to be intelligible to all foreigners. The humor is so broad that that may be true. Each show includes international attractions such as acrobats, clowns, dancers, magicians, and aerialists. There are special tables for smoking and drinking. Two shows are performed daily Monday to Saturday at 4 and 8pm and Sunday at 3 and 7pm. Prices are 40DM to 70DM ($20 to $35).

THE CLUB & MUSIC SCENE
JAZZ
Cotton Club. Alter Steinweg 10. ☎ **040/34-38-78.** Cover 8DM–25DM ($4–$12.50). S-bahn: Stadthausbrücke.

The legendary Cotton Club is the oldest (some 36 years) and best established of the Hamburg jazz clubs. Jazz and Dixieland bands come here from throughout Europe and the United States. Open Friday and Saturday 8pm to 1am and Monday to Thurs-day 8pm to midnight; September to April, also open Sunday 11pm to 3am.

Dennis' Swing Club. Papenhuderstrasse 25 (in Uhlenhorst). ☎ **040/2-29-91-92.** Cover 10DM–15DM ($5–$7.50); no cover Wed. U-Bahn:Hamburgerstrasse.

The completely informal Dennis' became legendary under the management of Dennis Busby, a transplant from Louisiana. After his death, the club was taken over by Jochen Marcus, a very well-known jazz drummer in the 1950s. Today the club features some of the finest jazz talent in the city and a bilingual German-English format that's very familiar with the jazz traditions of both Europe and the U.S. Open Tuesday to Sunday 8:30pm to 2am.

ROCK
Club Grosse Freiheit. Grosse Freiheit 36. ☎ **040/3177780.** Cover 6DM–40DM ($3–$20). S-bahn: Reeperbahn.

This club, now world-famous, is where the Beatles performed in their earliest days. Today, it's a free-for-all venue whose acts change almost nightly, and whose guests in the recent past have included Prince and Willie Nelson. Even the civic and municipal authorities of Hamburg view it as one of their preeminent cultural treasures. For recorded information about upcoming acts, call ☎ **040/3177-7811.**

Fabrik. Barnerstrasse 36 (5 min. from Bahnhof Altona). ☎ **040/39-10-70.** Cover 15DM–40DM ($7.50–$20). U-Bahn: Altona.

The Reeperbahn: A Walk on the Wild Side

Commercialized sex flourishes in many towns, but hardworking, entrepreneurial Hamburg has succeeded better than almost anywhere else at transforming it into a tourist attraction. The place where it all hangs out is the St. Pauli district (U-Bahn: St. Pauli; S-Bahn: Reeperbahn), just east of the center. St. Pauli's midsection—the "genital-zone," as it's sometimes called—is the Reeperbahn, a half-mile thoroughfare whose name literally translates as "rope street," referring to the massive amounts of hempen rope produced here during the 18th and 19th centuries for ships in Germany's biggest harbor.

In the 19th century, most forms of entertainment, including theaters, were banned from the city's more respectable medieval core. As one resident of the district remarked, "Bourgeois Protestants don't know how to have fun." Consequently, this neighborhood near the great port developed entertainment options of its own, and sailors from around the world were safely channeled into a neighborhood where their recreational activities were out of sight (and out of mind) of the city's sober business establishment. Hamburg's first theater opened on the Reeperbahn in 1842. By the 1860s, the question, "Whatch'a doing, sailor?" became the unofficial motto of an army of prostitutes who set up shop (with the legal sanction of municipal authorities) in the district.

The city's official line is that the Reeperbahn is Hamburg's second greatest attraction and asset (the first is the port itself). The authorities see their policies as a rare instance of civic and moral enlightenment unparalleled in any other city, except for Amsterdam's more sanitized sex scene. They make frequent references to their requirement that every officially sanctioned working girl submit to a medical examination every 2 weeks—and pay income tax on her profits. Hamburg's most talked-about police station, Davidwache, at the corner of the Davidstrasse and the Reeperbahn, provides highly visible and omnipresent police protection.

What are the rules of the game and what should you do to survive such an "in-your-face" neighborhood? Throw your sense of scheduling to the wind and take a nap on the day of your visit. Mornings in St. Pauli are burned-out, unenthusiastic times, when virtually everyone is recovering from the bacchanals of the night before. Midafternoons perk up a bit. But regardless of the fogs that roll in from the Baltic and the damp chill that's an inseparable part of the Hamburg experience, by 8pm the district's bars and theaters (legitimate and otherwise) are roaring away. Between midnight and 5am, you'll find thousands of women and female wanna-bes strutting their stuff along the turf. German enterprise has honored these women (and their reputation for a good time) by naming one of Hamburg's native beers in their honor—the famous "St. Pauli Girl."

This cultural center is similar in style to the Markthalle (see below). Originally it was an old ammunition depot (ca. 1830), until it burned down; later, it was reconstructed in the same style. Open 8pm to midnight (later on Saturday and Sunday), Fabrik is a nightclub beloved by those who survived the 1970s more or less intact. It offers a mixed program likely to feature African bands, jazz, and blues.

Finnegan's Wake. Börsenbrücke 4. ☎ **040/3-74-34-33.** Cover 5DM ($2.50) Sun–Thurs, 6DM ($3) Fri–Sat. U-Bahn: Hauptbahnhof.

There's a distinct pecking order among the working girls, based on the neighborhood, or street, where they're headquartered. The most exclusive and expensive area is **Herberstrasse,** where plate-glass windows allow the women to display their charms to window shoppers. This street is only open to men over the age of 18. Less-expensive rents can be found on the streets near Herbertstrasse: Gunterstrasse, Erichstrasse, Friedrichstrasse, Davidstrasse, and Gerhardstrasse. Lots of the women here are from the Eastern Bloc, and lately there's been a distressing trend for runaway teenagers to join their ranks. Cross-dressers, transsexuals, and "shemales" ply their trade here too.

If it's erotic theater you're looking for, you'll have to move a few blocks away to **Grosse Freiheit,** a street whose name appropriately translates as "Great Freedom." Any act of sexual expression, with every conceivable permutation except those that involve animals (bestiality is one of the few things expressly forbidden) is shown in these theaters. Be it joyful, be it disgusting, it's all here, often performed by artists whose barely concealed boredom sometimes permeates the setting in ways that anywhere else would be embarrassing, but here seems merely surreal.

You aren't likely to be solicited at a performance—municipal regulations forbid prostitution, or overt solicitation, inside erotic theaters. But there's nothing to prevent a member of the audience from suddenly deciding to be a performer—it's been known to happen, if rarely. And there's nothing that prevents performers setting up an off-premises rendezvous. In any event, *caveat emptor.*

If you're subject to sudden fits of guilt in places like this, municipal and religious authorities made provisions long ago. There always seems to be a church nearby, such as the early–18th-century **Kirche St. Joseph,** at 5 Grosse Freiheit. There's also a branch office of the Salvation Army, whose members are ready, willing, and able to fortify your resolve with a cup of coffee and some religious boosterism.

The district also contains the **Erotic Art Museum,** Nobistor 10A (☎ **040/ 31-74-757**). This institution is privately owned and funded, and closed to anyone under 16. It manages to present its displays in a way that's both academic and titillating, and it has a street-level gift shop featuring sexual toys and enhancements. Open daily 10am to midnight; entrance is 15DM ($7.50) adults, 10DM ($5) students.

Hamburg gay life, however, is centered west of the city's medieval core, within the St.-Georg district (see below). **Absolut,** Hans-Albers-Platz (☎ **040/ 317-3400**), is a St. Pauli bar that caters to a mixed/gay/lesbian crowd. The **Funky Pussy Club,** Grosse Freiheit 34 (☎ **040/31-42-36**), is mainly for lesbians. In the general free-for-all permissiveness that reigns in this neighborhood, however, sexual pigeonholing of visitors into specific gender preferences seems unnecessary.

This place is as Irish as it sounds. English speakers flock here for Guinness and Harp on tap, as well as shepherd's pie, chili, and sandwiches (food is available until 9pm). Every Thursday to Saturday, there's live music of some sort. The pub is open Sunday to Thursday 11am to 1am and Friday and Saturday 11am to 4am.

Kaiserkeller. Grosse Freiheit 36 (in the cellar of the Grosse Freiheit concert hall). ☎ **040/ 317-7780.** Cover 15DM–50DM ($7.50–$25). S-bahn: Reeperbahn.

Kaiserkeller functions both as a stage for live music by not terribly famous bands, and as a disco. Long-time aficionados of the Reeperbahn scene remember it, along with the now-defunct Star Club, whose empty premises stand across the street, as an early venue for performances by the Fabulous Four. The place has a different musical theme on different nights of the week (Sunday is oldies night). Open nightly 10pm to 4 or 5am.

Logo. Grindelallee 5. ☎ **040/4-10-56-58.** Cover 8DM–30DM ($4–$15). U-Bahn: Damtor.

Because of its position near Hamburg's university, this club attracts lots of college students, although many Big Chill survivors in their 40s and 50s gravitate here as well. It's a small, informal place that often features rock bands. Sometimes well-known singers appear in concert. Open daily 8pm (live music begins at 9pm) to 2 or 3am. Audiences often sit on the floor.

Markthalle. Klosterwall 49. ☎ **040/33-94-91.** Cover 20DM–40DM ($10–$20). U-Bahn: Hauptbahnhof.

This is one of the most visible live music venues in Hamburg, with a special emphasis on up-and-coming British groups and sometimes heavy metal and high-volume electronics. The building functioned early in the 20th century as a covered marketplace. Inside is an amphitheater with a stage and a large area for standing or sitting on notoriously uncomfortable benches. Performances usually begin at 8pm, with the ticket office opening about an hour before.

EROTIC SHOWS

Off-the-record theaters include **Safari,** Grosse Freiheit 24 (☎ **040/31-32-33;** S-bahn: Reeperbahn), where you're likely to find the press agent for the city of Hamburg entertaining foreign travel writers. Expect to pay a fixed price of around 45DM ($22.50) for one beer.

DRAG SHOWS

Pulverfass. Pulverteich 12. ☎ **040/24-97-91.** Cover 27DM–29DM ($13.50–$14.50); first drink 25DM ($12.50). U-Bahn: Steindamm.

The best-known drag show in town, Pulverfass is usually featured on the "Hamburg by Night" tours. This place is not for the timid. You might find the shows downright vulgar, especially if you know German. Female impersonators from all over Europe appear here. There are shows nightly at 8:30pm, 11:30pm, and 2:30am (Friday and Saturday only). Within the same building, with a view of the stage, there's a restaurant, **Teatro-café,** which is open daily 6am to 3pm, and where French- and German-inspired set-price menus cost 49DM ($24.50) each.

DANCE CLUBS

After Shave. Spielbudenplatz 7. ☎ **040/3-19-32-15.** Cover 10DM–15DM ($5–$7.50). S-bahn: Reeperbahn.

After Shave features funk, soul, jazz, and fusion. It's a place for dancing and for meeting people, and it attracts the 20s to 30s age group. The dance music is wide-ranging, featuring the latest imports but no hard rock or heavy metal. On Tuesday jazz is featured exclusively. Open 11pm to 4am Thursday, to 5am Friday, and to 6am Saturday.

Café Kesse. Reeperbahn 19–21. ☎ **040/31-08-05.** Cover 15DM ($7.50). S-bahn: Reeperbahn.

If you're a woman looking for a guy, Café Kesse features the so-called "Ball Paradox" whereby women have the right (and are encouraged) to ask the men to dance, drink, or whatever. There's a doorman who screens the entrance to keep out rowdies, and the place is highly legitimate and very visible on Hamburg's nightlife scene. Live bands alternate with disco, and it's open Wednesday to Saturday from 8:30pm to between 5 and 6am, depending on business.

Madhouse. Valentinskamp 46A. ☎ **040/34-41-93.** Cover 10DM ($5) Thurs–Fri, includes first drink. U-Bahn: Gansemarkt.

This dance club, the oldest in Hamburg, has been in business for 30 years, and in 1997 it was voted the best dance club in the city. Prince must agree; he's rented it out twice now. The music is a mix of rock, soul, funk, and house, played nightly 10pm until "whenever."

Mojo Club. Reeperbahn 1. ☎ **040/3-19-19-99.** Cover 12DM ($6). S-bahn: Reeperbahn.

Although located on the Reeperbahn, this nightclub and disco is devoted not to sex but to soul music and acid jazz. It attracts a crowd of mainly straight couples in their 30s. One local TV station called it "the best night club in Germany," but we think that's a bit of an exaggeration.

Molotow. Spielbudenplatz 5. ☎ **040/31-08-45.** Cover 5DM–18DM ($2.50–$9). S-bahn: Reeperbahn.

This is the place to dance to funk—George Clinton and Bootsy Collins have been elevated to god status here. Say you've seen Parliament-Funkadelic, and you may make lifelong friends. It opens Wednesday at 9pm, Thursday to Saturday at 11pm, and Sunday at 9pm; closing time depends on the energy of the dancers.

Top of the Town. On the 26th floor of the Radisson SAS Hotel Hamburg, Marseiller Strasse 2. ☎ **040/35020.** Cover 10DM ($5) Fri–Sat only; no cover for guests of the hotel. Bus: 102

This eagle's nest attracts a relatively youthful crowd, many of whom show up without jackets or neckties to dance, drink, and talk. A DJ spins out danceable tunes. This club isn't nearly as wild and crazy as those within less-restrictive parts of town, such as the Reeperbahn. Nonetheless, it can be fun, and there's a gorgeous panorama of North Germany's most dynamic city spread out in front of you. Open every night except Sunday, 9:30pm to around 4am.

GAY CLUBS

Hamburg, like Berlin, is one of the major gay havens of Europe, with a particularly dense concentration of gay boutiques and cafes along the Lange Reihe in St. Pauli. Try **Absolut,** Hans-Albers-Platz (☎ **040/317-3400;** S-bahn: Reeperbahn), a gay and lesbian bar, or the **Funky Pussy Club,** Grosse Freiheit 34 (☎ **040/314-236;** S-bahn: Reeperbahn)—no prize for guessing who this caters to. A little journal, *Dorn Rosa,* distributed at most gay and lesbian bars, lists the clubs, restaurants, bars, and events that cater to a gay, lesbian, and bisexual clientele.

Café Gnosa. Lange Reihe 93. ☎ **040/24-30-34.** U-Bahn: Hauptbahnhof.

More than any other eatery in Hamburg, this comes the closest to fulfilling the need for an official "gay restaurant." Set near the railway station, on a street noted for its gay clientele, it's open Tuesday to Sunday 11am to 1pm, and Monday 6pm to 1am. Platters of food range from 7.50DM to 16.50DM ($3.75 to $8.25) and feature all-day breakfasts, steaks, fish, salads, and all kinds of coffee and drinks.

Chocolate City. Heidenkampsweg 32. ☎ **040/23-25-23.** Cover 15DM ($7.50). U-Bahn: Damtor.

In 1997, this big-city bar and disco took over the premises of what had previously been an all-gay club, the Front. Since its takeover, music has included an engaging mixture of swing, soul, R&B, hip-hop, and reggae, and the clientele includes goodly numbers of gay men and women, who move easily (as they do in many clubs throughout Hamburg) within the permissive ambience. It's open Friday to Sunday 11pm to 5am.

Frauenkneipe. Stresemannstrasse 60. ☎ **040/43-63-77.** Cover 5DM–12DM ($2.50–$6). U-Bahn: Altona.

This bar is a major rendezvous point in Hamburg for women only—men are told to do their drinking elsewhere. The clientele is mainly lesbian, though there are a lot of straight women here, too. On the first Sunday of every month, there's ballroom dancing, with a 5DM ($2.50) cover, and Friday is disco night, with a cover of 8DM ($4). On other nights, this a good place to visit for a drink. Open Wednesday to Monday 8pm to 1am.

Pit Club-Saloon/Tom's Bar. Pulverteich 17. ☎ **040/280-30-56.** Cover 5DM ($2.50) for cellar leather bar; 10DM ($5) for street-level disco and first-floor "jeans bar." U-Bahn: Hauptbahnhof.

This is the best-established and most popular gay men's bar in Hamburg, known to virtually every gay male in town. Begin your night in the street-level disco, work your way up to a watering hole one floor above, and end your evening in the cellar, where leather is optional but encouraged. Women, if they come here at all (which is rare), usually remain in the street-level disco. At least one part of this place is open every night 10:30pm till dawn; every Wednesday to Sunday, additional sections open for greater space devoted to a leather bar/dungeon and a disco.

THE BAR SCENE

Bayrisch Zell. Reeperbahn 110. ☎ **040/31-42-81.** No cover Mon–Thurs; 10DM ($5) Fri–Sat, including first drink. S-bahn: Reeperbahn.

This beer hall, clearly an imitation of Munich's famed Hofbräuhaus, is one of the most popular places in the St. Pauli district. It may be on the Reeperbahn, but you could take your great-aunt here, especially if she likes to dance the polka. The place attracts couples young and old and has plenty of seats (1,200) for all. It also has good food, with meals ranging from 7.50DM to 20DM ($3.75 to $10). If someone catches your fancy from across the room, call him or her from your table—that's what those phones are for. Open 7pm to 3am daily.

Café Schone Aussichten. Gorch-Fock-Wall 4. ☎ **040/34-01-13.** U-Bahn: Gansemarkt.

This is a bar/restaurant/disco. On most nights, the 300-seat beer garden is full of students; if you get hungry, try the southeast Asian dishes. On weekends there's a breakfast bar. Hours are Sunday to Thursday 10am to 2am and Friday and Saturday 10am to 4am.

Gröninger Braukeller. Ost-West-Strasse 47. ☎ **040/33-13-81.** U-Bahn: Messberg.

Gröninger has been making and selling beer here since 1750; today the site consists of two brew pubs flanking a traditional German restaurant. One of the pubs opens at 11am, the other at 5pm, and both close at 1am. If you get hungry, the brewery restaurant serves meals 11:30am to 11:30pm.

La Paloma. Gerhardstrasse 2, at the corner of Friedrichstrasse. ☎ **040/31-45-12.** S-bahn: Reeperbahn.

This bar in the heart of the Reeperbahn has nothing to do with the sex trade going on around it. Instead, it's an artists' hangout where the wall space is used for art exhibitions. It's open Tuesday to Thursday 7pm to 1am, and Friday and Saturday 7pm to 4am.

Schwenders. Grossneumarkt 1. ☎ **040/34-54-23.** U-Bahn: Rödingsmarkt.

This is one of Hamburg's most venerated wine houses. The place today often attracts some 400 or more patrons to its belle époque setting, filled with nooks and crannies, even though there's room for only 200 to sit down. Musical entertainment might be anything from a Viennese operetta to cabaret, sometimes performed by local (often amateur, or temporarily out-of-work) musicians. Deli cold cuts and excellent cheese will do if you want something to eat with your drinks. Live classical music is played October to March. The bar is open daily 4pm to 3am.

Shamrock. Feldstrasse 40. ☎ **040/4-39-76-78.** U-Bahn: Altona.

The oldest Irish pub in Hamburg, the Shamrock has been in business for nearly 2 decades. It's a popular hangout for students and a transient English-speaking crowd that comes to soak up the Guinness, Kilkenney, Harp, and hard cider on tap. Open Sunday to Thursday 1pm to 2am, and Friday and Saturday 5pm to 4am.

A CASINO

Spielbank Hamburg. In the Hotel Inter-Continental, Fontenay 10. ☎ **040/44-70-44.** Cover 5DM ($2.50). U-Bahn: Stephansplatz.

This casino offers roulette, blackjack, and baccarat, played according to international rules. You can also enjoy a drink at the bar, taking in the panoramic view over the roofs and lakes of Hamburg. The minimum stake for roulette is 5DM ($2.50), for blackjack 10DM ($5). Men should wear jackets and ties. The casino is open daily 3pm to 3am.

17 Schleswig-Holstein

In this region of Germany, you can walk along the dunes and hear the roaring sea break fiercely on the rocks, or you can lie on a tranquil beach while tiny waves lap at your feet. Sound inconsistent? Not in Schleswig-Holstein. Germany's northernmost province borders both the turbulent, chilly North Sea and the smooth, gentle Baltic. And between these two bodies of water are rolling groves and meadows, lakes and ponds, and little fishing villages with thatched cottages. Fashionable seaside resorts dot both shorelines and nearby islands. Even in the coldest weather you can swim in heated seawater at the resorts of Westerland and Helgoland. In Kiel, you can wander around the harbor and explore Schleswig, with its Viking memories.

If you're flying, Hamburg (see chapter 16) is a good gateway to the region. After that, go to Lübeck, which is easily reached from Hamburg by train or by car, via the A1 Autobahn. Roads are only overcrowded in July and August. Where the trains end, local buses wait to take you the rest of the way, linking small towns and villages.

EXPLORING THE REGION BY CAR

Day 1 Leave Hamburg (see chapter 16) and take the E47 Autobahn to **Lübeck,** a distance of 66km (41 miles) to the northeast. Lübeck (see below), the old Hanseatic League capital, still retains its medieval aura, and deserves at least a day of your time.

Day 2 After visiting Lübeck, leave town on Route 207 and turn onto Route 76. This takes you to **Kiel,** a distance of 92km (57 miles). On the way, you pass through a region called Holsteinische Schweiz (Holstein Switzerland). The district is filled with nearly 150 lakes and many forests.

Day 3 After visiting Kiel, continue your motor tour northwest along Route 76 for 48km (30 miles) until you reach the Viking town of **Schleswig,** the oldest town in Schleswig-Holstein. Schleswig deserves an overnight stopover.

Day 4 From Schleswig, head to the long, narrow island of Sylt and its capital, **Westerland,** only 20km (13 miles) west of the border with Denmark. Go west along Route 201 toward Husum; then go north on Route 5 until Niebüll, where you must put your car aboard a train for the final journey to Westerland. After the short trip, you can explore the island by car.

1 Lübeck

92km (57 miles) SE of Kiel, 66km (41 miles) NE of Hamburg

It is said that nothing testifies to the wealth of an old European city as much as the size and number of its church spires. If this is so, Lübeck is rich indeed, for no fewer than seven towering steeples punctuate the skyline of this city. Lübeck was made a free imperial city in 1226. From the 13th century on, it was the capital of the Hanseatic League, the association of merchants that controlled trade along the Baltic as far as Russia. Even today the town retains the name Hansestadt Lübeck.

Today Lübeck is a city of high-gabled houses, massive gates, and strong towers. The Hanseatic merchants decorated their churches with art treasures and gilded their spires to show off their wealth. Many of these survivors of nearly 900 years of history stand side by side with postwar housing developments, and the neon lights of the business district shine on the streets and narrow passageways of bygone days.

Lübeck has had several famous sons, notably Thomas Mann and Willy Brandt. As a young man, Brandt, who later became West German chancellor and won the Nobel Peace Prize in 1971, opposed the Nazis so vehemently that he had to flee on a boat to Norway. Thomas Mann's novel *Buddenbrooks,* set in his hometown, catapulted the 27-year-old author to international fame in 1902. In 1929, he won the Nobel Prize for literature.

Lübeck's other claim to fame is that it's the world capital of marzipan. According to legend, Lübeckers, riding out a long siege, ran out of flour and started grinding almonds to make bread. So delighted were they with the results that they've been doing it ever since. To sample marzipan on its home turf, go to the Niederegger shop across from the Rathaus.

ESSENTIALS

GETTING THERE **By Train** The **Lübeck Hauptbahnhof** lies on major rail lines linking Denmark and Hamburg, and also on the Hamburg–Lüneburg–Lübeck–Kiel–Flensburg and the Lübeck–Rostock–Stralsund lines, with frequent connections. From Hamburg, 40 trains arrive daily (trip time: 40 min.), and from Berlin, 7 (trip time: 4 hr. 40 min.). For information, call ☎ **01805/99-66-33.**

By Bus Long-distance bus service to such cities as Berlin, Kiel, and Flensburg is provided by **Autokraft GmbH** (☎ **0451/89-97-283**).

By Ferry Ferryboat service from the region around Lübeck to Denmark lies astride the main railway lines between Hamburg and Copenhagen, and is therefore among the busiest in Europe. Service is offered by **ScandLines** (☎ **04371/86-51-61**), which has boats leaving across the sound every 30 minutes, 24 hours a day, every day of the year. The port on the German side is in Puttgarden; the one on the Danish side is in Rødbyhaven, a 2-hour train ride from Copenhagen. The trip takes about 75 minutes. Railway cars, trucks, and conventional automobiles are all taken on board. Round-trip transport for a car with up to four passengers averages 55DM ($27.50), with slight variations depending on the season.

TT Saga Line operates between the German port of Travemünde and the Swedish port of Trelleborg. Call ☎ **04502/80181** for bookings and departure times. And for transport by boat between Lübeck and the faraway Baltic port of Helsinki, **Finn Lines** (☎ **0451/1507443**) provides occasional service, usually favored by vacationers during midsummer.

By Car Access to Lübeck is via the A1 Autobahn north and south.

VISITOR INFORMATION For tourist information, contact the **Lübeck-Informations-Zentrum,** Breitestrasse 62 (☎ **0451/1-22-81-06**), Monday to Friday 9:30am to 6pm and Saturday and Sunday 10am to 2pm; or the **Touristbüro Beckergrube,** Beckergrube 95 (☎ **0451/1-22-1909**), Monday to Friday 8am to 4pm.

GETTING AROUND The Altstadt and the attractions outlined below can be reached by taking bus 5, 6, 7, 11, 14, or 16. Fare is 3.50DM ($1.75).

SPECIAL EVENTS Lübeck is the center of the **Schleswig-Holstein Music Festival,** with performances between the end of June and August every year. For more information, contact ☎ **0451/389-5731.** At the **Christmas market,** held mainly during the 3 weeks preceding Christmas, vendors from all over northwestern Germany descend on the town to sell their wares—many of them handmade. You can pick up deals on one-of-a-kind items from toys to pottery.

EXPLORING THE CITY

Lübeck's ✪ **Altstadt** is surrounded by the Trave River and its connecting canals, giving it an islandlike appearance. It suffered heavily during World War II, when about one-fifth of the city was leveled. Today, damaged buildings have been restored or reconstructed, and Lübeck still offers a wealth of historic attractions.

Just across the west bridge from the Altstadt, the **Holstentor (Holsten Gate)** is the first monument to greet visitors emerging from the Bahnhof. At one time it was the main town entrance, built in the 15th century as much to awe visitors with the power and prestige of Lübeck as to defend it against intruders. To the outside world the towers look simple and defiant, rather like part of a great palace. But on the city side they contain a wealth of decoration, with windows, arcades, and rich terra-cotta friezes. Within the gate is the **Museum Holstentor** (☎ 0451/1-22-41-29), housing a model of Lübeck as it appeared in the mid–17th century. The museum is open Tuesday to Sunday 10am to 5pm (to 4pm in winter). Admission is 5DM ($2.50) for adults, 3DM ($1.50) for students, and 1DM (50¢) for children 17 and under.

The **Salt Lofts (Der Salzspeicher)** viewed from the riverside, near the Holstentor, are among Lübeck's most attractive sights. In the 16th century, these buildings were used to store the salt from Lüneburg before it was shipped to Scandinavia. Each of the six buildings is slightly different, reflecting trends in Renaissance gabled architecture.

Rathaus, Rathausplatz (☎ 0451/1221005), traces its origins from 1230. It has been rebuilt several times, but there are remains of the original structure in the vaulting and Romanesque pillars in the cellar and the Gothic south wall. The towering walls have been made with open-air medallions to relieve the pressure on the Gothic-arcaded ground floor and foundations. Tours are conducted Monday to Friday at 11am, noon, and 3pm, costing 4DM ($2) for adults and 2.50DM ($1.25) for children.

✪ **Marienkirche (St. Mary's Church)** (☎ 0451/74901), across Marktplatz from the Rathaus, is the most outstanding church in Lübeck, possibly in northern Germany. Built on the highest point in the Altstadt, it has flying buttresses and towering windows that leave the rest of the city's rooftops at its feet. Some of its greatest art treasures were destroyed in 1942, but after the fire was put out, an earlier painted decoration on the walls and clerestory was discovered. The bells fell in a World War II air raid and embedded themselves in the floor of the church, where they remain to this day. Organ concerts take place during the summer months, carrying on the tradition established by St. Mary's best-known organist and composer, Dietrich Buxtehude (1668–1707).

Buddenbrookhaus, Mengstrasse 4 (☎ 0451/122-41-92), near Marienkirche, is the house where the grandparents of Thomas Mann (1875–1955) lived. It's a big, solid stone structure with a gabled roof and a recessed doorway. Above a leaded-glass fan over the heavy double doors is the date 1758. This is the house Mann described as the home of the family in *Buddenbrooks*. The museum also highlights Thomas's brother, Heinrich Mann (1871–1950), author of *Professor Unrat*, the source of the movie *The Blue Angel*. The house is open daily 10am to 5pm; admission is 7DM ($3.50) for adults, 4DM ($2) for students, and free for children under 14.

It's estimated that within an area of 5km² (2 square miles) around the Marktplatz stand 1,000 medieval houses. Nearby is **Petersgrube,** the finest street in Lübeck, lined with restored houses. A walk through the old streets of Lübeck reveals a continuing use of brick (the city insisted on this after fires in the 13th century). The effect is one of unity among all the houses, churches, shops, and guild halls.

Haus der Schiffergesellschaft (Seamen's Guild House), ont Breitestrasse, is one of the last of the elaborate guild houses of Hanseatic Lübeck, built in 1535 in Renaissance style, with stepped gables and High Gothic blind windows. It's worth seeing just for the medieval furnishings and the beamed ceilings in the main hall, now a restaurant (see "Where to Dine," below).

Museen Behnhaus/Drägerhaus, Königstrasse 9–11 (☎ 0451/1-22-41-42), was formed from two patrician houses, both entered on Königstrasse, north of Glockengiesser Strasse. Like many such houses in the town, they are tall and narrow, constructed that way to avoid heavy taxes based on frontage. The museum displays mostly German impressionists and paintings from around 1900. There is an outstanding collection of German Romantic and "Nazarene" paintings and drawings, especially by Johann Friedrich Overbeck and his school. The Behnhaus has a permanent exhibition of contemporary paintings, including Schumacher, Schultze, Rainer, Antes, and Kirkeby, along with such 20th-century artists as Kirchner, Beckmann, Lehmbruck, and Barlach. Both houses are open April to September, Tuesday to Sunday 10am to 5pm; October to March, Tuesday to Sunday 10am to 4pm. Admission is 5DM ($2.50) for adults, 3DM ($1.50) for children 6 to 18, and free for children under 6.

You can take an excursion boat around **Lübeck Harbor,** departing from Trave Landing, right in front of the Jensen hotel. In season, departures are every half hour, 10am to 6pm.

SHOPPING

Lübeck is a center for antiques stores. Two of the best are **Antique Center im Engelshof,** Engelsgrube 40 (☎ **0451/7-23-38**), and its competitor, **Antiquitäten Gunter Bannow,** Fleischhauerstrasse 87 (☎ **0451/7-73-38**). Both carry antique silver, crystal, porcelain, books, pewter, and English, Danish, and German furniture; any article can be shipped to your home. If you're in the market for antique books, head for the town's largest repository of antique books and folios, **Von Lingelsheim,** Breitestrasse 42 (☎ **0451/7-47-43**), which has everything from obscure volumes of Romantic poetry to arcane Protestant treatises. And if you're looking for souvenirs that celebrate Lübeck's rich maritime traditions, head for the town's most interesting handcrafts shop, **Kunsthaus Lübeck,** Königstrasse 20 (☎ **0451/7-57-00**), where tin, pewter, wood carvings, pottery, and antique books will help you remember your visit. **Breitestrasse,** a pedestrian walkway throughout most of the day, is the main shopping street in town. Much of Lübeck's Altstadt is banned to cars, which makes for a pleasant afternoon of wandering.

WHERE TO STAY
EXPENSIVE

Holiday Inn. Travemünder Allee 3, 23568 Lübeck (near the Burgtor entrance of the Altstadt). ☎ **0451/3-70-60.** Fax 0451/3-70-66-66. www.holiday-inn.com. 158 units. A/C MINIBAR TV TEL. 245DM–295DM ($122.50–$147.50) double; 495DM–520DM ($247.50–$260) suite. AE, DC, MC, V. Free outdoor parking; 12DM ($6) in garage. Bus: 12.

This chain hotel is first class. Until 1998, it was the Scandi Crown, and the Swedish aura remains. It's close to the ferry docks, and, as a result, attracts many Scandinavians as well as businesspeople. The medium-sized rooms are well maintained, with good beds and firm mattresses. Half are nonsmoking. There are also accommodations for people with allergies.

Dining: The restaurant offers not only north German dishes but regional Swedish seafood recipes as well.

Amenities: Laundry, room service, baby-sitting, pool, fitness center, and sauna.

Radisson SAS Senator Hotel Lübeck. Willy-Brandt-Allee 6, 23554 Lübeck (on the banks of the river, connected to the Altstadt by pedestrian bridge). ☎ **800/333-3333** in the U.S., or 0451/14-20. Fax 0451/1-42-22-22. www.radisson.com/lubeck.de. E-mail: jmh@lbczh.rdsas.com. 231 units. MINIBAR TV TEL. 230DM–320DM ($115–$160) double; 350DM–890DM ($175–$445) suite. AE, DC, MC, V. Parking 14DM ($7). Bus: 12.

This hotel is the best in town. It's well laid out and well run. Although the bulk of its clients are businesspeople, it has equal appeal to other visitors. The soundproof and medium-sized rooms are well kept and attractively furnished, with hair dryers and firm mattresses. The sleekly maintained baths come with a basket of toiletries.

Dining/Diversions: The Trave Restaurant, serving international cuisine, has distinguished itself since its opening. In addition, the Bierstube Kogge is a popular rendezvous, both for beer at night and afternoon tea or coffee, served with the luscious cakes for which Lübeck is well known. The hotel bar has good views of the Altstadt.

Amenities: 24-hour room service, 190-car garage, laundry, baby-sitting, fitness center with indoor swimming pool, solarium, sauna, steam room, and massage.

MODERATE

Hotel Excelsior. Hansestrasse 3, 23558 Lübeck (near Lindenplatz, opposite the central bus station and next to the train station). ☎ **0451/8-80-90.** Fax 0451/88-09-99. E-mail: ExcelsiorLuebeck@aol.com. 61 units. TV TEL. 140DM–210DM ($70–$105) double; 220DM–280DM ($110–$140) suite. Rates include buffet breakfast. AE, DC, MC, V. Free outdoor parking; 10DM ($5) underground. Bus: 11 or 12.

This is a good, functional hotel, and not a lot more. It's in a symmetrical baroque building with splendid proportions and an entirely renovated and modernized interior. It's especially convenient if you're traveling to Lübeck by rail. Rooms are small to medium, have shower or bath and a hair dryer, and some have a minibar. A few are designated for nonsmokers.

Jensen. An der Obertrave 4–5, 23552 Lübeck (near the Holstentor). ☎ **0451/70-24-90.** Fax 0451/7-33-86. www.hotel-jensen.de. E-mail: jensenhl@aol.com. 42 units. MINIBAR TV TEL. 170DM–210DM ($85–$105) double; from 300DM ($150) suite. Rates include buffet breakfast. AE, DC, MC, V. Parking 10DM ($5). Bus: 1, 3, or 11.

The Jensen is one of Lübeck's best moderately priced hotels, a good value if your expectations aren't too high. The small to medium rooms are modestly furnished in modern style and were recently renovated with new mattresses and upgraded plumbing. Some have fine views of the Hanseatic architecture across the canal. The buffet breakfast is served in a delightful room with picture windows overlooking the canal. The warmly decorated, tavern-style restaurant serves good lunches and dinners.

✪ **Kaiserhof.** Kronsforder Allee 11–13, 23560 Lübeck. ☎ **0451/70-33-01.** Fax 0451/79-50-83. www.kaiserhof-luebeck.de. E-mail: service@kaiserhof-luebeck.de. 60 units. MINIBAR TV TEL. 200DM–260DM ($100–$130) double; 380DM–450DM ($190–$225) suite. Rates include buffet breakfast. AE, DC, MC, V. Free outdoor parking; 12DM ($6) in garage. Bus: 2, 7, 10, 16, or 32.

The Kaiserhof, frankly, could probably demand a higher price for its rooms, as it ranks up near the top with the Senator. Two former patrician town houses outside the city center on a tree-lined boulevard have been remodeled into this hotel. The owner has created a fashionable yet homelike environment. Rooms come in various shapes and sizes, are individually furnished, and have firm mattresses. Some overflow guests are housed in a more sterile but still quite comfortable annex. Baths are compact and have hair dryers and plush towels. An elaborate and authentic Scandinavian sauna opens off the rear garden, and a large pool, a Roman vapor bath, a fitness center, and a solar studio are available.

Mövenpick Hotel. Willy-Brandt-Allee 1–3, 23554 Lübeck (across from the Holstentor). ☎ **800/111-2222** in the U.S., or 0451/1-50-40. Fax 0451/1-50-41-11. E-mail: hotel. luebeck@movenpick.com. 197 units. MINIBAR TV TEL. 215DM–250DM ($107.50–$125) double; 270DM–350DM ($135–$175) suite. Children under 16 stay free in parents' room. AE, DC, MC, V. Parking 10DM ($5). Bus: 1, 3, or 11.

This long-established hotel provides great value for the money. It stands by a canal, near the major attractions. Rooms are compact and furnished in a somewhat bland motel style, but each comes with a good bed and a firm mattress. Baths have plush towels and a hair dryer. Rooms for nonsmokers are available. Amenities include indoor and outdoor parking, Hertz reservation desk, concierge, room service, laundry, and dry cleaning. The restaurant, open 6:30am to 11pm, offers such Swiss specialties as *Rösti* and venison with lingonberries. The Lysia Bar opens daily at 5pm.

WHERE TO DINE

Das Schabbelhaus. Mengstrasse 48–52. ☎ **0451/7-20-11.** Reservations recommended. Main courses 30DM–42DM ($15–$21); fixed-price 4-course menu 58DM–63DM ($29–$31.50); menu à deux including wine 168DM ($84). AE, MC, V. Mon–Sat noon–3pm and 6–11pm. Bus: 5, 7, 11, 12, 14, or 16. NORTH GERMAN/ITALIAN.

A classic example of Hanseatic architecture on a medieval street, the Schabbelhaus is installed in two patrician buildings from the 16th and 17th centuries. A wooden staircase and balcony lead to two rooms devoted to Thomas Mann memorabilia. In the restaurant, ceiling-high studio windows overlook the small gardens. It's easy to get the impression that the setting competes with the food, but that's not entirely true. Although the cuisine isn't quite as good as the Wullenwever's (see below), it's skillfully prepared with fresh ingredients. Begin with Lübecker crab soup, the finest in town, and follow with one of the fresh fish items from the Baltic. If you wish, the chef will prepare a perfectly cooked steak to your specifications.

Haus der Schiffergesellschaft. Breitestrasse 2. ☎ **0451/7-67-76.** Reservations required. Main courses 18DM–38DM ($9–$19). No credit cards. Daily 10am–midnight. Bus: 1 or 2. NORTH GERMAN.

Entering this restaurant, with ship models and other nautical memorabilia, is like going inside a museum of Hanseatic architecture. The restaurant was once patronized exclusively by sailors. Today, good food (and lots of it) is served on scrubbed-oak plank tables with high-backed wooden booths carved with the coats of arms of Baltic merchants. Often, you must share a table. One of the most expensive items is an elaborate sole meunière (1 lb.) with salad. Many regional dishes are featured, such as baked black pudding with slices of apple and lamb's lettuce. Try the roast pork with fruit, pickled fried herring with home-fried potatoes, or Baltic plaice flavored with bacon. You might want to have a drink in the cocktail bar of the historical Gotteskeller, open Monday to Saturday 6pm to 2am.

Historischer Weinkeller. Heiligen-Geist-Hospital, Koberg 8. ☎ **0451/7-62-34.** Reservations recommended. Main courses 18DM–38DM ($9–$19). AE, MC, V. Daily noon–midnight. Bus: 1 or 3. INTERNATIONAL.

You'll find this first-class restaurant and 12th-century wine cellar in the basement of Holy Ghost Hospital. This is the number-three dining spot in town, topped only by the Wullenwever, which has better (and more expensive) food, and Das Schabbelhaus, which has a more refined atmosphere. You might begin with North Sea shrimp served with a quail egg and caviar or assorted fish in aspic. Soups can include mussel-cream soup with Pernod or clear soup prepared with Baltic fish. For a main dish, try fillet of cod gratinée with sauerkraut or poached haddock in a mustard sauce. North Sea sole is never better than when it's sautéed simply in butter. A few meat dishes are also featured.

In the basement is a potato cellar, where the potato-based menu items include baked potatoes and potato soufflé, served along with simple meat or fish selections. Main courses here cost 10DM to 22DM ($5 to $11).

✪ **Wullenwever.** Beckergrube 71. ☎ **0451/70-43-33.** Reservations required, as far in advance as possible. Main courses 28DM–48DM ($14–$24); fixed-price menus 88DM–135DM ($44–$67.50). AE, DC, MC, V. Tues–Sat noon–2pm and 7–11pm. Closed 2 weeks in Mar and Oct. Bus: 12. FRENCH/CONTINENTAL.

Sweet Treats

J.G. Niederegger, Breitestrasse 98 (☎ **0451/5-30-10;** bus: 5, 7, 11, 14, or 16), sells that "sweetest of all sweetmeats," famous Lübeck marzipan. It's been right across from the main entrance to the Rathaus since 1806. On the ground floor, you can purchase pastries to take away, or you can go upstairs to a pleasant cafe, where you can order dessert and the best brewed coffee in Lübeck. Ask for their pastry specialty, a nut torte resting under a huge slab of fresh marzipan. You'll pay around 56DM ($28) per kilo, which is about 26DM ($13) per pound. Open 9am to 6pm daily, no credit cards.

Roy Petermann, in his elegant 16th-century house, has established himself as one of the finest chefs in northern Germany. Scion of a distinguished culinary family, Petermann has brought a refined and imaginative cuisine to sleepy Lübeck. Chandeliers and oil paintings enhance the ambience, and in summer, tables overflow onto a flower-filled courtyard. Using only the best and freshest produce, his dishes have subtle depths of flavor and texture. Game is featured in the autumn, and seafood is always available. One recent memorable creation is baked pike perch fillets in a red-wine sauce.

Zimmermann's Lübecker Hanse. Am Kolk 3–7. ☎ **0451/7-80-54.** Reservations recommended. Main courses 28DM–45DM ($14–$22.50); fixed-price lunch 33DM–38DM ($16.50–$19); fixed-price dinner 35DM–60DM ($17.50–$30). AE, DC, MC, V. Mon–Fri noon–2pm and 7–11pm. Open Sat Nov–Dec. Closed Jan 1–6. Bus: 1, 3, or 11. FRENCH/GERMAN.

This is one of the most praised restaurants of Lübeck. It has an authentically weathered exterior, with dark paneling inside. French food, regional meals, and lots of fresh seafood are offered. You might want to confine yourself to the *plats du jour;* they are invariably fresh and well prepared. Fresh fish from the Baltic is another good choice. In season, wild game is featured.

LÜBECK AFTER DARK

Two newsletters, *Piste* or *Szene Journal,* free at most hotels, have news of local happenings.

Lübeck is known for its organ concerts, and about two a week are presented in various churches in the summer. The tourist office (see above) will provide complete details, or check with **Musik und Kongresshallen Lübeck,** Willy-Brandt-Allee 10 (☎ **0451/79-04-00**), about the many concert and theater opportunities in town. The most important venue is **Theater Combinale,** Huxstrasse 115 (☎ **0451/7-88-17;** bus: 11). Its plays range between the experimental and the classic. Performances are on Friday and Saturday August to June. Tickets are 20DM to 30DM ($10 to $15) for adults and 15DM to 22DM ($7.50 to $11) for students and children.

Finnegan, Mengstrasse 42 (☎ **0451/7-11-10;** bus: 12), won a 1997 award from Guinness as the best Irish pub in northern Germany. Naturally, there's Guinness on tap, as well as Kilkenny, other kinds of beers, and five or six whiskies. On Wednesday night, visiting bands play Irish music from 8pm to midnight. The pub is open Monday to Thursday 6pm to 1am and Friday and Saturday 6pm to either 3 or 4am.

Bräuberger, Alfstrasse 36 (☎ **0451/7-14-44;** bus: 12), is a restaurant and pub located in the oldest cellar in Lübeck, dating from 1225. Its beer, Zwickel, is brewed on the premises, and it also serves regional dishes and Bavarian specialties. Open Monday to Friday 5pm to 1am, and Saturday 6pm to 2am. Large mugs of beer are

5.10DM ($2.55) each. Don't overlook this place for a hearty, traditional platter of German food as an accompaniment for your beer. Platters cost 15DM to 18DM ($7.50 to $9) each.

2 Kiel

88km (55 miles) SE of the Danish border at Flensburg, 97km (60 miles) N of Hamburg, 92km (57 miles) NW of Lübeck

Everything about this city reflects the importance the sea has played in its growth and prosperity. Its perfect natural harbor at the end of a 16km (10-mile) extension of the Baltic Sea made Kiel a center for commerce with other northern European countries. The opening of the Kiel Canal in 1895 connected the Baltic with the North Sea and Western trade.

Although Kiel celebrated its 750th anniversary in 1992, there is little in the way of streets or buildings to make the casual visitor believe that the town was ever anything other than a modern city. Almost all its buildings were destroyed in World War II, after which the town was rebuilt in an admirable modern style. Kielers are proud of their broad streets, spacious squares, and green parks in the heart of town. Stretches of sandy beach in nearby resorts make this port a Baltic vacation spot as well.

ESSENTIALS

GETTING THERE **By Plane** **Lufthansa** has flights from Frankfurt to Kiel Sunday to Friday. There are also daily flights from Munich and Hamburg. Call ☎ **800/ 645-3880** for flight information. In Kiel, call the airport at ☎ **0431/32-36-56.**

By Train The **Kiel Hauptbahnhof** is on two major rail lines, the Neumünster–Hamburg and the Flensburg–Kiel–Lübeck–Lüneburg lines, with frequent connections. From Hamburg, there are 40 trains daily (trip time: 1 hr. 10 min.). For information, call ☎ **01805/99-66-33.**

By Bus Long-distance bus service to Berlin and Flensburg, as well as local and regional service, is provided by **Autokraft GmbH,** in Kiel (☎ **0431/66-60**). Buses pull into the Bahnhofplatz. The tourist office (see below) will provide you with schedules.

By Ferry Service between Kiel and Oslo, Norway, is provided by **Color Line GmbH,** in Kiel (☎ **0431/73000**). **Stena Line,** in Kiel (☎ **0431/9099**), offers service between Kiel and Gothenburg (Göteborg), Sweden.

By Car To reach Kiel from Hamburg, head north along the A7 Autobahn; from Lübeck, take Route 76 west.

VISITOR INFORMATION Contact **Tourist Information Kiel,** Andreas-Gayk-Strasse 31 (☎ **0431/67-91-00**). It's open October to April, Monday to Friday 9am to 6:30pm; May and August to September, Monday to Saturday 9am to 6:30pm; and daily 9am to 6:30pm in June and July.

GETTING AROUND Most attractions in Kiel center around the harbor, reached by bus 8 or 18. Fare is 3.40DM ($1.70).

SPECIAL EVENTS **Kiel Week (Kieler Woche),** held each June, celebrates the port's close ties to the sea. This week of special events, held for more than 100 years, includes a spectacular regatta in which more than 1,500 yachts race on the water of the Kieler Förde. In 1936 and 1972, the Olympic yacht races were held on the waters at Schilksee. For information, call the **Kieler Wochenbüro** at ☎ **0431/901-24-02**).

EXPLORING THE HARBOR & BEYOND

For the best overall look at the city and the harbor, go to the top of the **Rathaus**'s 107m (350-foot) century-old tower, much of which was restored after the devastating bombs of World War II. May to September, guided tours are offered Wednesday at noon and 6pm, and Sunday at noon, for 3DM ($1.50) per person. For an even closer view over the harbor, take a stroll along tthe **Hindenburgufer (Hindenburg Embankment)**, which stretches for 3km (2 miles) along the west side of the fjord, opposite the shipyards. Perches along this embankment are especially favored by spectators during regattas. Call tourist information for additional details.

If you'd like to go to the beach, take a short steamer trip to one of the nearby Baltic towns, such as Laboe, 16km (10 miles) to the north. Besides the beach, the town's main attraction is the restored World War II submarine **U-Boot 995,** Strandstrasse 92, Kiel-Laboe (☎ **04343/42700;** bus: 100 from the Kiel Hauptbahnhof). May to October, you can tour it every day 9:30am to 6pm (to 4pm November to April). Admission is 5DM ($2.50).

The open-air **Schleswig-Holsteinisches Freilichtmuseum,** Alte Hamburger Landstrasse (☎ **0431/659660;** bus: 502), lies 6km (4 miles) south of Kiel. Farms and rustic country homes, dating from the 16th to the 19th centuries, have been assembled here, and craftspeople operate shops while working animals perform their tasks. A half-timbered inn serves tasty lunches to visitors. The site is open November to March, Sundays and holidays 11am to 5pm; April to October, Tuesday to Sunday 9am to 6pm (July to September, also Monday 9am to 6pm). Admission is 8DM ($4) for adults, 4DM ($2) for children 6 and over, and free for children under 6.

WHERE TO STAY

Hotel Kieler Yacht Club. Hindenburgufer 70, 24105 Kiel. ☎ **0431/8-81-30.** Fax 0431/8-81-34-44. 58 units. MINIBAR TV TEL. 250DM–330DM ($125–$165) double. Rates include buffet breakfast. AE, DC, MC, V. Parking 15DM ($7.50). Bus: 8 or 18.

This yacht club offers unusually fine guest facilities. It's in an old classical building, standing back from the harbor, with an adjoining contemporary motel annex. Rooms are comfortable but unexciting. For style, we prefer those in the main building; however, all units have quality mattresses and neatly arranged baths. Mastenkeller, in the basement, is for beer drinking; the restaurant is recommended separately (see "Where to Dine," below).

Hotel Wiking. Schützenwall 1–3, 24114 Kiel. ☎ **0431/67-30-51.** Fax 0431/66-109-66. www.hotel-wiking.de. E-mail: hotelwiking@t-online.de. 42 units. MINIBAR TV TEL. 160DM–195DM ($80–$97.50) double. Rates include continental breakfast. AE, DC, MC, V. Parking 10DM ($5). Bus: 8 or 18.

The Wiking, in the center of town, offers well-furnished rooms for reasonable prices. The dark facade is ornamented with heavy-walled balconies painted a vividly contrasting white. Rooms are a bit small but well maintained, each equipped with a comfortable mattress on a good bed, plus a compact bath with shower stalls. The restaurant, Pfannkuchen Haus, and breakfast rooms have a warm Nordic ambience. The hotel has a sauna and solarium.

Maritim-Bellevue. Bismarckallee 2, 24105 Kiel. ☎ **0431/3-89-40.** Fax 0431/33-84-90. www.maritim.de. 89 units. MINIBAR TV TEL. 268DM–450DM ($134–$225) double; 600DM ($300) suite. Rates include buffet breakfast. AE, DC, MC, V. Parking 15DM ($7.50). Bus: 8 or 18.

Rated "superior first class," the Maritim-Bellevue is a well-appointed convention hotel opening onto the shore promenade of the Baltic. Its most serious rival, to which it plays second fiddle, is the Steigenberger Conti-Hansa (see below). The most expensive doubles are the luxurious corner rooms, but all—even the medium-sized ones—are well furnished and beautifully maintained.

Dining/Diversions: The hotel is known locally for its Baltic cuisine at two restaurants: the Stockholm and the Oslo. Drinks are served at the Maritim Nightclub.

Amenities: Room service, laundry, and dry cleaning are available.

Steigenberger Conti-Hansa. Schlossgarten 7, 24103 Kiel. ☎ **800/223-5652** in the U.S. and Canada, or 0431/431-51-150. Fax 0431/431-511-54-44. www.srs-worldhotels.com. 166 units. MINIBAR TV TEL. 300DM–355DM ($150–$177.50) double; 500DM–700DM ($250–$350) suite. Rates include buffet breakfast. AE, DC, MC, V. Parking 22DM ($11). Bus: 1 or 12.

Conti-Hansa, located between the edge of the harbor and a well-groomed city park, is Kiel's premier hotel. It's well maintained, modern, and solidly comfortable. The medium-sized rooms are outfitted in streamlined contemporary furniture; most look out over the harbor or the park. All have a trouser press and a hair dryer, and (if requested) air-conditioning.

Dining/Diversions: There's a formal dining room, the Restaurant Jakob (see "Where to Dine," below), as well as a bistro (the Avance) and a bar.

Amenities: Concierge, laundry, baby-sitting, whirlpool, solarium, sauna, car-rental kiosk, easy access to golf, horseback riding, tennis, and boat rentals.

WHERE TO DINE

Kieler Yacht Club. Hindenburgufer 70. ☎ **0431/8-81-34-42.** Reservations recommended. Main courses 28.50DM–39DM ($14.25–$19.50); fixed-price menu 39.50DM ($19.75). AE, DC, MC, V. Daily noon–3pm and 6–10:30pm. Bus: 8 or 18. CONTINENTAL.

This restaurant is found in the previously recommended hotel. The bar, a local hangout, attracts the yachting set. The food is solid and reliable, though not dazzling. The main attraction, naturally, is seafood. Try the fillet of haddock with mustard sauce and potatoes. Other chef's specialties are saddle of venison with savoy cabbage, roasted lamb in wine sauce with herbs, and an assortment of meal-sized salads.

Restaurant im Schloss. Am Oslokai. ☎ **0431/9-11-55.** Reservations required. Main courses 28DM–48DM ($14–$24); fixed-price menu 45DM ($22.50) for 3 courses, 98DM ($49) for 7 courses. AE, DC, MC, V. Year-round, Tues–Fri 11am–3pm; Mon–Sat 6–10:30pm. Sept–May also Sun noon–3:30pm. Bus: 1. CONTINENTAL.

The most elegant formal restaurant in Kiel offers superb cuisine, service, and wine. The Schloss, a stone building overlooking the harbor, looks like a museum set in a park. If you reserve, you can get one of the window tables opening onto the water. The cuisine has a creative and lighthearted style, using the freshest of produce. Many fish dishes are from the north German seas. Try, for example, terrine of salmon and zander in cream sauce, followed by fillet of lamb breast brushed with white bread crumbs and baked with fresh herbs.

Restaurant Jakob. In the Steigenberger Avance Conti-Hansa Hotel, Schlossgarten 7. ☎ **0431/5-11-54-07.** Reservations recommended. Main courses 25DM–35DM ($12.50–$17.50); fixed-price menus 55.50DM ($27.75). AE, DC, MC, V. Daily noon–3pm and 6–9:30pm. Bus: 1 or 12. CONTINENTAL.

Set on the lobby level of one of Kiel's most comfortable hotels, this restaurant boasts views over the harbor and a plush, modern decor. You might begin your meal with a crepe filled with Jacob mussels served on red lentils, or a soup—perhaps lobster soup with cognac. Main dishes range from the mundane (strips of turkey breast in a curry-and-yogurt sauce) to the sublime (saddle of boar with a juniper berry sauce). Try the fillet of pork medallions coated in bacon and served with a mustard sauce, or the calves' liver with asparagus and hollandaise. Dessert might be a slice of apricot cake with ice cream.

KIEL AFTER DARK

It's worthwhile just to take a stroll after dark through the salt air and fog of this sea-faring city, admiring the Hanseatic architecture and the ever-present sense of gloomy nostalgia. Along the way, you can stop at any of the small bars of the Altstadt, one of the best of which is **Nachtcafe,** Iggirstedtstrasse (☎ **0431/9-55-50;** bus: 8 or 12), which attracts night owls beginning at around 7pm. In the cramped basement, there's a bar and a dance floor, with recorded soul, funk, and garage music. Next door, under the same management (same phone) is the town's most popular disco, Velvet. No self-respecting Kieler would consider going into **Velvet** (whose red-and-green interior on two floors has velvet upholstery, as you'd expect) before 11pm. Entrance is 10DM ($5). Newer, and more intently geared to the developing (and sometimes cutting-edge) musical tastes of the under-25 crowd, is **Mex Musik Halle,** Eichhof Strasse 1 (☎ **0431/122-9944**). It's open only Friday, Saturday, and Sunday 11pm till dawn. Entrance costs 10DM ($5) per person.

One of the most visible old-fashioned nightlife options in Kiel is **Klosterbräurei,** Am Alten Markt (☎ **0431/906-290;** bus: 8), which brews and serves, on-site, a medium-dark beer that locals compare to the better-known Düsseldorfer. Most clients come just for the beer, but if you're hungry, head for the self-service cafeteria for heaping platters of sauerkraut, sausage, salads, and prepared meats (try the pig on a spit, tastefully rotating behind glass for your viewing pleasure), which a staff member will weigh for you and charge by the kilo. Expect to pay around 9DM to 22DM ($4.50 to $11) for a platter.

3 Schleswig

48km (30 miles) NW of Kiel, 34km (21 miles) S of Flensburg

This one-time Viking stronghold on the Schlei (an arm of the Baltic) is Schleswig-Holstein's oldest town, with some 1,200 years of history. Everything here is steeped in legend, even the seagulls. According to tradition, the birds nesting on Seagull Island in the middle of the Schlei are actually the fellow conspirators of Duke Abel, who in 1250 murdered his own brother, King Eric. The crime was discovered when the king's body, weighted with chains, washed ashore from the Schlei. The duke went mad, eventually died, and was impaled and buried in the Tiergarten. But his followers became seagulls, doomed to nest forever on Seagull Island. Today this sleepy town is visited mainly for its memories.

ESSENTIALS

GETTING THERE **By Train** The **Schleswig Bahnhof** is on the Flensburg–Neumünster–Hamburg and Westerland–Hamburg rail lines, with frequent connections. Trains from Hamburg arrive daily (trip time: 2 hr. 20 min.). For information, call ☎ **01805/99-66-33.**

By Bus Long-distance bus service to and from Hamburg, Flensburg, and Kiel is provided by **Autokraft GmbH** in Kiel (☎ **0431/71070**).

By Car Access by car is via the A7 Autobahn north or south.

VISITOR INFORMATION For information, contact **Tourist-Information,** Plessenstrasse 7 (☎ **04621/2-48-78**). Hours are May to September, Monday to

Friday 9am to 12:30pm and 1:30 to 5pm, Saturday 9am to noon; October to April, Monday to Thursday 9am to 12:30pm and 1:30 to 5pm, and Friday 9am to 12:30pm.

GETTING AROUND   A network of buses fan out from Königstrasse and Plessenstrasse, in the town center. Fare is 2DM ($1) to 10DM ($5). Buses operate every day 6am to 10pm.

EXPLORING THE TOWN

Dom St. Petri (St. Peter's Cathedral). Süderdomstrasse 1. ☎ **04621/96-30-54.** Free admission. May–Sept, Mon–Thurs and Sat 9am–5pm, Fri 9am–3pm, Sun 1–5pm; Oct–Apr, Mon–Thurs and Sat 10am–4pm, Fri 10am–3pm, Sun 1–4pm. Bus: 1, 2, 3, 4, or 5.

The jewel of Schleswig is St. Peter's Cathedral, a brick Romanesque-Gothic Hallenkirche (hall church) begun in the 12th century. Its towering spire makes the rest of the Altstadt seem like so many dollhouses by comparison. Inside is the outstanding 16th-century *Bordesholm Altarpiece,* a powerful work carved in oak by Hans Bruggeman for the convent at Bordesholm. Its elaborately carved Gothic panels contain nearly 400 figures. The cathedral and cloisters also possess art treasures, including the *Blue Madonna* by J. Ovens and 13th-century frescoes.

Schloss Gottorf. On a small island in the Burgsee, a bay at the west end of the Schlei. ☎ **04621/8130.** Admission (including both museums) 8DM ($4) adults, 4DM ($2) children. Mar–Oct daily 9am–5pm; Nov–Feb daily 9:30am–4pm. Bus: 1, 2, 3, 4, or 5.

A dam and a bridge connect the island with the town. As you walk around the harbor, the panorama of the Altstadt and the widening bay opens up behind you. The castle is the largest in Schleswig-Holstein. The foundations date from the original 13th-century ducal palace; the present structure was built mainly in the 16th and 17th centuries and has been reconditioned since 1948 to house two museums.

The **Provincial Museum of Archeology (Archäologisches Landesmuseum)** (☎ 04621/81-33-00) thas a most remarkable exhibit (in a separate building), the Nydam Boat, a 4th-century ship found in the Nydam marshes in 1863. In the same room are artifacts and weapons discovered with the ship and Viking corpses preserved in the moor, all adding up to one of the major archaeological finds in northern Germany.

Schleswig-Holstein State Museum (☎ 04621/81-32-22), also housed in the castle, contains an exceptional collection of fine and applied art from medieval times to the 20th century, including painting, sculpture, furniture, textiles, and weapons. Outstanding are the late Gothic King's Hall, the 17th-century ducal living rooms with rich stucco ceilings, and the Renaissance chapel with a private pew for the ducal family, decorated with intricate and elaborate carvings and inlays. Two buildings east of the castle house collections of contemporary art, including outstanding works of German expressionism and modern sculpture, plus the ethnological collection of implements and tools used by farmers, artisans, and fishermen.

Wikinger Museum Haithabu. Durchwahl, 2.5km (1½ miles) from Schleswig. ☎ **04621/81-33-00.** Admission 6DM ($3). Mar 3–Oct, daily 9am–5pm; Nov–Mar 2, Tues–Sun 10am–4pm.

Haithabu was one of the most prominent settlements of northern Europe during the Viking era. This Viking Museum, opened in 1985, contains the finds of archaeological excavations of the Viking-age town of Haithabu. Exhibits cover all aspects of daily life. There's even a Viking long ship.

In summer, you can reach this site by a scenic, 20-minute boat ride. Departures are from Stadthafen, the town quay in Schleswig, south of the cathedral. After you dock, it's a 10-minute walk to the museum. In winter you'll have to take a 3km (2-mile) walk from the rail station.

WHERE TO STAY

Hotel Waldschlösschen. Kolonnenweg 152, 24837 Schleswig-Pulverholz (a mile southwest of town). ☎ **04621/38-30.** Fax 04621/38-31-05. www.hotel-waldschloesschen.de. E-mail: reception@hotel-waldschloesschen.de. 121 units. TV TEL. 145DM–225DM ($72.50–$112.50) double; 370DM ($185) suite. Rates include buffet breakfast. AE, DC, MC, V. Free parking.

This elegant country hotel, finer than any of the in-town properties, is equipped with every convenience to make your stay interesting and comfortable. Rooms range from small to medium, each with a firm mattress on a comfortable bed, plus a compact bath. Many have a minibar and safe. Outside, there's a rock garden, a gabled house, an elongated annex, and lots of trees. The pool is centrally heated year-round. Other amenities include a bowling alley, sauna, whirlpool bathtub, and solarium. The restaurant serves a regional and continental menu at lunch and dinner, with complete meals costing 40DM ($20) to 75DM ($37.50).

Strandhalle. Strandweg 2, 24837 Schleswig. ☎ **04621/90-90.** Fax 04621/90-91-00. 25 units. MINIBAR TV TEL. 170DM–215DM ($85–$107.50) double. Rates include buffet breakfast. AE, DC, MC, V. Parking 12DM ($6). Bus: 1, 2, 3, 4, or 5.

Strandhalle may not be as good as the Waldschlösschen, but it has many winning features, especially for those who'd like to stay within Schleswig and absorb the atmosphere of this ancient town. Actually, this hotel is more of a holiday resort—right on the water, with its own rowboats and indoor pool. The owners maintain an informal atmosphere. Rooms are small but neatly kept, each with a firm mattress on a good bed, plus a small, somewhat cramped bath with shower stalls. Nonetheless, the hotel is good value for the area. Ask for a room opening on the water, with a view of the yacht harbor.

WHERE TO DINE

Olschewski's. Hafenstrasse 40 (near the waterfront). ☎ **04621/2-55-77.** Reservations required Fri–Sat. Main courses 20DM–40DM ($10–$20). AE, MC, V. Wed–Mon 11:30am–2:30pm; Wed–Sun 5:30–9:30pm. Bus: 1, 2, 3, 4, or 5. CONTINENTAL.

This cozy, well-managed restaurant is the best in town, superior to any of the hotel dining rooms. You can dine in either a glass-sided modern extension or an unpretentious dining room with views of the Schlei. Your choices may include fresh salad in almost any season, cream of tomato soup, salmon with a tangy cream base or a Riesling sauce, fillet of lamb with rosemary, or a perfectly cooked roast goose.

SCHLESWIG AFTER DARK

If you're looking for action, head for **Lollfuss,** running parallel to the Schlei between Schloss Gottorf and a north-side residential area. Many places here are cafes during the day and bars at night. The best and most popular pub of the lot is **Patio,** Lollfuss 3 (☎ **04621/2-99-99;** bus: 1 or 2), an intimate two-story structure that usually stays open between midnight and 1am (considered very late in this small town). It also has Schleswig's most popular outdoor terrace. If you get hungry, you'll find pastas, salads, pizzas, and steaks at 8DM to 21DM ($4 to $10.50).

4 The Island of Sylt

20km (13 miles) W of the German/Danish border, 193km (120 miles) NW of Hamburg

The long, narrow island of Sylt (pronounced *Zoolt*) and its capital, Westerland, form the northernmost point of Germany. Sylt lies in the North Sea off the coasts of Denmark and Schleswig-Holstein. It's the largest island of the Frisian archipelago, which stretches from Denmark to the Netherlands. The "Watt" is the name given to the eastern coast, facing the mainland. Pounding winter storms seem to take more and more of the coastline each year, and there are those who think that Sylt will one day disappear into the sea.

People come here to breathe the iodine-rich air and enjoy a climate the Germans call *Reizklima*. Sylt is today the most exclusive resort in Germany, and its hotel prices reflect its lofty status. Sylt also has a sizable gay and lesbian population, and is often called "The Fire Island of Europe." In the 1960s, Sylt became famous for "the rich and the naked," when the entire island was reportedly an ongoing bacchanalian frenzy. But it's quieted down since then. Temperatures in midsummer are usually in the low to mid 20s° C (low 70s° F), but rain can come at any minute, and winds on the beach are a constant. This has given rise to the Sylt "mink," or yellow oilskin, which chic visitors wear to protect themselves from the elements.

The spa here has facilities for the treatment of everything from heart disease to skin irritations. The basic therapy is sunshine, pure air, and seawater, but in recent years mud baths have also become a method of treatment. Some of the more remote sections of the dunes have been turned into nudist beaches for purists in the art of sunshine therapy. In addition to bathing, there are facilities in and around Westerland for horseback riding, surfing, golf, and tennis, as well as more sedentary entertainment, such as theater and concerts.

ESSENTIALS

GETTING THERE **By Plane** The nearest international airport is at Hamburg (see chapter 16). From there you can fly to the regional **Westland Airport** (☎ 04651/ 92-06-12). There's also regularly scheduled air service from Berlin, Munich, Frankfurt.

By Train The only link between the mainland and the island of Sylt is the railroad causeway running from the mainland town of Niebüll. If you wish to bring your car to the island, you'll have to load it on the train at Niebüll for the slow ride (see "By Car," below). No advance booking is necessary—you just arrive and take your chances. Passengers are carried free.

Westerland Bahnhof lies on the Westerland–Hamburg and the Westerland–Lübeck lines, with frequent connections. Seventeen trains arrive from Hamburg daily (trip time: 2 hr. 40 min. to 3 hr. 20 min., depending on the train). For information, call ☎ 01805/99-66-33.

By Car-Ferry An alternative way of reaching Sylt is to take a car-ferry between the Danish port of Havneby, on the island of Rømo (which is easily accessible via highway from Germany) and the German port of List, at the northern tip of Sylt. There are at least a dozen daily crossings between those points in summer, with a much-reduced schedule in winter. Reservations for your car are possible. For information, call the **Rømo-Sylt Line.** In List (Germany), its number is ☎ 04651/ 870475. In Havneby (Denmark), the number is ☎ 045/74-75-53-04.

By Bus The few buses that pull into Sylt are forced to ride the flatcars on the rail line across the Hindenburg Causeway for the final stretch of their journey. Many passengers prefer to get off their bus in Niebühl and transfer onto one of the passenger trains that make the frequent crossings to Westerland from other parts of Germany and Europe. Rail fare between Niebühl and Westerland costs 22DM ($11) per person, round-trip. The ride takes between 30 and 45 minutes each way.

By Car Construction of a conventional bridge from the mainland of Schleswig-Holstein to Sylt has never really been feasible. Therefore, cars headed to Sylt are loaded onto flatcars at the mainland railway junction of Niebühl and hauled out across the

A Disappearing Playground

Scientists warn that the western coast of Sylt is one of the most fragile ecosystems in Germany, and like New York's Fire Island, may one day be reclaimed by the sea. The entire island is little more than a strip, only 550m (1,800 feet) wide as its narrowest point, that's composed mostly of sand and very little rock. As such, it presents little resistance—especially after it's been stripped of its tenacious salt grasses—to the onslaught of erosion and deterioration. The sand dunes, warmed by the Gulf Stream, are forever shifting, and the winds sweeping in from the North Sea can move them by as much as a dozen feet in only a year. (Locals call these "wandering" sand dunes *Wanderdunen*.) Although the winter months in general, and storms at any time of the year, are highly destructive, it's during strong south winds that most erosion takes place, and on some mornings after violent storms, huge amounts of sand migrate from the beachfront out into the North Sea.

In the 1970s, a series of *tetrapoden* (four-legged concrete structures that look like giant jacks) were built on the sands of Westerland and Hornum beaches, in an unsuccessful attempt to hold back erosion. (They were later judged useless, and their construction discontinued.)

Today, everyone's favorite solution is one of the simplest: Whenever funds are allocated by the municipal budget, you'll see one or more barges moored off-shore, pumping sand from deepwater sites back onto beaches of Sylt. There are also severe penalties for anyone removing salt grasses and scrub from the beach-fronts, and severe restrictions against building new houses on any land that's deemed as fragile.

A Frisan we met took us for a day's walk to view the desertlike, forlorn beauty of the sand dunes. Deep, windless ridges were everywhere. "Look, the wind, the rain, and the sea are taking my island from me," the man said with a kind of despair. "One day—not in my time, perhaps—but one day it will be gone. The wind is actually blowing Sylt away. The crashing tides are claiming our coast."

If there is an air of desperation about the Germans who love and frolic in this North Sea playground, it may be because they know they won't be here forever.

Hindenburg Damm (Hindenburg Causeway) to the railway station of Westerland, on Sylt. Drivers remain in their cars, with the doors locked, eventually arriving at Wester-land 30 and 45 minutes later. For information on these and all other (conventional) trains between the German mainland and Sylt, call the **Deutsche Bahn** information service in Westerland at ☎ **01805/99-66-33.** Trains depart at 30-minute intervals daily 5am to 10pm. No reservations are accepted for hauling your car across. Round-trip transport for most cars costs 144DM ($72).

Access to Niebühl is possible via the A7 Autobahn north or south.

VISITOR INFORMATION   For information, contact the **Fremdenverkehrszentrale,** Am Bundesbahnhof Westerland (☎ **04651/99-80**). It's open May to October daily 9am to 8pm; November to April, Monday to Saturday 9am to 7pm.

SHOPPING   Few other holiday destinations in Germany are as frenetic about clothing as Sylt. Garments are removed and put on again with abandon on this island with fickle weather and an extremely clothes-conscious population. You'll find impres-sive inventories of expensively casual clothing on Sylt—items that are artfully simple, easy to don, easy to doff, and easy to look at. The island's best shopping streets are the **Friedrichstrasse,** in Westerland, and the **Stroewae,** in Kampen, both lined with boutiques associated with the great names of European fashion.

In Westerland, look for menswear at **The Camel Store,** Friedrichstrasse 32 (☎ **04651/8-25-00**), and **Heising,** Friedrichstrasse 22 (☎ **04651/2-27-65**); and women's wear at **Marco Polo,** Strandstrasse 3–5 (☎ **04651/61-11**), or at any of the dozens of chic hole-in-the-wall boutiques. In Kampen, on the northern side, both men and women will find the glossy and endlessly tasteful emporium of German luminary **Jil Sander,** Stroewae 7 (☎ **04651/4-54-56**).

The island's art galleries reflect the tastes and preoccupations of big-city Hamburg. One of the most interesting emporiums for dramatic modern art is **Galerie Sprotte,** Altdorfstrasse 1 (☎ **04651/4-24-13**), whose exhibition space is mostly devoted to the stylized and often riveting paintings of long-time Sylt resident Siegvard Sprotte. His renderings of the landscapes of Sylt have been influenced by everything from 16th-century Flemish portraits to early 20th-century impressionism.

WHERE TO STAY

Hotel Clausen. Friedrichstrasse 20, 25980 Westerland/Sylt (in Westerland's pedestrian zone, a 3-min. walk from the beach). ☎ **04651/9-22-90.** Fax 04651/2-80-07. 20 units. TV TEL. 180DM–280DM ($90–$140) double; 240DM–310DM ($120–$155) suite. Rates include buffet breakfast. AE, MC, V. Closed Jan 7–21. Parking 10DM ($5).

This four-story building was originally built around 1950 and radically modernized in 1992. Today, its congenial English-speaking owners occupy the upper (fourth) floor. On the building's lower stories is a series of small but tidily maintained rooms, each fitted with a quality mattress on a good bed. Baths are also small and have shower stalls. Breakfast is the only meal served, but many restaurants are nearby.

Hotel Miramar. Friedrichstrasse 43, 25980 Westerland/Sylt. ☎ **04651/85-50.** Fax 04651/ 85-52-22. www.hotel-miramar.de. E-mail: miramar-sylt@t-online.de. 104 units. MINIBAR TV TEL. 290DM–670DM ($145–$335) double; 460DM–1,200DM ($230–$600) suite. Rates include buffet breakfast. AE, DC, MC, V.

This hotel, on a bluff just above the beach, is the second best accommodation at Westerland, just below Stadt Hamburg (see below). The Miramar is surrounded by an arched veranda, and its public areas are graced with enormous arched windows with views of the sea. An octagonal light, left over from the building's 1903 construction, illuminates the salon from above. The high-ceilinged rooms are quite comfortable and were recently renovated; each comes with a luxurious bed and a recently renewed bath.

Dining/Diversions: Guests relax on the cafe-terrace overlooking the water. The bar is a chic rendezvous spot. The formal restaurant, serving both North German and international dishes, is among the finest on the island.

Amenities: The sunny indoor pool, near the sauna and fitness room, makes swimming an option even in winter. Also, room service, concierge, dry cleaning, laundry.

✪ **Stadt Hamburg.** Strandstrasse 2, 25980 Westerland/Sylt (next to the casino). ☎ **04651/85-80.** Fax 04651/85-82-20. www.relaischateaux.fr/stadthamburg. E-mail: hsh. sylt@t-online.de. 72 units. TV TEL. 325DM–490DM ($162.50–$245) double; 540DM–610DM ($270–$305) suite. AE, MC, V. Parking 15DM ($7.50).

This is the best hotel on the island, though it looks more like a well-appointed country home than a hotel. The gleaming white entrance is reached through a white picket fence, its rear windows overlook a well-kept lawn. Each spacious room is individually furnished, with homelike touches. Mattresses and linens are the island's finest, and the baths are state of the art, with hair dryers and toiletries.

Dining/Diversions: The charming breakfast room has a blue-and-white ceramic stove. Guests gather on cooler evenings around the open fireplace. The restaurant serves some of the best food at the resort (see below).

Amenities: Concierge, room service, dry cleaning, laundry, newspaper delivery.

Wunschmann Hotel. Andreas-Dirks-Strasse 4, 25980 Westerland/Sylt. ☎ **04651/50-25.** Fax 04651/50-28. 36 units. TV TEL. 206DM–396DM ($103–$198) double; 490DM–660DM ($245–$330) suite. AE. Closed mid-Nov to mid-Dec. Parking 12DM ($6).

This hotel is in the heart of the tourist belt of Westerland, yet only minutes from the sand dunes. Rooms are in a complex of modern buildings (with more than two dozen boutiques), but the hotel's interior exudes Old-World tranquility. The medium-sized and one-of-a-kind rooms are cheerful, with strong colors and firm mattresses. Two offer minibars.

Dining: The hotel restaurant serves adequate German and international fare for breakfast, lunch, and dinner.

Amenities: Concierge, 24-hour room service, dry cleaning, laundry service, in-room massage, twice-daily maid service, and baby-sitting. A health club is nearby.

WHERE TO DINE

Alte Friesenstube. Gaadt 4, Westerland. ☎ **04651/12-28.** Reservations required. Main courses 29.50DM–50DM ($14.75–$25). AE. Tues–Sun 11:30am–2:30pm and 6–10:30pm. Closed Jan. NORTHERN GERMAN/FRISIAN.

This restaurant is refreshingly down-to-earth amid the pretentiousness of Sylt. The thatched building housing this place was constructed in 1648. The menus are written on the wall in a dialect of low German, but someone will gladly assist you in deciphering the offerings, which include regional pork, fish, and beef dishes. Especially popular is duck with orange sauce, and a local saltwater fish (*panfische*) with roasted potatoes and mustard sauce. No one puts on airs, and the kitchen hardly follows trendy recipes, sticking instead to the robust fare the islanders have been eating for decades.

Hardy auf Sylt. Norderstrasse 65, Westerland. ☎ **04651/2-27-75.** Reservations required. Main courses 26DM–35DM ($13–$17.50). No credit cards. Tues–Sun 6pm–midnight. Closed Jan 15–Feb 15 and Nov 30–Dec 20. INTERNATIONAL/NORTHERN GERMAN.

This round, thatched restaurant has a nostalgic interior featuring furniture dating from about 1890. Finely worked columns, old oil portraits, beautiful glass lamps, and skillfully wrought candlesticks combine to create a relaxed, intimate feeling. The menu is adjusted seasonally. There's a fine selection of French and German wines.

✪ **Jörg Müller.** Süderstrasse 8 (a 5-min. walk from the center of Westerland). ☎ **04651/2-77-88.** Reservations required. Main courses 52DM–76DM ($26–$38); fixed-price menus 148DM–186DM ($74–$93). AE, DC, MC, V. Thurs–Mon 11:30am–2pm; Wed–Mon 6–10pm. Closed Nov 25–Dec 18. CONTINENTAL/FRENCH.

The most elegant dining on the island is at Jörg Müller. The brick building that contains this restaurant is almost a landmark in itself, thanks to its thatched roof, steep gables, and Frisian architecture. The restaurant's fame has eclipsed that of every competitor. Menu items change with the seasons and feature a blend of contemporary continental cuisine with imaginative variations of French recipes, which might include lobster salad with herb-flavored vinaigrette sauce, sliced and braised goose liver with segments of glazed apples, or roast salt-marsh lamb flavored with herbs and served with ratatouille-flavored cream sauce. You can also enjoy local oysters with compote of red shallots and champagne sauce or halibut baked in fennel. For dessert, you might order a compote of fresh fruits with pistachio nuts or feuilleté of chocolate served with both light- and dark-chocolate mousse.

◑ Restaurant Stadt Hamburg. Strandstrasse 2, Westerland. ☎ **04651/85-80.** Reservations recommended, especially if you're not a hotel guest. Main courses 44DM–62DM ($22–$31); fixed-price dinners 69DM–140DM ($34.50–$70). AE, MC, V. Daily 6–10pm. Bus: Centrale Omnibus Bahnhof. GERMAN/FRISIAN.

Top-rate cuisine is offered here in an attractive setting. The menu is so wide-ranging it may be hard to make up your mind, but among the à la carte listings, the smoothest beginning is the cream of lobster soup. Many seafood specialties are featured as main courses, such as pan-fried fresh North Sea sole and turbot medallions in saffron sauce with zucchini. Another good dish is the rack of lamb (raised on the salty grasslands of the island). For dessert, try homemade *rote Grütze*—different kinds of berries and cherries topped with vanilla ice cream.

Web Christel. Süderstrasse 11 (opposite Jörg Müller), Westerland. ☎ **04651/2-29-00.** Reservations recommended. Main courses 33DM–45DM ($16.50–$22.50); fixed-price menus 50DM–99DM ($25–$49.50). No credit cards. Fri–Wed 5–11pm. NORTH GERMAN.

Favored by local residents for its reasonable prices and cozy ambience, this restaurant occupies a century-old Frisian house set in the center of Westerland, opposite its more glamorous (and more expensive) rival, Jörg Müller. Menu items include a wide selection of fish, such as classic versions of turbot in an herb-butter-mustard sauce, and sole prepared in the meuniére style or grilled and served with hollandaise sauce. Roast duck with two different sauces is also available. The staff is warm and polite.

SYLT AFTER DARK

Two contenders on Sylt's nightlife circuit include **Disco Pony,** Strowae, in Kampen (☎ 04651/42182), where both indoor and outdoor bar areas encompass views of the sea and the scrub-covered coastline that flanks it. Attracting for the most part a clientele under 40, it's open nightly around 10:30pm. (It's closed on Monday and Tuesday October to April.) And for the closest thing to the kind of urban underground life you might have expected in Hamburg or Berlin, head for the **Airport Lounge,** a disco within some of the industrial-looking buildings at the Westerland airport (☎ 04651/92-06-12). Here, loud and highly danceable house and garage music is the norm every Wednesday to Sunday 10:30pm till at least 3am.

Unless you're a hard-core gambler, the island's bars, cafes, and restaurants are more interesting than its casino, **Spielbank Westerland,** Strandstrasse (☎ 04561/230450), which, ironically, occupies the same premises as Westerland's Rathaus (town hall). There's no maximum limit on how much you can bet, so the activities around the baccarat, roulette, and blackjack tables can get intense, depending on the crowd. Entrance costs 5DM ($2.50) per person. Men are encouraged to wear neckties. Hours are daily 5pm till at least 3am. You must present a passport to enter. On the premises is a sophisticated bar, open during the same hours as the gaming tables.

A Scenic Drive
Along the Baltic

The Baltic coast is saltier and windier and has a more international outlook than other regions of the former East Germany. Throughout the Cold War, this windswept seaside was a playground for the factory workers and bureaucrats of the now-defunct DDR. For centuries before that, the region thrived as the site of the busy ports of the Hanseatic League, whose lore still permeates the land. Other cultural influences came from the Swedish, Latvian, Lithuanian, and Polish ports with which for many centuries the League did much of its trading. Since reunification, the Baltic Coast has slowly emerged as a hot spot for Germany's beach-loving throngs, and the entire coastline has benefited from a major restoration of its historic structures, many of which were decaying.

The region is best visited by car, on any of several different driving routes. The ideal departure point for this exploration is Lübeck (see chapter 17). From Lübeck, drive east along Highway 105 (also known as E22). En route, you'll traverse the frontier that separated West from East Germany for more than 45 years and enter the medieval principality of Mecklenburg-West Pomerania. Your first stop will be Wismar.

1 Wismar

60km (37 miles) E of Lübeck, 53km (33 miles) W of Rostock

Wismar was once an elegant city of the Hanseatic League, the medieval capital of Mecklenburg-West Pomerania. The city became prominent in the early 1200s because of its port facilities. For long periods of its history it was part of the overseas empire of Sweden. Wismar contains the largest market square in Germany—1 ha (2½ acres). It's surrounded by elegant buildings with architectural styles ranging from 14th-century North German Gothic to 19th-century Romanesque revival. The square's focal point, and one of the town's most frequently photographed objects, is an elaborate wrought-iron fountain imported from Holland in the early 1600s. The silent filmmaker Friedrich Wilhelm Murnau used the twisting streets of Wismar's Altstadt as the backdrop for his classic vampire film, *Nosferatu.*

Unfortunately, your drive into this town's charming core will be dampened by a view of the socialist regime's endless concrete-sided suburbs. Sites to watch for in the historic city center include the pillared and gabled **Rathaus** (not open to visitors), built on the town's

Driving Along the Baltic

main square in the neoclassical style in 1819. A very old house on the square, **Alter Schwede (The Old Swede),** constructed around 1380, functions as a restaurant (see "Where to Dine," below). The town's most famous church is the **St. Nikolaikirche,** Hinter dem Chor (☎ **03841/21-36-24**), a Gothic brick structure whose high altar dates from 1430. It's open May to October, Monday to Saturday 10am to noon and 1 to 6pm, and Sunday 1 to 5pm; in the off-season only Saturday 11am to 3pm and Sunday 1 to 4pm. Admission is free.

For tourist information in Wismar, contact **Wismar-Informationen,** Am Markt 11 (☎ **03841/1-94-33**), open year-round daily 9am to 6pm.

WHERE TO STAY

Most visitors come to Wismar only for the day, moving on to overnight accommodations in either Rostock or Schwerin. However, if you choose to stay, try one of these hotels below.

Hotel Stadt Hamburg. Am Markt 24, 23966 Wismar. ☎ **03841/23-90.** Fax 03841/
23-92-39. www.wismar-service.de. E-mail: info@wismar-service.de. 102 units. TV TEL.
195DM–255DM ($97.50–$127.50) double. Rates include buffet breakfast. AE, DC, MC, V.

This well-managed hotel, recently renovated, is the best in town. It has three floors,
three restaurants, an English-speaking staff, and a desirable location on the main (and
most historic) square in Wismar. The no-frills rooms are comfortable and contemporary. Each is rather bandboxy, but all are fitted with comfortable mattresses. The
hotel's uppermost floor contains a health club that's free for residents but costs 12DM
($6) for a 2-hour session for nonresidents. The hotel's most formal restaurant is the
Pülergarten; more casual is a simple coffee shop (Café Am Markt). Our favorite spot
is the Tittataster (see below).

WHERE TO DINE
Bierkeller Tittataster. Am Markt 24. ☎ **03841/23-90.** Platters 14DM–35DM
($7–$17.50). AE, DC, MC, V. Mon–Sat 6:30-10pm. GERMAN/INTERNATIONAL.

This restaurant in the cellar of the Hotel Stadt Hamburg is workaday and deliberately
informal. The vaulting that rises above its battered wooden tables dates from the 14th
century. Menu items taste best when consumed with copious amounts of beer. They
include an array of snack-style platters and a hearty selection of salads, schnitzels, and
roasts. On some nights, the cellar hosts live jazz bands.

Restaurant Alter Schwede. Am Markt 20. ☎ **03841/28-35-52.** Reservations recommended in summer. Main courses 20DM–35DM ($10–$17.50); fixed-menu 38DM ($19).
AE, MC, V. Daily 11:30am–11:30pm. GERMAN.

Constructed in 1380, this building is one of the oldest and most historically evocative
in Wismar, so well known that many Germans drive from other parts of the Baltic just
to see it. Its name, "The Old Swede," refers to the Swedish invasions of the 1600s, but
luckily for sightseers, the building functions as a restaurant. In the high-ceilinged
dining room, an old-time staff in black-and-white uniforms bustles back and forth,
carrying steaming platters of traditional Germanic food. Menu items include sauerbraten with red cabbage and potatoes, a marinated pork roast known as *Rippenbraten,*
all kinds of wursts, salmon roasted in orange sauce, and lots of fish from the Baltic.

FROM WISMAR TO SCHWERIN
Our route now detours inland (south) toward the present-day capital of Mecklenburg-
West Pomerania. Drive out of Wismar along the main southbound artery (Highway
106) until you reach Schwerin.

2 Schwerin
30km (19 miles) S of Wismar

Lying inland from the Baltic coast, this town at the southwestern corner of Lake
Schwerin is set in a fertile, well-irrigated district of "lakelets." Schwerin is the industrial and cultural center of an important agricultural district, but it has more to offer
visitors than commerce.

This is a city of ancient history and well-entrenched civic pride. It was originally
established in the 11th century by Slavs, who fortified a settlement on the island now
occupied by Schwerin Castle. Henry the Lion, duke of Saxony, annexed their settlement and used the strategic site to establish the first German-speaking colony east of
the Elbe. In 1358, Schwerin was honored with a designation as seat of the ducal court
of Mecklenburg, a title it held until the closing days of World War I.

SEEING THE SIGHTS

There aren't many historic buildings in Schwerin, since most of the old structures were destroyed by fire and replaced during the 19th century. Worth a look are the **Arsenal,** set beside the Pfaffenteich (an artificial reservoir in the city center), the **Marstall** (royal stables), and the **Kollegiengebäude,** seat of civic government until 1945 and today a site of government offices. (None of these three buildings can be visited.)

Schweriner Schloss (Schwerin Castle), Lennestrasse 1 (☎ **0385/56-57-38**), is the most spectacular monument in town and a triumph of 19th-century civic architecture. This castle, the 19th-century seat of the Mecklenburg grand dukes, was spared from fires and bombings. It's set on an island that separates a small lake (the Burgsee) from a much larger lake (the Schweriner See), and is connected to the German mainland by a pair of bridges. Inspired by the Château de Chambord in France's Loire Valley, Schweriner Schloss is a pentagonal structure of many domes, towers, and turrets, built between 1843 and 1857. Its style incorporates elements of Gothic, baroque, and Renaissance architecture. The castle's chapel (built around 1560) is much older than the larger structure that contains it. The castle-museum is open Tuesday to Sunday 10am to 5pm (closes at 6pm April 15 to October 14). Entrance costs 6DM ($3) for adults and 3DM ($1.50) for children.

Even if the castle is closed, you'll still be able to appreciate the formal 18th-century **Schlossgarten** (park) that flanks it. Its architects incorporated terraced waterfalls, a battery of heroic statues, and a network of canals that divide the garden into a series of interconnected rectangles. Entrance to the gardens is possible anytime, and there's no admission fee.

On the mainland, a pair of imposing buildings stands in the former Alter Garten parade grounds. These include the neoclassical **Mecklenburgisches Staatstheater** (☎ **0385/53000**), where dramas, comedies, and operas are sometimes performed, and also the well-recommended **Staatliches Museum Schwerin-Kunstsammlunger,** Alter Garten 3, Werderstrasse (☎ **0385/59-580**), in a neoclassical building resembling a Roman temple, completed in 1785. Inside you'll find a worthy collection of 16th-century Dutch and Flemish paintings, as well as 18th-century paintings from France and the German-speaking world. Specific examples include *Drinking Boy* and *Boy Holding a Flute* by Frans Hals, and *Home Concert* by Frans van Mieris. There are also German medieval collections, including porcelain (especially Dresden china), 18th-century court paintings, and works by such modern artists as Max Liebermann. It's open Tuesday to Sunday 10am to 5pm. Admission is 7DM ($3.50) adults, 3.50DM ($1.75) students and children.

Schwerin's **Dom,** Am Marktplatz (☎ **0385/56-50-14**), was begun around 1248. The cathedral is a fine example of brick medieval architecture, designed in the Lübeck Hanseatic Gothic style. Highlights include a Gothic altarpiece, probably carved in Lübeck around 1480. If you'd like a panoramic view of the town and the lake, you can climb to the top of the 98m-high (320-foot-high) tower. The Dom is open June to September, Monday 10am to 1pm, Tuesday to Saturday 10am to 1pm and 2 to 5pm, and Sunday noon to 5pm. Other months, hours are Monday 10am to 4pm, Tuesday to Saturday 11am to noon and 2:30 to 4:30pm, and Sunday 2:30 to 4:30pm. You can enter the church free, but it costs 2DM ($1) to go up in the tower.

Several interesting trips are possible from Schwerin. You can take a boat trip (midsummer only) across the Schweriner See or, if you feel athletic, hike around the lake's southern shore. Information on attractions in and around the town can be obtained at the **City Tourist Office,** Am Markt 10 (☎ **0385/592-52-12**). It's open Monday to Friday 10am to noon and 1 to 5pm, and during summer (May to September), Monday to Friday 10am to 6pm and Saturday 10am to 2pm.

WHERE TO STAY

Crowne Plaza Hotel Schwerin. Bleicher Ufer 23, 19053 Schwerin (a 15-min. walk west of the town center). ☎ **0385/5-75-50.** Fax 0385/5-75-57-77. www.crowneplaza.com. 100 units. MINIBAR TV TEL. 230DM–250DM ($115–$125) double; 380DM ($190) suite. AE, DC, MC, V. Tram: 1 or 2. Bus: 10.

This hotel rises five floors above the shoreline of a freshwater lake (the Ostdorfer See). It's part of a modern office and residential compound. Rooms are modern and convenient, although rather bandboxy and furnished in a completely functional way, but the beds are comfortable with good mattresses. Some overlook the lake, others a verdant public park. Two of the five floors are reserved strictly for nonsmokers. On the hotel's premises is a health club with its own sauna, a bar, and a noteworthy restaurant, Marco Polo, which is open daily for lunch and dinner. Set menus cost 42DM to 60DM ($21 to $30).

Hotel Nordlicht. Apothekerstrasse 2, 19055 Schwerin (one-half mile from Marktplatz). ☎ **0385/55-81-50.** Fax 0385/5-57-43-83. www.all-in-all.com. E-mail: steiveo@t.dmx.de. 5 units. TV TEL. 145DM ($72.50) double. Rates include continental breakfast. MC, V. Free parking. Tram: Marienplatz.

This inexpensive establishment is more like a B&B than a conventional hotel. It's across from the pond (*Pfaffenteich*), which is encircled by walkways. The hotel, built in 1991, consists of only five rooms furnished in a simple but modern style, each with a good mattress and a cramped bath with a shower stall and thin towels. Hot food is served daily 11:30am to midnight in the restaurant or on the cafe-terrace.

Hotel Plaza Schwerin. Am Grünen Tal, 19063 Schwerin (near Schloss Schwerin, 5 min. from the center by car). ☎ **800/528-1234** in the U.S., or 0385/3-99-20. Fax 0385/3-99-21-88. 79 units. MINIBAR TV TEL. 150DM–200DM ($75–$100) double; 250DM ($125) suite. AE, DC, MC, V. Free parking. Tram: Zoo.

This hotel is outstanding in many respects, in spite of its unappetizing location in a sea of Sputnik-era apartment blocks. It's a favorite with vacationers and business travelers. Most of the contemporary rooms are spacious and all are designed for standard comfort with decent beds and compact little baths with shower stalls. Amenities include trouser presses, hair dryers, and fax outlets. There's also a sauna and fitness center, and room service and baby-sitting are offered. The hotel's much-awarded restaurant, Primavera, is one of the best along the Baltic (see "Where to Dine," below).

WHERE TO DINE

Primavera. In the Hotel Plaza Schwerin, Am Grünen Tal. ☎ **0385/3-99-20.** Reservations recommended. Main courses 22.50DM–32.50DM ($11.25–$16.25); fixed-price lunch 15.50DM ($7.75); fixed-price dinner 35DM–55DM ($17.50–$27.50). AE, DC, MC, V. Daily 11:30am–midnight. Tram: Zum Zoo. ITALIAN.

This restaurant, in the previously recommended hotel, has consistently been voted the best in the Mecklenburg area. The menu changes with the season. Italian dishes are featured, along with a small regional menu. The service is impeccable, and the food is always good. The fresh fish is often from the North Sea. Arrive early for dinner and enjoy music in the piano bar beginning at 6pm.

Weinhaus Uhle. Schusterstrasse 13–15 (near the castle and the cathedral). ☎ **0385/56-29-56.** Reservations recommended. Main courses 25DM–40DM ($12.50–$20); daily specials 16DM–20DM ($8–$10). Daily noon–11pm. INTERNATIONAL.

This wine house in the oldest part of town is set in a building dating from 1751. It's mostly decorated in Jugendstil (German art nouveau), but the second floor incorporates a traditional Rittersaal (Knight's Room) with large and ornate windows, metal replicas of knights, and heraldic coats of arms. The chef's specialty is a savory

Mecklenburger Ente (duck). A host of other regional dishes, as well as an international mixed grill, are also offered. A small band plays nightly.

A SIDE TRIP TO GÜSTROW

From Schwerin, strike out in a northeasterly direction along a secondary road (Route 104, but be aware that some sections along this road might also be called Route 192). Follow the signs to Brüel and then to the historic town of Güstrow, a distance of 69km (43 miles). En route, you'll pass through villages that haven't really changed very much since the days of the East German regime.

Güstrow holds one of the district's architectural gems, **Schloss Güstrow,** which rises in imposing 16th-century splendor amid formal French gardens. Also of interest is the town's cathedral, the **Dom** (Am Domplatz), whose decorative highlights are statues of the Apostles, sculptured in oak around 1530.

For information in Güstrow, contact the **tourist information office,** Domstrasse 9 (☎ **03843/68-10-23**). It's open May to September, Monday to Friday 9am to 6pm and Sunday 9:30am to 1pm; October to April, Monday to Friday 9:30am to 6pm.

Continue from Güstrow north along Autobahn 19 for another 42km (26 miles) into the heart of Rostock, one of the Baltic coast's most historic seaports. To get to Rostock from Schwerin, take route 106 north to Wismar, and then take Route 105 (E22) east.

3 Rostock

117km (73 miles) NE of Lübeck, 282km (175 miles) NE of Berlin.

Rostock is set on a wide and navigable estuary of the Warnow River. Throughout the Cold War, it was the largest and busiest seaport in East Germany, built on a scale to rival Hamburg. The town still bustles with maritime activity, though its importance has declined since reunification. Today visitors come to Rostock to wander its reconstructed Alstadt, which contains major sections of the town's medieval wall, and visit the town's museums and churches.

During the 13th and 14th centuries, Rostock was one of the most important cities of the Hanseatic League, trading and competing with ports in Sweden, Denmark, Estonia, Poland, and Lithuania. Its university (founded in 1419) was the first in any city along the Baltic, and its wealth and strategic location soon provoked the envy of the Scandinavians. Danes and Swedes occupied the city twice, first during the Thirty Years' War (1618–48), and again from 1700 to 1721. Later, the French, under Napoléon, occupied the town for about a decade until 1813. During World War II, Rostock was blasted by British bombers. The monuments and houses lining its principal street, Lange Strasse (Long Street), were completely demolished. Some historic buildings were restored, at great expense, from piles of little more than rubble.

SEEING THE SIGHTS

Some noteworthy historic buildings stand on Neuer Platz (also known as Ernst-Thalmann-Platz). Among the most prominent is the **Rathaus,** Neuer Markt (☎ **0381/14-16**), which manages to incorporate three late 13th- and early 14th-century houses and seven towers into a brick structure linked by an arcaded gallery. Its interior is devoted to municipal offices.

Beginning at the Rathaus's base and extending westward for several historic blocks is Rostock's most photographed street, **Kröpeliner-Strasse,** a pedestrians-only walkway lined with shops and restored buildings constructed between 1500 and around 1850. It runs parallel to the more banal, and much less charming, Lange Strasse,

Rostock's principal street. Of particular interest is the **step-gabled presbytery** (ca. 1480), from what used to be a hospital, at Kröpeliner-Strasse 82. The street ends at one of the most instantly recognizable features in town, the **Kröpeliner Tor,** a 14th-century brick gatehouse (the interior is closed to the public).

Among the buildings that survived war damage is the **St-Marien-Kirche (St. Mary's Church),** Am Ziegenmarkt (☎ **0381/4-92-33-96**), set on a narrow side street off Lange Strasse. It's one of the finest (and largest) ecclesiastical structures of the Baltic world. It began in the 1200s as a Romanesque Hallenkirche (hall church) and was enlarged and modified around 1398 into a cross-shaped basilica. The huge tower wasn't completed until the late 1700s. From the top there's a sweeping panorama over Rostock's wharves and dock areas. Inside the church is an enormous organ dating from 1770 and an astronomical clock originally built in the late 1400s and reconfigured in 1643. The Marien-Kirche is open Monday to Saturday 10am to 5pm. Sunday worship is at 10am. Admission for adults is 2DM ($1).

Other churches to be seen include the **Heilig-Kreuz-Kirche (Church of the Holy Cross),** a Gothic Hallenkirche with three naves (or aisles), built of brick in the 14th century. In the Cistercian convent associated with this church is the **Kultur-historisches Museum,** Universitätsplatz (☎ **0381/45-59-13**), containing medieval religious paintings and sacred art. It's open Tuesday to Sunday 10am to 6pm. Entrance is 4DM ($2) for adults, 2DM ($1) for children.

Schiffahrtsmuseum (Navigational Museum), August-Bebel-Strasse 1, at the corner of Richard-Wagner-Strasse (☎ **0381/25-20-60**), contains exhibits related to the nautical history of one of Germany's most important seaports, beginning with the Vikings and focusing on the great maritime developments of the 19th and early 20th centuries. It's open Tuesday to Sunday 10am to 6pm. Admission is 6DM ($3) for adults, 2DM ($1) students and children.

Rostock's **tourist office,** Schnickmannstrasse 13–14 (☎ **0381/49-79-90**), is open October to April, Monday to Friday 10am to 6pm and Saturday 10am to 2:30pm; May to September, Monday to Friday 10am to 6pm and Saturday and Sunday 10am to 4:30pm. The tourist office can provide information on any boat tours that might be offered at the time of your visit.

WHERE TO STAY

Radisson SAS Hotel Rostock. Lange Strasse 40, 18055 Rostock (a block from the Kröpeliner Gate). ☎ **0381/4-59-70.** Fax 0381/4-59-78-00. www.radisson.com/rostockde. E-mail: guest@zrozh.rdsa3.com. 352 units. MINIBAR TV TEL. 170DM–250DM ($85–$125) double; 380DM–480DM ($190–$240) suite. Rates include buffet breakfast. AE, DC, MC, V. Parking 12DM ($6) outdoors; 14DM ($7) in garage. Tram: Schröderplatz.

This eight-story high-rise in the center of the city is the largest hotel in town. It used to house the bigwigs of the DDR as well as vacationing East German workers. Rooms are done in a contemporary style, but are strictly functionally furnished, even though the beds are comfortable. The hotel offers two restaurants, the Malmö and the Captain's Corner, featuring both international and regional cuisine. Its bar, the Arkona, is one of the major rendezvous centers in town.

WHERE TO DINE

Mond und Sterne. Strandstrasse 85 (on the harbor). ☎ **0381/4-59-03-44.** Reservations recommended. Main courses 12.50DM–29DM ($6.25–$14.50). AE, MC, V. Daily 11am–midnight. Tram: Lange Strasse. NORTH GERMAN/FISH/GAME.

This establishment has flourished since 1992 because of its well-prepared cuisine and its no-frills, rib-sticking food, rich with the traditions of the Baltic. The decor is inspired by the old Hanseatic League, with timber beams and brass lighting fixtures.

The restaurant offers steaming bowls of *Leberknödel* (liver dumpling) soup and goulash soup, platters of fried schnitzels of pork or veal, and several preparations of herring and cod. A house specialty is *Laubskauf,* a fish hash traditionally made with whatever leftovers were in the larder—fish, potatoes, onions, eggs, and perhaps a trace or two of meat. Another chef's specialty is *Edelfischteller,* a platter of four Baltic fish, sautéed and then served with potatoes and chives. This traditional Baltic dish, popular in Denmark as well, is associated with civic and regional culinary pride.

Zur Kogge. Wokrenterstrasse 27 (on the harbor). ☎ **0381/4-93-44-93.** Reservations required at night. Main courses 15DM–32DM ($7.50–$16). AE, DC, MC, V. Daily 11:30am–11:30pm. Tram: Lange Strasse. GERMAN.

This is the oldest sailors' pub in Rostock. The restaurant is decorated with all kinds of nautical marine items, either placed on shelves or hanging from the ceiling. Wednesday to Saturday, there's live music—the German version of New England sea chanteys. Naturally, fish specialties are the chef's best items. Try the *Mecklenburger Fischsuppe* (fish soup) or the various versions of smoked fish.

FROM ROSTOCK TO STRALSUND

To continue our tour of Germany's Baltic coast from Rostock, drive northeast from the center of town along the E22 highway (also called Route 105), heading for the next major destination, Stralsund, about 80km (50 miles) away. Off the highway at any of about five different junctions are some half-dozen seafront towns, each permeated with the scents and salt air of the Baltic. Many are attractive and, to an increasing degree, open for resort business.

Consider breaking up your trip with a visit to one of the best of these towns, **Ribnitz-Damgarten,** about 26km (16 miles) northeast of Rostock, right beside the E22 highway. Its architectural highlight is the **Rostocker Tor,** an imposing tower that symbolized the town for many generations. Most visitors opt for only a brief exploration of Ribnitz before continuing on their journey. The **tourist information office** in Ribnitz-Damgarten is at Am Markt 1 (☎ **03821/2201**).

From Ribnitz, continue driving east along E22/ Route 105 until you reach Stralsund.

4 Stralsund

72km (45 miles) NE of Rostock

Stralsund has one of the best natural harbors in the Baltic. The town is separated from the island of Rügen by a narrow sea channel, the Strait of Bodden, and makes its living mainly from shipyards, fishing fleets, and, to an increasing degree, tourism. Stralsund boasts a picturesque network of canals, coves, and lakes, as well as more half-timbered 19th-century houses and a more intact sense of history than many other cities on Germany's Baltic coast.

During the 1200s, it was rivaled in the Hanseatic League only by Lübeck, and enjoyed a rich trade with many of the other cities around the Baltic basin. Perhaps because of its success, the town has been invaded repeatedly throughout its long history, by armies from Denmark, Sweden, Holland, Napoleonic France, Prussia, and, in May 1945, the Soviet Union. By the mid-1960s, much of the inner core of Stralsund had been faithfully rebuilt by the Communist local government, though some historic structures remain.

Many visitors use Stralsund as the takeoff point for the flat and sandy Baltic island of Rügen (see below), which is joined to Stralsund by a 2km (1¼-mile) bridge.

SEEING THE SIGHTS

Buildings of historic interest include a series of medieval defenses whose ramparts are best viewed on the town's western edge. Also important is the 13th-century **Rathaus,** Alter Markt (☎ 03831/25-20), one of the most imposing examples of the North German secular brick Gothic architecture.

Stralsund's other attractions are mostly ecclesiastical buildings. **St. Nikolaikirche,** Alter Markt (☎ 03831/29-71-99), with an entrance on Badenstrasse, whose design was based on models in Lübeck, has a very high nave built in the 13th and 14th centuries in the Hallenkirche style. It's open May to October, Tuesday to Saturday 10am to 5pm and Sunday noon to 5pm; November to April, Tuesday to Friday 10am to noon. Entrance is free. Also of interest is the **Marienkirche,** Neuer Markt (☎ 03831/29-35-29), with an entrance on Bleistrasse. It was begun in the late 1200s, and had a soaring tower added to it in the mid-1400s. Open Monday to Saturday 10am to 4pm and Sunday 11:30am to 4pm. If you don't mind climbing 349 steps, you'll be rewarded with a view of the old town, the coastline, and Rügen Island. It costs 2DM ($1) to climb the tower. Another church, the **Jacobikirche** on Böttchrstrasse, was transformed into a three-nave basilica in the 14th century. It has a high altar with baroque mountings and paintings by J. H. Tischbein, one of the foremost ecclesiastical artists of his day. The **Heiligengeistkirche (Church of the Holy Ghost),** on Wasserstrasse (☎ 03831/29-04-46), is noteworthy for its inner courtyard ringed with wooden galleries and is open July and August, Monday to Saturday 10am to noon and 3 to 6pm. Admission is free.

Stralsund's cultural museum, **Kulturhistorisches Museum,** Mönchstrasse 25–27 (☎ 03831/29-21-80), contains medieval sacred art and Stralsund-related historical exhibits. It's open Tuesday to Sunday 10am to 5pm. Admission is 6DM ($3). There's also the **Deutsches Museum für Meereskunde und Fischerei (Oceanographic Museum and Aquarium),** Mönchstrasse 25 (☎ 03831/26500), in a complex of buildings originally part of a 15th-century abbey, the Katharinenkloster. The museum features exhibitions pertaining to the sea life of the Baltic and the distillation of its seawater into salt during the Middle Ages. A very large 42,000l (11,000 gal.) aquarium, containing exhibitions of tropical fish, is housed in the cloister's medieval crypt. The complex is open November to April, Tuesday to Sunday 10am to 5pm; May, June, September, and October, daily 10am to 5pm; and July and August, Monday to Thursday 9am to 6pm and Friday to Sunday 10am to 5pm. Admission is 7DM ($3.50) for adults and 3.50DM ($1.75) for students.

For more information, contact the **tourist office,** Ossenrexerstrasse 1–3 (☎ 03831/ 2-46-90). It's open Monday to Friday 10am to 5pm and Saturday 10am to noon.

WHERE TO STAY

Hotel an den Bleichen Garni. An den Bleichen 45, 18435 Stralsund (a 10-min. walk west of the historic center). ☎ 03831/39-06-75. Fax 03831/39-21-53. 23 units. TV TEL. 125DM–145DM ($62.50–$72.50) double. Rates include buffet breakfast. AE, MC, V.

This 1993 hotel is a three-story, family-run establishment similar to many that have blossomed across Germany's eastern region since reunification. Rooms and baths are rather small but still quite comfortable; everything is neatly maintained by the hardworking on-site owners. No meals are served other than breakfast, but many restaurants are within a short walk, and there's a bar on the premises.

Norddeutscher Hof. Neuer Markt 22, 18439 Stralsund. ☎ 03831/29-31-61. Fax 03831/ 28-79-39. 13 units. TV TEL. 160DM ($80) double. Rates include buffet breakfast. AE, MC, V. Bus: 3.

This small and charming inn, built around 1900, is set in the heart of Stralsund's old town. On its street level, it contains a simple restaurant that's popular with local residents. Full meals are served every day at both lunch and dinner; the chef special-izes in Baltic cuisine. The small rooms are outfitted with old-fashioned furniture whose slightly battered look adds to the establishment's time-tested charm.

WHERE TO DINE

Wulflamstuben. Alter Markt 5 (within the Wulflamhaus). ☎ **03831/29-15-33.** Reserva-tions recommended. Main courses 15DM–24DM ($7.50–$12). AE, DC, MC, V. Daily 11am–11pm. Bus: 3. NORTH GERMAN.

This restaurant was established in 1991 within the historic walls of a town monument (the Wulflamhaus), originally built in 1370. It's set on the ground floor and features a carefully preserved decor of ornate carvings and old-fashioned engravings of local folklore and architecture. In many ways this place is a civic showcase of the town's culinary bounty. The focus is almost exclusively on the food of Mecklenburg and Lower Pomerania. Menu items include *Stralsunder Aal Suppe* (eel soup in the style of Stralsund), *Eisbein* (veal shank in the style of Berlin), stuffed goose in the style of Mecklenburg, and roast duckling stuffed with apples, black bread, and plums. There's also a choice of fish from local waters.

5 Rügen

4km (2¹/₂ miles) NE of Stralsund

Rügen is the largest island in Germany, but in many ways it's more Scandinavian than German in its climate, flavor, and feel. Riddled with saltwater lagoons and radically indented coves and harbors, it lies just off the northwestern coast of what used to be Pomeranian Prussia, joined to the town of Straslund by bridge. From north to south, it stretches 51km (32 miles), covering a landmass of 927km^2 (358 square miles)—mostly scrubland, windswept forests, and dunes.

Don't come here for monuments or museums; nature is the main attraction, as well as seaside bathing (often nude) in summer. Highlights include geological features such as the chalk cliffs of Stubbenkammer and the Königstuhl Rock on the island's north-eastern tip. Kap (Cape) Arkona, a Baltic Gibraltar, is the most northerly point of what used to be East Germany.

EXPLORING THE ISLAND

Of architectural interest is **Schloss Spyker (Spycher Castle),** Schlossallee, 18551 Spyker (☎ **038302/5-33-83;** fax 038302/53-386), a baronial building now func-tioning (somewhat erratically) as a restaurant and hotel. The island's most unusual building is Jagdschloss Granitz (Rügen)the **Jagdschloss Granitz (Granitz Hunting Lodge),** in the village of Binz (☎ **038393/22-63**), an ornate neofeudal castle built in 1836 by Prince Wilhelm Malte I of Putbus. One of its most unusual features is a corkscrew-inspired stone staircase winding gracefully up 154 steps to the top of the building's massive central tower. The lodge is open October to April, Tuesday to Sunday 9am to 4pm; May to September, daily 9am to 5:30pm. Admission is 5DM ($2.85) for adults and 3DM ($1.50) for children.

Although the island's capital is Bergen, most of the population is centered around the seasonal coastal resorts of Ostseebad Göhren, Ostseebad Baabe, Ostseebad Sellin, and Ostseebad Binz, all of which lie on the island's eastern edge. Of the above-mentioned villages, Ostseebad Binz (referred to locally simply as Binz) is the most interesting and most charming. Of special interest to bird-watchers are the shores of the island's vast inland sea, beautiful **Jasmunder Bodden.**

The coast of Rügen contains some of the island's finest scenic beauty. To get to Kap (or Cape) Arkona, the Baltic Gibraltar, go northeast from Bergen on Route 96, until you come to a small secondary road signposted Kap Arkona. A lighthouse stands at the cape, next to a restored watchtower, which you can climb for a view of the Danish island of Moen. Near the lighthouse stand the ruins of the ancient fortress of Jarosmarburg, constructed by the Slavs but destroyed by invading Vikings in 1168. All around the cape, chalky cliffs rise to 170 feet above the water.

After viewing the cape, drive back to Route 96, but instead of returning immediately to Bergen, follow this route east (it's signposted) to another end of the line, the towering chalky cliffs of Stubbenkammer, which lie 10km (6 miles) north of the small port of Sassnitz. Stubbenkammer is one of the most photographed sights on the island. From here, a steep trail leads down to a Baltic Beach.

For **tourist information** on the island, go to the office at Markt 11 in Bergen (☎ **03838/25-60-95**). June to October, it's open Monday to Friday 10am to 8pm and Saturday 10am to 2pm. Off-season hours are Monday to Friday 10am to 6pm.

WHERE TO STAY & DINE

Hotel Nordperd. Nordperdstrasse 11, 18586 Göhren-Rügen. ☎ **038308/70.** Fax 038308/ 71-60. www.top-hotels.de/travelcharme. 95 units. TV TEL. 160DM–310DM ($80–$155) double. Rates include buffet breakfast. AE, DC, MC, V.

This four-story hotel is unusual for the island in that it remains open all year, even after the vacationers have gone home. It offers modern design and simple comfort. Rooms in front have coastal views; all have streamlined furniture, including firm mattresses on comfortable beds. There's a restaurant on the premises that offers well-prepared regional food even when virtually everything else on Rügen is closed. It's open for dinner only, daily 6 to 10:30pm.

Steigenberger MAXX. Neddesitz 4, 18551 Sagard-Rügen. ☎ **038302/95.** Fax 038302/ 966-20. www.ruegen.max-hotels.com. 145 units. A/C MINIBAR TV TEL. 152DM–247DM ($76–$123.50) double; 399DM ($199.50) suite. AE, DC, MC, V.

One of the grander choices on island is this member of a first-class and deluxe chain hotel. The resort stands on its own 35ha (85-acre) site adjacent to Jasmund National Park, renowned for its chalk cliffs. It offers more facilities, including a full spa, than anything else on island. Rooms are attractively furnished, with good-sized baths spotlessly maintained.

Dining/Diversions: The hotel offers four excellent restaurants and two cozy bars. International food is featured in all of them, but your best bet is the regional cuisine of the Baltic, especially fresh fish.

Amenities: Indoor pool, outdoor pool, steambath, massage, fitness center, babysitting, kindergarten, laundry, dry cleaning, room service.

Vier Jahreszeiten. Zeppelinstrasse 8, 18609 Binz-Rügen. ☎ **038393/500.** Fax 038393/ 504-30. www.hotel-vier-jahreszeiten.de. E-mail: hotel-vier-jahreszeiten@binz.de. 77 units. TV TEL. 160DM–270DM ($80–$135) double; 220DM–350DM ($110–$175) suite. AE, V.

An elegant, stately, and white-painted villa, this landmark hotel enjoys a tranquil location at the beach along Lake Schmacht and is set against the backdrop of the Granitz Woods. Rooms are brightly furnished and generally spacious, each with good beds and windows opening onto views. On site is a good restaurant and wine bar, along with a fitness center, pool, sauna, and solarium, plus tennis. The hotel restaurant is elegantly appointed and serves some of the best food on island. Consider dining here even if you're not a guest of the hotel. Sample the Rugener fish soup and typical food of the Baltic. Lunch menus cost from 22DM to 28DM ($11 to $14), with fixed-price dinners ranging from 35DM to 110DM ($17.50 to $55).

Appendix A:
Germany In Depth

This appendix will introduce you to Germany's history, artistic and cultural traditions, and cuisine. We'll also recommend some books to help you get even better acquainted with this fascinating country.

1 History 101

EARLY DAYS

"A large build, very strong in the attack, but not suitable to the same extent for heavy work" was how Tacitus, the Roman historian, described the Teutons in A.D. 60. The Romans had been trying to push the borders of their empire up to the Rhineland, with mixed success, since 9 B.C., but the Teutonic tribes fought back ferociously. The first recognized German national hero was Arminius, who led his tribe (the Cherusci) in defeating three Roman legions near modern-day Bielefeld in A.D. 9.

After the deterioration of the Roman Empire, the Franks ruled much of what we now know as Germany. In 800, a Frankish king, Charlemagne, extended the Carolingian empire from the Pyrenees to Saxony and Bavaria. His rule marks the high point of cultural and political development of that period. He divided the empire into counties, each with an administrator directly responsible to him, and promoted education, scholarship, and the revival of Greek and Roman culture.

THE HOLY ROMAN EMPIRE

After Charlemagne's death, the Carolingian empire fell apart. In 843, the Treaty of Verdun granted the empire's eastern territory to Louis the German, marking the beginning of German history.

In 962, the pope officially recognized Otto I as Emperor of what was later called the Holy Roman Empire. This new political entity was formed both to impose unity on the European political world and to create a bulwark against the invasion of non-Christian tribes. It claimed direct links both to the grandeur of ancient Rome and to the more contemporary might of the Church.

Unity, however, did not prevail. The empire splintered into a bickering alliance of dukedoms, bishoprics, and principalities. The emperor's authority was often dependent on German nobles and the pope. A capital city that could have served as a center of power was never established—the monarch would simply move from one city to another, mustering an army and collecting revenue wherever he could—so the possibilities for dynastic intrigues were endless. In subsequent jockeying, the church itself was a voracious competitor for power. This power struggle broke out into open conflict in 1076, when Pope Gregory VII excommunicated the emperor Henry IV, who was forced to stand humiliatingly barefoot in the snow outside Canossa, awaiting a repeal.

To strengthen their position as the Holy Roman Empire declined, the emperors turned to alliances with the wealthy, independent trading ports to the north and east, under the federation of the Hanseatic League. Such German cities as Hamburg, Lübeck, and Bremen grew in both economic and political power. Eventually the league controlled trade as far as Novgorod in Russia.

THE REFORMATION & THE RELIGIOUS WARS

When an Augustinian monk, Martin Luther, nailed his theological and political complaints to a church door in Wittenberg in 1517, he set off a political and religious wildfire that spread across the landscape of Europe. He was not the first religious reformer; in the early 15th century, John Wyclif had translated the Bible into English, and Jan Hus of Prague had become a martyr to his beliefs at the Council of Constance. However, the fragmented political situation in Germany played into Luther's hands: For every prince who condemned him, he could find one to protect him. Luther's Reformation fanned the flames around Germany's political factions. The new conflict between Catholics and Protestants set the stage for the devastation of the Thirty Years' War (1618–48), which only entrenched the divided sensibilities of the splintered German nation.

The only powerful German state to emerge from these conflicts was the little kingdom of Prussia, in the northeast on the Baltic Sea. The rise of Prussian power continued throughout the 18th century until, led by that talented soldier and patron of the Enlightenment, Frederick the Great, Prussia became a major kingdom, with Berlin as its capital.

NAPOLÉON ARRIVES

After the French Revolution, Napoléon and his new political ideas swept across Europe. The

Dateline

- **9 B.C.–A.D. 9** Romans attempt to conquer Teutonic tribes.
- **486** Clovis founds Frankish kingdom, ruling from Paris.
- **496** Franks are converted to Christianity.
- **800** Pope crowns Charlemagne in Rome.
- **962** Pope crowns Otto I as Holy Roman Emperor.
- **1152–90** Frederick Barbarossa's reign leads to a greater centralization of power, but his invasion of Italy is beaten back by the Lombard League.
- **1158** Munich founded by Henry the Lion, duke of Saxony.
- **1241** Hanseatic League founded to protect the trade of such cities as Bremen, Hamburg, and Lübeck.
- **1432** Maximilian I, "last of the German knights," becomes Holy Roman Emperor, marking the beginning of the hegemony of the Hapsburgs.
- **1456** Johannes Guttenberg prints the first book in Europe using movable type.
- **1517** Martin Luther nails his "Ninety-Five Theses" to a church door in Wittenberg, beginning the Protestant Reformation in Germany.
- **1618–48** Thirty Years' War devastates Germany, as Protestant forces defeat Catholic Hapsburgs.
- **1740–86** Prussian might grows under Frederick the Great in the Age of Enlightenment.
- **1806** Armies of Napoléon invade Prussia, which is incorporated briefly into the French Empire.
- **1813** Prussians defeat Napoléon at Leipzig.

continues

- **1815** At the Congress of Vienna, the German Confederation of 39 independent states is created.
- **1862** Otto von Bismarck (1815–98) becomes prime minister of Prussia.
- **1870–71** Germany invades and defeats France in the Franco-Prussian War.
- **1871** Wilhelm I is crowned emperor of the newly created German Empire; Bismarck becomes chancellor.
- **1890** Bismarck is dismissed by Kaiser Wilhelm II, who launches an aggressive foreign policy.
- **1907** Russia, Great Britain, and France form the Triple Entente, against the Triple Alliance of Germany, Austria-Hungary, and Italy.
- **1914** Assassination of Archduke Franz Ferdinand launches World War I.
- **1918** Germany is forced to sign the Treaty of Versailles, accepting responsibility for starting World War I.
- **1923** Hitler's "Beer Hall Putsch," a rightist revolt, fails in Munich.
- **1925** Hitler publishes *Mein Kampf.*
- **1926** Germany is admitted to the League of Nations, in the heyday of the Weimar Republic.
- **1933** Hitler becomes chancellor.
- **1934** President von Hindenburg dies and Hitler declares himself *Führer* (leader) of the Third Reich.
- **1935** Nuremberg Laws deprive Jews of citizenship and forbid marriage between Jews and non-Jewish Germans.
- **1936** Summer Olympic Games held in Berlin; Winter Games held at Garmisch-Partenkirchen; Germany militarizes the Rhineland in violation of the Treaty of

continues

left bank of the Rhine came under French control. Under these pressures, the Holy Roman Empire officially came to an end in 1806. Around the same time, Napoléon's armies invaded Prussia, making it, for a brief time, a part of the French empire. But Napoléon was defeated at Leipzig in 1813, and two years later Britain and Prussia crushed him forever at the Battle of Waterloo.

BISMARCK & PRUSSIA

The Congress of Vienna (1814–15) redrew the map of Germany after Napoléon's defeat, giving more territory to Prussia, but making Austria the leader in a German Confederation. During this time, there was a rising spirit of nationalism, exploited to good effect by Prince Otto von Bismarck when he became Prussia's prime minister in 1862. Prussia triumphed in the Austro-Prussian War of 1866, and after the subsequent Franco-Prussian War (1870–71), when Prussia laid siege to Paris, Bismarck succeeded in his goal of unification. Wilhelm I was made emperor of all Germany in 1871, and a strong, unified Germany at last took shape. Under Bismarck's leadership, Germany adopted an advanced social welfare system and brought its military and industrial production, as well as technical and scientific achievements, to new heights.

WORLD WAR I

By 1907, Europe was divided into two armed camps: the Triple Alliance (Germany, Austria-Hungary, and Italy) and the Triple Entente (France, Great Britain, and Russia). The match that ignited the powder keg was struck at Sarajevo in 1914, with the assassination of Archduke Franz Ferdinand, heir to the throne of the Austro-Hungarian Empire. The subsequent German invasion of France launched the bloodiest war the world had ever seen. A new and particularly demoralizing form of battle known as "trench warfare" produced staggering casualties. On August 8, 1918, the Allies, now joined by the United States, penetrated German lines, and the German high command realized that the situation was hopeless.

In an attempt to get more favorable treatment from the Allies, the Germans voluntarily declared a parliamentary democracy, ending the reign of the kaiser. Despite that concession, in

1918 Germany was forced to sign the humiliating Treaty of Versailles, which demanded the surrender of strategic territories including Alsace-Lorraine, just west of the Rhine. The Allies—especially the French—also demanded huge monetary reparations.

WEIMAR REPUBLIC

In 1919, the National Assembly met in Weimar to draw up a new constitution, which at the time was hailed as the most progressive in the world. But in the defeated and humiliated postwar Germany, extremists from both the left and the right launched savage attacks against the inexperienced and idealistic government. The enormous payments demanded by the Allies crippled the German economy. When reparations from Germany couldn't be made, France retaliated by occupying the Ruhr, one of Germany's most valuable industrial resources. Inflation—perhaps the worst in history—destroyed what was left of the German economy.

THE RISE OF NAZISM

This was just the right climate for the rise of Adolf Hitler and the Nazi Party. The Nazis believed in the superiority of the Aryan race and blamed non-Aryan elements, particularly Jews, for Germany's woes. At first Hitler's anti-Semitic, nationalist ideas failed to gain popular support, even with right-wingers. Nazi membership in the *Reichstag* (parliament) dropped from 25 in 1925 to only a dozen following the elections of 1928.

In 1932, Hitler lost the electoral race for president against the compromise candidate of the democratic parties, war hero Paul von Hindenburg. Nevertheless, Hitler's power increased, and on January 30, 1933, Hindenburg submitted to right-wing pressure and appointed him chancellor. Upon Hindenburg's death in 1934, Hitler declared himself *Führer* (leader) of a new German empire he called the "Third Reich." Protected by hastily drafted laws and regulations, he made his power absolute.

The horrors of unchecked Nazi rule lasted until 1945. The Gestapo, or secret police, launched one of the most notorious reigns of terror in history. Anyone whom the Nazis considered enemies, or simply undesirables—which included Communists, Social Democrats, homosexuals, political dissidents, Gypsies, and many others—were persecuted. Jews were disenfranchised, terrorized,

Versailles; and Hitler signs agreements with Italy and Japan to form the Axis.
- **1938** Germany occupies Austria and the Sudetenland in Czechoslovakia.
- **1939** Hitler signs a non-aggression pact with the Soviet Union in August and invades Poland on September 1, launching World War II.
- **1940–45** After early successes, German armies are forced back by the Soviet Union in the east and Allied troops in the west; Germany is in ruins by 1945.
- **1945** The Yalta Conference divides Germany into zones of occupation.
- **1948–49** The Soviet Union attempts to exclude the Allies from Berlin by blockade; the city is saved by a massive airlift.
- **1949** Soviets establish the German Democratic Republic (East Germany); Konrad Adenauer becomes chancellor of newly established Federal Republic of Germany (West Germany).
- **1950** West Germany's "economic miracle" begins to take hold.
- **1958** West Germany becomes a founding member of the European Economic Community (now European Union).
- **1961** The Berlin Wall divides the city.
- **1985** West Germany joins the Group of Seven (G7) organization of the world's greatest industrial powers.
- **1989** Refugees from East Germany flood into West Germany; Communist power collapses in the east, and the Berlin Wall comes down.
- **1990** East Germany and West Germany unite.
- **1991** Berlin is chosen as the capital of the united Germany.

continues

- **1992** Unemployment and disillusionment sweep across the former East Germany as unification costs mount.
- **1995** Bundestag approves German participation in NATO Bosnia mission.
- **1997** German government and private companies tally up the cost of rebuilding eastern Germany: $1 trillion U.S. dollars to date.
- **1998** Chancellor Kohl is defeated in election, bowing to Gerhard Schröder.
- **1999** The German seat of government is returned to Berlin.
- **2000** Christian Democrats shaken by political scandals; Germany pledges $5.2 billion to aid Nazi victims.

deprived of property, and forced into ghettos and concentration camps.

On June 30, 1934, Hitler disposed of any opposing elements in his own party in the "Night of Long Knives," when hundreds were massacred, including Ernst Röhm, chief of his notorious Brownshirts. Heinrich Himmler's black-shirted *Schutzstaffel* (SS) became a powerful political force. Surrounded by adoring fans (or, at best, passive witnesses), Hitler now viewed his empire as a worthy successor to those of Charlemagne and Bismarck.

In 1936, Hitler remilitarized the Rhineland and signed agreements with Japan and fascist Italy, forming the Axis alliance. In 1938, he enforced the *Anschluss* (annexation) of Austria and marched triumphantly into the country of his birth. That same year, he occupied the German-speaking Sudetenland in Czechoslovakia, an act the other Western powers could not summon the will to oppose.

WORLD WAR II

In late August 1939, Hitler signed a non-aggression pact with the Soviet Union that gave him free reign to launch an invasion of Poland, which he did on September 1. France and Britain, honoring their agreements with Poland, declared war on Germany. Germany scored early victories, and in one of the most stunning campaigns of the 20th century, invaded and occupied France in June 1940. In 1941, Hitler turned on the Soviet Union. Meeting at the Berlin suburb of Wannsee in 1942, the Nazi leadership formulated the implementation of the "final solution" to the "Jewish Question," the systematic extermination of millions of Jews. The mass murders of homosexuals, Gypsies, Communists, Slavs, and other undesirables were less systematic but also numbered in the millions.

Following Japan's attack on Pearl Harbor, Germany declared war on the United States on December 11, 1942. But after defeats in North Africa in 1942 and at Stalingrad in 1943, the recurrent theme became one of Nazi retreat. The D-Day landings along the coast of Normandy on June 6, 1944, began the steady advance of the Allied armies from the west, while Soviet armies relentlessly marched toward Berlin from the east. Hitler committed suicide in Berlin in April 1945. His country, along with much of Europe, lay in ruins.

DIVISION OF GERMANY

At war's end, Germany and its capital city were divided. The nation shrank in size, losing long-held territories (among them East Prussia and Upper Silesia). The United States, Great Britain, France, and Soviet Union divided the country into four zones of occupation. Berlin, in the heart of the Soviet district, was also divided among the four powers. In the late 1940s, the Soviet Union tried to cut off all Allied access to Berlin, but a massive U.S.-sponsored airlift into the beleaguered city thwarted the attempt. In 1949, the Soviets established the German Democratic Republic (DDR) in their zone. In response, the Federal Republic of Germany was established in the American, British, and French zones. In 1961, the DDR sealed off its borders and erected the Berlin Wall, a stark symbol of the Cold War itself.

FALL OF THE WALL & UNIFICATION

1989 was a year of change and turmoil. In the wake of the collapse of Communist power across eastern Europe, the Berlin Wall also fell. The following year was perhaps the most significant in postwar German history. The two German nations announced economic unification in July, followed by total unification—with its thousands of inherent problems and headaches—on October 3, 1990. In 1991, Parliament voted to quit Bonn, seat of the West German government, and reestablish the once-mighty capital of Berlin.

After the first heady period of reunification, disillusionment set in, especially in eastern Germany, which was riddled with unemployment and unrealized expectations. Resentment against immigrant workers led in some instances to violent neo-Nazi marches, bombings, and physical assaults. However, most Germans rose up in revulsion to condemn the ultrarightists and the sporadic violence.

Psychic and emotional differences between the two zones were almost overwhelming, as were the vast disparities in industrial development. As the influential newspaper *Frankfurter Rundschau* editorialized, "The terms of east and west are not so much geographical expressions as they are descriptions of states of mind."

GERMANY TODAY

Political scandal and memories of the war dominated headlines in Germany in 2000. In the waning weeks of 1999, Germany sealed a historic agreement that resolved one of the gravest injustices left over from World War II, formally pledging to pay $5.2 billion in belated compensation to hundreds of thousands of Nazi-era slave workers and other victims of the Third Reich.

As the 21st century begins, Germany, despite the enormous costs of reunification, is an economic powerhouse in the center of Europe. As a member of the European Union, NATO, and the G7 group of the world's industrial powers, Germany's influence extends throughout Europe and across the globe.

2 In Pursuit of Artistic Excellence

ARCHITECTURE

ROMANESQUE German architecture first flowered in the 10th and early 11th centuries—an era called the Ottonian period, in honor of Emperor Otto I. German architects, virtually all anonymous, built churches on principles adapted from the basilicas developed centuries earlier by the ancient Romans. Noteworthy features included barrel vaults, rounded arches, very thick walls, and (usually) symmetrical, rather squat towers. Today, the few Romanesque buildings that remain intact are among the most cherished in Germany. Cologne contains many important examples (see chapter 13).

GOTHIC New developments in the Middle Ages such as "broken" (pointed) arches and flying buttresses permitted a world of new structural possibilities. Architects could now build bigger and more impressive buildings, higher and thinner walls, taller belfries, and spacious windows. This Gothic architectural style flowered in Europe, especially in northern France, between the 13th and 16th centuries.

The Romanesque influence remained pervasive, however, and Gothic design never established as strong a foothold in Germany as it did in France and England. Most representative of the German Gothic style is the hall-type church (*Hallenkirche*), which originated in Westphalia. It was characterized by aisles constructed at the same height as the nave, separated from the nave by tall columns. A good example is **St. Georgskirche (Church of St. George)** in **Nördlingen,** on the Romantic Road (see chapter 6).

Cologne Cathedral, the greatest of the German Gothic churches, was begun in 1284 but not completed until 1880 (see chapter 13). The High Gothic style is best represented by the cathedral at **Freiburg im Breisgau** (see chapter 10), famous for its pierced octagonal belfry crowned by a delicate openwork spire.

RENAISSANCE   In southern Germany, Italian-inspired Renaissance motifs were installed in **Augsburg** in the **funerary chapel** of **Fugger the Rich** (see chapter 6) and in **Munich** in **St. Michael's Church** (see chapter 7). Overall, however, the emerging Protestant principalities of northern Germany tended to reject Italian influences as being too closely tied to the Catholic sensibility. In the north, motifs from Flanders and Holland were much more popular. The finest German Renaissance towns are **Rothenburg** (see chapter 6) and **Celle** (see chapter 15). As the prosperity of the rich trading centers of the Hanseatic League grew, they adopted a distinctive design, the so-called "Weser Renaissance," almost never seen in the south

FROM BAROQUE TO NEOCLASSICISM   The Baroque style, an Italian import whose influence in Germany began around 1660 and continued into the 18th century, brought a different kind of renaissance to southern Germany, especially Bavaria. Architectural forms no longer followed regular patterns, as individual artists and craftsmen were granted increased freedom and more variety in design. **Würzburg** is one of Germany's most beautiful baroque cities (see chapter 6). The baroque movement eventually led to the greater freedom and gaiety of the rococo. Outstanding examples are **Kloster Ettal,** near **Oberammergau** (see chapter 8), and the **Cuvilliés Theater** and **Asamkirche** in **Munich** (see chapter 7).

By the 19th century, many members of the rising and prosperous middle class in Germany favored the **Biedermeier style** of furniture and decoration, with its lighter designs and carefully balanced symmetry. **Neoclassicism,** with its references to the grandeur of ancient Greece and imperial Rome, gained favor as well. Once again, the south of Germany brought a lighter touch to this style than did the north. Ludwig I of Bavaria built the **Alte Pinakothek** and the **Glyptothek** in **Munich** (see chapter 7), in an effort to make the city into a "new Athens."

ROMANTICISM   The romantic movement was full of implications for Germany's sense of national identity. For inspiration in this neo-Gothic era, architects looked back to a rose-colored image of Germany's medieval history, myth, and folklore. There was an almost obsessive rebirth of interest in Teutonic lore, as rediscovered by the Brothers Grimm and reinterpreted by Richard Wagner. The imitation Florentine loggia in **Munich,** the **Feldherrnhalle,** unites all these ideas.

The German architectural style of the late 1800s is often labeled **Historicism.** No one represented this flamboyant and eclectic movement better than Ludwig II of Bavaria. His unfinished **Neues Schloss** at **Herrenchiemsee** (see chapter 8), is an elaborate and romanticized interpretation of Versailles. But his completed palace, **Neuschwanstein** (see chapter 6), best represents the movement. Outrageously ornate, with all the fairy-tale ornamentation of a Teutonic version of Disneyland, it's one of the major tourist attractions of modern Germany.

FROM JUGENDSTIL TO MODERNISM By the end of the 19th century, the art nouveau movement—called Jugendstil in German, after the magazine *Jugend* (*Youth*)—was sweeping the country. Jugendstil, which was characterized by mass production and solid construction, marked the beginning of contemporary architecture. Its practitioners used such materials as glass, steel, and concrete, often shaping them into curved lines inspired by the sinuous forms of nature.

In the aftermath of World War I, Walter Gropius (1883–1969) gained prominence as leader of the **Bauhaus movement.** The primary aim of this movement was to unify arts and crafts within the context of architecture. Its appeal derived from the changing sensibilities of the Industrial Age, as well as from the need for inexpensive construction techniques in an era of rising costs and exploding demand for housing. Founded at Weimar and directed there by Gropius from 1919, the Bauhaus moved to Dessau in 1925. (Gropius eventually settled in the United States.) For a variety of personal and political reasons, the movement was formally dissolved in 1933, but not before its influence had been felt around Europe.

By 1935, the so-called National Socialist, or "Third Reich," style of architecture was virtually the law of the land. Under Hitler and such designers as Albert Speer, architecture became a propaganda tool. It was pompous, monumental, innately frightening, and devoid of any real humanity. After the war, cities scrambled to hide the origins of some of these buildings. A good example is **Munich's Haus der Kunst** (see chapter 7), which houses the State Gallery of Modern Art. Its angular fascist architecture seems curiously appropriate for the starkly modern painting it showcases today—ironically, everything now in it would have been anathema to Hitler.

DESTRUCTION & RENEWAL One of the legacies of World War II was the leveling of many of Germany's greatest architectural treasures by Allied bombing raids. Notable among these was the destruction of **Dresden,** until 1945 one of the most beautiful cities in Europe. More than 50 years after its firebombing by British and American planes, its loss is felt more poignantly than that of any other city, though some of its buildings have been restored.

In the years after the war, both Germanys, East and West, set for themselves the formidable task of rebuilding. In some cases, the architectural rubble of the past was swept away, never to be restored. However, many cathedrals, churches, town halls, and other buildings were laboriously (and expensively) reconstructed in the original style, notably **the Zwinger** in **Dresden** (see chapter 4). Other careful and tasteful city restorations were those of **Cologne** (see chapter 13) and of **Munich** (see chapter 7). Some cities, like **Düsseldorf,** opted to become strikingly modern (see chapter 13).

Berlin, once reduced to rubble, is today undergoing a massive rebuilding project. A previous restoration effort was made in 1957, when architects from 22 nations were invited to design homes, schools, and apartment buildings in Berlin's **Hansaviertel,** or Hansa Quarter (see chapter 3). The resulting works, by Gropius, Niemeyer, Duttman, and many others, created an exciting diversity.

MUSIC

Music is an important and pervasive facet of German life. German disunity over the centuries actually helped foster German music. The many small principalities and bishoprics that split up the German-speaking world meant that there were many courts to offer opportunities to musicians, both composers and instrumentalists. As a result, the German-speaking nations produced more composers of indisputable greatness than any other.

Today, the musical scene in Germany is as vibrant as ever. Every major city has an opera house and an orchestra, many of them world renowned. New composers are encouraged, and productions are often at the cutting edge.

MUSIC FESTIVALS   Major music festivals take place in the summer, but music lovers can pretty well take their pick all year of what they want to hear. The most famous festival, of course, is the **Bayreuth Festival,** instituted by Richard Wagner, which made the town of Bayreuth a musical landmark (unfortunately, tickets are very hard to come by). But all major cities, including Munich and Berlin, have music festivals throughout the year. Contact German tourist offices, within the country and abroad, for the latest information and dates.

Since reunification, **Dresden** has emerged as a major center for music. The Dresden Music Festivals, held each year at the end of May and the beginning of June, bring together not only local ensembles but prominent German and international artists. The Dresden Festival of Contemporary Music is presented in October. And a Dixieland Festival, a tradition since 1971, transforms Dresden into a city of jazz in May.

Other world-class festivals include the **Mozart Festival** at **Würzburg** in June, the **Berliner Festwochen** in September, and the **Jazz-Fest Berlin** in November.

MUSICAL MUSEUMS   The true devotee of German music may want to visit cities and towns where the masters lived and wrote their music. Some of the homes of former composers have been turned into museums, such as the home of **Franz Liszt** in **Weimar** and of **Richard Wagner** in **Bayreuth.** To see where the great **Beethoven** lived, head for **Bonn.** Considering how many famous musicians lived and composed in Germany, however, the country has surprisingly few museums devoted to these great artists. Blame it on wartime devastation.

A HISTORY OF GERMAN MUSIC

BAROQUE MUSIC   The greatest composer of the baroque era was **Johann Sebastian Bach** (1685–1750), who was a supreme master of all musical forms of his time. Bach produced many church cantatas, especially for St. Thomas's Lutheran Church in Leipzig (see chapter 4), where he served as cantor. His compositions were technically outstanding, vigorous, and profound. Little of his music was published during his lifetime, but after his death, his influence steadily grew, especially that of his organ works. The musical tradition in his large family was maintained by two of his talented sons, Carl Philipp Emanuel Bach (1714–88) and Johann Christian Bach (1735–82). The Brandenburg Concertos are highly recommended.

Bach's contemporary **George Frideric Handel** (1685–1759) was another great composer. He first rose to prominence as musician of the court of Hannover, a post that he left to become composer at the court of St. James of England. He was a leading composer of operas and instrumental music for the court. Listen to his oratorio: *Messiah.*

THE CLASSICAL PERIOD   **Wolfgang Amadeus Mozart** (1756–91), although an Austrian, cannot be omitted from any discussion of German music. His operas, with their contemporary themes and lively musical characterizations, paved the way for later composers. **Franz Joseph Haydn** (1732–1809), another Austrian, also exerted great influence on German music, especially instrumental music. Listen to: Mozart's *The Marriage of Figaro* and *Don Giovanni,* Haydn's "Drum Roll" Symphony no. 103.

THE 19TH CENTURY & ROMANTICISM   The 19th century was rich in musical genius. **Ludwig van Beethoven** (1770–1827) ushered in romanticism. His works included symphonies, piano concertos, piano sonatas, quartets, and many others. He greatly expanded and developed the orchestra. Tragically, he completely lost his hearing in 1819. However, the chamber music he wrote after this event shows an even greater depth and complexity than his previous compositions. Listen to: Symphony no. 5 and no. 9.

Other great composers of the era include **Franz Schubert** (1797–1828), **Felix Mendelssohn** (1809–47), **Robert Schumann** (1810–56), and **Johannes Brahms** (1833–97). Listen to: Schubert's *Lieder,* Mendelssohn's "Overture to 'A Midsummer Night's Dream,'" Schumann's "Scenes from Childhood," and Brahms's *German Requiem.*

The giant of the 19th-century opera world was **Richard Wagner** (1813–83). His theories of music drama exerted a tremendous influence on everyone who followed him, even his detractors. His influence can best be heard in the music of the later romantic composer **Richard Strauss** (1864–1949). Strauss's operas carry Wagner's ideas of character development to greater psychological depth. Listen to: Wagner's *The Ring of the Nibelungs,* Strauss's *Salome* and *Elektra.*

THE 20TH CENTURY   Musical experimentation flourished in early 20th-century Germany. Austrian-born **Arnold Schoenberg** (1874–1951) developed the 12-tone system of musical structure. **Kurt Weill** (1900–50) and **Paul Hindemith** (1895–1963) tried to reach a more popular audience. During the Nazi era, many composers fled Germany. Others, like **Hans Pfitzner** (1869–1949) and Richard Strauss, remained in an uneasy relationship with the Nazis. Listen to: Schoenberg's *Five Pieces for Orchestra,* Weill's *Threepenny Opera,* Hindemith's *Mathis der Maler.*

Today, at the end of the 20th century, important composers such as **Karlheinz Stockhausen** (1928–) and **Hans Werner Henze** (1926–) carry on the traditions of Germany's musical past. Listen to: Stockhausen's *Gesang der Jünglinge* (*Song of the Youths*).

3 A Taste of Germany

Traditional Germans like to eat, but don't like to count calories. Cholesterol-conscious Americans may recoil at the sight of heavy dumplings, *wurst* (sausages), and pastries. The beer that often accompanies meals is not in the "light" category, and helpings of food are not small. And even the heaviest meals do not keep many Germans from their cake and coffee break, considered a compulsory afternoon event.

However, Germans get German cooking at home, and so more and more restaurants are offering foreign foods and *neue Küche* (*cuisine moderne*). Young people are becoming increasingly health conscious and are eschewing the rich fare of their parents. Young chefs trained in Switzerland, France, or Italy are returning to Germany to open continental restaurants. Italians, many of whom originally came to Germany as "guest workers," have stayed to open up trattorias. Even health-food shops are beginning to pop up.

REGIONAL SPECIALTIES

Every region has its own specialties, ranging from *Aalsuppe* (eel soup) in Hamburg, to *Zwiebelbrot* (onion bread) in the Black Forest.

- **Bavaria & Franconia:** In southern Germany, you can feast on such hearty fare as *Leberkäs* (minced pork, beef, and liver prepared as a galantine); lots of *Knödel* (dumplings or soaked bread); gigantic *Haxen* (pork or veal trotters, most often consumed with sauerkraut); *Roastbratwürste* (small finger sausages); and *Leberknödel* (large liver dumplings in a clear broth). *Schweinwürstl mit Kraut* (pork sausages with sauerkraut) is another unforgettable local dish.

- **Lower Saxony & Schleswig-Holstein:** Here in northwest Germany, with its maritime tradition, one of the most typical local dishes is *Aalsuppe*, sweet and sour eel soup flavored with bacon, vegetables, and sometimes even pears and prunes (or perhaps other fruits). The eternal sailor's favorite is *Labskaus*, a ground-together medley of pork, salt herring, and beef, along with potatoes and beets. The traditional topping is a fried egg and a side dish of cucumbers. *Bruntes Huhn* is salt beef on a bed of diced vegetables, a robust winter favorite. *Rollmops*, pickled herring rolled in sour cream, is another local specialty, as is *Finkenwerder Scholle* (plaice) and oysters, raw or baked with cheese.

- **Berlin:** During those cold nights in old Prussia, Berliners took comfort in their soups, notably *Kohlsuppe* (cabbage soup) and *Erbensuppe* (pea soup), along with dark bread, especially Westphalia pumpernickel. *Hase im Topf* is a delicious rabbit pâté. Other favorites are *Bratwurst*, a pork sausage; and *Regensburger*, a spicy pork sausage. For dessert, Berliners like *Kugelhupf*, a marvelous coffeecake; and *Käsekuchen*, cheesecake. But probably the most ypical Berlin delicacy is *Eisbein*, pigs' knuckles.

- **Hassen & Westphalia:** Famed for its hams, this region of Germany eats food guaranteed to put hair on your chest. To go totally native, sample their *Sulperknochen*, made from the pig's trotters, ears, and tail, and served traditionally with peas pudding and pickled cabbage. Or try *Tüttchen*, a ragout of herb-flavored calf's head and calf's brains. Not into any of the above? You might settle for the local favorite *Pickert*, sweet potato cakes flavored with raisins.

- **Baden-Württemberg:** Here in southern Germany, in the region centered around Stuttgart, you can begin with such dishes as *Schneckensuppe* (snail soup), *spätzle* (egg-based pasta), or perhaps *Maultaschen* (ravioli stuffed with ground meat, spinach, and calf's brains). A main dish beloved in the area and widely consumed is *Geschnetzeltes* (slices of veal in a cream sauce). The favorite local dish in Stuttgart itself is *Gaisburger Marsch*, a beef stew. Another commonly served dish is *Roastbraten*, braised beef, invariably accompanied by *Sauerkraut*, or else *Linsen mit Saiten*, lentil stew cooked with sausages.

- **Saxony & Thuringia:** In eastern Germany, you can feast on everything from *Linsensuppe mit Thüringer Rotwurst* (lentil soup with Thuringian sausages) to *Rinderzunge in Rosinen-Sauce* (calf's tongue in grape sauce). *Kartoffelsuppe* (potato soup) remains a favorite of the district, as does a baked appetizer, *Quarkkeulchen*, made from curd, boiled potatoes, flour, sugar and raisins, topped with cinnamon, and served with applesauce. Each city in the district also has its own popular local dishes. Leipzig, for example, has its *Leipziger Allerlei*, a blend of carrots, peas, asparagus, cauliflower, mushrooms, crayfish, tails, bits of veal, and dumplings.

BEER & WINE

BEER For variety and quality, German beer is unmatched. The world's oldest brewery is in Bavaria, but other regions in Germany have proud beer-making traditions. Export beers and the rather more bitter *Pils*, the most popular type of beer, are also produced in Berlin, Hamburg, the Ruhr, Hesse,

The Best of the Wurst

The German love affair with *wurst* (sausage) dates from the dawn of history. Every region of Germany has its own specialty, but everybody's favorite seems to be bratwurst from Nürnberg, made of seasoned and spice pork. Germans often take their wurst with a bun and a dab of mustard (often smoky). White sausage, called *Weisswurst,* is a medley of veal, calves' brains, and spleen. Tradition has it that this sausage should be eaten only between midnight and noon. *Bauernwurst* (farmer's sausage) and *Knockwurst* are variations of the frankfurter, which originated (naturally) in Frankfurt. (Oddly enough, small frankfurters, which are called wieners or Vienna sausages in the United States, and *Wienerwurst* in Germany, are known simply as frankfurters in Austria.) *Leberwurst* is a specialty of Hesse. *Rinderwurst* and *Blutwurst* (beef sausage and blood sausage) are specialties of Westphalia and are often consumed with *Steinhager* (corn brandy).

and Stuttgart. *Altbier,* a very early product of the brewer's art, can be found today all over Germany. *Berliner Weisse* is made from wheat, like a Bavarian white beer, but with a dash of raspberry or woodruff syrup. Dark and sweet, malt beer contains hardly any alcohol, whereas "March beer" is also dark but considerably stronger.

In Germany, if you go into a beer hall and ask the bartender for *ein Bier,* you'll probably get the standard stock beer, *Vollbier,* which is 4% alcohol. More potent is *Export* at 5%, or *Bockbier* at 6%. *Helles Bier* is light and brewed from malt dried and baked by the local brewery, or *Brauerei.* When the malt has been darkly roasted and fermented for much longer, it becomes *dunkles Bier,* or dark beer. *Pils,* or *Pilsener,* beers are light and contain more hops. Dortmund has earned a reputation in this field.

Many inns today actually brew their own beer. In summer, Germans, particularly Bavarians, flock to beer gardens to enjoy their local brews, which are sometimes accompanied by white or red radishes and crisp pretzels.

WINE   Germany has produced delightful wines for centuries, but sometime in the 1970s German wine became the butt of jokes. The post-war German economic miracle had led to a boom in wine production. Many new vineyards sprung up suddenly, and quality was not always their first priority. Cheap, cloyingly sweet table wines flooded the market. One label in particular, Liebfraumilch, began to sully the reputation of the entire industry; the mere mention of its name to anyone in the know met with a knowing titter or contemptuous sneer. These days, however, German viticulture has been saved by smaller producers who have exploited their potential by producing excellent, unique wines.

Good German wine is renowned for its natural lightness and its delicate balance of sweetness and acidity. Most vineyards flourish on steep hillsides, protected from harsh winds by wooded neighboring hills, especially on the banks of the Rhine and the Mosel Rivers and their many tributaries. The vineyards profit from the warmth reflected off the sunlit water. The slow maturing of the grapes gives German wines their typical fresh, fruity acidity.

O' Zapfstisl ("The Barrel Is Tapped")

Much of the world seems to think that the Germans invented beer, but the drink has actually has been around for thousands of years, at least since the days of ancient Egypt and Babylon. But if the Germans didn't exactly invent beer, they certainly perfected the process of making it. Just ask them!

At Weilhenstephan, a former Benedictine monastery 30km (18 miles) northeast of Munich in Old Bavaria, stands the oldest brewery in the world. It dates from the year 1040, although there is evidence that a hop garden already existed near the grounds of the monastery in A.D. 768. The monks here brought beer to the masses in Europe. Even today, the oldest brewery within Munich itself, Augustiner, reflects brewing's monastic heritage.

Over the centuries monks brewed a strong beer for consumption during the fasting period of Lent, during which they were technically supposed to drink only water. The story goes that the pope heard about this custom and ordered that the beer be transported to Rome for him to sample. When the pope finally tasted the beer (which didn't have preservatives back then) after its long journey, he couldn't imagine why anyone would want to drink it and decreed that the beer was strong enough punishment for the Bavarian monks to drink it during Lent. Today, all Munich breweries brew this strong beer during Lent. The beer always ends with an "ator" in its name; *Salvator* and *Triumphator* are the best-known brands.

To go into a German beer hall and ask simply for a beer would brand you a beer illiterate. Connoisseurs specify the type of beer they want and

Germany does produce red wine, but as a rule it's better to stick to white or perhaps a rosé, if recommended. The words *trocken* (dry) or *halbtrocken* (semidry) are often given on the labels; look for them if you want to escape anything sweet. This avoidance, however, should not extend to the delicious dessert wines, which resemble nectar as opposed to syrup.

The overload of information on a German wine label is often puzzling to foreigners, but it's not really that hard to decipher. First of all, the grape variety should be indicated. Legally, German wines are only required to contain 85% of the declared variety. The classic is *Riesling,* which can range widely in taste from fruity to spicy. Other grapes include *Weisburgunder,* used to make dry wines, often with an aroma of melon or pear, and *Scheurebe,* which produces delicious, high-quality wine with the aroma of red currant. No grape reference on the label often means a poorly blended, inferior quality; these wines should be kept at an arm's length.

The term "vintage" refers to when the grapes were grown (not harvested). The question of origin is also something to keep an eye on. It's best if the label gives a single vineyard, but these can only be distinguished from the less specific vineyard zones if you are in the know or can consult a pocket guide, such as Johnson's.

Next, check for the level of ripeness. German law distinguishes between *tafelwein* (table wine) and *qualitatswein* (quality wine). QbA on a bottle means the wine is made from the approved grape varieties, which will give it the often the brewery. The following is a bit of beer vocabulary. *Dunkel* is a generic designation for all dark beers. *Doppelbock* is an extra dark beer with a 6% alcoholic content. *Hell*, believe it or not, is the name for light-colored beers. Many Germans, especially the citizens of Bamberg, like their beer "smoked." If that appeals to you, request *Rauchbier*. In nearby Bayreuth, Richard Wagner's old hometown, locals prefer a "steam beer" known as *Dampfbier*. The denizens of Düsseldorf and Frankfurt can often be heard requesting *Alt*, a brown, barley-malt brew. *Kolsch* is a light beer drunk mainly in Cologne in tall fluted glasses. *Hefe-Weizen* is a yeasty wheat beer consumed often with a squeeze of lemon. Finally, *Starkbierzet* is a powerful beer served when the barrels are opened after the post-Lenten celebrations in March. It has the highest alcohol content of them all.

What to consume with this brew? Germans prefer white and red radishes, chives on buttered bread, cold sausages, and, you guessed it, pretzels. What about a main course? One old Bavarian who starts drinking beer at 7 in the morning (and has ever since he was 16) says there is only one "acceptable" dish—ox from the spit with a potato and cucumber salad. Many Germans, especially Bavarians, see nothing wrong with drinking beer in the morning, often along with a hearty second breakfast of white sausage.

Although beer festivals are common around the world, none has ever equaled Munich's renowned **Oktoberfest.** This massive celebration lasts 16 days and lures some 7 million visitors yearly; some 1 1/2 million gallons of beer are consumed. Of course, if you attend the right beer party in Germany, any night can be Oktoberfest.

particular and traditional taste of its region. QmP refers to *qualitatswein mit pradikat* (wine with distinction) and carries one of six special attributes. These, in order of ascending price, are *Kabinett, Spatlese, Auslese, Berrenauslese* (BA), *Eiswein,* and the exclusive *Trockenbeerenauslese* (TBA).

As a classification, *Kabinett* was first used by Eberbach Abbey in 1712 to denote quality. This wine is especially good as an apertif with light snacks or veal. The mildly sweet and fruity *Auslese* from the Mosel-Saar-Ruwer region and the rich *Spätlese* are well suited to richer dishes such as duck, smoked fowl and oysters. Those *trocken* and *halbtrocken* Rieslings from the Rheingau and Mosel-Saar-Ruwer are perfect with pork, sausages, and sauerkraut as well as with mild cheeses. A fuller-bodied Riesling *Spätlese* and *Auslese Trocken* from Rheingau or Pfalz go excellently with wild boar and lobster. The rarest vintages, those sweet wines carrying the BA and TBA designations, are best left for anything oily or pungent in flavor, such as goose liver pâté or rich cheeses. They are also wonderful with desserts.

Many foreign visitors tour one of the wine-growing districts. Since reunification, a number of wine districts have emerged in eastern Germany; however, the traditional German wine country, stretching from the middle Rhine at Bonn down to Lake Constance on the Swiss border, is still the most charming, with its classic scenery of imposing castle ruins, elegant spas, and Brothers Grimm villages replete with spires and black-and-white gabled houses.

BIOGRAPHY

Riefenstahl, Leni. *Leni Riefenstahl: A Memoir.* St. Martin's Press, 1993. This auto-biography by the aging photographer and former film director has been both praised and condemned by critics. Known as the "Führer's moviemaker" because of her 1934 Nazi propaganda film, *The Triumph of the Will,* Riefenstahl has been the subject of lurid speculation concerning her personal and professional life. She answers her critics in this account of her life.

Taylor, A. J. P. *Bismarck: The Man and the Statesman.* Random House, 1967. This is the story of the "Iron Chancellor," who was instrumental in uni-fying the German states into the German empire.

Trevor-Roper, Hugh. *The Last Days of Hitler.* Macmillan, 1986. This is an insightful reconstruction of the twilight of the Third Reich.

FICTION

Goethe, Johann Wolfgang von. *The Sorrows of Young Werther.* Random House, 1990. This is required reading for every German schoolchild. Goethe explored the theme of suicide in this early epistolary novella.

Grass, Günter. *Dog Years* (Harcourt Brace Jovanovich, 1989), *The Tin Drum* (Random House, 1990), and *The Flounder* (Harcourt Brace Jovanovich, 1989). Grass's works deal with the German psyche coming to terms with the dreadful legacy of Nazism and World War II. His latest book, *The Call of the Toad* (Harcourt Brace Jovanovich, 1993), is a good read—part love story and part political lampoon.

Hesse, Hermann. *Narcissus and Goldmund.* Batman, 1981. This book tells the story of two monks in Germany in the Middle Ages.

Isherwood, Christopher. *The Berlin Stories.* New Directions, 1954. Isherwood lived in Berlin from 1929 to 1933. His most famous story was "Good-bye to Berlin," which became the source of the stage and film versions of *Cabaret.*

Mann, Thomas. *The Magic Mountain.* Random House, 1969. This is Mann's most celebrated masterpiece.

Nebenzal, Harold. *Café Berlin.* Avon, 1994. Nebenzal has attracted a lot of world attention with this kaleidoscopic work, his first novel. Its intrigue unfolds against the backdrop of the 1930s nightlife of Berlin.

Remarque, Erich Maria. *All Quiet on the Western Front.* Fawcett, 1987. This is a classic novel of World War I.

FOLKLORE & LEGENDS

Grimm, Jacob, and Wilhelm Grimm. *Complete Grimm Tales.* Pantheon, 1974. This is the world's most famous collection of folktales, with a cast of char-acters that includes everybody from Little Red Riding Hood to Tom Thumb.

The Nibelungenlied. Penguin, 1965. The great German epic.

HISTORY

Ash, Timothy Garton, *In Europe's Name: Germany and the Divided Continent.* Random House, 1993. This book tells a tale filled with paradoxes and ironies of how a divided Germany achieved unification. Ash, a British jour-nalist and scholar, drew part of his information from declassified files of East Germany's secret police.

Darnton, Robert. *Berlin Journal 1989–90.* W. W. Norton, 1991. This American scholar writes of the near-bloodless revolution that led to the unification of Germany.

Schneider, Peter. *The German Comedy: Scenes of Life After the Wall,* translated by Leigh Hafrey and Philip Boehm. Farrar, Straus & Giroux, 1992. Comic absurdities surrounding the collapse of the Wall fill this book, but Schneider (author of *The Wall Jumper*) also explores resurgent anti-Semitism and how Germans are coping with the flood of refugees from the east.

Shirer, William L. *The Rise and Fall of the Third Reich: A History of Nazi Germany.* Simon & Schuster, 1959–60. This story has never been told better—the complete saga of Hitler's empire from beginning to end.

West, Rebecca. *A Train of Powder.* Viking, 1955. This English novelist and historian covered the Nürnberg Trials for the *Daily Telegraph.* She provides a keen insight into the moral and legal judgments rendered there.

TRAVEL

Twain, Mark. *A Triumph Abroad.* Hippocrene Books, 1989. The American humorist's travels through Germany are humorously detailed here. Read also his comments on "The Awful German Language."

Appendix B: Useful Terms & Phrases

1 Glossary

GENERAL TERMS

Altstadt Old part of a city or town.

Anlage Park area.

Apotheke Pharmacy.

Bad Spa (also bath).

Bahn Railroad, train.

Bahnhof Railroad station.

Bergbahn Funicular (cable railway).

Hauptbahnhof Main railroad station.

Seilbahn Cable car.

Stadtbahn (S-Bahn) Commuter railroad.

Strassenbahn Streetcar, tram.

Untergrundbahn (U-Bahn) Subway, underground transportation system in a city.

Berg Mountain.

Brücke Bridge.

Brunnen Spring or well.

Burg Fortified castle.

Damm Dike, embankment.

Diet A policy meeting of church officials.

Dom Cathedral.

Domplatz Cathedral square.

Drogerie Shop selling cosmetics, sundries.

"Evergreen" Traditional alpine music.

Fleet Canal.

Gasse Lane.

Gastarbeiter Foreign worker.

Gasthof Inn.

Gemütlichkeit (adj. Gemütlich) Comfort, coziness, friendliness.

Graben Moat.

Gutbürgerliche Küche German home-cooking.

Hotelgarni Hotel that serves no meals or serves breakfast only.

Insel Island.

Jugendstil Art nouveau.

Kai Quay.

Kaufhaus Department store.

Kloster Monastery.

Kneipe Bar for drinking, may serve snacks.

Konditorei Cafe for coffee and pastries.

Kunst Art.

Marktplatz Market square.

Messegelände Exhibition center, fairgrounds.

Neue Küche Cuisine moderne.

Neustadt New part of city or town.

Oper Opera.

Platz Square.

Rathaus Town or city hall.

Altes Rathaus Old town hall.

Neues Rathaus New town hall (currently used as such).

Ratskeller Restaurant in Rathaus cellar serving traditional German food.

Reisebüro   Travel agency.
Schauspielhaus   Theater for plays.
Schloss   Palace, castle.
See   Lake *(der See)* or sea *(die See)*.
Spielbank   Casino.
Stadt   Town, city.
Steg   Footbridge.
Strasse   Street.

Tor   Gateway.
Turm   Tower.
Ufer   Shore, riverbank.
Verkehrsamt   Tourist office.
Weg   road.
Weinstube   wine bar or tavern serving meals.

ART & ARCHITECTURE TERMS

Apse   Domed or arched area at the altar end of a church.

Baroque   Ornate, decorated style of art and architecture in the 18th century; characterized by elaborate gilding and ornamentation.

Bauhaus   Style of functional design for architecture and objects, originating in the early 20th century in Germany.

Biedermeier   Solid, bourgeois style of furniture design and interior decoration in the mid-19th century.

Chancel   Part of a church that contains the altar, with seats for the clergy and choir.

Clerestory   An outside wall, rising above an adjoining roof, that contains windows.

Cloister   Covered walkway, usually enclosed by columns, around a quadrangle.

Finial   An ornament at the top of a column or some upper extremity in Gothic architecture.

Nave   The central part of a church.

Ottonian   A Romanesque style of the 10th and early 11th centuries, named for the first Holy Roman emperor, Otto I.

Reliquary   A container or shrine for sacred relics.

Retable   A raised shelf above an altar for a cross.

Rococo   A highly decorative development of baroque style.

Transept   The part of a Gothic cross-shaped church at right angles to the nave.

Vault   An arched structure of masonry forming a ceiling or roof.

Wilhelmian   Decorative style of the 18th century.

2 Menu Terms

SOUPS (SUPPEN)

Erbsensuppe   Pea soup.
Gemüsesuppe   Vegetable soup.
Kartoffelsuppe   Potato soup.

Gulaschsuppe   Goulash soup.
Linsensuppe   Lentil soup.
Nudelsuppe   Noodle soup.

MEATS (WURST, FLEISCH & GEFLÜGEL)

Aufschnitt   Cold cuts.
Brathuhn   Roasted chicken.
Bratwurst   Grilled sausage.
Deutsches beefsteak   Hamburger steak.
Eisbein   Pigs' knuckles.
Ente   Duck.
Gans   Goose.
Geflügel   Poultry.
Kalb   Veal.
Kassler rippchen   Pork chops.
Lamm   Lamb.

Leber   Liver.
Ragout   Stew.
Rinderbraten   Roast beef.
Rindfleisch   Beef.
Schinken   Ham.
Schnitzel   Cutlet.
Schweinebraten   Roast pork.
Truthahn   Turkey.
Wiener schnitzel   Breaded veal cutlet.
Wurst   Sausage.

FISH (FISCH)

Forelle Trout.
Hecht Pike.
Karpfen Carp.
Krebs Crayfish.
Lachs Salmon.

Makrele Mackerel.
Muschel Mussel.
Rheinsalm Rhine salmon.
Schellfisch Haddock.
Seezunge Sole.

EGGS (EIER)

Eier in der schale Boiled eggs.
Mit speck With bacon.
Rühreier Scrambled eggs.

Spiegeleier Fried eggs.
Verlorene eier Poached eggs.

SALADS (SALAT)

Gemischter salat Mixed salad.
Gurkensalat Cucumber salad.

Rohkostplatte Raw vegetable platter.

SANDWICHES (BELEGTE BROTE)

Käsebrot Cheese sandwich.
Schinkenbrot Ham sandwich.

Schwarzbrot mit butter Pumpernickel with butter.
Wurstbrot Sausage sandwich.

VEGETABLES (GEMÜSE)

Artischocken Artichokes.
Blumenkohl Cauliflower.
Bohnen Beans.
Bratkartoffeln Fried potatoes.
Erbsen Peas.
Grüne bohnen Green or string beans.
Gurken Cucumbers.
Karotten Carrots.
Kartoffel Potato.
Kartoffelbrei Mashed potatoes.
Kartoffelsalat Potato salad.

Knödel Dumplings.
Kohl Cabbage.
Reis Rice.
Rote Rüben Beets.
Rotkraut Red cabbage.
Salat Lettuce.
Salzkartoffeln Boiled potatoes.
Spargel Asparagus.
Spinat Spinach.
Steinpilze Boletus mushrooms.
Tomaten Tomatoes.
Vorspeisen Hors d'oeuvres.

DESSERTS (NACHTISCH)

Blatterteiggebäck Puff pastry.
Bratapfel Baked apple.
Käse Cheese.
Kompott Stewed fruit.

Obstkuchen Fruit tart.
Obstsalat Fruit salad.
Pfannkuchen Sugared pancakes.
Pflaumenkompott Stewed plums.
Torte Pastry.

FRUITS (OBST)

Ananas Pineapple.
Apfel Apple.
Apfelsine Orange.
Banane Banana.
Birne Pear.
Erdbeeren Strawberries.

Himberren Raspberries.
Kirschen Cherries.
Pfirsich Peach.
Weintrauben Grapes.
Zitrone Lemon.

BEVERAGES (GETRÄNKE)

Bier Beer.
Ein dunkles A dark beer.
Ein helles A light beer.
Eine tasse kaffee A cup of coffee.
Eine tasse tee A cup of tea.
Milch Milk.
Rotwein Red wine.

Saft Juice.
Schaumwein Sparkling wine.
Schokolade Chocolate.
Tomatensaft Tomato juice.
Wasser Water.
Weisswein White wine.

CONDIMENTS & TABLE ITEMS

Brot Bread.
Bötchen Rolls.
Butter Butter.
Eis Ice.
Essig Vinegar.
Flasche Bottle.
Gabel Fork.
Glas Glass.

Löffel Spoon.
Messer Knife.
Platte Plate.
Pfeffer Pepper.
Sahne Cream.
Salz Salt.
Senf Mustard.
Tasse Cup.
Zucker Sugar.

COOKING TERMS

Gebacken Baked.
Gebraten Fried.
Gedämpft Steamed.
Gefüllt Stuffed.
Gekocht Boiled.
Geröstet Boiled.
Gut durchgebraten Well done.

Heiss Hot.
Kaltes Cold.
Mittep Medium.
Nicht durchgebraten Rare.
Paniert Breaded.
Pochiert Poached.

Useful Terms & Phrases

Index

Aachen (Aix-la-Chapelle),
    482, 483
    accommodations,
        484–485
    bars, cafes, 486
    live music clubs, 486
    performing arts, 486
    restaurants, 485–486
    sightseeing, 6, 483–484
Aachen Cathedral, 6, 483
Abtai Kirche St. Maria
    (Amorbach), 223
Accommodations. *See also*
    specific cities and towns
    family-friendly hotels,
        261, 425, 570
    general information,
        44–45
    locator Web sites, 53,
        58
    luxury, recommended, 9
    recommended, 9–10
Addresses, street, in
    Munich, 253
Adventure travel, 25,
    52–53
Air travel
    airline Web sites, 53
    airlines, 33–36
    bargains, discounts,
        54–56
    discount fares, 34
    in Germany, 39
    online booking, 49–52
Airport Hamburg Fuhls-
    büttel, 562
Aix-la-Chapelle. *See* Aachen
Alamannen Museum
    (Kornhus), 361
Albertinum (Dresden), 168
Albrecht Dürer House
    (Nürnberg), 194
Alpengarten (Pforzheim),
    383
Alps. *See* Bavarian Alps
Alspitz, 328

Alsterpark (Hamburg), 582
Alte Nikolaikirche (Frank-
    furt), 433
Alte Pinakothek (Munich),
    4, 284, 630
Altenburg, 149
Alter Schwede (Wismar),
    614
Altes Museum (Berlin), 103
Altes Rathaus
    Bamberg, 187
    Göttingen, 554
    Hannover, 541
    Leipzig, 155
    Regensburg, 204
Altes Residenztheater
    (Munich), 301
Altes Schloss
    Meersburg, 5, 349
    Stuttgart, 408
Altes Schloss Ermitage
    (Bayreuth), 185
Altmühltal Nature Park,
    180
Altona, 11
Amorbach, 223
    accommodations/
        restaurants, 224
    sightseeing, 223
Amphitheater (Trier), 521
Antiques
    Berlin, 118
    Bonn, 477
    Düsseldorf, 503
    Leipzig, 157
    Lübeck, 598
    Munich, 295–296
Apple-wine taverns,
    Frankfurt, 431
Aquarium (Stralsund), 621
Archaeological digs, 361
Archäologisches Landes-
    museum (Schleswig), 606
Arnstadt, 149
Arsenal (Schwerin), 616
Art auction, Lindau, 343

Art galleries
    Berlin, 118–119, 124
    Bremen, 531
    Cologne, 491
    Island of Sylt, 610
    Mainz, 465
    Munich, 296
Asamkirche (Munich), 630
Aschaffenburg, 442–443
    accommodations, 444
    restaurants, 444
    sightseeing, 443–444
Assmannshausen, 471.
    See Rüdesheim/
    Assmannshausen
ATMs, banks, 20
Augsburg, 213, 240, 630
    accommodations,
        243–244
    nightlife, 245
    restaurants, 244–245
    sightseeing, 240–242
Augustiner Museum
    (Freiburg), 365

Bach, Johann Sebastian,
    140, 155, 632
    birthplace (Eisenach),
        152
Bach Museum (Leipzig),
    155
Bad Godesberg, 481–482
Bad Homburg, 8, 27
    448–449
    accommodations,
        450–451
    nightlife, 451
    recreational activities,
        sightseeing, 449
    restaurants, 451
Bad Kissingen, 27
Bad Mergentheim,
    224–225
    accommodations/
        restaurants, 225
    sightseeing, 224

Bad Nauheim, 8, 452
    accommodations, 452–453
    famous guests, 453
    restaurants, 453–454
Bad Pyrmont, 548
    accommodations, 549
    restaurants, 550
    sightseeing, 549
Bad Reichenhall, 8, 27, 318
    accommodations, 319–320
    activities, sightseeing, 318
    nightlife, 320–321
    restaurants, 320
    shopping, 319
Bad Wiessee, 323
    accommodations, 324–325
    activities, sightseeing, 324
    restaurants, 324–325
    shopping, 324
Bad Wildstein, 517
Bad Wildungen, 557
    accommodations, 557–558
    activities, sightseeing, 557
    nightlife, 558–559
    restaurants, 558
    shopping, 557
Baden-Baden, 16, 384
    accommodations, 9, 387–389
    casino, 385
    food specialties, 634
    golfing, 28
    nightlife, 391
    public transportation, 385
    recreational activities, 386
    restaurants, 389–390
    shopping, 386
    spas, 2, 8–9, 27
    special events, 391
    thermal baths, 385
Baden-Württemberg, 16
Badenweiler, 369
    accommodations, 370–371
    activities, sightseeing, 369–370
    restaurants, 371
Baiersbronn, 379–380

Ballet
    Frankfurt, 440
    Hannover, 545
    Stuttgart, 412
Ballooning, 310, 386
Baltic Sea, 17
Baltic Sea coast, driving tours, 613, 615
Bamberg, 13, 187
    accommodations, 189–190
    bars and clubs, 191
    beer gardens, 2
    performing arts, 191
    restaurants, 190–191
    shopping, 188
    sightseeing, 187–188
Banks. See ATMs, banks
Baron von Landenberg Castle (Cochem), 514
Baroque architecture, 630
Baroque music, 632
Bars, pubs. See also Cafes
    Aachen, 486
    Berlin, 132–134
    Bonn, 481
    Bremen, 534
    Cologne, 498–499
    Dresden, 175
    Düsseldorf, 508
    Frankfurt, 431, 441–442
    Freiburg, 368–369
    Göttingen, 556
    Hamburg, 592–593
    Hannover, 545
    Heidelberg, 402
    Koblenz, 474
    Leipzig, 160–161
    Munich, 305–307
    Regensburg, 206
    Stuttgart, 412
    Ulm, 212
    Würzburg, 221
Basilica (Trier), 521
Bauhaus movement, 145, 631
Bauhaus Museum (Berlin), 106
Bavaria, 309
    food specialties, 633
Bavarian Alps, 13
    Chiemsee (Bavarian Sea), 321
    Deutsche Alpenstrasse (German Alpine Road), 312–313
    driving tours, 7
    hiking, 2, 28, 309, 328

    Marienbrücke, 8
    Mittenwald, 7
    Partnachklamm Gorge, 7
    skiing, 309
    spas, 26
    Web sites about, 60
    winter sports, 29, 30
    wood carvings, 11
    Zugspitze, 2
Bavarian State Opera, 301
Bayerischen Staatsoper (Munich), 301
Bayerisches Nationalmuseum (Munich), 286–287
Bayerisches Staatsschauspiel (Munich), 301
Bayreuth, 13, 182–183
    accommodations, 185–186
    Festspiele, 183
    restaurants, 186
    sightseeing, 183–185
    special events, 24
Bayreuth Festival, 632
Beaches
    Baden-Baden, 386
    Eichwald Lido (Lindau), 340
    Hamburg, 583
    in the Bavarian Alps, 310
    Konstanz, 353
    Lake Titisee, 372
    Lindau, 343
    Meersburg, 350
Beautiful Fountain (Nürnburg), 194
Beer gardens (biergartens), 2
    Berlin, 132
    Munich, 278
Beer halls, taverns
    Cologne, 496
    Düsselkdorf, 508
    Göttingen, 11
    Hamburg, 11
    Heidelberg, 11
    Leipzig, 11
    Munich, 11
    ordering in, 635–636
    recommended, 11
Beer, types of, 634–636
Beethoven, Ludwig van, 633
    home of (Bonn), 476, 632
Beheiztes Freibad (Meersburg), 350
Beilstein, 515–516

Belchen mountain, 368
Berchtesgaden, 16, 313
    accommodations,
        314–315
    Berchtesgaden National
        Park, 28, 310
    restaurants, 315
    sightseeing, 313–314
Berchtesgadener Land, 309
Berghof (Obersalzberg),
    316
Berlin, 1, 12
    accommodations, 9,
        74–75, 78–86, 88–90
    architectural highlights,
        111–112
    average temperature/
        rainfall, 22
    bars, pubs, 132–134
    beer gardens, wine
        cellars, 132
    Berlin Wall, 104
    cabaret, 126–127
    cafes, 134–135
    casino, 135
    castles and palaces, 102
    cathedrals and
        churches, 111
    classical music,
        124–125
    dance clubs, discos,
        126–129
    drag shows, 129
    food specialties, 634
    gay and lesbian com-
        munity, 130–132
    guided tours, 114–115
    Jewish community, 29
    live music clubs, 129
    local transportation,
        71–72
    museums, 3, 103–104,
        106, 108–111
    neighborhoods, 66–67,
        70–71
    parks and zoos, 113–114
    rebuilding of, 64, 631
    recreational activities,
        116–117
    restaurants, 10, 90–100
    services, basic informa-
        tion, 72–74
    shopping, 112,
        117–124
    sightseeing highlights,
        100, 102–104, 106,
        108–114
    special events, 23–24,
        632

    street addresses, 67
    theater, 125
    traveling to, 63–65
    visitor information, 65
    Web sites about, 58–59
Berlin Wall, 1, 110, 629
Berliner Festwochen, 24
Bernkastel, 518–519
Bernkastel-Kues, 17
Bibliography, recommended
    books, 638–639
Bicycling
    in Berlin, 72, 116
    in Frankfurt, 437
    in Germany, 44
    in Konstanz, 353
    around Lake Con-
        stance, 8, 340
    around Lünenburg
        Heath, 8
    in Meersburg, 350
    in Munich, 8, 258
    in the Neckar Valley, 8
Bicycling tours, 8, 25
    Franconia, 180
    Munich, 294
    Neckar Valley Cycle
        Path, 395
    Romantic Road, 213
Biedermeier style, 630
Biergarten Chinesischer
    Turm (Munich), 278
Biergartens. See Beer
    gardens
Birkenkopf (Stuttgart),
    406
Bischöfliches Museum
    (Trier), 522
Bismarck, Otto von, 626
Black Forest (Schwarzwald),
    16, 28, 362
    driving tours, 7, 362
    hiking, 369, 376
    upper regions, 368
    winter sports, 30
Boat tours, cruises, 44
    Berlin, 115–116
    Bremen, 528
    Danube River, 25, 207
    Elbe River, 168
    to Germany, 39
    Hamburg, 582
    Konstanz, 353
    Lake Titisee, 372
    Lübeck harbor, 598
    Neckar River, 398
    Obersee, 316
    Rhine River, 17, 458
    Triers, 523

Boating
    Hamburg, 583
    on the Königssee, 2
    Lake Constance, 28,
        29, 340, 353
    Lake Titisee, 372
    Lindau, 343
Bodensee. See Constance,
    Lake
Bodensee Festival
    (Konstanz), 355
Bomann Museum (Celle),
    538
Bonn, 475, 632
    accommodations, 477,
        478
    bars, pubs, 481
    gay and lesbian bars,
        481
    live music clubs, 480
    performing arts, 480
    public transportation,
        475
    restaurants, 479– 480
    shopping, 476
    sightseeing, 476
    special events, 23, 480
    traveling to, 475
Bonner Summer Festival,
    480
Bookstores, English-language
    Berlin, 119
    Frankfurt, 422
    Hamburg, 565
    Munich, 258
Botanical Garden (Berlin),
    113
Böttcherstrasse (Bremen),
    530
Brahms, Johannes, 633
Breites Tor (Goslar),
    551
Bremen, 3, 17, 526
    accommodations, 9,
        531–532
    bars, pubs, 534
    gay and lesbian clubs,
        534
    guided tours, 528
    live music clubs,
        534–535
    performing arts, 534
    public transportation,
        528
    restaurants, 532–534
    shopping, 530–531
    sightseeing, 528–530
    traveling to, 526, 528
    Web sites about, 62

Index

Bremen Flughaven, 526
Breweries, in Miltenberg, 222
Bröhan Museum (Berlin), 103
Bromserburg Castle (Rüdenheim), 469
Buchenwald Concentration Camp, 145–146
Buddenbrookhaus (Hamburg), 597
Burg Eltz (nr. Cochem), 6, 514
Bus tours
  Berlin, 115
  Bremen, 528
  Dresden, 168
  Munich, 293–294
  Romantic Road, 213
Bus travel. See also Public transportation
  in Germany, 43
  to Germany, 37
Business hours, 45
  Berlin, 72, 118
  Hamburg, 565
  Munich, 258

Cabaret
  Berlin, 126–127
  Bonn, 480
  Bremen, 535
  Dresden, 176
  Leipzig, 161
  Nürnberg, 201
  Passau, 210
Cable cars (funiculars)
  in the Bavarian Alps, 328
  Dresden, 166
Cafes. See also Bars, pubs
  Berlin, 134–135
  Frankfurt, 441–442
  Munich, 269
Calendar of events, 23
Calw, 380
  accommodations, 381
  restaurants, 381–382
  sightseeing, 381
Camping, caravanning, 25
Car rentals, 42–43
  agencies, 72
  Frankfurt, 422
  Hamburg, 565
Car travel. See also Driving, parking
  to Berlin, 65
  driving rules, 43
  emergency services, 43

gasoline prices, 43
  in Germany, 42
  to Germany, 36
Caracalla-Therme (Baden-Baden), 385
Caravanning. See Camping, caravanning
Carl Hagenbeck's Tierpark (Hamburg), 580
Carnival (Mainz), 464
Casinos
  Bad Homburg, 451
  Bad Reichenhall, 320
  Baden-Baden, 385
  Berlin, 135
  Bremen, 534
  Garmish-Partenkirchen, 334
  Hamburg, 593
  Hannover, 546
  Island of Sylt, 612
  Konstanz, 355
  Lindau, 345
  Wiesbaden, 448
Castle Road (Burgenstrasse), 16
Castles. See also specific castles
  recommended, 4, 6
Cathedral of Our Lady (Munich), 291
Cathedrals, churches. See also specific cathedrals/churches
  recommended, 6
Celle, 538, 630
  accommodations, 9, 539
  restaurants, 539–540
  sightseeing, 538
Chapel of St. Bartholomew (Königssee), 316
Charlottenburg Palace and Museum complex (Berlin), 102–103
Checkpoint Charlie Museum (Berlin), 110
Chiemsee, 321–322
  accommodations, 322–323
  Frauenchimemsee island, 321
  Herrenchimemsee island, 322
  restaurants, 322–323
Children's activities
  Frankfurt, 436–437
  Hamburg, 582
  Munich, 293

Children, traveling with, 53
  discounts, 20
  family-friendly hotels, 78, 261, 425, 570
  family-friendly restaurants, 92, 273, 431, 575
Christmas fairs, markets
  Lübeck, 596
  Mainz, 24
Chunnel Tunnel, 37
Church of St. Severi (Erfurt), 150
Church of St. Ulrich and St. Afra (Augsburg), 242
Churches. See Cathedrals and specific cathedrals/churches
Circus performances, in Frankfurt, 436
Classical music
  Aachen, 486
  Baden-Baden, 391
  Bamberg, 191
  Bayreuth, 24
  Bayreuth Festival, 632
  Berlin, 24, 124–125
  Bonn, 480
  Bremen, 534
  Cologne, 497
  Dresden, 174–175
  Düsseldorf, 508
  Göttingen, 556
  Hamburg, 586
  Hannover, 545
  Koblenz, 474
  Konstanz, 355
  Leipzig, 160
  Meersburg, 352
  Munich, 300–302
  Passeau, 209
  Würzburg, 23
Climate, 22
Clocks. See Watches, clocks
Clothing. See Fashion
Coburg, 26
Cochem, 7, 512
  accommodations, 514
  castles and palaces, 6
  grape harvest, 17
  restaurants, 515
  special events, 513
Cologne, 17, 455, 487, 629
  accommodations, 10, 492–494
  bars, pubs, 498
  beer taverns, 496

Cologne (*cont.*)
churches and
cathedrals, 6, 488,
490–491
gay and lesbian clubs,
499
live music clubs,
497–498
museums, 4
performing arts, 497
public transportation,
488
rebuilding of, 631
restaurants, 494–495
shopping, 491–492
sightseeing, 488,
490–491
special events, 23
traveling to, 487
Web sites about, 61
Cologne Cathedral, 6, 488,
490, 630
Concentration camps
Buchenwald, 145–146
Dachau, 4, 308
Constance, Lake
(Bodensee), 7, 16, 340
bicycling, 8
golfing, 28
Mainau Island, 7
sailing lessons, 29
Web sites about, 60
Corpus Christi Festival
(Frauenchiemsee), 321
Council Building
(Konstanz), 353
Couven Museum (Aachen),
484
Credit cards, 20
Creglingen, 227
accommodations,
228
sightseeing, 227
Cruises. *See* Boat
excursions, cruises
Cuckoo clocks. *See*
Watches, clocks
Cuisine, local specialties
Frankfurt, 439
Munich, 268, 299
Nürnberg, 197
Currency, currency
exchange, 20
ATMs, banks, 20
Berlin, 73
credit cards, 20
currency converters, 57
euro, 20
Frankfurt, 423

German currency, 21
Hamburg, 565
Munich, 259
traveler's checks, 21
Customs regulations, 57
entering Germany, 18
returning citizens, 19
Cutlery, 11
Cuvilliés Theater (Munich),
301, 630
Cuvilliés, François, 301

Dachau Concentration
Camp, 4, 308
Dance clubs, discos
Aachen, 486
Berlin, 126–127, 129
Bonn, 480
Bremen, 534
Cologne, 497
Dresden, 176
Düsseldorf, 508
Frankfurt, 440
Göttingen, 556
Hamburg, 590–591
Hannover, 545
Koblenz, 474
Leipzig, 160
Regensburg, 206
Danube River, 13, 180
bicycle tours, 182
cruises, 2, 207
regional Web sites, 60
Department stores
Berlin, 120
Düsseldorf, 503
Frankfurt, 438
Munich, 297
Deutsche Alpenstrasse
(German Alpine Road),
7, 312–313
Deutsche Guggenheim
Berlin (Berlin), 106
Deutsche Weinstrasse
(Wine Road), 462–463
Deutsches Architekturmu-
seum (Frankfurt), 435
Deutsches Filmmuseum
(Frankfurt), 435
Deutsches Museum
(Munich), 3, 287, 293
Deutsches Museum für
Meereskunde und
Fischerei (Stralsund),
621
Deutsches Nationaltheater
(Weimar), 149
Deutsches Salzmuseum
(Lüneburg), 536

Deutsches Uhrenmuseum
(nr. Triberg), 376
Diebsturm (Lindau), 343
Dining. *See* Restaurants
Dinkelsbühl, 7, 213,
235–236
Diozesanmuseum St.
Ulrich (Regensburg), 203
Disabled travelers, resources
for, 31–32
Dixieland festival
(Dresden), 632
Doctors, dentists, 30
Berlin, 73
Frankfurt, 423
Hamburg, 565
Munich, 259
Documents, required, 18
Dom St. Bartolomäus
(Frankfurt), 433
Dom St. Kilian
(Würzburg), 217
Dom St. Maria (Augsburg),
242
Dom St. Peter (Worms),
460
Dom St. Peter's
(Regensburg), 202
Dom St. Peter's (Trier),
522
Dom St. Petri (Bremen),
529
Dom und Diözesan
Museum (Mainz), 464
Donauwörth, 239–240
Dornburg, 149
Drag shows
Berlin, 129
Cologne, 499
Hamburg, 590
Dresden, 13, 164
accommodations,
169–172
bars and clubs,
175–176
cathedrals and
churches, 166
destruction of, 631
guided tours, 168
museums, 3
performing arts,
174–175
public transportation,
166
restaurants, 172–174
shopping, 169
sightseeing, 166–168
special events, 632
traveling to, 164

Dresden Festival of Contemporary Music, 632
Drinking laws, 46
Driver's licenses, 43
Driving, parking. See Car travel
in Berlin, 72
in Munich, 258
Driving tours
Baltic coast, 613, 615
Castle Road (Burgenstrasse), 16
Deutsche Alpenstrasse, 312–313
Deutsche Weinstrasse, 462–463
Fairy-Tale Road, 13, 17, 559–561
Franconia, 182
Märchenstrasse, 3
Mosel Valley, 510, 513
Neckar River, 2
recommended routes, 7
Rhine Valley, 455–457
Romantic Road, 13, 213
Schleswig-Holstein, 594
Schwarzwald Hochstrasse, 362
Thuringian High Road, 149
upper Black Forest, 368
Wallberg Road, 324
Drug laws, 45
Dürer, Albrecht, 195
home of (Nürnburg), 194
Düsseldorf, 17, 455, 500
accommodations, 504–505
bars, beer halls, 508
gay and lesbian clubs, 509
live music clubs, 508–509
performing arts, 508
public transportation, 500
rebuilding of, 631
restaurants, 10, 506–507
shopping, 503–504
sightseeing, 502–503
special events, 23
traveling to, 500
Web sites about, 62
Düsseldorf International Airport, 500

E-mail. See also Internet access
checking, 58
E. T. A. Hoffmanhaus (Bamberg), 188
East Germany, 12, 32, 58, 140, 628
Web sites about, 60
Eau-de-Cologne (Cologne water), 492
Eberbach, 404
Eckbauer peak, 328
Egyptian (Ägyptishes) Museum (Berlin), 103
Eichwald Lido (Lindau), 340
Eisenach, 5, 151–152
Elbe River, 562
cruises, 2, 168
Meissen, 6
Elbe Valley, 178
Electricity, in Germany, 45
Embassies, consulates, 45–46
Emergency services, 46
Berlin, 73
Frankfurt, 423
Hamburg, 569
Munich, 259
Erfurt, 150–151
Erfurt Cathedral, 150
Erotic Art Museum (Hamburg), 589
Erotic theater, in Hamburg, 588, 590
Escorted tours, 38
Ettal, 339
Eurailpasses, 36, 42
Europass, 42
Events, seasonal, 23

Fairy-Tale Road (Märchenstrasse), 3, 13, 17
driving tour, 559–561
Fall Wine Festival (Zell), 516
Falls of Todtnau, 368
Fasching (carnival), 23
Fashion
Berlin, 120, 122
Bremen, 531
Düsseldorf, 504
Hamburg, 585
Munich, 298–299
Stuttgart, 408–409
Feldherrnhalle (Munich), 630
Fernsehturm tower (Stuttgart), 408

Ferries
Dresden, 166
Konstanz-Meersburg, 353
to Germany, 36
to Hamburg, 563
to Lübeck, 596
Festivals, 23, 632
Festspiele (Bayreuth), 183
Festspielhaus (Bayreuth), 183
Festung Ehrenbreitstein (Koblenz), 472
Festung und Schloss Pyrmont, 549
Feuerwehrmuseum (Creglingen), 227
Figurentheater (Rothenburg), 234
Film, cinema
Deutsches Filmmuseum (Frankfurt), 435
International Film Festival (Berlin), 23
Fingerhutmuseum (Creglingen), 227
Fishing, 26, 310
Flea markets. See Markets, outdoor
Flughafen Frankfurt/Main, 418
Flughafen Köln/ Bonn Konrad Adenauer, 475, 487
Folklore Museum (Calw), 381
Foreign language instruction, 56
Franconia, 13, 180, 182
food specialities, 633
Frankenwald forest, 180
Web sites about, 60
Frankenberg Kirche (Goslar), 551
Frankenwald, 180
Frankfurt, 418
accommodations, 423–428
apple-wine taverns, 431
average temperature/ rainfall, 22
bars, cafes, 441–442
dance clubs, discos, 440
gay and lesbian clubs, 442
live music clubs, 441
museums, 434–436

Frankfurt (*cont.*)
neighborhoods, layout, 419
parks and gardens, 436, 437
performing arts, 439–440
public transportation, 419, 422
recreational activities, 437–438
restaurants, 428–433
services, basic information, 422–423
shopping, 438
sightseeing, 433–434
special events, 23–24
taxis, 422
traveling to, 418–419
visitor information, 419
Web sites about, 61
Frankfurt Book Fair, 24
Frankfurter-Goethe-Museum, 434
Franz Josef Strauss Airport (Munich), 252
Franz-Liszt-Museum (Bayreuth), 184
Frauenchiemsee Abbey, 322
Fraueninsel, 321
Frauenkirche (Dresden), 166
Frauenkirche (Munich), 291
Freiburg Cathedral, 364
Freiburg im Breisgau, 16, 362, 364
accommodations, 365, 366
nightlife, 368–369
public transportation, 364
restaurants, 367
sightseeing, 364–365
special events, 24, 368
Freiburg Wine Tasting, 24
Freilichtmuseum Schwarzwälder (nr. Triberg), 376
Freudenstadt, 377–378
accommodations, 378–379
restaurants, 379
sightseeing, 378
Friedrichsbad (Baden-Baden), 385
Friedrichshafen, 346–347
accommodations, 347–348

restaurants, 348
sightseeing, 347
Friedrichswerdersche Kirche-Schinkelmuseum (Berlin), 108
Fuggerai (Augsburg), 240
Funiculars. *See* Cable cars
Füssen, 245–246
accommodations, 247
castles and palaces near, 5, 8, 248–251
restaurants, 247–248
sightseeing, 246

Garmisch-Partenkirchen, 2, 16, 23, 30, 310, 327
accommodations, 331–332
activities, sightseeing, 328–330
nightlife, 334
restaurants, 333
shopping, 330
Gay and lesbian travelers
Berlin, 130–132
Bonn, 481
Bremen, 534
Cologne, 499
Dresden, 175
Düsseldorf, 509
Frankfurt, 442
Göttingen, 556
Hamburg, 591–592
Hannover, 546
Leipzig, 161
Munich, 307
Nürnberg, 201
resources for, 32
Stuttgart, 413
Gay Pride Parade (Cologne), 499
Geigenbau- und Heimat-museum (Mittenwald), 326
Gemäldegalerie (Berlin), 3, 104
Georgenkirche (Children's Festival) (Dinkelsbühl), 235
German Alpine Road, 312–313
German Democratic Republic (DDR), 628. *See also* East Germany
German Museum of Masterpieces of Science and Technology (Munich), 287

Germanisches National-museum (Nürnberg), 194
GermanRail passes, 41
Germany, cultural heritage
architecture, 629–631
music, 631–633
Germany, history of
dateline, 625–628
early period, 624
German Renaissance, 192
Holy Roman Empire, 624–625
post-war division, 628
Reformation, 625
reunification, 629
Third Reich, Nazism, 627–628
unification, 625–626
Weimar Republic, 627
World War I, 626–627
World War II, 628
Glasmuseum (Passau), 208
Glockenspiel (Goslar), 551
Glossaries
art, architecture terms, 641
food, dining terms, 641–643
general terms, 640–641
Glyptothek (Munich), 630
Goethe Museum Düssel-dorf, 502
Goethe Nationalmuseum (Weimar), 143, 146
Goethe-Haus (Frankfurt), 434
Goethe-Schiller Mausoleum (Weimar), 145
Goethes Gartenhaus (Weimar), 144
Golf, golf courses, 27
Frankfurt, 437
Fremersberg, 386
Hamburg, 583
Goslar, 550–551
accommodations, 552
churches, 551
restaurants, 553
sightseeing, 551
Goslarer-Museum, 551
Gothic architecture, 629
Göttingen, 553–554
accommodations, 554–555
bars, pubs, 556
beer halls, taverns, 11
gay and lesbian clubs, 556

live music clubs, 556
performing arts, 556
public transportation, 554
restaurants, 555
shopping, 554
sightseeing, 554
student taverns, 556
Grevenburg Castle (Traben-Trarbach), 517
Grimm brothers (Jakob and Wilhelm), 3, 17, 559
Grosser Alpsee, 29
Grosser Garten (Dresden), 166
Günerturm (Ravensburg), 360
Güstrow, 618
Gutach Falls (Triberg), 375
Gutenberg Festival (Mainz), 464
Gutenberg Museum (Mainz), 4, 465

Hamburg, 562
accommodations, 9–10, 568–574
activities for children, 582
bars, pubs, 592–593
beer halls, taverns, 11
casino, 593
dance clubs, 590–591
gay and lesbian clubs, 591–592
guided tours, 582
live music clubs, 587, 590
museums, 4
neighborhoods, layout, 563–564
outdoor, recreational activities, 583
parks, gardens, 582
performing arts, 586–587
public transportation, 564–565, 568
restaurants, 574–578
services, basic information, 565, 568
shopping, 584–585
sightseeing, 579–580
special events, 23–24
taxis, 565
traveling to, 562–563
visitor information, 563
Web sites about, 62

Hameln (Hamelin), 546, 547
accommodations, 547
nightlife, 547
restaurants, 548
shopping, 547
sightseeing, 547
Hanau, 3, 17
Handcrafts, 11, 194, 197, 296–297
Handel, George Frideric, 632
Hang gliding, para gliding, 310
Hannover, 540–541
accommodations, 542–543
bars, pubs, 545
casino, 546
gay and lesbian clubs, 546
live music clubs, 545–546
performing arts, 545
public transportation, 541
restaurants, 543–545
shopping, 542
sightseeing, 541–542
Web sites about, 62
Hannover-Langenhagen International Airport, 540
Harz Mountains, 2, 23, 526, 550
Quedlinburg, 6
winter sports, 30
Hassen, 634
Hauptkirche St. Michaelis (Hamburg), 579
Haus de Geschichte der Bundesrepublik Deutschland (Bonn), 476
Haus der Bürgerschaft (Bremen), 528
Haus der Kunst (Munich), 631
Haus der Schiffergesell-schaft (Lübeck), 597
Haus der Wannsee-Konferenz (Berlin), 112
Haus zum Cavazzen (Lindau), 343
Havel River, 12
Hayden, Franz Joseph, 632
Health advisories, 56
Health conditions, traveling with, 30
Health insurance needs, 30

Health resorts. *See* Spas
Heidelberg, 16, 392, 394
accommodations, 10, 398–400
bars, pubs, 402
beer halls, taverns, 11
bicycling, 8
castles and palaces, 5
live music, 403
performing arts, 402
public transportation, 394
restaurants, 400–402
shopping, 396
sightseeing, 394–396
special events, 24
Web sites about, 61
Heidelberg Castle (Heidelberg), 5, 394–395
Heilbronn, 404–405
special events, 404
Heilig-Kreutz-Kirche (Rostock), 619
Heiligengeistkirche (Stralsund), 621
Heimatmuseum (Freudenstadt), 378
Heimatmuseum (Oberammergau), 335
Heimatmuseum (Ravensburg), 360
Heine, Heinrich, 503
Heinrich Heine Institut (Düsseldorf), 503
Heinrich-Hertz-Turm (Hamburg), 579
Hellabrun Zoo (Munich), 292–293
Henze, Hans Werner, 633
Herrenchiemsee, 630
Herrenhäuser Garten (Hannover), 541
Herreninsel, 322
Herrgottskirche (Creglingen), 227
Herzogschloss (Celle), 538
Hesse, Hermann, 378
birthplace (Calw), 381
Hiking, 28
in the Bavarian Alps, 2, 7, 309, 328
in the Black Forest, 369, 376
in Franconia, 180
in the Thuringian forest, 149
Hindemith, Paul, 633
Hindenburgufer (Kiel), 603

Hinterzarten, 374–375
Hirschhorn, 403–404
Hirschpark (Hamburg), 582
Hitler, Adolf, 316–317, 627–628
Hockzeitshaus (Hameln), 546
Hoffman, E. T. A., 188
Hofgarten (Düsseldorf), 502
Hohenschwangau castle (nr. Füssen), 5, 248, 251
Hölderlinturm (Tübingen), 414
Holidays, public, 22
Holstentor (Lübeck), 596
Honey products, 387
Honigschlecker statue (Meersburg), 350
Horse racing, 386
Hot lines/help lines, Berlin, 73
Hotels. See Accommodations
Housewares, kitchenwares, 504

Ice-skating, 294, 437
Ilm River, 142
Imperial Baths (Trier), 521
Imperial Cathedral (Aachen), 6, 483
Imperial Cathedral (Speyer), 458
Imperial Hall (Frankfurt), 433
Inns. See Accommodations
Insurance needs, 30
International May Festival (Wiesbaden), 23, 448
International Ski-Jumping (Garmisch-Partenkirchen), 23
International Spring Fair (Frankfurt), 23
Internationale-Bodensee-Kunstauktion (Lindau), 343
Internet access
    Berlin, 73
    Frankfurt, 423
    Munich, 259
    Net cafe locator, 56, 58
Isar River rafting, 295
Island of Sylt casino, 612

Jacobikirche (Stralsund), 621
Jacobkirche (Hamburg), 579
Jagdschloss Granitz (Rügen), 622
Jazz. See Live music clubs
Jazz festivals
    Berlin, 24, 632
    Dresden, 632
    Konstanz, 356
    Leipzig, 154
Jewelry, 122
Jewish Cemetery (Jüdischer Friedhof) (Berlin), 112
Jewish cemetery (Worms), 460
Jewish communities, 29
Jewish quarter (Worms), 460
Jogging, 437
    Berlin, 116
    Hamburg, 583

Kaiserburg (Nürnberg), 194
Kaiserdom (Bamberg), 188
Kaiserdom (Speyer), 458
Karl-Marx-Haus (Trier), 522
Karmeliteenklosterkirche (Ravensburg), 360
Käthe-Kollwitz Museum (Berlin), 108
Käthe-Kruse-Puppen-Museum (Donauwörth), 239
Katholische Hofkirche (Dresden), 166
Kaufhaus (Freiburg), 365
Kayaking, 310
KD River Cruises of Europe, 2
Kiel, 602
    accommodations, 603–604
    nightlife, 604–605
    restaurants, 603
    sightseeing, 603
    special events, 602
Kinderzeche (Children's Festival) (Dinkelsbühl), 235
Kirche St. Joseph (Hamburg), 589
Kirfstliches Palais (Trier), 521
Kloster Ettal, 339, 630
Kloster Maulbronn, 384

Kneipe. See Bars, pubs
Knives. See Cutlery
Koblenz, 3, 471–472
    accommodations, 472–473
    bars and pubs, 474
    live music clubs, 474
    performing arts, 474
    restaurants, 473–474
    sightseeing, 472
Kollegiengebäude (Schwerin), 616
Köln. See Cologne
Kölner Philharmoniker, 497
Königliche Porzellan Manufaktur (Berlin), 119
Königliches Schloss Berchtesgaden, 314
Königssee, 2, 315–316
Konstanz (Constance), 16, 352
    accommodations, 354
    nightlife, 355–356
    recreational activities, 353
    restaurants, 354–355
    shopping, 353
    sightseeing, 353
Konstanz Basilica, 353
Konstanz Stadttheater, 352
Krämerbrücke (Erfurt), 150
Kranziskanerkirche (Ümberlingen), 359
Kreuzkirche (Dresden), 166
Kriminal Museum (Rothenburg), 231
Kulturhistorisches Museum (Stralsund), 621
Kunst Halle Düsseldorf, 503
Kunst- und Kulturgeschichtliche Sammlungen (Regensburg), 203
Kunstgewerbemuseum (Berlin), 106
Kunsthalle (Hamburg), 4, 580
Kunstmuseum (Bonn), 476
Kunstmuseum Düsseldorf, 503
Kunstsammlung Nordrhein Westfaln (Düsseldorf), 502
Kunstsammlungen zu Weimar, 144
Kupark (Bad Pyrmont), 549

Kurhaus (Baden-Baden), 391
Kurpfälzisches Museum (Heidelberg), 396

Lake Constance. *See* Constance, Lake
Lake Constance Wine Festival (Meersburg), 349
Landesmuseum Mainz, 465
Langenargen, 346
Langenargen Stadtmuseum (Wasserburg), 346
Lapidarium (Mainz), 465
Leather goods, 439
Leipzig, 12, 152, 154
    accommodations, 158–159
    bars and clubs, 160–161
    beer halls, taverns, 11
    food specialties, 634
    performing arts, 160
    public transportation, 154
    restaurants, 159
    shopping, 157
    sightseeing, 154–157
    special events, 154
    traveling to, 154
    Web sites about, 59
Leipziger Jazztage, 154
Leipziger Stadtfest, 154
Liebfrauenkirche (Koblenz), 472
Liebfrauenkirche (Trier), 522
Liebieghaus (Frankfurt), 434
Liederhalle (Stuttgart), 406
Lindau, 7, 16, 342
    accommodations, 344
    casino, 345
    recreational activities, 343
    restaurants, 345
    shopping, 343
    sightseeing, 342–343
Liszt, Franz, 144, 184
    home of (Weimar), 144, 632
Live music clubs
    Aachen, 486
    Bamberg, 191
    Berlin, 129
    Bonn, 480
    Bremen, 534–535
    Cologne, 497–498
    Dresden, 176

Düsseldorf, 508
Frankfurt, 441
Freiburg, 368–369
Hamburg, 587, 590
Hannover, 546
Heidelberg, 403
Koblenz, 474
Leipzig, 160
Munich, 303–305
Stuttgart, 412
Trier, 525
Würzburg, 221
Lochgefängnis (Nürnberg), 196
Love Parade (Berlin), 128
Lower Saxony, 526
    Fairy Tale Road, 13, 17
    food specialties, 634
    Web sites about, 62
Lübbenau, 177
Lübeck, 18, 595–596
    accommodations, 598–599
    nightlife, 601–602
    restaurants, 600–601
    shopping, 598
    sightseeing, 596–598
    special events, 596
Lucas Cranach the Elder House (Weimar), 142
Ludwig II, 249
Ludwig Museum (Cologne), 490
Ludwig of Bavaria, 204
Lünenburg, 535
    accommodations, 536
    bicycling, 8
    nightlife, 537
    restaurants, 536–537
    shopping, 536
    sightseeing, 535–536
Lünenburg Heath (Lünenburger Heide), 8, 537
Luther, Martin, 152, 161, 459, 625
Lutherhalle Wittenberg, 161
Lutherhaus (Eisenach), 152
Lutherstadt Wittenberg, 161–162

Mail, post offices, 46
    Berlin, 74
    Frankfurt, 423
    Hamburg, 568
    Munich, 259
Main River, 7, 13, 215
    fishing, 26
Mainau Island, 352–353
    walking tours, 7

Mainfränkisches Fortress and Museum (Würzburg), 216
Mainz, 463–464
    accommodations, 466–467
    museums, 4
    nightlife, 467
    public transportation, 464
    restaurants, 467
    shopping, 465
    sightseeing, 464–465
    special events, 24, 464
Malls, shopping streets
    Baden-Baden, 386
    Berlin, 117–118, 124
    Bonn, 476
    Bremen, 530
    Dresden, 169
    Düsseldorf, 503
    Frankfurt, 438
    Hamburg, 584–585
    Heidelberg, 396
    Leipzig, 157
    Mainz, 465
    Munich, 295
    Stuttgart, 408
Mangturm (Lindau), 342
Mann, Thomas, 18, 597
Maps, sources for, 43, 56, 66
Marienbrücke, 8, 248
Marienkirche (Berlin), 111
Marienkirche (Lübeck), 597
Marienkirche (Stralsund), 621
Market Church (Hannover), 541
Markets, outdoor
    Berlin, 123
    Bremen, 531
    Cologne, 492
    Stuttgart, 409
Markgräfliches Opernhaus (Bayreuth), 184
Märkisches Museum (Berlin), 109
Marstall (Schwerin), 616
Martin-Gropius-Bau (Berlin), 109
Marx, Karl, birthplace (Trier), 520
Maulbronn, 384
Mäuseturm (Rhinegau area), 468
Mecklenburgishces Staatstheater (Schwerin), 616

Medical emergencies, 46
  Berlin, 73
  Frankfurt, 423
  Hamburg, 565
  handling, 30
  Munich, 259
Meersburg, 5, 349
  accommodations, 351
  nightlife, 352
  recreational activities, 350
  restaurants, 351
  sightseeing, 349–350
  special events, 349
Meersburg Chamber Music Festival, 352
Mehlsack Tower (Ravensburg), 360
Meissen, 6, 177–178
  accommodations, 179
  restaurants, 179
  shopping, 179
  sightseeing, 178–179
Melanchthon, Philipp, 161
Mendelssohn, Felix, 633
Mercedes-Benz Museum (Stuttgart), 408
Merheim, 10
Michaelskirche (Schwäbisch Hall), 416
Military figures/collectibles, 123
Miltenberg, 221–222
  accommodations, 222–223
  restaurants, 222–223
  sightseeing, 222
Mittenwald, 7, 16, 325–326
  accommodations, 326–327
  activities, sightseeing, 326
  restaurants, 327
  shopping, 326
  sightseeing, 326
Modern History Museum (Bonn), 476
Money. See Currency, currency exchange
Mont Royal (Traben-Trarbach), 517
Montfort Castle (Wasserburg), 346
Mosel River, 17, 510
Mosel Valley, 17, 510
  Cochem, 7
  driving tours, 7, 510, 513
  vineyards, 3

Mosel-Wein-Woche (Cochem), 513
Motorcycling, 28
Mountain climbing, 28, 386
Mozart festivals
  Augsburg, 245
  Würzburg, 23, 632
Mozart, Wolfgang Amadeus, 632
Münchner Philharmoniker (Munich), 302
Munich, 13
  accommodations, 9, 260–265, 268
  bars and pubs, 305–307
  beer gardens, 2
  beer halls, taverns, 11, 302–303
  bicycling in, 8
  cars and bicycles, 258
  castles and palaces, 5
  cathedrals and churches, 290–291
  coffeehouses, cafes, 269
  gay and lesbian clubs, 307
  guided tours, 293–294
  live music clubs, night clubs, 303–305
  museums, 3–4, 284, 286–290, 293
  neighborhoods, city layout, 253, 256
  Oktoberfest, 24
  parks and zoos, 291
  performing arts, 300–302
  pubic transportation, 256, 258
  recreational activities, 294–295
  restaurants, 10, 268–280
  services, basic information, 258–259
  shopping, 295–300
  sightseeing, 281, 284, 286, 291
  special events, 23
  taxis, 258
  traveling to, 252–253
  visitor information, 253
  Web sites about, 60
Münster (Hameln), 547
Münster (Ümberlingen), 358

Münster St. Maria and Markus (Reichenau island), 356
Museen Behnhaus/Drägerhaus (Lübeck), 597
Museum der Bildenen Künst (Leipzig), 155
Museum für Angewandte Kunst (Applied Art) (Cologne), 490
Museum für Hamburgische Geschichte, 580
Museum für Moderne Kunst (Frankfurt), 435–436
Museum für Neue Kunst (Freiburg), 365
Museum Holstentor (Lübeck), 597
Museum in der Runden Ecke (Leipzig), 156
Museum Mile (Bonn), 475
Museum of Books and Scripts (Leipzig), 157
Museum of Contemporary Art (Berlin), 109
Museum of Folklore (Ümberlingen), 358
Museum of Prehistory (Berlin), 103
Museums. See also specific museums
  about music, 632
  recommended, 3–4
Music. See Live music clubs; Classical music
Music stores, 123
Musical instruments, stringed, 326
Musikalischer Sommer Festival (Baden-Baden), 391
Musikinstrumenten Museum (Leipzig), 156

Napolean, 625
Naturschützpark Lünenburger Heide (Lünenburg), 537
Nautical Museum (Rostock), 619
Neckar River, 392
  cruising on, 398
Neckar Valley
  Castle Road, 16
  Cycle Path, 8, 395
  driving tours, 2
  Web sites about, 61
  wineries, 404

Index

Needlepoint, embroidery, 542
Neiderwald Monument (Rheingau area), 468
Neoclassical architecture, 630
Neubulach, 381
Neue Nationalgalerie (Berlin), 106
Neue Residenz (Bamberg), 188
Neuer Garten (Potsdam), 138
Neues Schloss
  Bayreuth, 184
  Herrenchiemsee, 322
  Meersburg, 350
  Stuttgart, 406
Neuschwanstein castle (nr. Füssen), 5, 8, 13, 248–251, 630
Neuweier, 390
New Synagogue (Berlin), 113
Nibelungen legends, 3, 455, 459
Niedersächsisches Landsmuseum (Hannover), 542
Nikolaikirche (Berlin), 111
Nikolaikirche (Leipzig), 157
Nikolausbrüke (Calw), 381
Nördlingen, 213, 237, 239
North Hesse, 526
  Fairy Tale Road, 13, 17
  Web sites about, 62
North Sea, 17, 594
Nuremberg. See Nürnberg
Nürnberg (Nuremberg), 13, 191–192
  accommodations, 197–199
  nightlife, 201–202
  public transportation, 193
  restaurants, 10, 199, 201
  shopping, 197
  sightseeing, 193–194, 196
  toys, 11
Nymphenburg Palace complex (Munich), 5, 249, 287, 289

Oberammergau, 5, 16, 334–335
  accommodations, 335, 337–338
  activities, sightseeing, 335
  restaurants, 335, 337–338
  wood-carvers, 335–336
Obersalzberg, 316–317
Obersee (Lake Constance), 316, 340
Oberstaufen, 28
Oceanographic Museum and Aquarium (Stralsund), 621
Oktoberfest (Munich), 24, 252, 637
Olympic Park (Munich), 292–293
Olympic Stadium (Berlin), 110
Oper der Stadt Köln, 497
Oper Frankfurt/Ballet Frankfurt, 440
Opera
  Bayreuth, 24, 183
  Berlin, 24, 124–125
  Bonn, 480
  Bremen, 534
  Cologne, 497
  Dresden, 174–175
  Düsseldorf, 508
  Frankfurt, 439–440
  Hamburg, 586
  Hannover, 545
  Leipzig, 160
  Munich, 300–302
  Passau, 209
  Stuttgart, 412
Optical products, 11

Package discounts, 39
Palaces. See also specific palaces
  recommended, 4, 6
Palatinate Museum (Heidelberg), 396
Palmengarten (Frankfurt), 436
Parking. See Driving, parking
Partnachklamm Gorge, 7, 329
Passau, 206–207
  accommodations, 9, 208–209
  Danube cruises, 207
  nightlife, 209–210
  public transportation, 207
  restaurants, 209
  sightseeing, 207–208
Passports, 18
Perfume, 123

Pergamon Museum (Berlin), 3, 104
Peterskirche (Erfurt), 151
Pets, traveling with, 46
Pewter toys, 300
Pforzheim, 382
  accommodations, 383
  restaurants, 383
  sightseeing, 382–383
Pharmacies, drugstores, 45
Pilatushaus (Oberammergau), 335
Police, 46
Pöllat Gorge, 8
Pompeianum (Aschaffenburg), 443
Porcelain, 11, 169
  Berlin, 119
  Frankfurt, 439
  Meissen, 178–179
  Munich, 299
Porzellan Manufaktur (Meissen), 178
Potsdam, 4, 12, 136–139
Predigerkirche (Erfurt), 151
Presley, Elvis, 453
Prostitution, in Hamburg, 588
Prussia, 626
Public transportation
  Berlin, 71
  Bonn, 475
  Bremen, 528
  Cologne, 488
  Dresden, 166
  Düsseldorf, 500
  Frankfurt, 419, 422
  Freiburg, 364
  Göttingen, 554
  Hannover, 541
  Heidelberg, 394
  Leipzig, 154
  Munich, 256, 258
Pump Room (Baden-Baden), 385
Punk memorabilia, 123
Puppet theater
  Bremen, 535
  Rothenburg, 234

Quedlinburg, 6, 162–163

Racquet sports, 295, 386, 437
  Berlin, 117
  Hamburg, 583
Rafting, 295, 310
Rail Europe passes, 41
Rail passes, 41–42

Rail travel
  in Germany, 39–41
  to Germany, 36–37
Rammelsberger Bergbau-
  museum (Goslar), 552
Raschi-Haus Museum
  (Worms), 460
Rathaus
  Aachen, 483
  Augsburg, 242
  Bremen, 530
  Dresden, 166
  Freiburg, 365
  Goslar, 551
  Hannover, 542
  Heilbronn, 404
  Lübeck, 597
  Lünenburg, 535
  Nördlingen, 237
  Passau, 208
  Ravensburg, 360
  Rostock, 618
  Rothenburg, 230
  Stralsund, 621
  Stuttgart, 406
  Ulm, 211
  Wasserburg, 345
  Wismar, 613
Ravensburg, 359–360
  accommodations,
    360–361
  restaurants, 361
  sightseeing, 360
Red Wine Festival
  (Assmannshausen), 23
Redoute Palace (Bad
  Godesberg), 481
Reeperbahn (Hamburg),
  588
Regensburg, 13, 202
  accommodations,
    204–205
  nightlife, 206
  restaurants, 205–206
  sightseeing, 202–204
Reichenau island, 356
  accommodations, 357
  restaurants, 357
  sightseeing, 356–357
Reichsburg castle
  (Cochem), 7, 512–513
Reichsstadtmuseum
  (Rothenburg), 230
Residenz
  Munich, 249, 286
  Würzburg, 5,
    216–217
Rest rooms, 46, 74, 259

Restaurants
  family-friendly, 273,
    431, 575
  recommended, 10–11
Rheingau area, 468–471
Rheingau- und
  Weinmuseum
  (Rüdenheim), 469
Rheinisches Landmuseum
  (Trier), 522
Rhine River, 455
  cruises, 2, 17, 458
Rhine Valley, 455
  Deutsche Weinstrasse,
    462–463
  driving tour, 455–457
  Rüdesheim, 7
  vineyards, 3, 468–471
  Web sites about, 61
Rhineland. *See* Rhine
  Valley
Ribnitz-Damgarten, 620
Richard Wagner Museum
  (Bayreuth), 185
Rieskrater Museum
  (Nördlingen), 238
Roadside services,
  emergency, 43
Rock. *See* Live music clubs
Rock Am See Festival
  (Konstanz), 356
Roman ruins
  Mainz, 465
  Regensburg, 203
  Trier, 520–521
Romanesque architecture,
  629
Romantic Road (Roman-
  tische Strasse), 13, 213
Romanticism, 630
Romantische Strasse. *See*
  Romantic Road
Römer (Frankfurt), 433
Römisch-Germanisches
  Museum (Cologne), 490
Rostock, 618
  accommodations, 619
  restaurants, 619–620
  sightseeing, 618
Rothenburg ob der Tauber,
  213, 228–229, 630
  accommodations, 9,
    231–233
  nightlife, 234
  restaurants, 233–234
  shopping, 231
  sightseeing, 230–231
  special events, 229

Rüdesheim/
  Assmannshausen, 7, 9,
    17, 469–471
  special events, 23
Rügen, 622
  accommodations, 623
  restaurants, 623
  sightseeing, 622–623
Ruprecht-Karl-University
  (Heidelberg), 392

Saale River, 149
Safety, personal, 32, 46
  Berlin, 74
  Dresden, 164
  Frankfurt, 423
  Hamburg, 568
  Munich, 259
Sailing schools, 28, 340
St. Georgskirche
  (Nördlingen), 237, 630
St. Jakob (Wasserburg), 345
St-Jakobskirche
  (Rothenburg), 230
St. Killian's Church
  (Heilbronn), 404
St.-Lorenz-Kirche
  (Nürnberg), 196
St-Marien-Kirche
  (Rostock), 619
St. Michael's Church
  (Munich), 630
St. Nikolaikirche
  (Stralsund), 621
St. Nikolaikirche (Wismar),
  614
St. Peter's Dom
  (Schleswig), 606
St. Petri Kirche (Hamburg),
  579
St.-Sebaldus-Kirche
  (Nürnberg), 196
St. Stephen's Cathedral
  (Passau), 208
St. Thomas Choir
  (Leipzig), 156
St. Thomas's Lutheran
  Church (Leipzig), 632
Salt Lofts (Der Salzspeicher)
  (Lübeck), 597
Saltmuseum (Bad
  Reichenhall), 318
Salzbergwerk
  Berchtesgaden, 314
Sammlung Berggruen
  (Berlin), 108
Sankt Michaelerskirche
  (Pforzheim), 382

Sans-Souci Palace
(Potsdam), 4, 137
Saxony, 12, 140. *See also*
Lower Saxony; East
Germany
food specialties, 634
Web sites about, 59
Schaezlerpalais (Augsburg),
242
Schiffahrtsmuseum
(Rostock), 619
Schillerhaus (Leipzig), 156
Schillerhaus (Weimar), 144
Schleswig, 605–606
accommodations, 607
nightlife, 607
restaurants, 607
sightseeing, 606
Schleswig-Holstein, 17, 594
driving tour, 594
food specialties, 634
Schleswig-Holstein Music
Festival (Lübeck), 596
Schleswig-Holstein State
Museum (Schleswig), 606
Schleswig-Holsteinisches
Freilichtmuseum (Keil),
603
Schloss Belvedere
(Weimar), 145
Schloss Bürgeln
(Badenweiler), 369
Schloss Cecilienhof
(Potsdam), 139
Schloss Charlotte
(Potsdam), 138
Schloss Charlottenburg
(Berlin), 102
Schloss Gotoff (Schleswig),
606
Schloss Johannisburg
(Aschaffenburg), 443
Schloss Linderhof (nr.
Oberammergau), 5,
338–339
Schloss Miltenburg, 222
Schloss Neuweier, 390
Schloss Nymphenburg.
See Nymphenburg Palace
complex
Schloss Sigmaringen
(nr. Ulm), 212
Schloss Spyker (Rügen), 622
Schloss Tiefurt (Weimar),
145
Schloss und Gartenver-
waltung (Würzburg), 216
Schloss Veitshöchheim
(nr. Würzburg), 217

Schloss Wartburg
(Eisenach), 5, 151
Schloss Weikersheim, 226
Schlossgarten (Schwerin),
616
Schlosskirche
(Friedrichshafen), 347
Schlosskirche (Wittenberg),
161
Schluchsee, 368
Schmuckmuseum
(Pforzheim), 383
Schnütgen Museum
(Cologne), 490
Schoenberg, Arnold, 633
Schöneberg Rathaus
(Berlin), 110
Schönefeld Airport
(Berlin), 63, 65
Schötting (Bremen), 528
Schubert, Franz, 633
Schulemuseum
(Friedrichshafen), 347
Schumann, Robert, 633
Schwäbisch Hall, 416
accommodations,
416–417
restaurants, 416–417
sightseeing, 416
Schwarzwald. *See* Black
Forest
Schwarzwald Hochstrasse,
362
Schwerin, 615
accommodations, 617
restaurants, 617
sightseeing, 616
Schwerin Cathedral, 616
Schweriner Schloss, 616
Seehotel Siber
restaurants, 10
Seepromenade
(Friedrichshafen), 347
Senckenberg Museum
of Natural History
(Frankfurt), 436
Senior travelers,
discounts/resources for,
32–33
Shopping
German specialties, 11
Ski jumping, 23
Skiing, Alpine, 295,
309–310
Skiing, cross-country, 310
Soccer
Berlin, 116
Hamburg, 583
Sorb country, 176–177

Spandau Citadel (Berlin),
70, 113
Spas, 2, 26
Aachen, 482–487
Bad Godesberg,
481–482
Bad Homburg, 8, 448,
450–451
Bad Mergenheim,
224–225
Bad Nauheim, 8, 452,
454
Bad Pyrmont, 548–550
Bad Reichenhall, 8,
318–320
Bad Wiessee, 323–325
Bad Wildstein, 517
Bad Wildungen,
557–559
Baden-Baden, 8,
384–391
Badenweiler, 369–371
Wiesbaden, 8, 445–448
Speer, Albert, 631
Speyer, 457
cathedrals and
churches, 6
hotels, restaurants, 459
public transportation,
457
sightseeing, 458–459
Speyer Cathedral, 6
Spiegelsaal (Meersburg),
352
Spielbank. *See* Casinos
Spielzeugmuseum
(Toy Museum)
(Nürnberg), 196
Spreewald, 176–177
Squash. *See* Racquet sports
Staatsbad, 318
Staatsgalerie (Stuttgart),
408
Staatsgalerie Moderner
Kunst (Munich), 4, 289
Staatsliches Museum
Schwerin-Kunstsamm-
lunger, 616
Städel Gallery (Frankfurt),
435
Stadtische Galerie im
Lenbachhaus (Munich),
4, 290
Stadtisches Museum
(Göttingen), 554
Stadtkirche (Bad
Wildungen), 557
Stadtkirche (Freudenstadt),
378

Stadtkirche (Wittenberg), 162

Stadtkirche St. Peter and Paul (Weimar), 145

Stadtmuseum Dresden, 168

Stadtpark (Hamburg), 582

Stadttheater Konstanz, 355

Stiftkirche St. Peter and St. Alexander (Aschaffenburg), 443

Stiftskirche (Berchtesgaden), 313

Stiftskirche (Tübingen), 414

Stockhausen, Karlheinz, 633

Stralsund, 620
    accommodations, 621
    restaurants, 622
    sightseeing, 621

Strauss, Richard, 633

Street Music Festival (Leipzig), 154

Struwwelpeter Museum (Frankfurt), 436

Student Jail (Heidelberg), 396

Student taverns, in Göttingen, 556

Stuppach, 225

Stuttgart, 16, 405–406
    accommodations, 409–411
    architectural highlights, 406
    bars, clubs, 412
    food specialties, 634
    performing arts, 412
    public transportation, 406
    restaurants, 411–412
    shopping, 408–409
    sightseeing, 406, 408
    Web sites about, 61

Stutthart Echterdingen Airport, 405

Subways. See Public transportation

Suermondt Ludwig Museum (Aachen), 484

Swimming pools
    Baden-Baden, 386
    Berlin, 116
    Hamburg, 583
    Meersburg, 350
    Munich, 294
    Titisee, 372

Sylt, Island of, 3, 18, 607
    accommodations, 610–611
    erosion, 609
    nightlife, 612
    restaurants, 611–612
    shopping, 609
    traveling to, 608

Taverns. See Beer halls, taverns

Taxes, 47

Taxis
    Berlin, 71
    Bremen, 528
    Düsseldorf, 502
    Frankfurt, 422
    Hamburg, 565
    Munich, 258

Technisches Museum (Pforzheim), 383

Tegel Airport (Berlin), 63–64

Telegrams/telefax, 423

Telephone, 47

Tempelhof Airport (Berlin), 63, 65

Tennis. See Racquet sports

Theater
    Bamberg, 191
    Berlin, 125
    Cologne, 497
    Dresden, 174–175
    Frankfurt, 440
    Göttingen, 556
    Hamburg, 586–588, 590
    Heidelberg, 402
    Koblenz, 474
    Konstanz, 355
    Leipzig, 160
    Munich, 300–302
    Nürnberg, 201

Theater am Goetheplatz (Baden-Baden), 391

Thomaskirche (Leipzig), 155–156

Thuringia, 12
    food specialties, 634
    forests in, 2, 149
    Web sites about, 59

Tiergarten (Berlin), 70, 109, 113

Time, 47

Tipping, 48, 74

Titisee, 371–372
    accommodations, 373
    activities, sightseeing, 372
    restaurants, 374

Tourism offices, 18
    Web listings, 56

Toys, 11, 196–197, 300, 439

Traban-Trarbach, 517–518

Train travel. See Rail travel

Travel advisories, 57

Travel tips, Web sites for, 56–57

Traveler's checks, 21

Traveling
    in Germany, 39–41
    to Germany, 33–34, 36–39

Treves. See Trier

Triberg, 16, 375
    accommodations, 376–377
    museums, 375–376
    restaurants, 377
    shopping, 375
    sightseeing, 375–376

Trier (Treves), 3, 17, 519–520
    accommodations, 10, 523–524
    boat tours, 523
    nightlife, 525–526
    public transportation, 520
    restaurants, 524–525
    Roman ruins, 520–521
    shopping, 520
    sightseeing, 521–523

Tübingen, 16, 413
    accommodations, 414
    nightlife, 415
    restaurants, 415
    sightseeing, 413–414

Überlingersee (Lake Constance), 340
    cuisine, local specialties, 633–635

Ulm, 210
    accommodations, 212
    nightlife, 212
    restaurants, 212
    sightseeing, 6, 211

Ulm Münster, 211

Ulm Münsterl, 6

Ulmer Museum, 211

Ümberlingen, 358
    hotels, restaurants, 359
    sightseeing, 358–359

Undeloh, 537

Untersee (Lake Constance), 340

Vacation packages, 53
Value-added taxes (VAT), 47
Variety shows. See Cabaret
Viking Museum (Schleswig), 606
Vineyards. See Wine, vineyards
Visas, 18

Wagner, Richard, 13, 24, 182–83, 633
   home of (Bayreuth), 632
Walhalla (Regensburg), 204
Walking tours, 25
   Berlin, 114
   through the Black Forest, 376
   Bremen, 528
   recommended, 7
   Trier, 520
Wallberg Road (Bad Wiesse), 324
Wallfahrtskirche, 350
Wallgahrtkirche Maria in der Tannen (Triberg), 376
Wallraf-Richartz Museum (Cologne), 4, 490
Wallringpark (Hamburg), 582
Walpurgis festivals, 23
Wasserburg, 345
Watches, clocks, 11
   Düsseldorf, 504
   Munich, 299
   Pforzheim, 383
   Triberg, 16, 375
Water quality, 30, 48, 74
Weather information, 22, 56
   Berlin, 74
Web sites
   airlines, 53
   Bavarian Alps, 60
   Berlin information, 58–59
   Franconia, Danube region information, 60
   Frankfurt , 61
   general travel information, 50
   Germany, general information, 57–58
   Hamburg, 62
   Heidelberg & Neckar Valley, 61

Lake Constance, 60
Lower Saxony, North Hesse, 62
Munich information, 60
online booking, 49–53
Rhineland, 61
Saxony/Thuringia information, 59
specialty travel sites, 52–53
tourist information, 18
travel advisories, 56
travel bargains, 54–56
travel discussions, 56
traveling aids, 56–57
Wedding House (Hameln), 546
Wedel, 580–581
Weill, Kurt, 633
Weimar, 12, 142
   accommodations, 9, 147–148
   nightlife, 148, 150
   restaurants, 148
   shopping, 146
   sightseeing, 142–146
   Web sites about, 59
Weinfest (Cochem), 513
Weingarten, 361
Weingarten Basilica, 361
Weser River, 3
Westphalia, 634
Wiesbaden, 445
   accommodations, 10, 446–447
   nightlife, 448
   public transportation, 445
   restaurants, 447–448
   shopping, 445
   spas, 8, 26
   special events, 23, 448
Wieskirche (nr. Füssen), 246
Wikersheim, 226
   accommodations, 226
   restaurants, 226
   sightseeing, 226
Wilhelm I, 626
Wilhelmine, Margravine, 184
Willkomm Höft (Wedel), 580
Windsurfing, 343
Wine cellars, in Berlin, 132

Wine Fair (Mainz), 464
Wine Festival (Meersburg), 349
Wine Road (Deutsche Weinstrasse), 462–463
Wine, vineyards, 635, 637. See also Apple-wine taverns
   Baden-Baden, 387
   Bodensee region, 357
   Deutsche Weinstrasse, 462–463
   Elbe Valley, 178
   Freiburg wine tasting, 24
   Heilbronn, 404
   Mosel Valley, 3, 7, 510, 513, 516, 520
   Red Wine Festival, 23
   Rheingau area, 468–471
   Rhine Valley, 3
Winter Dom (Hamburg), 24
Wismar, 613, 615
Wittenberg, 161–162, 625
Wittumspalais (Weimar), 145
Wood carvings, 11, 314, 335. See also Handcrafts
   Munich, 297
   Oberammergau, 336
Worms, 459, 460
   cathedrals and churches, 6
   hotels, restaurants, 460–461
   nightlife, 461
   performing arts, 461
   public transportation, 460
   sightseeing, 460
Worms Cathedral, 6
Würm River, 383
Wurst (sausage), 635
Würzburg, 5, 13, 213, 215, 630
   accommodations, 218–220
   nightlife, 221
   public transportation, 215
   restaurants, 10, 220–221
   sightseeing, 215–217
   special events, 23, 632

Index

Zavelstein, 381
Zell, 515–516
Zeltmusik Festival
    (Freiburg), 368
Zeppelin-Museum
    (Friedrichshafen), 347

Zoo, Hellabrun (Munich),
    292–293
Zoo, Tierpark (Hamburg),
    580
Zoo-Aquarium (Berlin),
    114

Zoologischer Garten
    Frankfurt, 437
    Leipzig, 157
Zugspitze, 2, 30, 330
Zugspitzplatt, 309
Zwinger Museum complex
    (Dresden), 3, 167–168, 631